A History of British Prime Ministers

A History of British Prime Ministers (Omnibus Edition)

Walpole to Cameron

Dick Leonard

palgrave
macmillan

First published 2014 by
First published in paperback 2015 by
PALGRAVE MACMILLAN

Palgrave Macmillan in the UK is an imprint of Macmillan Publishers Limited, registered in England, company number 785998, of Houndmills, Basingstoke, Hampshire RG21 6XS.

Palgrave Macmillan in the US is a division of St Martin's Press LLC, 175 Fifth Avenue, New York, NY 10010.

Palgrave Macmillan is the global academic imprint of the above companies and has companies and representatives throughout the world.

Palgrave® and Macmillan® are registered trademarks in the United States, the United Kingdom, Europe and other countries

ISBN: 978–1–137–33804–4   hardback
ISBN: 978–1–137–57438–1   paperback

This book is printed on paper suitable for recycling and made from fully managed and sustained forest sources. Logging, pulping and manufacturing processes are expected to conform to the environmental regulations of the country of origin.

A catalogue record for this book is available from the British Library.

A catalog record for this book is available from the Library of Congress.

For Irène, my partner and inspiration for more than 50 years

Contents

Part III   The 20th and 21st Centuries

List of Plates

Preface and Acknowledgements

Fifty-two men and one woman have held the post of Prime Minister (or, more technically, First Lord of the Treasury) since Sir Robert Walpole was appointed by George I in 1721. This book aims to provide a succinct account of their political careers, assess their achievements and, where appropriate, draw conclusions as to their relevance to the present day. It has been compiled over a period of ten years, and its contents have formed the basis of three earlier volumes, published in 2005, 2008 and 2011. Witten in reverse chronological order, these were, respectively, *A Century of Premiers: Salisbury to Blair*, *Nineteenth-Century British Premiers: Pitt to Rosebery* and *Eighteenth-Century British Premiers: Walpole to the Younger Pitt*. The present omnibus edition incorporates these three earlier volumes, very lightly revised, plus new chapters on Gordon Brown and David Cameron.

The present volume, which was first published as a hardback in 2014, is not based on a large amount of original research. It is based principally on a close reading of relevant historical works as well as of the main biographies of the personalities involved. For the later chapters in the work, this has been increasingly supplemented by my own observations of the political scene, during the course of a long career as a political journalist, and a much shorter one as an active politician and Member of Parliament. In these capacities I have had some personal contact with most of the Prime Ministers concerned, though I was never a close associate of any of them.

I may not, perhaps, have achieved the highest level of objectivity. Even though I have striven to avoid conscious bias, I cannot avoid unconscious ones, and it is right that the reader should know that mine come from a centre-left position. What I have tried to do is to judge the characters involved by the success or otherwise with which they have pursued their declared objectives, rather than whether I personally approve of these objectives. I have also made a serious effort not to apply twenty-first-century standards to the careers of the earlier Prime Ministers, who were operating according to the norms of the eighteenth, nineteenth and early twentieth centuries.

Short bibliographies are included at the end of each chapter. More general works, listed below, have also been of assistance. William Keegan, Mark Garnett, John Leonard and Mark Leonard have kindly read drafts of many of the chapters in this book, and made valuable suggestions for improvements. The chapter on Cameron has been revised and updated to take account of the result of the 2015 general election. The new material is included in a Postscript on pages xv–xix. Responsibility for any remaining errors or misinterpretations remains mine alone.

Dick Leonard

June 2015

Works consulted

Walter Bagehot, 1964, *The English Constitution*, Introduction by Richard Crossman, London, Watts.

F.W.G. Benemy, 1965, *The Elected Monarch,* London, Harrap.

Humphry Berkeley, 1968, *The Power of the Prime Minister*, London, Allen & Unwin.

Robert Blake, 1975, *The Office of Prime Minister* (1975), London, Oxford University Press.

Andrew Blick and George Jones, 2010, *Premiership: The Development, Nature and Power of the Office of the British Prime Minister*, Exeter, Imprint Academic.

Dermot Englefield, Janet Seaton and Isabel White, 1995, *Facts about the British Prime Ministers*, New York, H.W. Wilson.

Peter Hennessy, 2000, *The Prime Minister: The Office and its Holders Since 1945*, Allen Lane.

Dennis Kavanagh and Anthony Seldon, 1999, *The Powers Behind the Prime Minister*, London, HarperCollins.

Anthony King, ed., 1985, 2nd edition, *The British Prime Minister*, Basingstoke, Macmillan.

John P. Mackintosh, 1977, 3rd edition, *The British Cabinet*, London, Stevens.

Postscript, June 2015: Update to David Cameron – Plausible 'Front Man' (Continued from p. 851)

During 2013 there was a gradual improvement in the economic situation with unemployment steadily falling and a large number of new jobs being created, though many of these were low-paid or on zero-hours contracts. The improvement continued through 2014, and by the end of that year, with sharply falling oil and gas prices and inflation coming down to nearly zero, the average level of incomes finally reached and began to exceed the 2010 level. The Labour criticism of the coalition shifted from denial that there had been any recovery into asserting that the benefits had accrued only to a wealthy minority and that the living standards of the many had shown no improvement. This criticism had much resonance, and the Tories expressed dismay at what appeared to be 'a voteless recovery'. Their poll rating remained stuck at around 30 per cent, though the Labour lead over them declined to around 5 per cent in early 2014, the extra votes going not to them but to UKIP and, to a lesser extent, the Greens. UKIP's support soared, enabling them to win the largest number of seats in the European Parliament election in June 2014, pushing the Tories into third place behind Labour, while the Liberal Democrats were reduced to a single seat.

In September, the long-awaited referendum on Scottish independence took place. The opinion polls had fairly consistently predicted an easy victory for the 'no' side, with a likely margin of 60–40 per cent. But as the campaign moved to its closing stages, the gap dramatically narrowed, and a week before voting, a Yougov poll put the 'yes' side two points ahead. General panic broke out, but was calmed by a timely intervention by former Labour Prime Minister Gordon Brown, who retained his standing and popularity in Scotland, despite having lost it in other parts of the UK. He persuaded the three main parties to agree a promise of 'maximum devolution' to Scotland if it voted to remain in the Union. This did the trick, and on 15 September the Scots voted 'no', by 55.3 per cent to 44.7 per cent. Ominously for Labour, four of its strongholds, Dundee, Glasgow, North Lanarkshire and West Dunbartonshire voted for independence. Cameron issued a statement welcoming the result, and pledging to redeem the pledge of 'devomax', but said at the same time that legislation would be introduced to prevent Scottish MPs voting on English issues. The SNP expressed shock that Scottish MPs were to be treated as 'second class' members and protested loudly. Disheartened by their referendum defeat, this new grievance acted as a shot in the arm, and they began campaigning again with great vigour, recruiting a large number of new members. Within a few weeks, an independent committee, under the chairmanship of Lord Smith of Kelvin, a crossbench peer, produced a report listing a series of new powers, including proposals on taxation, which should be transferred to the Scottish Parliament. The report was generally welcomed, except by the new Scottish First Minister, Nicola Sturgeon, who said she was disappointed, and wanted further talks with the British government.

Later in the year, two sitting Tory MPs, Douglas Carswell and Mark Reckless, defected to UKIP, and retained their seats in subsequent by-elections, despite Herculean efforts by the Tories to defeat them. This led to near panic among the Tories as the general election approached less than six months later. Their election strategy had long been agreed, and was openly based on that of the 1992 election, in which Cameron had been intimately involved. That had two elements – depicting Labour as the party of soaring taxation, and its leader, Neil Kinnock, as not being up to the job of Prime Minister. This time Labour was stigmatised for 'creating the mess' in 2010, which the Tories claimed to have successfully cleared up by their 'long-term economic plan', while Miliband was vilified not only for his alleged incapacity but also for his supposedly extreme views, being dubbed as 'Red Ed' by most of the Tory-supporting press. The Tories had much earlier appointed the Australian election organiser Lynton Crosby to direct their election campaign, which he did with ruthless efficiency, insisting that all his candidates, even senior cabinet ministers, followed his instructions to the letter. Armed by a treasure chest, mostly subscribed by hedge funds and other business donors, at least three times as large as Labour's, and with the support of at least 85 per cent of the press, measured in terms of their circulations, the Tories had two principal fears. One was that the UKIP surge would continue, principally at their expense, and enable Labour to scrape an election victory with 35 per cent, or so, of the total vote. The other was a fear that Miliband would come off best in election debates with Cameron, and thus enable him to overcome his negative image. When the broadcasting authorities came up with plans to largely repeat the formula used in 2010, when Clegg had outshone his rivals, the Tories refused to participate, and the broadcasters eventually agreed to a 'compromise' arrangement for a couple of multi-party encounters, excluding a one-on one debate between Cameron and Miliband. This exposed Cameron to accusations of cowardice, but he evidently calculated that this would be a lesser risk than that of being outshone by the

Labour leader. Miliband in fact had an excellent campaign, and his poll ratings shot up, though still remaining worse than Cameron's. He made only one serious mistake, but that was an egregious one, A week before polling day, in a widely watched BBC Question Time programme, he, Clegg and Cameron were separately quizzed by a studio audience made up of equal numbers of party supporters and of undecided voters. Asked if he now regretted Labour's over-spend before the 2010 election, and whether he would now apologise for it, he defiantly answered 'no', and went on to boast of the benefits which this spending had produced. An audible murmur of disbelief then spread across almost all the audience, and at that moment – if not long before – Labour's defeat was assured.

The campaign had been dominated by the opinion polls, conducted by no fewer than 11 organisations. There were marginal differences in their findings, but they all told essentially the same story. This was that the Labour lead had almost evaporated by Christmas, and thereafter a virtual dead heat between Labour and the Conservatives was indicated, right up until polling day. The Scottish polls indicated that the SNP would make enormous gains, perhaps even wiping out Labour, which was defending 41 of the country's 59 seats. In compensation, it looked as though Labour would win perhaps 40–55 seats in England and Wales. Almost every single poll and the great majority of political commentators concluded that another 'hung parliament' would result, quite likely with the SNP holding the balance of power. Few doubted that they would decide to prop up a Labour government, even if the Tories finished up with the largest number of seats. Panic now gripped the Conservatives, who had been assured all along by Lynton Crosby that there would by then have been a large swing back of votes to them from Labour. They therefore, suddenly produced a flurry of promises of tax cuts and spending proposals, all of them unfunded, which threatened to undermine their reputation for fiscal responsibility. They even, through the mouth of Defence Minister Michael Fallon, launched a vicious personal attack on Ed Miliband, saying he had stabbed his own brother in the back, and would be willing 'to stab his country in the back' by scrapping the Trident missile system in order to secure the backing of the SNP. This was seen to be hitting below the belt and backfired on the Tories. But their message during the final days of the campaign, that a minority Labour government propped up by the SNP would lead to their being 'blackmailed' or 'held to ransom' was widely disseminated, notably by former Prime Minister, Sir John Major. It may well have had a significant effect on still-undecided voters.

On polling day, 7 May 2015, the reputation of the polls was rudely punctured by an exit poll, commissioned by the BBC and other broadcasting organisations, and released promptly at 10 pm, as the polling booths closed. It showed the Tories very far ahead of Labour, the Liberal Democrats almost eliminated, the Scottish Nationalists taking every seat bar one, and UKIP with few if any seats. Widely suspected to be an aberrant poll, as the night wore on it was seen to have been extremely accurate, except that it under-estimated the Conservative performance, which was good enough for them to have won an overall majority of 12 seats. The final result, in terms of seats, was as follows:

Conservatives 331, Labour 232, SNP 56, Liberal Democrats 8, UKIP 1, Greens 1, Others 21, Total 650. Con. majority 12.

The Conservatives had won a famous victory, proclaimed by Cameron the following day as 'the sweetest victory of all', made all the sweeter by the fact that his three rival party leaders – Miliband, Clegg and Farage – all stood down on the morrow of the poll, though Farage later withdrew his resignation. In reality, the Tories had not won the election, Labour had lost it, and the real victor had been the SNP and its dynamic new leader, Niola Sturgeon. She had destroyed the Labour Party in Scotland and fatally undermined its position in England, where it had confidently expected to win a large number of Tory and LibDem marginal seats, but fell short in many of them, probably due to fears of a minority Labour government depending on SNP support to keep them in power.

Cameron's second government may prove to be more precarious than the first. He has got rid of the Liberal Democrats, but the government's majority of 12 seats is distinctly less comfortable than the 76 enjoyed by the coalition. Cameron will be much more vulnerable to revolts by his right-wing and anti-European backbenchers, while he could see his majority being whittled away by by-election losses, as happened to the Callaghan government in the 1970s.

He now faces three great challenges – keeping the UK together in the face of the SNP challenge, keeping Britain in the EU and – perhaps the least difficult of the three – eliminating the deficit by his new target date of 2017–18, Cameron indicated during the election campaign that he would not fight another election, and that before then he would give way to a successor, listing George Osborne, Theresa May and Boris Johnson as likely runners. So far, at least, he has proved to be an acceptable face for the Conservative Party, at least for voters in southern England. A competent parliamentary performer, he is by nature a conciliator, too ready to give way to pressure from UKIP and his own backbenchers. He deserves credit for holding his coalition together through five difficult years, though he was over-dependent on his Chancellor (perhaps his Svengali?) for a sense of direction to his government. Despite his academic success at Oxford, he is no sort of intellectual, and his solid middle-brow tastes ensured that a majority of the public felt comfortable with him, which they never did with his more cerebral opponent, Miliband. His powers of persuasion should not be under-estimated: he and Osborne convinced the mass of voters that their economic record had been a success, while many eminent economists, such as Nobel Prize-winners Joseph Stiglitz and Paul Krugman, and commentators Martin Wolf (*Financial Times*) and William Keegan (*The Observer*), found it distinctly mediocre.

Behind his bland exterior, David Cameron is a single-minded and ruthless operator. What matters to him, above all, is to gain power, and he allows no sentiment to get into his way. In 2015, he turned on his coalition partners of five years and flooded their constituencies with money and personnel, and succeeded in winning every one of their seats in their south-western heartlands. It was a triumph of professionalism, which left both his Liberal and Labour opponents looking like a bunch of amateurs.

Works consulted

Bale, Tim (2015), *Five Year Mission: The Labour Party under Ed Miliband*, Oxford, OUP.

Bogdanor, Vernon (2011), *The Coalition and the Constitution*, Oxford, Hart Publishing.

Cameron, David and Jones, Dylan (2008), *Cameron on Cameron: Conversations with Dylan Jones*, London, Fourth Estate.

d'Ancona, Matthew (2013), *In It Together: The Inside Story of the Coalition Government*, Viking.

Elliott, Francis and Hanning, James (2012), *Cameron: Practically a Conservative*, London, Fourth Estate.

Gould, Philip (1998), *The Unfinished Revolution*, London, Little Brown.

Hasan, Mehdi and Macintyre, James (eds) (2011), *The Milibands and the Making of a Labour Leader*, London, Biteback Publishing.

Kavanagh, Dennis (2012), *Philip Gould: An Unfinished Life*, London, Palgrave Macmillan.

Kavanagh, Dennis and Cowley, Philip (2010), *The British General Election of 2010*, London, Palgrave Macmillan.

Lee, Simon and Beech, Matt (2011), *The Cameron-Clegg Government: Coalition Government in an Age of Austerity*, London, Palgrave Macmillan.

Shorthouse, Ryan and Stagg, Guy (eds) (2013), *Tory Modernisation 2.0: The Future of the Conservative Party*, London, Bright Blue Publishing.

Introduction – The Road to the Prime Ministership

Historians are agreed that Sir Robert Walpole should be accounted the first British Prime Minister, though he never held the formal title, and nor did any of his successors until Sir Henry Campbell-Bannerman, in 1906–08. (The actual post to which Walpole was appointed, and for which he was paid a salary, was First Lord of the Treasury, a post held by all but two of his successors – Lord Chatham and the Marquess of Salisbury). It was George I, the first Hanoverian king, who chose Walpole in 1721, but both he and all his royal predecessors had previously employed ministers (not always known as such) who had advised them and helped in the administration of the kingdom. For substantial periods, individual ministers had been able to eclipse their colleagues and effectively become the 'chief minister' of the monarch. Writing in the 1920s, Clive Bigham identified 27 individuals who had filled this role, between the reigns of Edred (946–955) and Anne (1702–14). They held various titles, including Justiciar, Chancellor, Treasurer, Admiral, High Steward, Lord President, Marshal, Lord Lieutenant and Lord Great Chamberlain.[1] Bigham estimates that these men, whose average tenure was about 12 years, held power for rather less than half the nearly 800 years which separated Edred and Anne. 'Strong rulers', he writes, 'such as William I, William III or Oliver Cromwell, could do without them; weak ones, like Stephen, Edward II or Richard II, could never maintain them' (Bigham, 1925, p. 4). Although these men wielded considerable, and sometimes arbitrary, power, they – with the partial exception of the last two or three names in the list – lacked many of the attributes which later became associated with the prime ministership, perhaps being more comparable to the vizier of a Moslem ruler. It required the developments of the previous half century –

---

[1] The 27 men were Dunstan, Godwin, Harold, Flambard, Roger, Becket, Marshall, de Burgh, de Montfort, Burnell, Stratford, Wykeham, Beaufort, Suffolk, Warwick, Morton, Wolsey, Thomas Cromwell, Somerset, Burghley (William Cecil), Salisbury (Robert Cecil), Buckingham, Strafford, Clarendon, Danby, Godolphin and Harley.

and particularly the Glorious Revolution of 1688–89 – to create the conditions which enabled Walpole, a man of considerable talent and resource, to fashion a new role for himself and his successors.

Politically, and constitutionally, the key achievement of the Glorious Revolution was the concept of a limited monarchy. Henceforth, the King (or Queen) would still govern the country, but only through and with the consent of Parliament. Even as naturally authoritarian a monarch as William III recognized this: his three successors – Queen Anne and the first two Georges – had little option, but to do so. A series of other developments, some of them preceding the Revolution, also contributed to the growing importance of Parliament, and the necessity for ministers to secure consistent support from both Houses if they were to survive in office. Chief of these was perhaps the emergence of political parties. This effectively dated from the reign of Charles II, and the attempt to exclude the King's younger brother, the Catholic James, Duke of York, from the succession. The opposition to James was led by the first Earl of Shaftesbury, whose Exclusion Bill failed to carry in 1680. His supporters were christened Whigs by their opponents, after the Whiggamores, Scottish Presbyterian rebels, who had opposed Charles I in 1648. The Whigs themselves happily accepted this appellation, claiming that Whig was an acronym for We Hope In God. They, in turn, branded their opponents, the supporters of the future James II, as Tories, after an Irish word meaning highwaymen or outlaws. It was largely the Whigs who presided over the replacement in 1688 of James II by his elder daughter, Mary II, and son-in-law William III, though the Tory Earl of Danby also played a significant role, and most Tories assented to the change. Party differences continued, however, mostly defined by attitudes to the monarchy, to religion and to foreign policy. It was the Whigs who were most in favour of limiting the monarchy, who believed most strongly in religious toleration, especially of Protestant Dissenters, and of prosecuting a warlike foreign policy, aimed at curtailing the ambitions of Louis XIV. The Tories retained a residual belief in the Divine Right of Kings. Though they accepted the accession of William, and later of Anne, they were divided about excluding the Stuart family from the succession after her death. They were fervent supporters of the Church of England, and opposed to any initiative to remove the disqualifications of Dissenters, let alone Catholics. Opponents of high taxation, they also emerged as the peace party, believing that the two long wars against France – the War of the Grand Alliance (1688–97), and the War of Spanish Succession (1701–13) – were ruinously expensive and were being fought more in the interests of the Netherlands than of Britain. There were social differences between the two parties – the Whigs were more aristocratic, while the Tories' strongest support came from the country gentry. The Whigs were less cohesive, being divided between the dominant 'court' faction, more interested in securing ministerial offices and other 'places' and the 'Country Whigs', whose interests often coincided with the Tories, though they were loath to cooperate with them.

Both Whigs and Tories lacked most of the attributes of modern political parties, but their development was fostered by the frequent electoral contests in the reigns of both William and Anne. Under the Triennial Act, passed in 1694, there were no fewer than ten general elections in the period up till 1715, after which the Septennial Act of 1716 brought the era of almost constant electoral activity to an end. Political activity was also fostered by the abolition of censorship in 1695, which led to the development of a lively periodical press, while the proliferation of coffee houses in London and the main provincial towns provided centres of debate for the growing intelligentsia. The fortunes of the parties fluctuated throughout the period – the Whigs gradually squeezing the Tories out of government during the reign of William III, but the accession of Anne, in 1702, giving the Tories a momentary boost. The largely apolitical Sidney Godolphin, who led the government until 1710, was supported predominantly by Whigs, notably John Churchill, the Duke of Marlborough, by far his most forceful colleague, whose influence was greatly bolstered by his stunning series of military victories over the French. His wife, Sarah, was a longtime favourite and confidante of the Queen, and constantly used her intimacy with her to promote her husband's interests, and those of his Whig allies. In the end, she over-did it, virtually browbeating Anne into appointing her son-in-law, Charles Spencer, Earl of Sunderland, as Secretary of State. Eventually, she fell out badly with Anne, who replaced her as her principal Woman of the Bedchamber by Sarah's cousin, Amelia Hill, who became Lady Masham, and a rather more discreet advocate for the Tories. In June 1710, the Queen girded herself up to dismiss both Marlborough and Godolphin, and a predominantly Tory administration was appointed, led by Robert Harley, later Earl of Oxford. In the subsequent general election, the Tories won a large majority in the Commons, though the Whigs were in control of the Lords. Harley proceeded to negotiate the Treaty of Utrecht, of 1713, ending the war with France, which the Whigs were in favour of continuing. On Harley's advice, the Queen took the unprecedented step of creating 12 new Tory peers in order to get the Treaty through the House of Lords.

The Tory triumph was short-lived: in the closing months of Anne's life, both Harley and his Tory colleague and bitter rival, Henry St. John, Viscount Bolingbroke, compromised themselves by entering into secret communications with James II's son, James Edward Stuart, the 'Old Pretender', trying in vain to persuade him to renounce Catholicism in order to succeed to the throne. On her deathbed, at the end of July 1714, Anne dismissed Harley and appointed the Duke of Shrewsbury as Lord Treasurer, who supervised the inauguration of the Elector of Hanover, George I, who arrived in England six weeks later. The Tories were irremediably tainted with Jacobitism, though most of them declared their loyalty to the Hanoverian dynasty. George immediately appointed a Whig administration, led by James, later Lord, Stanhope, and the Tories were condemned to opposition throughout his reign, and that of his son, George II, remaining in the wilderness until 1762, when the young George III appointed the Earl of Bute as Prime Minister.

Partly due to the expense of the wars which raged almost continuously during the reigns of William III and Anne, there was a constant need for Parliament to meet in order to vote Supply, which meant that the days when it met only occasionally – sometimes with a gap of several years – were long past. The monarch now had the need of a chief minister who would defend the policies of the government on a regular basis either in the Lords or in the Commons, which added a large new dimension to the role of the chief minister. Another important change was the development of cabinet government. From being individual advisers to the monarch, ministers were now summoned increasingly to meet together to give their collective view in a Council normally presided over by the monarch in person, though this was increasingly not the case with the accession of George I. Speaking little English, and often absent in his Hanoverian dominions, the cabinet, as it became known, met more and more often in his absence, with a leading minister in the chair, and this became the normal pattern when Walpole became First Lord of the Treasury in 1721. The fact that Walpole led his government from the Commons, rather than the Lords where most previous chief ministers had sat, both reflected and reinforced the growing predominance of the lower House of Parliament, which the Glorious Revolution had made possible. Walpole's long period in office – just short of 21 years – effectively bedded in the office of Prime Minister. Despite the fact that few of his successors were able to rival his qualities, all of them were expected to fulfill the various functions which he had accumulated – of being the monarch's chief adviser and administrator, of presiding over the cabinet and of ensuring majority support in both Houses of Parliament of the polices which the King wished to pursue.

The nation over which they ruled, earlier regarded as being a rather peripheral power, was poised to play an increasingly important role on the European and even the world stage. At the beginning of the eighteenth century, it was still an overwhelmingly rural country. The population of England and Wales, in 1700, was probably under 6 million, 85 per cent of whom lived in villages or small market towns. The population of Ireland was about 2.5 million and of Scotland, just over 1 million, making a total of around 9 million. Half a million of these lived in London, the second largest English town being Norwich with around 30,000 inhabitants, followed by Bristol with 20,000 and Newcastle with 15,000. Future major cities such as Liverpool, Manchester, Birmingham and Leeds, all had fewer than 10,000 inhabitants. In Ireland, Dublin had 60,000, while Edinburgh had 35,000 and Glasgow 12,000 inhabitants. The Act of Union of 1707 had united the parliaments and administrations of England and Scotland, though Scottish law and many of its customs remained distinct, with Presbyterianism being the established religion. Ireland retained its own Parliament and administration, but was effectively treated as a colony of England, and was dominated by its largely absentee Protestant Anglo-Irish aristocracy. Economically, Britain was now a fast developing country, though large-scale industrialization was still in the future. It was, however, already a major commercial and trading power, the union with Scotland making it the largest free trade area in Europe, while the establishment of the Bank of England, in 1694, greatly facilitated the raising of loans, for both government and private activity. Urbanization was to proceed rapidly throughout the century, so that by 1800 one-third of the population were town dwellers, though the big population growth of the major towns and cities was only just getting under way by then.

In 1700, already, Britain was becoming a significant imperial power, with its 13 North American colonies, a scattering of islands in the West Indies, a settlement in Gambia and an important presence in India, at Bombay, Madras and Calcutta. The treaty of Utrecht, in 1713, brought Hudson's Bay, Nova Scotia, Newfoundland, St Kitts, Gibraltar and Minorca under British rule, while the British Navy was probably already the most powerful in the world. Even its military strength was at its peak, with a large, standing army raised during the reigns of William and Mary, which was still nearly 150,000 strong at the accession of George I. It was then, however, rapidly run down, the country henceforth relying more on subsidizing the armies of its allies in the field, rather than employing large numbers of its own troops in the many European wars in which it engaged. Both politically and economically, Britain at the beginning of the eighteenth century was probably the most dynamic of the European powers. This was the inheritance that Sir Robert Walpole took over in 1721.

Works consulted

Bigham, Clive (1925), *The Chief Ministers of England 920–1720*, London, John Murray.

Cook, Chris and John Stevenson (1988), *British Historical Facts 1688–1760*, London, Palgrave Macmillan.

Cook, Chris and John Stevenson (1980), *British Historical Facts 1760–1830*, London, Palgrave Macmillan.

Eccleshall, Robert and Graham Walker, eds. (1998), *Biographical Dictionary of British Prime Ministers*, London, Routledge.

Englefield, Dermot, Janet Seaton and Isobel White (1995), *Facts about the British Prime Ministers*, New York, H.W. Wilson Company.

O'Gorman, Frank (1997), *The Long Eighteenth Century: British Political and Social History 1688–1832*, London, Arnold.

Turberville, A.S. (1964), *English Men and Manners in the 18th Century*, 2nd edition, New York, Oxford University Press.

Part I
The 18th Century

1
Robert Walpole, First Earl of Orford – 'All These Men Have Their Price'

Despite his many qualities, Robert Walpole was not a particularly nice man. This is hinted at by the somewhat unwieldy title of the latest biography of him to appear, *The Great Man: Sir Robert Walpole – Scoundrel, Genius and Britain's First Prime Minister* (by Edward Pearce), and is amply corroborated by its text. But being nice has not been highly correlated with competence in high office: if it were, Lord Aberdeen would now rank higher than Gladstone, Baldwin higher than Churchill. Walpole was coarse, venal, ruthless and, at times, vindictive. Yet the fact that he was the longest serving, as well as the first, of Britain's 53 prime ministers (to date) strongly suggests that he was also one of the more effective.

Walpole was descended from a long line of country squires, who had been landowners in North Norfolk for 400 years. It was never one of the more prominent Norfolk families, but Robert's grandfather, Edward Walpole, a strong Royalist, was knighted at the restoration of Charles II in 1660 and was elected to the 'Cavalier' Parliament. He died prematurely, in 1667, leaving a 17-year-old son, Robert, to manage and extend the family estate, which he did to good effect, raising the annual rent-roll from £750 to £2500 over his lifetime. The elder Robert, usually known as Colonel Walpole because of his service in the Norfolk militia, was also knighted like his father, and for the last 11 years of his life represented the nearby constituency of Castle Rising in the House of Commons, thanks partly to the sponsorship of the Duke of Norfolk and his brother, Thomas Howard, who largely controlled the nomination for the seat. A man of some learning, he built up a notable library at his house at Houghton, and his wife, Mary Burwell, the daughter of another – more affluent – Norfolk squire, also had intellectual tastes. They had 17 children, 8 of whom died in infancy. The younger Robert Walpole, who was the fifth child and third son, was born at Houghton on 26 August 1676. Intended, as a younger son, for the Church, he was sent to board at the age of six, with the Rev. Richard Ransome, who ran an elementary school at Great Dunham,

Norfolk, from where he proceeded to Eton, as a King's Scholar, at the age of 13, though his age was falsely listed as 12, so as to qualify for the scholarship. While at Eton, he became close friends with his cousin, Charles Townshend, the scion of a much grander Norfolk family, who inherited a viscountcy while still in his teens. Townshend was to marry Robert's sister, Dorothy, and was later to become an important influence in his brother-in-law's political career. In 1696, at the age of 20, Robert went up to King's College, Cambridge, but resigned his scholarship two years later, when his elder brother Edward died, and his father summoned him home to run the family estates. He was now his father's heir, the second son – Burwell, a naval cadet – having died in 1690, aged 14, at the Battle of Beachy Head, in which the French defeated the combined Anglo-Dutch fleet. All thoughts of entering the Church were now quickly forgotten, and when Colonel Walpole died suddenly, on 18 November 1700, his son moved quickly to ensure that he took over his parliamentary seat. Within a week he had secured the backing of Thomas Howard, for what was expected to be an early by-election. A general election intervened, however, and in January 1701, he and Howard were elected unopposed as the two MPs for the borough. Howard was a Whig, as Walpole's father had been, and the new 24-year-old MP wore the same party colours.

Six months earlier, Walpole had got married to the 18-year-old Catherine Shorter, daughter of a Baltic timber merchant, from Kent, who had aristocratic connections through her mother. It was effectively an arranged marriage, Colonel Walpole having searched far and wide for a suitable consort for his son, who would bring in a sizeable dowry, and consolidate his social position. Yet Walpole was undoubtedly in love with his new wife, who was described by Walpole's first biographer, Archdeacon Coxe, writing in 1797, as 'a woman of exquisite beauty and accomplished manners' (Taylor, 2004). It did not, however, turn out to be a successful marriage. Catherine's extravagant tastes matched those of her husband's, and he soon got deeply into debt, not least because soon after inheriting Houghton Hall from his father, he embarked on extensive improvements to the house, which he was later to pull down to erect a far grander Palladian mansion in its place. Most of the time, however, he spent in London, where the couple lived, initially, in an apartment in Berkeley Street, in the house of Catherine's grandmother, Lady Philipps, where they entertained on an impressive scale. Catherine produced two sons and two daughters during the first six years of their marriage, but after that they drifted apart, both having numerous affairs. It was widely suspected that Robert may not have been the father of Catherine's fifth child, Horace Walpole (the noted author and aesthete), born in 1717, though he acknowledged him as his son.

As a young MP, Walpole soon established himself as an up-and-coming man. He was rapidly accepted in leading Whig circles, largely through the influence of his schoolboy friend, Charles Townshend, already the Lord Lieutenant of

Norfolk, and of his wife's aristocratic relatives. He was also to benefit from his connection to Sir Charles Turner, who had married his elder sister Mary. Turner's father, Sir John, a wealthy wine merchant, was the 'proprietor' of the two King's Lynn parliamentary seats, which he jointly represented with his son, Charles. As a favour to the Turners, Walpole, who soon mastered the procedures of the House of Commons, undertook the arduous task of steering through Parliament a Private Bill establishing a workhouse at King's Lynn. This proved a farsighted move, when, in 1702, he was forced to seek a new constituency. He desperately needed to raise money to pay his debts, and required the consent of his Uncle, Horatio Walpole, who was a trustee of his father's estate, to sell family property in Suffolk. Horatio agreed to this only on condition that he could take over his seat at Castle Rising. To this, Walpole reluctantly agreed, even though Horatio was a Tory, but Sir John came to his rescue, standing down at King's Lynn, which enabled Walpole to share the borough's representation with Charles Turner. They were returned unopposed, as Walpole was on 16 subsequent occasions. At two general elections, those of 1701 and 1710, however, he also contested the much more prestigious county constituency of Norfolk, but lost each time to Tory opponents.

The general election of 1702 was consequent on the death of William III, and the accession of Queen Anne. Unlike William, who was predisposed to the Whigs, the new Queen was known to favour the Tories, who obtained a significant majority in the election, leading to the eviction of Whig ministers from the government, which continued to be led by the virtually non-party Sidney (now Lord) Godolphin, as Lord High Treasurer. As most of the more prominent Whigs – including the surviving members of the 'Junto' who had dominated the government for much of William's reign* – were in the House of Lords, there was a dearth of talent on the Whig benches of the Commons, and Walpole soon assumed a prominent role. This was not only because of his superior debating skills and his easy mastery of parliamentary procedure but also because of his high popularity, which spread far beyond his core following of Whiggish Norfolk squires. As the historian Geoffrey Holmes put it:

> The young Robert Walpole was a man of easy temper and almost limitless good humour, endowed with what James Brydges [Paymaster-General in 1705–13] once called 'the most friendly nature I have known'. (Holmes, 1967, p. 231)

Walpole became a particular protégé of one of the 'Junto' lords,* Edward Russell, Earl of Orford, and his already close relationship with the steadily rising

---

*The five 'Junto' lords, three of whom were unsuccessfully impeached by their Tory opponents in 1701, were the Marquis of Wharton, the Earl of Orford, the Earl of Sunderland, the Earl of Halifax and Lord Somers.

Lord Townshend was further consolidated when, in 1705, he and Catherine moved into larger premises, in Dover Street, and invited his younger sister Dolly, 20 years old and a noted beauty, to stay with them for the winter season. She immediately attracted the attention of a number of notorious rakes, including another 'Junto' lord, the Marquis of Wharton. Catherine quarrelled with her, and she took herself off to the Wharton household, where Lady Wharton was well known for condoning her husband's infidelities. A furious Walpole raced round to Wharton's house, and peremptorily removed his sister, lodging her instead with the Townshends. Lady Townshend died soon afterwards, and within two years Townshend made Dolly his second wife. Townshend was also responsible for enrolling Walpole into the exclusive Kit-Cat club, the apex of Whig 'High Society'.

In the 1705 general election, the Whigs made extensive gains, finishing up on nearly equal terms with the Tories. Some prominent Whigs joined the Cabinet, and Walpole had his first taste of junior office, being appointed a member of the Council of the Lord High Admiral. This cabinet post was held by Prince George of Denmark, the Queen's husband, though the fleet was actually commanded by Admiral George Churchill, the brother of the Duke of Marlborough who, as Captain-General was the most powerful figure in the government. This appointment carried a salary of £1000 a year, which – though welcome – did not go very far towards relieving the debts, which both Robert and Catherine had accumulated due to their continuing extravagance. However, it brought Walpole into closer contact with leading governmental figures, including both Godolphin and Marlborough, who were impressed by his appetite for administration, and the clear and forthright way in which he expressed his views. He also continued to be an effective debater for the Whigs in the House of Commons, though there was some cooling of his relations with the 'Junto', who resented their continued exclusion from the cabinet, and who feared that Walpole was becoming a mere creature of Godolphin's. However, both Walpole and the Junto proved to be beneficiaries of the Act of Union with Scotland, forced through in 1707 against some resistance from the Tories. In the ensuing general election, in 1708, the Whigs were victorious, partly owing to their sweeping successes in the Scottish constituencies, and the Junto Lords returned to the Cabinet after an eight-year interval, while Walpole was appointed to the important post of Secretary-at-War, on the strong recommendation of Marlborough. In January 1710, he was appointed simultaneously to the post of Treasurer of the Navy, potentially a highly profitable office. This time – or so she claimed – it was at the strong urging to the Queen of Sarah, Duchess of Marlborough. Walpole thus assumed parliamentary responsibility for both the armed forces at a crucial period during the War of Spanish Succession.

Walpole took a prominent part in the impeachment proceedings against Dr Henry Sacherevell, a High Church and High Tory clergyman, who, in November

1709, preached a fiery sermon in St Paul's Cathedral in which he was held to have challenged the legitimacy of the Glorious Revolution and appeared to be advocating the claims to the throne of the 'Old Pretender', James Edward Stuart, the Catholic son of James II. Heavily applauded by his fellow Whigs, he made by far the most effective speech against Sacherevell in the Commons debate, which led to his trial before the House of Lords. A major *cause célèbre*, the move proved to be a serious miscalculation by the overconfident Whigs. A backlash soon built up in Sacherevell's favour: the London mob rioted on his behalf, he was widely seen as a martyr and even his strongest critics regarded the Commons' decision as an overreaction. When the case reached the House of Lords, which then had a strong Whig majority, their lordships took fright, and though they found him guilty, imposed only the mildest sentence. Public opinion swung against the Whigs, who were already losing support because of their insistence in continuing an unpopular war, and this finally emboldened the Queen to take decisive action against her increasingly over-bearing ministers. She had already replaced her long-standing friend and confidante, the Duchess of Marlborough, as her Chief Woman of the Bedchamber by the Tory-supporting Mrs Masham, and, in August 1710, she dismissed both Godolphin and Marlborough, forming a new and almost exclusively Tory government, led by Robert Harley (soon to become Earl of Oxford), with Henry St John (later Viscount Bolingbroke) as a Secretary of State. Walpole lost his post as Secretary-at-War, but continued for a few months more as Treasurer of the Navy, before resigning in sympathy with his fellow Whigs. No sooner was he in office, than Harley began secret negotiations with France, which led eventually to the Treaty of Utrecht, bringing an end to the war nearly three years later. A general election, held soon after, led to a crushing victory for the Tories, and Walpole, who chanced his arm by contesting, for a second time, the Norfolk county constituency, came bottom of the poll, though he was re-elected at King's Lynn.

The Tory government, after having unsuccessfully tried to tempt Walpole away from his fellow Whigs, soon proved nasty, and launched an investigation into his financial probity. The commissioners of public accounts reported to Parliament that he had accepted bribes from a friend, the banker Robert Mann, to whom he had awarded, while War Secretary, two lucrative forage contracts for the army in Scotland. He was expelled from the House of Commons and committed to the Tower of London in January 1712, a fate which actually seems to have given his political career a significant boost, as the historian Stephen Taylor suggests:

> Imprisonment turned Walpole into a national political figure and a Whig martyr. He was visited daily by the leading Whigs, a ballad composed in his honour described him as 'the Jewel in the *Tower* ... and at the King's

Lynn by-election he was triumphantly returned, defeating a local Tory. The Commons promptly declared his re-election void. (Taylor, 2004)

He was released from the Tower in July 1712, and remained out of Parliament until the general election of 1713, when he was returned unopposed for King's Lynn. Whether he was guilty as charged is doubtful, but the fact that – like many other ministers in this period – he left office a much wealthier man than when he entered suggests that there were ample grounds for suspicion. On his return to Parliament, Walpole resumed his role as one of the leading Whig speakers, and was well placed to benefit from the discomfiture of the Tories, after the death of Queen Anne, in August 1714. The Tory leaders, including both Oxford and Bolingbroke, had compromised themselves by entering into correspondence with the Pretender, and George I was determined, from the outset, to govern only with the Whigs, pushing the Tories into opposition for a period which was to last for 48 years. His first administration was effectively headed by General James Stanhope, as one of the two Secretaries of State, the other being Townshend, Walpole's brother in-law. Three of the 'Junto' lords, Wharton, Halifax and Sunderland, were included in prominent posts, while Marlborough regained his position as Captain-General, and sat in the Cabinet as Master of the Ordnance. Largely due to Townshend's advocacy, Walpole secured the highly lucrative post of Paymaster-General.

The new government, with Walpole taking the lead, lost no time in settling scores with its Tory predecessors. Oxford, Bolingbroke and the Duke of Ormonde (who had succeeded Marlborough as Captain-General in 1710) were impeached for treason. Ormonde and Bolingbroke fled to France, where the latter served for some time as Secretary of State with the Pretender, but Oxford was committed to the Tower. He was eventually acquitted when he came up for trial in 1717. No sooner had the three Tory leaders been impeached, than the 1715 Jacobite rebellion, in support of the Pretender, broke out in Scotland and Lancashire. It was easily defeated – the Pretender attracting very little support in the face of his refusal to give up his Catholic religion. Six peers had, however, assisted in the uprising, and Walpole, who had been promoted to First Lord of the Treasury and Chancellor of the Exchequer in October 1715, strongly urged their attainment and execution. George I, however, was inclined to clemency, and eventually only two of their number, Lords Derwentwater and Kenmure, were beheaded. Walpole made his implacable opposition to Jacobitism a central theme of his political career, and in truth was something of a 'witch-hunter'. He saw Jacobite plots everywhere, and cynically used the issue to discomfort his opponents, implying that all Tories – even those most publicly loyal to the Hanoverian succession – were Jacobites at heart.

Walpole remained a minister for three years – from August 1714 to October 1717 – during which time he accumulated a large sum of money, estimated by

J.H. Plumb at over £100,000 (roughly equivalent to £20m today). He suddenly became one of the richest men in the country, paying off his enormous debts and later enabling him to pull down Houghton Hall and build a magnificent Palladian replacement, which he filled with a fantastic array of paintings and other artistic treasures. Most of these finished up in the hands of Catherine the Great of Russia, when his grandson, George, sold them off in 1779. Today, they form the core of the Hermitage collection in St Petersburg. Walpole was by no means the only minister in British history to make money for himself by managing the country's finances. Yet he did it on a more exorbitant scale than any of his predecessors or successors, and of Britain's 53 Prime Ministers, to date, he remains the only one who raised himself to plutocrat status by this means. During this period, Walpole was the principal ministerial spokesman in the Commons, especially after Stanhope took a peerage, becoming Viscount Stanhope of Mahon. Yet he was probably no higher than number five or six in the unofficial ranking order of ministers, coming behind Stanhope, Townshend, the Earl of Sunderland and perhaps one or two others. Due to ill health, he played little part in the passage of the Septennial Act, in 1716, though this legislation, which increased the parliamentary term of office from three years to seven, was later to prove a major factor in enabling him to remain in power as Prime Minister for a record 21 years.

Throughout his reign of nearly 13 years, George I, who remained Elector of Hanover, made lengthy periodic visits (seven in all) to his German dominions, causing some concern to his British subjects, many of whom felt he was subordinating British interests to those of Hanover. This was particularly true of the visit which he made between July 1716 and the following January, when he took Stanhope with him, and they were later joined by Sunderland. Hanover had joined Charles XII of Sweden in the Great Northern War against Peter I of Russia, Christian V of Denmark and Augustus of Saxony-Poland, as George was hopeful of annexing new territories to his Electorate. Anxious to protect his rear, he sought an alliance with Britain's traditional enemy France, whose Regent following the death of Louis XIV, the Duke of Orleans, was happy to comply. Stanhope sent instructions to Townshend to negotiate such an alliance, which would also include the Netherlands. Townshend, who doubted the wisdom of the move, was somewhat dilatory in carrying it out. Stanhope, prompted by Sunderland, who lusted after Townshend's position as Secretary of State, wrote to him saying that the King wished to relieve him of the post and offering instead the Lord Lieutenancy of Ireland. Townshend reluctantly accepted, but was dismissed from this post a few months later, in April 1717, when he voted against a government bill in the Lords. Walpole then resigned in sympathy with his brother-in-law; his post as First Lord of the Treasury and Chancellor of the Exchequer being taken by Stanhope, while Sunderland and the essayist Joseph Addison became the two Secretaries of State. This was effectively a new government, known to history as the Stanhope-Sunderland administration. It was thoroughly Whig, but the Whigs were now split, as Townshend and Walpole carried their own faction, which included Lord Orford, William Pulteney, Paul Methuen and the second Duke of Devonshire, all former ministers, into opposition with them. The following three years were marked by growing bitterness between Walpole and Stanhope and Sunderland. He did everything he could to undermine their power in the hope of forcing his own return to office, while carefully avoiding giving gratuitous offence to the King.

In opposing the government, the Walpolites did not disdain from cooperating with the Tories on several occasions. They also benefited from the support of the Prince of Wales, the future George II, who was at odds with his father, and who encouraged his own band of supporters in the Commons to vote with the 'opposition Whigs'. One issue on which they succeeded in defeating the government was on the repeal of the Corporation and Tests Acts, dating from the reign of Charles II, which barred Protestant Dissenters (later known as Non-Conformists) from public office. The Whigs had traditionally been supporters of religious toleration, and Stanhope proposed a Bill to restore the Dissenters' rights, but Walpole – nothing if not an opportunist – calculated that the weight of opinion of the Church of England (which was vehemently opposed to repeal) was very much greater. He therefore sided with the Tories in opposing the government's measure, which it was forced to withdraw. A much more serious defeat for Stanhope's government was over the Peerage Bill of 1719. This was an attempt by Stanhope and his associates to perpetuate their rule by freezing the current membership of the House of Lords, where they enjoyed a comfortable majority. In perhaps the outstanding parliamentary performance of his entire career, Walpole rallied the Commons to stand up for its own rights, which he maintained would be prejudiced by creating a permanent oligarchy in the Upper House, responsible to nobody, neither the electors nor, indeed, the King. Perhaps his conclusive argument, so far as many MPs were concerned, was his appeal to their own self-interest and ambitions. Walpole had already published a swingeing attack on the Bill in a pamphlet entitled *Thoughts of a Member of the Lower House,* in which he quoted the words of a typical 'country' Member: 'Shall I consent to the shutting the door upon my family ever coming into the House of Lords?' He returned to this theme in his speech. The result was a humiliating rebuff to Stanhope, whose Bill was defeated by 269 votes to 177, with the aid of numerous defections from normally loyal supporters of the government.

Stanhope concluded that in order to safeguard his ministry, he would have to lure back the opposition Whigs, and, in June 1720, both Townshend and Walpole, and a handful of their supporters, rejoined the government. Several of their prominent followers, however, notably William Pulteney, who had been Walpole's able 'lieutenant' in the Commons, were left out, much to their chagrin. Even Townshend and Walpole had to content themselves with more menial offices than they had held before. Townshend now became Lord President of the Council, but Walpole was fobbed of with the Paymaster-Generalship, a lucrative but not very senior post. Their position in the government was not a strong one – they were deeply distrusted by both Stanhope and Sunderland, and also – to some extent – by George I.

It now appeared as if Stanhope, who enjoyed the full confidence of the King, was set to remain in power for many years. If this had been the case, he – and not Walpole – would almost certainly have gone down in history as Britain's first Prime Minister. It was not to be – largely because of the events which came to be known as the 'South Sea Bubble'. The South Sea Company had been established in 1711, with the support of Harley (Oxford), and was initially seen as a Tory rival to the Whig-sponsored Bank of England and East India Company. It was assured of large profits by the Treaty of Utrecht (1713), which awarded Britain the *assiento* (the monopoly of the slave trade with Spanish America) and the right to send one ship a year to trade with the Spanish colonies. In

February 1720 Parliament approved a measure, promoted by Stanhope and Sunderland, designed to reduce the rate of interest on the National Debt, which had become a heavy burden as a result of the two long wars against France. The proposal was that three-fifths of the debt should be converted into South Sea Company stock, the remainder being held by the Bank and the East India Company. The directors of the South Sea Company proceeded to 'talk up' the value of their stock, which led to a feverish bout of speculation, in which many other new companies of doubtful provenance were formed, and their shares also were snapped up by large numbers of people anxious to get rich quick. Many already wealthy people, including George I, who invested, and lost, the enormous sum of £56,000 (over £11million in today's money), also bought into the Company, seeing their investments rise to dizzy heights, and then fall vertiginously when, inevitably, the bubble burst. The directors of the company paid bribes to ministers and court officials on a large scale and were undoubtedly guilty of a wide range of fraudulent practices.

Thousands of people were ruined, and some, at least, of those who had profited illegally from their transactions now had to face the reckoning. The House of Commons took the lead in demanding retribution, not least on those who were themselves Members of the House. Chief among these was the Chancellor of the Exchequer, John Aislabie, who was expelled from the House and sent to the Tower of London, after the passage of a motion that he had been guilty of 'most notorious, dangerous and infamous corruption'. He was stripped of all his ill-gotten gains, though he was eventually allowed to keep all the property he had owned before becoming Chancellor, and retired to live quietly on his estate in Yorkshire. The Postmaster-General, James Craggs the elder, committed suicide when faced with criminal charges, while his son, James Craggs the younger, one of the two Secretaries of State, who was also deeply implicated, fortuitously died of smallpox at the same time. William Stanhope, the Secretary of the Treasury, escaped censure by only three votes after George I had intervened on his behalf. His cousin James Stanhope, the effective leader of the government, was less lucky. Though himself innocent of any wrong-doing, he faced fierce criticism in the House of Lords, and burst a blood vessel while making an impassioned speech in his own defence, dying of a stroke shortly afterwards.

The chief beneficiary of the 'Bubble' was undoubtedly Walpole, who had originally strongly opposed the scheme to sell off the National Debt to the Company, though he had then unwisely invested in it and narrowly avoided financial ruin when his banker failed to act on his instructions sharply to increase his stake a few days before the final crash. He was called in by George I to resume his earlier posts as First Lord of the Treasury and Chancellor, and calmly proceeded to introduce measures to restore some stability to financial markets. Their apparent success greatly added to his reputation, and he was now seen for the first time as one of, if not yet *the*, leading ministers of the King. Walpole did not restrict himself to trying to restore the damage to the national finances, but also sought, wherever possible, to protect the reputations of fellow ministers and royal courtiers suspected of accepting bribes from the Company. Chief among these was his great rival, John Spencer, the Earl of Sunderland, who aspired to take over James Stanhope's role at the head of the government. Sunderland was very close to the King, and Walpole presumably calculated that it would do him no harm in the King's eyes if he threw him a lifebelt. Accordingly, when Sunderland was charged with corruption before the House of Commons, Walpole sprang to his defence, and in a brilliant speech – on 15 March 1721 – secured a vote for acquittal by 233 votes to 172. For this, and several other efforts which he made to 'screen' suspected villains, Walpole acquired the nickname of 'Skreenmaster-General'. This did him no good with the more high-minded Whigs, but won him invaluable support in high places. Then in April 1722, Sunderland suddenly died, which removed another serious rival from his path. There were now only two other ministers who might challenge his seniority in the government. These were the two Secretaries of State, Townshend and John, Lord Carteret, the very able former Ambassador to Sweden, who had negotiated an end to the Great Northern War in 1719–20. An excellent linguist, Carteret was on the inside track with George I, with whom he was able to converse in fluent German.

Traditionally, Walpole's period as 'Prime Minister' has been dated from his appointment, for the second time, as First Lord of the Treasury, on 3 April 1721. By this reckoning, his total time as PM was almost 21 years. In reality, his primacy was established only later, perhaps after both these ministers had resigned, or been ejected from the government, Carteret in 1724, and Townshend in 1730, though the death of Sunderland, on 19 April 1722, has also been suggested as a plausible date (see Plumb, 1956, p. 378, and Taylor, 1998, pp. 3–5). Where Walpole was pre-eminent, right from the beginning, was in the House of Commons, where he had no rival. (Indeed, throughout his period in office he was either the only Cabinet minister in the Commons, or – at most – shared this distinction with only one other.) Walpole was adamant that he must lead the government from the Commons, and strongly resisted pressure from George I to accept a peerage. In 1724, however, he persuaded the monarch to bestow the honour instead on his eldest son, Robert, who became Baron Walpole of Walpole.

Initially, Walpole's relationship with George I was rather distant, but he set himself assiduously to earn the goodwill of his monarch. This was greatly assisted by his assiduity in pursuing Francis Atterbury, the Bishop of Rochester, who was involved in a plot to assist a Jacobite invasion in 1722, led by the Duke of Ormonde. The plot came to nothing, and the case against Bishop Atterbury was too slender for him to be prosecuted for treason. Instead, Walpole introduced a 'bill of pains and penalties' into Parliament, for the passage of which it was only necessary to secure a parliamentary majority rather than submitting the partly manufactured evidence, which Walpole had assembled, to a court of law. The vote went against Atterbury, and he was stripped of his bishopric and exiled to Brussels, and then to France, where he shortly entered the service of the Pretender, thereby virtually acknowledging his guilt. Within the ministry, a largely silent struggle began for influence with the King, pitching the Townshend–Walpole faction against the followers of the late Earl of Sunderland, of whom the effective leader was Carteret. The two Secretaries of State, Townsend and Carteret, were jointly responsible for foreign policy and fierce rivalry opened up between them. They openly quarrelled over relations with both France and Russia, and particularly over plans to marry off the daughter of the King's mistress, the Countess Von Platen, into a leading French aristocratic family. Carteret's protégé, the British Ambassador to the French court, Sir Luke Schaub, was blamed by George I for mishandling the negotiations and was dismissed in April 1724, and replaced by Walpole's younger brother Horatio, while Carteret himself was sacked two months later, but was compensated by being appointed Lord Lieutenant of Ireland.

William Pulteney, who had been Walpole's chief supporter in the House of Commons was grievously disappointed not to have been appointed to replace Carteret as Secretary of State, and bitterly blamed Walpole for not using his influence on his behalf. Instead, Walpole successfully pushed the claims of the young Duke of Newcastle, whose initial appeal to Walpole rested largely on his control, as a landed grandee, of a string of several parliamentary constituencies.

Walpole's neglect of Pulteney, as well as his hostility to Carteret, has often been attributed to his unwillingness to accept men of high talent as his colleagues, fearing that they would become serious rivals to him. Instead, he preferred men of rather lesser ability, on whose personal loyalty he could rely. Newcastle, and his more able younger brother, Henry Pelham, both of whom held senior posts throughout the remainder of Walpole's long period in office, were the most prominent of these. As for Pulteney, he became completely estranged from Walpole, and set himself up as the leader of a growing group of 'opposition' or 'country' Whigs, who consistently harassed the government in a similar fashion to Walpole's own conduct against Stanhope's administration in 1717–20. Pulteney received heavyweight support from Bolingbroke, who returned to Britain with a royal pardon in 1723, having broken with the Pretender. Walpole succeeded in maintaining Bolingbroke's exclusion from the House of Lords, but he remained an influential figure through his writings, particularly in the magazine *The Craftsman*, to which Pulteney was also a leading contributor, and which ceaselessly and pungently criticized the 'corruption' of Walpole's administration.

The corruption of which they complained was, above all, linked to his successful methods for obtaining and keeping control of the House of Commons. Every possible inducement was offered to those prepared to sell their votes – either at a constituency level – or within the Commons. As his latest biographer puts it:

> There had been places and placemen before, but Walpole was the most systematic and unfastidious player of that game electorally and inside the House of Commons itself ... He operated a species of private interest/public expenditure mini-welfare state for anyone able to elect a Member or persuade one to vote right. (Pearce, pp. 207, 383)

Nor did Walpole neglect the House of Lords, over whom he, in practice, exercised greater control than he was ever able to achieve in the Commons. Large number of peers were granted places or pensions either for themselves or for their relatives or friends, and Walpole for long achieved conspicuous success in 'fixing' the election of Scottish Representative Peers, who contributed 16 of the 200-odd members of the Upper House. Another 26 seats were held by Archbishops and Bishops, and Walpole was able to ensure, through his adviser on ecclesiastical appointments, Bishop Edmund Gibson, that virtually all bishoprics and other senior Church appointments went to convinced Whigs. By this means, Walpole was also able to counteract the influence within the Church of the lower clergy, the great majority of whom were Tories. The more ambitious of these soon learnt on which side their bread was buttered and moderated or dissimulated their opinions.

The expression 'every man has his price' has been widely attributed to Walpole, who was undoubtedly a cynic of a high order. His actual words, referring to a specific group of opposition MPs were 'All these men have their price.' In partial mitigation, it should be remembered that this was nearly 200 years before MPs were paid a salary, and long before peers received attendance allowances. Many upright citizens at that time took the view that it was acceptable for them to make some profit from their political activities. It would be a mistake, however, to conclude that it was only through corruption that Walpole was able to maintain his parliamentary primacy for so long. At no time did he have an assured majority in the Commons, where a substantial number of Members did not have any firm party allegiance or venal motive for supporting the government. Time and again Walpole was able to win the support of a majority of these 'independent' members, through his persuasive if seldom brilliant oratory, his commonsense arguments and the trouble he took to maintain good relations with even the humblest of MPs. Most of these were country squires, and Walpole presented himself as a typical plain, blunt Norfolk squire, more interested in hunting and shooting than in intellectual pursuits.

Walpole characterized himself as 'no saint, no Spartan, no reformer'. His policy objectives were relatively modest, and have been best summarized as 'security, stability and low taxation' (O'Gorman, 1997, p. 80). The key to all three of these was, in Walpole's view, peace, and the need to keep Britain out of foreign conflicts, following the almost continuous two decades of war against France after the 'Glorious Revolution', which had left the country a heavy burden of debt. Throughout the 1720s, Townshend as Secretary of State was primarily responsible for conducting foreign policy, but initially at least, he and Walpole were at one in their desire to maintain peace and to prioritize the pursuit of friendship with Britain's traditional enemy France, with whom a treaty of alliance had been signed, under Stanhope, in 1717. The maintenance of peace enabled Walpole to concentrate on economic and financial improvements, and to abate the heavy level of taxation which he had inherited. Deft management of the national debt (including the establishment of a 'sinking fund', some half a century before the Younger Pitt adopted the same device to help reduce the large accumulated debts from the American War of Independence) allowed him to reduce the interest paid by the government from 5 per cent to 4 per cent. During his ministry the total debt was reduced by £6.25 million, and the annual interest charge fell from £2.57 million to £1.89 million (Taylor, 2004). He was particularly anxious to reduce the Land Tax, which bore heavily on his own class of country landowners, and he sought to achieve this by reducing public expenditure, cracking down on smuggling and transferring the tax burden from direct to indirect taxation. In 1731–32, he was able to bring the Land Tax down to 1s. in the pound, the lowest it had ever been since its introduction under William III. (Prior to this it had fluctuated between 2s. and 4s. in the pound.) He was only able to achieve this by re-imposing a salt duty, which affected everybody, but bore down most heavily on those with the smallest incomes.

In the final years of George I's reign, he came more and more to depend on Walpole, and their relations became much warmer. In 1725, he was made a Knight of the Bath, and two years later, of the Garter, the large star of which he proudly bore on his breast in all the numerous portraits which were painted of him. By contrast, however, the Prince of Wales, who was often (like most Hanoverian heirs to the throne) at loggerheads with his father, and ran an 'alternative' court based at Leicester House (the site of the modern Leicester Square), became increasingly hostile to him. Walpole, however, was careful to build up a good relationship with his shrewd and highly intelligent wife, Caroline of Brandenburg-Anspach. Other ambitious politicians made the mistake of cultivating instead the Prince's mistress, Henrietta Howard, whose influence over the Prince did not extend beyond the bedchamber. When George I unexpectedly died, aged 67, during a visit to Hanover, on 11 June 1727, the general expectation, shared by Walpole himself, was that the new King George II would rapidly dispense with his services. This seemed to be confirmed when he received a cold message from the King to 'Go to Chiswick and take your directions from Sir Spencer Compton.' Compton, who was more of a courtier than politician, was Speaker of the House of Commons, and had been Treasurer to the Prince of Wales. It was certainly the King's intention to appoint him in Walpole's place, but he failed abysmally to live up to expectations. Asked to draft the King's declaration to the Privy Council on ascending the throne, he found this beyond his capacity and called in Walpole to do it for him. The King also sought Walpole's advice on seeking parliamentary approval for a new Civil List, and was delighted when Walpole proposed that he should ask for £800,000 a year – £100,000 more than what his father had received – plus £100,000 for the Queen. Within three weeks, Compton threw in his hand, and Walpole's government was confirmed in office, with Compton (who was created Lord Wilmington), later becoming Lord Privy Seal, and then Lord President of the Council. Walpole's survival was generally attributed to Caroline's spirited pleas to her husband, who – spurning her as a lover – was the more disposed to follow her advice on public affairs.

The early years of George II's reign proved to be the zenith of Walpole's power and influence. One mark of this was his eclipse of Townshend, who, from being his close friend and sponsor, had sometimes become a fractious rival, particularly the death of Dolly Townshend, in 1726, severed their warm familial relationship. Walpole is reported by Lord Macaulay as saying: 'The firm is now going to be the firm of Walpole and Townsend, and not the firm of Townshend and Walpole as it used to be.' On one occasion the two men actually came to blows and even put their hands on their swords, only to be restrained by onlookers. Their views on foreign policy also began to diverge gradually, Townshend believing that the new alliance with France should take preference over all other considerations, even to the extent of siding with her against Britain's traditional ally, Austria. This Walpole, and Townshend's fellow Secretary of State, the Duke of Newcastle, refused to do, and they succeeded in over-ruling him, with the support of the Queen, leading to Townshend's resignation in 1730. He retired to his Norfolk estate, where he spent the eight remaining years of his life in pioneering experiments in crop rotation, earning himself the nickname of 'Turnip Townshend'. Walpole seized his opportunity, and persuaded George II to appoint one of his own cronies, Lord Harrington, in his place. He even prevailed upon the reluctant King to dismiss Carteret from his post as viceroy (Lord Lieutenant) of Ireland, and from now on the ministerial team consisted predominantly of Walpole's men. His closest collaborators were the Pelham brothers – the Duke of Newcastle continuing as the other Secretary of State, and Henry Pelham, the only other cabinet minister in the Commons, as Paymaster-General. It was now that Walpole became a popular public figure, much better known than any other politician, and his features became generally familiar, owing to the new vogue of publishing prints, whose display in shop-windows meant that they were seen by many more people than actually purchased them. He was widely dubbed as 'the Great Man', not altogether an ironic comment on his wide girth, and the term of 'Prime Minister', previously employed pejoratively by his critics, and those of earlier dominant ministers, such as Godolphin and Harley, now became a more neutral description, used as much by his friends as his enemies.

George II, essentially a lazy man, who took little interest in administration, and who was mainly interested in military and foreign affairs, as well as in his beloved Electorate of Hanover, came to depend heavily on Walpole, and strongly backed him, despite his initial dislike. One of their few disagreements was over the War of Polish Succession, which broke out in 1733, with France backing the claims of Stanislaw

Leszcynski, the father-in-law of Louis XV, while Austria and Russia supported Augustus II of Saxony. Britain was obliged to go to the support of Austria, under the Treaty of Vienna, signed in 1731, and George II was anxious to do so, sensing the possibility of adding to his German dominions at the expense of other German states allied to France. There was also considerable backing in Parliament for British intervention, not only from Tories but also from many Whigs. Yet Walpole was adamant that no British interest was involved in the conflict, and succeeded in carrying the point. When the War ended within two years, Walpole was able to boast that 50,000 had been slain during the conflict, but that not a drop of British blood had been spilled. Augustus was confirmed as King of Poland, but France and Spain both made territorial gains at Austria's expense, including the Duchy of Lorraine, which was given to Stanislaw as compensation for the loss of his throne, but was to revert to France on his death.

Up until 1733, Walpole's reputation rested largely on his handling of financial affairs, and his success in reducing taxation. In that year, however, he overreached himself with his proposal to end customs charges (largely circumvented by smuggling) on tobacco and wine and the substitution of excise duties. This was substantially based on his much earlier legislation concerning tea, coffee and chocolate. The proposal was that all imports should be put into bonded warehouses and only released when excise duties were collected. He estimated that government revenue would increase by some £300,000 a year, helping him to keep the Land Tax low. Yet he seriously underestimated the degree of opposition which his proposal would provoke. The tobacco merchants, many of whom were deeply implicated in fraud, organized a spirited campaign against his Tobacco Excise Bill, claiming it would lead to a massive expansion of the Excise Service, with 'arbitrary powers of search', which would be an attack on 'English liberties' (Taylor, 2004). Their arguments resonated with many MPs, and Walpole saw his parliamentary majority (normally over 100) plunge to a mere 17 votes on a motion to receive a petition against the Bill from the City of London. He promptly dropped the Bill, a personal humiliation, from which he extricated himself with some skill. He remained in office for a further eight years, but in retrospect it appears as the first in a long series of setbacks which eventually led to his downfall.

In the subsequent general election, of 1734, Taylor writes: 'There is little doubt that, in what was one of the most contested elections of the century, most of the electorate voted against Walpole's ministry' (Taylor, 2004). He was saved by the fact that most of the 'rotten boroughs', in particular those in Cornwall and Scotland, returned MPs who were his supporters. His majority – just over 90 – remained substantially intact, but the opposition was clearly strengthened in the new Parliament, where it was reinforced by the election of several forceful younger MPs, such as William Pitt (later Lord Chatham) and his brother-in-law, George Grenville, both later prime ministers. It nevertheless remained seriously divided, and was seldom able to mount an effective challenge to Walpole in the Commons. Even on those occasions when it was able to pass Bills restricting the number of placemen in Parliament, Walpole was able to reverse the decision when the Bills reached the Lords.

Outside Parliament, the government's critics (both Tories and Opposition Whigs) had greater success in denting its reputation and that of Walpole, in particular. Their periodicals, notably but not only *The Craftsman*, were more lively and better written than those, often helped by lavish government subsidies, which supported Walpole, while most of the leading authors of the time, joined in lampooning the over-mighty Prime Minister, including Defoe,

Swift, Pope, Fielding and Dr Johnson. He was ridiculed both as Peacham, and MacHeath in John Gay's *The Beggar's Opera*, and as Flimflam in *Gulliver's Travels*. They largely succeeded in implanting the notion that Walpole's rule was based on corruption, and dubbed his system of government 'the Robinocracy'. Nevertheless, some of Walpole's most inveterate enemies began to tire of the struggle. Bolingbroke packed up and went back to France in 1736, while Pulteney hedged his bets by hinting at a willingness to end his differences with Walpole in exchange for being re-admitted into the government. Despite this, no deal was, however, concluded.

In 1736, the system of personal support which Walpole had painstakingly constructed began to unravel. In arithmetical terms, the most serious was the undermining of his previous dominance over the Scots, which contributed largely to his majority in both Houses of Parliament. The trigger for this was a riot in Edinburgh, which had been forcefully put down by Colonel John Porteus, the commander of the Edinburgh city guard, whose soldiers fired on and killed six demonstrators. He was subsequently tried, found guilty of murder and sentenced to death, but received a royal reprieve. A mob then stormed the gaol in which he was held, seized him and hanged him in the street. Ministers then drew up a 'bill of pains and penalties' to punish the city of Edinburgh, which was toned down by Walpole, so that the only penalty actually imposed was the barring from office of the City Provost, Andrew Wilson. In the process, however, Walpole fatally alienated the Duke of Argyll and his brother, the Earl of Ilay, on whom he had previously relied for organizing the Whig electoral interest in Scotland.

Almost equally serious was the alienation of Frederick, Prince of Wales, who – like his father before him – was at daggers' drawn with both the King and the Queen – and was organizing an alternative court at Leicester House, to which opposition politicians flocked. His main disagreement with his father was over what he regarded as a mean provision for himself in the Civil List, but he widened this out into general opposition to government policies. As Duke of Cornwall, he controlled a large number of parliamentary boroughs in the county, whose MPs normally deferred to his wishes in casting their votes. In the same year, Walpole fell out with his close collaborator on Church affairs, Edmund Gibson, now Bishop of London, and with several other bishops, on whose support in the House of Lords he had previously depended. They were upset by three government bills, with which they disagreed, particularly the Quaker Tithe Bill, which was designed to give limited relief to members of the Society of Friends who suffered because of their conscientious objection to paying tithes to the Church of England. The Bill was defeated in the House of Lords, with all the bishops present voting against, and Gibson promptly resigned as Walpole's ecclesiastical adviser. The following year, Queen Caroline, who had been his strongest and most consistent supporter at Court, died. George II continued to favour Walpole, but no longer so firmly as hitherto. Another death occurred in 1737 – that of Walpole's long-estranged wife Catherine. After the minimum 'decent' interval – a mere six months – Walpole married a second time, to his long-time mistress, Molly Skerrett, who had borne him a daughter, Maria, 13 years earlier. Walpole was devoted to Molly, but they were to enjoy barely three months of marital bliss. She died in childbirth, in June 1738, aged 36. Walpole was devastated, and never fully recovered from his loss.

Yet the main factor leading to Walpole's eventual loss of power was the breakdown of his 'peace at any price' policy, which had left Britain dangerously isolated in Europe, after his refusal to take sides in the War of Polish Succession. In the following years tension built up between Britain and Spain, whose coastguards in the Caribbean enforced the right of search over British ships suspected of smuggling or piracy. Often the searches were carried out in a brutal fashion, with damage to British lives and property. British merchants began to petition the House of Commons for support, amid strident demands, led by the opposition Whigs, for war on Spain. The pressure became almost irresistible, when a Captain Robert Jenkins appeared before a committee of the House brandishing his own severed ear, which he alleged had been cut off by Spanish coastguards who had boarded his ship. Walpole sought to head off the demands by seeking an amicable settlement with Spain, which resulted in the Convention of Pardo, negotiated in January 1739. This was only narrowly passed in both Houses of Parliament. When the Convention broke down, with neither side having fulfilled all its obligations, Walpole could no longer resist pressure from his Cabinet colleagues and acquiesced in a declaration of war, in October 1739. The 'War of Jenkins' Ear', as it was popularly known, soon merged into the War of Austrian Succession, in which France, Spain and Prussia contended with Austria and Britain. It lasted until 1748, and ended with the inconclusive Treaty of Aix-la-Chapelle, the main consequence of which was the confirmation of 'great power' status for Prussia. Walpole grumpily refused to take responsibility for prosecuting the war, saying to the Duke of Newcastle, 'This war is yours, you have had the conduct of it, I wish you joy of it.' Nevertheless, the early stages of the war went very badly, and this inevitably contributed further to the attrition of Walpole's authority.

If there was a dominant issue in the general election which took place in the early summer of 1741, it was for or against 'Robin' Walpole. Heavy losses in Cornwall and Scotland, influenced respectively by the Prince of Wales and the Duke of Argyll, cut heavily into the government's nominal majority, which was now estimated at 16, with 23 seats vacant or contested, and to be determined by the Commons itself. The House was not due to meet until December, but already by the autumn there were credible rumours that senior ministers, notably Newcastle and Lord Hardwicke, the Lord Chancellor, were negotiating with Carteret and Pulteney to form a broader government, excluding Walpole.

When Parliament did meet, Walpole with 'an impressive and memorable speech' (Taylor, 2004) just held off a motion for a secret committee to investigate the conduct of the war, which was effectively a motion of no confidence. But the margin was only 253 votes to 250, and within a couple of weeks he resigned, on 11 February 1742, following two defeats on an election petition concerning the Chippenham constituency. He had accepted a peerage, becoming the Earl of Orford, a title which he took over from his former 'Junto' mentor, who had died without surviving issue in 1727. He soon made clear his lack of esteem for the Upper House: meeting up with Pulteney who had been ennobled shortly after, he said 'My Lord Bath, you and I are now two as insignificant men as any in England' (Turberville, 1957, p. 220).

Nevertheless, he used his influence with the King to secure a warrant recognizing the legitimacy of his daughter by Molly Skerrett, who was henceforth known as Lady Maria Walpole, and subsequently married into the Churchill family.

The removal of Walpole after more than two decades in office was an event of the highest public significance. The intrigues leading up to it were almost certainly parodied in the famous nursery rhyme, *Who killed Cock Robin?* the first written record of which dates from 1744 (Opie and Opie, pp. 130–3). George II reverted to Sir Spencer Compton, now Lord Wilmington, his first choice in 1727, to replace Walpole as First Lord of the Treasury. He became the nominal head of the new government, but the dominant figure was Carteret, who reclaimed his place as a Secretary of State. Otherwise, the main posts continued to be held by Walpole's senior ministers. Pulteney, now the Earl of Bath, declined for the moment to serve, in the evident hope that he would eventually be asked to form a government of his own. Walpole retired to Houghton to live among the splendours of his art collection, but continued to bombard his former close associates, notably the Pelham brothers, with advice as to how they should conduct the government, and in particular on how to ensure that the succession, as Wilmington's health rapidly deteriorated, went to one of them rather than to Pulteney. In return, they exerted themselves to head off parliamentary enquiries designed to arraign the former Prime Minister for abuses of power and for enriching himself at the public expense. His health was not good, he suffered from kidney stones and he was weakened by responding to an appeal from the King to travel to London to advise him during a cabinet dispute between Carteret (now the Earl of Granville) and the Pelhams, which was resolved, before his arrival, by Granville's resignation, in November 1744 (see Chapter 3). Too ill to return to Norfolk, Walpole died at his London home in Arlington Street, Mayfair, from kidney failure, on 18 March 1745.

Modern readers instinctively recoil from Walpole's methods, but few would now deny that – within the limits he set himself – he was remarkably successful in achieving his aims of peace, stability and economy. He left the country – and the Hanoverian dynasty – in a much stronger position than he had found it. The relative ease with which it met the greatest challenge it had faced in several decades – the 1745 rebellion of the Young Pretender – within a few months of his death is a tribute to the soundness of his policies. His claim to be accounted as the first Prime Minister has on occasion been questioned, but few can deny that he re-moulded and largely enhanced the office so that he was able to play the dual role of representing the King in Parliament and Parliament 'in the [royal] closet' (Holmes, 1974, p. 46). His long tenure set a pattern which was to be followed by all his successors, even though few of them were as dominant as he. Perhaps the most perceptive estimate of his qualities was that made by a much later Prime Minister, and one who was far less successful, the Earl of Rosebery. Writing in his biography of the Elder Pitt, he wrote of Walpole:

> He had the advantage of being brought up as a younger son to work, and thus he gained that self-reliance and pertinacious industry which served him so well through long years of high office. From the beginning to the end he was primarily a man of business. Had he not been a politician it cannot be doubted that he would have been a great merchant or a great financier. And, though his lot was cast in politics, a man of business he essentially remained ... His first object was to carry on the business of the country in a business spirit, as economically and as peacefully as possible ... a hard-working man with practical knowledge of affairs and strong common sense; a sagacious man who hated extremes. He had besides the highest qualities of a parliamentary leader ... he had dauntless courage and imperturbable temper. (Rosebery, 1910, pp. 144–6)

Works consulted

Black, Jeremy (2001), *Walpole in Power,* London, Sutton Publishing.

Cannon, John (2004), 'George II (1683–1760)', *Oxford Dictionary of National Biography,* Oxford, OUP.

Hill, Brian W. (1989) *Sir Robert Walpole: 'Sole and Prime Minister',* London, Hamish Hamilton.

Holmes, Geoffrey (1967), *British Politics in the Reign of Anne,* London, Palgrave Macmillan.

Holmes, Geoffrey (1974), 'Sir Robert Walpole', in Herbert Van Thal (ed.), *The Prime Ministers,* Volume I, London, Allen & Unwin.

O'Gorman, Frank (1997), *The Long Eighteenth Century,* London, Arnold.

Opie, Iona and Opie, Peter (1973), *The Oxford Dictionary of Nursery Rhymes,* Oxford, Clarendon Press.

Pearce, Edward (2007), *The Great Man: Sir Robert Walpole – Scoundrel, Genius and Britain's First Prime Minister,* London, Jonathan Cape.

Plumb, J.H. (1956), *Sir Robert Walpole: The Making of a Statesman,* London, Cresset Press.

Plumb, J.H. (1960), *Sir Robert Walpole: The King's Minister,* London, Cresset Press.

Plumb, J.H. (1967), *The Growth of Political Stability in England 1675–1725*, London, Palgrave Macmillan.

Rosebery, Lord (1910), *Chatham*, London, A.L. Humphreys.

Taylor, Stephen (1998), 'Robert Walpole, First Earl of Orford', *Biographical Dictionary of British Prime Ministers*, London, Routledge.

Taylor, Stephen (2004), 'Walpole, Robert, First Earl of Orford (1676–1745)', *Oxford Dictionary of National Biography*, Oxford, OUP.

Turberville, A.S. (1957), *English Men and Manners in the 18th Century*, New York, OUP.

Wilson, Harold (1977), *A Prime Minister on Prime Ministers*, London, Weidenfeld & Nicolson.

2
Spencer Compton, First Earl of Wilmington – 'George II's Favourite Nonentity'

The man usually credited with having been Britain's second Prime Minister is a somewhat shadowy figure. No full-length biography of him has ever appeared, and most accounts of his career have largely depended on passing – and usually acerbic – references in the memoirs of such contemporaries as Horace Walpole, Lord Hervey, Lord Chesterfield and Mr Speaker Onslow. The almost unanimous conclusion has been that he was not really up to the job, and that he owed his preferment almost entirely to the inflated view which King George II held of his abilities.

Spencer Compton was born in 1673 – the exact date is unknown – at the family seat at Compton Wynyates, in Warwickshire. His father, James Compton, was the third Earl of Northampton, his mother being his second wife, Mary Noel, daughter of the third Viscount Camden. Altogether, there were ten children from the two marriages, most of whom died in infancy. Spencer was the youngest child, and of his siblings only his elder brother, George (who became the fourth Earl) and a sister, Mary, who was to marry the sixth Earl of Dorset, reached adulthood. The third Earl came from a wealthy family, long established in both Warwickshire and Northamptonshire, who were strong Royalists during the Civil War and afterwards. A fervent Tory, he died in 1681, but subsequent events pushed members of his family in the direction of the Whigs. One of the Earl's brothers became Bishop of London under Charles II, but joined in the movement to exclude the Catholic James, Duke of York, from the succession. When James II came to the throne, he suspended Bishop Compton, but he was reinstated under William III and Mary, and indeed was responsible for crowning the new King and Queen, when the Archbishop of Canterbury refused to take the oath of allegiance. Meanwhile, Spencer's brother, George Compton, the fourth Earl, had married into a leading Whig family, becoming the brother-in-law of Henry Fox (later the first Lord Holland, and the father of Charles James Fox). So the young Spencer grew up in a family with strong Tory roots, but with some at least of his close relatives now having Whig connections.

Very little is known of Spencer's childhood and youth. He was educated at St Paul's School, and Trinity College, Oxford, and enrolled at the Middle Temple, becoming a barrister. Aged 22, he contested the 1695 general election, as a Tory, at East Grinstead, but came bottom of the poll. Three years later, while travelling on the Continent, in an early version of the 'Grand Tour', he was elected unopposed, still as a Tory, in a by-election in the Suffolk constituency of Eye. This was a 'pocket' borough controlled by the Cornwallis family, and Spencer continued to represent it until 1710, though in 1701 he switched his allegiance to the Whigs, soon hitching his wagon to that of the rising young star, Robert Walpole, three years his junior.

A poor and pedantic speaker, Compton's parliamentary career soon prospered, however, due to the assiduity with which he mastered Commons procedures, his strong aristocratic connections and his ingratiating manner. In 1705, he was appointed chairman of the important Elections and Privileges Committee of the House of Commons, a key position as he was expected by the government, then led by Lord Godolphin, to ensure that the many disputed elections were normally settled in favour of the government's candidates. Two years later, while retaining the chairmanship, he achieved office as Paymaster of the Queen's Pensions, which he doubled up with acting as Treasurer to the household of Prince George of Denmark, the Queen's husband, who sat in the Cabinet as Lord High Admiral. In 1709, he was appointed, together with Walpole, to draw up the articles of impeachment against Dr Henry Sacheverell (see Chapter 1). Normally a mild-mannered man, he attacked Sacheverell with the greatest severity in several speeches, so much so that even his friends felt he had gone rather 'over the top'. One person who was displeased by Compton's performance was Lord Cornwallis, who withdrew his support in the Eye constituency, which meant that he was unable to contest the 1710 general election. So he was out of the House for three years, though the predominantly Tory government led by Robert Harley (later Lord Oxford) allowed him to retain his Paymaster's office. His other post with Prince George had lapsed, when the latter died in 1708.

Compton returned to Parliament in the 1713 general election, being returned unopposed for the East Grinstead constituency of Sussex, in which county he had recently acquired an estate. Two years later, in the general election following George I's accession, he contested one of the county seats, and – coming in second place – was elected as one of the two county MPs – more prestigious than sitting for a borough. Compton was disappointed not to be included in the Whig ministry appointed by the new Hanoverian king, but received ample compensation when he was chosen as Treasurer of the household of the Prince of Wales (later George II), as well as being elected as Speaker of the House of Commons, on 17 March 1715. This was largely a reward for his earlier work as Chairman of the Elections and Privileges Committee and a tribute to his mastery of parliamentary procedure. He continued as Speaker for 12 years, presiding with great dignity and punctiliousness and not a little self-importance. His much more distinguished successor as Speaker, Arthur Onslow, described him as 'very able in the chair ... but [he] had not the powers of speech out of it' (Hanham, 2004). He was remembered for a famous put-down, when a Member complained of noisy interruptions, and claimed the right to be heard. 'No Sir', replied the Speaker, 'You have a right to speak, but the House have a right to judge whether they will hear you.'

Compton was put in a potentially invidious position in 1717, when a violent dispute between the Prince of Wales and his father coincided with a split in the Whig Party, leading to the exit from the government of Lord Townshend, Robert Walpole and several other leading figures, who then set themselves up as a Opposition faction, with the support of the Prince. Despite his position in the Chair, Compton proclaimed himself a supporter of the Opposition Whigs, but this did not seem to affect the acceptance of his authority by MPs as a whole. In 1721, Walpole was restored to office as First Lord of the Treasury and Chancellor of the Exchequer, but the Prince's feud with his father continued, and he again became openly hostile to the king's ministers, including Walpole. He made no secret of his intention to replace him, as Prime Minister, by his loyal treasurer when he should succeed to the throne. In the meantime, Walpole tried to buy Compton off, by supporting his re-election as Speaker in 1722, and appointing him, in addition, as Paymaster-General, a highly lucrative office, from which Compton was reputed to have made £100,000 over the next eight years. He was also appointed, on Walpole's recommendation, as a Knight of the Bath, in 1725.

When George I died during a visit to Hanover on 11 June 1727, it seemed as though Compton's hour had come. As recounted in Chapter 1, Walpole hastened to Richmond to inform the Prince of Wales, bowing deeply and saying, 'I am come to acquaint your Majesty with the death of your father.' He was received coolly by the new monarch, whose only reply was: 'Go to Chiswick and take your directions from Sir Spencer Compton.' This Walpole did, and according to the memoirs of Lord Hervey, addressed Compton with great humility, saying:

> I put myself under your protection, and for this reason I expect you to give it. I desire no share of power or business; one of your white sticks, or any employment of that sort, is all I ask as a mark from the Crown that I am not abandoned to the enmity of those whose envy is the only source of their hate. (Sedgwick, 1931, vol. 1, p. 23)

Compton proved himself incapable of rising to the opportunity which now opened out before him. Instructed by the new King to draft his declaration to the Privy Council on assuming the throne, he felt unequal to the task, and asked Walpole to do it for him. As his most distinguished biographer put it, 'Walpole took up the employment immediately retiring to another room, and naturally slipped in a charming and appreciative tribute to the ability of the late ministry' (Plumb, 1960, p. 165). The first issue which had to be settled under the new reign was the size of the Civil List, for which Parliamentary approval would be sought. The King consulted Compton, who displeased him by suggesting that the new Queen's allowance should be set no higher than £50,000. He then discussed it with Walpole, who proposed to double the amount, and the King concluded that the retiring Prime Minister would have a better chance of obtaining a generous settlement from Parliament than his projected successor. Queen Caroline herself had spared no effort in persuading the King both of Walpole's abilities and of Compton's shortcomings, and within three weeks Compton concluded that the game was up, and withdrew himself from the King's counsels. He felt humiliated, and bore a lasting grievance against Walpole, which he was careful to conceal until the closing stages of Walpole's premiership more than a decade later.

Reinstated as the King's chief minister, Walpole hastened to placate Compton by nominating him for a peerage, and he became Baron Wilmington, which title was upgraded to an earldom in 1730. He was also made a Knight of the Garter, in 1733. He joined Walpole's cabinet as Lord Privy Seal, in May 1730 – probably at the King's behest, and on the last day of that year became Lord President of the Council, a post he held until 1742. Punctilious in his duties, in a low-key manner, he was outwardly loyal, but privately intrigued against Walpole on several occasions. A now wealthy bachelor, Wilmington never married, though, according to Horace Walpole's memoirs, he was 'a great lover of private debauchery'. He was reputed to have fathered several illegitimate children, one of whom – a daughter – was to marry James Glen, a Governor of South Carolina. His sister, Mary, was married to Charles Sackville, the sixth Earl of Dorset, who was close to him and apparently anticipated (wrongly) that he and his family would inherit Wilmington's fortune. Dorset's three sons were all in the House of Commons and, together with their father, constituted the bulk of the small parliamentary faction personally loyal to Wilmington. Despite Wilmington's ministerial office, he remained much more of a courtier than a politician, and his basic loyalty was to the King rather than Walpole. Indeed, he privately expressed the view that Walpole's use of his powers was excessive, and that 'the true interest of England was to have no chief minister ... that every great office should be immediately dependent on the king and answer for it' (Egmont Diary, quoted by Hanham, 2004). Nevertheless, he continued to brood on his earlier humiliating failure and felt increasingly that if there had to be a chief minister it should be him.

When Walpole finally resigned, in February 1742, it was a severe blow to George II, an essentially lazy man who had grown used to his heavy dependence on the man who had been his chief minister throughout the (then) nearly 15 years of his reign. He was shocked that there was no longer a stable parliamentary majority available for Walpole, but wished to continue with his administration with the least possible disruption. He therefore resolved to keep the bulk of his ministers in place, but to recruit from the opposition sufficient additional support for them to retain power. Determined to maintain the exclusion of the Tories, he focused on two distinct groups of opposition Whigs – those associated with Lord Carteret and William Pulteney, and the followers of his estranged son, Frederick, Prince of Wales, with whom he now sought an accord. On the advice of the Duke of Newcastle, the senior of his two Secretaries of State, and of Lord Hardwicke, the Lord Chancellor, the post of First Lord of the Treasury was offered to Pulteney, who reluctantly declined, feeling bound by his previous declarations that he had not sought office for himself in pursuing his opposition to Walpole. Nevertheless, he agreed to cooperate in the formation of a new, broadened government, and evidently hoped that after a decent interval he would himself take over its leadership. Carteret had expected that Pulteney would support his own claims, but – recognizing his general unpopularity – he declined to do so, and George seized the opportunity of offering the post to the man who had long been dubbed his 'favourite nonentity'. Wilmington thus became First Lord of the Treasury, and nominal head of the government, but this role was effectively played by Carteret, who became – with Newcastle – a Secretary of State. The most able and decisive man in the cabinet, Carteret had the additional qualification of being close to the King, with whom he was able to converse in fluent German. Proud and disdainful, Carteret had a low opinion of the House of Commons, in which he had never served. The additional support in the Commons, from Pulteney's followers and those of the Prince of Wales (who had been bought off by an increase in his Civil List provision) amounted to 43 MPs, who became known as 'New Whigs'. No member of the Cabinet now sat in the Commons, and the effective leader of the House became Newcastle's younger brother, Henry Pelham, who was Paymaster-General. After a little while it was apparent that close liaison with the Commons was essential to the government's survival, and Pelham was invited to attend Cabinet meetings and became, in effect, one of its most influential members. Pulteney then made the crucial blunder of accepting a peerage, becoming the first Earl of Bath. His previous standing owed much to his being perhaps the most effective debater in the Commons, and his influence soon declined, as Walpole shrewdly anticipated, with his transfer to the Upper House. Moreover, he was now cut off from his former followers in the Commons, and many other 'opposition Whigs' were resentful that he had not also brought them into the governmental fold, so that they could share in the 'spoils'.

Wilmington himself had been in favour of a more 'broad-bottomed' government, bringing in not only all the Whig factions, but leading Tories as well, a view strongly held by the Duke of Argyll, previously a strong Walpolite and the leader of the Scottish Whigs, who had violently fallen out with his leader following the Porteus riots in Edinburgh in 1736 (see Chapter 1). Wilmington protested to the King about the narrowness of the government's base, and the promotion of Carteret without his being consulted, even threatening to resign, but without avail, and quietly reconciled himself to being merely a figurehead Prime Minister. Even his powers as the chief Treasury Minister were effectively removed from him, with the appointment of Samuel (later Lord) Sandys as Chancellor of the Exchequer (previously Walpole had combined both posts). Already 69, and in poor health – he suffered from kidney stones – his government had few achievements to its credit. The only significant Bill to be passed was the Place Act, of 1742. In a bid to restrict the government's powers of corrupting MPs, this excluded Members of Parliament from being appointed to various public offices.

Otherwise, apart from the passage of the Spirituous Liquors Act, of 1743, which increased the duties on spirits in an attempt to combat public drunkenness, overwhelming priority was given to Britain's participation in the War of Austrian succession. This had broken out in 1740, following the death of the Hapsburg Emperor, Charles VI. He had left no male heir, and his daughter, Maria Theresa, while recognized as Queen of Hungary, was not eligible to be elected Holy Roman Emperor, which title had been monopolized by the Austrian Arch-Dukes since the fifteenth century. In the hope of wresting Hapsburg territories in Germany and Italy, France, Spain, Prussia and Bavaria promptly attacked Austria, whose allies were Britain and Holland. George II took a keen interest in the war, his main concerns being to protect his Hanoverian electorate from French or Prussian attacks and his own desire for military glory. Skilful diplomacy by Carteret succeeded in establishing that Hanover would remain neutral in the conflict, but a large military force, known as the 'Pragmatic Army' made up of British, Austrian, Dutch, Hanoverian and Hessian troops was assembled in the Netherlands, under the personal command of George II. It crossed the Rhine and defeated the French army at Dettingen, in June 1743. George II, who exposed himself to great personal danger while fighting on foot, emerged as a hero from the battle, while Carteret discreetly observed the conflict from the comfort of his heavily upholstered coach at a respectful distance. Despite this victory, the war continued, with many ups and downs, for another five years, before it ended inconclusively, with the Treaty of Aix-la-Chapelle in 1748 (see Chapter 3).

Wilmington played no part in these stirring events. He was already a dying man, and expired at his house in St James's Square, while still in office, five days after the battle, on 2 July 1743. He was probably aged 70. Altogether, he had served for one year and 136 days. He was unlamented by most of his contemporaries, who seem to have had little respect for him, Lord Hervey's view being not untypical:

> A plodding heavy fellow with great application but no talents, and vast complaisance for a court without any address; he was always more concerned for the manner and form in which a thing was done than about the propriety or expediency of the thing itself. His only pleasures were money and eating; his only knowledge form and precedents; his only insinuations bows and smiles. (Bigham, 1924, p. 30)

Nor has posterity been much kinder in its verdict. As previously noted, there has been no biography, but the fullest appreciation was penned, as long ago as 1924, by Clive Bigham, whose words of extenuation were strictly limited:

> Yet Wilmington filled for nearly thirty years the four highest places in the State to which a layman can aspire. He seems to have been honest, conscientious, well-meaning and precise, perhaps even loyal as the times went, but as to character and talents he was little more than a cipher. (Ibid., p. 31)

In Britain, he is a totally forgotten figure, though in the United States there remain small sparks of fame. There are three places called Wilmington – in Massachusetts, North Carolina and Delaware. It is doubtful if many of their inhabitants know anything at all about the man after whom their home towns were named.

Works consulted

Bigham, Clive (1924), *The Prime Ministers of Britain 1721–1924*, London, John Murray.

Cannon, John (2004), 'George II (1683–1760)', *Oxford Dictionary of National Biography*, Oxford, OUP.

Cruickshanks, Eveline (1998), 'Spencer Compton, First Earl of Wilmington', in *Biographical Dictionary of British Prime Ministers*, London, Routledge.

Hanham, A.A. (2004), 'Compton, Spencer, Earl of Wilmington (c. 1674–1743)', *Oxford Dictionary of National Biography*, Oxford, OUP.

Hill, Brian W. (1989), *Sir Robert Walpole: 'Sole and Prime Minister'*, London, Hamish Hamilton.

O'Gorman, Frank (1997), *The Long Eighteenth Century*, London, Arnold.

Owen, John B. (1957), *The Rise of the Pelhams*, London, Methuen.

Plumb, J.H. (1960), *Sir Robert Walpole: The King's Minister,* London, Cresset Press.

Romney, Sedgwick (ed.), (1931), *Some Materials towards Memoirs of the Reign of King George II,* by John, Lord Hervey, three volumes, London, Eyre & Spottiswoode.

Van Thal, Herbert (1974), 'The Earl of Wilmington and the Carteret Administration under Wilmington', in Herbert Van Thal (ed.), *The Prime Ministers,* Volume I, London, Allen & Unwin.

3

Henry Pelham – Pragmatic Heir to Walpole

Henry Pelham is invariably listed as Britain's third Prime Minister, but a case can certainly be made that he was virtually the second, given the ineffectiveness of his predecessor as First Lord of the Treasury, the Earl of Wilmington (see Chapter 2). The offspring of a landed family based mainly in Sussex, which had sent representatives to Parliament continually since Elizabethan times, he was born in London on 25 September 1694. His father, Thomas, the first Baron Pelham, was married twice, and fathered 11 children, two from his first marriage, and nine from the second. Henry was the third son, and ninth child. The first son, John, was to die in infancy, but the second, also named Thomas, who was only 14 months his senior, was to play a crucial, and indeed determining, role in his life and career. Their mother, formerly Lady Grace Holles, was the daughter of the third Earl of Clare, and sister of John Holles, Duke of Newcastle. The brothers were unusually close and loved each other dearly, though this did not prevent them from having many disputes, or Thomas from becoming obsessively jealous of Henry, later in life.

Both brothers were educated at Westminster School, but Thomas then proceeded to Cambridge, while Henry enrolled at Hart Hall, Oxford, in September 1710, which he was to leave without taking a degree. Both his parents died when he was still young, his mother in 1700, when he was nearly five, and his father, in 1712, when he was not yet 18. His father left him £5000 and some small annuities, but the bulk of his large estate went to Thomas, who had already inherited a substantial fortune from his uncle, the Duke of Newcastle, on condition of changing his name to Pelham-Holles. Thomas was to inherit the Pelham barony from his father and later the Earldom of Clare from his grandfather. He provided Henry with an additional annuity of £1000 a year, and was to settle further sums on him on several subsequent occasions. The Pelham family were staunch Whigs, and strongly supported the accession of George I in 1714. The two brothers raised a troop of horse in Sussex during the Jacobite rebellion of 1715, and Henry went off to fight at the Battle of Preston. As a reward, the Newcastle dukedom, which had lapsed with his uncle's death without a direct male heir, was revived in Thomas's favour, and he attained the highest rank of the peerage at the age of 22. He was related by blood or marriage to many of the great Whig families, including that of Robert Walpole, and he consolidated these links in 1717, by marrying Lady Henrietta Godolphin, the granddaughter both of the Duke of Marlborough and of Queen Anne's former chief minister, Sidney Godolphin.

Thomas, who had immediately taken his seat in the House of Lords within days of his twenty-first birthday, now held property in no less than 11 counties, which gave him a strong influence in the representation of a large clutch of parliamentary constituencies. He lost no time in providing a 'pocket borough' for Henry, who was returned unopposed for the Sussex constituency of Seaford in a by-election in February 1717, at the age of 22. Henry, who had returned from an early version of the 'grand tour' to fight the seat, thus owed the opportunity of a political career entirely to his brother, and his wider family connections. His rapid promotion up the political ladder was also due primarily to the continued support of Thomas, who had quickly established himself as a leading Whig magnate.

Newcastle joined the government, jointly led by James Stanhope and the Earl of Sunderland, in April 1717, as Lord Chamberlain of the Royal Household, and in this capacity was able to appoint his brother as Treasurer of the Chamber, a junior ministerial post, three years later. This brought Pelham into close contact with Robert Walpole, who was Paymaster-General and later First Lord of the Treasury and Chancellor of the Exchequer. Walpole appointed Pelham as a Lord of the Treasury in 1721. He was deeply impressed by Pelham's administrative abilities, his discretion and his ability to argue the government's case in the House of Commons, virtually all the other ministers, apart from Walpole himself, being in the Lords. Something of the quality of the relationship which was to grow up between the two men was caught in the usually caustic memoirs of Lord Hervey, who – together with Horace Walpole – was one of the two leading contemporary chroniclers of politics during the reign of George II. 'Mr. Pelham', he wrote,

> was strongly attached to Sir Robert Walpole, and more personally beloved by him than any man in England. He was a gentleman-like sort of man, of very good character, with moderate parts, in the secret of every transaction, which, made him at last, though not a bright speaker, often a useful one; and by the means of a general affability he had fewer enemies than commonly falls to the share of one so high a rank. (Newman, 1974, p. 63)

Both Newcastle's and Pelham's position was greatly strengthened in 1724, when Walpole succeeded in evicting the ambitious Lord Carteret from his post as one of the two Secretaries of State (see Chapter 1). These positions, regarded as the most senior posts in the government, after that of First Lord of the Treasury, were mainly concerned with Foreign Affairs, the Northern Department being responsible for relations with countries in Northern and Central Europe, and the Southern with the Mediterranean powers. Newcastle replaced Carteret (who was exiled to become Lord Lieutenant of Ireland), as Secretary of State (South), and became effectively the number three man in the government, after Walpole and Lord Townshend, who was Secretary of State (North).

Pelham was promoted to the post of Secretary at War, one of the most senior posts outside the Cabinet. Steps were also being taken at this time to ensure his financial security, and diminish his dependence on his brother. In the words of his biographer:

> As early as 1723 the solution was decided upon: Henry Pelham was to marry someone who would bring him a dowry of £30,000 in cash, which he could exchange for the family estates in Lincolnshire. Such a marriage was arranged in 1726 with the Duke of Rutland, who gave the required sum with his daughter, Lady Katharine Manners. The Lincolnshire estates, thus obtained, were the main financial resources of Henry Pelham and his family for the rest of his life, though the Duke of Newcastle often supplemented the income of his brother. It is interesting to observe that the marriage, contracted in this calculating manner, proved to be a supremely happy one.
> (Wilkes, 1964, p. 3)

It was to produce six daughters and two sons, both of whom were to die, on successive days in 1739, from a throat infection, at the ages of ten and three – the greatest tragedy in Pelham's life.

Pelham was to remain a member of Walpole's administration for the whole of his period in power, becoming personally closer to him than any other minister. Walpole acted as his mentor, as well as his friend, and taught him everything he knew, so much so that by the time that he finally resigned in 1742, his pupil had completed, in his biographer's view, 'the most thorough preparation for office of any man of the eighteenth century'(Wilkes, p. 25). In 1730, when Walpole reconstructed his ministry following the resignation of Lord Townshend (see Chapter 1), Pelham was appointed Paymaster-General to the Forces, a post he continued to hold until 1743. Traditionally, its holders used the office greatly to enrich themselves, which Pelham conspicuously failed to do. This earned him a reluctant tribute, after his death, from his long-time enemy, Horace Walpole (Sir Robert's putative son), who wrote: 'He lived without abusing his power, and died poor' (Wilkes, p. 214). Although he remained outside the Cabinet, Pelham eventually became one of the most influential of Walpole's ministers, along with his brother, Newcastle, and Philip Yorke, Earl of Hardwicke, the Lord Chancellor. He was also his most loyal follower, opposing him only once during his 21 years as a minister, on the issue of reforming the national debt in 1737. Nor, unlike Newcastle (see Chapter 4) and other leading ministers, did he engage in any intrigues with opposition figures trying to displace Walpole during his declining years. Indeed, it was only through his gentle mediation between Walpole and Newcastle (both of whom trusted him implicitly) that he was able to prevent a breach between the two men.

Pelham was notably lacking in charisma, and came across as a pleasant, mild man, well organized and skilful in his handling of parliamentary colleagues. Beneath his bland exterior, lay steely determination and moral and physical courage. He almost fought a duel with William Pulteney after an altercation in the Commons, in 1732, and 'the next year he came boldly forward when quite alone and protected Sir Robert [Walpole] from the attack of a crowd of his opponents outside the House. He drew his sword and stood out, saying, "Now, gentlemen, who will be the first to fall?" ' (Bigham, 1924, p. 36). It was he who took the lead in defending Walpole from censure motions in the House of Commons in the final year of his premiership, and in heading off subsequent attempts to impeach him.

When Walpole finally resigned, in 1742, and was replaced by the ineffective Lord Wilmington as First Lord of the Treasury, Pelham was the only senior minister sitting in the House of Commons, and when Pulteney unwisely accepted a peerage, as the Earl of Bath, became its uncontested leader. He was still, initially, outside the Cabinet, and Carteret, who as Secretary of State (Northern), and an intimate of George II, dominated the government, strongly resented his growing influence. On one occasion, he expostulated: 'He [Pelham] was only a chief clerk to Sir Robert Walpole, and why should he expect to be more under me, I can't imagine: he did his drudgery and he shall do mine.' Nevertheless, as the man whose task it was to present the Cabinet's policies to the Commons it was illogical for Pelham not to be a member, and he was soon to be admitted, despite Carteret's objections. Within the Cabinet, he formed part of a triumvirate, along with his brother and Lord Hardwicke, who provided the strongest resistance to the overbearing Carteret. It was only a matter of time before there would be a decisive showdown between these three, supported from the outside by Walpole (now Lord Orford), who still had the King's ear, and Carteret, who was his undoubted favourite. A crucial moment came when Wilmington died, in July 1743. For almost two months, George II hesitated about appointing a successor as First Lord of the Treasury. Bath, backed by Carteret, aspired to the post, but the choice eventually fell on Pelham, the King having reluctantly decided that it was better to have somebody from the Commons. Newcastle outwardly supported his brother's promotion, but was clearly in two minds about it.

He regarded himself as the leader of the 'Old Corps' of Whigs who had dominated the Walpole government, and he did not enjoy the prospect of having to play second fiddle to his brother.

Pelham was appointed on 27 August 1743, but it was another year or two before he came to be regarded as 'Prime Minister', in the sense that Sir Robert Walpole had been. Before that could happen, two further conditions had to be met. He had to assert his dominance over Lord Carteret, and to win the full backing of George II. The first objective was made easier by the insensitivity of Carteret, who became the Earl of Granville, in October 1744. Basing himself entirely on his close relationship with George II, with whom he was able to chat cosily in German, he totally failed to build up a reservoir of parliamentary support and unnecessarily antagonized many would-be supporters by his apparent disdain. His conduct of the War of Austrian Succession, which Britain had joined in 1741, as a consequence of its existing struggle with Spain and France in the War of Jenkins' Ear (see Chapter 1), brought him great unpopularity, especially among landowning MPs. They blamed him for the high taxation which this brought, and also because they believed he was giving too much weight to the King's Hanoverian dominions at the expense of Britain's own interests. Granville's policies were relentlessly criticized in the Commons by, among others, William Pitt the Elder, the greatest orator of his day, and Pelham and his colleagues believed that it would no longer be possible to maintain a parliamentary majority unless he was removed from the Government. In November 1744, they persuaded a deeply reluctant George II to agree to the dropping of his favourite, and Pelham, who by now had – like Walpole before him – added the post of Chancellor of the Exchequer to that of First Lord of the Treasury was given (almost) a free hand in restructuring the government. He determined to form a 'broad bottomed' administration, bringing in as many weighty figures as possible from the former Opposition in order to ensure that – unlike under Walpole – the government's position would not be progressively undermined by parliamentary attrition. He even brought in a few Tories, mostly into fairly junior posts, but mainly he was instrumental in bringing in 'dissident' Whigs, including the followers of such influential grandees as the Duke of Bedford, the Earl of Chesterfield and Lord Cobham. Pelham wanted to include William Pitt, but George II, inflamed by his earlier attacks on Hanover, refused to countenance this.

The King greatly resented the formation of a government containing so many of his erstwhile critics, and withheld full confidence from them, continuing to consult with Granville, whom he hoped to be able to restore to office at an early date.

It was this government which had to contend with the 1745 Jacobite uprising. This began on 22 June 1745, with the landing on the Hebridean island of

Enniskay of 'Bonnie Prince Charlie', the elder son of the Old Pretender, James Edward Stuart. Accompanied by seven followers, and a consignment of arms and ammunition supplied by the French, he made his way to the mainland and soon raised mass support among the Highland clans, capturing Edinburgh on 17 September, and defeating a British force under Sir John Cope at Prestonpans four days later. The Scottish authorities, led by the Secretary of State, Lord Tweeddale, the only supporter of Granville remaining in the Cabinet, grossly underestimated the danger and totally failed to take adequate steps to contain the uprising. General panic now afflicted the government, as fears raged of a French invasion across the Channel in support of the Jacobites, but Pelham kept his head and calmly decided that salvation would come through the withdrawal from Flanders of the powerful British army led by the King's younger son, the Duke of Cumberland. The Duke was highly reluctant, but eventually returned with ten battalions and marched north to face the troops of the Pretender. By then Charles Stuart had squandered his great opportunity by wasting several weeks in elaborate celebrations in Scotland, before crossing the border into England. It was 4 December before his exhausted troops reached Derby, a mere 128 miles from London, but – disheartened by the absence of either an English uprising or a French invasion – they then turned back in the hope of consolidating Stuart rule in Scotland. Cumberland set off slowly in pursuit, and despite reverses at Penrith on 18 December, and Falkirk on 17 January 1746, totally routed the Pretender's army at Culloden, on 16 April 1746. Earning himself the sobriquet of 'Butcher' Cumberland, the Duke then proceeded brutally to suppress the Highland clans, one of the most disreputable episodes in British military history. Pelham strongly disapproved of Cumberland's actions, but was determined to prevent any recurrence of Jacobite activity north of the border. He embarked on a programme of 'carrots' and 'sticks', the former being a policy of clemency towards the survivors of the uprising, the latter a substantial centralization of the Scottish legal system, depriving clan chiefs of their hereditary jurisdictions. Only two treason trials were held of the Pretender's chief supporters. One was of the Earls of Kilmarnock and Cromarty, and of Lord Balmerino. All were found guilty, but Cromarty was reprieved as a sign of the King's mercy. A separate trial was held later for Simon, Lord Lovat, who had earlier been reprieved for his role in the 1715 uprising. This time he was less lucky. Found guilty by a unanimous vote of the House of Lords, by 117 votes to 0, he was the last person in Britain to suffer death by beheading. With his death, the Jacobite cause expired, and an issue which had lingered on for nearly six decades was finally laid to rest. One consequence was a boost to the standing of the Tories, who had long suffered from the taint of Jacobitism, sedulously spread by Walpole and other leading Whigs. The fact that not a single prominent Tory declared for the Pretender meant that this was no longer a tenable accusation.

In February 1746, Pelham and his closest colleagues had decided that it was now essential to reinforce the government by including William Pitt, preferably as Secretary at War. When George II, egged on by Lord Bath, refused to contemplate this, the Cabinet decided, at a secret meeting on 9 February 1746 to force the issue by collective resignation. Next day, Newcastle and his fellow Secretary of State, Lord Harrington, submitted their resignations, followed by Pelham and a bevy of other ministers a day later. The King responded by appointing Bath to replace Pelham, and Granville in place of both Newcastle and Harrington, and invited the two men to form a new government. Their attempt to do so proved farcical – they failed to recruit men of sufficient standing to fill the other Cabinet offices, their following in the Commons was derisory and the City of London made it clear that little financial support would be forthcoming for a government not led by Pelham. The 'Bath government' was stillborn, and within two days George II was pleading with Pelham and his colleagues to come back. A contemporary satire, entitled *A History of the Long Administration,* concluded with the words:

> And thus endeth the second and last part of this astonishing Administration which lasted 48 hours and 3 quarters, seven minutes and eleven seconds; which may truly be called the most honest of all administrations; the minister to the astonishment of all wise men never transacted one rash thing; and, what is more marvellous, left as much money in the treasury as he found in it. (Wilson, 1977, p. 11)

In a masterstroke, Pelham and his colleagues insisted that they resumed office on their own terms, and not those of the King. In a secret meeting on 13 February, held in the house of the Duke of Dorset, the Lord President of the Council, they drew up a memorandum to present to the King, a copy of which, in the handwriting of the Lord
Chancellor, Lord Hardwicke, is in the archives of the British Library. It is in the following terms:

> That, out of Duty to the King, & Regard to the Public, It is apprehended that His Majesty's late Servants cannot return into his Service, without being honour'd with that degree of Authority, Confidence, & Credit from His Majesty, which the Ministers of the Crown have usually enjoy'd in this country, & which is absolutely necessary for carrying on his Service.

> That His Majesty will be pleas'd entirely to withdraw his confidence & countenance from those Persons, who have of late, behind the Curtain, suggested private Councills, with ye view of creating difficulties to his Servants, who are responsible for every thing, whilst those Persons are responsible for nothing.

That His Majesty will be pleased to demonstrate his Conviction of mind that Those Persons have deceiv'd or misled Him by representing that they had sufficient Credit & Interest in the Nation to support & carry on the public affairs, & that he finds They are not able to do it.

That in order to these Ends, his Majesty will be pleas'd to remove [Granville's followers] ... .

That he will be graciously pleased to perfect the Scheme lately humbly propos'd to Him for bringing Mr. Pitt into some honourable Employment, & also the other persons formerly nam'd with him.

That His Majesty will be pleased to dispose of the vacant Garters in such manner, as to strengthen, & give a public mark of his Satisfaction in, his Administration.

That, as to foreign affairs, His Majesty will be pleased not to require more from His Servants than to support the Plan, which He has already approved. (Wilkes, p. 144)

Modern readers may be astonished at the temerity of Pelham's ministers in presenting such a document to the King, and even more surprised that he meekly accepted it. Nor did this hitherto rather slippery customer subsequently attempt to renege on the assurances which he had given. The previously unpretentious Pelham now emerged as one of the strongest characters ever to hold the role of Prime Minister, and the extent of his power now rivalled or exceeded that of Walpole in his prime. He had demonstrated that, with a largely united Cabinet and solid support in the House of Commons, a Prime Minister could have his way over a reluctant monarch. This was an important precedent for the future, though one which George II's headstrong grandson and successor, George III, was able to ignore on a number of occasions, notably in 1783 (see Chapter 13) and in 1807 (see Chapter 13).

The immediate consequence was that Pelham, who returned to office on 14 February 1746, was able to take even further his desire to form a broad-bottomed administration, bringing in Pitt as Paymaster-General, Pitt's brother-in-law, George Grenville, as a Lord of the Admiralty, and a little later, the fourth Duke of Bedford as one of the two Secretaries of State, along with Newcastle. Bedford had been the leader of a large dissident Whig faction, and his adhesion to the government – though he proved an ineffective minister – greatly helped to boost its parliamentary majority. Pelham moved sharply to consolidate his advantage by springing a snap election – one year before it was due under the Septennial Act, in June 1747, catching the opposition off guard, and substantially increasing his majority. There was now – apart from the Tories, who were much reduced in numbers – no significant opposition grouping left in the Commons, apart from the faction supporting the interest of Frederick, Prince of Wales, who – permanently at odds with his father – was constantly stoking discontent. His following was considerable, partly because of the large number of 'pocket' boroughs he controlled, notably in the Duchy of Cornwall, but mainly because, as his father grew older and in less than splendid health, ambitious politicians increasingly looked forward to his succession to the throne to further their own fortunes. This 'Reversionary interest' was a recurrent factor under each of the first three Hanoverian kings, all of whom had bad relations with their eldest sons. Pelham acknowledged the difficulty he often faced from Frederick, and his 'Leicester House circle', saying in a letter to Newcastle, in May 1750:

> The House of Commons is a great unwieldy body, which requires great Art and some Cordials to keep it loyal; we have not many of the latter in our power; the Opposition is headed by the Prince, who has as much to give in the present as we have, and more in Reversion. This makes my task an hard one, and if it were not for that I should sleep in quiet. (Newman, 1974, p. 68)

The 'Cordials' which Pelham mentioned referred to the system of patronage and bribery, which Walpole had perfected during his long period in power. Although both Pelham and Newcastle personally refrained from enriching themselves from the public service (apart from drawing their ministerial salaries), they had few scruples in continuing with Walpole's methods, though they did it more discreetly and on a somewhat smaller scale. Frederick's unexpected death, in 1751, at the age of 44, removed this particular difficulty, as his group of followers rapidly disintegrated, many of them hastening to make peace with the government. Henceforward Pelham had no difficulty whatever in controlling the Commons, as the leader of the House, Henry Fox (later the first Lord Holland), indicated in a letter in November 1751: 'There never was such a session as this is likely to be …. A bird might build her nest in the Speaker's chair, or in his peruke; There won't be a debate that can disturb her' (Hanham, 1998, p. 23).

As a faithful disciple of Walpole, Pelham shared most of his objectives, notably the desire to bring peace and stability to the country, and to lower taxation. As Prime Minister, he had little direct control over foreign affairs, in which the King took great interest, and which was the special concern of the two Secretaries of State, of whom the more influential was his brother, Newcastle. Pelham earlier took the view that Britain had little to gain from a continuation of the War of Austrian Succession, which was a serious drain on the country's finances. Yet the King still hankered after military glory, following his personal participation in the Battle of Dettingen, in 1743 (see Chapter 2), a rare victory over France in continental Europe, and Newcastle rashly promised renewed subsidies to Britain's allies to keep them in the war. Yet it continued to go badly, with the French Marshal Saxe gaining a series of striking victories at Fontenoy, Roucoux and Lauffield in 1745, 1746 and 1747, and the only British successes being at sea. Pelham eventually had his way, and the compromise Treaty of Aix-la-Chapelle concluded the war in October 1748. Only France's ally Prussia, which retained its conquests of Silesia and Glatz, emerged with any significant gains. Britain had little to show for its participation, other than belated recognition by France of the Hanoverian succession.

Partly driven by the cost of the war, Pelham was determined to reform the national finances, and to reduce the burden of the national debt. By 1748, this had risen to the then regarded astronomical sum of £76 million, the interest thereon absorbing some 44 per cent of the annual budget. 'Over the next two years', according to a parliamentary historian,

> He succeeded in scaling down government expenditure from £12 million to £7 million. This was greatly facilitated by the cutting of the army back from 50,000 to its peacetime level of 18,850 men, and the navy from 51,550 to 8,000. His wholesale reduction in the size and cost of the government's fiscal bureaucracy was probably the most extensive undertaken by an eighteenth-century prime minister. (Hanham, 1998, p. 26)

This enabled him to cut the land tax from four shillings in the pound in 1749 to three, and again to two shillings in 1752, a highly popular move among land-owning backbenchers. Even more important were his fiscal reforms, which allowed interest on the national debt to be reduced from 4 per cent to 3.5 per cent in 1750, and down to 3 per cent in 1757. Among those who expressed their admiration for Pelham's achievement was the King, who in conversation with Newcastle, in 1752, compared him favourably to Walpole. 'With regard to money matters', he said, 'your brother does that, understands that, much better' (Hanham, p. 22). It had taken the King some time to warm to Pelham, whom he had initially disliked. But within a year or two of Pelham's *démarche* in 1746, he had become so dependent on him to deliver quiet and orderly government that he had utterly lost any desire to replace him. Much of the power had soon slipped away from the Cabinet as a whole, whose meetings became little more than a formality. Almost everything was settled by Pelham, in close consultation with Newcastle and the Lord Chancellor, Lord Hardwicke. The ever-jealous Newcastle even began to complain that he was left out of the loop, complaining to Hardwicke in September 1751: 'The truth is everything passes through my brother's hands, and I am with regard to the King as much a stranger as if I was not in the ministry' (Hanham, p. 24). Newcastle constantly quarrelled with his brother, and it was up to the ultra-conciliatory Hardwicke to patch things up. In fact, Pelham, though intensely irritated by his unreasonable attitude, deferred to Newcastle on numerous occasions. For years – against his better judgment – he tolerated Newcastle's policy of paying subsidies to German states, such as Bavaria and Saxony, in order to ensure that they would vote for the Austrian Hapsburg candidate for the Holy Roman Emperor, despite substantial parliamentary opposition. He also eventually supported Newcastle's campaign to enforce the resignation of his fellow Secretary of State, the Duke of Bedford, and very reluctantly agreed, in 1751, to the readmission to the Cabinet of Granville, as Lord President of the Council. Newcastle represented that he was now a 'changed man', and would not represent a threat to their primacy. So it proved, and Granville remained a member of successive governments until his death in 1763, though his now ingrained alcoholism largely undermined his effectiveness. Despite their frequent quarrels, the mutual love and affection of the two brothers continued until the end. The childless Newcastle was devoted to Pelham's young family, and arranged for his own title to pass, on his death, to the Earl of Lincoln, who married Pelham's eldest daughter, Catherine, in 1744.

Apart from his financial policies, Pelham left no great reputation as a reformer. Nevertheless, a number of useful pieces of legislation were enacted under his leadership. Most important may have been the overdue proposal of the Earl of Chesterfield to adopt the new Gregorian calendar, which had replaced the Julian calendar in most of the rest of Europe as long ago as 1582. Under this Act, the New Year was to begin on 1 January, instead of 25 March, and 11 days were omitted between 2 and 14 September 1752, provoking mob riots with the slogan 'Give us back our eleven days.' Another reform was the Marriage Act of 1753, proposed by Lord Hardwicke, which prohibited clandestine and runaway marriages. This caused great controversy, and seriously upset the leader of the Commons, Henry Fox, who had himself eloped with a Duke's daughter. Subsequent generations of scholars, and armies of tourists, have had reason to be grateful to Pelham's government for passing an Act in 1753, establishing the British Museum.

It said much for Pelham's religious toleration, and perhaps also for his gratitude to Jewish financiers who helped in the restructuring of the national debt, that he sponsored the Jewish Naturalization Act of 1753. It said rather less for his courage that he later agreed to its repeal in the face of anti-Semitic agitation in advance of the general election scheduled for April 1754. He did not live to fight the election, dying, while still in office, on 6 March 1754, aged 59. He had served for 10 years and 191 days, succumbing finally to an attack of the inflammatory disease, erysipelas. His health had not been good since 1748, when he suffered a severe attack of shingles, and three years later had proposed to retire from office and take a sinecure. George II would not hear of this, and he had carried on, declaring only a few weeks before his death that 'I am now, thank God, as well as I ever was in my life' (Kulisheck, 2004).

Newcastle was devastated by Pelham's death, and 'was sunk for several days in violent grief, unable and unwilling to attend to any business at all' (Newman, p. 70). Within a week, however, he was able to exert himself sufficiently to ensure that he would be his brother's successor. As for George II, his first words, as recorded by Horace Walpole, were 'Now I shall have no more peace.' Prophetic words, for the stability which Pelham had been able to establish did not long survive his departure from the scene. Of the many tributes he received from his contemporaries, that from the *Memoirs* of the second Earl of Waldegrave seems most apposite:

> Mr. Pelham died in March 1754; and our tranquility, both at home and abroad, died with him.

> He had acquired the reputation of an able and honest minister, had a plain, solid understanding, improved by experience in business, as well as by a thorough knowledge of the world; and without being an orator, or having the finest parts, no man in the House of Commons argued with more weight, or was heard with greater attention.

> He was a frugal steward to the public, averse to continental extravagance and useless subsidies; preferring a tolerable peace to the most successful war; jealous to maintain his personal credit and authority; but nowise inattentive to the true interest of his country. (Wilkes, p. 215)

Squeezed between the premierships of Walpole and the Elder Pitt (Chatham), Pelham's achievements have often been overlooked. Infinitely less flamboyant than either of these rivals, he nevertheless must share with them the credit of having been one of the three most effective political leaders of the eighteenth century.

Works consulted

Bigham, Clive (1924), *The Prime Ministers of Britain 1721–1924*, London, John Murray.

Browning, Reed (1975), *The Duke of Newcastle*, New Haven, Yale University Press.

Hanham, Andrew (1998), 'Henry Pelham', in Robert Eccleshall and Graham Walker, eds., *Biographical Dictionary of British Prime Ministers*, London, Routledge.

Kulisheck, P.J. (2004), Pelham, Henry (1694–1754), *Oxford Dictionary of National Biography*, Oxford, OUP.

Newman, A.N. (1974), 'Henry Pelham (1743–54)', in Herbert Van Thal, ed., *The Prime Ministers*, Volume I, London, Allen & Unwin.

Owen, John B. (1957), *The Rise of the Pelhams*, London, Methuen.

Wilkes, John W. (1964), *A Whig in Power: The Political Career of Henry Pelham*, Evanston, Northwestern University Press.

Wilson, Harold (1977), *A Prime Minister on Prime Ministers*, London, Weidenfeld & Nicolson and Michael Joseph.

4
Thomas Pelham-Holles, Duke of Newcastle – Mighty Panjandrum, Feeble Premier

Britain's roll-call of 53 Prime Ministers, to date, contains two sets of fathers and sons (Pitts and Grenvilles), but only one pair of brothers. Thomas Pelham's case was the more unusual, in that he was to succeed his *younger* brother (Henry Pelham). As recounted in the previous chapter, they were the two surviving sons of Thomas, first Baron Pelham, and his second wife, Lady Grace Holles, the sister of John Holles, Duke of Newcastle-upon-Tyne. The Duke had no male children, though he had a daughter, and several other nephews who were older than young 'Tommy' Pelham, but he took a fancy to him and made him his heir, much to the chagrin of his widow, his daughter and other potential inheritors. When he was 18, Tommy was to change his name to Pelham-Holles, in accordance with the terms of this legacy. He was born in London on 21 July 1693, and lost his mother at the age of 7, and his father when he was 18. His childhood, however, was hardly a lonely one – he had seven sisters or half-sisters and a younger brother – Henry. Moreover, he was educated at a day school – Westminster – before moving on to Clare Hall (later Clare College), Cambridge, which – like Henry, at Oxford – he was to leave without taking a degree. According to his biographer, he was 'In fine, no scholar, but in light of his later facility with French and his ability to conform to the epistolary standards of the age by invoking relevant classical allusions, neither was he a dunce' (Browning, 1974, p. 2).

Tommy was to remember Cambridge with great affection, and eagerly accepted nomination as University Chancellor in 1748, having induced George II to persuade the rival candidate, Frederick, Prince of Wales, to withdraw from the contest. By the time he left the University his life and financial circumstances had changed beyond recognition. The death of his father, in 1712, left him as the second Baron Pelham, and the inheritor of the larger part of his father's estate, after provision had been made for Henry and each of his five surviving sisters. A year earlier, he had received a far larger inheritance from his uncle. The Duke's will was fiercely contested by his widow, the Dowager Duchess, and by his daughter, Lady Henrietta Holles. Together with other relatives – some quite distant – they fought a long, but losing legal battle for several years, but Thomas was anxious to reach a compromise settlement, even expressing his willingness to marry Lady Henrietta. This offer was not accepted, but after the death of the Dowager Duchess in 1716, the daughter, now married to Lord Harley, son of the Earl of Oxford, formerly Queen Anne's chief minister, struck a deal giving her Welbeck Abbey, the great Nottinghamshire estate, and numerous other lands, but leaving Pelham-Holles with the great bulk of his uncle's holdings, which – together with his father's legacy – yielded him an annual income of some £32,000 a year (perhaps equivalent to £6.4m in modern terms). According to Browning (1975, p. 5), 'this figure placed him somewhat below the rank of the wealthiest landlords in the kingdom'. It should, however, have been sufficient for him to live a life of luxury, with no material cares, but the new Duke, as he became in 1715, was recklessly extravagant, abnormally generous and an extremely bad manager of his own resources. He was in debt for the greater part of his long life, and by the time of his death, in 1768, his income had shrunk to barely £6000 a year and his debts amounted to £114,000.

As Lord Pelham, Thomas took his seat in the House of Lords, a few days after his twenty-first birthday in August 1714, and it immediately became clear that he was interested in following a political career. An ardent Whig, and follower of the new Hanoverian monarch, George I, he bribed a London mob to demonstrate noisily in his favour on the day of his proclamation, and the new monarch was not tardy in repaying his debt. Two months later he was raised in the peerage to become Viscount Houghton and Earl of Clare, both titles previously held by his uncle, and was appointed Lord Lieutenant of both Middlesex and Nottinghamshire. In the general election, which followed George's accession to the throne, he threw his weight behind the new Whig ministry, in which his brother-in-law, Lord Townshend, was a Secretary of State. Thomas was now a landowner in no less than 11 counties, and in 3 of these – Sussex, Nottinghamshire and Yorkshire – he had significant influence in the choice of MPs. In this election, in January 1715, he was credited with securing the election of no fewer than 14 MPs, which made him the biggest 'boroughmonger' in the country. An impressed George I once more showed his gratitude, by restoring the Dukedom of Newcastle-upon-Tyne, and bestowing it on Thomas, shortly after his twenty-second birthday, in August 1715. A month later, the Jacobite Rebellion of 1715 broke out, and Newcastle, as he was now known, hastened to organize militia in both Middlesex and Nottinghamshire, as well as in his native Sussex, and dispatched his brother Henry to take part in the Battle of Preston, where the supporters of the Old Pretender, Prince James Edward Stuart, were decisively defeated.

The final step which Thomas took in his progress towards becoming a grandee was his marriage, on 2 April 1717, to Lady Harriet Godolphin: he was 23, she 16. This united Newcastle with two of the grandest Whig families, one of Harriet's grandfathers being Lord Godolphin, the chief minister during most of Queen Anne's reign, and the other, the Duke of Marlborough. It was, in fact, Marlborough's wife, Sarah, who negotiated the marriage of her granddaughter. She offered to provide a dowry of £10,000, but the already cash-strapped Newcastle demanded £30,000. Eventually a figure of £20,000 was agreed, and the fact that the normally avaricious Sarah agreed to part with this sum 'suggests that [she] was pleased to get her dull and unattractive granddaughter married off so well' (Browning, 1975, p. 12). A chronic invalid – or at least a hypochondriac – Harriet hardly proved an asset to her husband's career. Yet, he was devoted to her, and apparently – highly unusually for a Whig magnate at this period – remained entirely faithful to her. His hopes of siring progeny descended from the great Duke of Marlborough were not, however, to be realized. Harriet had a miscarriage shortly after the marriage, and was not thereafter able to conceive. Newcastle compensated for his childlessness by quite extraordinary devotion to other members of his family, particularly the children of his brother, Henry, but also extending it to a wide network of cousins, nephews and nieces, many of whom became beneficiaries of the extensive patronage which he was later able to dispense.

Newcastle's perpetual financial worries have been attributed to the large sums he expended in order to ensure the election of his nominees in Parliament for the constituencies (varying between 14 and 17, over a period of 40 years), where his influence was predominant (see Ray A. Kelch, 1974). In fact, he spent far more on endless improvements to his many houses, notably Claremont, the fine Surrey mansion built by John Vanbrugh. Both here, and in his grandiose London residence, Newcastle House, in Lincoln's Inn Fields, he embarked on a ceaseless round of entertainment for his large number of friends and associates of every kind. Everybody who was anybody benefited at one time or another from the Duke's hospitality.

Newcastle's political career took off in 1717 when, still at the age of 23, he was appointed Lord Chamberlain, with responsibility for George I's household – then an important political office, though outside the Cabinet. This brought him into frequent contact with the King, and a close friendship developed between the two men. When, later in the year, a son was born to the Prince of Wales (later George II), the King insisted that Newcastle should be named as his godfather. The younger George had other ideas and had a violent argument with the Duke when he personally conveyed the message to him, leaving Newcastle with the impression that he was challenging him to a duel. This was, apparently a misunderstanding, due to the Prince's inadequate knowledge of the English language, but the King angrily banished his son from the Court, and relations between the Lord Chamberlain and the heir to the throne remained extremely frosty for some years.

When the Cabinet split later in the same year, with the eviction of his brother-in-law, Lord Townshend, and of Robert Walpole (see Chapter 1), Newcastle sided with their opponents – Lord Stanhope and the Earl of Sunderland. Yet he was able to mend his fences with them, when they returned to power, with Walpole becoming First Lord of the Treasury and Townshend, Secretary of State (North), in 1721. This enabled Newcastle to appoint his brother, Henry Pelham, as Treasurer of the Chamber, and the two brothers now both became close associates of Walpole. So far as the latter was concerned, Newcastle's greatest assets were his closeness to the King, his great assiduity in carrying out his duties and his willingness (indeed, eagerness) to take on any additional task that might be assigned to him, his unquestioning acceptance of Walpole's judgment and – not least – his control of more than a dozen parliamentary constituencies. When Walpole succeeded in removing his rival, Lord Carteret, from the post of Secretary of State (South) and banishing him to the Lord Lieutenancy of Ireland, the general expectation (certainly shared by Pulteney himself) was that he would propose to the King the appointment of William Pulteney, his chief supporter in the House of Commons. But Pulteney was a man of independent judgement, and very considerable ability, and thus a new potential rival, so Walpole played safe by proposing Newcastle instead. This was to make a deadly enemy out of Pulteney, but bound Newcastle to him with ties of steel.

The two Secretaries of State shared responsibility for foreign affairs, and there were often serious disagreements and rivalry between them. Yet – at least in the early years – Newcastle readily accepted his junior status in relation to Townshend and goodnaturedly deferred to him, allowing him to set the broad outlines of foreign policy. Townshend gave over-riding priority to fostering good relations with France, after 20 years of almost continuous warfare between the two traditional enemies, and – with the close co-operation of Cardinal Fleury, France's chief minister during the minority of Louis XV, an informal alliance was formed, somewhat to the detriment of Britain's long-standing association with Austria. In 1725, however, the unexpected conclusion of an alliance between Austria and Spain, under the Treaty of Vienna, posed an added threat to British interests. On the one hand, Austria, through its development of ports in the newly acquired Austrian Netherlands, and the creation of an aggressive new trading company, based in Ostend, was beginning to present a direct challenge to the East India Company. On the other hand, Spain was blockading Gibraltar, and represented an ever-present threat to British possessions in the Caribbean. Townshend and Newcastle were agreed that the new alliance must be broken up, but disagreed strongly about how to go about it. Townshend regarded the Austrian threat as more serious, and advocated taking a pacific approach towards Spain to detach her from her new ally. Newcastle was adamant that Spain represented a far greater danger, and strongly urged the reconstitution of the earlier close ties with Austria.

Meanwhile, in 1727, the sudden death of George I threatened to put an immediate end to Newcastle's ministerial career. The new King, George II, initially intended to dismiss Walpole and his fellow ministers, and install a rival team under Spencer Compton, later Lord Wilmington (see Chapter 1). Partly persuaded by Queen Caroline, however, he soon changed his mind, and Walpole, together with both Newcastle and Townshend, resumed office, the King not seeming to harbour any resentment against Newcastle from their contretemps of ten years earlier. His disagreement with Townshend over relations with Austria and Spain now re-surfaced, and Walpole exerted himself to resolve the issue. His formerly close family ties with Townshend had been loosened by the death in 1726 of his favourite sister, Dolly (the second Lady Townshend), and he came down decisively on Newcastle's side. A disillusioned Townshend resigned, to spend the remainder of his life conducting agricultural experiments on his Norfolk estate.

Townshend's replacement as Secretary of State (North) was the inoffensive Lord Harrington, who readily accepted that Newcastle should henceforth play the dominant role in foreign policy. 'With this latest ministerial reshuffle, Newcastle was the second most powerful politician in the kingdom' (Browning, 2004). His influence was to grow even greater as the 1730s and 1740s progressed and, as he amassed an unprecedented degree of patronage. This covered not only the bulk of appointments in the diplomatic service and in the colonies, but also in Scotland, for which he had assumed responsibility for the administration after the suppression of the post of Secretary of State for Scotland, and ecclesiastical appointments, which he controlled after Bishop Edmund Gibson felt out with Walpole in 1736 (see Chapter 1). In addition to this was his ability to provide parliamentary seats for those who sought his favour. He also acted as leader of the House of Lords, where he was the government's chief spokesman. In fact, Newcastle became the Grand Panjandrum of the Walpole administration, with his finger in every pie, and his willingness to spend long hours in boring administrative duties. He was fussy and pompous, and regarded by many as a figure of fun, but both Walpole and the King came to see him as an indispensable wheel in the government machine. His main weakness was an inability to say no, which arose in part from his genuine good nature. This meant that though he had many critics he had very few enemies, of whom Horace Walpole, his leader's putative son, was the most persistent. Never an easy colleague, he was extremely touchy, and inclined to be jealous of others' success, including his brother, who eventually surpassed him, partly due to greater ability, but also because – like Walpole until his last years – he chose to remain in the House of Commons rather than accept a peerage. One of Newcastle's saving graces was that, though he was more than willing to use his vast patronage powers for political purposes, he was – like his brother Henry Pelham – personally incorruptible, and never used his 40-year-long ministerial career to enrich himself, despite his chronic shortage of cash.

Throughout the greater part of his long career, Newcastle's closest associate was Philip Yorke, later the first Earl of Hardwicke. A promising and highly ambitious young lawyer, two years his junior, Yorke was first elected to Parliament in 1719, under Newcastle's aegis for the Sussex borough of Lewes, transferring to another seat in the Duke's gift – Seaford – three years later. As a strong Walpolite, he became successively Solicitor-General, Attorney-General, Lord Chief Justice, and, finally, in 1737, Lord Chancellor, a post he was to hold for almost 20 years. During the final years of Walpole's rule, he formed, with Newcastle and Henry Pelham, a triumvirate of 'Old Corps Whigs' who contested the ministerial succession with such formidable rivals as Lord Carteret (later the Earl of Granville) and William Pulteney (later, Earl of Bath). An exceptionally level-headed man, Hardwicke was the sheet-anchor of this alliance, mediating between the two brothers who were often quarrelling, and also between them and King George II, who blew hot and cold in his relations with the two men. Newcastle, in particular, came to rely heavily on Hardwicke for advice, which was freely given and almost always sound.

Newcastle remained Secretary of State, first of the Southern, then of the Northern Department, for 30 years – from 1724 to 1754 – a record unlikely ever to be equalled. For all of this period, except for the first half dozen or so years when he was subordinate to Lord Townshend, he was the dominant influence in determining British foreign policy – only the Prime Minister or, of course, the King, being in a position to over-rule him. One such occasion was the outbreak, in 1733, of the War of Polish succession, which pitched Austria and Russia against an alliance between France, Spain and Piedmont-Sardinia, who were supporting Stanislaus Leszczynski (the father-in-law of Louis XV), against the rival claims of Frederick Augustus II of Saxony. Newcastle, who had negotiated the Treaty of Vienna two years earlier, which pledged mutual support in war between Britain and Austria, felt that Britain was now obliged to intervene on the Austrian side. Walpole, however, who felt that no important British interest was at stake, was determined to keep out of the war, and succeeded in imposing his view, even though many, including the King, sympathized with Newcastle's opinion. The Duke was resentful, feeling, not without some justification, that Austria would, in its turn, be reluctant to support Britain in any future conflict.

Newcastle, however, supported Walpole's efforts to reach a peaceful agreement with Spain over the mounting number of maritime disputes between the two countries. With the negotiation of the Convention of Pardo (see Chapter 1), in January 1739, it seemed that they had succeeded. Yet the failure of both sides fully to implement it, and the incessant pressure by British trading companies and sea captains, led to an overwhelming public demand for war, which Newcastle and a majority of his Cabinet colleagues felt unable to resist. The

War of Jenkins' Ear began in October 1739, Walpole, having resisted to the last, saying to Newcastle: 'This war is yours, you have had the conduct of it, I wish you joy of it.' In his biographer's words, 'this transformed Newcastle from *de facto* foreign minister to *de facto* minister of defence' (Browning, 2004). Under his guidance, the war did not go well – an initial success with the British capture of Porto Bello being over-shadowed by the failure of an attack on Cartagena, with heavy loss of life. The following year the death of the Emperor Charles VI, without a male heir, led to the War of Austrian Succession, in which Britain sided with Maria Theresa (Charles's daughter) in her war against Frederick the Great of Prussia, and his Bourbon allies, France and Spain. The War of Jenkins' Ear was merged with this greater struggle, which continued spasmodically until 1748 (see Chapter 3).

During the last couple of years of Walpole's premiership, there was a certain cooling of relations between the two men, and Newcastle was suspected of conspiring with opposition Whigs, notably Lord Carteret and William Pulteney, in moves to displace the Prime Minister. That he had contacts with them (as did many other Cabinet ministers) is undeniable, but it is doubtful if he did anything actively to undermine his chief. When Walpole finally resigned, in February 1742, having effectively lost his parliamentary majority, Newcastle remained as Secretary of State (South) in the administration formed by the Earl of Wilmington, which included Carteret as Secretary of State (North). Newcastle accepted with reasonable grace that Carteret's influence on foreign and defence policy should be greater than his own, but – with encouragement from Walpole (now retired as Earl of Orford) – worked together with his brother, Henry Pelham, and the Earl of Hardwicke to prepare for what they regarded as an inevitable showdown with their brilliant but erratic rival. Newcastle certainly regarded himself as the leader of the 'Old Corps' of Whigs, and as Walpole's political heir. With the death of Wilmington, in July 1743, he found it difficult to reconcile himself to the fact that his brother's appointment as First Lord of the Treasury made him, at best, only the number two man in the government, which he effectively became, with the ousting of Carteret, in November 1744 (see Chapter 3). Throughout the ten years of Pelham's premiership, they had a difficult relationship, with Newcastle being openly jealous of his brother's superiority and trying to act on the basis that the government was really a diarchy. Pelham was greatly irritated, but often deferred to his brother – especially on foreign policy issues, and the conduct of the War of Austrian Succession – even against his own better judgment. Although they frequently quarrelled, there was a deep bond of love and affection between the two men, and when Pelham died, on 6 March 1754, the Duke was devastated.

Within a week, however, he was persuaded (or persuaded himself) that as the unchallenged leader of the Whig party it was his duty also to take charge of the government. He might have preferred to do this while remaining Secretary of State, but as the post of First Lord of the Treasury had effectively become synonymous with the Prime Ministership, he determined to take it himself. 'With that decision taken', his biographer writes, 'a major problem loomed, for three vacancies needed filling' (Browning, 1974, p. 195). There were highly capable candidates for each of the three posts involved, but Newcastle declined to choose them, thereby in large part contributing to the disastrous failure of his own premiership. The most important of the posts was the leadership of the House of Commons, and, according to Horace Walpole, there were three outstanding candidates for the post – William Pitt, Henry Fox and William Murray, the Solicitor-General. Newcastle, however, was chary of awarding the post to a man of the highest ability, lest he should emerge as a rival leader to himself, and chose instead the mediocre Sir Thomas Robinson, who doubled up as Secretary of State (South), the second of the two vacancies to be filled. Before this could be effected, however, Newcastle had to contend with the difficulty that both King George II and majority parliamentary opinion clearly expressed a preference for Fox. Newcastle and Hardwicke accordingly 'devised the plan of offering him a restricted leadership, with conditions such as to make likely his rejection of the offer' (Browning, 1975, p. 197). An emissary, Lord Hartington (later the fourth Duke of Devonshire), 'was dispatched to Fox on 12 March to offer him the post of southern secretary with direction of affairs in the Commons'. Fox enthusiastically accepted, but when he met Newcastle the following day, he learnt that he would have no right to nominate people for office and would have no knowledge of which MPs were in receipt of secret service money (essential for maintaining a majority in crucial divisions). He angrily withdrew his acceptance, and asked, instead, to retain his previous post of Secretary at War.

As Chancellor of the Exchequer, a much more significant position when the First Lord of the Treasury was in the Lords, he chose Sir William Lee, a clearly inadequate choice, whom he replaced a month later with Henry Bilson Legge. Legge was a competent figure, but Newcastle withheld authority from him, and the effective head of the Treasury was one of the under-secretaries, James West, a crony of Newcastle. Having grossly mishandled his major ministerial appointments, on 16 March 1754 Newcastle embarked on his first premiership, which lasted for some two-and-a-half years. By general consent, it proved to be a catastrophe, not least because, under Newcastle's feeble leadership, Britain slipped into what became known as the Seven Years' War, utterly unprepared for the struggle.

It was the young Colonel George Washington who fired the first shots in the war, on 3 July 1754, even though Britain and France were still at peace. With the encouragement of the British governor of Virginia, he led a force of 350 troops in an ill-judged attack on Fort Duquesne (later renamed Pittsburgh), a French fortress dominating the Ohio valley. Defeated and captured by the French, his humiliation led Newcastle to conclude that a major reinforcement of British forces in North America was necessary. Vice-Admiral Edward Boscowen and Major-General Edward Braddock were dispatched, after much hesitation, but the former was unable to prevent the landing of French troops at Louisbourg, in Nova Scotia, while the latter was killed, fighting alongside Washington, in yet another abortive attack on Fort Duquesne, in July 1755.

It was only in May 1756 that war was officially declared between the two countries, in what to most Britons appeared as a continuation of the War of Austrian Succession, which had come to an end eight years earlier. There had, however, been a substantial *renversement des alliances*, largely due to maladroit diplomatic initiatives by Newcastle, who succeeded in alienating Britain's former ally, Austria, and the newly powerful Russia under Catherine the Great. France abandoned its earlier alliance with Protestant Prussia in favour of Catholic Austria, its traditional foe. These two countries now joined Russia, Sweden and Saxony in a struggle against Prussia and Great Britain. At first, the war went very badly for Britain, an early setback being the French conquest of Minorca, which had been under British rule since 1708.

Newcastle, and his ministers, now faced severe criticism, led by William Pitt in a series of coruscating speeches in the House of Commons, which Sir Thomas Robinson and other government spokesmen were quite unable to combat. In desperation, Newcastle made another approach to Henry Fox, who in November 1755 accepted the post of Secretary of State (South), combined with the leadership of the Commons. Though hardly Pitt's equal as an orator, he was an effective parliamentary performer, and under his guidance the government's business in the Commons began to proceed more smoothly. Outside Parliament, however, the barrage of criticism of ministers over the loss of Minorca continued unabated. Newcastle did everything he could to deflect it to Admiral John Byng, the unfortunate commander of the naval force which had been sent to relieve the siege of the island. Byng was accused of dilatoriness in arriving at the scene and of failing to engage the French forces with sufficient commitment. When a deputation from the City of London visited Newcastle to complain about Byng's conduct, he said to them: 'Oh! Indeed he shall be tried immediately – he shall be hanged directly' (Browning, 1975, p. 236). In what Browning describes as 'the most shameful chapter of his personal life', Newcastle hastened to convene a court-martial, taking good care to suppress the presentation of evidence which might have exonerated Byng. The admiral was acquitted of cowardice and disaffection, but was found guilty of neglect of duty and condemned to death, with a recommendation of mercy. George II refused to exercise clemency, and Newcastle made no attempt to persuade him to do so. Byng was executed aboard ship by firing squad on 14 March 1757. This sordid incident gained added notoriety from Voltaire's famous comment in *Candide* that 'In England it is thought well to kill an admiral from time to time to encourage the others.'

By the time of Byng's execution, Newcastle was no longer in office. The scapegoating of the admiral had not sufficed to ease the criticism of the Duke for his inept conduct of the war, and William Pitt's repeated oratorical onslaughts led to the gradual attrition of his parliamentary support. Eventually, in October 1756, Henry Fox decided he had had enough, and resigned his post to join Pitt in opposition. Unable to find an effective replacement, and belatedly recognizing that Pitt was now the inevitable war leader, Newcastle himself resigned a month later. To his great distaste, George II – who had consistently refused to give high office to him – was now forced to appoint Pitt as Secretary of State (South), with the fourth Duke of Devonshire as a figurehead Prime Minister.

It looked as though Newcastle's political career was now over. His premiership was almost universally seen as a disaster. An indispensable support – as a number two – to Walpole and then to Pelham, he had proved incapable of providing leadership himself. Chronically afraid of accepting responsibility, he was also too jealous of the success of others to devolve power to those who might have been able to use it to good effect. Yet the one extraordinary talent which he did possess – his mastery of patronage – was sorely needed by the incoming Devonshire government, which collapsed after less than eight months, in June 1757 (see Chapter 5). The King toyed with the idea of appointing the Earl of Waldegrave, but after three days abandoned the attempt, and turned again to the Duke, being reluctantly persuaded that he needed not only Pitt, but also Newcastle, if a stable government was to be formed. So, on 29 June 1757, he again became First Lord of the Treasury, and thus at least nominally Prime Minister. The government, however, is known to history as the Pitt-Newcastle government, with Pitt undoubtedly seen as the senior partner. Yet it was a true partnership – with Pitt triumphantly directing the war effort (see Chapter 9), while Newcastle, with the assistance of able colleagues in the Treasury, raising unprecedented sums to finance Pitt's expensive campaigns, as well as using his patronage powers to assure strong support for the government in both Houses of Parliament.

Newcastle's principal means of maintaining control of Parliament was the payment of bribes or pensions to peers and MPs, or to their family connections, out of Secret Service funds. Newcastle kept assiduous notes of the payments made, and accounted for every penny spent in periodic reports which he made directly to the King. These reports were to be a principal source for Sir Lewis Namier's groundbreaking work, *The Structure of Politics at the Accession of George III*, first published in 1957. This included a 56-page appendix setting out every payment made during Newcastle's two terms as Prime Minister. Typical examples are the payments made during the month of May 1759:

		£
May 2d	To Mr. Martin towards Camelford election	300
8th	To Mr. Medlycott for one year	600
11th	To Lord Saye and Sele, one year to Lady Day	600
	To Mr. Hamilton, the late Duke of Hamilton's relation, ½ a year due at Lady Day	100
	To Mr. Henry Fane, for Lyme as usual	100
17th	To Sir Francis Poole, one year due at Christmas	300
18th	To Mr. Dodd, one year	500
25th	Retained to myself by Your Majesty's special command, one quarter	1050
	To Lord Malpas, remainder	300
29th	To Orford, rent, ½ a year due at Midsummer last	100
	To Mr. Offley, ½ a year to Christmas	200

(Namier, 1957, p. 457)

On most issues Newcastle was obliged to defer to Pitt, and though they had occasional disagreements, their partnership worked extremely well, while Pitt's energetic direction of the war led to a series of major victories in Canada, India, Germany, the Caribbean, West Africa and the high seas. The year 1759, dubbed the 'year of victories', was without doubt the most successful in British military history. There seemed no reason to believe that the Pitt-Newcastle government would not be set for a long and glorious tenure. Then, on 25 October 1760, George II died suddenly, just short of his 77th birthday. Newcastle had never been close to him, but – after many misgivings – George had come to depend on him as an anchor of stability for his government during his final years. On his death, Newcastle wrote to Hardwicke's son, Joseph Yorke, that he had lost 'the best king, the best master & best friend that ever subject had' (Browning, 1975, p. 271). His tribute may not have been totally sincere, but perhaps betrayed a fear that his relationship with his successor would be a great deal less satisfactory. So it was to prove.

George III was 22 years old, and had very different ideas on how to reign than his grandfather, George II, and great-grandfather, George I. He considered that they had supinely allowed royal prerogatives to be appropriated by a Whig oligarchy, and was determined to put the process into reverse. He had been influenced by the Tory philosopher and former politician, Lord Bolingbroke, whose work *The Idea of a Patriot King* had fostered in him a deep aversion to party politics. He regarded parties as divisive, if not subversive, but his particular dislike was focused on the Whigs. Ministers should be appointed, in George's view, because of their 'virtue' not their political views. Devoted to his former tutor, the Earl of Bute, to whom he invariably referred as 'my dearest friend', he was determined to promote this royal favourite to the highest ranks of his administration. Initially, he was appointed to the largely honorific post of the Groom of the Stole, which hardly did justice to the great influence which he wielded from the day of George's accession. It should have been evident to both Pitt and Newcastle that the eruption of Bute was likely to undermine the position of both men, and that in self-defence they should work closely together. Unfortunately, Newcastle appeared not to realize this, and – in the hope of ingratiating himself to the King and to Bute – he connived in the appointment of the latter as the Secretary of State (North), without previously consulting Pitt, who was far from amused. Sharp differences now appeared between Pitt and Newcastle on the continuation of the war. Newcastle, acutely aware of the costs of the conflict was in favour of negotiating a quick peace with France, on the basis of the great territorial gains which had already been made. Pitt, however, was determined to continue the struggle until Britain's hereditary enemy had been brought to its knees. Bute was able to play off each of them against the other, and the government became seriously split on the issue, and also on the priority which should be given to waging the war in Germany, which was no longer a great royal concern, as George III placed much less value on his Hanoverian possessions than his predecessor.

The issue came to a head over the determination of Pitt to extend the war to Spain, which had recently concluded a treaty of alliance with France. Pitt believed that Spain would eventually come in on the French side, and that it was better for Britain to make a preemptive strike before its forces were properly mobilized. He was over-ruled by his Cabinet colleagues, led by Bute, and, declaring that 'I will be responsible for nothing that I do not direct' flounced out of the government in October 1761. With Pitt gone, Newcastle's position soon became untenable. He grumbled that 'My advice or opinion are scarce ever ask'd, but *never* taken. I am kept in, without confidence, and indeed without communication' (Browning, 1975, p. 283).

He submitted his resignation in May 1762. The King, who had taken a thorough dislike to him and had been heard to remark 'The more I know of this fellow the more I wish to see him out of employment', was delighted, and offered him a pension. Newcastle proudly refused, saying that if his fortune had suffered in service to the royal family 'it was my honour, my glory and my pride' (Browning, 1975, pp. 288–9).

Newcastle was now nearly 69, and a comfortable retirement might well have beckoned. But the still energetic Duke's whole interest in life centred on politics and administration, and he did not think for a moment of giving up. Grossly over-estimating his own continuing influence, he calculated that 'over 40 per cent of the House of Lords and thirty-five per cent of the members of the House of Commons would stand with him' (Browning, 1975, p. 291), and set himself the task of either controlling the government from the outside, or of evicting the new Prime Minister, Bute, from power. He was soon to be disillusioned. In October 1762, Bute dismissed the Duke of Devonshire, a close associate of Newcastle's, from his post as Lord Chamberlain. An enraged Newcastle then called on all his presumed followers to resign from office in protest. Few of them did so, and Bute, encouraged by Henry Fox, who was now again Leader of the House of Commons, sensing Newcastle's impotence, moved against his remaining supporters – in what became known as 'the slaughter of the Pelhamite innocents'. A goodly number of officials, high or low, who owed their initial appointments to one or other of the Pelham brothers, were peremptorily dismissed, while Newcastle himself was unceremoniously stripped of his Lord Lieutenancies of Middlesex and Nottinghamshire.

Altogether, Newcastle served for 7 years and 204 days as Prime Minister, but his total ministerial career was one of the longest in British history, some 46 years, including 30 continuously as a Secretary of State, and effectively number two or three in the government. Only Palmerston, who served – rather less continuously – for a total of 47 years has surpassed his record. The surprising fact about Newcastle is that he was able to survive for so long, when contemporary views of him were so negative. These views have been conveyed by the three principal chroniclers of the reign of George II – Horace Walpole, Lord Hervey and the Earl of Waldegrave. All three, however, were rival (and less successful) politicians, and each had a personal grudge against him, as the historian H.T. Dickenson has pointed out (Van Thal, Vol. I, 1974, p. 75). Walpole, he writes, described Newcastle as:

> A Secretary of State without intelligence, a Duke without money, a man of infinite intrigue, without secrecy or policy, and a Minister despised and hated by his master, by all parties and Ministers, without being turned out by any.

Waldegrave's view was just as damning:

> Talk with him concerning public or private business, of a nice or delicate nature, he will be found confused, irresolute, continually rambling from the subject, contradicting himself almost every instant.

Another contemporary politician, with literary inclinations – Lord Chesterfield – saw matters more in perspective. His view is cited by Lewis Namier, and goes a long way towards explaining why, despite his many faults, Newcastle was long regarded as being indispensable by those who worked with him:

The public put him below his level: for though he had no superior parts, nor eminent talents, he had a most indefatigable industry, perseverance, a court craft, and a servile compliance with the will of his sovereign for the time being. (Namier, 1961, p. 7)

Perhaps the final word should go to Reed Browning, who set out fairly the case for and against Newcastle in his distinguished biography of 1975. Writing a generation later, he was forced to conclude that 'Newcastle was not always guilty of poor judgment. But, leaving longevity aside, it is hard in surveying the entirety of his career to find substantive arguments for regarding it as anything other than an exercise in political mediocrity' (Browning, 2004).

Works consulted

Bigham, Clive (1924), *The Prime Ministers of Britain 1721–1924*, London, John Murray.

Black, Jeremy (1998), 'Thomas Pelham-Holles, Duke of Newcastle', in Robert Ecceleshall and Graham Walker, eds, *Biographical Dictionary of British Prime Ministers*, London, Routledge.

Brooke, John (1972), *King George III*, London, Constable.

Browning, Reed (1975),, *The Duke of Newcastle*, Newhaven, Yale University Press.

Browning, Reed (2004), 'Thomas Pelham-Holles, Duke of Newcastle (1693–1768)', in *Oxford Dictionary of National Biography*, Oxford, OUP.

Clark, J.C. D. (1982), *The Dynamics of Change; The Crisis of the 1750s and English Party Systems*, Cambridge, CUP.

Dickinson, H.T. (1974), The Duke of Newcastle (1754–56; 1757–62) in Herbert Van Thal, ed., *The Prime Ministers*, Volume I, London, Allen & Unwin.

Kelch, Ray A. (1974), *Newcastle: A Duke without Money*, London, Routledge & Kegan Paul.

Nulle, Stebelton H. (1931), *Thomas Pelham-Holles, Duke of Newcastle: His Early Political Career 1693–1724*, Philadelphia, University of Pennsylvania Press.

Namier, Lewis (1957), *The Structure of Politics at the Accession of George III*, London, Macmillan.

Namier, Lewis (1963), *England in the Age of the American Revolution*, 2nd ed., London, Macmillan.

Owen, John B. (1957), *The Rise of the Pelhams*, London, Methuen.

Turberville, A.S. (1929), *English Men and Manners in the 18th Century*, 2nd edition, New York, Galaxy Books, OUP.

5

William Cavendish, Fourth Duke of Devonshire – 'I Have No Motive but the King's Service'

Although he came from the very highest ranks of the aristocracy, surprisingly little is known of the early years of Britain's fifth Prime Minister. His date of birth was not recorded, though it was almost certainly in 1720, the year in which he was baptized (in St. Martin-in the Field Church on 1 June), nor is there any information about his schooling. It is assumed that he was educated at home by private tutors, and there is no record of his attending a university. William Cavendish was the second child and eldest son in a family of four boys and three girls. His father, the third Duke of Devonshire, was descended from a family which derived from the small town village of Cavendish Overhall in Suffolk – one of his ancestors, Sir John Cavendish, was Lord Chief Justice under Edward III, and was beheaded by a mob during the Peasants' Revolt, in 1381. The family came into great prominence in Tudor times, and the Earldom of Devonshire dated from 1618. It was the fourth Earl of Devonshire, one of the original 'Whigs' who tried to exclude the Catholic Duke of York (James II) from the throne, who established the family as a political dynasty. When James ascended the throne in 1685, he set out to ruin Devonshire, fining him £30,000, and exiling him from his court to his stately home at Chatsworth (Derbyshire). The Earl soon had his revenge, being one of the seven notables who invited William III to invade England, and himself seized the city of Nottingham in William's interest. The new King showed his gratitude by creating him the first Duke, and he and his son and grandson all held office in Whig administrations. William Cavendish also had distinguished Whig ancestry through the female line, his grandmother, being the daughter of Lord William Russell, revered as the first 'Whig martyr', being beheaded in 1683 for his alleged participation in the Rye House Plot against Charles II. His own mother, Catherine Hoskins, came from less eminent or adventurous stock. She was the daughter of a steward to the Duke of Bedford, and William's father may well have been thought to be marrying 'beneath' himself, in choosing her in an evident love-match.

64

With this background, it is no surprise that William Cavendish grew up as a very committed Whig, and a strong supporter of the Hanoverian monarchy. When he was nine years old, in 1729, his father became the third Duke, and subsequently held high office under Robert Walpole, successively as Lord Privy Seal, Lord Steward of the Household, and – for the unusually long period of seven years – as Lord Lieutenant of Ireland. William, who was now known by the courtesy title of the Marquess of Hartington, departed on the Grand Tour in his late teens, returning to be elected, very shortly after his coming of age, as one of the two MPs for Derbyshire, a family seat. This was in the April 1741 general election, and he was to remain an MP for ten years. A strong supporter of Robert Walpole, Hartington transferred his loyalties to the Pelham brothers (Henry Pelham and the Duke of Newcastle), who were his kinsmen, when Walpole was forced to resign in February 1742. Henry Pelham, who became Leader of the House of Commons, under Walpole's successor, Lord Wilmington, invited Hartington to move the loyal address after the King's Speech at the opening of Parliament in October 1742, a clear sign that the young Marquess was already being seen by the Whig hierarchy as having a promising political future.

On 27 March 1748, the 28-year-old Hartington married Lady Charlotte Elizabeth Boyle, aged 16. It was a good match. His bride was the daughter and heir of the third Earl of Burlington, and was also a peeress in her own right, as Baroness de Clifford. Her inheritance brought to Hartington vast landownings in Yorkshire, including Bolton Abbey and Londesborough, and equally large holdings in Ireland, including Lismore Castle, in County Waterford, as well as both Chiswick House and Burlington House in London. It boosted the Devonshires' already great political influence, and gave them control of 'pocket' boroughs in both the London and Dublin parliaments. The marriage had been arranged several years earlier by the third Duke, when Lady Charlotte was still a child. Hartington's mother, who had married for love, did not approve, and left her husband for a period, subsequently boycotting the marriage and remaining on distant terms with her son and his wife. Nevertheless, the marriage turned out to be a happy one, and four children were born in the seven years until Lady Charlotte (who never became the Duchess of Devonshire) died from smallpox, at the age of 23, in December 1754.

Hartington did not appear to be a very active Member of Parliament, but from the outset mixed freely with the most senior Whigs, becoming a close friend of Henry Fox and on good terms with William Pitt, though remaining somewhat wary of him. In 1749, following his marriage, he was translated to the House of Lords, assuming one of his father's subsidiary titles, as Baron Cavendish of Hardwicke. Around this time, he was sounded out about becoming tutor to the young Prince George, whose father, Frederick, Prince of Wales, had recently died. Devonshire declined, which had serious consequences, as the prince was instead to fall under the nefarious influence of the Earl of Bute (see Chapter 6). Two years later, he joined Henry Pelham's cabinet as Master of the Horse, and was sworn of the Privy Council. Pelham died in March 1754, to be succeeded by his brother, the Duke of Newcastle, who, the following year rewarded Cavendish with the prestigious post of Lord-Lieutenant of Ireland. It was an unusual appointment, as his father had recently served in the same capacity, and it was not customary to choose a major Irish landowner to the post. In fact, Hartington (who became the 4th Duke of Devonshire the following year, on the death of his father), proved an ideal choice. He had close family connections with each of the two factions vying for control of the Irish Parliament and administration. By a mixture of firmness and tact, he was able to reconcile the factions – at least temporarily – and when he returned to England, in October 1756, he was acclaimed as a successful viceroy, who had succeeded in putting the Irish administration on a firmer basis.

Now a widower, who had been devastated by the death of his young wife, and left with four young children to bring up, Devonshire did not expect – nor indeed did he aspire to – any other senior appointment. But his return came at a very convenient moment for George II. The war with France was going badly, the Newcastle government had just collapsed, and Henry Fox's attempt to form an administration had failed. The King was reluctantly persuaded that William Pitt, who had been his *bête noire*, must play a major role in any new government, in order to dynamize the war effort, but was unwilling to appoint him as Newcastle's successor. Pitt himself proposed the answer: who better to take the lead than the charming and unambitious Devonshire, whom everybody liked and who had all the right political connections? George II leaped at the suggestion, but Devonshire was highly reluctant, refusing to commit himself to serve beyond the end of the current parliamentary session. It was on this basis that, on 16 November 1756, he became First Lord of the Treasury, with Pitt, as Secretary of State (South), acknowledged as the dominant figure in the government, with responsibility for prosecuting the Seven Years War, which pitched Britain and Prussia against France, Austria, Russia, Sweden, Saxony and Bavaria.

Newcastle, who commanded the allegiance of a majority of Whig MPs, remained in opposition, so the parliamentary position of the new government was precarious from the outset. It could, however, rely on at least the benevolent neutrality of the Tories, who admired Pitt's ultra-patriotic stance, and of the Leicester House faction – the supporters of the late Frederick, Prince of Wales, who under the leadership of the Earl of Bute, had transferred their loyalty to his son, the young Prince George, still a minor but widely courted as the heir to the throne. On this basis, the new government's ambitions were strictly limited. It could attempt no controversial legislation, and confined itself to holding the ring until such time as the three dominant political actors, Pitt, Henry Fox and the Duke of Newcastle, should have resolved which of them – or what combination – would take control of the nation's affairs. Newcastle, in particular, was in no hurry to bring matters to a head. Hanging over him and his former colleagues (including Fox, who sought to dissociate himself as far as possible from them) was the threat of a parliamentary enquiry into their conduct of the war against France. Newcastle was determined that Admiral John Byng should be the main, or if possible, the sole scapegoat for the disasters which occurred under his premiership, and wanted to wait until after his trial and punishment before mounting any challenge to the Pitt-Devonshire government, as it was widely dubbed.

The principal significance of this government, which lasted only for 225 days – the shortest term during the eighteenth century – was the opportunity it gave to Pitt to show his mettle as a war leader. In short order, 'America was set forth as a strategic priority, a militia for home defence was established, a continental army was assembled, and naval raids against the French coast were organized' (Schweizer, 2004). It was widely noted that Pitt had dropped his earlier opposition to a major British commitment on the European continent and to the payment of subsidies to Britain's Prussian ally. Lord Lyttelton reported in a letter to a kinsman that Pitt's contribution to the debate on the King's speech in December 1756 was 'modest and discreet ... In short, he spoke like a minister; and unsaid almost all he had said in opposition' (Clark, p. 305). Nevertheless, Pitt proved himself less than a totally satisfactory colleague to most of his fellow ministers. He was a firm decision-taker, but was reluctant to consult with them. His health was bad, and he was frequently absent through attacks of gout. Sometimes their reality was doubted, and it was suspected that he used them as a pretext to avoid entering into discussions. Devonshire was largely a figurehead leader, and his chief functions seemed to be liaising with the King through their frequent meetings in 'the closet', and the tactful way in which he kept his rather heterogeneous team of ministers in reasonable harmony.

The first three months of the government were dominated by the trial of Admiral Byng for his alleged responsibility for the fall of Minorca to the French (see Chapters 4 and 9). Public opinion – and George II – was strongly against Byng, but the government itself was deeply divided, with Pitt and his brother-in-law, Lord Temple, the First Lord of the Admiralty, confidently expecting him to be acquitted, and then exerting themselves to persuade the King to exercise clemency, in the face of the unanimous recommendation by the judges that their mandatory death sentence should not be carried out. Pitt and Temple's concern was probably only partly motivated by humanitarian considerations: they wished to pin the blame firmly on to Newcastle and his associates, and did not want to see the Admiral used as a scapegoat. George II did not take kindly to their efforts. In a letter to the Duke of Newcastle, Baron Münchausen, the Hanoverian representative in London, reported that he was 'horrid angry' and resented personally any challenge to the court-martial's decision; from the outset he was determined to confirm it (Clark, p. 324). Byng was duly executed on 14 March 1757. Three weeks later, the King demanded the resignations of Pitt and Temple, his anger against them having been reinforced by the refusal of his favourite son, the Duke of Cumberland, to take over command of the British forces in Germany so long as Pitt remained as a minister.

Pitt's dismissal broke the back of Devonshire's government, and both he and George II soon accepted that it could not continue much longer. George eventually asked Henry Fox to draw up an alternative list of ministers, which he attempted to do, but failed to persuade a sufficiently senior team to serve with him, especially as 'public opinion' loudly demanded the return of Pitt, who resolutely refused to serve under his rival. The King then invited Earl Waldegrave to form a government (see Chapter 9), but his efforts collapsed after three days, by which time a deal had finally been struck between Pitt and Newcastle. They agreed together to form a government, which took office on 29 June 1757, with Newcastle as First Lord of the Treasury, and Pitt resuming his earlier post as Secretary of State (South), and acknowledged as 'war minister'. Fox was bought off with the lucrative post of Paymaster-General and the award of a peerage for his wife. Devonshire was happy to make way, and joined the Pitt-Newcastle government as Lord Chamberlain, a post he held until 1762. He remained a highly respected figure, was regarded as the effective leader of the Whigs and a trusted counsellor of George II. Some indication of the influence he continued to wield is revealed in the fragmentary diary which he kept during the years between 1759 and 1762. This was published in a scholarly edition in 1982 (Brown and Schweizer). A valuable historical document which throws much light on the inner machinations of the Pitt-Newcastle government, it reveals Devonshire as a shrewd observer but not very active participant. It shows him as a man who was primarily concerned to serve the King's interest, even in ways not wholly appreciated by the monarch himself. Indeed, he quotes himself as saying to the King's mistress, Lady Yarmouth, 'I have no motive but the King's service'. The occasion was a determined attempt to persuade the King to make Lord Temple, Pitt's brother-in-law, a Knight of the Garter in order to deter him (and probably also Pitt) from resigning their ministerial posts at a critical time. The King loathed Temple, but eventually accepted the force of Devonshire's unasked for advice, and the resignations were averted (Brown and Schweizer, pp. 9, 24–38).

Devonshire's cosy relationship with the monarchy came to an abrupt end on 25 October 1760, with the death of George II. His grandson and successor, George III, had a deep-seated aversion to leading Whig politicians who had served his predecessor, and though Newcastle was the principal target of his ire, Devonshire was not far behind. He was never to enjoy the confidence of the new King, despite his earnest desire to serve him. The arrival of Lord Bute as the new King's closest adviser, followed by appointment as First Lord of the Treasury, in succession to Newcastle, in May 1762, convinced Devonshire that he no longer had a useful role to play, and he ceased attending cabinet meetings, though he did not resign his post. In October 1762, George III wanted him to attend a meeting of the Privy Council to discuss the final peace terms being negotiated with France. Devonshire declined, on the grounds that he was insufficiently informed on the subject. A few days later, the King's coach overtook Devonshire's on the way to London, and George mistakenly assumed that he was on his way to cabal with other Whig dignitaries against the government. When Devonshire came to the Court to take his leave of the King before travelling north to Chatsworth, the King refused to see him, and dismissed him from office. A few days later he personally erased Devonshire's name from the list of privy councillors.

Shortly afterwards, Bute, and Henry Fox, now again leader of the House of Commons, began the 'slaughter of the Pelhamite innocents', in which a large number of officials who had been appointed by Newcastle or his brother, Henry Pelham, were peremptorily dismissed from office (see Chapter 4). Among the victims were Newcastle himself, the Marquess of Rockingham and the Duke of Grafton, who were dismissed from their Lord Lieutenancies respectively of Middlesex and Nottinghamshire, the North and West Ridings of Yorkshire, and the county of Suffolk. In sympathy with them, Devonshire immediately resigned as Lord Lieutenant of Derbyshire, bringing to an end a half century in which this post had been held by three successive Dukes of Devonshire. This was effectively the end of his political career, though he did host a dinner party of senior Whigs opposed to the introduction in March 1763 of a Cider Tax by Bute's government (see Chapter 6). Bute got his Bill through, but its unpopularity was a major factor in his decision to resign a few days later. Devonshire's health then began to deteriorate. He suffered from dropsy, and the following year he travelled to Spa, in Germany, to take the waters, in the hope of a cure. He died there on 2 October 1764. The editors of his diary (Brown and Schweizer, p. 18) speculated that 'his death at the age of 44 may have been hastened by the ingratitude of the young Sovereign whose family owed so much to the House of Cavendish'. He was a man of limited abilities, but a high sense of duty, who did his best to oil a system of government whose equilibrium was shaken by the machinations of coarser and more ambitious men.

Works consulted

Bigham, Clive (1924), *The Prime Ministers of Britain 1721–1924*, London, John Murray.
Brown, Peter D. and Schweizer, Karl W. eds. (1982), *The Devonshire Diary*, London, Royal Historical Society.

Brooke, John (1972), *King George III*, London, Constable.

Clark, J.C.D. (1982), *The Dynamics of Change: The Crisis of the 1750s and English Party Systems*, Cambridge University Press.

Howat, G.M.D. (1974), 'The Duke of Devonshire', in Herbert Van Thal, ed., *The Prime Ministers*, Volume I, London, Allen & Unwin.

Lawson, Philip (1998), 'William Cavendish, Fourth Duke of Devonshire', in Robert Eccleshall and Graham Walker, eds., *Biographical Dictionary of British Prime Ministers*, London, Routledge.

Schweizer, Karl Wolfgang (2004), 'Cavendish William, Fourth Duke of Devonshire', in *Oxford Dictionary of National Biography*, Oxford University Press.

6

John Stuart, Third Earl of Bute – the King's 'Dearest Friend'

John Stuart, third Earl of Bute, was the first Scotsman to become Prime Minister, the first Tory and the first, and perhaps the only one, to owe his appointment exclusively to his role as a royal favourite. He was the scion of a not particularly distinguished Scottish aristocratic family, his grandfather, the first Earl, serving as a Privy Councillor during the reign of Queen Anne. His father, the second Earl, lived only till the age of 33, and died, having risen no further than becoming the Lord Lieutenant of the County of Bute (an island abutting the Firth of Clyde), and for the last two years of his life a Lord of the Bedchamber to George I. The second Earl, however, made a rather grand marriage, to Lady Anne Campbell, daughter of the first Duke of Argyll, whose two brothers, the second Duke, and the Earl of Islay, were to become the most influential figures in Scotland, during the long premiership of Sir Robert Walpole. The young John Stuart was to inherit his father's title at the age of nine, and his two uncles were largely responsible for his upbringing, and Islay, in particular, greatly influenced him.

John was born in Edinburgh, on 11 May 1713, the eldest son and the second of eight children. He was one of the first Scottish nobles to attend Eton, where his contemporaries included two other future Prime Ministers, George Grenville and William Pitt, as well as Horace Walpole, the putative younger son of Robert Walpole. A scholarly figure, he went on to the University of Leyden, in the Netherlands, in 1728, graduating in Civil Law, four years later, at the age of 19. By 1732, accordingly to Professor McKelvey, 'Bute had become a stranger to Scotland, even his vacations from school having been spent at the English estate of his uncles. By education and inclination the young earl was a member of the English aristocracy' (McKelvey, p. 4). A further break from his Scottish background was his marriage in 1736 to Mary Wortley Montagu, the only daughter of the famous and eccentric traveller and writer, Lady Mary Wortley Montagu, and 'her miserly husband Mr Wortley' (Ibid.). Edward Wortley Montagu may have been a miser, but he was the owner of immense estates in Yorkshire, which his daughter was to inherit, and Bute's marriage provided him with the firmest of financial bases. After his graduation he had gone to live on the family estate at Mount Stuart, in Bute, where he was now able to make major improvements. Most of his time, however, was spent on pursuing his studies in a wide variety of fields, but particularly in botany, becoming in due course an acknowledged authority on British plants. His uncles, however, foresaw a political future for him, and in 1737, Lord Islay secured his election as a Scottish representative peer, when a vacancy arose from the death of the Earl of Orkney. He also obtained a lucrative sinecure as a commissioner of police for Scotland, and in 1738, he was made a Knight of the Thistle. 'As a personable and well connected young nobleman, Bute had every reason to assume that the future would provide still greater rewards' (McKelvey, p. 5). The following year, however, his political career came to a juddering halt, when his two uncles found themselves on different sides on the question of whether Britain should go to war with Spain (see Chapter 1). Argyll was all for war, but Islay supported Robert Walpole's effort to avoid conflict by negotiating the Convention of Pardo with Spain. Argyll joined in the revolt against Walpole on the issue, and Bute supported him, but Walpole was able to win the critical parliamentary division and Argyll and Bute were forced into opposition, Bute losing his seat as a representative peer in the subsequent election, in 1741. It was 20 years before he was able to return to the House of Lords.

Bute retired for five years to live on his estate, where he began to raise a large family, consisting eventually of five sons and six daughters. Life in a Scottish backwater, however, eventually began to pall, and in 1746 he bought a half share in Kenwood House, adjoining Hampstead Heath, from his uncle, Lord Islay, who had now succeeded his elder brother, becoming the third Duke of Argyll. The following year a chance encounter totally changed the future course of his life. He had gone to a race meeting at Egham, which was attended by Frederick, Prince of Wales, the disaffected son and heir to George II. The two men were unacquainted, but when it started to rain the bored Prince retired to a tent, and called for a game of cards. 'There was no one of sufficient quality to take a hand with him until an equerry recollected that he had seen Lord Bute on the course. Bute was brought in, presented, and sat down at the table' (Bigham, 1924, p. 119). They hit it off very well, and soon became inseparable companions, Bute becoming a fixture at Leicester House, the Prince's London residence, where opposition politicians met to plot and carouse. The Prince found him good company, but had no very elevated opinion of his talents, describing Bute to Lord Waldegrave as 'a fine showy man who would make an excellent ambassador in a court where there was no business' (Ibid., p. 120). Frederick's wife, Princess Augusta, however, was completely taken by this handsome and erudite Scottish noble, who became her principal adviser after the death of the Prince in 1751. A frightened woman, Augusta's fears centred on the risk of George II dying before her son, Prince George, came of age. This would necessitate the appointment of a regent, and though she herself was scheduled for this role, she feared that the Duke of Cumberland, George II's second son, would be substituted in the event. In her fanciful mind, it was then just a short step to her imagining Cumberland behaving like Richard III, who was regent to his young nephew, Edward V, and whom he murdered, together with Edward's younger brother, in the Tower of London, and had himself proclaimed King. Augusta communicated her fears to her son, who became physically afraid of his uncle. Cumberland was not a very nice man, as his reputation as the 'Butcher of Culloden' showed, but he was devoted to serving his nephew's interests, and none of his actions gave the slightest justification for his sister-in-law's paranoia. Bute should have firmly told Augusta that her fears were groundless, but he chose not to do so. A rumour, put about by Horace Walpole, that they were lovers, was given almost universal credence. It was, indeed, the basis of a devastating retort delivered to the princess by one of her maids of honour (later the notorious Duchess of Kingston) whom she had reproved for her promiscuity, asking her 'les raisons de cette conduite'. 'Ah, Madame', she replied, 'chacun a son but' – an obvious pun on Bute's name (Bigham, p. 120). Modern scholars, however, have expressed doubts. John Brooke, for example, the author of a much admired biography of George III, wrote:

> Two persons less likely to engage in a love affair than Bute and the Princess could hardly be imagined. In 1755 Bute was forty-two, happily married to an attractive and devoted wife, and the father of a large family. He had never been suspected of gallantry. The Princess was thirty-six, the mother of nine children, and more famed for her discretion and good conduct than for her beauty or sexual charms. Everything we know of the character of either is evidence against a love affair. (Brooke, 1972, p. 48)

Whatever the truth of the matter, there is no doubting the closeness of Bute's relationship to the Princess or the enormous confidence that she had in him. She used all her wiles on a reluctant George II to get him to appoint Bute as tutor, and later Groom of the Stole (effectively head of the Prince's household) to her son, the future George III, and his tutorship began in1755, when the still immature and impressionable prince was barely 17. In addition to his duties with the Prince, Bute became the acknowledged leader of the Leicester House faction, and represented its interests in his dealings with the Court and with other politicians, his greatest *coup* being to recruit William Pitt, in an alliance which led indirectly to the resignation of the Duke of Newcastle as Prime Minister in 1757. Pitt was fiercely opposed to the government's policy of paying subsidies to continental allies in the war against France and Austria, and this was a view shared by Bute and his Leicester House cohorts. Bute,

Princess Augusta and the young Prince George all felt that Pitt was now unreservedly attached to their cause, and – when he later joined the governments of Devonshire and the second Newcastle administration – were aghast when he promptly reversed his earlier stance over the payment of subsidies, and failed to consult Bute over important government decisions. They came to regard him as a fair weather friend, and reacted hostilely to him.

Prince George had had several other tutors before Bute, and none of them had regarded him as a very satisfactory charge. Sullen and indolent (by his own later admission), he had failed to take advantage of the knowledge which a series of learned and distinguished men had done their best to impart. With the arrival of Bute, all that was to change. The lonely and refractory boy, who had largely been excluded from the company of his own generation, had seldom before encountered an adult to whom he was able to relate. His father, whom he adored, had died when he was 12, and he was desperately in need of a 'father figure' to whom he could look up as a role model. Bute fulfilled this part to perfection. Twenty-five years older than the prince, and a former associate of his father, he 'represented all the qualities in which the prince was so deficient – handsome, self-assured, well educated' (McKelvey, p. 54). George immediately responded to him, and resolved to put his indolence behind him. The very close relationship which they soon built up is reflected in the series of letters which the prince wrote to his tutor, and which were published under the editorship of Romney Sedgwick in 1939 (*Letters from George III to Lord Bute, 1756–1766*). He invariably addressed Bute as 'My dearest Friend', and was to write 'I am young and unexperienc'd , and shall exactly follow your advice, without which I shall inevitably sink', adding 'I daily return Heaven thanks, for having met with such a friend as you' (Ibid). Later, in June 1756, when George II, and leading ministers (including Newcastle) resolutely opposed Bute's appointment as Groom of the Stole, and he himself suggested that 'the simplest solution might be for him to leave Leicester House', he wrote imploring him not to do so:

> It is true that the Ministers have done everything they can to provoke me, that they have call'd me a harmless boy, and have not even deign'd to give me an answer when I so earnestly wish to see my Friend about me … I know few things to be more thankfull for to the Great Power above, than for its having pleased Him to send you to help and advise me in these difficult times. I do hope that you will from this instant banish all thoughts of leaving me. (Ibid., p. 41)

Eventually, the Duke of Newcastle, not wishing to alienate a young man who might ascend to the throne at any time, withdrew his opposition, and persuaded George II to agree to Bute's appointment, and his closeness to, and influence over, the prince grew even greater.

As a tutor, Bute was nothing if not thorough. He gave George an extensive grounding in history, constitutional law, finance, sciences and the arts, setting him to write lengthy essays, sometimes more than 50 pages long, which are preserved in the Royal Archives in Windsor, complete with Bute's often pedantic annotations. If he had left it at that, this would have been an excellent preparation for the future king's reign. But he also imbued his young charge with his own deep political beliefs and prejudices. These were largely based on the writings of Lord Bolingbroke, the former Tory (and sometime Jacobite) politician and philosopher, particularly his *chef d'oeuvre*, *The Idea of a Patriot King*. A key theme, as interpreted by Bute, was that the two first Hanoverian monarchs had been derelict in allowing many of their prerogatives, preserved under the Glorious Revolution settlement, to be expropriated by a corrupt Whig oligarchy, which had governed in its own interest rather than for the public good. They should now be reclaimed by a monarch, whose moral authority would be such that nobody would doubt that he was acting in the interest of the country as a whole rather than any party or faction. This king would appoint as his ministers only men of 'virtue' rather the general run of politicians, most of whom, Bute implied, were knaves or worse. Bute proceeded insidiously to poison the mind of the young Prince against all the leading Whig politicians of the day, reserving much of his venom for Pitt, whose achievements as a war leader, he consistently downplayed, emphasizing instead the 'enormous debts' which his policies incurred. George showed how completely he had absorbed Bute's lessons by composing an essay on the British political system, which is copiously quoted in Brooke's biography:

> Let the day come in which the banner of virtue, honour and liberty shall be displayed, that noble actions and generous sentiments shall lead to the royal favour, and prostitution of principle, venality and corruption meet their just reward, the honest citizen, the zealous patriot, will lift up their heads, all good men will unite in support of a government built on the firm foundations of liberty and virtue, and even the degenerate mercenary sons of slavery will suppress their thoughts, and worship outwardly the generous maxims of a prince, while they in secret detest his maxims and tremble at his virtues. Power, wealth, and honours still remain the favourite objects, but let the royal fiat change, the road revive, the long untrodden path, and crowds of all denominations will soon frequent it, and a generous reformation will ensue…The prince once possessed of the nation's confidence, the people's love, will be feared and respected abroad, adored at home by mixing private economy with public magnificence. He will silence every clamour, be able to apply proper remedies to the heavy taxes that oppress the people, and lay a sure foundation for diminishing the enormous debt that weighs this country down and preys upon its vitals. (Brooke, p. 65)

A thoroughly idealistic young man, George took seriously Bute's insistence on the necessity for a high moral character, and resolved to shape his life accordingly. In this, he was largely successful, being, for example, the only one of the five Hanoverian kings not to keep mistresses. A high-minded man, as Bute himself was, he was unable, also like Bute, to avoid becoming self-righteous. Bolingbroke had written that the Patriot King 'must begin to govern as soon as he begins to reign ... His first care will be ... to purge his court and call into the administration such men as he can assure himself will serve on the same principles on which he intends to govern' (quoted by Bigham, p. 121). It seems to have been explicitly agreed between Bute and the Prince, long before the long-awaited day of George II's decease, that he should become the first Prime Minister of the new reign.

Yet, when on 25 October 1760, word came of the King's sudden death, Bute's nerve failed him. He sensed that to dismiss Newcastle and Pitt at a time when their popularity was soaring after an unprecedented series of victories in the Seven Years War would be tempting Providence, and he advised George to await a more opportune moment. Meanwhile, he was content to act and to be seen as the power behind the throne. When Newcastle went to see the new King, he was told: 'My Lord Bute is your very good friend. He will tell you my thoughts at large'. What George intended was that though – for the time being – Bute was not to become First Lord of the Treasury, he would be the dominant force in the administration, equal or superior to both Newcastle and Pitt. The former was relatively relaxed about this prospect, concluding that if he humoured the new King by accepting Bute's projected role with equanimity it would protect his own influence and position. Pitt, however, sensed from the outset that this new constellation would not work, and that the King would soon have to choose between him and his former tutor.

Initially, Bute did not become a minister, and – if he had his constitutional position would have been anomalous, as he was not a member of either House of Parliament. As it was, some eyebrows were raised when he apparently attended the first Privy Council of the new King's reign, on 25 October, and his name was left out of the list of those attending published the following day in the *London Gazette*. He was sworn in as a member on 27 October. It was he who had drafted the King's address to the Council, and Bute may well have influenced George when he inserted into his first speech to Parliament the famous words 'Born and educated in this country, I glory in the name of Britain.' This was meant to emphasize the difference between him and his two predecessors, who continued to be viewed as foreigners throughout their reigns. It was certainly Bute, a Scot, who suggested substituting 'Britain' for 'England' in George's original wording. After five months, during which he held only the Court post of Groom of the Stole, but was in daily contact with the King, who constantly sought his advice, Bute's position was 'regularised' by his appointment to the cabinet as Secretary of State (North) on 5 March 1761. A week later, Lady Bute was created Baroness Mount Stuart of Wortley in the peerage of Great Britain, while Bute himself was elected as a Scottish representative peer, in May, returning to the Upper House after an interval of 20 years. Bute's appointment was resented by most of the Whig members of the Cabinet, who rightly perceived him as a 'cuckoo in the nest', not least by Pitt, who had not been consulted, and who felt that Newcastle, who had, should have objected strongly, instead of quietly acquiescing in a move which was likely to undermine his own position, as well as Pitt's. Once in the Cabinet, Bute played a dominating role in all its discussions, though he did not attempt to question Pitt's direction of the war. In the summer of 1761, he played a leading part in formulating the British position in peace negotiations with France, which proved abortive. Instead, the French King, Louis XV, agreed to renew a 'family compact' with his first cousin, Charles III of Spain, which many saw as a prelude to Spanish entry into the war on the French side. Pitt was vehemently of this view, and proposed a pre-emptive strike against Spain, in the form of an attack on the annual 'treasure fleet' on its way from South America. Bute strongly opposed this in the Cabinet, and his arguments won round all the other members, with the exception of Pitt's brother-in-law, Lord Temple. Pitt, unwilling to be over-ruled on any issue concerning the war, immediately resigned, on 5 October 1761, declaring 'I will be responsible for nothing that I do not direct' (see Chapter 9).

With Pitt gone, there was no one to challenge Bute's dominance, and he took over running the war effort, scaling back Britain's participation in the war in Germany, and its subsidy to Prussia, in a bid to reduce the 'enormous debts' which so worried him and the King. This alienated Frederick the Great, who henceforth saw Britain as an unreliable ally, and sought instead an alliance with Russia, to the great consternation of Pitt, who accused Bute of leading Britain into isolation. Meanwhile, the evidence grew that Spain was preparing to intervene in support of France, and on 4 January 1762 Bute himself took the initiative of declaring war, despite his earlier stance. He was now to rival Pitt's earlier energy in prosecuting the war, at least in its maritime dimensions, and 1762 became another 'year of victories', with both Havana and Manila being seized from Spain, and Martinique, Grenada, St. Vincent, St. Lucia and Tobago from France. Meanwhile, in May 1762, Newcastle, feeling that he had become a mere cipher in his own government finally resigned, leaving the way open for Bute to become First Lord of the Treasury, and thus the nominal as well as the actual head of the administration. George Grenville, a younger brother of Earl Temple, and brother-in-law to Pitt, from whom he was estranged, succeeded him as Secretary of State (North), while Henry Fox, who remained as Paymaster-General, became Leader of the House of Commons, assuring by his none too scrupulous means that a solid majority was maintained for Bute's policies, despite his growing unpopularity. It was Fox who initiated the so-called 'massacre of the Pelhamite innocents', in October 1762, when George III wrongly suspected Newcastle and Devonshire of plotting a 'coup', and stripped them of their lord lieutenancies, while dismissing a wide range of their followers from more junior posts (see Chapter 5). Bute and the King were now determined to bring the war to an end as quickly as possible, in order to end the drain on Britain's finances, and the Duke of Bedford was despatched to France to negotiate the best terms he could get. This did not prove difficult, as both France and Spain, following their new round of defeats, were in no mood to extend the struggle, while France's allies – Russia, Austria and Sweden – had already signed separate peace agreements with Prussia, restoring the ante-bellum situation in Central Europe. On 10 February 1763, the Treaty of Paris was signed between Britain, France, Spain and Portugal. Its main provisions included the cession by France to Britain of Canada, Cape Breton Island and the Middle West as far as the Mississippi, but it retained the islands of St. Pierre and Miquelon and a share in the Newfoundland fisheries. In the West Indies, Britain also obtained the islands of Grenada, Dominica, St.Vincent and Tobago, while annexing Florida from Spain. In Africa it acquired Senegal, while its dominant position in India was assured by the defortification of all the remaining French enclaves. In Europe it recovered possession of Minorca, and France was compelled to evacuate and restore the territories it had conquered in Hanover, Hesse and Brunswick.

Most historians have concluded that this was an honourable peace which brought a fair reward for the achievements of British arms, but it was heavily criticized by Pitt who claimed that the French had been let off too lightly. Thanks to the efforts of Henry Fox, the peace treaty had little difficulty in winning parliamentary approval, but Pitt, who was widely regarded as a martyr, largely won the battle for public opinion, and Bute (whose nickname was 'Jack Boot') became wildly unpopular, being the target of many demonstrations where jackboots and petticoats (an allusion to his rumoured affair with Princess Augusta) were burnt. Bute was also subjected to savage attacks in the press, John Wilkes founding his famous publication *The North Briton*, of which 45 issues appeared between June 1762 and April 1763, for the specific purpose of hounding Bute and the many Scottish associates whom he was believed to have brought into office. Altogether, at this period, Bute 'was lampooned in over 400 prints and broadsheets' (Schweizer, 2004). Bute became unnerved, fearing assassination. 'On 25 November [1762], on his way to the opening of Parliament, he was hissed and pelted by the mob, and if the Guards had not been summoned his life would have been in danger' (Brooke, p. 100). Unfamiliar with the capricious ways of the London mob, Bute concluded that it must have been bribed to attack him by his political opponents, and told George III that he wished to resign as a minister, and revert to his previous status as a privileged courtier controlling the government from behind the scenes. George, not lacking courage himself when faced by a hostile mob, was disappointed, but sympathized with Bute and believed that his fears were justified. Bute agreed, however, to remain in office at least until the Treaty of Paris had been ratified. This happened in March 1763, by which time the government was involved in a heated controversy over a proposal by the Chancellor of the Exchequer, Sir Francis Dashwood, to impose a tax on cider. Its critics maintained that 'the collection and enforcement of [this tax] would have threatened personal liberty through the intrusion of inquisitorial officials into private dwellings', while 'the measure was portrayed by Bute's opponents as part of an odious scheme to introduce a "general excise" similar to that envisaged by Walpole in 1733' (Schweizer, 2004). The measure proved intensely unpopular, but Bute strongly defended the Bill in the House of Lords, and it received royal approval on 1 April 1763. The effort finally un-nerved Bute, and he resigned eight days later, recommending the King to appoint Henry Fox in his place. George III baulked at this, regarding Fox as a man of insufficient 'virtue', whereupon Bute proposed his own protégé, George Grenville, in the belief that he would be happy to act as his puppet. He was to be grievously disappointed. Bute had been less than a year in office, 317 days, the first of a series of short-lived premiercies, reflecting the impatience and immaturity of the young monarch. Altogether, George III ran through six different Prime Ministers in the first ten years of his reign, before settling on Lord North, in 1770, who was to serve for twelve years.

Bute retained his position as Keeper of the Privy Purse, but otherwise was now a simple courtier. Nevertheless, both he and the King intended that he should still have the overall direction of the government, but this was to underestimate the determination of Grenville and his fellow ministers to be their own masters. As recounted in Chapter 7, Grenville consistently outmanoeuvred him, and the King was eventually obliged to dispense with Bute's services, and to promise not to meet him privately. After George III peremptorily dismissed Grenville, in July 1765, Bute and his close associates were much involved in the comings and goings which led to the formation of the governments of Lord Rockingham, and subsequently of William Pitt, now Lord Chatham, in July 1766. Bute and his friends were deeply disappointed at not being included in Chatham's government, and Bute wrote a letter of bitter complaint to the King. George, however, who had by now become thoroughly disillusioned about Bute's political judgment, returned a cold reply, and the friendship, which George had often said would continue for the rest of their days, was at an end. This breach, however, was not known to the public, and for several years afterwards Bute was widely believed to wield a secret and malign influence on the King. His reputation as a bogyman continued to haunt him up to and beyond his death, which did not occur until 1792, nearly 30 years after he had ceased to be Prime Minister.

The death of Bute's father-in-law, Edward Wortley Montagu, in 1761 had left Bute as one the richest men in the country. His family's wealth was further increased by the grand marriages which several of his children were to make. Bute acquired the magnificent estate of Luton Hoo, in Bedfordshire, and commissioned Robert Adam to build a grand London residence in Berkeley Square. This was to be known as Bute House, but before it was finished he sold it off to the Earl of Shelburne, and it was subsequently renamed Lansdowne House. He also built a villa at Highcliffe, in the Isle of Wight, where he was to spend his declining years. He also became a major patron of both the arts and the sciences, being a particularly generous benefactor of several Scottish universities. He continued his interest in botany, publishing in 1785 a nine-volume work entitled *Botanical Tables Containing the Families of British Plants*, containing 654 hand-coloured plates, which won him the approbation of such international scholars as Linnaeus and Albrecht von Haller. He may have been pompous and narrow-minded, and was certainly pedantic, but there was no doubting the seriousness of his scholarship. His poor historical reputation is at least partly due to the fact that most history was written by Whigs, including such contemporaries of Bute's as Horace Walpole and the Earl of Waldegrave. Recently, there has been an attempt at least partially to rehabilitate him, led by Professor Karl Wolfgang Schweizer. Writing in the *Oxford Dictionary of National Biography*, he concluded:

> Ultimately, however, Bute is more than a symbol of the aberrations conventionally associated with George III's early reign. Though brief and turbulent, his tenure as secretary of state and as prime minister was not without success. While his plans for political reform remained unfulfilled, Bute showed himself generally capable of leading a ministry in time of domestic stress and international conflict. For all his limitations, he implemented a coherent political strategy, one that consolidated Britain's imperial achievement and projected a minimalist continental policy at a time of intensifying national concern over the financial consequences of war. Altogether, he was a responsible, cautious minister who maintained his concentration on the most important issues and had a clear sense of political priorities. (Schweizer, 2004)

There is something in this, but Bute's principal contribution was to act as a Svengali to a future monarch. He was largely responsible for moulding the man who came to the throne in 1760. A better man, and far more conscientious, than the other Hanoverian rulers, he was unfortunately to prove a worse king. Bute must bear much of the blame for this.

Works consulted

Bigham, Clive (1924), *The Prime Ministers of Britain 1721–1924*, London, John Murray.

Brooke, John (1972), *King George III*, London, Constable.

McKelvey, James Lee (1973), *George III and Lord Bute: The Leicester House Years*, Durham, North Carolina, Duke University Press.

Pares, Richard (1953), *George III and the Politicians*, Oxford, OUP.

Rudé, George (1962), *Wilkes and Liberty*, Oxford, Clarendon Press.

Schweizer, Karl W. ed. (1988), *Lord Bute: Essays in Re-Interpretation*, Leicester, Leicester University Press.

Schweizer, Karl (1998), 'John Stuart, Third Earl of Bute', in *Biographical Dictionary of British Prime Ministers*, London, Routledge.

Schweizer, Karl Wolfgang (2004), 'John Stuart, Third Earl of Bute' (1713–1792), in *Oxford Dictionary of National Biography*, Oxford, OUP.

7

George Grenville – Able Premier, Undermined by His Own Prolixity

George Grenville was a reluctant politician, but once he had committed himself to a political career, he gave it his all, and mastered the details of both Parliament and administration more comprehensively than any of his contemporaries. Horace Walpole described him as 'the ablest man of business in the House of Commons, and, though not popular, of great authority there from his spirit, knowledge, and gravity of character'. Although he rose to be Prime Minister, he did not enjoy the success which his talents deserved. Caught between his rivalry with his elder brother, Lord Temple, and his brother-in-law, William Pitt, and the impatience of the young George III, his ambitions were circumscribed, and he finished up by being more respected than influential. Born in London on 14 October 1712, the second of five sons and a daughter, his father, Richard Grenville, was descended from a Norman family who had been local landowners in Buckinghamshire since the twelfth century, with an estate at Wotton Underwood. Although he, and several of his ancestors, had been Members of Parliament for Buckinghamshire constituencies, they had never amounted to very much on the national political scene. The family's importance greatly increased, however, through inter-marriage with the much grander Temple family, their neighbours in Buckinghamshire, with their magnificent estate at Stowe. Richard Grenville had married Hester Temple, whose brother, Viscount Cobham, was immensely wealthy, and controlled a string of parliamentary constituencies. This meant that, in the course of time, all five of Richard Grenville's children were able to take up seats in the House of Commons.

Very little is known of George's childhood, as all the family papers were destroyed in a great fire at Wotton in 1820. All his biographer is able to say about it was:

George enjoyed a happy childhood, with devoted parents and a closely knit family providing all the amusement and stimulus he required. At Eton and

Christ Church, Oxford, he proved a conscientious, hard-working scholar; he did not gamble or drink heavily and left no hint of scandal behind him. (Lawson, 1984, p. 3)

As a second son, George realized that he would have to earn his own living, and set his sights on a legal career, joining the Inner Temple in 1729, and being called to the bar in 1735, aged 23. During this period, he was dependent for financial support on his elder brother, Richard (later Lord Temple), and though he inherited £3000 from his father, in 1727, this too was administered by his brother. Philip Lawson comments: 'He endured this period of dependence with good grace but in his later years economy and thrift became the *modus vivendi* of George's family life. These restraints coloured his attitude to personal finances and eventually those of the nation too' (Ibid., p. 4).

George was doing well in the law, and had no thought of switching professions. But, in 1741, when he was 28, his uncle drafted him in to fill a vacancy in one of his 'pocket' boroughs – Buckingham – where the electoral role contained only 13 voters. Cobham had become a man with a mission. A strong Whig, and previously a loyal supporter of Sir Robert Walpole, he had fallen out with the Prime Minister in 1733, when he fiercely opposed his plans to introduce a general excise duty (see Chapter 1). Walpole responded by stripping Cobham of the colonelcy of his regiment, and Cobham planned to take his revenge, bringing into Parliament, in the 1734 general election, four relatives sworn to oppose Walpole, including George's elder brother, Richard, and William Pitt. This group, all of whom took an ultra-patriotic line, were mockingly referred to by Walpole as 'the boy patriots', but were otherwise known as 'Cobham's Cubs'. All four of them made a mark in the House by the virulence of their attacks on Walpole, and Pitt quickly won a reputation as a much-feared debater. By 1741, Walpole's position had weakened and he appeared vulnerable because of the lukewarm way in which he was prosecuting the 'War of Jenkins' Ear' (see Chapter 1). Cobham called for reinforcements, bringing into the House not only George Grenville, but his younger brother, James. Grenville's aunt, Christian Lyttelton, thought it a great pity that her nephew should abandon 'so promising a legal career' to become an opposition politician. 'A bold stroke for so young a lawyer to begin with being against the Crown', she told her son, the Bishop of Carlisle, and blamed his friends and relatives for 'putting him on so hazardous a point'.

George's election passed without incident – he was unopposed, and his expenses came to a modest £58 12s 7d. He hadn't sought to get into Parliament, but he made an instant mark. His maiden speech, on 21 January 1742, supporting a motion by William Pulteney to investigate Robert Walpole's conduct of the war caught the attention of Horace Walpole, who wrote in a letter: 'There were several glorious speeches on both sides; Mr. Pulteney's two,

W. Pitt's and Grenville's ...' (Ibid., p. 8). Grenville very soon went on to establish himself as a highly effective parliamentarian. He lacked Pitt's bravura as an orator, but his speeches were always well prepared and well informed, and he soon developed a mastery of parliamentary procedure unrivalled by any other MP. It was an extremely rare event for him to come off second best in a debate. It was not long before Grenville was recognized as the effective number two to Pitt among Cobham's group of opposition Whigs in the House of Commons. When, in 1744, the group was brought into the government of Henry Pelham, Grenville became a member of the Admiralty Board, and its chief spokesman in the House of Commons, the First Lord, the Duke of Bedford, being in the House of Lords. After three years, he was promoted to be a Lord of the Treasury, and became the secondary spokesman for Treasury affairs in the Commons, where Pelham himself combined the posts of First Lord of the Treasury and Chancellor of the Exchequer. He held this post for seven years, proving himself a first class administrator, as well as a highly effective parliamentarian. Temperamentally, he was ideally suited to these twin roles, his cousin, Thomas Pitt, recalling that he was:

> a man born to public business, which was his luxury and amusement. An Act of Parliament was in itself entertaining to him, as was proved when he stole a turnpike Bill out of somebody's pocket at a concert and read it in a corner in despite of the efforts of the finest singers to attract his attention. (Thomas, 1974, p. 118)

Grenville's salary at the Admiralty Board was £1000 a year, which was increased to £1400 at the Treasury. This was sufficient for him to lead a decent but unostentatious life, but he was always very careful with money to avoid having to becoming over-dependent on his brother who had inherited large fortunes from their uncle, Lord Cobham, and his wife, who died respectively in 1749 and 1752. Lady Cobham had been a viscountess in her own right, and Richard Grenville inherited the title, becoming the second Viscount Temple. He also took over the family seat of the Cobhams at Stowe, vacating the Grenville estate at Wotton in George Grenville's favour. Grenville himself also received a series of (relatively small) legacies from his father, who died in 1727, his younger brother, Thomas, a naval captain who died in battle in 1747 and from Lord Cobham, in 1749. He scrupulously declined to make any money, other than his official salary, from his ministerial posts throughout his career, and he carried over into his administration of public finances the same frugality he showed in handling his own affairs.

In May 1749, at the age of 36, Grenville, was married to the 29-year old Elizabeth Wyndham, daughter of the former Tory leader, Sir William

Wyndham, and grand-daughter of the snobbish sixth Duke of Somerset, who showed his disapproval of the forthcoming match, by bequeathing Elizabeth a humiliatingly small legacy of £100 a year. This was, Horace Walpole observed, 'Just such a legacy as you would give to a house keeper to prevent her going into service again' (Lawson, 1984, p. 56). The bride was no great beauty, her looks having been blemished by a bout of smallpox, so much so that Lady Bolingbroke opined that 'she looked more like 49 than 29' (Thomas, p. 117). Nevertheless, the marriage proved a triumphant success; they became a devoted couple, producing nine children, one of whom was himself to become Prime Minister (William Grenville), while Mrs. Grenville was a committed and astute supporter of her husband in all his activities. She was much later to be described by one of Grenville's friends as 'the first prize in the marriage lottery of our century' (Lawson, 1984, p. 56). Grenville also gained by acquiring two brothers-in-law – Charles, Earl of Egremont, and Percy, later Earl of Thomond, who became important political supporters.

When Pelham unexpectedly died, in March 1754, it was a distinct setback for the Cobham-Pitt faction. The new Prime Minister – Pelham's elder brother, the Duke of Newcastle – was much less well-disposed to them than Pelham had been. Newcastle became First Lord of the Treasury, but the Chancellorship of the Exchequer was reserved for a member of the House of Commons. George Grenville, who had by this time built up a formidable mastery of Treasury affairs, rightly believed that he was the best-qualified person to take over the position. Instead, it was given, in rapid succession over a period of 18 months, to Sir William Lee, Henry Bilson Legge and Sir George Lyttelton, Grenville having to make do with the non-cabinet post of Treasurer of the Navy, though he was appointed to the Privy Council, and his salary increased to £2000. He swallowed his disappointment, but began to wonder whether William Pitt, who was about to become his brother-in-law on his marriage to his sister, Hester, and his own elder brother, Richard, now Viscount Temple, might not have used their influence to press his claims more strongly. Whatever, his feelings, however, Grenville remained outwardly loyal to Pitt, who continued as Paymaster-General in Newcastle's government, but also began to establish links with the Leicester House faction, associated with the 'alternative court' of the young Prince George and his mother Princess Augusta (see Chapter 9). This brought Grenville into touch with the Earl of Bute, the leader of the faction, who formed a high opinion of his abilities and marked him down as a valuable potential ally.

In November 1755, Pitt, losing all patience with Newcastle, who had consistently refused to promote him to the leadership of the House of Commons, and was indeed preparing to give the post to his great rival, Henry Fox, launched a massive attack on the government in the debate on the King's speech. He focused on the policy of paying subsidies to Russia and the German state of Hesse in an attempt to draw them into the looming war against France. Pitt maintained that this policy was to the benefit of George II's electorate of Hanover rather than of Britain, and saw no reason why the British Treasury should foot the bill. Grenville backed up Pitt in a well-argued speech, which was, however, a great deal less provocative in its tone. This did not save him from the ire of Newcastle, who – having assured himself of massive majorities in the two parliamentary divisions on the motions moved by Pitt – promptly dismissed the two men from their government posts. Pitt, according to Grenville's biographer, 'was not in the least dismayed at the prospect of opposition; indeed he felt more comfortable that his antagonism towards Newcastle could now have free rein' (Lawson, 1984, p. 84). Grenville was less happy, feeling keenly the loss of his ministerial salary. Nevertheless, alongside their new Leicester House allies, he joined Pitt in mounting a sustained campaign against involving the country in 'continental entanglements', and in advocating that the war against France, which was formally declared in May 1756, should be fought on a maritime basis, and in particular in defence of the North American colonies, rather than on European soil.

Grenville continued to interest himself in naval matters and made a powerful speech in favour of abolishing the practice of 'press gangs' in the recruitment of sailors, which he described as 'inhumane and a most inefficient means of guaranteeing naval personnel in times of war' (Lawson, 1984, p. 85). He spoke with authority as a former Admiralty minister, but his arguments fell on deaf ears. Nor did he and Pitt enjoy much success in rallying opinion against Newcastle, who kept a tight grip on his parliamentary following. Things began to change, however, with the outbreak of war, and the serious setbacks suffered by British forces, notably the loss of Minorca and of Fort Oswego in Canada, and the 'Black Hole of Calcutta' incident in India. Newcastle found it progressively harder to find spokesmen in the Commons to defend his policies, and when Henry Fox threw in his hand, and resigned as Leader of the House in October 1756, he realized the game was up, and a month later submitted his resignation to George II, advising that Pitt should be asked to form a new government (See Chapters 4 and 9). The King was not willing to accept Pitt as Premier, but agreed to the appointment of the Duke of Devonshire, with Pitt, who became Secretary of State (South), recognized as the dominant figure in the government. Grenville hoped to be appointed Paymaster-General, the post held earlier by Pitt, but was persuaded to resume his position as Treasurer of the Navy. He was disgruntled by his failure to win promotion, particularly as for most of the period of the Devonshire government he had to deputise for the often ill Pitt as Leader of the Commons.

Grenville's second term as Treasurer of the Navy lasted for only five months. As an Admiralty minister, he took it upon himself to advise the King to exercise clemency, after Admiral Byng had been sentenced to death for his alleged failure fully to exert himself in resisting the French invasion of Minorca (see Chapters 5 and 9). His brother, Lord Temple, who was First Lord of the Admiralty, also made representations on Byng's behalf, as did William Pitt, and an exasperated George II peremptorily dismissed both men on 6 April 1757. Three days later, in solidarity with them, Grenville submitted his own resignation. The King, however, had over-reached himself – and the outburst of public support for Pitt soon convinced him – and the majority of leading politicians – that Pitt's presence in the government was indispensable. It took another three months of wrangling and intrigue before a much-broadened government was installed, with the return of the Duke of Newcastle, as Prime Minister, and Pitt back in his former post of Secretary of State (South), and more dominant than ever. He was not able, however, to secure the post of Chancellor of the Exchequer for Grenville, in the face of determined resistance by the King, and in the end Grenville agreed to efface himself in order that the administration could be formed. So, for a third time, he became Treasurer of the Navy, and was to serve for five years. During this time, he won a high reputation for efficiency, and also as a reformer, his Bill to improve the pay and conditions of sailors passed into law, despite strong opposition in the House of Lords, at the second attempt, in 1758. He continued to deputise for Pitt in the Commons throughout this period, and in February 1761, was finally admitted to the cabinet, while continuing to serve as Treasurer of the Navy. During this period, however, his close relations with Pitt, and to some extent with Temple, began to deteriorate. He undoubtedly felt that they should have exerted themselves more strongly in support of his own promotion, and policy differences between them began to appear. These notably concerned finances, where the ever frugal Grenville was aghast at the insouciance with which Pitt allowed the national debt to soar upwards as a result of his ambitious military and naval operations. Grenville also stayed close to Lord Bute and the Leicester House faction, who had turned against Pitt, believing that he had used them as a lever to bring himself to power, and had subsequently neglected to consult or inform them on government policies.

The death of George II, October 1760, and the accession of George III, with Bute becoming the King's closest adviser, and later Prime Minister, proved to be a turning point in Grenville's career. When, in February 1761, Arthur Onslow, decided to stand down, after 33 years as Speaker of the House of Commons, there was a great deal of support for Grenville, now widely recognized as a distinguished and assiduous parliamentarian, to succeed him. Feeling that he had reached his ceiling, as a minister, Grenville was happy to accept the post, but Lord Bute, and the King himself, dissuaded him, implying that they had higher plans in view. It did not take long for these to materialize. The following October Pitt, having been over-ruled by the Cabinet, egged on by Lord Bute, on the issue of declaring war on Spain, promptly resigned. He was joined by Lord

Temple, now Lord Privy Seal, and Grenville's younger brother James, who held a junior ministerial post. Grenville conspicuously declined to follow them, and Bute sent for him, and proposed that he should take Pitt's place as Secretary of State of the Southern Department. Fearing a family split, and the risk of being attacked by his brother-in-law in parliamentary debates, Grenville declined, but recommended his wife's brother, the Earl of Egremont instead. Bute agreed, but ten days later offered Grenville the leadership of the House of Commons, which he accepted, causing an immediate breach with his family, the childless Temple cutting Grenville's sons out of his will and refusing all communication with him.

Grenville proved to be an able leader of the House, and a valuable ally of Bute's within the Cabinet. After attempts to appease Spain had broken down during the autumn of 1761, Bute, who had led the resistance to Pitt's proposal only three months earlier, declared war on 2 January 1762. Immediately the question arose, as to how great a priority should be given to pursuing operations against this new enemy. Bute, supported by Grenville, wanted to divert money raised to continue operations in Germany, to finance naval attacks on Spanish possessions in the Caribbean and the Far East. They therefore proposed to cut the £5 million subsidy promised to Prussia, a suggestion hotly contested by the Prime Minister, the Duke of Newcastle. At a series of Cabinet meetings, held in April 1762, Newcastle was outvoted on the issue, and the following month resigned, feeling that he had become a mere cipher within his own Cabinet. He was succeeded by Bute, who was now the nominal as well as the actual head of the government. His and Grenville's view seemed to have been triumphantly vindicated when British forces seized both Havana and Manila later in the year. This quickly led to the signing of a peace treaty with both France and Spain, in February 1763, bringing an end to the Seven Years War. On the other hand, the decision led to the ending of the alliance with Frederick the Great's Prussia, which left Britain dangerously isolated on the European continent.

If Bute had expected Grenville to be a docile follower, he had an unpleasant surprise, when he came to form his government. He offered him the post of Chancellor of the Exchequer, which he had long hankered after, but Grenville's appetite for power had grown during his long years of waiting. He turned down the offer, and insisted on being appointed as a Secretary of State, assuming control of the Northern Department, which Bute himself was vacating on becoming Prime Minister. Both he and George III were taken aback by Grenville's demand, and did their best to argue him out of it. As his brother-in-law, Lord Egremont, was already Secretary of State (South), it was inappropriate, the King suggested, for Grenville to hold the parallel post. When Grenville still insisted, Bute proposed a compromise, moving Egremont to become Lord Lieutenant of Ireland. An enraged Grenville 'refused to take any part in this proposition, and said it was impossible for him to take the seals, to have a personal affront given at the same moment to Lord Egremont' (Lawson, 1984, p. 133). At this, the King relented, and Grenville was sworn in as Secretary of State (North) on 28 May 1762, his brother-in-law remaining in charge of the Southern Department. Lawson cites the Grenville family biographer, L.M. Wiggin, enumerating the qualities which Grenville had used in reaching high office as 'hard work, ability, and at the last stubbornness' (Wiggin, 1958, p. 264).

Grenville's term as Secretary of State was brief and unhappy. Almost from the outset, he found himself at odds with Bute and the King. Both of them were desperate to end the war as soon as possible, in order to reduce the heavy burden on public finances. Consequently, they gave private assurances to French peace negotiators, that they would make concessions beyond those already agreed by the Cabinet. In particular, they promised the return to France of the Caribbean island of St. Lucia, captured early in 1762. When word came from the French Foreign Minister, the Duc de Choiseul, that France was now ready to accept the British peace terms, Bute reported this to the Cabinet, expecting general acceptance. Grenville, however, no less eager for peace, believed that appeasing the French was not the right way to go about it. He strongly opposed the cession of St. Lucia, and rallied a majority of the Cabinet against the proposal. Nevertheless, Bute sent the Duke of Bedford to France with a mandate to complete the negotiations, to the horror of both Grenville and Egremont, who felt that he was too weak a figure to stand up to the wiles of French diplomacy. When Bedford's first dispatches arrived from France, Egremont forwarded them to Grenville, who was in the country, with a covering note saying 'you will see that silly wretch has already given up two or three points in his conversation with Choiseul, and that his design was to have signed without any communication here' (Lawson, 1984, p. 138). Grenville joined in the criticism of Bedford, and he and Egremont both insisted that the British terms should be stiffened after the news arrived on 29 September of the conquest of Havana. Bute was forced to concede the point, but began to wonder whether Grenville could be relied on to steer the anticipated peace treaty through the House of Commons, when he was so lukewarm about its terms. He sought out Henry Fox, an accomplished, and none too scrupulous, parliamentary performer, who agreed to resume the post of Leader of the House, which he had earlier held in 1755–56. There followed two unpleasant interviews between Grenville, and first, Bute, and then, George III, at which they spelled out their intentions for him. He was relieved of his post as Secretary of State, after less than five months, and instead was offered the First Lordship of the Admiralty, at a salary of £2500, less than a third of what he had been receiving.

It was a humiliation, but Grenville felt obliged to accept his fate. His breach with Temple meant that he had no alternative source of revenue, and desperately needed his ministerial salary, even if it was substantially reduced.

Nor did he relish the prospect of again putting himself under William Pitt's leadership to campaign against the peace terms. So, writes Lawson, 'he took the admiralty, ate humble pie and nursed his grievances in the hope of settling the score at some future date' (Ibid., p. 141). George III was greatly disappointed in him, telling Bute, in March 1763, that Grenville 'had thrown away the game he had two years ago' (Beckett and Thomas, 2004). Yet, less than a month later, he invited Grenville to form a new government, replacing that of Bute, who resigned shortly after Parliament ratified the Treaty of Paris, bringing the Seven Years War to an end (see Chapter 6). Bute had been un-nerved by the violent protests against him, and the calumnies which had been spread about his alleged affair with the King's mother, Princess Augusta, and was determined to relinquish the premiership. George III reluctantly accepted his resignation, but was resolved to keep him as his principal adviser, who would control the new government from behind the scenes. Bute advised him to appoint Henry Fox, a proposal which the King found highly distasteful, on account of his 'bad character' and corrupt ways. Nevertheless, he wrote to Bute, if this was the only solution that Bute could propose, he would accept it, adding 'but I own from the moment he comes in I shall not feel myself interested in public affairs and shall feel rejoiced whenever I can see a glimmering hope of getting quit of him' (Brooke, 1972, p. 101).

Fox was duly offered the Treasury, but aware of his own unpopularity, and fearful of assuming the responsibility, he declined, preferring to hold on to his lucrative post as Paymaster-General, and finally securing his peerage, as the First Baron Holland, though he had hoped for an earldom. Fox suggested Grenville, and George III – concluding that he would otherwise be forced back on Newcastle or Pitt – agreed.

So Grenville became First Lord of the Treasury and Chancellor of the Exchequer on 6 April 1763. He was somewhat surprised at his sudden elevation, and it has been suggested that he accepted the post under the most humiliating conditions, with Bute handpicking his ministers, and the King making it clear that he held his new posts only on sufferance. He wrote to Bute about his new ministers in the most contemptuous terms, saying 'I care not one farthing for these men I have now to do with. [They] are mean in their manners of thinking as well as their actions. They forget what they owe me, but I shall not, therefore sooner or later they shall suffer for it' (Ibid., p. 102).

In further letters to Bute, he complained of Grenville's 'tiresome manner' and 'selfish disposition'. When the new Prime Minister made a trivial error, forgetting to make an appointment for Lord le Despenser (the former Sir Francis Dashwood) to kiss hands on his succession to a his peerage, he gave him a quite disproportionate dressing down. Nevertheless, Grenville was able to insist on a number of conditions – the retention of his brother-in-law, Lord Egremont, as a Secretary of State, appointments or sinecures for several of his supporters and relatives, and the promise of a pension of £3000 for when he left office. In their entry on Grenville, in *The Oxford Dictionary of National Biography*, J.V. Beckett and Peter D.G. Thomas comment that the 'Duke of Newcastle knew little of this, but shrewdly perceived that Bute had chosen the wrong man if he wanted a puppet minister'.

Initially, Grenville made his way carefully, and his government was widely seen as a 'triumvirate', in which he shared power almost equally with the two Secretaries of State, Egremont, and the Earl of Halifax, a highly experienced minister, whose earlier achievements included the foundation of a colony in Nova Scotia, whose capital, Halifax, was named after him. The three men worked well together, and were united in their resentment that the King insisted on continuing to consult with Bute on public business. Bute himself was hardly to blame for this, taking himself off to Harrogate to take the waters, and then retiring to his country seat at Luton Hoo, declaring that 'he was determined to be a private man for the rest of his days, never to intermeddle in Government' (Lawson, 1984, p. 156). Yet the King refused to let him go, constantly writing to him, and insisting on receiving his advice. He also secretly authorized Bute to sound out opposition politicians with a view to replacing Grenville as Prime Minister, and lied to Grenville when he taxed the King about it.

Meanwhile, Grenville worked hard at consolidating his position in the House of Commons, where he attracted considerable support because of his efficiency and his ready responsiveness to Members' views and interests. On most occasions, he dominated the House, though he once fell victim to the ready wit of his brother-in-law, the Elder Pitt. Speaking on the cider tax, which was the final act of the Bute government, he admitted its unpopularity, but asked where else he could raise the money. 'Tell me where', he repeated several times, and Pitt who was sitting opposite, started to hum the opening lines of a well-known hymn, 'Gentle Shepherd tell me where.' The House dissolved in laughter, and the nickname 'Gentle Shepherd' stuck to Grenville for the rest of his life (Bigham, p. 104). After four months, the ministry felt strong enough to deliver an ultimatum to the King. Either he must give the Cabinet his full support, and cease to depend on Bute or he must seek a new government. George III chose the latter alternative, and – despite his earlier hostility to Newcastle and Pitt – put out feelers to them. But Pitt, in particular, set his demands too high, in a two-hour interview with the King, and George III came scurrying back to Grenville, asking him to stay on, saying, according to an account written up in Mrs. Grenville's diary:

> that he wished to put his affairs into his hands; that he gave him the fullest assurances of every support and every strength that he could give him towards the carrying his business into execution; that he meant to take his

advice, and his alone, in everything: that it was necessary the direction should be in one man's hands only, and he meant it should be his. (Lawson, 1984, p. 169)

Had the King been sincere in making these declarations, and had Grenville believed in his sincerity, all might have been well, but, as Lawson put it, 'the basis of trust and mutual understanding…had crumbled away during the summer months' (Ibid.). Grenville did not believe that Bute had finally been shown the door by the King, and was constantly on his guard, periodically lecturing the King (at considerable length) on his duties during his audiences, which only reinforced the deep dislike that the King had for him. Nevertheless, an early governmental reshuffle was harmoniously agreed between the two men. It was occasioned by the deaths of two ministers – Lord Egremont, who quite unexpectedly succumbed to an apoplectic fit, and the Earl of Granville (formerly Lord Carteret), the veteran Lord President of the Council. Egremont's place at the Southern Department was filled by the Earl of Halifax, whose post as Northern Secretary was taken by the Earl of Sandwich, previously First Lord of the Admiralty. Granville's place was more difficult to fill, but it was eventually assumed by the Duke of Bedford, who commanded the support of around 20 MPs, and whose entry into the government sensibly increased its parliamentary majority. Bedford and Sandwich assumed that they would form a new 'triumvirate' with Grenville, but after his trial of strength with the King he was determined to be master of his own house, and, with the King's support, refused to agree to this.

Although, the principal mark he made during his premiership was in greatly improving the efficiency of the government machine and its financial structures, Grenville is chiefly remembered for two events – the early stages of the John Wilkes affair and the passage of the Stamp Act, widely blamed as the seminal cause for the rebellion of the North American colonies ten years later. John Wilkes was a radical MP, who had set up an opposition newspaper, *The North Briton*, partly financed by Lord Temple, for the express purpose of criticizing the government of the Earl of Bute, who was attacked in its pages with great venom. After Grenville became Prime Minister, it continued to attack the government, though in less personal terms. Issue number 45 of the paper, published in April 1763, however, contained what ministers regarded as a serious libel, and the Earl of Halifax, whose department included powers and responsibilities held in modern times by the Home Office, issued a general arrest warrant for un-named persons associated with the publication. Some 48 persons were arrested, including Wilkes, who was thrown into the Tower of London, but a week later was released by order of the Lord Chief Justice, Charles Pratt, on the grounds that his arrest was a breach of parliamentary privilege. Wilkes and his associates then launched a legal action against Halifax, which resulted in the award of damages to them, and a definitive ruling that the issue of 'general warrants' (that is those not naming individuals) was illegal. The government, however, was not prepared to let matters rest, and parliamentary resolutions were passed declaring issue 45 a 'seditious libel' and a satirical work published by Wilkes, entitled *Essay on Woman*, an 'obscene and impious libel'. Then, on 20 January 1764, ministers carried a motion in the Commons expelling him from the House so that he could face trial on these charges. Wilkes fled to Paris, but was tried in his absence the following month, found guilty, and later was declared an outlaw for impeding justice. Grenville did not take the initiative in the moves against Wilkes, which were promoted by Halifax and Sandwich, and was content that the law courts had declared general warrants illegal (they were never again used), but he ably defended the government's conduct in the Commons, winning crucial votes of confidence against opposition motions strongly backed by Pitt. This might have seemed the end of the matter, so far as politics was concerned, but the issues raised by the Wilkes case, which had important consequences both for the freedom of the press and the rights of MPs, kept recurring over the next dozen years, involving the premierships of Rockingham, Chatham, Grafton and North.

Grenville was much more directly involved in the introduction of the Stamp Act of 1765. Determined to reduce the national debt, which had ballooned during the recently concluded Seven Years War, he was resolved that the North American colonists, on whose behalf the war had largely been waged, should make some contribution towards paying off the debt, and in particular to financing the large British garrison which was being maintained as a safeguard against possible French moves to regain the territorial losses they had suffered during the war. Grenville considered alternative methods of raising money, but concluded that the levying of stamp duties, which had been in force in Britain since 1671, would be the most efficacious. It would be 'the least exceptionable means of taxation', he told the Commons in his budget speech on 9 March 1764, 'because it requires few officers and even collects itself' (Lawson, 1984, p. 200). Under the proposal, which met little opposition in the Commons, stamp duty would be imposed on all colonial commercial and legal papers, newspapers, pamphlets, cards, almanacs and dice. Grenville allowed for a year's delay in applying the Act, in order that the views of the colonists on the actual implementation could be heard, but he did not at all anticipate the barrage of complaints that soon materialized. Indeed, he believed that his Act was an extremely moderate measure, calculated to raise only one-third of the cost of the British garrison, whereas many MPs felt that the colonists should contribute the full amount. Grenville had lost office by the time that the effects of the American boycott of the Act were felt, and the new Rockingham administration hastened to repeal it (See Chapter 8). But the damage had been done, and the cry of 'No taxation without representation' was heard throughout the length and breadth of the 13 colonies. None of Grenville's four successors over the next decade were able or willing to accept the full consequences of the new American militancy, and it was probably only a matter of time before open conflict broke out between the colonists and their 'motherland'.

Grenville was supreme in the Commons, but his relations with the King continued to deteriorate, exacerbated by Grenville's stubborn insistence on controlling official appointments, even those – like Keeper of the Privy Purse – which had previously been regarded as personal appointments by the monarch. In this case, he proposed the appointment of the Earl of Guildford, father of the young Lord North MP, who was a member of Grenville's Treasury Board. The King held out for his own choice, Sir William Breton, a close friend of Lord Bute's, and Grenville gave way with very bad grace after a prolonged argument. There were also periodic conflicts about patronage in Scotland, which was controlled by Bute's brother, James Stuart Mackenzie, who was Lord Privy Seal for Scotland. Grenville endeavoured, with only moderate success, to win precedence for his own nominees. The King came to dread his audiences with his Prime Minister, complaining, 'When he has wearied me for two hours, he looks at his watch to see if he may not tire me for an hour more' (Brooke, p. 108). George III was not the only person to be annoyed by Grenville's prolixity. His cousin and devoted political supporter, Thomas Pitt, described him as 'to a proverb tedious... he was diffuse and argumentative, and never had done with a subject after he had convinced your judgment', while Horace Walpole noted that his favourite occupation was talking, and 'brevity was not his failing' (Ibid., pp. 107–8).

In March 1765 the King, who had not quite reached his twenty-seventh birthday, fell ill with recurrent coughs and fevers, and fears were widely expressed that he might die within a year. He himself proposed a Regency Bill, to provide for that contingency, which would have resulted in the young Prince George, then aged nearly three, coming to the throne. The King declined to name the Regent in the draft Bill, apparently leaving himself the option of making a nomination after it became law, if his illness then took a more serious turn. This led to a widespread suspicion that he intended to choose his mother, the Princess Augusta, who was known to be very close to the Earl of Bute, and it was feared that this was a roundabout way of restoring the King's former favourite to power. This was far from being the King's intention, but he failed to take Grenville into his confidence as to his reasons for not wanting to name the intended Regent in the Bill. After a parliamentary revolt, he was forced to agree to the naming of Queen Charlotte, which had always been his intention, but he had not wished to upset his own brother, Edward, Duke of York, who had strong nominal claims, but in whom George III had little confidence. The King's failure to consult his ministers over the affair did nothing to improve the existing poor relations between monarch and Prime Minister. The Bill was eventually passed, in May 1765, with Queen Charlotte's name added, but by then the King had recovered his health, and it became a dead letter.

On the very day the Regency Bill received the Royal Assent, fierce riots broke out in London, led by silk workers protesting at the Government's failure to control the importation of silk. The King blamed Grenville for the riots, and saw this as an opportunity to dismiss him, and summoned Pitt to form a new administration. But Pitt unexpectedly refused the offer unless his other brother-in-law, Lord Temple, would agree to serve with him. But Temple had recently had a highly emotional reconciliation with Grenville, and refused to be party to his ejection from office. So once again the King was thwarted, and had to come cap-in-hand back to Grenville to beg him to stay on. Sensing the weak position of the King, Grenville and his Cabinet then imposed humiliating conditions on him before they agreed to resume office. The King wriggled, tried to induce Newcastle and his friends to take office, but they refused to do so without Pitt, and then after two agonizing discussions with his Uncle, the Duke of Cumberland (who had by then effectively replaced Bute as his most intimate adviser) concluded that he had no choice but to submit. The terms imposed by Grenville and his colleagues were that the King should have no more contact with Bute or his brother, James Stuart Mackenzie, that they should have complete control over patronage, and that, in particular, the Marquess of Granby should be appointed as Commander-in-Chief, Lord Holland (the former Henry Fox) should be dismissed as Paymaster-General, and that a Lord Lieutenant of Ireland should be appointed 'by the full approbation and recommendation of the ministers'. After a long day of consultations, on 24 May 1765, George III summoned Grenville at 11 o'clock at night, and agreed to the conditions, seeking only to soften the blow to Mackenzie. He agreed to strip him of patronage powers in Scotland, 'but begged that he should be allowed to retain the sinecure office of Lord Privy Seal of Scotland which the King had promised him for life' (Brooke, 1972, p. 119). But Grenville, completely insensitive to the King's personal feelings, was adamant: Mackenzie must go. The King replied, in words he repeated to the Earl of Egmont, who was First Lord of the Admiralty and his only unconditional supporter in the Cabinet, that:

> He saw evidently that they were not satisfied with his parting with his power, but that nothing would content him but his parting with his honour too – bid him take notice what he told him – and earnestly and in great anger take notice of this – more than once – that he had forced him to part with his honour – that as a King for the safety of his people he must submit – but that nothing induced him to this but the danger of the crisis. (Ibid.)

Grenville and his Cabinet were jubilant at their triumph at the King's expense, and fatally assumed that they were now assured of a prolonged spell in government. They could hardly have been more wrong. For as the King's biographer, John Brooke, put it: 'From 22 May 1765 to the day of Grenville's death on 13 November 1770 the King's politics revolved round two aims: first to get Grenville out of office, and next, to make sure he never came back ... and he never did' (Ibid.) So determined was George III to oust Grenville, that he turned to two men whom he had earlier utterly despised to do the dirty work for him. One was his uncle, the Duke of Cumberland, whom he and his mother had once feared would murder him, to become King himself (as the future King Richard III had done to his two nephews, 'the princes in the Tower'). The other was the Duke of Newcastle, the senior Whig whom he had blamed for the widespread corruption which he believed had infested Government and Parliament during the reign of his predecessor, George II. Less than a month after his humiliation on 22 May, the King commissioned Cumberland to recruit a government which would allow him to get rid of Grenville. Cumberland immediately sounded out Pitt, but he refused, sensing that Cumberland would be the real head of the government, and that he would be only a figurehead. Cumberland then approached Newcastle, who – aged 72 and with 40 years of senior ministerial office behind him – now felt unable to bear the burden of supreme responsibility. He therefore suggested his young protégé, the Marquess of Rockingham, who was highly congenial to Cumberland, who shared his passion for horse-racing. Newcastle accepted the post of Lord Privy Seal, but otherwise the Rockingham government, which took office on 13 July 1765, was an inexperienced and untested team, largely manned from the ranks of the Jockey Club. It looked even more light-weight when, a few months later, Cumberland unexpectedly died, at the age of 44. George III was not worried; he had got rid of his *bête noire*, having told a friend of Horace Walpole that he 'would rather see the Devil in his closet than Mr. Grenville' (Brooke, p. 119).

Grenville emerged from his premiership a much bigger figure than when he had entered, and now led a large and loyal band of parliamentary followers. He was the outstanding opposition figure during the largely unsuccessful ministries of Rockingham, Chatham (the elder Pitt) and the Duke of Grafton, which governed for the next five years, but the King resolutely refused to employ him again as a minister (let alone as Premier), and over-looked him again, in January 1770, when he despairingly turned to Lord North. A few months later his health began to decline, and he died of a blood disorder on 13 November 1770, at the age of 58.

He was Prime Minister for 2 years and 85 days, but if he had known to keep his mouth shut and show a minimum of tact in the presence of the King, he might well have had a much longer and more successful tenure. As it was, he set a new – and much higher – standard of ministerial efficiency than any of his predecessors and most of his successors, and he won the grudging admiration of Edmund Burke, who had been a political opponent, but who was to say of him after his death:

> Undoubtedly Mr. Grenville was a first-rate figure in this country. With a masculine understanding; and a stout and resolute heart, he had an application undissipated and unwearied...If he was ambitious, I will say this for him, his ambition was of a noble and generous strain. It was to raise himself, not by the low, pimping politics of a court, but to win his way to power, through the laborious gradations of public service, and to secure to himself the well-earned rank in parliament, by a thorough knowledge of its constitution and a perfect practice in all its business...this country owes [him] very great obligations. (Lawson, 1984, p. 1)

Works consulted

Beckett, J.V. and Peter D.G. Thomas (2004), 'George Grenville (1712–1770)', in *Oxford Dictionary of National Biography*, Oxford University Press.

Bigham, Clive (1924), *The Prime Ministers of Britain 1721–1924*, London, John Murray.

Brooke, John (1972), *King George III*, London, Constable.

Lawson, Philip (1984), *George Grenville: A Political Life*, Oxford, Clarendon Press.

Lawson, Philip (1998), 'George Grenville', in Robert Eccleshall and Graham E. Walker, eds., *Biographical Dictionary of British Prime Ministers*, London, Routledge.

Rudé, George (1962), *Wilkes and Liberty*, Oxford, Clarendon Press.

Thomas, Peter D.G. (1973), 'George Grenville', in Herbert Van Thal, ed., *The Prime Ministers*, Volume 2, London, Allen & Unwin.

Wiggin, L.M. (1958), *A Faction of Cousins: A Political Account of the Grenvilles 1733–1763*, Newhaven, Yale University Press.

8
Charles Watson-Wentworth, Second Marquess of Rockingham – the Conscience of the Whigs

If George Grenville is blamed for first having provoked the rebellion of the North American colonists, and Lord North condemned for waging an unsuccessful war against them, the second Marquess of Rockingham may fairly be remembered as the man whose wise counsels, had they been heeded, might well have prevented the War of Independence from taking place. Yet his two periods in office were extremely brief – only 1 year and 113 days in all – and during the interim period of 16 years, during which he led a principled and consistent opposition, his warnings were just as consistently ignored.

A descendant of Thomas Wentworth, Earl of Strafford, chief adviser to Charles I, who was executed by order of Parliament, in 1641, Charles Watson-Wentworth was born on 13 May 1730, the fifth son and eighth child in a family of ten. His four elder brothers died in infancy or childhood, leaving him the heir to his immensely wealthy parents. His father, Thomas, the largest landowner in Yorkshire with extensive holdings also in Northamptonshire and County Wicklow, was an MP and a leading supporter of Sir Robert Walpole, which enabled him to make spectacular advances in the peerage, after being successively created a knight, a baron, a viscount and an earl, the Earl of Malton. At this stage, Walpole was reported to have remarked 'I suppose we shall soon see our friend Malton in opposition, for he has had no promotion in the peerage for the last fortnight' (Bigham, 1924, p. 139). It was left to a later Premier, Henry Pelham, to go one step further, in 1746, when Malton was created a Marquess, the first and for a long time, the only one in the English peerage. Charles's mother, Lady Mary Finch, also came from a great Whig family, her father being the second Earl of Nottingham. To emphasize his eminence as a great territorial and political magnate, the first Marquess transformed his ancestral residence of Wentworth Woodhouse, near Rotherham, into a vast palace, with 240 rooms, and the longest country house façade in Europe (185 metres). It is still standing over 250 years later, and remains by far the largest privately owned residence in the United Kingdom.

Fears were expressed that Charles would not long survive his elder brothers, and he was much coddled as a young child. Yet by the age of 13, he had survived a number of serious aliments, and according to his uncle, Lord Winchelsea, 'the young man is of a pretty healthy strong constitution' (Hoffman, 1973, p. 3). Known by the courtesy title of Viscount Higham, he attended Westminster School as a day pupil, living with his family at number 4 Grosvenor Square, his father's London residence, bought in 1741. At Westminster, from which he later transferred briefly to Eton, he was known particularly for his participation in adventurous pranks and in amateur theatricals. In 1745, when the Jacobite rebellion took place, the family seat at Wentworth Woodhouse was threatened by Prince Charles Edward's troops on their way south to Derby, and Lord Malton raised three regiments of militia, to one of which he appointed the 15-year-old Lord Higham as Colonel. By December 1745, the danger had passed, as the Young Pretender's forces were in full retreat in Cumberland. The militia was discharged, but the young Colonel, quietly slipped away, and under an assumed name rode to Carlisle, where he put himself at the disposal of the army of the Duke of Cumberland, who was in hot pursuit of the rebels. The Duke received him kindly, and was impressed by his youthful ardour, but having been forewarned by letters from Higham's anxious father, sent him back home, where he greatly feared the reaction of his parents. He need not have worried:

> Charles' devoted sister Mary tried to shelter him from parental wrath; but the need was probably slight. As his safety was assured, the more becoming did his adventure appear in the heir to a great name. Charles' spirit and courage won general applause; his ingenuity brought more guarded admiration; and his family feared only lest his 'military eagerness' should persist. The army was not the place for an only son. (Guttridge, 1952, p. 4)

In the aftermath of the final defeat of the Pretender, at Culloden, in April 1746, Higham's father finally received his marquessate, and the young Charles became known as the Earl of Malton. To complete his education, Charles was despatched to Geneva, under the charge of George Quarme, who had been a captain in his militia regiment, where he applied himself to learning both French and Italian, as well as more traditional subjects, such as Greek and Latin. He was at one stage mildly rebuked by his father for his extravagance, and for accepting a gift of £100 from a dubious source. He wrote back full of remorse, and promised to reform his conduct, while Mr Quarme wrote that he was now applying himself diligently to his studies. He returned to England early in 1748, and preparations were then made for his departure on a 'grand tour', beginning in the summer, shortly after his eighteenth birthday. Few young noblemen could have embarked on a grander tour than the Earl of Malton.

First of all, he made a round of visits to all 'the most considerable places in England', and then embarked, together with a new tutor, Major James Forrester, who had been released from his military duties on the express leave of the King and the Duke of Cumberland, for a two year stay, mostly in Italy, but also taking in visits to several of the principal royal courts of Europe. Everywhere he went, despite his shyness and modesty, he proved to be a great social success, a later visitor, Lord Stormont, reporting that 'never was any visitor so loved and esteemed in Florence, where every lady made frequent enquiries after him' (Guttridge, p. 6). This, however, hardly had a beneficial effect on his health. According to S.M. Farrell:

> Although he had had several childhood illnesses, it may also have been in Italy, through at least one sexual liaison, that he contracted what was probably a persistent problem in his urogenitary system. His 'old complaint', as he called it, caused him frequently recurring bouts of debilitating sickness and may have made him impotent, though some contemporaries regarded him as a hypochondriac. (Farrell, 2004a)

In many places he visited, he purchased works of art to be sent back to Wentworth Woodhouse. One acquisition was a fine harpsichord intended for the use of a Miss Mary Bright, to whom he was already apparently unofficially engaged, even though she was still barely 14. Malton concluded his grand tour with visits to four royal courts – those of Austria, Prussia, Brunswick and Hanover.

At Vienna, he was royally received, being seated next to the Emperor at dinner, and came away, he wrote to his father, 'violently fond of our allies the Emperor and Empress from conviction of it's being thoroughly the interest of England to keep up that alliance'. It was a different matter at Berlin, Britain and Austria's opponent during the recently concluded War of Austrian Succession. Here Frederick the Great declined to speak to Malton 'but talked ostentatiously to an unknown visitor from Denmark'. The rebuff in Berlin was compensated by 'ten delightful days at the court of Brunswick', but the highlight of the tour was undoubtedly Hanover, where George II was holding court as the Elector. His reception, he told his father, was 'not only extremely courteous but had an air of satisfaction at seeing a person of whose loyalty and fidelity his Majesty had a very good opinion...I constantly went to court both in the morning and evening and his Majesty did me the honour of speaking to me more or less every day. In short, my lord, you could not have wished a more gracious reception for your son'. The good impression he had made was confirmed by George II himself, who on his return to London told Malton's uncle, Henry Finch 'that he had never seen a finer and more promising youth than Lord Malton' (Guttridge, pp. 8–9). Moreover, the Duke of Newcastle, the Prime

Minister's brother and eventual successor, had also been in attendance at the court, and insisted on dining and supping with him each day. Malton was now indeed seen as a 'gilded youth', enjoying the good opinion of both the Monarch and the most senior of the Whig leaders. He was also well regarded by the King's favourite son, the Duke of Cumberland, with whom he shared a passionate interest in horse-racing.

Charles was never to see his father again. From Hanover, he had proceeded to Paris, when word came that the Marquess had died, at the age of 57, on 14 December 1750. Malton, still only 20, succeeded to the title and became one of the richest men in England. He came of age on 13 May 1751, and immediately received a letter from Newcastle informing him that he had been appointed to the offices held by his father, as Lord Lieutenant of the West and North Ridings of Yorkshire and *custos rotulorum* (or chief magistrate) of the North. A week later he took his seat in the House of Lords, 'and became assiduous in his attendance, especially when matters of interest to Yorkshire were being discussed' (Guttridge, p. 11). Like his father before him, he immediately attached himself to the 'Old Whigs', under Newcastle, and was seen from the outset as their major ally in Yorkshire, where he controlled a string of parliamentary seats. His dominance in the county was further enhanced by his marriage, on 26 February 1752, to the now 16-year-old Mary Bright. She had inherited a fortune of £60,000, including two substantial estates near Sheffield, from her late father, Thomas Bright MP, and these were added to her husband's already large holdings in the county. Rockingham took his responsibilities as a landowner very seriously. He constantly sought to improve his estates, and was a pioneer of new agricultural techniques, being elected a Fellow of the Royal Society for his services in agriculture. His estimated annual income in rents at the time of his inheritance was £20,000: this had at least doubled by the time of his death 30 years later.

Soon after taking his seat in the House of Lords, Rockingham was appointed as a Lord of the Bedchamber to George II, which gave him a position of dignity in the court. In the House, Rockingham was seen as a nervous and hesitant speaker, but so greatly was he esteemed by the Whig leadership that he was invited to move the Loyal Address at the opening of Parliament in 1753. He declined, being – at least at that stage – unambitious for high office, preferring to concentrate on his responsibilities in Yorkshire. Here he made a false start, when he attempted to terminate a long-standing 'gentleman's agreement' between Yorkshire landowners that the two county MPs should be equally divided between the two parties. Rockingham proposed his friend Sir George Savile as a rival candidate to the sitting Tory MP in the 1754 general election. This went down badly with his fellow Whig landowners, who were desperate to avoid what would certainly prove a highly expensive election campaign, due to the very large electorate in Yorkshire. Savile might well have been elected had he run, but Rockingham bowed to the wishes of his fellow grandees, and withdrew Savile's candidature, offering him instead one of his own 'pocket boroughs'. But Savile yearned for the much greater prestige of being a county Member, and preferred to wait until the next general election, when the sitting Whig MP was expected to retire. (He, in fact, died in 1758, and Savile was returned unopposed in a by-election) Rockingham's reputation was damaged both by his rashness in proposing Savile, but also for his pusillanimity in withdrawing him when he met with resistance. He was reproved, in no uncertain terms, by his uncle, the highly influential Solicitor-General, William Murray (later the famous Lord Chief Justice, Lord Mansfield), who was his political mentor. Subsequently, he showed much more tact and better judgment in his electoral management of England's largest and most populous county, and succeeded, over the years, in turning it into a predominantly Whig preserve. By 1768, 26 of the 30 seats in the county were held by Whigs.

When the Seven Years War broke out in 1756, with British arms facing a series of setbacks, there was lively fear of a French invasion. As Lord Lieutenant of Yorkshire, Rockingham distinguished himself by raising record numbers of recruits both for the regular army, and for local militias, of which he formed three regiments within the county, one of which was commanded by Sir George Savile. Newcastle, who was now Prime Minister, following the death of his brother, Henry Pelham, in 1754, was delighted, and his already good opinion of the young Marquess soared. Alongside his public duties, Rockingham played a major role in the development and control of horse-racing, both in Yorkshire and nationally. He was a founder member, and one of the leading spirits, of the Jockey Club, and built imposing new stables at Wentworth Woodhouse, which produced a string of winners of classic races, notably the famous horse Whistlejacket, immortalized in one of George Stubbs's greatest paintings, acquired by the National Gallery in 1997. Rockingham was a regular visitor to race meetings at York, Doncaster and Pontefract, as well as at Newmarket. These meetings were frequented by many of the leading

Whig aristocrats, as well as by the Duke of Cumberland (a fellow steward of the Jockey Club), and much political wheeler-dealing undoubtedly took place in the intervals between races. Rockingham was supported in all his activities, by his wife, who acted as his political secretary, and often gave him shrewd advice. More activist in her approach than her somewhat languorous husband, she took charge of his correspondence, and often herself replied to letters which he had neglected to acknowledge. 'An intelligent, quick-witted, and musical woman, Lady Rockingham had eccentric habits and an engaging sense of humour – which some found too frivolous – and enjoyed a happy married life, despite having no children' (Farrell, 2004b).

Rockingham remained staunchly loyal to the old Whigs, and to George II personally, and in 1756 turned down an offer from Frederick, Prince of Wales, then at odds with his father, to become his Master of the Horse. He became very close to Newcastle and to the fourth Duke of Devonshire, the other leading Whig grandee, who was briefly Prime Minister in 1756–57. He was duly rewarded, in May 1760, being made a Knight of the Garter (a sure sign of the monarch's approval) six days before his thirtieth birthday. The accession of George III, five months later, and his promotion of the Tory, Lord Bute, represented the greatest challenge to the Whig supremacy in over 40 years, and Rockingham was determined to stand shoulder-to-shoulder with his political associates. When George III peremptorily dismissed Devonshire as a privy councillor, in November 1762, (see Chapter 5), he went straight to the King to resign his place at court, recounting their meeting in a letter to his wife, written the same day:

> I had an audience this morning of the King in which I acquainted him, with how much uneasiness & regret I had seen the tendency of all the late domestic measures, that I looked upon the last event of the Duke of Devonshire, as a further explanation & illustration of all the foregoing, that I was grieved to see that all persons, who had long been steadily attached to his Majesty's family etc, were now the mere objects of his Majesty's displeasure than of his favour, that the pursuit of such counsels had given much alarm, & that as I felt the whole so strongly in my mind I beg'd leave not to continue a Lord of the Bedchamber, lest my continuance should carry with it the appearance of approbation. (Hoffman, pp. 42–3)

It was typical of Rockingham's high-mindedness and the sense of independence which his wealth and high social position gave him that he was prepared to speak to the King with such frankness. It had little effect on the monarch, who, according to Hoffman, heard him out 'with cold indifference'. But he set an example, which a number of followers of the Duke of Newcastle who held official appointments tried to emulate, by beginning a wave of 'rolling resignations', which they hoped would force Bute's removal from power. But there were too few of them to carry weight, and Bute found no difficulty in finding willing candidates to take their place. Aided and abetted by Henry Fox, then the Leader of the House of Commons, he struck back with the famous 'Massacre of the Pelhamite innocents', in which large numbers of supporters of the Duke, and of his late brother Henry Pelham, who had preceded him in the premiership, were systematically rooted out of their public appointments, both honorific and material. Rockingham was not spared: his Lord-lieutenancies of the West and North Ridings and other important posts he held in Yorkshire were taken from him. At the same time, both Newcastle and the young Duke of

Grafton, a rising star in the Whig firmament, lost their own Lord-lieutenancies, though Devonshire was kept in place as the Lord Lieutenant of Derbyshire. He promptly resigned in sympathy with his fellows.

During the next two to three years, under the governments of Bute and George Grenville, Rockingham emerged as a major opposition politician, rarely speaking, but working energetically to marshal the forces of the Whigs, in both Houses of Parliaments. He was to be dubbed 'the Whip of Whiggery' (Hoffman, p. 31). Then, in July 1765, the hand of destiny fell on him. George III, having become totally exasperated by Grenville, who he felt had failed to treat him with due respect, decided to get rid of him, come what may (See Chapter 7). Having failed to reach an accommodation with William Pitt, he turned in desperation to his uncle, the Duke of Cumberland and asked him to form a government. Cumberland was willing, but felt it inappropriate, as a Royal Duke, to assume the post of First Lord of the Treasury, so he turned to the Newcastle Whigs to provide a suitable candidate. Newcastle was now 72, and though anxious to play a leading role in the new government, was hesitant to push himself forward. Devonshire, having died some months earlier at the age of 44, was no longer available, while the Dukes of Grafton and Portland, not yet 30, were considered too young. This left Rockingham as the only major Whig grandee available. There was, nevertheless, considerable surprise that the choice should fall on a man who had no previous ministerial experience (in fact he remains only one of four Prime Ministers of whom this was true – the others being two Labour premiers of the twentieth century – James Ramsay MacDonald and Tony Blair, and most recently, David Cameron in 2010). Rockingham himself wrote to a colleague in Ireland:

> It must surprize you to hear that I am at the head of the Treasury...but indeed the necessity here made it necessary that some thing should be done, & therefore howsoever unsuitable I might be for that office from my health and inexperience in the sort of business, yet I thought it incumbent on me to acquiesce in the attempting it, rather than throw any fresh confusion into the negotiation. (Hoffman, pp. 78–9)

The truth is that Rockingham did not see himself as becoming the head of the government, rather to act as chief lieutenant to Cumberland. The Duke was generally seen as being the 'real' prime minister, and it was in his houses – Cumberland Lodge in Windsor Great Park, and in Upper Grosvenor Street, Mayfair – that the cabinet meetings were held. It was during a meeting in his London residence on 31 October 1765 that he had a sudden seizure, and died at the age of 44. Rockingham, who had expected to be a mere deputy, found himself less than four months later carrying the ultimate responsibility. Not only was he inexperienced himself, but the same was true of most of his

Cabinet, of whom only the Duke of Newcastle had a long period of ministerial service behind him. Newcastle thought that he should be running the show, but found himself shunted into the mainly honorific post of Lord Privy Seal. Most of the other ministers were chosen among the personal friends of Cumberland and Rockingham, mostly from among the racing fraternity. The principal members of the government were the young Duke of Grafton and General Sir Henry Conway, a nephew of Sir Robert Walpole, as the two Secretaries of State, and William Dowdeswell as Chancellor of the Exchequer. Dowdeswell was an expert on taxation, but as a former Tory was still feeling his way in what was a very self-consciously Whig government. Perhaps as significant, in the long run, as any of the ministerial appointments was Rockingham's choice of Edmund Burke to act as his private secretary. For the rest of the Marquess's life, he was to remain his right-hand man, giving him shrewd advice, and using his elegant pen to refine and project the political principles which motivated his master. Like the preceding Grenville government, at least in its early days, Rockingham's administration was effectively led by a triumvirate, consisting of himself, Grafton and Conway. John Brooke, the biographer of George III, is withering in his criticism of the government, describing it as: 'a constitutional anomaly. It is the strangest cabinet in British history.... It is the only one formed round the principal members of the Jockey Club' (Brooke, 1972, p. 122).

At the outset, the government received warm support from the King, only too happy to have got shot of George Grenville. Yet its parliamentary position was weak, and it was in sore need of finding reinforcements. There were two possible alternative sources – the friends respectively of Lord Bute, and of William Pitt, either of whom would have assured Rockingham of a stable majority. The King was especially keen on an agreement being reached with Bute and his followers, in particular to secure the return of Bute's brother – James Stuart Mackenzie – as Lord Privy Seal for Scotland. He was nursing a bad conscience about having reluctantly agreed with Grenville on Mackenzie's dismissal, despite having previously given him an assurance that he could keep his post for life (see Chapter 7). But Rockingham and his colleagues refused point-blank to agree to this, and insisted on treating Bute and all his faction as pariahs. Their attitude to Pitt was quite different, but the government was badly split on how to deal with him. All the ministers would have welcomed Pitt's parliamentary support, but there were differing opinions about recruiting him, and/or some of his followers, into the government. On the one hand there were those, such as the Duke of Grafton, who were unreserved admirers of the 'Great Commoner' and who wished him not just to join the government, but to take over its leadership from Rockingham. Others remembered how dictatorial he had been as the dominant force in Newcastle's second government during the Seven Years War, and feared for their own authority if he were to become a colleague. There were also great reservations about Pitt's associates, particularly his two brothers-in-law – Lord Temple and George Grenville – whom Pitt might well insist on bringing into the government with him, were he to join. The King was horrified at the prospect of 'the family' as he called them, being brought back to power, and made it clear that Pitt would only be acceptable, if at all, without them. Ministers never reached agreement on how to deal with Pitt, and their continuing split on the issue progressively weakened the government.

Rockingham's government remained in office for barely a year, during most of which time it was chiefly involved in undoing some of the work of the two preceding governments. Most significantly, it repealed the Stamp Act of 1765 (see Chapter 7), which had imposed direct taxation on the American colonists for the first time. It had – quite unexpectedly – led to massive protests, only some of which were peaceful, such as the 'Stamp Act Congress' convened in New York in October 1765, and attended by representatives of nine colonies. They agreed on resolutions of 'rights and grievances' and agreed to petition both King and Parliament to repeal the Act and other objectionable measures. Meanwhile, there were widespread riots, stamp burning and intimidation of colonial stamp distributors, as well as an outright refusal to use the stamps, accompanied by a highly organized boycott of British imports. British manufactures and exporters took fright and lobbied the government to repeal the Act, which Rockingham – who was keen to conciliate the colonists – was readily persuaded to do. It took some time, however, to convince his fellow ministers, and even longer, the King, who at first argued for modification rather than outright repeal of the Act. He eventually agreed, however, and Rockingham felt aggrieved when the repeal was opposed in Parliament, not only by George Grenville and his followers, but by many self-proclaimed 'friends of the King' (Lord Bute's followers), leading Rockingham to believe that they were being privately encouraged by the King. He had it out with the monarch, and the obstuctionism ceased, but the basis of mutual trust between King and Prime Minister was badly shaken. In order to get the repeal through Parliament, however, Rockingham was forced to accompany it with a so-called 'Declaratory Act', based on earlier legislation concerning Ireland. This Act specifically spelled out the superiority of the British Parliament over the various legislative bodies in the colonies, and asserted its authority to pass binding laws on the colonies 'in all cases whatsoever'. The effect of this was to replace the Americans' current concerns over the Stamp Act with a permanent grievance that their interests could be arbitrarily over-ruled by a distant Parliament in which they were unrepresented. Rockingham did not intend that the Declaratory Act should actually be applied: he was in favour of a 'sleeping sovereignty' or 'salutary neglect', under which the colonies should largely be left to their own devices. Unfortunately, his successors had other ideas.

Two other noteworthy legislative measures were carried by Rockingham's government. One was to repeal the unpopular Cider tax, the last measure enacted by Lord Bute, and to replace it by a Window tax. The second was a resolution by the House of Commons declaring general warrants (that is arrest warrants not naming specific individuals) illegal. They had been used, under the Grenville government, for the arrest of John Wilkes and some 47 of his associates in the production of the dissident newspaper, *The North Briton* (see Chapter 7).

Pitt had supported the repeal of the Stamp Act, but was not ready to give consistent backing to the government, though he expected them to consult him before taking important initiatives. In April 1766, after receiving petitions from various mercantile interests, the cabinet considered introducing a Free Port Bill for the West Indies, as part of Rockingham's policy to foster free trade in the colonies. Rockingham suddenly remembered that no word of this had been made to Pitt, and he despatched Burke to see him and to acquaint him with the government's plans. He reported that he found the Great Commoner in a 'peevish and perverse mood', and he reacted unfavourably to a maladroit attempt by Burke to get him to spell out the 'conditions on which he would come into the King's service' (Hoffman, p. 116). The haughty Pitt maintained that only the King himself should put such questions to him. A few days later, he 'appeared in the House and captiously seized on a routine motion touching the militia to declare open hostility toward the administration' (op. cit.). In so doing, he lit a fuse which rapidly led to the disintegration, and then the dismissal, of the government. The Duke of Grafton felt that he could not remain in an administration to which Pitt was hostile. He urged Rockingham that ministers should collectively give advice to the King to invite Pitt to form an administration. Rockingham refused and according to a letter written by Grafton to Conway, added that 'he saw no reason why the present Administration (if they received assurances from the king that people in office were to hold their posts at the good will of the ministers) should not carry on very well and with honour to themselves the King's business' (Grafton, 1898, pp. 71–2).

But the ever impatient King was becoming increasingly disillusioned with Rockingham, whose capacity he had never rated very highly, once having remarked, according to Horace Walpole, that 'I thought I had not two men in my bedchamber of less parts than Lord Rockingham' (Bigham, p. 141). When Grafton resigned, the King left to his ministers the choice of his successor, but was then aggrieved that they chose the Duke of Richmond, like Grafton an illegitimate descendant of Charles II. The King had a low opinion of Richmond, and only very grumpily acquiesced in his appointment. The last straw, so far as George III was concerned, was when Rockingham failed to bring forward proposals to Parliament to make financial provision for three of the King's younger brothers, who had recently come of age. The King intended that the money previously paid to the Duke of Cumberland, under the Civil List, should be applied to this purpose. Several ministers objected to the proposal being put to Parliament at the tail end of the session, when many MPs had retired to the country and it could not be properly debated, and Rockingham decided that it should be held over until the new session began much later in the year. The King, who had noted with approval a speech made by Pitt, on 24 April 1766, in which he had indicated that his own views on the proper role of government more or less coincided with his own, summoned 'the Great Commoner' to an audience on 12 July, at which they agreed that Pitt should form a government on 'as broad a basis as possible'. This meant that some of Lord Bute's followers would be included, and though several of Rockingham's ministers would be retained, neither he nor Newcastle should continue. The King also insisted that no place should be found for Pitt's brother-in-law, George Grenville. On 30 July 1766, Rockingham's first government came to an end, after one year and 17 days. His successor became the first Earl of Chatham, and unwisely chose to lead his government from the House of Lords, assuming the post of Lord Privy Seal rather than First Lord of the Treasury, another fateful decision (see Chapter 9).

Rockingham had been blithely unaware of the extent to which he had annoyed the King, and had naively assumed that he was in no imminent danger. As his biographer comments:

> If Rockingham was so deluded... his delusion was honourable. He had car-ried all his measures and served his King well, restoring stability to empire (or so it appeared) and prosperity to commerce. There was abundant evi-dence of public satisfaction with what had been done. Why should Majesty withdraw support from so successful an administration? (Hoffman, p. 23)

The answer was surely that Rockingham was more interested in being a good Whig, and sticking to his principles, than being Prime Minister. The jibe made against many Liberal American presidential aspirants that 'He'd rather be right than President' was never more apt than in his case. He consistently refused to bend his views to suit the King's prejudices, to indulge in empty flattery or to consider for a moment agreeing to the appointment of any of Lord Bute's friends, which would have mollified the King and made his own task of governing easier. He paid the price.

Rockingham had been the youngest ever Prime Minister, and now became an ex-Premier at the age of 36. For the next 16 years, he was, effectively, to act, albeit somewhat spasmodically, as Leader of the Opposition, though no such post existed at the time. During most of this period – between 1770 and 1782 – a Tory government, led by Lord North MP was in power. Rockingham did not lead a united Whig opposition, but his faction was the largest and much the most coherent. The 'Rockingham Whigs', as they became known, have some claim to be regarded as the first modern political party. The other factions were largely made up of the personal followers of leading politicians. A strong group of supporters of George Grenville, largely disintegrated after his death in 1770, while Pitt's (Chatham's) followers mostly transferred their allegiance to the Earl of Shelburne when he died in 1778. The Rockingham Whigs were strongly represented in the House of Lords, while in the Commons the oratory of Edmund Burke, and later of Charles James Fox, a brilliant younger son of Henry Fox, the first Baron Holland, made them a force to be reckoned with. The publication, in 1770, of Burke's pamphlet, *Thoughts on the Cause of the Present Discontent*, provided intellectual justification for the positions taken up by the Rockingham Whigs. The pamphlet argued that George III's attempts to create a more active role for the monarchy were not only against the letter but also the spirit of the constitution, which derived from the 'Glorious Revolution' of 1688–89. This pamphlet was also notable for Burke's justification of the role of 'party', which he defined as 'a body of men united on public principle, which could act as a constitutional link between king and Parliament, providing consistency and strength in administration, or principled criticism in opposition'.

A nervous, and initially ineffective speaker, Rockingham gradually overcame his inhibitions and spoke more frequently in the Lords, where he was listened to with some respect because of his status as a great grandee, his geniality and his apparently spotless character. It was regarded as noteworthy, and more than a shade eccentric, that he appeared more interested in pursuing a consistent line than on gaining office. On more than one occasion he declined invitations to join subsequent governments because he disagreed with their policies. Issues on which he felt strongly and opposed the government of the day included the repeated exclusion of John Wilkes from the House of Commons despite his being returned by his loyal electors in Middlesex, (see Chapters 9, 10 and 11), the use of secret service money to influence elections, attempts to restrict the freedom of the press, and the Royal Marriages Act of 1772, personally promoted by George III to give himself control over the marriages of his descendants and siblings. He proved an advocate of religious toleration, a very moderate supporter of electoral reform and sympathetic to the aspirations of Irish Catholics. Like Burke, he was convinced that George III was exceeding his constitutional powers in intervening so actively in government and in manipulating Parliament, and he also believed that the King was still under the active influence of the Earl of Bute, though there had been no contact between the two men for many years. In 1780, John Dunning, a leading Rockinghamite MP, caused a stir by carrying a parliamentary resolution stating that 'The influence of the crown has increased, is increasing and ought to be diminished'. Most notably, Rockingham was a firm and consistent advocate of conciliation towards the American colonists, strongly opposed Lord North's prosecution of the war against them, and as early as 1778 called for the immediate granting of American independence. In this, he went further than either Chatham or Shelburne, both of whom were highly critical of government policy but still believed it would be possible and desirable to reconcile the 'rebels' to continued British rule. His voice was not heard, and he and his friends were widely attacked as 'unpatriotic'. It was only after the news of General Cornwallis's defeat and surrender at Yorktown reached England, in November 1781, that the bulk of both parliamentary and public opinion began to swing to his side. Lord North realized that the game was up, and sought to resign, but it was only four months later, in March 1782 that George III reluctantly let him go, and – on North's advice – invited Rockingham to form his second government.

George III was initially averse to taking this step, and first approached the Earl of Shelburne, the leader of the Chathamites. But Shelburne declined, aware that he was unlikely to be able to command majority support in the Commons. The King, however, not wishing to deal directly with Rockingham, insisted on using Shelburne as a go-between, and also demanded that he should hold a senior post in the government. This was the only concession which Rockingham was to make – all the other important offices went to Whigs, mostly of the Rockinghamite connection. The only survivor from the previous government of Lord North was the Lord Chancellor, Lord Thurlow, a 'Vicar of Bray' character who succeeded in retaining office in several governments of highly different political complexions. Rockingham intended that his government would be a reforming administration, putting into practice all the policies which he had advocated while in opposition – a novel concept for eighteenth century politicians. One change which he implemented was to alter the designations of the two Secretaries of State, who, apart from their other responsibilities, had been in charge of foreign policy, being respectively heads of the Northern and Southern Departments. Rockingham proceeded to appoint Charles James Fox as Foreign Secretary, and Shelburne as Home Secretary, the first two men to hold these specific posts. Unfortunately, this did not have the intended effect of putting one person unequivocally in charge of foreign policy, as the Home Department was responsible for the colonies, which had great relevance, in particular, to the peace negotiations which were pending with the American colonists. Fox assumed that he would be responsible and was horrified when Shelburne, who was a great deal less sympathetic to the American cause, insisted on interfering. The other main ministers included Lord John Cavendish, as Chancellor of the Exchequer, the Duke of Grafton, as Lord Privy Seal, the Duke of Richmond as Master-General of the Ordnance and Edmund Burke, as Paymaster-General. John Dunning, now Lord Ashburton, became Chancellor of the Duchy of Lancaster.

Rockingham did not prove to be a strong leader of his government. His health was poor, his energy not over-abundant and he was hindered by the fact that the King insisted on treating Shelburne as at least his co-equal, and even taking clandestine steps to assure him the eventual succession to what he evidently hoped would be only a short-lived premiership. Nevertheless, he was determined to implement the policies which he and his followers had fervently preached for many years past. Foremost of these was the determination to curb the King's ability to control Parliament through the use of patronage and bribery, notably by the creation of 'placemen' among MPs. Three Acts of Parliament were rushed through to help bring this about. Two of these ('Clerke's Act' and 'Crewe's Act') had repeatedly been introduced by Rockinghamite MPs, during Lord North's long premiership, and had been voted down. Now produced as government measures, they at last reached the Statute book. The first disfranchised revenue officers, and the second excluded government contractors from the House of Commons. The third act, introduced by Burke, the Civil Establishment Act, imposed strict controls over government expenditure, to prevent it from being used for electoral purposes. The combined effect of these three measures was markedly to reduce the role of corruption in British politics, but – due to disagreement among the leading ministers – the government did not attempt any electoral reform measures which the more radical of them would have liked to push forward. These had to wait until the Younger Pitt briefly but unsuccessfully took up the challenge (see Chapter 14) a few years later, and were not, in fact, enacted until the passage of the 'Great Reform Bill' in 1832.

Rockingham, who was an absentee, but nevertheless enlightened Irish landlord, who kept himself well informed about Irish grievances, also acted to free the Dublin Parliament from its subordination to the Parliament in Westminster. His government repealed parts of the famous 'Poynings Act' of 1494, as well as the Irish Declaratory Act of 1720, ushering in a period of almost two decades during which Ireland became substantially self-governing. The Wolfe Tone rebellion of 1798, followed by the Irish Act of Union in 1800, brought this happy state of affairs to an end (see Chapter 14). Yet it was the peace negotiations to end the War of Independence which dominated the short life of the second Rockingham government. It declared an immediate end to hostilities in North America, and embarked on two parallel sets of negotiations, one with the American colonists and the other with the governments of France, Spain and the Netherlands which had intervened on the American side. Fox proposed to concede recognition of independence from the outset, while Shelburne, encouraged by the King, wished to hold it back as a bargaining chip during the talks. At a Cabinet meeting on 26 June 1782, held in the absence of Rockingham, who was away ill at his home in Wimbledon, Fox was outvoted, and – threatening to his friends to resign – left the meeting in high dudgeon. After a further meeting, on 30 June, when he was again outvoted he declared that he would in fact resign, as soon as Rockingham was well enough to deal with the matter. The following morning, 1 July, news arrived that Rockingham was dead – his second ministry having lasted a mere 96 days, and was already on the verge of collapse. Rockingham's death, at the age of 52, was attributed to influenza, though the underlying cause was most probably the long-term effects of the urogenitary disease he had contracted over 30 years earlier. The King lost no time in appointing Shelburne as his successor, but his government was weakened from the outset by the refusal of Fox and the majority of the Rockinghamites to take part (see Chapter 12).

Rockingham was a man of only modest abilities, but of great wisdom and integrity. He saw his mission as being to maintain and rejuvenate Whig traditions derived from the 'Glorious Revolution' at a time when they were threatened by rampant opportunism and unremitting pressure from the Throne. Historically, he can be seen as having been on the 'progressive' side on most of the issues of his day, though he was certainly no advanced democrat, believing that government should be the business of an enlightened aristocracy. His immediate legacy was a strong parliamentary party, led by Charles James Fox, which was however condemned to long frustrating years in opposition as it was outmanoeuvred by the King and the Younger Pitt, and then fatally split by its response to the French Revolution (see Chapter 14). It was not until half a century after his death that a new generation of Whigs, led by Earl Grey and Lord John Russell, were able to take over the baton and lead governments inspired by his own principles. They revered Rockingham as a great precursor, but most historians have tended to neglect Rockingham and under-estimate his importance.

Works consulted

Bigham, Clive (1924), *The Prime Ministers of Britain 1721–1924*, London, John Murray.

Bloy, Marjorie (1998), 'Charles Watson-Wentworth, Second Marquess of Rockingham', in Robert Eccleshall and Graham Walker, eds., *Biographical Dictionary of British Prime Ministers*, London, Routledge.

Brooke, John (1972), *King George III*, London, Constable.

Farrell, S.M. (2004a), 'Wentworth, Charles Watson-, second Marquess of Rockingham', in *Oxford Dictionary of National Biography,* Oxford, OUP.

Farrell, S.M. (2004b), 'Wentworth, Mary Watson-, Marchioness of Rockingham', in *Oxford Dictionary of National Biography,* Oxford, OUP.

Henry Augustus, Third Duke of Grafton, (1898), *Autobiography and Political Correspondence*, edited by Sir William R. Anson, London, John Murray.

Hoffman, Ross J.S. (1973), *The Marquis: A Study of Lord Rockingham, 1730–1782*, New York, Fordham University Press.

Langford, Paul (1973), *The First Rockingham Administration, 1765–1766*, Oxford, OUP.

Langford, Paul (1974), 'The Marquis of Rockingham', in Herbert Van Thal, ed., *The Prime Ministers,* Volume I, London, Allen & Unwin.

Norris, John (1963), *Shelburne and Reform*, London, Macmillan.

9

William Pitt, the Elder, First Earl of Chatham – 'I am Sure That I Can Save This Country, and That Nobody Else Can'

For 250 years, the Elder Pitt has been revered as an exemplary, and highly successful, war leader – the forerunner and inspiration of Winston Churchill, whose life and career resembled his in a number of ways. He was, without doubt, a remarkable man, but recent scholarship, (and particularly the writings of the New Zealand academic Marie Peters), has confirmed that he was an erratic and deeply flawed character, whose achievements were a great deal more mixed than his reputation would suggest.

Pitt's family were minor gentry from Dorset, whose status was transformed by his grandfather, Thomas Pitt, who made a fortune as a trader in India, rising to the position of Governor of Madras, under the East India Company. He held this post from 1688 to 1709, returning to England, with an abnormally large diamond, which he sold at a considerable profit, earning himself the nickname of 'Diamond' Pitt. He purchased several West Country estates, the largest being at Boconnoc, in Cornwall. He also succeeded in marrying off all his five surviving children into titled families. His eldest, rather undistinguished son, Robert Pitt, was married to Harriet Villiers, granddaughter of the fourth Viscount Grandison. Thomas Pitt's estates gave him a commanding influence in three parliamentary constituencies, and Robert Pitt was to represent each of these in turn, during a parliamentary career of 22 years, culminating in his appointment as Clerk to the Household of the Prince of Wales (later George II).

William was the fourth child, and second son, of the seven children born to Robert and Harriet. Together with his chronically bad health, his position as a younger son was to prove a handicap to him, financially and psychologically, and was a contributory factor in his late arrival as a politician of the first rank. Like 10 of the first 26 Prime Ministers (Black, 1992, p. 2), he was educated at Eton, an experience he detested, and was later to say to his ministerial colleague, the Earl of Shelburne, that 'he scarce observed a boy who was not cowed for life at Eton'. Jeremy Black comments:

The public schools of the period were certainly violent, characterised by bullying, buggery and the bottle. It is unclear whether the strain of life at Eton was responsible for the onset of Pitt's ill-health. He suffered there from gout, but as that illness in his case had definite psychosomatic aspects, it may well have reflected his response to the school. (Black, p. 3)

Pitt was determined not to subject his own children to similar treatment, and had them all educated at home by private tutors. Consequently, the Younger Pitt is probably the only one of Britain's 53 Prime Ministers (to date) not to have been to school. The elder William may not have enjoyed Eton, but seems to have done quite well there, unlike his elder brother, Thomas. His teacher, William Burchett, wrote to his father: 'Your younger son has made a great progress since his coming hither, indeed I never was concerned with a young gentleman of so good abilities, and at the same time of so good a disposition, and there is no question to be made that he will answer your hopes' (Ibid., p. 3).

William proceeded to Trinity College, Oxford, where he remained only for a year, during which time he experienced difficulty keeping up with the conspicuous expenditure of his fellow students, most of whom came from wealthier families. His father originally intended him for the Church, where he could have provided one of the several livings on his estates, but changed his mind, shortly before his unexpected death in May 1727. The following year, William, then aged 19, transferred to the University of Utrecht, at that time probably a more distinguished seat of learning, though there is no information about the content of his studies there. In 1730, unsure of what to do with his life, he returned disconsolately to Boconnoc, now inherited by his brother Thomas, where time hung heavily on his hands, writing to a friend: 'I grow more and more out of temper with the remoteness of this cursed hiding place' (Ibid., p. 5). His only income was a legacy of £100 a year from his father, and he resented being otherwise dependent on his elder brother, to whom he was not close.

In 1731, he was rescued by an old school-friend, George Lyttelton, who introduced him to his uncle, the influential peer, Richard, first Viscount Cobham. Cobham was the commander of the King's Own Regiment of Horse, generally known as Cobham's Own. He offered Pitt a cornetcy in the regiment, which cost £1000, a sum which the family found difficult to raise. The Prime Minister, Sir Robert Walpole, is believed to have come to the rescue, and provided the money in the expectation of parliamentary support from Thomas Pitt and the MPs representing the pocket boroughs he controlled (Peters, 2004). In the event, Walpole was to be grievously disappointed (see below).

William departed with enthusiasm for what was soon to become, despite his best intentions, a tedious life in a series of dreary garrison towns. Evidently more intelligent and serious-minded than most of his fellow officers, it is clear from his letters to his favourite sister, Ann, that he soon fell in with their favourite pastimes of heavy drinking and whoring. This evidently exacerbated his gout, and possibly, Jeremy Black speculates on the basis of a letter which Pitt wrote to a nephew 20 years later, led to his being infected by a venereal disease. If so, he writes, 'that may have played a role in his late marriage, though other factors, principally his relative poverty, may have been responsible' (Ibid., p. 8). His brother, Thomas, was to marry at the age of 26; William remained a bachelor until he was 46.

After two years of this life, he took time out to depart on what was an abbreviated version of the Grand Tour, taking in only a brief visit to Paris, before proceeding to more lengthy stays in Besançon and Luneville, and shorter visits to Marseilles, Montpellier, Lyons, Geneva and Strasbourg, not being able to spare the time, or the money, to go on to Italy, usually the high point of such tours. In Besançon, he briefly fell in love with the beautiful younger daughter of a local squire, about whom he wrote to his sister Ann. He seems to have considered marriage to her, but rejected the idea because of her lowly background. Not long after his return to England, William's life abruptly changed, with his election to Parliament for the quintessential 'rotten borough' of Old Sarum (5 voters). This was one of the three seats now controlled by his brother Thomas, who had previously sat for it himself, before transferring to the somewhat larger borough of Okehampton (300 voters), also under his control. Thomas had hesitated about bringing William in, flirting with the idea of selling the seat to somebody else, a move which William strongly opposed. Eventually Thomas gave way, and on 18 February 1735 William was elected unopposed in a by-election, at the age of 26.

At this time, Pitt seems to have had no fixed political opinions, and it is possible that, initially, he saw his election primarily as a means of furthering his military career. He regarded himself as a Whig, but chose to align himself not with Walpole, but with the dissident Whigs who formed the liveliest element of the Opposition, the Tories being somewhat dormant. Even so, the Opposition Whigs were divided among themselves, the largest faction being led by William Pulteney in the Commons, and by Lord Carteret in the Lords. Pitt, however, joined a smaller group, mostly of younger MPs with family or personal connections with Lord Cobham, who came to be known as 'Cobham's Cubs'. Cobham was fiercely opposed to Walpole, and – taking his cue from him – Pitt made a number of trenchant speeches criticizing the Prime Minister and his policies. Walpole, aghast at the temerity of one whom he had benefited, promptly responded by cancelling Pitt's commission, and in April 1736 his soldiering days came to an abrupt end after five years, without his having seen any action.

There were compensations. Pitt became a frequent visitor to Stowe, the magnificent country seat of Lord Cobham (now the site of a famous 'public' school). Here he consolidated his friendship with George Lyttelton, now also an MP, and various members of the Grenville family, including four brothers, all of whom were to sit in Parliament. The eldest, Richard Grenville (later Earl Temple) was Cobham's heir, and the second, George Grenville, was to precede Pitt as Prime Minister, in 1763–65 (see Chapter 7). The brothers had a younger sister, Hester, whom, much later, in 1754, Pitt was eventually to marry. Meanwhile, Cobham had transferred the loyalty of his group to Frederick, Prince of Wales, now openly opposed to his father, George II, and running an 'alternative' court from his residence at Leicester House (the site of the present Leicester Square). The Prince appointed Pitt as Groom to his Bedchamber, at a salary of £400 a year, which was a welcome addition to the £300 a year, from successive legacies from his father, mother and grandfather, which made up his sole income.

Over the next few years, Pitt emerged as the most effective opposition critic of Walpole and his government, his speeches, invariably trenchant, and sometimes recklessly offensive, became parliamentary occasions not to be missed. He acquired numerous admirers, but also implacable enemies, who later obstructed his passage to power. Pitt carried his party identification lightly, presenting himself primarily as a 'patriot', whose over-riding objective was to increase national power and prestige. He strongly opposed Walpole's pacific attitude to Spain, and his attempt to avoid war by negotiating the Convention of Pardo, in January 1739. In a coruscating speech, he described the Convention as a 'national ignominy...odious throughout the kingdom', and condemned the proposed payment of financial reparations to Spain as 'a public infamy' (Peters, 1998, p. 22). The virulence of his intervention appalled Walpole's supporters, but won him a public kiss from the Prince of Wales, still vehemently opposed to his father and his ministers. When the Convention broke down, and Walpole was forced against his will to launch the 'War of Jenkins' Ear' (see Chapter 1), Pitt transferred his attack to the government's ineffectual prosecution of the struggle. This soon merged into the wider War of Austrian Succession, pitching Britain and Austria against France, Spain, Prussia, Saxony and Bavaria.

After the resignation of Walpole, in February 1742, Pitt played a leading role in efforts to hold him to account for his alleged corruption and misuse of power, making two powerful parliamentary speeches in support of the appointment of a committee of enquiry into his conduct as Prime Minister. Pitt was appointed to the committee, which met in secret, but skilful manoeuvring by Henry Pelham, now leader of the Commons, under Lord Wilmington, prevented it from pursuing its work to a conclusion (see Chapter 1). Meanwhile, Pitt stepped up his criticism of the war effort, focusing on Lord Carteret's forward policy in Germany, which he argued was much more in the interest of George II's electorate of Hanover than of Britain. He railed against the agreement to take

16,000 Hanoverian soldiers into British pay, saying that this was yet another example of the way in which 'this great, this powerful, this formidable kingdom is considered only as a province to a despicable electorate' (Peters, 2004). George II was deeply upset, and resolved never to employ Pitt as one of his ministers. Though critical of Carteret's policy, Pitt enthusiastically backed the war, but argued for a 'maritime strategy', asserting that the powerful British navy was more than a match for France and Spain, from both of whom it could expect 'easy pickings', in the Caribbean and North America, whereas there was, he believed, little to gain from engaging the formidable French forces on the Continent. Though alienating the King, Pitt's position, and his eloquent advocacy, brought him great popularity 'out of doors' (that is outside Parliament, in eighteenth century parlance), and increasingly with Tories and Opposition Whigs in the House of Commons.

Meanwhile, the death of Lord Wilmington, in July 1743, exacerbated divisions in the government, and precipitated a power struggle between the King's favourite, Lord Carteret, Secretary of State (North), and the trio of 'Old Corps Whigs', who regarded themselves as the political heirs to Robert Walpole. They were Henry Pelham, who became First Lord of the Treasury, his brother, the Duke of Newcastle, who was Secretary of State (South) and the Earl of Hardwicke, the Lord Chancellor. Pitt, now 36 years old and anxious to achieve ministerial office himself, sought to throw in his lot with the Pelhamites, and began to modify his criticisms of the government, focusing them almost exclusively on Carteret. In October 1744, he received a welcome financial boost, with the death of Sarah, Duchess of Marlborough, the widow of the great General. Herself a doughty opponent of Walpole, she had been charmed by Pitt's attacks on the former Prime Minister and his corrupt ways. In her will she left Pitt £10,000 'upon account of his merit in the noble defence he has made for the support of the laws of England, and to prevent the ruin of his country' (Black, p. 58). A month later, however, Pitt was to suffer a considerable disappointment. Pelham and his associates succeeded in forcing the resignation of Carteret, and proceeded to bring into the government a number of former opposition Whigs. Yet, as Black remarks, 'Pitt was the sole leading opposition Whig who did not gain office' (Black, p. 58). Pelham was anxious to include him, but Pitt probably pitched his demands too high, seeking the post of Secretary at War, which George II adamantly refused to grant him. Pelham privately assured Pitt that he would work on the King in the hope that he might later relent his implacable aversion to one who had made such bitter attacks on his beloved electorate of Hanover. Meanwhile Pitt went out of his way to support Pelham's government in his parliamentary speeches, even endorsing their decision to increase British military involvement in Germany. This disappointed some of his 'patriot' supporters who felt, that he was trimming his views in the hope of achieving office. It paid dividends, however, in 1746, when the Pelham government, by threatening resignation, successfully forced the King to cease his private consultations with Carteret (now the Earl of Granville) and secured the dismissal of almost all of his followers from their posts. One of the conditions, which Pelham and his colleagues imposed on the King, was 'That he will be graciously pleased to perfect the Scheme lately humbly propos'd to Him for bringing Mr. Pitt into some honourable Employment' (see Chapter 3).

George II reluctantly complied, appointing him to the very junior post of Joint Vice-Treasurer of Ireland, but three months later, in May 1746, he became Paymaster-General, a post he retained for over nine years, until November 1755. This was outside the Cabinet, but a highly sought position, as the holder traditionally was able to profit from the use of the very large sums of money which passed through his hands. Henry Pelham, who was Paymaster-General between 1730 and 1743, was one of very few eighteenth century holders of this office not to enrich himself in this way, but Pitt, despite his relative poverty, followed his example rather than that of most of his other predecessors. This certainly helped to foster his reputation as an incorruptible politician. Throughout his period as Paymaster-General, Pitt was seen, and saw himself, as something of an 'outsider' within the administration. He was not there because of great wealth or family connection, but had forced his way in because of his power as a parliamentary orator, and his rising popularity 'out of doors'. His ministerial colleagues wanted him in the government so that his debating powers could be exercised on their behalf in the House of Commons, rather than hammering them from the opposition benches. In the typically inelegant words which President Lyndon Baines Johnson used about FBI chief J. Edgar Hoover, two centuries later: 'Better to have him inside the tent pissing out, than outside pissing in.'

Pelham formed the highest opinion of Pitt's character and abilities, writing to his brother that he was 'The most able and useful man we have amongst us; truly honourable and strictly honest. He is as firm a friend to us, as we can wish for, and a more useful one does not exist' (Peters, 1998, p. 57). He made no attempt, however, to promote him to the Cabinet, and Pitt was to continue as Paymaster-General for the remainder of Pelham's Premiership. He soon won a reputation as an energetic and efficient administrator, despite his periodic bouts of ill-health, and an able defender of the government's policies in Parliament. These included the compromise peace of Aix-la-Chapelle, which brought an end to the War of Austrian Succession, without achieving many of Britain's announced war aims. The previously highly belligerent Pitt admitted to the House of Commons that he had changed his views, saying: 'I have upon some former occasions, by the heat of youth and the warmth of a debate, been hurried into expressions, which upon cool reflection, I have heartily regretted' (Peters, 2004).

An additional reason for Pitt to feel obliged to conform to government policies, which he might earlier have hastened to condemn, was that he had become dependent on the patronage of the Duke of Newcastle. The Duke had provided him with pocket boroughs of his own at the 1747 and 1754 general elections, when Pitt's elder brother Thomas had withdrawn support from him at Old Sarum. When Pelham died in March 1754, to be succeeded by his brother, Newcastle, Pitt felt that the time had come for him to be promoted to a more senior position, having in mind the Secretary of State (North) post which Newcastle vacated on becoming Premier. He was to be grievously disappointed: Newcastle instead chose the ineffectual Earl of Holderness, while as Secretary of State (South), combined with the leadership of the House of Commons, he appointed the even more mediocre Sir Thomas Robinson. When Robinson proved totally inadequate, Newcastle still did not turn to Pitt, but to his great rival, Henry Fox, who succeeded Robinson in November 1755 (see Chapter 4). Well before this, Pitt began to loosen his ties with the administration, renewing contact with the 'alternative court' of Frederick Prince of Wales, only to be thwarted by the Prince's sudden death in March 1751. Pitt proceeded once again to alienate George II, by paying extravagant tribute to the Prince (who had been deeply estranged from his father), and began again to attack government policies in increasingly vehement Commons speeches, despite the fact that he remained a government minister. Fox, no mean parliamentarian himself, was to comment on Pitt's somewhat wayward conduct, 'He is a better speaker than I am, but thank God! I have more judgment' (Peters, 2004). The rivalry between the two men foreshadowed the more famous, and much more prolonged, struggle between their respective sons, the Younger Pitt and Charles James Fox (See Chapter 14).

In November 1754, Pitt finally got married, at the age of 46. His bride was the 36-year-old Lady Hester Grenville, the younger sister of the three Grenville brothers – Richard (now Earl Temple), George and James – who had been his fellow 'Cobham cubs' and were now his parliamentary allies. He had known her since she was in her teens, but the two had met again two months earlier during Pitt's annual visit to Stowe, where he began a whirlwind courtship. It was a love-match, on both sides, and the marriage brought continuing solace to Pitt among all his later disappointments, and provided him with a family life, with their three sons and two daughters, which he found deeply satisfying. In the judgment of his latest biographer, Marie Peters, 'Certainly, without Hester's unstinting devotion and skills of family management, Pitt's chronic ill health, financial irresponsibility and personal arrogance might well have wrecked, rather than merely hampered, his later career' (Peters, 2004). As it turned out, the marriage was the immediate prelude to the most productive, and constructive, seven years of his life, during which he rose to the peak of his fame and acclaim.

A year into his marriage, Pitt took the decisive step of breaking with the Newcastle government. He had already been highly critical of Newcastle's failure to take energetic action to oppose French encroachments on territory claimed by Britain in North America, and his negotiation of subsidy agreements with Hesse-Cassel and Russia, which Pitt believed was more in the interests of Hanover than of Britain. In November 1755, his impatience and indignation boiled over during an all-night debate on the annual Queen's Speech, reported on admiringly by the normally caustic Horace Walpole, in a letter to a friend (General Henry Conway): 'He spoke at past one, for an hour and thirty-five minutes: there was more humour, wit, vivacity, finer language, more boldness, in short, more astonishing perfections than even you, who are used to him, can conceive...'

Pitt concluded by calling for a war to be fought for the 'long forgotten people of America', a war to be fought by 'our proper force', the navy (Peters, 2004). This speech earned Pitt, as he must have foreseen, instant dismissal from the government, which released him to mount from the opposition benches a hail of attacks as Britain slid unprepared into the Seven Years War, and a series of disasters, of which the loss of Minorca, in June 1756, was only the most conspicuous. Pitt now totally dominated the House of Commons, where his only rival as an orator, the Attorney-General, William Murray, was removed to the House of Lords in 1756, on his appointment as Lord Chief Justice (he became Lord Mansfield). Unable to mount an effective response to Pitt, Henry Fox threw in his hand, and resigned, in October 1756, and Newcastle, despairing of finding an adequate substitute to lead the House of Commons, followed a month later. George II then summoned Fox and invited him to form an administration, which, over a four-day period of complex negotiations with rival political figures, he attempted to do. Fox was determined that Pitt should join his government, which he adamantly refused to do. It was open to Fox to proceed without 'the great commoner', as Pitt was now known, on board, but he was loath to do so, fearing that his administration would not long survive. His ambition, also, was not so great that he was willing to risk everything for the highest post. He decided instead to set his sights on the Paymaster-Generalship, which he rightly believed would enable him to amass a large fortune. He achieved this objective a few months later, and served for eight years before retiring, with great pomp, but very little honour, as the First Baron Holland.

Newcastle's resignation, and Fox's failure of nerve, had demonstrated to George II that it was impossible at that time to proceed without Pitt's support. The King was still unwilling to have him as his chief minister, but Pitt indicated that he was ready to serve under the fourth Duke of Devonshire, provided that he played a decisive role in the government and that places were found for his own leading supporters, notably his brother-in-law, Earl Temple, who became First Lord of the Admiralty (see Chapter 4). The new government was formed on 16 November 1756. Devonshire, who had only succeeded to his title a few months earlier, came from one of the most powerful Whig families, and was highly popular in both Court and political circles largely because of his apparent lack of personal ambition. He accepted the post of First Lord of the Treasury with some reluctance, making it clear from the outset that he did not expect to continue in office for very long. This was just as well, for the government lacked a parliamentary majority. The previous general election, in 1754, had been a triumph for Lord Newcastle, and the majority of MPs still looked to him for leadership, even though he was now in opposition. Only a minority of Whigs regarded themselves as supporters of the Devonshire-Pitt administration, though it did attract support from the Tories and the supporters of the 'Leicester House' faction, who looked to the 'alternative court' of the King's grandson and heir apparent, George, Prince of Wales. The Prince was still a minor, but his tutor, the Earl of Bute, was a highly influential figure on his behalf (see Chapters 4, 5 and 6).

Pitt's office was Secretary of State (South), coupled with the leadership of the House of Commons. It was understood from the outset that he would have overall direction of the war effort, which could not have been going more badly. There is no doubt that, at this juncture, Pitt saw himself as a 'man of destiny', saying to Devonshire, 'My Lord, I am sure that I can save this country, and that nobody else can' (Macaulay, 2004, p. 317). Despite being heavily afflicted with gout, Pitt entered into his new responsibilities with great vigour, planning substantial reinforcements for America and naval support for the East India Company, which was locked in conflict with France. Despite his earlier opposition to the Treaty of Westminster, signed with Prussia in January 1756, he insisted on the payment of a large subsidy to Frederick the Great, Britain's only ally on the Continent, whose forces were facing the formidable combination of France, Austria and Russia. He also made preparations for the deployment of a large military force in northern Germany to aid the Prussian king. The two men soon formed something of a mutual admiration society, with Frederick saying of Pitt: 'England has been a long time in labour, but she has at last brought forth a man'.

The early months of the Devonshire administration were, however, dominated by the controversy over Admiral Byng and his alleged responsibility for the loss of Minorca to the French (see Chapters 4 and 5). Newcastle, anxious to divert from his own responsibility, had insisted that he be court-martialled, and the trial duly opened on 27 December 1756, ending a month later, with a verdict of guilty on the charge of 'not doing his utmost' to engage the French fleet during the siege of Minorca. The court imposed a mandatory death sentence, but coupled this with a unanimous plea for mercy. Public opinion was howling for Byng's blood, but many MPs felt that both the verdict and the sentence were unjust. Pitt was strongly of this opinion, and (together with Temple) urged the King to exercise the prerogative of mercy. George, however, was determined that the sentence should be carried out, and on 14 March 1757 the admiral faced a firing squad on the deck of HMS *Monarch* in Portsmouth Harbour. A few weeks later, on 6 April, both Pitt and Temple were peremptorily dismissed from office. It was not just the King's anger at Pitt's pleading for Byng that caused his demise. He had also deeply offended the King's younger and favourite son, the Duke of Cumberland ('The butcher of Culloden'), who was refusing to take over command of the armed forces so long as Pitt remained a minister. It was also the case that Pitt had been effectively out of action for around a month, with one of his periodic attacks of gout, and had been almost *incommunicado* at Bath.

Whatever motivated George II, he was totally taken aback by the public reaction. The City of London was up in arms, and 13 other cities in a 'golden rain', in Horace Walpole's words, showered the dismissed Secretary of State with the their freedoms and compliments. No doubt there was an element of manipulation by Pitt's followers, but it certainly appeared to be a rare example of spontaneous support by 'out of doors' opinion for a politician denied royal favour. Not only that, the entire government machine ground to a halt, with Devonshire anxious to throw in the sponge, and a ceaseless round of negotiation and intrigue began, as George II tried in vain to secure a stable government without calling on the services of Pitt. Among other intermediaries he employed, was the pleasure-loving second Earl of Waldegrave, whom he actually appointed as First Lord of the Treasury, on 8 June 1757. After three days, the Earl concluded that his task was hopeless, and he advised the King to send for Pitt. (By some reckonings, Waldegrave qualifies as the second shortest serving Prime Minister, after William Pulteney, Lord Bath, who unsuccessfully tried to form a government in February 1742, but gave up the attempt after two days. Neither man however, has been credited by historians as having actually been in power, and both have been excluded from most roll calls of British Premiers).

If Pitt was now seen as indispensable, so was the Duke of Newcastle, who still commanded majority support in the Commons. Henry Fox, who was Cumberland's leading supporter, was also seen as somebody who needed to be accommodated if a new government was to prove viable. After performing a seemingly endless series of minuets around each other, these three men finally agreed to come together, with Newcastle becoming First Lord of the Treasury, and nominal head of the government, Pitt resuming his post as Secretary of State, but acknowledged as the War Minister and dominant figure in the government, and Fox securing his coveted role of Paymaster-General.

The new government took office on 29 June 1757, almost three months after Pitt's dismissal. The general course of events during the so-called Pitt-Newcastle government, which lasted for nearly five years (the final eight months without Pitt), is described in Chapter 4. Although the two men had their differences, they got on surprisingly well, with Pitt allowed an increasingly free hand in running the war, and Newcastle assuring consistent parliamentary support and raising prodigious amounts in taxation and loans to pay for his ambitious strategy. The war that Pitt waged was the first to be conducted on something approaching a world-wide scale, involving campaigns in North America, the Caribbean, West Africa, Germany, the French coast and India. Pitt was not in a position to plan all these campaigns down to the closest detail, though the instructions to commanding officers, written in his own hand, left little room for their own initiatives. The vast distances involved, and the slowness of communication meant that things seldom worked out precisely in the way that Pitt intended. Nor was his military judgment invariably sound. The series of raids on the French coast which he insisted on, in an effort to relieve pressure on the allied forces in Germany, had very little effect and the resources committed to them could almost certainly have been employed with greater profit elsewhere. What Pitt contributed was his aggressive spirit, his overwhelming commitment to victory, his energy (despite his ill-health) and his ability to impose his dynamic will on all his colleagues and subordinates.

It did not take long for Pitt to turn the war round, and for the setbacks of 1756 and 1757 to be followed by a run of successes in 1758, including the capture of two great French fortresses in North America – Louisbourg on Cape Breton (the 'gateway to Canada') and Fort Duquesne in Pennsylvania, which the victorious British general, John Forbes, promptly renamed Pittsburgh. But it was in 1759, the so-called 'Year of Victories' and still regarded as the most successful year in the whole of British military history, that Pitt's renown as a great war leader reached its apex. In May a prize French possession, the sugar island of Guadeloupe, was captured, followed by Fort Niagara in June. In August, the French army was heavily defeated at Minden by a largely Anglo-Hanoverian force commanded by the Prussian General, Prince Ferdinand of Brunswick, while Admiral Edward Boscowen overwhelmed the French fleet in the Battle of Lagos Bay. In September, Quebec was taken after a titanic struggle in which both the British and French commanders, General James Wolfe and the Marquis de Montcalm, were killed. The year, which also saw the complete expulsion of the French from their West African territories in Senegal and Gorée Island, was rounded off by yet another naval victory, by Admiral Edward Hawke, in the Battle of Quiberon Bay. The following year, 1760, saw the surrender of Montreal to the British and the effective end of French rule in Canada. Meanwhile in India, the defeat at Wandiwash of the Comte de Lally (who finally surrendered his forces at Pondicherry in January 1761) marked the triumphant end of a campaign, in which the turning point had been Robert Clive's famous victory at Plessey, in June 1757. The French dream of becoming the dominant force in India was well and truly over.

During these years church bells were constantly ringing to celebrate the news – often belated – of one success after another. So much so that the ever caustic Horace Walpole was to write that 'we are forced to ask every morning what victory there has been for fear of missing one' (Turberville, 1929, p. 255). Pitt's reputation and popularity soared, and it seemed that there was no limit to the scope and span of his power. Then, on 25 October, 1760, George II died, a week short of his seventy-seventh birthday. Long resistant to Pitt, and forever wary of Newcastle, he had warmed to both men as the flow of victories continued, and was more than content that they should remain indefinitely in office. Not so, with his grandson and successor, George III. The new King, barely 22 years old, headstrong and impatient, was determined to govern in his own way and not subordinate himself to a Whig oligarchy, as he believed the first two Georges had done. Influenced by the writings of Lord Bolingbroke, particularly *The Idea of a Patriot King*, he saw it as his duty to rise above political factions and represent the nation as a whole. He therefore despised Newcastle, whom he saw as the epitome of factional government, and had also formed a low opinion of Pitt, who he believed had joined the Leicester House circle for opportunist reasons and drifted away when it no longer appeared to be a useful vehicle for his own ambitions. George wanted to displace the Pitt-Newcastle government and install his former tutor, the Earl of Bute, but realized that he could hardly do this in the midst of a war the course of which was bringing the government great popularity. Instead, he resolved to insert Bute into the administration, with special and direct access to himself, in a manner which he must have known would undermine the position of both of his most senior ministers (see Chapters 4 and 6). Initially, Bute held no higher formal office than Groom to the Stole, but in March 1761 he was appointed Secretary of State for the Northern Department, in succession to the Earl of Holderness. This put him, in formal terms, in a position of equality to Pitt, and he began increasingly to challenge Pitt's previous ascendancy within the Cabinet. One point at issue was the continuation of the war against France. Pitt was in favour of carrying it on until Britain's traditional enemy had been brought to its knees, but others felt that sufficient territorial gains had already been made to secure a favourable peace settlement, and bring an end to the heavy financial sacrifices of which the country was beginning to weary. In France, too, pressure was building up for a negotiated peace, and Pitt was forced to agree to the opening of negotiations in May 1761. Pitt was not alone in taking a fairly hard line, particularly in seeking to exclude France, which had in any event lost Canada, from the lucrative Atlantic fisheries waters off Newfoundland, but he argued his case more petulantly, which upset many, including the French Foreign Minister, the Duc de Choiseul. This was not, however, the reason that the negotiations failed, the Duc becoming convinced that he could secure a better deal if the hitherto neutral Spain could be induced to enter the war on the French side.

When the two Bourbon monarchs, Louis XV and Charles III, who were first cousins, renewed the 'Family Compact' between their kingdoms in August 1761, this appeared to be an imminent possibility, and Pitt argued strongly for a preemptive attack on Spain, and the seizure of the annual treasure fleet which sailed from South America. When he put this to the Cabinet, only his brother-in-law, Earl Temple, the Lord Privy Seal, supported him. An angry Pitt, flounced out of the government, on 5 October 1761, declaring: 'I will be responsible for nothing that I do not direct'. His self-removal from power left Bute the effective leader of the government, and within eight months, Newcastle, feeling that he had become a mere cipher, also resigned, enabling the King to appoint Bute as First Lord of the Treasury and the head of a reconstructed government. Although Bute had led the opposition to war with Spain, he himself was to announce the declaration of war only three months later (see Chapter 5). Few of Pitt's fellow ministers were sad to see him go, having grown tired of his arrogance and dictatorial ways. Bute, however, wanted to soften the blow for him, and with George III's blessing offered Pitt the governor-generalship of Canada or the largely sinecure appointment of Chancellor of the Duchy of Lancaster. Pitt declined, but accepted a pension of £3,000 a year for his own lifetime and that of his wife Hester and eldest son, John. He refused a peerage for himself, but Hester was created Baroness Chatham. These actions disappointed some of Pitt's own supporters, and – for a time at least – he lost some of his popularity, while his wife was lampooned as 'Lady Cheat'em'.

Despite Pitt's withdrawal from office, the war continued to go well for Britain, with sensational victories over Spain, notably the conquest of both Havana and Manila during 1762. On the continent, however, Frederick the Great was almost overwhelmed by a combination of his Russian, Austrian and Swedish adversaries, but was saved by the fortuitous death of the Tsarina Elizabeth, in January 1762. Her successor, Tsar Peter III, promptly halted all operations, enabling Frederick to negotiate peace treaties which preserved his territories, including Silesia, which he had annexed from Austria in the earlier War of Austrian Succession. With both Britain and France being abandoned by their allies, the two countries, together with Spain, met in Paris early in 1763, and agreed peace terms, under which Britain gained Canada, Cape Breton, the Mid-West as far as the Mississippi, four West Indian islands and Senegal from France, while confirming its dominant position in India. From Spain it gained Florida, while regaining possession of Minorca, which had been occupied by France.

Out of office, Pitt retired to the country, saying he 'hoped never to become a public man again', and determined to devote himself primarily to his young family, in which he took great delight. However, he was drawn back by the parliamentary debate on the preliminary terms of the peace treaties with France and Spain. Although very ill, swathed in white flannel, hobbling on a crutch and supported in the arms of his servants, he spoke for 3 hours and 25 minutes, denouncing the terms as 'inadequate, dishonourable and dangerous'. They were also, he said, 'insecure because they restored the enemy to her former greatness'. Pitt was particularly critical of the restoration of Guadeloupe and Martinique to France, and her retention of the islands of St. Pierre and Miquelon, off the Newfoundland coast, which enabled her to retain her share of fishing rights in the North Atlantic. It was not one of Pitt's finest speeches, and it was poorly delivered and had little effect on the Commons, which voted by 319 to 65 in favour of the government's proposals. But it helped to sustain Pitt's reputation as a patriot, and in later years when France was able to offer crucial support to the American revolutionaries, his judgment seemed to be retrospectively vindicated. For the next five years, Pitt led a restless existence, seemingly unable to decide whether to live a quiet life of contemplation or to plunge back into political controversy. He was not an easy person to cooperate with. As a young man, he had been congenial, if not gregarious. But years of ill-health and frustrated ambitions had coarsened his character, and he became increasingly irritable, self-centred and, at times, paranoid. He quarrelled with two of his brothers-in-law, George Grenville (who became Prime Minister in 1763) and Earl Temple, something he could ill afford to do, as his personal following among leading politicians was very small. A true manic depressive, he alternated between brief spurts of enthusiasm, and long periods of inactivity, during which he became reclusive. Only marriage and his young family – two daughters and three sons born between 1755 and 1761 – seemed to give him lasting satisfaction: he spent long hours with them, especially with his second son, William, whom he coached in oratory from a very young age, and whom he appeared to be consciously grooming for a political career which would surpass his own. In 1765, Sir William Pynsent, an admirer whom he had never met, left him his splendid estate at Burton Pynsent, in Somerset, and Pitt was henceforth able to play the role of country gentleman which he did with great panache, building a new wing to the house and a range of classical farm buildings, where he personally but not very successfully supervised the dairy herd, and erected a column in memory of his benefactor (Black, 1992, pp. 20–1). He acquired other properties, both in town and country, and adopted a style of life, complete with liveried servants, he could ill afford, falling grievously into debt, and often having to resort to mortgages and loans from wealthy friends.

Between May 1762 and July 1766, George III went through three Prime Ministers – Bute, Grenville and Rockingham – none of whom was able to serve him for long to his satisfaction (see Chapters 6–8). Pitt remained in opposition, though his appearances on the political scene were spasmodic, due largely to his fluctuating health and frequent bouts of depression. Among his more notable parliamentary interventions was his fierce opposition to the imposition of the Stamp Act on the American colonies and support for John

Wilkes' campaign for civil liberties (see Chapter 8). On several occasions he was approached to join one or other government, or to form one of his own, but the demands he made proved unacceptable either to the Prime Minister or the King. His own stance fluctuated wildly – sometimes he took an anti-party line like the King, deprecating all factions, and 'connexions', and at other times claimed to be a true Whig who could only work with those who adhered most strictly to the precepts of the 'Glorious Revolution'. By July 1766, however, when Rockingham's government appeared to be breaking up, Pitt's appetite for power had returned, and he had fewer scruples in accepting an invitation from George III to form an administration of his own.

George's action had been prompted by a speech which Pitt had made on 24 April 1766, in which he had indicated that his own views on the proper role of government more or less coincided with those of the King. On 12 July the two men met, and agreed on the formation of a government on 'as broad a basis as possible', but both men had firm views on those individuals they wished to exclude (Black, p. 261). George III wished particularly to do without the services of George Grenville, whom he had peremptorily sacked as Prime Minister one year earlier, and was pleased to hear that Pitt had decisively broken with his brother-in-law. For his part, Pitt did not wish to have as colleagues anyone who had previously served as Prime Minister, in order that his own pre-eminence would not be challenged, which meant that no place could be found for either Newcastle or Rockingham, who had succeeded the Duke as the effective leader of the 'Old Corps' Whigs.

In forming his administration, Pitt made two decisions which, with the benefit of hindsight, could be seen as virtually guaranteeing its failure. He decided not to take the post of First Lord of the Treasury, or as one of the Secretaries of State, but the non-executive position of Lord Privy Seal. Harry Harris MP, a protégé of Henry Fox (who was not included in the ministry) shrewdly commented: 'Pitt, having by this arrangement a cabinet place void of business, interferes in measures just as far as he pleases, while both the responsibility of office and the drudgery of it fall totally upon others' (Black, p. 262).

Pitt's other – more fatal – error was to abandon the House of Commons, and to accept the title of Earl of Chatham. In doing so, he gave up one of his trump cards – his total mastery of debates in the lower House, which was by no means balanced by his entry into the House of Lords, where the atmosphere was less amenable to his style of oratory. In fact, Chatham was to speak in the Lords on only two occasions during the more than two years of his premiership. It was not just the facility of speaking in the Commons that Chatham lost – his reputation as 'the great commoner' went with it, and he lost much of his popularity by his apparent eagerness to take a peerage. The example of Walpole and Pelham, his two most effective and long-serving predecessors – both of whom insisted on governing from the Commons – seem to have been lost on Pitt. As Black points out, 'Before the time of Lord Liverpool [1812–27] there was not to be a single Lords-led Hanoverian ministry that endured any time' (Ibid., p. 264). Lord North, who joined Chatham's government as a junior minister, and who later took care to remain in the Commons throughout the whole 12 years of his own premiership, wrote to his father, the Earl of Guildford, already on 31 July 1766, describing Chatham's move as foolish, and commenting: 'I should have thought administration more steady with him in the House of Commons' (Ibid., p. 263).

The government which Chatham formed, on 30 July 1766, was hardly a cohesive team, but rather an *ad hoc* collection of individuals, some more talented than others. The key post of First Lord of the Treasury, went to the youthful Duke of Grafton, an illegitimate descendant of Charles II, whose good intentions hardly made up for his inexperience. The two secretaries of state were General Henry Conway and the Earl of Shelburne, both close political associates of Chatham. The Chancellor of the Exchequer was Charles Townshend, probably the best speaker in the House of Commons, but notably unreliable and willful. He was to die suddenly, in October 1767, when he was succeeded by Lord North.

Pitt had taken the peerage, and chosen to be Lord Privy Seal, because of concerns about his health and whether it would stand up to the strain of leading the Commons and shouldering the most demanding office in the government. In doing so, however, he surrendered much of his authority, and he had great difficulty in controlling the administration which he headed. During the Pitt-Newcastle government, he had been able to call on the sense of national unity, which the war with France engendered, and his lack of skill in man management was less apparent as he had the Duke to smooth over differences with colleagues. Now he was on his own, and – as Black comments – 'His strong will had become increasingly imperious as a consequence of his successful role in the Seven Years War, while his subsequent political isolation had made him more aloof'. He quotes the opinion of John Pringle MP, written as early as December 1766:

> Nothing can prevent the system being effectual but the risk there is of the ministers disagreeing amongst themselves, which may possibly happen as it is said Lord Chatham is very absolute and [has] little communication with the best of them. I will have this done, is the language used; no reply, not one iota shall be altered. These are the answers said to be made to some of the ministers on their remonstrating against some measures proposed, and, mortifying to tell, they were obliged to support them in the House though some of them did it very awkwardly. (Ibid., p. 266)

Unlike during the Pitt-Newcastle government, when his energies had been exclusively focused on the war effort, Chatham had no over-arching objective during his own administration, and took a very uneven interest in the main issues which confronted it. His attention was principally directed to foreign affairs, and in particular to renewing the alliance with Frederick the Great's Prussia, which he blamed Lord Bute for allowing to lapse during his premiership in 1762. Frederick had turned instead to Russia, with whom he had forged an alliance in 1764. Chatham, then in opposition, had urged in vain that Britain should propose turning this into a 'triple alliance' linking all three countries. As soon as he came to power, he commanded the British ambassador in Berlin, Sir Andrew Mitchell, to make a formal approach to Frederick along these lines. Mitchell, a veteran on the Berlin diplomatic circuit, and well informed about Frederick's intentions and the detailed nature of his relationship with Russia (now ruled by Catherine the Great, after the murder of her husband, Peter III, in 1762), was highly sceptical, but carried out Chatham's instructions, and reported back that the Prussian King was not interested. The British Prime Minister was dissatisfied, and ordered Mitchell to make a second approach two months later. This, he did, on 1 December 1766, with no greater success. The Duke of Grafton, effectively the number two figure in the government, was later to comment in his *Autobiography* 'Mr. Pitt's plan was Utopian, and I will venture to add, that he lived too much out of the world to have a right knowledge of mankind' (Grafton, 1898, p. 91).

Chatham had no greater success in his plans for dealing with India and the American colonies in the aftermath of the Seven Years War, when he was outmanouvred by his Chancellor of the Exchequer, who favoured quite different policies. Chatham was opposed to the East India Company enjoying revenues from the territories acquired during the war, which he wished to utilize to finance the defence of India. He therefore proposed a parliamentary enquiry into the affairs of the company accompanied by a declaration that the revenues should revert to the British government. Chatham was over-ruled by the Cabinet in favour of Townshend's proposal that an amicable agreement, under which an annual grant would be paid to the government, should be sought with the company. Chatham's health broke down in early 1767, and he retired for long intervals to Bath or to Burton Pynsent, where he was unable to attend to public business for long periods. In his absence a Revenue Act, was drawn up by Townshend, imposing customs duties on a number of goods, including tea, which was exported from India by the East India Company. The imposition of this Act led to continuing difficulties with the American colonists, culminating in the 'Boston Tea Party' in 1773 (see Chapter 11).

Had Chatham been in good health, it is just possible that, despite his largely self-imposed difficulties, he could have made a success of his government. George III was now extremely well disposed to him, and was ready to give him a great deal of support. But in January 1767, he suffered what can charitably be described as a prolonged nervous breakdown, though some observers felt that he was actually going mad. He lost all control of the government, and failed to give a lead on policy issues, saying that they should be left to the 'wisdom' of the House of Commons. Insofar as there was an effective leader of the government, it was the Duke of Grafton, but he lacked natural authority and was also isolated in the House of Lords, so other ministers and the Commons itself were largely left to go their own ways. Chatham's last meeting with the King was in March 1767, though he continued in office for another 18 months. The King for long refused to believe that Chatham had become incapable of directing his government, and sent Grafton down to see him in Somerset in July 1767, even though Chatham had refused a visit from him the previous month. Grafton reported that Chatham was able to discuss politics, but 'his nerves and spirits were affected to a dreadful degree...his great mind bowed down, and thus weakened by disorder'. The following month he legally signed over the care of his private affairs to his wife, while his old friend, George Lyttelton was reported as telling James Harris MP:

> Pitt disabled by dejection of spirits almost approaching to insane melancholy...[London Lord Mayor] Beckford offered him a Letter of Business, which threw him into agitation on the sight of it, and he would not open it...scarce any one sees him but Lady Chatham...criminal to ask how he does – servants turned off for inquiring. (Black, p. 274)

Chatham's doctor, Anthony Addington, the father of a later Prime Minister (Henry Addington, Lord Sidmouth), a specialist in mental health, was confident that he would recover, and prescribed alcohol, plenty of meat and little exercise. Chatham appears to have offered his resignation, in January 1768, but the King refused to consider it, writing to him that 'your name has been sufficient to enable my administration to proceed' (Ibid., p. 275). Nevertheless, in February 1768, his office of Privy Seal was placed into commission, and in the following October, Lady Chatham was to write that 'the very weak and broken state' of her husband's health had 'reduced him to the necessity of asking the King for permission to resign' (Ibid., p. 275). By now, even George III was forced to admit that Chatham's government had been a fiasco, and he resolved never to employ him as a minister again. The government was reconstructed, with Grafton, who continued as First Lord of the Treasury, now confirmed as Prime Minister (see Chapter 10).

In the months following his resignation Chatham slowly recovered from his mental illness, and he returned to court, in July 1769, reinvigorated, and apparently anxious to regain office. He made common cause with the Rockinghamite Whig opposition, setting himself up as an arch-defender of civil liberties and of constitutional reform (including many issues arising out of the Wilkes affair – see Chapters 6 and 7) and a powerful advocate of concessions to the American colonists, who were chafing against the imposition of 'taxation without representation'. When Grafton's government fell, in January 1770, their hopes of taking power were disappointed, when the King turned instead to Lord North, whom he found the most tractable of his Prime Ministers, and one of the best at keeping control of the House of Commons. (He was to serve for 12 years, and George III was most upset when he finally insisted on resigning in 1782, after the defeat of the British forces in the American War of Independence.)

Chatham celebrated his sixtieth birthday a month after leaving office, and he was to live for another nine and half years. They were largely years of political frustration to him, but much private happiness, as he luxuriated in his young family, at Burton Pynsent, and indulged himself in a passion for landscape gardening. He lived well beyond his means, and was constantly having to mortgage his properties or seek loans from wealthy friends, and his health remained precarious. There was no recurrence of his mental illness, but he continued to suffer periodically from gout. His alliance with the Rockinghamites broke down after two years, and henceforth he was a rather isolated figure, withdrawing for long periods from parliamentary activity, and keeping close touch with only one other senior figure, the Earl of Shelburne. Shelburne had been a Secretary of State in Chatham's government, and remained a devoted supporter. Even John Wilkes, whose cause he had earlier backed with passion, turned against him, when Chatham failed to support his more radical claims.

After 1774, the only issue which aroused him was the dispute with the American colonists. He combined a strong sympathy with their demands with a conviction that the British Parliament should remain the sovereign authority over the colonies. Thus, he consistently called for concessions to be made to them in the period before hostilities broke out at Lexington in April 1776. Thereafter, he just as consistently advocated a generous peace settlement, which would allow the Americans effectively to be responsible for their own affairs, subject only to their recognizing the ultimate authority of the British crown and Parliament. On 33 May 1777, he rose from his sickbed, and hobbled into the House of Lords, resting on a crutch, to make an impassioned appeal for peace. 'You cannot conquer the Americans', he said, 'I might as well talk of driving them before me with this crutch'. As the war went increasingly badly, with the news, in December 1777, of the surrender of General Burgoyne and his army to the Americans at Saratoga, demands began to be made that the former great war leader should be recalled to office. Lord North repeatedly asked to resign, and in March 1778 implored the King to appoint Chatham in his place.

George III very reluctantly agreed that an approach should be made, but refused to meet with him. The proud Chatham replied that he was willing to form his own ministry, but would only negotiate this directly with the King, who, however, declined to take the matter further, and insisted that North should continue in office. He was reported as declaring that he 'would rather lose his throne than submit to [Chatham] as minister' (Peters, 1998, p. 238). Meanwhile, the French recognized American independence, and prepared to send both naval and military support to the rebels. Fearing that the war was effectively lost, the Rockingham Whigs now urged that peace negotiations should be sought on the basis of recognition of American independence. This was too much for Chatham, who despite his long-standing sympathy for the American cause, was too much of an imperialist to contemplate a complete cession of British rule over the 13 North American colonies. His last visit to the House of Lords was on 7 April 1778, when, swathed in flannel and clearly in a weak physical condition, he rose to make a dramatic but largely incoherent speech opposing a resolution by the third Duke of Richmond to let the colonies go their own way. The man who had once said 'If I were an American, as I am an Englishman, while a foreign troop was landed in my country, I never would lay down my arms – never! never! never!', now declared: 'If the Americans defend independence they will find me in their way.' When Richmond replied to his arguments, he intervened a second time, but collapsed in a sudden fit, and was carried out of a shocked Chamber by his two grief-stricken sons and a son-in-law. A famous painting recording the scene, by John Singleton Copley, and sometimes misleadingly entitled *The Death of the Earl of Chatham*, hangs in the National Portrait Gallery. In fact, he lingered on for just over a month, dying on 11 May, at Hayes Place, his suburban home near Bromley.

The House of Commons voted on the day of his death that there should be an official funeral and that a memorial to him should be erected in Westminster Abbey. It also agreed to pay off all his debts. George III King was surprised, and not best pleased, but acquiesced in their decision, and modern visitors to the Abbey may read the following words:

Erected by the King and Parliament
As a Testimony to
The Virtues and Ability
of
WILLIAM PITT EARL OF CHATHAM
During whose Administration
In the Reigns of George II and George III
Divine Providence
Exalted Great Britain
To an Height of Prosperity and Glory
Unknown to any Former Age
Born November 15, 1708; Died May 11, 1778

Together with Robert Walpole, the Elder Pitt has been seen as one of the two outstanding British political leaders of the eighteenth century. They came from a similar social background; both were Etonians and both Whigs, but otherwise they were very different men, and their political careers could hardly have been more dissimilar. What they undoubtedly shared was an exceptional appetite for power. Walpole was able to satisfy this for the unprecedentedly long span of almost 21 years during which he was Prime Minister. Pitt, however, was only able to get his hands near the levers of power for two relatively brief periods: in 1756–61 (when he was at least nominally junior to the Dukes of Devonshire and Newcastle), and in 1766–68, for most of which time he was an impotent 'passenger' in his own administration, which was ineffectively led by a third duke, the Duke of Grafton. For one of his remarkable talents, the remainder of his career can only be seen as a sad story of relative failure. This is partly attributable to bad health, but also to his character and temperament. In truth, the Elder Pitt was a very indifferent politician, compared not only to Walpole, and his own younger son, William, but also to much more mundane figures such as the Duke of Newcastle. He was notably deficient in man management, and greatly blighted his own prospects by the gratuitous offence he caused to the successive monarchs under whom he served, George II and George III. Pitt unfortunately combined the greatest obsequiousness in the royal presence, where it was said that 'he used to bow so low, you could see the tip of his hooked nose between his legs' (Peters, 1998, p. 237), with unthinking public attacks on policies and causes the kings were known to favour. Pitt also upset many ministerial colleagues by the dictatorial way in which he imposed his will, without any pretence of discussing the pros and cons. He was too much of a loner to bother to build up any considerable band of personal supporters, and foolishly quarrelled with his influential brothers-in-law, George Grenville and Earl Temple. In the political arena, at least, Pitt seemed incapable of friendship. The most damning testimony in this respect came from the Earl of Shelburne, his closest political associate, who wrote that he was 'never natural ... constantly on the watch, and never unbent ... I was in the most intimate political habits with him for ten years ... without drinking a glass of water in his house or company, or five minutes conversation out of the way of business' (Ibid., p. 243).

As an orator, and more especially in the House of Commons, Pitt far exceeded any of his contemporaries, who came to regard him as a modern Demosthenes. Few verbatim texts of his speeches have survived, as parliamentary reporting was not permitted, so it is difficult to judge the quality of his argumentation. It is evident that his style was very different from that of his son, William Pitt the Younger, who was to impress by the logical, step-by-step way in which he built up his case. The Elder Pitt appears to have been a much more emotional speaker, who depended more on the striking phrase, the use of paradox, his flashing eyes and dramatic and theatrical gestures. Horace Walpole favourably compared him to David Garrick, the leading actor of the day. The fear and admiration which his speeches provoked were eventually to carry him to high office, despite the manifold and partly self-inflicted handicaps which he bore. It was not enough however, to sustain him at the pinnacle for long, particularly after he had abandoned his favoured arena, the House of Commons. He was often accused of hypocrisy because of the aplomb with which he trimmed his views in the hope of achieving office. Yet there is no doubt that his consistent advocacy of 'patriotic' policies was absolutely genuine and sincere. This lay behind his implacable conduct of the Seven Years War, when, in Horace Walpole's words, he seemed determined 'that his administration should decide which alone should exist as a nation, Britain or France' (Ibid., p. 246). Walpole bracketed his personal ambitions with his aspiration for his country, concluding, he 'aspired to redeem the honour of his country, and to place it in a point of giving law to nations. His ambition was to be the most illustrious man of the first country in Europe' (Ibid., p. 246). For a time at least, he succeeded in his objectives, but he was to die a disappointed – if not despairing – man.

Works consulted

Bigham, Clive (1924), *The Prime Ministers of Britain 1721–1924*, London, John Murray.
Black, Jeremy (1992), *Pitt the Elder*, Cambridge, CUP.
Brooke, John (1972), *King George III*, London, Constable.
Clark, J.C.D. (1982), *The Dynamics of Change: The Crisis of the 1750s and English Party Systems*, Cambridge, CUP.
Henry, Augustus Third Duke of Grafton (1898), edited by Sir William R. Anson, *Autobiography and Political Correspondence*, London, John Murray.
Lord Macaulay (1904), *Critical and Historical Essays, Vol. 3*, London, Methuen.
Pares, Richard (1953), *King George III and the Politicians*, Oxford, OUP.
Peters, Marie (1998), *The Elder Pitt*, London, Longman.
Peters, Marie (2004), 'Pitt, William, first earl of Chatham [Pitt the elder] (1708–1778), *Oxford Dictionary of National Biography*, Oxford, OUP.

10
Augustus Henry Fitzroy, Third Duke of Grafton – Well-Intentioned Dilettante

Augustus Henry Fitzroy was the great-great grandson of Charles II, to whom he bore a certain physical resemblance, and of one of his more long-term mistresses, Barbara Villiers, Duchess of Cleveland. Born on 28 September 1735, he was the elder surviving son of Lord Augustus Fitzroy and of Elizabeth Cosby, daughter of Colonel Cosby, a former governor of New York. His father, a naval officer, died of fever in Jamaica, aged 25, when Augustus was five years old. The death of his uncle, Lord Euston, in 1747, left him as the heir to his grandfather, the second Duke. Augustus's mother remarried in 1747, and he and his younger brother Charles were largely brought up by the Duke. From 1747, Augustus himself bore the courtesy title of the Earl of Euston.

The young Lord Euston was educated, first at Hackney School, in East London, then at Westminster, and finally at Peterhouse, Cambridge. Meanwhile, 'as a boy he met the famous William Pitt at Lord Cobham's seat at Stowe, and conceived a strong admiration for him' (Bigham, 1924, p. 58). It would be more accurate to say that, from that moment onwards, he hero-worshipped the 'Great Commoner', and this was the key to his own political career. After leaving Cambridge, he embarked on the 'grand tour', accompanied by a Swiss tutor, a Monsieur Alléon, of Geneva, whom he described as 'a real gentleman, and a man of great honor, with much knowledge of the world; but who was more fitted to form the polite man than to assist, or encourage any progress in literary pursuits' (Grafton, 1898, p. 3). M. Alleon's deficiency in that respect was more than compensated by Lord Albemarle, the British ambassador in France, in whose house he stayed for a lengthy period, giving him 'the opportunity of seeing the best company in Paris, which I cultivated much to my satisfaction.' In Albemarle's library, he was able to pursue his love for history, and

> to study those principles of government which were ever present to my mind from the time I first read the sound system of Mr. [John] Locke. I lost

no opportunity of improving myself in that science, on which the most essential interests of mankind in this world depend. (Grafton, p. 4)

Not long after his return, Euston married Anne Liddell, the daughter and heir of a wealthy Northumberland coal owner, Baron Ravensworth, in January 1756. He was 20, and she 18. The following December, he was elected unopposed to Parliament in two by-elections, one in a pocket borough controlled by the Duke of Newcastle, the leader of the Whigs and currently Prime Minister, and a week or two later for his family's borough of Bury St. Edmunds, which he chose to represent. In the meantime, he had been appointed as a Gentleman of the Bedchamber to the young Prince George (the future George III). Euston remained an MP for less than five months, as the death, on 6 May 1757, of his grandfather, left him as the 3rd Duke of Grafton. The second Duke had been a great favourite of George II: he was, according to the *Memoirs* of the Earl of Waldegrave:

a few days older than the King; had been Lord Chamberlain during the whole reign and had a particular manner of talking to his master on all subjects, and of touching upon the most tender points, which no other person ever ventured to imitate. He usually turned politics into ridicule; had never applied himself to business; and as to books was totally illiterate; yet from long observation, and great natural sagacity, he became the ablest courtier of his time; had the most perfect knowledge both of King and ministers; and had more opportunities than any man of doling good or bad offices. (Bigham, p. 59)

The new duke thus started off on a good footing with the monarch, recalling in his *Autobiography:*

When I waited on His Majesty at Kensington, and was admitted into the closet, in order to deliver the ensigns of the Order of the Garter of my late grandfather, the King, after a few common questions, said, and with tears evidently rising his eyes, 'Duke of Grafton, I always honoured and loved your grandfather, and lament his loss. I wish you may be like him; I hear that you are a very good boy.' (Grafton, pp. 10–11)

Grafton played little part in politics or in the House of Lords over the next few years, though he counted himself as a strong supporter of the Pitt-Newcastle government, which took office in June 1757. He spent the bulk of his time at his country estates, at Euston Hall, Suffolk and Wakefield Lodge, in Northamptonshire. His great passions were hunting and the turf (he bred racehorses which three times won the Derby and twice the Oaks). but he also took much interest in farming, and in collecting and talking about books. His marriage to Anne Liddell was not a happy one, and they quarrelled incessantly. Four children, of whom only two survived – a boy and a girl – were born during the first five years of their marriage, but in 1761 they left on a prolonged continental tour, ostensibly because of Anne's ill health, but perhaps in an attempt to patch up the marriage. They returned a year later in no better humour with each other, and though another son was born in 1764, their union was effectively over. In 1763, Grafton had met the famous courtesan, Nancy Parsons, whose outstanding beauty was immortalized in a portrait by Joshua Reynolds (now in the Metropolitan Museum of Art, in New York), and began a passionate affair with her, openly disporting her as his mistress at the Ascot races and installing her in a secluded property on his estate at Euston Hall. He was formally separated from Anne in 1765, and – in the evident hope of exchanging one duke for another – she began what seemed to be a promising affair with the young Duke of Portland (another future Prime Minister), who then humiliated her by unexpectedly announcing his engagement to a daughter of the fourth Duke of Devonshire. Anne then lowered her sights and eloped with a mere Irish peer, eight years her junior – John Fitzpatrick, the Earl of Upper Ossory. They had a child in 1768, but were only able to marry after she and Grafton were divorced by an Act of Parliament in 1769.

On his return to England in 1762, Grafton became active in politics, as the leader of a group of 'young friends' of the former Prime Minister, the Duke of Newcastle. He made a strong speech in the House of Lords against the peace proposals which the new Prime Minister, George III's favourite, Lord Bute, was proposing to end the Seven Years War. Regarded as an effective parliamentary debater, he was marked down as a likely candidate for office if Newcastle or Pitt were to return to power. When Bute, and his ally Henry Fox, launched their purge of Whig notables in December 1762 (see Chapter 5), he was stripped of his Lord-lieutenancy of the county of Suffolk. The resignation of Lord Bute, in April 1763, led to the appointment of George Grenville as his successor, and Grafton remained in opposition, working closely with Lord Temple and with William Pitt – Grenville's brother and brother-in-law respectively – who were estranged from him. At Temple's urging, Grafton visited John Wilkes who had been committed to prison in the Tower of London, under a controversial 'general warrant', for alleged seditious libel (see Chapter 7). Grenville's ministry lasted just over two years, by which time he had so exasperated George III (see Chapter 7) that the monarch arbitrarily dismissed him, and invited his uncle, the Duke of Cumberland, to form a new administration. Cumberland did not want formally to head the government, but persuaded the Marquess of Rockingham to take the post of First Lord of the Treasury, and – as recounted in Chapter 8 – selected the remaining ministers primarily from his friends in the Jockey Club, of which Grafton was a leading member. With few exceptions, the new Cabinet was thus made up of very inexperienced politicians, including the 29-year-old Grafton, who assumed the post of Secretary of State for the Northern Department – one of the three key posts in the government – without any previous ministerial record. Grafton was far from pushing himself forward, and only accepted office on the basis that every effort would be subsequently made to bring the Elder Pitt into the government in a leading role.

The government took office in July 1765, but the sudden death of Cumberland four months later, left it under the direction of a trio of neophyte politicians – Rockingham, as First Lord of the Treasury, Grafton and General Sir Harry Conway, who was Secretary of State of the Southern Department. In practice, Grafton's main contribution was to act as *de facto* leader of the House of Lords, given Rockingham's poor qualities as an orator and his reluctance to speak in the House. Grafton's performances were generally regarded as satisfactory. Rockingham's premiership, which lasted for just over a year, was punctuated by periodic negotiations with Pitt to determine whether, and on what terms, he would join the government, or to lend his parliamentary support. Pitt proved a difficult interlocutor, sometimes being unwilling to commit himself and at other times putting forward unrealistic demands. Grafton, who strongly believed that Rockingham should make way for Pitt, became increasingly frustrated, and when, in May 1766, Rockingham refused point blank to do this, and Pitt responded by attacking the government, felt he could no longer remain as a minister (see Chapter 8). His resignation destabilized the government, and led indirectly to its fall two months later. His replacement was his remote cousin, the Duke of Richmond, another descendant of Charles II, through Louise de Kéroüalle, Duchess of Portsmouth, and the last *maitresse en titre* of his reign. George III only reluctantly agreed to Richmond's appointment, and when – shortly afterwards – Rockingham angered him by delaying the submission to Parliament of a proposal to make financial provision for three royal princes – abruptly withdrew his support and, in July 1766 invited Pitt to form a government 'on as broad a basis as possible'.

Pitt retained many of Rockingham's minsters and, to please the King, included several former supporters of the Earl of Bute. Unwisely, however, he declined to become First Lord of the Treasury, preferring the non-departmental post of Lord Privy Seal, and to go to the House of Lords as the Earl of Chatham. He offered the post of First Lord to his brother-in-law, Richard Grenville, Earl Temple, but Temple refused when Pitt made it clear to him that he would not exercise the full powers previously associated with that post. Pitt then approached Grafton, who, doubting his own capacity and almost entirely lacking in ambition, also refused. At this, according to his *Autobiography*:

> Mr. Pitt, shewing strong marks of disappointment, rose from his chair, and declared that he must fairly tell me that his whole attempt to relieve the

country and His Majesty was at an end; and that he must acquaint the king, that he was once more frustrated in his endeavors to serve him; and that he should recommend to His Majesty to employ others; for that he could do nothing if he had not my assistance at the Treasury. (Grafton, p. 90)

Chatham clearly wanted to have somebody who was his unconditional supporter, and who would do what he was told, in this key post. With the greatest of reluctance, and deeply regretting that he could not get back to his horses and hounds, and his ravishing mistress, Grafton allowed himself to be persuaded, little realizing what he was letting himself in for.

For the first seven months or so of the government, Grafton found himself virtually playing the part of errand-boy to Chatham, receiving precise instructions on what to do and whom to appoint, and not daring to undertake anything under his own initiative. Then, from March 1767 onwards, there was an almost total change in his situation, with Chatham retiring to Bath or to his country estate, breaking off all communications with his ministers and leaving them effectively to their own devices (see Chapter 9). He was suffering from a severe nervous breakdown, or even incipient madness. As First Lord of the Treasury, Grafton was expected to act as Prime Minister, but lacked the authority and self-confidence to do so, and made only feeble attempts to coordinate the activities of his fellow ministers. Nor did his 'private life' add to the respect in which he was held. Marital fidelity was by no means regarded as *de rigueur* for Whig grandees of the eighteenth century, but Grafton showed altogether too little respect for public sensibilities by entertaining at his London house in the company of Nancy Parsons, and taking her to an opera performance in the presence of the Queen. He was also widely criticized for neglecting his duties, Horace Walpole described him as 'an apprentice, thinking the world should be postponed to a whore and a horse race', while former Premier George Grenville wrote in a letter: 'The account of the Cabinet Council meeting being put off, first for a match at Newmarket, and secondly because the Duke of Grafton had company in his house, exhibits a lively picture of the present administration' (Bigham, p. 62).

Periodically, Grafton wrote rather pathetic letters to Lady Chatham, begging to be allowed to visit her husband to discuss government business with him, to no avail. However, the King gave him warm encouragement to carry on, and to seek to bolster the government's parliamentary position by opening it out to other factions. The death of the mercurial Charles Townshend, in October 1767, led to the appointment of Lord North, as Chancellor of the Exchequer, in October 1767. North also assumed the role of leader of the House of Commons, where he was to show consummate skills as a parliamentary manager. Less satisfactory was the recruitment of two prominent supporters of the Duke of Bedford, in January 1768, Viscount Weymouth replacing General Conway as

Secretary of State of the Northern Department, and the Earl of Hillsborough becoming a third Secretary of State, with responsibility for the colonies. Finally, in October 1768, Chatham resigned, and Grafton became Prime Minister in his own right, though he refused to use the title, and forbade his family from referring to him as such.

His cabinet was virtually unchanged, except that the Earl of Bristol replaced Chatham as Lord Privy Seal, while Lord North, having proved himself an effective leader of the Commons, was now more clearly seen as the number two figure in the government. Grafton was far from being a dominant figure, seldom giving a clear lead over divisive issues. More 'liberal' than most of his colleagues, he was on several occasions out-voted within the Cabinet, and calmly accepted defeat without any thought of resigning or fighting to reverse the decision. The most difficult issue with which he had to contend was how to deal with the re-emergence of John Wilkes, who had been living as an outlaw in France since his expulsion from the House of Commons in January 1764, and his conviction for publishing 'seditious, obscene and impious' libels (see Chapter 7). Wilkes had returned to England in February 1768, and offered himself as a candidate for London in the general election the following month, coming bottom of the poll. Unperturbed, he immediately transferred his candidacy to Middlesex, where he fought a rousing campaign, under the slogan 'Wilkes and Liberty' against the two sitting Members, and horrified 'respectable opinion' by coming top of the poll in a constituency which had a much wider electorate than usual. He then surrendered himself to the Court of King's Bench to answer the charges on which he had been convicted four years earlier, and was fined £1000 and sentenced to 22 months' imprisonment, from which he sought a royal pardon. Ministers were divided about how to react, with Grafton himself being highly reluctant to take any action against Wilkes. But more hard-line ministers, strongly pressed by the King, insisted on proposing his renewed expulsion from the House of Common, which was carried on 3 February 1769. The irrepressible Wilkes stood, and was elected unopposed, in the subsequent by-election, on 16 February, and again on 16 March, after a further expulsion, despite a Commons resolution that he was 'incapable of being elected to serve in the present Parliament'. Finally, and in despair, the ministry found a candidate to oppose him in a third by-election, on 13 April. On this occasion, Wilkes secured 1143 votes, and his opponent, Colonel Henry Luttrell, only 296, but the Commons declared Lutrell duly elected. Nobody was particularly proud of this outcome, but it settled the issue for the time being, though Wilkes later staged a comeback, being elected Lord Mayor of London, and when he was again elected for Middlesex in the 1774 general election, he was allowed to take his seat.

Like Rockingham, Grafton was a consistent believer in seeking conciliation with the American colonists, and had opposed the imposition of tea and other duties by Charles Townshend, as Chancellor of the Exchequer, in 1767. When, in 1769, harsh measures were proposed by the Colonial Secretary, Lord Hillsborough, in response to widespread disturbances following the imposition of the Townshend duties, Grafton opposed them, but was outvoted in the Cabinet by five votes to four. Grafton also wanted to repeal the duties on tea, but was over-ruled. On Irish issues, he had more success in promoting a more liberal line. He passed the Octennial Act, requiring elections every eight years, whereas previously there had been general elections in Ireland only on the death of the monarch. He also laid down that the Lord Lieutenant should be resident in Dublin, whereas previously – like most of Ireland's Protestant landlords – he had spent most, if not all, of his time in England.

Meanwhile, there were significant changes in Grafton's private life. In 1769, following the birth of a son to his estranged wife Anne, by her lover, the Earl of Upper Ossory, he sued her for divorcé, which required an Act of Parliament, passed on 23 March. Three days later, Anne married Upper Ossory, and there was much speculation that Grafton would now wed Nancy Parsons. But she had recently started a passionate affair with the handsome 24-year-old Duke of Dorset, and Grafton abruptly terminated his own liaison with her. Within three months, now aged 33, he married Elizabeth Wrottesley, the highly respectable 23-year-old daughter of Sir Richard Wrottesley, a clergyman and former MP, who was the Dean of Worcester. Described as 'not handsome, but quiet and reasonable, having a very amiable character', her marriage to Grafton appears to have been a happy one. They had 13 children, and Grafton – who some 30 years later wrote his *Autobiography* in the form of a series of letters to his eldest son – said of Elizabeth that her 'merit as a wife, tenderness and affection as mother of a numerous family, and exemplary conduct thro' life, need not be related to you' (Grafton, p. 235). As for Parsons, she remained with Dorset for seven years, and then left him for another young aristocrat, the second Viscount Maynard, whom she married, and then began an 'odd *ménage à trois*' with him and the 19-year-old fifth Duke of Bedford (Hanham, 2004). As Viscountess Maynard, she lived till the age of 80, being buried in Paris in the winter of 1814–15, having devoted her old age 'to pious good works'.

Grafton continued to be subjected to criticism for not applying himself whole-heartedly to his duties, and spending altogether too much time on the hunting field and the race track. Some of the most ferocious assaults on him were penned by the anonymous writer, 'Junius', whose cutting and witty letters in the leading London newspaper, *The Public Advertiser*, between 1768 and 1773, became required reading for all who had any serious interest in politics. Some 60 individuals were suspected at one time or another as being the author, but modern scholarship, based on textual analysis, points a finger pretty conclusively at Sir Philip Francis, a leading civil servant (Cordasco, 2004). Francis had no known motive for the extraordinary venom he showed towards Grafton, but it is possible he might have been put up to it by Lord Temple, who never forgave Grafton for accepting the First Lordship of the Treasury in 1768, after he had turned it down (see above). A sensitive man, Grafton was on more than one occasion tempted to resign in the face of such provocation, but worse was to come with the recovery from mental illness of his erstwhile hero, Lord Chatham. He returned to court on 7 July 1769, 'when his manner towards Grafton was particularly cold and ungracious' (Durrant, 2004). It soon became apparent that he was working to discredit the government in the hope of being recalled to office by the King. In Parliament he cooperated with the Rockinghamite opposition, and the government's majority fell dangerously low in several divisions. In January 1770, Chatham's two strongest supporters within the government, the Lord Chancellor, Lord Camden (formerly Charles Pratt), and the Master of the Ordnance, the Marquis of Granby, both tendered their resignations. In an effort to bolster his tottering administration, Grafton, with the King's strong backing, appealed to Charles Yorke, son of the former Lord Chancellor, Lord Hardwicke, to take Camden's place. This had always been Yorke's ambition, but as a Rockinghamite he felt cross-pressured and hesitated to take the post. The outcome of his indecision is poignantly described by George III's biographer, John Brooke:

> The King had no patience with hesitation at such a moment, and told Yorke that if he refused this time he should never again have the offer. What with the King's threats, his brother's warning, and Rockingham's reproaches, poor Yorke hardly knew which way to turn. After three days' agony of mind and body he kissed hands, went home and took to his bed. On 20 January he died. Rumour had it that he had committed suicide in an agony of remorse; but contemporary accounts by his wife and brother indicate that he died a natural death, probably from the bursting of a blood vessel. (Brooke, 1972, p. 157)

Grafton, who believed the suicide rumour, was deeply shocked, and tried to get the Attorney-General, William de Grey, to take the post. When he declined, he submitted his own resignation. George III always referred to this subsequently as a 'desertion', but his personal relations with Grafton remained good. Nor did he find it difficult to find a satisfactory successor. He lost no time in approaching Lord North, who suited him very well – remaining in office for 12 years, whereas the previous six premiers during the reign had only managed 10 years between them.

Grafton had served as Prime Minister for 1 year and 106 days. He remains to this day the second youngest Premier, after the Younger Pitt, having succeeded his father, Lord Chatham, at the age of 33. He was to live another 45 years, serving on two occasions as Lord Privy Seal, first under Lord North, from whose government he resigned in 1775 in protest against its hard-line policy against the American colonists, and again in the governments of Lords Rockingham and Shelburne, in 1782–83. In none of these governments did he play a very active role. When the younger Pitt became Premier in December 1783, he was again offered the same post, but chose instead to retire to his country pursuits, and never held office again, though he retained his somewhat dilettante interest in politics. When he was still Prime Minister, he had been appointed as Chancellor of Cambridge University, and he played an active part in university affairs, associating himself particularly with a group of liberal churchmen in Cambridge. He himself took an increasing interest in theological matters, writing two books, and becoming an active adherent of the Unitarian church. He lived on until 1811, dying at the age of 75. In 1804, he was to write a series of letters to his son, which were put together by Sir William Anson, the Warden of All Souls College, Oxford, in 1898, and published, with a commentary, as his *Autobiography*. It was notable both for the brevity of the references to his personal life, and the magnanimity which he showed to his opponents and critics. Apart from this volume, no other biography has yet appeared, which makes him almost unique among British Prime Ministers. To the best of my knowledge, only the Earl of Wilmington has suffered comparable neglect by later authors. The best assessment of his political career was written as long ago as 1924, by Clive Bigham, later the second Viscount Mersey. His summing up appears eminently judicious:

> Grafton was a fair example of a Stuart; well-intentioned loyal and honourable, not without capacity and taste, but bored by business, lacking in industry and determination, and overmuch given to sport and pleasure. His high rank and early promise brought him great place, but want of endurance and the misfortunes of the times made him fail in it. A competent colleague in ordinary circumstances, he was called upon to act as a leader in days of difficulty and for this he had neither the character, the energy nor the courage. (Bigham, p. 66)

He does not lack geographical memorials. In London NW1, Grafton Street, Fitzroy Square and Euston Road and Station are all named after Grafton or members of his family, while in the United States, there is a Grafton, Vermont and a Grafton town and county in New Hampshire.

Works consulted

Bigham, Clive (1924), *The Prime Ministers of Britain 1721–1924*, London, John Murray.
Black, Jeremy (1992), *Pitt the Elder*, Cambridge, CUP.

Bloy, Marjorie (1998), 'Augustus Henry Fitzroy, Third Duke of Grafton', in *Biographical Dictionary of British Prime Ministers*, London, Routledge.

Brooke, John (1972), *King George III*, London, Constable.

Cordasco, Francesco (2004), 'Junius (fl. 1768–1773)', in *Oxford Dictionary of National Biography*, Oxford, OUP.

Durrant, Peter (1974), 'The Duke of Grafton (1768–70)', in Herbert Van Thal, ed., *The Prime Ministers*, Volume I, London, Allen & Unwin.

Durrant, Peter (2004), 'Fitzroy, Augustus Herbert, third duke of Grafton', in *Oxford Dictionary of National Biography*, Oxford, OUP.

Henry, Augustus Third Duke of Grafton (1898), *Autobiography*, ed. by Sir William Anson, London, John Murray.

Hanham, A.A. (2004), 'Parsons, Anne [Nancy] married name Anne Maynard, Viscountess Maynard', in *Oxford Dictionary of National Biography*, Oxford, OUP.

Kilburn, Matthew (2004), 'Anne, Countess of Upper Ossory [other married name Anne FitzRoy, duchess of Grafton]', in *Oxford Dictionary of National Biography*, Oxford, OUP.

Rudé, George (1962), *Wilkes and Liberty*, Oxford, Clarendon Press. 11

11

Frederick North, Styled Lord North – Outstanding Parliamentarian, Pity about the Colonies. ...

In British political folklore, Lord North has long held the distinction of being regarded as the worst Prime Minister the country has ever had. It would be a bold person who tried to reverse this verdict as it was undeniably during his premiership that the 13 British colonies in North America were lost. Yet this should not obscure the fact that North was one of the abler men to hold the top office, and possessed many good qualities.

Frederick North was born on 13 April 1732 in Albemarle Street, off Piccadilly, in London. He was the first child of Francis North, (third Baron, and later first Earl of Guilford) and his first wife, Lady Lucy Montagu, daughter of the Earl of Halifax. Guilford, who was descended from a long line of 'courtiers, lawyers, politicians and writers' (Whiteley, 1996, p. 1) had been appointed a Gentleman of the Bedchamber to Frederick Louis, Prince of Wales, the estranged son of George II, two years earlier. The Prince of Wales became the godfather of the infant Frederick, who was named after him, and it was not long before he started good-humouredly to tease Guilford with how similar to him was his godson. If the prince had indeed cuckolded Guilford, he apparently did not suspect this at the time, but his later treatment of his daughter, Lucy, who was born two years after Frederick, was peculiar, to say the least. Her mother died in child-birth, aged 25, and Guilford packed their daughter off to his late wife's family, and put it about that she also had died. (In fact, she lived until 1790, marrying a tradesman, Thomas Bradley, and living in Preston). That Prince Frederick Louis was a renowned libertine, who fathered several illegitimate children, makes his paternity of both children appear more probable.

In 1736, the Prince married Princess Augusta of Saxe-Gotha, and the following year she gave birth to their first son, George, the future George III, a putative half-brother to Frederick North, who was five years his senior. There was never a public scandal involving the Prince, who died in 1751, when Frederick North was 19 and the future King 14, but many years later, when North was Prime Minister, there were a number of innuendoes in the press and even occasionally in parliamentary interventions. In the absence of any DNA evidence, the question is never likely to be definitively resolved, but the pictorial evidence points strongly to the prince being North's real father. It was presented in 1979 in a profusely illustrated book (Smith, 1979, pp. 25–67). Most significantly, the book contains portraits from respectively, the National Portrait Gallery and the Courtauld Institute, of Prince Frederick Louis and Frederick North, both painted when young men in their 20s, which show an extraordinary resemblance. By contrast, a portrait of the Earl of Guilford, again from the Courtauld Institute, shows absolutely no similarity at all to that of his supposed son. The book also includes portraits of Frederick North and George III, in their mature years, again taken from the National Portrait Gallery and the Courtauld Institute (Ibid., pp. 107–8), which also show a marked resemblance.

Whatever suspicions he may have had – and despite his rejection of his daughter, Lucy – Guilford brought up the young Frederick himself, and integrated him into the largish family which he accumulated during his two subsequent marriages. The first of these, to Elizabeth Legge, the Dowager Viscountess Lewisham, in 1736, produced a son and three daughters, while she brought three step-children from her previous marriage into the family. Her marriage to Guilford was a happy one, but she – too – died in childbirth, in 1745. Six years later, Guilford was to marry a third time – to Katherine, Dowager Countess of Rockingham. This marriage brought no further children, but a great deal of money to the previously cash-strapped Guilford. He proved an affectionate if somewhat strict father to all his brood, and Frederick grew up in a happy family atmosphere, and was to remain on good terms with his 'father' throughout his long life (he was to die only two years before Frederick, in 1790). The only thing that marred the relationship was the tight-fistedness of Guilford, who kept him on a very short rein, leaving him to get deeply into debt.

Frederick's step-brother, William Legge (later the second Earl of Dartmouth), who was only one year older than him, became his inseparable friend and companion throughout their lives. They, however, were to attend different schools, William going to Westminster, and Frederick to Eton, where he proved a highly competent if rather slovenly student, very popular with both boys and teachers and much remarked upon for his high moral standards. When he left Eton, at 17, Guilford, who had received glowing reports from his teachers, wrote him a letter, saying, 'My dear Man, or rather Boy: It gives me great pleasure to find you have left a very good name behind you, & I hope you will preserve it at Oxford....Believe me my Dear, Your Very Affectionate Father' (Whiteley, 1996, p. 8)

At Oxford, he enrolled at Trinity College, where his step-brother had already been since the previous year. Both boys replicated the high reputations they had gained at their schools, excelling in their studies and setting a high moral example to their fellow students. When they left, in 1751, the President of Trinity wrote to Guilford, referring to them as those 'most amiable young gentlemen whose residence was a very great advantage as well as an ornament to the College (Ibid.). Peter Whiteley, North's most recent biographer, comments:

> North's time at school and university can clearly be considered well-spent, but there is something lacking. There is never any hint of rebellion or wish for independence, a trait that appears at least briefly in most adolescents. He seldom found it easy to challenge authority whether represented by his father or the King. His precocious virtue, however, never turned stale or tiresome as he grew older; it was fortunately leavened with a ready wit. He had an unpompous ability to accept jokes at his own expense and to respond to humour in others. (Ibid., p. 9)

The year 1751 proved to be a most significant one in the life of Frederick and his family. Guilford had continued to work in the service of the Prince of Wales, and since 1749 had acted as Governor to his eldest son, Prince George. But then, on 20 March 1751, Frederick Louis, who had been nursing a cold, died quite unexpectedly, and Guilford was out of a job. King George II took over responsibility for his grandson, and appointed Lord Harcourt in Guilford's place. Guilford had suddenly lost his salary, and – whether or not in consequence of this – married a very wealthy widow, Katherine, the Dowager Countess of Rockingham, less than three months later. Thus newly endowed, he was in a position to send Frederick North and William Legge off on a very extensive grand tour, mostly in Germany and Italy, which kept them occupied for almost three years. In 1752, Guilford was compensated for the loss of his court appointments by being promoted to an earldom. Frederick consequently assumed the courtesy title of Lord North, by which he was known for almost the whole of his adult life. William Legge had meanwhile become the second Earl of Dartmouth, on the death of his grandfather. The two young milords were accompanied on their grand tour by a Mr. Golding, their chaperon/tutor, but rarely can such an appointment have proved so unnecessary, given the notorious piety and serious-mindedness of his two charges. Their time was mostly spent sight-seeing, and in the social round, but they did not neglect the educational opportunities available to them, in particular acquiring fluency in German, Italian and, especially French. 'This acquirement', North's youngest daughter, Lady Charlotte Lindsay, was later to write 'together with the observations he had made upon the men and manners of the countries he had visited, gave him what Madame de Stael called *l'esprit européen*, and enabled him to be as agreeable a man in Paris, Naples and Vienna, as he was in London' (Whiteley, pp. 14–15). Whiteley himself comments:

Agreeable is a term well justified in describing North. He returned from his Grand Tour a man of the world, cultivated, unobtrusively amusing and at ease in the best circles. Though not profound or given to original or abstract thought, he possessed a good, clear mind that was frequently underrated by his opponents. His confidence in his social position never made him arrogant or quick to take offence and he remained throughout his life a very enjoyable companion. (Ibid., p. 15).

Very soon after their return to England both young men took their seats in Parliament, Dartmouth in the House of Lords, and North in the Commons. He was elected unopposed for the Banbury constituency, on 15 April 1754, two days after his twenty-second birthday. Banbury was unusual in being a single-member constituency, the vast majority of English seats returning two members. It was not exactly a 'pocket' borough of Lord Guilford's – the electors being the 18 members of the borough corporation – but he was the main landlord in the area, and they usually did his bidding. North was to represent Banbury for 36 years until he entered the House of Lords, only two years before his death, when he inherited the earldom of Guilford. He was elected, altogether, on 11 occasions, never facing any opposition. Largely for conventional reasons, North stood unofficially as a Whig, but Whiteley quotes one of his descendants as saying that 'his tendencies were Tory; he came from a Tory family and he never attached himself to the interests of any of the Whig houses'. He also pointed out that Horace Walpole, in his *Memoirs of the Reign of George III*, 'stated flatly that he was a Tory, underlying the words for emphasis' (Ibid., p. 24). Later historians have followed Walpole's lead, North's government invariably being described as Tory. Despite this, it was a very leading Whig, the Duke of Newcastle, who gave North his first leg up in politics. A distant cousin, he invited his kinsman to second the address in reply to the King's speech, in December 1757, apparently his maiden speech, though he had already been in the House for over three years. He was warmly commended by Lord Guilford, and wrote back:

I am extremely obliged to your Lordship for your repeated congratulations to me & to my Friends for all the kind things they have written on my behalf. I possessed myself & spoke I believe with a loud voice & a tolerable manner & to that much more than my matter I owe my reputation. (Smith, p. 71)

In fact, the 25-year-old North was being over-modest. His speech was widely acclaimed as an outstanding success, and he was immediately seen as a likely candidate for ministerial office. His uncle the Earl of Halifax, who was President of the Board of Trade, wrote to him that he 'could now conscientiously regard him as having first claim to a vacancy on the Board of Trade' (Ibid., p. 72). A month later, he received an offer from Lord Newcastle to head the Embassy in Turin, the capital of the Kingdom of Sardinia. North consulted Guilford before rejecting the offer, writing 'I have observed that most men who have passed their youth in foreign employments make no great figure in Parliament at their return (Ibid., p. 72). Meanwhile, on 20 May 1756, he had got married to the 16-year-old Anne Speke, daughter of a West country landowner. It was widely observed that Anne was far from good-looking, but as North was no oil painting himself it could be judged that they were well matched. (Horace Walpole was to describe the corpulent North in the following terms: 'two large prominent eyes that rolled about to no purpose, for he was utterly short-sighted, a wide mouth, thick lips and an inflated visage gave him the air of a blind trumpeter') It was generally believed that Anne was a considerable heiress, but in fact she brought with her only a modest estate, Dillington House, Ilminster, in Somerset, and her expectations of being left a far more considerable property by her uncle, Sir William Pynsent, were to be dashed (see below). The marriage, which was to produce four sons and three daughters, seems to have given great satisfaction to both partners. Their youngest daughter, Lady Charlotte Lindsay, in her own old age, wrote about her mother in a letter to Lord Brougham, saying that she:

> was plain in her person, but had excellent good sense, and was blessed with singular mildness and placidity of temper. She was also not deficient in humour, and her conversational powers were by no means contemptible; but she, like the rest of the world, delighted in her husband's conversation, and being by nature shy and indolent, was contented to be a happy listener…Whether they had been in love when they married I don't know, but I am sure there never was a more happy union than theirs during the thirty-six years that it lasted. I never saw an unkind look, or heard an unkind word pass between them; his affectionate attachment to her was as unabated as her love and admiration of him. (Whiteley, p. 17)

In June 1759, North was appointed as a Lord of the Treasury, with a salary of £1400 a year, a welcome addition to his income of around £2000, on which he was finding it increasingly difficult to live. This may have been a reason why he clung to office, in May 1762, when Newcastle and his closest associates resigned, leaving the Earl of Bute in charge of the government. North did not get on with Bute, and his first inclination was also to resign, but he was dissuaded by Lord Guilford and by his uncle, Lord Halifax, who became a Secretary of State. North was probably highly relieved when Bute left office less than a year later, and was succeeded by George Grenville, a man he respected though he was never personally close to him. Grenville increasingly used North to present government policies in the House of Commons, where he spoke on some 50 occasions in the next two parliamentary sessions. In particular,

North took the lead in presenting the case against John Wilkes (see Chapter 7), including moving the motion, in January 1764, to expel him from the House of Commons. The same month, however, found him speaking against government policy, when he opposed the repeal of the unpopular cider tax, introduced under Lord Bute. This was to cost him dear, as the cider tax was particularly abominated by West country landowners, including Sir William Pynsent, his wife's uncle. Pynsent apparently had never met William Pitt, but admired him greatly (see Chapter 9), and as North phlegmatically wrote in a letter to Lord Guilford: 'Our neighbour Sir Wm Pynsent has left all his estate to Mr. Pitt. It is reported, and from pretty good authority that he left it all to me but alter'd his will in consequence of the Cider Tax' (Ibid., p. 17).

When Grenville's government was peremptorily dismissed, in July 1765, North was the only member of the Treasury Board not turned out, and the new Rockingham government would have liked him to stay, but he insisted on resigning out of loyalty to Grenville, even though he had no personal attachment to him, and also perhaps because of his anger that his uncle, the Earl of Halifax, had been dismissed along with Grenville. Several Cabinet members were particularly anxious, however, to recruit him, not least for his debating power in the Commons, when the new Prime Minister was in the Lords. Charles Townshend, for example the Paymaster-General, wrote to Lord Newcastle that 'there is no one belonging to the late administration whose talents would be more use to the present' (Thomas, 1976, p. 16). Eventually, the Earl of Dartmouth, who was President of the Board of Trade, was authorized to approach his step-brother with the offer of the post of Joint Vice-Treasurer of Ireland, at a salary of £2000 a year. North declined, and took his place on the Opposition benches. A strong supporter of the Stamp Act, he vigorously opposed its repeal by the Rockingham government, and, in May 1766, repulsed a further offer of ministerial office. Two months later, however, when the government was dismissed and replaced by one led by Lord Chatham, he accepted the lucrative post of Joint Paymaster-General. Within six months he was sworn of the Privy Council, and was occasionally summoned to Cabinet meetings. In March 1767, he was offered the post of Chancellor of the Exchequer, in place of Charles Townshend 'who was proving a difficult colleague' (Thomas, 2004). He declined, and when Townshend died unexpectedly four months later was still reluctant to take his place, despite being personally invited by the King and by the Duke of Grafton, who was acting premier in the absence of Lord Chatham. One reason may well have been financial – the salary was £2500, as against the £3500 he was currently receiving. Eventually, after consulting his 'father', he accepted the post. By then, he was widely seen as a 'coming man'. Townshend himself was reputed to have said a few weeks earlier: 'See that great, heavy, booby-looking, seeming changeling. You may believe me when I assure you as a fact that if anything should happen to me, he will succeed to my place, and very shortly after come to be First Commissioner of the Treasury' (Thomas, 1976, p. 20).

Around the same time, Grenville had told a friend: 'North is a man of great promise and high qualifications, and if he does not relax his political pursuits he is very likely to be Prime Minister' (Ibid.). North became Chancellor of the Exchequer on 6 October 1767; it was not very long before the appointment was being widely acclaimed as a success. North's six-year experience on the Treasury Board had been excellent preparation for the post, and he quickly showed himself to be both competent and decisive, as well as being utterly loyal to Grafton. The latter, as First Lord of the Treasury, soon excused himself from attending the twice-weekly meetings of the Treasury Board, allowing North to preside over them in his absence. Within three months of his appointment, North also assumed the unofficial role of leader of the House of Commons, a key position when the Prime Minister (and also Lord Grafton, who was acting in his place) was in the House of Lords. He soon established almost complete mastery of the House, after a number of skilful interventions, including handling the dodgy issue of excluding John Wilkes from the Commons, despite his repeated election for the Middlesex constituency in the spring of 1769 (see Chapter 10). By this time, Grafton had replaced Chatham as Prime Minister, and he retained North as his principal spokesman in the House of Commons. George III noted with approval how well he was succeeding in managing the House, and in December 1769, when the Grafton ministry appeared to be tottering, sent North a note saying 'Lord North – I wish to see you about eight this Evening' (Whiteley, p. 77). At the ensuing meeting, the King appears to have offered North the reversion in the event of Grafton resigning. North seems to have given a non-committal answer, but five days later wrote to his 'father' 'my pride…has by the late offer been gratified to the utmost of its wish' (Thomas, 1976, p. 33).

A month later, when Grafton threw in his hand, George III had little difficulty in persuading North to take up the challenge. The positive reason for asking him was North's mastery of the Commons. The negative one, as the King explained to the outgoing Secretary of State, Sir Harry Conway, was that he was absolutely determined not to go back to either of the three previous Premiers – Chatham, Rockingham and Grenville, all of whom he had found to be unsatisfactory. He would sooner abdicate his Crown, he said (Brooke, 1972, p. 158). North became First Lord of the Treasury on 28 January 1770, aged 37, and was to serve for 12 years and 58 days. His premiership may be divided into three periods, each of roughly four years. In the first period – up to 1774 – the country was at peace, and he was seen as a diligent and largely successful premier. In the second – until late in 1777 – it drifted into war with the American colonists, and the government was strongly supported by a wave of patriotic fervour. In the final period, up till March 1782, it gradually dawned on Parliament and the public – and sooner than most on the Prime Minister himself – that the War was likely to be lost, and North spent a vast deal of time and effort trying to persuade a highly reluctant King that he should let him resign.

In the first year or two of his premiership, North was concerned, above all, with consolidating his position – in his Cabinet (which was not of his choosing, but was substantially made up of survivors from the Grafton government), in Parliament, and with the King, who, though encouraging, was not yet convinced that North was the ideal answer to his problems. The first test he faced was over the Falkland Islands, where – in June 1770 – Spanish forces had seized a British military base at Port Egmont, and attempted to assert their sovereignty over the islands. The Cabinet was divided over how to respond, with Viscount Weymouth, the belligerent Secretary of State for the Southern Department, who was the responsible minister, advocating war on Spain unless the British base was reinstated. But North took a coldly realistic view, realizing that the British fleet had been substantially run down since the end of the Seven Years War in 1763. It was now heavily outgunned by the combined forces of Spain and her Bourbon ally, France, still led by the Duc de Choiseul, who was itching for an opportunity to avenge his country's defeats. North encouraged secret negotiations with the French, which were facilitated by the action of Louis XV in dismissing de Choiseul, who had run foul of his new mistress, Madame du Barry. The outcome was that the Spaniards evacuated the British base, but received confidential assurances that Britain would quietly relinquish it after a decent interval (in fact, in 1774). Weymouth resigned in disgust, and North won a stunning vote of confidence in the House of Commons by 275 votes to 157. The subsequent government reshuffle, following the departure of Weymouth, enabled him to reshape the Cabinet much more to his own design. Two years later, he was able to bring his step-brother, Lord Dartmouth in, as a third Secretary of State, with responsibility for the American colonies.

In the Commons, North soon established a near impregnable position. This he achieved by his great assiduity, and by his good nature, which assuaged the hostility even of those who opposed his policies. He was a living exemplar of the biblical adage that 'a soft answer turneth away wrath'. It was said of North that though he had plenty of opponents, he never had any enemies. Every day that the House met, he took his place on the Treasury bench, and remained there until it rose, often late into the night. As Peter D.G. Thomas comments:

> This was more than mere form…During his first five sessions as prime minister, from 1770 to 1774, he made about 800 speeches and interventions in debate…He was the leading administration speaker on government business, whether or not he moved the proposals himself, for he

was 'the minister', and many of these speeches lasted an hour or more. North never prepared formal orations and seldom spoke from notes, for his prodigious memory enabled him to put the government case and refute points made against it. His speeches were distinguished by clarity. When he spoke every squire understood the subject of debate, whether foreign policy, the national finances, or the constitution, or at least thought he did. (Thomas, 2004)

One of North's most potent rhetorical weapons was humour, which he often turned against himself. Once, when he appeared to have dozed off during a debate, an enraged opponent, who was in the midst of an interminable speech, exclaimed 'Even now, in the midst of these perils, the noble Lord is asleep'. Without opening his eyes, North said wearily: 'I wish to God I was' (Bigham, 1924, p. 131). Although he was not a great orator, North was an outstanding parliamentarian, and this was the basic reason why he was able to continue as Prime Minister for so long. It has been noted more than once that – with the exception of Newcastle who served for seven years – none of the eighteenth century Prime Ministers from the House of Lords remained in power for any length of time. By contrast, all the commoners, apart from Grenville, who upset the King, served for long periods – Walpole nearly 21 years, Pelham 10, North 12 and the Younger Pitt 19. The underlying reason was that MPs – especially the large swathe of country gentlemen with no fixed political allegiances – needed constant sympathetic attention from the Prime Minister, in order to keep them on board. This attention was impossible to apply from the Upper House, and no Prime Minister was ever more approachable and ready to pass the time of day with a cheery word than Frederick North.

North also benefited from the increasing impotence of the Opposition. The death of George Grenville, in November 1770 removed a considerable figure from the House, and North moved swiftly to win the backing of a majority of his followers, who felt bereft without their leader. The Earl of Suffolk became Lord Privy Seal, and Alexander Wedderburn Solicitor-General, while places or pensions were obtained for several other Grenvillites. The remaining two sizeable opposition groups – the followers respectively of Rockingham and Chatham – were only able to act together on spasmodic occasions and were seldom in a position to mount an effective challenge. George III was delighted with North's performance during his first year or two in office, and hastened to express his appreciation. When, in June 1771, his uncle, the Earl of Halifax, was dying, the King wished to appoint him to the Earl's post of Ranger of Bushy Park, which involved a salary and a handsome house, near Twickenham, to the west of London. The post, however, was an 'office of profit under the Crown', and therefore not available to an MP, so North requested that his wife should be appointed instead. For the rest of his life, Bushy House proved a highly agreeable and convenient place for him to relax in the bosom of his family at the weekends, and periodically for longer stretches. An even more significant indication of the King's approval was the bestowal, in June 1772, of the Order of the Garter, a rare distinction for a commoner, Robert Walpole being the only other one to be so honoured throughout the whole of the eighteenth century. Subsequently, North was often referred to during parliamentary debates as 'the noble lord in the blue ribbon' (Thomas, 1976, pp. 51–2).

As Premier, North was in receipt of an avalanche of requests for patronage, which he dealt with reasonably conscientiously, and always with great courtesy, though he found it difficult to refuse, in as many words. This sometimes led to misunderstandings, or accusations of broken promises, and eventually he felt constrained to give an explanation to the Commons, as reported in the *London Evening Post* on 25 February 1772:

> It was the etiquette of the Minister, if he could not grant the favour asked of him, at least to send home the person refused in good humour. This was well understood by courtiers; but for such ignorant honest country gentlemen as the Honourable Member, he thought it right to explain, that, when he only nodded, or squeezed the hand, or did not absolutely promise, he always meant No; which produced a great and long laugh. (Thomas, 2004)

On becoming Premier, North retained his post as Chancellor of the Exchequer, and so was in complete charge of the Treasury. This was a heavy call on his time and energy, as Thomas explains:

> The Treasury board met usually twice a week, and this demand on North's time became burdensome...between 1775 and 1782 he missed only 23 of 670 such meetings. In the House of Commons, three days a week were set aside, in form at least, for the two finance committees, supply to decide expenditure and ways and means to meet the cost by taxes and duties. Budget day was already an annual occasion for the presentation of the nation's accounts, and in the early 1770s North made it a great political occasion, and an opportunity for a review of the year's events. (Ibid.)

North proved himself adept at handling the nation's finances, and he applied himself, in his early years, to reducing the national debt, which stood at the historically high figure of £140 million. In five years he succeeded in reducing this by £10m, cutting the annual interest burden by £500,000. He mainly achieved this by an ingenious use of the annual lottery, but he also introduced some tax changes which prefigured the more famous tax reforms of the Younger Pitt a dozen years or so later.

Although his government had its ups and downs during its first four years, it was generally seen as successful, and North's personal prestige was high in 1774, when the dormant issue of British taxation of the American colonies again came to a head, and with it the overall right of the British Parliament to legislate for the colonies. North already had a track record as being unsympathetic to the grievances of the colonists. In 1769, when Chancellor of the Exchequer, under Grafton, he had resisted the proposal to rescind the duties on tea imposed by Charles Townshend in 1767. His was the determining vote in a 5–4 decision, which over-ruled the wishes of the Prime Minister. The Americans largely avoided paying the duty through the large-scale smuggling of tea from the Netherlands, but in 1772, in response to an appeal from the East India Company, which had accumulated large stocks of tea which it found difficult to sell, the government approved proposals which would enable the tea to be 'dumped' in North America at prices which would undercut the Dutch smugglers, even after the tea duty had been paid. When this was put to the House of Commons, it faced heavy resistance, with widespread calls for the tea duties to be abolished, but North refused, saying, of the colonists, that 'the temper of the people there is little deserving favour from hence' (Thomas, 1976, p. 74).

The American response was the famous 'Boston Tea Party', of 16 December 1773, when, disguised as Indians, a group of dare-devil colonists boarded a British ship, under cover of darkness, and destroyed a valuable shipment of tea belonging to the East India Company. Whether from choice, or because of overwhelming pressure both from the House of Commons and the King, North resolved on a robust response, proposing a series of punitive measures, known to the colonists as the 'Intolerable Acts'. These included the Boston Port Act, which closed the city's harbour until such time as restitution was paid for the destroyed tea. Equally obnoxious to the Americans was the Massachusetts Government Act, sharply reducing the degree of self-government which this colony had previously attained. Then, there was the Quebec Act, which placed all the previously French-controlled territory between the Ohio and Mississippi rivers under the control of the province of Quebec, threatening to close it off to settlement or exploitation by the American colonists. Warned that the Acts might provoke the Americans to armed resistance, North laughed this off, saying that the despatch of 'four or five frigates' would be sufficient to deal with any trouble. The opposition – Rockinghamites and Chathamites – agreed that a firm response was necessary, but were critical of the Massachusetts legislation and urged that some conciliatory move should also be made, notably the repeal of the tea duty. Their arguments went unheard in a House which was becoming gripped with patriotic fervour, as conflict threatened. The 'Intolerable Acts', passed in the spring of 1774, led to the convening of the First Continental Congress, attended by all the colonies except Georgia, which met in Philadelphia on 5 September 1774. This denounced taxation without representation and the maintenance of a British army in the colonies without their consent, adopted a declaration of personal rights, declared a boycott of British imports and petitioned the Crown for a redress of grievances accumulated since 1763. Meanwhile the British Governor of Massachusetts, cowed by the increasing militancy of the local population, submitted his resignation, and was replaced – in an act of intended firmness – by the Commander-in-chief of the British forces in North America, General Sir Thomas Gage. The Earl of Dartmouth, as Secretary of State for the American Colonies, however, made an attempt to achieve conciliation, proposing the sending of a Commission to America 'to examine into the disputes'. North put his step-brother's proposal to the Cabinet, but it was turned down after the King had remarked that sending a commission would look like 'the Mother Country being more afraid of the continuance of the dispute than the Colonies' (Thomas, 1976, p. 83).

A week later, North made his own conciliatory move, persuading the Cabinet to agree that Britain 'would promise not to tax the colonies if in return they agreed to pay the cost of their own civil governments, courts of law, and defence' (Ibid., p. 83). Too late! A year or two earlier this might have sufficed to reconcile the colonists, but the scale of their demands had now grown so great that it was seen almost as an irrelevance. So, the drift to war began, with the British sending over more troops, mainly German mercenaries, and the colonists recruiting their own militias, particularly in Massachusetts. In April 1775, the first skirmishes occurred at Lexington and Concord, Massachusetts, followed in July by the Battle of Bunker Hill, outside Boston, technically a British victory though a pyrrhic one, as the heavy British casualties were twice as high as on the American side. Full-scale war now appeared inevitable, though the British Parliament agreed to the despatch of peace commissioners, who were expected to negotiate with the rebels. When they duly arrived, however, they revealed that they were authorized only to accept the submission of the rebels and to offer pardons to those who repented their actions. In the meantime, the Declaration of Independence had been approved by the Second Continental Congress, in July 1776, and George Washington had been placed in command of a newly raised Continental Army.

So the die was cast, and Lord North, bolstered by a wave of patriotic fervour, which embraced King, country and a clear majority of the House of Commons, prepared for war *à l'outrance*, confident of success. His step-brother, Lord Dartmouth, had no stomach for directing operations against the population for whom he had previously been responsible, and asked to stand down as Secretary for the Colonies, becoming instead Lord Privy Seal. His replacement was a distinguished soldier, Lord George Germain, previously known as Lord George Sackville. Sackville had been unjustly court-martialled and disgraced for alleged disobedience during the Battle of Minden, in 1759. His reputation had, however, subsequently been rehabilitated. North recognized that he himself had no interest in, nor aptitude for, military strategy and left the direction of the war in Germain's hands. His intention was to repeat the winning formula in the Seven Years War, when the Elder Pitt had directed the war effort, and the Duke of Newcastle had taken charge of the other Prime Ministerial duties, notably – as First Lord of the Treasury – raising sufficient funds to pay for the military and naval campaigns. Germain may have lacked the dynamic energy of the Elder Pitt, but he proved himself to be a sound strategist and an efficient administrator. If the campaigns he planned did not yield the success he hoped for it was due more to the shortcomings of the generals in charge, and in particular their failure to press home their advantage on several occasions after winning significant victories.

For the first two years of the war, the British forces generally held the upper hand, and American morale sank, until it was revitalized by Washington's successful Trenton-Princeton campaign, launched on Christmas night 1776. In the summer of 1777, Germain launched his master-stroke, sending General Burgoyne with a powerful army down the Hudson Valley from Canada to link up in New York, with another army led by General Sir William Howe, brother of Admiral Lord Howe, who was commanding the British fleet. The objective was to cut off the rebellious New England colonies from the southern states, where loyalist sentiment was more strong, enabling the British to re-establish themselves there, before concentrating all their forces to subdue the North. Unfortunately for the British, this did not go according to plan. Burgoyne met with greater and more effective resistance than expected, as he slowly made his way down the Hudson, and Howe, impatient of waiting for him, set off southwards himself, and occupied the American capital of Philadelphia. After suffering several defeats, and despairing of being reinforced by Howe, Burgoyne surrendered his entire army, when it became surrounded at Saratoga, on 17 October 1777.

This proved to be the turning point of the war – though few people realized it at the time, apart from Lord North. He despaired of victory, certainly under his own leadership, and during the next four years, on literally dozens of occasions, begged George III to allow him to stand down. One of his most fervent appeals was in March 1778, when he suggested that the King should send for Lord Chatham in the desperate hope that he would be able to repeat his achievements during the Seven Years War. But the King, remembering only too well the fiasco of his premiership during 1766–68, refused to countenance this. A few weeks later Chatham collapsed, making his final speech in the House of Lords (see Chapter 9), and died shortly after. Unabashed, North then tried to pass the poisoned chalice to a member of his own Cabinet, writing to the King that 'The person best qualified for that station appears to him to be

Lord Suffolk'. No sooner was this suggestion made, than Suffolk keeled over and died at the age of 39 (Cannon, 1974, p. 178). Meanwhile, North continued to dominate the House of Commons, successfully defending the government policies against increasing clamour from the opposition – from Chathamites (now led by Lord Shelburne), critical of the conduct of military operations, and Rockinghamites, who were openly calling for recognition of American independence. There were rare defeats in parliamentary votes, most notably on a famous motion by John Dunning, on 6 April 1980, that 'The Influence of the Crown has Increased, is Increasing, and Ought to be Diminished'. This was passed by 233 votes to 215, and North, once again, offered his resignation, only to see it refused. In practice, there was little risk of defeat on a confidence motion, until such time that the House became convinced that the war was definitively lost. This was still a year or two ahead.

The costs of the war placed an enormous strain on government finances, and put an end to North's earlier successful efforts to run down the National Debt. Like Newcastle before him, during the Seven Years War, North succeeded in getting the bills paid, partly by tax increases but mainly by negotiating a series of large loans, though the rate of interest demanded increased as the years of war went on. North's own finances were also under pressure, as Lord Guilford continued to make only the meanest of provisions for him. By September 1777, his debts totalled some £16,000, and the King got to know of this, and wrote to him, offering to pay them off. His letter concluded: 'You know me very ill if you do not think that of all the letters I have ever wrote to You this one gives me the most pleasure, and I want no other return but Your being convinced that I love You as well as a Man of Worth as I esteem you as a Minister' (Whiteley, p. 169). The following year he helped to put North's finances on a firmer permanent basis by appointing him as Lord Warden of the Cinque Ports, with a salary of £1000 a year when Prime Minister, and a nominal £4000 thereafter. Peter D.G. Thomas comments: 'These rewards had the political consequence that North felt himself unable to resign without the King's permission; and that he was never able to obtain. The bond had become a chain' (Thomas, 1976, p. 168).

What was the basis of this 'bond' between King and Prime Minister? There is little doubt that the King felt more comfortable dealing with North than with any other of his premiers, even Lord Bute. He was more successful than any of the others in getting his policies through the House of Commons, and he was much the most agreeable to deal with. North treated him with great respect, but was never obsequious. His opponents regarded him as a mere creature of the King, willing to accept anything the monarch demanded. In fact, his views genuinely coincided with the King's on a wide range of issues, and could be characterized, in more modern terms, as generally right-wing or reactionary. Their instinctive reactions were often similar, if not identical. The question is did the 'bond' go any further than that? Did the King have any inkling that North might be his own half-brother? We shall never know, but – in any event – their friendship went back a very long way. They had been brought up in the same princely household, and Prince George might well have looked up to the young Frederick as a sort of 'elder brother' figure, even if no blood relationship was suspected.

The surrender of the British army at Saratoga, in October 1777, not only unnerved North, but greatly encouraged the Comte de Vergennes, the French foreign minister. Already France had been covertly helping the rebels, but he now recommended Louis XVI to declare war on Britain, and send an army and navy to fight on the American side. Spain, too, entered the war in the hope of recouping its loss of Florida in the Seven Years War, despite an unsuccessful attempt by North to buy it off with an offer to cede Gibraltar. Finally, in an act of gross folly, Britain itself declared war on the Netherlands, thus bringing all three of the strongest European maritime powers into the conflict on the other side. Hitherto, the greatest advantage which Britain held was its control of the sea, which enabled it to transport its troops along the American coast, so that they could strike at any time and place against the rebel forces. Now it lost this advantage, and the French fleet, under Admiral de Grasse, was able to perform the same service for the Americans, and in particular for the 6000-strong army under General Rochambeau, which the French had shipped across the Atlantic in 1780. After Saratoga, the British ceased all operations in New England, and fighting was restricted to the southern states, and the West Indies. British efforts were also undermined by the loss of control of the English Channel to the combined fleets of France, Spain and the Netherlands. There was a lively fear of a Franco-Spanish invasion, and this meant that the dispatch of further troop reinforcements to North America could not be contemplated.

In the four years following Saratoga, despite periodic British successes in the more southern states, hopes of a final British victory over the Americans began to fade, and the government's majorities in crucial parliamentary divisions gradually declined to about half the level previously achieved. The young Charles James Fox effectively became the leader of the Rockinghamites in the Commons, and he and Edmund Burke made a formidable debating team harrying the government. In June 1780, in an attempt to broaden his government, North approached Rockingham with a proposal that he and his leading supporters should form a coalition with him. But Rockingham's terms, which included negotiating a peace with the Americans on the basis of independence, were quite unacceptable to the King, even if, which was unlikely, North had been able to bring himself to agree. Instead, in September 1780, North risked calling a general election, a year before it was due under the Septennial Act. Although he lost some seats, the result was reasonably satisfactory for him, and in the first division in the new Parliament the ministry had a comfortable majority, with 212 votes to 130. The election was a costly affair for the government, which expended an estimated £62,000 (Whiteley, p. 188) in the customary inducements to electors and the patrons of 'pocket' boroughs to ensure the election of its own supporters. Such expenditure was normally met from secret service funds, but there was a shortfall of some £30,000, and –believing he had the King's full authority – North borrowed this amount in his own name from the royal banker, Henry Drummond, and spent a further £2754 of his own money.

Meanwhile, on the other side of the Atlantic the conflict was gradually approaching its endgame. In October 1781 a British army under Lord Cornwallis found itself cooped up in the port of Yorktown, and besieged by superior forces led by Rochambeau, Washington and Lafayette. Expected help from a British fleet, laden with reinforcements, which set sail from New York failed to arrive, after it had been defeated in a battle with the French Admiral de Grasse, whose ships then began to bombard the British positions. A despairing Cornwallis then surrendered his entire army, virtually bringing the war to an end, though a British fleet led by Admiral Rodney was later able to defeat de Grasse in the Battle of the Saints, in April 1782. When news arrived in London of Cornwallis's surrender, a stricken North cried out 'Oh God, it's all over' – a judgment which was shared by most of his Cabinet and by a clear majority of parliamentarians. Germain, however, was determined to continue the war, while George III resolutely set his face against conceding independence to the Americans. It took another five months before he was prepared, with the greatest reluctance, to face reality. During this time the opposition made a series of determined attempts to force the North government out of office, which were beaten off with steadily declining majorities. The last one to be put to a vote, on 8 March 1782 was defeated by a mere nine votes, and North then received a deputation from 'a group of independent MPs', who informed him that they were withdrawing their support from him, being 'of opinion that vain and ineffectual struggles tend only to public mischief and confusion'. Realizing that defeat was inevitable in a further no-confidence motion due on 20 March, and wishing to avoid the opprobrium of being condemned by the House of Commons, North at last summoned up the resolution to insist on his resignation. He wrote what has become a famous letter to the King, gently explaining to him his constitutional responsibilities, saying, *inter alia*:

> Your Majesty has graciously and steadily supported the servants you approve, as long as they could be supported. Your Majesty has firmly and resolutely maintained what appeared to you essential to the welfare and dignity of this country, as long as the country itself thought proper to maintain it. The Parliament have altered their sentiments, and as their sentiments whether just or erroneous must ultimately prevail, Your Majesty, having persevered so

long as possible, in what you thought right, can lose no honour if you yield at length, as some of the most renowned and most glorious of your predecessors have done, to the opinion and wishes of the House of Commons. (Thomas, 1976, p. 132)

North had been loyal, perhaps over-loyal, to the King, but he never had any doubt that his greater loyalty was to Parliament. When he announced his resignation to the House, on 20 March, in a speech of great dignity, he thanked MPs for:

the very kind, the repeated and essential support he had for so many years received from the Commons of England, during his holding a situation to which he must confess he had at all times been unequal. And it was…the more incumbent upon him to return his thanks in that place because it was that House which had made him what he had been. (Cannon, 1974, p. 182)

The King did not take kindly to North's determination to resign, and accepted it only with the greatest reluctance after an interview of over an hour. According to Horace Walpole, 'the King parted with him rudely without thanking him, adding "Remember, my Lord, that it is you who desert me, not I you"' (Thomas, 1976, p. 132). Thereafter, he often treated North in a spiteful or vindictive way, notably over the payment of the election expenses incurred in 1780. He refused to honour the full debt of £30,000 owed to his banker, Henry Drummond, paying only £13,000, and insisting that North should accept responsibility for the balance. (It was only several years later, in 1786, that he relented, and reluctantly paid off the debt, which the impoverished North had been unable to discharge).

At the time of his resignation, North was still only 49, and was the leader of a substantial body of MPs, the second largest grouping in the Commons. His prospects of staging a comeback, and enjoying a renewed period of power, after a decent interval, must have appeared quite good. In fact, although he continued to be active politically, almost until his death, aged 60, in 1790, he was to enjoy only a brief period of less than nine months in office, in the so-called 'Fox–North coalition', led by the Duke of Portland, in 1783 (see Chapter 13). Thereafter, he continued to cooperate with Charles James Fox, in opposing the government of the Younger Pitt, and proved himself to be still one of the most effective debaters in the House, until 1788, when his 'father' finally died, aged 86, and he inherited the earldom of Guilford. Now, at last, he became a very rich man, with property in five counties. But by then his health had badly deteriorated, and in his last years he became totally blind. Cosseted by his loving family, he continued to receive constant visits from a host of friends, who still enjoyed his highly congenial company, both at his London home in Grosvenor Square and at Bushy Park. The historian Edward Gibbon was later to recall: 'The house in London which I frequented with the most pleasure was that of Lord North; after the loss of power and of sight, he was still happy in himself and his friends' (Whiteley, p. 15). Early in 1792, he became fatally ill, and dropsy was diagnosed. He died on 5 August 1792, at Grosvenor Square, shortly after confiding to his daughter Catherine that he feared that his posthumous reputation would be irredeemably tainted by his responsibility for the loss of the colonies. It proved to be a prescient prediction.

So, was Lord North the worst ever British Prime Minister? Having now surveyed the careers of all 53 premiers over three centuries, from Walpole to Cameron, this author, at least, is convinced that he was not. He can think of a number of stronger candidates, both from the eighteenth century and later, for that dubious honour. What is certain is that North was the wrong person to be Prime Minister during most of the 12 years that he held that office. In 'normal' times, he would have made an effective premier, with a distinctly conservative bent, as he in fact showed during his first four years in office. What he was assuredly not cut out to be was a war leader. It is arguable that had Rockingham been Prime Minister during these years the war might have been prevented. If Chatham had been premier it would have been prosecuted with more vigour and perhaps with greater success. What is equally certain, with the benefit of hindsight, is that independence for the 13 colonies was inevitable, and would have come at some point during the second half of the century, with or without a war. A serious clash of interest with the metropolitan power was bound to come, and it would have been impossible to withhold independence from such a thrusting and enterprising people as the American colonists. This judgment does not absolve North from his own serious responsibility in provoking the conflict, notably for having blocked the repeal of the tea duties, which were the proximate cause of the war. But this was a responsibility which he shared with a majority of the Cabinet, with the mass of parliamentary and public opinion and, above all, with George III, who was the most pig-headed and inveterate opponent of any concession, however timely, being made to American demands. A descendant of Lord North's, the ninth Earl of Guilford, asked one of his biographers, Professor Charles Daniel Smith, 'if it was true that my ancestor was responsible for the loss of the American colonies?' Smith replied; 'Well, let's put it this way: he had a lot of help!' (Smith, p. 11).

Works consulted

Bigham, Clive (1924), *The Prime Ministers of Britain 1721–1924*, London, John Murray.
Brooke, John (1972), *King George III*, London, Constable.
Cannon, John (1969), *The Fox-North Coalition*, Cambridge, CUP.

Cannon, John (1974), 'Lord North (1770–82)', in Herbert Van Thal, ed., *The Prime Ministers*, Volume I, London, Allen & Unwin.

Simms, Brendan (2007), *Three Victories and a Defeat: The Rise and Fall of the First British Empire, 1714–1783*, London, Allen Lane.

Smith, Charles Daniel (1979), *The Early Career of Lord North the Prime Minister*, London, The Athlone Press.

Thomas, Peter D.G. (1976), *Lord North*, London, Allen Lane.

Thomas, Peter (1998), 'Frederick North, styled Lord North 1752–90, Second Earl of Guilford', in Robert Eccleshall and Graham Walker, eds., *Biographical Dictionary of British Prime Ministers*, London, Routledge.

Thomas, Peter D.G. (2004), 'Frederick North, second Earl of Guilford, known as Lord North, 1732–1790', in *Oxford Dictionary of National Biography*, Oxford, OUP.

Whiteley, Peter (1996), *Lord North: The Prime Minister who Lost America*, London, The Hambledon Press.

12

William Petty, Second Earl of Shelburne – Too Clever by Half?

John Quincy Adams was probably the cleverest man ever to be President of the United States, but also the most disliked. This was largely responsible for abridging his political career, and he served only one term at a period when the norm was two. William Petty, the second Earl of Shelburne, has a good claim to be regarded as his nearest British equivalent. Born in Dublin, on 2 May 1737, his parents, who were first cousins, were John Fitzmaurice (later Petty) and Mary Fitzmaurice, both of whom were descended from a family which had dominated the western Irish county of Kerry, since the twelfth century. The head of the family when William was born was his grandfather, the first Earl of Kerry, who ruled the roost with unbridled tyranny. William's father, who was an MP in both the Dublin and Westminster Parliaments, changed his surname in 1751, after inheriting great wealth and large estates, both in England and Ireland, from his uncle, Henry Petty. He became an Irish peer, as the first Earl of Shelburne, in 1753, and Baron Wycombe, in the peerage of Great Britain, in 1760, which gave him a seat in the House of Lords. William clearly felt that his mother was the dominant partner in the marriage, saying of her that she was a foolish woman, but:

> one of the most passionate characters I ever met with, but good natured and forgiving when it was over – with a boundless love of power, economical to excess in the most minute particulars, and persevering, by which means she was always sure to gain her ends of my father…. If it had not been for her continual energy my father would have passed the remainder of his life in Ireland and I might at this time be the chief of some little provincial faction. (Norris, 1963, p. 3)

William grew up as a neglected son. 'A poor school [Dr Ford's Academy, in Dublin], the intermittent attentions of a cheap French Huguenot tutor, and a year of penurious idleness in London at the age of fifteen were almost the sum of his early formal education' (Ibid.). The care and attention which he was denied at his home, which he characterized as 'domestic brutality and ill-usage' (Cannon, 2004), was, in part at least, compensated by his aunt, Lady Arabella Denny. 'Shelburne believed that it was due to her that he was able to read, write and speak, and attributed his later success to her…she instilled in him an exaggerated respect for methodical habits (though he lacked these himself) and a strong sense of duty' (Norris, p. 3).

William's parents, newly enriched by their great inheritance, at least found the money to send him to Christ Church, Oxford, where he matriculated on 11 March 1755. He now held the courtesy title of Viscount Fitzmaurice, and stayed there for a further two years, imbibing, according to his own reminiscences, an eclectic mix of 'natural law and the law of nations, some history, part of Livy, and translations of Demosthenes', a mixture enlightened by 'Blackstone's early lectures and a good deal of indiscriminate reading in religion' (Ibid., p. 3). This led him into a great deal of scepticism concerning orthodox Christianity, 'and in later years he held to an austere Deism strongly coloured by dislike for the Anglican clergy' (Ibid., p. 4). He left Oxford, without taking a degree, and his experience left him with a passionate intellectual curiosity, but also a conviction that he was poorly educated, and he long continued to feel an inferiority complex towards many less gifted but more polished contemporaries. Deeply discontented with his lot, he later wrote 'it became necessary for me to take some resolution for myself; home detestable, no prospect of a decent allowance to go abroad, neither happiness nor quiet' (Cannon, 2004). He determined to join the Army, and his father was persuaded by Henry Fox, his political mentor and a distant relative, to purchase him a commission in the twentieth Regiment, then commanded by Colonel James Wolfe, a very able officer, who was later to meet a glorious death leading his troops to a famous victory at Quebec in 1759.

In the Army, the young Lord Fitzmaurice thrived, not least because of the support he received from Wolfe who encouraged him to continue his private studies in philosophy, as well as a range of military subjects, and he became a popular figure in the regiment. He took part in the raid on Rochefort, in 1757, one of the first engagements in the Seven Years War. When Wolfe left for Canada, he was transferred to the third (Scots) Guards, and posted in Germany, where he distinguished himself at the battles of Minden and Kloster Kampen. He was decorated for bravery and, in 1760, was recommended by the British commander, the Marquis of Granby, for promotion to Colonel and appointment as *aide-de-camp* to the new King, George III. In the same year, his father received his barony, which meant that he relinquished his parliamentary seat at Wycombe, on entering the House of Lords. While still serving in Germany, Fitzmaurice was elected unopposed to take his place as the MP for Wycombe, and was re-elected for the same seat in the general election of

March 1761, both for this seat, and for the constituency of Kerry in the Irish Parliament in Dublin. He was never, however, to sit in the House of Commons, for two months later, in May 1761, his father died, and Fitzmaurice inherited both of his father's titles, and took his seat in the House of Lords. Henceforth, he was known as the Earl of Shelburne.

At the age of 24, Shelburne now appeared as a very grand figure indeed. One of the richest men in the country, with splendid residences at Bowood House, in Wiltshire, Wycombe Abbey in Buckinghamshire and Lixnaw in County Kerry, his royal appointment and his high military rank, the world seemed to be at his feet. But the political career to which he aspired proved to be a chequered one. This was partly due to flaws in his character, but largely to ill luck, and the misfortune that his earliest political associates turned out to be two of the most unpopular figures of the time – the Earl of Bute and Henry Fox. The former was despised as a royal favourite, and the latter deeply distrusted as an opportunist, and for having made a large personal fortune through holding the office of Paymaster-General (see Chapters 5 and 6). Shelburne also undoubtedly suffered from not having sat in the Commons, and learning there the tough trade of competitive politics before being promoted to the more sedate benches of the Upper House.

He was also the victim of envy. One of the more influential of the younger Whig leaders was the Duke of Richmond, who took against Shelburne because he had been promoted over the head of the Duke's younger brother, Lord George Lennox, in obtaining his colonelcy. Richmond convinced himself – wrongly – that this had been the result of political intrigue, and resigned his post as a Gentleman of the Royal Bedchamber in protest. He then proceeded to blacken Shelburne's reputation with his fellow Whig grandees, including the Duke of Devonshire and the Marquess of Rockingham. This meant that Shelburne, a natural Whig, was put on the wrong foot, from the outset, with what must have seemed his likeliest future political allies.

For the moment, however, he was involved with Bute and Fox, who had been his father's political sponsors. Bute, who became Prime Minister in May 1762, was anxious to recruit Henry Fox as Leader of the House of Commons, in order to force through the peace treaty terms which he was negotiating with France, about which the current leader, George Grenville, was distinctly lukewarm. He used Shelburne as a go-between with Fox, who was playing hard to get. Holding the highly lucrative post of Paymaster-General, Fox's main concern was to secure a cast-iron assurance that he would receive a peerage, preferably an earldom, as soon as he had completed his mission in the Commons. Bute and George III were ready to concede this, but assumed that Fox would be willing to relinquish the Paymastership when he went up to the Lords. This was not Fox's intention, and he was later annoyed with Shelburne for putting it about that it was, describing him as 'a perfidious and infamous liar' (Norris, p. 12). Fox, however, did not for long hold this against him. More serious for Shelburne was that he upset the King on a number of occasions. The first was as early as March 1761, when he applied to become Controller of the Royal Household. George III evidently regarded this as highly presumptuous for a young man of 24 who had only recently become his *aide-de-camp*, and Shelburne was forced to make abject apologies through Bute. The King, and Bute, were also irritated when he made a speech deploring any continuation of the war in Germany and voted against a motion which Bute had moved in the House of Lords. Despite this, Bute was eager to appoint Shelburne to a ministerial post, and Fox urged him 'to get your harness on immediately' (Cannon, 2004). Shelburne, however, evidently regarded the post he had in mind as too insignificant, and declined to accept. Throughout his career, as a very wealthy man, he was completely indifferent to the 'emoluments' of office, and this made him reluctant to accept any post which was not completely to his liking, and all too ready, if he did not get his way, to resign. Despite his refusal to join Bute's government, he was long to remain an object of suspicion to the leading Whigs, who regarded him as an acolyte of the King's favourite. This suspicion was further aroused when he purchased Bute's house in Berkeley Square (now known as Lansdowne House) as his London residence.

When Bute resigned as Premier in April 1763, he, Bute, continued to enjoy the King's confidence, and was largely responsible for recruiting ministers for the government of his successor, George Grenville. He greatly valued Shelburne for his high intelligence and his formidable debating skills in the House of Lords, and recommended his appointment as Secretary of State for the Southern Department, which would have meant displacing the Earl of Egremont, Grenville's brother-in-law, and a much more experienced politician. It was not to be:

> The King refused to consider it and Grenville, under no illusion but that it was intended to use Shelburne as Bute's agent and spy in the new government, compromised by offering the Board of Trade. Shelburne's first reaction was to refuse, but…he demanded the full powers of policy and patronage which had been enjoyed by the Earl of Halifax at the Board of Trade between 1752 and 1761. Egremont objected to this, and as a compromise Shelburne was allowed cabinet rank. But when Shelburne kissed hands for his first office on April 20, 1763, it was as the subordinate of the Secretary of State. Far from ruling the cabinet for Bute, Shelburne was only a hostage in the Grenville camp. (Norris, p. 13)

It was an inauspicious start, and things only got worse during the barely four months which ensued before he resigned in a huff. During this brief period, he amply demonstrated 'his inability to work with others in a ministerial team.

He was touchy and interfering as a subordinate, uncooperative as an equal and secretive when in command' (Stuart, 1981, p. 247). Shelburne had shown himself to be a skilled and assiduous administrator, thoughtful and forward-looking in his policies, but arrogant and highly impatient in his dealings with his colleagues. They were unsurprised, and – on the whole – relieved, when he threw in his hand, leaving office on 2 September 1763. Two months later he strongly opposed a government motion to expel John Wilkes from the House of Commons, and Grenville complained to George III, who promptly dismissed him as his *aide-de-camp*, describing him as 'a worthless man' (Cannon, 2004). Shelburne, however, continued with his army career, eventually rising to the rank of General, in 1783. Yet it seems to have been very much a part-time commitment, and he never again saw any military action. Shelburne had collected a small but devoted parliamentary following, based, initially, on the Members he returned for the two 'pocket boroughs' he controlled, Wycombe and Calne. It included such highly able figures, as Colonel Isaac Barré, John Calcraft and Richard Rigby. More generally, however, his reputation among politicians had sunk to a low level. He was regarded as awkward, sententious, insincere, self-seeking and – above all – devious. He was dubbed the 'the Jesuit of Berkeley Square', a comment not on his religious views, which were very far from Catholicism, but on his alleged methods, with an oblique reference to his association with the Earl of Bute. Yet his evil public reputation was in almost complete contrast to how he was viewed by those closest to him. As Charles Stuart was to write in a perceptive essay: 'Everything we can learn of Shelburne, from his published letters and papers, from his first wife's diary or from his friends shows him to have been, in private life, considerate, unselfish and amiable with, above all else, a wholly disinterested and dedicated regard for truth' (Stuart, 1981). Shelburne became somewhat less maladroit in his public life as he grew older, but he was never able to live down the largely unjustified reputation he early acquired. Give a dog a bad name...

For the next three years, Shelburne was in opposition, and fell under the spell of the Elder Pitt. He was to remain a follower and close collaborator with him until Pitt – now Chatham – died in 1778. But he was never personally close to him, to Shelburne's great regret. In his old age, he was to write:

> I was in the most intimate political habits with him for ten years, the time when I was Secretary of State included, he Minister [*i.e.* Prime Minister], and necessarily was with him at all hours in town and country, without drinking a glass of water in his house or company, or five minutes conversation out of the way of business. (Norris, p. 17)

Meanwhile, he occupied himself with making extensive improvements to his various properties, employing Capability Brown to construct a lake at Bowood and Robert Adam to enlarge the house, and modernizing his somewhat run-down estates at Wycombe. On 3 February 1765, aged 27, he married the 19-year-old Lady Sophia Carteret, the only child of Earl Granville, the former John Carteret, and great rival to Sir Robert Walpole, and to his successors, the Pelham brothers. This marriage further augmented his extensive landholdings, bringing to him large estates near Bath, centred on Lansdowne Hill, from which he – much later – took his title, on becoming the Marquess of Lansdowne. The marriage lasted only six years, Lady Sophia dying in childbirth in January 1771, at the age of 25. They had had two sons, one of whom was to die in childhood. According to John Norris:

> Lady Shelburne's diary shows her to have been amiable and intelligently observant of the world of affairs. She was apparently devoted to her husband, tolerating his restlessness and conforming to his odd evangelical enthusiasms. His letters to her are surprisingly cold in tone, but when she died...he sank into a depression and had to go abroad for a season to recover. (Ibid., p. 6)

George Grenville's government was dismissed by the King in the summer of 1765, and the new Premier, Lord Rockingham, offered Shelburne his former post back, as President of the Board of Trade. He declined, citing 'a real consciousness of my own inability in so active an office, to which the domestic habits I have lately fallen into add not a little' (Cannon, 2004). In truth, Shelburne was by now a pretty unconditional supporter of Pitt, and was unwilling to serve in an administration from which he was excluded. His loyalty was rewarded a year later, when Pitt, now translated to the House of Lords as the Earl of Chatham, was asked to form a government, and proposed him as Secretary of State for the Southern department, where his responsibilities also included India, Ireland and America. This was the most senior post in the government, after Chatham and the Duke of Grafton, who was First Lord of the Treasury. Shelburne, who was now 29, was not to make a success of it.

During the first six months or so, Chatham very carefully supervised Shelburne's work. The position changed dramatically during the spring of 1766, when he retired to Bath, and later to his country estate, suffering from a severe nervous breakdown, and virtually abandoning his prime ministerial duties. Of all the ministers, Shelburne was politically closest to him and the most clearly in accord with his views. Now, he felt himself alone, and progressively fell out with all his colleagues. His greatest difficulties were with the Chancellor of the Exchequer, Charles Townshend, who was determined to raise significant sums of money by taxing the North American colonists. Shelburne, who had voted against both the Stamp Act, when it was introduced in 1765, and the Declaratory Act of 1766 (see Chapter 7), was convinced that Townshend's proposals would unnecessarily inflame American opinion, and vainly sent a message to Chatham asking him to intervene. Eventually, against Shelburne's opposition, the cabinet agreed on the imposition of import duties on china, glass, paper and, most famously tea. Shelburne went into a sulk, and for a time boycotted cabinet meetings. He was to clash again with Townshend over revenues from India, where there was general agreement that the East India Company should not enjoy all the gains accruing from the newly conquered territories, but that at least part of it should go to the British government. Shelburne, who had a financial interest in the company, nevertheless proposed taking a hard line against it, calling for 'a searching review which would lead to a measure of government control and a substantial subsidy to the exchequer' (Cannon, 2004). Townshend favoured a softer approach, suggesting direct negotiations with the company's directors, and his view carried the day. Townshend's sudden death in September 1767 ended his rivalry with Shelburne, but the feud continued with his elder brother, Viscount Townshend, who was Lord Lieutenant of Ireland, which came under Shelburne's authority. The two men were constantly at odds, with Shelburne, who favoured a more 'liberal' approach to Irish problems, continually over-ruling his decisions.

As well as his colleagues, Shelburne succeeded, once again, in alienating the King, who wrote to Chatham that 'he and Grafton regarded Shelburne as "a secret enemy" and suggesting his removal' (Ibid.) Chatham did not agree, but Shelburne suffered the humiliation of seeing the American colonies taken away from him, and given to a newly appointed Secretary of State for the Colonies, Lord Hillsborough. Difficulties also arose over determining the government's attitude to Wilkes's election for the Middlesex constituency in the 1768 general election, with the King and most ministers in favour of ejecting him, while Shelburne strongly opposed this step. The King evidently hoped that Shelburne would resign, but he refused to do so, putting his faith in Chatham's return. When Chatham himself eventually resigned in October 1768, Shelburne followed suit, leaving Grafton to reorganize the government without his participation.

Shelburne was now 31, and left office a deeply chastened man. He now embarked on what turned out to be a period of 13 years in opposition, 12 of them against the predominantly Tory government led by Lord North. He held himself aloof from the main Whig opposition, led by Rockingham, but became the most influential figure in the much smaller group of Chathamite supporters, and their acknowledged leader after Chatham's death in 1778. Shelburne has been described as 'perhaps the most brilliant intellectual in politics in the second half of the eighteenth century after Burke' (O'Gorman, 1974, p. 185). O'Gorman goes on to say:

> He took few ideas for granted and subjected prevailing ideas and institutions to constant analysis...He must have been one of the very few eighteenth-century statesmen to have enjoyed the services of what the twentieth

century would term a 'think tank' in the little coterie of intellectuals which he patronised at Bowood, and to have established a formal secretariat to facilitate his political activities. (Ibid.)

His circle at Bowood included the eminent utilitarians, Jeremy Bentham, Richard Price and Joseph Priestley, while among his friends were Benjamin Franklin, who spent five years in London representing the colony of Pennsylvania, Dr Samuel Johnson and Sir Joshua Reynolds. On a visit to Paris in 1771, following the death of his first wife, he met a number of the leading *Philosophes*, including D'Holbach, Turgot, Trudaine and, in particular, Morellet, whose views on free trade greatly influenced him.

During his lengthy period in opposition, Shelburne thought long and deeply about the problems facing Britain, and evolved a programme of reforms which, in many respects, were a great deal more radical than those espoused by the Rockingham Whigs. An exception was Shelburne's approach to the conflict with the American colonies, by far the most contentious issue throughout the period of Lord North's government. Shelburne argued consistently for a conciliatory approach to the Americans, for a cessation of hostilities and a negotiated settlement on generous terms. In a speech, in January 1775, supporting a motion of Chatham's to withdraw British troops from Boston, he condemned 'the madness, injustice and infatuation of coercing the Americans into a blind and servile submission'. Yet he was strongly against the recognition of American independence, saying – even after the surrender at Yorktown – that 'he would never consent, under any given circumstances, to acknowledge the independency of America' (Cannon, 2004). 'Without America', he argued, 'Britain would be but a petty state' (Ibid.). Shelburne's solution was a 'federal union' between a largely self-governing America and the United Kingdom, under the British Crown. This somewhat resembled the dominion status achieved by Canada, Australia and New Zealand a century or more later. Had he been in a position to offer this to the Americans some years before, it is highly likely that they would have accepted it, which would have brought the war to an end far sooner, or even prevented it in the first place. Even after peace had been negotiated and independence ceded, Shelburne continued to argue for a free trade area with the newly formed United States, but by then he was out of power, and his voice was unheeded.

Partly through his support for John Wilkes, Shelburne was drawn into close contact with a group of Radicals in the City of London. Subsequently, he advocated a series of 'economical reforms', loosely based on their demands and designed, in part, to reduce the power of the Crown, and government ministers, to corrupt the electoral system. Thus, Shelburne advocated the reduction of the parliamentary term from seven to three years, and a moderate measure of electoral reform, based on awarding a third member to each county (where the franchise was generally wider than in the boroughs and therefore more 'democratic', though that is not a term which he would have used). He also advocated the abolition of a great range of 'fees' (some dating from Medieval times) paid to government officials, in addition to their salaries, a policy he had started to implement in his own ministry, during his two brief periods in office.

By 1778, when Shelburne had been a widower for seven years, his younger son, William, died aged nine, and soon afterwards, his engagement was announced to Frances Molesworth, described as 'a young, attractive and wealthy heiress' (Cannon, 2004). But, according to Horace Walpole, it was not long before she began complaining that 'Shelburne did nothing but talk politics to her', and the engagement was called off. In 1789, however, he married Lady Louisa FitzPatrick, daughter of the Earl of Upper Ossory, who was 18 years his junior. Her family were close to Charles James Fox, and this alliance might have brought Shelburne closer to the Whig mainstream, but Lady Louisa's brothers took a great aversion to him, so the link bore no political fruit. She and Shelburne had two children, the elder of whom, Henry, third Marquess of Lansdowne, was to have a distinguished political career as a senior member of several Whig governments in the first half of the nineteenth century. Lady Louisa was praised by Jeremy Bentham for 'her beauty, her reserve and her kindness' (Norris, p. 6). The marriage was to last only 11 years, before she died at the age of 34. 'Shelburne felt her death in 1789 perhaps more than he had done that of his first wife. It left him alone in the world in his later middle age, when he was in the political wilderness without the distraction of pubic affairs (Ibid.). On 22 March 1780, Shelburne was to fight a duel, in Hyde Park at 5 a.m., with a Scottish MP, Lieutenant-General William Fullarton, who had taken exception to 'some characteristically sharp remarks' which Shelburne had made in a parliamentary debate (Cannon, 2004). Shelburne was lightly wounded in the groin, but was admired for his courage, and the incident brought him much acclaim, with several towns conferring their freedom upon him, because the Scots were even more unpopular than he was.

During the 12 years of Lord North's ministry, the two largest opposition groups were able to work together only spasmodically, due largely to personal differences between Rockingham and both Chatham and Shelburne, and the deep distrust in which the latter was held by the Rockinghamites. These were more important than the actual policy differences between them. Like Chatham, Shelburne placed little store on party allegiances, while the Rockinghams regarded them as essential. Rockingham and his followers were convinced that the King was bent on securing unlimited power, and felt that he could only be constrained by a disciplined party with a consistent policy, which they aimed to impose on the monarch by virtue of their parliamentary power. Their objective, in contemporary terms, was 'to storm the closet' – that is, to force the King to appoint ministers of their, and not his own choosing, and accept whatever policies they proposed. Shelburne, by contrast, believed that the Royal Prerogative to choose his own ministers was an essential element of the 'Glorious Revolution' settlement, creating a balanced division of power between King and Parliament. It was only after the surrender of Lord Cornwallis's army, at Yorktown in October 1781, that the two groups came together to launch a determined effort to oust the government of Lord North.

It took five months for them to achieve this objective, and when North – faced with imminent defeat in a confidence vote – insisted on resigning, the King had no alternative but to seek a new Prime Minister from among the opposition. Rockingham and Shelburne were the only feasible choices. Despite his earlier hostility to Shelburne, the King found him greatly preferable, partly because of his continued opposition to American independence. George III offered the post to Shelburne, but realizing that he could not command a majority in the Commons, he declined. The King, with the greatest reluctance, and only after vainly exploring other possibilities, finally agreed to Rockingham forming a government, but refused to deal with him personally, insisting on using Shelburne as an intermediary, and that he should hold a senior post. He, in fact, became Home Secretary (replacing the former Southern Department), and the King underlined his new confidence in him by appointing him to the Order of the Garter. Charles James Fox was appointed Foreign Secretary (replacing the Northern Department), Lord John Cavendish, a leading Rockinghamite, became Chancellor of the Exchequer and Edmund Burke, Paymaster-General.

The new government was an uneasy coalition between Rockinghamites and Chathamites. Rockingham had much the larger parliamentary following, but Shelburne enjoyed the confidence of the King, who regarded him as the joint head of the government, and wanted to channel patronage through him rather than through the First Lord of the Treasury. During the brief three months of Rockingham's premiership, Shelburne was constantly at odds with him over patronage and other issues, and with Fox over the conduct of peace negotiations with the Americans and their European allies. With the backing of the King, who treated Rockingham with disdain and who was violently hostile to Fox, Shelburne gradually strengthened his position. The main legislative battle was over the issue of 'economical reform'. Burke's Bill to reform the Civil List, removing or reducing a large number of sinecures, pensions or fees, was the centre-piece. The King was willing to let the Bill proceed, but insisted that he – rather than Parliament – should be responsible for implementing parallel reforms in the Royal Household. Shelburne, whose obsequiousness to the King now knew few bounds, managed to amend the Bill accordingly. He also began to forge alliances with former close supporters of Lord North, such as Henry Dundas, Charles Jenkinson and John Robinson. His greatest catch, however, was the young William Pitt, then only 22, but already seen as a rising star.

The main business of the Rockingham government was to attempt to negotiate peace with the American colonists, and with their three allies – France, Spain and Holland. Fox assumed that as Foreign Secretary, he would be the minister responsible, but Shelburne's department was responsible for the colonies, and he too claimed responsibility. The ludicrous outcome was that they both sent separate representatives to Paris, to negotiate with Benjamin Franklin, the US plenipotentiary in France. The two men were also divided over the terms to offer the Americans. Fox, backed by Rockingham, believed that independence should be granted unconditionally at the outset of the official talks: Shelburne, acutely aware of the King's continuing reluctance to face reality, argued that recognition should be held back, and used as a bargaining counter during the negotiations to extract concessions from the US, notably over the treatment of 'loyalists' who had supported Britain during the war. At two successive Cabinet meetings, held on 26 and 30 June 1782, in the absence of Rockingham, who was away ill, Fox was narrowly outvoted on this issue, and petulantly announced that he would resign, as soon as Rockingham returned. Unfortunately for him, Rockingham died the following day (see Chapter 8). The Rockinghamites quickly met and chose the young Duke of Portland as their new leader, proposing him as the next Prime Minister. Yet George III was having nothing of this; he had already been in close touch with Shelburne, even before Rockingham's death, and now asked him to form a new government. Fox refused to serve, and hoped that his fellow Rockinghamites would follow his example, and thus abort Shelburne's appointment. It was not to be – Lord John Cavendish, the Chancellor of the Exchequer, Edmund Burke and a few more junior ministers decided to quit, but the rest agreed to stay. The decisive voice was that of Fox's uncle, the Duke of Richmond, who agonized over his conflicted loyalties, but eventually held on to his post, as did most of his colleagues. Fox was deeply disappointed, but a clear majority of the Rockinghamite MPs rallied to his side, and went into opposition.

So Shelburne became Prime Minister on 4 July 1782, at the age of 45. His government was substantially the same as Rockingham's, except that Lord Grantham replaced Fox as Foreign Secretary and the now 23-year-old William Pitt came in as Chancellor of the Exchequer. Shelburne rewarded some of his own followers with more junior posts: Isaac Barré replaced Burke as Paymaster-General and his new ally, Henry Dundas, became Treasurer of the Navy. Thomas Townshend, later Lord Sydney, took over Shelburne's post as Home Secretary, and also acted as Leader of the Commons. Yet in this latter role, he proved scarcely adequate, and he was soon effectively replaced by William Pitt, the only minister capable of matching such formidable opposition debaters as Fox, Burke and North. Pitt soon became Shelburne's closest collaborator, and was seen by many – including George III – as his likely successor. The parliamentary position of Shelburne's government was hazardous from the first. He had no assured majority, and it was estimated that, of the three largest factions in the Commons, Shelburne 'would have 140 followers, North 120 and Fox 90' (Cannon, 1969, p. 30). This left over 200 Members uncommitted, but strongly suggested that if Shelburne wished to remain in power he should seek to make an arrangement with either Fox or North. Isolated in the House of Lords, and by his congenital inability to work on a basis of mutual confidence with his ministerial colleagues, Shelburne remained woefully ignorant of the flow of parliamentary opinion, and only realized very late in the day the necessity of dealing with one or other of his rivals.

The principal task of his government was to pursue the peace negotiations with the US, and its allies, in the hope of being able to present a peace treaty which would be acceptable to a majority of the House of Commons. This was no easy mission, as the war was well and truly lost, and the British nego- tiating position was very weak. It was, however, somewhat improved by the British victory over the French, in the final battle of the war, when Admiral Rodney defeated the Comte de Grasse in the Battle of the Saintes, securing Britain's precarious position in the West Indies. In the event, the Americans got their way on virtually every issue, securing unconditional recognition, a very favourable territorial settlement, giving them control of all the land between the Mississippi, the Ohio and the Great Lakes, with only Canada remaining in British hands and without promising restitution to 'loyalists' who had lost their property during the war. In addition, Britain restored Senegal and Gorée to France, and ceded Tobago, while the two countries restored to each other the various islands which they had occupied during the war. To Spain, Britain ceded Florida and Minorca, though it kept control of Gibraltar, which had survived a determined Spanish siege. It was not a very appetizing proposition to put to the House of Commons, and Shelburne began to sniff danger when it appeared that Lord North's followers, in particular, were enraged by the failure to secure the position of the 'loyalists'. Believing, however, that North was a pure creature of the King, he got George III to send him an admonitory letter. The King duly obliged, beginning:

Lord North has so often whilst in office assured me that whenever I could consent to his retiring he would give the most cordial support to such an administration as I might approve of … my strongest wishes that he will give the most active support … to the administration formed with my thor- ough approbation on the death of Lord Rockingham, and that during the recess he will call on the country gentlemen who certainly have great atten- tion for him to come early and show their countenance by which I may be enabled to keep the constitution from being entirely annihilated, which must be the case if Mr. Fox and his associates are not withstood … (Cannon, 1969, p. 28)

It was obtuse, in the extreme, for the monarch to write such a letter to his former Prime Minister so soon after he had mortified him by refusing to foot the bill for government expenses during the 1780 general election (see Chapter 11). North wrote back an evasive reply, saying:

> that it was true that he had, while in office, received the support of several independent country gentlemen, but he did not know whether he could venture to ask them to support the present ministry, and he was afraid that 'he might give them some offence if he were to attempt it'. (Ibid.)

North was at the same time receiving unexpected attentions from another quarter. His great parliamentary critic during his ministry had been Charles James Fox, but Fox now approached him saying that he did not believe there were any irreconcilable differences between them, and that they and their followers should work together to ensure the defeat of Shelburne, over the peace preliminaries, which had been agreed with the Americans in November 1782. Their opposition, and that of their supporters, came from different sources. Fox thought that Shelburne had grossly mishandled the negotiations by unrealistically resisting recognition of independence for far too long, while North and his friends bitterly resented that the 'loyalists' had been let down. What potentially united the two factions was the desire to get back into office, and this was to prove sufficiently strong to overcome hesitations on both sides. Meanwhile, Shelburne was finding it increasingly difficult to keep his government together. There were serious divisions within the Cabinet over both 'economical' and parliamentary reform, as well as on policy towards both Ireland and India, while many ministers constantly complained about his failure to consult. In January 1783, the Duke of Richmond and Lord Keppel, the First Lord of the Admiralty, resigned, and Shelburne, for the first time, began to scent the possibility of defeat. Very late in the day, he concluded that it would be necessary to conclude a deal with either North or Fox to secure the acceptance of the peace terms. He made contact with North's supporters, who insisted that he should be brought into the government as the price for giving their support. Shelburne might have been willing, but the Younger Pitt, who was now the main prop of the government, declared that he would find this utterly unacceptable. He blamed North for the eclipse of his father, and said, in effect, 'it is either him or me'. So Shelburne sent Pitt to see Fox to find out what his terms would be. The interview did not last long: Fox insisted that Shelburne would have to stand down, and Pitt left the room, saying 'I did not come here to betray Lord Shelburne' (see Chapter 14). On 14 February Fox and North met, and formally agreed on an alliance.

It was soon put to the test, the peace proposals being presented to Parliament on 18 February. In the Lords, Shelburne offered 'a rather rambling and theatrical defence but carried the day, in a very full house, by seventy votes to fifty-nine' (Cannon, 2004). In the Commons, there was much confusion, but eventually the government was defeated, on a procedural motion, by 224 to 208. This was a rather better result for Shelburne than might have been expected; he was backed by a majority of the independent Members of the House. Yet despite defections, and a great deal of cross-voting among the different factions, the agreement between Fox and North largely held firm. The House met three days later, to vote on a motion of censure on the government. The debate was dominated by a magnificent speech by Pitt extolling Shelburne's virtues, but to no avail – the government lost by a similar margin, 207 votes to 190. Unwilling to recognize his own shortcomings, Shelburne blamed the King for letting him down, bitterly complaining that he had betrayed him by surreptitiously helping his enemies. There were no grounds for his suspicions, and the main reason for his failure was his neglect in building up a sufficient basis of party support for himself. As Cannon puts it: 'He had always professed contempt for parties and political organisation, and was to pay dearly for it' (Cannon, 1969, p. 31). He submitted his resignation two days later, but remained in office until 26 March, when the King finally acknowledged that he had no alternative to appointing a government dominated by Fox and North (see Chapter 13).

He had been Prime Minister for a mere 266 days, and – at the age of 45 – might well have expected further opportunities to serve in government during the remaining 23 years of his life, during all of which he remained active in politics. It was not to be. As Cannon comments, 'No politician who held office with Shelburne wished to do so again' (Ibid., p. 59). Even the Younger Pitt, who owed so much to Shelburne's patronage, was not prepared to risk including him in his government, which came into power in December 1783 and remained in office for 17 years. Perhaps he had a bad conscience about this: at the end of 1784 he recommended George III to advance him in the peerage, and Shelburne became the first Marquess of Lansdowne. As such, he continued to plough his lonely furrow in the House of Lords, becoming progressively more radical as he grew older. He welcomed the French Revolution, and was strongly opposed to Britain joining with Austria and Prussia in attempts to suppress it. Thereafter, he consistently campaigned for a compromise peace agreement, and fiercely opposed the repressive legislation introduced by Pitt during the 1790s. This brought him closer to Charles James Fox, and when – much later in 1801 – George III fell ill and a regency was threatened, the Prince of Wales had the two men pencilled in as Secretaries of State in the government which he hoped to form under Lord Moira (Cannon, 2004). George's recovery within a few weeks aborted this prospect and Lansdowne remained in opposition, making his last speech on 23 May 1803, opposing the resumption of war with Napoleon. He died two years later at the age of 68.

Despite his high intelligence and manifold gifts, his political career had been a failure, and he was only too aware of this. It was partly due to ill luck, but more to faults in his personality and judgment. His parents and his grand-father had much to answer for. Their brutality and neglect helped to mould his suspicious and secretive nature, which made him such a difficult colleague to deal with. Moreover, in many respects his ideas were ahead of his time, and were more appreciated by later generations. One of his greatest admirers was Benjamin Disraeli, who devoted several pages of his novel *Sybil* to a panegyric of the man he called 'the ablest and most accomplished minister of the eighteenth century'. Somewhere between this soaring assessment, and the scorn of many of Lansdowne's political contemporaries, will lie a truer estimate of his abilities and achievements.

Works consulted

Bigham, Clive (1924), *The Prime Ministers of Britain 1721–1924*, London, John Murray.

Black, Jeremy (1998), 'William Petty, Second Earl of Shelburne', in *Biographical Dictionary of British Prime Ministers*, London, Routledge.

Cannon, John (1969), *The Fox-North Coalition*, Cambridge, CUP.

Cannon, John (2004), 'Petty, William, second earl of Shelburne and first marquess of Lansdowne (1737–1805)', in *Oxford Dictionary of National Biography*, Oxford, OUP.

Norris, John (1963), *Shelburne and Reform*, London, Macmillan.

O'Gorman, Frank (1974), 'The Earl of Shelburne (1782–83)', in Herbert Van Thal, ed., *The Prime Ministers*, Volume II, London, Allen & Unwin.

Stuart, Charles (1931), 'Lord Shelburne', in eds. Hugh Lloyd-Jones etc., *History & Imagination: Essays in honour of H.R. Trevor-Roper*, London, Duckworth.

13

William Henry Cavendish-Bentinck, Third Duke of Portland –Twice a Figurehead Premier

The Duke of Portland had the singular distinction of leading both a predominantly Whig and a Tory administration. Twenty-five years separated his two governments, and in each case he was a mere figurehead, the government being dominated by more powerful nominal subordinates. In between his two brief premierships, however, Portland played a prominent political role.

William Henry Cavendish-Bentinck was born on 14 April 1738, the eldest son and third child of the second Duke of Portland and of Margaret Cavendish-Holles-Harley, granddaughter of Robert Harley, Earl of Oxford, a prominent minister under Queen Anne. William's great-grandfather, Hans William Bentinck, had come over from the Netherlands with William III, in 1689, and was his closest friend and most influential adviser, being created Earl of Portland, and awarded extensive estates in several English counties. The title was upped to a dukedom by George I in 1716, and the family holdings were further enlarged, when the second Duchess inherited Welbeck Abbey and an income of £12,000 a year from her mother and her cousin, the third Earl of Oxford. The second Duke is described by the historian, A.S. Turberville, as 'retiring, unambitious, inconspicuous, a much less remarkable personality than his wife...but wise, gentle and kindly' The Duchess was a much stronger personality, who outlived her husband by 23 years, and – through her control of the family purse-strings – was something of a restraining influence on her elder son up till and even after his first premiership.

William was educated at Westminster School and Christ Church, Oxford, qualifying Master of Arts in 1757. He seems to have been an adequate but not outstanding student, and at the age of 19 set out for the Grand Tour, spending three years, mostly in Italy, but also visiting Hamburg, Prussia and Warsaw. Judging from his portraits, an exceptionally handsome young man, known by his courtesy title as the Marquis of Titchfield, he soon acquired a reputation as a philanderer and rapidly got into debt. His parents gave him an allowance of £2500 a year, which they regarded as more than adequate for his needs, but he wrote plaintively to his father asking for this to be increased to £5000. When this was refused, he addressed himself to his two elder sisters, one of whom, Elizabeth, was married to Viscount Weymouth, with no greater success. William aspired to a diplomatic career, hoping for a cushy post in a European capital, but his family doubted if he had sufficient experience, and his sister Elizabeth wrote to him suggesting that a political career might be more appropriate. Her husband controlled the Herefordshire constituency of Weobley, and, in March 1761, shortly before his twenty-third birthday, and even before his return from the continent, he was elected unopposed as one of its two MPs.

He sat in the Commons for exactly one year, and there is no record of any activity on his part. But in March 1762, his father, who had played no part in politics, died. The young Lord Titchfield became the third Duke, immediately taking his seat in the House of Lords, and attaching himself to the largest of the Whig factions, led by the ageing former Prime Minister, the Duke of Newcastle. Newcastle's protégé, the Marquess of Rockingham, was poised to take over and Portland, in turn, became his protégé and close associate.

A poor and infrequent speaker, Portland may appear to have been an indifferent recruit to Newcastle's ranks, but his high social standing made him a prize catch. Dukes (other than royal dukes) were thin on the ground and to find one who was young, personally agreeable, keen and prepared to give generously of his time and money in organizational activities, including the financing of elections, was an unlooked for opportunity. In a very short space of time, Portland was accepted as one of the leading Whig peers.

On his return from the continent, he was also seen as a highly eligible bachelor, but before settling down he embarked on love affairs with two ladies who would have been unlikely to commend themselves to the Dowager Lady Portland as suitable marriage mates for her son. One was a beautiful young widow, Maria Walpole, the illegitimate daughter of Sir Edward Walpole, and niece of the writer, Horace Walpole. Married to the Earl of Waldegrave, who was twice her age, she was left with three young children while still in her early twenties. Portland wooed her passionately, but she set her cap at even higher prey. As Horace Walpole put it, in his Memoirs, 'the young Duke of Gloucester, who had gazed at her with desire during her husband's life, now openly shewing himself her admirer, she slighted the subject and aspired to the brother of the crown'. She became his mistress, and later his wife, much to the fury of George III, who introduced the Royal Marriages Act into Parliament, shortly afterwards, one of his own brothers, the second Duke of Cumberland, also having contracted an unsuitable match (Turberville, 1939, p. 44).

Disappointed by Maria, Portland now directed his attention to Anne Liddell, the estranged wife of the Duke of Grafton, who was himself to be Prime Minister in 1768–70. He lavished presents on her, including two horses, and her surviving letters to him reveal that she more than reciprocated his feelings. Suddenly, however, Portland's side of the correspondence grew more distant, and, in March 1766 he wrote announcing his engagement to Lady Dorothy Cavendish, daughter of the fourth Duke of Devonshire. Judging from her portrait, the future Duchess of Portland was a great deal less attractive than either of her rivals, and she was certainly less vivacious. She was, however, universally seen as a suitable match and their marriage, which took place the following November, seems to have been a happy one. The advantage to Portland was obvious, He was marrying into one of the greatest aristocratic and political families of the realm and his new brother-in-law, the fifth Duke of Devonshire, obligingly lent him Burlington House, in Piccadilly, as his London residence, an ideal venue for political entertaining (Turberville, pp. 44–51). As for the Duchess of Grafton, she did not remain broken hearted for long. She soon took up with the Earl of Upper Ossory, bearing him a son in 1768 and marrying him as soon as her marriage to Grafton had been dissolved by Act of Parliament in 1769. (It is intriguing that another future Prime Minister, Harold Macmillan, was to marry a Lady Dorothy Cavendish, daughter of the ninth Duke of Devonshire, over 150 years later, in 1920).

What sort of man was the Third Duke of Portland, and what beliefs and principles underlay his political career? First and foremost, he was an almost perfect exemplar of the creed of *noblesse oblige*, as was illustrated by a letter he addressed to his wastrel younger brother, Lord Edward Bentinck, urging on him his duty to accept nomination as a Member of Parliament:

> Since I have been able to exercise my reason, I never could persuade myself that men were born only for themselves. I have always been bred to think that Society has its claims on them, & that those claims were in general proportioned to the degrees of their fortunes, their situation, and their abilities...(Turberville, p. 68)

Secondly, Portland was a strong party man, and the party he had chosen was the Whig party, which he saw as the natural protector of the Bill of Rights of 1689. This prescribed a limited monarchy, and parliamentary government, and it was the duty of the Whig aristocracy, in Portland's view, to ensure that this doctrine prevailed. Throughout the reigns of the first two Georges, they had successfully carried out this mission, but the young George III, who ascended the throne in 1760, had lost little time in challenging it, effectively turning out of office a Whig government led by the Duke of Newcastle, and substituting one led by a royal favourite, the Earl of Bute.

Portland, a mild-mannered man, was nevertheless capable of strong emotions and conceived a deep aversion to Bute and a keen distrust of the King. For his part, George refused to accept that he was acting against either the letter or the spirit of the Bill of Rights. He believed that his right to appoint or dismiss ministers at his will was underwritten by this Act, and that it was only the laziness of his great grandfather, George I and his grandfather, George II, which had allowed this power to be usurped by a Whig oligarchy. He was doing no more, he believed, than reclaiming the powers awarded to William III by the 1689 Act.

Despite, his Whig principles, Portland was no democrat and in general held highly conservative views. He was opposed to parliamentary reform, to Catholic emancipation and the abolition of slavery. This might have brought him into conflict with Charles James Fox, the undisputed leader of the Whigs in the House of Commons, but in fact the two men acted in almost complete harmony for many years and were only driven apart by the impact of the French Revolution, in the years after 1789. The basis of Portland's influence was his position as a great territorial magnate, with estates in Buckinghamshire, Cumberland, Hampshire and Soho. Yet he was constrained by two factors – his relationship with his mother, and his own spendthrift ways. The Dowager Duchess of Portland loved her elder son dearly, but was fiercely protective of her own rights. The Cavendish interest, including large estates in Nottinghamshire and Derbyshire and a grand London residence, which she had inherited from her mother, remained hers until her death in 1785, while Portland only controlled the Bentinck inheritance until then. The Dowager chose, however, to make her home at Bulstrode, in Buckinghamshire, the main Bentinck residence, allowing her son, in exchange, to live in Welbeck Abbey, the Nottinghamshire base of her branch of the Cavendish family, conveniently close to Portland's new Cavendish in-laws, the Devonshires, at Chatsworth. There were periodic conflicts between mother and son over the control and management of the different estates and in addition sharp political differences, as the Dowager was an intimate friend of Lady Bute and had many close contacts with courtiers of the King. In addition, Portland's brother-in-law, Lord Weymouth, who had provided him with his parliamentary seat, was a Tory, who served for many years, without distinction, in Lord North's government.

Portland was a benevolent landlord and was regarded as an 'easy touch' by many of his large circle of friends and dependents. He was continually bailing out Lord Edward Bentinck, described by Horace Walpole as his 'idle and worthless younger brother', and lent as much as £56,000 to his rakish friend George Byng (Lord Torrington), which he never got back. In addition, he recklessly spent large sums of money in the general election of 1768 in a determined attempt to win parliamentary seats in Cumberland, where he was a large landowner, from the control of the notorious 'boroughmonger', Sir James Lowther. In the short-term, he was notably successful, doubling the number of seats he directly controlled in the House of Commons, from four to eight, but in the long-term it was ruinous to his finances. Lowther retaliated by launching a lawsuit against Portland, challenging the legality of his Cumberland holdings which had been granted to his great grandfather by William III. Lowther was immensely wealthy and boasted 'I would at any time spend £20,000 to make the Duke of Portland spend fifteen, for I know I can hold out longer than he can, and my meaning is to ruin the Duke of Portland.' The case dragged on for ten years, at enormous expense, and though Portland eventually prevailed, 'it proved a joyless victory, which resulted in the sale of most of his Cumberland estates' (Wilkinson, 2003, p. 24). Wilkinson points out that, though Portland was by most measures a very wealthy man, his assets palled in comparison with those of other territorial magnates. Prior to his mother's death, in 1785, his net income was some £9000 a year, which then rose to £17,000. 'These figures should be compared with fellow grandees, such as the Duke of Devonshire and the Marquis of Rockingham, whose net incomes were in the region of £40,000 p. a.' (Ibid., p. 61).

Portland did not have long to wait to win ministerial office. In July 1765, three years after he succeeded to the dukedom, the King ejected George Grenville, Bute's successor, from office, and turned once again to the Whigs to form a government. The Marquess of Rockingham became Prime Minister at the age of 35 and invited Portland, then 27, to become Lord Chamberlain, outside the Cabinet. The duties were not very arduous, and were largely routine, such as the organization of 'state ceremonies, the preparation of apartments for royal visits, the redecoration of ballrooms, the purchase of new furniture and similar topics' (Turberville, p. 88). Portland found it all rather boring, but proved efficient at his post, and when the King dismissed the Rockingham government, after just over a year, he was one of a number of ministers asked to stay on in the new government led by the Earl of Chatham (the elder Pitt). Portland was not an admirer of Chatham, whom he referred to as 'Lord Cheat'em', and had no qualms in resigning after a few months, when Rockingham called on his supporters to quit the government. In opposition, he stayed close to Rockingham and remained so for the ensuing 16 years until Rockingham was again asked to form a government, in March 1782. This was in succession to Lord North, whose 12 years in office came to an end with the collapse of the British position in the American War of Independence. Rockingham nominated him as Lord Lieutenant, or 'viceroy' of Ireland, but less than three months after his arrival in Dublin the sudden death of the Prime Minister brought the government to an abrupt end.

The Rockinghamites met to appoint a successor, whom they optimistically assumed would be asked by George III to form a new government. Much the most able of the Whig peers was the Duke of Richmond, an illegitimate descendant of Charles II, who had served with distinction in both the Rockingham governments and would dearly have loved to be chosen. Yet, in Horace Walpole's words, quoted by Turberville, 'with a thousand virtues, he was nevertheless exceedingly unpopular'. One reason was his ardent advocacy of Parliamentary reform, which did not go down well with many of the Whig magnates, who feared the loss of their 'pocket' boroughs. What, asked Turberville, of the party's

> most active and brilliant representative in the Lower House – Fox? It is exceedingly doubtful whether this most intensely aristocratic of all political connexions would ever have selected a commoner as its head: but there was a fatal objection apart from that – Fox was anathema to the King. It was Fox himself who proposed the solution which found general favour – the election of the Duke of Portland. (Turberville, p. 180)

So it was that one of the least qualified people ever to lead a British political party was chosen. As his grandson, the nineteenth century diarist, Charles Greville, also quoted by Turberville, put it:

> My grandfather was a very honourable, high-minded but ordinary man; his abilities were very second-rate, and he had no power of speaking, and his election to the post of leader of the great Whig party only shows how aristocratic that party was…they would never have endured to be led by a Peel or a Canning. (Ibid., pp. 180–1)

George III never seriously considered asking Portland to become Prime Minister and hastened to appoint the Earl of Shelburne, formerly a close associate of the Elder Pitt, who asked Portland to stay on as Lord Lieutenant of Ireland. Soon afterwards, however, he resigned, joining the bulk of the Rockinghamites in opposition, and beginning a long and harmonious partnership with Fox, who was the undisputed Whig leader in the Commons. As recounted in Chapter 12, Shelburne's ministry did not last long, being defeated in February 1783, in a House of Commons vote on the American peace terms, due to the coming together of the forces of Fox and of Lord North MP, the former Tory Prime Minister. The King, with great reluctance, agreed that they should form the next government, but insisted that someone else should be Prime Minister. His preference was the young William Pitt, then only 23, but he was unwilling and in any case was unacceptable to both Fox and North, who both insisted that Portland should be chosen. He agreed to take office, but the new government, installed on 2 April 1783, was totally dominated by Fox, as Foreign Secretary, and North as Home Secretary, both being in the House of Commons. In effect, Portland's role was principally to act merely as Leader of the House of Lords, but he enjoyed excellent relations with both of his nominal subordinates, and seemed quite comfortable to be seen as a figurehead.

From the outset, George was determined that the government, to whom he refused all patronage, should be of brief duration and his resolve was only strengthened when it proposed to him a generous formula for clearing the debts of the spendthrift Prince of Wales and substantially increasing his official allowance. The King expressed his 'utter indignation and astonishment' at so large a sum being proposed (far larger than *he* had enjoyed as heir apparent), and charged the Duke with 'neglecting the interests of the Sovereign and of the public to gratify the passions of an ill-advised Young Man'. Portland replied with an emollient letter proposing a compromise, which the King accepted, and – untypically – apologized to Portland for his earlier ill temper. Despite this apparent reconciliation, George was still determined to remove the Portland government at the earliest opportunity, which – as described in Chapter 14 – occurred when Fox enthusiastically pushed through the Commons a Bill, drafted by Edmund Burke, sharply curtailing the independence of the East India Company and transferring its powers of patronage to parliamentary commissioners. In a plot carefully contrived with the former (and future) Lord Chancellor, Lord Thurlow and with the Younger Pitt, the latter's cousin, the second Earl Temple, was authorized to tell members of the House of Lords that the King would regard any of them who voted for the Bill as his 'personal enemy'. Rumours of what was afoot reached the government and Portland referred obliquely to them in his speech proposing the Second Reading of the Bill in the Lords. Perhaps there was nothing to be done about it, but Portland badly mishandled the situation, making no serious attempt to persuade peers of the merits of the Bill and then bungling the parliamentary procedure for its approval. The Bill was defeated by 19 votes, but the government, which still enjoyed a large majority in the Commons, refused to resign. It was then unceremoniously dismissed by the King, who sent personal messengers at midnight to the homes of Portland, Fox and North to demand the return of their seals of office. Portland's premiership, which came to an end on 18 December 1783, had lasted a mere 260 days. The King's intervention was described, by the leading historian of this period, as 'indefensible according to both the constitutional theory and practice of his own day' (Cannon, p. xiii). Portland received no blame from his colleagues for his maladroit performance. He was regarded by them as a martyr for the Whig cause, and 'it became impossible to conceive of the return of the whigs without his reinstatement [as Prime Minister]' (Wilkinson, 2004).

Such a return seemed probable late in 1788, when the first bout of madness of George III appeared to open the way to the appointment of his son (later George IV), a bosom friend of Fox and other leading Whigs, as Prince Regent. The King's recovery, the following March, before a regency bill had been passed, forestalled this possibility and the main body of the Whigs were to remain in the wilderness for many years to come. Portland, however, was restored to office, though not to the premiership, some five years later.

The French Revolution, in 1789, had opened up deep divisions within the Whig Party, with Fox enthusiastically welcoming it, and Edmund Burke reacting sharply against. Portland's initial reaction was mildly favourable, but as the excesses mounted up, he, together with many other Whig aristocrats, began to fear for his property if French revolutionary ideas were to cross the Channel. When war broke out with France, in 1792, he became even more concerned and succumbed to the patriotic fervour whipped up by Pitt's supporters. He was, however, deeply reluctant to break with Fox, who was opposed to the war, and for long refused to respond to feelers from Pitt to join his government, as Lord Loughborough, the leading Whig lawyer, had done, in becoming Lord Chancellor in January 1793. It was another 18 months before he was prepared to take the plunge, finally, as recounted in Chapter 14, becoming Home Secretary in July 1794. He was accompanied by four other conservative Whig defectors, who joined the cabinet at the same time and he succeeded in bringing over to the government side more than half of the Whig representation in the Commons. This greatly bolstered Pitt's majority and left Fox in charge of a diminishing rump of largely demoralized supporters.

The Portlandites also obtained numerous peerages and other honours, as well as appointments to non-cabinet posts, of which the most important was the Lord Lieutenancy of Ireland. This went to Earl Fitzwilliam, Rockingham's nephew and a close friend of Portland's. On his arrival in Dublin, Fitzwilliam embarked on a purge of government officials, replacing supporters of Pitt with Irish Whigs and without obtaining Cabinet approval, expressed his sympathy for Catholic emancipation. Portland was horrified and immediately recalled Fitzwilliam, offering, however, as a token of friendship, to resign as Home Secretary and telling Fitzwilliam that the King had agreed to his appointment to a Cabinet post as compensation for his dismissal, provided he affirmed his support for the ministry. With all the pride of a leading Whig magnate, Fitzwilliam rejected this offer out of hand and his friendship with Portland was at an end. As Home Secretary, Portland continued to be responsible for Irish affairs and following the unsuccessful United Irish uprising, led by Wolfe Tone, in 1798, took a leading role in the moves to incorporate the Irish Parliament into the British Parliament at Westminster. This was only achieved by the massive employment of patronage and outright bribes to Irish MPs to induce them to vote their own Parliament out of existence. This policy was carried through by the men on the spot in Dublin, the Marquis of Cornwallis, as Lord Lieutenant, and Viscount Castlereagh MP, as Chief Secretary. When Portland left office, in 1801, there were substantial funds missing from the Home Office accounts, which was promptly covered up. For nearly 200 years, Portland, who was known to be in financial difficulties at the time, was suspected of having diverted the money (more than £30,000) for his own purposes. It was only with the release of the Home Office secret service papers, in the 1990s and sharp detective work by the historian, David Wilkinson, that it was revealed that the missing money had, in fact, been illegally transmitted to Dublin to grease the palms of Irish Protestant legislators (Wilkinson, 2003, pp. 148–58).

Portland's Whiggish instincts did not long survive his recruitment to the Pitt government and his previous animus against Pitt, who had usurped his premiership a dozen years earlier and against George III, soon evaporated. Indeed, he became a fervent admirer of Pitt, whom he found a considerate colleague and of the King, with whom he developed good relations and whom he came to see as a model patriotic monarch. For all intents and purposes, Portland became a Tory, though he never described himself as such, and his record as Home Secretary showed him to be one of the most hard-line of Pitt's ministers. He was largely responsible for introducing and implementing the oppressive legislation directed against alleged supporters of the French Revolution and of parliamentary reform and he did not scruple to use secret service informers and *agents provateurs* to harry their activities. Nor did he show himself sympathetic to those suffering from serious food shortages, following a series of bad harvests, setting his face against proposals to fix food prices or make government purchases of imported grain. Only on two occasions, in 1795 and 1800, did he relent, in the face of strong pressure from other ministers.

When Pitt resigned, along with other leading cabinet ministers, in February 1801, in protest against George III's vetoing of Catholic emancipation, Portland did not join them. He carried on as Home Secretary in Henry Addington's government, later switching to become Lord President of the Council, a position he retained in Pitt's second ministry, formed in May 1804. The following year, he relinquished the post to make room for Addington (now Lord Sidmouth), but remained in the Cabinet as Minister without Portfolio. He went into opposition when Lord Grenville formed his 'Ministry of All the Talents', on Pitt's death in February 1806, becoming the nominal leader of the Pittites, who were excluded, or excluded themselves, from the government because of their incompatibility with the Whigs, who formed the largest element in Grenville's team. The Pittite group included such strong characters as George Canning, Spencer Perceval, Lord Hawkesbury (the future Lord Liverpool) and Viscount Castlereagh, whose mutual rivalry was assuaged by their common agreement to unite under the emollient Duke.

Portland was now an elderly man and his health was far from good and it looked as though his ministerial days were at an end. Yet when, in early 1807, George III once again came into conflict with his ministers on the issue of Catholic emancipation), Portland wrote an ill-advised letter to the King urging him to stand his ground. Grenville and his leading colleagues agreed to withdraw their Bill granting the rights of Catholics to hold senior positions in the Army and Navy, but refused to promise the King never to raise the issue again. Thereupon, he peremptorily dismissed them and appealed to Portland to take Grenville's place. With evident misgivings, Portland complied, forming what was effectively a Tory government, with the leading positions all filled by Pittites. On paper, at least, it was a strong team, with Spencer

Perceval as Chancellor of the Exchequer, George Canning as Foreign Secretary, Lord Hawkesbury (shortly to succeed to the Earldom of Liverpoool) as Home Secretary and Viscount Castlereagh MP as Secretary for War and the Colonies. In practice, it proved a great deal weaker than the sum of its parts. This was because of the lack of direction which it received from Portland, who attended cabinet meetings only spasmodically, and hardly ever the House of Lords, where he remained silent throughout his premiership. Wilkinson did not put it too bluntly, when he wrote: 'Portland was worse than useless as prime minister. Not only did he fail to direct policy, he also bungled the lesser role of conciliator' (Wilkinson, 2003, pp. 164–5). Contemporary comment, especially from Whig supporters, who felt betrayed by him, was even more unkind. Wilkinson quotes, at length, a poem published in the *Morning Chronicle*, and beginning:

> He totters on a crutch;
> his brain by sickness long depressed,
> has lost the sense it once possessed,
> though that's not losing much. (Ibid., p. 137)

The government faced serious problems, not least in promoting the war against Napoleon, where the campaign in Spain and Portugal was going badly and the expedition to the Dutch island of Walcheren, with the aim of seizing Antwerp, planned by Castlereagh, went disastrously wrong. They were compounded by a scandal involving the King's brother, the Duke of York, who was Commander-in-Chief, and whose mistress was accused of selling army commissions. The worst feature of Portland's government, however, was the intrigues conducted by individual ministers against their colleagues. The main culprit was George Canning, who – sensing that the Portland ministry would not last long – endeavoured to manoeuvre himself into a position where he would be well placed to succeed him. His main rival was likely to be Perceval, but the man he had in his sights was Castlereagh, and he approached Portland, threatening to resign if Castlereagh was not removed from the War Office and replaced by Lord Wellesley, the elder brother of General Sir Arthur Wellesley, later the Duke of Wellington. Portland agreed, in principle and squared the matter with the King, but insisted that the change could not be made until after the outcome of the Walcheren expedition was known and that until then the decision should be kept from Castlereagh so as not to undermine him. He also suggested that the bad news should ultimately be conveyed to Castlereagh by Earl Camden, the Lord President of the Council, who was his uncle, and who nobly offered to give up his own post in his nephew's favour, in order to soften the blow. Yet when the time came, after the failure of the Walcheren expedition, his nerve failed him and shortly afterwards Portland had an apoplectic seizure while on his journey from London to Bulstrode and was taken out of his carriage 'speechless and insensible. He made a partial recovery of both mind and speech, but no hopes were entertained of his ultimate restoration to health' (Turberville, p. 301). His family wanted Portland to retire immediately, and when Perceval also recommended him to do so, he decided to call it a day, a decision which alarmed Canning, as he thought it had come too early for his own chances of the succession. When Castlereagh learned of Canning's conduct, he was outraged, and immediately demanded satisfaction. The two men met on Putney Heath for a duel, in which Canning was slightly wounded and the scandal added to the ignominy of the collapse of Portland's government.

Portland resigned on 4 October 1809, after a premiership of two years and 187 days. This was more than three times as long as his first premiership, but whereas he had played a useful role as a mediator the first time round, he was almost a complete passenger in his second administration. Perceval went on to form a government from which both Canning and Castlereagh were excluded and the former had to wait another 13 years before he was restored to office. Portland agreed to continue in Perceval's cabinet as Minister without Portfolio, but died three weeks later, after a second apoplectic attack, on 30 October 1809, aged 71. He left debts of £500,000 and it was only by effecting painful economies, including the sale of the main Bentinck estate at Bulstrode, that his son, the fourth Duke, who eschewed any political participation, was able to mend the family fortunes.

Portland's long political career had seldom risen above the level of mediocrity. As opposition leader in the 1780s, he lent respectability to the otherwise somewhat raffish Whigs and his patience and affability helped to hold the party together in a difficult period. A conscientious, if reactionary, Home Secretary between 1794 and 1801, he would probably have been wiser to bow out of politics at that stage, and devote his evidently waning powers to the management of his still extensive estates. Yet a misguided sense of duty, and a desire to please the King, to whom he was now devoted, forced him to carry on. His historical importance lies chiefly in his action in 1794 of bringing the more conservative Whigs over to Pitt. He thereby paved the way for a reconstituted Tory party, which was to become the dominant political force in the first three decades of the nineteenth century.

Works consulted

Cannon, John (1969), *The Fox-North Coalition*, Cambridge, Cambridge University Press.
Derry, John W. (1990), *Politics in the Age of Fox, Pitt and Liverpool*, Basingstoke, Macmillan.
Smith, E. Anthony (1973), 'The Duke of Portland', in Herbert Van Thal (ed.), *The Prime Ministers*, Volume I, London, Allen & Unwin.

Stephens H.M. (H.M.S) (1885), Article in *Dictionary of National Biography*.

Turberville, A.S. (1939), *A History of Welbeck Abbey and its Owners*, Volume II, London, Faber and Faber.

Wilkinson, David (2003), *The Duke of Portland: Politics and Party in the Age of George III*, Basingstoke, Palgrave Macmillan.

Wilkinson, David (2004), Article in *Oxford Dictionary of National Biography*.

14
William Pitt, the Younger – Peacetime Prodigy, Less Successful in War

If ever anybody was pre-programmed to be Prime Minister, it was William Pitt the Younger. He was born, in Kent, on 28 May 1759 – the very year in which his father gained lasting renown as a war leader in the Seven Years War. The elder Pitt (later Lord Chatham) was not, then, actually Prime Minister, but he planned and directed Britain's military and naval operations, which saw France driven out of its possessions in both Canada and India and worsted in conflicts in West Africa and the West Indies. Although his subsequent term as Prime Minister, in 1766–68, was a disappointment, his achievements in 1759, combined with his passionate patriotism, rare incorruptibility and soaring oratory established him as Britain's outstanding eighteenth century political leader.

The elder Pitt came from a well-established landed family, with a tradition of public service, whose fortune derived from his grandfather, Thomas Pitt, a trader in India, who became Governor of Madras. William the Elder married Hester Grenville, whose brother, George Grenville, was also to be Prime Minister (in 1763–65), so the young William grew up in a family which was deeply political on both sides. William was the second son and fourth child (out of five) in the family, but from the outset his father had marked him out as the one to carry forward the flame of his own burning ambition. Partly because of his delicate health, but also because of the elder Pitt's unpleasant memories of Eton, which he described as 'a stultifying and brutal place' (Turner, p. 6), William was educated at home by a private tutor, but his father took a very active role in his instruction. He coached him in oratory, getting him to translate, verbally and at sight, passages from Greek and Latin authors and hearing him recite. By the age of seven, William was already looking forward to following in his father's footsteps. Very quick to learn he was judged at 14 to be the equal or superior of most 18-year-olds and started to study at Pembroke Hall, Cambridge, with the Rev. George Pretyman (whom he was much later to nominate as Archbishop of Canterbury, only to be over-ruled by George III) as his tutor. His health soon broke down and he spent much of the next three years at home, suffering, among other ailments, from gout. His doctor, Anthony Addington (father of his successor as Prime Minister, Henry Addington), prescribed a bottle of port every day as a cure. It seemed to work, but it left William with a heavy dependence on alcohol, which was to do him no good in the long run.

As an undergraduate, he lived a solitary life, meeting few people other than his tutor, Pretyman. He proved a diligent student of Latin and Greek, showed a taste for mathematics and learned French, but no other modern languages and showed little interest in contemporary culture. In 1776, still aged only 17, he graduated as a Master of Arts, without taking an examination. He stayed on in Cambridge and his social life at last took off, bringing him into contact with a group of well-bred young men, several of whom were later to become his political associates. One of these was William Wilberforce, the famous campaigner for the abolition of the slave trade, who left a record of Pitt's life at Cambridge, describing him as being always 'remarkably cheerful and pleasant, full of wit and playfulness' (Ehrman, Vol. I, pp. 17–18). This view was corroborated by others, including Pretyman and he was undoubtedly very popular with his fellows but at the same time he was remarked as being gawky and awkward and painfully shy with strangers. He was in no doubt that politics was his vocation and travelled frequently to London to listen to parliamentary debates, on one occasion being introduced to Charles James Fox, the leading Whig orator, who commented favourably on his lively intelligence. He attended the House of Lords on 7 April 1778, to hear his father's last speech, a passionate appeal to make peace with the American rebels, and when the Earl collapsed before reaching his peroration, helped to carry him out of the Chamber. Chatham died a month later and – in the absence of his elder brother, John, who was on military service overseas – Pitt was left to make the funeral arrangements and attempt to sort out his father's tangled financial affairs. He was deeply in debt, having – unlike most of his contemporaries – refused to enrich himself from his ministerial duties, and though Parliament voted to pay off the debts and to establish an annuity of £4000 attached to the Earldom (which went to his brother), Pitt received no legacy and himself went into debt, which – with ups and downs – continued for the rest of his life.

It was necessary to earn a living and Pitt now started eating dinners at Lincoln's Inn, with the intention of working at the bar. He qualified in June 1780, and in August went to work on the Western circuit. In September, however, a general election was called and he hastily returned to Cambridge, where he was nominated as a candidate for one of the University seats. He was just over 21 years old and wrote enthusiastically to his mother that it was 'a seat of all others the most desirable, as being free from expense, perfectly independent and I think in every respect extremely honourable' (Turner,

p. 13). The only disadvantage was that Pitt, despite his long residence in Cambridge, had very little support. He came bottom of the poll, in fifth place with less than 14 per cent of the votes. In order to secure election at such an early stage, it would be necessary, he concluded, to surrender some of the independence he (like his father) so craved. When he was approached by a notorious 'boroughmonger', Sir James Lowther, to take over, with all expenses paid, the representation of Appleby (in Westmorland) – one of his string of 'rotten boroughs', which had become immediately vacant – he accepted with little hesitation. Lowther was an admirer of his father, and as Pitt explained to his mother:

> No Kind of Condition was mentioned, but that if ever Our Lines of Conduct should become opposite, I should give Him an Opportunity of chusing another Person. On such Liberal Terms, I should certainly not hesitate to accept the Proposal, than which Nothing could be in any respect more agreeable. (Ehrman, I, p. 26)

Accordingly, on 8 January 1781, Pitt was returned unopposed at a by-election, without setting foot in the constituency.

The Parliament to which Pitt was elected was divided as much by faction as by party. The historical division between Whigs and Tories had become somewhat blurred during the 20 years that George III had occupied the throne. The long domination of the Whigs throughout the reigns of the first two Georges, which had seen the Tories steadily decline in both numbers and influence, was a thing of the past. The Whigs still saw themselves as the guarantors of the Glorious Revolution of 1688–89, believing in a limited monarchy, the supremacy of Parliament, a vigorous and basically anti-French foreign policy, free trade and relative religious tolerance. Led by an oligarchy of enlightened aristocrats, they tended to be arrogant, self-satisfied and to behave as though they were born to rule. The main Whig factions were led by three peers – the Marquess of Rockingham, the Earl of Shelburne and the Duke of Portland, with Charles James Fox the dominant figure in the House of Commons.

The Tories, representing primarily the gentry, were strong supporters of the royal prerogative and the Church of England, tending to believe in the divine right of monarchs, and were long tainted by suspicions of Jacobitism, though this was less of a factor after the failure of the 1745 uprising of Bonnie Prince Charlie. They were also protectionist, and more isolationist in international affairs, putting their trust in the British Navy to keep the nation out of danger. Their long eviction from power was ended by the accession of George III, who distrusted the Whig oligarchs and was determined to assert his own personal role. In 1762, he installed a Tory, the Earl of Bute, a personal favourite, as Prime Minister, but his ministry lasted for less than a year. There followed four short-lived Whig governments, one of them led by the elder Pitt as Earl of Chatham, but in 1770, George succeeded in imposing a second Tory administration. This was led by Lord North MP, a much more substantial politician than Bute, who was to continue in office for 12 years. When Pitt was elected, his long rule was nearing its end, and he was largely discredited by the disasters of the American War of Independence.

Pitt's entry into Parliament aroused great interest, almost entirely because of his father, to whom he bore much physical resemblance, with his long, thin face and tall body, though at six feet his was longer and more ungainly than his father's. He also made much of his adherence to his father's principles, of putting patriotism before party advantage and of refusing to enrich himself at the public expense. He did not disappoint the high expectations: after hearing his maiden speech, which made a deep impression on the Commons, Edmund Burke declared 'he is not a chip of the old block, he is the old block himself' (Duffy, p. 4).

Like the Elder Pitt, William described himself as an 'independent Whig', and loosely attached himself to the faction led by the Earl of Shelburne, who had been one of the two Secretaries of State in his father's administration. He proved himself an incisive critic of the North government, making a powerful speech, on 12 June 1781, in favour of Fox's motion for peace with the American colonies. A year later, with his reputation as an up-and-coming force already well established, and the government clearly on its last legs, he rashly declared that he would 'never accept a subordinate situation' in any successor administration. North resigned a few days later and the Marquess of Rockingham was summoned to form a new Whig government, in which Shelburne became Home and Fox, Foreign Secretary. Pitt was offered the post of Vice-Treasurer of Ireland, which his father had briefly held in 1746. It carried a salary of £5000, which Pitt could well have done with, but he felt trapped by his earlier words and declined, choosing instead to support the new government from outside. Pitt now moved swiftly to assert himself as an advocate of electoral reform, moving a resolution to appoint a select committee to consider the state of representation, supporting one to shorten the duration of parliaments and a bill to check bribery. Pitt's efforts failed, but he resolved to return to the charge on a more auspicious occasion. Meanwhile, the Rockingham government lasted a mere three months, the Prime Minister dying suddenly of influenza in July 1782. The King chose Shelburne as his successor and Fox, who had quarrelled with him over the peace negotiations with America and France, declined to serve under him and resigned his post, as did Burke, who had been Paymaster-General. Shelburne, the bulk of his Cabinet being peers, was desperate to recruit debating strength in the Commons to counter these two formidable adversaries and offered Pitt the post of Chancellor of the Exchequer. This was not then as senior a post as it subsequently became, as the First Lord of the Treasury (i.e., the Prime Minister) was primarily responsible for financial and fiscal affairs; nevertheless it was a stunning promotion for a man of 23 with no previous ministerial experience.

Pitt's period as Chancellor lasted a mere eight months, during which he made his mark by reorganizing customs duties, cutting out wasteful expenditure and reducing the extent of jobbery in public offices. Meanwhile, Shelburne, a highly intelligent man but lacking in political skills, was having great difficulty in seeking approval for the peace terms which had finally been negotiated with the Americans. An unholy alliance was formed between the followers of Fox, the leader of the 'advanced' Whigs and the main critic of the American War and the Tory Lord North, who had been responsible for its conduct. Shelburne realized that he would have to break up this alliance if his policy and his ministry were to survive. He made overtures to some of North's supporters who, however, insisted that North should be included in the government, which Pitt was not prepared to countenance. Shelburne then sent Pitt to see Fox to invite him to rejoin the government. Fox refused, saying that for a new coalition to be formed, Shelburne would have to resign. Pitt stormed out, saying, 'I did not come here to betray Lord Shelburne', and the two men, who previously had been mutual admirers, were never to meet in private again (Turner, p. 43). The Commons passed a censure motion against the peace terms, by 207 to 190 votes, on 22 February 1783 and Shelburne resigned two days later, much to the King's chagrin. In the final Commons debate, Pitt had made an extraordinarily eloquent appeal on Shelburne's behalf and castigated the opportunism of the two previously sworn enemies, Fox and North, who were clearly putting themselves forward as joint heads of a new government. 'If this ill-omened marriage is not already solemnised', he said, 'I know a just and lawful impediment, and, in the name of public safety, I here forbid the banns' (Duffy, p. 10).

George III made a last desperate effort to avoid giving office to the pair, one of whom was his most inveterate critic, and the other whom he felt had abandoned him by insisting on resigning after the collapse of the British position in North America. He offered the premiership to the 23-year-old Pitt, on Shelburne's recommendation and renewed the offer twice more over the succeeding six months. In Duffy's words, Pitt's 'refusals show a great degree of political maturity and *judgment* in being able to control his ambition'. Pitt was clear in his own mind that he could not hope to form a viable government without being able to command a majority in the House of Commons, and this he could only do with the cooperation, or at least the acquiescence, of Lord North, a man he held 'responsible for the misuse of Crown influence to corrupt Parliament, and for the confrontation with the colonies which had hastened the death of his father, who had exhausted himself in battling against it, and resulted in the loss of America' (Duffy, pp. 12–13).

Eventually, the King had to agree to the Fox–North coalition, which was nominally led by a Whig grandee, the Duke of Portland, with Fox resuming his tenure of the Foreign Office and North becoming Home Secretary. It took office on 2 April 1783, but from the beginning George III was determined to overthrow it at the earliest opportunity, and refused point-blank to sustain the government with the powers of royal patronage normally put at the disposal of his ministers. The King, however, had to act with some circumspection, as the new government enjoyed a comfortable majority in the House of Commons. He seized his opportunity towards the end of the year, when the government introduced legislation to bring the East India Company, which governed territories whose population greatly exceeded that of Britain itself, under closer control. It proposed that the management and patronage of the company should be transferred to parliamentary commissioners appointed for a four-year term. The King and Pitt, thought that Fox would use the extensive patronage of the Company to the government's advantage, to compensate for the royal patronage which it lacked. They also recalled that Fox's father, Henry, the first Lord Holland, had used the patronage at his disposal, when he had been Paymaster-General in 1757–65, to build himself a large fortune, and were determined to block the Bill.

Fox appeared to have little difficulty in getting it through the Commons, and though George was insistent on his right to veto legislation, this power had not been used since the reign of Queen Anne, and it was widely thought to have fallen into desuetude. In a plan cooked up with Lord Thurlow, a former and future Lord Chancellor, in which Pitt was complicit, it was resolved to use the House of Lords to defeat the measure. The King authorized Lord Temple, a cousin of Pitt's, to tell peers that anybody who voted for the India Bill 'was not only not his friend, but would be considered by him as an enemy' (Duffy, p. 18). The Lords duly obliged, defeating the Bill, on 17 December 1783, by 95 votes to 76. Both Pitt and George III had expected the government to resign immediately, but it decided to cling to office, not least because it secured 2–1 majorities in votes in the House of Commons attacking the use of the King's name and those who advised its use in the Lords. The King waited a further day, and then sent messengers at midnight to Portland, Fox and North requiring them to surrender their seals of office. Pitt was appointed First Lord of the Treasury on 19 December, with Lord Thurlow as Lord Chancellor, but few other men of any standing were prepared to associate themselves with a government which had been brought to power in such an underhand way and Pitt was attacked for forming a government of mediocrities. Few people expected it to survive for long and it was quickly dubbed the 'mince pie government', on the assumption that it would not last beyond Christmas. In such inauspicious circumstances began a premiership which was to last for over 17 years (and almost 19 years, in all, including Pitt's second ministry in 1804–06). Pitt was aged 24 years, 205 days – almost nine years younger than any other British Prime Minister – his closest rival, the third Duke of Grafton, being just over 33 on his appointment in 1768.

Pitt endured a scary few months, being repeatedly defeated in votes in the House of Commons, but – to Fox's exasperation – refused to resign, secure in the knowledge that he retained the King's confidence. During this period, however, his personal stock rose sharply, due to the skill with which he defended himself in parliamentary debates. The burden on him was considerable, as his entire cabinet was made up of peers, and he had to act as the government's spokesman on every conceivable issue. Pitt's reputation also grew outside Parliament, partly because of his forbearance in declining to appoint himself to a sinecure office, the Clerkship of the Pells, worth £3000 a year, which was in the Prime Minister's gift. He also gained from public revulsion at an attack on his carriage by a Foxite mob on his return from receiving the Freedom of the City of London. Salvation came with the dissolution of Parliament in March 1784 – three-and-a-half years before the end of its term. Pitt knew that the odds were overwhelming that he would emerge with a comfortable majority from the election. He had already made deals with 'borough mongers', and the full weight of royal patronage (and Treasury money) was at his disposal. Indeed, throughout the eighteenth century, no sitting government was ever to lose an election. It was the King who gave ministers their marching orders, not the electors, who were few in number and largely influenced by a relatively small number of aristocratic landowners. The general election of 1784 was no exception: no detailed breakdown of the results has survived, but it was generally estimated that the government secured a majority of around 120 in a House of 558. The opposition was divided between about 130 MPs committed to Fox and 70 to North, who had been the main loser in the election and whose support subsequently fell away (Derry, p. 52). For Pitt, the election brought another cause for satisfaction: he was able to exchange his 'pocket' borough of Appleby for his first love – Cambridge University – where this time he came top of the poll and was easily elected, retaining the seat for the rest of his life.

With his solid parliamentary majority and the renewed support of the King, Pitt no longer seemed vulnerable and he settled in for a long innings in Downing Street, though nobody foresaw that it would prove quite as long as it did. His cabinet was still devoid of parliamentary talent and he himself chose to retain the office of Chancellor of the Exchequer throughout his premiership, but he was able to bring along two close associates of high ability, who were eventually to fill the most senior posts. These were his cousin, William Grenville, son of a former Prime Minister, who was to rise successively to Home and Foreign Secretary and Henry Dundas, a formidable political 'fixer' from Scotland, who became his chief 'trouble shooter', and was also to be Home Secretary and later Secretary for War and the Colonies. His main handicap was that the King insisted on choosing the ministers himself, and ruled that Lord Thurlow, a man whom Pitt found highly uncongenial and disloyal, should continue as Lord Chancellor. Thurlow's relationship to George III was much closer and warmer than his own, which Pitt resented but was unable to do anything about.

Across the floor of the House of Commons, he had regularly to face Fox, now the undisputed leader of the Whigs, and his only rival and perhaps superior, as a parliamentary orator. Always credited by history with both his forenames, he was invariably known as Charles or Charley during his lifetime. Ten years older than Pitt and himself the second son of a distinguished political father, Fox was also known for his precocity, having first been elected to Parliament at the age of 19. This was two years below the legal limit, but in the less rule-bound ways of the eighteenth century, nobody objected when he took his seat. His own political career was to be blighted by Pitt's rise to power and by George III's unrelenting hostility. He was effectively to be the leader of the opposition (though the title did not then exist) for 23 years, and his sole periods in Cabinet office were three stints as Foreign Secretary, each lasting only a few months, in 1782, 1783 and 1806. On more than one occasion, Pitt sought to include Fox in his government but Fox demanded that they should both serve under a nominal superior, such as Portland, while Pitt invariably insisted on retaining the premiership. The two leaders' long rivalry prefigured that of Gladstone and Disraeli nearly a century later and they were an equally contrasting pair, both in appearance and character. Pitt was tall, stiff and withdrawn; Fox fat, warm and gregarious. Pitt was cautious, calculating and conservative; Fox radical, impulsive, untidy. Pitt's political judgment was excellent, and he never (except on Ireland much later in his career) attempted to push hard for policies that had little chance of being acceptable to Parliament or – more importantly in his eyes – the King. Fox's *judgment* was poor, and though he was capable of wild opportunism, consistently pursued policies calculated to alienate the King. Fox was dissolute – a gambler and womanizer, who eventually contracted a happy marriage with a former courtesan, Elizabeth Armistead. Pitt was highly disciplined, had little apparent interest in women, and has – on the basis of rather slender evidence – become something of a gay icon (see p. 239, below). Nearly everybody loved 'Charley', whose charm was a by-word. Except for a few bosom friends, with whom he was able to unbend in moments of alcoholic revelry, Pitt was respected but not greatly liked. They had some causes in common – electoral reform and the abolition of the slave trade – and in other circumstances their complementary talents could have drawn them together and made a formidable team. But raw ambition drove them apart in 1782–84 and they were never to be reconciled. Indeed, Pitt revealed a vindictive streak in his character, following his sweeping victory in the 1784 election, when he persisted for several months in an attempt to get Fox unseated from his Westminster constituency on – by eighteenth century standards – relatively minor evidence of irregularities. He was only finally dissuaded from this course when he was defeated on the issue by a House of Commons vote. (It was by no means unusual for the government to lose parliamentary votes, at a time of weak or non-existent party discipline, and when those in general support of the government, or even cabinet ministers, felt no particular obligation to deliver their votes except on major issues.)

Pitt's over-riding objective during his first years in office was to restore national confidence, and the declining economy, after the setbacks and disasters of the American War. His purpose was to stimulate trade – particularly with Europe to offset the loss of North American markets (which was to prove only temporary) – to improve the public finances and to usher in a period of political stability. On any reckoning, he was largely successful in his endeavours and within a relatively short time, not only King George but a large proportion of the 'political' class, came to view him as the indispensable head of government. One of Pitt's principal tools was his annual budgets but he did not make a name for himself, at least in his earlier years, as a tax pioneer. He relied on traditional forms of taxation and did not noticeably expand the tax base, concentrating as Ehrman convincingly argues (Ehrman, Vol. I, pp. 250–6) primarily on increasing the yield from existing taxes, by improving methods of collection and by cracking down more effectively on smuggling. His most important innovation, in 1786, was to establish a sinking fund, with the objective of eventually paying off the national debt, which had doubled to around £213 million as a consequence of the American War. Pitt's proposal was well received, and steady progress was to be made in reducing the debt over the first half dozen years, but the outbreak of war with France in 1793 meant that it rapidly resumed its upward trend. Pitt was also active in cutting out wasteful expenditure, and, wherever possible, reducing or terminating the award of pensions and sinecures, though he was not above using such means for *political* purposes, including to strengthen the government's position in the House of Lords.

Pitt was also successful in his efforts to promote trade, though he suffered a setback in 1785, when he was forced to withdraw proposals for free trade between England and Ireland. He had more success with a commercial treaty, negotiated with France, in 1786, which led to a sharp increase in trade between the two traditional enemies. Pitt was to return to his earlier campaign for electoral reform, introducing a bill, in April 1785, which provided for a very modest extension of the franchise in county constituencies, while granting one million pounds to compensate the electors of 36 rotten boroughs which were to be disfranchised, while the 72 seats thus made available were to be transferred to London, Westminster and the more populous counties. Neither the King nor several of his ministerial colleagues approved of the measure, and nor did Lord North and his followers, though Fox supported the Bill. The King did not try to prevent its introduction, but insisted that it should be introduced in Pitt's personal capacity rather than as a government measure. Pitt made a powerful speech seeking leave to introduce the Bill, but it was defeated by 248 to 174 votes. A disappointed Pitt decided to cut his losses, and never again raised the issue, indeed opposing reform bills introduced by private members on three occasions in the 1790s and 1800s. So parliamentary reform had to wait nearly another half century until the 'great' Reform Bill of 1832. Nor did Pitt's enthusiasm for reform extend to support for the repeal of the Test and Corporation Acts. These two measures, dating from the mid-seventeenth century, had the effect of excluding Protestant dissenters (later known as Nonconformists) from membership of municipal corporations or from holding a wide range of public offices or commissions in the army and navy. Although these acts were only enforced in a spasmodic manner, they remained a standing grievance, particularly to the business community, in which many dissenters had gained prominence. Pitt appeared to have no strong views on the subject and consulted the Archbishop of Canterbury, who informed him that only two out of 16 bishops favoured reform (Hague, p. 239). Unwilling to alienate the Church of England, Pitt threw his weight against the proposed repeal, which was duly defeated, in March 1787, by 176 votes to 98. Pitt was a strong supporter of the abolition of the slave trade and encouraged his friend Wilberforce to bring motions before the House of Commons to secure this objective. On one occasion, in April 1792, he made what was regarded as one of the greatest speeches of his career in support of Wilberforce's demand for 'immediate' abolition but the House preferred to adopt an amendment tabled by Dundas, substituting the word 'gradual', which stripped the motion of any practical effect. William Hague describes Pitt's inability to secure the final abolition of the trade as his 'greatest failure'. He writes:

> The sincerity of his opposition to this dreadful trade was all too plain, but so is the fact that he lost the energy, focus and will to pursue the matter to a successful conclusion...The fact that abolition was so speedily secured by Grenville and Fox soon after Pitt's death suggests that he too could have secured it if he had marshalled his forces to do so. (Hague, p. 589)

By the late 1780s, an increasingly frustrated Fox followed the course pursued by earlier opposition leaders in the reigns of George I and George II, by transferring his allegiance to the court of the Prince of Wales, who was at daggers' drawn with his father. More intelligent and much more cultured than the philistine King, the future George IV was far from being an admirable character. Dissolute, vain, extravagantly self-indulgent, lacking in judgment and profoundly untrustworthy, Fox and his fellow Whigs would have been well advised to keep him at arms-length. Instead, Fox and he became bosom companions, and few doubted that the first act of young George if he were to succeed his father would be to dismiss Pitt from power and restore Fox and Portland to their former posts. In 1788 George III was 50 years old, and had already reigned for 28 years. Given the average expectation of life, it was not fanciful to suppose that before long the Prince of Wales would ascend the throne. His – and Fox's – opportunity seemed to have arrived in November 1788, with the Regency crisis, brought on by the onset of George III's first serious attack of porphyria, a little understood hereditary illness, whose symptoms included temporary insanity. The King's principal doctor, Warren, declared that he was incurable and unlikely to live for long. The Whigs, in Fox's absence on holiday in Italy, were persuaded by Richard Sheridan, the Irish playwright and leading Foxite MP, to demand the immediate installation of the Prince as regent. Pitt, sensing the great danger he was in, played for time, insisting that all the relevant precedents should be studied and that an Act of Parliament should be passed setting out the terms of the regency. He also consulted his own former doctor, Anthony Addington, who gave a much more favourable prognosis, saying that he had seen worse cases than the King make a full recovery. Pitt's regency bill sharply curtailed the powers of the regent, in particular, preventing him from granting peerages and making official appointments (except on a temporary basis), and placing the King's person and property wholly in the Queen's hands. Fox, who had hastened back to London, in a poor physical state, stricken with dysentery, then made a crucial blunder. The self-proclaimed 'tribune of the people' declared in the House of Commons that the Prince had an hereditary right to the regency, implying that Parliament had no business in seeking to define the limits. Pitt immediately seized his chance, whispering to his neighbour 'I'll unwhig the gentleman for the rest of his life', and proceeded to point out that this went directly against the long-standing Whig principle of parliamentary sovereignty. Despite, the disloyalty of his Lord Chancellor, Thurlow, who was negotiating behind his back with the Foxites and the Prince, to ensure that he kept his own post in the event of a change of government, Pitt was able to rally his Cabinet and a majority of the House of Commons, who adopted the Bill on 5 February 1789. It then went to the Lords, but further progress was made unnecessary by the King's sudden recovery.

The outcome of the Regency crisis was as great a triumph for Pitt and a disaster for Fox, as the overthrow of the Fox–North coalition in 1783. The King's inveterate hostility to Fox became even greater and his gratitude to Pitt knew few bounds. He sought to make him a Knight of the Garter, which Pitt declined, suggesting instead that the honour went to his elder brother, the second Earl of Chatham, who was currently First Lord of the Admiralty. A couple of years later, he finally overcame Pitt's reluctance to accept a sinecure office, appointing him as Warden of the Cinque ports, worth £3000 a year, and with a fine residence, Walmer Castle, to go with it. Pitt's stout defence of the King's position, against the intrigues of his eldest son, also increased his own standing with the public.

Unlike his two Hanoverian predecessors, who were disliked as foreigners who made little effort to endear themselves to their new countrymen, George III was widely popular, despite his authoritarian tendencies. He looked and behaved like an English country squire, and fully shared the tastes and prejudices of a majority of his subjects.

Pitt's advantage over Fox was consolidated by the general election of 1790, where his supporters improved even further on their major success in 1784, with 340 seats going to the government, 183 to the opposition and 35 'others' (Turner, p. 118). Meanwhile, Pitt had begun to make his mark on the international stage, reducing his ineffectual Foreign Secretary, the Marquis of Carmarthen (later, Duke of Leeds) to little more than a cipher. He chanced his arm by ordering mobilization in 1787, when France threatened to intervene in the Netherlands on the side of the Republicans in their struggle for power with the *Stadhouder*, the Prince of Orange. Together with the King of Prussia, who was the Prince's brother-in-law, he threatened a military riposte, and Prussian troops actually crossed the Dutch border, whereupon the Republicans' resistance collapsed. The French then hastily backed down, and Pitt was able to claim a triumph without firing a shot. Three years later, he was able to repeat the trick with Britain's other traditional enemy – Spain – over the Nootka Sound dispute. This concerned the establishment of a British trading post on Vancouver Island, in territory long claimed by Spain. The Spanish reacted by stopping a British ship and arresting the traders, while demanding that the British should recognize Spanish sovereignty over the entire west coasts of the American continents. The British cabinet prepared for war, and called on Spain to compensate the arrested traders. Spain proved obdurate until it transpired that its long-time ally and fellow Bourbon kingdom, France, distracted by the early phases of the Revolution, was in no mood to go to war on its behalf. It then smartly climbed down, agreed to compensate the traders and conceded that British subjects could enter areas not actually settled by the Spanish and fish in the Pacific.

Pitt had followed up his Dutch success by concluding a 'Triple Alliance' between Britain, Holland and Prussia, and now aspired to expand this into a general 'Concert of Europe', whose purpose would be the peaceful settlement of disputes and the confirmation of European boundaries as they had existed in 1787. In particular, he aimed to associate Austria and Russia with the project, which would leave France isolated if it declined to participate. This grand design, which prefigured the system imposed after the Congress of Vienna in 1815, collapsed at its first test, in 1791, when Catherine the Great of Russia proclaimed the annexation of the fortress of Ochakov (Odessa), which had been captured during a war with Turkey. Britain and Prussia sent an ultimatum to Catherine that she should return it to the Turks, and Pitt prepared to send British fleets to the Black and Baltic seas to add to the pressure. But the Austrians declined to join in and Catherine showed herself to be unexpectedly obdurate.

Pitt also faced strong parliamentary and cabinet opposition and – deeply humiliated – sent a message to the Prussians to withdraw the ultimatum, telling Joseph Ewart, the British Ambassador to Berlin, 'with tears in his eyes, that it was the greatest mortification he had ever experienced' (Ehrman, II, p. 24). His projected 'Concert' was dead and two years later he looked on helplessly as Russia, Prussia and Austria proceeded to the second of their three partitions of Poland. The Duke of Leeds resigned as Foreign Secretary, in protest against his handling of the Ochakov affair, which caused Pitt no anguish, as it enabled him to promote his cousin, and close associate, William Grenville, in his place.

The storming of the Bastille on 14 July 1789 marked a watershed in Pitt's long premiership. Before then he had been a highly successful peacetime Prime Minister and a moderate reformer. Later he was to be a markedly less successful war leader and what might be most accurately described as a moderate reactionary (if that is not a contradiction in terms), though it was to be nearly another four years before Britain was actually at war with France. Initially, Pitt welcomed the early stages of the French Revolution, as did the great majority of Britain's political class. It came in the midst of the hundredth anniversary celebrations of the 'Glorious Revolution' of 1688–89, and the general feeling was that France was at last catching up with Britain and would develop into a constitutional monarchy with enhanced liberties for its citizens. Even as disorders spread, Pitt remained sanguine, as he believed that this would weaken France as a great power, which would be to the British advantage. His attitude hardened after the September massacres of 1792 and the execution of Louis XVI the following January, yet he still resisted pressure to join Austria and Prussia in their war against France. Eventually, it was France which declared war, in April 1793, after Britain had objected to its invasion of Holland.

Meanwhile, serious splits developed within the opposition. Fox had welcomed the Revolution unequivocally, exclaiming after the fall of the Bastille, 'How much the greatest event it is that ever happened in the world!, and how much the best!'. Many of his younger supporters, including a future reformist Prime Minister, Charles Grey, were inspired to seek to revive the movement for parliamentary reform, which was largely dormant since the failure of Pitt's Bill in 1785. They founded a body called Friends of the People, and argued for much more thoroughgoing changes, including Household suffrage. This, however, fell well behind the demands of more rank-and-file bodies, such as the London Correspondence Society, led by a shoemaker, Thomas Hardy. These included universal male suffrage, the abolition of the property qualification for MPs, equal electoral districts, the payment of MPs, annual parliaments and the secret ballot. These demands horrified the more conservative Whigs, including Portland, who regarded their advocates as no better than 'Jacobins', and feared for the defence of their own property. They were even more appalled by the publication, in 1791, of Thomas Paine's *Rights of Man*. The earliest and most painful defector from Fox was Edmund Burke, formerly his closest friend and collaborator. Showing extraordinary prescience, Burke, at an early date, foresaw all the more nefarious consequences of the Revolution – the growth of fanaticism, the descent into chaos and civil war, the destruction of liberty and the military adventurism, which would plunge Europe into a generation of war. He spelled out his fears in his pamphlet, *Reflections on the Revolution in France*, published in November 1790, and advocated immediate action to forestall them. Pitt himself was by no means convinced and for more than another two years maintained a policy of strict neutrality towards the events in France.

Once war was joined, however, in 1793, he became fully committed to conducting it to a successful conclusion. This did not, in his view, necessarily involve the restoration of the monarchy, which most of his allies wished to proclaim as a war aim, but it did mean that France should cease to be a constant threat to the security of its neighbours. Pitt was emphatic that only he should lead the government but was anxious to strengthen its position by recruiting heavyweight figures from the opposition who were prepared to sever their connections with Fox. An opportunity had already arisen, in January 1793, when Thurlow had finally exhausted Pitt's – and the King's patience – by attacking the government's fiscal policies in the House of Lords. Pitt successfully demanded his resignation and was able to replace him as Lord Chancellor by the Whigs' leading lawyer, Lord Loughborough. Detailed negotiations then followed with Portland and other leading Whigs, but they were not yet already to abandon Fox. Eighteen months later, however, in July 1794, Pitt pulled off a considerable coup, when Portland, who became Home Secretary, and four of his leading colleagues, joined the cabinet, bringing a large parliamentary following with them. The Portlandites drove a hard bargain: 'The alliance could not have been arranged without Pitt's generous offer of five places in the cabinet, five peerages and one promotion in the peerage, a pension for Burke, two offices in the royal household, the lord lieutenancy of Middlesex and the promise of the lord lieutenancy of Ireland' (Turner, p. 118). Some of Pitt's supporters criticized him for ceding too much, fearing that he would lose control over his own cabinet, 6 of whose 13 members were now his former political opponents. But Pitt was careful to keep the main portfolios connected to the war effort in the hands of his own loyalists, and the effect of the whole exercise was to hamstring the opposition. Portland was able to bring 62 MPs over to the government's side, 'leaving the Foxites in the Commons as a small and isolated party of about fifty-five members' (Turner, p. 132). In any event, the cabinet, as a whole, seldom played a significant role in determining war policy. Pitt was in the habit of settling decisions with his two closest collaborators – Grenville, the Foreign Secretary, and Dundas, War Secretary, and provided these three were of one mind there was little chance of their being successfully challenged. The only other person of great influence was the King, who liked to be consulted and was not bashful about making his own suggestions. On some occasions he was to over-rule Pitt, but most of the time the Prime Minister got his own way.

Pitt's reputation as a reformer did not long survive the onset of war. Backed by his new Home Secretary, Portland, he introduced a series of repressive measures which, while ostensibly aimed at would-be violent supporters of the French Revolution, were, in practice, employed against the essentially peaceful advocates of electoral reform, such as the leaders of the London Correspondence Society, who were actually arraigned in a treason trial which carried the threat of the death sentence. Fortunately, a London jury had the good sense to acquit them, though in Edinburgh one man was hanged on similar charges, and others imprisoned or sent to Botany Bay. Pitt himself took part in the cross-examination of several of those arrested, but was highly embarrassed when he was subpoenaed to appear as a witness in the trial of the noted radical, John Horne Tooke. Here he was forced to admit the similarity between the views attributed to Tooke and his own advocacy ten years earlier. Pitt's measures, which included the suspension of *habeus corpus* for several periods, were bitterly opposed in the Commons by Fox and his depleted band of supporters, but were carried by large majorities. Fox denounced them as a concerted attack on liberty, but the historian John Derry attempted to put them in perspective when he wrote:

> But Pitt and Portland did not preside over anything like a reign of terror. Something like a total of 200 prosecutions over a period of ten years hardly merits such a description. Many of the cases ended in acquittal or the charges being dropped and the proceedings discontinued. The pressure of convention and the weight of public opinion achieved more in damping down radicalism than either the Seditious Meetings Act or the Treasonable Practices Act. With the ascendancy of loyalism and the popular identification of radicalism with Jacobinism, radicals suffered more from the prejudices of the community than from the force of law. (Derry, p. 97)

Pitt's war strategy closely paralleled that of his father during the Seven Years War, utilizing Britain's naval supremacy to facilitate attacks on France's overseas possessions, while subsidizing European allies to bear the brunt of military operations on the continent. Consistently, however, he failed to match the achievements of the elder Pitt. While most of the French possessions in the Caribbean were over-run, British troops had great difficulty in consolidating their conquests and were decimated by tropical diseases. They had more success in their operations against France's allies, Spain and Holland, conquering Trinidad from the former and the Cape Colony and Ceylon (Sri Lanka) from the latter. On the continent, however, direct British military operations – against Toulon, the Vendée (in support of French royalists) and Flanders – all ended in disaster. Nor did Britain's allies – either in the First coalition (1792–97), or the Second (1798–1801), fare any better. Whereas his father had had the good fortune to ally himself with a military genius – Frederick the Great – none of the Younger Pitt's more numerous allies revealed conspicuous fighting qualities, their armies being regularly rolled over by French generals, from Carnot to Bonaparte. They then hastened to make peace, often on humiliating terms, leaving the British to fight on alone. The British troops, also, were poorly led, notably by Frederick, Duke of York, the favourite son of George III, whose ineffectiveness as commander during the Flanders campaign has been immortalized in the famous song, *The Grand Old Duke of York*. Virtually the only successes Pitt had to celebrate were periodic victories by the Navy, a deserved recompense for the assiduity he had shown in modernizing and expanding the fleet throughout the 1780s.

Pitt was to prove persistently optimistic in his conduct of the war but failed – despite his Herculean labours – to pursue a consistent path, while his organization of public business was chaotic. Nor did his close personal alliance with Grenville and Dundas remain untroubled. The former was critical of his readiness to strike at France at any time and at any place, whenever an opportunity arose, believing that the available forces should be concentrated and only used in carefully planned and well-resourced campaigns which offered a good prospect of success. He also became exasperated at Pitt's continuance in paying subsidies to Prussia at a time when it was proving to be an inactive and unreliable ally, much more interested in carving up Poland, in successive partitions, with Austria and Russia, than in fighting against the French. Dundas proved an efficient organizer but was inclined to defeatism and favoured an essentially defensive policy, giving priority to forestalling the probably exaggerated fears of a French invasion. Pitt had never anticipated a prolonged war, believing that the French economy would quickly collapse under the strain and was distressed to find that it was the British economy which appeared to suffer most, with recurrent food shortages, labour unrest and the national debt reaching unprecedented heights. Periodically he was tempted to seek a negotiated peace but George III was reluctant to agree. On two occasions, however, in 1796 and 1797, serious talks began, with Pitt essentially offering a deal on the basis of the return of the conquered French colonies in exchange for a withdrawal from the Low Countries. This was not sufficient bait to attract even the more moderate members of the *Directoire*, which replaced the terror regime in 1795. Pitt's wisdom in sticking to these conditions may be questioned. Certainly, Fox and Pitt's friend Wilberforce, firmly believed that a continuation of the war was not in Britain's interest and that a perfectly reasonable settlement could have been reached if the British negotiators had been more flexible. It could also be argued that the continuation of the war led to what Britain most feared – a permanently aggressive and expansionist France, which was assured by the rise to power of Napoleon, a direct result of his victories in the War of the Second Coalition, which Pitt organized after 1798.

Pitt wore himself out and largely destroyed his health through his wartime exertions, becoming more and more dependent on alcohol. While attempting to supervise every detail of the war effort, he was also single-handedly running the Treasury, having retained his post as Chancellor of the Exchequer throughout his premiership. He found it increasingly difficult to finance the war, balancing tax increases with very extensive borrowing, but he continued to show tenacity and ingenuity in introducing his annual budgets. One of these, in 1798, was to introduce Income Tax for the first time. Intended only as a temporary measure, and initially raising far less than he had envisaged, it was eventually to become the principal resource on which subsequent Chancellors of the Exchequer have depended to fill the coffers of the state. He continued to carry a heavy load as Leader of the House of Commons, all his senior ministers, with the exception of Henry Dundas, being in the Lords, which meant that he had continually to speak for the government on a very wide range of subjects.

He was an increasingly isolated figure. Both his sisters, to whom he was devoted, had died in childbirth, his younger brother, James, a naval captain, had perished at sea, and his brother-in-law, Edward Eliot, who became his closest companion, died in 1791. Devoted associates of his youth, such as William Wilberforce, gradually drifted away, and he found it difficult to cultivate new friends. Although he remained throughout his career a masterly presence in the House of Commons, he did not use it as a means to build up a circle of close personal supporters. He was the object of immense respect, but little warmth, among his fellow MPs. A much-quoted account by the great parliamentary diarist, Sir Nathaniel Wraxall, describing his first appearance in the House as Prime Minister, is revelatory of the general disdain with which he treated them:

> From the instant that Pitt entered the doorway, he advanced up the floor with a quick and firm step, his head erect and thrown back, looking neither to the right nor the left, not favouring with a nod or a glance any of the individuals seated on either side, among whom many who possessed £5,000 a year would have been gratified even by so slight a mark of attention. It was not thus that Lord North or Fox treated Parliament.

With a few of his ministers he enjoyed greater intimacy, particularly Henry Dundas, who became his main drinking companion and whose home, close to his own house at Holwood in Kent, he often visited. Also nearby lived Lord Auckland, the former William Eden, a distinguished former ambassador, who had negotiated Pitt's commercial treaty with France. Pitt spent much time at his home in the autumn of 1796, relaxing with Auckland and his extensive family, not least his eldest daughter, the attractive 19-year-old Lady Eleanor Eden. Pitt made no declaration but apparently Eleanor and both her parents assumed he was working up to a proposal of marriage, a prospect which gave them enormous pleasure. Rumours began to spread and even reached the newspapers, and in January 1797 Pitt felt constrained to send an embarrassed letter to Auckland, disclaiming any such intention, and saying that, however, desirable such a union would be, there were 'decisive and insurmountable' obstacles. Auckland apparently concluded that these were of a temporary and financial nature and wrote back suggesting that Pitt should come round 'and talk about the whole at leisure and again and again' (Hague, p. 391). Pitt was therefore forced to write a further and less circumspect letter, making it brutally clear that his mind was 'unalterably' fixed.

This episode, which caused a considerable stir, is discussed in detail by Pitt's most exhaustive biographer, John Ehrman and more recently by former Tory leader William Hague. Both are disinclined to believe that Pitt's main motivation in backing off was the chaotic state of his financial situation (over which he exercised none of the conscientious care which he lavished on the nation's finances as First Lord of the Treasury), though this could have been a subordinate factor. Both conclude that, when it came down to it, Pitt simply could not face the prospect of marriage, either with Eleanor or any other woman, given his apparent lack of carnal interest in the opposite sex. Ehrman does not believe that he was actively homosexual. 'If he had any homosexual "potential" it would seem to have been very mild', he writes, 'and it is much more likely that he had no strong sexual inclinations at all' (Ehrman, I, p. 109). Ehrman does, however, add that 'If there was a homosexual relationship in Pitt's life, Canning might appear the most obvious candidate' (Ehrman, III, p. 94). The future Foreign Secretary, and briefly Prime Minister, was one of a number of young junior ministers – among them Castlereagh, Huskisson. Perceval and the future Lord Liverpool – with whom Pitt enjoyed friendly and relaxed relations, but Canning was clearly his favourite and he was reported to be in a 'trance' when he attended his young protégé's wedding. That there was mutual affection is clear, but there is only the slightest evidence that it took a physical form. Ehrman quotes Pitt as having told his niece, Lady Hester Stanhope, many years later, that he must stay 'a single man for my King and country's sake'. 'He stood apart', he concludes, 'untouched as a priest stands untouched at the centre of his avocations; a priest in this instance of politics and government!' (Ehrman, III, p. 97).

Lonely, in failing health, depressed by the continued lack of success in the war, as the eighteenth century drew to its end, Pitt began to show occasional signs of losing his grip. In May 1798, he provoked a duel with an opposition MP, George Tierney, after carelessly impugning his patriotism in a parliamentary exchange. It took place on Putney Heath, both men fired twice, but neither was injured, Pitt firing his second shot into the air. More seriously for his survival as Prime Minister, he failed to keep George III regularly informed of the government's intentions. This had fatal consequences in 1801, when Pitt proposed to his Cabinet colleagues that legislation should be brought in to enable Catholics to vote in parliamentary elections and to be appointed to public office. Intended as a *quid pro quo* for the Union of the British and Irish Parliaments, which had been approved the previous year (though only after extensive bribery of Irish MPs to vote their own chamber out of existence), the proposal fell foul of several of Pitt's colleagues, notably the Lord Chancellor, Lord Loughborough. He hastened to inform the King of what was proposed and George angrily declared that he could not approve the measure which was a breach of his Coronation oath to defend the Protestant religion. Pitt feeling himself morally bound to proceed with the legislation, in the light of informal assurances which had been given to Irish Catholics, promptly offered his resignation to the King. Perhaps he hoped that George would not accept it and would acquiesce in Catholic emancipation in order to keep the services of the man who had loyally served him for 17 years. But George had grown tired of Pitt's growing independence, and – crucially – now had an acceptable candidate for the premiership in view and was no longer fearful of opening the way to Fox, whose influence in Parliament had sharply declined since the defection from him of the Portland Whigs. He turned to Henry Addington, the popular Speaker of the House of Commons and a friend of Pitt's, many of whose ministers (but not Grenville or Dundas) were willing to serve under him. Pitt himself was happy to lend his support to Addington, whom he probably thought was in a better position than himself to seek a peace treaty with France, which he now believed to be necessary.

Addington duly succeeded in negotiating the Peace of Amiens, within a year of assuming the premiership. Described by Canning as 'the peace everybody was glad of and nobody was proud of' (Derry, p. 121), it broke down after 14 months, after both sides had breached its terms, Napoleon by invading Switzerland and the British by refusing to evacuate their troops from Malta. War resumed in May 1803, and Addington quickly revealed himself as a less than inspiring war leader. Agitation soon arose for the return of Pitt, celebrated in a song composed by Canning as 'The Pilot that weathered the Storm', and Addington twice attempted to recruit him to his government. Pitt made it clear, however, that he would come back only as Prime Minister, and in May 1804, Addington, bowing to the inevitable, tended his resignation. George welcomed Pitt back with a clear conscience, his new Prime Minister having promised him that he would not raise the subject of Catholic emancipation again during the King's lifetime.

The government which Pitt formed, in May 1804, was not the one he intended. He had wanted to form a 'grand coalition', uniting all the significant parliamentary factions in a patriotic government pledged to resist the threat of a French invasion which, with Napoleon massing his forces outside Boulogne, seemed a much more serious threat than at any time since 1793. In particular, he wished to include Fox and his supporters, as well as those of his cousin, Grenville, from whom he had become estranged, partly because of the pledge he had given the king over Catholic emancipation, and who, together with Fox, had led the opposition to the Addington ministry. The King was perfectly prepared to accept Grenville in the government, but drew the line at Fox, whereupon Grenville himself refused to participate. The result was that Pitt's government was largely composed of Addington's ministers, plus a few of his own strong supporters, notably George Canning. Dundas, who had been ennobled as Viscount Melville, returned as First Lord of the Admiralty, but was soon forced to resign when he, by the casting vote of the Speaker, was impeached for alleged malversation of funds during his earlier service as Treasurer of the Navy. Tears were reported to have rolled down Pitt's cheeks 'in one of the rare occasions on which he lost control of his feelings in public...at the destruction of his old and loyal colleague' (Derry, p. 131). Melville was ultimately acquitted, but his removal was a heavy blow to Pitt, an exhausted, seriously ill and depressed man, who showed little of the resilience of 20 years earlier, when he had formed his first administration.

With infinite difficulty, Pitt now managed to construct the Third Coalition, luring Austria and Russia to put large armies into the field, with Prussia also limbering up. In October 1805, Nelson's great victory at Trafalgar, destroying the cream of the French and Spanish fleets and removing the threat of invasion, restored Pitt's spirits and his customary over-optimism, only for these to be smashed by Napoleon's comprehensive defeats of the Austrians and Russians at Ulm and Austerlitz. When news of Austerlitz reached Pitt, in December 1805, he pointed to a map of Europe and said: 'Roll up that map; it will not be needed these ten years', a prescient estimate of how long it would take before Napoleon's final defeat at Waterloo. A month later, on 23 January 1806, Pitt was dead. The cause was long suspected to be cancer, but, according to Hague, who consulted expert medical opinion, the most probable cause was a peptic ulcer. 'Two hundred years later he would have been cured in a few days by therapy with antibiotic and acid-reducing drugs. In 1806, there was nothing that could be done for him' (Hague, p. 577).

The Younger Pitt was a new kind of Prime Minister, compared to whom the great majority of his predecessors were amateur dilettantes. No premier before, and few since, has dedicated his life so completely to his calling, working exceptionally long hours, suppressing most of his other interests and possible sources of pleasure, and establishing such a command over the political scene. He was able to expand the informal, if not the formal powers of the premiership, establishing his authority, at least to a limited extent, over other departments than the Treasury, which was the only one where the writ of previous premiers had actually run, though most of them had had considerable influence over foreign policy and defence issues. Partly because he had to deal with an exceptionally opinionated and stubborn monarch, whom he was reluctant to challenge directly, Pitt was never able to establish his own right to appoint, shift or dismiss ministers, nor to be accepted as the only minister to have direct access to the King and the sole right to advise him. Nevertheless, the fact that he was known to seek these objectives made it easier for his successors to pursue them from more pliable monarchs, though it was not until the end of the reign of Queen Victoria that these were unequivocally conceded.

Though not particularly efficient in his own working methods, being notoriously unwilling to reply to letters and tending to postpone decisions on routine matters until they reached crisis point, he was concerned to improve the overall performance of the administration and was always on the lookout for improvements, if not fundamental reforms, to be introduced. He was always exceptionally cautious, if not conservative, in constitutional matters, and became more so as he grew older, tending to conform to George III's own view that the British constitution, as defined by the legacy of the Glorious Revolution, was a perfect instrument and should not be tampered with. Pitt was singularly concerned about his own reputation, wishing to be seen as a selfless public servant, always putting the national interest above any narrow party or factional interest and utterly incorrupt in all his dealings. These principles he claimed to have inherited from his father and he could certainly be said to have followed them exceptionally closely, even to the extent of leaving behind him massive debts – largely caused through his being systematically swindled by servants and tradesmen – which had, like his father's, to be posthumously redeemed by a vote of the House of Commons. He was a far more successful politician than his father, and much better at handling his relations with George III than the Elder Pitt had been with either him or George II. Pitt was not a party man, and never called himself a Tory, though history has so assigned him and the modern Conservative Party has recognized him as one of its founding fathers. He could fairly lay claim, nearly 200 years before Harold Wilson, to the title of the Great Pragmatist and was the first Prime Minister who actively sought to mould public opinion to reinforce his position in Parliament and with the Court.

He was perhaps a less great man than his father, and infinitely less capable as a war leader. Indeed, one modern historian, A.J.P. Taylor, has argued that it was wrongheaded of Pitt to get involved in war in the first place. 'What was the war about?', Taylor asked. 'Pitt claimed to be fighting for the liberties of Europe. What he was fighting for was the liberties of princes and for the aristocracy. The decision to go to war with revolutionary France in 1793 was a catastrophe for free principles' (Taylor, p. 22). This was, of course, the view that Fox took at the time, and it is one of history's great might-have-beens to ponder what would have happened if he, rather than Pitt, had been George III's choice as his Prime Minister.

Works consulted

Ayling, Stanley (1991), *Fox*, London, John Murray.
Derry, John W. (1990), *Politics in the Age of Fox, Pitt and Liverpool*, Basingstoke, Macmillan.
Duffy, Michael (2000), *The Younger Pitt*, London, Longman.
Ehrman, John (1969), *The Younger Pitt: I The Years of Acclaim*, London, Constable.
Ehrman, John (1983), *The Younger Pitt: II The Reluctant Transition*, London, Constable.
Ehrman, John (1996), *The Younger Pitt: III The Consuming Struggle*, London, Constable.
Hague, William (2004), *William Pitt the Younger*, London, HarperCollins.
O'Gorman, Frank (1997), *The Long Eighteenth Century*, London, Arnold.
Oxford Dictionary of National Biography, London, 2004, Oxford University Press.
Taylor, A.J.P. (2000), *British Prime Ministers and Other Essays*, London, Penguin.
Turner, Michael J. (2003), *The Younger Pitt: A Life*, London, Hambledon and London.

Part II
The 19th Century

15

Henry Addington, 1st Viscount Sidmouth – Better Than His Reputation?

Whoever succeeded the Younger Pitt was likely to be regarded as something of an anti-climax, and this was certainly the fate of Henry Addington, whose premiership lasted from March 1801 to May 1804, bridging the period between Pitt's two administrations. The butt of a spiteful jibe by George Canning that 'Pitt is to Addington as London is to Paddington', he was long dismissed as ineffectual, though his reputation was, very belatedly, partially restored by a perceptive biography by Philip Ziegler, appearing only in 1965. This argued that he led his government with some ability, and that his major – and fatal – shortcoming was one of communication.

Addington was the first middle-class Prime Minister. He was descended from a long line of yeoman farmers, whose fortunes had been transformed by his grandfather, who, thanks to two advantageous marriages, was able to educate his son, Anthony, at Winchester and Trinity College, Oxford. Anthony became a physician, specializing in mental illness, and ran a private lunatic asylum next door to his house in Reading. After some years, he took the risky step of transferring his practice to London, becoming a Fellow of the Royal College of Physicians, and eventually acquiring a string of fashionable patrons, of whom the most distinguished was the first Earl of Chatham, the Elder Pitt, to whom he became a family friend as well as physician. Dr Addington was to have six children, of whom the fourth, and the elder son, was Henry, born 30 May 1757. This was two years before the birth of the Younger Pitt, whom he got to know as a child, and to whom, at the age of 17, Dr Addington prescribed a bottle of port a day in an apparently successful attempt to cure him of gout (see Chapter 1).

Henry, a placid, congenial and moderately intelligent child, was sent to a top-drawer 'prep school' at Cheam, and subsequently followed his father to Winchester and Oxford, where he was enrolled in one of the more scholarly colleges – Brasenose. At Cheam and Winchester, he was regarded as a model pupil, but – according to Ziegler – had the misfortune to fall at Winchester under the influence of a fanatically narrow-minded and reactionary tutor, the

Reverend George Huntingford, whom he was to reward with the Bishopric of Gloucester when he became Prime Minister. Huntingford quite possibly had homo-erotic feelings for the young Henry, but if so was apparently able to suppress them: it was Henry's mind rather than his body which was corrupted by the association. Friendly by nature, Henry's main ambition in life was to be liked by his fellows, and in this he was largely successful. He made close friends at both his schools, and was later to include several of them in his government, while at Oxford much of his time was taken up by what would now be called networking. In particular, he was able to win the friendship of two of the grandest young men in the University – William Grenville, himself the son of a Prime Minister and first cousin to William Pitt, and Lord Mornington, later Marquess Wellesley, whose younger brother, Arthur, was to become the Duke of Wellington.

Addington graduated in February 1778, but stayed on at Oxford for another year, largely for social reasons, only establishing himself in London, to read for the bar, in the autumn of 1780. In the meantime, he had spent much of the summer at Devizes, with his wealthy brother-in-law, James Seaton, who was one of the two local MPs. Seaton may already at this time have indicated to Addington that he intended to promote him as his successor for the seat. This duly occurred in 1784, when Addington, a Tory, was returned unopposed for the constituency, which he continued to represent until 1805, when he took a peerage as Viscount Sidmouth. In the meantime, Addington had acquired a wife, Ursula Mary Hammond, the daughter and joint heir of a local Cheam businessman of gentle birth. They married in September 1781, when Henry was 24 and Ursula 21. It was a genuine love match, which had the added attraction that the bride brought an income of £1,000 a year. It proved a happy marriage, which lasted until Ursula's death, in 1811 at the age of 51, and produced four daughters and four sons, one of whom was to die in infancy.

Addington's parliamentary career began very quietly; he made no attempt to speak during his first two sessions, but continued his practice of networking, making a wide circle of friends, mostly among the country gentry. Then, in January 1786, he was asked by Pitt to second the address at the beginning of the parliamentary session, an honour usually reserved for bright, up-and-coming young backbenchers, a description which hardly fitted the rather stodgy, if still youthful, MP for Devizes. He performed the task adequately but without distinction, and the few subsequent speeches he made during his first Parliament did little to suggest that he was destined for higher things. Normally a consistent and uncritical follower of Pitt, he was however – due to the now deeply ingrained conservatism he had first imbibed from the Rev. Hungerford – unable to bring himself to support the very moderate bill for parliamentary reform, which his childhood friend unsuccessfully introduced in April 1785. If Pitt was disappointed by his abstention, he did not hold it against him for long, as four years later he plucked him from obscurity, and proposed him as Speaker of the House of Commons. Pitt was motivated not just by friendship: he wanted a docile supporter of his government in the Chair, and one who was prepared if necessary to use his casting vote on the government's side; no nonsense about choosing an impartial arbiter.

Pitt's choice was widely criticized by MPs who thought a more senior and more distinguished candidate should have been chosen, but Addington was duly elected thanks to the large Pittite majority in the House. Those who opposed his election were in for a pleasant surprise. Addington turned out to be an excellent Speaker, with a good grasp of parliamentary procedure, the patience to endure long hours of tedious debate without losing his good humour and notably fair in his treatment of the Foxite opposition. He soon became popular in all quarters of the House and gained the trust of the great majority of MPs. This did not prevent him being treated with condescension by the more aristocratic Members, who looked down on his humble origins and referred to him, disparagingly, as 'the Doctor'. As Speaker he was expected to do a lot of entertaining, which, as a man of modest means, he was ill equipped to do. The House responded by voting him a salary of £6,000 a year and the provision of an official residence within the parliamentary precincts. Addington became ever closer to Pitt, who got into the habit of dining with him at the Speaker's House, together with his closest ministerial colleagues, William Grenville, Henry Dundas and the Lord Chancellor, Lord Loughborough. Here they discussed the government's problems in a frank and informal manner, and Addington offered sage and commonsense advice, which Pitt clearly appreciated. Such a close association with ministers would be regarded as highly improper for a modern Speaker, but – though it was generally known – it did not appear to affect adversely Addington's growing reputation for fair-mindedness. Nor did his highly conservative views on most political (and religious) issues mean that his mind was closed to the need to make parliamentary procedures more flexible. When the Clerk of the House tried to prevent evidence on the slave trade being presented to a special committee on the grounds that it would break with precedents, he over-ruled him, saying 'It does not follow that because a mode is new it must therefore be improper' (Ziegler, p. 73). Addington further endeared himself with MPs by turning down an offer, in 1793, by Pitt to make him Home Secretary, preferring to continue as Speaker. This was favourably compared to the action of his predecessor, William Grenville, who had abandoned the Speakership after a mere few months in order to accept the same Cabinet post.

Two events, in 1797 and 1798, underline his increasingly warm personal relationship with Pitt. It was to Addington that the Prime Minister chose to confide his difficulties in backtracking from his wooing of Lady Eleanor Eden. A year later, Addington rode out to Putney Heath to observe, from a discreet distance, Pitt's duel with the Foxite MP George Tierney. This was an act of friendship and moral support, but it may also be a sign of a bad conscience that he had not intervened more decisively from the Chair to get Pitt to withdraw the aspersions he had cast on Tierney's patriotism during a parliamentary debate. Then, in 1800, when Pitt's health temporarily broke down, it was to Woodley, Addington's small estate near Reading, that he retired to recuperate (Cookson, p. 304).

It was Addington, too, who, in 1798, when Pitt was at a loss to find additional sources of finance to sustain the war effort, suggested that taxpayers should be invited to make voluntary contributions, in excess of the sums for which they had been assessed. The project was remarkably successful, at least in its first year of operation, when it yielded over £2.8 million, including £20,000 from the King, and £2,000 each from Pitt, Dundas and Loughborough. Addington also subscribed £2,000, just over one-fifth of his total income, saying that 'the strict fifth would have given too much the appearance of minute *calculation*' (Ziegler, p. 79). Altogether, Addington was to serve as Speaker for over 11 years, the longest term since the legendary Arthur Onslow, who served for over 33 years, until 1761, and he succeeded in restoring the dignity and authority to the Chair, which it had lost under Onslow's successors. On Addington's own career, however, it had one malign effect. According to Ziegler,

> Addington's years as Speaker destroyed whatever chance there might have been that he would become a competent parliamentary debater. The freedom from interruption, the invitation to pomposity and prolixity, the need for objectivity which went far to rule out any form of dramatic expression or emotional appeal: all these ensured that his delivery remained pedestrian and his matter so displayed as to appeal neither to the imagination nor the intellect. (Ziegler, pp. 74–5)

This was to prove a severe deficiency when Addington succeeded to the Premiership, and proved incapable of defending his policies effectively in the House of Commons, in marked contrast to his predecessor.

It was in 1797 that the first suggestion was made that Addington should take over the premiership. Pitt, depressed after the failure of peace negotiations, thought of retiring for a while, and installing Addington as a temporary successor, who would keep the seat warm until he was ready to return. He discussed the possibility with George III, who was ready to go along with it, but Pitt's spirits suddenly returned and he decided to labour on. Four years later, when he somewhat impetuously offered his resignation to the King, after he had vetoed Pitt's proposals for Catholic emancipation (see Chapter 1), neither he nor George III considered any other possible person for the premiership. There was, however, a difference in their attitudes. Pitt still saw Addington as only a stand-in; the King, who had tired of Pitt's growing independence and his increasing tendency not to confide in him, now saw Addington (an opponent of Catholic emancipation) as a contender for office in his own right. What is clear, however, is that Pitt genuinely encouraged Addington to accept the King's commission, and called on his friends and supporters to rally to the new government, and that Addington was still in awe of Pitt and was far from wishing to supplant him. He showed a marked reluctance to become Prime Minister, but responded when the King said to him 'Lay your hand upon your heart, and ask yourself where I am to turn for support if *you* do not stand by me'. When Addington finally agreed, the King embraced him, saying 'My dear Addington, you have saved your country' (Zeigler, pp. 93–4).

Despite Pitt's goodwill, several of his closest associates refused to join Addington's government. The most prominent was Grenville, a convinced supporter of Catholic emancipation, who subsequently had a fierce row with Pitt when the latter promised George never to raise the issue again during the King's lifetime. Other devoted Pittites, such as George Canning, were so distressed at their master's fate that they could not bring themselves to serve under Addington, whom they regarded as a usurper. George Rose, who had been Pitt's Secretary to the Treasury for 17 years, was even heard to remark that he would 'as soon assent to the prostitution of his daughter as remain in office' (Ziegler, p. 98). Addington peremptorily dispensed with Loughborough, the Lord Chancellor, whom he rightly regarded as an unscrupulous intriguer, but was distressed when other central figures of Pitt's administration, such as Henry Dundas, Earl Spencer and William Windham, declined to continue in office. Their replacements were, for the most part, a mediocre lot, including several old school friends of Addington's, his brother Hiley, and brother-in-law, Charles Bragge. Among the more able were the new Foreign Secretary, Lord Hawkesbury (later Lord Liverpool) and the Solicitor-General, Spencer Perceval, both future Prime Ministers. The biggest shortcoming of Addington's new government was its dearth of parliamentary orators, which – given the Prime Minister's own deficiency in this department – was to prove a grievous handicap.

Addington's first, and over-riding priority – with which Pitt was in full agreement – was to negotiate a peace treaty with France. The war had reached a total stalemate, with France, now led by Napoleon Bonaparte as First Consul, seemingly unbeatable on the European continent, and Britain, with its naval supremacy, dominant elsewhere, having captured a string of French and Dutch colonies, as well as the Spanish island of Trinidad. The nation was suffering from war weariness and the new Prime Minister could conceive of no possible advantage in continuing hostilities. Yet he had few illusions that a lasting peace was obtainable, given his well-founded suspicions that Napoleon's imperial ambitions were by no means fully satisfied. The country, however, needed a breathing space, in which to recuperate its economy, and which would leave it in a stronger position if, unfortunately, it proved necessary to resume the war at a later date.

After Addington had been in office for almost exactly a year, on 25 March 1802, the Treaty of Amiens was signed, ending war with France, Spain and Holland. The terms which Addington's negotiators had been able to obtain were, perhaps, marginally inferior to those which Pitt had rejected during the earlier abortive negotiations in 1796 and 1797, but in the meantime Britain's continental allies had been decisively defeated in the War of the Second Coalition. In these circumstances, Addington drove as hard a bargain as could realistically be expected. Under the terms agreed, all the conquered French and Dutch colonies were returned, with the exception of Ceylon, while the island of Malta was to be handed back to the Knights of St. John. Britain was to keep Trinidad, while the French were to withdraw from Naples, and relinquish their claim to the Ionian islands. Nobody in London thought the peace terms glorious, but they were grudgingly accepted, while Pitt (who privately regretted the return of the Cape Colony to the Dutch) enthusiastically endorsed them, and they were carried with large majorities in both Houses of Parliament. In the country, as a whole, the response was more positive, and Addington gained greatly in popularity as the man who had finally brought peace after ten dispiriting years of conflict.

Within a month of the signing of the treaty, Addington produced his first peacetime budget, abolishing Pitt's income tax, which had proved highly unpopular and inefficient, and which he believed was no longer justified as the war had come to an end. His proposals also contributed markedly to tidying up the government's finances. Despite the gross nepotism which Addington, untypically, then displayed, in appointing his 16-year-old son, Henry, to the lucrative sinecure of Clerk of the Pells, he retained his popularity, and in July 1802, had no difficulty in maintaining his majority in a general election, without resorting, his biographer reported, 'to the morass of bribery and abuse, blackmail and threats which made up the traditional pattern of a British general election' (Ziegler, p. 160). Addington was also able to strengthen his ministerial team, by bringing back Castlereagh, who had been Irish Secretary under Pitt, while the Whig, George Tierney, who had fought a duel with Pitt four years earlier, was a welcome addition to the government's feeble debating strength in the Commons. Tierney had hoped to bring over other leading Whigs with him, but in the end they decided to remain loyal to their party leader, Charles James Fox, who was now working closely with Grenville in opposition.

Addington's relations with the King could hardly have been better. George much preferred his cordiality to Pitt's icy correctness, and gave many signs of his personal favour, notably assigning his Prime Minister the use of a prestigious residence, White Lodge, in Richmond Park. If peace could only have been maintained, there was every prospect that his 'stop-gap' government could have settled in to a lengthy and moderately successful term of office. Yet relations with France soon began to deteriorate, exacerbated by Napoleon's invasion of Switzerland and Britain's refusal to evacuate Malta under the terms of the Amiens Treaty. In the end, it was a British decision to resume the conflict, in May 1803, and the very unmartial-looking Addington made a complete fool of himself by dressing up in the uniform of the Berkshire militia and going down to the House of Commons to announce the declaration of war in a bombastic statement. From that moment, it became clear, possibly even to Addington, that it was only a matter of when, rather than whether, Pitt would replace him as the wartime leader. Pitt was only too willing to assume the burden, but a certain fastidiousness held him back from plunging the knife into the back of his former protégé. It is a fascinating exercise to trace the gradual development of his relations with Addington and his government, as he slipped almost imperceptibly from warm encouragement to benevolent neutrality to disdainful indifference and, in the final weeks, to active hostility. Right from the beginning, he was urged by his closest followers, notably George Canning, who conducted a poisonous campaign of calumniation against Addington, to deliver the *coup de grace*, but Pitt held back and did his best to restrain the ardour of his supporters. Addington was not lacking in his own loyalists, who were strongly represented on the government backbenches, and included many distinguished men in public life, notably Admiral Lord Nelson. He also possessed his own 'spin-doctor', in his younger brother, Hiley Addington, who was highly successful in manipulating the press, including, in particular, *The Times,* which was always ready to accept articles written anonymously by him, defending his brother and attacking Pitt and his followers.

As Prime Minister, Addington grew in self-confidence, and lost much of his awe for Pitt, though he recognized that his government would be immensely strengthened if he could entice him to join. Even before the war was resumed, he made overtures to Pitt in a series of three meetings in January 1803. Pitt made it clear that he would not be willing to serve under Addington, and a few weeks later Addington proposed that he and Pitt should effectively share power by serving under a figurehead premier, whom, he suggested, might be Pitt's elder brother, the 2nd Earl of Chatham. Pitt again refused, using the occasion to give his own definition of the requisites of the premiership:

There should be an avowed and real minister possessing the chief weight in council and the principal place in the confidence of the King. In that respect there can be no rivality or division of power. That power must rest in the person generally called the First Minister; and that minister ought, he thinks, to be the person at the head of the finances. (Quoted in Hague, p. 505)

Addington then made the extraordinary offer of standing down in favour of Pitt, and accepting a subsidiary position himself in the government, provided his cabinet colleagues agreed. Even this was not good enough for Pitt, who insisted on forming an entirely new government, ejecting most of Addington's supporters and including Grenville and other figures from the opposition. Addington, he suggested, should leave the government altogether, and take on an honorific role, such as Speaker of the House of Lords, a post which, he said, had once existed and could be reconstituted. This was too much for the Addington cabinet to stomach, whereupon Pitt broke off negotiations, saying that he would only return to power at the express request of the King. His personal relations with Addington then sharply deteriorated.

Canning convinced himself, and the bulk of Pitt's supporters, that, as soon as war was declared, an overwhelming public demand would ensure his early return to power. In the event, the force of the demand was limited, while George III felt no necessity to rid himself of a Prime Minister whom he valued highly, and who was conducting his government with reasonable competence. Addington remained in office for a full year after the resumption of hostilities, introducing a wartime budget, restoring income tax, but putting it on a much sounder footing than Pitt had done. Pitt had relied on voluntary compliance, and his tax had brought in a great deal less than had been estimated. Addington insisted that the tax should be deducted at source, the basis of direct taxation both in Britain and all other modern countries until the present day, and the yield dramatically increased. Pitt and his friends were not amused that Addington was proving himself a more successful Chancellor of the Exchequer than his predecessor.

Addington's war aims were distinctly unheroic and commonsensical, but were probably better suited to the situation in 1803–1804 than the more active strategy adopted by Pitt both before and after. In Addington's view, there was a stalemate between Britain and France, with the former supreme at sea and the latter on the land. The only way in which this could be broken, given the failure of successive coalitions against France, would be to tempt Napoleon to try to invade Britain, and hope to destroy his army either at sea or on the beaches. He therefore determined to build up a massive force of militias and regular forces to ensure the defeat of any invasion, and to rely upon the assurances of his friend, Nelson, that the bulk of Napoleon's forces would not make it across the Channel. In the meantime, the British proceeded, once again, to mop up the bulk of the French and Dutch colonies, facing very little resistance. Addington's government can be absolved of making any really fundamental mistakes, but there were inevitably organizational muddles in recruiting a large militia force in a relatively short period, and this caused a great deal of discontent. His real failure was in rousing the spirit of the nation – the series of fumbling and pedestrian speeches which he made in Parliament during the first year of war were inevitably compared unfavourably with the orations of Pitt. Gradually, Addington's parliamentary support began to crumble, particularly after Pitt moved into open opposition in the spring of 2004. In successive divisions in the Commons, his majority fell from 58 to 52 to 37. The personal pressure on Addington, a sensitive man, became unbearable. 'By 1804', wrote his biographer, 'the affable and complacent figure who had presided so urbanely in the Speaker's chair had been reduced to a haggard neurotic, sleeping badly, short-tempered, scenting insults and hostility even when there were none, doubting his own capacities and pathetically uncertain even of his closest friends...the last few months in office had come close to destroying his spirit' (Ziegler, p. 219). On 29 April 1804, he told George III that his position was 'hopeless', and on 10 May he resigned, the King immediately sending for Pitt. 'On the whole his government's record on finance, foreign policy and national defence was a good one', according to the latest authoritative assessment (Cookson, p. 310). Yet many of his contemporaries, and much later opinion, regarded him as a failure. According to Ziegler, there were three reasons for this 'He was not an aristocrat, he was not an orator and he was not William Pitt' (Ziegler, p. 110). There was another, perhaps more fundamental reason – his long post-Prime Ministerial career. Addington was just under 47 when he resigned, becoming Viscount Sidmouth soon after. He was to live nearly another 40 years, for 14 of which he served as a Cabinet Minister, under four Prime Ministers – Pitt, Grenville, Perceval and Liverpool. During this period, he deservedly acquired the reputation of an arch reactionary, particularly during his ten years as Home Secretary in the Liverpool government, when he was blamed for the 'Peterloo massacre', and much repressive legislation (see Chapter 6). His long period in office ended in 1824, when he resigned in protest against the diplomatic recognition of the revolting Spanish colonies in South America. He continued to oppose reform in the House of Lords, voting both against Catholic emancipation in 1828 and the Great Reform Bill in 1832. He thus became something of a bogy figure to 'progressive opinion', which refused to accept that he could have been anything but a disaster as Prime Minister. This unjust verdict has been largely qualified by modern scholarship, which has also concluded that, despite his unfortunate political record, he had many admirable human qualities. Ziegler's conclusion has substantially been borne out by later scholars:

> He was not a great man, let alone a great Prime Minister. He was almost as convinced a reactionary as he has been depicted. His talents were in no way extraordinary...Yet I am left in no doubt that he has been monstrously misused by history. As a Minister he was responsible, conscientious and far from ineffectual. As a man he was kindly, courteous and sincere. His honour

and his integrity would be remarkable in any age and any profession. Less can be said for many men whose reputation stands immeasurably higher. (Ziegler, p. 11)

Works consulted

J.E. Cookson, 2004, Article in *The Oxford Dictionary of National Biography*, Oxford, Oxford University Press.
John W. Derry, 1990, *Politics in the Age of Fox, Pitt and Liverpool*, Basingstoke, Macmillan.
William Hague, 2004, *William Pitt the Younger*, London, HarperCollins.
W.H., 1885, Article in *The Dictionary of National Biography*, London, George Smith.
Philip Ziegler, 1965, *Addington*, London, Collins.

16
William Grenville, 1st Baron Grenville – Not Quite 'All the Talents'

Only two men in British history have had the distinction of following their own fathers in the top office. One was William Pitt; the other, his first cousin, William Grenville. Like Henry Addington's, William Grenville's career was largely shaped by his relationship with Pitt, his almost exact contemporary. Yet Grenville was a more independent character, and was never so much in awe of Pitt, even though he became his closest associate and a leading ministerial colleague throughout most of Pitt's long first premiership. Thereafter, the two men drifted apart, and Grenville largely transferred his loyalty to Pitt's great rival, Charles James Fox.

William Wyndham Grenville was born on 24 October 1759, the third son and sixth child of George Grenville and Elizabeth Wyndham, two of whose nine children were to die in infancy. The Grenvilles were descended from a Norman family, who had been landowners in Buckinghamshire since the twelfth century, living at Wotton, near Aylesbury. Their fortunes had taken a distinct change for the better at the beginning of the eighteenth century, through inter-marriage with the neighbouring and more powerful Temple family, with their magnificent residence at Stowe. The Temples amassed considerable wealth and political influence, controlling a number of parliamentary seats, which enabled members of both branches of the family to embark on political careers. This 'cousinhood' was extended in 1754 into the Pitt family, when George Grenville's sister Hester married the elder Pitt. George preceded Pitt (later the Earl of Chatham) into the premiership, in 1763. He proved to be an able administrator and reformer of the public finances, but was an indifferent manager of men and soon became unpopular, not least because of the alacrity with which he, like other members of the Temple clan, availed himself of valuable sinecures. His premiership lasted a little over two years, after which 'the King [George III] took the opportunity of ridding himself in 1765 of a prime minister he came to regard as a self-opinionated bore' (Jupp, 1985, p. 8).

Whatever his failings as a public man, George Grenville was a fond father to William and his siblings, and established a happy home environment at Wotton, together with his wife Elizabeth. She also came from a political family, her father having been the leader of the Hanoverian Tories in the House of Commons under George I and George II (The Temples and the Grenvilles were Whigs). Little is known, in detail, about William's childhood, which effectively came to an end at the age of 11 when, shortly after his arrival at Eton, both his parents died within a year of each other. He was later to describe this as 'a misfortune which every subsequent period of my life has given me fresh occasion to lament'. His eldest brother, George, who was soon to inherit the title Earl Temple from his uncle, assumed the role of head of the family at the age of 17, and became a sort of surrogate father to William. He continued to be the largest, if not the controlling, influence in his life until William was at least in his late twenties and was already a senior politician in his own right. By then, it was already clear to most observers, if not to themselves, that the younger brother was far superior to his elder, both in intelligence and judgement. There was an intermediate brother, Tom, who was less dependent on, and less influenced by, Earl Temple.

William, who of the three was the most similar to his father in character and outlook, had also inherited his probing intelligence and addiction to hard work. After Eton, he proceeded to Christ Church, Oxford, where he proved to be an outstanding student, excelling in the classics, English and mathematics, winning the Chancellor's Prize for Latin Verse and achieving a very good grasp of modern languages, particularly French. He went on to read for the bar at Lincoln's Inn, but never practised, his brother, Earl Temple, drafting him in as MP for one of the family boroughs – Buckingham – in place of his brother-in-law, Richard Aldworth Neville. He was 22 years old, and was returned unopposed in a by-election in February 1782. It was in the dying days of Lord North's government, and Grenville immediately allied himself with the Whig opposition, led by the Marquess of Rockingham, as had his two elder brothers and the entire Temple-Grenville clan. When North resigned, one month later, Rockingham formed his second administration, in which Temple was disappointed not to make the cabinet. Instead, he was fobbed off with the Lord Lieutenancy of Buckinghamshire, while Tom Grenville joined the new Foreign Secretary, Charles James Fox, who sent him to Paris as plenipotentiary in the peace negotiations with France and the United States.

The new government was not a happy team, Fox soon falling out with the Home Secretary, the Earl of Shelburne, who insisted on butting in on the peace negotiations on the pretext that the colonies came under his department. On 29 June, an exasperated Fox precipitately offered his resignation, a maladroit move whose effects were exacerbated by the totally unexpected death, from influenza, of Rockingham, on 1 July. The King called on Shelburne to take over the premiership, and Fox insisted on resigning, being supported by the great mass of Rockingham's supporters, including Tom Grenville. Temple, however, who now aspired to being appointed to one of the great two Secretaryships of State, now vacated by Fox and Shelburne, rallied to the support of the latter, as did William Grenville. Shelburne was hard pressed to form a viable government, in the absence of the Foxites, but declined to include Temple in his cabinet, offering him instead the Lord Lieutenancy (or 'viceroy') of Ireland. Temple accepted, and set off for Dublin, taking William Grenville with him as Chief Secretary. Grenville thus achieved significant office at the age of 22 years and nine months, and after only five months in Parliament. His cousin, William Pitt, only five months older, did even better: he was appointed Chancellor of the Exchequer.

As soon as Grenville had found his bearings in Dublin, he was despatched to London by his brother to act as his eyes and ears, and general fixer, in the imperial capital. He was Temple's main means of communication, albeit unofficially, with the government. Temple was actually subordinate to the Lord President of the Council, Earl Camden, a veteran minister who was not particularly energetic or interested in Irish affairs. Grenville soon proved himself highly effective, and his role became even more important when a decision in a court case put in doubt the sovereignty of the Irish Parliament, subject only to its allegiance to the King. This caused an uproar in Dublin, and – at Temple's prompting – Grenville began to lobby hard for the passage of a 'Renunciation Bill' disclaiming the right of the House of Commons to over-rule decisions of the Irish Parliament. He personally drew up a bill, and managed to overcome strong opposition within the cabinet to its introduction. The motion to approve the bill was moved in the Commons by the Home Secretary, Thomas Townshend, but Grenville was allowed to second it, and made a powerful impression with his speech, which was only the second time he had addressed the House. The whole affair redounded greatly to his credit, fostering the belief that he was 'a coming man'.

Shelburne's government, however, lasted only for eight months, being defeated in a Commons vote, as recounted in Chapter 1, in March 1783, when the supporters of Fox and Lord North united to reject the peace terms agreed with the American colonists. George III was furious, but felt himself impotent to prevent the formation of a Fox–North coalition, under the nominal leadership of the Duke of Portland. He resolved, however, to take the first opportunity that presented itself to unhorse the new government. In this resolution, he was supported by William Pitt, and by two of the three Grenville brothers, who declared themselves 'king's men'. Tom, once again, went his own way, continuing to support Fox. The fact that Temple and William Grenville decided to throw in their lot with the King was remarkable, in view of their undoubted resentment at his action 18 years earlier in peremptorily dismissing their father, George Grenville, from the premiership. One reason for their decision may have been the loyalty they felt to the Earl of Shelburne, but Temple, in particular, whose appetite for office, honours and fat sinecures was known to be insatiable, may have calculated that his long-term prospects would be better served by sucking up to the King. Grenville's appetite, while far from negligible, was more moderate, and he may well have followed Temple out of fraternal regard and a desire to promote the broader family interest.

George III did not have to wait long before seizing the opportunity to dispense with the Portland government, and Temple, together with William Pitt, was the chief actor in the *dénouement*. The occasion, as recounted in Chapter 14, was the introduction of the India Bill, in the autumn of 1783, fiercely opposed by the East India Company and other city interests. The bill easily passed the Commons, but the King then authorized Temple to tell his fellow peers that anybody who voted for the bill 'was not only not his friend, but would be considered by him as an enemy'. Sufficient peers took the hint for it to be defeated by 95 votes to 76, and the King promptly dismissed the Portland–Fox–North ministry, after only 260 days in office, even though it still commanded a large majority in the Commons. Pitt, who had earlier twice refused the premiership, this time accepted eagerly, but had difficulty in forming a cabinet as few senior statesmen were prepared to associate themselves with what they held to be unconstitutional conduct by the King. As a result, Pitt took the extraordinary step of appointing Temple to both Secretaryships of State, Home and Foreign Affairs. This caused such an outcry in the Commons that Temple was forced to resign within a few days, and Pitt scraped around to fill his cabinet, which few expected to last for long, with essentially 'second eleven' figures, all from the House of Lords.

Temple's reputation was severely damaged by the episode, and he was never again to be seriously considered for cabinet office, though he did serve a second term as Lord Lieutenant for Ireland in 1787–89. He also, like his father before him, had demanded and received the extremely valuable sinecure office of Teller of the Exchequer, worth £14,500 a year (Jupp, 1985, p. 428). Temple felt that the King owed him more recompense than this for the service he had rendered, and lobbied hard for a dukedom. George III, however, considered that new ducal creations should be restricted to royal princes, and was not prepared to go beyond a marquessate, which Temple, nursing a strong sense of grievance, reluctantly accepted, becoming the 1st Marquess of Buckingham. There was nothing unusual in politicians of the eighteenth and early nineteenth centuries seeking sinecures or honours for themselves, or patronage for their relatives and friends, nor was the practice generally regarded as reprehensible. The two William Pitts, father and son, were, in fact, seen as being rather eccentric in failing to enrich themselves or their families in this way. The Grenvilles, by contrast, were regarded as being altogether too greedy, and as pushing the system beyond its acceptable limits.

William Grenville had played no significant role in the plot to replace Portland by Pitt, but he was to become one of the main beneficiaries. Henceforth, he was progressively to replace his brother as the most influential figure in the 'Grenville connection', which counted up to 30 adherents, by no means all family members, in the two Houses of Parliament. Crucial to his advance was his relationship with Pitt. They had hardly known each other as children, and were only distant acquaintances when Grenville reached the House of Commons in February 1782, one year after his cousin. They then became close friends, and Pitt formed the highest opinion of Grenville's capacity and readiness to involve himself in complex and difficult issues. Grenville was to benefit also from the mediocre quality of Pitt's cabinet, which led the Prime Minister more and more to seek help from, and devolve responsibilities to, more junior figures who held only subordinate government posts. Together with Henry Dundas, a Scottish lawyer, he became Pitt's closest associate, and general workhorse, during the early years of his ministry, becoming joint Paymaster-General, and a member of the Board of Control and the Board of Trade.

In 1784, Pitt proposed to make him Governor-General of India, a sure route to fame and riches, and a remarkable temptation to the 24-year old younger son of a landed family who was determined to make his own way in the world and relieve himself of his dependence on his brother, who had provided his parliamentary seat, and in whose London house he felt obliged to live. Although their personal relations were good, Grenville obviously felt uncomfortable about his situation, having described 'dependence', in a letter to a friend, as ' the greatest curse in nature' (Jupp, 1985, p. 15). However, one of Grenville's most marked characteristics, along with his sharp intelligence, was an ingrained caution, and he regarded the internal situation in India as so unpredictable that he was not prepared to take the risk of failure.

Though not lacking in self-confidence, Grenville did not set his personal ambitions at the highest level. He defined them, in a letter to Buckingham, in 1786, 'as a cabinet post which would not involve topics of great parliamentary interest and, in addition, a sinecure for life'. Earlier he had written to a friend of the difficulty 'of carrying off an heiress', which suggests that he was not looking exclusively to public service as a way of securing his fortune. He was to tell the same friend, 'I have treasured up in my mind a saying…which was repeated to me frequently by my uncle…that there is nothing within the compass of a reasonable man's wish he may not be sure of attaining provided he will use the proper means' (Jupp, 1985, p. 15).

Grenville had a number of close friends, with whom he was able to unbend, and who described him as a warm and charming companion. But his public persona was more forbidding. He was regarded as stiff and haughty and completely lacking in small talk. Nor did his personal appearance do him any favours. He had bulging eyes, an over-sized head and a more than ample posterior, was untidily dressed and short-sighted, which meant that he wore spectacles, or an eye-glass, from an early age. He soon became the butt of cartoonists, such as James Gillray, and acquired the nickname of Bogy, or Bogey, on account of his goblin-like appearance. In his biography, Peter Jupp cites a much quoted piece of verse, which first appeared in a scandal sheet when Grenville was in his mid-twenties:

> Lord Bogy boasts no common share of head;
> what plenteous stores of knowledge may contain
> The spacious tenement of Bogy's brain.
> Nature in all her dispensations wise,
> who formed his head-piece of so vast a size,
> Hath not, 'tis true, neglected to bestow
> Its due proportions on the part below;
> and hence the reason, that to secure the State
> His top and bottom may have equal weight.

Grenville also suffered from a certain diffidence which inhibited him from putting himself forward. Thus, when Pitt invited him, in 1783, to move the acceptance of the peace terms with America in the House of Commons, he declined, saying: 'I do not like to stand forth so conspicuous in public questions, which I had always rather follow than lead...'. It was this quality which made Grenville, for all his abilities, a natural number two rather than a leader, and Pitt never seems to have felt any danger that his talented supporter would turn into a rival. In most respects, he was in fact Pitt's equal if not superior, though he fell far short of him as an orator, despite developing into a very competent parliamentary debater.

It was to Grenville that Pitt turned in 1787, when a difficult situation arose in the Netherlands, with Dutch Republicans, supported by the French government, vying for power with the hereditary *stadhouder*, the Prince of Orange, whose brother-in-law, the King of Prussia was threatening to intervene on his behalf. Pitt was anxious to prevent the growth of French influence in the Low Countries, but did not want lightly to run the risk of renewed war, and wanted an assessment of first the level of support for the Prince in the Netherlands and second of how likely the French would be to take to arms in the event of Britain and/or Prussia providing him with military help. Grenville travelled first to the Hague, and then to Paris, having detailed discussions in both capitals and was able to report back that the Prince's position was retrievable, while the French had little appetite to involve themselves in armed hostilities. This encouraged

Pitt to take a robust attitude, and when the Prussians sent an army across the Dutch border they met little resistence, and the French stood idly by while the Republicans were routed.

Pitt was delighted with Grenville's conduct of a difficult diplomatic mission, and resolved to bring him into his cabinet at the earliest opportunity. He offered to make him First Lord of the Admiralty in 1788, but Grenville declined, partly on the grounds that he was poorly informed and poorly qualified for this post, and preferred to wait until something more attuned to his talents became available, evidently having the Home Office, currently occupied by Lord Sydney (the former Thomas Townshend), in mind. It seems to have been agreed between him and Pitt that he should have the reversion of this post, as soon as an appropriate occasion arose for moving Sydney. Before this happened, however, Pitt once again called on his services to meet a short-term contingency. This arose during the Regency crisis, beginning in November 1788 (see Chapter 1), when Pitt was desperately anxious to prevent the House of Commons voting to grant the Prince of Wales unlimited powers as Regent. The sudden death of the Speaker came as a severe embarrassment to him, and he resolved to appoint one of his most faithful supporters in an attempt to keep the House in line and to steer the conduct of their debates. His choice fell on Grenville, who at the age of 29 became the youngest Speaker since Medieval times. There was strong resistance to his election from the Foxite opposition, but he was chosen by 215 votes to 144 on 5 January 1789. Eleven days later, he made a lengthy and highly persuasive speech, from the Chair, in favour of the government's proposals for sharply circumscribing the powers of the proposed Prince Regent, and Pitt was more than satisfied with his performance. The recovery of George III from his illness, in early March, removed the necessity for him to preside over the Commons, and on 5 June, he duly resigned the Speakership and was immediately appointed Home Secretary – a move bitterly resented by many MPs, who thought their House had been made a mere convenience of the government. Grenville, however, who some months earlier had been appointed to the sinecure post of Chief Remembrancer of the Exchequer (worth £2,400 a year), was able to congratulate himself on achieving the two main ambitions he had previously confided to his brother, Buckingham, and that while he was still on the right side of 30.

Grenville regarded the Home Office as the ideal post for his interests and talents, and looked forward to a lengthy tenancy, which, however, was not to be. His main impact on the Office, which was responsible for control of the colonies, as well as a wide range of domestic responsibilities now shared by up to half a dozen different ministries, was drastically to overhaul its antiquated practices. He instituted, his biographer recalls, 'the practice of having précis made of all incoming and outgoing correspondence ... [and] established a register for letters that were circulated amongst cabinet ministers for information' (Jupp,

1985, pp. 89–90). The chief piece of legislation for which he was responsible was the 1791 Canada Act. This divided the territory into two provinces, Upper and Lower Canada (the modern provinces of Ontario and Quebec), providing each of them with bicameral representative assemblies, the upper house hereditary and the lower subject to popular election, with a wider franchise than existed in Britain at the time. These constitutional arrangements remained in force for some 40 years, and were a clear improvement on what went before, but, according to Jupp, it worked only 'moderately well'. Yet Grenville's role in government was by no means confined to his responsibilities as Home Secretary. He had by now clearly emerged as the number two man in the government, a fact underlined by his promotion to the cabinet ahead of Pitt's two other close advisors – Henry Dundas and Lord Hawkesbury (later the Earl of Liverpool). Most of the cabinet were still in the House of Lords, and Grenville became, after Pitt, the government's main spokesman in the Commons, speaking on a wide range of subjects, including foreign affairs, for which he had no ministerial responsibility He was dubbed as 'Pitt's Vice-Chancellor' by Richard Sheridan, the Irish playwright and leading Whig MP.

Grenville's tenure of the Home Office came to an end after two years – in June 1791 – when he reluctantly accepted Pitt's request that he should take over the Foreign Office. The vacancy had occurred through the resignation of the Duke of Leeds, over the Ochakov affair (see Chapter 14), when Britain had threatened war with Russia, and then rather ignominiously backed down. Grenville had accepted a peerage some months earlier, due to Pitt's desire to strengthen his position in the upper house, of which Grenville became the leader. Although Grenville's long-term ambitions had included a peerage, he was far from certain that his removal from the Commons at this stage would not hinder his subsequent political career. Nor did he share the vainglorious aspirations of his brother, Buckingham, settling without argument for a barony, the lowest rank in the peerage, and not seeking a territorial title, styling himself simply Lord Grenville. He was 31 years old, and became one of the longest-serving Foreign Secretaries, continuing for nearly ten years in the office, combining it for the whole period with the leadership of the House of Lords, in which capacity he was universally recognized as being outstandingly successful. It was an extremely arduous period in his life, dominated from start to finish by the conflict with revolutionary France. As noted in an earlier chapter, he became, with Pitt, and Henry Dundas (who succeeded him as Home Secretary) part of a triumvirate which was jointly responsible for framing war policy, subject to spasmodic interference by George III. For the first year and a half of his Foreign Secretaryship, Britain was neutral in the war against France conducted by Austria and Prussia, a policy which he strongly supported, secure in the conviction that the two Germanic powers would prove victorious, and unwilling to commit Britain to making the restoration of the Bourbons an objective of its policy. However, the French occupation of the Austrian Netherlands and threat to invade Holland convinced him that French expansionism must be resisted, and the stiffening of the British attitude provoked a French declaration of war in February 1793. From then onwards, it became his firm conviction that no peace with France would be acceptable until she disgorged her conquests in the Low Countries.

By this time, a major change had occurred in Grenville's personal life. On 18 July 1792, he had married a cousin, Anne Pitt, the 19-year-old daughter of the first Lord Camelford, a wealthy nephew of the Elder Pitt. He had first proposed to her two years earlier, in what would effectively have been an arranged marriage, both Camelford and the Marquess of Buckingham being strongly in favour of the match. But the feisty 17-year-old had turned him down, largely on the grounds that she hardly knew him. Grenville had persisted in his wooing, and she became more and more attracted to him as she got to know him better, and after a long wait Grenville's patience was rewarded. Jupp comments that he had been 'completely smitten by a teenager who, although not a beauty, possessed considerable intelligence and, like his mother and himself, was a devout Anglican. It is possible that this was his first physical relationship with a woman and it was certainly his last' (Jupp, 2004). Part of her original attraction to him was undoubtedly her father's wealth, and she brought him a dowry of £20,000. The long-term benefit of the union was to be even greater, putting Grenville's finances permanently on a solid footing. Anne's brother, the dissolute second Lord Camelford, was killed in a duel in 1804, and the family's spacious Cornish estate, Boconnoc, reverted to her as well as the equally grand Camelford House, which Grenville was to make his London home. The dowry had partly been used to help Grenville buy a small estate in Buckinghamshire, Dropmore Park, which became their principal home. Grenville's marriage delighted his friends, who thought it had had a very beneficial effect on his persona. Lord Mornington, the future Marquess Wellesley, who had been his fellow student at Oxford, wrote to him, in October 1792,

> I cannot tell you with how much pleasure I saw your ménage. I told Pitt that matrimony had made three very important changes in you which could not but affect your old friends, 1). a brown lapelled coat instead of the eternal blue single breasted, 2). strings in your shoes, 3). very good perfume in your hair powder.

The marriage appears to have brought lasting happiness to both partners, though it was not to be blessed with children.

At the Foreign Office, Grenville lost little time in imposing a marked improvement in practices and administration, as he had earlier at the Home Office. In this, he was following in the footsteps of his father, George Grenville, who had implemented comparable improvements at the Treasury 30 years earlier. The two Grenvilles may justly claim to have been among the most *efficient* ministers until modern times. With one notable exception, Grenville did not engage in much personal diplomacy, preferring to operate through a voluminous correspondence and the use of ambassadors and special envoys, including his brother, Tom. The exception was the negotiation of the so-called Jay Treaty, signed in London in November 1794. Britain had been on the verge of renewed war with the United States, owing to disputes concerning the American-Canadian border, frontier posts, debts, trade with the West Indies and the British demand to be able to seize and search neutral ships trading with France. President George Washington sent Chief Justice John Jay to London in an attempt to negotiate a settlement of all these disputes, and after overcoming their initial distrust, the two men, both distinguished intellectuals, hit it off in a big way, and were able to reach compromises on all the questions at issue. By and large, the Americans came out best on the territorial issues, while the British view prevailed on the right of search. Historically, the main importance of the Jay Treaty was the precedent it set for the use of arbitration in the settlement of territorial disputes. Otherwise, the almost exclusive focus of Grenville's activities as Foreign Secretary was the continuous search for allies in the war against France, and the offering of inducements to keep their armies in the field. The principal objects of Grenville's attention were the trio of Austria, Prussia and Russia, but he also paid close attention to Spain and the Netherlands, as well as smaller powers, such as Denmark, Portugal, the kingdoms of Sardinia (Piedmont) and the Two Sicilies, many of the smaller German states, and even Turkey. As noted in Chapter 1, although the three ministers responsible for directing the war effort worked together in general harmony, they did have their differences of approach. Grenville was critical of Pitt's impulse to attack France on any and every occasion, believing that it was preferable to strike only when numerical superiority was assured. He did not, however, share Dundas's preference for a wholly defensive war, with British efforts reserved for overseas expeditions, where its naval dominance should ensure success. On the question of internal security, Grenville fully supported the repressive efforts of Pitt and of Lord Portland, who succeeded Dundas (who became War Secretary) as Home Secretary in 1794. It was he who moved the Habeus Corpus Suspension Bill in the Lords, in 1794, and the Treasonable Practices and Seditious Meetings bills two years later.

As the 1790s proceeded, with the successive defeats of the First and Second Coalitions against France, Grenville's disagreements with Pitt over war policy became stronger. He objected to Pitt's insistence on continuing to pay subsidies to Prussia long after it had ceased to be an effective ally against France, and put his faith instead in a closer alliance with Austria and Russia, where the unpredictable Tsar Paul, had succeeded his mother, Catherine the Great, in 1796.

Normally exceedingly cautious, Grenville took the lead, in 1799, in organizing a pincer movement to overwhelm the French occupiers of the Low Countries, by an Austrian attack from the east and an Anglo-Russian invasion of Holland, which, he wrongly predicted, would be supported by a mass uprising. In the end, the Austrian thrust proved ineffective, the Russians sent fewer troops than promised and the uprising failed to materialize. The invasion turned out to be a fiasco, the only compensation being the capture of the Dutch fleet, and the Russian forces had to be ignominiously evacuated to the Channel Islands, where they sat out until the following year, when the Tsar withdrew from the war, and recalled his troops. A chastened Grenville concluded that he was no strategist, and concentrated instead on trying to ensure that Britain was not forced into peace negotiations with France at a time of military weakness. He was not able to prevent preliminary talks taking place with the French, in 1796, 1797 and 1800, but was able to insist on a stiffening of the British terms sufficient to make them unacceptable to the French negotiators. It seems likely that without his energetic intervention, Pitt would have been prepared to settle for rather less, and a peace agreement comparable to that reached at Amiens, in 1802, would have been possible. By then, of course, Grenville, as well as Pitt himself were out of office.

They had resigned, as recounted in Chapter 14, in February 1801, when George III had vetoed cabinet proposals for Catholic emancipation. Grenville had been one of the strongest advocates of this measure, partly because of his belief in religious toleration, but more importantly because his experience of dealing with Irish affairs had convinced him that it was a necessary means to assure solid Irish backing for the war effort. He then fell out with Pitt, when the latter – possibly in the hope of an early recall to office – gave the King an assurance that he would not raise the issue again in his lifetime. Grenville refused to serve in Henry Addington's government, which took office in March 1801, and watched with growing dismay as he negotiated a peace treaty with France, which left it in control of the Low countries and provided for the return of most of Britain's colonial conquests. He was the most senior politician to denounce the treaty, which was accepted as an unfortunate necessity by the great majority, including Pitt, and brought short-term popularity to Addington from a war-weary nation. Grenville became the leader of a 'new opposition' to Addington, which included most of the Portland Whigs (but not the Duke himself), in contrast to the 'old opposition', a more numerous body still headed by Charles James Fox. Gradually, the two oppositions began to coordinate their activities in Parliament, despite their strong differences over war and peace. To a large extent, Grenville fell under the potent charm of Fox and the two men became close associates and friends. There was a third opposition grouping, the Pittites – led by George Canning – who were unable to accept the fact that their hero had been supplanted by Addington. After the war with

France resumed, in May 1803, Grenville became convinced that it could only successfully be pursued under a government of national unity – a 'Ministry of All the Talents' – led by Pitt, but including the Addingtonians and all three elements of the opposition. This was also now Pitt's preference, and when he resumed the premiership, in May 1804, he asked to include both Grenville and Fox in his team. George III had no objection to Grenville, but firmly vetoed Fox, at which Grenville said that he himself would not serve, despite Fox saying that he would not stand in his way. This offer of self-abnegation by Fox greatly touched Grenville, and bound them even more closely together, the 'new' and 'old' oppositions virtually combining their forces. This new constellation was greatly helped by a visit which Fox had made to France, during the 14 months' peace, when he had had an interview with Napoleon. He was offended by his imperious attitude, and the growing evidence of his dictatorial excesses, and returned much less of an advocate of 'peace at any price' than he had previously been.

The death of Pitt, at the age of 46, in January 1806, came at a particularly bleak moment in the resumed war against France. If the battle of Trafalgar, the previous October, had made Britain safe from invasion, the more recent victories of Napoleon at Ulm and Austerlitz had shattered the Austrian and Russian armies and destroyed the Third Coalition. George III was presented with an unwelcome choice. His strong preference was that Pitt's government should continue, with the members of the cabinet proposing a new Prime Minister from amongst their number. They were, however, unwilling to do this, and firmly recommended to the King that he should instead appoint Grenville, as much the most experienced and respected figure who had been in government over the previous 20 years. George realized he had no choice in the circumstances, and invited Grenville to propose a government 'with no exclusions', an acknowledgment that he was no longer in a position to block Fox's return to office. Grenville was in no hurry to accept, proposing instead that Earl Spencer, a leading Whig peer, should be Prime Minister. It was not only diffidence, and a sense of weariness which made him hesitate, but also a concern for his own income, despite the fact that the death of his brother-in-law two years earlier had left him a very wealthy man. Writing to his brother, Buckingham, he complained that he would have to give up his sinecure post of Auditor of the Exchequer, and that 'I should in fact receive no addition to my present income and must incur a very great additional expense'. Fox removed this difficulty for him by agreeing to introduce a bill placing the auditorship temporarily in the hands of a trustee, and Grenville went ahead and drew up a list of ministers to present to the King. Although his government became known as The Ministry of All the Talents, only three of the four main party formations were, in fact, included – hostility between the Whigs (who had been in the wilderness for a generation) and the Pittites (now generally regarded as Tories) preventing them from working together. So the government was made up of the Grenvillites, the Whigs, led by Fox and the young Charles Grey, and the Addingtonians, whose leader had become Viscount Sidmouth. Grenville would have liked to find posts for the abler Pittites, notably Canning, Castlereagh, Perceval and Hawkesbury (later Lord Liverpool), and hoped it would be possible for some of them to join the government at a later stage, but this did not happen.

The result was that he was to lead a largely inexperienced team, which was particularly weak in debating power in the Commons, apart from Fox, who was to die within seven months. Grenville's being in the Lords was to prove a major disadvantage, particularly after Fox's death. Unlike Pitt and Addington, Grenville did not choose to combine the Premiership with the Chancellorship of the Exchequer, to which post he appointed the 26-year-old Lord Henry Petty (later the Marquess of Lansdowne). Sidmouth became Lord Privy Seal; Earl Spencer, Home Secretary; Fox, Foreign Secretary; Grey, First Lord of the Admiralty and William Windham, War Secretary. Predictions that the government would soon split due to foreign policy differences between Grenville and Fox proved groundless, and though Fox attempted to negotiate peace with the French, he agreed to seek a joint negotiating position with the Russians, Britain's only remaining ally. This precluded any agreement being reached with the French. Ill-advised and badly conducted military operations were then undertaken against France and her allies, in such diverse locations as Buenos Aires, the Dardanelles, Sicily and Alexandria. None was successful, and Britain was henceforth to adopt Grenville's own 'defensive and husbanding system', which effectively meant a policy of armed vigilance, while waiting for Napoleon to commit the mistakes which would ultimately lead to his downfall. It was to be a long wait, but Grenville would live to see it as a still semi-active politician, but one who had been out of power for eight years.

Grenville had clear ideas about his government's objectives, but was less certain about the means to be employed, and was largely deficient (as he himself was to admit) in the skills required to galvanize his fellow ministers into effective action. According to Jupp, the 'central features' of Grenville's plan for a 'systematic government' included:

> First, a reorganization of the armed services which Grenville, in the company of others, had been urging since the renewal of the war with France. Second, a reform of national finances so as to deal with the recurring problem of raising enough money to pay for the war. Third, a policy of 'conciliation' towards Ireland in terms of both political management and measures. (Jupp, 1974, p. 260)

For Grenville, an essential element in this 'conciliation' was progress towards Catholic emancipation, a conviction which was inevitably to set him on a course of conflict with his monarch. The clash, when it came, was made worse by Grenville's less than tactful handling of his relations with the King. This particularly concerned his demand to hold a general election in October 1806, ostensibly to legitimize the reconstruction of the government, following Fox's death. Grenville's purpose was to boost his own authority, and to demonstrate to the Pittites, who now formed the opposition, the strength of his support in the country. George III considered the election unnecessary, as the government already enjoyed a large majority in Parliament, and very reluctantly agreed, while refraining from making the customary royal financial contribution to the government's electoral expenses. Grenville's initiative was successful, in so far as he succeeded in increasing his majority by between 20 and 30 seats, but the cost to him of alienating the King was disproportional. Thereafter the King was wary of his Prime Minister, and this was exacerbated by Grenville's lack of the ready charm which had, for example, made Addington so adept at handling his prickly sovereign. In this – as in many other respects – Grenville's government was irreparably weakened by Fox's death. Against all expectations, Fox had got on famously with the King once he had admitted him into government, and George was heard to confess after his death that he had never thought 'he would miss him so much' (Derry, p. 133).

From Dublin, the demand for progress towards Catholic emancipation grew ever stronger, and Grenville and his leading colleagues (with only Sidmouth dissenting) felt that the minimum concession to the agitation should be the introduction of a Bill throwing senior posts, in both the Army and Navy, open to Catholics. This was similar to, but went rather further than, a Bill to which the King had given his consent in 1793, which applied only to service within Ireland, and excluded the Navy. Grenville and his colleagues unwisely concealed from the King the extent to which the new Bill differed from its predecessor. When the King was informed of this by Sidmouth, he reacted angrily, and demanded that the Bill be withdrawn. To this the government reluctantly agreed, but then the King went further and demanded an assurance from all his ministers that they would never again raise the question of Catholic relief in his lifetime – the same demand to which Pitt had acceded in 1801. Grenville and Grey, who had succeeded Fox as Foreign Secretary and leader of the Whigs, refused, and the government was effectively dismissed. Grenville had been Prime Minister for one year and 42 days, almost exactly half as long as his father, also dismissed by George III some 42 years earlier, after 2 years and 85 days.

Grenville's government was largely a failure – with one shining exception. Almost entirely due to the personal efforts of Grenville and Fox, it had pushed ahead with measures to abolish the slave trade, which despite all the efforts of William Wilberforce, and the encouragement of Pitt, who had however lacked the final commitment to force it through, had languished as a political issue for a generation. The abolition bill obtained the royal assent on the very day that Grenville and his ministers handed in their seals of office. Grenville was not sorry to retire from office, having found the experience of leading a government dispiriting, and doubting his own competence to do it. Shortly before, he had written to Buckingham that he longed 'daily and hourly... for the moment that my friends will allow me to think that I have fully discharged (by a life of hitherto incessant labour) every claim they, or the country can have upon me'. He added: 'I want one great and essential quality for my station and every hour increases the difficulty... I am not competent to the management of men. I never was so naturally, and toil and anxiety more and more unfit me for it' (Jupp, 1985, p. 409).

Grenville was still only 47, but his thoughts now lay in a quiet retirement at Dropmore, where he could relax with his wife, carry on with his classical and literary studies and indulge his passion for landscape gardening. His reaction to a request from Charles Grey to attend a meeting to discuss co-ordinating opposition to the incoming government, led by the Duke of Portland, was most discouraging. 'I feel very repugnant to any course of very active opposition', he wrote, 'having been most unaffectedly disinclined to take upon myself the task in which I have been engaged, and feeling no small pleasure in an honourable release, I could not bring myself to struggle much to get my chains on again'. However, Grey, who shortly afterwards inherited an Earldom from his father, joining Grenville in the Lords, was adamant: Grenville must lead the opposition, even though his parliamentary faction was much smaller than his own, and Grenville became the acknowledged leader of the Whig Party until 1817. For Grenville, this was very much a part-time activity, from which he probably derived far less satisfaction than from the Chancellorship of Oxford University. He succeeded to this post after Portland's death in 1809, but only after a fierce election campaign in which he engaged with a great deal more energy than he had ever shown in fighting parliamentary elections. His narrow victory was all the sweeter because his principal opponent was no other than Lord Eldon, Lord Chancellor in Perceval's government and a noted anti-Catholic, who was widely suspected of having influenced George III in his dismissal of Grenville's government.

Although Grenville's political activity was now spasmodic, his influence over his followers was considerable, for example, converting them to the importance of free trade, leading them to oppose the Corn laws in 1815, and he was expected to negotiate on their behalf whenever an opportunity arose for returning to office, either in coalition with the Pittites or replacing them, should arrive. There were no fewer than five occasions, between September 1809 and June 1812, when this seemed possible, but on four of these the terms proposed were unacceptable to the Whigs. The exception was in February 1811, when the renewed madness of the King led to the Prince of Wales taking over the regency, which he retained until George III's death in 1820, when he succeeded him as George IV. The Regent was keen to turn out the Perceval government, and restore his Whig friends to power, but Grenville botched his exploratory meetings with him and exasperated his colleagues by once again making an issue about retaining his sinecure office should he become premier. The Prince Regent lost heart and allowed the Perceval government to continue, confirming it in office, under the Earl of Liverpool, when Perceval was assassinated in 1812. Grenville continued to lead the Whigs until 1817, when he bowed out of active politics, leaving Earl Grey as the undisputed leader. It was not quite the end: he continued to attend the House of Lords occasionally, and in November 1820, was approached by the new King with an offer to form a government to replace Liverpool's administration, with which he was at loggerheads over the treatment of Queen Caroline, whom he wished to divorce. Much to the chagrin of the Grenvillites, and particularly his nephew, the second Marquess of Buckingham, who saw in this approach the restoration of their own political fortunes, Grenville turned the King down on the spot, and advised him to compose his differences with his ministers. Grenville's last speech in the House of Lords – generally reckoned to be one of his greatest – was in favour of yet another unsuccessful Catholic Emancipation Bill. He suffered a debilitating stroke, the first of several, in 1823, but was delighted to be able to vote by proxy in 1829 for the Bill finally carried by the Duke of Wellington's administration. 'I may now say', he said to his nephew, Buckingham, 'that I have not lived in vain'. He died five years later, at Dropmore, aged 74.

Although his premiership was to be short and lacking in achievement, Grenville was a leading political actor over a spread of some 40 years, during which his influence was arguably exceeded only by Pitt and Fox. An essentially conservative figure, he had a high intelligence and an exceptionally clear mind, and was noted for his strong sense of personal loyalty, which he exhibited successively to his eldest brother, to Pitt, and to Fox. Despite sharing the venal instincts of other members of the Grenville clan, he was essentially a man of integrity who showed remarkable consistency in his views and commitments, whether it was the abolition of slavery, Catholic emancipation or the obstinate refusal to condone a peace with France which did not guarantee Britain's essential interests, as he saw them. Highly effective as a departmental minister, and as Leader of the House of Lords, he was to lack some of the qualities, not all of them admirable in themselves, which might have made him equally successful as a Prime Minister.

Works consulted

John W. Derry, 1990, *Politics in the Age of Fox, Pitt and Liverpool*, Basingstoke, Macmillan.
John Ehrman, 1969, *The Younger Pitt:I The Years of Acclaim*, London, Constable.

John Ehrman, 1983, *The Younger Pitt: II The Reluctant Transition*, London, Constable.

John Ehrman, 1996, *The Younger Pitt: III The Consuming Struggle*, London, Constable.

Peter Jupp, 1985, *Lord Grenville 1759 –1834*, Oxford, Oxford University Press.

Peter Jupp, 1974, 'Lord Grenville' in Herbert Van Thal, (ed.), *The Prime Ministers*. Vol. One, London, Allen & Unwin.

Peter Jupp, 2004, Article in *Oxford Dictionary of National Biography*, London, Oxford University Press.

17
Spencer Perceval – Struck Down in His Prime

Spencer Perceval has gone down in history as one of the least known of nineteenth century Prime Ministers, being remembered – if at all – as the only one to have been assassinated. Otherwise, he has been noted for his fervent evangelical Christianity and for being one of very few practising lawyers to have made it to 10 Downing Street. Yet, he had an unusual political career, and – after a tentative beginning – was at the height of his powers when he was killed in 1812. Had he lived, he might well have served for a lengthy term, perhaps for much of the 15 years that his successor, the 2nd Earl of Liverpool, was to occupy the post.

Although he came from an aristocratic and highly political background, Perceval had largely to make his own way in the world. Born on 1 November 1762, he was the second son, of the second marriage of his father, the second Earl of Egmont, who was First Lord of the Admiralty under George Grenville and in the first administration of the Marquess of Rockingham, in 1763–6. He was to die, when the young Spencer was only eight years old, leaving seven children from his first marriage, and nine from the second, of whom Spencer was the fifth born. Spencer's mother, Catherine Compton, was related to the Earls of Northampton, and was the great-niece of Spencer Compton, the Earl of Wilmington, who had been the second British Prime Minister, in 1742–3, and after whom Perceval was named. She became a Baroness in her own right (in the Irish peerage, as Baroness Arden), in 1770, the title being inherited by Spencer's elder brother Charles, together with a considerable fortune, while his much older half-brother John, became the third Earl of Egmont. Spencer himself was to inherit an income of only £200 a year, and his whole career was to be dominated by his need to earn enough money to maintain his own large family of six sons and six daughters.

Spencer was under-sized, and sallow if not sepulchral in appearance, an effect that was exacerbated by his always being dressed in black. He was known at school, and frequently in later life, as 'Little P'. At Harrow School, his headmaster, Joseph Drury, was to recall many years later, 'hard work and singleness of purpose were his cardinal virtues', while he succeeded in avoiding the temptations of 'desultory reading which could only vitiate his taste and confuse his ideas' (Gray, p. 4). Already at Harrow, Perceval was noted, together with his close friend Dudley Ryder (later Lord Harrowby) for his strong commitment to evangelical Anglicanism, which was to dominate his life. He won many prizes at school, and in 1780, proceeded to Trinity College, Cambridge, where he graduated MA two years later. The University was then known as a centre for hard drinking and general riotousness, but Perceval held aloof, devoting himself to his studies and associating mainly with a small group of fellow Evangelicals. 'Perceval', wrote his biographer, 'was undoubtedly studious; perhaps, for most tastes, he was a little too serious-minded [and] may sound too good to be true'. Yet, he added, 'there was a lighter side', referring to his 'guileless, guiltless jokes', and his fondness for hoaxes (Gray, p. 6). It was probably this which saved him from acquiring a reputation for priggishness, though he was famously described by Sydney Smith as 'an odious evangelical'.

When he left Cambridge, Gray records, 'there was no money for the usual grand tour of Europe', and he enrolled at Lincoln's Inn to read for the bar, also joining a debating society, meeting at the *Crown and Rolls* public house in Chancery Lane, where he honed his public speaking skills which were to prove invaluable at the bar, and much later in the House of Commons. He qualified as a barrister in 1786, and attached himself to the Midland circuit, where, however, money and clients were hard to come by. An anonymous contemporary memoir, quoted by Gray, refers to him hiring a horse to travel from town to town rather than buying his own, and how he would keep a careful note 'of the shilling spent on his dinner at a wayside inn, or of the florin which covered both dinner and breakfast, of the sixpenny tip to the chambermaid and the hostler, and of the cost of oats for his horse'. Somewhat lacking in self-confidence, and with an 'excess of modesty, which, at that period, almost amounted to timidity', he eventually became the leader of the circuit, and proved a popular figure. The eminent barrister, Sir Samuel Romilly, recalled in his *Memoirs* how 'With very little reading, of a conversation barren of instruction and with strong invincible prejudices on many subjects, yet by his excellent temper, his engaging manners and his sprightly conversation he was the delight of all who knew him'.

In 1787, the still penniless barrister was to fall in love. Revisiting, with his brother, Charles, the old family home in Charlton, Kent, which had been sold to Sir Thomas Wilson, an old soldier who had fought at the battle of Minden, they were immediately attracted by two of his daughters. Charles, now Lord Arden, an MP and a Lord of the Admiralty, with a large income, was warmly welcomed by Sir Thomas as a suitor, and was soon to marry the elder sister, Margaretta, in the private chapel of Charlton House. Spencer had less luck in courting the younger daughter, Jane, who was 18 years old, and her father refused point-blank to consent to her marriage to a young man of such poor prospects. The couple decided to bide their time for three years until she came of age.

Perceval's precarious finances received some modest relief by his appointment as Deputy Recorder of Northampton, in 1790, obtained through the influence of his maternal grandfather, the Earl of Northampton, and a year later he obtained two small sinecures at the Royal Mint, worth a little over £100 a year. By then, he and Jane were married, possibly having eloped, she arriving for the ceremony in her riding habit. Sir Thomas's anger was soon appeased, and he accepted his new son-in-law with good grace, assuring him that his daughter's eventual dowry would be no less than if she had wed with his consent.

Yet the young couple were certainly a great deal poorer than most of their social equals, setting up home in lodgings over a carpet shop in London's Bedford Row. Perceval was now 27, and the couple lost little time in establishing a family, six children being born in the first six years of their marriage, and another six over the subsequent decade. It was a happy marriage and Spencer doted over his wife and children. To bring them up in comfortable circumstances, he needed to maximize his income, and he made steady progress at the bar, becoming a King's Counsel in 1796, and a Bencher at Lincoln's Inn, his legal fees rising to about £1,000 a year. Through his brother, Lord Arden's influence, he also became counsel to the Board of Admiralty, and he was also appointed a commissioner in bankruptcy. In 1791 and 1792, he took the first tentative steps towards a political career by publishing, albeit anonymously, two pamphlets, one on the impeachment of Warren Hastings, the former governor-general of India, the other arguing for more repressive action to be taken against sympathizers of the French Revolution. The latter pamphlet attracted the favourable attention of the Prime Minister, William Pitt, and Perceval was appointed as junior counsel for the prosecution in the trials of two leading radicals, Thomas Paine and John Horne Tooke, in 1792 and 1794.

Despite his urgent need of money to sustain his family, Perceval throughout his life made generous charitable gifts, usually anonymously. He regarded this as his simple Christian duty, which also made him a fierce critic of hunting, gambling, drunkenness and adultery, and a fairly strict sabbatarian. Wilberforce said of him that 'Perceval had the sweetest of all possible tempers, and was one of the most conscientious men I ever knew; the most instinctively obedient to the dictates of conscience, the least disposed to give pain to others; the most charitable and truly kind and generous creature I ever knew', while a fellow Evangelical, William Roberts, is quoted by Gray as describing him as 'Christianity personified'. 'Perceval's spotless private life', Gray comments, 'was one of the greatest assets in his later political career…he set a new standard in fair-dealing and candour in politics, even at times to the detriment of his own interests'. Perceval's instincts, however, were deeply conservative, which led to an exaggerated deference to existing practices and a horror of innovation. He was, nevertheless, a fervent supporter of the abolition of slavery, and a believer in reform within the Church of England, where he campaigned for the restriction or abolition of absentee appointments to clerical livings, the payment of decent salaries to curates and the building of new churches in industrialized areas. His strong Anglicanism, however, made him an implacable opponent of Catholic emancipation, while his close study of the more prophetical books of the Bible laid him open to some of the more absurd millenarian superstitions which took hold in the late 1790s. In 1800, he was to publish a pamphlet entitled *Observations intended to point out the application of a prophecy in the eleventh chapter of the Book of Daniel to the French Power*. It is perhaps going too far to describe Perceval as a religious bigot, but he was not far off.

In January 1796, Perceval was surprised to receive a letter from the Prime Minister, William Pitt, offering him the vacant post of Chief Secretary to the Irish government. The new Lord Lieutenant, the Earl of Camden, had proposed his nephew, Viscount Castlereagh MP, but Pitt and the Home Secretary, the Duke of Portland, both felt that his Northern Irish connections would prove prejudicial to his acceptance in Dublin. Taking account of Perceval's financial worries, the offer included a promise of 'some provision of a permanent nature' and implored Perceval not to refuse because of 'misplaced diffidence'. Immensely flattered by the offer, which he described as 'so vastly beyond anything I could have imagined would ever have been submitted to my choice', Perceval nevertheless immediately wrote back declining, because of his family responsibilities. He ruled out the prospect of accepting the implied offer of a lucrative sinecure, saying that such terms 'would be so much too great for any service I could offer to the public, that you could not grant them with any degree of credit to yourself, or indeed without the imputation of inexcusable profusion of the public money' (Gray, pp. 13–14). Thus did the high-minded Evangelical exclude himself from an arrangement which would have been regarded as absolutely normal by the vast majority of contemporary politicians without large private means. Pitt made no further effort to persuade him, and Castlereagh duly embarked upon his own long and distinguished ministerial career.

Perceval's own entry into politics was not, however, long delayed. As the Deputy Recorder of Northampton, he had given some useful advice to the local corporation in a dispute over the town's charter in the spring of 1796, and when shortly afterwards one of the town's two MPs, his cousin Charles Compton, inherited his father's seat in the House of Lords, Perceval, aged 33, was returned unopposed in the ensuing by-election. Within less than a month, however, he was compelled to fight a vigorous campaign to hold the seat in a general election. Northampton had a reputation for fiercely fought election campaigns, having a relatively wide franchise with 1,000 voters on the electoral roll, and three rival interests usually competing for the two seats. The three groups were, respectively, the Compton family interest, the local corporation and the Whigs. Perceval received the support of the first of these, the new Earl of Northampton paying his election expenses, and easily topped the poll in a three-cornered contest, the second seat going to a Whig. Perceval, who proclaimed himself a supporter of Pitt, was returned unopposed in six further contests, and represented the borough for the rest of his life.

Perceval made an immediate impact upon the House of Commons, largely by a rollicking speech roundly attacking Charles James Fox, which left the opposition squirming. It was described by Pitt as 'in all respects one of the best I ever heard'. A year or so later, when Pitt fought his duel with Tierney (see Chapter 14), his second, Dudley Ryder, posed the delicate question of who should succeed if he were killed. He was astonished at Pitt's reply that 'he thought that Mr Perceval was the most competent person, and that he appeared the most equal to Mr Fox' (Gray, p. 41). Certainly, Perceval soon established himself as the most effective parliamentary debater on the government side, apart from Pitt. He was not asked to join the government, but in 1798 was appointed Solicitor-General to the Queen and solicitor to the Board of Ordnance. When Pitt resigned, in January 1801, the new Prime Minister, Henry Addington hastened to add Perceval to his team, largely to boost its debating strength in the Commons. Perceval became Solicitor-General, and a year later was promoted to Attorney-General. In this capacity, he successfully conducted two important prosecutions – one against Colonel Edward Despard, who was executed for high treason, the other against Jean Peltier, a French exile, who was found guilty of a criminal libel against Napoleon Bonaparte, during the Peace of Amiens. Perceval was able to continue with private legal work, transferring his practice from the King's Bench to Chancery. Within a year his fees had doubled, reaching almost £10,000 by 1804. 'For the first (and only) time in his life he felt free from private financial worries' (Gray, p. 47). Perceval continued as Attorney-General in Pitt's second ministry, in 1804–1806, and showed himself unexpectedly liberal in several of his decisions. He refused to interpret the anti-trade union Combination Acts in the interests of the employers, and tried to extend the scope of the elder Peel's Cotton Manufacturing Apprentices Bill, which sought to protect young workers. When Pitt died, he declined to join the 'Ministry of All the Talents', formed by Lord Grenville, in February 1806.

He went into opposition, along with the great majority of those who regarded themselves as 'the friends of the late Mr Pitt', but who were seen by their opponents as Tories. They included a number of men of great ability, but mutual jealousies were so strong that they were unable to agree among themselves on who should be chosen as party leader. They fell back on the unsatisfactory solution of acknowledging the ageing Duke of Portland, who a generation earlier had led a predominantly Whig government, as their titular chief, but nobody was designated to lead them in the House of Commons. Neither Canning nor Castlereagh, the most able of them, were prepared to serve under the other, while the third of the trio of former senior ministers, Robert Jenkinson, who was to succeed to the title of Earl of Liverpool in 1808, was already in the House of Lords, having been created Baron Hawkesbury in 1803. Perceval slowly emerged as the *de facto* leader in the Commons, and proved by far the most effective spokesman. The most dramatic incident involving Perceval during his period in opposition was the appointment by the King of a Commission to consider the alleged misconduct of Princess Caroline, the separated wife of the Prince of Wales, who was rumoured to have become pregnant by a commoner.

This enquiry, known as the 'Delicate Investigation' failed to substantiate the most serious charges against the Princess, and the Cabinet accordingly recommended to the King that she should again be received at Court, though a Cabinet minute warned her that she 'must be more circumspect in her future behaviour'. The Princess's principal legal adviser throughout the process was Perceval, and the 156-page letter he drafted in her defence was widely hailed as a masterful effort, described by Gray as 'the last and greatest production of Perceval's legal career' (Gray, p. 83). The episode undoubtedly enhanced his reputation, though he risked permanently alienating the Prince of Wales (the future Prince Regent), who had hoped to use the enquiry as a basis for a divorce action. By now, the Grenville government, fatally weakened by the death of Fox, in September 1806, was coming to its end, and Perceval helped it on its way by strongly opposing its Bill to make concessions to Irish Catholics. Perceval's stand, which was supported by the bulk of opposition MPs, probably emboldened George III to insist on the dropping of the Bill and then to present his ministers with an ultimatum to renounce any future initiatives along similar lines or face instant dismissal. Grenville and Grey and their leading colleagues then refused to give such an undertaking, and the King invited Portland to form a government, which was to consist exclusively of the 'friends of Mr Pitt'. The most important offices went to Canning, as Foreign Secretary, Castlereagh as Minister for War and the Colonies, Hawkesbury as Home Secretary and Perceval, as Chancellor of the Exchequer and Leader of the House of Commons. Perceval was highly reluctant to take on this double portfolio, preferring to resume his previous role as Attorney-General, or alternatively to take the Home Office. He pleaded his ignorance of financial matters, but his real objection was that he could not afford to take on the Chancellorship of the Exchequer, with its relatively small salary of less than £3,700 a year, compared to £6,000 for the Home Secretary and the assurance of large legal fees to supplement the Attorney-General's salary. He finally agreed under pressure from his colleagues to accept the additional post of Chancellor of the Duchy of Lancaster, during the King's pleasure, which would considerably augment his salary.

In accepting these posts, Perceval was taking on an enormous double burden. In facing the 'Talents' across the floor of the House, he was encountering one of the strongest opposition teams – both in numbers and debating power – for many years, with relatively little supporting strength at his own disposal. As Chancellor, he was not only handicapped by his lack of experience, but by the effective absence of a First Lord of the Treasury, who normally took the major responsibility for Treasury policy and administration, with the Chancellor playing only a subsidiary role (comparable, perhaps, to the modern post of Chief Secretary to the Treasury). The Duke of Portland, who was a mere figurehead as Prime Minister, took no part in the Treasury of which he was the nominal head, leaving Perceval to run the most important department of the government virtually single-handed.

Perceval's main challenge as Chancellor of the Exchequer was to raise enough money to continue the war against Napoleonic France, which threatened to become a crippling burden. In 1807, the retiring Prime Minister, Lord Grenville, had told his closest associates that Britain was capable only of waging a defensive war. Any major continental campaign was, he said, beyond our means. Yet, wrote Perceval's biographer: 'Over the succeeding five years, the Portland and Perceval administrations maintained British garrisons in all parts of the world, subsidised Austria, Portugal, Sicily and Sweden, launched the Walcheren expedition, and supported Wellington's lengthy and expensive campaigns in the Peninsula' (Gray, p. 323).

The Peninsular War was sparked off by Napoleon's ill-considered action, in March 1808, of deposing the Portuguese and Spanish dynasties and installing his brother, Joseph, as King of Spain. This provoked national uprisings in both countries, providing Britain for the first time with an opportunity of military intervention with significant support from the local population. Despite initial success, it proved a far longer and more hazardous commitment than was originally conceived, but it was to play an important part in Napoleon's eventual downfall. The Walcheren expedition (see Chapter 4), by contrast, was to prove a humiliating failure. Perceval played no direct part in the planning of either operation, which was primarily the role of Castlereagh, yet it was his efforts which made them possible. Perceval's budgets were not particularly innovative, but he managed to raise unprecedented sums to finance the war effort, without raising taxes. This he achieved by careful administration, cutting out unnecessary expenditure, and by raising large sums through long-term loans at very favourable rates of interest. The confidence he created by his own evident integrity undoubtedly influenced bankers to advance larger sums than they would otherwise have been inclined to do.

In Parliament, Perceval faced constant harassment from the Whig opposition, confident that the government's hold on power was increasingly precarious. The three issues on which they concentrated were Catholic emancipation, the conduct of the war and the linked questions of government patronage, corruption and parliamentary reform. On the Catholic issue, Perceval, to the delight of George III, gave no quarter. In the by-election, in the event unopposed, which he fought in April 1807, caused by his appointment as Chancellor of the Exchequer, he adopted the slogan 'No Popery', a stance he maintained on all the subsequent occasions on which the issue was raised in Parliament. On other issues, he showed a more subtle approach, seeking by amendment to weaken the impact of bills, such as that introduced by the leading Whig, J.C. Curwen, in 1809 to abolish the practice of selling parliamentary seats. The most difficult issue with which Perceval had to deal was the concerted effort to secure the dismissal of the Commander-in Chief of the Army, the Duke of York, following the scandal over the alleged sale of commissions by his former mistress, Mary Anne Clarke (see Chapter 13). The Duke had been hopeless as a field commander in the Flanders campaign a decade earlier, but was an effective administrator and was very popular with the troops because of his evident concern for their welfare. Moreover, there was no serious evidence that he had been involved in corruption. Perceval made a brilliant speech in the House defending the Duke, managing – against all expectation – to secure the defeat of the principal motion against him. Yet the Duke's enemies were not prepared to relent, and a further motion, backed by William Wilberforce and his group of high-minded Christians known as 'the Saints', and with whom Perceval was himself often associated, was tabled calling for his removal on account of his 'immoral conduct'. Combined with the Whig and Grenvillite opposition, this was almost certain to be carried, and Perceval succeeded in convincing an unwilling Duke, and his father, George III, that the only way to salve the situation would be for the Duke to resign, leaving open the possibility that he might be re-appointed when the excitement died down. (This is what in fact happened two years later, when Perceval as Prime Minister, recommended the Prince Regent to restore his younger brother, on the retirement of his elderly replacement, General Sir David Dundas).

The final months of the Portland government were darkened by the intrigues of the Foreign Secretary, George Canning to evict the War Secretary, Lord Castlereagh from office, and to prepare the way for his own succession or that of another figurehead Prime Minister, in the form of the Earl of Chatham (the Younger Pitt's elder brother), whom he would hope to manipulate (see Chapter 13). Perceval held himself aloof from the intrigue, and Canning overplayed his hand, repelling his colleagues by his conduct, while Chatham's prospects of the leadership evaporated with his inept conduct of the Walcheren campaign, of which he was the military commander. The consequence was that the bulk of the cabinet concluded that Perceval was the most suitable candidate for the Premiership, a view with which George III heartily concurred. The King was attracted by Perceval's anti-Catholic views, and expressed the opinion that he was 'perhaps the most straightforward man he had ever known'. The Cabinet doubted, however, that with the resignations of Canning and Castlereagh, it would be strong enough to carry on without reinforcement from the other side of the House. With the King's consent, Perceval and Liverpool therefore approached Lord Grenville and Grey to discuss the possibility of their co-operating in the formation of a new government. Perceval, who had no driving ambition to be Prime Minister, contemplated that this post would probably fall to Grenville, and hoped to take over the Home Office himself. Grenville and Grey, however, deeply distrustful, did not realize that a wide coalition, in which they would play a very considerable role, was intended. They assumed that the object was to split the opposition by offering only a few token places in what would continue to be a Pittite government, and declined to respond. They no doubt believed that, without their support, the new government would collapse, and that they would soon be called back to office. In fact, they missed their best opportunity, and condemned the Whigs to another 21 years in opposition.

In fact, it was only with the greatest difficulty that Perceval, aged just under 47, was able to construct his government. Conscious of his weak position in the House of Commons, he made an attempt to attract the support of Lord Sidmouth (formerly Henry Addington) and of Lord Melville (the former Henry Dundas), each of whom commanded the support of a significant *bloc* of MPs. Aware, however, that each of them was personally unpopular, and that their inclusion in the government might alienate other potential allies, he did not want to offer either of them cabinet posts. Instead, he sought their consent, or at least acquiescence, to an approach being made to their own leading supporters, such as Melville's son, Robert Dundas, whom he wished to appoint as Secretary for War and the Colonies. Most people in Perceval's position would have attempted to camouflage their motives, but he wrote candidly to both men setting out exactly the difficulty he was in. Neither of them reacted positively, so Perceval had to proceed initially without their support, though Robert Dundas later joined the government in a more junior capacity, while Sidmouth became Lord President of the Council over two years later. Perceval also found it impossible to find a suitable successor to himself as Chancellor of the Exchequer, a post he was most anxious to relinquish. Altogether, he approached no fewer than five possible candidates, including the young Lord Palmerston, but none of them was willing to serve. Eventually, he agreed to continue in the post, though he insisted on giving up the salary, which he was entitled to receive in addition to that of the First Lordship of the Treasury. It had taken him six weeks to form his cabinet of nine members, seven of whom were in the House of Lords.

The principal offices were filled by Richard Ryder, younger brother of his friend Dudley Ryder, as Home Secretary; the Earl of Liverpool as Secretary for War and the Colonies, Lord Eldon as Lord Chancellor and Marquess Wellesley (elder brother of the future Duke of Wellington) as Foreign Minister. Apart from Liverpool, it was not a strong team, and Perceval found that he had to carry an even heavier burden than he had under Portland. During his first year of office, he was under particular stress: his government was defeated six times in major parliamentary divisions, and it was only the stubborn support of George III, which enabled it to survive.

Several of the government defeats arose over the parliamentary enquiry into the failure of the Walcheren expedition, which had been forced by the Opposition. The government was gravely embarrassed by the attitude towards the enquiry of the Earl of Chatham, the expedition's military commander, who served in the cabinet as Master-General of the Ordnance. It was only his very belated resignation which saved the government from losing the crucial vote condemning the whole conduct of the expedition, which would certainly have led to the resignation of the government as a whole. Perceval won praise for his handling of an extremely tricky situation, but he was himself mainly to blame for the next crisis to hit the government – the arrest of the radical MP, Sir Francis Burdett.

Burdett, one of the Members for the City of London, had addressed an open letter to his constituents criticizing the House of Commons for its 'arbitrary and tyrannical use of privilege'. This followed a vote, from which Burdett had been absent through illness, committing to prison the secretary of a radical debating society, which had described the decision to exclude the public from the debates on the Walcheren enquiry as 'an insidious and ill-timed attack upon the liberty of the press, as tending to aggravate the discontents of the people, and to render their representatives objects of jealous suspicion'. Despite the view of many of his colleagues that a reprimand at the bar of the House would be a sufficient punishment for Burdett, Perceval insisted that he should be committed to the Tower of London, and forced through a motion to this effect, by 189 votes to 152. The attempt to arrest Burdett provoked the most serious street riots in London since the Gordon riots of 1780. Burdett was eventually arrested in his own home, where he was calmly teaching his son to translate the *Magna Carta*, and was transported to the Tower, where he was held from April to June 1810, when he was quietly released after Parliament had gone into recess. This episode reflected no credit at all on Perceval, but was consistent with the strong support he had given in the 1790s to the repressive actions taken against radical organizations by the Pitt government.

In October 1810, Perceval faced perhaps his greatest challenge, when the King finally plunged into insanity. The Prince of Wales, supported by all his younger brothers, exerted strong pressure to be appointed without delay as

Prince Regent, with no strings attached. But Perceval refused to be hurried, and insisted on introducing a parliamentary bill, which was a replica of Pitt's measure of 1788–9, in particular severely limiting the Regent's powers of patronage during the first 12 months of his regency. Fully aware that the Prince was most likely to turn him out of office in favour of the Whigs as soon as he was appointed, Perceval refused all opportunities to appease him, and succeeded in carrying his Bill though both Houses of Parliament. It came into effect in February 1811. Then, to general surprise, after a great deal of coming and going with the main opposition leaders, Lords Grenville and Grey, the Prince Regent changed his mind about a change of government, and confirmed Perceval in office. It seems clear that Grey and Grenville, the latter in particular, mishandled their relations with the Regent, who found them less willing to defer to his wishes than he had expected. More likely, though, he had been influenced by reports from his mother that the King was well on the way to recovery, and feared what his father would do if he resumed his powers after a short interval and found that his son had dismissed his ministers for no good reason. In the event, there was no recovery; the King lived for another nine years, during which the regency continued. After 12 months, the restrictions on the Regent expired, but – an essentially indolent man – he was loath to face the disruption which a change in administration would bring. He was disappointed by his old Whig friends, and found he had more in common than he had expected, with Perceval, whose anti-Catholic views now chimed in well with his own, which more and more resembled his father's, as he grew older.

The vexed question remained of the Prince Regent's Privy Purse and what financial provision should be made for the Queen and for the now much-restricted circle of courtiers of the King. The Regent petulantly dismissed the government's proposals, demanding separate establishments for the Queen and for each of the royal princes and princesses and that Parliament should be invited to discharge his own accumulated debts, which he estimated at £522,000. Perceval would have none of this, and, after consulting the cabinet, wrote to one of the Prince's advisers to the effect that

> it was, in his opinion, best for the real dignity of the Prince Regent and 'for the maintenance of his popularity and high estimation in the country' that he should accept a scheme by which his debts 'should be discharged by means of his own privations and not by means of fresh burdens on the people'. (Gray, p. 438)

The cabinet's united front was, however, broken by Wellesley, the Foreign Secretary, who had already proved himself a most unsatisfactory colleague. Putting on the grandest airs, while grievously neglecting his routine duties, and justly suspected of intriguing behind their backs with Canning, he now saw an opportunity of ingratiating himself with the Prince Regent, in the hope of himself supplanting Perceval as Prime Minister. He therefore let it be known to the Regent that he was in favour of a more generous settlement, and when he was brought to book by an otherwise united cabinet announced his intention to resign. After much toing and froing, the Prince Regent finally acceded to the bulk of the government's proposals, and Wellesley departed from the government, to the general relief. Perceval seized the opportunity to strengthen his team by bringing in Castlereagh to succeed him, while Lord Sidmouth (Addington) finally joined the government as Lord President of the Council. The embittered Canning was left out, and sourly commented that, like measles, every one had to have Sidmouth once. (The former Prime Minister, in fact, succeeded in joining the governments of no fewer than five of his successors – Pitt, Grenville, Portland, Perceval and Liverpool). Finally, the death of the first Lord Melville left the way open for his son and heir, Robert Dundas, to take the senior post of First Lord of the Admiralty. It looked as though Perceval's government had at last reached calmer waters, and that he could look forward to a long and secure tenure of his office. Then, without warning, on the afternoon of 11 May 1812, he was shot dead in the lobby of the House of Commons. He was 49 years old, and had been Prime Minister for two years and 221 days.

His assassin, John Bellingham, was unknown to him. A merchant's clerk, working in Archangel for a Liverpool firm, he had fallen into debt, and had spent five years in a Russian prison. Convinced that the British Ambassador in St. Petersburg, Lord Granville Leveson-Gower, had done nothing to facilitate his release, he repeatedly petitioned the British government on his return to Britain for financial compensation, and worked himself up into a mania, when none of his attempts proved successful. He was determined on revenge for what he believed was a gross injustice, and thought first of killing Leveson-Gower, now a leading politician, but at the last moment decided to target the Prime Minister. As Perceval entered the lobby, he rushed up to him, held a pistol against his breast and discharged a single shot. Perceval staggered forward, cried out 'I am murdered, murdered', and fell down dead. Bellingham quietly sat down, beside his smoking pistol, and waited to be arrested. A shocked House of Commons met the next day, and voted an annuity of £2,000 for Perceval's widow and a grant of £50,000 for her children. Bellingham was tried three days later at the Old Bailey. A plea of insanity was made on his behalf, but he addressed the jury for two hours with such lucidity, saying amongst other things that he wished in retrospect that he had killed Leveson-Gower instead, that it was not seriously entertained. The jury took only ten minutes to convict him of murder. He was hanged on 18 May, a week after the assassination.

Perceval was not a great Prime Minister, but – with all his limitations – was remarkably successful in achieving what he set out to do. Assuming the premiership, which he had not consciously sought, in extremely difficult circumstances, he succeeded in rallying all the disparate factions which had supported the Younger Pitt, with the exception of the Canningites. He achieved a mastery of the House of Commons, pursued the war against France more fruitfully than any of his predecessors, handled the nation's finances with dexterity and, without appeasing the self-indulgence of the Prince Regent, managed to establish a reasonable *modus vivendi* with that difficult and unpredictable character. At the time of his death, his government had achieved more authority, and seemed more stable, than any of its predecessors since the first administration of the Younger Pitt. A highly conservative figure, he nevertheless showed surprising flexibility in handling controversial issues, with the exception of Catholic emancipation, to which his rocklike opposition was second only to that of George III. The main criticism that historians have made of Perceval is that he was too rooted in the past, and to the ideas of the Younger Pitt, to set Britain on a fresh path, and enable it to grasp the new opportunities presented by the opening years of the nineteenth century. Nor was that task adequately fulfilled by his immediate successors over the following two decades. It was, essentially, left to later leaders, both Whig and Tory, who came to power only in the 1830s, such as Grey, Melbourne and Robert Peel.

Works consulted

John W. Derry, 1990, *Politics in the Age of Fox, Pitt and Liverpool*, London, Macmillan.
Norman Gash, 1984, *Lord Liverpool*, London, Weidenfeld and Nicolson.
Mollie Gillen, 1972, *Assassination of the Prime Minister*, London, Sidgwick & Jackson.
Denis Gray, 1963, *Spencer Perceval: The Evangelical Prime Minister 1762–1812*, Manchester, Manchester University Press.
J.A. Hamilton, 1895, Article in *Dictionary of National Biography*, London, Murray.
Lucille Iremonger, 1970, *The Fiery Chariot*, London, Secker & Warburg.
Peter Jupp, 2004, Article in *Oxford Dictionary of National Biography*, Oxford, Oxford University Press.

18

Robert Banks Jenkinson, 2nd Earl of Liverpool – Keeping the Show on the Road

The third longest-serving British Prime Minister was the second Earl of Liverpool, who took over the leadership of Spencer Perceval's government, following his assassination in 1812, and remained in office until April 1827. He was, effectively, the product of a one-parent family, his mother dying one month after his birth and his father not remarrying until he was 12 years old. Robert Banks Jenkinson was born in London on 7 June 1770. His father, Charles Jenkinson, was descended from a long line of baronets going back to the reign of Charles II, but whose fortune dated back to Anthony Jenkinson, a sea captain and merchant venturer in the reign of Queen Elizabeth, who had finished up as her ambassador to the Tsar of Russia and the Shah of Persia. Charles Jenkinson was a successful politician, who had become the leader of 'the King's friends' in the House of Commons, and a minister under both Lord North and the Younger Pitt. In 1769, at the age of 41, he made a financially beneficial marriage to the 18-year-old Amelia Watts, the partly Indian daughter of William Watts, a former governor of Fort William in Bengal, who had made a considerable fortune as one of the more rapacious associates of Robert Clive. She was to die, from the delayed effects of childbirth, at the age of 19, on 7 July 1770. Robert was brought up in his father's household, but spent his holidays near Winchester, either in the house of his grandmother Amarantha Cornwall, or his Aunt Elizabeth, whose husband, Charles Wolfram Cornwall, was Speaker of the House of Commons in 1780–9. Charles Jenkinson, who was to become one of the closest associates of Pitt, was created Baron Hawkesbury in 1786, and Earl of Liverpool, in 1796. He also inherited the family baronetcy in 1789, becoming the 7th Baronet. He was to marry, for a second time, in 1782, to Catherine, the wealthy widow of Sir Charles Cope. Two children were born to this marriage, Charlotte, in 1783, and Charles Cecil, in 1784.

The older Jenkinson was an able administrator, and a learned, if rather pedantic man, who wrote several scholarly works. Immensely ambitious for his son, he carefully supervized his education, which began at Albion House, a private boys' school at Parsons Green, Fulham, and continued, as a boarder, at Charterhouse, a 'public' school then located in the heart of London, near Smithfield and the Old Bailey. His father plied him with advice, both on his studies, and his manners and his personal appearance, writing on one occasion that he and the rest of the family 'look forward with anxiety to the figure you will hereafter make in the world'. He added that the chief happiness he expected to enjoy in his declining years would be derived from his son's 'prosperity and eminence' (Gash, 1984, p. 12). At 16 he left school, to enrol at Christ Church, Oxford. Though somewhat emotionally under-developed, he was better educated and much better informed than the vast majority of his fellow undergraduates, having met and conversed with such famous figures as Pitt, Edmund Burke and Lord Chancellor Thurlow at his father's dinner table. Jenkinson, who applied himself with great diligence to his studies, was admired and looked up to by many of his fellow students. These included the young George Canning, who came up to Christ Church seven months after Jenkinson, and wrote to his uncle that he was 'very clever and very remarkably good natured'. Canning and Jenkinson became very close friends, being known among their fellows as 'the inseparables', and were leading members of a small debating society, in which Jenkinson argued from a Tory, and Canning from a Whig point of view. They were, indeed, very different characters: Jenkinson, sober and industrious, distinguished himself by actually spending less than his annual allowance of £200 in his first year at Oxford. Canning, wild, witty, malicious, had a much quicker mind than his friend and rival, but was nevertheless greatly influenced by him, soon shedding his own Whig views. Jenkinson was regarded by many as being stiff and pompous, but was generally well liked; Canning soon acquired an incorrigible reputation for levity, and his mercurial temperament won him adoring friends and bitter enemies in almost equal numbers. Both of them were highly ambitious, but Jenkinson was much the more skilful at concealing this.

Jenkinson interrupted his undergraduate career after only 26 months to embark on the first stage of the Grand Tour, which was a common feature of the lives of young aristocrats in the late eighteenth and early nineteenth centuries. This took him to Paris in July 1789, where his father had arranged for him to meet a range of dignitaries, and where he planned to perfect his already good knowledge of French. A week after his arrival, on 14 July, he happened to be, his biographer recalls, among 'the great crowd of Parisians who watched the storming of the Bastille and saw the rioters, including numbers of women, at their horrid work of destruction and slaughter. It was a spectacle which gave him a distaste for revolutions' (Gash, 1984, p. 16). He returned to Oxford in October, and the following May, being excused, as the son of a peer, from taking the BA examination, was proclaimed as a Master of Arts. Within a month, he had been elected a Member of Parliament, in the June 1790 general election, won easily by the Pitt government. His father arranged for him to stand in two constituencies, Appleby in Cumberland, controlled by the famous borough-monger, Lord Lonsdale (formerly Sir James Lowther) and Rye, in Kent, a pocket borough controlled by the Treasury. In both constituencies he was elected un-opposed, but chose to represent Rye, which continued to elect him unopposed until 1803, when he was elevated to the peerage. Jenkinson was just 20 years old, and did not attempt to take his seat until a year later, when he attained the legal minimum of 21. Instead, he embarked on the second stage of his Grand Tour, which took in Rome, Naples and Florence.

Jenkinson's maiden speech was given in February 1792. A confident per-formance, lasting over an hour, it was devoted to foreign affairs, discussing the European balance of power, the value of the Prussian alliance and the apparent military weakness of France. By contrast, he was highly critical of the growing strength of Russia, which he foresaw would represent a serious threat to the European balance. The speech was favourably received, being praised by Pitt in his reply to the debate, and also in his written report to the King. Thereafter, Jenkinson spoke only sparingly in the House, on one occasion opposing Wilberforce's motion to abolish the slave trade. It was an unconvincing speech, probably made to please his father, now Lord Hawkesbury, who was a leading opponent of abolition in the House of Lords.

When the House rose for the summer recess, in June, Jenkinson resumed his continental travels, leaving for Holland, Germany and France. He visited the Austrian and Prussian forces now massing to cross into France in the confident hope of squashing the French revolution, and sent back letters to his father shrewdly assessing their relative competence, being much more impressed by the Prussians. News of the visit by this well-connected young MP soon spread, and in French circles it was widely believed that Jenkinson had been personally sent by Pitt in order to make contact with their enemies. This seems improb-able, but Jenkinson certainly returned from his travels in a much more hostile mood towards France. Relations between the two countries were fast deterior-ating, and the opposition, led by Charles James Fox and Charles Grey, tabled a resolution urging the dispatch of a mission to Paris to negotiate a settlement of all outstanding difficulties so as to prevent the slide to war. Jenkinson fiercely attacked the motion, saying that it would be 'infamous' to send an ambassador to 'bow his neck to a band of sanguinary ruffians'. Jenkinson's attitude was shared by the bulk of the House of Commons, and Fox's motion was negatived without a division. Hostilities with France began in February 1793, and when Fox moved a set of resolutions condemning the outbreak of war, Jenkinson was put up by the government to move the previous question, bringing the debate to a premature end. Pitt was, again, mightily impressed, and wrote to George III described his speech as one of 'uncommon ability and effect' (Gash, 1984, p. 24). Two months later, he created a less favourable impression in a debate on the unsuccessful operations at Toulon and Dunkirk, suggesting that the 'soundest military strategy would be to strike at the heart of the enemy and march on Paris itself'. This seemed a far-fetched notion to a generation brought up on eighteenth century principles of warfare and he was widely ridiculed for his supposed naivety. Gash points out, however, that this was to be precisely the strategy soon to be followed against his enemies by Napoleon, with devastating effect, and that it might well have been the best course for Britain to take in 1793 (Gash, 1984, p. 24).

Jenkinson resumed his friendship with Canning, and almost certainly was instrumental in drawing him to the attention of Pitt. This may well have helped Canning's own search for a parliamentary seat, and in June 1793 he was returned unopposed at a by-election in Newtown, Isle of Wight (the first of no fewer than seven constituencies which he was to represent in a tumultuous parliamentary career). They then again became almost as inseparable as they had been at Oxford, dining frequently together at Jenkinson's house in Conduit Street, before proceeding together to the House of Commons. While the friendship was wholehearted on Jenkinson's side, Gash suggests that

> Canning's feelings towards Jenkinson still had an element of contempt of a kind not uncommon in a clever, witty young man towards a duller, loyal companion. It was an example followed by many of Canning's friends and admirers ... His moral seriousness, his slightly odd physical appearance, made him something of a butt among the bright, amusing, somewhat malicious young men who gathered round Canning. (Gash, 1984, pp. 25–6)

Although tall, Jenkinson did not present an impressive figure. He had a melancholy air, a conspicuously long neck, and an awkward, shambling gait, much parodied by cartoonists. To the young Canningites, Gash adds, 'it was vexing that such an unmodish figure should be ahead of them in the parliamentary race'. Jenkinson did not have to wait long before Pitt offered him preferment. In June 1793, shortly after his twenty-third birthday, he was appointed to the Board of Control set up to supervise the affairs of the East India Company. The other members were all senior figures, including Pitt himself, Henry Dundas, Lord Grenville and Lord Mornington (the future Marquess Wellesley). At Pitt's urging, too, Jenkinson, who had already enrolled in the militia organized in the face of the threat of a possible French invasion, assumed a colonelcy in the Cinque Ports Regiment of Fencible Cavalry, organized by the Prime Minister himself. He took his duties extremely seriously, and much of his time was now absorbed by military activity, despite the mockery of Canning, who once reduced Jenkinson to tears by mercilessly lampooning him in the company of their friends. The ever-forgiving Jenkinson soon made it up with him, after an estrangement lasting several weeks. It was at about this time that

Jenkinson fell in love. The object of his affections was Lady Louisa Hervey, the youngest daughter of the eccentric 4th Marquess of Bristol, an inveterate traveller after whom the numerous Bristol hotels in European cities were named. A former Bishop of Derry, who had unexpectedly inherited the marquessate after the death of his two elder brothers, he promptly separated from his wife of 30 years' duration, leaving her to bring up Louisa in a very strait-laced household in the country. His two, much older, elder daughters both made disastrous marriages, and then attained notoriety by their promiscuousness, so the whole family was living under something of a cloud. Louisa, who was three years older than Jenkinson, shared neither the eccentricities of her father nor the vices of her sisters, but was nevertheless regarded by the elder Jenkinson (now Lord Hawkesbury) as an unsuitable wife for his son. He did not want his family to be associated with that of Lord Bristol, who, apart from his other shortcomings, was a Whig. It was only after Pitt, and even George III, had personally remonstrated with him that he gave his consent to the marriage, which took place on 25 March 1795. He then soon forgot his earlier opposition and warmly welcomed Louisa into the family fold. Jenkinson was then 24; he and Louisa became a devoted couple, though they were to remain childless.

In 1796, his father was created the 1st Earl of Liverpool, and Jenkinson assumed the courtesy title of Lord Hawkesbury, by which he was known until he inherited the earldom in 1808. Three years later, he was appointed Master of the Mint, previously a sinecure, but now involving a number of duties, for which he was offered the salary of £2,500 a year, which, at his father's prompting, he negotiated up to £3,000. With this appointment came membership of the Privy Council, and it seemed only a matter of time before Pitt would bring him into his government. Instead, Pitt resigned in 1801, when the King vetoed his proposals for Catholic emancipation. Pitt urged his friends to carry on and support the new Prime Minister, Henry Addington, but many refused to do so, including Lord Grenville, the Foreign Secretary, Henry Dundas, Lord Spencer and William Windham, from the cabinet, and Castlereagh, Canning and Granville Leveson-Gower from more junior posts. When Addington offered the 30-year-old Lord Hawkesbury the Foreign Office, his father, who was also in the cabinet, was delighted; Hawkesbury, over-awed by his lack of experience, rather less so. He would probably have preferred a less dazzling promotion at this stage, but having assured himself of Pitt's goodwill, nevertheless accepted. His immediate brief was to negotiate peace terms with France, but Addington, himself a poor parliamentary performer, was also desperately in need of his debating power in the House of Commons, his other cabinet ministers all being in the House of Lords.

It was not easy for the young Hawkesbury to take control of the Foreign Office. Many of the senior diplomats, loyal to Lord Grenville throughout his long tenure as Foreign Secretary, found it difficult to adjust to a younger and inexperienced chief. Grenville himself, though initially giving Hawkesbury friendly encouragement, became more and more critical as the peace negotiations (with which he fundamentally disagreed) proceeded. Hawkesbury was also, understandably, the object of jealousy from contemporaries (including Canning and his circle) who felt he had been promoted beyond his merits. Nevertheless, he created a favourable impression by his parliamentary speeches, and the negotiations continued until, in March 1802, the Treaty of Amiens was signed (see Chapter 2). It proved widely popular in a war-weary nation, and was welcomed by virtually all political leaders with the exception of Grenville. Some of them, however, privately felt that too much had been conceded to the French negotiators, who were led by the wily Talleyrand.

The peace gradually unravelled over the following 14 months, largely because of Napoleon's continued intervention in the affairs of neighbouring states, including Switzerland, and Holland, and the British reluctance to withdraw from Malta under the terms of the Treaty. The British ambassador to Paris reported that the payment of a large bribe to the Bonaparte family might secure agreement to the British annexation of the island, suggesting £2 million, as an appropriate sum. Hawkesbury responded with an offer of a mere £100,000, and nothing came of the proposal. A last minute offer from the Tsar of Russia to mediate between the two countries was rejected, causing anger to the Tsar, a possible ally in the renewed war which Britain declared in May 1803. In retrospect, Hawkesbury and his colleagues have been criticized both for their handling of the peace negotiations and for precipitating the renewed outbreak of war. As Gash put it, 'having been too conciliatory in 1801–2, they were too inflexible in 1802–3' (Gash, 1984, p. 48). The consequence was that when the Addington government finally resigned, in May 1804, to make way for Pitt's second administration, Hawkesbury's tenure of the Foreign Office was not seen as an unmitigated success. He had shown himself a good administrator, and his parliamentary performances had been impressive, but his political judgement and general 'feel' for the situation left something to be desired. Nevertheless, having spent three years holding very senior office, he emerged from the government with a greatly enhanced status. He had also ceased to be a member of the House of Commons, being created Baron Hawkesbury, in his own right, in November 1803, to become Leader of the House of Lords. It was not a move he welcomed, but he loyally agreed when Addington told him it was essential to counter the growing opposition from Lord Grenville, who was a dominant figure in the upper house. In any event, he was destined for the Lords on the death of his father, who was still President of the Board of Trade, but seldom attended cabinet meetings because of ill health. In fact, he was to live for another five years.

When Pitt formed his second government, he was determined to retain the services of Hawkesbury, but not as Foreign Secretary. This he gave to Lord

Harrowby, the former Dudley Ryder, and Hawkesbury reluctantly accepted the less senior and, in his eyes, less interesting post of Home Secretary. This was, nevertheless one of the most important posts in the government, and Hawkesbury retained his position as Leader of the Lords. He was undoubtedly one of the pivotal members of the cabinet, which was made up in almost equal parts by survivors from the Addington administration and by Pitt's personal followers. These, to his chagrin, did not include the impatient George Canning, who, with ill grace, had to content himself with the non-cabinet post of Treasurer of the Navy. When Harrowby was forced to relinquish his office through ill health, Canning brashly volunteered himself as a successor, only to be rebuffed by Pitt, who excused himself by saying he did not want to hurt Hawkesbury's feelings. He nevertheless did not restore him to his former post, but instead appointed the relatively uncontroversial Lord Mulgrave. The resentful Canning then proceeded to intrigue against Hawkesbury, which strained their friendship to the limit. Hawkesbury's tenure of the Home Office was uneventful, but he showed his qualities as a thoroughly reliable team player, while the post brought him into close contact with George III, who formed the highest opinion of his abilities.

When Pitt died, in January 1806, Hawkesbury was the King's first choice as his successor. Believing that he would not be able to form a viable government, Hawkesbury declined, but the King then pressed on him the valuable sinecure of Warden of the Cinque Ports, which had been held by Pitt. This was worth £5,000 a year, which, together with an increased allowance from his father, enabled him fully to maintain his income when the King next turned to Lord Grenville and invited him to form his 'Government of All the Talents'. This, as recounted in Chapter 3, did not include the Pittites, and Hawkesbury went into opposition for the first time since his election to Parliament. He then formed part of a quartet of experienced former ministers, along with Castlereagh, Perceval and Canning who, under the nominal leadership of the Duke of Portland, were responsible for organizing the parliamentary opposition in both Houses. They did not have to wait long to return to office. Just over a year after being sworn in, the Grenville government was sent packing by George III for refusing to give an undertaking not to revive the issue of Catholic emancipation during the King's lifetime. The Duke of Portland was asked to form a new government, in which Hawkesbury returned to the Home Office, Perceval became Chancellor of the Exchequer and Leader of the House of Commons, Canning Foreign Secretary and Castlereagh Secretary for War and the Colonies. Hawkesbury, who retained the leadership of the House of Lords, was a pivotal member of the Cabinet, and – together with Perceval – was responsible for whatever degree of co-ordination there was between ministries in what, under the feeble leadership of Portland was essentially a 'government of departments' rather than a centralized team. When he learnt of Canning's intrigues against Castlereagh (see Chapter 3), he was appalled, and he threw his weight decisively in favour of Perceval when he and Canning appeared to be the most likely candidates to succeed Portland as Prime Minister. The scandal of the duel between Canning and Castlereagh in the dying days of the Portland government, in any event, put both of them out of the running for inclusion in the new government, which Perceval formed in October 1809. By then, Hawkesbury had succeeded to the Earldom of Liverpool, on the death of his father the previous year, and in Perceval's government he succeeded Castlereagh as Secretary for War and the Colonies. The new Home Secretary was Richard Ryder (Lord Harrowby's younger brother), and the Foreign Secretary was Marquess Wellesley.

Liverpool continued to act as Leader of the House of Lords, and was now generally regarded as the number two man in the government. His over-riding concern as War Minister was to sustain the up-and-down campaign of the British forces in the Iberian Peninsula. The commander, now known as Viscount Wellington, was much the ablest of the British generals, but was notoriously grumpy and difficult to deal with. He had a low opinion of politicians, with the exception of Castlereagh, whom he regarded as the only minister who had ever given him solid support. He therefore did not initially welcome Liverpool's appointment, but gradually warmed to him, as he discovered that the new minister was determined to fight his political battles for him, and would do all he could to maximize the flow of reinforcements, supplies and financial support, while leaving him a maximum of flexibility in military strategy. Liverpool did not, of course, have an entirely free hand; not only the Treasury, but also the Commander-in-Chief and the Master-General of the Ordnance were intimately involved in many of the decisions which needed to be taken. His biographer probably understated Liverpool's problems in writing: 'With the Treasury, controlled by politicians like himself, Liverpool's relations were close; with the two successive commanders in chief, first Sir David Dundas and then, from May 1811, the Duke of York, they were correct; with the Ordnance, distant and sometimes difficult' (Gash, 1984, p. 82).

Liverpool, however, whose diplomatic skills were formidable, usually managed to get his way, and by the time he left the War Office, in June 1812, the ultimate success of the Peninsular campaign seemed no longer in doubt. A month later, Wellington's great victory at Salamanca sealed all his efforts. By then, Liverpool was ensconced in 10 Downing Street, a transition which had been far from smooth. The assassination of Perceval, on 11 May 1812 left the cabinet devastated, but they rapidly came to two conclusions. One was that the only possible successor, among their midst, was Liverpool. The second was that it would be difficult, if not impossible, for the government to remain in office unless it was reinforced by at least one of the opposing groups in Parliament. Their preference was to approach Canning and Wellesley rather than Grenville and Grey, the leaders of the Whigs. These conclusions were reported to the Prince Regent, who authorized an approach to Canning and Wellesley, both of whom rejected the offer to serve under Liverpool, Canning on the ostensible grounds of the government's refusal to consider Catholic emancipation, while Wellesley, who still hoped to secure the premiership for himself, advanced a number of objections. Soundings with Grenville and Grey were no more encouraging, and the Regent then invited Wellesley to form an administration, but the existing cabinet was unanimous in refusing to serve under him, as were Grenville and Grey. Wellesley then threw in the towel, and the exasperated Regent then passed the commission on to Lord Moira, a professional soldier and long-time favourite of the Prince. The best he could come up with was a sort of 'second eleven' of Pittites, with himself as a figurehead Prime Minister and Canning as First Lord of the Treasury and Leader of the House of Commons. The Regent was sensible enough to see that this would not do, and told Moira to 'settle it all with Eldon [the Lord Chancellor] and Liverpool', leaving them a free hand as to ministerial appointments. This was not the way his father, George III, had conducted his cabinet-making.

Liverpool became Prime Minister on 8 June 1812, the day after his forty-second birthday. Two months earlier, he had personally persuaded Lord Sidmouth to join Perceval's cabinet as Lord President of the Council, and he now decided that the best way to strengthen the government was to give him a more central role, thus cementing the support of the sizeable Addingtonian group in the Commons. Sidmouth thus became Home Secretary, his brother-in-law, Charles Bragge, Chancellor of the Duchy of Lancaster, and his leading supporter, Nicholas Vansittart, Chancellor of the Exchequer. Castlereagh remained Foreign Secretary and Leader of the House of Commons, and Lord Eldon continued as Lord Chancellor. A year later, in June 1813, he made another attempt to persuade Canning to join his government, offering him the post of Foreign Secretary, which Castlereagh was prepared to relinquish. Yet Canning, as so often, overplayed his hand, demanding that he should also become Leader of the House of Commons – something which Liverpool was not prepared to concede.

Liverpool's first three years in office were dominated by the concluding stages of the Napoleonic Wars, victory in which was his over-riding priority. Napoleon's retreat from Moscow had fatally weakened him, and Liverpool responded by enabling Wellington to step up the pressure in Spain, leading to the victory at Vitoria, in June 1813, and the crossing of the Pyrenees into France on 1 August. The final battle in the campaign was won at Toulouse, in April 1814. Meanwhile, Liverpool's resourceful Foreign Secretary, Viscount Castlereagh MP, was equally active on the diplomatic front, successfully offering subsidies to Prussia, Sweden and Austria to join Russia, and re-enter the war against Napoleon's depleted forces. Their decisive victory at Leipzig, in the so-called Battle of the Nations, in November 1813, foreshadowed Napoleon's final defeat, though it was only in the following April that he abdicated and surrendered to the allied forces.

The victory, after so many years, was celebrated with great enthusiasm and pageantry in London, which welcomed the visits of the Tsar Alexander, the King of Prussia, and Marshal Blücher, in June 1814, while Wellington received a dukedom, and both Liverpool and Castlereagh were invested as Knights of the Garter. Liverpool then despatched Castlereagh to Vienna, where the rulers of the victorious powers were to be engaged for many months in redrawing the map of Europe. As with Wellington, in the Peninsular War, Liverpool gave Castlereagh maximum flexibility, having agreed with him, and the cabinet, in advance on Britain's principal aims. These included the re-establishment as independent powers of Portugal, Spain and the Netherlands (now to include Belgium), and the restriction of France to its borders of 1790, without, however, stripping her of any of her ancient territories. Liverpool feared that if this were to happen it would so weaken the authority of the restored Bourbon monarchy that it would be vulnerable to a further Revolution, probably led by Jacobins. All these objectives Castlereagh was able to achieve, but the restoration of Poland, another British aim, was beyond even his powers of negotiation. In fact, the main business of the Congress was an uninhibited struggle to grab territory between the three main eastern allies, with the future of Poland and Saxony being the main bones of contention. On Poland, the issue was essentially whether Russia should be permitted to swallow up the whole country, with Austria and Prussia being compensated by gains further to the west, including Alsace and part of Lorraine from France. The alternative was that the three countries should each retain the parts of Poland, which they had annexed in three successive partitions between 1772 and 1795. Castlereagh considered that this was the lesser of two evils and threw his influence behind this arrangement, which was eventually agreed, though the Russian share of the spoils was substantially increased. The Kingdom of Saxony had been an ally of Napoleon, and both Austria and Prussia sought to annex it outright. At one point, the two Germanic powers were on the brink of going to war over the issue, but cooler heads eventually prevailed and, though truncated, it was awarded to neither power, preserving a precarious independence, which lasted until 1871, though formally until 1918.

No sooner was Castlereagh back in Britain than Napoleon escaped from Elba, and Liverpool and his government were adamant that he should be prevented, at all costs, from re-establishing himself. A Commons motion moved by the radical MP, Sir Francis Burdett, that Britain should follow a policy of non-intervention, attracted a mere 37 votes. It was clear that the government's determination was supported by an overwhelming majority of the public. Wellington, who happened to be in the Netherlands on a visit, was instructed to remain, and prepare a new British army around the small garrison already stationed there, which was immediately reinforced by the dispatch of several regiments from Ireland. Between April and June, the force was increased from

4,000 to over 32,000 men. Castlereagh sent instructions to the British delegation in Vienna to offer yet further subsidies to the allied powers to accelerate
their own military preparations. That Napoleon's comeback was definitively
halted at Waterloo, on 18 June, was as much due to Liverpool's urgent reaction
as it was to the soldiers of Wellington and Blücher. When Napoleon surrendered to a British ship a month later, Liverpool insisted that there should be no
question of negotiating with him, and that he should this time be exiled to an
island under British control, much more remote and better guarded than Elba.
He was duly dispatched to St. Helena in the warship *Northumberland* less than
two months after the battle. At the resumed Congress of Vienna, Castlereagh
revived an old vision of the Younger Pitt's, by successfully seeking agreement
that the great European powers should establish a 'concert of Europe', consulting
on a regular basis on how to maintain peace and resolve international conflicts.
Four other congresses were held between the four powers, until 1822, when
the British walked out of the Congress of Verona, in protest against a decision
by the other three powers to authorize a French intervention in Spain to quell
a revolt against the restored Bourbon monarchy. Nor did Britain formally adhere to the Holy Alliance, advocated by the Tsar Alexander and enthusiastically
endorsed by Austria and Prussia, which soon degenerated into an instrument to
maintain the *status quo* by intervening in the affairs of sovereign states to prevent political change. A final congress was held in St. Petersburg, in 1825, not
attended by Britain, and the congress system was then abandoned.

Liverpool and his government emerged from the war with greatly enhanced
prestige, though this soon evaporated, as post-war problems built up, and
an economic recession set in. Unemployment, boosted by a precipitate
demobilization of the armed forces, soared, and civil disorders abounded. A
prominent element was the Luddite movement of hand-workers displaced by
new machinery. They banded together to smash up the machines, but were
met by savage repression from the government, including numerous hangings
and transportations. By 1818 the Luddite movement was effectively destroyed,
but its place had been taken by an upsurge in political radicalism, with the
formation of numerous political clubs and societies. They presented renewed
demands for electoral reform, going far beyond the relatively modest demands
supported by the Whig opposition. The government, thoroughly alarmed,
feared that revolutionary violence would soon break out, and responded by
reactivating some of Pitt's repressive legislation of the 1790's, including the
suspension of *habeas corpus*. The so-called Peterloo massacre, in August 1819,
when local magistrates sent cavalry in to break up a mass open-air meeting
in St. Peter's Fields, Manchester, address by the radical orator, Henry Hunt,
causing 11 deaths and 400 hundred injuries, was the worst act of repression,
and prompted the Whigs to organize mass protest meetings throughout the
country. One of these, in Yorkshire, was sponsored by the great Whig magnate,

Earl Fitzwilliam, the Lord Lieutenant of the county, who was promptly dismissed by the government from his post. The government then brought in even harsher legislation, known as the 'Six Acts', which Liverpool admitted in the House Lords was 'odious' to him, but which he regarded as a temporary necessity. In practice, the Acts were applied very sparingly, but this did not prevent his government from being labelled as one of the most reactionary in British history. Much of the blame was attributed to Castlereagh, who carried the legislation through the House of Commons, and was famously stigmatised in a poem by Shelley:

> I met Murder on the way
> He had a mask like Castlereagh

The real authors of the Six Acts, however, were Lords Sidmouth and Eldon, who had to be restrained by their Cabinet colleagues from introducing even more draconian measures. It is easy to categorize Liverpool's government as paranoid, seeing non-violent advocates of reform as bloodthirsty Jacobins. Not all the revolutionary plots dreamed up by informers and *agents provocateurs*, however, were imaginary. The Cato Street conspiracy, of 1820, was a plan to murder the entire Cabinet, while it dined at the house of Lord Harrowby, the Lord President of the Council, and subsequently to seize control of London. The conspirators, led by the extreme radical, Arthur Thistlewood, were arrested just in time; five were hanged and five transported for life.

At no time during his premiership was Liverpool (whose position was made more difficult by his membership of the House of Lords) in command of a solid majority in the House of Commons. The membership was fragmented, and though the Pittites (most of whom now recognized themselves as Tories) and the Whigs were the two largest factions, there was a large number of uncommitted MPs, mostly country gentry, who though they usually voted with the government could never be taken for granted. The great majority of MPs were landed aristocrats, or their nominees, and in the post-war period they had two overwhelming objectives. The first was to reduce taxation, in particular the hated income tax, and the other was to secure the landed interest in a time of recession. Also the support of the monarch was not anything like as potent a force as in earlier times. George III may have had strong prejudices and little patience with ministers who were unwilling to follow his will, but he was, on the whole, a popular figure in the country and the object of deep respect and deference from almost the entire political class. If he wished to sustain even an unpopular ministry he had many ways, including the generous use of patronage, to keep it in power. With the Prince Regent (later George IV), it was a different matter. Regarded as a lazy voluptuary, he enjoyed neither popularity in the country, nor respect from his ministers. His available powers of patronage had, moreover, been greatly reduced by reform legislation under Pitt, Grenville and Perceval which had led to the abolition of many sinecure posts, including even that held by Liverpool himself, the Wardenship of the Cinque Ports, or at least the salary attached to it.

The consequence was that, in order to placate MPs, Liverpool had to take two painful decisions, which went very much against his own convictions. Alarmed at the high level of the national debt, after more than 20 years of conflict, he wished to continue with the temporary wartime expedient of income tax for at least a few years, in order to help reduce the size of the debt. The House of Commons would have none of this, and, in March 1816, roundly defeated the government's proposal by 238 votes to 201. In consequence the government was forced to abolish the tax, borrow an additional £5–6 million from the Bank of England, and embark on successive rounds of expenditure cuts, gravely weakening the armed force in the process. Even before this, in order to protect the prosperity of the agricultural interest, the government felt compelled to introduce the notorious 'Corn law', under which foreign grain could not be imported unless the price of wheat climbed to over 80s. a quarter. Liverpool, a close student of the works of Adam Smith, was a convinced free trader, and tried to water down the government's bill, proposing a sliding scale, rather than an inflexible cut-off point at 80s. He was not able to convince his colleagues. The original proposal went through, guaranteeing protectionism for agriculture for over 30 years, and laying up trouble for his protégé, Sir Robert Peel, when he became Prime Minister in the 1840s (see Chapter 24).

By 1820 economic recovery had set in, and the government's position seemed a great deal more secure. But the death of the old, blind, mad King, after 60 years on the throne, presaged a major political crisis. Now that he was on the throne in his own right, George IV determined to secure a divorce from his Queen, the former Princess Caroline, who had lived abroad since 1814. Having appointed his own three-man commission to investigate the apparently ample evidence of her sexual misdemeanours, George pressed the cabinet to introduce a 'Bill of pains and penalties' to strip the new Queen of her title and to end her marriage by act of Parliament. The government, rightly fearing that the proceedings would be infinitely damaging to George himself, as it would inevitably throw the spotlight on his own multiple infidelities throughout the 25 years of their marriage, was highly reluctant to take this step. George thereupon promptly invited Lord Grenville to form a new government, an offer which the former Prime Minister of 'the government of the all the talents' abruptly declined (see Chapter 16). Liverpool and his colleagues then agreed, in August 1820, to introduce the Bill in the House of Lords. Known popularly, if inaccurately, as the Trial of the Queen, who sat in the public gallery throughout its proceedings, it was one of the most dramatic and sensational events in parliamentary history. Huge numbers of people tried to attend the debates, which were reported by a press overwhelmingly sympathetic to the Queen and hostile to the King, as was virtually the whole of the opposition. The proceedings went extremely badly for the King, and the Bill only scraped through the House with a majority of nine votes. Realizing that there was no possibility of it passing the House of Commons, given the state of public opinion, Liverpool announced on 10 November that he was withdrawing the Bill. The Queen became something of a national hero, but her popularity did not last long. At George's coronation, to which she was not invited, in July 1821, she tried to force her way into Westminster Abbey, but her way was barred, and she was heartily booed by the crowd. A current epigram reflected the fickleness of public favour:

> Most Gracious Queen, we thee implore
> To go away and sin no more
> But, if that effort be too great
> To go away at any rate. (Smith, p. 147)

Within less than a month, Caroline was dead, struck down by an intestinal complaint.

Liverpool was constantly on the alert for possibilities of strengthening his Cabinet, and in 1816 at last succeeded in recruiting Canning, who – by now desperate to regain office – accepted the relatively junior post of President of the Board of Control, effectively the minister for Indian affairs. He represented a considerable reinforcement of the government's debating power in the Commons. Two years later, he carried off an even greater coup by persuading the Duke of Wellington to join the cabinet as Master-General of the Ordnance. His prowess as a parliamentary debater was less obvious, but his enormous prestige added greatly to the general standing of the government. Of all Liverpool's colleagues, the key figure during his first 10 years in office, was Castlereagh. He carried the double burden of Foreign Secretary and Leader of the House of Commons. In both tasks, he was a conspicuous success. Not an outstanding orator, by unfailing courtesy and quiet diligence, he commended himself to his fellow MPs, and the government consistently did far better than expected in the division lobbies. Castlereagh was highly valued by Liverpool, who undoubtedly saw him as his favoured successor. Yet he was probably a manic-depressive, and the accumulated strain of performing two such demanding jobs for so long eventually got the better of him. In August 1822, a year after he had succeeded his father as the 2nd Marquess of Londonderry, he cut his throat with a penknife, after receiving a blackmail threat over his alleged, but far from substantiated, homosexuality. Liverpool was devastated, but soon concluded that the only possible successor would be Canning, who was about to leave for India to take up the appointment of Governor-General. The problem was that Canning had become *persona non grata* to George IV, who regarded him with as much hostility as George III had shown to Charles James Fox. But the younger George lacked his father's iron will, and when Liverpool firmly insisted on the choice of Canning, he reluctantly gave way. Canning took over both of Castlereagh's posts, carrying on the general lines of his foreign policy, but with rather more *panache*. In the Commons, he was markedly less conciliatory, but proved a more effective expositor of government policy. Also, in 1822, a significant promotion brought the 30-year-old Sir Robert Peel to the Home Office, replacing Sidmouth, who remained in the cabinet, though without portfolio. At this time, Liverpool brought off another notable feat, by cementing an alliance with the Grenvillites, who had broken off their alliance with the main opposition Whigs some years earlier. Lord Grenville himself was no longer interested in office, but Charles Wynn joined the cabinet as President of the Board of Control, and a dukedom was offered to Grenville's nephew, Lord Buckingham, an honour that his father had vainly sought on several occasions from George III. With the adherence of the Grenvillites, Liverpool had finally succeeded in reuniting all the factions which had supported the Younger Pitt. In January 1823, there was a further reconstruction of the government, when Frederick Robinson replaced Vansittart as Chancellor of the Exchequer and William Huskisson became President of the Board of Trade. Both these men were supporters of Canning, and their appointment reflected his growing influence in the government. These changes set the pattern for the final years of Liverpool's ministry.

In June 1821, Liverpool's wife, Louisa, who had been in bad health for some time, died at the age of 54. He was severely affected, but sought to bury himself even more deeply in his work than before. Eighteen months later, at the age of 52, he was to marry a second time. His 46-year old bride was Mary Chester, a long-time close friend of his first wife. There were no children from either marriage. Liverpool's health, also, began to decline at this time; he suffered from a painful form of thrombophlebitis in his left leg, and often had to take the waters at Bath. Though basically a calm man, he became more irritable, and was described by one of his ministers as 'a great fidgett'. Despite his failing health, the beginning of the 1820s marked the most successful period of his premiership. The post-war difficulties were effectively over, with the economy now booming and the upsurge of radicalism on the wane. In 1819, Liverpool had geared himself up to make a stand against the incessant demands of the Commons for tax cuts, and presented a budget involving some £3 million in new taxes, with the aim of producing an annual surplus of £5 million. He made it clear that this was a matter of confidence, telling his fearful Lord Chancellor that 'If we cannot carry what has been proposed, it is far, far better for the country that we should cease to be the Government' (Gash, 2004). Despite a fierce onslaught by George Tierney, the leader of the Whigs in the Commons, a large majority of MPs swallowed their dislike of the new tax proposals and backed the government in what proved a turning point in their economic policies. From then onwards, there was a steady surplus in the national accounts, and the national debt began to fall. By the middle of the decade, when tax cuts became a realistic possibility, Liverpool insisted that these should be directed at the reduction of tariffs, encouraging home consumption and lowering the cost of raw materials. 'The budgets of 1824 and 1825 constituted the first free trade budgets of the century', according to Gash (2004). He thus established a claim to be considered as a forerunner of Cobden and Gladstone, as a pioneer of free trade. The fortunate presenter of these two budgets, the Chancellor of the Exchequer, Frederick Robinson, collected most of the credit for their immediate beneficial effects, and was accorded the sobriquet 'Prosperity' Robinson.

Yet apart from its later budgetary and free trade policies, Liverpool's government could in no sense be categorized as a reforming ministry. It was essentially a conservative administration, and it largely chose to ignore the two most pressing *political* issues with which it was faced: the twin demands for electoral reform and Catholic emancipation. Liverpool was opposed to both, though in a less stubborn way than, for instance, Perceval or Sidmouth (Addington). In each case, he was prepared to countenance minor concessions in order to stave off more far-reaching changes. Thus, while firmly opposing all the general reform bills presented by opposition MPs, he acquiesced in the demand to disfranchise one of the most notorious 'rotten boroughs'. In 1821 Lord John Russell had carried a bill in the House of Commons to take away the two seats from Grampound, after a case of gross corruption, and award them to the fast-growing city of Leeds, which had no separate representation. When the Bill reached the House of Lords, Liverpool rejected the award of the seats to Leeds, and successfully amended the proposal to grant them to the County of Yorkshire, then the most populous constituency in the country, with 20,000 electors. Henceforth it was to have, uniquely, four members.

Similarly, on Catholic emancipation, Liverpool was prepared to accept Catholics on the electoral roll but not as Members of Parliament. The Catholic issue was evenly more divisive and explosive than political reform. George IV was not such a hard-line opponent as George III had been, but largely shared his father's views and would not lightly have consented to legislation. The political world, including Liverpool's own government, was deeply split, and the only way that Liverpool could hold his team together was by declaring government neutrality on the issue, leaving individual members free to express their own views. Initially, the division of opinion within the Cabinet was fairly even, but with the passage of time, and especially after Canning joined the cabinet, the proportion of pro-Catholics grew steadily, until eventually only Liverpool and his Home Secretary, Robert Peel, were opposed. Meanwhile, during the 1820s – partly under the stimulus of Daniel O'Connell's campaigning Catholic

Association in Ireland – pressure for change reached boiling point. In 1821, for the first time, a bill was passed in the House of Commons for the enfranchisement of Roman Catholics. Prompted by a hostile speech by the Duke of York, heir presumptive to the throne, it was defeated by the House of Lords.

The following year, the Commons backed a bill, proposed by Canning (temporarily out of the government), to admit Catholics to the House of Lords, by a majority of 12. Again it was reversed by the Lords, and Liverpool thought that the writing was on the wall. He now concluded that emancipation was inevitable, but that his would not be the administration to bring it in. When a third Bill, proposed by Sir Francis Burdett, passed the Commons in 1825, he and Peel both decided to resign unless, which they did not expect, it was rejected in the Lords by a wide margin. This would have opened the way to a new government pledged to carry the measure. The cabinet, alarmed by this prospect, rallied round, and despite the objections of Canning, helped to ensure its defeat, by the substantial majority of 48 votes. Both Peel and Liverpool then agreed to carry on, but Liverpool's health was now fast declining, and few expected him to wait much longer before quietly bowing out. In fact, the end of his premiership came abruptly, when, on 17 February 1827, he had a massive cerebral haemorrhage, and was temporarily paralysed. The King waited for a decent interval, and then sent for Canning to form a new government. Liverpool had served for 14 years and 305 days, a term only exceeded by Robert Walpole and the Younger Pitt. He recovered partially, and was to outlive his immediate successor, who died the following August. He lingered on, a mere shadow of his former self, until 4 December 1828, when he died aged 58.

Liverpool has hardly received his due from posterity. Too facilely dismissed by Disraeli as an 'arch mediocrity', he has been strangely neglected by historians. The only full-length biography appeared as long ago as 1868, though Norman Gash's much shorter life, which appeared in 1984, is highly informative and perceptive. What emerges from his picture is a man who was not highly gifted, but possessed a multitude of small talents, which together made him an extremely effective politician. Pre-eminent among these was his ability to win the confidence of his colleagues. At all times, his cabinet contained powerful and controversial figures, along with the normal complement of non-entities, yet he managed to harness their energies in such a way that it worked together as a cohesive team, perhaps more so than any of its predecessors. He effectively established the principle of collective cabinet responsibility, to which the Younger Pitt had unsuccessfully aspired. This greatly strengthened him in his dealings with the Prince Regent, who soon discovered that there was no point in trying to intrigue with individual ministers in order to undermine the Prime Minister. If, as was often the case, he was tempted to dispense with Liverpool's services, he was aware that the whole cabinet would resign with him, and that he would have to look to the Whigs to form an alternative administration, a prospect which became increasingly unattractive to him as he became older and more set in his ways.

Technically, Liverpool was undoubtedly one of the most proficient of British Prime Ministers. Vastly experienced before he took office, having occupied each of the three Secretaryships of state, he kept a firm overall control over decision-making, while allowing his colleagues a very free hand in running their departments. Immensely patient, pragmatic, a good listener, and regarded even by his opponents as being exceptionally fair-minded in debate, never attempting to misrepresent their arguments, it is not difficult to understand how he was able to win the fierce loyalty of his colleagues. Not expected at the outset, either by himself or by others, to serve a lengthy term, he managed to keep the show on the road for almost 15 years. The strength of this achievement can be measured by what came afterwards – the rapid disintegration of the Pittite coalition, which he had so painfully reconstructed. Half his cabinet refused to serve under Canning, who was forced to include the Whigs in his government, while 'Prosperity' Robinson, now ennobled as Viscount Goderich, who was to succeed Canning after his death four months later, was himself able to survive in office only for a further four months before his own exceptionally argumentative government collapsed around him.

Works consulted

John W. Derry, 1990, *Politics in the Age of Fox, Pitt and Liverpool*, London, Macmillan.
John Ehrman, 1983, *The Younger Pitt: III The Consuming Struggle*, London, Constable.
Norman Gash, 1984, *Lord Liverpool*, London, Weidenfeld & Nicolson.
Norman Gash, 2004, Article in *Oxford Dictionary of National Biography*, Oxford, Oxford University Press.
Denis Gray, 1963, *Spencer Perceval: The Evangelical Prime Minister 1762–1812*, Manchester, Manchester University Press.
Lucille Iremonger, 1970, *The Fiery Chariot*, London, Secker & Warburg.
E.A. Smith, 2005, *A Queen on Trial; the Affair of Queen Caroline*, London, Sutton Publishing.

19

George Canning – in the Footsteps of Pitt

The shortest-serving Prime Minister in British history was George Canning, whose premiership lasted a mere 119 days, before he died in office. The irony is that he could well have been one of the longest-serving – if it was not for his unbridled ambition and apparent passion for intrigue, which alienated both the King and his Cabinet colleagues, he might have been appointed 18 years earlier. On the other hand, the wonder was that somebody from his own unconventional background reached high office at all. Born in London, on 11 April 1770, of Protestant Irish descent, his father's family were minor gentry who had been established in co. Londonderry since 1618. His father – also George – was a raffish figure, who had been a barrister, radical pamphleteer and a failed wine merchant in London, before being disinherited by his own father. He had married Mary Ann Costello, a ravishing beauty, also from Ireland, in 1768, and rapidly had three children, of whom only George survived, before dying in 1771, on George's first birthday, leaving his still only 24-year old wife destitute, with an allowance from his grandfather of only £40 a year to bring up the young George. A resourceful woman, she decided to seek her fortune on the stage, but after an unsuccessful debut at the Drury Lane Theatre, tried her luck in the provinces, where she did rather better. She became the mistress of a dissolute actor, Samuel Reddish, by whom she had five illegitimate children (including two pairs of twins), of whom only three survived infancy. She then married again, to Richard Hunn, a draper, and went on to have five more children. George spent his infancy travelling round with his mother, and her increasing ménage, staying in cheap theatrical lodgings, until – at the age of eight – he was plucked out of poverty and obscurity by his uncle, Stratford Canning, a merchant banker, who became his guardian, and took him into his own home. Soon after, he sent George to a prep school in Hampshire, and four years later to Eton. Part of the bargain was that he would not see his mother, except with his guardian's consent, though he kept in touch by letter, and was devoted to her. It was, in fact, eight years before he was to see her again.

At Eton, George proved a precocious scholar and at the age of 16 distinguished himself by producing, with three friends, *The Microcosm*, a superior kind of school magazine, published weekly in Windsor, and of which both King George III and Queen Charlotte became devoted readers. Much the most brilliant of the contributions, signed merely 'B' or 'Gregory Griffin', were written by Canning himself. Non-political in content, they were highly satirical in tone, and included a number of poems of good quality. Canning's uncle was well in with the Whigs, and at his house he met such luminaries as Charles James Fox, Edmund Burke and Richard Sheridan. When he went up to Christ Church, Oxford, in 1787, he was a convinced Whig. By this time, his guardian had died, and the role had been taken over by his business partner, William Borrowes, though the Rev. William Leigh, a wealthy clergyman married to George's Aunt Elizabeth, also took a close interest in his welfare. George, who wrote to his mother that he 'loved them very much' (Hinde, p. 16), spent his holidays with them, and looked to them for his main source of guidance and advice. His paternal grandmother had also died, bequeathing him a small estate in Ireland, which gave him an uncertain income of £400 a year, £50 of which he directed should be paid to his mother. In his first term in Oxford, Canning took the lead in setting up a small private debating society, consisting of only six members, the most prominent of whom, Robert Banks Jenkinson, was the son of the President of the Board of Trade in Pitt's government. They had a fine conceit of themselves, wearing a distinctive uniform, with buttons labelled D, C, P and F – after Demosthenes, Cicero, Pitt and Fox, whom they regarded as the greatest orators of all time. Word of their activities soon spread – and in particular of Canning's enthusiastic advocacy of Whig causes, and the Dean of Christ Church, Dr Cyril Jackson, who had become a warm admirer and supporter of Canning's, thought it was time to have a quiet word in his ear. He seems to have put it to him diplomatically that it was all very well for wealthy aristocrats, like his fellow members, to play at politics and even to aspire to a parliamentary career, but that Canning had his own way to make in the world, and that it would be better to look to the law, or some other profession to make his fortune. In the meantime, too open an association with politics might do his prospects harm. Canning took the hint, and promptly resigned from the club, much to the chagrin of his fellow members. He remained friendly with Jenkinson, who, however, soon left the University to embark on his Grand tour, and Canning made new friends.

One of these, Lord Granville Leveson Gower, was the son of the Marquess of Stafford, the Lord Privy Seal, and he soon invited Canning to visit the family seat at Trentham. Here he met many leading Tory politicians and their wives, nearly all of whom were charmed by this lively, witty, intelligent and handsome (he had inherited his mother's dark good looks) friend of the youngest son of their host. Meanwhile, Canning was becoming a figure of note within the University, winning the Chancellor's Medal for Latin Verse, and being pointed out by the former Prime Minister, the Earl of Shelburne (now the Marquess of Lansdowne), as a likely future premier. In 1789, at Dr Jackson's instigation, he was elected to a fellowship at his college, which, while the stipend was low, gave him an excellent position and free lodgings. He now decided to concentrate on reading for the bar, being in no position to accompany his wealthy friends, such as Leveson Gower, on a year-long Grand tour. The most he could manage was a short tour of the Netherlands, just after going down from Oxford in 1791. He then enrolled at Lincoln's Inn, and took chambers in Paper Buildings, but the lure of politics was too great, and he set his heart on getting quickly into Parliament, without waiting to get established as a lawyer. Yet before he could seek election, he had to decide under whose colours he would stand. Torn between his Whiggish background and his new Tory friends, he took some time to decide, before throwing in his lot with the latter. His motives were almost certainly mixed. On the one hand, personal advantage probably lay with shifting his allegiance. The Whigs were overwhelmingly an aristocratic group, and without family interest or a large private income it was unlikely that he would prosper in their ranks. Moreover, they were in opposition, and had no access to patronage. The Tories, by contrast, were less uniformly aristocratic, and could offer the prospect of ministerial or other official appointments.

On the other hand, Canning found himself less and less in sympathy with the Whigs, and in particular his friends, Sheridan and Fox, as a result of their response to the French Revolution. Canning had shared their initial enthusiasm, but as the excesses of the revolutionaries grew found himself more and more alienated. When Burke, one of his heroes, broke with Fox over the issue, he had much sympathy for him. Canning's attitude to the French republic was that it was 'an interesting experiment', and republicanism might well be a preferable system for some other countries, but not his own. Writing to a friend in 1792, he said:

> As to this country, though I am not so enthusiastically attached to the beauties of its constitution, and still less so determinedly blind to its defects, as to believe it unimprovable – yet I *do* think it much the best practical Government that the world has ever seen ... I do think it almost impossible to begin improving now. (Hinde, 1973, p. 24)

He therefore concluded that he was, broadly, in favour of the *status quo*, and reacted unfavourably when Fox's young lieutenant, Charles Grey, formed the Association of the Friends of the People, to campaign for a radical scheme of parliamentary reform. It was this which finally prompted him, he later recalled, to sit down on 26 July 1792 and write a letter to the Prime Minister, William Pitt, whom he had never met. Pitt, however, was well aware of Canning's existence, and may well have been forewarned by Jenkinson, who had been a Pittite MP since 1790, and was himself highly regarded by the Prime Minister. The letter from the 22-year-old Canning could hardly have been more brash. He wrote asking permission to call on the Prime Minister, saying that 'although he was on terms of familiar friendship with some of the more eminent members of the opposition, he was not in any way committed to them politically. He also made it clear that although he wanted to enter Parliament, he lacked the financial resources to bring himself in' (Hinde, p. 25). Pitt immediately replied in the most courteous terms, and a meeting was arranged for 15 August. Here, Pitt, obviously charmed by his young visitor and on the look-out to poach a promising recruit from the opposition,

> explained that the amount of patronage directly at his disposal was tiny, but that sometimes owners of seats were prepared to dispose of them simply at his recommendation. Canning replied that this would be acceptable so long as it was clear that he owed the seat to Pitt's recommendation and not to the owner's choice. He also expressed the hope that he would be allowed to make up his own mind on issues that were not of major importance to the government, like the Test Act on which he knew he and the prime minister disagreed. Pitt accommodatingly replied that thinking men could not always be expected to agree, especially on 'speculative subjects' and that what he hoped for from Canning was a 'general good disposition towards Government'. (Hinde, p. 27)

Canning did not have to wait long before his *chutzpah* was rewarded. The following June, the MP for Newtown, Isle of Wight, Sir Richard Worsley, indicated to the government that he was willing to give up his seat in exchange for a government post. Pitt immediately informed Canning that, at no expense to himself, he could have the constituency 'exactly in the manner which will be agreeable to your wishes as you explained them in your letter and when I had the pleasure of seeing you' (Hinde, p. 28). A week later, he was returned unopposed, without visiting the constituency, and his political career was launched. Most of his Whig friends concluded that he had turned his coat for dishonourable reasons, but several of them, notably Sheridan, maintained amicable relations. Canning's arrival in the House of Commons was not widely seen as an extraordinary event. His maiden speech was well received, but it took a little time before he became – as he undoubtedly did – one of the most effective debaters in the House, perhaps excelled only by Fox and Pitt. On the other hand, he was immensely gratified by the reception he received from Pitt. On his very first night in the House, he was invited to dinner with the Prime Minister and with other senior cabinet ministers, including the Foreign Secretary, Lord Grenville and Henry Dundas, the Secretary for War. Thereafter, Pitt frequently had him over for dinner or supper, often à *deux*, and could not have been more friendly or encouraging. Meanwhile, he continued fitfully with his law studies, but by the summer of 1795 had to take a serious decision on whether to commit himself to the bar. He decided against, but needed to earn some money, and was most disinclined to seek a sinecure post. It would be discreditable, he wrote in his journal, to give up the law for 'an office of mere income and idleness'. He consulted Pitt, who immediately responded by saying that ministerial office would solve his problem, but that, unfortunately, no vacancy existed at the moment (Hinde, p. 41). Within a few months, however, he contrived to find a post for Canning as one of two Under-Secretaries at the Foreign Office, to serve under Grenville. He took up the post in January 1796, at the age of 25.

His fellow Under-Secretary was frequently away on diplomatic missions, while Grenville preferred to work much of the time at his country residence at Dropmore, so Canning was often effectively in control of the Office, and handled the bulk of the routine work. A workaholic, he revelled in his new responsibilities, even though they made heavy inroads into his busy social life. His greatest difficulty arose during the two unsuccessful bouts of peace negotiations, in 1796 and 1797, when he was responsible for liaising with Lord Malmesbury, the chief British negotiator at meetings in Lille and Paris. Canning's – and Malmesbury's – problem was that, whereas Pitt genuinely wished the talks to succeed, Grenville (and George III) did not, and his loyalties were often stretched. He solved the problem by ensuring that Grenville did not see some of the more sensitive dispatches, but in spite of this both sets of negotiations failed, mainly due to intransigence on the French side.

Canning's ministerial and parliamentary duties did not exhaust all his energies. At the beginning of the 1797–8 parliamentary session, he agreed with Pitt to launch a pro-government newspaper, which would combat the 'lies' told by the opposition press and counter radical views by proclaiming a vigorous patriotic message. It was supposed to be anonymous, but it soon got around that Canning himself was the principal contributor, with Pitt chipping in with the odd article. Entitled *The Anti-Jacobin*, it ran for 35 weekly issues, and obtained a healthy circulation of some 2,500 copies, which its proprietors implausibly boasted represented a readership of 50,000. A high-class propaganda sheet, it pulled few punches, and its final issue was devoted to a long epic poem, largely composed by Canning, ridiculing the lack of patriotism of the radicals. This included the couplet 'A steady patriot of the world alone/ The friend of every country – but his own'. It is, however, mostly memorable for containing the most famous words Canning ever wrote, which have since appeared in numerous anthologies:

> But of all plagues, good Heav'n, thy wrath can send,
> Save, save, oh! Save me from the *Candid Friend*.

The *Anti-Jacobin* was discontinued at the end of the parliamentary session, in June 1798, most of its contributors, including Canning, moving on to the Tory *Quarterly Review*. Canning's period as Under-Secretary came to an end in March 1799, when he was appointed a member of the Board of Control for India, which effectively supervised the activities of the East India Company. The Board was presided over by Dundas, who regarded it as almost a full-time job added to his responsibilities as War Secretary (it was soon to be made a cabinet post in its own right). Canning seemed to consider the post as something of a resting place, to broaden his experience, before Pitt was ready to bring him into his cabinet. This impression was strengthened by his appointment as a Privy Councillor and Joint Paymaster-General of the Forces in March 1800. Canning was not Pitt's only young protégé, but there is no doubt Canning was his favourite. Their relationship became exceptionally close, and Canning wrote to a friend, in 1796, saying 'I could not love or admire him more, even if I had no obligations to him'. Pitt's feelings for Canning are unrecorded, but his actions spoke louder than words – and – at least up to Canning's marriage, in July 1800, he showed him exceptional favour. The question inevitably arises whether part of Canning's attraction to him was sexual. The author of the most thorough, indeed monumental, biography of Pitt – extending to three long volumes – John Ehrman, thinks it is improbable that there was a homosexual relationship, but expressed the view that if Pitt did have a male lover Canning was the most obvious candidate. In fact, the only evidence pointing to this was a single occasion when Canning was seen to put his hand familiarly on Pitt's shoulder (Ehrman, p. 94).

Whatever Pitt's sexual predilections, there is little doubt that Canning's were heterosexual. The first person with whom he was believed to be involved was Princess Caroline, the estranged wife of the Prince of Wales. A notorious sexual predator, like her husband, she made a dead set at Canning, when he met her at Lord Palmerston's house. He was obviously strongly attracted to her, as he revealed in a letter to his aunt, Mrs Leigh, four days later, without, however, revealing her identity, but he was also fearful of the consequences of getting involved with her. It was, after all, a capital offence to have carnal relations with the wife of the heir to the throne. The probability is that they never became lovers, though the future George IV believed that they did, and this accounts for his prolonged hostility to Canning, and his great reluctance to accept him as a member of Lord Liverpool's cabinet many years later. What is clear is that they became close friends, and she later became godmother to Canning's eldest son. Canning was, perhaps, saved from succumbing to her charms by falling deeply in love with a wealthy heiress he met soon after. This was Joan Scott, the youngest of three daughters of General John Scott, who had made a fortune through gambling, and when he died left £100,000 to each of them.

He set out to woo her, though very circumspectly, as he was only too aware that, given his lower social status and lack of means, he would be suspected of trying to marry her for her money. An added difficulty was that her eldest sister was married to the Marquess of Titchfield, the son and heir of the Home Secretary, the Duke of Portland, and that she regarded him as acting *in loco parentis*. Titchfield was not in favour of the match, but Canning was not without powerful allies. These included Pitt, whom he took into his confidence, and who helped plan his marital strategy with him, and Lady Jane Dundas, the wife of the War Secretary, whose husband was related to Joan Scott, and who was more than happy to put a word in on his behalf. Eventually Joan made it clear that she wanted to marry Canning, and he then tackled Titchfield directly and succeeded in winning him over. They were married in London, on 8 July 1800, and Pitt, whose emotions were almost certainly mixed, was reported as being in a 'daze' throughout the ceremony. The marriage turned out to be totally satisfactory from Canning's point of view. He may not have acted from pecuniary motives, but from now on his income was assured, and provided a firm base for his political career. Moreover, Joan proved to be a perfect partner for him, acting as his secretary, following his career with great interest, offering unending support and usually good advice, while herself avoiding the limelight. It was a very happy union, which produced three sons and a daughter, though unfortunately the eldest son, George Charles, was afflicted with ill health, and was to die before his nineteenth birthday.

On the morrow of his marriage, at the age of 30, Canning's prospects could hardly have appeared brighter. Utterly confident in Pitt's continuing goodwill, and believing that promotion to the cabinet was only a matter of time, he had already built up his own following among the younger Pittite MPs, and was widely acknowledged to be the most able of Pitt's lieutenants. He had good grounds for believing that, if all went well, he would emerge as his political heir and eventual successor. There were, however, some clouds on the horizon. One was represented by his mother. Although a keen theatre-goer, Canning was only too aware that acting was not regarded as a respectable profession, and was always badgering his mother to give it up. If not, he was determined that she should remain in the provinces, rather than coming to live in London, as she threatened to do once her marriage to Mr. Hunn broke up. Canning was generous to her, sending as much money as he could, even when he himself was still hard up, and putting himself out to help his numerous half-siblings. In practice, she was only a minor embarrassment to him, but Canning's love for her was blended with an extreme wariness. Much more damaging to him was his unwillingness to suffer fools gladly, and his propensity to include a large proportion of mankind in that category. He was apt to make witty and malicious remarks at their expense, which not unusually got back to them, creating unnecessary enmities. His friends were very aware of this, and some of them remonstrated with him to be more careful in future. He resolved to do so, but was all too often unable to live up to his resolution. This, coupled with envy and resentment at the excessive favours he received from Pitt, meant that his numerous admirers were balanced by a perhaps equal number of critics.

Then, in March 1801, the bottom fell out of Canning's world, with the sudden resignation of Pitt as Prime Minister. This followed the refusal of George III to agree to his policy of Catholic emancipation. Canning insisted on also resigning, despite Pitt's plea to him to carry on in support of the new premier, Henry Addington. In doing so, and in becoming Addington's unremitting scourge throughout the three years of his ministry, Canning proved himself more royalist than the King, more Catholic than the Pope, or more precisely, more Pittite than Pitt. Although Pitt eventually joined in the criticism of Addington, and was happy to return to office in May 1804, he was immensely embarrassed by Canning's activities, genuinely believing that Addington should be given a fair chance to succeed. When he formed his second administration, he included two of Canning's contemporaries, in senior posts – Jenkinson as Home Secretary and Castlereagh as Secretary for War and the Colonies – much to his disgust, Canning had to put up with the non-cabinet position of Treasurer of the Navy. Even this post, he threatened to resign, in protest against the inclusion of Addington (now Viscount Sidmouth) in the cabinet. Pitt persuaded him to stay, but Canning made an enduring enemy of Sidmouth, who was to remain an influential political figure for another two decades. Subsequently, he was rebuffed by Pitt when the Foreign Secretary, Lord Harrowby, was forced to stand down temporarily because of ill-health. Canning, believing that his previous experience as Under-Secretary made him well qualified for the post, volunteered to stand in for him, without, he told Pitt, insisting on either the title or the salary. Pitt appeared to receive the suggestion well, without committing himself, but when, shortly afterwards, Harrowby insisted on resigning for good, he overlooked Canning, and appointed Lord Mulgrave, the Chancellor of the Duchy of Lancaster, in his place.

Canning was mortified, and bitterly resented having to be, after Pitt, one of the main spokesmen in the House of Commons for policies approved by the cabinet, of which he was not a member. It was only ten months later, in October 1805, when Pitt suddenly invited him to dinner, that he had an opportunity to pour out to the Prime Minister the full extent of his frustrations. Pitt immediately responded, by promising Canning that he would join the cabinet the following January, either keeping his present post of Treasurer of the Navy, or

– if he preferred – becoming President of the Board of Control. Canning was delighted, and felt that all his old intimacy with Pitt would now be restored, as it indeed was over the following weeks. These, however, were a period of immense strain and disappointment for Pitt, with the unravelling of the Third coalition against France, which he had laboriously put together, with Napoleon's rout of the Austrian and Russian armies at Ulm and Austerlitz. The triumph at Trafalgar, which guaranteed Britain against invasion, was a welcome relief, despite the death of Lord Nelson, but it only fleetingly lifted the transcendental gloom into which Pitt was descending in the final months of 1805. He was to die in office, in January 1806, before carrying out his promised cabinet reshuffle.

Canning was devastated by Pitt's death, and was unprepared for politics without him, though he had taken a small step towards asserting his independence at the 1802 general election, when he relinquished the seat he held at Pitt's behest, and purchased an Irish rotten borough, at Tralee, for the rumoured price of 4,000 guineas. 'The friends of the late Mr Pitt', as they styled themselves, were excluded from the new government formed by Lord Grenville, who had foreseen an administration of 'All the Talents', but had no room left for them after he had provided places for his own followers, the Whigs led by Charles James Fox, and the supporters of Lord Sidmouth. The Pittites could not agree on who should be their leader, but settled on the elderly Duke of Portland as their nominal head. In practice, Jenkinson, now Lord Hawkesbury and soon to become the Earl of Liverpool, led them in the Lords, while Canning, together with Perceval and Castlereagh, formed an uncomfortable triumvirate in the Commons. It was not long before Grenville began to regret the omission of the Pittites, and particularly of Canning, whose abilities he greatly admired. He made two separate approaches to him, in July and August 1806, with pressing invitations to join the cabinet, which Canning would have loved to accept, but he felt constrained to consult his colleagues, and then replied that he would only be willing to accept if the entire cabinet was reconstructed to bring in all the leading associates of Pitt. This Grenville was unwilling to do, as it would almost certainly provoke the resignation of Sidmouth and his associates, whom he regarded as an essential element in his coalition. Then, in September, came the death of Charles James Fox, his Foreign Secretary and Leader of the House of Commons, which left a gaping hole in his government. Charles Grey was appointed to fill his posts, but his father, the 1st Earl Grey, was believed to be a dying man, which meant that he would soon be wafted into the House of Lords and no longer able to lead the Commons. This was an absolutely crucial post when the Prime Minister was in the Lords, and Grenville made a tentative approach to Canning to enquire whether he would be willing to accept it – if as expected – Grey went up to the Lords. This offer was so tempting that Canning might well have done so, despite the obligation which he felt towards his fellow Pittites. Before the issue arose, however, Grenville was out of office, sacked by George III, in March 1807, because his government refused to give a pledge not to revive the issue of Catholic emancipation (see Chapter 16).

George III was tempted to appoint the Earl of Chatham, the Younger Pitt's elder brother, as Prime Minister, but was strongly advised by the leading Pittites to choose the Duke of Portland. This elderly, ineffective grandee, who a generation earlier had led a predominantly Whig government, was incapable of giving any direction to his ministers, who, in Perceval's words, became 'a government of departments'. The chief posts went to Liverpool, as Home Secretary and Leader of the House of Lords, Perceval as Chancellor of the Exchequer and Leader of the Commons, Castlereagh as Secretary for War and the Colonies, and Canning as Foreign Secretary. In this post, he was – initially at least – supremely happy, despite, the difficult international situation, as the war against Napoleon continued to go badly.

Within three months of his appointment came the disaster of the Battle of Friedland, which knocked Russia and Prussia out of the war, and was followed by the meeting at Tilsit between Napoleon and Tsar Alexander I, at which the latter effectively became an ally of Napoleon. He agreed to join his Continental System, aimed at blockading Britain by closing all continental ports to British shipping and commerce. Canning, probably the keenest 'hawk' in the cabinet, in his determination to carry on the war as vigorously as possible, was especially concerned about rumoured secret clauses to the Tilsit treaty which he suspected included plans to bring the neutral state of Denmark into the war on the French side. He sent a large fleet to Copenhagen, with a threat to bombard the City if the Danes did not hand over their fleet to Britain for the duration of the war. The Danish Regent refused and a three-day bombardment commenced, resulting in 2,000 deaths and the destruction or damage of a third of the buildings in the city, before the Danes yielded. The British then seized the Danish fleet and sailed it back to Britain. The action was strongly criticized by the Whig opposition, but was popularly received within the country, and added to Canning's fast-growing reputation, despite the fact that it had the inevitable consequence of bringing Denmark into the war on the opposing side. Canning thereupon decided on an equivalent response on the southern extremity of Europe, where, following a French invasion, there was a severe risk of the powerful Portuguese fleet falling into enemy hands. An ultimatum was sent to Prince John, the Portuguese Regent, to go into exile in Brazil, and take his fleet with him, or face an attack from British ships blockading Lisbon's harbour. A few hours before Marshal Junot's forces reached Lisbon, a reluctant Prince John sailed off to Portugal's largest colony, escorted on his way by the British ships.

The French invasion of Portugal, followed by Napoleon's action the following year, in deposing the Spanish king and imposing his brother Joseph in his place, marked the beginning of the Peninsular War. The spontaneous Spanish insurgency against their French occupiers provoked an excited response in London, and a determination by Canning and his colleagues to do everything they could to assist their new Spanish allies. A British army, with General Sir Arthur Wellesley (later the Duke of Wellington) in temporary command, was sent to Portugal, and routed the French forces, under Junot, at the battle of Vimeiro. On the morrow of the battle, two more senior generals, Sir Hew Dalrymple and Sir Henry Burrard arrived from Britain and took over command from Wellington. They then proceeded to negotiate an armistice with the French – the Convention of Cintra – which provided extraordinarily generous terms for their defeated enemy. Under its provisions, the British agreed to repatriate the French troops to France in their own ships; there was no restriction on these troops re-entering the war; the French were guaranteed their 'property' (most of which had been plundered from the Portuguese), and any reprisals against the pro-French party in Portugal were forbidden. Canning was furious and raged against all the generals, including Wellesley, and demanded their recall. Under the influence of Castlereagh, a great admirer of Wellesley, the cabinet, however, more wisely decided only to sanction Dalrymple, who was later to be rebuked by a Court of Inquiry. Neither he nor Burrard were ever to be employed again. The frustrations of Portugal were soon to be amplified by the outcome of the British intervention in Spain. An army under the command of General Sir John Moore, found it impossible to liaise effectively with the scattered and divided forces of the Spanish insurgency, and after manoeuvring indecisively for several months concluded that its position had become untenable, and set out for the long march, through wild and inhospitable country, from central Spain to the northern port of Corunna to be evacuated back to Britain. Pursued by Napoleon's forces, it repelled a French attack on the outskirts of Corunna, in which Moore was killed, an action celebrated in a famous poem by Charles Wolfe. Moore's somewhat bedraggled army then sailed away.

Canning added to his growing reputation as an orator by his forceful speeches defending these events in the Commons, but he was deeply dissatisfied with their outcome. It was, perhaps, because of this that, in March 1809, he sat down and wrote a letter which was to have the most injurious effect on his own subsequent career. It was addressed to the Prime Minister, and listed a series of complaints about the conduct of the war. He subsequently met Portland at his country seat at Bulstrode for several days of discussions, during which he made the blunt demand that Castlereagh should be removed from the direction of the war. If not, Canning insisted, he himself would resign. A deeply embarrassed Portland discussed this with other cabinet ministers, and then with George III, all of whom agreed that it was essential to prevent Canning's resignation. It was also agreed that the best plan would be to offer Castlereagh an alternative post, perhaps in the House of Lords, but that no change should be made until after the outcome of the Walcheren expedition (see Chapter 3), which had been planned by Castlereagh, was known. The Lord President of the Council, the Earl of Camden, who was Castlereagh's uncle, agreed to break the news gently to him, and even offered to relinquish his own post to make way for his nephew. When it came to the point, however, he could not face telling Castlereagh, and already regretted his impetuous offer to make way. So weeks, and months went by, without Castlereagh having the merest suspicion that his days were numbered, while virtually all the other cabinet ministers became aware of what was afoot. Then, on 15 August, Portland had an apoplectic fit, and the whole question of Castlereagh's replacement got caught up in the manoeuvring for the prime ministerial succession. In this, Canning clearly overplayed his hand, and his position was severely weakened by his apparent plotting against Castlereagh, though it had not been his idea to keep Castlereagh in ignorance and he was not to blame for the long delay in putting his plan into effect. He had a frank discussion with Perceval, saying that in his view the new Prime Minister must come from the House of Commons, and that he and Perceval were the only feasible candidates. While he had the deepest personal respect for Perceval, he hoped he would understand that it would be impossible for him to serve under him, and suggested that Perceval should go to the House of Lords, possibly as Lord Chancellor. Perceval replied that he, too, would be unwilling to serve under Canning, and proposed that both of them should keep their present posts, and that another Prime Minister should be appointed from the Lords, whom they would both find acceptable. Canning retorted that it was essential for the premier to be in the Commons. The following day he had an audience with George III, which went disastrously badly, as recounted by one of his biographers. Canning told the King that:

> There is no substitute for Portland, for 'he is not one of a species, he is an individual, the last of his species – there is nothing like him to be found'. As to alternative prime ministers in the Lords, Chatham, who had once seemed obvious, was ruled out by his apparent mishandling of the Walcheren expedition. He renewed his threat to retire if Perceval was chosen, but told the King that if the Government failed to stand he would have an alternative in Canning and his friends. The King told Perceval later that this was 'the most extraordinary' conversation he had ever heard. Edward Cook, Castlereagh's Under-Secretary, called it 'the most insolent proposition that was ever obtruded upon a Monarch by a presumptuous Subject'. (Dixon, 1976, p. 136)

It was not surprising that the only effect of this conversation was to convince the King that his already existing preference for Perceval was fully justified. Soon after this, Castlereagh finally heard from his uncle the details of

Canning's proposal to supplant him, and after brooding on it for 12 days, sent an angry letter to Canning demanding satisfaction:

> You continued to sit in the same Cabinet with me, and to leave me not only in the persuasion that I possessed your confidence and support as a colleague, but you allowed me, tho' virtually superseded, in breach of every principle both public and private to originate and proceed in the Execution of a new Enterprise of the most arduous and important nature [Walcheren], with your apparent concurrence and ostensible approbation. (Dixon, p. 136)

The following day, Canning, who had never fired a pistol in his life, met Castlereagh on Putney Heath at 6 a.m., and each man fired two shots. Castlereagh was uninjured, but Canning was lightly wounded in his left thigh. The damage to his reputation was much worse. Castlereagh was also criticized for his pride and apparent desire for revenge, but Canning was almost universally condemned for provoking the quarrel. Both men were left out of the government formed by Perceval a few weeks later, though Castlereagh was welcomed back, as Foreign Secretary in 1812, and continued in this office, which he doubled up with the leadership of the House of Commons, for another ten years under Lord Liverpool. Canning was twice invited to join Liverpool's government – in 1812 – and was even offered the Foreign Secretaryship, but again grossly overplayed his hand, demanding the leadership of the Commons as well. He consequently remained in the wilderness until 1816, when, swallowing his pride, he accepted the much more junior post of President of the Board of Control (of India).

The general election of October 1812 provided a new experience for Canning. It was his tenth parliamentary contest, but on each previous occasion he had been returned unopposed for a pocket or rotten borough. This time, he was one of two Tory candidates facing opposition from Whigs in Liverpool, a borough with a large parliamentary franchise, and a long history of fiercely fought partisan contests. He had been invited to fight the seat, at no expense to himself, by the local Tories, led by John Gladstone, father of the future Liberal Prime Minister. It was a genuinely uncertain contest, with two strong rivals, in Henry Brougham, the leading Whig orator and future Lord Chancellor, and Thomas Creevey, the famous diarist. In the end, Canning headed the poll, with his fellow Tory in second place. He had finally tasted the rough-and-tumble of a pre-Reform Bill election and had found it exhilarating, and was by no means better disposed to reform than he had previously been. During the course of the campaign, he made a remarkable declaration of his continuing loyalty to Pitt, and of his independence from all other politicians: 'To one man, while he lived, I was devoted with all my heart and all my soul. Since the death of Mr. Pitt I acknowledge no leader...I have adhered and shall adhere to [his] opinions as the guides of my public conduct' (Dixon, p. 164).

From now on, his relationship with his constituency was to be transformed, with large numbers of constituents expecting favours, and no question of his getting away with never setting foot in the borough he represented in Parliament. During the next couple of years, he pursued an uncertain political course. Together with his small band of rather over a dozen supporters, he alternated between supporting the government and backing initiatives by Whig MPs. He was a deeply frustrated man – watching his great rival, Castlereagh, emerge as an international statesman and the star of the Congress of Vienna, with the knowledge that he himself could have played the same role, and that it was his own fault that it had been denied him. He had conceded this in a letter to his old friend Granville Leveson-Gower, in which he wrote: 'I am afraid no possible combination of circumstances can place me again where I stood...and it is no use to reflect where I might have been now had that time been taken at the flood' (Rolo, p. 93).

For at least 10 years, Canning, and his wife, had been desperately anxious about the health of their dearly loved eldest child, George Charles. who was lame in one leg and almost perpetually ill. In 1807, they had moved house to the distinctly unfashionable town of Hinckley, in Leicestershire, 100 miles from London, purely because of the presence there of a Mr Chesher, who was known to have effected some remarkable cures of other lame children. Joan and the other children went to live there, which meant that they were separated for long periods from Canning, who, of course, spent most of his time in London. By 1814, little George had got a lot worse, and his parents became convinced that he needed to live in a warmer climate. The Prime Minister, his old friend, Lord Liverpool, came to their aid, suggesting that Canning might like to take up the post of Ambassador to Lisbon. It was expected that the Regent, Prince John, later King John VI, who had withdrawn to Brazil at Canning's instigation in 1807, was about to return, and it was thought fitting that Canning should be in Lisbon to welcome him back. So, in November 1814, Canning duly took up the post, and established his family in the grand ambassadorial residence. Yet John showed himself in no hurry to return, and Canning had a frustrating time dealing with the Portuguese government, who constantly had to wait weeks or months before committing themselves while instructions were awaited from Rio de Janeiro. His son's health did not improve, and Canning needed no persuasion when, in June 1816, on the death of the Earl of Buckinghamshire, Liverpool offered him the vacant cabinet post of President of the Board of Control. This time, Canning made no awkward conditions, and returned to the cabinet a much chastened man, in a post far junior to that he had previously held.

He had to fight a by-election, which was vigorously contested by a radical candidate, before he could take up his position. The opposition made much of supposed corruption involved in Canning's appointment to Lisbon, circulating the ditty:

> Fourteen thousand a year is a very fine thing
> For a trip to a Court without any King. (Dixon, p. 182)

Canning was elected with a good majority, and took up his new post, which consisted of overseeing the East India Company. Within the cabinet, he managed to work with Castlereagh, and even Sidmouth, in tolerable accord. In the Commons, Canning provided heavy reinforcement to the government's debating strength, while in his own department, he worked with quiet efficiency and unwonted tact. His relations with the governor-general, the Marquess of Hastings (formerly Lord Moira), however, never got beyond the stage of formal correctness. An appalling snob, Hastings resented being responsible to man he regarded as a parvenu. Canning remained at his post for four years, until 1820, when the government reluctantly agreed, at the behest of the new King, George IV, to introduce a bill enabling him to divorce Queen Caroline (see Chapter 18). As a personal friend of the Queen, Canning felt that he could not be associated with a move against her, and proffered his resignation. Liverpool, thinking that this was, in reality, a bid by Canning to secure a more senior post, offered him the Home Secretaryship, in succession to the ageing Lord Sidmouth. Canning, however, declined, writing to Liverpool that 'Lord Sidmouth's office is just the one upon the daily details of which this unhappy question must operate with the most sensible and constant effect' (Rolo, p. 102). So Canning retired, with the unspoken understanding that he would return to office once the divorce issue was out of the way. Yet when, a year later, with the withdrawal of the Bill and the subsequent death of the Queen, Liverpool proposed to bring him back, George IV vehemently objected. When it was suggested that Canning should instead go to India as governor-general, in succession to Lord Hastings, there was a barrage of dissent, led by Hastings himself, who argued that the Indian princes would never accept someone of such low birth. The King, however, anxious to get Canning as far away from his court as possible, enthusiastically accepted the nomination, and Canning prepared to pack his bags to depart for Calcutta, reflecting that the ample emoluments would at least permit his wife to replenish her somewhat depleted fortune. Both of them had been devastated by the death of young George Charles, in March 1820, which had knocked the raw edge off Canning's political ambitions, and perhaps predisposed them to the prospect of starting a new life together in the Far East. But, shortly before they were due to sail, the hand of God struck: in August 1822, Castlereagh committed suicide (see Chapter 18).

Liverpool was now adamant that Canning must return to the cabinet as Castlereagh's successor, both as Foreign Secretary and Leader of the Commons.

The King, still hostile, made indirect inquiries to see whether the Prime Minister would regard his refusal as a resigning matter, and – not being prepared to take the risk – very reluctantly agreed. He told the Lord Chancellor, Lord Eldon (a firm opponent of Canning) that he had been called upon to make 'the greatest personal sacrifice that a sovereign ever made to a subject, or indeed, taking all *the circumstances*, that man ever made to man' (Rolo, p. 113). At the age of 52, Canning finally regained the position he was in 1809, the intervening 13 years being largely wasted in terms of his political advance. Yet he was an older and a wiser man – more patient, less arrogant and much less inclined to intrigue. In fact, during the five years of his second Foreign Secretaryship, he was much more intrigued against than intriguing. The main intriguers were the King himself, and the ultra-Tory element in the Cabinet, which comprised virtually all the ministers in the House of Lords with the exception of Liverpool himself, who was his firm and constant ally. Although temperamentally very different from his predecessor, and fellow Irishman, Castlereagh, their views were rather similar. Both of them, though Protestants themselves, were strongly in favour of Catholic emancipation, and both of them believed in following what might be described as a 'liberal' foreign policy. This principally meant dissociating themselves from the Holy Alliance powers of Austria, Prussia and Russia, who were bent on intervening in smaller states to suppress liberal or nationalist movements. Canning effectively carried on with Castlereagh's policies, though he enunciated them far more clearly and defended them with great oratorical effect in speeches both in the House of Commons and on public platforms. The effect of these speeches was to greatly increase his popularity in the country, while mitigating the hostility of the Whigs, who broadly approved, while up-setting many of his fellow Tories.

His most effective opponent within the cabinet was the Duke of Wellington, who became the chief spokesmen of the 'ultras', and whose standing was boosted by his close relations with the King. George IV, who sympathized with the Holy Alliance, actively plotted with the 'ultras' to undermine Canning, egged on by their ambassadors, who were frequent visitors to his Court. A notable intriguer was the Princess Lieven, whose husband was the Russian Ambassador, but who, more significantly, was the mistress of the Austrian Chancellor, Metternich. She was to leave a vivid picture of the machinations around the court and government in her letters to Metternich and other personalities, published long after her death. With Liverpool's backing, Canning was able to see off all the plots against him, but meanwhile worked hard to overcome the King's hostility. In this, he was to be helped by the current, and last, of the long line of royal mistresses, Lady Conyngham, with whom the King was completely besotted. Canning offered a vacant Under-Secretaryship in his department to her son, Lord Francis Conyngham, which pleased the King mightily. He was even more delighted when Canning recommended the appointment, as Ambassador to the newly established republic of Buenos Aires (later Argentina), of Lord Ponsonby, a previous lover of Lady Conyngham, whom George IV wished to be sent as far away as possible. As both Foreign Secretary and Leader of the Commons, Canning was necessarily in frequent contact with the King, who, easily bored with public affairs, was surprised to find him a much more congenial inter-locutor than the great majority of his colleagues. He was charmed by Canning's wit and candour, and began to develop some of the affection for him that he had felt for Fox, when he was a young man, 40 years earlier. From being a fer-ocious opponent, he became a strong supporter of Canning, and lent no further countenance to those plotting against him.

The first crisis that Canning had to deal with, which he inherited from Castlereagh, was the determination of the Holy Alliance to use French troops to intervene in Spain, to suppress a liberal constitution and enforce the dicta-torial rule of the new Bourbon monarch, Ferdinand VII. Canning used every means he could to discourage this venture, but when the French invasion began, in April 1823, it was clear that the only recourse left to him was to go to war with France, with Britain's recent allies firmly lined up on the other side. Canning might conceivably have stayed the French hand by the mere threat of war, but – though sorely tempted – he refrained from doing so, partly at least because it was far from clear that he would have been supported by the King and his cabinet colleagues if he had attempted this. Acutely conscious that he had suffered a setback, he determined that, if France had regained con-trol over Spain, she should not also be allowed to extend her influence to the New World by helping to restore Spanish control over her revolted colonies in Latin America. He made it clear that the British Navy, which he also employed (with only very partial success) to help suppress the international slave trade, would prevent this from happening. This – together with the proclamation of the Monroe doctrine by the US President in January 1823 – effectively guar-anteed the independence of the newly established states. Independence was one thing, diplomatic recognition quite another, and Canning had a long and difficult struggle before he was able to persuade the King and his cabinet col-leagues to extend it. It was only in 1825 that the first Latin American ambas-sador, from Colombia, was able to present his credentials. Canning's prime motivation was undoubtedly to further British interests by opening up the whole of Latin America to British trade and investment, but he successfully dressed up his policies in liberal and internationalist rhetoric, famously de-claring, in a parliamentary speech in December 1826: 'I resolved that if France had Spain, it should not be Spain with the Indies. I called the New World into existence to redress the balance of the Old.'

Canning became a popular hero throughout Latin America, and to this day his statue dominates many city squares, and there is hardly a major town which does not have a street named after him. In Greece, he is less celebrated, unlike Byron, whose death at Missolonghi in 1824, during the Greek national uprising against the Ottoman Turks, brought him lasting renown. Arguably, however, Greek independence, recognized by the great powers in 1829, owed much more to Canning's subtle diplomacy. This aimed equally at stopping the Turks from brutally suppressing the uprising and at forestalling Austrian and Russian military intervention. It did not prevent an eventual war between Russia and Turkey after Canning's death, but it gave vital breathing space to the Greeks and set at least a temporary limit to Russian expansion into the Balkans. Canning's final foreign policy success was in Portugal, following the death of John VI in 1826. His legitimate successor was his eldest son Dom Pedro, who preferred to remain in Brazil, where he had been proclaimed Emperor four years earlier. He abdicated in favour of his eight-year-old daughter, Maria, appointing his sister Isabella as Regent, and granting the country a liberal constitution. Yet Dom Pedro's younger brother Miguel, claimed the throne for himself, and amassed an army of right-wing sympathizers on the Spanish side of the frontier, ready to invade his country with the backing of the Spanish government, egged on by the French ambassador. Miguel's forces crossed into Portugal in November 1826, but Canning reacted with commendable dispatch, and immediately mobilized 5,000 troops to send to Lisbon, whose arrival galvanized the Portuguese resistance, and Miguel's troops were driven out by the following January. Canning achieved one of his great debating successes, when he defended his action in Parliament, on 12 December, saying: 'We go to Portugal, not to rule, not to dictate, not to prescribe constitutions, but to defend and preserve the independence of an ally. We go to plant the standard of England upon the well-known heights of Lisbon. Where that standard is planted, foreign domination shall not come' (Dixon, p. 250).

This intervention, and this speech, foreshadowed many made two or three decades later by Lord Palmerston, who was already a junior member of Liverpool's government, and who counted Canning as his mentor. Doubling up his Foreign Secretaryship with the leadership of the House of Commons put enormous strain on Canning, as it had on his predecessor, Castlereagh. He had to spend long hours listening to virtually every debate in the House, and was the government's principal spokesman on a wide range of issues, which had little or no connection with foreign policy. He once admitted that the two jobs ought not to be combined, but said that 'he would rather die' than consent to 'their separation in his person' (Dixon, p. 254). He suffered severely from gout, and his health deteriorated sharply during the five years of his second term as Foreign Secretary. The climax came in January 1827, when he caught a severe chill attending the funeral of the Duke of York, when he quixotically lent his coat to the ailing Lord Chancellor, Lord Eldon, one of his fiercest cabinet opponents, and never really recovered.

Less than a month later, Lord Liverpool suffered the cerebral haemorrhage which led to his retirement from the premiership. The only serious candidates to succeed him, from within the cabinet, were Canning and a somewhat reluctant Wellington. After some vacillation, George IV invited Canning to take over the government, but immediately half the cabinet, including Wellington, announced their resignation, as did no fewer than 41 office holders. It was estimated that around half of them were opposed to Canning because of his championship of Catholic emancipation and the other half because they objected to him personally. It was immediately clear that Canning would be unable to form a purely Tory government, but he secured the King's permission to approach the Whigs to see whether they would be willing to participate in a coalition. The Whig leader, Charles Grey, now the 2nd Earl Grey, was firmly opposed. Despite his progressive views on such subjects as parliamentary reform, he declared himself unalterably opposed to having 'the son of an actress' as Prime Minister. Other Whigs, however, were more forthcoming, notably the 3rd Marquess of Lansdowne, the son of the former Prime Minister, Lord Shelburne. Protracted negotiations eventually led to Whigs taking over almost half the cabinet portfolios, with Lansdowne as Home Secretary, the Duke of Devonshire as Lord Privy Seal and Lord Lyndhurst as Lord Chancellor. Canning became Prime Minister, and Chancellor of the Exchequer, on 10 April 1827. His cabinet was not completed until 16 July. On 8 August, he died, after five days of intense pain caused by inflammation of the liver and lungs. He was 57 years old, and had served for only 119 days. Almost his entire premiership had been taken up with the formation of his government, though he did introduce a budget on 1 June, and was able to complete the parliamentary passage of the Corn Amendment Bill (somewhat liberalizing the Corn Law), which he had earlier introduced, and on which he made his last speech in the Commons, on 21 June. He was buried in Westminster Abbey, fittingly alongside Pitt, and his widow was made a Viscountess by a deeply grieving George IV.

Canning was, without doubt, one of the most gifted politicians of the nineteenth century. As a young man, he showed tremendous promise: a fine speaker, persuasive in argument, decisive in action, enormously intelligent, he lacked only patience and discretion. These came to him later in life, perhaps after he had missed his best chances of progressing to the top. Whether he would have made a great Prime Minister, we shall never know. As it is, he is principally remembered as one of our most effective foreign secretaries.

Works Consulted

Derek Beales, 2004, Article in *Oxford Dictionary of National Biography,* Oxford, Oxford University Press.
Peter Dixon, 1976, *Canning:Politician and Statesman*, London, Weidenfeld & Nicolson.

John Ehrman, 1996, *The Younger Pitt: The Consuming Struggle*, London, Constable.
Norman Gash, 1984, *Lord Liverpool*, London, Weidenfeld & Nicolson.
Denis Gray, 1963, *Spencer Perceval: The Evangelical Prime Minister 1762–1812*, Manchester, Manchester University Press.
Wendy Hinde, 1973, *George Canning*, London, Methuen & Co.
Lucille Iremonger, 1970, *The Fiery Chariot*, London, Secker and Warburg.
Wilbur Devereux Jones, 1967, *'Prosperity' Robinson*, London, Macmillan.
P.J.V. Rolo, 1965, *George Canning: Three Biographical Sketches*, London, Macmillan.

20
Frederick John Robinson, Viscount Goderich, 1st Earl of Ripon – Inadequate Stopgap

Andrew Bonar Law, who was Prime Minister for barely seven months in 1922–3, was dubbed the 'Unknown Prime Minister'. A better candidate for this dubious honour might have been Viscount Goderich, who lasted a mere four months in 1827–8. He had the added handicap of relative anonymity. For most of his long life he was known either as Frederick Robinson or the Earl of Ripon. It was only for a six-year stretch, which included his premiership, that he was known as Goderich. He was born on 30 October 1782, the second of three sons of the 2nd Baron Grantham, and his much younger wife, Lady Mary Jemina Grey Yorke, daughter of the 2nd Earl of Hardwicke. Both Lord Grantham, who as Foreign Secretary had negotiated the peace terms with the American colonies in 1782, and his father had been cabinet ministers, and another kinsman, Lord Malmesbury, was also a prominent politician and diplomat. So, the young Frederick John Robinson came from a very well connected family, who were heirs to several titles and vast estates. Unfortunately, however, all these went to his elder brother, Thomas, even though there was only ten months between their ages. Robinson was to be one of the more obvious examples of younger sons deciding on a political career as their route to fame or fortune. (Of the 53 Prime Ministers to date, only 13 were only sons or the first born in a family).

Lord Grantham was a very fond father, and it was a devastating loss to Frederick and his brothers (the younger of whom was not to survive infancy), when he died, aged 41, shortly before Frederick's fourth birthday. From an early age, Frederick, whose first education was received at the hands of his parents, proved much more able than his brother, and was an excellent, but not outstanding scholar, both at Harrow School and at St. John's College, Cambridge, from which he graduated in 1802. An extremely amiable, popular and rather studious young man, he enrolled at Lincoln's Inn to study law, but did not persist for very long with his studies. The Peace of Amiens, in 1802, enabled Robinson to visit France in a party led by Lord and Lady Bessborough, a leading Whig couple who were family friends. Several members of the party were presented to Napoleon, but, his biographer recounts, 'whether or not Robinson met the man whose career he followed with a mixture of fascination and distaste is unknown' (Jones, p. 10). The following year, he had intended to go on the Grand Tour, but the resumption of hostilities made this impossible. Instead, he set off for Ireland, where his cousin, the 3rd Earl of Hardwicke, had become Lord Lieutenant in the Addington government. In his pocket, he carried a letter written by his brother, now the 3rd Lord Grantham. This explained that

> It was necessary to find him some 'proper occupation' pending the next election, when he would be returned to Parliament, and that he hoped ... 'some situation under you might present itself, which tho' at present rather subordinate, might be an extremely proper situation, for one with an inclination, and I can say without vanity with abilities to appear in [the] future in a higher one. (Jones, p. 11)

Lord Hardwicke knew his family duty, and promptly appointed Robinson as his confidential secretary. Robinson was to spend more than two years working for Hardwicke, and acting as his personal representative in visits to ministers in London. He then, as his brother had predicted, became a Member of Parliament in the 1806 general election. None of the seats which his broader family controlled was vacant, so he had, perforce, to purchase a 'rotten' borough, the Irish constituency of Carlow near Dublin, under the control of the Earl of Charleville. The price he paid is unknown, and it is not clear who put up the money. He was 24 years old, and a very personable young man, with blue eyes and blond hair, though by no means as good-looking as his elder brother. Robinson did not appear to have strong political views at the time, and it was initially unclear which party he would support. He was, in fact, cross-pressured by his family connections – Hardwicke leaning towards the new Prime Minister, Lord Grenville, and the Whigs, while Lord Malmesbury was a strong Pittite. In fact, throughout his life, moderate without any deep partisan commitments, he would probably have preferred to pursue an independent line. Malmesbury, however, was ambitious for his kinsman, and when the Portland government was formed, in March 1807, managed to secure for him a nomination to the Admiralty Board. To no avail, as he recounted in his diary:

> In the morning I spoke to Fred. Robinson about his accepting the Admiralty; he doubtful, with no good reason, but influenced by the Yorkes, and his own family. Spoke to Lady Grantham; she irresolute, and, though not saying so, manifestly against his taking office, under an Administration she did not think would last. (Jones, p. 16)

Nevertheless, Robinson did throw in his lot, though very loosely, with the Tories, and his adherence was strengthened by his change of seat in the 1807 general election. He was elected for Ripon, a Yorkshire constituency which was to return him unopposed in eight further contests. It was controlled by his distant cousin, Elizabeth Sophia Lawrence, a strong Tory and a spinster, who was reputedly in (unrequited) love with his very handsome elder brother, Thomas. Robinson was not a frequent performer in parliamentary debates, but created a good impression as a relatively open-minded MP who spoke clearly and always with moderation. Then, in December 1808, he received a letter from the Leader of the House, Spencer Perceval, inviting him to move the address at the opening of Parliament in 1809. Robinson waited several days to reply, realizing that this would be tantamount to a formal declaration of support for the Portland government. He then wrote to Hardwicke saying that 'this step may possibly not meet with your entire approbation', and asking for his indulgence. Hardwicke's reply has not survived, but as he continued to correspond cordially with his cousin, it must be assumed that he was not too upset. Having thus finally nailed his colours to the mast, he soon acquired a powerful patron in Viscount Castlereagh, the Secretary for War and the Colonies, who invited him to become an Under-Secretary in his department, the following April. He remained in office for less than six months, until October 1809, when the Portland government resigned, and Castlereagh was excluded from the succeeding Perceval government. Perceval pressed Robinson to stay on, but both Hardwicke and his brother, Charles Yorke, who had been a supporter of Portland, advised him not to, as they believed that the new government would not long survive. Robinson followed their advice, but Yorke himself subsequently became First Lord of the Admiralty in Perceval's government, and offered him a post as one of the Lords of the Admiralty, with a salary of £1,000 a year, which Robinson gratefully accepted.

During this period Robinson became associated with a group of serious-minded youngish Tory MPs, who dined together at the Alfred Club, and were known as the Alfred Club Set. All of them came from an aristocratic or wealthy background, all represented pocket or rotten boroughs and most of them had been at university together, either at Oxford or Cambridge. Apart from Robinson, they included two future Prime Ministers – Sir Robert Peel and Lord Palmerston. They shared a common political outlook, but their unanimity (though not their friendship) was shattered, in 1812, when Canning successfully proposed a motion in the Commons advocating Catholic emancipation. Robinson was among those who voted in favour, despite the strong opposition of Malmesbury and of Miss Lawrence, to whom he wrote a careful letter of justification, explaining that emancipation would conciliate Ireland and yet would not 'endanger the perfect security of the Protestant establishment'. The vote was significant as perhaps the first sign that Robinson was following his own independent judgement, and was leaning towards the 'liberal' side of the Tory party. It did him no harm at all with Castlereagh, who shared his views, and hastened to bring Robinson into the Liverpool government, of which he was the most influential member, when it was formed after the assassination of Perceval. The post he obtained for Robinson was Vice-President of the Board of Trade, where he was immediately immersed in the minutia of waging economic warfare against the French. In lieu of a ministerial salary, Castlereagh secured two sinecures for him, though he apparently only drew the emoluments of one of them.

When Castlereagh left London, in December 1813, with plenipotentiary powers, to meet with the sovereigns of Russia, Prussia and Austria, in the closing stages of campaign against Napoleon, and to negotiate a peace treaty with the restored Bourbon government, he took Robinson with him, as a counsellor and friend, and the ties between them grew even stronger. At Liverpool's urgent request, Robinson returned in May, after the signing of the Treaty of Paris, to report back to Parliament, and to prepare for the visit of the crowned heads of Europe to London the following month. He received a rapturous welcome, something of the glory of the victory achieved after so many years of struggle was reflected upon him, and his popularity soared. Four months later, this 31-year-old impecunious bachelor surprised his family and friends by getting married, apparently after a whirlwind courtship. Ten years earlier, his brother, Thomas, had married the 'transcendently beautiful' daughter of the Earl of Enniskillen. Frederick Robinson was also to marry an earl's daughter, but she was notably devoid of either charm or beauty. She was, however, the sole heir to a very considerable fortune, and the world drew what seemed to be the appropriate conclusion. Lady Sarah Hobart was the daughter of the 4th Earl of Buckinghamshire, President of the Board of Control for India in Liverpool's government, and was also a kinswoman of Castlereagh. She was to prove a very serious handicap to Robinson, being demanding, neurotic and hypochondriacal, but the couple remained devoted to each other through all their vicissitudes, so perhaps the world was mistaken.

The first important parliamentary duty which Robinson was to perform after peace was restored was to move the adoption in the Commons of the famous 'Corn Law', the President of the Board of Trade being in the Lords. As Robinson was later to be credited, along with William Huskisson, as an architect of the free trade measures adopted during the final years of the Liverpool government, it is paradoxical that he was at least nominally responsible for the most notoriously protectionist measure to be adopted during the nineteenth century (see Chapter 18). In fact, Robinson seems to have been extremely lukewarm about the measure, carefully setting out both the case for, and the case against, during his parliamentary speeches. This did not save him from being a target of a London mob, furious at a measure which they believed would push bread prices through the roof. Fearing that his house in Old Burlington Street was about to be attacked, he evacuated his wife and himself to her father's residence, leaving his servants to protect his property, and their own lives, with the help of some soldiers supplied by the Home Secretary at Robinson's request. In the ensuing melee two unfortunate bystanders, one a widow, were fatally wounded, one at least of the shots being fired by Robinson's butler, James Ripley. A conscience-stricken Robinson subsequently recounted the incident in a speech in the Commons, but was so overcome by emotion that he burst into tears, earning him the nickname of 'the Blubberer'. He was unable to shake this off, as this was to be only one of a number of occasions when his emotions got the better of him. The effect on Robinson's wife, who was pregnant at the time, was a great deal worse. She was reported to have reacted 'in a most extreme manner', while W.D. Jones comments: 'Lady Sarah's fears seem to have grown gradually from morbid anxiety to positive obsession during the next decade, haunting, nagging fears, destructive to her own peace of mind, as well as that of her husband' (Jones, p. 64).

Robinson served as Vice-President for six years, but effectively was in charge of the department because the President, the Earl of Clancarty, took his duties extremely lightly. In 1818 he retired and Robinson took over, serving for a further four years, and joining the cabinet. He was thus responsible for trade policy over a full decade. During this period, he showed himself an effective administrator, and a true disciple of Adam Smith, whose works, and those of other economists, such as David Ricardo (who sat in the Commons on the opposition benches), he had closely studied. Conscious as he said, on more than one occasion, that Britain could not hope to sell its products in foreign markets if their traders were unable to export goods to Britain in return, he set his face against prohibitive tariffs, and was always on the look-out to reduce, or remove them, when the opportunity arose. He also worked hard to restore trading relations with the United States, which had been broken by the 1812–14 War, leaving a legacy of renewed bitterness between the two sides. The Americans were extremely touchy about negotiations, having long experience of condescension by British ministers, and were therefore delighted when both Robinson and Castlereagh showed themselves more forthcoming than their predecessors. The result was the Commercial Convention between the two countries, signed on 3 July 1815, and eight years later two Acts of Parliament, sponsored by Robinson, opening up a large number of harbours in the West Indies and Canada, as Free Ports, open to American ships and those of all other nations. The US Congress passed a reciprocal act in the following year. The US Ambassador in London, Richard Rush, a 'radical democrat', later left his impressions of the two British ministers with whom he had to deal. His verdict on Castlereagh was 'that he was dangerous to all the remaining liberties of England', but at the same time called him 'the British statesman who was most interested in promoting Anglo-American goodwill'. On Robinson, he wrote several years later: 'We are amongst those who think very favourably of Lord Goderich' He called him a 'clear-headed, diligent and efficient man of business', and especially noted his 'fine education' and 'admirable temper', concluding that Robinson was 'an intellectualised version of Lord Liverpool' (Jones, p. 86).

The suicide of Castlereagh. in August 1822, deprived Robinson of his patron, but in the subsequent government reshuffle, he was promoted Chancellor of the Exchequer. From this time onward, he was generally seen as a supporter of Canning, but did not enjoy particularly close relations with him. However, his role as Chancellor, at a time when Britain was strongly emerging from the postwar depression, established him as a major political figure, and one who, largely because of his great amiability, had virtually no enemies. He benefited from the budgetary policy of his predecessor, Nicholas Vansittart, who bequeathed him booming tax revenues. For the first time in many years, the budget was in surplus, and it continued to be until his final year at the Exchequer. In addition, he was the beneficiary of a large windfall, when Austria quite unexpectedly repaid an old debt of £ 2.2 million, which had practically been written off as a loss. The result was that for the first three years, he was able to deliver expansionary budgets, abolishing many of the more pernickety taxes, including those on 'windows, male servants, wheeled vehicles, occasional house servants, occasional gardeners, certain ponies and mules, horses and mules engaged in agriculture and trade, on clerks and shopmen of traders, and some other items of a similar nature' (Jones, p. 101). He flanked his tax cuts, with sweeping tariff reductions, which led to his being hailed as the author of the first real Free Trade budgets in British history. Some later scholars have questioned whether he was their true architect, suggesting that his contribution was less than that of William Huskisson, his successor as President of the Board of Trade. Nevertheless, it was Robinson who claimed the credit, and was rewarded with the nickname of 'Prosperity Robinson'. His stock rose very high, but was somewhat dented during his last year as Chancellor, when he was judged to have badly mishandled a financial crisis, and it seemed probable that Robinson's next budget would show a deficit. He became the object of unaccustomed criticism, though, as his biographer makes clear, it was of a far more gentle nature than another chancellor might have experienced. This was due, he recounted, to Robinson's popularity, on both sides of the House, which was 'the reward not only for his liberal policies , but for the essential kindness, honesty and integrity of his character, which made him a sort of special person whom the customs of the House protected from personal invective' (Jones, p. 122). Stories abounded of Robinson's geniality, lack of side and ability to laugh at himself.

One famous incident, related by the political diarist and MP, John Wilson Croker, is quoted by W.D. Jones:

> Everyone knows the story of a gentleman's asking Lord North who 'that frightful woman was?' and his lordship's answering, that is my wife. The other, to repair the blunder, said I do not mean *her*, but that monster next to her. 'Oh!' said Lord North, 'that monster is my daughter'. With this story Fred. Robinson, in his usual absent enthusiastic way, was one day entertaining a lady whom he sat next to at dinner, and lo! the lady was Lady Charlotte Lindsay – the monster in question.

Nevertheless, Robinson found it hard to bear the strain of even mild criticism at a time of considerable upheaval in his private life. By this time his wife was suffering from severe mental illness, which led her to believe that she was dying, even though there was no objective reason for this belief. Her condition was then made much worse by the prolonged illness of their beloved daughter, Eleanor, who died, aged 11, in October 1826, their other child, a son, having died ten years earlier, aged only two days. Lady Sarah reacted from their loss by forming excessive fears about the health of her husband, being extremely reluctant to let him out of her sight As a result, Robinson wrote to the King, requesting permission to be absent from 'the approaching *early* session of Parliament', so that he could take his wife to their country estate in Lincolnshire. The King warmly responded in the affirmative, and Lady Sarah then aged 33, determined that they should have another child, who was to be born a year later, in October 1927. (Unlike his two siblings, George Frederick Samuel Robinson was to enjoy a long life, dying only in 1909, after a long and distinguished political career of his own). Two months later, in December 1826, Robinson wrote a further letter, this time to the Prime Minister, Lord Liverpool, in which he suggested that he should go up to the House of Lords, and occupy a less arduous position in the government. Liverpool replied that the government's position was extremely fragile, and that it was inexpedient to make any ministerial changes at that juncture, and Robinson agreed to carry on for the time being.

Liverpool was to suffer a cerebral haemorrhage, in February 1827, and shortly afterwards retired as Prime Minister. George IV momentarily considered Robinson as Liverpool's successor, in order to avoid having to choose between Canning and Wellington, but eventually decided on the former. Canning offered Robinson the post of Secretary for War and the Colonies, combined with leadership of the House of Lords, to which he was appointed as Viscount Goderich. Goderich served for too short a time to have a measurable effect in his department, but his leadership of the Lords left a great deal to be desired. It is doubtful if the Canning government enjoyed a majority in the Upper House – no confidence vote was called during its four months in office. What was soon apparent was that its enemies were more cohesive than its friends. Goderich had to face fierce attacks from right-wing Tories, who wanted nothing to do with Canning, and from the main body of Whigs, under Earl Grey, whose object was to replace his administration with a purely Whig government. A third element of dissension was a faction around Charles Stewart, the third Marquess of Londonderry, the half-brother of Castlereagh and a former friend of Goderich's. He now bitterly attacked him for having transferred his loyalties to Canning – Castlereagh's earlier foe – even though the two men had long since patched up the quarrel which had led to their duel many years earlier. Goderich never succeeded in imposing himself on the House and was humiliated when a government bill to ameliorate the worst effects the Corn Law was effectively shredded by a hostile amendment pro- posed by the Duke of Wellington. Goderich's short spell in the Lords cast serious doubts upon his leadership qualities, but George IV lost no time in sending for him to succeed Canning, when the latter died on 8 August 1827. Goderich, who was 44, would have been well advised to refuse the King's offer to form a government, particularly under the restrictive conditions which were imposed. He had already told colleagues that he doubted whether a coalition between liberal Tories and only a minority faction of the Whig party could long survive, or one which was not at liberty to proceed with Catholic emancipation.

Yet these were just the conditions on which George IV was insisting, and he also imposed a veto over the personnel of the Cabinet. Thus he declined to accept Lord Holland, Charles James Fox's nephew and political heir, who would have greatly boosted political support for the government, and insisted – against Goderich's advice – on the appointment of the ultra Tory, John Charles Herries, as Chancellor of the Exchequer. It is fairly clear that George IV had little confidence in Goderich, but chose him as a stopgap – to avoid, or post- pone, a painful choice between appointing a Tory government under the Duke of Wellington or a Whig one under Lord Grey.

So, the government started on an uncertain note and never developed any rhythm. While there were some changes in personnel, its composition was similar to that of Canning's government, an uneasy coalition between moderate Tories and moderate Whigs, with the Prime Minister, the most mod- erate of them all, actively regretting the mere existence of party distinctions. His closest associate in the government was Huskisson, Secretary for War and the Colonies, but more importantly also leader of the House of Commons. Conscious that they would soon have to meet Parliament, they began pre- paring the draft of a King's speech setting out a government programme for the next session. One idea which Goderich was working on was for a new property tax which would replace a range of indirect taxes, and which in fact foreshadowed Sir Robert Peel's introduction of the first peace-time income tax in 1842. But ministers' attentions, and unity of purpose, were distracted by dramatic news which arrived from Greece. Before his death, Canning had negotiated a treaty with Russia and France that the three countries should jointly endeavour to secure a peaceful end to the struggle for Greek independence by attempting to secure a separation of the belligerent forces. On the Turkish side, this largely consisted of a force which had been sent from its vassal state of Egypt, under the command of Ibrahim Pasha, and which was currently terrorizing the Morea. A naval force, under the British Admiral Codrington, had been sent to the Aegean and was monitoring the Egyptian and Turkish fleets, which were lying in the harbour of Navarino. A dispatch was drawn up to send to Codrington urging him to act with great circumspection and not on any account to provoke hostilities. Due to the length of time it took to consult too many ministers and officials, there was a delay in sending it out, and, in the meantime, Codrington had taken affairs into his own hands and, on 20 October 1827, sailed his warships into Navarino, mooring them provocatively close to the Turkish and Egyptian vessels. It was never established who fired the first shots, but by the end of the afternoon 60 of the 89 Turco-Egyptian ships had been sunk, with a loss of 8,000 men, while the much smaller allied fleet had lost no ships and suffered no more than 200 casualties. The Battle of Navarino was to go down in history as the last major engagement between sailing ships. The steam age was about to emerge.

The cabinet was completely split on whether to proclaim Codrington a national hero or have him court-martialled, and there was considerable apprehension that the country would find itself in a totally unwanted war against Turkey. There were anguished discussions on how the issue should be handled when Parliament met in January 1828. At this stage a row broke out between ministers on a relatively trivial issue – the chairmanship of a finance committee to be set up in the Commons. After consulting several colleagues, Huskisson approached a Whig MP, Lord Althorp, to ascertain whether he would be willing to accept this post. Herries then protested, on the grounds that he, as Chancellor of the Exchequer, should be responsible for the nomination, but when the majority of the cabinet backed Huskisson appeared to acquiesce. Partly because of these quarrels, Goderich now determined that the cabinet must be strengthened before the beginning of the parliamentary session. Together with Huskisson and Lord Lansdowne, the leading Whig minister, he agreed that he should tell the King, when he met him on 8 December, that it was now essential to bring Lord Holland into the government and balanced this with the suggestion that the former Tory Foreign Secretary, Marquess Wellesley, should also be brought in. Goderich was under exceptional pressure at this time, not only because of the cabinet splits, but because of the mental state of his wife. She had successfully given birth to their second son, on 24 October, but was now suffering from an extreme form of post-natal depression and was behaving in a most unreasonable way towards her husband. Huskisson referred to this in a letter he wrote at this time, saying that Goderich was 'in a most pitiful state...his spirits are worn out...he has lost his powers of decision'. He attributed this not to the new cabinet crisis, but to 'constant worry in which he has been kept by his all but crazy wife' (Jones, p. 189). Goderich's interview with the King was far from satisfactory. George IV was quite happy to accept Wellesley, but refused point blank to have Holland. Goderich indicated that this would be unacceptable to his cabinet colleagues. The three men then wrote a formal letter to the King, stressing the need for more 'solid and united support', They proposed that the Duke of Wellington or Lord Hill should be made Master of the Ordnance, that Wellesley should become Lord President of the Council and that Holland should be brought into the Cabinet. The alternative, they implied, was resignation. Then, unknown to his colleagues, Goderich added a postscript to the letter, in the following terms:

> Lord Goderich cannot conclude this statement without venturing to add, how deeply he feels his own inadequacy to discharge the great duties of the situation to which your Majesty's far too favourable opinion called him. His own natural infirmities have been aggravated by a protracted state of anxiety during the last two years; his health is enfeebled, and above all he fears that the health of one dependent upon him for support and strength is still in a state of such feebleness and uncertainty as to keep alive that anxiety to a degree not easily compatible with the due discharge of duties which require the exertion of the energies of the strongest mind. (Iremonger, 1970, p. 80)

Goderich certainly did not intend this to be taken as a letter of resignation. It was merely a plea for more understanding from the King of the difficulties which he was in. George IV, however, construed it as such, sending a cold reply, which contained the words: 'The King can only regret that Lord Goderich's domestic calamities unfit him for his present situation, but over this the King unhappily has not control' (Jones, p. 19). He then sent for the Earl of Harrowby, a former Foreign Secretary and Lord President of the Council, and invited him to form a new government. Harrowby eventually declined, recommending the King to persist with Goderich. Goderich's reprieve did not, however, last long. Herries, possibly egged on by the King's private secretary, Sir William Knighton, who was anxious to see the back of the Goderich government, renewed his objection to the appointment of Lord Althorp to head the Finance committee of the Commons, and said that he would resign if the appointment went ahead. Huskisson thereupon declared that he would resign if it did not.

The King, concluding that the Prime Minister was incapable of controlling his ministers, told Goderich when he saw him on 8 January 1828 that he considered the government as dissolved. According to one account, Goderich, very upset, dissolved in tears, and the King lent him his handkerchief. Two weeks later, Wellington accepted an invitation to form a government, in which the majority of Goderich's ministers retained their posts. Goderich had served for a total of 130 days, and his was the only government in modern British history not to present itself to Parliament.

Despite this humiliation, this was by no means the end of Goderich's ministerial career, which was one of the longest in British history. Altogether, he served for 30 years, 20 of them as a Cabinet minister. He was also to establish something of a record as to the number of different party labels under which he served. Starting off as a Tory, he was to join the Whig government of Lord Grey, in 1830, as Secretary for War and the Colonies, and later, as Lord Privy Seal, becoming the Earl of Ripon in 1834. In 1841, he was back in Sir Robert Peel's Conservative government, for a further term as President of the Board of Trade, with the young Gladstone as his deputy. His final post , also under Peel, was as President of the Board of Control of India, in 1843–46. When the Conservative Party split over the abolition of the Corn Law, he became a Peelite. Living until 1859, he died at the age of 76. His wife, whose mental health was to recover remarkably quickly once he had left the premiership, outlived him by eight years.

Goderich was valued as a Cabinet colleague as somebody who was conscientious, reliable and easy to deal with. His very amiability, however, proved a fatal weakness as head of government. There was neither enough steel in his character to assert his will over awkward colleagues, nor enough firmness to enable him to deal effectively with a blustering but essentially weak-willed monarch. His career is an illustration of the 'Peter Principle', enunciated, in 1966, by the Canadian author Laurence J. Peter. He argued that, in any hierarchical organization, people are promoted until they reach their level of incompetence. In Goderich's case that level was very high indeed – the premiership.

Works consulted

Norman Gash, 1984, *Lord Liverpool*, London, Weidenfeld & Nicolson.

Wendy Hinde, 1973, *George Canning*, London, Purnell Book Services.

Lucille Iremonger, 1970, *The Fiery Chariot*, London, Secker & Warburg.

Wilbur Devereux Jones, 1970, *'Prosperity' Robinson: The Life of Viscount Goderich 1782–1859*, London, Macmillan.

Peter Jupp, 2004, Article in *Oxford Dictionary of National Biography*, Oxford, Oxford University Press.

21

Arthur Wesley (Wellesley), 1st Duke of Wellington – Military Hero, Political Misfit?

The war hero, who takes up politics and rises effortlessly to the top, is a familiar figure in American history. At least eight presidents – George Washington, Andrew Jackson, William Henry Harrison, Zachary Taylor, Ulysses S. Grant, Benjamin Harrison, Theodore Roosevelt and Dwight Eisenhower – conform to this stereotype. The only British Prime Minister to have followed a similar route is Arthur Wellesley, 1st Duke of Wellington, and even he is somewhat different, as he already had a fair amount of political experience before his military triumphs. Born Arthur Wesley, in Dublin, on 1 May 1769 (the same year as Napoleon), he was the fifth son and sixth child of nine children. His father, the 1st Earl of Mornington (in the Irish peerage), was a composer and Professor of Music at Trinity College, Dublin. His mother, the former Anne Hill, was the eldest daughter of the 1st Viscount Dungannon. Both of his parents were products of the Protestant ascendancy in Ireland. Arthur grew up a solitary child, closer to his father than his mother, and showed no promise whatsoever, either academically or at games, other than at playing the violin, at which he seems to have inherited something of his father's skill. (That is, if the first Lord Mornington was, indeed, his father. According to the historian L.G. Mitchell, Arthur later came to doubt his mother's fidelity, and believed his actual father may have been a gardener on the Wesleys' Irish estate – Mitchell, p. 183). The family moved to London, where they lived in rented rooms in Knightsbridge, Lord Mornington now being quite heavily in debt. When Arthur was 12, Lord Mornington suddenly died, and the following year, Arthur and his younger brother Gerald were sent to Eton by his eldest brother, Richard, nine years his senior and now the 2nd Lord Mornington. Richard had to mortgage the family estate in County Meath in order to pay the school fees. Richard himself had been a brilliant scholar at Eton and had gone on to win the Chancellor's prize for a Latin ode at Christ Church, Oxford, but neither of his younger siblings made any sort of mark at the school; the only memorable event being recorded by the school's historian was a fight Arthur had with Robert Smith, the brother of the well-known clergyman and wit, Sydney Smith.

After only three years, he was taken away from the school, in order to save money, by his mother, Anne, who not only did not lavish her son with love but seems to have actively disliked him. She took him to live in Brussels, where she hoped to live more economically than in London, and set him, with only mediocre results, to learn French. Yet Arthur showed little aptitude for this, and spent most of his time lounging around, his only interest being playing the violin, 'the only species of talent that the young man appeared to possess', according to a fellow lodger (Hibbert, 1997, p. 6). Anne soon returned to London, leaving Arthur to fend for himself in Brussels, but when her youngest son, Henry, decided to join the army, concluded that her 'ugly son Arthur', also, was 'good for powder and nothing more', and packed him off to a military academy for young noblemen at Angers, in western France. Here he learnt fencing and ballroom dancing, and how to sit properly on horseback. He also greatly improved his French, developed a taste for gambling, and most probably lost his virginity in a local brothel. He much impressed the academy's director, Marcel de Pignerolle, who was reported as saying that he had 'one Irish lad of great promise, of the name of Wesley' (Longford, 1969, p. 21). He returned to London, aged 17, in 1786, ready to take advantage of the patronage of his brother Richard, now an MP in the Irish House of Commons, and a Junior Lord of the Treasury in the government of the Younger Pitt. Shortly before his eighteenth birthday, he became an ensign in the 73rd (Highland) Regiment of Foot, and was soon promoted Lieutenant and appointed as aide-de-camp to the Marquess of Buckingham, the Lord Lieutenant of Ireland. His duties were extremely light, and it soon became apparent that his role was intended to be that of a courtier rather than filling any administrative or military function.

It was a lazy and corrupt court, and Lieutenant (later to be Captain, Major and Lt.-Colonel) Wesley, who periodically bought promotion with money advanced by his brother Richard, spent much of his time playing cards, getting into debt and visiting brothels, in one of which he was arrested and fined for assaulting a French client with a stick. There was a more serious side to him, however; he regretted not having been to a university, and a visitor to his home was surprised to find him reading John Locke's *Essay concerning Human Understanding*. In April 1790, he became a Member of the Irish House of Commons, for the family seat of Trim and was elected unopposed. He was not yet 21 and had to wait for two years before making his maiden speech. In 1792, he began courting Lady Kitty Pakenham, the 20-year-old daughter of the 2nd Earl of Longford, described both as a 'beauty' and 'bookish'. In 1793, he proposed marriage, only to be rejected because her elder brother, Thomas, soon to become the third Earl, considered that neither the income nor the prospects of a captain in the 18th Light Dragoons would be sufficient to keep his sister in the life to which she had become accustomed. Mortally offended, Arthur determined to turn his back on Ireland and go to war against the French, with whom hostilities had finally broken out four years after the storming of the Bastille. At the same time, he resolved to take his own life in hand, to exercise the maximum of self-discipline, to become a real professional soldier instead of a part-time dilettante. Gone would be the endless hours playing cards, gone his ineffectual entry into politics, gone his beloved music – he was to burn his violin with his own hands in the summer of 1793. Nevertheless, it was to be another year, before he was able to join the British army in Flanders, sailing from Cork in June 1794, as a Lieutenant-Colonel. Before he left, he wrote a final letter to Kitty, summarized in the first of two enthralling biographical volumes written by Elizabeth Longford, the wife of a lineal descendant of Kitty's brother, Thomas:

> He could not accept that all was over. As Lord Longford's decision was founded upon 'prudential motives', an improvement in Arthur's situation could alter everything. There followed a sentence of which the last phrase was decisively to alter Arthur's life. If something did occur to make Kitty and her brother change their minds – 'my mind will still remain the same'. To an honourable man, those seven words would be binding. (Longford, 1969, p. 36)

The campaign which Wesley was to join in Flanders was one of the least glorious in British military history. Commanded by the ineffectual Duke of York, the British troops were made mincemeat of by their much more motivated and better-led French adversaries. In Lady Longford's words, Colonel Wesley:

> saw the effects of a divided command, of a winter campaign in a bitter climate, of no properly organized food supply or winter clothing, of local inhabitants who preferred the enemy to their allies, and above all of a prolonged and undisciplined retreat. In short, as he told [the Earl of] Stanhope forty-five years later when his friend was suggesting that the Dutch campaign must have been very useful to him: 'Why – I learnt what one ought not to do and that is always something'. (Longford, 1969, p. 37)

Lieutenant-Colonel Wesley was, however, one of very few British officers whose reputation was enhanced by the campaign, being congratulated by headquarters on an action he had fought at Boxtel, in Holland, the first military engagement in his life, in which, thanks to the iron discipline which he imposed on his troops, they had repulsed a French charge. After returning to Dublin,

Wesley then had to wait another dispiriting year before receiving command of the 33rd Regiment of Foot, with orders to sail to India. Still heavily in debt, he resolved to spend the long voyage out in self-improvement, purchasing a library of well over 100 books, including works on military history, law, economics, philosophy and theology. In the course of her voluminous research, Elizabeth Longford was able to establish that five of the books purchased by Wesley also appeared in the *Bibliothèque du camp* which accompanied Napoleon Bonaparte on his 1798 campaign (Longford, 1969, p. 44n.) After arriving in Calcutta, and later Madras, Wesley soon settled again into the desultory round of self-indulgent regimental life, which he had known in Dublin, embarking on numerous affairs, mainly with the wives of fellow officers. Of only medium height, with a too prominent nose, Wesley was neither blessed with the appearance of a matinee idol, nor did he possess any small talk. Yet his conversation was interesting, and by this time he exuded great self-confidence, and already a certain charisma which marked him out from his fellows. His position in India was transformed by the arrival a year later of his eldest brother, Lord Mornington, as Governor-General, accompanied by a younger brother, Henry, as his private secretary. Some years earlier, Mornington had abandoned the use of his surname, Wesley, in favour of an older spelling 'Wellesley', which sounded more aristocratic and removed any suspicion that he might be connected with the recently established religious movement of Methodism, of which the brothers John and Charles Wesley were the leading spirits. Colonel Arthur Wesley now followed suit, while Mornington was shortly advanced in the peerage and became known as Marquess Wellesley.

The governor-general's main objective in India was vastly to expand the territory under British control and to extirpate any French influence within the peninsula. Ignoring claims of military seniority, he blatantly used his brother as the main instrument of his ambitions, giving him successive military commands in campaigns against the Sultan of Mysore, Tipu Sultan, and then the powerful Maratha confederacy in central India. He won all his battles, with the exception of a night-time skirmish in woods outside the great fortress of Seringapatam, which he was able to reverse the following day. His greatest victory, against the odds, was at Assaye, in September 1803, when his 7,000 men defeated a 50,000-strong force of Marathas in a battle in which Arthur Wellesley had two horses shot from under him. The extent of his victories wiped out any criticism of his brother's favouritism, and he returned home in 1805, with a knighthood, the rank of Major-General and £42,000 in war booty to his credit.

He was now 36, appeared to have the world at his feet, but – encouraged by a mutual friend and would-be matchmaker – promptly fired off a renewed proposal to Kitty Pakenham, with whom he had had no contact in 12 years. The passing years had not enhanced her attractions. 'By 1802, Kitty had decided that the affair was over, became engaged to another man, broke it off, and suffered a nervous breakdown which destroyed her youthful charm and self-confidence' (Gash, 2004). She wrote back to Wellesley accepting his proposal, but suggesting that they should meet again before he finally committed himself. Wellesley demurred, and set in hand the arrangements for the marriage to be celebrated in Dublin on 10 April 1806. He was soon to regret his impetuosity, whispering at the altar to his brother, the Rev. Gerald Wellesley, who performed the ceremony, 'She has become ugly, by Jove!' (Iremonger, p. 89). Many years later, he explained to his friend, Harriett Arbuthnot, 'I married her because they asked me to, and I did not know myself. I thought I should not care for anybody again, and that I should be with my army, and, in short, I was a fool' (Ibid.). One does not need a Ph.D. in psychology to conclude that what motivated him was his injured pride: that he wanted to demonstrate to the Longfords that they had been grievously wrong in undervaluing him a dozen years earlier. It did not take long before both partners concluded that the marriage had been a mistake, finding that they had few interests in common and derived no pleasure from each other's company. Two sons were, however, born within the first two years; after that they spent a minimum of time together, and Wellesley did not once come home on a visit during five years he was away fighting the Peninsular War. Largely at the suggestion of Lord Grenville, the Prime Minister, who had replaced Pitt on his death in Janury1806, Wellesley now resumed his political career, though at a much higher level. He was elected to the House of Commons for Rye, in April 1806, and, the following year was appointed Chief Secretary for Ireland in the new government formed by the Duke of Portland. He accepted the post on condition that it should not be allowed to interfere with his army career. He proved himself brisk and efficient in the performance of his duties, and gained general respect, but his heart was not really in it. Later,when in the summer of 1808 an expedition was sent to Copenhagen to seize the Danish fleet, he successfully applied to participate, and was awarded the command of a division which routed a Danish force sent to relieve the siege of the capital.

Back in Dublin, he resumed his duties, but for less than a year, when, with the outbreak of the Peninsular War, he was put in temporary charge of an expeditionary force sent to resist the French invasion of Portugal. He sailed from Cork, with 9,000 men, landing in Portugal on 1 August 1808, and within three weeks had inflicted two crushing defeats on the French army led by Marshal Junot. The French sued for an armistice, but by then two more senior generals had arrived from London, who took over command from Wellesley, and negotiated ridiculously generous terms with Junot's representatives, the so-called Convention of Cintra. Wellesley was appalled, but counter-signed the agreement, which led to his being bracketed with his two seniors in a subsequent parliamentary enquiry, which exonerated him. A year later he was back in Portugal, in charge of the British army after the death of Sir John Moore. He was not to return to Britain until June 1814, following the apparent final defeat of Napoleon. The largest contributory factor to the Emperor's downfall was obviously his disastrous invasion, and subsequent retreat, from Russia, in 1812–13, but historians have generally attributed second place to the Peninsular War, known as 'Napoleon's Spanish ulcer'. In this, Wellesley had held down vastly superior French forces, depriving Napoleon of their use elsewhere, and had then – together with Spanish and Portuguese auxiliaries – succeeded in expelling them from the Peninsula. He pursued them into France, gaining a final military victory at Toulouse in April 1814, four days after Napoleon's abdication, news of which had not yet reached the south of France. Wellesley's command had gained him great renown, he won all the pitched battles which he fought, was created successively an earl, a viscount and finally Duke of Wellington, and voted £400,000 by a grateful House of Commons, as well as being awarded estates in Portugal, Spain and the Netherlands by the monarchs of these newly restored countries. He used the parliamentary grant to purchase two imposing residences – at Stratfield Saye, in Hampshire, and Apsley House, at Hyde Park Corner in London.

But before he could enjoy them, he was called back for foreign service – as Ambassador to the restored Bourbon court in Paris. Arriving in August 1814, he cut a glittering social figure, with legions of attractive young women throwing themselves at his feet. Among his amours were at least two of Napoleon's former mistresses, one of whom was later to recall that 'M. le duc était beaucoup le plus fort' (Longford, 1969, p. 375). He also had at least one assignation with the famous courtesan, Harriette Wilson, with whom he had consorted more than a decade earlier in London, and who later tried to blackmail him, in exchange for expunging his name from her notorious memoirs. The Duke's response was immediate: 'Publish and be damned', he wrote to her egregious publisher. The unhappy Kitty, who belatedly joined her husband in Paris, with their two sons, was severely embarrassed by his conduct and was the recipient of many pitying glances. The Duke undoubtedly added lustre to the British representation, none of the Austrian, Prussian or Russian representatives being able to compete with his renown, but his many distractions left him little time to concentrate on serious diplomacy. This may have been one reason why, in February 1815, when Lord Castlereagh, the Foreign Secretary and Leader of the House of Commons, was recalled from the Congress of Vienna to resume his parliamentary duties, Wellington was sent to replace him. Another reason why Wellington was removed from Paris was a lively fear of assassination attempts by disgruntled Bonapartists. Within a month of his arrival in Vienna, however, Napoleon escaped from Elba, and the four principal powers represented at the Congress – Britain, Austria, Russia and Prussia – promptly appointed him commander-in chief of the allied armies, and Wellington set out for Brussels to prepare for the final showdown with the restored Emperor.

The climax was the battle of Waterloo, fought on 18 June 1815, which he was to describe as 'a damned close run thing...I was nearly beat'. On the day, he showed himself a better general than Napoleon, marshalling his forces more intelligently, showing greater flexibility and more actively inspiring his troops. Was Wellington a military genius? No, if measured against the achievements of Alexander, Julius Caesar, Frederick the Great or Napoleon. Yes, if 'genius' is defined, as it was by Thomas Carlyle, as the ability to take infinite pains, or, more vulgarly, 'nine tenths perspiration, one tenth inspiration'. Wellington was essentially a defensive general, and as such had few equals. No general took as much trouble as Wellington in securing logistical support and adequate weaponry and supplies for his troops, cultivating the goodwill of local inhabitants in foreign campaigns, spying out battlefields in advance, choosing the best defensive positions for his troops and actively directing the flow of battle by ceaselessly riding round from unit to unit during the course of a conflict. He also had a healthy respect for his opponents. He never met Napoleon in battle before Waterloo, but he was heard to say that if he learnt that the Emperor was about to take personal command of his troops it would be more fearful news than if 40,000 French reinforcements were on their way. By contrast, Napoleon was by no means in awe of his British opponent, blaming French defeats in Portugal and Spain on his marshals rather than on Wellington's skill. On the morning of Waterloo, he said to Marshal Soult: 'Just because you have been beaten by Wellington you regard him as a great general. I tell you that Wellington is a bad general, that the English are bad troops and that this battle will be a picnic. We have ninety chances in our favour and not ten against' (Hibbert, pp. 177–8). Wellington was a harsh disciplinarian, who became known as the Iron Duke, though he himself on several occasions showed scant respect for the orders of his superiors. Though often grumpy and short tempered, he was invariably straightforward and honourable in his dealings. He was popular with his troops and was customarily known as 'Nosey', a comment on his appearance rather than his curiosity. If Wellington had a fault as a general, it was in his reluctance to give credit to his subordinates. He mortally offended the family of his second-in-command at Waterloo, Lord Uxbridge, whose leg was shot off as he rode at Wellington's side, by giving him only the most perfunctory of mentions in the dispatch which he sent to the Secretary for War after the battle. He has subsequently been criticized for his alleged attempts to downplay the role of Marshal Blücher and his Prussian army, without whose timely arrival the battle would undoubtedly have been lost. That said, Wellington was far from glorying in his victory. 'Nothing except a battle lost can be half so melancholy as a battle won. I hope to God that I have fought my last battle', he told his friend, Lady Shelley, 'It is a bad thing to be always fighting' (Ibid., p. 185).

His wish was granted, but Waterloo was by no means the end of either his military or his broader public career. He returned to Paris, no longer as ambassador but commander-in-chief of the 150,000 strong allied army of oc cupation which was to remain in France until the defeated nation had paid off the reparations which had been imposed by the Congress of Vienna. After three years he was recalled to join the cabinet of Lord Liverpool's government. The attraction of this for Liverpool was obvious. His government was highly unpopular and going through a bad patch. Its standing could only be improved by the recruitment of so eminent a figure as the Iron Duke. Wellington was more hesitant: he did not wish to label himself as a party politician, though his Tory views were obvious enough. He consented to join only after being persuaded by Castlereagh, who had appointed him to his command in the Peninsular War, and supported him through thick and thin against his many critics. Even so, Wellington insisted on the condition that he should not be counted as a political supporter of the government and would be free to go his own way if it subsequently fell, without being committed to opposing any alternative ministry. The original plan was that he should be appointed as a minister without portfolio, but Lord Mulgrave offered to relinquish the post of Master-General of the Ordnance in his favour, which was regarded as a highly suitable post because of his military experience.

Wellington took great care over the running of his department, and showed himself an outstanding administrator, but played little part in general cabinet discussions for the first three to four years, until the death of Castlereagh, in 1822. He then played a significant role in persuading George IV to accept the appointment of George Canning as Foreign Secretary and leader of the Commons. The King was highly reluctant (see Chapters 18 and 19), but when Wellington added his great influence to that of Liverpool, he finally gave way. It was not long before Wellington regretted having helped bring Canning back on board. He gradually emerged during the succeeding five years as his main opponent within the Cabinet both on foreign and domestic affairs. In foreign policy, he unsuccessfully opposed, together with the ultra Tory peers, Canning's championship of independence for Spain's Latin American col-onies and his opposition to the Holy Alliance (of Russia, Prussia and Austria) in Europe. On the domestic front, he was against Liverpool and Canning's Liberal Tory policies, and in particular Canning's determination to press for Catholic emancipation. This was to lead to a misunderstanding which was later to cost Wellington dear. Unlike the Tory ultras, he was not opposed to Catholic emancipation as such; his private views were little different from Canning's. What he was against was bringing the issue to a head at that par-ticular time. The Tory ultras did not appreciate the difference, and he was de-cidedly their candidate for the succession when Liverpool's health broke down early in 1827. Wellington himself professed reluctance, and told the House of

Lords that he 'felt disqualified from the post of prime minister and lacked the capacity to fill it', adding: 'My Lords, I should have been worse than mad if I had thought of such a thing' (Gash, 1990, pp. 122–3). In the event, George IV chose Canning, and Wellington and half of the Cabinet promptly resigned, leading Canning to seek Whig support in order to form an administration. In January 1827, Wellington had been appointed Commander-in-Chief of the army, on the death of the Duke of York. He resigned in a huff, in April, when Canning became Prime Minister, but he was persuaded to resume the post when Canning died, and was replaced as Prime Minister by Lord Goderich, in August 1827.

Goderich lasted barely four months before he was effectively dismissed by George IV, who, this time, unhesitatingly sent for Wellington as his successor. George IV was now determined to have a purely Tory government, having a marked aversion to the Whig leader, Lord Grey. Sir Robert Peel, the Tory leader in the Commons, who had been Home Secretary in the previous three governments, would have been an obvious alternative, but the King did not like him either. Despite Wellington's earlier diffidence, he accepted without demur. He was 58 years old, and took office on 22 January 1828. There was an immediate crisis due to Wellington's pigheaded determination to retain his post as commander-in-chief. He refused to see any constitutional impropriety in combining the two posts, and only backed down, with exceedingly bad grace, in the face of the opposition of his entire cabinet. George IV's hope was that Wellington would succeed in restoring the sort of balance within the Cabinet that Lord Liverpool had enjoyed. The Whigs were excluded, and the posts were divided up between the more traditional Tories, mostly peers, and those who were regarded as Liberal Tories or Canningites, of whom the most prominent was William Huskisson, the Secretary for War and the Colonies. The other Canningite ministers were Lord Palmerston MP, as War Secretary, Charles Grant as President of the Board of Trade and the Earl of Dudley as Foreign Secretary. The Chancellor of the Exchequer was Henry Goulburn, a far from assertive personality, who was described as having 'the self-effacing habits of a good civil servant'. Robert Peel returned to his earlier post as Home Secretary, which he combined with the leadership of the Commons, and was clearly the number two man in the government. On the question of Catholic emancipation, the most divisive political issue of the day, the Cabinet was almost evenly divided, with seven pros and six antis, and a general agreement not to push the issue in the face of the King's known opposition. On parliamentary reform, of which the Duke himself was a resolute opponent, there was a clear majority against, though the Canningites were more sympathetic.

Although Wellington started off by enjoying the affection and goodwill of nearly all his colleagues, it was not long before difficulties began to arise. Naturally authoritarian by temperament, he had long grown used to having his decisions accepted unquestionably by his military subordinates, and he found it hard to accept any disagreement or criticism from his cabinet colleagues. The daily round of compromise and negotiation which was meat and drink to most politicians and senior officials was wholly alien to his character. He also did not appear to have any serious misgivings about his own abilities to lead. When the Princess Lieven, the wife of the Russian ambassador and a notorious intriguer, especially among the upper ranks of the ultra Tories, suggested to him that his lack of practice as a parliamentary speaker would be a handicap, he replied: 'No...to begin with, I can learn; if I want it, it will come back to me. And, even if I can't, the Duke of Portland had no more idea of speaking than I have, and yet he was at the head of the administration' (Gash, 1990, p. 125). Nevertheless, he confessed in a private letter to the Prince of Orange, immediately after his appointment, that it was an office 'for the performance of the duties of which I am not qualified, and they are very disagreeable to me' (Ibid., p. 119).

It was therefore predictable that he would have a bumpy ride, and in the process upset many of his supporters. The first to feel aggrieved were the ultra Tories, who did very badly out of the Duke's initial cabinet appointments; in particular, Lord Eldon, the former Lord Chancellor, was left out, much to his chagrin. Wellington's own family was also grievously disappointed. His eldest brother Richard, Marquess Wellesley, who had previously held the posts of Governor-General of India, Foreign Secretary and Lord Lieutenant of Ireland, had wrongly assumed that he would be included, while the second brother, William Wellesley-Pole, who had married into great wealth and was a former minister under Lord Liverpool, also had his hopes dashed.

The ultras were further put out by one of the earliest pieces of legislation introduced by the Wellington government. This was a long overdue measure to repeal the Test and Corporation Acts, excluding Protestant dissenters (that is, Quakers and members of nonconformist churches, such as Methodists, Congregationalists and Baptists) from holding various public offices. These acts had long been a source of vexation to important sections of the business community, even though they were seldom applied in practice. Wellington had not himself been in favour of repeal, but when the government was defeated in the Commons on a motion moved by Lord John Russell, he concluded – as a military man – that the government's position was untenable and that a healthy retreat was required. He therefore pushed through a government bill repealing both pieces of legislation. The ultras were horrified, not so much because of the minor damage which this did to the status of the Church of England, but because they saw it as the thin edge of the wedge for Catholic emancipation. They began to lose all confidence in Wellington. It was, however, the Canningites who were the first to withdraw their support, and this was due to the other major controversial issue – parliamentary reform. The trigger was a debate on the disfranchisement of two parliamentary boroughs on account of gross electoral corruption. These were the Cornish borough of Penryn and the Nottinghamshire seat of East Retford. The issue, so far as East Retford was concerned, was whether its representation should be transferred to the fast growing city of Birmingham, which had no parliamentary seats at all, or merely amalgamated with the neighbouring district of Bassetlaw. The government decided to choose the amalgamation option, but when a division was called in the Commons by the opposition, two government ministers, Lord Palmerston and William Huskisson, decided to abstain and remained in their seats. Peel, as leader of the House was totally unprepared for this, and, Joseph Planta, the Tory chief whip firmly admonished Huskisson for his 'disloyalty'. Huskisson, a proud and over-sensitive man, went home and wrote a letter to Wellington offering his resignation. He did not mean it to be accepted – 'his ill-conceived letter was meant as an *amende honorable* for his demonstration of the night before' (Gash, 1976, p. 99) – but Wellington and Peel took it at face value, and started to look for a successor. When alarmed Canningites sought to intervene on Huskisson's behalf, they were told that if he did not mean to re-sign he should formally withdraw his letter, which he was too proud to do. So, after five days, Wellington informed Huskisson that arrangements had been made to appoint a successor, and the other three Canningite cabinet minis-ters resigned in sympathy with him, as did William Lamb (the future Lord Melbourne), who was Chief Secretary for Ireland.

Wellington's stiff-necked response was a major political blunder, and fundamentally weakened his government over a very peripheral issue. Henceforth, it enjoyed no stable majority in the House of Commons, and had a greatly weakened front bench. It also, inadvertently, brought to a head the Catholic issue, which the government had vainly hoped to keep in abeyance. The government reshuffle did Wellington no good at all. In place of Huskisson, Palmerston, Dudley and Grant, he brought in, respectively, Sir George Murray, Sir Henry Hardinge, the Earl of Aberdeen and Vesey Fitzgerald. The first two were generals from the Peninsular War, which led to accusations that Wellington was inaugurating a military dictatorship, but the appointment which brought him real problems was that of Fitzgerald. He was MP for the Irish constituency of Clare, and in accordance with the law at the time was forced to resign his seat and fight a by-election before taking up his ministerial post. Normally such proceedings were a mere formality, with the retiring MP being returned unopposed or with a large majority after only token opposition. This time, however, the leader of the Catholic Association, the brilliant lawyer, Daniel O'Connell, caused a sensation by offering himself as a candidate, despite the fact that, as a Catholic, he would be ineligible to take his seat. The franchise in County Clare was wider than in many constituencies, being open to '40 shilling freeholders'. This meant that a large number of peasant farmers, most of them Catholics, could vote, and vote they did, returning O'Connell with 2,057 votes to 982 for Fitzgerald.

Once again, the old soldier concluded that he was in an indefensible position that it would cause an uncontrollable wave of discontent in Ireland if O'Connell was deprived of his seat and Catholic emancipation was not granted.* He therefore determined finally to corner George IV and insist that the appropriate legislation should be tabled. This was far from being an easy task. The King, at best a slippery customer, was fast declining after a life of unrestrained excess. He was seriously ill, his mind wandering, so much so that there were serious fears that he would follow his father into insanity. Wellington had several audiences in his bedchamber, with the King anxious to discuss any issue except that of emancipation. He railed at Wellington, claimed that he himself had fought at the battle of Waterloo and earlier, at Salamanca, where he had led 'a magnificent charge of dragoons disguised as General Bock' (Hibbert, p. 271). George's resistance was stiffened by the presence of his younger brother, the Duke of Cumberland, normally resident in Hanover, of which he later was to become King, a fanatical anti-Catholic who threatened to put himself at the head of popular protest marches. Probably only Wellington could have persuaded the King to give way. He finally succeeded in doing so, though only after having threatened to resign if Cumberland was not sent back to Hanover.

Wellington's own thoughts on this episode, and on many others throughout his premiership, and generally in the period between 1820 and 1832 have been preserved for posterity in the political diaries of his *confidante* Harriett Arbuthnot, published only in 1950. The much younger second wife of Charles Arbuthnot, a senior Foreign Office official and later a cabinet minister, she and Wellington used to walk arm-in-arm together in Birdcage Walk and in St. James's Park, while he recounted to her all the details of the daily political round. It was widely assumed that she was his mistress, but this was apparently not the case. Charles was almost as close to Wellington as his wife, and when she died of cholera in 1834, at the age of nearly 41, he gave up his own home and went to live with Wellington in Apsley House for the following 16 years until his own death in 1850.

Wellington long had been anxious to resolve the Catholic issue, and in 1825 had submitted a memorandum to the Liverpool government, advocating a concordat with the Pope and the licensing of priests, who would in future receive a stipend from public funds, as a *quid pro quo* for admitting

---

*In an interesting historical parallel, in 1961, the Labour MP, Tony Benn, who had inherited a peerage, successfully contested a by-election in his Bristol constituency, but was then unseated in favour of the Tory runner-up. The government, however, hastened to bring in a bill enabling hereditary peers to disclaim their titles, and the Tory MP subsequently graciously resigned his seat in Benn's favour.

Catholics into Parliament. His memorandum, which was not published at the time, failed to win the approval of his ministerial colleagues, notably Peel, and it was Peel in particular who influenced the content of the Bill which the Cabinet put before Parliament in March 1829. It was to pass both Houses and receive the royal assent within six weeks. The Catholic Relief Bill differed greatly from Wellington's earlier proposal. It opened up the House of Commons, and all but a tiny list of senior public offices (of which the most important was the Lord Chancellorship) to Roman Catholics, provided for an amended parliamentary oath which they could take and balanced these concessions by two measures designed to promote security in Ireland and to limit the political influence of the Catholic majority. These were the banning of the Catholic Association as a subversive body, and the raising of the property qualification for voting in Irish constituencies to £10, rather than 40s. The Bill's parliamentary passage was remarkably smooth, being supported by the opposition Whigs and Canningites, and opposed only by the Tory ultras. Daniel O'Connell was delighted with the result, and exclaimed to his wife: 'Who would have expected such a bill from Peel and Wellington!' (Quoted in Gash, 1990, p. 158). The ultras now, however, regarded Wellington as their bitter enemy, and he was grossly libelled by the Earl of Winchilsea. When he refused to withdraw his allegations, Wellington demanded satisfaction, and they met on Battersea Fields on the morning of 21 March 1829. Both deliberately shot wide, after which Winchilsea belatedly offered an apology, which was accepted by Wellington, who then calmly rode off, to report on the affair to Mrs Arbuthnot (Hibbert, p. 294).

George's health continued to decline, and few believed his death could be long delayed. In the early summer of 1830, Wellington, tiring of the wear and tear of office and the long working hours which he, a conscientious man and stickler for detail, imposed upon himself, drafted a memorandum to Peel. In this he suggested that the approaching end of the reign would be an appropriate moment for him to retire and for Peel to take over the premiership. But he never sent it off, perhaps suggests Norman Gash, 'because of the objections made by his over-partial friends the Arbuthnots' (Gash, 2004). But George's death, on 26 June 1830, at the age of 67, undoubtedly hastened Wellington's departure.

The ensuing general election, occasioned by William IV's accession, was largely fought on the issue of parliamentary reform, and produced substantial gains for the opposition Whigs and Canningites. It seemed likely that the government would be defeated on the first occasion that an issue of confidence was voted on. Some very tentative approaches were made to the Canningites to see whether they could be drawn back into the government, and Wellington himself travelled up to Liverpool, Huskisson's constituency, for the grand opening ceremony of the new Liverpool–Manchester railway line. Ensconced in a luxury carriage, Wellington was chatting amiably with Huskisson through the carriage window, when a warning went up that the famous steam engine, George Stephenson's *Rocket*, was approaching on the other track, where Huskisson was standing. He made a clumsy effort to get out of the way and was fatally struck by the engine; he died a few hours later. Wellington was ever after to have a visceral dislike of the railways, but the more immediate effect of the tragedy was to forestall a formal approach to the Canningites, of whom Huskisson was the undisputed leader. Wellington then effectively sealed his fate as Prime Minister by a rabidly anti-Reform speech, which he made – for no good reason – in the House of Lords, on 2 November 1830. This not only united the opposition, virtually driving the Canningites into the arms of the Whigs, but upset many on his own side, including senior ministers, who would have preferred to produce their own moderate Reform Bill to head off the prospect of a more radical measure being carried by their opponents.

Wellington might have hoped that the previously disaffected ultra Tories would be encouraged by his speech, in which he said in as many words that the existing system of electoral representation was as near perfect as could be devised by mankind, that he was not prepared to bring forward any measure of reform, and would 'always feel it my duty to resist such measures when proposed by others'. But their venom against him was now so strong that many of them were consumed by the desire to drive him out of office, whatever the issue involved. Virtually everybody else was dismayed by the evidence that Wellington was totally out of touch with a growing groundswell of opinion in the country (see Chapter 22) that the time had at last come to grasp the nettle of reform, which all governments had studiously avoided since the Younger Pitt's unsuccessful efforts in the 1780s.

The Whigs were preparing to propose a reform measure on 16 November, and it was widely expected that this would lead to a government defeat. There was already a sense of crisis in the air: Wellington, however, was utterly confident that he would prevail. He was cocooned in his own overwhelming self-confidence, reinforced by his inability to consult freely even with his most senior ministers. Peel was to tell the diarist Charles Greville that 'the Duke was never influenced by men, though he was by women and the silliest women at that' (Hibbert, p. 290). In truth, however, the government had lost control of the Commons, and, on the day before the Reform measure was to be debated, fell to an unexpected ambush, provoked by a Tory malcontent, on a vote on the Civil List, going down by 233 votes to 204, with 34 Ultras voting with the Opposition. Wellington, now seriously disillusioned with the experience of governing, took this as a cue to throw in his hand, and promptly resigned. William IV, who did not share his brother's aversion to Lord Grey, summoned him to form a new government. This he was able to do without difficulty, blending Whigs and Canningites, and even including the former Tory Prime Minister, Lord Goderich.

Wellington's government had lasted for two years and 298 days. Despite its shambolic demise, it was not without its achievements. Apart from Catholic relief, and the repeal of the Test and Corporation Acts, it had passed a Bill (largely the work of Robert Peel) establishing a Metropolitan Police Force for the first time and had amended the Corn Laws in a liberalizing direction. In foreign policy, it had veered away from the liberal policies pursued by Canning, withdrawing the British troops guaranteeing constitutional rule in Portugal and adopting a more pro-Turkish position in the Balkans. This did not, however, preclude the establishment of Greek independence in 1829. Following his resignation, the Duke retired to his Stratfield Saye estate in Hampshire, where he was Lord Lieutenant of the county, and energetically applied himself to the restoration of order in the county, which was much affected by the so-called 'Captain Swing' riots and nocturnal burnings of hayricks provoked by growing rural unemployment caused, it was believed, by the introduction of mechanization. He also involved himself more in family affairs, adopting the three abandoned children of his scapegrace nephew, William, and placing them in the care of his Duchess, Kitty. This led to a late reconciliation between them, and a revival of his affection for her. He was to care for her devotedly in her final illness (possibly cancer), which led to her death on 24 April 1831, at the age of 59. The Duke was to outlive her by 21 years. He was regarded as a highly eligible widower, but never married again, though there was no shortage of ladies who would have been only too happy to take Kitty's place. One of these was the famous philanthropist and banking heiress, Angela Burdett-Coutts, who actually proposed to him, when she was 30 and he, 76. He good-naturedly declined and preferred to keep her as one of several ladies, with whom he enjoyed an intimate and probably chaste friendship comparable to, but less intense than, his earlier relationship with Harriett Arbuthnot, who had died in 1834. Another such *confidante* was the young Lady Salisbury, mother of the future Prime Minister.

The somewhat undignified collapse of his government was not the end of Wellington's political career, though he had little appetite for opposition politics. He unsuccessfully attempted to form a second government in May 1832, when Grey resigned because of a dispute with the King over the Reform Bill, and Grey resumed office. Later, when William IV agreed with Grey to create a sufficient number of new Whig peers to carry the Bill through the House of Lords, Wellington persuaded enough Tory peers to abstain to make this unnecessary, even though he remained a fervent opponent of reform. Once again, this demonstrated the determination of a military man not to die in the last ditch when the battle was clearly lost. Then, in November 1834, on the fall of the Melbourne government (see Chapter 23), he again became Prime Minister, but only for three weeks before handing over to Peel, who had been away in Rome. He continued to serve, under Peel, as Foreign Minister, until the following April, when the government fell, and he was Leader of the Opposition in the Lords for the following six years. Returning to office in 1841, as Minister without Portfolio under Peel, he loyally stuck with his chief and helped to push the abolition of the Corn Laws through the Lords, in 1846, even though he did not agree with the policy. He had resumed his position as Commander-in-Chief in 1842, and held this office until his death ten years later, his last public role being to organize massive cover for the police during the last great Chartist demonstration in 1848, the 'year of revolutions'. To general relief, the demonstration passed off peacefully and the troops were not needed. He was to die four years later, at the age of 83, and was buried with great pomp in St. Paul's Cathedral, London. For the last three to four decades of his life, Wellington held a unique place in British society. He was regarded as the first subject of the monarch; indeed George IV treated him as a near equal, addressing him familiarly as 'Arthur'. His appearance was known to virtually the whole population, nobody's face appeared in more cartoons or prints during the first half of the nineteenth century, and once when he was approached in the street by a stranger, who said 'Mr. Jones?' he famously replied 'If you believe that, Sir, you'll believe anything'. (In fact, Wellington bore a marked resemblance to George Jones, the Keeper of the Royal Academy). He carried with him the aura of a 'Great Man', and even those who did not accept this valuation conceded that he was, at least a 'great character', if not a 'national treasure'. His views were widely regarded as anachronistic, or just plain wrong, but he was respected for the sincerity with which he held them. Above all, he was credited – justly – with acting out of a strong sense of duty. His earlier enormous popularity did not endure among all social classes. He was widely reviled for his opposition to Reform and his house was attacked more than once by London mobs, while there was some booing at his funeral. His political career, as a whole, cannot be counted as a success, but he had one great achievement to his name, somewhat in spite of himself, that of Catholic emancipation. This finally laid to rest a controversy which had festered and poisoned political life for the previous three decades.

Works consulted

Norman Gash, 1990, (ed.), *Wellington: Studies in the Military and Political career of the First Duke of Wellington*, Manchester, Manchester University Press.

Norman Gash, 2004, Article in *Oxford Dictionary of National Biography*, Oxford, Oxford University Press.

Christopher Hibbert, 1997, *Wellington: A Personal History*, London, HarperCollins.

Richard Holmes, 2002, *Wellington: The Iron Duke*, London, HarperCollins.

Lucille Iremonger, 1970, *The Fiery Chariot*, London, Secker & Warburg.

Elizabeth Longford, 1969, *Wellington: The Years of the Sword*, London, Weidenfeld & Nicolson.

Elizabeth Longford, 1972, *Wellington: Pillar of State*, London, Weidenfeld & Nicolson.

L.G. Mitchell, 1997, *Lord Melbourne 1779–1848*, Oxford, Oxford University Press.

Edward Pearce, 2003, *Reform!: The Fight for the 1832 Reform Act*, London, Jonathan Cape.

22
Charles Grey, 2nd Earl Grey – In the Footsteps of Fox

If Earl Grey is a household name, it is less through his political accomplishments, than because a popular brand of tea has been named after him. Nevertheless, he must be reckoned as one of the more significant of Nineteenth-century premiers, as the architect of the 'Great Reform Bill', of 1832, an important staging post on the long road to parliamentary democracy. Charles Grey was born on 13 March 1764. He was the second of nine children, but effectively the eldest, as his elder brother Henry died a few days after his birth. His father, Sir Charles Grey, was a general, who distinguished himself as commander-in-chief in the West Indies during the American War of Independence, and a sizeable landowner in Northumberland, where the family had been established since the fourteenth century. His mother, Elizabeth Grey, was possibly a distant cousin of his father. Of great significance in young Charles's life was his uncle, Sir Henry Grey, a bachelor who made him his heir. He was Sir Charles's elder brother, and his estate, at Howick, was rather grander than the former's at Fallodon.

Very little is known about Charles's childhood. He was sent to a school at Marylebone in London, where he was apparently lonely and unhappy. His most traumatic experience as a child was inadvertently witnessing the public hanging of several forgers at Tyburn. This was to cause severe nightmares, which afflicted him periodically throughout his life. He went on to Eton, where he was to remain for eight years until 1781. He was not much happier there, forming no great affection for the school, and, like the Elder Pitt, declined to educate any of his own children at a 'public' school. He learned to write competent Latin verse, but, according to his own account, little else. He went on to Trinity College, Cambridge, where he lived an active and enjoyable social life, but left the University – like many other aristocrats at the time – without bothering to take a degree. He left for the Grand tour, but while he was away a vacancy occurred in the Parliamentary representation of Northumberland, due to Lord Algernon Percy inheriting a peerage. His Uncle Henry, a former MP for the county, lost no time in pushing the nomination of his 22-year-old nephew, who was returned unopposed in a by-election in July 1786. Sir Henry had promoted Charles as 'one who would follow in his own footsteps and who would be agreeable to the local country squires as a quiet backbencher of conservative instincts' (Smith, 1990, p. 9), fully expecting that he would be a loyal supporter of the Younger Pitt. Grey, however, an extremely handsome young man, very vain and with a high estimation of his own intellectual abilities, had other ideas. He soon fell in with the Whigs, captivated by the personality of Charles James Fox, and even more so by the leading Whig hostess, the glamorous Georgiana, Duchess of Devonshire. The daughter of the first Earl Spencer, and a collateral ancestor of Princess Diana, with whom she has been much compared, she and Grey soon became lovers and she bore him an illegitimate daughter. Her 'dull middle-aged husband' packed her off to the Continent, accompanied by his own mistress (and later second wife), Lady Elizabeth Foster, to give birth to the child, who was then entrusted to Grey's parents, who brought her up themselves, passing her off as Grey's much younger sister.

Grey's relationship with Georgiana did not last for more than a few years. His commitment to Fox, however, was to endure, as E.A. Smith recounts:

> Within a year, perhaps two at most, Grey had become what he was to remain for the rest of his life: a disciple of Fox's brand of liberal, populist yet basically conservative Whiggism, an advocate of 'civil and religious liberty all over the world', yet a political realist ever ready to temper idealism with expediency, a pragmatist who never lost sight of reputation and consistency, at once ardent and cautious, idealistic and calculating. (Smith, 1990, p. 10)

Highly ambitious, Grey was soon recognized as one of the finest speakers in the House of Commons, with an exceptionally clear style, though not quite able to match the oratorical heights of Pitt or Fox. He aspired to being recognized as Fox's chief lieutenant and collaborator; his principal rivals being the Irish-born playwright, Richard Brinsley Sheridan, a brilliant wit whose political judgement, however, left much to be desired, and, somewhat later, Fox's own nephew, the 3rd Lord Holland. Two years after the birth of his daughter, Grey, then aged 30, married the 18-year-old Mary Elizabeth Ponsonby, daughter of a leading Whig peer, in November 1794. It was a happy marriage, blessed with 16 children, and Grey became a devoted father, though this did not prevent him from having numerous affairs while he was away in London, including with Sheridan's second wife, Hecca, and, much later, when he was in his 60s, with Princess Lieven, the promiscuous wife of the Russian Ambassador and notorious intriguer at the court of George IV.

Grey's rise in the Whig hierarchy was hastened by the split in the party provoked by the French Revolution and its aftermath. The first to defect from

Fox was Edmund Burke, the Revolution's fiercest critic, but two years after war broke out between Britain and France, the Duke of Portland, the nominal leader of the party, took almost half of its parliamentary strength with him in joining Pitt's government, in July 1794. In the much depleted ranks of the Foxites, Grey now stood out as the brightest star. He had already established himself as the party's chief advocate of parliamentary reform, launching a popular movement entitled the Society of Friends of the People, in April 1792. This sounded a more extreme body than it actually was. Grey, no supporter of democracy, rejected the Radical demand for manhood suffrage, and restricted himself to calling for the elimination of 'pocket' and 'rotten' boroughs, most of which were represented by Tories, and a modest extension of the franchise in borough constituencies. Nevertheless, Fox hesitated to support the new organization, fearing the loss of support by the more conservative Whigs, and only reluctantly backed his protégé's initiative. When Grey introduced a parliamentary motion in support of reform, in May 1793, it was defeated by 282 votes to 41. His second attempt, four years later, was again defeated, by 256 votes to 91, leading to the 'secession' from Parliament of Fox, Grey and their supporters, who boycotted the House for 18 months. Throughout the 1790s, Grey and Fox had stoutly resisted the Pitt government's repressive measures against dissidents, arguing strongly against the suspension of *habeas corpus* and the restriction of the rights of assembly and of the press, while advocating peace with France. This alienated them from 'respectable' opinion, and the Whigs lost more and more parliamentary and popular support. Grey took up the issue of Catholic emancipation as well as parliamentary reform and was a strong opponent of the Act of Union with Ireland, passed in 1800.

Two events in 1801 had a marked personal effect on Grey. His father accepted a peerage, without consulting him, becoming the first Baron Grey. Grey was furious, as he realized that he would have to give up his seat in the Commons, when his father died, and that this would be a setback to his political career. He was much happier at the decision of his uncle, Sir Henry Grey, to give up living at Howick and to offer it to Grey as a residence for his own family. Grey, who eventually inherited the property in 1808, came to love Howick, where he luxuriated in the company of his rapidly growing family, and became more and more reluctant to travel to London to carry out his parliamentary duties. When his father was promoted to an Earldom in 1806, Grey assumed the courtesy title of Viscount Howick, but continued to sit in the Commons.

Also in 1801, Pitt resigned as Prime Minister, following George III's refusal to agree to Catholic emancipation, and this had the effect of ending the isolation of the Foxites. Pitt's Foreign Secretary, Lord Grenville, a strong advocate of emancipation, refused to join the incoming Addington government, and rapidly became one of its strongest critics (see Chapter 15). This brought him into contact with Fox and Grey, and they began to co-operate closely in opposition.

When Pitt returned to power in 1804, Grenville declined to resume office unless Fox was also admitted into the government, which George III vetoed. Grey and the other Foxites then refused to serve in the absence of their chief. Pitt's death in January 1806 left George III with little alternative but to appoint Grenville in his place, and to swallow his pride by accepting Fox as his deputy, as Foreign Secretary and Leader of the Commons. This enabled the Whigs to return to office, for the first time since 1783, as the leading element in Grenville's 'Ministry of all the Talents'.

In the new government, Grey was First Lord of the Admiralty, and, after Fox, the government's leading spokesman in the Commons. It was he who carried through the Commons the Bill abolishing the slave trade, the short-lived government's greatest achievement. At the Admiralty, he proved an energetic and effective minister, though he was over-ruled by his cabinet colleagues when he resisted pressure to authorize an attack on the Spanish colony of Buenos Aires, which – after initial success – proved a failure. After the death of Fox, in September 1806, he was preferred to Lord Holland (Fox's own choice) as Foreign Secretary and also became Leader of the Commons, and effective head of the Whig party. The government was swept from office when it tried to legislate to enable Catholics to achieve senior rank in the Army and Navy (see Chapter 16). George III forced the government to withdraw the Bill, and then insisted that no further measures of Catholic relief should be put forward during his lifetime, a pledge which the ministers were unwilling to give. The King then dismissed the government and replaced it, in May 1807, with a Tory administration, headed by the Duke of Portland. Grey, whose Foreign Secretaryship had lasted a mere six months, then suffered a further setback when Portland called an election, and he was unceremoniously removed from his Northumberland county seat, which he had represented for 21 years, by the Duke of Northumberland, who insisted on putting forward his own son, Lord Percy. An infuriated Grey regarded this as rank treachery by his previous friend and sponsor, and withdrew from the contest, having to make do instead with the pocket borough of Appleby, provided by his friend, Lord Thanet. Grey was now universally recognized as the leader of the opposition in the Commons, and made a powerful speech attacking the circumstances (a 'court intrigue') under which the Portland ministry had been brought to power, and pledging his continuing enmity. As the most talented debater in the House, he threatened to be a thorn in the government's side, but the death of his father a few weeks later removed him from the scene of all his earlier triumphs and condemned him to serve in what he regarded as the much less congenial atmosphere of the House of Lords. He wrote to his wife after his first speech in the chamber: 'What a place to speak in! With just enough light to make darkness visible, it was like speaking in a vault by the glimmering light of a sepulchral lamp to the dead. It is impossible I should ever do anything there worth speaking of' (Smith, 2004).

In the Lords, he largely deferred to Lord Grenville, who was now widely accepted as the notional leader of the Whig party, even though his parliamentary faction was much smaller than the Foxites, led by Grey. The two men were bracketed together in the public's perception as being joint leaders of the opposition, though no such post formally existed at that time. Thus began a dispiriting period of nearly a quarter of a century, during which the Whigs were to languish in opposition, and for the most part not offering a very inspiring alternative to the governments in power. For most of this time, the Whigs were badly led in the Commons, and neither Grey nor Grenville were consistent attenders in the House of Lords, preferring to spend the bulk of their time on their country estates. On several occasions – notably in 1809, when Portland resigned and was succeeded by Spencer Perceval – they muffed opportunities to return to government, insisting that a predominantly Whig administration should be formed, rather than being (as they perhaps wrongly assumed) merely junior partners in a coalition. Their hopes of achieving office when the Prince Regent assumed power in 1811 were to prove illusory. The Prince was initially forthcoming, but found their demands too exigent, and feared the reaction of his father if he were to return to sanity, and find out that he had ejected the Perceval government for no good reason.

Grey's subsequent career was to parallel Fox's to a remarkable extent, spending over 20 continuous years as Opposition leader, largely as result of his own insistence on maintaining the purity of his Whig principles. Like many other Whigs his attitude to the war against France was ambiguous. He no longer believed in peace at any price, seeing Napoleon as a dictator and aggressor, yet he was consistently pessimistic about the military prospects and downplayed Wellington's achievements in Spain. His earlier fierce ambition gradually waned, and for long periods he was inactive, springing back to life in 1820, when he emerged as one of the strongest and most effective opponents of George IV's attempt to divorce his wife, Queen Caroline. He made one of the finest speeches of his life, denouncing the Bill of Pains and Penalties in the Lords, and when the government dropped the Bill the new King's resentment against Grey was so great that there appeared little chance that he would ever again serve as a minister so long as George remained King. An opportunity did, however, arise, in 1827, when the already dying George Canning became Prime Minister in succession to Lord Liverpool, and was immediately abandoned by half the members of the Cabinet. With the permission of George IV, Canning applied to the Whigs to fill the vacant places, to be met with a blunt refusal by Grey, still the party leader (Grenville having given up in 1817). Grey regarded Canning as an unprincipled adventurer, but was apparently also influenced by his aristocratic disdain for his low birth, as the son of an actress. Other Whigs, led by Lord Lansdowne, were less fastidious, and agreed to serve (see Chapter 20), but the death of Canning after four months, and the dismissal of Lord Goderich's ministry after a similar period, led to the formation, in January 1828, of a purely Tory government under the Duke of Wellington.

Lord Grey was now 63 years old, and it looked as though his political career was gliding gently to its close. Yet three developments over the next couple of years enabled him to re-establish himself in the forefront of politics and to compensate for the many years of frustration by a final burst of achievement. These were the death, in June 1830, of George IV, and the succession of his brother, William IV, who had no ill-feelings towards Grey; the inability of Wellington to hold his government together, and the sudden surge of public opinion in favour of parliamentary reform. The surge had been long in coming. The Parliamentary system had remained virtually unchanged since the middle of the seventeenth century, and more and more anomalies had built up. These were well described by an American historian, Frank Woodbridge:

> There were rotten boroughs, in which the population had dwindled to little or nothing, and pocket (or nomination) boroughs, where one or very few men controlled elections, in effect appointing Members of Parliament. The Report of the Society of the Friends of the People indicated that 154 individuals sent 307 (out of 658) Members to the Commons. In the late 1820s, Croker, a Tory opposed to reform, concluded that at least 276 (out of 489) English Members were returned by patrons. There was a very uneven distribution of Members in relation to population. For example, more Members were elected in the two counties of Cornwall and Wiltshire than in the five counties of Middlesex, Somerset, Warwickshire, Worcester and Yorkshire, though the latter had a combined population of more than ten times the former. The franchise, with few exceptions, was very limited. Even in Westminster, generally considered a very democratic constituency, less than one quarter of adult males could vote. (Woodbridge, 1974, p. 344)

When Wellington resigned the premiership, in November 1830, William IV, who was himself convinced of the necessity of parliamentary reform, had no hesitation in sending for Grey, now aged 66. He would have preferred to lead a purely Whig administration, but in order to secure a parliamentary majority was compelled to appoint several Canningites and even one ultra Tory, the Duke of Richmond. It was an overwhelmingly aristocratic government, whose members, Grey was to claim, controlled more acres than any previous administration. In a letter to Princess Lieven, he justified his choices:

> In these times of democracy and Jacobinism it is possible to find real capacity in the high Aristocracy – not that I wish to exclude merit if I should meet with it in the commonality; but given equal merit, I admit I should

choose the aristocrat, for that class is the guarantee for the safety of the state and of the throne. (Smith, 1990, p. 259)

His government was also well stocked with his own relatives and in-laws, no fewer than seven of whom, including his eldest son, Viscount Howick MP, held government posts, while Lord Althorp MP, the Chancellor of the Exchequer and leader of the Commons – a key figure – was the nephew of his long dead former mistress, Georgiana. Apart from Althorp, the most senior posts were held by Viscount Melbourne (Home Secretary), Viscount Palmerston MP (Foreign Secretary), Lord Lansdowne (Lord President of the Council) and Lord Durham, known as 'Radical Jack' and Grey's son-in-law (Lord Privy Seal). The colleague whom he had the greatest difficulty in placing was the leading Whig lawyer and orator, Henry Brougham, whose views on Reform and other contentious issues were far more radical than his own. Grey feared he would dominate any proceedings in the House of Commons, to the embarrassment of the government, and to avoid this – after tricky negotiations – made him an offer he couldn't refuse. He became Lord Brougham and Vaux, and, by general consent, one of the greatest of Lord Chancellors. The government included a former Prime Minister, Lord Goderich, who became Earl of Ripon, and no fewer than four future ones – Melbourne, Lord John Russell, Edward Stanley (later Earl of Derby) and Palmerston.

Before it could get into its stride, the Grey government was faced by two urgent crises, one foreign, the other domestic. In August 1830, the Belgian uprising against Dutch rule posed a direct challenge to the postwar settlement agreed at the Congress of Vienna in 1815, and also to perceived British interests. Grey and Palmerston reacted promptly, determined that it should lead neither to international conflict nor to the re-absorption of Belgium by France, which was the evident desire of many French-speaking Belgians. They convened the London Conference, of December 1830–January 1831, attended also by Austria, France, Prussia and Russia. This recognized Belgian independence and guaranteed its permanent neutrality. At the same time, the British leaders applied strong pressure on the new French King, Louis Philippe, to withdraw the candidature of his second son, the Duc de Nemours, for the Belgian throne. Instead, the British successfully advanced the claims of Prince Leopold of Saxe-Coburg, the widower of Princess Charlotte, the former heiress to George IV, who had died in childbirth in 1817. Leopold then diplomatically proposed marriage to Louis Philippe's elder daughter, Louise-Marie, and the couple subsequently became the first sovereigns of the new Belgian kingdom. Grey's and Palmerston's success was to be hailed as a diplomatic masterstroke.

Nearer home was the problem of rural unrest, manifested by the wave of rick-burnings and destruction of agricultural machinery, sweeping southern England and known popularly as the 'Captain Swing' riots. Despite the consistent resistance of the Whigs to the repressive legislation brought in by Pitt in the 1790s, and by the Liverpool government after 1815, Grey and his colleagues, with Home Secretary Melbourne to the fore, did not hesitate to introduce the harshest measures to put down the disturbances. They set up special commissions to try the suspects, which handed down stern punishments – 644 imprisonments, 481 transportations and 19 executions (O'Gorman, 1997, p. 362). The tough line appeared to pay off – in little over a year the protest movement petered out.

Nearly four decades earlier, Grey had first proposed a parliamentary motion in favour of Reform, and his views had changed little in the intervening period. Then and now, he had been a moderate reformer, anxious to remove the anomalies in the existing system rather than to develop it radically in a democratic direction. An aristocrat to his finger-tips, he believed that the landed interest should be the predominant influence in Parliament and had no patience with those who were advocating universal (or even manhood) suffrage, annual parliaments or secret ballots. Yet he was convinced that it was dangerous to leave the rising manufacturing, trading and professional classes without an effective voice, fearing that this would drive them to make common cause with radical or even revolutionary forces. A judicious extension of the franchise, and the removal of the more indefensible and corrupt features of the electoral process would, on the contrary, effectively co-opt them to the governing class of, as he saw it, enlightened aristocrats.

One of Grey's first acts as Prime Minister was to establish a committee of four ministers, the most influential being Durham and Lord John Russell, not yet a member of the Cabinet, to draw up detailed proposals for Reform. Within a month, they produced three draft bills, for England and Wales, Scotland, and Ireland. Presented to the House of Commons by Russell, in March 1831, the Bills proposed the disfranchisement of 60 boroughs with populations of less than 2000, while 47 other boroughs with populations between 2,000 and 4,000 were each to lose one of their two members, while the borough of Weymouth and Melcombe Regis was to go down from four to two. Altogether, 168 seats were to be eliminated, but – in a smaller House of Commons – 105 of these were to be redistributed, mostly among English counties (55 seats) and 42 urban constituencies, including the previously unrepresented cities of Manchester and Birmingham, and four London boroughs, which were to receive two members each. Most people were taken aback by the scale of the proposed redistribution. There were few defenders of such ultra-rotten boroughs as Gatton (two electors) and Old Sarum (seven), but not many had anticipated that the overall clear-out would be quite so wholesale. The proposals concerning the franchise were much more limited in their scope. The previously widely differing voting qualifications in borough constituencies were consolidated in a single requirement – to be a male householder of property worth £10 a year. In the counties, the £10 copyholder and £50 leaseholder were to be enfranchised, in addition to the 40s freeholder. The net effect of these changes would have been to increase the overall number of qualified electors from around half a million to something over 700,000, or seven per cent of the adult population.

The provisions of the bills were very much in line with Grey's own views, and he remained closely in control of the parliamentary proceedings, even though – as a member of the upper house, he was not able personally to present the case to the Commons or to gauge the reactions of individual MPs. His first – and essential move – was to clear the proposals with the King, whom he visited in Brighton, on 30 January 1831. It proved more difficult to get the proposals through the House of Commons, which had been elected during Wellington's premiership and where the government enjoyed only the narrowest of majorities. After a furious debate, the English Bill passed its second reading by a single vote (302 votes to 301). Grey sought a dissolution in order to secure the election of a House more favourable to Reform, but the King refused. A month later, on 30 April, the Opposition carried a 'wrecking amendment' during the Committee Stage by 299 votes to 291. Grey then threatened resignation if he did not get a dissolution, and William IV reluctantly gave way. The resulting general election, in May 1831, was a triumph for Grey and a humiliating rout for the Tories. The Bill was reintroduced, in an only slightly modified form, and rapidly made its way through the House of Commons. It then went up to the Lords, which was to prove a much stiffer hurdle. The House had been stuffed with Tories, during the long first premiership of the Younger Pitt, who in 17 years persuaded George III to create no fewer than 140 new peers. It was they, or their inheritors, who now presented an almost insurmountable barrier to the Bill. On 8 October, despite a powerful speech by Grey, the Lords rejected the Bill on its second reading by 41 votes.

The Lords' action provoked widespread revulsion in the country, with huge protest meetings being held in many towns and cities. Most of these were entirely peaceful, but in several places order broke down. In Derby the army was called in to suppress a riot, in Nottingham the castle was burned down by a mob, while in Bristol a mob went on the rampage for three days. The Cabinet was divided about how to proceed, with Palmerston and Melbourne urging delay, and Durham – much the most radical minister – in favour of raising the stakes. Grey was firmly against any significant watering down of the Bill, but authorized negotiations with the more moderate Tories (known as 'the waverers') to see whether some minor amendments might reconcile the Lords to letting the Bill through. These came to nothing, and the question then arose of asking William IV to create a sufficient number of new Whig peers to force the measure through. The only precedent was in 1712, when Queen Anne created 12 new Tory peers to carry through the Treaty of Utrecht, which brought the War of Spanish Succession to a close. This time a much larger creation – of perhaps 60 new peers – might well be necessary in order to secure the passage of the Reform Bill. Grey discussed this tentatively with William IV, who was horrified at the prospect, and indicated that he would not wish to increase the size of the Lords by more than two or three, and that beyond that any new creations should be confined to the heirs to existing peerages, many of whom were currently in the Commons, which would create a rash of by-elections, something the government was anxious to avoid.

The government then withdrew the Bill, but reintroduced it, with only minor changes, into the Lords, who passed it on second reading by a majority of nine votes, in April 1832. A month later, in committee, it voted to postpone the most crucial clauses in the Bill, by 35 votes, and the Cabinet decided formally to ask William IV to create sufficient peers to carry the Bill through. William refused, and Grey promptly submitted his government's resignation. William then summoned the Duke of Wellington, and asked him to form a government, with the objective of carrying a more moderate measure of Reform. Within a week, Wellington, after extensive consultations with his Tory colleagues, returned to tell the King that he had been unable to do so. This was mainly because of the determined refusal of Sir Robert Peel, the Tory leader in the Commons, to serve. The King then threw in the sponge, asked Grey to carry on, and finally agreed to create whatever number of new peers should prove necessary. In the event, Wellington absolved him of the need for such action. When the Bill came up for its third reading, on 4 June 1832, he left his seat in the Chamber, and followed by a hundred Tory peers, allowed it to pass by 106 votes to 22. Three days later, it received the royal assent.

Neither Grey nor any member of his cabinet (with the exception of Durham) saw the Reform Act as a forerunner of future legislation further enlarging the franchise. They saw it rather as a final settlement, removing the imperfections which had appeared in the constitutional arrangements bequeathed by the 'Glorious Revolution' of 1688–9. One of Grey's strongest supporters, Lord John Russell, who had pioneered a series of earlier unsuccessful attempts at Reform, earned himself the nickname of 'Finality Jack', when he declared, in 1837, that no further changes were necessary. In fact, the initial impact of the Act was rather modest. It increased the franchise only from around 5 to 7 per cent of the adult population, and though the amount of bribery and corruption was undoubtedly reduced, the failure to provide for a secret ballot meant that landlords and employers were still able to exert undue influence over their tenants and employees. The predominance of the 'landed interest' was to continue for at least another three or four decades. The Act's significance lay in the precedent it set for future legislation which, in Bills passed in 1858, 1867, 1872, 1883, 1884, 1911, 1918 and 1928, paved the way, in easy stages, to the eventual adoption of universal suffrage. Predictions that the adoption of the 1832 Bill would open the way to chaos or Jacobin revolution were wide of the mark, but, according to John Derry, 'the Duke of Wellington and Peel were right when they said that Grey's reform of Parliament was opening a door which there was no prospect of closing' (Derry, p. 192).

Grey's own contribution to the passage of the Bill was crucial. He showed a cool nerve, and great firmness, in that, while he was willing to be flexible over details, he was resolved not to tolerate any watering down of the central features of the Bill, insisting when the second and third drafts were produced that they should be no less 'efficient' in their effect than the original version. Probably only he could have persuaded a timorous and reluctant William IV to persevere with the measure, while his own highly respectable and conservative image undoubtedly reassured many doubters who might have shied away if the lead role had been taken by a more obviously radical figure, such as Brougham, Durham or, even, Lord John Russell. The Bill's large body of supporters outside Parliament, led by Francis Place, William Cobbett, 'Orator' Hunt and – most effectively – Thomas Attwood, whose Birmingham Political Union was the best organized and most widely supported of the many grass-roots organizations pressing for Reform (always spelled with a capital 'R'), would have liked a more radical measure, at least incorporating household suffrage. Yet, as John Derry emphasizes: 'the real alternatives to Grey's Bill were either a more limited bill … or no bill at all … there was no chance of a democratic measure being accepted by [a still unreformed] Parliament' (Derry, p. 185).

No sooner was the Act passed, than Grey moved swiftly to consolidate the government's position. He called a general election, in December 1832, and the enlarged electorate duly expressed their thanks, giving the Whigs a handsome majority. Together with their Radical and Irish allies, they secured no fewer than 479 seats, against 179 for the Tories. The government went on to introduce a series of measures on which is based its claim to be the first of the great reforming governments of the nineteenth century. These included, notably, the abolition of slavery throughout the British Empire (completing the work done by the 'Talents' ministry, in 1806, when Grey had played a leading part in the abolition of the slave trade). Another important measure was the Factory Act, of 1833, limiting the working hours of children and creating a factory inspectorate. The Poor Law Act, of 1834, was a less benign measure. It went some way to ameliorating rural poverty, but totally failed to tackle the more widespread misery in the towns, instituting a harsh regime of workhouses to replace the 'outdoor relief' for which paupers were previously eligible. Other new bills removed the trade monopoly of the East India Company, introduced elected local government into Scotland and reformed the banking system.

Yet, with Reform successfully accomplished, Grey undoubtedly felt a sense of anti-climax and – approaching his seventieth year – began to lapse into the 'despondent indolence' which, in the words of John Derry, had characterized his long years in opposition. He no longer possessed the energy or patience to deal with awkward and quarrelsome ministers, and was particularly vexed by disagreements on how to deal with Irish problems, which were still high on the political agenda, despite the granting of Catholic emancipation in 1829. Three interlocking issues dominated the debate – rural unrest, the privileged position of the Anglican Church and the continued campaign by Daniel O'Connell for the rescinding of the Act of Union of 1800 and the restoration of a separate Irish Parliament. A feud soon developed between Lord Anglesey, the Lord Lieutenant, and the Chief Irish Secretary, E.G. Stanley (later the 14th Earl of Derby). Anglesey, whom Grey had inherited from the Wellington government, was a pronounced liberal, sympathetic to Irish demands, while Stanley, who was a member of the Cabinet, was a strong advocate of coercion as well as being a diehard supporter of Church privileges. Anglesey (previously Lord Uxbridge, who lost a leg at the Battle of Waterloo) threatened to resign on several occasions, and was eventually transferred to another post, but subsequently Stanley also resigned, and this effectively brought the government to an end. The point at issue was the payment of tithes, predominantly and unwillingly by Catholic farmers, to the Church of Ireland. An enquiry revealed that the revenues raised were far in excess of the legitimate needs of the Church, and Lord John Russell introduced a bill to apply the surplus to secular purposes, mainly for education. His action split the Cabinet down the middle, and four ministers – Stanley, the Duke of Richmond, the Earl of Ripon and Sir James Graham, the First Lord of the Admiralty – walked out of the government. Shortly afterwards, Lord Althorp MP (shortly to succeed his father, as the third Earl Spencer) resigned on another issue, which proved the last straw for Grey, who followed suit.

He relinquished the premiership on 9 July 1834, after serving three years and 229 days, giving one of his finest orations in his resignation speech in the House of Lords, which was widely applauded. William IV turned to the Tories to form a new government, but Wellington and Peel, whose supporters were only a small minority in the Commons, were unable to do so. William invited the Home Secretary, Lord Melbourne, to take over the reins from Grey, who would, in fact, have preferred to be succeeded by Althorp. He had lost all appetite for office, but had a strong desire to control the Melbourne government from the outside. Melbourne, a diffident man, deferred to Grey's advice in many of his early decisions, but with growing self-confidence became more independent and less inclined to seek guidance from his former leader. His government was short-lived, being turned out by William IV after four months (see Chapter 23). The succeeding Tory government, under Sir Robert Peel, did not last much longer, resigning in April 1835, after a series of parliamentary defeats, and William was obliged to turn back to the Whigs. Grey was strongly pressed to resume the premiership, or to serve as Foreign Secretary, but firmly declined, and Melbourne returned and remained Prime Minister for another six years. During this time, he received only lukewarm support from Grey, who grew more and more impatient at what he saw as his undue dependence on the Radicals, and, in particular, on Daniel O'Connell (whom he saw as a dangerous demagogue). He was also deeply offended that Melbourne had not appointed his eldest son, Viscount Howick MP, as Chancellor of the Exchequer, and had fobbed him off with a relatively junior Cabinet post. Grey became more and more conservative as he grew older, saying that he now had no significant differences with Wellington and Peel, for whom he had the greatest personal respect. When Howick finally resigned from the government, in 1839, Grey withdrew from politics altogether, ceasing to attend the House of Lords, and retiring to his beloved Howick, where he lived out a relatively tranquil old age, dying on 17 July 1845, aged 81.

Grey might well be compared with a Prime Minister of more modern times – Edward Heath. He also had a long but largely unsuccessful political career, crowned with one great achievement which offset all his failures – bringing Britain into the European Economic Community. Grey, however, was more lucky than Heath, in not being repudiated by his own party. He continued to be honoured by them for many years, both before and after his death. His greatest admirers were, perhaps, his fellow Northumbrians, who erected a large column on which his statue still stands, dominating the centre of Newcastle. According to Edward Pearce, a recent chronicler of the struggle to pass the Reform Bill, he is the only British civilian to be memorialized on a column.

Works consulted

John W. Derry, 1992, *Charles, Earl Grey: Aristocratic Reformer*, Oxford, Blackwell.

Frank O'Gorman, 1997, *The Long Eighteenth Century*, London, Arnold.

Edward Pearce, 2003, *Reform!: The Fight for the 1832 Reform Act*, London, Cape.

E.A. Smith, 1990, *Lord Grey 1764–1845*, Oxford, Clarendon Press.

E.A. Smith, 2004, Article in *The Oxford Dictionary of National Biography*, Oxford University Press.

George, Woodbridge, 1974, 'Earl Grey', in Herbert Van Thal, (ed.), *The Prime Ministers*, Vol. I, London, Allen & Unwin.

23

William Lamb, 2nd Viscount Melbourne – Mentor to a Young Monarch

Of Britain's 53 Premiers, two were undoubtedly born illegitimately. One – Ramsay MacDonald – was brought up in extreme poverty by his mother and grandmother, and had a fierce struggle to establish himself in life. The other – William Lamb – grew up in great luxury in an aristocratic home, was educated at Eton and Cambridge and inherited a peerage from a man who was certainly not his father. Yet he appeared to have suffered some psychological damage, and though gifted and highly intelligent he grew up chronically indecisive and directionless, which, among other things, led him into a disastrous marriage. Born on 15 March 1779, he was the second of six surviving children born to Elizabeth Lamb (née Milbanke), Lady Melbourne. Only the eldest of these – Peniston – appears to have been fathered by her husband Peniston Lamb, the First Viscount Melbourne (originally in the Irish peerage). A complaisant husband, he allowed all six to be brought up in the family home and did not openly question their parentage. The first Lord Melbourne was a pleasant nonentity, without ambition, speaking only once during his 40 years in Parliament. The only official post he ever held was as a Gentleman of the Bedchamber to the Prince of Wales. Lady Melbourne, the daughter of a wealthy Yorkshire baronet, was of sterner stuff. Intelligent, vivacious and beautiful, she established herself as a leading Whig hostess (third only to the Duchess of Devonshire and Lady Holland), and held regular soirées in Melbourne House, in Piccadilly (now the site of the Albany), which she had taken over from the Holland family, when they had moved to Holland Park. A highly ambitious and promiscuous woman, who was caricatured in Sheridan's play *The School for Scandal* as 'Lady Sneerwell', she had many lovers, including the Prince of Wales (the probable father of her fourth son, George). The identity of William's father is unknown, though he was generally believed to be George Wyndham, the third Earl of Egremont, the eccentric and immensely wealthy owner of Petworth House, in Sussex, one of the grandest of family seats. Egremont, a notorious roué, was certainly the longest-standing of Lady Melbourne's 'admirers', and evidently believed that William was his son. He was also probably the father of William's brother Frederick and his sister Emily.

So William was brought up in the heart of the high Whig aristocracy – clannish, worldly, amoral and united politically – by little more than by their belief that they were the natural rulers of the country and their enduring distrust of the monarchy. In William's case, this was complicated by close family ties with two successive monarchs, George IV and William IV. The former was the father of his favourite brother, George, while the latter's illegitimate son was married to William's half sister, an illegitimate daughter of Lord Egremont.

William had a happy childhood, being doted on by his mother, whose favourite child he was, and getting on very well with all his siblings. His relations with his nominal father were perfectly amiable and correct, but – not surprisingly – the first Lord Melbourne reserved his warmest feelings for his own son, Peniston. In addition to their London home, the Melbournes had an estate, Melbourne Hall in Derbyshire, and another seat at Brocket Hall, in Hertfordshire, which had been more recently built and where they stayed more often, while Lord Egremont allowed the children a pretty free run at Petworth, where they were frequent visitors. Bookish and highly intelligent, though not particularly hard-working, William was taught at home by a governess and a local clergyman until the age of nine, when he was sent to Eton (the almost *de rigueur* school for eighteenth- and nineteenth-century premiers). Here, he was reasonably happy, enjoying the freedom and the privileged status accorded to aristocrats and managing to survive without too much difficulty the endemic bullying. As one of his biographers was to note:

> William himself disliked any kind of rough and tumble tinged with malice, or brutality that so often among boys produced a fight about a trifle. Why get hurt unnecessarily for something quite unimportant? Fights could not always be avoided even by young William but, as he told [Queen] Victoria later, if he found he was getting the worst of it he gave up and walked away, deterred by no false shame, declaring that it was a silly business. (Marshall, 1975, pp. 8–9)

His behaviour as an adult followed the same pattern. 'Throughout his life Melbourne never confronted unpleasantness, but always fled before it' (Mitchell, 1990, p. 27). He early developed an extraordinary detachment, perhaps too easily seeing both sides of a question, and finding it hard to commit himself to any cause or course of action. William left Eton in 1796, without having obtained any particular distinction, though he was steeped in classical learning. At Trinity College, Cambridge, he had a thoroughly good time, but the University having declined, at that period, into little more than a finishing school for young aristocrats before they departed on the Grand tour, he did very little organized studying, though he continued to read widely, He did, however, win the University prize for an oration on 'The Progressive Improvement of Mankind', which, to his great satisfaction, was read by the Whig leader, Charles James Fox, and commended by him in a speech in the House of Commons. He left after two years, but the Grand tour was now out of the question because of the continuing war with France. Some family friends of the Melbournes suggested that he should, instead, round off his education by going for a couple of years to the University of Glasgow, which in contrast to Cambridge was then at its height as a centre of learning. So, with his younger brother, Frederick, William Lamb travelled north to board with Professor John Millar, one of the University's finest scholars and a disciple of two of Scotland's greatest seers, David Hume and Adam Smith. Here the two brothers were subjected to the discipline of long periods of hard work and study, but Lamb found time to write light-hearted verse and to lead an active social life, dining with the Earl of Minto, who described him as 'a remarkably pleasant, clever and well-informed young man' (Marshall, p. 13). Glasgow did not dramatically change him, but enlarged his fund of knowledge, and confirmed him in the sceptical rationalism which had already become one of his hallmarks. Intellectually, he was interested in religion, but was probably not a believer, though he always counted himself as supporter of the Church of England, telling his mother in a letter: 'If we are to have a prevailing Religion, let us have one that is cool and indifferent and such a one we have got' (Mitchell, 1997, p. 36).

Politically, he was a Whig, more out of tribal reasons than from intellectual conviction, though for a time at least he paraded fairly extreme views, including a marked sympathy for France in its war against Britain. At the age of 21, he returned to London and entered 'society', or more precisely, Whig society, becoming an *habitué* not only of his mother's functions, but also those at Devonshire House, Holland House and above all, Carlton House, the home of the extravagantly hospitable Prince of Wales. The Prince was at odds with his father, George III, and revelled at surrounding himself with the King's political enemies, above all Fox and his circle. Lamb soon became a popular figure – good-looking, amusing, and obviously attractive to women, though notably discreet in any affairs which he may have conducted. There seemed to be only one thing lacking: as a younger son, he had no money and little prospects. What was he to do with his life? Apart from appointment to a sinecure, which his mother's connections might conceivably have been able to secure, there were, in Dorothy Marshall's words, four options, 'the Army, the Navy, the Church and the Law' (Marshall, p. 17). The first three having no appeal to Lamb, he moved into Chambers in 1801, and was called to the Bar three years later, joining the Northern Circuit. He is recorded as having received only one brief, for which he earned precisely one guinea, before his life was transformed by the sudden death of his elder brother Peniston, at the age of 35. A distinctly unpromising young man, his father had purchased a parliamentary seat for him, at the age of 23, but his main interests in life were gambling and horse-racing. Lord Melbourne was devastated by his son's death, and unhappy that William was now his heir. He cut the allowance of £5,000 a year, which he had been paying to Peniston, to £2,000, but nevertheless set in train arrangements to send him into Parliament. In January 1806, at the age of 26, William Lamb was elected unopposed in a by-election for the Herefordshire constituency of Leominster, a 'pocket borough' which he represented by courtesy of the Scottish peer, Lord Kinnaird, an old school friend.

Already before his election, Lamb had taken another portentous step: in June 1805, he got married to the 19-year-old Lady Caroline Ponsonby. He had apparently already been in love with her for four years, but was unable to contemplate marriage before his prospects dramatically improved. The daughter of the Earl and Countess of Bessborough, and niece of the famous Georgiana, Duchess of Devonshire, Caroline had had a wayward and undisciplined childhood, and was virtually uneducated, though she had a lively intelligence and undoubted charm. Views differed as to whether she was beautiful, with her androgynous figure, but she had little difficulty in attracting admirers. Highly strung and impetuous, she had, already at the age of 12, announced that she was in love with Fox, but a year later had transferred her adoration to Lamb. The marriage was to lead to one of the great scandals of the century, which is recounted with immense verve by Lord David Cecil in his brilliant book, first published in 1939, *The Young Melbourne*. Here we are concerned only with its effect on Lamb, whose life and career were blighted for over 20 years by this *mésalliance*, from which he never emotionally recovered. That, however, was some time in the future. At the beginning of his marriage Lamb was blissfully happy, and embarked on his life as a parliamentarian in good spirits. With his well established connections at the apex of the Whig world, he received the warmest of welcomes in the House of Commons, being already on terms of intimacy with Fox and other leading Whigs. When the Whigs joined the Grenville government, after nearly 23 years 'in the wilderness', in February 1806, only a week or two after his election, it was taken for granted that he would soon be considered for office. As a newly elected MP, however, he could hardly expect an immediate appointment.

In fact, Grenville's government lasted barely a year, before being turned out by George III and replaced by a Tory ministry under the Duke of Portland (see Chapter 16). So Lamb's early years in Parliament were spent mostly in opposition, though he was hardly a typical opposition MP. To the consternation of many of his Whig friends, he refused to toe a party line, and got into the habit of considering every issue which came up on its merits, which often led him into supporting measures proposed by the government, especially concerning the war effort, having long since abandoned his pro-French views in the face of

Napoleon's growing despotism. In particular, he formed a growing admiration for the Tory Foreign Secretary, George Canning, which was ironic in view of the fact that some ten years earlier, while still at Cambridge, he had written and published a rebuttal, in verse, of a poem written by Canning attacking the Whigs for their alleged lack of patriotism (see Chapter 19). Now, he found much to agree with in Canning's progressive Toryism, and while retaining his Whig affiliation, privately came to regard himself as a Canningite, though he did not particularly like the man and did not have close relations with him. He dreamed of an inter-party coalition, preferably led by Canning, in which he could honourably participate, without abandoning the Whigs. When the Prince of Wales became Regent, in 1811, it looked for a time as if such an outcome might be possible (see Chapter 5), but the future George IV became disillusioned with his former Whig friends and confirmed the Perceval government in office. His personal wish, however, was to further Lamb's career and, in February 1812, he persuaded Perceval to offer him the post of a Lord of the Treasury. Lamb turned it down, probably out of loyalty to the Whigs, though it has been suggested (Mandler, 2004) that he felt insulted at the meanness of the offer. Had he been offered a cabinet post, he might well have been more tempted.

Difficulties in his marriage, however, were already upsetting Lamb, and perhaps sapping his political ambition. Four pregnancies in as many years had led to two miscarriages, a still-born daughter and the birth of an apparently healthy son, Augustus, who later turned out to be mentally handicapped. The strain on Lady Caroline Lamb, whose grasp of reality was slender at the best of times, was considerable, and she proceeded to act in a more and more irrational manner, with frequent tantrums and rages, often involving the destruction of much valuable crockery. William showed great patience, but his essentially passive nature and horror of facing unpleasantness made him ill-equipped to deal with the situation. Caroline, who had fantasized that her William was a strong and forceful figure, was deeply disappointed, and soon sought comfort elsewhere. She began a liaison with Sir Godfrey Webster, the son of Lady Holland by her first marriage, and then appeared to transfer her affections to his younger brother, Harry. The Holland family strongly disapproved, and their relations with the Lambs were strained, damaging William's political prospects. Adultery, even serial adultery, was readily condoned in Whig circles, but Lady Caroline seemed to go out of her way to flout the unwritten rules, which both her mother, Lady Bessborough, and her mother-in-law, Lady Melbourne, had scrupulously observed in their many amours. These were that affairs should be conducted with a measure of decorum, and above all that their spouses should not be subjected to public humiliation.

If Lady Caroline had been indiscreet in her relations with the Webster brothers, this was as nothing compared to her next adventure. At a ball, in April 1812, she met Lord Byron, fresh from the triumph of the publication of the first volume of *Childe Harold*, which made him the new darling of London society. She famously noted in her journal that he was 'Mad, bad and dangerous to know', but this did not prevent her the following day from throwing herself at him, and beginning a wild, passionate and very public affair which lasted for some 14 months, before ending with a terrible scene at another ball where she slashed herself with broken glasses. All three principals emerged with their reputations in threads: Byron was regarded as a cad, Caroline a slut and William Lamb a wimp (though that term was not yet in current usage). There were many (including Caroline herself) who thought that the least he could do would have been to challenge Byron to a duel, but this would have been wholly out of character, and the best he could manage was to present himself as a long-suffering husband. He was, however, deeply wounded, hardly able to bear the realization that he was mocked in every club and tavern as a cuckold, and wanting nothing more than to withdraw himself from society and hide away at Brocket Hall.

Subconsciously at least, this probably also influenced his decision not to contest the general election in October 1812, though there were certainly other reasons. One was his acute lack of money, his father still not having increased the £2,000 a year he had set seven years earlier. Lamb felt he could not afford the cost of buying and maintaining a parliamentary seat. Portarlington, for example, the Irish constituency which he represented from 1807 to 1812, had been purchased for £5,000. He felt inhibited from approaching his parents, currently struggling to pay off gambling debts, for assistance. He was also not willing to go cap in hand to Whig proprietors of pocket boroughs who would let him have a seat for nothing, but only if he undertook to vote in accordance with their wishes. He had some hopes that his friend, Lord Holland, might be able to use his great influence to find him a constituency with no strings attached, but Holland was currently upset with him and did not exert himself. So at the age of 33, after six years in the Commons, it looked as though his political career was over. If truth be told, it had not been a glorious one: he was a nervous and hesitant speaker, and a poor attender at the House, and his influence owed much more to his social position than to any other factor. Nevertheless, he felt the keenest disappointment, writing to his mother that: 'It is impossible that any Body can feel the being out of Parliament more keenly than I feel for myself. It is actually cutting my throat. It is depriving me of the greatest object of my life at the moment' (Mitchell, p. 109).

Outside the House, there was little respite from his marital troubles. Caroline continued to act in an unpredictable way, with fearful rows alternating with tearful reconciliations. She was dropped from respectable society and instead started to ingratiate herself with the intellectual world and with fringe figures who had also been excluded. She had a series of affairs with 'unsuitable' – and usually very young – men, including the young Bulwer Lytton and an illegitimate son of the Duke of Bedford, and was frequently drunk. Lamb's family took strongly against her, and put enormous pressure upon him to agree to a judicial separation, but at the last moment he could not bring himself to sign the papers. By 1816, just as he was beginning to feel that he had put the scandal behind him, Caroline published a *roman-à-clef*, in which the whole affair was regurgitated in the most sensational way. It was only in 1824, that Lamb finally agreed to a separation, though he continued to visit and correspond affectionately with her until her death, from dropsy, in 1828, aged 42. Lamb returned to Parliament in 1816, for the borough of Peterborough, switching to Hertfordshire in 1819. He carried on more or less as before, retaining his Whig affiliation, but frequently casting his vote in favour of government measures. This did not endear him to his colleagues. He had written to Lord Holland, already, in 1815 , declaring that he supported: 'The Whig principles of the [Glorious Revolution of 1688–89]…the irresponsibility of the crown, the consequent responsibility of ministers, and the preservation of the dignity of Parliament as constituted by law and custom. With the modern additions, interpolations, facts and fictions, I have nothing to do' (Ziegler, 1982, p. 70).

Lamb's mother died in 1818, and after that he seemed to drift on aimlessly, his ambition all but extinguished. He remained an insatiable reader, and spent his time thinking about the world, and eating and drinking well, while remaining faithful to Caroline, despite all her transgressions. He felt a nagging frustration at the emptiness of his life, and started to write a biography of Sheridan, whom he had known well, and who had died in 1816. Yet the effort seemed too great, and after a while he handed the project over to the popular Irish poet, Thomas Moore, who duly published a volume in 1825. The nadir of Lamb's fortunes came in 1826, when – accustomed to being returned unopposed in his parliamentary contests – he unexpectedly faced a Tory challenger in his Hertfordshire constituency. Lamb, who did not believe in democracy, and was at best a lukewarm supporter of Reform, found the whole business of canvassing for votes extremely unpleasant, and, when his opponent started to drag up the Byron-Lady Caroline Lamb affair, abruptly withdrew from the contest. Once again, outside of Parliament, it looked as though his political career was finally over. Then, it was rescued by a totally unexpected sequence of events. In early 1827, Lord Liverpool, who had governed for nearly 15 years, was incapacitated by a stroke, and George Canning, already a dying man, was appointed by George IV to succeed him (see Chapter 7). When half of Liverpool's cabinet, and many other Tories, refused to serve under him, Canning was desperate to find suitable people to fill a large number of government posts. He appealed to the Whig leader, Earl Grey, to join a coalition, but Grey refused, though other Whigs agreed to serve on an individual basis. Canning then offered Lamb the vacant post – outside the cabinet – of Chief Secretary for Ireland. Lamb accepted, and departed for Dublin, delighted that he now, at the age of 48, finally had a real job to do. (Canning was also able to find him a pocket borough – Newport, Isle of Wight – for which he was returned unopposed in a by-election in April 1827).

Lamb remained at his post until June 1828, under three Prime ministers – Canning, Goderich and Wellington. As L.G. Mitchell relates:

> In these fifteen months, he showed a capacity for hard work that surprised his family and may have surprised himself. By September 1827, he was writing letters that suggested a mastery of such Irish problems as tithes, education, customs, and land reform. Though there were topics like 'police, gaols, hospitals, penitentiaries' which he had 'little or no taste for', he worked away at them and modestly thought his situation 'enough for me, who have been for so long used to doing nothing'. (Mitchell, p. 113)

Lamb got on well with both the Lord-Lieutenants with whom he served, the touchy Marquess Wellesley and his successor, the more amiable Marquess of Anglesey, but his great success was with the majority Catholic community. Previous Chief Secretaries had mixed only with the Protestant Ascendancy, but Lamb, a great believer in religious toleration, refused to distinguish between the affiliations of those he met, and dined as often with Catholics as with Protestants, while making himself equally available to all-comers at his office, receiving a constant stream of visitors, without hiding behind secretaries or attendants. At this stage – but not later – he liked and admired Daniel O'Connell, the Irish nationalist leader, and had no difficulty with his campaigning for the rights of Catholics and tenants, so long as it was done peacefully. If, however, violence was threatened, he was determined to deal with it with a firm hand.

Lamb now regarded himself more than ever as a Canningite and this inclination was reinforced by family connections. His cousin, William Huskisson, was a leading Canningite minister, while his sister Emily, who was married to Lord Cowper, was the long-time mistress of Lord Palmerston MP, another Canningite, and was to marry him after her husband's death. When Huskisson resigned from Wellington's cabinet in May 1828 (see Chapter 21), the other Canningite ministers, including Palmerston, also left in sympathy with him. Lamb felt he should do the same, though he did not agree with Huskisson over the issue on which he resigned, and returned from Dublin with his reputation as a serious politician largely restored. His nominal father died a month later, aged 83, leaving him a large fortune and extensive estates. As the second Viscount Melbourne, he was now at last a man of substance, and was to cut a rather more impressive figure in the House of Lords than he ever had in the Commons. It was thus no surprise that Earl Grey sought to include Melbourne in the government he formed in 1830, essentially a coalition between Whigs and Canningites, with a mandate to introduce electoral reform.

What had not been expected, however, was that he should be offered so senior a post as Home Secretary. The probability was that Grey wished to balance the appointments of radical figures such as Lord Brougham, the Lord Chancellor, and Lord Durham, his son-in-law and Lord Privy Seal, with somebody of more conservative views. Apart from the ultra Tory, the Duke of Richmond, who became Postmaster-General, no member of the new government was more conservative than Melbourne.

Melbourne remained at the Home Office throughout Grey's ministry of nearly four years. Of chief interest are his attitudes and actions concerning two policy areas – the Reform Bill, and law and order, for which he had overall Cabinet responsibility. On Reform, he was, in L. G. Mitchell's words: 'virtually invisible. He spoke on the issue rarely, had no part in drawing up the measure, and had to be carried along like a dead weight by his more enthusiastic colleagues' (Mitchell, p. 130).

Melbourne's difficulty was that, though he recognized the necessity of the Bill, in view of the state of public opinion, he found it highly distasteful. In his view, politics was a matter to be determined by men of property and taste, not by the broad masses, and he had a particular dislike for those likely to benefit from the Bill. 'I don't like the middle classes', he was recorded as saying, 'the higher and lower classes, there's some good in them, but the middle class are all affectation and conceit and pretence and concealment' (Cecil, 1954, pp. 161–2). So he was never more than a lukewarm supporter of the Bill, and with Palmerston, was in favour of shelving it when it was first defeated by the Lords. He was particularly opposed to swamping the House of Lords with new members in order to get the Bill through, and only ten days before its final passage threatened to resign if this should be resorted to. As recounted in Chapter 22, it proved unnecessary due to the mass abstention of Tory peers, led by the Duke of Wellington, at the conclusion of the Third Reading debate.

On law and order, Melbourne was very firm in insisting that laws should be obeyed, but he was extremely reluctant to extend the scope of the law, especially (in this respect, being a good Whig) if this would curtail the liberties of citizens. Thus he cracked down hard on the 'Captain Swing' disturbances of 1830–31, involving a great deal of arson and destruction of farm machinery, setting up commissions to try the offenders, who imposed heavy sentences, including 227 of death, all but 19 of which were commuted to imprisonment or transportation. Nevertheless, he refused impassioned appeals from landowners for the widespread use of troops to protect their estates and for even more coercive laws to be passed, taking the view that their best protection would be to act as model landlords and employers, which very few of them were.

He took the same attitude during the protests provoked by the defeat by the House of Lords of the first version of the Reform Bill. He refused to legislate against the creation of 'political unions' campaigning for a more extreme reform measure, or against the holding of mass demonstrations – both of which – he said were perfectly legal, and would be tolerated if they did not break the existing law. He used his own influence to mediate with protest leaders, such as the Chartist William Place, who had once worked for him as a tailor, to ensure that their followers were law-abiding. He regarded the demands of certain Tory peers for more extreme measures as hysterical, writing to the Duke of Buckingham, saying that 'it is impossible to guarantee any one against broken windows'. The ultra-Tory Duke of Newcastle, whose property was destroyed during riots in Nottingham, received an even dustier reply: 'Melbourne refused to put him on a commission to try the rioters, thought his claim for damages exorbitant, since his house was nothing but an 'old ruin' anyway and resolutely refused to allow him the use of arms' (Mitchell, p. 129).

Equally, Melbourne declined to re-impose restrictions against the forming of trade unions, which had been repealed in 1824, though he regarded unions as pernicious organizations, inevitably doomed to failure. When ten Dorset agricultural workers, known to history as the Tolpuddle Martyrs, broke the law in 1834, by administering oaths, he refused to intervene against the sentences of transportation passed on them by local magistrates. They were shipped to New South Wales, but two years later, when Melbourne was Prime Minister, they were allowed to return after mass protests on their behalf.

Grey soon became dissatisfied with Melbourne's performance, regarding him as indolent, and, in 1831 proposed to move him to a less senior post. He was dissuaded by Lord Holland, who argued that his apparently casual ways were deceptive, and that he was, in fact, a hard-working and assiduous minister, who carefully read his briefs and replied promptly to his correspondence. If, in any particular matter, Melbourne decided not to take action it was because in his view it could only make matters worse and that inactivity was the better option. So Melbourne remained in place, though Grey was not really convinced. When Grey resigned in July 1834 – he did not see Melbourne as a likely successor – his own preference would have been Lord Althorp MP, who had been his Chancellor of the Exchequer and Leader of the Commons. Melbourne too did not have any expectation of succeeding, or any evident desire to do so. The choice was made by King William IV, who wanted to appoint a Tory, but in deference to the situation in the House of Commons, went for the next best thing, a highly conservative Whig, which was how Melbourne was then seen. This was acquiesced in by Melbourne's cabinet colleagues because, in the words of Lord Durham, the very radical Lord Privy Seal, 'he was the only one of whom none of us would be jealous'. Melbourne himself expressed no enthusiasm, as recounted by the diarist, Charles Greville:

> When the King sent for him he told Young [his private secretary] 'he thought it a damned bore, and said he was in many minds what he should

do – be Minister or no'. Young said, 'Why damn it, such a position never was occupied by a Greek or Roman, and, if it lasts only two months, it is well worth to have been Prime Minister of England.' 'By God that's true,' said Melbourne; 'I'll go'. (Hibbert, ed., 1981, p. 120)

So, he became Prime Minister, on 16 July 1834, at the age of 55. He reappointed all the members of Grey's cabinet, adding only his brother-in-law, Viscount Duncannon MP, as his own successor as Home Secretary. With some difficulty, he persuaded Lord Althorp MP, who had just resigned as Leader of the Commons, to stay on. The death of Althorp's father, the second Earl Spencer, whose title and seat in the House of Lords he inherited, sounded the death knell of the government only four months later. Melbourne travelled down to Brighton to discuss with William IV a replacement for Althorp, having in mind Lord John Russell MP, who happened to be the King's *bête noire*. William said he would sleep on the matter, and invited Melbourne to stay overnight. In the morning, he abruptly dismissed the government, and said that he would invite the Duke of Wellington to form a Tory administration. Wellington demurred, in favour of Sir Robert Peel, who was away in Italy, but acted as Prime Minister for three weeks until Peel's return. William IV was taking a gamble in dismissing a government which still enjoyed a majority in the Commons, something which his father, George III, had done several times, but which was now widely seen as a constitutional outrage. Peel called a general election within two months, and tried to gild his party's colours by renaming it the Conservative Party, and indicating that it now fully accepted the Reform Act, as well as Catholic emancipation. He made extensive gains, but not enough to achieve a parliamentary majority. When, inevitably, he was defeated on a major parliamentary vote a few months later, in April 1835, he immediately resigned, and the king was forced to swallow his pride and send again for the Whigs. Since then no monarch has ever dared to turn out a government with a Commons majority.

The Whigs were angry with Melbourne for having given up office without a fight, and strongly appealed to Grey to come back as Prime Minister, which he firmly refused. Melbourne was then invited to form a government, but this time he insisted on making his own ministerial appointments, and – to their great chagrin – excluded the two most radical members of Grey's government, Lords Brougham and Durham. He also wished to move Palmerston, whose brash conduct of foreign affairs had annoyed many foreign rulers, but he refused to accept any other post. Melbourne then, most reluctantly, reappointed him as Foreign Secretary. Russell now became Home Secretary and leader of the Commons, while Thomas Spring-Rice was Chancellor of the Exchequer and Lord Holland (the acknowledged 'keeper of the Whig conscience') returned to his former post as Chancellor of the Duchy of Lancaster. The Marquess of

Lansdowne was Lord President of the Council, and Melbourne's deputy as leader of the House of Lords. The general expectation was that Melbourne's second government would not last long. In fact, it managed to stagger on for nearly seven years. The main reason for this was Melbourne's lack of ambition. He had few objectives other than keeping his government together, which meant that he seldom took political initiatives, and proposed a minimal amount of legislation, which limited the possibilities of defeat.

There were objective reasons for Melbourne's caution. The King was hostile, while his government was in a small minority in the House of Lords, where the Tory majority had little hesitation in blocking government bills or hamstringing them by wrecking amendments. In the Commons, the Whigs (who had by now successfully incorporated the Canningites, apart from those who, led by E.G. Stanley, had defected to the Tories in 1834) were far short of being a majority. They could only survive with the support of the Radicals and/or the Irish nationalists led by Daniel O'Connell. Melbourne heartily disliked both factions, and was most unwilling to treat with them, but they reluctantly kept him in office solely to keep the Tories out. Even the Tories, themselves, led by Wellington and Peel, were for long in two minds about the desirability of defeating Melbourne. In order to form a government of their own, they knew that they would have to include a large swathe of 'ultras' determined to put the clock back, both on Reform and Catholic emancipation. For them also, at least until 1839 or thereabouts, a Melbourne government was the lesser of two evils.

Melbourne's team was by no means homogenous. It included strong and mutually unsympathetic characters, who were only kept together by Melbourne's charm and his resolute determination to avoid the taking of unpleasant decisions. Each minister was left in virtually unchallenged control of his own department; cabinet meetings were infrequent and parliamentary recesses long. The reforming era ushered in by the Grey government was stopped short in its tracks. The only important reform for which Melbourne was prepared to fight was the Municipal Corporations Act of 1835. This provided for triennial elections by ratepayers in 178 boroughs and cities, each of which was to have a mayor, alderman and councillors. They replaced a largely corrupt system of self-perpetuating corporations, most of which were Tory controlled, perhaps a reason why Melbourne promoted the measure, which was a logical consequence of the 1832 Reform Act. A minor but useful measure was the Registration of Births, Deaths and Marriages Bill, which for the first time provided for secular records to be kept of matters which had previously been left in the hands of parish clergy, who carried out this duty with widely varying efficiency.

Although he might appear to have been a 'do nothing' premier, Melbourne was by no means idle. He was conscientious to a fault in such matters as recommending the appointment of bishops, despite his own absence of religious beliefs. He was anxious to ensure that only able nominees were chosen, being careful to exclude those too infected with sectarian enthusiasms. He also kept up his voracious reading habits, amazing acquaintances with the breadth of his knowledge in a wide range of fields and continued to be an enthusiastic diner-out, particularly, but by no means exclusively, at the table of Lord and Lady Holland. He refused to move into 10 Downing Street, preferring to remain in his house in South Street, Mayfair, which he had bought in 1828, after selling off Melbourne House. Melbourne's emotional life was fairly bleak, and was not improved by the death of his backward son Augustus, on whom he had lavished much care, in 1836. Yet he was not lacking in female company, having a number of (mostly married) women friends, with whom he consorted, but without forming deep attachments. He had the misfortune to be cited in court cases by two aggrieved husbands, the first of whom, Lord Branden, he managed to pay off, but the second actually came to court while he was Prime Minister, causing a sensation. The plaintiff was George Norton, the blackguardly husband of Caroline Norton, the beautiful and intelligent grand-daughter of Sheridan, who succeeded precariously in maintaining herself, and supporting her young family, by novel-writing. There was no doubt that Melbourne had been highly indiscreet, but when the case came to court he was dismissed from the action due to lack of convincing evidence. After these scrapes, Melbourne cold-heartedly refused any further contact with the two women concerned, though he continued to support them financially, and remembered both of them in his will. His biographer, L.C. Mitchell, had little doubt of the cause of the older Melbourne's inability to form a deep relationship:

> He had loved and trusted Caroline Lamb, and the result had been such public humiliation and misery, that he had been forced into terrible introspection. He determined never to love or trust anyone again. ... women were to be taken on as friends only on terms. He much prized their company, but he wanted nothing more. (Mitchell, p. 231)

If there was one exception to this, it could only have been the young Queen Victoria. Certainly, his association with her gave him a new purpose in life, and for three to four years he gave every indication of being a happy and fulfilled man. She succeeded her uncle, William IV, on 20 June 1837, when she was barely 18. Her father, Edward, Duke of Kent, had died when she was less than two, and she had been brought up in semi-seclusion by her mother, the former Princess Victoria of Saxe-Saalfeld-Coburg, with whom she was on bad terms. She suspected her mother of scheming with the Comptroller of her Household, Sir John Conroy, to take control of the monarchy, reducing her to a mere puppet. Her first action on becoming Queen was to summon the Prime Minister to tell him that she had no intention of changing any of her ministers, and Melbourne, 'handsome and resplendent in full court dress' (Marshall, p. 126) kissed hands on his re-appointment. That night the Queen recorded in her journal that her first minister was 'straightforward, clever, honest and good'. This was the first of a long series of flattering references to her 'good friend', whom she rapidly came to accept as the father she had never had. He was, in fact, the first adult who had taken her seriously and given her good, disinterested advice, with the partial exception of her Uncle Leopold, the King of Belgium, who wrote her encouraging letters, but for the most part was far away in Brussels. On his part, Melbourne was fascinated to have this young, lively, naïve, yet alert and strong-willed girl – forty years his junior – hanging on his every word, as he endlessly recounted the ups and downs of his life and of politics and society over the previous half-century. He told her a great deal about such characters as Fox, Pitt, Liverpool and Canning, and about her grandfather, George III, and her two regal uncles George IV and William IV, while imparting to her a straightforward Whig account of history and injunctions over how a constitutional monarch should behave. It was not long before he became her private secretary, as well as Prime Minister, and got into the habit of spending nearly all his time at the court, either at Windsor or Buckingham Palace.

Nearly always he gave her good advice, with two notable exceptions. One was over the Lady Flora Hastings affair, concerning a lady-in-waiting of the Queen's mother, whose stomach became swollen and rumours swiftly travelled round the Court that she was pregnant, by – evil tongues suggested – no other than Sir John Conroy. This she vehemently denied, but Victoria insisted that she should submit to a medical examination, which revealed that she was a virgin. She died soon afterwards, and the post-mortem revealed that the swelling had been caused by an enormous liver tumour. Melbourne was at fault in not deterring the Queen from forcing Lady Flora to submit to humiliation, and also for trying to cover up the affair, when her brother, Lord Hastings, vehemently objected. Victoria emerged with her reputation damaged. The other occasion occurred in 1839, when Melbourne's government resigned, after its parliamentary majority fell away to a mere five votes in a parliamentary debate over a rebellion in the colony of Jamaica. Victoria was distraught to lose her Prime Minister, but, on Melbourne's advice, sent for Sir Robert Peel to form a new government. This Peel agreed to do, but in submitting his list of proposed appointments, included nominations of some Tory women to replace the Ladies of the Queen's Bedchamber, all of whom had been Whigs. The Queen was flabbergasted, and consulted Melbourne, who advised her that she could insist that these were personal appointments, and that she could not agree to Sir Robert's proposals. Melbourne's action was undoubtedly unconstitutional – as he had resigned as Prime Minister he had no business in offering advice on appointments. When Sir Robert heard the Queen's response, he said that the Tories were unwilling to form a government under such conditions, and Melbourne resumed as Prime Minister, somewhat shame-facedly, as he almost certainly realized that he had erred in proffering advice.

The diarist Charles Greville has left a graphic description of how Melbourne's daily routine was dominated by his attendance on the Queen:

> He is at her side for at least six hours every day – an hour in the morning, two on horseback, one at dinner, and two in the evening...Month after month he remains at the Castle, submitting to this daily routine...he is always sitting bolt upright; his free and easy language interlarded with 'damns' is carefully guarded and regulated with the strictest propriety, and he has exchanged the good talk of Holland House for the trivial, laboured, and wearisome inanities of the Royal circle. (Hibbert, pp. 163–4)

Melbourne could only spend so much time with the Queen by grievously neglecting his duties as Prime Minister, and effectively abdicating from any supervision of his ministers. In particular, Lord Palmerston, who had recently become Melbourne's brother-in-law on marrying his sister Emily, established himself as the absolute ruler of the Foreign Office. In 1840, this almost led to a disastrous war with France, for which the nation was utterly unprepared. The occasion was the rebellion of the ruler of Egypt, Mehemet Ali, against his Turkish overlords. Strongly encouraged by the French government, led by Adolphe Thiers, he had seized Syria and Palestine, and was threatening to march on Constantinople. Palmerston reacted with extraordinary belligerence, to the horror of several of his cabinet colleagues, notably the pro-French Lord Holland. Melbourne failed to take energetic steps to restrain him, and it was only the downfall of the Thiers government, and his replacement by the anglophile François Guizot, which prevented hostilities from breaking out (see Chapter 27).

Melbourne's position at Court was transformed in February 1840 by the marriage of the now 20-year-old Queen to Prince Albert of Saxe-Coburg-Gotha, after a whirlwind courtship. Albert took over the role of Victoria's secretary, and though he continued to have close access to her as Prime Minister, her emotional dependence on him quickly faded, so besotted was she with her new husband. The political difficulties of his government now also greatly increased. The Tories had made further gains in the 1837 general election, and Peel – now the most effective debater in the Commons – began to press the government much harder, particularly on financial and economic issues, with the government seemingly unable to control a mounting budget deficit. Relations between ministers began to deteriorate – the chief would-be reformer, Lord John Russell became increasingly frustrated; while, in September 1839, Earl

Grey's son, Viscount Howick MP, who had constantly been threateningly to resign, finally did so. His replacement as War Secretary was T.B. Macaulay, who proved to be far less effective as a politician than as a historian. Against his better judgement, Melbourne was forced to dismiss another cabinet minister, Lord Glenelg, the Colonial Secretary, after several other ministers had threatened to leave unless he did so. The government was deeply split over two political issues which were assuming increasing importance – the Corn Laws and the secret ballot. Agitation to repeal the protectionist Corn laws (see Chapter 24), led by two Radical MPs, Richard Cobden and John Bright, built up strongly during 1839, and Melbourne, who was personally opposed to repeal, had to agree that it would be regarded as an 'open issue', with Cabinet ministers free to argue on either side, though he was adamant that there was no immediate possibility of legislation. On the secret ballot, of which Lord John Russell was a strong advocate, Melbourne refused to budge, not even to the extent of allowing this also to be recognized as an open issue. The government appeared increasingly care-worn and ineffective, and there was little surprise when it went down to defeat in the 1841 general election, of which the result was:

Conservatives   368
Whigs and allies   290

Melbourne resigned soon after, on 30 August 1841, with evident feelings of relief. The only thing he regretted was the loss of his close proximity to the Queen. Despite increasingly clear hints from Albert and others that they were unwelcome, he continually bombarded Victoria with letters proffering advice on a wide range of questions. The Queen responded in a kindly way, but her replies became more and more infrequent, and Melbourne was forced to the sad conclusion that he had outlived his usefulness to her. In Mitchell's view, his ultimate rejection by 'the young Victoria, who became a surrogate daughter' was almost on a par with his betrayal by Lady Caroline Lamb, and gave a 'bitter edge to his last years' (Mitchell, p. 276). He survived his premiership by some seven years, but after suffering a stroke, in October 1842, his health sharply deteriorated, and he was confined mostly to Brocket Hall. Despite devoted care by his sister Emily, whose Palmerston family estate was nearby, his brother Frederick and his young Austrian wife and the widow of his brother George who had died in 1834, after having served under Melbourne as Under-Secretary at the Home Office, he was lonely and miserable, finding it difficult to accept that Russell had now effectively replaced him as leader of the Whigs. He died on 24 November 1848, at the age of 69.

As Prime Minister, Melbourne's performance was, at best, mediocre. As guide, counsellor and friend to the young queen, he excelled himself. It would be idle to contend that she invariably showed wisdom and good judgement throughout her long reign. Yet without his gentle tutelage, it is highly improbable that she would have coped as well as she did in treading the difficult and unfamiliar path of being a constitutional monarch in an age of unprecedented upheaval.

Works consulted

Lord David Cecil, 1948, *The Young Melbourne*, London, Pan Books.

Lord David Cecil, 1954, *Lord M: The later life of Lord Melbourne*, London, Constable.

Christopher Hibbert, 1981, (ed.), *Greville's England: Selections from the diaries of Charles Greville 1818–1860*, London, The Folio Society.

Lucille Iremonger, 1970, *The Fiery Chariot*, London, Secker & Warburg.

Peter Mandler, 2004, Article in *The Oxford Dictionary of National Biography*, Oxford, Oxford University Press.

Dorothy Marshall, 1975, *Lord Melbourne*, London, Weidenfeld & Nicolson.

L.G. Mitchell, 1997, *Lord Melbourne 1779–1848*, Oxford, Oxford University Press.

Philip Ziegler, 1982, *Melbourne*, New York, Athenaeum.

24
Sir Robert Peel – Arch Pragmatist or Tory Traitor?

Robert Peel came from a different social background from all his predecessors as Prime Minister and, for that matter, from nearly all his successors. His father and grandfather, both also called Robert, were northern manufacturers, self-made men who rose from the yeoman class.

His grandfather, who had started life as a dealer in linen, opened up a small calico printing factory at Oswaldtwistle in Lancashire in the early 1760s, together with two associates who put up most of the capital. They had the good fortune to employ James Hargreaves, the inventor of the spinning jenny, whose invention he was able to exploit. Known as 'Parsley' Peel, because of his success in marketing a simple parsley leaf design, within a few years he became one of the leading figures in the Lancashire cotton industry. His son Robert chafed at working at his father's side and, in 1772, at the age of 22 was given £500 to set up on his own. Within a very few years, he had outstripped his father, and by 1784 was employing at least 6,800 people, directly or indirectly, which by the end of the century had increased to 15,000. By then, he had far outgrown his Lancashire roots, transferring much of his manufacturing activity to Staffordshire, where he bought an estate, Drayton Manor, from the Marquess of Bath, in the vicinity of Tamworth, for which he became MP in 1790, and served for 40 years. A loyal supporter of the Younger Pitt, he was made a baronet in 1800.

In 1783, he had married Ellen Yates, the much younger daughter of his business partner, and, on 5 February 1788, their eldest son, Robert, was born. He was the third of eleven children, having five brothers and five sisters, the two youngest of whom were to die in childhood. Sir Robert Peel, Bart, was ambitious for all his children, though initially he had the highest hopes for his second and third sons, William and Edmund. Nevertheless, it was to Robert that he – only semi-jocularly – remarked, as the latter was to recall late in life, 'Bob, you dog, if you are not prime minister some day, I'll disinherit you' (Gash, 1976, p. 6). He was determined that they should grow up to be 'gentlemen' rather than merely mill-owners like himself and his father. The young Robert was duly enrolled at Harrow, where he arrived in 1800, at the age of 12.

At Harrow, Robert, who was initially looked down upon by his aristocratic schoolfellows as a rough provincial (he was to retain a Lancashire accent throughout his life) became something of a solitary. He avoided organized games, preferring to roam alone the ten-mile stretch of open country between Harrow and the metropolis, carrying his shot guns, and often returning with rabbits for the cooking pot. He was a first-class shot. Apart from a thrashing from a senior pupil for whom he refused to fag, Peel avoided being bullied, being a large, well-built young man, who looked as though he was well able to take care of himself. Nevertheless, he was extremely sensitive, and became more so after a tragedy befell his family, when he was 15, with the sudden death of his mother, at the age of 37. His father almost immediately remarried – to a woman to whom he had proposed and been rejected over 20 years earlier, before his first marriage. This second marriage was a total failure, and soon broke up, leaving a vacuum in the household, instead of the loving stepmother that Sir Robert had hoped to provide for his children. Robert grieved deeply over his mother, and it may be significant that almost the only close friend he made at Harrow was the young Lord Byron, his exact contemporary at the school, who had lost his father at a very young age. Academically, he was an ideal pupil, more than fulfilling his father's ambitions for him. His tutor, Mark Drury, was in the habit of saying to his classmates, to Robert's deep embarrassment, 'You boys will one day see Peel Prime Minister' (Iremonger, p. 99). He avoided unpopularity among his fellows, by being extremely generous in helping the less gifted with their exercises.

Robert left Harrow at the end of 1804, aged nearly 17, and spent several months living at his father's London house, preparing to go up to Oxford the following October. He often went to the House of Commons to listen to debates, and his father introduced him to the Prime Minister, William Pitt, though the highlight of this visit was to listen to one of the finest speeches ever made by his great rival, Charles James Fox. It was on Catholic emancipation, and over 20 years later he was to recall that 'he had never heard a speech which made a greater impression on his mind than that delivered by Mr Fox during that debate' (Gash, 1976, p. 9). At Oxford, he came under the supervision of Cyril Jackson, the famous Dean of Christ Church, through whose hands had earlier passed two other future prime ministers – Charles Jenkinson (Lord Liverpool) and George Canning – as well as Henry Fox (Lord Holland), the nephew of Charles James Fox and his political heir. He was heard to remark that 'Harrow has sent us up at least one scholar in Mr Peel', and Robert was not to let him down, exceeding all his other students in his achievements. The Oxford degree curriculum had recently been divided into two separate schools – *Literae Humaniores* and Mathematics – and students had to choose between them when being examined for their degree. Peel chose to do both, and was the first person ever to achieve a double First Class result, a tribute not only to his intelligence, but the enormous hard work he had put in. According to his brother William, he read 'eighteen hours in the day and the night. I doubt if anyone ever read harder than Robert for the two or three terms before he passed his examinations' (Gash, 1976, p. 11). He had a more rounded time at Oxford than at Harrow, abandoning his solitary ways and taking part in such sporting activities as rowing and cricket. He also became quite a popular figure, with his handsome physique, and dressing for a while in a dandyesque way. He made a number of good friends, the closest being Henry Vane, later Earl of Cleveland.

His father, now an enormously wealthy man, lost no time in rewarding him for his tremendous effort. Robert left Oxford in March 1809, having just passed his twenty-first birthday. Within a month, he was to become Member of Parliament for the Irish pocket borough of Cashel, his father having already begun negotiations to purchase the seat, through the good offices of General Sir Arthur Wellesley (later the Duke of Wellington), who was at the time the Chief Secretary for Ireland. He joined his father in the House, and like him aligned himself with the Pittite faction, who were by now generally recognized as Tories. The elder Peel had already made his mark as a respected and active MP. His large fortune derived, at least in part, from the exploitation of child labour, and he now sought to make amends by improving the employment conditions in his own factories, and by carrying through Parliament the first piece of factory legislation – 30 years before the Factory Act of the Grey government. This was the Health and Morals of Apprentices Act of 1802, which was far from pleasing to most of his fellow Lancashire manufacturers. The younger Peel was not yet definitely set on a political career. With his father's encouragement, he had taken chambers at Lincoln's Inn, and began studying for the Bar. But the decision was soon taken out of his hands. His maiden speech, seconding the reply to the King's Speech, on 23 January 1810, was a triumphant success, prompting the Speaker to declare that it had been the best maiden speech since the Younger Pitt's.

Four months later, Lord Liverpool, the Secretary of State for Colonies and War, and one of the leading figures in the Perceval government, snapped him up to be one of two under-secretaries in his department. Liverpool, a fellow alumnus of Christ Church, had picked him out as the most promising of the newer pro-government MPs. At just over 22, he was beginning his ministerial career even younger than William Pitt, who became Chancellor of the Exchequer at the age of 23. His post, which he was to hold for two years, gave him excellent administrative and parliamentary experience. The other under-secretary was responsible for military matters, while Peel was left to deal with the whole range of colonial issues, in which Liverpool took little interest and left him largely a free hand. These covered everything, 'from Botany Bay to Prince Edward Island' as he himself put it. He was also responsible for the administration of secret service money. Moreover, as the only minister in the department in the Commons, he was responsible for answering in Parliament for all questions concerning the war effort, including the ongoing campaigns in the Iberian peninsula, and was thus one of the government's most frequent spokesmen in the lower House. He worked hard, mastered his briefs with little difficulty, and spoke with great confidence in the House. He was soon seen as a rising star, and when Liverpool became Prime Minister, after Perceval's assassination in 1812, there was little surprise when he rewarded Peel with a senior post. This was as Chief Secretary for Ireland.

He was there for six years – an exceedingly lengthy incumbency for this post – and made his mark on the island as it did upon him. The position was an exceptionally testing one for a young politician. He virtually acted as Prime Minister of Ireland (with the Lord Lieutenant effectively playing the role of a constitutional monarch). Peel was formally responsible to the Home Secretary, Lord Sidmouth, who took little interest in Irish affairs. Peel, who crossed the Irish Channel no fewer than 15 times during his period in office, acted as his own chief spokesman in the House of Commons, where, he once remarked, 'Most MPs knew as much about Ireland as they did of Kamchatka' (Gash, 1976, p. 39). On arrival, he was extremely depressed by what he saw, particularly as he ventured out from Dublin. He was shocked at the level of poverty, the chronically bad relations between the (often-absentee) Protestant landowners and their Catholic tenants, the high level of violence and disorder, the low quality of the local administration and the prevalence of corruption and jobbery. He set himself to reform the Dublin administration, weeding out inefficient officials and ensuring, as far as he was able, that their successors were chosen on merit. He sadly concluded that it was impossible to achieve anything comparable at local level – the powers of patronage of the country landowners were so entrenched that there was no means of over-riding them without enraging the entire Protestant ascendancy, on which the British government depended for the maintenance of the union with England. Nevertheless, despite the feeble implements at his disposal, Peel soon acquired a reputation as a first-class administrator. His work methods are well described by his principal biographer, Norman Gash:

> Few things are more striking in his dealings with his Irish subordinates than his insistence on precise, factual information, a commodity not easy to obtain in Ireland. Facts to Peel were the basis of sound administration; facts were the best arguments to lay before the legislature. 'There is nothing like a fact' he observed '... facts are ten times more valuable than declamations'. In administration this was an admirable attitude; in politics, where much

depends on appearances, it was not always to be so infallible a guide. (Gash, 1976, p. 445)

Peel was well aware of what was expected of him during the two general elections which occurred during his time in Ireland. This was, as he delicately put it, 'to secure the Government's interest if possible from dilapidation, but still more to faint with horror at the mention of money transactions' (Gash, 1976, p. 20). He was able to secure a handful of net gains during the 1812 election, and rather more in that of 1818, when it was estimated that 71 of the 100 Irish Members elected were Tory supporters. Peel was resistant to the claims of the Catholic majority, both as regards to emancipation and the repeal of the 1800 Union Act. He fell out badly with Daniel O'Connell, the leader of the Catholic agitation, with whom he traded notable insults, leading, in 1815, to a challenge to a duel, which the participants agreed should be held on the neutral ground of Ostend. This could have had the most disastrous consequences, as both men were first-class marksmen, and O'Connell had already killed an opponent in another duel earlier the same year. Word of the projected duel got round, however, and on his way to Belgium O'Connell was arrested in London, eventually sending Peel a formal apology nine years later. Peel claimed not to have any animosity to Catholics as such, and 'appears to have felt that in the long run the best hope for the country would be that popery was something which a more prosperous people would grow out of' (Prest). He privately felt contempt for the Ulster Protestants, but publicly was seen as their champion, and the nickname of 'Orange' Peel, which O'Connell had bestowed on him, stuck. Even more so, after the great debate on Catholic emancipation, which took place in the Commons on 9 May 1817, on a motion tabled by the Irish Whig Henry Grattan. The pro-Catholics had been expected to carry the day, and that they did not do so was attributed almost entirely to a rumbustious speech by Peel – long regarded as one of the greatest of his parliamentary orations – winding up the debate. He became an instant hero to the many Anglicans who were fundamentally opposed to emancipation. Nowhere was the Church of England interest stronger than at the University of Oxford, one of whose prestigious seats in Parliament was currently vacant. It had been kept warm for George Canning, but – as a pro-Catholic – his supporters now abandoned him and approached Peel instead. Canning withdrew his name, and Peel was returned unopposed on 10 June 1817, giving up his Chippenham constituency, to which he had transferred from Cashel in 1812. Now, whether he liked it or not, Peel was seen as an arch Protestant, which was to have portentous consequences in his later career.

In Ireland, he made no reputation as a reformer, but as a firm and fair administrator. Two achievements in his final two years there ensured, however, that he would leave the country (to which he would never return) with an enhanced reputation. One was his energetic response to the failure of the Irish potato crop in 1817, when he exerted himself to obtain money and alternative supplies of food, which probably saved the country from widespread famine. The other was the creation of the beginnings of a national police force for Ireland, foreshadowing his action ten years later in creating the Metropolitan Police. His purpose was to minimize the use of troops in responding to disorder, and though his embryo force, nicknamed the 'Peelers', left a great deal to be desired, it was undoubtedly an improvement on what went before. Peel worked exceptionally hard during his six years as Chief Secretary, taking only one holiday – in 1815, when he visited Paris and dined with the Duke of Wellington, who gave him a first-hand account of his recent victory at Waterloo. By 1818, he felt exhausted, and submitted his resignation, spending the next three-and-a-half years as an influential backbencher. As such, he was chosen as the chairman of a high-powered House of Commons committee, including all the senior ministers in the lower house, to consider the complex question of whether Britain should return to the 'gold standard', after having printed a substantial amount of paper money during the course of the Napoleonic wars. Peel tackled the task with his customary assiduity, and eventually produced a magisterial report which argued in favour, largely on the grounds of curbing inflation. His recommendations were immediately accepted by the Government.

His period out of office was marked by two events of great significance in his private life. On 8 June 1820, he got married to Julia Floyd, daughter of General Sir John Floyd, who had been the commander-in-chief of the British army in Ireland during his Chief Secretaryship. He was then 32, and his bride 24. Beautiful and warm-hearted, but – according to Wellington – 'not a clever woman', she had little interest in politics or intellectual pursuits, but she was utterly devoted to Peel, and he to her, and their marriage appears to have brought total satisfaction to both parties. It produced seven children, several of whom went on to have distinguished careers of their own, three serving as government ministers, one of them finishing up as Speaker of the Commons, while another son was to win a VC in the Crimean War. The other development was that Peel, who had an acute artistic sense, began to build up his fine art collection, which gave him immense satisfaction throughout the remainder of his life. Backed by his father's wealth, he made a number of shrewd acquisitions, starting with a Rembrandt, which he picked up at a sale in Dublin for a mere 59 guineas, but culminating in Rubens' magnificent portrait 'Chapeau de Paille', which cost him the considerable sum of £2,725. Peel became a trustee of the National Gallery, which was established in 1824, when he was Home Secretary, and at his death he bequeathed to it his entire collection of over 300 works.

Liverpool was keen to bring Peel back into his government, as indeed was the King, but the only vacant Cabinet post which he had to offer was President of the Board of Control (of Indian affairs), which Peel twice declined, in 1820 and 1821. A proposal to appoint him as Chancellor of the Exchequer, which Peel would almost certainly have accepted, was blocked by the already ailing Lord Castlereagh MP, who feared that Peel's presence would undermine his own position as leader of the House of Commons. So Peel had to wait until January 1822, when a general reconstruction of the government included the retirement of Lord Sidmouth as Home Secretary, a post which Peel was happy to accept. Eight months later, the suicide of Castlereagh led to another reconstruction, which brought Canning back into the government to take over both of Castlereagh's functions, as Foreign Secretary and leader of the House. Peel, who might well have staked a claim to the latter post, declined to do so, in the interest of restoring harmony to the Cabinet, and of easing Canning's return (see Chapter 18).

The reconstructed Cabinet was a finely balanced affair between 'liberal Tories' open-minded about reform measures, generally in favour of free trade and sympathetic to nationalist and liberal movements in South America, the Iberian peninsula and Greece, and the 'ultras', highly protectionist, opposed to all reform measures and in favour of aligning British foreign policy with the authoritarian governments of the Holy Alliance powers – Russia, Prussia and Austria. The first group consisted largely of the ministers sitting in the House of Commons, led by George Canning, and including Fredrick Robinson (later Lord Goderich), the Chancellor of the Exchequer, and William Huskisson, the President of the Board of Trade. Peel, who was the senior minister in the Commons, after Canning, naturally gravitated to this group, which also normally received the support of the Prime Minister, Lord Liverpool. The 'ultras' were concentrated in the House of Lords, where their most influential representative was the Duke of Wellington, but their intellectual leader was the Lord Chancellor, Lord Eldon. The other divisive issue within the Cabinet was over Catholic emancipation, which was treated as an 'open question'. The majority, pro-Catholic faction was led by Canning, but on this issue Peel found himself in general agreement with the 'Ultras', along with Liverpool. Indeed, he and the Prime Minister were the most fervent opponents of emancipation within the government.

Peel served as Home Secretary, under Liverpool, for nearly five years, until April 1827, and then, again, from January 1828 to November 1830, under Wellington, seven and a quarter years in all, and according to a later Prime Minister, Harold Wilson, 'was undoubtedly the greatest reforming Home Secretary of all time' (Wilson, 1977, p. 45). His two most notable achievements were the complete re-codification of English criminal law (with the purpose, he said, 'of simplification, consolidation and mitigation') and the establishment of the Metropolitan Police Force. The first exercise involved the examination of thousands of separate laws, some dating as far back as the thirteenth century. Altogether, 278 Acts were repealed, and the remainder consolidated into eight statutes. Peel was especially concerned to cut down on the number of offences for which the death penalty was prescribed (more than 200 in all, including for stealing a lamb), and to substitute lesser and more realistic penalties, as many criminals were being let off scot-free because juries were becoming more and more reluctant to convict. The immediate result was not a reduction in the number of criminals hanged (that had to wait until the return of more merciful Whig governments in the 1830s), but a marked increase in the rate of convictions, as punishments such as transportation, whipping, the treadmill and prison sentences of varying length were imposed. Peel's Act of Parliament establishing the Metropolitan Police, passed in 1829, created for the first time a reliable and efficient police force for the capital city, without – as had been feared – opening the way to an oppressive means of political control, such as had occurred in Paris and other continental cities. As in Ireland, a decade earlier, the members of the force became known as 'Peelers' or more commonly, 'Bobbies', after the first name of their founder.

Peel was in many ways the outstanding member of Liverpool's cabinet from 1822 onwards, even though Canning was more prominent. Extraordinarily hard-working, always the master of his brief, he dominated all the parliamentary debates in which he participated. His principal worry was the mounting discontent in Ireland, for which he now had governmental responsibility, and which, unlike many previous Home Secretaries, he took extremely seriously. His task was made no easier by the new Lord-Lieutenant of Ireland, the haughty, lazy and uncommunicative Marquess Wellesley, elder brother of the Duke of Wellington. Peel was disconcerted by the growing demand for Catholic emancipation, which not only affected Ireland, but increasingly British public and parliamentary opinion and also his Cabinet colleagues. He began to have private doubts as to whether continued resistance was realistic, but he was seen as the principal government advocate for the status quo, and was put up to speak as such whenever the question was aired in Parliament. In March 1825, a Bill proposed by the Radical MP, Sir Francis Burdett, passed the Commons. Peel felt his position was untenable and offered his resignation, but the Lords rejected the Bill, and Liverpool persuaded him to stay on. A year later, it looked as though Burdett's bill would again pass the Commons, this time with an increased majority, and both Peel and Liverpool proposed to resign if this happened, leaving the King with no alternative but to appoint a Whig government, or one led by Canning, to carry the measure through. Yet, on 17 February 1826, Liverpool was incapacitated by a stroke (though he did not resign until 9 April), and when, in March, Burdett's resolution came up before the House, where it was debated for two full nights, it was to general surprise defeated by the narrow margin of four votes – 276 to 272. This owed much to a brilliant speech by Peel.

Nevertheless, he was to resign a month later, when Liverpool gave up the premiership, and George IV asked Canning to succeed him. As recounted in Chapter 7, half the Cabinet – the ultra Tories – refused to serve under the new premier. Peel, who on most policy issues was extremely close to him, might have been expected to stay on, but advanced his own opposition to Catholic emancipation as his reason for refusing to serve. This was a fateful decision: Peel was essentially a natural 'Canningite', and had he stayed with him he would very probably have ended up in the Liberal Party, like most of the other Canningites, and eventually become its leader. As it was, he was to become leader of the Tories, a party with which he had little in common, and for whose natural supporters, the country squires, he felt only contempt.

Peel sat out Canning's government, and also that of Lord Goderich, each of which lasted a mere four months, but returned as Home Secretary, and also as leader of the House of Commons, when Wellington formed a purely Tory government in January 1828. He was now clearly the number two man in the government and was extensively consulted by Wellington about its composition. Peel wanted it to be a centrist coalition, and insisted that all the leading Canningites should be included, and that several of the hard-line Tory 'ultras', such as Lord Eldon, should be left out. It was thus as much Peel's construction as Wellington's, but the whole balance of the government was destroyed, when Wellington clumsily provoked the resignation of the Canningites in May 1828 (see Chapter 21). The subsequent reconstruction of the government inadvertently brought the issue of Catholic emancipation to a head, resulting in the fall of the government and gravely damaging Peel's already bad relations with the 'ultras'. One of the Canningites who resigned was Charles Grant, the President of the Board of Trade, and Wellington nominated as his successor William Vesey Fitzgerald, a Protestant Irish landowner who, under the law at the time, was required to resign his parliamentary seat and fight a by-election before taking up his post. Fitzgerald, a popular figure in his constituency of County Clare, where he was regarded as a model landlord, and who was personally in favour of Catholic emancipation, had every expectation of being returned unopposed. Yet, Daniel O'Connell, the leader of the Catholic Association, decided to contest the seat, even though, as a Catholic, he was disqualified from sitting in the House of Commons. The electorate was made up predominately of Catholic farmers, who were insistently urged by their priests to vote for O'Connell. He was triumphantly returned with more than two-thirds of the vote. Peel immediately concluded that the game was up, so far as further resistance to emancipation was concerned. In his view, civil war in Ireland could only be averted by the taking of early steps to enable O'Connell to take up his seat in the House. Yet he did not want to be the instrument for bringing forward a reform which he had resisted so tenaciously for so long. He resolved to urge his Cabinet colleagues, and King George IV, of the necessity of acting without delay, but fully intended to resign from the government so that he should have no responsibility for the legislation which would be brought in. Wellington, also a long-term opponent of emancipation, though not so publicly associated with the Protestant cause as Peel, had drawn the same conclusions from O'Connell's triumph. He set himself to persuade the ailing and highly reluctant King that there was no alternative to ceding the Catholics' claim, which he only succeeded in doing by threatening the resignation of the whole Cabinet. The Duke, however, felt incapable of carrying the necessary Bill through Parliament without the help of Peel, who out of loyalty to a chief whom he profoundly admired, though their personal relations were never close, very reluctantly agreed to carry on. It was thus he who was responsible for introducing the Bill in the Commons and carrying it though all its stages, until it finally received the Royal Assent on 13 April 1829. In Gash's words: 'A more prudent, a more timid, a more selfish man would have left Wellington to deal with the situation as well as he could; Peel chose to remain' (Gash, 1976, p. 123).

The personal consequences for him were considerable. He was vigorously criticized by some of his Oxford University constituents, and felt constrained to resign his seat and seek a vote of confidence in a by-election. In this, he was humiliatingly defeated, in a poll in which it was reported by the diarist Charles Greville that 'an immense number of parsons' had taken part. The government could not afford his absence from the House and immediate steps had to be taken to find him a new seat, the Member for the pocket borough of Westbury, Sir Manasseh Lopez, being induced to make way for him. Many of the ultra Tories openly treated Peel as a 'traitor', one of them declaring that he should henceforth be known not as 'Orange' Peel, but as 'Lemon' Peel because of the bitterness his action had caused. Some of them did not have to wait long before seeking revenge on him and on Wellington. The accession of William IV, the following year, led to a general election, in which the opposition (of Whigs and Canningites) improved their position, without gaining a majority in the House. They hoped to defeat the government over the issue of parliamentary reform, for which public support was sharply rising, encouraged by the July Revolution in France, which brought down the authoritarian Bourbon monarchy. Even before the Commons voted on a motion for Reform, however, the government was defeated, on 16 November 1830 in a division on the Civil List, in which 29 ultra Tories voted with the opposition to bring the government down (see Chapter 21). Wellington immediately resigned and the King called on Earl Grey to form a Whig government. This marked the end of Peel's long period as a departmental minister, which had occupied all but five of the 21 years of his parliamentary career so far. He was to serve for another 20 years, all but five of them in opposition, and the only ministerial post in which he was to serve was as Prime Minister. The year 1830, during which he celebrated his forty-second birthday, was a watershed in one other important respect. His father, the first Sir Robert Peel, died on 3 May, aged 80, and Peel inherited the baronetcy, an income of £40,000 a year, and the estate of Drayton Manor, where he proceeded to build a new and much grander house, incorporating every modern innovation. He also took over his father's parliamentary seat of Tamworth, which he was to represent for the rest of his life.

With the installation of Lord Grey's government, Peel became leader of the opposition in the Commons. His first challenge was how to respond to the Reform Bill which the government introduced early in 1831. Peel was personally a moderate supporter of Reform, believing that limited steps should be taken to remove the most obviously corrupt features of the existing system. But he was quite unprepared for the sweeping proposals included in the new Bill (see Chapter 10), and concluded that the only course open to him, and his party, was to seek its total defeat. He almost succeeded, when, on 22 March 1831, it passed its Second Reading by a single vote (302–301). He lost his temper (a rare event for such a well disciplined man) in a subsequent debate when the Government had successfully sought a dissolution in order to get a popular mandate for the Bill, and engaged in a shouting match with the Speaker. This was only concluded when the King arrived to announce the dissolution in person. The subsequent general election, which produced a strong majority for the Whigs, convinced Peel that further resistance to the Bill would be fruitless, but he refused to take steps to facilitate its passage. A year later, when the Lords had defeated the Bill, and the King had refused Grey's request to create sufficient new peers to force it through, the government resigned. The King invited Peel to form a government with the object of bringing in a more limited measure, but Peel declined, saying that it would be far preferable for the Whigs to carry through the Reform which they had demanded. After his experience with Catholic emancipation, he refused to do his opponents' work for them. The King then made the same proposal to Wellington, which he was willing to attempt, but the firm refusal of Peel and other leading Tories in the Commons to join his government meant that he was unable to proceed. The King then recalled Grey, and gave him the assurance which he had previously refused. As recounted in Chapter 22, the leading Tory peers, led by Wellington, then abstained on the Third Reading vote, and the Bill was finally passed, on 4 June 1832, by 106 votes to 22.

In the subsequent general election, the Tories suffered their worst ever defeat, and Peel found himself leading a much-depleted group of 179 Tory MPs against 479 Whigs, Radicals and Irish followers of Daniel O'Connell. It looked as though the Tories would be condemned to many years in opposition, but only two years later they once again had an opportunity to govern. This was in November 1834, when Peel had taken his wife and elder daughter to Italy for a rare holiday. William IV peremptorily dismissed Lord Melbourne's Whig government, only four months after he had succeeded Lord Grey, and determined instead to install a Tory administration (see Chapter 23). He had Peel in mind as Prime Minister, but in his absence offered the post to Wellington who, however, accepted only on a temporary basis, pending Peel's return. When Peel returned, three weeks later, he realized that he had no choice but to accept the premiership, but he made two conditions. One was that he should not be restricted to known Tories in proposing his Cabinet, the other was that he should be granted dissolution in order to bid for a parliamentary majority. His primary target for new recruits was the Stanleyite group of former Canningites, who had resigned from Grey's government, in June 1834, on the issue of Irish tithe reform. He therefore invited both Edward Stanley (the future 14th Earl of Derby) and his close associate, Sir James Graham, to join the Cabinet. Both were sympathetic, but they were not yet ready to throw in their lot with the Tories, so Peel had to make do with what was effectively a rerun of the Wellington cabinet of 1827–30, with the Duke now acting as Foreign Secretary. Even before the general election, Peel had to present himself again to the electors of Tamworth to confirm his nomination as Prime Minister, and he took this as an opportunity to re-make the image of the Tory Party, whom he now renamed the Conservatives. He issued his famous 'Tamworth Manifesto', formally an appeal for support from his constituents, but intended as a programme on which Conservative candidates could fight the general election – an unprecedented step.

The manifesto made it clear that the Conservatives had finally accepted both Catholic emancipation and the Reform Act as irreversible, and henceforth saw themselves as the representatives of 'that great and intelligent class of society...which is far less interested in the contentions of party, than in the maintenance of order and the cause of good government'. He pledged a 'careful review of institutions, both civil and ecclesiastical and the correction of proved abuses and the redress of real grievances'. Caution and good sense were the keynotes of Peel's manifesto, which was an accurate reflection of his own longstanding attitudes. It was meant to convey reassurance to the new body of electors enfranchised by the Reform Act, and its initial impact was largely favourable. The Conservatives made substantial gains in the general election, becoming the largest party in the House of Commons. They remained in a minority, however, only because of the success of Daniel O'Connell's followers who swept up the great bulk of the Irish seats. Within a few weeks of the general election the O'Connellites linked up with the Whigs and Radicals to defeat the government and, on 18 April 1835, Lord Melbourne was able to return to office at the head of a Whig government, to the humiliation of William IV. Peel, now aged 47, had been in office for a mere 119 days.

For the next six years, Peel was again leader of the opposition, and proved to be the dominant figure in the House of Commons. Shy and often awkward in his personal contacts, he was a fluent and authoritative public speaker, and the larger the audience the more confident he became. A tall, imposing figure, the contrast between him and the diminutive Lord John Russell, the leader of the Commons, and his frequent opponent in debate, was striking. He was less successful in establishing warm relations with his followers, a natural reserve being reinforced by his acute sensitivity abut his social inferiority. He was always over-anxious that he should be seen to act like a gentleman, but was quick to take offence, and on more than one occasion was only dissuaded from fighting duels with other politicians by the good sense of their 'seconds'. Nevertheless, Peel showed great patience in marshalling his forces, particularly in the House of Lords, where the ultra Tory element was still strong and he could not always rely on Wellington to keep them under control. He had to fight hard to prevent the Lords, where the Tories had a large majority, from throwing out the Municipal Corporations Act of 1835, which he regarded as an essential measure of local government reform. Otherwise, the Lords effectively put an end to the timid reforming instincts of Melbourne's government, voting down several other measures including the Irish Tithes Bill, which would have expropriated the excess revenues of the Anglican Church in Ireland for educational purposes. Peel continued to woo the Stanleyites, but refused to countenance any moves to co–operate with the Radicals or O'Connellites in what he regarded as premature efforts to dislodge the government. He was wary of any repeat of his experience in 1834–5, of trying to govern without a majority of his own, while the accession of the openly pro-Whig Queen Victoria, in June 1837, removed any possibility of preferential treatment by the monarch. Even so, he came near to resuming office, in May 1839, when Melbourne resigned after his parliamentary majority fell to five votes in a division arising over the rebellion in Jamaica. As recounted in Chapter 23, Melbourne advised the deeply unhappy Queen to send for Peel, whom she received in a foul temper, making 'it clear that she would not agree to a dissolution of parliament, that she wished Wellington to be a member of the new administration, and that she intended to continue her friendship with her late prime minister' (Gash, 1976, p. 186).

Peel, always awkward in the presence of women and lacking Melbourne's easy charm, was taken aback by the abrupt manner of his 20-year-old sovereign, but meekly agreed to her conditions. He did, however, emphasize the difficulty of his parliamentary position and asked the Queen for some public sign of her confidence, suggesting that this might be shown by *some* changes in her Household appointments, all of which were currently held by Whig women, some of them the wives of prominent Whig politicians. Victoria was incensed, telling Melbourne untruthfully that Peel had demanded the dismissal of *all* the Ladies of the Bedchamber. Melbourne, no longer Prime Minister, should have refrained from offering advice on the matter, but nevertheless suggested to her that she should tell Peel that these were personal appointments, not subject to governmental decision. Victoria thereupon informed Peel that she would make no changes to her Household, and the incoming Cabinet decided that in these circumstances it could not take office. The outcome of the 'Bedchamber episode' as it became known, was that a delighted Victoria was able to reappoint Melbourne, who remained in office for a further two years.

During this time the economic situation in the country deteriorated, and the government seemed quite unable to prevent a sharp rise in the budget deficit. Peel, whose grasp of economics was formidable, regularly worsted ministers in debates on these issues, and the government's standing fell sharply. In the general election of 1841, Peel's patience received its reward, the Conservatives securing an overall majority of 77 seats. It was a truly historic victory: the first time in British history that 'a party in office enjoying a majority in the Commons had been defeated in the polling booths by an opposition previously in a minority' (Gash, 1976, p. 207). At last, Peel's hour had come, and he embarked on what is widely regarded as his great administration. Even before the election, the ground had been laid for Peel's accession to power by a private initiative of Prince Albert. He sent his private secretary, George Anson, to see Peel to suggest a discreet compromise over Household appointments, in order to avoid any repetition of the 'Bedchamber affair'. This was to the effect that the three leading Whig ladies, and any others to whom Peel took objection, should be privately persuaded to resign, and that the Queen herself should announce the appointment of their replacements, although Peel would communicate to her the actual names. Thus began an increasingly close and warm relationship between Peel and Albert, who in the course of time succeeded in thawing out the *froideur* of his wife towards her new Prime Minister. It was not long before their relations became perfectly amicable, though there was none of the intimacy which she had shown to Melbourne. Peel led a 12-man Cabinet, of whom two were widely seen as 'passengers', appointed for reasons of political balance. These were the Duke of Buckingham, as Lord Privy Seal, and Sir Edward Knatchbull, as Paymaster-General. The former was regarded as representing the agricultural interest, the latter the ultra Tories. Both Edward Stanley, as Secretary for War and Colonies, and Sir James Graham, as Home Secretary, agreed to join the government, signifying their integration into the Conservative Party, while Lord Aberdeen became Foreign Secretary and Henry Goulburn, Chancellor of the Exchequer. Wellington joined the Cabinet as Minister without Portfolio, but also resumed his earlier post as Commander-in-Chief. The Earl of Ripon, who had been Prime Minister, as Lord Goderich, in 1827–8, became President of the Board of Trade, with the young William Gladstone as his deputy. Among the many disappointed office-seekers was Benjamin Disraeli, MP for Shrewsbury, who wrote him an obsequious letter, which Peel ignored, to his later cost.

Peel himself took a close interest in foreign policy, refusing to allow the mild-mannered Aberdeen anything like the autonomy which Palmerston had enjoyed under Melbourne. The main external distractions during the course of his government were strained relations with the United States and France, and problems in India. The Governor-General, Lord Ellenborough, nominally employed by the East India Company, pursued a forward policy, leading to a hazardous military campaign in Afghanistan, and the annexation of the Sind, neither of which were in accord with Peel's wishes. Ellenborough, difficult to control at such a distance, then added to his misdemeanours by writing directly to Victoria, suggesting that she should proclaim herself Empress of India, a proposal which Peel strongly deprecated, though it was to be adopted by Disraeli over 30 years later. When, in 1844, Ellenborough proceeded to yet another unauthorized annexation, that of Gwalior, he was eventually dismissed, and Sir Henry Hardinge, a cautious old soldier, and a trusted intimate of Peel's, was sent out in his place. With both the United States and France, Peel insisted on pursuing a firm but conciliatory policy. This eventually led to a settlement of the long-standing border dispute with the United States, with the signing of the Oregon treaty, retaining British control of Vancouver. With France there were numerous quarrels, including disputes over Tahiti, Morocco and Syria, and naval rearmament, but the main British concern was to forestall French dynastic ambitions in Spain, where Louis-Philippe was suspected of designs to marry off one of his younger sons to the adolescent Queen Isabella. He was eventually dissuaded, though the Duc de Montpensier did in fact marry the Queen's younger sister, Lucia, after Peel had left office, to the great dissatisfaction of the British court and government.

Yet Peel's main concern was with 'the Condition of England', as it was described in a famous pamphlet by Thomas Carlyle, published in 1840. This described the misery caused by one of the worst depressions of the nineteenth century, with widespread unemployment and poverty, particularly in towns such as Bolton and Paisley, where starvation was barely kept at bay. The nation was in tumult, with mass meetings by the Chartists and the Anti-Corn Law League constantly threatening public order, while the ten-hour day campaign by Lord Ashley (later the Earl of Shaftesbury) was infuriating industrialists. Meanwhile the accumulated national deficit had grown to £7½ million, an unprecedented level in peacetime. Peel came to power with two clear objectives. One was to create a budget surplus. The other – closely allied – was to reorganize the taxation system so as to permit a progressive transition to free trade, lowering the price of food and raw materials, which would both ease poverty and stimulate demand, thus giving an upward push to economic growth. To achieve a surplus, he suggested what no previous government had dared since 1816, when the temporary wartime income tax introduced by Pitt had been swept away by a backbench revolt in the Commons. He proposed a rate of 7d in the pound, for incomes over £150, to run for a three-year period. He probably had a shrewd idea that this period would be extended, and so it has proved, with income tax being the mainstay of the government's revenue ever since. It took some doing to persuade the Cabinet, with Stanley and Graham being particularly sceptical, but he gradually won them round, and the tax formed the central element in the budget which Peel personally introduced in March 1842, the Chancellor, Henry Goulburn, having deferred to him. Much of the surplus obtained through the tax was disbursed through a large range of tariff reductions, focussed on food and other essential items. Peel would have liked to remove all duty from corn, but fearful of the strong agricultural lobby, extremely well represented on the government benches largely peopled by country squires, he proposed instead only a marginal liberalization of the Corn Laws. Even this was too much for his Lord Privy Seal, the Duke of Buckingham, who was President of the Agricultural Protection Society. He resigned after only five months in office.

Within a year or two, Peel's tax policies were clearly having an effect, with employment rising, the budget showing a healthy surplus and the level of public discontent sensibly easing. Before this happened, though, there was continuing fear of public disorder, and even of revolution, with both the Chartists and the Anti-Corn Law League stepping up their activities. There was great alarm in January 1843, when Peel's Private Secretary, Edward Drummond, was assassinated while walking down Whitehall, and it was evident that he had been mistaken for the Prime Minister. There was some relief, however, when it appeared that the assassin was a man of unsound mind, pursuing a private grievance, rather than being politically motivated. With his government getting into its stride, all now seemed set fair for Peel, when the failure of the Irish potato crop in 1845 led to the greatest crisis of his political career. Estimated to have caused over a million deaths, and massive emigration to the United States and elsewhere, Peel immediately realized that it would be necessary to suspend the operation of the corn laws in order that cheap grain, mainly from Canada, could be imported in large amounts. He also concluded that it would be politically impossible to re-impose the laws once they had been suspended, and decided that the only honest thing to do was to repeal them altogether. He found it impossible, however, to persuade his own Cabinet, only three of whom, including the Home Secretary, Sir James Graham, initially supported him. In the meantime, the leader of the opposition, Lord John Russell, had launched a stirring call for abolition, in an open letter issued in Edinburgh. Peel composed no less than five memoranda arguing the case to the Cabinet, in the period between 31 October and 4 December 1845, and when the Cabinet met on that date, two members, Stanley and the Duke of Buccleuch, declared that they would resign rather than back Peel's proposal, for which he received only lukewarm support from the majority of his other colleagues. Peel then decided to resign, recommending that Lord John

Russell should be invited to form an administration to carry through the policy which he had publicly recommended.

The Queen promptly summoned Russell, who tried to form a government, but failed due to the inability of his leading colleagues to agree on the allocation of ministerial posts, in particular whether Palmerston should be permitted to resume the Foreign Secretaryship. Peel would much have preferred Russell to have succeeded, so as to prevent a re-run of the events of 1829, when he had had to carry through, with Whig support, a measure (Catholic emancipation) of which the great majority of his fellow Tories disapproved. Yet, when the Queen appealed to him not to abandon her, he readily agreed to resume as Prime Minister. His decision was welcomed by his Cabinet, with the exception of Stanley, who insisted on resigning, and Buccleuch, who asked for time to consider his position, but eventually agreed to carry on. Peel was greatly encouraged by Wellington's strong support, even though the Duke had previously been a supporter of the Corn laws. Gladstone was promoted to fill Stanley's position as Secretary for War and Colonies.

On 27 January 1846, Peel introduced his Bill to repeal the Corn Laws, allowing three years before the Bill would take full effect. He was spectacularly abandoned by the great bulk of his own party, only 112 Conservative MPs voting for the second reading, and 231 against. His opponents were rallied by Lord George Bentinck, a younger son of the Duke of Portland and a prominent member of the Jockey Club, who had sat for 20 years as a silent MP, but: 'who now brought to the Protectionist cause the ruthless determination and single-mindedness which he had formerly shown in hunting down dishonest trainers and crooked jockeys on the Turf. Violent and unscrupulous by temperament, he made up for his political inexperience by tenacity and force' (Gash, 1976, p. 275).

If Bentinck provided the organizational drive for the Protectionists, it was Benjamin Disraeli, still bitter at his exclusion from office by Peel, who supplied the debating skill, launching a series of merciless attacks on the Prime Minister, which greatly wounded him. When Peel expostulated that Disraeli had begged to be included in his government, Disraeli brazenly denied it, gambling on the probability that Peel would not have his letter to hand. Disraeli effectively knocked the stuffing out of Peel, whose only desire now was to get the Bill through as quickly as possible, with Whig support, and then to insist on resigning. On 25 June 1846, the Bill was finally passed by the House of Lords. On the same day the government was defeated in the Commons on its Irish coercion bill, and Peel resigned four days later. His party was irremediably split, the majority eventually choosing Stanley (later the 14th Earl of Derby) as their leader. The minority, who included most of the more able figures, became known as Peelites, most of whom, including Gladstone, later joined with the Whigs, who, under Russell, united with the Radicals to form the Liberal Party.

On the day he resigned, Peel went down to the House of Commons and made was what probably his greatest ever speech. The peroration was long remembered, and acted as his political epitaph:

> I shall leave a name execrated by every monopolist who … clamours for protection because it accrues to his individual benefit; but it may be that I shall leave a name sometimes remembered with expressions of goodwill in the abodes of those whose lot it is to labour, and to earn their daily bread by the sweat of their brow, when they shall recruit their exhausted strength with abundant and untaxed food, the sweeter because it is no longer leavened by a sense of injustice. (Wilson, p. 60)

Peel's hope was handsomely fulfilled: he remains the only Conservative peacetime leader to be widely revered by the working class. By contrast, the Conservative Party, of which he was the founder, has largely airbrushed him out of its history, blaming him rather than Bentinck or Disraeli for the 1846 split in the party, which condemned it to spending the best part of a generation in opposition. It has preferred to regard either the Younger Pitt or Disraeli as its true source of inspiration. Peel's offence was his pragmatic response to the Great Irish famine, choosing, as in 1829, to do what the situation clearly demanded, rather than to follow the prejudices of the mass of his party colleagues. The question remains whether he could have achieved his objectives without losing their support. A less arrogant, less prickly, more clubbable man might have pulled it off, it is sometimes suggested, but this seems highly unlikely. Yes, he might have been able to win round a few more of his opponents if he had shown more tact and made more of a personal effort, but the size of the majority against him in his party strongly suggests that any such effect would have been marginal. Peel's intensely unflattering assessment of the mass of his fellow Tory MPs is a sufficient explanation of why he disdained to make a more serious attempt to woo them:

> How can those who spend their time in hunting and shooting and eating and drinking know what were the motives of those who are responsible for the public security, who have access to the best information, and have no other object under Heaven but to provide against danger, and consult the general interests of all classes! (Hilton, 1998, p. 147)

In the general election of 1847, Lord John Russell's Liberals, and their Irish allies, won 323 seats against 321 Conservatives, though the latter were divided between around 225 Protectionists and just under 100 Peelites. There was thus no question of the Liberal government being defeated, and it was not long before it became clear that there would be no healing of the Conservative split. Peel, though only 59, concluded that his ministerial career was over, and made no effort to organize a parliamentary opposition, regarding himself henceforward as an elder statesman, and confining himself to occasional, well thought-out speeches on major issues. His last speech, on 28 June 1850, was a magisterial critique of Palmerston's aggressive foreign policy, provoked by the storm created by the Don Pacifico affair (see Chapter 16). The day after, while riding his horse on Constitution Hill, it stumbled, throwing its rider and then falling on top of him. Peel suffered fatal injuries, from which he died at his London home in Whitehall Gardens four days later. He was 62, and had been Prime Minister, taking his two terms together, for a total of five years and 57 days. For those who put party loyalty above all other considerations, he was the object of scorn and derision. Others have rightly regarded him as one of, if not *the* greatest of Nineteenth-century Premiers.

Works consulted

Norman Gash, 1961, *Mr Secretary Peel: The Life of Sir Robert Peel to 1830*, London, Longman.

Norman Gash, 1972, *Sir Robert Peel: The Life of Sir Robert after 1830*, London, Longman.

Norman Gash, 1976, *Peel*, London, Longman.

Christopher Hibbert, 1981, (ed.), *Greville's England*, London, Folio Society.

Boyd Hilton, 1998, 'Robert Peel' in Robert Eccleshall and Graham Walker, (eds.), *Biographical Dictionary of British Prime Ministers*, London, Routledge.

Douglas Hurd, 2007, *Robert Peel: A Biography*, London, Weidenfeld & Nicolson.

Lucille Iremonger, 1970, *The Fiery Chariot*, London, Secker & Warburg.

John Prest, 2004, Article in *Oxford Dictionary of National Biography*.

Harold Wilson, 1977, *A Prime Minister on Prime Ministers*, London, Weidenfeld & Nicolson.

25
Lord John Russell, 1st Earl Russell – from Whig to Liberal

It is an open question whether Lord John Russell should be considered the last of the Whigs or the first of the Liberals. He has an equal claim to both distinctions. His upbringing could hardly have been more Whiggish. The third son of the 6th Duke of Bedford, he was brought up to believe that Charles James Fox (whose life he was later to write in three volumes) was the fount of all wisdom. He was the first person to describe his party as Liberal rather than Whig, and he should perhaps be regarded as the first Liberal Prime Minister, though Palmerston is usually accorded this honour. Born on 18 August 1792, two months prematurely, John Russell was a sickly child, who was to remain unhealthy and short of stature throughout his life, never quite reaching five foot, five inches. His father, then known as Lord John Russell, was a Whig MP, who later rose to be Lord-Lieutenant of Ireland. He was the younger brother of the 5th Duke of Bedford, and unexpectedly succeeded to the title in 1802, when his still unmarried brother was killed in a riding accident. Young John's mother, Georgiana Elizabeth Byng, was a daughter of the 4th Viscount Torrington, and had already borne her husband two sons. Her new-born baby was undoubtedly her favourite, and she lavished care and attention upon him, delighting in his early signs of maturity, writing to her husband:

> It is not in my power to express the merits of that child. His sense, his cleverness, his quietness, and the sweetness of his temper and disposition surpass all I've ever witnessed. His attentions to me are those of a grown person of superior sense. His active mind makes him attempt everything. (Scherer, 1999, pp. 13–14)

This included teaching himself Latin, while still in his infancy, and reading *Plutarch's Lives* to his mother, before he was belatedly sent to school for the first time, at the age of eight. This was what he later described as 'a very bad private school at Sunbury', and a year later he was devastated by the death, on 11 October 1801, of his mother – from unknown causes – though she had been an invalid more or less continuously since his birth. Soon afterwards his Uncle Francis died, and his father succeeded to the dukedom, moving into the grand family seat of Woburn Abbey, which now became his home. Young John was now known as Lord John, and in June 1803 his father married again, once more to a Georgiana. This was Lady Georgiana Gordon, a 21-year-old daughter of the Duke of Gordon. She tried to be a good stepmother to John, but as she went on to have seven sons and three daughters of her own, she had little time to spare for him. John was forced more and more into the company of his two elder brothers. The elder of these, Francis (known as Lord Tavistock and, much later, the 7th Duke), treated him with condescension, but the middle brother, William, two years his senior, became a close companion. When he was 11 he was sent to Westminster School, traditionally patronized by the Russell family, but life there was soon regarded as being too boisterous for such a frail child, and – at his stepmother's suggestion – he was withdrawn from the school in July 1804, and privately tutored for six months by the chaplain at Woburn, Dr Edmund Cartwright, the inventor of the power loom. He was later sent to a small private boarding school, run by a clergyman in Kent, where he remained until he was 15. Here he made a number of close friends, including Lord Clare, who shared with him the handicap of being under-sized, and for whom he felt a great deal of empathy. The school's curriculum was undemanding, but Lord John was a voracious reader.

His father achieved high office in the 'Ministry of All the Talents', led by Lord Grenville, in 1806–1807, being appointed Lord-Lieutenant of Ireland, and the young Lord John met many leading Whig politicians who visited their home, or the Vice-regal lodge in Dublin, nearly all of whom were impressed by his intelligence and precocity. The Duke of Bedford lost office in March 1807, when George III dismissed Grenville's government, and he decided to spend more time with his children, particularly Lord John. He took John, together with his wife, on a three-month tour of Scotland, and in the autumn of that year, John left school for the last time, after Lord Holland, the leading Whig peer, had offered to take him with him on a tour of Spain and Portugal, where the Peninsular War was now raging. The visit lasted until August of the following year, and proved a hazardous venture, Holland's party being caught up in a British retreat against superior French forces, while John caught a fever which delayed their return. During the visit he met most of the leaders of the Spanish revolt against the French, and grew very close to Holland, and, particularly his wife, who 'became virtually a second mother to Lord John' (Scherer, p. 17).

On his return, he was anxious to go up to Oxford or Cambridge, but Bedford, dismayed that his eldest son, Tavistock, had learnt nothing at Cambridge beyond becoming a playboy, insisted that he should instead go to Edinburgh, which he regarded as a far more serious university. This proved a wise decision, and though Lord John declined, like many other aristocrats at the time, to take a degree, he had a thorough grounding, particularly in more 'modern' subjects, such as mathematics, chemistry and physics. His tutor, Professor Playfair, described him as 'one of the most promising young men I have ever met with' (Scherer, p. 17). A valuable experience for Russell, which helped to prepare him for a political career, was his membership of the Speculative Society, whose 30 elected members met every week to read essays and conduct debates. He thoroughly enjoyed his time at Edinburgh, and made frequent visits to the city throughout his later life. He left in 1812, and instead of the Grand Tour, made impossible by French occupation of most of Western Europe, departed with two friends for a tour of the Mediterranean. He left them for a while, to visit his brother, Lord William, who was fighting in Spain, and had been wounded at the Battle of Talavera. It was a dangerous trip, in which he narrowly avoided capture by French forces, but he rejoined his friends and sailed with them to Majorca, intending to go on to Greece, Egypt, Palestine and Syria. But word reached him there that, on 4 May 1813, he had been elected unopposed to Parliament in a by-election in the 'family seat' of Tavistock, caused by the death of the sitting member, Richard Fitzpatrick. He was not yet 21, and only took his seat several months later, when he had come of age.

Russell was later to be regarded as a great parliamentarian, but his first term in Parliament was distinctly patchy. He revealed himself immediately as an 'advanced Whig', particularly strong on libertarian issues, devoting his maiden speech, on 12 May 1814, to attacking the decision in the peace settlement to transfer Norway from Danish to Swedish rule, against the wishes of the Norwegians, and to cede Parga, on the Greek Adriatic coast and formerly ruled by Venice, to the Turks. But his attendance was fitful – he took part in only three divisions out of 32 –, and spent much of his time travelling on the Continent, including a visit to Elba, where he had an interview with Napoleon. Later, after Napoleon's escape, he attacked the decision to renew the war against France, describing it as 'impolitic, unjust and injurious...' (Scherer, p. 26). He soon lost interest in debates dominated by the large Tory majority, and, in 1817, announced his withdrawal from Parliament, accepting the Chiltern Hundreds. He later changed his mind, and stood for re-election at Tavistock, in the 1818 general election, though for the next few years he devoted most of his time to writing, turning out a biography, a novel, a five-act play in verse and a history of the English constitution, all during a three-year span. It was only in the early 1820s that he started seriously to devote himself to politics, taking up the issue which was later to bring him lasting fame – parliamentary reform. He had felt strongly about the issue for a long time. When he was barely 18, in August 1810, he had written to Lord Holland, complaining at the lack of 'zeal', which the Whig leader, Earl Grey, was displaying on the question of reform. He scathingly commented: 'He still seems to think of himself as a Whig, and I am afraid the Tory Opinions which he wears under that cloak will bring the name into great discredit' (Prest, 1972, p. 12).

Nobody could make the same complaint about Lord John. He seized on the issue like a terrier, raising it on every possible occasion, and giving greater thought to the practical details than any other politician. His first initiative came in the 1820–21 session, when he proposed the disfranchisement of Grampound, a rotten borough, for 'gross corruption', and that its two seats be transferred to the (unrepresented) city of Leeds, or another large town. Grampound duly lost its seats, but – at the government's insistence – they were transferred instead to the county of Yorkshire, which henceforth returned four members. He returned to the charge in 1822, when he proposed a motion in favour of a more comprehensive reform measure, proposing that one member should be taken away from each of 100 small boroughs, and that 60 of these seats should be transferred to the counties and 40 to the large towns. In a stirring speech, which made his reputation as a parliamentary orator, he asserted: 'At the present period the ministers of the crown possess the confidence of the House of Commons, but the House of Commons does not possess the esteem and reverence of the people' (Prest, 2004).

The House divided, largely upon party lines, and Russell's motion was defeated by 269 votes to 164, and when he tried again, four years later, he was defeated by a wider margin. He had more success with a motion to curb bribery in elections, which he won, by the Speaker's casting vote, after a tied division in the Commons. This, however, led indirectly to a personal setback, when he lost his seat in the ensuing general election, of June 1826. Together with his brother, Lord Tavistock MP, he high-mindedly resolved not to do any canvassing, or to spend money on entertainment or the transportation of voters. The money which ordinarily would have been devoted to election expenses was instead donated to local charities. This had a disastrous effect on their election results. Tavistock held on to his seat, but came in second in a contest in the 'family borough', where he would normally have been expected to head the poll, while Russell was defeated in Huntingdonshire, to which he had transferred in 1820. He was out of Parliament for six months, until December 1826, when he was returned unopposed in a by-election for the pocket borough of Bandon.

By now, Russell was recognized as one of the most forceful and active MPs on the Whig side of the House. In February 1828, he tabled a resolution to repeal the Test and Corporation Acts, which restricted the civic rights of members of nonconformist churches. He succeeded in winning over 15 of the ultra-Tories, and his motion was carried by 237 votes to 193, leading the Wellington government to introduce its own repeal measure (see Chapter 21). Earlier, Russell had taken the lead in pressing for Catholic emancipation, urging his fellow

Whigs to join the short-lived Canning and Goderich governments in exchange for a pledge for early action on this issue. It was at this time that Russell began to take a close interest in Irish affairs, and he became a long-term advocate of measures to appease the grievances of the Catholic majority. Despite his high level of parliamentary activity, Russell continued to be a frequent visitor to the Continent, and maintained his prolific literary output, publishing three major historical works in the decade after 1822 – the two-volume *Memoirs of the Affairs of Europe from the Peace of Utrecht* (1824, 1829), *Establishment of the Turks in Europe* (1828) and *Causes of the French Revolution* (1832). He also spent much time in the company of writers, including the Irish poet Thomas Moore (whose letters he was later to edit in an eight-volume collection), Lord Byron, Sir Walter Scott and Charles Dickens. As his latest biographer comments: 'Far from their equal as an author, Lord John was nevertheless a skillful writer for a full-time politician. He continued to publish a substantial quantity of work throughout his career' (Scherer, p. 36).

If Russell made steady progress, both as a politician and an author, during the 1820s, his private life was a series of embarrassing setbacks. He was painfully shy, and physically unprepossessing, and – despite his advanced views – was vain of his Russell ancestry, and very much aware of his position as the son of a duke. He was, however, a younger son, which did much to diminish both his financial and matrimonial prospects. Moreover, he lacked social graces, and many young women were put off by his over-intellectualized approach. He was to remain unmarried until after his fortieth birthday, which led his friend Lady Holland to lament to her son, Henry Fox, that 'he was making himself almost ridiculous by his frequent proposals' (Scherer, p. 23). The first of these had been back in 1817, when, aged 25, he had proposed to the society beauty Elizabeth Rawdon, only to discover that she had become engaged to his brother William just a few hours before. This was a lucky escape, as William was to find her a most unsatisfactory wife. Lord John was to be turned down by a long list of other aristocratic ladies during the 1820s, and he settled instead for a long-running affair with a married Italian lady, Louise Durazzo, which greatly impressed young Henry Fox, who wrote in his journal: 'I was extremely delighted with the beauty, pretty manners, simplicity and agreeable conversation of Madame Durazzo. Little Johnnie Russell has made an excellent choice. I never saw a woman more calculated to captivate one than she is ... M. Durazzo (her husband) is a little, sulky disagreeable man' (Scherer, pp. 44–5).

Other women known to have attracted Russell during this time, included Henry Fox's sister Mary and Lady Elizabeth Vernon, with whom the entire Russell family was reputed to have been in love at one time or another. In his biography, John Prest suggests that he proposed in 1829 to the 19-year-old Lady Emily (known as 'Minnie') Cowper, but that she turned him down in favour of the Tory peer and factory reformer Lord Ashley, later the Earl of Shaftesbury

(Prest, 1972, p. 71). Scherer disputes this, and suggests that there may have been a confusion with another 'Emily', one of three daughters of Nelson's captain at Trafalgar, Sir Thomas Hardy, two of whom Lord John is known to have wooed unsuccessfully a year or two later.

So Lord John was still a bachelor in 1830, when Earl Grey formed a Whig government, and he began his ministerial career, at the age of 38. He was appointed Paymaster-General of the Forces – to his great disappointment, outside the Cabinet. Yet, because of his long interest in the subject, he was immediately co-opted, to a committee of four, appointed by Grey to prepare a Reform Bill. Russell was to go on to a long and distinguished political career, during which he was twice Prime Minister, but this was undoubtedly his finest hour. He was the dominant member of the committee, providing, according to his own estimate, 90 per cent of the input into the draft Bill, which followed – though on a much more ambitious scale – the principles of the Bill which he had twice unsuccessfully introduced while in opposition. It provided for a wide-ranging cull of 'pocket' and 'rotten' boroughs, without any provision for financial compensation for their 'proprietors', in contrast to the million pounds which the Younger Pitt had proposed in his unsuccessful measure of 1785 – the last serious attempt at Reform. In addition, Russell proposed a modest extension of the franchise, particularly in borough constituencies

The long and complicated story of the eventual passage of the Bill is summarized in Chapter 22, but here we are concerned primarily with Lord John's role, which was second only to that of the Prime Minister's, Earl Grey. It was Russell who set out the full details of the Bill, in a marathon speech on 1 March 1831, which stunned the House by the unexpected ambition of the government's proposals, and made an instant hero of Lord John, in all but the most conservative ranks of the Whig party, as well as among the small group of Radicals in the House. For the remaining 15 months until the Bill's final adoption in June 1832, he was the principal spokesman for the government in all the lengthy debates in the Commons, which dominated the timetable of the House. He effectively became the joint-leader of the House, with Lord Althorp MP, who was a vital ally in piloting the bill through. Within the Cabinet, which he joined in June 1831, he was, together with the Radical, Lord Durham, the strongest advocate for pressing ahead, when fainter hearts were tempted to compromise or abandon the Bill altogether. In the process, he deeply upset the King, William IV, by strongly pressing the demand, which William eventually conceded with great reluctance, to create as many new peers as necessary to overcome the veto of the House of Lords. In the general election which followed the passage of the Bill, in which the Whigs, with their Radical and Irish allies, won an overwhelming majority, Lord John was returned for the new county constituency of South Devon.

In the new Parliament, while retaining his portfolio as Paymaster-General, which was little more than a sinecure, he greatly expanded the range of his interests, in particular taking up the question of Irish grievances, which soon brought him into conflict with his cabinet colleague, Edward Stanley, the Irish Chief Secretary, who was much more interested in introducing coercive measures than in taking constructive steps to remove the causes of discontent. Stanley, a scion of an ancient Whig family, and heir to the Earldom of Derby, was seen as a rising figure in the party, being one of its most effective parliamentary performers, described by Edward Bulwer-Lytton as 'the Rupert of debate'. He was regarded by many as the future party leader, and this may well have sharpened Russell's sense of rivalry, as his own ambitions ran in the same direction. The issue which split them apart was the payment of tithes to the Church of Ireland (the Anglican church), which claimed the allegiance of only 10 per cent of Irishmen, the remainder being either Catholics or Presbyterians, who bitterly resented being forced to pay. Despite Earl Grey's strong discouragement, Russell insisted on backing a proposal to expropriate the 'excess' proceeds of the tithe system for general educational purposes in Ireland, to which Stanley, as a fanatical Anglican, was fundamentally opposed. When a majority of Whigs supported a Bill proposed by Russell, Stanley, together with three other cabinet ministers resigned, and stormed out of the party, joining the Tories several years later. (Whether by design, or otherwise, Lord John had got rid of a dangerous rival, though his Bill was to be defeated in the House of Lords). This episode indirectly led to Grey's resignation, two months later, his place being taken by Lord Melbourne, the Home Secretary.

Melbourne took over the Grey government, with only minimal changes, but the death of Lord Althorp's father, Earl Spencer, four months later, in November 1834, led to his elevation to the House of Lords leaving a vacancy in the leadership of the House of Commons. As related in Chapter 11, Melbourne proposed to William IV that Russell should be appointed to the post. The King, whom Lord John had grievously offended, took this as an opportunity to dismiss the Melbourne government, appointing a Tory administration in its place. The incoming Prime Minister, Sir Robert Peel, sought to win a majority in the subsequent general election, in January 1835, but though he made extensive gains, he fell short of the combined total of seats won by the Whigs, Radicals and Irish Nationalists, and he was forced to resign three months later, when – largely at Lord John's initiative, the three opposition groups came together and inflicted repeated defeats on the government in parliamentary divisions. Lord John had had little difficulty in defending his seat, and during the course of the campaign met the recently widowed Adelaide, Lady Ribblesdale, who was living in Torquay. Aged 27, the mother of four young children, she and Lord John, now aged 42, were immediately attracted to each other, and were married three months later, at St. George's, Hanover Square, in London. Adelaide was generally acclaimed as being 'pretty, charming, amiable' and 'clever' and shared with Russell the attribute of being diminutive. As Lord John's friend, the cleric and wit, Sydney Smith, put it, no doubt with some exaggeration, 'she was about three feet high; his late love Miss Hardy was seven feet'. 'To the surprise of many', his biographer records: 'Russell made an excellent husband and father. He was extremely devoted to his stepchildren, and retained their love and respect throughout their lives' (Scherer, p. 80).

A week into his marriage, Russell (who acquired a new nickname as 'The Widow's Mite') became a minister again, but this time at a much more senior level. Melbourne, who became Prime Minister for the second time, on Peel's resignation after a series of defeats in Commons' votes, appointed him both Home Secretary and Leader of the House, effectively the number two man in the Government. He was generally seen as the only realistic choice within the Whig party, though many – including his father, the Duke of Bedford – doubted whether his health would stand the strain, and regretted the appointment. In the event, he was to lead his party in the Commons for over 20 years, a record only rivalled in the post-Reform Bill period by Clem Attlee, who led the Labour Party from 1935 to 1955. During the six years of Melbourne's second government, from April 1835 to August 1841, Russell was easily the most dynamic minister, and was the moving force behind its relatively few successes. He was constantly prodding the Prime Minister into attempting new reform measures, despite the continual obstruction of the Tory-dominated House of Lords, which threw out a series of Bills passed by the Commons, especially those relating to Ireland, where Russell's repeated attempts to 'appropriate' the surplus yield of tithes for secular purposes were given short shrift. Russell, however, was able to use his executive authority, as Home Secretary, to implement a wide range of measures which did not require legislation. These included the recruitment of Catholics into the police force, the appointment of Catholics to public offices, including the judiciary, and ceasing the practice of using troops to collect the tithe, which effectively meant it was not paid at all in many areas. The result of Russell's efforts was a marked improvement in law and order, and a sharp reduction in the intensity of the agitation to end the Union. Daniel O'Connell (whom Russell had unsuccessfully urged Melbourne to appoint to the Cabinet) warmly approved of his decisions, and his followers gave consistent support to the government in the Commons, where the Whigs were in a minority, and depended on them as well as the Radicals to keep themselves in power.

As Home Secretary, he proved himself a vigorous law reformer, carrying a series of bills drastically reducing the large number of crimes for which the death penalty was imposed. Henceforward, only treason, murder and arson against buildings or ships with persons inside, were subject to capital punishment. He also gave a sharp forward push to the development of state support for education by forcing through an Order in Council providing financial support for teacher training and apprenticeships programmes after he had been forced to abandon a more general education bill due to Anglican hostility.

In November 1838, Russell suffered a grievous blow with the death of his wife, Adelaide, shortly after having given birth to their second daughter, after less than four years of marriage. He was to re-marry, three years later, to Lady Frances Elliot, daughter of the Earl of Minto, and 23 years his junior. Described by the Cambridge historian Jonathan Parry, as 'his protective, unworldly and cloyingly religious second wife' (Parry, p. 155), she was to present him with three sons and a daughter, and helped to bring up his own two children and four step-children. Russell appeared to be happy with her, though her health was bad, and she lacked the self-confidence and skills to act as a political hostess, tending to cut him off from his political associates, which undoubtedly had a deleterious effect on his later career. Already, while leader of the House, he had offended many of his own MPs by his cold and distant attitude towards them. His father, the Duke of Bedford remonstrated with him in a letter, in August 1838: 'You give great offence to your followers...in the H. of Commons by not being *courteous* to them, by treating them superciliously or *de haut en bas*, by not listening with sufficient patience to their solicitations, remonstrances, or whatever it may be' (Prest, 1972, p. 134).

Bulwer Lytton wrote of him, in his political poem, *The New Timon*:

> Like or dislike, he does not care a jot.
> He wants your vote, but your affection not.

Russell's insouciant attitude to his followers was partly due to his personal shyness, but many people detected in him the traditional haughtiness of the Russell family, who, according to a later Duke, the 13th, 'have always thought themselves rather grander than God' (John Robert Russell, 1959, p. 17). In 1839, while retaining the leadership of the Commons, he swapped jobs with the Colonial secretary, Lord Normanby. His main achievement in his new office was to settle the future constitutional arrangements for Canada, following the rebellions of 1837 and the short but stormy governor-generalship of Lord Durham, the irascible Radical peer. Durham's influential Report, following his impetuous resignation, is often credited with paving the way for future Canadian independence, but it was Russell who was the architect of the short-term programme of reforms, which were ably implemented by the new Governor-General Charles Poulett Thomson (later Lord Sydenham). When the Melbourne government finally resigned, following its defeat in the 1841 general election, it was Russell who emerged with the greatest credit from its six-year span of office. He had been responsible for almost all the reforms which it had been able to carry through, despite the unrelenting hostility of a Tory-dominated House of Lords, and – in the Commons – he had successfully kept both the Radicals and the Irish followers of Daniel O'Connell in line, despite their impatience with Melbourne's lack of reforming zeal. Few now doubted that if a new Whig administration were to be formed in the foreseeable future it would be led by Lord John. Any doubt on this point was removed in October 1842, when Melbourne suffered a severe stroke, and it was obvious to everyone (apart from Melbourne himself) that his political career was over.

Now Russell became once again leader of the opposition in the Commons, and given Peel's large majority and his commanding presence in the House of Commons, it looked as though he would have a long wait before returning to office. Then – in 1845 – came the Irish famine, and what appeared to Peel to be the imperative need to repeal the Corn Laws, despite the resistance of the bulk of his own party. In November 1845, without consulting his own followers, Russell launched a stirring appeal for complete free trade in an open letter sent from Edinburgh, where he was on a visit, to his constituents in the City of London, which he had represented since the 1841 election. When Peel, within a few days, failed to persuade his Cabinet to back a Bill repealing the laws, he submitted his resignation to Queen Victoria, who promptly called upon Russell to form a new government (see Chapter 12). Russell, accepted, and then – humiliatingly – was forced a few days later to report that he could not do so. This was because he was unable to impose himself on his potential cabinet colleagues. Several of them, led by Lord Howick, son of the former Prime Minister Earl Grey, refused to serve if Lord Palmerston MP was reappointed as Foreign Secretary, after having effectively pursued his own personal foreign policy throughout the period of the Melbourne government. For his part, Palmerston obstinately refused to accept any other post, and Russell felt – given the minority position of the Whigs and their allies in the Commons – that he would not be able to take office without him.

This episode perhaps foreshadowed that when he subsequently did become Prime Minister he would be weak and ineffective, and incapable of fulfilling his earlier promise. There were a number of reasons for this. One was his inability, as already mentioned, to develop a warm relationship with his followers. Second, his lack of stature, compared to the commanding presence of Peel. When colleagues such as Henry Fox could casually refer to him as 'little Johnnie Russell', it hardly suggests that they saw him as a figure of authority. Third, Russell regarded himself, in a phrase later made famous by Margaret Thatcher, as 'a conviction politician'. Not for him, an earnest search for consensus: when a problem arose he was in the habit of asking his conscience what was right, and reacting precipitately without bothering to consult his followers. All too often, they refused to follow where he led, and he was forced to backtrack.

He did not have to wait that much longer, however, before moving into 10 Downing Street. As recounted in Chapter 24, Peel carried the repeal of the

Corn Laws, with Whig support, but against the votes of the majority of his own party, and he was almost immediately afterwards defeated on a vote on the Irish Coercion Bill. He resigned on 26 June 1846, and Russell took office four days later, leading a minority government, but in the hope that Peel and his followers would support him in crucial parliamentary votes. He had some difficulty in forming his cabinet, but Howick (now the 3rd Earl Grey, on the recent death of his father) withdrew his earlier objection to Palmerston's resumption of the Foreign Office and accepted the post of War and Colonial Secretary. The other leading posts were filled by Sir George Grey as Home Secretary, Sir Charles Wood as Chancellor of the Exchequer and Lord Lansdowne as leader of the Lords. Russell also found room in his Cabinet for his father-in-law, the Earl of Minto, who became Lord Privy Seal. It was noted how beholden Russell felt towards the Grey family, as Sir George was the new Earl Grey's cousin and Sir Charles was his brother-in law. Of this trio, only Sir George really pulled his weight, and Russell embarked on his first premiership at the head of a weak and quarrelsome team. It was almost immediately to be faced with the most painful challenge of any government during the century, when, one year after the failure of the Irish potato crop in 1845:

> there was a second and even more complete failure, and the cereal crops, which had been good in 1845, were poor all over Europe. Peel had got out just in time. In bare outline, a population of ten millions faced the winter, spring, and early summer of 1846–47 with no more than four-fifths of their normal food supply. Within that population, 2m were normally unemployed, and one-third lived off their potato patches at subsistence level. These groups were already enfeebled by the first failure, and had no reserves to face the second successive dearth. The truth will never be known, but in round figures 1m or more people perished in the two years after Lord John took office, and another 1m emigrated between 1847 and 1850. It was 'an evil unknown in the history of modern Europe', or as Lord John said in a famous phrase, it was like a famine of the thirteenth century acting on a population of the nineteenth century. (Prest, 1972, pp. 234–5)

Russell, whose sympathy with the Irish masses was long-standing, was anguished by the human suffering involved, and took what steps he could to ameliorate the situation. These included an easing of the Irish poor law, public works programmes, the provision of soup kitchens, assisted emigration and very limited government purchase of food supplies. His efforts were, however, inhibited by adherence to the prevailing doctrines of *laissez-faire*, obstruction by Treasury officials and by the presence in his Cabinet of major Irish absentee landlords, such as Lord Lansdowne and Lord Palmerston MP, who actively sought to defend their own class interests. Scherer concludes:

There is no reason to lavish praise upon the Russell government for its handling of the Irish famine. The Treasury, which controlled most relief efforts, was doctrinaire, harsh, and parsimonious. Nevertheless, the Whigs did about as well as an average government of the time would have done, limited by the attitudes of its era. (Scherer, p. 175)

In his domestic programme, Russell did rather better, attempting to continue with, and expand, the range of reform measures for which he had been responsible during the Grey and Melbourne governments. He was inhibited by his lack of a parliamentary majority, in either House, but succeeded in passing a very important Public Health Act, repealing the navigation laws, which were a severe inhibition on free trade, introducing further educational reforms, including a long overdue review of Oxford and Cambridge universities, legislating to enable practising Jews to sit in Parliament (though this was blocked by the House of Lords) and granting self-government to the Australian colonies. Russell's firm but sensitive handling of the last great Chartist demonstration in 1848 was credited by some observers with having saved Britain from the wave of revolutions which swept across Europe during that year.

Despite these successes, Russell himself steadily lost support among his fellow Whigs, while being unable to recruit the leading Peelites into his government, though, in 1851, he managed to persuade Peel's second son, Frederick, to accept an under-secretaryship. He upset the more conservative Whigs by his continuing zeal for reform, by his constant efforts to remove disabilities from Dissenters, Catholics and Jews – to the chagrin of many of his fellow Anglicans – and by a number of serious misjudgements. One of these concerned his appointment to the vacant bishopric of Hereford of Dr R.D. Hampden, the Regius Professor of Divinity at Oxford, who was widely accused of heresy. This uniquely succeeded in simultaneously upsetting both the High and Low Church factions. Then, in 1850, he grievously offended his previously loyal Irish supporters (who contributed substantially to his parliamentary strength) by his intemperate reaction to a Papal Bull creating 12 Roman Catholic bishops in Britain, and allocating them territorial titles. Russell roundly condemned this in a widely publicized letter to the Bishop of Durham, and he promptly introduced the Ecclesiastical Titles Act, which made it a criminal offence for Catholic priests to accept geographical titles. For a man who had previously been regarded as a beacon of religious toleration, it was a sad aberration, which later cost him dear.

At about the same time, Lord John, who in 1838 had won himself the nickname 'Finality Jack' for declaring that the 1832 Reform Act had settled the suffrage question for all time, became convinced that it was now essential for an extension of the franchise to take in a much larger proportion of working class voters. Yet he had great difficulty in persuading his cabinet and MPs to act.

Lord John's final misfortune was to fall out seriously with his Foreign Secretary, Lord Palmerston MP. The fault was almost entirely Palmerston's, but it was Russell who was ultimately to be more damaged by their quarrel. Palmerston had grown used to running the Foreign Office, with virtually no control by the Prime Minister, in his earlier stint under Lord Melbourne, and he continued to do so under Russell. An imperious character, he treated foreign governments, and even monarchs, with little concern for diplomatic niceties, which Russell deprecated but which caused consternation to Queen Victoria and Prince Albert. Russell attempted to shuffle him out of the Foreign Office, by offering to go up to the Lords himself and making Palmerston leader of the Commons. This he flatly refused to discuss – his public and parliamentary reputation having been greatly boosted by the Don Pacifico affair (see Chapter 16) – but he reluctantly acquiesced in the Queen's demand that he should in future submit all proposed actions and dispatches for her approval before implementing them. Then, in December 1851, he went too far, by publicly endorsing Louis-Napoleon's *coup d'etat*, over-throwing the Second French republic, after the government had agreed to take a neutral stance. Russell's patience finally snapped, and he peremptorily dismissed Palmerston, who got his 'tit-for-tat' two months later, in February 1852, when he moved a hostile amendment to the government's Militia Bill, securing its defeat in a parliamentary vote, which led to its immediate resignation. The Queen called on the Tory leader, Lord Stanley (who had recently succeeded his father as the 14th Earl of Derby), to form a new government.

Russell went into opposition, confident that he would soon be back, correctly surmizing that Derby's government would not last long. Derby secured a dissolution, and the ensuing general election brought substantial Tory gains and Peelite losses, but still left him short of a majority. After less than 10 months in office, he was forced to resign, and, in December 1852, his government was replaced by a coalition of Whigs and Peelites. Russell had assumed that, as the Whigs greatly outnumbered the Peelites, he would be Prime Minister, but he had become so unpopular in his own party (and especially among his former Irish supporters) that they were unwilling to push his claim. The Queen's first choice was Lord Lansdowne, the Whig leader in the Lords, but he declined, and the choice then fell on the Earl of Aberdeen, a former Foreign Secretary, who had led the Peelites since Peel's death in 1850.

Russell was now 60 years old, and his health being poor, he might have been well advised to retire from politics altogether or at least go to the Lords as an elder statesman. He chose, however, to battle on for another 14 years, during which he was to serve twice as Foreign Secretary and for a second period as Prime Minister, but his achievements were slight, and – if anything – subtracted from, rather than added to, his reputation. Russell's ambivalent attitude towards the Aberdeen government did nothing to further his own influence or popularity.

Deeply resentful at being supplanted by someone he clearly regarded, with justification, as his inferior, he failed to develop a considered view on whether he really wanted to serve in the government, or if so, in what post. In the end, he accepted the Foreign secretaryship, only to renounce it after two months in favour of leading the Commons, without a department of his own. The government lasted for just over two years, and proved deeply frustrating for Lord John. He was, nominally, the number two man, but his influence was largely disregarded, and his continued efforts to persuade his colleagues to agree to the introduction of a new Reform Bill came to nothing, as they appealed neither to the more conservative Whigs nor to most of the Peelites.

Aberdeen's government was dominated by the Crimean War (see Chapters 27 and 28). It was an unwanted and unnecessary conflict, largely caused by the failure of Aberdeen and Palmerston (now Home Secretary, but retaining his proprietorial interest in foreign policy) to agree on the so-called Eastern Question. The crisis was provoked by Russian demands on Turkey to oversee the Holy Places in Palestine, and, more generally, to be accepted as the guarantor of the rights of Christians throughout the Ottoman Empire. Tsar Nicholas I ordered his troops to occupy the two Romanian principalities of Moldavia and Wallachia, in October 1853, and refused to withdraw them unless the Turkish sultan accepted his claims. Aberdeen favoured appeasing Russia and pressurizing the Turks to give way, while Palmerston argued for a robust support of Turkey, threatening war on Russia if it did not withdraw from the two principalities, which were under Turkish suzerainty. Either policy, if consistently followed, might have brought peace, but Britain wavered between the two, and eventually, in March 1854, the Turks declared war on Russia, and Britain and France followed suit. Russell, who tended to support Palmerston, found that his views were virtually ignored. Aberdeen's shortcomings as a war leader were soon apparent, and in January 1855, Russell resigned, rather than defending his conduct of the war in a parliamentary debate. This precipitated Aberdeen's own resignation, and he was succeeded as head of the coalition by the more warlike Palmerston.

Russell did not initially rejoin the government, but was sent by Palmerston to a conference in Austria, whose purpose was to seek a compromise peace with Russia, in view of the bloody stalemate which had developed before Sebastopol, or – alternatively – to induce Austria to enter the war on the allied side. Russell showed great patience as a negotiator, despite the apparent intransigence of the Russian delegate, Prince Alexander Menshikov, and considered that a reasonable settlement was possible, but neither the French, who still hoped for a military victory, nor Palmerston, now in hock to the fervour worked up by a jingoistic press, was prepared to accept the terms available. Nor were the Austrians prepared to join in the war, so the conference ended in failure. Russell, who had accepted the post of Colonial Secretary, returned to London, but did not stay long in office, resigning in July 1855, after he had been widely attacked for his alleged willingness to accept a humiliating settlement at Vienna. Palmerston's government managed very well without his services, and won a greatly increased majority in the 1857 general election, benefitting from Palmerston's war leadership and the eventual capture of Sebastopol, which brought the Crimean War to a victorious conclusion. Yet the government was dominated by the most conservative elements of the Whig and Peelite parties, and Russell gradually reclaimed his popularity with their younger and more progressive supporters by his continued advocacy of reform. Meanwhile, parliamentary support for Palmerston began to crumble, following the Indian mutiny and the Orsini plot, planned in London, to assassinate Napoleon III (see Chapter 28). Palmerston responded by introducing the Conspiracy to Murder Bill, to mollify French anger, but this was defeated in the Commons, on 18 February 1858, and the government resigned, leaving the way open for the Earl of Derby to form a Conservative administration for the second time. In opposition, the Whigs, Peelites and Radicals, together with their Irish supporters, finally agreed to amalgamate, forming the Liberal Party, at a meeting, in June 1859, attended by 274 MPs.

Russell was the main architect of the new alignment, and would probably have been its first choice for Prime Minister, if a vote had been taken. Yet when the Derby government, having done badly in the 1859 general election, resigned shortly afterwards, Queen Victoria sent for Lord Granville, the Liberal leader in the Lords, and when he failed to form a government, sighed that she would have to choose between the 'two terrible old men'. Inevitably, she picked Palmerston, as Russell's views were much too radical for her liking. Russell and Palmerston were now thoroughly reconciled to each other, and Russell demanded and received the Foreign secretaryship. Thus began a partnership of more than six years, during which their relations remained remarkably good. Russell accepted an earldom in 1861, and Palmerston, now well into his seventies, unexpectedly left him a remarkably free hand, intervening only on major issues, and, even then, often deferring to his colleague's views. Four issues dominated – Mexico, the US Civil War, Italian unity and Denmark (the Schleswig-Holstein question). These are discussed in some detail in Chapter 28, but here it may be noted that the first three were handled relatively well, producing outcomes which were generally acceptable from a British point of view, but the fourth resulted in public humiliation (partly because of unwanted interference by Queen Victoria).

In July 1865, Palmerston, almost 82 years old, again led the Liberals to a general election triumph, but he did not live to face the new House of Commons, dying the following October, after having caught a chill while out driving. Victoria had no real choice, but to ask the 73-year-old Russell to take over the leadership of the government, which he did with great enthusiasm, feeling that the time had at last arrived to complete his mission of again reforming the British electoral system. He made very few ministerial changes, confirming the former Peelite, William Gladstone, as Chancellor of the Exchequer, and appointing him also as leader of the Commons and effective deputy premier. Lord Clarendon, who had been Foreign Secretary in 1853–8, now replaced him in that post. Russell lost little time in introducing his Reform Bill, which provided for a substantial widening of the franchise, though falling well short of manhood suffrage. It was vigorously attacked by the Tory opposition, supported by many right-wing Liberals (dubbed the 'Cave of Adullum' by the arch-reformer John Bright), and to Russell's great chagrin was defeated by 11 votes in a crucial division during the Committee Stage. The government resigned, in June 1866, after 240 days in office, and Lord Derby became Prime Minister for the third time. Despite this defeat, Russell was the moral victor, as the new momentum he had created for Reform proved unstoppable. A year later, the 1867 Reform Bill, designed by Disraeli 'to steal the Whigs' clothes while they were bathing', and going substantially further than Russell's own measure, was passed. It gave the vote to all heads of households in borough constituencies (see Chapter 29).

Russell lived another 12 years, declining office in Gladstone's first government formed in 1868, but continuing to be active in the House of Lords almost until his death, aged nearly 86, on 28 May 1878. Undoubtedly the smallest of the nineteenth-century Prime Ministers, 'Little Johnnie Russell' made a bigger impact than most. Almost single-handedly, he enlarged the objectives of the Whig Party from a narrow desire to curb the prerogatives of the monarch and to protect ancient liberties, into a much wider social concern, and a mission to subject not only Parliament but all elements of public life to critical scrutiny and reform. 'Above all', in the words of one of his biographers, 'he was absolutely without fear of change (only of no change)' (Prest, 2004). Despite not commanding a parliamentary majority, and much obstruction from the House of Lords, the legislative record of his first government, in 1846–52, surpassed that of any other administration between Gray's government of 1830–34 and Gladstone's of 1868–74, though he could undoubtedly have done more had it not been for the conservatism of many of his own supporters. His legacy was a Liberal Party which, under the leadership of Gladstone, and later of Campbell-Bannerman, Asquith and the younger Lloyd George, was prepared to lead the nation in new and more radical directions. Another gift he left to posterity was his grandson, Bertrand Russell, whose restless mind reflected that of his distinguished ancestor.

Works consulted

J.B. Conacher, 1968, *The Aberdeen Coalition 1852–1855*, Cambridge, Cambridge University Press.
Lucille Iremonger, 1970, *The Fiery Chariot*, London, Secker & Warburg.

Jonathan Parry, 1993, *The Rise and Fall of Liberal Government in Victorian Britain*, New Haven, Yale University Press.

Jonathan Parry, 1998, 'Lord John Russell, First Earl Russell', in Robert Eccleshall and Graham Walker (eds.), *Biographical Dictionary of British Prime Ministers*, London, Routledge.

John Prest, 1972, *Lord John Russell*, London, Macmillan.

John Prest, 2004, Article in *Oxford Dictionary of National Biography*.

John Robert Russell, 1959, *A Silver Plated Spoon*, London, Sphere Books.

Paul Scherer, 1999, *Lord John Russell*, Selinsgrove, Susquehanna University Press.

26
Edward Stanley, 14th Earl of Derby – 'The Brilliant Chief, Irregularly Great'

Lord Derby was the first person ever to become Prime Minister three times, but he failed to live up to his early promise, and his posthumous reputation is shadowy, being almost entirely eclipsed by those of his principal opponents and by his leading follower, and successor, Benjamin Disraeli. Born Edward George Geoffrey Smith Stanley, on 29 March 1799, he was the scion of an ancient Whig family, whose title dated back to 1485. His father, the 13th Earl, was mostly known for the impressive zoological collection which he built up at the family seat of Knowsley Hall, in Lancashire. He had married his cousin, Charlotte Hornby, a clergyman's daughter. Edward was their first child, and they went on to have two other sons and four daughters.

The young Edward was little influenced by his father, who sat for many years as an inactive and ineffective Whig MP, but from his mother he inherited a strong devotion to the Church of England. The dominant figure in his early life was his grandfather, the 12th Earl, an ardent Whig and a close friend and admirer of Charles James Fox. A widower, he married a second time to a young actress, Elizabeth Farren, and their children were of a similar age to Edward. Indeed, one of Edward's contemporaries at Eton was his uncle, James Stanley, who was a year younger than himself, and who was to die at the age of 17. Edward was to be noted at Eton as 'clever' and 'scholarly' and 'full of self-assurance'. From Eton, he went on to Christ Church, Oxford, where he distinguished himself for his classical scholarship, winning the Chancellor's prize for Latin verse. He disgraced himself one night by leading a drunken group of undergraduates, who pulled down from a plinth in the college's Great Quadrangle a figure of Mercury, erected in 1695, but he was generally seen as a figure of great promise, though wilful and resentful of personal criticism. According to one biographer, his 'precocity was so rare among members of his class that Stanley was sometimes mentioned as the only 'brilliant eldest son produced by the British peerage for a hundred years' (Jones, 1956, p. 6). His family was immensely wealthy, being major territorial magnates in Lancashire, and owning estates in several other English counties, as well as in Limerick, Ireland.

Leading Whigs came to see him as a potential 'great catch' for their party, and his grandfather was induced to buy a 'pocket borough' for him, at the age of 23. The sitting MP for Stockbridge, duly made way for him, and he was returned unopposed in a by-election in July 1822. He waited nearly two years before making his maiden speech, on the unpromising subject of the Manchester Gas Light Bill, but – despite feeling an acute sense of failure when he sat down – was astonished to find that his speech was widely hailed as an oratorical triumph. Three months later, he decided to take a prolonged leave of his parliamentary duties, sailing for New York for a nine-month tour of the US and Canada, and shortly after his return, in May 1826, got married, at the age of 26, to Emma Bootle-Wilbraham, the 20-year-old daughter of a Tory MP, who later became the first Lord Skelmersdale. Little is known about their courtship, but it was apparently a successful marriage, which produced two sons (one of whom, later the 15th Earl of Derby, was himself to serve as both Colonial and Foreign Secretary) and a daughter. Emma acted from time to time as Stanley's secretary, and became an active political hostess.

It was not long before Stanley came to be seen as the finest speaker in the House of Commons, with no rival after the death of Canning in 1827. A political opponent, Lord Campbell, wrote of him that: 'Stanley is a host in himself. He has a marvellous acuteness of intellect and consummate power in debate. There is no subject which he cannot master thoroughly and lucidly explain. His voice and manner are so good that no one can hear him without listening to him' (Jones, p. 51).

Campbell's verdict was typical of many of his contemporaries, including Daniel Webster, reputedly the greatest of American orators, who heard him speak in the Commons in 1839, and declared it to be the best speech he had ever heard. He was not, however, without his critics. Many MPs regarded him as a most appalling snob, who treated his non-aristocratic colleagues with un-disguised disdain, while others – noting his independent views – came to doubt the orthodoxy of his Whiggism. Stanley was one of the first Whigs to rally to the support of George Canning, when many leading Tories refused to join his government in April 1827. Canning appealed to the Whigs to fill the vacant places, and – despite the discouragement of the Whig leader, Earl Grey – several took up the offer, including Stanley, who became a junior Lord of the Treasury, and went on to serve as under-secretary for the Colonies in Goderich's equally short-lived government of 1827–8. When Earl Grey formed his Whig government, in 1830, Stanley, now aged 31, obtained the important post of Chief Secretary for Ireland, initially outside the Cabinet.

Stanley then suffered the first setback in his promising political career. In order to be confirmed in his new post, he had to resign his seat at Preston, to which he had transferred at the 1826 general election, and fight a by-election. He was disconcerted to be challenged by Henry 'Orator' Hunt, the radical campaigner who had been the speaker at the 'Peterloo massacre' meeting, in 1819, and Hunt succeeded in winning the seat, by 3,392 votes to 3,370. There followed a desperate search to find Stanley another seat, and the new King, William IV, came to his rescue by offering the pocket borough of Windsor, which he personally controlled. He was returned unopposed nine weeks later, after the sitting MP was bought off by being appointed Commander of the Forces in Ireland. Stanley embarked on his new duties with enthusiasm, but before he could give Ireland his undivided attention, he was much in demand as a parliamentary speaker during the long series of debates on the Reform Bill. Grey and most of his senior ministers were in the Lords, and Lord John Russell, who was in charge of the Bill in the Commons, badly needed debating support in the Lower House. Stanley was hardly a born reformer, and he was reported to have roared with laughter when he first heard the details of the Bill, which went so much further than he or most of his colleagues had expected. But he buckled down, and in a series of brilliant speeches swept the floor with his Tory opponents.

His record as Irish Secretary was a mixed one. He promoted a number of reforms, notably the Irish Education Act of 1832, which provided for secular schools open to children from all religious denominations. Yet he was determined to give over-riding priority to the restoration of law and order, and the protection of private property, and introduced a number of coercive measures, which upset several of his cabinet colleagues, who thought it more expedient to concentrate instead on removing Irish grievances. He also made a bitter enemy of Daniel O'Connell, dubbed 'the Liberator' for his successful leadership of the campaign for Catholic Emancipation, who was now himself ensconced in the House of Commons, and became his most intransigent critic. Stanley joined the Cabinet in June 1831, and was a close ally of Grey in opposing his more radical colleagues, but during his entire time in Ireland was at loggerheads with the Lord Lieutenant, the Marquess of Anglesey, who, as Lord Uxbridge, had been Wellington's second-in-command at Waterloo, where he had lost a leg in the battle. Anglesey was a pronounced liberal, and his relations with Stanley became so bad that, in 1833, Grey decided to shift both of them out of their jobs. Stanley was promoted to Secretary for War and the Colonies, and Anglesey was replaced by Marquess Wellesley, elder brother of the Duke of Wellington.

The outstanding event during the 14 months that Stanley spent in his new post was the abolition of slavery in the British Empire, a logical sequel to the legislation carried, in 1806, by the predominantly Whig government of Lord Grenville, which brought an end to the slave trade. Stanley was responsible for the Bill, which provided for compensation of some £20 million for the slave-owners, and laid down a fixed seven-year apprenticeship for adult slaves before they would be finally freed. The Bill was opposed by the West Indian 'planters', whose influence in the House of Commons, where they had controlled many 'pocket boroughs' was greatly diminished by the Reform Act, and by Radical MPs who objected to the scale of the compensation and the compulsory apprenticeships, but Stanley's action was generally applauded, and his reputation soared. Many years later, Disraeli was to recall an intriguing conversation he had had at this time with Lord Melbourne, then Home Secretary, from whom he had sought advice about promoting his own nascent political career. He brashly mentioned his ambition to become Prime Minister, and Melbourne replied: 'No chance of that in our time. It is all arranged and settled...Nobody can compete with Stanley...you must put all these foolish notions out of your head; they won't do at all. Stanley will be the next Prime Minister, you will see' (Cromwell, 1998, p. 163).

Melbourne was wrong: it was he, himself, who unexpectedly succeeded Grey as Prime Minister, in 1834, but it might well have been Stanley (then 35) if he had not disagreed with his colleagues over Ireland, and resigned from the government a few weeks earlier. All would have been well, if Stanley had not continued to take a close interest in Irish affairs after taking up his new post. However, he put himself at the head of the opposition to the move by Lord John Russell to expropriate, for secular purposes, the excess yield of the tithes paid to the Anglican church in Ireland (see Chapter 25). For Stanley this was an intolerable attack on the perquisites of the Church, and, in June 1834, when Russell obtained cabinet approval to introduce a bill, he abruptly resigned from the government, saying 'Johnnie has upset the coach' He took with him, the Earl of Ripon (Lord Privy Seal, and a former Prime Minister, as Lord Goderich), Sir James Graham (First Lord of the Admiralty) and the Duke of Richmond (Paymaster-General). Their departure destabilized the Grey government, and while not the proximate reason for the Prime Minister's own resignation a month later, was undoubtedly a contributory factor.

Stanley still considered himself a Whig, but on policy issues felt far closer to Sir Robert Peel, who was about to relaunch the Tories as the Conservative Party. When Peel formed his first government, in December 1834, he was anxious to include both Stanley and Graham, but they were not yet willing to break their ties with the Whigs, and declined to serve. In the general election which followed, in January 1835, the Stanleyites put up a significant number of candidates, hoping to win the balance of power between Whigs and Tories and form the basis of a new centre party. The results were a great disappointment to them, only about half a dozen of Stanley's supporters were elected, and the Whigs were returned by a substantial majority, though smaller than in 1832. Peel's government resigned shortly afterwards, and Melbourne, who had been arbitrarily dismissed by William IV (see Chapter 23), triumphantly returned to power.

It was at this time that Stanley first became afflicted with gout, a disease which seemed to be hereditary in the Derby family, and which periodically incapacitated him throughout the remainder of his life. His biographer comments that 'with the onset of this illness, Stanley became increasingly cautious in political affairs, and the impetuousness of his youth rapidly became a fading memory' (Jones, p. 71). Stanley's little group, contemptuously referred to by O'Connell as 'the Derby Dilly, carrying six inside',* tried for some time to maintain an independent existence, but in 1838 both Stanley and Graham formally joined the Conservative Party, and Stanley became one of Peel's leading associates. When Peel formed his second government, following the Conservative victory in the 1841 election, both took senior posts, Graham as Home Secretary, and Stanley as Secretary for War and the Colonies and effectively the number two minister in the Commons. The Earl of Ripon also joined the government, as President of the Board of Trade, with the young William Gladstone as his deputy, and, two years later, successor. Scowling on the government backbenches was Disraeli, bitterly disappointed to have been left out of the government, despite the passionate plea he had made to Peel to be included (see Chapters 24 and 29).

Peel regarded Stanley as his most able colleague, but they never became personally close, perhaps because Peel, acutely sensitive about his relatively humble origins, sensed the scarcely concealed superiority which the proudly aristocratic Stanley felt towards him. As War and Colonial Secretary, Stanley had to confront a wide range of issues. These included winding up the first 'Opium War' with China, which led to the annexation of Hong Kong, about which he was personally unenthusiastic; the negotiation, in conjunction with the Foreign Secretary, Lord Aberdeen, of the Webster-Ashburton treaty with the United States; demarcating the boundary between Canada and the state of Maine, the passage of the Canadian Corn Bill; allowing preferential imports from Canada; the annexation of Natal and Sind, and troubles arising from the recent establishment of the colony of New Zealand, for which the governor was largely to blame but for which Stanley was much criticized. In November 1844, he accepted a peerage, becoming Lord Stanley of Bickerstaffe. This was at his own request, following a renewed attack of gout, and he thought he would have a more relaxing time in the Upper House. It was also the case that the Duke of Wellington, the Tory leader in the Lords, was badly in need of additional debating power on the government side. Peel, who may always have felt a trifle uneasy about sitting side by side with him in the Commons, was probably somewhat relieved, but it is highly doubtful if the change was in Stanley's own long-term interest, even though he was bound to end up in the Lords on the death of his father. This did not, however, occur until seven years later.

---

*The reference was to a poem by Canning describing the Derby Dilly (or diligence carriage) making its way through the Derbyshire hills.

Within a year of joining the Lords, Stanley was faced with the most difficult choice of his entire career, when Peel, faced by the Irish famine, determined to repeal the Corn Laws to permit the importation of cheap foreign grain (see Chapter 24). Stanley was not oblivious of the need to assist the Irish, but was adamantly opposed to Peel's decision. He regarded the landed interest as the bedrock of British society and was not prepared to put its prosperity at risk by allowing it to be undercut by foreign suppliers, which he felt would have a devastating effect on the English countryside. He also felt that Peel and his government had been elected on a Protectionist mandate and that it would be a betrayal of their own supporters for them to act in this way. If the Corn Laws were to be repealed, Stanley thought, it would be far better to make way for a Whig government to do the dirty deed. 'We can't', he said, 'do this as gentlemen' (Jones, p. 114). He therefore insisted on resigning, even though the rest of the Cabinet, including even the Duke of Buccleuch, who led the Scottish landed interest, agreed to support Peel, although most of them had initially been opposed to him.

Peel felt he could not continue in the face of Stanley's resignation, and the opposition of the majority of Tory MPs, and submitted the government's resignation to the Queen. He considered recommending her to send for Stanley to try to form a protectionist government, but thought that he would be unable to succeed, and that public opinion would not tolerate an aristocratic government deliberating forcing up food prices. So he suggested that Lord John Russell, the opposition leader, should be appointed instead, and promised his full support in carrying the repeal. When Russell failed to form a government, he unhesitatingly accepted to carry on, determined to push the measure through in the teeth of his own party's resistance. Stanley was saddened that Sir James Graham, formally his own closest supporter, was foursquare behind Peel, and equally committed to repeal. When Graham came to see him to try to talk him round, he was cut to the quick by a remark of Graham's which he took to imply that he was opposing Peel in the hope of replacing him as Premier. This may sub-consciously have been true, and certainly accorded with the wishes of his wife Emma, but Stanley was never prepared to admit it, and his friendship with Graham abruptly ceased.

So far from aspiring to the premiership, Stanley gave some indication at that time that he was thinking of giving up politics altogether. Writing to his former cabinet colleague, Lord Ellenborough, at Christmas 1845, he said: 'Though it is difficult to foresee the future, my own opinion is that my official life is over, and I am well content that it should be so. The political current seems steadily setting in a direction which leaves me high and dry on the beach' (Stewart, 1971, p. 55).

Had he still been in the Commons, Stanley would have faced irresistible pressure to put himself at the head of the protectionist forces, and his biographer

Wilbur Devereux Jones speculated that his great debating power might have been sufficient to ensure the defeat of the Repeal Bill. As it was, he found himself 'in the wrong house of Parliament' (Jones, p. 107), and the leadership of the protectionists fell into the unskilled hands of Lord George Bentinck, with Disraeli as his main lieutenant (see Chapter 24). They secured the backing of two-thirds of the Tory MPs, but with Whig support the Bill was carried through. After much hesitation, Stanley agreed to oppose it in the Lords, and made a fine speech in the second reading debate which won the support of a majority of the peers in the Chamber. But the Duke of Wellington, who decided to back Peel despite his own opposition to repeal, had succeeded in collecting enough proxy votes to carry the day. The Bill was finally passed on 25 June 1846. Four days later Peel resigned, his government having been defeated in the Commons on the Irish Coercion Bill, when many of the protectionists voted with the Whigs, leading to the formation of a new Whig government under Lord John Russell.

Stanley was chosen as leader of the Conservative peers, and later succeeded Bentinck as the overall leader, and his main concern now became to prevent the split in the party from becoming permanent. He took a moderate stance in the 1847 general election, and afterwards declared that the electorate had clearly given a mandate for free trade, as a majority had voted either for the Whigs or the Peelites. He therefore saw the question as settled, at least for the time being, and saw no reason why the Conservative Party should not now be reunited. He was disconcerted by the continuing hostility of Peel's main supporters, who included nearly all the most able figures of the party. When he himself had left the Whigs, he had continued to have good personal relations with his former colleagues, notably Lord John Russell, and throughout his life maintained that political differences should not be allowed to take precedence over friendly intercourse (at least between social equals!). He was amazed at the depth of hostility which arose between former party allies. Disraeli narrowly avoided fighting a duel with Peel's brother Jonathan, while Peel himself was only restrained from challenging Bentinck, when Lord Lincoln threatened to call in the police. Lincoln himself, a leading Peelite, became totally estranged from his father, the 4th Duke of Newcastle, because of their opposing views over protectionism, and they were only reconciled on the Duke's deathbed in 1851.

Bentinck resigned the Tory leadership in December 1847, dying the following year at the early age of 46, and Stanley exerted himself to prevent the election of Disraeli as the new Tory leader in the Commons. He wanted to ensure that he would be fully consulted on tactics in the Commons, and he disapproved of Disraeli on social grounds, regarding him as an opportunistic *parvenu*. He also feared that Disraeli's leadership would forestall any possibility of reunion with the Peelites, who had been appalled by the vehemence of his attacks on Peel. He therefore agreed with Bentinck that the new leader should be the

Marquess of Granby MP, an unexceptionable Tory aristocrat, and he was duly elected by the protectionist MPs. But Granby was lacking in self-confidence, and refused to serve, which meant that for the whole of the 1848–9 session, the party was leaderless in the Commons. Despite the fact that Disraeli was, by a wide margin, the most able of the MPs (and, by an even wider margin, the most ambitious!), Stanley continued to look elsewhere, and proposed John Herries, a veteran ex-civil servant, who had briefly served in Peel's 1834–5 government. Yet Herries, too, was diffident about assuming the leadership, and Stanley eventually acquiesced in an agreement that the party should be led in the Commons by a triumvirate of Granby, Herries and Disraeli. The latter, however, comported himself as if he were the sole leader, and the other two quietly effaced themselves, but it was only late in 1851 that Stanley was prepared to accept him as leader, and another two years before he brought himself to invite him to a house party at Knowsley Hall, where other leading protectionists had been regular visitors over a long period. Despite this unpromising beginning, Stanley and Disraeli were to work together, as respective party leaders in the two Houses, with surprising harmony for the best part of two decades.

Stanley insisted that the Protectionist party should resume the name Conservative Party against the wishes of most of his leading colleagues, who preferred to be known as Tories. Because of his high social standing, and his unmatched oratorical abilities, his own leadership was unchallengeable in a party largely made up of country squires, but he was to be constantly criticized for his apparent lack of commitment and the self-described tactic of 'masterly inactivity' with which he opposed a series of Whig or coalition governments, preferring to wait for them to make mistakes. He absented himself for long periods to Knowsley Hall, where he was a fanatical hunter and shooter, but his main interest was in horseracing, and he was a familiar figure at racetracks throughout the country. He regularly left the impression that he would rather win the Derby (a race named after his own family) than be Prime Minister. He never did, but it was a great day in his life when, in 1848, he became Steward of the Jockey Club. Some years later, a Tory backbencher, Lord Henry Lennox, was to write to Disraeli complaining that 'as a leader of a party, [Stanley] is more hopeless than ever!! Devoted to whist, billiards, racing, betting, & making a fool of himself with [the Ladies] ...' (Blake, 1966, p. 369). Some of his many interests were more intellectual: he was to publish a translation of *The Iliad*, which was widely admired in its day. The writer and Tory MP, and much later minister in Derby's third government, Sir Edward Bulwer-Lytton, summed up both his virtues and shortcomings in his political poem *The New Timon*:

> The brilliant chief, irregularly great,
> Frank, haughty, rash, the Rupert of Debate.

He was drawing on a parliamentary speech of Disraeli's, in 1844, when, referring to Stanley, he had said: 'The noble lord in this case, as in so many others, is the Prince Rupert of parliamentary discussion; his charge is resistless; but when he returns from pursuit he always finds his camp in the possession of the enemy' (Hansard, 24 April 1844).

The first occasion on which Stanley seriously disappointed his followers was in February 1851, when Russell's government resigned, after being defeated in a parliamentary vote on electoral reform. Painfully aware of the lack of potential ministerial talent among the Tories, Stanley made strenuous attempts to recruit leading Peelites to his team, and even put out feelers to Palmerston, whom he correctly identified as the most conservative of the Whigs. He had particular hopes of attracting Lord Aberdeen, who was personally very friendly to him and who he hoped to make Foreign Secretary, and Gladstone, to whom he offered the choice of any other post in the government. Both, however, declined, as did all their colleagues, partly because of the continuing Tory commitment to reimpose tariff duties on corn, even though these would be at a moderate level. It was still open to Stanley to form a minority government, but after reviewing the talent available to him, and particularly when Herries proved reluctant to take the Chancellorship of the Exchequer, he threw in his hand, and the Queen invited Russell to resume power.

Four months later, Stanley's father died, aged 76, and on 30 June 1851, he became the 14th Earl of Derby. He was now 52, and within eight months he unexpectedly became Prime Minister for the first time. The opportunity arose, as described in Chapter 25, because of Lord Palmerston's action in turning out Russell's government, following his own dismissal as Foreign Secretary. This time Derby realized that he must take office, even without Peelite support, but he had high hopes of recruiting Palmerston to his colours, though negotiations with him proved abortive. As for the Peelites, of whom Gladstone seemed the most likely to join up, there were two insuperable objections. One was the lingering Tory commitment to protectionism, which Disraeli was quite ready to abandon, but which Derby could not bring himself to do, at least until he had fought another election on the issue. The other Peelite objection was to Disraeli's leadership of the Commons, but Derby, having reluctantly accepted him in that role a year earlier, was not prepared to let him go at the first sign of trouble. So he had to make do with the meagre talent available to him in his own party. Disraeli became Chancellor of the Exchequer and leader of the Commons, and the second Earl of Malmesbury, his favourite shooting companion at Knowsley, Foreign Secretary, but most of his other appointees were virtually unknown. Indeed, the government became known as the Who? Who? Government, after the hard-of-hearing Duke of Wellington had repeatedly queried the unfamiliar names when a list of the cabinet members was read out to him. Derby had to put up with a great deal of ridicule about some of his more obscure choices. Lady Clanricarde, the wife of a rather raffish Whig peer, asked him at a dinner party: 'Are you sure, Lord Derby, that Sir John Pakington [the new Colonial Secretary] is a *real* man?', and was disconcerted when he coolly replied 'Well, I think so – he has been married three times.'

So Derby became Prime Minister on 23 February 1852. It was a minority government, but Derby was reasonably confident that – given the serious dissensions within the ranks of the opposition – it would not be turned out in a hurry. His objective was to govern calmly in a non-controversial manner, in the hope of building up confidence with the electorate and winning a majority at the subsequent general election, to which he was committed during the summer of 1852. The election was duly held in July, and the Conservatives made numerous gains, largely at the expense of the Peelites but remained in a minority. In a memorandum to Prince Albert, Derby analysed the membership of the new House of Commons, as follows: '286 Conservatives, 150 Radicals, 120 Whigs, 50 in the Irish Brigade, and 30 Peelites'. A major effort was now mounted to recruit the Peelites, with particular attention being paid to Lord Aberdeen and William Gladstone, who had pursued a policy of benevolent neutrality towards the government prior to the election. Derby now made the grand gesture of renouncing protectionism. Speaking in the House of Lords, in November 1852,

> Derby admitted that a very large majority of the British people, including many from agricultural districts, no longer sought a reimposition of the Corn Laws, and that he himself saw there might be advantages to the nation as a whole in retaining Free Trade. Derby added: 'on the part, then, of myself and my colleagues, I bow to the decision of the country'. (Jones, p. 173)

Derby's concession came too late. The Peelites were no longer interested in reuniting the Conservative Party. They had received a better offer from the Whigs – of a coalition government – in which they would secure the Prime Ministership and almost half the cabinet seats. This, to the chagrin of the former Whig Prime Minister, Lord John Russell, who found himself forced to play second fiddle to Lord Aberdeen. The government was duly defeated on a vote on Disraeli's budget, and resigned on 17 December 1852, after a mere 292 days in office.

Derby was replaced as Prime Minister by the Peelite leader, Lord Aberdeen, but might well have had a second innings two years later, when Aberdeen resigned after losing what amounted to a confidence vote on his conduct of the Crimean War. There were widely seen as three possible candidates for the succession – Derby, Russell and Palmerston. It was, perhaps, Derby's misfortune that the Queen sent for him first. Ignoring the earnest plea of his colleague, Lord Ellenborough ('Don't leave the room without kissing hands'), Derby temporized, and said that because of the strong public support for Palmerston it would be necessary to include him in the government. He declined to accept office until he had discussed the situation with Palmerston and the leading Peelites, but finding them unco-operative returned the next day to tell the Queen that he could not proceed. The probability is that Derby was confident that neither Russell nor Palmerston would be able to form a government, and that the Queen would then turn to him again, as a last resort. Victoria then summoned Russell, who – as predicted – failed to assemble enough support, but, against all expectations, the much older and frailer Palmerston succeeded in reconstructing the previous coalition, minus Aberdeen and the 5th Duke of Newcastle (formerly Lord Lincoln), who had been War Secretary. To the ill-disguised fury of Disraeli, the Conservatives were condemned to continue in opposition, with no likely early prospect of a return to power.

Over the next three years, Derby, isolated in the House of Lords from the main forum of political combat, grew more and more conservative in his outlook. He fiercely opposed any whisper of parliamentary reform, concentrating his energies on ecclesiastical affairs and the protection of the rights of hereditary peers, and strongly discouraging efforts by Disraeli (aided and abetted by Derby's much more liberal eldest son, Edward) to find common cause with the Radicals in harassing the government. Derby still considered the Peelites as the only acceptable source of additional support. He again began to woo Gladstone (who had resigned from the Palmerston government in March 1855), but nothing came of it, and the Peelites were virtually wiped out in the 1857 election, which was a triumph for Palmerston. So far from winning new recruits, Derby nearly lost one, when Palmerston offered his son, Edward, the Colonial secretaryship. Lord Stanley, as he now was, hastened to consult his father, and then declined, explaining in a letter to Disraeli that 'I shall never during my Father's public life, connect myself with a party opposed to his' (Jones, p. 214).

Then, quite unexpectedly, the Palmerston government collapsed, due to the dissastisfaction of its Radical supporters and manouvring by Lord John Russell, still smarting from his displacement as leader of the Whigs. The occasion was the attempted assassination of Napoleon III, in January 1858, by an Italian republican, Felice Orsini, who had plotted his conspiracy in London, where he had acquired the bomb with which he killed many bystanders, but not the Emperor. The French government sent an insultingly provocative note demanding that the British government took steps to prevent a recurrence of the outrage, and Palmerston, normally quick to repulse any foreign interference, meekly introduced the Conspiracy to Murder Bill, which was explicitly designed to meet the French protest. The Radicals, deeply disappointed in Palmerston because of his indifference to Reform, put down a no confidence motion, which was backed by Russell. Derby and Disraeli, sensing that the government was in danger, ordered their troops to vote in favour of the motion, which was carried by 19 votes.

Derby went on to form his second government, taking office on 20 February 1858, with substantially the same personnel as the first, though they were now older and more experienced, and appeared more authoritative. Lord Stanley now became Colonial Secretary, and Peel's younger brother, General Jonathan Peel, served as War Secretary, though none of the leading Peelites responded to Derby's approaches. They passed several important bills, notably the India Act, which took over the government of the sub-continent from the East India Company, following the suppression of the Indian Mutiny, and they supported measures to remove the property qualification for MPs and to allow practising Jews to sit in the Commons. Yet the centrepiece of their legislative programme was a Reform Bill, Derby having finally been convinced that a moderate measure, slightly enlarging the franchise, would forestall the introduction of a much more democratic Bill by his opponents. The gamble did not come off: 40 ultra conservatives, including two ministers who resigned from the Cabinet, declared their opposition, while the Bill did not go nearly far enough to attract much support from the other side of the House. The Bill was sunk, when a hostile motion moved by Lord John Russell, on 1 April 1859, was carried by 330 votes to 291. Derby immediately sought a dissolution, and the Conservatives gained seats in the subsequent general election, but still emerged as a minority, with 306 seats. Before the new Parliament met, the Whigs, Peelites and Radicals came together to form the Liberal Party (see Chapter 13), and on 10 June 1858 defeated the government on a no confidence motion by 323 votes to 310. Derby immediately resigned; his second government had lasted rather longer than the first: one year and 111 days.

There followed eight dispiriting years in opposition, during which his health gradually declined and he appeared increasingly elderly and out of touch. Periodically he thought of retiring from the leadership, but declined to do so, as he saw no generally acceptable candidate for the succession. The only two possibilities were Disraeli and his own son, Edward. Yet the former was widely distrusted, and the latter was regarded as too liberal in his views to be acceptable to the mass of Tory supporters. So he ploughed on, and these years saw a late blossoming of his social conscience. He had always prided himself on being a good landlord, but his sympathies broadened out to include the entire working class of his native Lancashire, when the US Civil War, which cut off cotton supplies from the South, had a devastating effect on employment in the textile industry which dominated the county. Derby threw himself with great vigour into the relief effort, serving as chairman of the Lancashire Relief Committee to which he devoted at least a day a week of his time, contributing generously to its funds and persuading other wealthy aristocrats to do the same.

He had the slenderest hopes of returning to the premiership, but it was the reform issue which created the opportunity for Derby's third and last government. In 1866 Lord John – now Earl – Russell, and Prime Minister for the second time, sought to crown his own career by passing a more radical Bill, but could not carry all his Whig supporters who, as recounted in Chapter 13, joined with the Tories in voting it down. The Queen invited Derby to form a new administration, and this time he accepted without hesitation, though again seeking to enlarge his parliamentary support by recruiting ministers from outside the Tory Party. On this occasion, he targeted the 'Adullamites', the right-wing Liberals who had voted against Russell's Reform bill, but they declined to serve, and Derby formed an entirely Conservative government. It was, however, stronger than its two predecessors, including some promising newcomers, notably Lord Cranborne, a future Prime Minister as the Third Marquess of Salisbury, while Lord Stanley became Foreign Secretary.

He took office on 28 June 1866. There now occurred the most extraordinary transformation in his attitude. Having been a fervent long-time opponent of parliamentary reform, he now decided that it had become imperative to pass a Bill, and moreover that it had to be more radical than Russell's abortive measure if it was to have any hope of settling the issue for the foreseeable future. Russell had proposed reducing the property qualification for voters in borough constituencies from £10 to £7 a year, while his more Liberal supporters wanted to go down to £6. Derby brooded on the question, asking himself whether he should propose £5 or some lesser sum, but finally concluded that the only logical conclusion was household suffrage, that is, that every head of household should have the vote whatever his income. His experience in dealing with the unemployed in Lancashire had convinced him that, so far from being potential revolutionaries they were, on the whole, moderate and reasonable men. Moreover, his friend Lord Malmesbury had concluded that, whereas the better off members of the working class were more likely to be Liberal voters, the really poor tended to be deferential to the wealthy, and were thus an untapped source of Tory support. Lord Cranborne, however, did some rapid calculations, and concluded that if Derby's proposal was implemented, it would give the working class a 2:1 majority in the electorate, and that this would pose an unacceptable risk. Derby then came up with what he regarded as a masterstroke, proposing a plurality of votes for the wealthier and better educated.

Disraeli, who later got the credit for what became the 1867 Reform Act (see Chapter 29), was extremely sceptical at the outset, but hastened to do his master's bidding. He was in charge of the Bill in the Commons, under close direction by Derby until the later stages when the Prime Minister's health began to fail, while Derby himself steered it through the Lords, with assistance from Malmesbury. During the parliamentary passage the plurality proposals were defeated, but Derby determined to persist with the Bill, despite a Cabinet revolt which led to the resignation of Cranborne, the Secretary of State for India, and two other ministers, the Earl of Carnarvon and General Peel. It led to a very large extension of the electorate, from 7 to 16 per cent of the adult population, a far bigger enlargement than the more famous measure of 1832. Derby gave his own summing up at the conclusion of the Lords' debates:

> No doubt we are making a great experiment and 'taking a leap in the dark', but I have the greatest confidence in the sound sense of my fellow countrymen, and I entertain a strong hope that the extended franchise which we are now conferring on them will be the means of placing the institutions of this country on a firmer basis, and that the passing of this measure will tend to increase the loyalty and contentment of a great portion of Her Majesty's subjects; (House of Lords Hansard, 6 August 1867)

With the passage of the Bill concluded, Derby had no thoughts of early retirement, but successively severe attacks of gout gradually weakened him, and the following February he made way for Disraeli, whom he nominated as his successor. He lived on until October 1869, making one last spirited speech in the House of Lords, in June 1869, in defence of his beloved (Anglican) Church of Ireland, which the newly elected Gladstone government was determined to disestablish. He failed, and predicted that this would herald the end of the Union with Ireland. For some 20 years, he had led the Conservative Party, most of the time in opposition, but for rather less than four years, in total, in government, always in a minority. He had been a dignified and usually moderate leader, who had always commanded respect, but it is doubtful whether his long tenure of the leadership did his party much good. He failed to secure a re-union with the Peelites and did little to improve the electoral prospects of his party. The elements that he represented most strongly – the landed interest and the Church of England – were in relative decline, and he failed to make much impact on the rising industrial and middle classes, or the nonconformist churches. Only his belated conversion to parliamentary reform provided the opportunity for extending the Tories' appeal to newly enfranchised sections of the electorate, and it was left to his successors, Disraeli and Salisbury, to reach out to what became an essential element in Conservative electoral success over the next 100 years – the deferential working-class voter.

Works consulted

Robert Blake, 1966, *Disraeli*, London, Eyre & Spottiswoode.
James Chambers, 2004, *Palmerston: The People's Darling*, London, John Murray.
J.B. Conacher, 1968, *The Aberdeen Coalition 1852–1855*, Cambridge, Cambridge University Press.

Valerie Cromwell, 1998, 'Edward George Geoffrey Smith Stanley, 14th Earl of Derby', in Robert Eccelshall and Graham Walker (eds.), *Biographical Dictionary of British Prime Ministers*, London, Routledge.

Angus Hawkins, 2004, Article in *Oxford Dictionary of National Biography*, Oxford University Press.

Christopher Hibbert, 2005, *Disraeli, A Personal History*, Harper Perennial, London.

Wilbur Devereux Jones, 1956, *Lord Derby and Victorian Conservatism*, Blackwell, Oxford.

Robert Stewart, 1971, *The Politics of Protection: Lord Derby and the Protectionist Party 1841–1852*, Cambridge, Cambridge University Press.

27

George Gordon, 4th Earl of Aberdeen – Failure or Scapegoat?

Lord Aberdeen is unusual among Prime Ministers in never having been a Member of the House of Commons. Many other peers became Prime Minister, but nearly all of them had served an earlier apprenticeship in the Lower House. During the past two centuries, only Aberdeen and Lord Rosebery spent their entire political careers in the House of Lords. It is perhaps no accident that they have long been regarded as being among the least successful of British premiers.

George Gordon (later Hamilton-Gordon) was born on 28 January 1784, to a life which was to be repeatedly marked by tragedy. He came from a long line of Scottish aristocrats who had been the largest landowners in Aberdeenshire for several centuries, though his belief that he was a direct descendant of Bertrand de Guerdon, whose fatal arrow had killed Richard the Lionheart at the siege of Chalus in 1199, was probably erroneous. Less fanciful was the literally shotgun marriage contracted by his grandfather, the 3rd Earl. He seduced a blacksmith's daughter, who, when he visited her a second time, produced a loaded pistol and threatened to shoot him unless he married her. The eldest son of this union was Lord Haddo, who at the age of 18 married Charlotte Brand, the sister of a Scottish general. George was the eldest of seven children (one born post-humously) that Haddo fathered before dying, aged 27, in a riding accident. Charlotte soon quarrelled with her father-in-law and took her seven children off to London, where she herself died four years later.

George, aged 11, was now the heir to a large fortune and estate, which his grandfather was busy diminishing by making generous provisions for his many mistresses and illegitimate children. Together with his six siblings, he was now taken into the London household of one of his father's friends. This was no other than Henry Dundas (later Lord Melville), the most powerful politician in Scotland, and a close friend and associate of the Prime Minister, William Pitt, in whose government he was to serve as Home Secretary and War Minister for over a decade. George and his brothers were sent to Harrow School, where he was a contemporary of two other future Prime Ministers, Palmerston and Goderich. At the age of 14, under Scottish law, he was permitted to nominate his own guardians. He chose Dundas and Pitt, and lived alternately with them. 'In a sense', wrote his biographer, 'his whole later political career sprang from those critical years' (Chamberlain, 1983, p. 26). Indeed, it seems improbable that he would have gone into politics at all if it had not been for the strong influence on him of his two guardians. There was no recent political tradition in his family; he had a poor temperament for politics, and strong intellectual and artistic interests which would most likely have led him into different directions if it had not been for these circumstances.

Despite his grandfather's expressed desire that he should be educated in Scotland, George (now known as Lord Haddo) proceeded from Harrow to St. John's College, Cambridge, in 1800, his fees possibly being paid by Pitt. Here he proved to be a dedicated scholar, immersing himself in Renaissance and classical studies, and falling in with a set of like-minded friends, all with literary ambitions. In August 1801, his grandfather died, and he became the 4th Earl of Aberdeen (in the Scottish peerage), though he was unable to take charge of his estates until his coming of age four years later. He did, however, travel up to Scotland, and was appalled at their run-down condition, and the considerable debts which his grandfather had incurred in providing for his illegitimate progeny.

Like other aristocrats at the time, he left Cambridge without taking a degree, and in 1802 embarked on the Grand Tour, which was made possible by the Peace of Amiens, which provided a break of 14 months in the long-running war with France. Pitt provided him with letters of introduction to many eminent personages, and he dined with Napoleon (who impressed him very much) at Malmaison, and with the widow of Bonnie Prince Charlie, the Young Pretender, in Florence. But the highlights of his journey were his visits to Greece and Constantinople, during which he participated in important archaeological excavations, bought several valuable artefacts which are now in the British Museum, and made extensive notes which he hoped to write up later for publication. He hoped to buy the 'Elgin marbles' from the Parthenon, but found that he had been pre-empted by his fellow Scottish peer. In Constantinople, he accompanied the British ambassador, William Drummond, who became a close friend, in an interview with the Sultan, but formed a very low opinion of the way that the Ottoman Empire was governed. This undoubtedly influenced his later attitude to the recurring 'Eastern question', both as Foreign Secretary and Prime Minister. The war with France having resumed, Aberdeen, now aged 20, returned to England in the summer of 1804, via Venice, Vienna and Berlin. Back in London, he was instrumental in founding the Athenian Society, and subsequently contributed a learned article about Troy, the probable site of which he had visited, for the *Edinburgh Review*. He was to establish a reputation for himself as an authority on antiquity, but was referred to, sarcastically, in a poem by his cousin, Lord Byron (whom he physically strongly resembled) as 'The travell'd thane, Athenian Aberdeen'.

Aberdeen came of age in January 1805, and hastened north to take possession of his estates, and the splendid, if neglected, Palladian mansion, Haddo House, which was his country seat. He immediately set in motion schemes to pay off the accumulated debts, to establish new and improved leases with his tenants, who, with their families included, came to over a thousand, to introduce modern methods of farming, and to renovate and modernize his home. He then repaired to London, where he effectively entered society for the first time, becoming an habitué at the endless series of receptions given by the Duchess of Devonshire, Lady Holland, and the Marquess of Abercorn. The latter, a Tory peer with vast estates in Ireland, held court at Bentley Priory, a mansion some distance from central London, at Stanmore, in Middlesex. He was immediately seen as a highly eligible bachelor, and the Duchess of Gordon marked him out as a likely suitor for her daughter Georgina. But Aberdeen showed no interest, and she was married off instead to the widowed Duke of Bedford, becoming, at the age of 20, stepmother to the young Lord John Russell. Aberdeen set his cap at the Duchess of Devonshire's daughter, Harriet, who played hard to get, and was then mortified when Aberdeen took up with Lady Catherine Hamilton, the beautiful and spirited eldest daughter of Lord Abercorn. They fell deeply in love, and were married a few months later, in July 1805, both aged 21.

Under the influence of Dundas and Pitt, Aberdeen was convinced that he should follow a political career, and Pitt, who resumed the premiership in 1804, promised to recommend him for an English peerage, which would enable him to enter the House of Lords (Scottish peers did not have an automatic right to do so, and were precluded – unlike Irish peers – from standing for the House of Commons). Before Pitt could make good on his promise, however, he died, in January 1806, at the age of 46. Aberdeen, who was very fond of Pitt, was deeply distressed, and not only because he was bereft of the launching pad for his intended career. Nevertheless, he was determined to obtain entry to the House of Lords, and decided to offer himself for election as one of the 16 Scottish representative peers, who were chosen in each Parliament by the whole body of Scottish peers, who then numbered 57. In the 1806 election, the 'Government of all the Talents', led by Lord Grenville, from which the Tories were excluded, put up its own slate of 16 peers. This did not include Aberdeen, who was nevertheless encouraged to run by Dundas, now Lord Melville, and his father-in-law, Lord Abercorn. Aberdeen established himself in Edinburgh, and began energetically canvassing, offering to trade his own votes with several other nominated candidates, and succeeded in coming out in fifteenth place, the only candidate not backed by the government to be elected.

Aged 22, Aberdeen made a far from glorious début in the upper house. The government bill to abolish the slave trade deeply divided the opposition, but Aberdeen decided to support it in his maiden speech. Yet when the time came for him to rise from his place, his nerve failed him, and he left the Chamber. He finally spoke some months later, on the occasion of the installation of the new Tory government, under the Duke of Portland, when he declared his support, and attempted to justify the action of George III in turning out the 'Talents' government, even though it maintained its Commons majority (see Chapter 3). It was a badly delivered speech, and throughout his long career Aberdeen failed to master the art of speaking in the Lords, and always dreaded doing so, though he was apparently able to speak passably well at other venues. Despite this poor effort, Portland offered Aberdeen a minor post in his government, a Lordship either at the Treasury or the Admiralty. Palmerston, a newly elected MP, received a similar offer, and accepted it with alacrity, but Aberdeen declined, apparently believing it was too junior for somebody of his rank. He hoped, instead, to receive an ambassadorial appointment, but for this too, he was extremely choosy, and had to wait for several years before being made an acceptable offer. He twice turned down the ambassadorship to Russia, and prevaricated over the post of British Minister to Sicily, hoping instead to be offered Constantinople, which was not then available, though he turned it down several years later. Over the next six years, he devoted himself mainly to running his estates, and to his scholarly pursuits, being elected a Fellow of the Royal Society in 1808, and President of the Society of Antiquaries in 1812. Three daughters, on whom he doted, were born in successive years, but in November 1810, the long-awaited son died less than an hour after his birth. His mother, Catherine, was to survive him for just over a year, succumbing to tuberculosis, in February 1812. Aberdeen was totally devastated: he wore mourning for the rest of his life, and transferred his perhaps extravagant devotion to his three daughters, all of whom were, in turn, to follow their mother to their graves before reaching their twentieth birthday.

In 1813, he finally accepted a diplomatic appointment, proposed by his friend, Lord Castlereagh MP, the Foreign Secretary. This was to go to Vienna, to re-establish diplomatic relations, which had been broken off in 1809, and to persuade the Austrians to join Russia and Prussia in a renewed war against Napoleon, following his retreat from Moscow. He had some doubts whether to accept, and did not want to stay away from his daughters (who were left in the care of his sister-in-law, Maria) for more than a short time, but decided to go, at least partly because it had been hinted to him that if he succeeded in his mission an English peerage would surely follow.

Before Aberdeen could reach Austria, the Emperor Francis I had already taken the plunge, and declared war on France. Putting himself at the head of his armies, he had established himself at Teplice, in northern Bohemia, where he had been joined by Tsar Alexander and Frederick William III, the King of Prussia. Aberdeen hastened there, via Berlin and Prague, travelling at full speed, his coach overturning one night, and he suffered from concussion, which he blamed for the recurrent headaches which plagued him for the rest of his life. On arrival, he soon succeeded in ingratiating himself with the Austrian Emperor, and with his Foreign Minister, Prince Metternich, so much so that he was later to be criticized for falling under the spell of this master of intrigue. His own position at the allied camp was awkward, as he was – much to his chagrin – technically junior to two British army officers, Lord Cathcart and Sir Charles Stewart (Castlereagh's half-brother), who were the ambassadors at the Russian and Prussian courts. As the three of them had widely diverging views, it was difficult for any of them to present a coherent view of British policy. However, Aberdeen largely succeeded in preventing the three allied powers from presenting a purely 'continental' peace proposal to Napoleon's unofficial emissary, which ignored British interests in the Low Countries and the Iberian Peninsula, and her maritime interests. Even the document finally agreed was less than totally satisfactory from a British point of view, but Napoleon, still confident of his eventual success, rejected the terms with disdain. Shortly afterwards, in October 1813, the combined armies of Austria, Prussia, Russia and Sweden, who outnumbered the French by two-one, inflicted a comprehensive defeat, in the three-day battle of Leipzig, on Napoleon, who withdrew his forces to the Rhine in great disorder. Aberdeen, who witnessed the aftermath of the battle, was appalled by the extent of the slaughter, writing to his sister-in-law, Maria:

> For three or four miles the ground is covered with bodies of men and horses, many not dead. Wretches wounded unable to crawl, crying for water amidst heaps of putrefying bodies. Their screams are heard at an immense distance, and still ring in my ears... Our victory is most complete. It must be owned that a victory is a fine thing, but one should beat a distance. (Chamberlain, 2004)

Apart from Wellington, Aberdeen was the only British Prime Minister of the nineteenth century to witness war at first hand. This did not make him a pacifist, as some have suggested, but may well account for the pacific approach which he consistently brought to foreign policy issues, in sharp contrast, for example, to Palmerston. Following Napoleon's retreat, the allied powers established themselves at Frankfurt-am-Main, where again peace proposals were drawn up, and communicated to Napoleon through the brother-in-law of the French foreign minister. Aberdeen again did his best to temper the document to take account of British interests, with only partial success. It offered France the prospect of keeping its 'natural' frontiers of the Rhine, the Alps and the Pyrenees, rather than having to withdraw to its pre-war boundaries of 1793. Once again, the over-confident Napoleon turned it down, and the final campaign to overthrow his regime began, with Wellington entering France from the south, and the Austrians, Prussians and Russians from the east. At Christmas 1813, Castlereagh, fed up by the perpetual bickering between the three British ambassadors, hastened to join the three eastern monarchs at their new headquarters at Langres, in the Champagne country, and take personal charge of the negotiations. Aberdeen's last task was to attend the conference at Chatillon-sur-Seine, in the spring of 1814, which was meant to draw up the final peace terms to be imposed on the soon-to-be defeated French. The conference was terminated by a sudden collapse of the French resistance, and the abdication of Napoleon on 11 April 1814, and Aberdeen accompanied Castlereagh to Paris, where he seconded him in negotiating the first Treaty of Paris, which, so they believed, brought the War to an end. Aberdeen declined Castlereagh's offer to accompany him to the Congress of Vienna, and instead returned to London, carrying with him the first copy of the Treaty. He had been away for nearly a year, more than enough for him, and he desperately wanted to rejoin his daughters, following the death, in January 1814, of his sister-in-law Maria, who had been looking after them. Like her sister, and – later each of the three children – she died from tuberculosis, which also cost the life of her brother, Lord James Hamilton, Abercorn's son and heir, whose death followed soon after.

Aberdeen's debut as a diplomat took place in difficult and frustrating, and even dangerous, circumstances, and on the whole he acquitted himself well. An English viscountcy, which guaranteed him a permanent place in the House of Lords, was duly bestowed on him, providing a firmer basis for his political career. This, however, trod water for more than a decade, as he concentrated his energies on family affairs, his intellectual pursuits and the running of his estates. It was not until 1828, when he was appointed Chancellor of the Duchy of Lancaster in the Duke of Wellington's government, that he again held public office. Muriel Chamberlain, in her definitive biography of Aberdeen, describes the ten months of his diplomatic mission as by far the most important formative influence in his career.

Aberdeen had decided some time earlier that he should marry a second time, partly, at least, to provide an acceptable stepmother for his daughters. He was attracted by Anne Cavendish, a niece of the Duke of Devonshire, but wooed her in a very low-key and spasmodic manner, perhaps because her parents disapproved of the match. He was also paying court to Susan Ryder, the very young daughter of his friend, Lord Harrowby, a leading minister in Lord Liverpool's government, but it was his father-in-law, Lord Abercorn, who acted as matchmaker. He suggested to Aberdeen that he should instead wed his daughter-in-law, Lady Harriet Hamilton, the 23-year-old widow of his only

were only released through the intervention of a sympathetic militia commander, and reached Charenton after several hours' delay. The party then proceeded at full speed to Switzerland, where they were happy to relax in the company of Edward Gibbon at his beautiful villa at Lausanne. They then went on to Naples where they spent the ensuing two winters, as part of large group of aristocratic English friends centred round the elderly British ambassador, Sir William Hamilton, and his young wife Emma, shortly to succumb to the fatal attractions of Lord Nelson.

When Harry returned to England, shortly before his tenth birthday, in October 1794, he spoke excellent French and Italian, which was to be a major asset in his future career. Soon afterwards, he was enrolled at Harrow School, then the most fashionable choice for aristocrats, temporarily having put Eton in the shade. Coming from a happy family background, clever, good-humoured, handsome, and excelling at games and in his studies, he was popular both with the masters and his fellow pupils. His housemaster, Dr Bromley, described him as 'a most charming boy and very quick at his books', while his 'fag', Augustus Clifford, recalled in old age, when he was a retired Rear-Admiral, that 'he was reckoned the best-tempered and most plucky boy in the school, as well as a young man of great promise' (Chambers, 2004, pp. 19–20). Harry's father withdrew him from the school at the age of 16, believing that it had already taught him all it could, and proposed to send him to a university to prepare for a career in diplomacy. Yet he was too young to go to Cambridge – his first choice – and he was sent instead to Edinburgh, at that time a more distinguished centre of learning. He spent three fruitful years there, studying a wide range of subjects, and was particularly influenced by the lectures on political economy given by his tutor, Dugald Stewart, the biographer of Adam Smith, the author of *The Wealth of Nations*, whose free trade views he strongly reflected. He was an assiduous student, and showed great self-discipline, abstaining from the riotous drinking habits of most of the other aristocratic students. He led an active social life but took no part in the debates of the Speculative Society (the equivalent of the Oxford and Cambridge Union societies), a remarkable omission, as it was to be a training ground for all of the other distinguished future statesmen who passed through the university at this period. Generally, however, Palmerston kept his views – if he had any – on current political issues to himself. Perhaps he was inhibited by being a nominal Tory in a generally Whiggish *ambience*, but – more likely – he had yet to develop a taste for politics.

When he had been at Edinburgh for nearly two years, in April 1802, his father died suddenly of cancer, aged 62. Devoted to both his parents, Harry took his loss very hard and also that of his mother, who died three years later, at the age of 50. At the age of 17, he inherited both the title and a sizeable amount of debt from his father, and two guardians, the Earls of Malmesbury and Chichester, were appointed to look after him. The former, a distinguished ambassador, and close associate of the Younger Pitt, guided Harry's early career path, ensuring that he enrolled, as his father had intended, at St. John's College, Cambridge, to complete his studies. Before going up, he returned to Edinburgh for a third year, and then made a tour of the Scottish Highlands and Wales, where he fell in love for the first time. Apart from the fact that she was a redhead, little is known of the affair. At Cambridge, where he got to know scions of all the main political families, he was – as a nobleman – not supposed to take any examinations, being assured an honorary MA at the end of his course. Yet he insisted on taking them, obtaining first class results in each of his three years there, from 1803–1806. He led a very active social life, having numerous affairs, but his favourite pursuits were riding and hunting. In the face of the threatened French invasion, in 1805, he joined the local militia in Hampshire, as a Lieutenant Colonel. Under Malmesbury's influence, he also became more interested in politics, and when Pitt, who was one of the two MPs for Cambridge University, died in January 1806, he was pressed by Malmesbury, and by his college tutor, to offer himself as the Tory candidate in the ensuing by-election. He was 21, and had only just ceased to be an undergraduate, but had some hopes of success as the Whig vote was split. Both his opponents were recent Cambridge men, and only a little older than himself, but both were already MPs, anxious to exchange their 'pocket' boroughs for the more prestigious Cambridge University seat. The official Whig candidate was Lord Henry Petty, aged 25, who had just become Chancellor of the Exchequer in the 'Government of all the Talents', while the Radical candidate was Viscount Althorp, aged 24, son of Earl Spencer, who was Home Secretary in the new government. Althorp's chances were discounted, and it was generally reckoned (including by Lord Byron, then a Cambridge undergraduate, who wrote a mocking poem on the subject) that the contest would be between Petty and Palmerston. In the event, Palmerston was pushed into third place, the 600 or so Cambridge graduates who participated dividing their votes as follows:

Petty	331
Althorp	145
Palmerston	128

Lord Malmesbury lost no time in seeking another seat for Palmerston to fight at the general election which followed later in the year, and hit on the constituency of Horsham, supposedly in the gift of Viscountess Irwin, to whom Palmerston paid £1,500, plus the promise of an extra £3,500 if he was elected. Much to Palmerston's (and the Viscountess's) consternation, however, another local landowner, the Duke of Norfolk – a leading Whig – moved in and presented two candidates of his own, who finished up winning more votes than the two Tories. The returning officer refused to discriminate between two local grandees, and declared all four candidates elected, leaving it to the (now Whig dominated) House of Commons to decide to whom to award the seats. So it was back to square one for Palmerston, but the indomitable Malmesbury quickly found him another pocket borough, Newport, Isle of Wight, for which he was returned seven months later, in the 1807 general election, on condition that he paid £4,000 and promised never to set foot in the constituency. At the same time, Palmerston had another go at Cambridge, where – this time – he lost by only three votes, after honourably insisting that his supporters (each of whom had two votes) should not renege on a mutual agreement with his fellow Tory candidate not to 'plump' their votes.

So – after an unexpectedly bumpy ride – Palmerston became an MP, at the age of 22. He had already become a junior member of the Duke of Portland's government, having been appointed a month earlier as a Lord of the Admiralty. He was to continue in this post – the duties of which were fairly nominal – for over two years, until October 1809, when the Duke retired, and Spencer Perceval was appointed in his place. The new Premier astonished Palmerston by offering him the post of Chancellor of the Exchequer – not such an important post as it later became, as the Prime Minister's duties as First Lord of the Treasury were still considerable – but still a very great promotion. Palmerston turned it down – not through lack of ambition, but through fear of tripping up in a post for which he had few qualifications, and probably remembering that the young Lord Henry Petty's short term in that office a few years earlier had badly damaged his reputation. Instead, he accepted the post of War Secretary, outside the Cabinet, in the belief – backed by Malmesbury – that if he performed well he would 'soon' win more merited promotion. Had he known how long he would stay in this post – over 18 years – it is doubtful if he would have accepted it. He was not the minister primarily responsible for defence – that was the Secretary of State for War and the Colonies, currently Lord Liverpool – who was his departmental superior. Palmerston's role, according to his latest biographer, was to act as 'the government's auditor' – a tedious and time-consuming job, which Palmerston carried out with heroic thoroughness, poring over some '40,000 regimental accounts in arrears, some of them dating back as far as the end of the War of American Independence in 1783' (Chambers, p. 62). Palmerston was soon seen as a first-class administrator, but his parliamentary performances were very variable. Highly authoritative when he kept to his script, he was ponderous and stilted when he had to ad lib. He also exhibited immense will-power, insisting on having his way in dealings with colleagues, and fighting a successful battle to establish the point that, as a civilian minister, he was senior to the Commander-in-Chief, who for much of the time was no other than the prickly Duke of York, the favourite son of George III.

Palmerston had been seen for several years as a highly eligible bachelor, but had skillfully avoided committing himself, though he continued be a great social success with the ladies, some respectable, others rather less so. He was soon dubbed 'Lord Cupid', but fell deeply in love with Lady Emily Cowper (formerly Lamb), sister to William Lamb (later Lord Melbourne), and a flighty society beauty. They had become lovers probably as early as 1809, and while Emily's first son, born in 1805, was almost certainly sired by Earl Cowper, her boring, drunken and neglectful husband, nobody doubted that Palmerston was the father of her three later children, one of whom was stillborn. Despite their mutual devotion, their association was by no means an exclusive one. In 1816, Palmerston fathered another child on a Mrs Emma Murray, whom he had set up in a flat in Piccadilly. He was called Henry John Temple Murray. Palmerston had earlier conducted simultaneous affairs with another society beauty, Lady Jersey, and probably also with Princess Lieven, the highly promiscuous wife of the Russian ambassador. Emily openly flaunted other lovers, including an Italian count, who for four years vied publicly with Palmerston for her affections, but the issue was finally decided in Palmerston's favour in 1818, when he survived an assassination attempt by a deranged ex-soldier, with a grievance. Palmerston suffered only superficial wounds, and taking pity on his penniless assailant, paid for the services of a lawyer to defend him in his trial. Clearly mad, he escaped the death penalty, but was committed to Bedlam 'during His Majesty's pleasure'.

When Spencer Perceval was assassinated, in 1812, he was succeeded as Prime Minister by the Earl of Liverpool, whose place as Secretary for War and Colonies was taken by Earl Bathurst, who remained Palmerston's superior throughout the 15 years of Liverpool's premiership. Palmerston was unlucky not to be promoted during all this time, but his relations with the Prime Minister were not good. His views were more liberal, and during the period, roughly between 1815 and 1822, when the government imposed a range of repressive and reactionary measures, he kept his head down, and refrained from supporting them in public. Also, on the divisive issue of Catholic emancipation, he took the pro-Catholic side, which did not commend him to the stoutly Protestant Prime Minister. In 1822, Liverpool tried to get rid of Palmerston, by offering him successively, an English peerage coupled with an appointment as Commissioner of Woods and Forests, and then the glittering post of Governor-General of India, but Palmerston declined, and chose to remain in his relatively junior government post. Yet he was not happy in this role; his former genial self became more and more abrasive, and he spared neither his ministerial colleagues nor his officials in his constant stream of acerbic remarks. The former 'Lord Cupid' became known as 'Lord Pumicestone'. His private life too did not give him much pleasure: possibly tiring of Emily's constant infidelities, he twice proposed marriage in 1823 and 1825, to Lady Georgiana Fane, the younger sister of Lady Jersey. Not willing to tie herself to one of her sister's castoffs, she turned him down both times. Then, in 1826, the more right-wing and anti-Catholic members of the government, with Liverpool's scarcely concealed connivance, intrigued to deprive him of his parliamentary seat. This was at Cambridge University, where Palmerston had finally succeeded in getting elected in 1811, and which he had represented ever since. The Tories nominated two new candidates, both fervent anti-Catholics, for the seats at the general election that year, and depended on the large number of clergymen who were Cambridge graduates to vote against Palmerston, whom they labelled a 'Papist'. Palmerston was only saved from imminent defeat by the decision of the Whigs not to put up any candidates of their own, and indeed instructed their supporters to vote for Palmerston. He survived, and may well have concluded that, as most of his best friends were Whigs, and his mistresses the wives or daughters of Whigs, he was perhaps in the wrong party. There were, however, other 'Liberal Tories', including Canning, who had become Foreign Secretary and leader of the Commons in 1822, and for whom Palmerston felt a growing affinity.

When Canning succeeded Liverpool as Prime Minister, in 1827, he renewed the offer of the Indian Governor-Generalship, which Palmerston again declined, but then appointed him to the cabinet, retaining the post of War Secretary, and he was also appointed as acting Commander-in-Chief, following the death of the Duke of York. When Canning died four months later, the new Prime Minister, Viscount Goderich, wanted to appoint Palmerston as Chancellor of the Exchequer, but George IV objected, and Palmerston remained at the War Office, and carried on when the Duke of Wellington succeeded Goderich after another four months. Yet, in May 1828, when the 'Canningite' ministers resigned (see Chapter 9), Palmerston quit with them, and went into opposition. Now, for the first time, he had the opportunity to shine in the House of Commons. Instead of speaking on 'dry' subjects, such as the purchase of military supplies or the details of army organization, he was able to let his imagination fly, and he made a series of masterly orations criticizing the foreign policy of the Wellington government, castigating it for its failure to stand up for Greece in its struggle against Turkey and for its appeasement of the Miguelite regime in Portugal, which had temporarily overthrown the more liberal administration of Queen Maria. Palmerston's speeches were warmly received by the Whigs, but were heard in stony silence by Tory MPs. He was the first politician to make a practice of sending his speeches to the newspapers in advance, which greatly extended his audience. Normally they read far better in the papers than they sounded, for Palmerston's delivery was often poor, and his reputation in the country became far higher than in the Commons.

When, in November 1830, Wellington's government was defeated, in a division in which the Canningites joined with the Whigs, it was no great surprise that the incoming Whig Prime Minister, Lord Grey, made Palmerston his Foreign Secretary. He was not the first choice – this was Lord Henry Petty (now the Marquess of Lansdowne), his former rival for the Cambridge

University seat. But Lansdowne declined, advising Grey to appoint Palmerston, whose claims were also strongly pressed by Princess Lieven, now an intimate friend of Grey's.

He was now 46, and could be seen as a 'late developer' in politics. But, having belatedly arrived in the front rank he remained there, for the next three and a half decades, serving three times as Foreign Secretary, once as Home Secretary and twice as Prime Minister, dying in office two days short of his eighty-first birthday, just after having been triumphantly re-elected. He has the all-time record for service as a minister – 48 years, a total unlikely ever to be exceeded. Having been among the most liberal Tories, Palmerston soon showed himself to be among the most conservative Whigs. Only a lukewarm supporter of the Reform Bill, he was one of the most strenuous advocates of compromise within the government, when it ran into fierce opposition from the House of Lords. When compromise failed, however, and he sensed that public opinion was overwhelmingly in favour of the passage of the Bill, he switched his position, and formally proposed in the cabinet that the King should be pressed to create enough new peers to assure its passage. Throughout his subsequent career, Palmerston was careful to keep public opinion on his side, and seldom failed to modify his policies if they encountered widespread opposition. Palmerston's support for Reform, however moderate, cost him his seat at Cambridge University in the 1831 general election, in the face of strong Tory opponents, who denounced him as a turncoat. He quickly returned to Parliament for a pocket borough (Bletchingly) in Surrey, but when this seat was abolished by the Reform Bill, switched to the South Hampshire constituency, which included his own country seat, at Broadlands. (He was to lose this constituency three years later, but then transferred to Tiverton, which he held for the remainder of his long life).

As Foreign Secretary, Palmerston soon revealed himself to be a worthy successor to two great predecessors – in Castlereagh and Canning. Like them, he vigorously pursued what he regarded as British interests, and set himself to counter the influence of the three 'Holy Alliance' powers, Russia, Austria and Prussia, who were bent on restoring absolutist rule throughout the European continent. By contrast, Palmerston strongly backed liberal or nationalist movements in Spain, Portugal and Greece. His attitude to France was equivocal, seeing her as a potential rival and military and naval threat, but also, on occasion as a useful ally, and believing that, under the Orleanist monarchy, she had much in common with Britain as a constitutional monarchy based on parliamentary institutions. Conversely, though he feared Russian expansionism, he was on occasion perfectly prepared to co-operate with the Tsar's government in curbing French pretensions. He famously justified his attitude in a speech in the House of Commons, in March 1848, declaring: 'We have no eternal allies and we have no perpetual enemies. Our interests are eternal and perpetual, and those interests it is our duty to follow' (Hansard, 1 March 1848).

His first challenge was to chair the London conference, attended by Holland and the five great powers of Europe – Britain, France, Austria, Prussia and Russia – to seek a settlement, following the Belgian rebellion against Dutch rule in 1830. Palmerston showed himself a master of diplomacy and intrigue, playing on the hopes and fears of all the participants, with whom he constantly played hot and cold, in order to achieve his own objects. These were to prevent a French takeover of Belgium, to avert a Dutch reconquest of the territory, and to prevent the three eastern powers from intervening on behalf of the Dutch King. He succeeded in all these objectives, by a judicious mixture of promises and threats. When the Belgian Parliament chose Louis Philippe's younger son, the Duc de Nemours, as their King, he put enormous pressure, with a none too subtle threat of war, on his father to withdraw the nomination, and he then successfully pushed a British nominee, Leopold of Saxe-Coburg, the widower of the former heiress to the British throne, Princess Charlotte. The French were appeased by the marriage of Leopold to Louis Philippe's daughter, Louise-Marie. The Dutch anger was then placated by compelling the Belgians to withdraw from the Grand Duchy of Luxembourg and the eastern part of Limburg province, which were restored to the Dutch king. It took nine years for Palmerston to achieve a generally acceptable settlement, but when he did so it was almost universally applauded as a diplomatic triumph – perhaps the greatest achievement of his whole career. The Treaty of London, finally signed in 1839, established the Kingdom of Belgium as 'an independent and perpetually neutral state', under the collective guarantee of Britain, France, Austria, Prussia and Russia. It was Germany's breach of this guarantee, in 1914, which brought Britain into the First World War, or, at least, was the justification claimed by the British government at the time.

Palmerston was also successful in preventing the Holy Alliance powers from intervening in the Iberian Peninsula. In both countries the relatively liberal legitimate monarchs – Isabella II in Spain and Maria de Gloria in Portugal – were challenged by male pretenders who wished to restore authoritarian rule. Palmerston persuaded the two governments to join with Britain and France in the Quadruple Alliance, of 1834, which successfully prevented any foreign intervention on behalf of the rebellious claimants. In 1834, Earl Grey, who had insisted on being kept fully informed of Palmerston's activities, resigned and was succeeded by Lord Melbourne, who tended to leave him to his own devices. This was partly because he was lazy, but also because he was chary of obstructing his sister Emily's lover. Lord Cowper died in 1837, and Palmerston, immediately proposed to her. They were finally married two years later, and still appeared a very handsome and youthful-looking couple, though he was 55, and she, 52. The snobbish Melbourne felt that Emily, the widow of an Earl, was lowering herself by marrying a mere Viscount (and an Irish one at that), but acquiesced in the match, and was now even less inclined to interfere with his brother-in-law's decisions, much to the chagrin of other cabinet ministers, who regarded the Foreign Secretary as a dangerous law unto himself.

Within the Foreign Office, Palmerston proved more forceful and more imperious than any of his predecessors. He issued exemplarily clear instructions to all his subordinates and expected them to be carried out with the utmost diligence. Working exceptionally long hours himself, he required his officials, who had grown used to 'knocking off' at teatime, to remain in the Office until late in the evenings, playing havoc with their social lives. Chronically unpunctual himself, he cheerfully turned up late at royal functions, and thought nothing of keeping such important visitors as the French ambassador, Talleyrand, waiting for hours before he condescended to see them. It was not surprising that he was highly unpopular with his staff, and the only colleagues whom he treated with any pretence of equality were his ambassadors in Paris, Vienna, St.Petersburg and Constantinople, all of whom came from the highest social circles. Talleyrand had considerable respect for Palmerston, writing in his memoirs, that he 'is certainly one of the most able, if not the most able, man of business that I have met in my career'. However, he added:

> One feature in his character dissipates all these advantages, and prevents him, in my opinion, from ranking as a real statesman. He feels passionately about public affairs, and to the point of sacrificing the most important interests to his resentments. Nearly every political question resolves itself into a personal question in his eyes, and in appearing to defend the interests of his country, it is really the interests of his hate and vengeance that he satisfies. (Ridley, pp. 120–1)

The wily French diplomat may just have been lamenting that Palmerston's cynicism was not equal to his own, but his criticism – though exaggerated – was, perhaps, not all that far from the mark.

There was a short break in Palmerston's foreign secretaryship in November 1834, when Melbourne's government was dismissed by William IV, but he was back five months later when Melbourne returned to office, and – if anything – proved even more independent than before. He also grew more reckless, unjustifiably – in the eyes of many of his colleagues – risking war with both the United States and France, and actually getting into wars with China and Afghanistan. In the words of one biographer, 'He tried to pursue the policy which is now known as "brinkmanship" by going as far as he could with impunity, but no further' (Ridley, p. 96).

The gravest risks that he ran were with France, particularly over the affair of Mehemet Ali. An Albanian adventurer, who became the Ottoman Sultan's viceroy in Egypt, in 1805, he showed great military ability, and built up the strength of the Egyptian forces to such an extent that he effectively became independent of his Ottoman overlords. In 1833, he invaded Syria, and the Sultan was forced to cede the province to him. In 1839, the Sultan unwisely resumed the war, and Mehemet Ali's son Ibrahim decisively defeated the Ottoman Army at the Battle of Nezib. At this point, Sultan Mahmud II died, and his successor – the youthful Abdul Mecid I, fearing that Mehemet Ali would advance on Constantinople and take over the whole empire – appealed to the European great powers for assistance. The French refused any help, and – anxious to expand their own influence in the Middle East and North Africa – actively encouraged Mehemet Ali. Palmerston, however, took the lead, and resolved not only that Mehemet Ali should be prevented from taking Constantinople, but should be forced to give up Syria, and retire back to Egypt. He signed a treaty with Austria, Russia and Prussia to use whatever force was necessary to expel Mehemet Ali from Syria. The French government was furious, and threatened war, and many of Palmerston's Whig colleagues – traditionally pro-French – were aghast, and tried in vain to get Melbourne to curb Palmerston, or switch him to another post. Palmerston held his ground, but the French King, Louis-Philippe, lost his nerve and sacked his bellicose Prime Minister, Louis Thiers. He was replaced by the less belligerent and more pro-British François Guizot. Mehemet Ali was left in the lurch, and was – humiliatingly – forced to withdraw, his army being repatriated to Egypt by the British fleet. The only sop he received was to be granted the hereditary 'pashalik' of Egypt, his heirs continuing to rule the country, first as Khedives later as Kings, until 1952, when King Farouk was forced to abdicate. Palmerston was jubilant: he had been utterly convinced that there would be no war, telling the British consul in Alexandria that:

> France would, indeed, oppose a hostile coalition of [the Great Powers] if those Powers were to threaten to invade France, to insult her honour, or attack her Possessions; but France will not go to war with the other Great Powers in order to help Mehemet Ali, nor has she the means of doing so. (Ridley, p. 235)

He would, no doubt, have made a great poker player. In his time, Britain was not a first-rank military power, but her assets included an invincible navy and the strongest economy in the world. On this basis, Palmerston almost invariably played an aggressive hand – not least in his dealings with non-European powers. He was an arch exponent of gunboat diplomacy, provoking the first Opium War with China, in 1835. When Chinese officials seized and destroyed opium belonging to British merchants, which they were endeavouring to smuggle into China, he made extravagant demands for compensation, which the Chinese refused to meet. Palmerston promptly dispatched a fleet which bombarded Canton and occupied the island of Hong Kong, which was ceded to Britain, under the Treaty of Nanking, in 1842, negotiated by Melbourne and Palmerston's Tory successors, after they had left office the previous year. The Tories were also left to clear up the mess of the first Afghan War, which began in 1838, when Palmerston – in a pre-emptive strike – sent a British army to Kabul to dethrone the pro-Russian Emir and replace him with a British puppet. Despite initial success, the expedition proved a total disaster, only a tiny handful of survivors of the 4,500 troops (and their 12,000 camp followers) making it back to India when the retreat was ordered in January 1842.

The widespread fear that Palmerston might provoke war with the United States – a much more formidable potential opponent – was almost certainly greatly exaggerated, but there was no doubt that relations between the two countries became extremely bad towards the end of the 11 years of his first period as Foreign Secretary. The still unresolved border disputes continued to fester, and when the United States arrested, and put on trial for murder, a drunken Canadian, who falsely claimed to have participated in a raid on US territory in which an American citizen had been killed, he instructed the British minister in Washington to warn the US government that his execution: 'would produce war, war immediate and frightful in its character, because it would be a war of retaliation and vengeance' (Chambers, p. 199).

Fortunately, the man was acquitted, and was whisked back to Canada before a lynch mob could get at him. But by now a new, and more serious, dispute had arisen, as a result of Palmerston's laudable attempt to suppress the slave trade. Following the abolition of slavery in British territories in 1834, Palmerston had energetically pursued a policy of using the British navy to prevent other nations from trading in slaves and had negotiated treaties with several other maritime states permitting the British navy to stop and search vessels flying their flags to ensure that there were no slaves on board. No such treaty had, however, been signed with the United States, and slave traders from other countries were escaping detection by the unauthorized use of the American flag. In his usual forceful way, Palmerston demanded that the US government should agree to a 'right of visit' by British naval captains to boats carrying their flag, and when the US authorities temporized, he sent an impatient note to the American minister in London saying that it was unacceptable 'that a merchantman can exempt himself from search by merely hoisting a piece of bunting with the United States' emblems and colours upon it'. To refer to 'Old Glory' as a 'piece of bunting' caused great offence in Washington, but on the very day that Palmerston sent the note, Melbourne's government resigned, and Palmerston was out of office. His Tory successor, Lord Aberdeen, hastened to patch up the quarrel, and went on to negotiate a treaty settling the border between Canada and the state of Maine (see Chapter 27). Palmerston was furious, and attacked the treaty in the Commons, regretting that the conduct of foreign policy was left to a 'flock of geese'. His words were coolly received on both sides of the House, and several leading Whigs resolved that he should never again hold the post of Foreign Secretary.

This resolve was put to the test in December 1845, when Sir Robert Peel's government resigned, as he was unable to convince his colleagues to repeal the Corn Laws. The Whig leader, Lord John Russell, was invited to form a government, but the 3rd Earl Grey (son of the former Prime Minister), and several other potential cabinet ministers, refused to serve unless Palmerston was switched to a different portfolio. Palmerston adamantly refused any other post, and in the circumstances Russell was unwilling to risk forming a minority government, and Queen Victoria then invited Peel to resume office (see Chapter 24). Six months later, however, when Peel's government was defeated, and Russell was again invited to become Prime Minister, Grey and his colleagues meekly accepted the posts which they were offered, even though Palmerston again became Foreign Secretary, holding the position for a further five-and-a-half years.

In 1848, the 'year of revolutions', Palmerston actively encouraged liberal forces in Italy, Germany, Poland and Hungary, but refused to lift a finger to help them when they were crushed by Austrian and Russian military intervention. In France, he welcomed the February revolution, and the subsequent election of Louis Napoleon Bonaparte, an anglophile, as President, and in Switzerland he succeeded in discouraging Austrian intervention on the Catholic side in the brief civil war, which started in November 1847. Whether Palmerston, if left with a free hand, would have done any more to help the beleaguered revolutionaries, is doubtful, but he was, in any event, constrained by his cabinet colleagues, and by the royal couple, who sought constantly to clip his wings. Queen Victoria had first formed a low opinion of Palmerston some years earlier – in 1839 – when he was a house guest at Windsor Castle and at dead of night had crept into the bedroom of one of the Ladies in Waiting, Mrs Brand. Fearing rape, she had raised the alarm, and Palmerston rapidly retreated. The more worldly-wise Prince Albert assumed that he had made an assignation with another lady, and had, in the ill-lit corridors of the Castle, blundered into the wrong room, but Victoria was deeply shocked, and it required all the tact of the Prime Minister, Lord Melbourne, to persuade her to cover up the incident. Both Victoria and Albert were abashed at the high-handed way in which Palmerston conducted the country's foreign policy, and sought to curb him by insisting that all his dispatches should be submitted to the Queen before they were sent. Palmerston reluctantly agreed, but in practice kept only spasmodically to his undertaking. The Prime Minister, Lord John Russell, made ineffectual attempts to persuade Palmerston to exchange his post for another senior position in the government (see Chapter 25), but he refused to consider the matter.

Palmerston's critics, both royal and political, were waiting for an occasion when he would over-reach himself, and that moment seemed to have arrived in 1850, with the Don Pacifico affair. A Portuguese Jew, born in Gibraltar, and thus a British subject, his house in Athens had been burnt down in an anti-Semitic riot, with police standing idly by. Don Pacifico, a businessman with a more than shady reputation, sued the Greek government for an excessive amount of compensation and appealed to the British government for support. Palmerston promptly ordered a naval squadron to blockade the Greek coast, until the government paid up, provoking strong protests from the French and Russian governments which, with Britain, were guarantors of Greek independence. Palmerston was formally condemned by the House of Lords for his impetuosity in risking war over a comparatively trivial amount of money owing to a man whose claims on British protection were negligible. When a confidence motion was put to the House of Commons, Palmerston was faced by a concerted attack from the finest speakers in the House – Peel, Gladstone, Disraeli and the leading Radical, Richard Cobden – and it seemed all was up for him. Rising to heights of oratory of which he had never previously shown himself capable, Palmerston spoke for four hours with hardly a note, and made a rumbustious defence of his actions, culminating in a much quoted peroration, asking the House to decide:

> whether, as the Roman, in days of old, held himself free from indignity when he could say *Civis Romanus sum*; so also a British subject, in whatever land he may be, shall feel confident that the watchful eye and the strong arm of England will protect him against injustice and wrong. (Hansard, 25 June 1850)

Large numbers of MPs, led by a phalanx of Radicals (but not by Cobden and John Bright), rose to applaud Palmerston with enthusiasm, and at the end of the debate, the Government had a comfortable majority of 46. Palmerston's speech was extensively reported in the press, and met with overwhelming approval from his readers. His brash patriotism struck a chord with the public at large, and henceforward he was by a wide margin the most popular politician in the country. Victoria and Albert, who had been unsuccessfully pressing Russell to dismiss his Foreign Secretary, were discomfited, but 18 months later got their way, in December 1851, when Palmerston rashly congratulated Louis Napoleon Bonaparte on his *coup d'Etat*, which destroyed the Second Republic and paved the way for his proclamation as Emperor. The government was officially neutral, and several other ministers, including Russell himself, approved of Louis Napoleon's action. But Palmerston had acted without authority from either the cabinet or the Queen, and Russell took the opportunity to rid himself of an over-mighty colleague, softening the blow by offering him the Lord-Lieutenancy of Ireland.

This, Palmerston politely declined, quietly preparing his revenge. This came only two months later, when he moved an amendment to the government's Militia Bill. Many Radicals joined with the Tories in defeating the government, by 13 votes, and Russell promptly resigned. Palmerston coolly wrote a letter to his brother, saying 'My dear William, I have had my tit-for-tat with John Russell, and I turned him out on Friday last' (Ridley, p. 401).

Palmerston was now in the anomalous position that – in a period in which no political party enjoyed a majority in the House of Commons – only his presence could ensure stability for any government that was formed, given his enormous popularity. Yet most leading politicians – and the royal couple – were determined that he should not again be Foreign Secretary. When the Earl of Derby was invited to become Prime Minister, following Russell's resignation, he tried long and hard to persuade Palmerston to join his minority Tory government as Chancellor of the Exchequer and leader of the House of Commons. Palmerston was tempted, but was not willing to break his ties with the Whigs, and declined. Derby had to make do with Disraeli instead, and his government did not last long, resigning when Disraeli's budget was rejected by the Commons in December 1852, less than ten months after taking office. It was replaced by a coalition of Whigs and Peelites, led by Lord Aberdeen, in which Palmerston was offered any post he chose...other than the Foreign Office. Now 68-years-old, he was persuaded to accept the Home Office, explaining in a letter to his brother that: 'I should, in any case, much prefer the Home Office to going back to the immense labour of the Foreign Office' (Chambers, p. 349).

At the Home Office, Palmerston again proved himself to be a hard worker, and a moderate social reformer, influenced by his son-in-law, the Tory factory reformer, Lord Shaftesbury, who had married Lady Minnie Cowper, Emily's daughter by Palmerston. Yet one reform to which Palmerston was adamantly opposed was any extension of the electoral franchise, and Palmerston submitted his resignation, when Lord John Russell proposed to introduce a Reform Bill. Within a week, he was persuaded to withdraw the resignation, and Russell watered down the Bill, which was later withdrawn after the outbreak of the Crimean War.

The origins of this war are described in Chapter 27. Palmerston, who felt no inhibition whatever about intervening in foreign affairs, insisted from the outset that a robust attitude should be taken to the Russian demands on Turkey, and argued forcefully that a British and French fleet should be sent to the Black Sea as a deterrent. His colleagues did not, at first, agree, but his angry interventions undermined Aberdeen's patient attempts to find a peaceful settlement, and when the Russians sank a Turkish fleet at Sinope, in November 1853, Palmerston persuaded the cabinet, against Aberdeen's wishes, to adopt a more aggressive stance. This inevitably led to war with Russia, which was declared by both France and Britain in March 1854. Palmerston now effectively took over the direction of the war, urging an attack on the Russian naval base at Sebastopol, simultaneously with a naval blockade in the Baltic, leading to the seizure and destruction of a Russian base in the Aaland Islands. His initial war aims were boundless, including the liberation of both Finland and Poland from Russian control, but he eventually restricted them to neutralizing her influence in the Black Sea area and propping up the Ottoman Empire, which he improbably argued was now 'a more enlightened and reformed country than Russia' (Chamberlain, 1998, p. 181).

Palmerston was not directly to blame for the disastrous conduct of the war in its initial stages, and when Aberdeen was forced to resign, in January 1855, after losing a confidence vote in the Commons, Queen Victoria was forced by the overwhelming pressure of public opinion to appoint her *bête noire* as his successor, after both Derby and Russell had failed to form an administration. Palmerston had great difficulty in forming a cabinet, as all the leading Peelites refused to serve, out of loyalty to Aberdeen. The Queen herself then pleaded with Aberdeen to talk them round, to which the pliable ex-Premier agreed. So Palmerston took over the previous government with minimal changes, excluding only Aberdeen and the War Secretary, Lord Newcastle, though within a few months Gladstone and two other Peelites resigned and were replaced by Whigs. Palmerston initially intended to include his Tory son-in-law, Lord Shaftesbury, in the government, but changed his mind, and when he later renewed the offer, the ever hesitant Christian evangelist made such a meal out of his struggle with his conscience over whether to accept that the post was eventually given to someone else. Lord John Russell was at first excluded, and sent instead as a delegate to an abortive peace conference convened by Austria, but later became Colonial Secretary, only to resign in a huff five months later.

Palmerston's great popularity owed much to his consistent wooing of the press, which gave him the affectionate nickname of 'Pam'. He thought nothing of leaking sensitive information to sympathetic newspapers, and often wrote anonymous articles himself which they were delighted to print. Several newspapers were effectively in his pocket, including the *Morning Post, The Globe, the Morning Advertiser, The Daily News* and the newly launched *Daily Telegraph*. Only *The Times* remained impervious to his appeal, and, under its formidable editor, John Delane, was a fierce critic for many years. Palmerston owed much to his marriage. The still beautiful Lady Palmerston inherited a large fortune from her brother, Lord Melbourne, in 1848, which – together with some shrewd investments which Palmerston had made – enabled them to move from their relatively modest home in Carlton Gardens to the magnificent no. 94 Piccadilly, formerly owned by the Queen's uncle, the Duke of Cambridge. Here Lady Palmerston held receptions every Saturday during the parliamentary sessions, to which the flower of London's social and political life flocked. Lady P introduced a significant innovation, which no other hostess had ever attempted. Her receptions were thrown open also to 'the gentlemen of the press' to the horror of the bulk of high society, but not wishing to be left out, the great majority held their noses and continued to come. Among the grateful journalists who received invitations was John Delane, who, greatly flattered, and impressed by Palmerston's jingoistic appeal during the War, finally succumbed, and added his newspaper to the new Prime Minister's circle of friends.

Palmerston assumed office on 6 February 55. At 71, he was the oldest person to become Prime Minister for the first time. Despite this, he was able to inject a new energy into the prosecution of the war. His insistence led to a great improvement in the provision of logistical support for the troops, and he strongly backed the efforts of Florence Nightingale (a near neighbour to his Broadlands estate) to improve the rudimentary medical services. Yet it was Britain's French allies that brought the war to a successful conclusion, when they stormed the Malakoff fortress in September 1855, and the Russians abandoned the city of Sebastopol, after setting fire to it. Palmerston was eager to continue the War, but the French – having secured their moment of glory – had had enough. The new Russian Tsar, Alexander II, who had succeeded to the throne after his father, Nicholas I, had caught a fatal chill while inspecting his troops in the rain, was more than ready to settle.

A peace treaty was signed in Paris, in March 1856. The terms were far worse than Palmerston had hoped, but he presented them as a great triumph to a grateful Queen and Parliament, and was rewarded with the Order of the Garter, whose sash he proudly wore at his wife's weekly receptions. Britain did not remain long at peace, due to Palmerston's customary aggressive response to provocations from weaker states, and the second Opium War was successfully waged against China in 1856, while an army of 7,000 men was sent into Afghanistan to defeat a Persian force which had occupied the province of Herat. Palmerston was defeated in a parliamentary vote over his China policy in 1857, but promptly called a general election, which was effectively a referendum on his conduct of affairs. It was a major success, the Whigs and their allies making a net gain of 50 seats.

Yet an improved position in Parliament did not yet constitute a stable majority, and Palmerston fell to an ambush in the following year. An assassination attempt on Napoleon III by Italian nationalists, who formulated their plot and acquired their weapons in London, led to a demand from the French to tighten British laws against international conspirators. Palmerston considered the request reasonable, and promptly introduced the Conspiracy to Murder Bill, which made it a felony, instead of a misdemeanour, to plot in England to kill somebody abroad. He was taken aback when he was fiercely attacked by his Radical allies for surrendering to French pressure. Disraeli, prompted by Lord Derby, sensed an opportunity to defeat the government, and when a division was called on a hostile amendment, took his followers into the division lobby along with the Radicals, and the amendment was carried by 234 votes to 219. Palmerston was completely wrong-footed, and was too proud, or too misadvised, to resort to the expedient of calling a vote of confidence, which he would most probably have won. Instead, he promptly resigned, and Lord Derby, for the second time, took office at the head of a minority Tory government.

Derby did not survive for long, despite calling a general election, in which the Tories gained 26 seats – not enough to give them a majority. Disraeli's budget was duly defeated, and Derby resigned after 15 months in office. In the meantime, the Whigs, Radicals and assorted allies had come together to form the Liberal Party, and Palmerston and Russell had made up their lengthy quarrel, each agreeing to serve under the other if invited by the Queen to do so. Victoria was not anxious to choose either of 'these terrible old men', and instead approached Lord Granville, the Liberal leader in the Lords. When he failed to form a government, she gritted her teeth and invited Palmerston back to office. So, now aged nearly 76, he returned to power with a more cohesive government than he had had before, with Russell at the Foreign Office and Gladstone at the Exchequer.

During his second term, which lasted for more than six years, the emphasis of his government was almost entirely on foreign affairs, the amount of legislation passed being minimal. Palmerston imposed an absolute block against any measure of parliamentary reform, and other reform measures were distinctly thin on the ground. Indeed, almost the only significant measure passed in either of his premierships was the Matrimonial Causes Act of 1857, which abolished the jurisdiction of ecclesiastical courts and established secular divorce courts in their place. (Six years later, it caused a sensation when Palmerston himself, then aged 79, was cited as a co-respondent in a divorce case, and his popularity undoubtedly increased in many quarters, while Lady Palmerston was vastly amused. When the case came to court, however, it was an anti-climax. The petition was dismissed on the grounds that the plaintiff, a journalist called O'Kane, was unable to establish that he was legally married to his wife, and it transpired that he had tried to blackmail Palmerston for £20,000 not to bring the action. The lady concerned then acknowledged that she had never slept with the Prime Minister).

Apart from yet another war against China, in which an Anglo-French force captured Peking and burned down the Emperor's summer palace, the main issues of contention concerned the struggle for Italian unification, the US Civil War and the Schleswig-Holstein dispute. Palmerston and Russell worked closely on each of these, and had remarkably few disagreements. The balance of their successes and failures was, at best, a narrow one. Over Italy, Palmerston was broadly supportive of the Nationalists. As he himself put it, the problem was essentially one of getting the Austrians out, without letting the French in.

In this aim, he was only very partially successful. Austria was driven out of Lombardy in the bloody war which it fought against Sardinia and France in 1859–60, but was left in control of Venetia, as Napoleon III, sickened by the appalling bloodshed at the Battle of Solferino, negotiated an armistice, to the disgust of the Sardinians, before the job was fully done. The French, nevertheless, acquired Savoy and Nice, and ended up with a garrison in control of Rome, protecting the Pope's diminished domains. It was left to the Prussians to complete the work of unification, after Palmerston's death, by their defeats of Austria, in 1866, and of France, in 1870.

In the US Civil War, Palmerston – like most of the British ruling class – was sympathetic to the Confederates, and two disputes with the Federal side involving naval actions might well have led to hostilities. The first involved the stopping by a US warship of the British vessel *Trent*, which was carrying two Confederate diplomatic representatives on their way to France and Britain, and their forcible removal. They were subsequently released by the US government, but only after the British threatened war. The second incident involved the *Alabama*, a privateer secretly built in Britain for the Confederates, which was allowed to leave Liverpool by the port authorities, and later sank or captured no fewer than 93 Federal ships, mostly merchantmen. Palmerston and Russell haughtily rejected American claims for compensation, but eventually they were referred to arbitration, and Britain finished up by paying $15.5million in gold, long after Palmerston's death.

The Schleswig-Holstein affair was singularly complicated – Palmerston himself famously said that there were only three people who had ever understood it – the Prince Consort, who was dead, a Danish politician who was in an asylum, and himself, who had forgotten about it. Yet there was no mystery about the outcome – it was the most staggering humiliation that he ever suffered. The two duchies had been governed by Kings of Denmark, as their Duke, since the Middle Ages, though the majority of their inhabitants were German. When the Danish King, Frederick VII, died in 1863, his successor, Christian IX, was descended through the female line, and was thus ineligible to rule over the duchies, which came under the Salic Law. Under this law, the rightful heir to the dukedoms was the Duke of Augustenburg, and his claims were backed by the two leading Germanic states, Prussia and Austria. Christian, however, refused to accept this, and took steps to incorporate the territory into his kingdom. When Austria and Prussia threatened war, Palmerston declared in the House of Commons that if it came Denmark would not fight alone, which gave the Danes the confidence to reject the Prusso-Austrian ultimatum. The Prussian Chancellor, Otto von Bismarck, promptly called Palmerston's bluff, and Prussian and Austrian troops crossed the frontier. Apart from Queen Victoria, who was – as ever – strongly pro-German, British opinion was predominantly on the Danish side, and pro-Danish feeling was strengthened by the arrival in London of the popular Danish Princess Alexandra to marry the Prince of Wales. Yet, Palmerston knew that he had been outsmarted by Bismarck, and

> That there was nothing that he could do to help Denmark. For four hundred years, Britain had not fought a war in Europe except as the ally of a major European power; and there was now no such ally available to help her in a war against Austria and Prussia. (Ridley, p. 527)

A formal appeal from Denmark for help received no answer, and in two short campaigns the Danish resistance was overwhelmed, Austria annexing Holstein and Prussia, Schleswig. (Two years later the victors fell out over the spoils, and Prussia claimed both duchies after defeating Austria at the battle of Sadowa). Palmerston was now extremely vulnerable, and was censured in a House of Lords debate. The Commons looked like following suit, General Peel, the brother of the former Prime Minster, saying: 'Is it come to this, that the words of the Prime Minister of England, uttered in the Parliament of England, are to be regarded as mere menaces to be laughed at and despised by foreign powers?' (*Hansard*, 8 July 1864).

Palmerston's back was to the wall, but he was not too proud to call in favours, and scrambled for votes in all corners of the House, where he could hope to find them. Finally, it was the pacifist section of the Radicals, led by Richard Cobden, which came to his rescue, and he saw off the Opposition censure motion by 313 votes to 295. He was looking his age now, pushing 80, and his health was beginning to fail, but he had not lost his appeal to the voters. He called a general election in July 1865, and the Liberals were triumphantly returned with an increased majority. He did not, however, live long enough to meet the new Parliament, when it was summoned in October 1865. He caught a chill while out driving earlier in the month, and died on 18 October, two days short of his eighty-first birthday. The legend that his last words were 'Die, my dear Doctor, that's the last thing I'll do' is unfortunately not true.

Palmerston was a controversial figure in his day, and has remained so ever since. He was the object both of extravagant praise and of intense denigration. Often described as a Liberal abroad and a Tory at home, he was also categorized as a bully to the weak and a coward to the strong, reflecting the many occasions in which he had reacted in a violent way to petty provocations from smaller states, while backing off when confronted by one or more of the great powers. The only occasion when he was prepared to go to war with one of these was in the Crimea, where he was assured of the support of France and, at least, the benevolent neutrality of Austria, while the Russians were without any potential allies. As a diplomat, he had shown great resource and subtlety during his earlier periods as Foreign Secretary, but as he grew older, and his self-confidence and public support grew, he began to lose his touch, and emerged all too often as a loud-mouthed braggart. For many years he was seen in the chancelleries of the three great absolutist powers of Russia, Austria and Prussia as a dangerous demagogue and revolutionary. Yet his support for the nationalist movements which they oppressed, in Germany, Italy, Poland and Hungary, was confined to gestures, and he extended no practical help to the revolutions of 1848, or the successive uprisings of the Poles against their Russian masters. Nor, though he had welcomed the French revolutions of both 1830 and 1848, did he oppose the actions of Louis Napoleon Bonaparte, when he overthrew the democratic republic which had been established, by his *coup d'Etat* in 1851. Indeed, he went so far as to congratulate him, which led to his own removal as Foreign Secretary.

The one common thread which linked every action of Palmerston, both as Foreign Secretary and as Prime Minister, was his extreme patriotism. He regarded England as the best country in the world, and the best governed, and always put the interests of England, as he perceived them, first. Gladstone, a powerful critic of Palmerston in his day, in his own old age, summed up his basic attitude in an anecdote, which is recorded in most of the many biographies which have appeared. 'A Frenchman', he recalled in a letter to a friend: 'thinking to be highly complimentary, said to Palmerston: "If I were not a Frenchman, I should wish to be an Englishman"; to which Pam coolly replied: "If I were not an Englishman, I should wish to be an Englishman"'.

Works consulted

Muriel Chamberlain, 1998, 'Lord Palmerston' in Robert Eccleshall and Graham Walker, (eds.), *Biographical Dictionary of British Prime Ministers*, London, Routledge.
Muriel Chamberlain, 1987, *Lord Palmerston*, Cardiff, University of Wales Press.
James Chambers, 2004, *Palmerston: The People's Darling*, London, John Murray.
Jasper Ridley, 1970, *Lord Palmerston*, London, Constable.
Donald Southgate, 1966, *The Most English Minister... The Policies and Politics of Palmerston*, London, Macmillan.
David Steele, 2004, Article in *Oxford Dictionary of National Biography*.
A.J.P. Taylor, 2000, 'Lord Palmerston' in *British Prime Ministers and other essays*, London, Penguin Books.

1 Sir Robert Walpole, by John Faber Jr., after Sir Godfrey Kneller © National Portrait Gallery, London

2 Spencer Compton, Earl of Wilmington, by Peter Pelham, after Sir G. Kneller © National Portrait Gallery, London

3 Henry Pelham, by William Hoare © National Portrait Gallery, London

4 Thomas Pelham-Holles, Duke of Newcastle, by Peter Pelham, after Sir G. Kneller © National Portrait Gallery, London

5 William Cavendish, 4th Duke of Devonshire, by Thomas Hudson © Government Art Collection

6 3rd Earl of Bute, by Sir Joshua Reynolds © National Portrait Gallery, London

7 George Grenville, by Richard Houston, after William Hoare © National Portrait Gallery, London

8 2nd Marquess of Rockingham, after Sir Joshua Reynolds © National Portrait Gallery, London

9 William Pitt, 1st Earl of Chatham, by Jonathan Spilsbury, after William Hoare © National Portrait Gallery, London

10 3rd Duke of Grafton, by James Watson, after Pompeo Batoni © National Portrait Gallery, London

11 Frederick North, 2nd Earl of Guilford, by Nathanial Dance © National Portrait Gallery, London

12 William Petty, 1st Marquess of Lansdowne (Lord Shelburne), by S.W. Reynolds, after Sir J. Reynolds © National Portrait Gallery, London

13 3rd Duke of Portland, by S.W. Reynolds, after Sir J. Reynolds © National Portrait Gallery, London

14 William Pitt, The Younger, by studio of John Hoppner © Tate [2013] on loan to the National Portrait Gallery

15 Henry Addington, by Sir William Beechey © National Portrait Gallery, London

16 William Grenville, by John Hoppner © National Portrait Gallery, London

17 Spencer Perceval, by George Francis Joseph © National Portrait Gallery, London

19 George Canning, by Sir Thomas Lawrence © National Portrait Gallery, London

18 2nd Earl of Liverpool, by Sir Thomas Lawrence © National Portrait Gallery, London

20 Frederick John Robinson, Viscount Goderich, by Charles Turner, after Lawrence © National Portrait Gallery, London

21 1st Duke of Wellington, by Thomas Goff Lupton © National Portrait Gallery, London

22 2nd Earl Grey, by Samuel Cousins, after Lawrence © National Portrait Gallery, London

23 2nd Viscount Melbourne, by Sir Edwin Henry Landseer © National Portrait Gallery, London

24 Sir Robert Peel, by George Baxter, after Lawrence © National Portrait Gallery, London

25 John Russell, 1st Earl Russell, by Sir Francis Grant © National Portrait Gallery, London

26 14th Earl of Derby, by William Walker & Sons © National Portrait Gallery, London

27 4th Earl of Aberdeen, by John Partridge © National Portrait Gallery, London

28 3rd Viscount Palmerton, by Francis Cruikshank © National Portrait Gallery, London

29 Benjamin Disraeli, by Sir John Everett Millais © National Portrait Gallery, London

30 William Ewart Gladstone, by Sir John Everett Millais © National Portrait Gallery, London

31 3rd Marquess of Salisbury, by Sir John Everett Millais © National Portrait Gallery, London

32 5th Earl of Rosebery, by Elliott & Fry © National Portrait Gallery, London

33 Arthur James Balfour, by Henry Walter Barnett © National Portrait Gallery, London

34 Sir Henry Campbell-Bannerman, by George Charles Beresford © National Portrait Gallery, London

35 Herbert Henry Asquith, by George Charles Beresford © National Portrait Gallery, London

36 David Lloyd George, by Sir William Orpen © National Portrait Gallery, London

THE RIGHT HON. A. BONAR LAW, P.C., M.P.

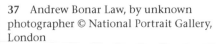

37 Andrew Bonar Law, by unknown photographer © National Portrait Gallery, London

38 Stanley Baldwin, by Bassano © National Portrait Gallery, London

39 James Ramsay MacDonald, by Bassano © National Portrait Gallery, London

40   Neville Chamberlain, by Bassano
© National Portrait Gallery, London

41   Winston Churchill © David Cole/
Alamy

42   Clement Richard Attlee, by Howard
Coster © National Portrait Gallery, London

43 Anthony Eden, by Walter Stoneman © National Portrait Gallery, London

44 Harold Macmillan, by unknown photographer © National Portrait Gallery, London

45 Alexander Frederick Douglas-Home, by Rex Coleman © National Portrait Gallery, London

46   Harold Wilson © David Cole/Alamy

47   Edward Heath, by Rex Coleman
© National Portrait Gallery, London

48   James Callaghan, by Bernard Lee
Schwartz © National Portrait Gallery,
London

49 Margaret Thatcher © David Levenson/Alamy

50 John Major © David Gordon/Alamy

51 Tony Blair © Alan Wylie/Alamy

52 Gordon Brown © James Davies/Alamy

53 David Cameron
© Allstar Picture Library/
Alamy

29
Benjamin Disraeli, Earl of Beaconsfield – Climbing 'the Greasy Pole'

The two best known Prime Ministers of the nineteenth century were probably Benjamin Disraeli and William Gladstone. They were notable opponents, and very dissimilar characters, but they had one thing in common – both of them switched their party affiliation. Gladstone started off as a Tory, but went on to become the most distinguished of Liberal Prime Ministers. Disraeli launched his political career as an 'Independent Radical', but it was as a Conservative that he achieved fame and fortune, and he is still revered today as one of the party's most formative influences.

Very little in his background and early life would have pointed to such a destiny. Disraeli (or Dizzy, as he became universally known) was without a doubt the most improbable character ever to have become Prime Minister. Indeed, when one considers the various obstacles which he had to overcome – some due to the accident of birth, but mostly erected by his own youthful folly – it seems a miracle that he ever managed to climb to the top of 'the greasy pole', as he himself described it. Benjamin Disraeli was born in London on 21 December 1804, the second child and eldest son of Isaac D'Israeli and his wife, Maria Basevi. Isaac was a scholar and dilettante, who, as a result of receiving a legacy while still a young man, had sufficient means to spurn a business career and devote himself to the literary life, spending much of his time in the British Museum Reading Room, and consorting with writers, artists and publishers. His speciality was collecting literary gossip and anecdotes, and his most successful work, *Curiosities of Literature*, first published in 1791 and going through 12 editions, was much admired by Lord Byron, Sir Walter Scott and the publisher, John Murray, all of whom became his friends. The young Benjamin loved and admired his father, but nursed a lasting grievance against his mother, whom he felt withheld the affection from him which she lavished on his younger brothers. He greatly embroidered his father's lineage in later accounts, maintaining that he came from an aristocratic line of Sephardic Jews, who left Spain in 1492 and established themselves in Venice for several centuries, before Isaac's father emigrated to England in 1748. Actually the family, originally known as Israeli, almost certainly came from the Levant, and went not to Venice but to Cento, a minor town in the Papal States. Ironically, his mother (unknown to Benjamin, but established by modern scholarship) had comparable antecedents to those which he attributed to his father. She was a direct descendant of Isaac Aboab, the leader of the Jewish community in Castille, who in 1492 led 20,000 followers into exile in Portugal (Blake, p. 7). Her family had lived in England since the seventeenth century.

Isaac D'Israeli was a member (but an inactive one) of the Bevis Marks Sephardic synagogue in London, and was disconcerted when he was elected a Warden of the synagogue. When he refused to serve, he was fined £40, which he refused to pay. He later resigned from the congregation, and – though not converting himself – had his three sons and his daughter baptized into the Church of England. Benjamin was 12 at the time, and his father's action had a crucial effect on his later career. Jews were not eligible to sit in the House of Commons, and this disability was not removed until 1858. It is scarcely conceivable that Disraeli would ever have become Prime Minister if he had had to wait until late middle age before entering Parliament. As it was, he undoubtedly suffered from anti-Semitic prejudices at various stages in his life, and he remains the only person of Jewish descent to become prime minister.

Benjamin was deeply interested in, and immensely proud of, his Jewish heritage, which he had a strong impulse to glamourize. Despite the evident affluence of his father, which enabled him to grow up in a spacious and comfortable home, with a fair number of servants at his beck and call, Benjamin's education was badly neglected. Not only was he – apart from Wellington – the only nineteenth century Premier not to have gone to a university, but the only one not educated at a 'public' school. Instead, he was sent to a 'dame school' in Islington, and then to two little known private schools run by clergymen, in Blackheath and Walthamstow. This, despite the fact that his two obviously less intelligent younger brothers were both enrolled at Winchester. At the age of 15, Benjamin left school and spent the next couple of years luxuriating in his father's well-stocked library, reading widely, but in an undisciplined fashion, and acquiring a good stock of Latin tags, with which, as was the custom of the day, he later embellished his parliamentary speeches, but he had no solid knowledge of the classics. Some idea of Disraeli's schoolboy experiences may be gained from his two thinly-disguised autobiographical novels, *Vivien Grey* and *Contrarini Fleming*. From these it appears that he felt a profound sense of difference between himself and his fellow pupils, whom he felt to be both less intelligent and less sensitive than himself. As Robert Blake commented: 'It is certain that throughout his adult life he was conscious of dwelling apart from other men and it is probable that this awareness first came upon him when he was a schoolboy...To the end of his days he remained an alien figure' (Blake, p. 17).

Part of the difference was no doubt due to his physical appearance; he did not look a typical Anglo-Saxon, as most of his schoolfellows probably did. Benjamin may not have gone to a 'public' school, but he did not miss out on at least some of the experiences usually associated with them. He appears to have fallen deeply in love with one of his fellow pupils at Walthamstow, though whether the relationship was physically consummated is not clear. Disraeli certainly had feminine traits in his character, and may perhaps have been bi-sexual. One of Disraeli's biographers refers to 'the latent homosexual element in Disraeli's friendships with younger men' and refers specifically to Lord Henry Lennox, an amusing but essential frivolous younger son of a duke who was unsuccessful both as a politician and as the would-be husband of an heiress, once lamenting to Disraeli that 'It is always the same thing; either the lady has too little money or I am too old'. Disraeli for long appeared to be besotted with Lennox, whom he habitually addressed as 'beloved' in his many letters, and once wrote 'I can only say I love you'. Even so, Sarah Bradford concludes that 'the relationship was almost certainly not physical' (Bradford, pp. 215–219).

Benjamin was allowed to sit in at his father's regular dinner parties, and he impressed the guests with his intelligence, precocity and gift for repartee, though not all of them accepted his self-evaluation as a genius. John Murray, in particular, took Benjamin very seriously, and began to send him manuscripts which he was considering for publication for his opinion, which elicited sharp, witty and pertinent comments. When he was 17, Isaac suggested that he should go to Oxford, but Benjamin demurred, and he was instead articled to the solicitors' firm of Swain, Stevens, Maples, Pearce and Hunt. One of the partners, Maples, was a close friend of Isaac's, and it seems to have been agreed between the two families that Benjamin and his daughter should eventually be married. Nothing came of this arrangement, and – though he appeared to give satisfaction to his employers, and made many useful contacts through his work – Benjamin's desire to become a solicitor soon waned. It was generally agreed that he should aspire to higher things, and in November 1824, not quite 20, he was admitted to Lincoln's Inn to read for the bar. Even then, Disraeli – who had by now dropped the apostrophe from his name – did not give the impression of having his heart set on the law. He had already sent Murray the draft of a novel which he had written, but when he received no early response, concluded that Murray was too embarrassed to tell him that it was no good, and so sent him a message to burn it. Now he set out self-consciously to present himself as a Bohemian, dressing in a very dandyish style, modelling himself on Byron, while attempting to build a quick fortune by gambling on the stock exchange, with money he didn't have. He drew friends, including Murray, into his speculations, particularly in South American mining shares, and though their value soared precipitately, they later collapsed, and all of them were out of pocket. Despite this, Murray responded enthusiastically to a proposal from his 20-year-old friend to launch a new newspaper, as a rival to *The Times*, for which Murray agreed to put up 50 per cent of the capital, the remainder to be supplied equally by Disraeli and a merchant called Powles. Disraeli promptly left for Scotland, with a laudatory letter of recommendation from Murray, to seek support from Sir Walter Scott, and – if possible – to recruit his son-in-law as editor of the new paper which, on Disraeli's suggestion, was entitled *The Representative*. Disraeli made extravagant – and quite unrealistic – promises to them, and to many others whom he sought to associate with the paper. It was launched two months behind schedule, in January 1825, was a total failure from the start, and crashed the following June, leaving Murray £26,000 the poorer, Powles on his way to bankruptcy and Disraeli with debts, which he had still not fully discharged a quarter of a century later. Desperate to make some money – *any* money – Disraeli now embarked on writing – at double-quick speed – a *roman-à-clef*, in which he mercilessly satirized his leading collaborators in the affair, including the long-suffering Murray. The novel, entitled *Vivien Grey*, appeared anonymously, but with the false suggestion that its author was a leading figure in high society. It was, initially, a *succès de scandale*, but when its true authorship emerged, it attracted universally hostile reviews, and the lasting enmity of Murray and of many others, who felt they had been duped by Disraeli. He made £750 from the book, but the whole episode had done him enormous damage, as Blake recounts: 'He acquired a reputation for cynicism, double-dealing, recklessness and insincerity which it took him years to live down' (Blake, p. 48).

   Disraeli responded by having a nervous breakdown, from which he partially recovered through making a short 'grand tour', on borrowed money, to France, Switzerland and Italy. He was still feeling low, however, on his return, and Isaac D'Israeli thought a spell of country air would do him good, and moved the whole family to a beautiful Queen Anne house at Bradenham, near High Wycombe. Here Benjamin remained for some time, making only occasional furtive trips to London, fearful of running into creditors who would dun him for his debts. He continued his legal studies, but only fitfully, and soon embarked on another novel – one of his slightest – *The Young Duke*, which was moderately well received, and earned him £500. He then embarked, together with his sister Sarah's fiancé, William Meredith, on a far more ambitious foreign journey, which took him to Spain, Malta, Albania, Turkey, Palestine and Egypt. Altogether, he was away for 16 months, and it would have been longer if it had not been for the tragic death of Meredith, in Egypt, which prompted him to return home to comfort his sister, who henceforth devoted her life almost exclusively to her brother's interests. For Disraeli, this encounter with 'the gorgeous east' fired his imagination, reawakened all his fanciful dreams about the exotic origins of his family and installed a lasting prejudice in favour of the Turks and against the Greeks, which was to be reflected in his later policies as Prime Minister. He lapped up the luxury and the indolence of the Turkish court, writing home:

> To repose on voluptuous ottomans and smoke superb pipes, daily to indulge in the luxury of a bath which requires half a dozen attendants for its perfection; to court the air in a carved caique, by shores which are a perpetual scene; this is, I think, a far more sensible life than all the bustle of clubs, all the boring of drawing rooms, and all the coarse vulgarity of our political controversies...I mend slowly but I mend (Hibbert, 2005, p. 53)

His general health and sense of well being did indeed improve markedly during the journey, with one unfortunate exception. On his return, he had to undergo painful treatment for a venereal infection. He soon published two further novels, finally renounced the bar, and began to form political ambitions, beginning the slow process of trying to re-ingratiate himself with respectable society. He suffered the indignity of being blackballed by several London clubs, including the Athenaeum and the Travellers', but his friend and fellow novelist Edward Bulwer-Lytton invited him to several of his wife's receptions, where he enjoyed only partial success, repelling many by his exotic dress, especially his penchant for 'green pantaloons'.

By this time, Disraeli had convinced himself that the route to the great future to which he aspired lay through the House of Commons. He resolved to present himself as a candidate for High Wycombe, where his new family home, Bradenham House, was situated. His main problem was to decide in which political interest he should stand. He had formed a marked aversion to the Whigs, but otherwise had no settled political convictions. As the latest of his many biographers put it:

> Realising that it might prove fatal to attach himself to a falling star, he shied away from the Tories, whose influence was rapidly waning; and he made up his mind to present himself as a Radical. 'Toryism is worn out', he told [a friend], 'and I cannot condescend to be a Whig...I start in the high Radical interest'. (Hibbert, 2005, pp. 66–67)

Disraeli fought High Wycombe twice in 1832, once in a by-election, and the second time in the general election following the passage of the Reform Bill, which greatly enlarged the electorate. Each time he was defeated by Whig opponents, whom he confidently expected to beat, flattering himself – no doubt justifiably – with being a vastly better orator, and certainly possessing a great deal more chutzpah. He was to try again, in 1835, still as an 'Independent Radical', when he came no closer to winning. By now it had occurred to Disraeli that, if he was to prosper in politics, he needed to find a powerful political patron, and with this in mind, he began to penetrate the lower reaches of society, gradually moving up the scale as he received invitations to more and more grand houses. His progress was mixed; for every one who was charmed by his conversation and impressed by his vitality there were others who were appalled by his brashness and conceit. He made more impression on women than on men, and one of these was Lady Henrietta Sykes, a young married woman with three children and a complaisant husband. Disraeli began a passionate affair with her, later memorialised in his novel, *Henrietta Temple*. It was through her that he met Lord Lyndhurst, a veteran Tory politician, who was to be three times Lord Chancellor. Lyndhurst took him up, and was repaid when Disraeli readily agreed to share Henrietta's charms with him, and later passed her on to him when his own ardour began to cool. He now proclaimed himself as a Tory, for the first time, joining the Carlton Club, and fighting a by-election at Taunton, in April 1835, where he was soundly beaten by the Whig, Henry Labouchere. One person who reacted angrily to Disraeli's switch from Radical to Tory was the Irish nationalist Daniel O'Connell. He had written a letter of commendation to him when he had fought High Wycombe, and now read a newspaper report which alleged that Disraeli had branded him as 'an incendiary and traitor'. In fact, Dizzy was not giving this as his own opinion, but was citing an earlier accusation of the Whigs, who had now formed a parliamentary alliance with O'Connell. O'Connell reacted with extreme violence, describing Disraeli at a meeting in Dublin as 'a vile creature', 'a living lie', 'a miscreant' and 'a reptile'. He continued:

> His name shows that he is of Jewish origin. I do not use it as a term of reproach; there are many most respectable Jews. But there are as in every other people some of the lowest and most disgusting grade of moral turpitude; and of those I look upon Mr Disraeli as the worst. (Blake, p. 125)

Disraeli felt he had no alternative but to challenge O'Connell to a duel, but the Irishman had once killed an opponent and had vowed never to fight another. So Dizzy challenged his son, Morgan O'Connell, instead, and added the provocation of publishing an open letter to his father returning all his insults with interest. Morgan was not at all anxious to fight, but the police intervened and Disraeli was arrested and bound over to keep the peace. He seemed very pleased with himself, writing in his diary 'Row with O'Connell in which I greatly distinguished myself' (Blake, p. 126).

Disraeli went on to write his first political book, entitled *A Vindication of the English Constitution in a Letter to a Noble and Learned Lord* [Lord Lyndhurst], by 'Disraeli the Younger', an action which delighted his father, Isaac. He also wrote a series of articles, notable for the venom with which they attacked leading Whigs, under the pseudonym, *Runnymede*, which appeared in *The Morning*

Post. He continued these in *The Times*, and – while he unconvincingly denied authorship – his fame spread and also his approval rating with the Tories. He lived extravagantly, contemplating moving into Byron's former chambers in The Albany, but he was always only one step ahead of his creditors, his debts now exceeding £20,000 (perhaps £600,000 in today's money). He was in daily dread of being thrown into a debtors' prison, and once had to hide down a well when a sheriff's officer came to arrest him, and on another occasion bribed the officer to go away. He importuned many of his friends and acquaintances for help, with varying degrees of success, and more than once called on his father to bail him out, while concealing the full extent of his debts. Then, in 1837, King William IV died, precipitating a general election, and he received a large number of invitations to stand as a candidate for the Conservatives. From at least nine possibilities, he chose Maidstone, which turned out to be an inspired choice. The other Tory candidate was one of the retiring members, Wyndham Lewis, a wealthy landowner, who was entranced by Disraeli, and took him under his wing, paying the bulk of his election expenses. Mrs Wyndham Lewis was even more impressed, describing him in a letter to her brother as 'one of the greatest writers and finest orators of the day – aged about 30' (Hibbert, p. 106). He was actually 32. The result, in a two-member constituency, was:

Lewis (Con)	707
Disraeli (Con)	616
Thompson (Radical)	412

Disraeli lost no time in making his maiden speech, and was determined to take the House by storm. It did not work out like that, being described by the diarist Charles Greville in the following terms: 'Mr Disraeli made his first exhibition the other night, beginning with florid assurance, speedily degenerating into ludicrous absurdity, and being at last put down in inextinguishable shouts of laughter' (Hibbert, ed., 1981, p. 49).

Disraeli's first mistake was in the choice of subject matter. MPs normally chose non-controversial subjects for their first appearance, but Disraeli was determined to pursue his vendetta against O'Connell, who was the immediately preceding speaker. He launched into an elaborate assault on the electoral malpractices of the O'Connellites in the general election, accusing them of 'majestic mendicancy', and it was hardly surprising that he was soon the object of 'hisses, hoots, laughter and catcalls' from a claque of O'Connell's supporters. So extravagant was Disraeli's rhetoric and so bizarre his attire, that the bulk of the House soon joined in the merriment, and Disraeli could no longer make himself heard. He abruptly broke off his speech, with the defiant words: 'Though I sit down now, the time will come when you will hear me' (Blake, p. 149).

This has gone down as one of the most famous – if least successful – maiden speeches in history. It was not quite a total disaster: some good came from it in the shape of sage advice which was given to Disraeli by R.L. O'Sheil, a veteran Irish MP, who was not one of O'Connell's men. 'Now, get rid of your genius for a session', he said: 'Speak often, for you must not show yourself cowed, but speak shortly. Be very quiet, try to be dull ... and in a short time the House will sigh for the wit and eloquence which they know are in you' (Blake, p. 150).

Disraeli was sensible and humble enough to agree to follow O'Sheil's counsel. Within a month or two of this fiasco, however, an event occurred which had a profound effect on his future prospects – the unexpected death, in March 1838, of his fellow Member for Maidstone, Wyndham Lewis. Lewis left his widow, Mary Anne, a life interest in his London home, in Grosvenor Gate, and an income of £5,000–6,000 a year. A good-natured, but ill-educated woman, who was a notorious chatterbox, she was – at 45 – Disraeli's senior by 12 years, yet within four months he proposed to her. He was on record as having said that 'I may commit many follies in my life, but I shall never marry for "love"' (Hibbert, p. 79), and it was almost universally believed that his motive was pecuniary. He made no very strenuous effort to deny this, but it was also evident that he was genuinely fond of her, and may well also have been looking for a mother-substitute. Mary Anne insisted on waiting a year until after her husband's death before giving him an answer, but they were duly married at St. George's, Hanover Square, on 28 August 1839. Against expectations, it turned out to be a successful marriage; they became a devoted couple, and Disraeli was devastated when she died nine years before him. This, however, had not prevented him from embarking on a number of extra-marital affairs, and he appeared to have fathered two illegitimate children during the 1860s (Weintraub, pp. 419–36). As for her money, it turned out not to be enough to settle all of Dizzy's debts, though Blake estimates that, altogether, she shelled out some £13,000 to his creditors (Blake, p. 161). This, at least, considerably eased the pressure on him, while as an MP he was now safe from arrest for debt.

In the 1841 general election, Disraeli switched his constituency, and was elected for Shrewsbury. The election was a triumph for Sir Robert Peel's Conservatives, and when Lord Melbourne subsequently resigned, he became Prime Minister. Disraeli wrote him an obsequious letter begging to be included in the new government, saying that to be left out would be 'an intolerable humiliation'. Unknown to him, Mary Anne had written an equally sycophantic letter on his behalf. Peel, who was besieged by similar importunities from many other MPs, wrote back civilly, saying he regretted that he was not in a position to: 'meet the wishes that are conveyed to me by men whose co-operation I should be proud to have, and whose qualifications and pretensions for office I do not contest'.

There is some slight evidence, however, that Peel would have been ready to include Disraeli, had it not been for the objections of his leading colleague, Lord Stanley (later the 14th Earl of Derby). Stanley had a long-standing quarrel with Disraeli, concerning a scrape in which his brother had been involved, and which he – probably unjustifiably – blamed on Dizzy. Stanley is cited as having declared that: 'If that scoundrel [were] taken in [he] would not remain [himself]' (Hibbert, p. 148).

Bitterly disappointed, Disraeli took himself and Mary Anne off to Paris, where (at least in his own account in a sheaf of letters to his sister), they were the stars of 'the season', being taken up by leading politicians such as Guizot and Thiers, writers such as de Tocqueville and Victor Hugo, Count Walewski (Napoleon's illegitimate son, and a future Foreign Minister), and not least by King Louis Philippe, who spent long hours with him, regaling him with stories of what he called his 'life of great vicissitude' (Hibbert, p. 155). It cannot be doubted that Disraeli responded with the diet of treacly flattery, which he later used with such effect on Queen Victoria.

Back home, he applied himself with energy to rebuilding his political career. Hitherto, he had been widely (and largely justifiably) seen as a brilliant, but unprincipled opportunist, with no abiding political philosophy. He now set out to formulate one, based on a deeply romantic view of the historic role of the aristocracy, which he came to see as the receptacle of all that was noble and generous in British society. He combined this with a total disdain for the money-grubbing middle class and sympathy for the poor and the workers. He discerned a community of interest between the landed and labouring classes, and – by extension – between the Tories and the Radicals, which justified his own peregrination between these two parties, which others saw as mutually contradictory. His elevated view of aristocrats was not just theoretical, but was based on actual models, in the shape of a small band of youthful MPs, all of whom had been educated together at Eton and Cambridge, known as Young England, which would – in modern terminology – be best described as a left-wing Tory pressure group. The three stalwarts of this group were Alexander Baillie-Cochrane (later Lord Lamington), MP for Bridport, the Hon. George Sydney Smythe, MP for Canterbury, and Lord John Manners, MP for Newark and son of the Duke of Rutland. All three were extremely attractive and congenial young men. Initially, they may have looked upon Disraeli as a *parvenu*, but they were deeply impressed by his gifts, and he was welcomed into the group, and soon recognized as its effective leader.

Disraeli now embarked on writing the trilogy of political and social novels – *Coningsby, Sybil (or The Two Nations),* and *Tancred* – which appeared between 1844 and 1847, and on which his reputation as a literary figure essentially rest. He attempted to weave his own political ideas into the novels, in which the

Young England trio and many other political figures appear in scarcely disguised forms. It was in *Sybil* that the famous passage occurs:

> 'Two nations between whom there is no intercourse and no sympathy; who are ignorant of each other's habits, thoughts, and feelings, as if they were dwellers in different zones or inhabitants of different planets; who are formed by a different breeding, are fed by different food, are ordered by different manners, and are not governed by the same laws'. 'You speak of-' said Egremont hesitatingly, 'THE RICH AND THE POOR'. (Penguin Books edition, 1954)

Disraeli was to say 'My works are my life' and that anyone wishing to know him would find him there. The first two volumes in particular, sold extremely well, and were highly popular. By this time, too, his parliamentary reputation had soared, and he was seen as one of – if not the very best – speakers in the House of Commons. He was at his most impressive in the debates on the repeal of the Corn Laws in 1846 (see Chapter 24). Although the Tory Party revolt against Sir Robert Peel's initiative had been led by Lord Stanley in the Lords, and Lord George Bentinck in the Commons, it was Disraeli who made much the most effective – and personally wounding – attacks on the Prime Minister. Without his passionate interventions, which provoked enormous enthusiasm among the serried ranks of country squires who made up the bulk of Conservative MPs, it is unlikely that a large majority of them could have been mobilized to vote against their hitherto greatly respected Prime Minister, or to turn him out of office, at the first opportunity after repeal had been carried, with the assistance of Whig, Radical and Irish votes.

Disraeli was never a hard-line supporter of protectionism as such: he based his opposition to Peel on the necessity of political parties not betraying their principles, and as most Conservative MPs had been elected on a platform of maintaining the Corn Laws, it would be dishonourable, he argued, for them now to support repeal. He backed this up with a fierce defence of the landed interest, which he asserted was the backbone of the country's constitution and of its prosperity. There can be little doubt, however, that the bitterness of his invective against Peel was inspired – at least in large part – by his disappointment that he had not been rewarded with office. Peel had previously been cowed by the ferocity of his repeated onslaughts, but after Disraeli had said, during the third reading debate, that 'his whole life had been one of political larceny', he rose in his place to enquire why, if this was so, he had been 'ready, as I think he was, to unite his fortunes with mine in office?' (*Hansard*, 15 May 1846). With breathtaking audacity, Disraeli angrily denied that he had ever sought office. Peel, who, according to his colleague, Lord Lincoln, actually had Disraeli's letter of 1841 in his dispatch-case (Blake, p. 239), was too fastidious or too honourable to reveal the contents of a private letter, and Disraeli escaped unscathed from what would have been a highly damaging and humiliating revelation. The Conservative Party, which was fatally split by the Corn Law issue, has chosen to blame it retrospectively on Peel, who was promptly dropped from its pantheon of heroes. More objective observers, however, might conclude that Disraeli carried a greater responsibility, not only for the split in 1846, but for the fact that it led to a permanent fracture of the party.

Disraeli's performance in 1846 was the determining event of his whole career. It had two momentous consequences. It was to be another 28 years before a Conservative government was again elected with a clear majority in the House of Commons, and – by driving out virtually all the other MPs with ability – he greatly increased the chances that he himself would eventually become leader of the Conservative Party. As recounted in Chapter 26, it took some time before Stanley (now Lord Derby) could bring himself to accept Disraeli as the undisputed Tory leader in the House of Commons. Yet by 1850 Disraeli was firmly in place, but not before he had adjusted himself to the role of frontbench spokesman, projecting a gravitas which had previously eluded him. Gone was his flamboyant attire: from now on 'he wore a suit of impeccable black, instead of the gorgeous colours of the past, and he spoke in a more weighty manner, avoiding the extravagance, the vituperation, and the imagery of his great philippics' (Blake, p. 256).

Moreover, this quintessentially urban figure attempted to turn himself into a country gentleman, exchanging his Shrewsbury constituency for the county seat of Buckinghamshire in the 1847 general election, which he went on to represent for the next 29 years, and buying a country house and estate in the county, Hughenden Manor. This cost £35,000 – far more than Mary Anne could afford, and much more than the legacy he received from his father, Isaac, who died in January 1848. He accepted a generous loan of £25,000 from the wealthy Bentinck and his two brothers, probably believing that he would never be called upon to repay it. But Bentinck was to die suddenly, within a year, and in 1857, his eldest brother, Lord Titchfield, who had become the Duke of Portland, suddenly called the loan in, putting Disraeli in severe difficulties and having to resort again to extortionate money-lenders to keep himself afloat. Relief finally came in 1863, when an elderly political admirer, Mrs. Brydges Willyams, died, leaving him a legacy of £40,000, on condition of being buried in his vault at Hughenden. A wealthy widow, of Jewish descent, both Disraeli and his wife had been carefully cultivating her for years, in the apparent hope of eventually benefiting from her friendship.

For the best part of two decades, Disraeli was to lead the Tories in the Commons, under the tutelage of Derby, who came to value him highly, despite his initial misgivings. They had plenty of disagreements along the way, though Dizzy always treated him with deference, and conceded with good grace whenever the

14th Earl insisted on having his way. A frequent cause of contention was on the tactics to be pursued in trying to unseat the Whig, coalition or Liberal governments, which were in power for the bulk of this period. Disraeli was keen to make common cause with the Radicals, and even the Irish (after O'Connell's death in 1847) in parliamentary ambushes, which Derby frequently vetoed. He was much keener on effecting a reunion with the Peelites and was constantly wooing Lord Aberdeen and Gladstone, as well as Palmerston, whom he correctly identified as the most conservative of the Whigs. He might well have succeeded, had he been willing to abandon protectionism at an earlier stage than he actually did (in 1852), but the presence of Disraeli as his deputy acted as a severe deterrent to the Peelites. They hated him almost to a man because of the savage way in which he had attacked Peel in 1846–7. Disraeli was also widely unpopular for other reasons. He had not entirely lived down his earlier unsavoury reputation, was looked down upon by many aristocrats in his own party, as well as among the Peelites, and also suffered from anti-Semitic prejudices, which were only exacerbated by his strong support for the removal of the disqualification of Jewish MPs. One of Disraeli's severest critics in his own party was a future Prime Minister, Lord Robert Cecil MP (later the 3rd Marquess of Salisbury), who described him as 'an adventurer, a mere political gangster...without principles and honesty' (Hibbert, p. 231).

That he was able to maintain his position as Tory leader in the Commons throughout this period was due to three factors: the support of Derby, the absence of any plausible rival and – above all – his effectiveness. He was a master of parliamentary tactics, and dominated the House in debates, his only rival as an orator being Gladstone, who was certainly his superior as a platform speaker but perhaps not quite his equal as a parliamentary debater. In each of Derby's short premierships – in 1852, 1858–9 and 1866–8 – he served as Chancellor of the Exchequer and Leader of the Commons, and each time he was the key figure in the government. When Derby became Prime Minister for the first time, leading a minority government of almost unknown faces, Disraeli was far from keen to take the chancellorship, telling Derby that he had no knowledge of the subject. Derby brushed his misgivings aside, saying: 'You know as much as Mr Canning did. They give you the figures'.

The Treasury did indeed give Disraeli the figures, but when he came to prepare his budget, in the autumn of 1852, he did not much like what he saw. He had a tricky exercise to prepare, and – if he were to provide for a budget surplus, which was regarded as essential – he had very little margin of manoeuvre. His first priority was to satisfy his own supporters on the Tory benches, who were crying out for tax reductions favouring the landed interest, which had suffered as a result of the repeal of the Corn Laws. In order to do this, he would have to put up other taxes or cut public spending, which would not be popular. Yet he also needed to make other concessions which would appeal to the Radicals, whose votes he also needed to secure a Commons majority. He managed, with considerable ingenuity, to put a package together which might just conceivably have reconciled these conflicting objectives, when he was presented with a last-minute increase in the defence estimates, occasioned by a war scare with Napoleon's III's France. The adjustments he then had to make to bring in extra revenue destroyed the balance of his proposals, and when he presented them to the House, it soon became clear that he would not be able to win many votes from the Opposition benches. His discomfiture became complete when, after he had given what he thought would be the closing speech in the budget debate, William Gladstone rose to his feet. In a masterly oration, he coolly dissected all the inconsistencies in Disraeli's proposals, delivered a magisterial rebuke to him for the intemperance of his remarks, and staked his own claim for the chancellorship, to which he was duly appointed by Lord Aberdeen a few days later. When Gladstone sat down, the House divided, and the government was defeated by 305 votes to 286. Derby immediately resigned, and the government came to an end after less than a year in office. The date was 17 December 1852, and this also marked the effective beginning of the long rivalry between Disraeli and Gladstone, which was to dominate British politics for the next 28 years.

Disraeli, who had loved being in office, now faced the prospect of many more dreary years in opposition. He was furious with Derby, who had been summoned to the premiership by Queen Victoria in 1855, on the resignation of Aberdeen during the Crimean War, and had declined to take office, when Palmerston refused to serve under him. Then, quite unexpectedly, in 1858 Palmerston was forced from office as a result of Count Orsini's assassination attempt on Napoleon III (see Chapter 28), and Dizzy again became Chancellor and Leader of the Commons, in Derby's second government. This government was regarded as a distinct improvement on that of 1852, and lasted a little longer. Disraeli appeared more on top of his job as Chancellor, but shone more as Leader of the House, through which he successfully piloted the India Bill, which – following the suppression of the Indian mutiny – effectively wound up the East India Company, transferring its functions to the Viceroy and his administration. The principal piece of legislation presented, however, was a Reform Bill, carefully drafted by Disraeli to ensure that its effects would be more favourable to the Tories than their opponents. Its main provision was to equalize the franchise between borough and county constituencies, with a property qualification of £10 a year. It also introduced a system of plural voting (or 'fancy franchises', as they were called by the Radical leader, John Bright), giving additional votes to 'those who had an income of £10 a year from the Funds [government bonds], on possession of £60 in a savings bank; on persons receiving government payments of £20 a year; on doctors, lawyers, university graduates, ministers of religion, and certain categories of schoolmasters' (Blake, pp. 399–400).

It all seemed a bit too clever by half, and many Tories were alarmed by how far their party seemed to be prepared to enter into what had previously been regarded as Whig or Radical territory. The Liberal leader, Lord John Russell, cleverly moved an amendment which could be supported equally by those who felt the Bill had gone too far, as well as those who thought it did not go far enough. It was carried by 330 votes to 291, and, instead of resigning, Derby asked the Queen for a dissolution. The election – held in April 1859 – was won by the newly created Liberal Party. Lord Palmerston, who had politely rejected an extraordinary offer put privately to him by Disraeli, that he should assume the leadership of the Conservatives, with both Derby and Disraeli bowing out in his favour, became Prime Minister for the second time, serving for over six years until his death in 1865.

By this time, Disraeli, now aged 55, beginning to feel his years, much affected by the death of his sister Sarah, in December 1859, and irritated by continuing criticism from the more traditional Tories, momentarily thought of retiring from the fray. Yet there was no viable successor in view, apart from Derby's son, Lord Stanley MP, who was by now his closest collaborator in the Commons. But Stanley was mistrusted by many Tory MPs because of his left-wing views, and his father was not keen to promote him as his deputy. So Dizzy carried on, and was still leading the Tories in the Commons when Russell (now in the House of Lords) again became Prime Minister, on Palmerston's death in October 1865. Russell was determined to round off his political career by carrying a Reform Bill, which would lower the property qualification for voters (see Chapters 25 and 26). Disraeli skillfully led the opposition to the Bill in the Commons, and succeeded with the aid of right-wing Liberals (known as the Adullamites), in securing its defeat, which led to the resignation of Russell's government in June 1866. For the third time, Derby became Prime Minister of a minority government, with Disraeli as Chancellor and Leader of the House. Stanley became Foreign Secretary.

It was the Prime Minister, Lord Derby, who decreed that the first priority of his government would be to introduce a reform bill of its own, which went beyond that which had just been defeated (see Chapter 14). Disraeli, at first sceptical, was given the task of steering it through the House of Commons, where the government was in a minority of some 70 seats. His challenge, given that there were sure to be some rebels on his side of the House, including notably Lord Robert Cecil (now Lord Cranborne), was how to attract rather more than 70 votes from among the Liberals and Irish Members, to carry the Bill, whose principal provision was to extend the vote to all householders in borough constituencies, irrespective of their income. The Bill was heavily amended during its passage, notably by the exclusion of all the 'fancy franchises', on which Derby had insisted, in order to dilute the influence of the large number of working-class voters who would be added to the electorate. But Disraeli showed immense tactical skill in organizing *ad hoc* majorities for each of the Bill's other main provisions, leaving him with a clear majority of MPs who were prepared to support the bill as a whole, when it emerged from its Committee Stage.

During the later stages of the Bill's passage, Derby (who shepherded it through the Lords) suffered increasingly from ill-health, and in February 1868 submitted his resignation, advising the Queen to appoint Disraeli (now 63), rather than his own son, Lord Stanley, as his successor. Victoria was happy to do so, despite once having described him as 'detestable, unprincipled, reckless and not respectable', while Prince Albert had said that there was 'not one single element of the gentleman in his composition' (Hibbert, p. 269). Yet that had been long ago, and Dizzy had subsequently worked long and hard to win her favour, beginning with his tribute to Albert on the Prince Consort's death. This greatly surpassed all others, and brought much comfort to the stricken Queen. Now as Prime Minister, he set out to consolidate his relationship with her. He took more time and trouble over his daily reports to her of parliamentary proceedings than any of his predecessors, seeking to turn them into minor literary masterpieces, and to entertain as well as inform his monarch. He followed to the full the advice which he gave to Matthew Arnold that 'Everyone likes flattery, and when you come to Royalty you should lay it on with a trowel'. When she published her *Leaves from the journal of our life in the Highlands,* in 1868, he delighted her by saying 'We authors, Ma'am'.

Disraeli made few changes to Derby's cabinet, replacing himself as Chancellor of the Exchequer with George Ward Hunt, a little-known barrister. He tried to lure Cranborne (the future Lord Salisbury), who had resigned over the 1867 Reform Bill, back into the government, but to no avail. His government was to last for 278 rather uneventful days, the main controversies being over a small war in Abyssinia (Ethiopia) and the proposal to endow a Catholic University in Ireland. Gladstone, now leader of the opposition, attacked this with great ferocity, coupling it with a demand to disestablish the (Anglican) Church of Ireland, to the great delight of the Non-Conformist churches. Disraeli called a general election in November 1868, hoping that the large number of new working-class voters enfranchised by the 1867 Act would show their gratitude by voting Tory. He was disappointed; the election produced a majority of over 100 for the Liberals, and Disraeli resigned without waiting to be defeated in a Commons vote. Victoria was mortified by having to accept Gladstone, whom she abominated, as Disraeli's successor, and was anxious to show her appreciation of her retiring Prime Minister by bestowing an important honour on him. He declined to accept, but asked instead for a peerage for his wife, who became Viscountess Beaconsfield.

For the next six years, Disraeli had a frustrating time, while his great rival Gladstone, presided over one of the great reforming governments of the nineteenth century. Mary Anne's health rapidly declined, and she died in December 1872, aged 80. Disraeli felt bereft, and paid her a heartfelt tribute, saying: 'There was no care which she could not mitigate, and no difficulty which she could not face. She was the most cheerful and the most courageous woman I ever knew'.

With her death, he also lost her private income and their London home at Grosvenor Gate, which reverted to her first husband's heirs. For a year, he moved into a suite in Edward's Hotel, telling his friends that living in lonely hotel rooms was like 'a cave of despair'. He later acquired a small house in Whitehall Gardens. Many years before her death, Mary Anne had written to Disraeli a letter urging him to re-marry, and not to live alone. He was more than ready to follow her advice. 'At the age of sixty-eight he fell head over heels in love with Lady Bradford, who was fifty-four and a grandmother' (Blake, p. 531). Unfortunately, Lady Bradford was married to a Tory peer, so Disraeli proposed instead to her elder sister, Lady Chesterfield, then over 70 years of age, and recently widowed. 'She refused him, of course, well aware that he would have asked her sister instead, had not Lady Bradford been married already' (Hibbert, p. 298). Disraeli was to pursue the two sisters for the last eight years of his life, constantly seeking their company, and bombarding them with letters (some 1,100 to Lady Bradford and 500 to her sister). These were published in two volumes in 1929, and have been a major source for all his recent biographers. They were kind and sympathetic to him, but – though several other aristocratic ladies made it fairly clear that they regarded him as an eligible widower – neither of these sisters saw him in this light.

In the early 1870s, Disraeli, to general astonishment, resumed his career as a novelist, publishing *Lothair*, in 1870, the first novel written by a former Prime Minister. It was a great success, leading his publisher – Longman's – to produce a collected edition of Disraeli's novels some of which – notably the semi-autobiographical *Vivien Grey* and *Contrarini Fleming* – Dizzy had bowdlerised, in order not to reopen ancient controversies. Altogether, Disraeli made some £10,000 from the exercise – a welcome addition to his now diminished income. After his wife's death, he absorbed himself more and more in politics, showing a renewed dedication , and throwing off the lethargy induced by Mary Anne's long terminal illness, and his own bouts of ill-health. He instituted a thorough overhaul of the Conservative Party, establishing the National Union of Conservative Associations, ensuring that there was a functioning branch of the party in every single constituency, equipped to appeal to the greatly increased electorate created by the 1867 Act. This effort bore fruit in 1874, when Gladstone unexpectedly called a general election one year ahead of time. Disraeli fought the election largely as a stout defender of the Anglican Church, but the result – a majority of more than 50 for the Conservatives – was much more due to 'reform fatigue' induced by the great burst of legislative action by the Liberal government (see Chapter 18). Like other reforming administrations, it found that while the majority who benefited from its reforms took them for granted, those who had been disadvantaged were spurred into furious opposition, determined to defeat the government which had dared to challenge their privileges.

The government which Disraeli formed, on 20 February 1874, was markedly stronger than his administration in 1868. Lord Cranborne (now the 3rd Marquess of Salisbury) was induced to overcome his distaste for the new Prime Minister, and resumed his former post as Secretary for India, Sir Stafford Northcote became Chancellor of the Exchequer and Lord Stanley (now the 15th Earl of Derby) was again Foreign Secretary. The new Lord Derby, formerly a close associate of Disraeli, was now often at odds with him, his increasingly left-wing views making him seem to have more in common with the Liberal Party (to which he was later to defect, in 1880). As Home Secretary, Disraeli appointed a middle-class protégé of Derby's, R.A. Cross. 'Disraeli was a ceremonious, slightly remote, but patient and unassertive chairman of cabinet, which conducted its business with laxity' (Parry). He concerned himself mainly with foreign affairs and matters concerning the monarchy, and it was Derby and Cross who took the initiative in promoting the domestic legislative programme. They were determined to carry on the reforming policies of Gladstone's government, to prevent the Conservative Party being seen, once again, as a reactionary force, and to increase its appeal to centrist opinion. It was due to them that, during 1875, a whole host of social reform measures were carried, including two Trade Union Acts, the Public Health Act, the Factory Act, the Sale of Food and Drugs Act and the Conspiracy and Protection of Property Act, which legalized peaceful picketing. Disraeli's posthumous reputation as a social reformer owes much to the efforts of these two colleagues. He took little interest in the passage of these Bills, and Derby complained in his diary that he 'detests the class of business which he is apt to call parochial' (Parry, 2004).

In May1876, Disraeli performed his supreme act of flattery to Queen Victoria, by having her proclaimed as Empress of India, despite widespread parliamentary opposition. Three months later, she returned the compliment by creating him Earl of Beaconsfield, and he subsequently led the government from the Lords, his health no longer permitting him to spend the long hours in the Commons to which he had become accustomed. At about the same time, Gladstone announced his own retirement as leader of the Liberal Party, and it appeared that the days of their duels were over. In November 1875, Disraeli had taken his first major step in foreign policy, which indicated his ambition to play a more forceful part on the international stage, and to take over from Palmerston the role of forcefully defending perceived British interests throughout the world. His success in doing this led to the Tories acquiring the reputation of being 'the patriotic party', which greatly increased their electoral appeal, particularly among working-class voters. The ruler of Egypt, the Khedive Ismail, facing bankruptcy, offered to sell his minority 40 per cent stake in the Suez Canal to French financial interests, which would have left the canal totally in French hands. Disraeli moved sharply in, made an improved offer, and bought the shares for the British government, with the aid of a large loan from the Rothschilds. The impression was created that Britain now controlled the canal, which proved a highly popular move. At about this time, several revolts against Turkish rule broke out in Bulgaria and Bosnia-Herzegovina, and, when the Ottomans moved to crush them, Russia threatened war against the Turks. Stories of brutal Turkish massacres of Bulgarians caused great indignation, and forced Gladstone out of his retirement, to lead a stirring campaign to drive the Turks 'bag and baggage' out of Europe. Beaconsfield, as he now was, dismissed the massacre stories as 'exaggerated' and was much more concerned with preventing Russian encroachments into the Balkans than in reprimanding the Turks, for whom he retained his youthful sympathy. He proposed a conference of the great powers of Europe (Austria, Britain, France, Germany, Italy and Russia), to try to persuade the Russians to hold their hand and the Turks to introduce long-overdue reforms in their subject territories.

To this, he sent Lord Salisbury, rather than Derby, the Foreign Secretary, from whom he was becoming increasingly estranged. The Conference, held in Constantinople, was a failure (see Chapter 31), but it had the totally unexpected effect of turning Salisbury into an international statesman of great renown. Russia now declared war on Turkey, and – after overcoming stubborn and prolonged resistance before the Bulgarian town of Plevna – its forces swept to the gates of Constantinople, where they imposed the humiliating Treaty of San Stefano on the Turks, stripping the country of large parts of its territory. Beaconsfield then ordered the mobilization of troops to put pressure on Russia, leading to the resignation of the peace-loving Derby, and his replacement by Salisbury, who – as recounted in Chapter 31 – now took a leading role in forcing the Russians to back down. They agreed to attend a Congress in Berlin, presided over by the German Chancellor, Bismarck, but where Beaconsfield created a tremendous impression, with his charm and panache, though most of the serious negotiation was conducted by Salisbury. Dizzy got on brilliantly with Bismarck, who made the famous comment 'Der alte Jude; das ist der Mann'. The result of the Congress was that Russia was forced to disgorge most of its gains, while the Turks handed over the island of Cyprus to Britain, as an east Mediterranean base. Beaconsfield and Salisbury returned in triumph to London, claiming to have brought back 'Peace with Honour'. Victoria wished to honour her favourite Prime Minister by making him a Duke. He declined, but accepted the Garter, on condition that it was also bestowed on Salisbury.

Dizzy remained Prime Minister for nearly another two years, basking in the glory of Berlin, but not attempting many fresh political initiatives. His health was not good – he suffered from gout, asthma and, perhaps, Bright's disease, a kidney disorder. Then – in March 1880 – misled by two Tory victories in by-elections, he called a general election, a year before it was due. It was a disaster: the Liberals won 414 seats, and the Tories only 238. Beaconsfield had hoped that his foreign policy successes would bring him victory, but more relevant to the voters was the bleak position of the economy, after six successive bad harvests and an industrial recession. His previously popular imperialist policies also cost him some support, following humiliating British defeats in Zululand and Afghanistan.

A rejuvenated Gladstone replaced him as Prime Minister, and Disraeli settled down to finish a further novel – *Endymion* – on which he had been working over many years. Lightly based on his own early political career, it was well received, and netted him another £10,000. Five months later – on 19 April 1881 – he died at his newly purchased London home in Curzon Street, after a severe attack of bronchitis, aged 76. A greatly concerned Queen Victoria had proposed to visit him during his last days, but Disraeli, whose mordant humour had not yet deserted him, replied 'No it is better not. She would only ask me to take a message to Albert'.

Altogether, Disraeli led his party in Parliament, first in the Commons, later in the Lords, for rather over 20 years, for less than seven of which he was Prime Minister. He was a supremely accomplished parliamentarian, but hardly a great Prime Minister. He was to lead a moderately reformist government, which had one major success in foreign affairs, the Congress of Berlin, for which he must share the credit with his Foreign Secretary, Lord Salisbury. Disraeli's greatest contribution was the legacy which he left to the Conservative Party. It had been effectively smashed by him in the 1840s, but he slowly rebuilt it, and left behind him a party which was to be an extremely successful competitor for many years to come, under the newly enlarged electorate, which he had created by his 1867 Reform Bill. Disraeli was not, in practice, a notable social reformer, but – more because of his writings, *Sybil* in particular, than the legislation for which he was responsible – he acquired a durable reputation of being one. This has continued to inspire Conservative leaders, with some notable exceptions, including Margaret Thatcher, until the present day. His concept of bridging the gap between the 'two nations' has been a potent rallying cry, even though subsequent Tory governments have seldom shown great assiduity in pursuing it.

Works consulted

Robert Blake, 1969, *Disraeli*, London, Methuen.
Sarah Bradford, 1982, *Disraeli*, London, Weidenfeld & Nicolson.
Benjamin Disraeli, 1954, *Sybil or The Two Nations*, Harmondsworth, Penguin Books.

Christopher Hibbert, 1981, (ed.), *Greville's* England, London, Folio Society.

Christopher Hibbert, 2005, *Disraeli: A Personal History*, London, Harper Perennial.

Dick Leonard, 2013, *The Great Rivalry: Gladstone & Disraeli, A Dual Biography*, London, I.B. Tauris.

André Maurois, 1978, *Vie de Disraeli*, Paris, Gallimard.

W.F. Monypenny and G.E. Buckle, 1910–1920, *The Life of Benjamin Disraeli, Earl of Beaconsfield*, 6 vols, London, John Murray.

Parry Jonathan, 2004, Article in *Oxford Dictionary of National Biography*.

D.C. Somervell, 1926, *Disraeli and Gladstone*, New York, Garden City Publishing.

John Vincent, 1990, *Disraeli*, Oxford University Press.

Stanley Weintraub, 1993, *Disraeli*, London, Hamish Hamilton.

30
William Ewart Gladstone – From 'Stern Unbending Tory' to 'the People's William'

For nearly three decades – from 1852 to 1881 – two men – Benjamin Disraeli and William Gladstone – were to dominate British politics. To say that they did not get on would be a monumental under-statement. They came to hate each other with a visceral fury. Nor was this attenuated by any respect for each other's personal qualities. For Gladstone, Disraeli was nothing more than a 'charlatan', while Dizzy regarded Gladstone as a 'humbug'.

Of the two, Gladstone came from a much more conventional background. His parents were Scottish Presbyterians, transplanted to Liverpool, where they joined the Church of England, favouring its more Evangelical wing. William Ewart Gladstone was born on 29 December 1809, the fifth child and youngest son of John Gladstone and his second wife, Anne Mackenzie Robinson. A self-made man, John Gladstone (originally Gladstones, he dropped the final 's' before his arrival in England), made a fortune as a trader with America and the West Indies, dealing in sugar, cotton and slaves. In Liverpool, he became a pillar of the local Tories and was instrumental in persuading George Canning to stand for the constituency in 1812. John Gladstone himself was also elected to the Commons, serving 'from 1818 to 1827 for a series of corrupt boroughs' (Matthew, 1986, p. 4). He was, according to Matthew, a classic Samuel Smiles character, 'mixing duty, probity and religion with materialism, initiative and a strong drive for worldly success' (Ibid.). Matthew goes on to describe the home atmosphere in which the young William grew up. It was:

> moderately Evangelical, with the Evangelicals' strong emphasis on the reading of the Bible and on personal duty, family obligation, sin and atonement. Religion brought joy to the Gladstone women, but it weighed heavily on the men, and especially upon William... William's mother believed that he had been 'truly converted to God' when he was about ten. (Ibid., p. 6)

William was heavily influenced by his mother, and his elder sister, Anne, both of whom were very – but cheerfully – pious, and were regarded by him as saints. Anne was to die, still unmarried, at the age of 26. She and her mother possessed

> the Evangelical religious assurance, repose and sense of grace which Gladstone never throughout his life gained. For him, awareness of sin ... was always uppermost, never its atoning opposite. His mother and sister represented to him, therefore, a quality of holiness which both inspired him and intensified his sense of inadequacy. (Ibid., p. 7)

Following the example of the elder Sir Robert Peel, who, having 'made his pile', determined that his children should enjoy the privileges and opportunities open to the aristocracy, John Gladstone sent three of his four sons to Eton, the two daughters being educated at home by governesses, while the remaining brother – at his own insistence – went to the Royal Naval College at Portsmouth. Neither of William's brothers distinguished themselves at the school, but, in Roy Jenkins's words, 'William took to Eton like a duck to water' (Jenkins, 1995, p. 12). A tall, good-looking and ferociously hard-working young man, who felt no sense of inferiority to his aristocratic schoolmates, he was a notable success, both academically and socially. He was soon co-opted to the school elite, becoming a member of the Eton Society (later known as 'Pop'), where, from the outset, he acquired a formidable reputation as a debater. Yet, comments Jenkins,

> For an outstanding orator, which he was already on the way to becoming, he was singularly lacking in neatness of phrase ... His force depended essentially on his flashing eyes and the physical authority of his presence. Thus the printed records of his speeches do not compare with those of Chatham [the Elder Pitt], or Burke or Canning or Abraham Lincoln, or even with the contrived epigrams of Disraeli, whose flippancy was so antipathetic to Gladstone. (Jenkins, p. 13)

He made a number of close friends, one of whom – Lord Lincoln, the heir to the dukedom of Newcastle – was later to be instrumental in launching his political career. He also had a highly charged 'on-off' relationship with Arthur Hallam, the brilliant and dangerously attractive son of a constitutional historian, who was two years younger than Gladstone but was generally held to outshine him. Hallam was to die tragically at the age of 22, and was the subject of Tennyson's famous poem *In Memoriam*. Jenkins commented that 'there is no evidence of any homosexual behaviour', but 'what was most remarkable, however, was that, as Professor Robert Martin's life of Tennyson points out, 'sixty years after his [Hallam's] death the Prime Minister and the Poet Laureate were still jealous of each other's place in his affections' (Jenkins, p. 18).

In his fourth year at Eton – on 16 July 1825 – he wrote the first entry in the diary which he was to continue until he was 85. His purpose, he later wrote, was to 'tell, amidst the recounting of numberless mercies...a melancholy tale of my own inward life' (Matthew, 1986, p. 7). In fact, it is largely a catalogue of the books which Gladstone read – over 20,000 in all – the events he attended, and the people he encountered – some 22,000 – in his long life, interspersed with agonizing introspections as to whether he was truly acting out God's purpose in his life. The entire diary, brilliantly edited by M.R.D. Foot and, in particular, H.C.G. (Colin) Matthew, was published in 14 volumes, between 1968 and 1994, under the title *The Gladstone Diaries with Cabinet Minutes and Prime-Ministerial Correspondence*. Thanks to this Herculean effort, more is known of the private and public life of Gladstone than of any other nineteenth-century politician.

Gladstone did not find the teaching at Eton very inspiring, and later wrote that the one thing the school taught him was the importance of strict accuracy in everything he attempted. Otherwise, according to Matthew, it made him: 'proficient in Greek and Latin, competent in French, barely adequate in mathematics, and largely ignorant of the sciences. Yet his self-education in English literature, history and theology was already considerable, and the school had achieved his father's objective of grafting him onto the metropolitan political elite' (Matthew, 2004).

In October 1828, Gladstone, aged nearly 19, went up to Christ Church, Oxford, then – and for much of the nineteenth century – the most intellectually distinguished of Oxford colleges. Here he excelled himself, taking double firsts in *Literae Humaniores* and Mathematics, in the autumn of 1831, 22 years after Robert Peel had performed the same feat (see Chapter 24). Yet studying was perhaps merely incidental to Gladstone's life at Oxford; it was a major formative influence both in his religious and political development. In religion, he drifted away somewhat from his Evangelical roots, and associated himself more with High Church figures such as Edward Pusey, John Keble, F.D. Maurice and John Henry Newman, several of whom – to Gladstone's dismay – later joined the Roman Church, as did another future cardinal with whom he became acquainted, Henry Manning, who was at that time rather Low Church. Some, at least, of Gladstone's fellow students found him an intolerable prig, and late one evening his rooms at Christ Church were invaded by a group of college 'hearties', who proceeded to beat him up. Gladstone recorded the occasion in his diary, in these words:

Here I have great reason to be thankful to that God whose mercies fail not...1) Because this incident must tend to the mortification of my pride, by God's grace...It is no disgrace to be beaten for Christ was buffeted and smitten...2) Because here I have to some small extent an opportunity of exercising the duty of forgiveness. (Jenkins, 1950, p. 21)

At about this time, Gladstone thought seriously about offering himself for ordination as a priest, and wrote to his father asking permission to do so. The elder Gladstone had much grander ambitions for his son, and wrote back strongly discouraging him, and Gladstone – possibly secretly relieved – readily complied and seems never to have had any regrets. Gladstone, who had already shone at Eton, was by a wide margin the best debater of his time at Oxford. He honed his skills in an essay club which he founded along with a group of Old Etonian friends. Intended as a counterpart of the Cambridge Apostles (of which Arthur Hallam was a member), it was known as the Weg (after Gladstone's initials). Unlike the Apostles, it did not survive the departure from the University of its founders. Yet Gladstone's finest performances were reserved for the Oxford Union, founded only five years earlier. Elected its President, his most notable speech, on 17 May 1831, was a vehement attack on the Reform Bill, then making its troubled way through Parliament. He spoke for 45 minutes, and carried the resolution against the Bill by 94 votes to 38. Also speaking on the same side in the debate, though with far less impact, was his Old Etonian friend, the Earl of Lincoln. He was deeply impressed by Gladstone's performance.

Gladstone left the university at the end of 1831, and two months later set off for the 'Grand Tour', ending up in Rome in July 1832. In the meantime, the Reform Bill was passed, and preparations were made for the general election of the reformed House. One of the strongest opponents of the Bill was the Duke of Newcastle, who was the proprietor of a series of rotten or pocket boroughs. Several of these had been eliminated by the Bill, but he still had a predominant influence in the Nottinghamshire constituency of Newark. At the urging of his son, Lord Lincoln, the Duke wrote to John Gladstone asking whether William would be interested being one of the two Tory candidates. John Gladstone thought the offer was a bit premature, but wrote to his son in Rome, who accepted it with enthusiasm. The following December, he was duly elected, heading the poll, with 887 votes, against 798 for his fellow Tory, and 726 for the sole Whig candidate. He was just short of his twenty-third birthday. He made his maiden speech on 3 June 1833, and his choice of topic was unfortunate. He was opposing the government's Bill to abolish slavery in the British Empire, which he did not object to in principle, but questioned the provisions for compensating the slave-owners, who included his father, who owned plantations in Jamaica. In his subsequent speeches, Gladstone made a considerable impression on the House, and was soon seen as a 'coming man', the historian Macaulay referring to him in an article as 'the rising hope of those stern and unbending Tories' (Matthew, 1986, p. 29). When Peel formed his minority Tory government in December 1834, Gladstone, aged just 25, was included as a Junior Lord of the Treasury. Within a month he was promoted to Colonial Under-Secretary, in which post he served for less than three months before the resignation of the government in April 1835.

In opposition, Gladstone's main concern was the protection of the role of the Anglican Church against what he saw as Whig attempts to undermine its privileges, particularly in Ireland, where Lord John Russell unsuccessfully sought to divert part of its tithe income to secular purposes (see Chapter 13). At this time, Gladstone held semi-theocratic views, believing that the state had a duty, through the established Church, to impose a Christian morality on its subjects. He argued the case for this in two books, *The State in its Relations with the Church* (1838) and *Church principles Considered in their Results* (1841). He became closely involved with the Tractarian movement (also known as the Oxford Movement) of High Church Anglicans, attended Church daily and, in 1838, drew up proposals for what he called a 'Third Order', a lay brotherhood of persons in public life. This was never formally established, but Gladstone with a number of like-minded friends later set up a small private all-male group, which they called 'the Engagement'. They met regularly together for prayer sessions and discussions on the religious life, committing themselves to devote a proportion of their incomes, and a great deal of their spare time, to charitable activities.

During the late 1830s, Gladstone made proposals of marriage to three aristocratic ladies. He proved himself an awkward and unpersuasive suitor, and was given short shrift by Caroline Farquhar, a society beauty who later married a son of Earl Grey, and by Lady Frances Douglas, daughter of the Earl of Morton. He had more success with Catherine Glynne, the sister of Sir Stephen Glynne, who had been with him both at Eton and Christ Church, and who was the owner of the Hawarden castle and estate in North Wales. They were married on 25 July 1839, at Hawarden parish Church, when Gladstone was 29 and Catherine, 27. She shared his strong Christian beliefs, but their characters were very dissimilar, she being much more informal, vague and untidy, in contrast to her husband's methodical and meticulous ways. Gladstone proved himself an uxorious husband, and the marriage was largely successful, though they tended to drift apart in later years. In the first 12 years of their marriage, four sons and four daughters (one of whom died in infancy) were born.

Sir Robert Peel was deeply impressed by Gladstone, whom he saw as a young man very much in his own image, and when he again became Prime Minister, this time of majority Tory government, in 1841, he appointed Gladstone Vice-President of the Board of Trade. The President was the Earl of Ripon, a former Prime Minister under the name of Viscount Goderich. A veteran politician who had rather run out of steam, the effective head of the department was Gladstone. Two years later Ripon retired, and Gladstone took his place, joining the Cabinet at the age of 33. Strongly influenced by Peel he became a fervent advocate of free trade, and carried a major piece of legislation – the Railways Act – through the Commons. His reputation as a hard-working, decisive and formidably well informed minister soared, and he was tipped by John Stuart Mill to become Peel's successor as Tory leader. Publicly successful, he went through a deep religious and sexual crisis during these years. It began painfully to dawn upon him that his theocratic ideas were impracticable, and his attitude to the Conservative Party insensibly changed. Formerly, he had seen the party as the chosen instrument of God's will for the nation, but increasing familiarity with his fellow Tory MPs slowly disillusioned him.

Now he viewed the party more in terms of being marginally preferable to the Whigs and much more so to the Radicals, rather than a thing apart. He also suffered from acute sexual frustration. According to Matthew, he was almost certainly a virgin at the time of his marriage, but was highly sexed, and found it difficult to abstain from sexual relations with Catherine during her repeated long periods of pregnancy when, according to Victorian custom, intercourse was strongly disadvised. He sought relief in furtive reading of pornography, but was driven more and more to his 'night-time work' of attempting to rescue 'fallen women'. This he had begun in 1840, as his chosen charitable work within the Engagement group, but – despite the meagre success of his efforts – he estimated that only one of the first 80 or 90 women he took up with was redeemed, he now stepped up his activities, which continued, including during his premierships, until his old age. He made little effort to conceal what he was doing, often taking the women he had encountered back to his house for a meal with Catherine, who approved her husband's activities, though it is doubtful if she knew their full extent. For Gladstone was physically attracted by many of them, and often succumbed to temptation, and then flagellated himself in atonement, signifying the occasions with a symbol resembling a whip in his diary. It is doubtful if he ever went 'the whole way' and indeed 17 months before his death he wrote a solemn declaration to his son, the Rev. Stephen Gladstone, now the Rector of Hawarden, assuring him that he had never 'been guilty of the act which is known as that of infidelity to the marriage bed' (Matthew, 1986, p. 93). Nevertheless, his diaries make it clear that he felt a very strong sense of having sinned on a number of occasions. Many of Gladstone's friends and colleagues became aware of his midnight prowls, and were concerned that they might cause a scandal, but not a mention appeared in the press until well after his death. This side of Gladstone's life was virtually ignored in the famous three-volume biography written by his friend and colleague John Morley, and it was only in 1927, during the course of a libel action between his son Herbert and a scurrilous author called Captain Peter Wright, that it became known to the general public. The jury in this trial, giving judgement in favour of Herbert Gladstone, added a note to the effect that the evidence had 'completely vindicated the high moral character of the late Mr W.E. Gladstone' (Jenkins, p. 106). It was not until the publication of Gladstone's diaries in the final third of the twentieth century that the full extent of Gladstone's nocturnal activities and his own sense of shame became known to scholars.Gladstone's cabinet career was interrupted in February 1845, when he resigned in protest against the decision to make a small grant to Maynooth College, in Dublin, a seminary for the training of Catholic priests. He felt that, as a stalwart defender of the Church of England, he could not be associated with this action. It amazed many of his colleagues that this apparently highly ambitious minister should risk his career over such a trifle, but it was not the first sign he had given of an over-sensitive conscience. Peel, however, was determined to bring Gladstone back to his team, and when he reconstructed his cabinet, after the defection of Lord Stanley over the projected repeal of the Corn Laws, the following December (see Chapter 24), he persuaded Gladstone to accept the post of Colonial Secretary. This obliged him to resign his seat, and fight a by-election, but the Duke of Newcastle – a strong supporter of the Corn Laws – refused to back him as a candidate for Newark. This put Gladstone in the anomalous and historically unique position of serving in the Cabinet without being a member of either House. As Colonial Secretary, Gladstone showed himself to be a strong advocate of home rule for the inhabitants of British colonies, particularly in Canada and New Zealand.

Gladstone was again in opposition after July 1846, when the Peel government was defeated on the morrow of the repeal of the Corn Laws. He had unhesitatingly backed Peel in the party split, and appeared not to find the division in the party especially painful, probably because he had already lost his faith in its divine mission. He remained out of Parliament until the 1847 general election, when he was returned as one of the two Members for Oxford University, which he represented for the next 18 years. He now had to concern himself very much with family problems. One arose from the collapse of the business activities of his brother-in-law, Stephen Glynne, who was facing bankruptcy, putting his continued ownership of the Hawarden estate at risk. Gladstone, who on his marriage had taken up residence there with Catherine, now moved sharply to take over control of Glynne's affairs, and over a period of years managed to re-establish them, with financial help from John Gladstone. In the process, he gradually – if gently – squeezed Stephen out of his position as the head of the household of Hawarden. Gladstone also discouraged Stephen's younger brother, the Rev. Henry Glynne, from embarking on a marriage, which might have produced an heir, in the apparent hope that the eventual ownership of the estate would fall to his own eldest son, Willy.

Gladstone was also deeply concerned over the delicate health of his infant daughter Mary and took her to Naples for four months between October 1850 and February 1851. In Naples he attended the trial of a leading liberal opponent of the Bourbon régime and visited a notorious prison, where political prisoners were kept in appalling conditions. On his return to London, he published two indignant *Letters to Lord Aberdeen*, a former Foreign Secretary who, since the death of Peel in July 1850, was the recognized leader of the Peelites, condemning the Kingdom of the Two Sicilies as 'the negation of God erected into a system of government'. Gladstone's published letters deeply embarrassed Aberdeen, who had no wish to be involved in the controversy, but they gave Gladstone an overnight international reputation. He was seen by conservatives throughout Europe as a dangerous supporter of revolutionaries, but was heroised by liberals. It was the first of many passionate pronouncements by Gladstone on foreign affairs, which sat ill with his domestic reputation as a cautious politician, who still considered himself a Conservative.

In December 1851, John Gladstone, who had been made a baronet in Peel's resignation honours in 1846 – more a tribute to the son than the father – died at his Scottish home, four days short of his eighty-seventh birthday. William was at the bedside of his formidable father, and recorded in his diary that 'I thrice kissed my Father's cheek & forehead before & after his death: the only kisses I can remember' (Matthew, 2004). His mother had died 16 years earlier, at the age of 64. Henceforth Gladstone regarded himself as the head of the family, though he was the fourth of four brothers. He was particularly concerned about the fate of his younger, unmarried sister, Helen, who became addicted to alcohol and drugs, and – perhaps worse in Gladstone's eyes – converted to Catholicism. They were estranged for many years, but were reconciled before her death in 1881.

When Lord John Russell's Whig government was defeated in a parliamentary vote in February 1852, Gladstone was invited to join the minority Tory government led by Lord Derby. He was tempted, but declined – for three reasons – the unwillingness of Derby at this stage to renounce protectionism, the failure to include all the leading Peelites in the invitation and – perhaps crucially – Gladstone's determination not to serve in a subordinate role to Disraeli, the Tory leader in the Commons. While Dizzy would have been prepared to efface himself if Palmerston – also targeted by Derby – had been willing to join the government, there was no question of his making way for Gladstone. Had Gladstone accepted Derby's invitation, he might well have emerged as his eventual successor and a future Tory Prime Minister. His refusal opened the way – though it was far from clear at the time – to a quite different destiny.

A decisive step in this new direction was Gladstone's speech – a great parliamentary triumph – condemning the budget which Disraeli, as Derby's Chancellor of the Exchequer, presented in December 1852 (see Chapter 29). Showing complete mastery of the subject, and extraordinary forensic power, Gladstone effectively destroyed the whole intellectual basis on which the budget had been constructed and removed any remaining possibility that it would be accepted by a majority of MPs. The dramatic effect of his intervention was enhanced by a fierce thunderstorm which raged outside, with frequent flashes of lightning visible through the windows of the Chamber. The government was defeated in the ensuing vote, and immediately resigned, being replaced by a coalition of Peelites and Whigs, led by Lord Aberdeen. It was no surprise after this performance that Gladstone was appointed Chancellor of the Exchequer in the new government, and on 28 December 1852, he began the first of his four chancellorships.

It is an open question whether Gladstone was the greatest man ever to be Britain's Prime Minister. Roy Jenkins thought he was, when he concluded his biography, but later changed his mind and awarded the palm to Churchill. Yet his primacy as Chancellor of the Exchequer has never been challenged. He effectively created the post, as it has existed in modern times, and none of his successors has rivalled the impact which he made. His first period in this office opened with an unedifying quarrel with his predecessor, Disraeli. The Chancellor's official robes, first worn by the Younger Pitt, had been passed on to each of his successors, who bought them from their own predecessors, but Disraeli insisted on keeping them (they are still on display in his home at Hughenden Manor, now owned by the National Trust), and a disgruntled Gladstone was forced to have a new set made at his own expense. This dispute, and a parallel one about paying for furniture at the Chancellor's official Downing Street residence, only served to confirm the extremely low opinion each of them had already formed about the other.

Gladstone presented his first budget on 18 April 1853. His speech, which lasted for four and three-quarter hours was every bit as much a triumph as his destruction of Disraeli's budget four months earlier, and it set the new Aberdeen government off to an encouraging start. It was as if he was carrying on where Peel left off – the centre piece of the budget was another large step towards free trade, removing tariffs altogether from 123 items, and reducing them on another 133. This was to be financed by broadening the base of income tax, which he described as 'an engine of gigantic power for great national purposes' and extending it for a further seven years, an unheard proposition for what was regarded only as a temporary tax, renewable – if at all – only on a yearly basis. Nevertheless, he proposed a steady diminution of its rate, and that it should be finally phased out by 1860 – a proposal rendered impracticable by the outbreak of the Crimean War two years later. Gladstone's performance in 1853 can be seen as the first modern budget. He instituted the practice of presenting it with a detailed annual account of the nation's finances, and made this presentation one of the central occasions of the parliamentary year. His chancellorship marked the effective ending of the Prime Minister's functions as First Lord of the Treasury, and clearly established that the Chancellor should normally be seen as the second man in the government, even though the office continued – in formal terms – to be junior to those of the Secretaries of State. Altogether, Gladstone introduced eleven budgets during his two chancellorships in the 1850s and 1860s, and, in the words of a later Chancellor (Roy Jenkins) gave them 'such a sweep and force that their presentation became a fixture of the national life comparable with Derby Day or the State Opening of Parliament' (Jenkins, 1998, p. 6). Apart from 1853, his most notable budgets were in1860 and 1861. In the first of these, he proposed the abolition of paper duties (which had made newspapers prohibitively expensive) only to have his proposal thrown out by the Lords. The following year he tried again, but this time presented it, together with all his other proposals, in a consolidated Finance Bill (the first time this had been done), and challenged the Lords to reject it – an action which they never again contemplated until – with fateful results – they threw out Lloyd George's 'People's Budget', in 1909. One of Gladstone's persistent aims as Chancellor was 'retrenchment'. He had a horror of what he regarded as unnecessary public expenditure, and once famously said that 'No Chancellor of the Exchequer is worth his salt who is not ready to save what are meant by candle-ends and cheese-parings in the cause of his country' (Speech at Edinburgh, 29 November 1879).

Apart from his budgets, Gladstone's main activity during the Aberdeen government was in overseeing parliamentary bills designed to reform the two ancient universities. As an MP for Oxford University, he took a close interest in their contents and managed to ensure that they were moderate in their scope, preserving the collegiate structure of the universities. Perhaps more significantly, he commissioned the Northcote-Trevelyan Report on recruitment to the Civil Service, which led to meritocracy replacing patronage as the basis for future appointments. Gladstone initially supported the Crimean War, despite his strong disapproval of the Turkish regime, and took energetic steps to raise revenue to pay for it, in an attempt to prevent the national debt from rising steeply. His close friend Lord Lincoln, who was now the 5th Duke of Newcastle, was Secretary for War and was more directly involved in the military preparations. When Aberdeen was forced to resign over the conduct of the war, Newcastle left with him. Gladstone and most of the other Peelites joined Palmerston's new government, but resigned after a few weeks, partly because they saw little point in continuing the war after the initial pretext – the Russian occupation of the two Romanian principalities – had come to an end.

Gladstone spent the next four years in opposition, and risked political isolation. He immersed himself in classical studies, publishing the first of several works on Homer in 1857, and for the remainder of his life produced a steady stream of articles and books, as well as translations, of classical authors, notably Horace, Homer and Dante. He pursued his course with enormous energy: his diary records that he read the *Iliad* 36 times during the course of his life.

When Lord Derby again became Prime Minister of a minority Tory government in 1858, he approached Gladstone once again to join his administration, but once more he declined. He did accept, however, an offer to go to the Ionian Islands, a former Venetian territory, which had been a British protect-orate since 1815, as Lord Commissioner Extraordinary, a decision regarded as eccentric by his political supporters. Gladstone's mission which lasted four months was not a success, and bordered on being a fiasco. He was intended to investigate the state of opinion within the islands and to advise on their future. He undertook this with his customary diligence, but he did not endear himself to the overwhelmingly Greek population by addressing them either in Italian or in ancient Greek, which was quite incomprehensible to them. The predominant feeling was in favour of *Enosis* (union with Greece), with which Gladstone was not unsympathetic, but he thought it premature, and recommended instead accelerated progress towards Home Rule. His own mission ended prematurely, when difficulties arose over his membership of the House of Commons, which was deemed incompatible with his role as Lord Commissioner, and Governor-designate. He hastened back to London to reclaim his Oxford University seat in an uncontested by-election. He travelled back through North Italy, stopping to have dinner with Count Cavour, the Piedmontese Prime Minister, on the eve of Napoleon III's war with Austria, which was intended to deliver the whole of North Italy into Piedmontese (Sardinian) hands. This journey served to reignite Gladstone's enthusiasm for Italian unity, which had first been sparked by his earlier visit to Naples in 1850–1.

Within three months of his return, the Derby–Disraeli government was defeated in a parliamentary vote, in which Gladstone perversely voted on the Tory side, while the other Peelites sided with the Whigs. In the ensuing general election, the Tories (while making up some ground) came a clear second to the newly created Liberal Party. This had been hurriedly established at a meeting at Willis's Rooms, on 6 June 1859, and brought together the Whigs, Radicals and Peelites (see Chapters 25 and 28). Gladstone did not attend this meeting, but despite this, he was immediately invited to join the government which Lord Palmerston formed following the election. Gladstone thoroughly disapproved of Palmerston, who was second only to Disraeli as his *bête noir*, but during the election campaign Palmerston had come out strongly in favour of Italian unity, which now came high on Gladstone's list of priorities. This and Palmerston's hostility to parliamentary reform, about which Gladstone was still at this stage highly sceptical, was enough to bring them together. Gladstone peremptorily demanded the chancellorship, saying he would accept no other post, and Palmerston acceded, glad to have a firm hand at the Treasury to underpin his adventurous foreign and imperial policies. Gladstone never got on well with 'Pam', but served out the whole seven years of his premiership, which only ended with his death in 1866, without once threatening to resign – quite a feat for him.

Joining Palmerston's government put an end to Gladstone's political isolation, and set him firmly on the road to the Liberal leadership and eventual premiership. He was not the second person in the government – that was Russell, the Foreign Secretary, who claimed seniority as a former Prime Minister, but he was already elderly. Moreover, Gladstone's potential rivals among the ex-Peelites nearly all died off during this period – Aberdeen in 1860, Sidney Herbert and Sir James Graham in 1861 and Newcastle (Lincoln) in 1864. In addition, the most able of the younger Whigs, George Cornewall Lewis, the Home Secretary, was to die, aged 57, in 1862. The reaper was ruthlessly clearing the way for Gladstone's advance. Not that Gladstone was particularly backward in pushing himself forward. He was the acknowledged author of one of the most significant achievements of Palmerston's second government, the Anglo-French Trade Treaty, negotiated in Paris by Richard Cobden in 1860. Four years later, he made himself the hero of the Radicals by reversing his previously negative attitude to extending the franchise to working-class voters. In a Commons speech, responding to a Private Member's Bill, he said: 'I venture to say that every man who is not presumably incapacitated by some consideration of personal unfitness or of political danger is morally entitled to come within the pale of the constitution' (Hansard, 11 May 1864).

This was taken to be an endorsement of universal manhood suffrage, which was perhaps rather further than Gladstone really intended to go, at this stage. He also set about building up for himself a mass following outside Parliament, speaking at packed public meetings throughout the country. He was the first politician to take advantage of the opportunities presented by the railway age. It was noted that he was particularly effective speaking to meetings of working men, and he was dubbed 'the People's William' by the *Daily Telegraph*, then a Liberal newspaper, which, like several others, had been able to reduce its price to one penny, following Gladstone's abolition of the paper duties, and whose circulation had then expanded rapidly, overtaking that of *The Times*. Other papers had benefited in the same way, and their proprietors were grateful to Gladstone, and rewarded him with an exceptionally favourable press. They reported his speeches word for word, which meant that their impact far exceeded their original audience. Other politicians, notably Disraeli, belatedly attempted to emulate Gladstone, but none of them enjoyed anything like his success.

In the 1865 general election, Gladstone lost his seat at Oxford University, having upset many of its graduates over his support for university reform, as well as on details of Christian theology and by joining the Liberals. He took the precaution of also standing for the South Lancashire constituency, a three-member seat, where he sneaked in in third place behind two Tories. The overall result was a Liberal triumph, but before Parliament could meet, Palmerston died, and was replaced as Prime Minister by Earl Russell. Gladstone continued as Chancellor, and also became Leader of the Commons. Russell, now 73, had only one ambition for his second government, which was to carry a new Reform Bill, having been restrained from introducing one earlier by Palmerston's stubborn opposition. The main provision of the measure, which it was Gladstone's task to carry through the Commons, was to reduce the property qualification in borough constituencies from £10 to £7 a year. The Bill, as it stood, had few supporters in the Commons. The Radicals thought that the threshold should be reduced to £6, or lower, the Tories were solidly opposed to the Bill, and so were the right-wing Liberals (or 'Adullamites'), who refused to accept any extension of the franchise. In the Commons proceedings, Disraeli completely out-manoeuvred Gladstone, and succeeded in defeating the Bill, leading to the government's resignation, in June 1866. Lord Derby then became Prime Minister for the third time, again leading a minority, and Gladstone suffered the mortification of seeing his arch-rival, Disraeli, carry through a measure which went significantly further than his own Bill, providing household suffrage in borough constituencies (see Chapters 26 and 29). Nevertheless, Gladstone was to be the first beneficiary of the 1867 Reform Bill, as the Liberals won the subsequent general election, in November 1868, with a majority of 112, and Disraeli, who had succeeded Derby in the premiership 10 months earlier, promptly resigned. Gladstone had lost his Lancashire seat in the election but was returned for Greenwich instead. Given that Russell had earlier announced that he would not seek office again, he was the only conceivable choice as Prime Minister.

A telegram was duly delivered to Hawarden, announcing the imminent arrival of Queen Victoria's private secretary, General Charles Grey, with a commission inviting him to form a government. It was an intriguing detail that Grey was the husband of Caroline Farquhar, who had turned Gladstone down 30 years earlier, but this did not appear to have caused either man much embarrassment. Gladstone was busy felling a tree on the estate – a frequent occurrence in which he took both pride and pleasure – when the news arrived. He paused to read the telegram, famously declared 'My mission is to pacify Ireland', and carried on with his axemanship. Gladstone had recently become obsessed with Ireland, currently the scene of a rash of terrorist incidents by the Fenians, and concluded that two steps were urgently necessary to remove the justified grievances of the Catholic majority. One was a major programme of land reform, at the expense of the largely absentee landlords of the Protestant ascendancy. The other was the disestablishment and disendowment of the Anglican Church in Ireland, a measure which he had strongly resisted when Lord John Russell had made some tentative steps in this direction in the 1830s. He now resolved to make them the two priority items in his government's programme.

Gladstone was a few weeks short of his fifty-ninth birthday when he became Prime Minister for the first time on 3 December 1868. The government he formed was rather over-weighted by Whig grandees, though it included the leading Radical, John Bright, as President of the Board of Trade, and younger, more reformist ministers such as Edward Cardwell (War Office) and W.E. Forster (Education). His somewhat surprising choice as Chancellor of the Exchequer was Robert Lowe, leader of the 'Adullamites', who had scuppered Russell's Reform Bill in 1866. Gladstone was to be disappointed by Lowe's performance, and switched him to the Home Office in 1873, taking on the chancellorship himself. The Foreign Office was entrusted to the experienced hands of Lord Clarendon, who had twice served before as Foreign Secretary. He was to die in 1870, and was replaced by Lord Granville, the Leader of the House of Lords, and perhaps Gladstone's closest colleague. One leading Whig who was disgruntled to be fobbed off with a relatively junior office was the Marquess of Hartington (later the 8th Duke of Devonshire). He became Postmaster-General, having served as Secretary for War in Earl Russell's Cabinet in 1866. After two years, he was switched by Gladstone to become Chief Secretary for Ireland – again a post which he did not relish.

Gladstone started his premiership with great *brio*, determined to mark each session with a major Bill, which he would himself carry through all its stages in the Commons, and which would act as a shop-window for his administration. For the first session he chose the Irish Church Bill, a highly complicated and controversial measure, whose purpose was to disestablish and disendow the Church in Ireland, though it made no provision, as some had argued, for endowing the Catholic and Presbyterian Churches, to which the great majority of Irish adhered. He got it through the Commons, with majorities of over 100 at all its stages, but had to compromise on its financial terms to carry it through the Lords, where the Tory majority threatened to veto the Bill. Gladstone freely admitted during the parliamentary debates that he had changed his views on disestablishment, but clothed his explanation in such lofty terms that he left little doubt in the minds of his listeners that he believed his present position was divinely inspired. This led the Radical politician Henry Labouchere to make his famous remark, often wrongly attributed to Disraeli, that he didn't object to Gladstone always having the ace of trumps up his sleeve, but merely to his belief that the Almighty put it there.

The Liberals saw the passage of the Bill as a great triumph, and Gladstone sought to consolidate his success with a repeat performance in the 1870 session, with the Irish Land Bill. His original aim had been to extend traditional tenants' rights in Ulster to the whole 32 counties of Ireland, but fierce resistance by Whig landowners in his cabinet forced him to backtrack. The Bill as it was presented, and passed, merely gave statutory force to these rights in Ulster, but for the remainder of Ireland, while it provided for compensation to tenants who made improvements to the farms which they rented, it did not greatly improve their position vis-à-vis their landlords. The Bill was passed and though it had some beneficial effect in Ireland, it did little to remove the causes of rural discontent. Meanwhile, other ministers were primarily responsible for carrying measures which contributed to Gladstone's 1868–74 government being seen as a great reforming administration. Chief among these were W.E. Forster's Elementary Education Act of 1870, Cardwell's Army reforms, abolishing the purchase of commissions, and the Ballot Act of 1872, finally establishing the secret ballot in elections, thereby protecting tenants and employees from intimidation by their landlords or bosses. This measure was twice rejected by the Lords – in 1870 and 1871 – but at the third time of asking they reluctantly gave way. Another measure, about which Gladstone was initially sceptical, but which he ended up by introducing himself in the Commons was the University Tests Bill, which removed most of the remaining restrictions on non-Anglicans holding posts in the universities of Oxford and Cambridge.

In foreign policy, Gladstone gave a strong impetus to the cause of international Arbitration by agreeing to refer the festering dispute with the United States over the *Alabama* affair (see Chapter 28) to an international tribunal in Geneva. This set the amount of compensation to be paid at £3.25m, about one-third of the US claim. This was an unpopular move with the voters, but it put Anglo-American relations back on a good footing, and probably relieved Gladstone's conscience for the strongly pro-Confederate speech he had made at the outset of the Civil War, and which he later regretted. When war broke out between France and Prussia in 1870, he saw merit on both sides, and was resolutely resolved to stay neutral, though he signed a treaty with both powers to recognise Belgian neutrality, and prepared to send an expeditionary force if 30,000 men if either side reneged. It was this treaty which was cited in 1914 to justify Britain's declaration of war on Germany. When the 1870 war ended, Gladstone was appalled by Germany's annexation of Alsace-Lorraine, without a plebiscite being held, but was over-ruled by his Cabinet when he proposed to organize a joint protest with other neutral countries. Gladstone was even more upset by the declaration of papal infallibility at the Vatican Council in 1870, which he largely blamed on his former Oxford friend, Cardinal Manning, who had become a leader of the extreme 'ultramontane' faction in the Roman Catholic Church. Gladstone attempted to mobilize diplomatic opposition by other European governments to the declaration, but had little success.

Gladstone overshadowed all his ministerial colleagues, but was by no means the unchallenged master of his own house. Roy Jenkins aptly described him as pre-eminent, but not predominant, and over several issues he was over-ruled by his Cabinet. He also experienced difficulties in his dealings with Queen Victoria, whom he tried to chivvy into playing a more active and public role, believing that her decade-long period of grieving for Albert was harmful both to the country and the monarchy. He also tried, with little success, to get her to allow the Prince of Wales to play an active part in public affairs, for example as Viceroy of Ireland. Although he invariably treated her in a respectful way, she soon tired of hearing the earnest arguments which he put to her, and complained that he addressed her like a public meeting. She pined for her beloved Disraeli. After the early bout of legislation, by 1872, the government was beginning to run out of steam, and was internally divided on many issues. The opposition Conservatives took heart and Disraeli in a famous speech in Manchester, in April 1872, excoriated the government, saying:

> As I sat opposite the Treasury bench the ministers reminded me of one of those marine landscapes not very uncommon on the coasts of South America. You behold a range of exhausted volcanoes. Not a flame flickers from a single pallid crest. But the situation is still dangerous. There are occasional earthquakes , and ever and anon the dark rumbling of the sea. (Blake, p. 523)

Even Gladstone's titanic energy seemed to be wilting, and for a time he was seriously distracted by what Jenkins describes as 'an infatuation' and Matthew as 'a platonic extra-marital affair'. This was with Laura Thistlethwayte, a former courtesan, who had made an advantageous marriage to a wealthy, but otherwise uninteresting gentleman. Gladstone quickly got into the habit of writing long letters to her, and seeking out her company, showing no regard for discretion. The relationship was at its most intense in 1869, but it dragged on spasmodically for several more years. It has been compared to Asquith's infatuation with Lady Venetia Stanley, to whom he wrote several letters a day at the height of his wartime premiership (see Chapter 35, below), but Gladstone managed to keep his feelings under tighter control. One consequence of his relationship with her is that his night-time activities with street prostitutes tailed off considerably during this period.

If Gladstone's first government began with a bang, it sadly ended with a whimper. He was largely responsible for creating his own troubles. Against the wishes of most of his Cabinet, he insisted on bringing in a third Irish measure, the Irish Universities Bill, whose main aim was to open them up to Catholic students. He handled the issue maladroitly, succeeding in antagonising not only the powerful lobby of Trinity College, Dublin, but also many secular educationalists and, fatally, the Roman Catholic hierarchy. When the Bill came up for its second Reading, on 13 March 1873, a large number of Liberals, mostly but not exclusively Irish Members, voted against, or abstained, and the government was defeated by three votes. Gladstone immediately resigned, and with perhaps indecent haste, Queen Victoria invited Disraeli to take his place. Yet the wary Tory leader declined. He had no wish to emulate Lord Derby's experience, on three occasions, of leading a minority government, and was by now confident enough to believe that if he held off until the next general election he would gain an elected majority. It was the last occasion in British history when an opposition leader refused to accept office.

The government limped on for nearly another year, but repeated Conservative successes in by-elections gave it little confidence that it would survive the general election. This was not due until 1875, but Gladstone decided on a bold stroke and sought dissolution early in 1874. He made the abolition of income tax the central feature of the Liberal election platform. He managed to persuade himself that it was justified on economic grounds, but, in reality, it was no more than a blatant electoral bribe, which sat ill with the high moral tone which he habitually adopted. Nor was it successful: Disraeli instantly followed suit, but when he assumed office found it utterly impractical, and the tax has remained the main source of government revenue ever since. During the election campaign, Gladstone was extraordinarily passive, speaking at only three meetings, all of them in, or near, his Greenwich constituency, which he had represented since 1868. The election result was a majority of 50 for the Tories, while Gladstone suffered the indignity of coming in second place at Greenwich, behind the leading Tory candidate who was a brewer. This election marked the beginning of a long tradition, still continuing, of massive financial support from the brewing industry for the Conservative Party, and Gladstone wrote to his brother that 'we have been borne down in a torrent of gin and beer' (Mathew, 2004). This was a direct consequence of the government's unsuccessful attempt to bring in a Licensing Bill in 1871.

Gladstone, now 64, assumed that his political career was virtually over, and had no desire to lead the Liberal Party in opposition. At the earliest opportunity, he handed over the leadership in the Commons to the Marquess of Hartington MP, while Earl Granville continued to lead in the Lords. Gladstone determined to devote what he saw as the few remaining years of his life to writing on classical and ecclesiastical topics, though he retained his seat in Parliament. Whether it would have proved possible for such a driven and restless character to remain for long out of the political limelight is highly doubtful. The revolts against Turkish rule in 1876 in Bulgaria and Bosnia-Herzegovina, and subsequent Turkish atrocities, settled the issue for him. Outraged at the indifference of Disraeli's government to the growing slaughter of Orthodox Christians by the Ottoman Turks, he published his most famous pamphlet, *The Bulgarian Horrors and the Question of the East*, and launched a massive campaign of public meetings throughout the country, at which he demanded that the Turks be expelled 'bag and baggage' from their European territories. Letting it be known that he would not be fighting his Greenwich seat again, he arranged – partly through the good offices of the young Scottish Liberal peer, the Earl of Rosebery – to contest the Midlothian constituency, then regarded as a safe Tory seat. The Liberal leadership, and many leading right-wing Liberals, were deeply embarrassed by the fury of Gladstone's campaign, but rank-and-file Liberals, mostly non-Conformists suddenly warmed to this High Church Anglican who articulated so well their own feelings, responded to him with great enthusiasm, and he was hailed as a hero wherever he went. He expanded his target to include the whole range of Disraeli's foreign and imperial polices, which he denounced as 'Beaconsfieldism', following Dizzy's elevation to the peerage. By this, he meant unprincipled adventurism. In the 1880 general election he was easily elected for Midlothian, ousting the Earl of Dalkeith, the son and heir of the Duke of Buccleuch, his former colleague in Sir Robert Peel's cabinet.

Nationally, the Liberals were returned to power, with a majority of nearly 200, including their large band of Irish supporters. It is doubtful whether Gladstone's campaign played more than a marginal part in the overall Tory defeat, which was largely due to economic issues (see Chapter 29), but he was very widely given the credit. Queen Victoria desperately sought to avoid appointing him as Prime Minister, preferring either Hartington or Granville, but Gladstone firmly persuaded both of them to advise her that he was the only possible choice, in the country's interest.

The Gladstone who returned to office in 1880 was a different character from the one who had been defeated in 1874. In the words of the Gladstonian scholar Eugenio Biagini, his 'semi retirement', in 1875, had 'marked a watershed in his career from the executive politician of the Peelite tradition to the charismatic leader of a new and more democratic age' (Biagini, p. 201). Gladstone's later career was, in fact, the prototype on which Max Weber based his famous theory of charisma in politics. Previously, essentially a cautious politician, Gladstone now increasingly threw caution to the winds, depended more and more on his own whims rather than on the counsel of colleagues, and became much more 'left wing', as he grew older, though still insisting that he was not an egalitarian. His reputation with the poor, and the working class soared, but he was increasingly seen by 'men of property' as a dangerous demagogue.

He again chose to be his own Chancellor of the Exchequer, though relinquishing the post to Hugh Childers, in 1882. Granville was again Foreign Secretary, and Sir William Harcourt became Home Secretary. The Radical leader, Joseph Chamberlain, became President of the Board of Trade, while Hartington was appointed Secretary for India, moving on to the War Office after two years. In 1882, also, the 15th Earl of Derby, a former Foreign Secretary, who had crossed the floor from the Tory benches, joined the government as Colonial Secretary. Unlike his first administration, Gladstone's second government was not hailed as a great reforming ministry, though it did pass the 1884 Reform Bill, which effectively completed the work of the 1867 Act, by introducing male household suffrage to county as well as borough constituencies. Lord Salisbury, formerly a stubborn opponent of reform, who had succeeded Disraeli as the Tory leader, threatened to defeat the Bill in the Lords, but after negotiation with Gladstone agreed to let it through, provided it was accompanied by a redistribution of seats, which saw the replacement of almost all the two-member seats by single-member constituencies. As he foresaw, but the Liberals did not, this proved greatly to the advantage of the Tories (see Chapter 31).

At the outset of the government, the now 70-year-old Gladstone, who initially saw his premiership as only a stopgap arrangement for a year or two at most, concentrated on foreign affairs, determined to put an end to Beaconsfield's adventurism and to curb the excesses of his imperialism. Gladstone's mentor in foreign affairs had been Lord Aberdeen, whose pacific approach to potential conflicts, based on a strong preference for diplomatic negotiation rather than sword-rattling, had greatly influenced him. He had, accordingly, set out six principles of correct international behaviour in a speech in Midlothian, on 27 November 1879 (Mathew, 2004). In practice, he found these principles more difficult to apply than he had imagined, and his determination to prevent further imperialist expansion proved elusive. Nowhere more so than in relations with Egypt, where British influence continued to grow following Disraeli's purchase of the Suez canal shares, so that it was fast becoming a British protectorate, though it remained technically part of the Ottoman empire. Gladstone initially encouraged nationalist sentiment in Egypt, but reluctantly agreed to the bombardment of Alexandria by a British fleet in June 1882, after riots had broken out, and then to a full-scale invasion, after it had been demanded by all his cabinet ministers except John Bright, who resigned in protest. The country was completely in British hands by September 1882, and the nationalist leader, Arabi Pasha, was deported and imprisoned in the Seychelles. Unfortunately, the British commitment did not end there. Sudan, an Egyptian dependency, was the scene of a rebellion by a fanatical Moslem leader, known as the Mahdi, and General Charles Gordon was despatched with a small force to rescue isolated Egyptian garrisons in the country, and evacuate them. Gordon, a war hero from the Crimean and Chinese Wars, exceeded his instructions, and established himself in Khartoum, where he hoped to keep the Mahdi's army at bay. Instead, he was besieged there, and his situation became progressively more hopeless. For long, Gladstone resisted pressure to send a relief force, but when he finally agreed it was too late, and the force arrived in Khartoum two days after it had been over-run, and Gordon and all his troops killed. Gladstone's reputation was badly damaged; he survived a Commons censure motion by only 14 votes. The Tories gleefully reversed the acronym GOM (Grand old Man), by which he was becoming widely known, to MOG (Murderer of Gordon).

When Gladstone returned to power in 1880 he had not expected that Ireland would again be the dominant issue facing his government, but so it proved to be. His 1870 Irish Land Act had failed to dampen discontent, and rural violence had greatly increased. Meanwhile, Charles Stewart Parnell, the Protestant leader of the predominantly Catholic Nationalist movement had built up a formable electoral machine, which had made a virtual clean sweep of the Irish constituencies outside Ulster, with an insistent demand for Home Rule. Gladstone's response was two-fold; he introduced another Land Bill, which went a great deal further to meeting Irish demands than his earlier measure, and accompanied this with a Coercion Bill, giving the Viceroy powers to detain people indefinitely, without bringing them to trial. Parnell and several of his associates were arrested, and held in Kilmainham jail for several months. Then in May 1882, Lord Frederick Cavendish, the Irish Chief Secretary, who was married to Catherine Gladstone's niece, was murdered by Fenians in Phoenix Park, Dublin, together with his Permanent Under Secretary, T.H. Burke. Gladstone was severely shaken by this event, but probably concluded about this time that Home Rule was the only viable long-term solution, though he did not reveal this to any of his colleagues. In the meantime, an even stronger coercion bill was passed. This upset Parnell and his party, previously allied to the Liberals, and in June 1885 they voted with the Tories to defeat the budget. Gladstone immediately resigned, and Lord Salisbury formed a minority Tory government. A relieved Victoria then offered Gladstone an earldom, which he unhesitatingly rejected. In November 1885, Salisbury called a general election, in which he failed to win a majority, but remained in office with the support of the Parnellites. At around this time, Gladstone approached Arthur Balfour, Salisbury's nephew, to see whether a bipartisan agreement on some measure of Home Rule might be reached (see Chapter 31). Salisbury flatly refused, and Gladstone's youngest son, Herbert, then leaked to the press that his father was converted to Home Rule.

This was good enough for the Parnellites, and they promptly abandoned their temporary alliance with the Tories, defeating the government in the Queen's Speech debate on 27 January 1886. Salisbury resigned, and Victoria, anxious to avoid a third Gladstone government at all costs, put out feelings to George Goschen, a former Liberal cabinet minister, who now often voted with the Tories, to see if he would head a coalition government. Goschen refused, and after three days, she bowed to the inevitable, and sent her secretary to call on Gladstone with 'the Queen's Commission', which, as he recorded in his diary 'I at once accepted'. He had difficulty in forming the government: several prominent Whigs, led by Lord Hartington, whom Gladstone had treated most insensitively in the past, and including both Derby and Goschen, refused to serve, because of their strong opposition to Home Rule. Two leading Radicals, Joseph Chamberlain and Sir George Trevelyan, accepted office, but resigned soon after for the same reason. Victoria continued to make difficulties, turning down Gladstone's first two choices for the Foreign Office, Lord Granville and the Earl of Kimberley, and insisting instead on the young Earl of Rosebery. Undeterred, Gladstone pressed ahead, and introduced his Home Rule Bill, in April 1886. After 16 days of debate, it was defeated by 30 votes on the Second

Reading, on 8 June 1886, with only two-thirds of Liberal MPs voting with the government. Gladstone immediately asked for, and was granted a dissolution, and went down to heavy defeat in the subsequent general election, which produced the following result:

Conservatives	316
Liberals	190
Liberal Unionists	79
Irish Nationalists	85

The Liberal Unionists, who included a large element of the former Whigs as well as Joe Chamberlain's formidable Birmingham-based group of Radicals, threw in their lot with the Conservatives, with whom they eventually merged to form the Conservative and Unionist Party. Gladstone's third government had lasted a mere 169 days, and Lord Salisbury became Prime Minister for the second time, with a large majority. Many of the Liberals who stayed loyal nevertheless blamed Gladstone for the recklessness with which he had split his party. They agreed with him in principle on Home Rule, but did not believe that its importance outweighed all other considerations. They felt that he should not have sprung the issue on the party, without spending a great deal more time in gentle persuasion. This, however, was not the way of the older Gladstone, who, in Lord Randolph Churchill's words, had become 'an old man in a hurry'.

The now 76-year-old Gladstone had no thought of retiring, but sat out the six years of Salisbury's term, continuing to make Home Rule his over-riding priority, and forming a close alliance with the Irish Nationalists, sometimes using Parnell's mistress, Kathy O'Shea, as a go-between. When Kathy's husband, Captain W.H. O'Shea MP, cited Parnell as a co-respondent in his divorce case, Gladstone sanctimoniously threw up his hands in horror, though he was well aware of what had been going on. He urged Parnell to retire temporarily from public life, and withheld his support when Parnell's Catholic supporters turned on him. Parnell, a broken man, died within the year, aged 46. The GOM's abandonment of Parnell, and the consequent fatal split in the Irish Nationalist party was highly damaging to the Home Rule cause. A string of by-election successes had led to high hopes of a massive Liberal victory at the forthcoming general election, with a majority large enough to secure not only the passage of a Bill through the Commons but also to deter the Lords from applying a veto. In the event, some 355 supporters of Home Rule were returned in the 1892 election, and 315 opponents – a clear majority, but a bitter disappointment after the earlier high hopes. Salisbury resigned, and in August 1892, aged 82, Gladstone embarked on his fourth government. His cabinet included three subsequent Liberal Prime Ministers – Rosebery, Henry

Campbell–Bannerman and H.H. Asquith, but his closest associate was John Morley, the Irish Chief Secretary, who was later to write his biography in three extensive volumes. His last premiership lasted for one year, and 199 days, and was totally dominated by the issue of Home Rule. Gladstone received little support from his Cabinet colleagues, only two of whom – Morley and Lord Spencer, a former Irish Viceroy – were wholeheartedly behind his efforts. The two most senior figures – Harcourt, the Chancellor of the Exchequer, and Rosebery, the Foreign Secretary – were determinedly obstructive, while most of the rest of the cabinet were sullenly resentful that what they regarded as a quixotic enterprise should take precedence over all other government business. Gladstone himself was far from optimistic about the outcome, and, now half blind as well as half deaf, had serious misgivings about his own his own capacity, confiding to his diary: 'Frankly from the condition (*now*) of my senses, I am no longer fit for public life; yet bidden to walk in it. "Lead thou me on"' (Jenkins, p. 585).

Yet, he rose sublimely to the occasion, Jenkins commenting that: 'Even among his bitterest opponents, there was a sense of witnessing a magnificent last performance by a unique creature, the like of whom would never be seen again' (Ibid., p. 603).

Virtually single-handedly, Gladstone assumed the entire burden of carrying the Bill through the Commons, speaking frequently and impressively at all stages – nine days of debate at Second Reading, 53 days for the Committee stage, nine for the Report stage, and three for Third Reading, altogether the greater part of 82 sittings of the House. In the end, the Bill was passed by a majority of 34. The House of Lords was not impressed, and certainly not over-awed. It spent only four days on the Bill, and then rejected it by 419 votes to 41, one of the most one-sided votes in its entire history. They did not stop at that, going on to defeat or truncate several other Liberal Bills over the following months. Gladstone was indignant that the Tory leader, Lord Salisbury, should take such liberties with the programme of a recently elected government, and proposed to his colleagues that an immediate election should be fought on a 'Peers versus People' prospectus, and that – in the event of victory – the Bill should be re-introduced. The Cabinet, sensing – probably correctly – that this was a recipe for electoral disaster, unanimously turned him down. Gladstone resigned his premiership shortly afterwards, having been overwhelmingly defeated in a cabinet vote on Naval rearmament, which he strongly resisted. The Queen, who treated Gladstone in the churlish way to which she had become accustomed, did not ask his advice on the succession. If she had, he would have proposed Lord Spencer; the choice of Liberal MPs would probably have been William Harcourt. Showing crass misjudgement, she chose instead the Earl of Rosebery, who turned out to be one of Britain's least successful premiers (see Chapter 31). Gladstone left office on 2 March 1894, in his 85th year. In total, he had been Prime Minister for 12 years and 126 days, then the fourth longest in British history, though he was subsequently overtaken by Salisbury. Gladstone lived on for another four years, dying of cancer on 19 May 1898, aged 88.

Gladstone was one of the most remarkable men ever to serve in 10 Downing Street. The sheer length of his political career was in itself daunting. Over 62 years as an MP (narrowly second only to Churchill among Prime Ministers), 27 years as a minister, he spanned the period between George Canning, whom he knew as a young man, and Asquith, who served in his last Cabinet. He transformed the office of Chancellor of the Exchequer, was the first politician to campaign actively throughout the whole country and was the virtual creator of the modern Liberal Party. He then badly split it, by driving out most of the former Whigs, while compensating by building up a great bond of trust among working-class voters. The effect of this was probably to delay the creation of a viable Labour or Socialist party until after his death, while this development occurred notably earlier in most other Western European countries. Regarded as 'mad' by Queen Victoria, many of his Liberal colleagues thought that he had lost all sense of proportion over Ireland, and that the strength and persistence of his commitment to Home Rule was a grave error. Nevertheless, if his efforts had been crowned with success, more than a century of turmoil, including two long periods of terrorist, and counter-terrorist, violence would have been avoided, and Ireland would conceivably have remained within a devolved United Kingdom. Gladstone was, more than any other British leader, strongly and publicly motivated by his Christian beliefs which were undoubtedly sincere, though he was not above cutting corners and indulging in sharp practice, from time to time. Disraeli should not be taken at his word when he complained that 'he did not have a single redeeming defect'. It would also not be true to picture Gladstone as consistently solemn and humourless. He had a lively sense of fun, and his speeches, though over-long, were enlivened by flashes of wit, which were not, however, the equal of those of his more mercurial rival. Perhaps, above all, Gladstone should be seen as an archetypal figure of the Victorian age, though he was never appreciated by its figurehead, whose interests he had tried so devotedly and so unrewardingly to serve.

Works consulted

Eugenio Biagini, 1998, 'William Ewart Gladstone', in Robert Eccleshall and Graham Walker (eds.), *Biographical Dictionary of British Prime Ministers*, London, Routledge.

Robert Blake, 1966, *Disraeli*, London, Eyre & Spottiswoode.

Peter Clarke, 1992, *A Question of Leadership: From Gladstone to Thatcher*, London, Penguin Books.

Roy Jenkins, 1998, *The Chancellors*, London, Macmillan.

Roy Jenkins, 1995, *Gladstone,* London, Macmillan.

Dick Leonard, 2013, *The Great Rivalry: Gladstone & Disraeli, A Dual Biography,* London, I.B. Tauris.

H.C.G. Matthew, 1986, *Gladstone 1809–1874,* Oxford, Clarendon Press.

H.C.G. Matthew, 1995, *Gladstone 1875–1898,* Oxford, Clarendon Press.

H.C.G. Matthew, 2004, Article in *Oxford Dictionary of National Biography.*

31

Robert Cecil, 3rd Marquess of Salisbury – Skilful Opponent of Reform

The third Marquess of Salisbury was one of the longest-serving of British Prime Ministers. His three terms of office stretched to 13 years and 252 days, a total exceeded only by three of his predecessors (Walpole, the Younger Pitt and Liverpool), and by none of his successors. He also had a distinguished record as Foreign Secretary – a post he continued to hold during the greater part of his time as Prime Minister – and he was, together with Gladstone, the dominant political personality during the final three decades of the nineteenth century. Yet he quickly became an almost forgotten and disregarded figure. It is only recently – 100 years after his death – that the full extent of his (largely negative) achievements has come to be widely recognised. At the beginning of the twenty-first century, he is at last being given the recognition that he was denied during the 20th. This is partly, but not entirely, due to the publication, in 1999, of the mammoth biography by Andrew Roberts, *Salisbury: Victorian Titan*, written with full access to the voluminous Salisbury papers, preserved at his stately home at Hatfield House.

Superficially, Salisbury strongly resembled the long series of aristocrats who led the majority of British governments throughout the eighteenth and nineteenth centuries. Educated at Eton and Oxford, elected to a 'family borough' while still in his early twenties, inheriting a peerage and large estates in his forties, his c.v. matched those of such predecessors as the Earl of Derby, Viscount Melbourne and Earl Grey. Yet, temperamentally, he was far from falling into this mould. Born on 3 February 1830, the third son of the second Marquess of Salisbury – a direct descendant of Lord Burghley and Robert Cecil, the chief ministers of Elizabeth I and James I – he was a sickly and unsociable child who had no appetite for the favoured pastimes of his class. He detested games, and throughout his life abstained alike from hunting, shooting and fishing. Instead, he spent long hours in the well-stocked library of Hatfield House, his ancestral home, and developed marked intellectual tastes from an early age. This did him no good at Eton, where he was so badly and incessantly bullied that his father agreed to take him away at the age of 15 and entrust him to a private tutor.

At 17, Lord Robert Cecil, as he was then known, went up to Christ Church (Oxford), where he felt more at home than at Eton, and showed a keen interest in politics, becoming successively secretary and treasurer of the Union, where he made his mark as a stern and orthodox Tory. But his health broke down after two years and he had to leave prematurely, being awarded an honorary Fourth Class degree in Mathematics. In view of the sad fate of his elder brothers, one of whom had died in infancy, while the other (Lord Cranborne) was a permanent invalid, his father agreed in July 1855 to send him on a long voyage to recover from what his doctor described as 'the complete breakdown of his nervous system.'

This voyage, which lasted 22 months and included lengthy stays in South Africa, Australia and New Zealand, was the making of Cecil. Not only did it permanently strengthen his health, but, according to a biographer, A.L. Kennedy, it

> broadened his mental outlook, afforded him close contact with types of humanity he would not otherwise have met, and gave him one or two of the permanent characteristics of his statesmanship, not the least of which was a profound belief in the Empire, by no means common among his contemporaries. (Kennedy, pp. 14–15)

Yet the man who returned from the voyage had little confidence that he would make anything of his life. Writing to his father, he discussed dismissively the prospects of a career in politics, the Church or the bar:

> 'My chances of getting into the House of Commons are practically nil ... [Holy] Orders is the profession I should place next to it [politics] in usefulness: but from my uncertain health and my inaptitude for gaining personal influence I am as little fitted to it as any man I ever met', he wrote, adding that 'I am as likely to attain eminence in it [the bar] as I am to get into Parliament'. (Kennedy, p. 16)

Only three months elapsed, however, from his return from New Zealand, in May 1853, before he was elected MP for Stamford. Effectively a pocket borough, it was in the gift of his cousin, the Marquess of Exeter. Cecil was unopposed in the by-election which followed the death of the previous Member, and he never had to fight a contest during the 15 years that he represented the seat. His father, who was himself later a Tory Cabinet minister in the second Derby government, used his influence to secure him the candidacy, and must have hoped that Cecil would now conform more closely to the accepted pattern of life for a country gentleman of high birth. He was due for two grievous disappointments. In April 1855 the colonelcy of the Middlesex militia fell vacant. As Lord-Lieutenant of the county, the appointment was in the Marquess's hands, and he resolved to confer it on his son, writing to offer it to him in the most enthusiastic terms. Cecil's blankly refused, saying 'I detest all soldiering beyond measure' and that his usefulness for the militia command was 'ludicrously glaring' (Kennedy, pp. 27–8).

Worse was to follow. Cecil might not have been generally considered a particularly eligible bachelor. 'A tall, stooping, myopic intellectual recluse, he was also an untidy unprepossessing man' (Taylor, p. 4), but it was taken for granted that he would eventually make an appropriate match with the daughter of another aristocratic house. When Cecil announced in 1856 that he was to marry Georgina Alderson, the dowerless daughter of a judge, his father promptly forbade the marriage. Cecil was obdurate, and his father eventually relented, though setting his allowance at so meagre a level that he was forced to seek a supplementary source of income – journalism.

This proved a blessing in disguise. For the type of journalism to which Salisbury devoted himself was at the highest intellectual level – long articles (33 in all), each of 20,000 words or so, for the *Quarterly Review*, supplemented by over 600 shorter pieces for the weekly *Saturday Review*, edited by his brother-in-law, Alexander Beresford-Hope. Such articles required a great deal of research, and Cecil expended much energy in informing himself and thinking through his position on all the major issues of the day. Although the majority of the articles dealt with domestic politics, the most trenchant are undoubtedly on foreign policy, including two brilliant historical studies of the Younger Pitt and Castlereagh, whom Cecil clearly regarded as appropriate role models (several of these articles are reprinted in Paul Smith (ed.), see below).

Perhaps the most significant of all his articles, which appeared in April 1864, was a critique of the policies carried out by the then Foreign Secretary, Earl Russell, and the Prime Minister, Lord Palmerston. He was especially scathing about their nonchalance in encouraging Denmark to stand up to Prussian and Austrian demands over Schleswig-Holstein, but then leaving the Danes in the lurch when it was clear that the two Germanic powers were bent on war. 'Peace without honour is not only a disgrace, it is a chimera', he wrote, in words which almost precisely prefigured the Munich agreement of 74 years later.

In a survey covering the eight years between 1856 and 1864, Cecil discerned a pattern of British bullying of weak countries (six examples), while using only menacing language against more powerful countries (first Russia, then Prussia, then the United States), followed by a hasty retreat when it became clear that they were in earnest. The conclusion he drew was that provocative words should only be used when there was a firm intention to back them up with action. Theodore Roosevelt's later dictum – 'Speak softly but carry a big stick' – surely encapsulated the lesson which Salisbury drew from his study of Russell and Palmerston, and it was one he faithfully applied on most occasions during his subsequent conduct of foreign policy.

If his financial dependency had the beneficial effect of preparing him intellectually much more thoroughly for ministerial office, its cause – his 'inappropriate marriage' – had no less happy an effect. Lord Blake describes it as:

> one of the wisest decisions in his life ... [Georgina Alderson] was of the same High Church persuasion as he was. Religion played a vital part in both their lives. She also had a similar sense of humour. But unlike Cecil she was sociable, gregarious and extrovert. She was highly intelligent and ready to talk about all the topics of the day; she suffered from none of the nervousness, the introspection, the shyness which afflicted him from his youth, but which evaporated to a great extent as their married life went by. She was his prop and invaluable support for forty-two years till she died in 1899. (Blake and Cecil, p. 3)

Although Cecil's articles were contributed anonymously, the identity of the author rapidly became known among political circles. He soon gained renown as a sceptical, shrewd and informed commentator whose views, though firmly based on Conservative principles, were not bound by narrow party political considerations. It was his writing, rather than his rather fitful and idiosyncratic parliamentary activity which gradually built up Cecil's political reputation during the 1850s and early 1860s. He was, however, overlooked by Lord Derby when he formed his short-lived Conservative administration of 1859–60, in which Cecil's father served as Lord President of the Council.

Still feeling under keen financial pressure, with a rapidly growing family to support, Cecil resolved to give up politics and seek an office of profit under the Crown. The most promising vacancy was for a Clerk to the Privy Council, now in the gift of his father. The second Marquess was willing to appoint him, but was over-ruled by the Cabinet who balked at this act of nepotism. So Cecil redoubled his journalistic efforts, but his situation was transformed in June 1865, with the death of his elder brother, Lord Cranborne. From being a mere younger son, he became the heir to the marquessate and to one of the largest estates and fortunes in the country. His father substantially increased his allowance, and his days of relative penury were over.

Cranborne, as he now became, had strongly criticized Benjamin Disraeli, whom he regarded as a mountebank, in several of his articles, but the Conservative leader in the Commons did not hold it against him. When Lord Derby again became Prime Minister in 1866, Disraeli readily agreed to the appointment of Cranborne as Secretary of State for India, and went out of his way to be friendly to him.

Cranborne's first cabinet post lasted for less than nine months. In March 1867 he resigned, with two other colleagues, in protest against the terms of the second Reform Bill, which extended the vote to all heads of households in urban constituencies. Cranborne made it clear that his objection was as much to what he regarded as Disraeli's unprincipled manipulation as to the actual terms of the bill, which was duly voted into law. Cranborne's resignation was no sudden fit of pique. No great believer in democracy, he appeared to feel that the settlement reached under the 1832 Reform Bill had produced an almost perfect balance between the different classes of society. The untrammelled power of the aristocracy had been trimmed, and representatives of the middle classes had been admitted into the decision-making process. Cranborne had no objection to working class representatives also being involved, but he did not wish them to be admitted in such numbers as to swamp the interests of the propertied classes. His quasi-Marxist analysis led him to conclude that giving power to the workers would inevitably lead to the despoliation of the other classes. His favoured solution – which was incorporated in the original draft which Disraeli presented to the Cabinet – was that the extension of the franchise should be balanced by plural voting rights for the propertied and better educated.

On his own account, Cranborne was notably disinterested, but not so on behalf of his class or of his party. He regarded the ownership of property as an essential basis for political leadership, and his opposition to the 1867 Reform Bill owed much to a study which he undertook of its likely political consequences. These, he concluded, would be injurious to the Conservatives, particularly in the smaller boroughs (Clarke, pp. 48–9).

Cranborne's resignation did little, if any, harm to his reputation. Rather, it confirmed him, at least in Conservative circles, as a man prepared to put principle before his own political career. Nor did Disraeli take offence, inviting him to rejoin the Cabinet when he succeeded Derby as Prime Minister in January 1868. Yet Cranborne was adamant, writing at this time:

> If I had a firm confidence in his principles or his honesty, or even if he were identified by birth or property with the Conservative classes in the country – I might...work to maintain him in power. But he is an adventurer and I have good cause to know he is without principles or honesty'. (Taylor, p. 28)

At this stage, he once again thought of abandoning politics, writing to a Liberal friend (John Coleridge): 'my opinions belong to the past, and it is better that the new principles in politics should be worked by those who sympathise with them heartily' (Kennedy, p. 64).

In April 1868 his father died, and he inherited his seat in the House of Lords as well as the family estates. The new Marquess's character and beliefs had long been fully formed. At their root was a strong Christian faith. Salisbury was no less committed a Christian than Gladstone – indeed had been strongly influenced by the teachings of the same Bishop Butler, whose works Gladstone was to edit and annotate. Yet, whereas Gladstone's Christian faith tormented him, Salisbury's brought him calm and reassurance. It also made him a profound pessimist, with few illusions about the perfectibility of man. Yet Salisbury was also a utilitarian, influenced by Jeremy Bentham with his doctrine of the greatest happiness of the greatest number. He was a very English character, who took it for granted that English ways were best, though he was sharply critical of signs of racial superiority exhibited by British colonists and administrators in South Africa or India. No social snob, he was more aware of the responsibilities than the privileges of the landed class, and considered public service an inescapable duty. Painfully shy in private, he never flinched from playing a public role. The natural authority which he exhibited may have owed much to his social position in an age of deference, but it was also due in part to his strength of character and the unaffected candour of his speech. His conservatism did not take the form of a blind resistance to change, indeed he regarded change as inevitable and beneficial. What he was against was sudden, revolutionary upheaval; change he believed should be something organic, as in nature. Nor did he believe in dying in the last ditch even against changes which he considered objectionable; they should instead be accepted as an accomplished fact, and energies should thereafter be directed to making them work out with the least undesirable consequences. This was certainly the spirit in which he accepted the 1867 Reform Bill once it had been passed, and it greatly influenced his attitude, as we shall see, to the subsequent Bill of 1884.

His new position led to a considerable broadening of his interests: he took his duties as a landowner and farmer extremely seriously, and showed a benevolent and highly practical interest in the welfare of his many tenants. As a keen amateur scientist, he set up his own laboratory at Hatfield House, which became one of the first private houses in England to be connected with electricity, or to have a telephone. He became an accomplished photographer, and even contributed a learned article on the subject to the *Quarterly Review*. In 1869 he became Chancellor of Oxford University, while a year earlier he became chairman (and effective general manager) of the Great Eastern Railway – a post which he successfully held for four years, and which gave him invaluable experience of business and commerce.

And there was the House of Lords, a chamber not especially revered by Salisbury, who once described it as 'the dullest assembly in the world'. Yet he played a considerable part in its proceedings during the six years of Gladstone's first government, which lasted until 1874. His position was somewhat anomalous. Easily the most effective debater in the House, he played no formal role in the Conservative opposition. Though he usually sided with them in debate, he continued to show the same independent streak that he had in the Commons. On one notable occasion, he rounded on Tory peers who had sought to modify the trust deeds of a charitable bequest intended to provide doles for old people. They had argued that it was bad for the poor to receive money without working for it. 'Lord Salisbury, furious and sarcastic', a biographer wrote 'mocked the hypocrisy of a House, which, living for the most part on inherited wealth, was denying the solace of an unearned pittance for the poor' (Kennedy, p. 76).

Salisbury continued to regard Disraeli with contempt, and it was ironic that he owed the resurrection of his political career entirely to his sustained patronage and support. Without this, he would only be remembered now – if at all – as an eccentric grandee and intellectual maverick.

When Disraeli unexpectedly won the 1874 election, and embarked on his second ministry, one of his first concerns was to recruit Salisbury to his Cabinet. Salisbury showed extreme reluctance, writing to his wife that the prospect of having to serve again 'with this man' was 'like a nightmare'. The wily Disraeli used Salisbury's step-mother, now married to the 15th Earl of Derby (son of the former Prime Minister and himself Foreign Secretary in the new government), as a go-between. Her urging and that of Salisbury's few intimate friends proved sufficient to overcome his doubts, though he still spent three days making up his mind. He returned to his previous post in the India Office, and from then onwards his distrust of Disraeli gradually diminished and something approaching friendship developed between the two men.

The decisive moment in Salisbury's political career came two years later, in 1876. Uprisings in Herzogovina and Bulgaria against Turkish rule, which had been suppressed with the utmost barbarity, had stirred consciences throughout Europe, especially that of Gladstone, who embarked on his missionary campaign to turn the Turks 'bag and baggage' out of Europe. Disraeli, fearful that if no action was taken, Russia – which had already vastly extended its territories by the virtual annexation of Turkmenistan, Khiva and Bokhara – would undertake this task for its own aggrandisement, proposed a conference of the great powers of Europe (Austria, Britain, France, Germany, Italy and Russia) to persuade the Turks to reform their administration. The Russian government was unexpectedly willing to go along with this proposal, and itself convened a conclave at its embassy in Constantinople to which the other powers were invited.

The obvious British representative was the Foreign Secretary, Lord Derby. But he was increasingly at odds with Disraeli, who chose Salisbury to go in his place. The consequence was to turn Salisbury from a little-known British politician into a statesman of international renown. He set off for Constantinople in

November 1876, stopping off on the way at the main European capitals to discuss the situation. In Berlin he met Bismarck, the German Chancellor, and the Emperor, William I, and in Paris, Vienna and Rome had long discussions with the leading political figures. No British politician since the Congress of Vienna 60 years earlier had had such extensive contact with his foreign counterparts. Salisbury's private views at this stage were not very different from Gladstone's; he was pre-disposed to a pro-Russian viewpoint, unlike Disraeli (now Lord Beaconsfield) and a majority of his Tory colleagues. At Constantinople he made common cause with the amiable but artful Russian representative, General Ignatiev, though he subsequently realised that he had been manipulated by him. The conference itself went remarkably smoothly, and an agreed list of demands was presented to the Sultan, Abdul Hamid II. These he promptly rejected, and the plenipotentiaries returned home feeling that the venture had been a failure. So, in substance, it had, but for Lord Salisbury it had been a triumphant success, putting him on the map internationally, and he returned home, to his amazement, to a hero's welcome.

The subsequent war between Russia and Turkey, which broke out in April 1887, led to Salisbury becoming more and more critical of Russia, as the threat increased of its occupation of Constantinople and the conversion of the whole of Turkey's European possessions into virtual Russian satellites. He repeatedly demanded a British show of force – such as sending a fleet to the Dardanelles – to warn the Russians off, but the majority of his cabinet colleagues were reluctant, and only finally agreed in February 1878 when the Russian troops were at the gates of Constantinople. The following month the Turks were induced to sign a peace treaty with Russia at San Stefano.

This treaty carved a large Bulgarian state out of Turkey's European territories, extending from the Danube to the shores of the Aegean, from the Black Sea to the Albanian border. Nominally under Turkish suzerainty, the terms of the treaty made it clear that it would, in fact, be a Russian satellite. The British government's reaction was that the Treaty breached the terms of the Treaty of Paris, which ended the Crimean War, and that it should not be ratified unless its terms were approved by all the signatories of the earlier treaty. When Russia sent an evasive reply, the Cabinet decided to transport troops from India to the Mediterranean to be in a position to intervene, if necessary, on behalf of the Turks. This decision provoked the resignation of Derby, to the relief of Beaconsfield, and Salisbury was the inevitable successor. He did not wait until his formal appointment, on 2 April 1878, before taking the most decisive step in his career. On the night of 29 March, returning to Hatfield from a dinner party, he retired to his study, and without any help or consultation with Foreign Office staff, composed a circular, which a subsequent Prime Minister, Lord Rosebery, described as one of the 'historic State papers of the English language'. Approved by the Cabinet the next day, it went out to the capitals of the other five European powers – St. Petersburg, Vienna, Berlin, Paris and Rome.

The circular made clear that each and every one of the provisions of the San Stefano Treaty must be re-examined at a congress of the European powers, and left little doubt in the minds of its readers that British military intervention would follow if Russia did not agree to this. Salisbury followed up the circular with secret negotiations with the Turks for the transfer to Britain of Cyprus, to provide a suitable base for such intervention either immediately or in the future. The circular had the effect of stiffening the other powers, notably Austria-Hungary, and Russia climbed down and agreed to the summoning of the Congress of Berlin. Here Bismarck was able to pose as an 'Honest Broker', and Beaconsfield basked in the limelight of what proved to be the twilight of his premiership. Yet it was clear to all the participants, as Beaconsfield generously conceded, that Salisbury was the real architect of the Congress and its settlement (which greatly reduced the size of the new Bulgaria, restored conquered territories to Turkey and confirmed the British take-over of Cyprus), and that without his decisive initiative the Russian war gains would have remained intact. In the words of A.L. Kennedy, 'The discomfiture of Russia at San Stefano was probably the most single-handed achievement in the whole long history of British diplomacy' (Kennedy, p. 137).

In retrospect, it appears less of an unmitigated triumph. Salisbury himself later came to question the wisdom of cutting Bulgaria down to size, the collapse of the Ottoman Empire was deferred rather than averted, and Britain was saddled with a new colony that proved less of a strategic asset than it appeared and which stored up troubles for the future. Less transitory were the benefits (primarily to his own party) of his two great contentions in domestic politics with Gladstone during the following decade.

After Beaconsfield's death, in 1881, Salisbury led the Tories in the Lords, but shared the party leadership with Sir Stafford Northcote, who was the leader in the Commons. The determining event which resulted in his supplanting Northcote as the most likely choice for a Tory Prime Minister was the 1884 Reform Bill, which extended the principle of household suffrage to the Tory heartland – the county constituencies. Salisbury was not above threatening to veto the bill in the House of Lords, and rather than provoking a Lords vs. Commons showdown, Gladstone invited the Tory leaders to a meeting with the objective of negotiating a bi-partisan compromise. At this meeting, Salisbury played the dominant role, entirely putting the passive Northcote in the shade. In exchange for letting the Reform Bill through, he insisted, there must be a general redistribution of seats, in order to maintain the influence of the rural and suburban areas against those of the larger towns, which formed the core of Liberal support. This objective he achieved, and in particular he secured the virtual ending of the long-established system of two-member constituencies.

Henceforward, the great majority of seats would return only a single member, which turned out to be a significant disadvantage to the Liberal party. This party embraced a wide range of interests, ranging from right-wing Whigs to left-wing radicals. A great many local Liberal associations had followed the practice of offering a 'balanced ticket' by nominating both a Whig and a Radical candidate, and this option would no longer be open to them.

Ever since Disraeli had split the Conservative Party in 1846, and the subsequent link-up of the Peelites with the Liberals, the Tories had been very much the minority party, winning only one election (that of 1874) in a 40-year period. It was Salisbury's long-term objective to reverse this situation by luring the Whigs away from the Liberals, to form a 'moderate' alliance with the Tories, embracing the centre and right of the political spectrum, confining a Radical-dominated Liberal Party to the left. Salisbury's handling of the 1884 Reform Bill was directed towards this end, but it was the Irish Home Rule crisis of 1885–6 which provided the catalyst.

The crucial moment came towards the end of Salisbury's first, minority, premiership, which lasted from June 1885 to January 1886. Gladstone, who was already convinced of the necessity of Home Rule, approached Salisbury, through his nephew, Arthur Balfour, with a proposal that the Irish question should be settled on a non-partisan basis. In practice, this could only take the form of some kind of all-Ireland assembly, with guarantees for the Protestant minority, and reserve powers for the Westminster Parliament. Salisbury rejected the approach out of hand. He was already on record as a convinced opponent of Home Rule, but it must also have occurred to him that such a settlement would divide his own party. The alternative – of leaving Gladstone himself to legislate for Home Rule – would be far. more likely to lead to the very split in the Liberal Party which he had long sought.

This is precisely what happened the following year when Gladstone introduced his first Home Rule Bill and was abandoned – not only by the Whigs under Lord Hartington, but by Joseph Chamberlain's Radicals as well. Salisbury's tactful handling of the Liberal Unionists led to their permanent detachment from the Liberal Party and their eventual absorption into the Conservative and Unionist Party.

Salisbury's own recipe for Ireland was to combine firm government ('coercion') with measures designed to remove the economic causes of discontent. In 1887 he appointed his nephew as Chief Secretary for Ireland with a mandate to carry out this policy, which he accomplished with limited success, earning the sobriquet 'Bloody Balfour' in the process.

Salisbury's three terms as Prime Minister (1885–6, 1886–92, 1895–1902) were hardly notable periods for domestic reform, though a number of useful bills were passed. The two most significant were probably the Education Act of 1891, which provided for free primary schooling, and the Local Government

Act 1888, which established elected county councils. Other Local Government Acts provided for elected authorities in Ireland, Scotland and London boroughs, while there were a number of other legislative measures concerning Irish land tenure, safety in coalmines, working-class housing and, in particular, improving the lot of agricultural labourers.

In large part, however, Salisbury was more interested in providing calm and efficient administration rather than in innovation. He proved himself a skilful cabinet-maker, promoting effective colleagues such as Hicks-Beach, W.H. Smith and C.T. Ritchie to senior posts and then, on the whole, leaving them to get on with their jobs with a minimum of interference. His major personnel problem was in handling the popular, energetic but disloyal Lord Randolph Churchill, whose burgeoning ambitions clearly represented a threat to Salisbury's own leadership. He comprehensively outmanoeuvred Churchill, whose impetuous resignation as Chancellor of the Exchequer, in December 1886, effectively ended his political career. Thereafter Salisbury's domination over his cabinets was virtually complete until his final years in office when his authority was visibly failing.

For 11 of the nearly 14 years of his premiership, Salisbury combined the office with the Foreign Secretaryship, something no subsequent Prime Minister has attempted, apart from Ramsay MacDonald in 1924. It was the principal focus of his interest, and it has even been suggested that Salisbury's only, or at least main interest in being Prime Minister was that it meant he could run his own foreign policy without having a senior colleague looking over his shoulder and restricting his freedom of action. Salisbury put the furtherance of the interests of the British Empire at the head of his priorities, but his preferred method of settling disputes was by international negotiation, actively seeking to revive the Concert of Europe.

He was firmly against embroiling Britain in permanent alliances, believing that national security depended, above all, on the strength of the British navy. He was the originator of the 'Two Power Naval Standard', that is, that the British fleet should be equal in strength to that of the combined forces of the next two biggest navies. He maintained particularly good relations with Germany, especially until the fall of Bismarck in 1890, but he rebuffed approaches to turn them into a formal treaty of alliance, either on a bilateral basis, or with the Triple Alliance of Germany, Italy and Austria-Hungary. The last attempt to formalize a treaty with Germany, strongly pressed by Joseph Chamberlain, was killed stone dead by a magisterial memorandum composed by Salisbury in May 1901.

With France his relationship was more difficult because of a multitude of conflicting interests in various parts of Africa, culminating in the Fashoda incident in 1898, which brought the two countries to the brink of war. Salisbury took an exceptionally firm line, insisting that the French should back down, which they did, but then negotiated a *modus vivendi*, leaving Britain a free hand in the Nile Valley, in exchange for French expansion in West Africa.

Eight years earlier he had agreed a comparable *quid pro quo* with Germany, ceding Heligoland (in spite of the reluctance of Queen Victoria) in exchange for British hegemony in Zanzibar, Uganda and Kenya. Salisbury, who remained cool towards the aspirations of Joseph Chamberlain and Cecil Rhodes to establish an unbroken British north–south link between Cairo and the Cape, nevertheless was vigilant to prevent any other colonial power, whether France, Germany, Belgium or Portugal, establishing an east–west trans-continental link. He was able to avert this possibility by a series of diplomatic negotiations, and though the 'scramble for Africa', which substantially coincided with Salisbury's periods in office, resulted in many crimes and horrors, these did not include any wars between the European colonial powers. This was largely Salisbury's achievement.

He has been pictured as a reluctant imperialist, adverse to British annexations, much preferring indirect to direct rule and hesitating for years before approving the reconquest of the Sudan, culminating in the Battle of Omdurman in September 1898. Yet the fact remains that under his premiership, as A. L. Kennedy points out, the British Empire expanded 'by six million square miles, containing populations of about a hundred million – a record – which no other Prime Minister in British history since the elder Pitt could approach' (Kennedy, pp. 341–2).

Salisbury's handling of the Fashoda incident was almost the last occasion on which he was able to demonstrate his leadership abilities. From then onwards it was downhill almost all the way. His physical and mental powers were in decline – he failed to recognise cabinet colleagues and on one occasion had a lengthy conversation with the African explorer Sir Harry Johnson under the misapprehension that he was the Commander-in-Chief of the British army, Lord Roberts. There was a major reshuffle of the government in 1900, when Salisbury relinquished the Foreign Office to Lord Lansdowne, but packed his ministry with so many relatives that it was caricatured as the Hotel Cecil.

More serious still had been the general lassitude which had afflicted him during the long-drawn-out illness and death of his wife, in 1899. During this period Britain had drifted into the Boer War, much against Salisbury's instincts, but he had lacked the ability or the will to control the actions of his bellicose Colonial Secretary, Joseph Chamberlain or of Lord Milner, the British commissioner in the Cape Colony. Had he still been at the height of his powers, it is scarcely conceivable that the war would have broken out nor that it would have been prosecuted with such little sense of purpose.

Yet, even when Queen Victoria died in 1901, Salisbury did not take the obvious opportunity of standing down, but laboured on for nearly two more years. His clinging to office was not the least paradox of his career, for he had been genuinely unwilling to take office, seeking to excuse himself on each of the first two occasions when the Queen had summoned him to take charge. By this time however, his fine intellect was blunted, his natural scepticism was suspended, and he allowed himself to succumb, as do many long-serving leaders, to the illusion that he was indispensable. Or, as his younger son, Lord Robert Cecil, put it more charitably in an article contributed anonymously to the *Modern Review*, shortly after his death:

> Probably the greatest trial of his patriotism and courage was reserved for the end of his career. Only those in his most intimate circle know how distasteful office had become to him in his later years. He hated war, and his hatred of it grew as he grew older. He was borne down with domestic grief and physical weakness; and yet he felt himself unable to lay down his burden lest the enemies of his country should take courage from the ministerial and electoral difficulties that might, and indeed did, follow his resignation. He remained at his post. (Kennedy, p. 328)

By hanging on into the twentieth century, Salisbury severely damaged his reputation. Had he died or resigned in 1898 or 1899, he might well have been assessed as one of the most successful leaders ever to have held the top office. Yet, three developments, in particular, owe more to him than any other single person. First, the dominance during most of the twentieth century of the Conservative Party, of which he – rather than the more celebrated Disraeli – was the main architect. Second, the persistence of the Irish problem until our own day, which may well be traced back to his refusal to agree a bi-partisan policy with Gladstone over Home Rule. Third – but more contentiously – his veto of an Anglo-German alliance, as late as 1901, has been blamed, notably by Julian Amery in his biography of Joseph Chamberlain, as leading to the First World War and, by implication, to all the horrors which came after (Amery, p. 158).

Salisbury could be regarded as the ultimate High Tory, and it is perhaps appropriate that what will almost certainly come to be regarded as his definitive biography has been written by a High Tory historian, Andrew Roberts. Roberts wrote that:

> Early in life Salisbury recognised that the institutions he cherished were coming under grave threat. The Established Church, the British Empire, the House of Lords, High Tory and High Church Oxford, Crown prerogatives, the rights of property, the landed aristocracy, the Act of Union – all that he regarded as the very foundations of English governing society... His was consciously a lifelong rearguard action. (Roberts, p. 851)

His stubborn efforts to hold back what others regarded as the march of progress are lauded by Roberts. Another renowned High Tory, however, believed that he rather overdid his resistance to change. Lord Curzon, one of his more distinguished successors as Tory leader in the Lords, was to describe him, in a rather bemused tone, as 'that strange, powerful, inscrutable and brilliant obstructive deadweight at the top' (Midwinter, p. 130).

Works consulted

Julian Amery, 1969, *The Life of Joseph Chamberlain*, Vol. IV, London, Macmillan.

Lord Blake and Hugh Cecil (eds.), *Salisbury: The Man and his Policies*, 1987, London, Macmillan.

Peter Clarke, 1992, *A Question of Leadership: From Gladstone to Thatcher*, Harmondsworth, Penguin.

A.L. Kennedy, 1953, *Salisbury, 1830–1905, Portrait of a Statesman*, London, John Murray.

Andrew Roberts, 1999, *Salisbury: Victorian Titan*, London, Weidenfeld & Nicolson.

Paul Smith, 1972, (ed.), *Lord Salisbury on Politics*, Cambridge, Cambridge University Press.

Paul Smith, 2004, Article in *Oxford Dictionary of National Biography*.

Robert Taylor, 1953, *Lord Salisbury*, London, Allen Lane.

Eric Midwinter, 2006, *Salisbury,* London, Haus Publishing.

32
Archibald Philip Primrose, 5th Earl of Rosebery – Seeking 'the Palm without the Dust'

Archibald Primrose, the fifth Earl of Rosebery is reputed to have said as a young man that he had three ambitions in life – to win the Derby, to marry a great heiress and to be Prime Minister (McKinstry, p. 43). He obtained all three objectives, indeed winning the Derby three times, but much of his life can be accounted a long-drawn-out failure, and his achievements during his short premiership were virtually nil, despite his undoubted gifts.

The blame for this has been attributed by one writer (Iremonger, pp. 147–156) almost entirely to his severe deprivation of parental love during his childhood. He was born on 7 May 1847, the eldest son and third child of Lord Dalmeny, also named Archibald Primrose, and the heir to the Rosebery earldom, and his wife, Lady Wilhelmina Stanhope, a beautiful and highly cultivated, but intensely selfish woman. The young Archie was doted on by his father, who unfortunately died when he was only three, but was almost totally neglected by his mother, who instead lavished whatever love she was capable of giving on his younger brother, Everard.

Archie himself became Lord Dalmeny on the death of his father, and was to inherit the earldom from his grandfather when he was just short of 21. Three years after his father's death, Lady Wilhelmina married for a second time, to Lord Henry Vane, later the Duke of Cleveland, an amiable but ineffectual grandee, who nevertheless failed to establish a close relationship with any of his four stepchildren. Archie proceeded to Eton when he was 13, where he impressed both the masters and his fellow pupils not only by his intellectual precocity and social assurance, but also by his apparent indolence. He was taken up by William Johnson, a highly erudite teacher and poet (the author of the words of the Eton Boating Song), who was scarcely able to conceal his homo-erotic interest in the boy. He wrote a series of letters to the Duchess of Cleveland, as she now was, recording the progress of her son, who, he said, had 'in himself wonderful delicacy of mind, penetration, sympathy, flexibility, capacity for friendship – all, but the tenacious resolution of one that is to be great' (Rhodes James, 1963, p. 30).

Writing to a fellow Eton schoolmaster, Johnson made an even shrewder remark, which presciently foreshadowed the young Lord Dalmeny's later career: 'He is one of those who like the palm without the dust' (McKinstry, p. 20). Dalmeny was by no means the only schoolboy who attracted Johnson, who, ten years later, was forced to leave Eton under a cloud, changing his name to Cory.

From Eton, Dalmeny proceeded, in 1866, to Christ Church, Oxford. Here he mixed with a boisterous crowd of Etonians, including Lord Randolph Churchill, who became for a time a close friend, joined the Bullingdon club, renowned for its drunkenness and general loutishness and infuriated his tutors by his unwillingness to conform. According to the recollections of a fellow student: 'His patrician hauteur was unmistakable. Not an offensive hauteur but that calm pride by which a man seems to ascend in a balloon out of earshot every time he is addressed by one not socially his equal' (McKinstry, p. 18).

For many he appeared a conundrum. Highly intelligent and considered physically attractive, though baby-faced and not very tall, he was extraordinarily sensitive, and unable to abide criticism. He appeared to neglect his studies, but read widely, often appeared boorish, but could light up a room by a sudden smile, and – when he could be bothered – was a scintillating conversationalist. Moody, capricious, for long periods he would prefer his own company to anyone else's, but would then ingratiate himself with his fellows by conspicuous displays of bonhomie. Aged 20, he inherited the earldom on the death of his grandfather, and with it two grand residences in Scotland, and an income of at least £30,000 a year, which he proceeded to spend at a great rate, gambling and losing vast sums on horse racing. He bought his own racehorse, named Ladas, which he confidently predicted would win the Derby. Despite all his distractions, he achieved First Class results in his preliminary examinations, and his tutors expected him to obtain a First in his final degree. It was not, however, to be. The University authorities discovered a regulation forbidding the ownership of racehorses by undergraduates, and gave Rosebery an ultimatum to get rid of the horse or be sent down. To their amazement, he haughtily refused to comply, and left the University without taking a degree. He was later to regret this, particularly when the Derby was run, and Ladas came in last.

Rosebery took his seat in the House of Lords within a week of his twenty-first birthday, in May 1868. Coming from a Whig family, he naturally sat on the Liberal benches, though he had been approached a year earlier by Darlington Tories who wanted him as their parliamentary candidate. He had no great respect for the House, where the Liberals were in a permanent minority, describing it as 'a gilded dungeon', and there is little doubt that his subsequent political career suffered from his never having been an MP. Winston Churchill, who started life as a great admirer of Rosebery, was later to lament: 'I feel that if I had his brain I would move mountains. Oh that he had been in the House of Commons! There is the tragedy. Never to have come into contact with realities, never to have felt the pulse of things – that is what is wrong with Rosebery' (McKinstry, pp. 36–7).

In the following years, Rosebery was moderately active in the Lords, but preferred speaking to public meetings, where his wonderfully melodious speaking voice made him a great attraction, and he was soon seen as a 'coming man' in the Liberal Party, where – at this stage – his views veered very much towards the Radical wing of the party. Though strictly paternalist, he showed great sympathy with working-class people, exposing the exploitation of children in the Glasgow brickfields, becoming President of the Edinburgh United Industrial School and calling in 1871 for 'a union of classes without which power is a phantom and freedom a farce' (Davis). Gladstone was much taken with him, and wanted to recruit him for office, but felt strongly that he – like other promising young recruits – should serve an apprenticeship in more menial roles before moving to a senior post. There thus began a long series of incidents when Rosebery was offered appointments and turned them down, ostensibly because he felt himself poorly qualified, but in reality because he thought they were beneath his dignity. Gladstone and other senior Liberals found this intensely irritating, but rank-and-file Liberals were thoroughly seduced by his glamour, and he rapidly became, after Gladstone, the most sought-after public speaker in the party, particularly in Scotland.

What gave Rosebery's political career a crucial upward push was his immediate support of Gladstone, when he emerged from his 'retirement', in 1876, to campaign against Turkish atrocities in the Balkans (see Chapter 18). Gladstone effectively swept back into the Liberal leadership, unceremoniously thrusting aside Lords Hartington and Granville, who had been elected respectively as leaders in the Commons and the Lords. Yet having declared that he would not fight again in his Greenwich constituency, he needed another seat to contest, and Rosebery exerted himself to obtain a nomination for him in Midlothian, a county constituency surrounding Edinburgh, where his residence at Dalmeny, overlooking the Firth of Forth, was situated. When Gladstone launched his famous Midlothian campaign in advance of the 1880 general election, he based himself at Dalmeny, and Rosebery footed the bill for the campaign. This, he estimated, amounted to £50,000; a figure which one of his biographers reckons was exaggerated (Rhodes James, 1975, p. 149). Rosebery was not content to act just as Gladstone's quartermaster. He himself played a very active part in the campaign, speaking to numerous meetings, where he invariably electrified the audience. He was one of the best 'stump' speakers of his day.

Rosebery was very attractive to women, and was regarded as a supremely eligible bachelor – many were the aristocratic ladies who saw him as the ideal mate for their daughters. So there was general consternation – which was felt at least equally in the Jewish community – when his engagement was announced to Hannah de Rothschild, the heiress of the fabulously wealthy

Baron Meyer de Rothschild. No great beauty, being plump and rather gauche, she had a very pleasant disposition and much commonsense (which her new husband notably lacked). He had originally met her ten years earlier, when she had been introduced to him by Disraeli. They married in March 1878, when he was nearly 31, and she 27. Neither she nor Rosebery (a Presbyterian) changed their religion. The marriage brought to Rosebery the enormous Rothschild residence of Mentmore, in Buckinghamshire, stuffed with art treasures, to add to his two Scottish homes, his London residence in Berkeley Square, and the Durdans, a country house near Epsom, which he had bought in 1872. It was obvious that Hannah totally adored Rosebery, but he tended to treat her in a rather offhand manner. They had two daughters, followed by two sons, in less than five years, but in 1890, after 12 years of marriage, Hannah was to die of typhoid, at the age of 39. It was only then that he fully appreciated her, and he entered a deep depression, which lasted for over a year, during which he withdrew himself from almost all human society, and from which he perhaps never fully recovered.

Forming his second government, following the 1880 election, Gladstone offered Rosebery the Under-Secretaryship at the India Office. Disappointed not to be included in the Cabinet, he declined, saying he did not want to appear to be receiving a pay-off for his role in the Midlothian campaign. He did, however, accept the post of Under-Secretary at the Home Office, with a brief to handle Scottish affairs, in August 1881, only to resign less than two years later. His reasons for resigning, according to John Davis:

> combined the principled and the petty: his belief that London habitually neglected Scottish business and his fear that this neglect would spawn a Scottish home-rule movement; his overreaction to criticism of the Home Office in the Commons; his difficult relationship with the Home Secretary, Sir William Harcourt; and the fact that he was bored with his work. (Davis)

Perhaps his incompatibility with Harcourt, which was later to blight his premiership, was the determining factor. Gladstone did not give up on him, offering him the post of Minister for Scotland, created under the Local Government Board Act of 1883. Rosebery demurred, partly it seems because it was not in the Cabinet, and departed in a huff for a tour of the United States and Australia. While on this tour, he made a famous speech at Adelaide calling for the British Empire to be converted into a 'commonwealth of nations', the first time that this phrase had been used. On his return he took the first of several initiatives to reform the House of Lords, proposing the appointment of a Select Committee to look into its efficiency. His motion was defeated. In November 1884, Gladstone finally offered him a cabinet post: that of Commissioner of Works, perhaps the least glamorous office in the government. Rosebery again declined, but three months later changed his mind, when the post was combined with the title of Lord Privy Seal. He was to serve out the remaining four months of Gladstone's second government, until it resigned in June 1885, after the Irish Nationalists ganged up with the Tories to defeat it on the budget.

During the short interim of the first Salisbury government (June 1885–January 1886), Gladstone's conversion to Home Rule in Ireland had a devastating effect on the unity of the Liberal Party. Lord Hartington MP, and other senior Whigs, refused to serve in the third Gladstone government, while the Radical Joseph Chamberlain agreed to do so, but resigned shortly afterwards. Furthermore, another leading Radical, Sir Charles Dilke, much fancied as a potential Foreign Secretary, was involved in a sensational divorce case at this time, and the ensuing scandal effectively destroyed his political career. This left something of a vacuum at the top end of the party, and this greatly facilitated Rosebery's rise. Lord Granville, who had been Foreign Secretary in Gladstone's first two administrations, was becoming increasingly decrepit, and Queen Victoria refused to accept him for a third term. She then opposed Gladstone's choice of the Earl of Kimberley, and strongly pressed for Rosebery, who had charmed her almost as much as her late lamented Disraeli. Gladstone thought Rosebery, then 38, too young for the post, but nevertheless offered it to him. Rosebery made his customary noises about being unfit for the office proposed, writing to Gladstone:

> I have absolutely no experience of the Foreign Office, which I have never entered except to attend a dinner. My French is I fear rusty. I have never had to face anything like what you would call hard work. I have no knowledge of diplomatic practice or forms and little of diplomatic men. And I am sensible of many deficiencies of temper and manner. Moreover the Foreign Office is usually considered, and I think justly so, to be the chief of all offices. I should gladly have climbed into it in ten or twenty years, had I been fit for it then. But I know very well that I am not fit for it now. (McKinstry, p. 147)

Nevertheless, he accepted the offer, and was clearly as pleased as punch at the prospect. It was noteworthy that, this time, it took only a few hours for him to overcome his qualms rather than months or years, as on previous occasions. In the event, Rosebery's first tenure of the Foreign Office proved to be a notable success, and perhaps the apogee of his political career. He was in office for just over five months, Gladstone's third government going down to a heavy electoral defeat, following the rejection of its Home Rule Bill, and the defection of most of the Whigs and the Chamberlainite Radicals from the Liberal Party. But during this short time, he proved himself to be firm and decisive, and revealed an unexpected talent for administration. Not all his fellow Liberals were delighted, however, that he aimed at pursuing a bipartisan policy, and was determined to achieve a maximum of continuity with his Tory predecessor, Lord Salisbury. 'The second rate foreign policy which is continuous', he later said, 'is better than the first rate foreign policy which is not' (Davis). The only potential crisis with which he had to deal concerned Bulgaria, which in 1885 annexed the neighbouring Turkish province of Eastern Roumelia, after defeating a Serbian army at the Battle of Slivnitsa. This could easily have sparked a wider Balkan War, in which Russia would have been directly involved, but Rosebery's cool handling of the issue, enabled it to be settled with a minimum of international discord. Gladstone was delighted, and wrote warmly congratulating him. When he left office, Queen Victoria said to him: 'You have a great political future ahead of you' (McKinstry, p. 159), while Gladstone in a speech at this time said: 'I say to the Liberal Party that they see the man of the future'.

Rosebery was far from being an enthusiastic supporter of Home Rule, and remained in the party largely out of loyalty to Gladstone, whom he greatly admired. He was, however, greatly distressed by the exit of the great majority of his fellow Whigs, which – in particular – left the Liberals in an even smaller minority in the House of Lords than before. This only confirmed Rosebery in his view that the composition of the House of Lords was in urgent need of reform, and over the years he launched a series of initiatives with this in view, including the appointment of life peers. None of his proposals came near to being adopted. On one occasion, he even contemplated contesting a seat in a by-election to put to the test the established view that a peerage was incompatible with membership of the Commons (a step actually taken by Tony Benn some 70 years later), and consulted a former Liberal Lord Chancellor, who advised him against taking this step. Instead, he stood for election to the newly established London County Council, in 1889, and being successful was immediately elected as the first chairman of the Council. The Liberals were in a majority in the Council, and Rosebery quickly acquired a reputation as a municipal reformer, collaborating closely with Fabians, such as Sidney Webb, in promoting a wide range of progressive policies, particularly in housing and education.

Rosebery was now widely seen as Gladstone's probable successor as Liberal leader, but the sudden death of his wife, Hannah, in November 1890, completely disoriented him. He dropped all his political activities, and spent long periods alone in his castle at Barnbougle, mourning inconsolably. The insomnia, which had periodically afflicted him since his youth, became chronic. He determined never to be a minister again, and expressed deep disdain for party politics, but again fought the London County Council (LCC) election in 1892, and resumed the chairmanship of the Council. He was gloomy about Liberal prospects for the general election in the same year, but out of loyalty to Gladstone agreed to speak at a number of meetings, some of his reported speeches indeed upsetting

Queen Victoria by their Radical tone. As usual, Gladstone, now an elderly and rather decrepit figure, made Dalmeny his base for the campaign, but found his host moody and uncommunicative. The election result was a deep disappointment to Gladstone, who had looked forward to winning a clear majority, but found himself some 40 seats adrift of the Tories, and able to govern only with the aid of the 81 Irish Nationalists, themselves deeply split by the disgrace and death of their former leader, Charles Stewart Parnell (see Chapter 30).

The Liberal leader gathered his leading supporters around him in London, urgently discussing how they might form a government in anticipation that Lord Salisbury would soon resign, which he did a month after the election. All this time Rosebery dawdled in Scotland (Achilles in his tent!), letting it be known that in no circumstances would he consider entering the government. Meanwhile virtually all his former colleagues, including his arch-rival Sir William Harcourt, convinced themselves that his presence was a *sine qua non*, and that almost any price should be paid to secure his agreement. It was only after John Morley had been dispatched to Dalmeny, where he begged almost on his knees for Rosebery to come to see Gladstone in London, that he agreed to do so, still determined to tell the GOM that he would not serve. At the meeting Gladstone failed to obtain an acceptance from Rosebery, who did, however, agree that he should tell the Queen that he wished Rosebery to be appointed. Gladstone left for his appointment with the Queen, who was at Osborne, her Isle of Wight residence, and Rosebery departed for a two-day visit to Paris where he communed alone. Informed by telegram that the Queen had agreed to his appointment, he sent back a cryptic reply 'So be it, Mentmore [the name of his Buckinghamshire home]'.

Rosebery resumed the Foreign Secretaryship with mixed feelings, but on one thing he was determined; that he should run his own policy, and permit only a minimum of consultation with his cabinet colleagues. The policy he intended to pursue was, however, not likely to commend him to the majority in his party. Determined, as before, to keep in step with his predecessor Salisbury, he was far more of an imperialist than most of the other leading Liberals, Gladstone in particular. Two major incidents occurred, in both of which Rosebery was at odds with majority Liberal opinion. The first concerned Uganda, where the British East Africa Company was effectively in control of the territory. It was threatened with bankruptcy, and Rosebery, backed by his Under-Secretary, Sir Edward Grey, and the Tory opposition, proposed to take it over and declare a British protectorate. This was too much for Gladstone, and Rosebery reluctantly agreed a compromise under which the company was kept afloat by an interim subsidy. He, however, prepared plans for annexation, which went ahead in 1894, after Gladstone's retirement.

The second flowed from the British occupation of Egypt, which had continued for ten years, following the decision, which Gladstone had taken with great reluctance in 1882, to impose a virtual protectorate on the country, which was still technically part of the Ottoman Empire. The effective ruler was the British proconsul, Sir Evelyn Baring (later Lord Cromer), an over-bearing figure who, for 24 years from 1883–1907, thought nothing of issuing detailed instructions to the Khedive on how to man and manage his administration. Gladstone, still keen to secure the withdrawal of British troops, responded encouragingly to an informal approach by the French ambassador suggesting that the two governments should jointly consider the problem of the future control of Egypt. Rosebery hit the roof, saying that it was a grave diplomatic solecism for the ambassador to by-pass the Foreign Secretary in seeking a meeting with the Prime Minister. Gladstone meekly apologized, and the ambassador was withdrawn soon afterwards. Nothing more was heard of Anglo-French co-operation, and when Cromer requested a further reinforcement of British troops, Rosebery arranged for a battalion of the Black Watch en route for India to be diverted to Port Said. In his second term as Foreign Secretary, he appeared to be a commanding figure, and his international reputation soared. He also received a glowing press in Britain, and his popularity reached fresh heights. Yet his relations with Gladstone seriously deteriorated, and were not improved by his failure to give strong support to the Prime Minister in his struggle to carry the Irish Home Rule Bill, which was the central objective of his last government. Nor were many of his Cabinet colleagues enthralled by his imperious ways. The Queen, however, was a different matter, and – in August 1893, he recorded in his diary a 'long and curious talk' he had had with her at Osborne, in which she said that: 'It was ridiculous for a man of 83 to be Prime Minister. "You ought to be there, Lord Rosebery, I wished you to be there and I hope you will be there. You are the only one of the Ministry with whom I can talk freely"' (McKinstry, pp. 258–9).

When Gladstone resigned six months later, in March 1894, there were at least two senior Liberals in the House of Commons who had good claims on the premiership, notably Sir William Harcourt, the Leader of the House and Chancellor of the Exchequer, but also, John Morley, the Irish Secretary, and Gladstone's closest colleague. Yet, without any consultation, Victoria sent unhesitatingly for Lord Rosebery. It is doubtful if she was doing him a favour, and certainly not the Liberal Party or the country as a whole. Rosebery himself had his usual qualms about taking office, though he immediately accepted when the Queen invited him to form a government. He had, however, set out in a private memorandum the reasons why he thought it a mistake. One of these was the great difficulty that a Liberal Prime Minister would have in leading a government from the Lords, where there were now only about 20 Liberal peers in a House of 560, following the mass defection of Whigs over Home Rule. In many ways, Rosebery would have preferred to remain as Foreign Secretary, and serve under Harcourt, despite their sharp differences, but was aware that Harcourt was deeply unpopular within the Cabinet, despite his large following among Liberal MPs as a whole. Harcourt's supporters, led by his son Lewis, universally known as 'Loulou', had waged an energetic campaign to secure the premiership for him, but had been blocked by Morley, formerly an ally, who came out strongly in support of Rosebery, partly it seems because he had hopes of succeeding him as Foreign Secretary. Harcourt was furious when Rosebery was named as Prime Minister, and he was tempted to refuse to join the government in the hope that Rosebery would be unable to proceed without him. But he held back, perhaps because Victoria might, in these circumstances, have sent for Lord Salisbury, rather than himself. Instead, he insisted on onerous terms, including the retention of both his posts, freedom to express his views publicly on any subject and the right to be fully consulted on all foreign policy issues, as well as on patronage. Rosebery, sensing that this would effectively mean a joint premiership, agreed with the greatest reluctance. Unlike Harcourt, Morley was in no position to drive a hard bargain. Rosebery declined to make him Foreign Secretary, insisting on choosing a fellow peer, the inoffensive Earl of Kimberley, who shared Rosebery's imperialist instincts, whereas Morley was a prominent advocate of the 'Little Englander' views, predominant among rank-and-file Liberals. Morley was not even able to secure the India Office as a consolation prize, and was forced to continue as Irish Secretary.

The government took office on 5 March 1894, when Rosebery was nearly 47. It got off to the worst of starts, with its three leading members deeply disgruntled and hardly on speaking terms with each other. Within less than a week, the new Prime Minister committed an appalling blunder, which upset the great bulk of his own supporters. Replying casually to a point made by Lord Salisbury, the Leader of the Opposition, he agreed that Home Rule would not be practicable until a majority of English, as distinct from British, MPs were in favour. He also tactlessly referred to England as the 'the predominant partner' in the Union, which deeply offended Scottish, Welsh and Irish MPs, the great majority of whom were Liberals or Nationalists. The deeply divided government was unable to present a coherent programme of intended legislation, offering instead a series of minor, if often contentious proposals, of which the most notable was a Bill to disestablish the Anglican Church in Wales. Its first important piece of business was the budget, which needed to raise considerably more revenue to pay for the expensive programme of naval rearmament, of which Rosebery had been a strong advocate, and which was the proximate cause of Gladstone's resignation (see Chapter 30). Harcourt proposed to raise the bulk of the extra £5 million he needed to balance the budget by the introduction of graduated death duties, which appalled Rosebery who, apart from any personal considerations, feared that this would drive away from the Liberal Party the few wealthy landed supporters that it retained. He sent a detailed memorandum to Harcourt setting out his objections, which the Chancellor of the Exchequer contemptuously rejected. Not wishing to be depicted 'as a rich man who disliked being taxed', as his son-in-law and first biographer, Lord Crewe, put it (Walker, p. 227). Rosebery refrained from challenging Harcourt within the Cabinet and was then mortified when the Chancellor achieved a great parliamentary triumph in carrying his proposals through. The government then suffered a considerable international humili-ation, when it negotiated an Anglo-Belgian treaty, leasing to King Leopold II substantial tracts of land in the Upper Nile basin in order to forestall French infiltration into the area. The treaty infuriated anti-imperialist feeling in the Liberal Party, and then had to be abandoned when the Belgian King, fearing French retaliation, refused to ratify it. Meanwhile, the government seemed to be drifting aimlessly along with no co-ordination between its leading members, and the conspicuous absence of any leadership from Rosebery. The one striking event, which – temporarily at least reignited Rosebery's flagging popularity – was when his horse, Ladas II, won the Derby in June 1894. (He repeated this achievement the following year with another horse, Sir Visto).

Even this, however, did not go down at all well with the influential Non-conformist elements in the Liberal Party, while Rosebery was rebuked by Queen Victoria for the frivolous tone of several of his speeches. He at last attempted to give his government some direction by calling for a bill to restrict the veto powers of the House of Lords, which he intended to make the centrepiece of the Liberal Party's next election manifesto. But there was little enthusiasm for this; the Lords had not made themselves unpopularr by blocking Home Rule, which was not supported by the majority of English voters. He was heavily crit-icized in debates in the House of Commons, and very little attempt was made by Liberal ministers, notably Harcourt as Leader of the House, to defend him. Rosebery petulantly summoned a meeting of the Cabinet in February 1895, at which he announced that he would resign because of their lack of support. He withdrew the threat two days later after receiving protestations of support from his leading colleagues, though they continued to grumble about him behind his back. In April 1895, he had a serious attack of influenza followed by an almost complete nervous breakdown, which effectively put him out of action for several months. Given his hyper-sensitive temperament, the break-down could well have been caused by the strain of leading a fractious govern-ment in unfavourable conditions, but it seems probable that it was also brought on by Rosebery's fear of being exposed in a homosexual scandal – the Oscar Wilde affair, which was reaching its climax in April and May 1895. There is no direct evidence that Rosebery was homosexual, but it was widely assumed in 'society' that he was, on the basis of certain effeminate traits, his apparent lack of interest in seeking a second marriage, and his habit of surrounding himself with attractive young men as his secretaries and assistants. One of these had been Viscount Drumlanrig, the 25-year-old heir to the mad 5th Marquess of Queensbery, whom he appointed as his Private Secretary, when he was Foreign Secretary in 1892. Queensberry, already disgusted by the relationship of his younger son, Lord Alfred Douglas ('Bosie'), with Wilde, convinced himself that Rosebery, whom he referred to as a 'snob queer', had seduced his heir. He followed Rosebery to Bad Homburg, where he was on holiday, intending to horse-whip him, but was apprehended by local police and deported. Two years later, in 1894, Drumlanrig had become engaged to be married, and then went off to join an aristocratic shooting party. He became separated from the group, who heard a single shot fired, and found him dying in a neighbouring field. The inquest verdict was that he had accidentally shot himself, but the general belief was that it was suicide, and it was suspected that he was being black-mailed about his alleged relationship with Rosebery.

The government's law officers were terrified that Rosebery's name would be mentioned in Wilde's libel action against Queensberry, or in the subsequent first trial of Wilde for gross indecency. The jury failed to agree, and the harsh and unexpected decision of the law officers to subject him to a second trial has been attributed to their fear that if they did not press the charges it would be seen as a cover-up to protect Rosebery. In the event, Wilde was convicted and given two years with hard labour, an effective death sentence, while Rosebery emerged unscathed.

He resumed his government duties, but the inter-ministerial squabbling con-tinued unabated, and the feeling spread that the government was doomed. In June 1895, the government was unexpectedly defeated in a parliamentary am-bush during a debate on the alleged shortage of cordite for the army. The War Secretary, Sir Henry Campbell-Bannerman insisted on resigning, and though the vote could easily have been reversed on a confidence motion, the Cabinet unanimously decided instead on collective resignation. As Asquith, the Home Secretary, rhetorically asked: 'Is there any member of Rosebery's Cabinet, in either House, who wishes to see it assembled again for any purpose under heaven?' (McKinstry, p. 378).

As for Rosebery himself, he felt the profoundest relief, saying a few years later: 'There are two supreme pleasures in life. One is ideal, the other real. The ideal is when a man receives the seals of office from his Sovereign. The real pleasure comes when he hands them back'.

His premiership had lasted a mere year and 109 days. The Queen immediately sent for Lord Salisbury, who requested, and was granted, a dissolution. In the subsequent general election, the Liberals went down to a resounding defeat, the Tories emerging with an overall majority of 152, the largest since the 1832 Reform Act. Among the Liberal losses were those of Harcourt and Morley, to Rosebery's ill-concealed satisfaction. He had taken no part in the campaign, instead going for an extended cruise in his yacht. He welcomed the extent of the Liberal defeat, saying it had been 'purged as with fire', and now had the opportunity of regrouping itself on what Rosebery regarded as a more realistic basis. He carried on as party leader for another 15 months, but resigned in October 1896, when Gladstone emerged from his retirement to make a fiery speech in Liverpool attacking Armenian massacres by the Turks. Rosebery felt this was undermining his own position, and with few regrets handed over the leadership to Harcourt. He was still under 50, and was to live another 33 years, until 1929. Yet his political career was virtually over, though it did not appear so at the time. He retained a strong following, particularly among younger Liberals, and those who supported his imperialist approach. Among these were three of the abler younger ministers in his government, Asquith, Sir Edward Grey and R.B. Haldane. This trio formed the core of the Liberal Imperialist faction, who strongly supported the Tory government's conduct of the Boer War, and who looked forward to Rosebery's return, perhaps at the head of a coalition government committed to imperialism abroad and social reform at home. Every now and then, Rosebery would make a well-publicized speech full of bright ideas, which would dominate the headlines for a few days or weeks, but he never had the patience or consistency to follow them up with an organized campaign. In his book *Great Contemporaries*, Winston Churchill charted the waning enthusiasm of his followers: 'At first they said, "He will come." Then for years "If only he could come;" And finally, long after he had renounced politics for ever, "If only he would come back" '.

The end of the Boer War, in 1902, and the recovery of Liberal unity under Campbell-Bannerman, effectively ended the possibility of Rosebery's return to the leadership even if he had desired it. It was perhaps in recognition of this that he declared in a long-anticipated speech at this time that 'I must plough my furrow alone'. Nevertheless, he appeared to be disappointed, when Campbell-Bannerman formed his government in December 1905, not to be given the opportunity of declining a Cabinet post. One was offered to him by Lloyd George in his coalition government in 1916, but by then all remnants of his political ambition had long been extinguished. The following year he had a debilitating stroke, and though he survived for another 12 years, it was as a sad, lonely and pitiful invalid.

For one who had aroused such strong hopes among so many people, his career was a bitter disappointment. No subsequent writer has been able to make out a case that he had any solid achievements to his credit, and most of them have been highly critical of his self-indulgence and dilettantism. The cruellest verdict was that of Philip Guedalla, who, in his book, *The Gallery*, published in 1924, wrote that Rosebery's: 'long career has been a painfully prolonged adolescence. Sometimes he would play quietly with his toys for years together. But at intervals, swept by those dark impulses which devastate a nursery, he dashed them on the floor and went off to mutter in a corner'.

This was perhaps a bit hard, but in truth Rosebery should never have tried his hand at politics. He had altogether the wrong temperament: he was much better suited to be an artist rather than a politician. He had wide cultural interests and was a gifted writer, publishing perceptive biographical studies of Chatham, Pitt, Napoleon and Lord Randolph Churchill. These were all decisive and ruthless men, everything in fact that Rosebery might have wished to be, but all too evidently was not.

Works consulted

John Davis, 2004, Article in *Oxford Dictionary of National Biography.*

Lucille Iremonger, 1970, *The Fiery Chariot*, London, Secker & Warburg.

Leo McKinstry, 2005, *Rosebery: Statesman in Turmoil*, London, John Murray.

Matthew Parris, 1995, *Great Parliamentary Scandals*, London, Robson Books.

Robert Rhodes James, 1963, *Rosebery*, London, Weidenfeld & Nicolson.

Robert Rhodes James, 1975, 'The Earl of Rosebery', in Herbert Van Thal, (ed.), *The Prime Ministers, Vol. II*, London, Allen & Unwin.

Graham Walker, 1998, 'Archibald Philip Primrose, Fifth Earl of Rosebery', in Robert Eccleshall & Graham Walker, (eds.), *Biographical Dictionary of British Prime Ministers*, London, Routledge.

Part III
The 20th and 21st Centuries

33

Arthur James Balfour – Bob's your Uncle

The most civilised, and perhaps the most intelligent, of twentieth-century Prime Ministers was Arthur Balfour. He was also, by common consent, one of the least effective. Cynics may conclude that there was a direct connection: that the rough-and-tumble of democratic politics is not designed for finer spirits. Yet Balfour successfully held high ministerial office, both before and after his premiership, and left his mark in several important areas of public policy. Indeed, it is a little known fact that Balfour's career as a Cabinet minister was the longest in British history. He served under four very different Prime Ministers, a clear indication that his contribution was highly valued. Balfour's record, compared in length of years with other long-serving statesmen, is listed by his most recent biographer as follows: Balfour 27, Churchill 26, Liverpool 25, Gladstone 24, Palmerston 23, the Younger Pitt 22 (Mackay, 1985, p. 354).

Arthur James Balfour, later 1st Earl of Balfour (1848–1930), was born with a 'silver spoon' in his mouth – that was, in fact, the heading of the first chapter in Kenneth Young's biography (Young, 1963, p. 1). He was the third child, and the eldest son, of James Maitland Balfour, a country landowner and local Tory MP who had inherited a large fortune and estate (Whittingehame in East Lothian) from his own father, who had made a fortune as a contractor in India. James Maitland Balfour died at the age of 36, when Arthur was only seven, and he was brought up by his strong-minded mother, Lady Blanche Balfour, sister of Lord Salisbury, who at the age of 31 was left with eight young children to raise. Lady Blanche devoted herself entirely to the educational and moral instruction of her children, widening their intellectual horizons, fostering their curiosity and giving them a firm basis of religious belief. Though a devoted evangelical Christian, she was no narrow sectarian, and brought up her children as members of both the Church of England and of Scotland, a membership which Balfour retained throughout his life.

Lady Blanche's declared intention, once she had completed the tuition of her eight surviving children, was to move to London's East End and devote herself to the poor, but this ambition was thwarted by her early death at 47. This left Arthur, whose education had continued at Eton and Cambridge, though without his achieving any particular distinction, as the head of the family. At 24, with a fortune probably exceeding £1 million (equal to at least £75 million today), surrounded by an adoring family circle of brothers, sisters and cousins (several of them of high intelligence and intellectual distinction), he had the world at his feet. Handsome, clever, charming, witty, he was also immensely well connected (his Uncle Robert, the future Prime Minister, was a trustee of his estate and seems to have felt more affinity with the young Arthur than with any of his own large brood of children). His own family was supplemented by the interlocking Lyttelton and Gladstone families, with whom Balfour became associated through his Cambridge friendship with Spencer Lyttelton and his younger brother, Alfred. There were eight Lyttelton brothers and four sisters in all, and their Gladstone cousins, with whom they were on intimate terms, were also numerous.

Both families were effectively co-opted to the Balfour circle. An unending carousel of visits ensued between Balfour's Whittingehame estate, and the country houses of Hagley Hall (Lytteltons) and Hawarden (Gladstones). The young Balfour much impressed William Gladstone, who seems to have regarded him as a possible future Liberal MP and a more than possible son-in-law, his daughter Mary being clearly enamoured of him. She became a close friend of Balfour's, but he evinced no romantic interest and she eventually married a local parson.

Surrounded by this large and admiring circle of intelligent and discriminating young people, who merged into a wider group of young and mostly aristocratic people of both sexes, known as 'the Souls' on account of their love of elevated conversation, and of playing both physical and intellectual games, Balfour was the undoubted centre of attention, being known variously as 'Prince Arthur' or 'King Arthur'. The absence of any struggle in his life, in contrast to his Uncle Robert who had fierce disputes with his father and had to work hard as a young man to earn his living, had a profound and not entirely positive effect on his temperament. He grew up as a wonderfully tolerant man, with an exceptionally open mind, a lively curiosity and a wide range of interests, but also prone to self-indulgence and a marked inability or unwillingness to commit himself.

This was very evident in his personal life. Balfour remained unmarried, the only bachelor Prime Minister of the twentieth century apart from Edward Heath. There is absolutely no evidence that he was homosexual, despite his acquiring the nickname of 'Pretty Fanny' at Cambridge, because of the alleged effeminacy of his artistic tastes. Balfour was, in fact, exceptionally fond of female company, and had a number of very close women friends, but few, if any, affairs.

The biggest tragedy in Balfour's life appears to have been the sudden death, aged 24, of May Lyttelton, the sister of his friends Spencer and Alfred, in March 1875. There had been no previous indication that they were romantically involved, but Balfour exhibited profound grief, sending her brother Edward an emerald ring which had belonged to his mother to put in May's coffin, and claiming that they had talked of marriage. If so, he had proved himself a hesitant and undemonstrative wooer.

Thereafter, he never seems to have contemplated marriage, though he had an intimate friendship over many years with a young married woman, Mary Wyndham, the wife of Lord Elcho, later Earl of Wemyss. They corresponded with each other for over 30 years, but the exact nature of their relationship is far from clear. One of Balfour's biographers, Kenneth Young, states bluntly that Mary Elcho was his mistress, and remained so for many years. This book caused great offence to the Wemyss family, who withdrew the Balfour–Elcho correspondence from the collection of Balfour papers in the British Museum, and later writers have doubted whether there was an actual physical relationship. Much later the correspondence was edited for publication by Jane Ridley and Clayre Percy, whose judgement is worth recording:

> Were they lovers? we wondered, as so many people have wondered at the time and since. At first we thought not. To begin with, the letters give little away. Then it became plain that something was going on; this was not a platonic friendship. But lovers in the conventional sense they were probably not. Which makes their relationship all the odder. It was an *amitié amoureuse* that lasted for well over thirty years. It never compromised Balfour's political career; and it did not threaten Mary Elcho's marriage. Yet for both of them it was the most important relationship in their lives. (Ridley and Percy, 1992, p. viii)

Whatever the truth, Balfour was notably circumspect in his correspondence. There is not one word of endearment in the several hundred letters which have survived, nor does he once address Mary Elcho by her Christian name.

This disinclination to commit himself is the key to both Balfour's strength and his weakness as a politician. On the one hand, he was exceptionally gifted as a drafter of memoranda setting out with crystal clarity the pros and cons of any proposed line of action. This made him an extremely useful member of a cabinet, a committee of inquiry or other public body. Yet his lack of passion precluded him from giving a decisive lead one way or the other, which was a fatal flaw in a Prime Minister, and was one reason why his government of 1902–05 broke up around him.

As a young man in his mid-twenties, Balfour was widely seen as no more than a gifted dilettante, as an anonymous poem preserved by Mary Elcho well illustrates:

Playful little Arthur, he
Plays with things so prettily
To him everything's a game
Win or lose it's all the same
Plays with politics or war
Trivial little games they are -
Plays with souls and plays at golf -
This must never be put off.
Plays with deep philosophies,
Faiths and minor things like these,
Plays with praise and plays with blame
Everything is but a game
Win or lose, it's all the same.
Playful little Arthur, he
Cannot take things seriously.   (Ridley and Percy, 1992, p. 20)

Yet at times, Balfour did want to take things seriously. At Cambridge he had thought of giving up his inheritance to a younger brother, and devoting himself to philosophy. He had been dissuaded by his mother, who wrote to him: 'You will have nothing to write about by the time you are 40' (Young, 1963, p. 10). When he was 26, his Uncle Robert came to his rescue, suggesting a political career. He provided him with a safe seat, close to his Hatfield estate, and Balfour was elected unopposed for Hertford in the 1874 election, which led to the formation of Disraeli's government.

Balfour was in no hurry to make his mark, waiting for two years before making his maiden speech, and remained a fairly obscure backbencher until 1878 when Salisbury again gave him a push up, taking him with him to the Congress of Berlin as his private secretary, an invaluable experience for a (much) later Foreign Secretary. In the short term, however, it did little to stimulate his political ambition. Instead, he resumed his earlier interest in philosophy, publishing in 1879, *A Defence of Philosophic Doubt*.

When the Tories lost the 1880 election, Balfour belatedly began to play an active role in the House of Commons, associating himself with the so-called Fourth Party, a small group of freebooters who tried to inject a more vigorous opposition to Gladstone's first government than was provided by the lacklustre leadership of Sir Stafford Northcote, the Tory leader in the Commons. The dominant figure in the Fourth Party was Lord Randolph Churchill, and the only other members were John Gorst and Sir Drummond Wolff. Balfour was the most detached member of the four – largely because he soon detected in Churchill a likely rival to Uncle Robert as the future Conservative leader.

Yet his detachment probably owed as much to his regarding parliamentary tactics as a fascinating game, rather than having a deeper purpose. As Mackay writes: 'He was motivated partly by genuine sympathy with the wish for a more lively opposition to the government and partly by his constant desire to improve his debating skills, as an end in itself rather than through ambition for ministerial office' (Mackay, 1985, p. 29). This desire paid off: from being an uncertain and hesitant speaker, Balfour progressed to being one of the most effective debaters in the House.

His languorous appearance and apparent frivolity still meant that few took him seriously, and his appointment as President of the Local Government Board by Lord Salisbury, when he formed his first government in June 1885, was uniformly attributed to family favouritism. The term 'Bob's your Uncle' entered the English language around this time, almost certainly as an ironic explanation for Balfour's preferment. When Salisbury again became Prime Minister in July 1886, Balfour was appointed to the newly created post of Secretary for Scotland, becoming a member of the Cabinet a few months later. He did not serve for long: in March 1887 Sir Michael Hicks Beach resigned because of ill health from the far more important and controversial post of Chief Secretary for Ireland. To the general amazement, the Prime Minister appointed his nephew in his place.

Few appointments had appeared more outlandish since Caligula made his horse a consul. That this dandyish, effete figure would match up to the demands of the toughest job in the government, which had broken the health of his predecessor, and only five years before had cost the life of Lord Frederick Cavendish, assassinated in Dublin's Phoenix Park, strained the bounds of credulity. The immediate reaction was one of hilarity, while the formidable Irish Party in the House of Commons, smarting from their recent setback over Home Rule, sharpened their sabres in the easy expectation of carving him up in parliamentary debate.

Only his uncle seemed to believe that Balfour had it in him to rise to the occasion, and he was not disappointed. Showing quite unexpected vigour, and the ability to work for long hours and apply himself to enervating detail, Balfour succeeded in calming down a potentially revolutionary situation in Ireland, while gaining the upper hand over the Irish parliamentary party in a series of blistering skirmishes. His twin objectives in Ireland were to restore law and order through a ruthless application of recently enacted coercive legislation, while seeking to remove the economic causes of discontent by Land Reform Acts forced through Parliament despite the opposition of Tory landowners. On the first count, he was largely successful, but not before three rioters had been shot dead by police at a mass demonstration in Mitchelstown, County Cork, which earned him the nickname of 'Bloody Balfour'. His attempts to pacify Irish land hunger also led to a falling away of agitation, though the deceptive peace which descended on Ireland for 20 or so years after his stewardship ended perhaps owed as much to the decline and premature death of Charles

Stewart Parnell. At best, he secured a respite while doing nothing to prevent the eventual resurgence of nationalist demands.

In 1891 Salisbury rewarded Balfour by making him Leader of the House of Commons, in succession to W.H. Smith, who had died. Unusually, he was also First Lord of the Treasury, as the Prime Minister did not need this title as he was already a secretary of state as Foreign Secretary. He had also assigned 10 Downing Street, first to Smith and then to Balfour, preferring to live in his own houses in Arlington Street and at Hatfield. On this occasion, nobody laughed and nobody uttered the word 'nepotism'. Balfour was acknowledged to have been the most capable and successful of the Tory ministers, and he was now widely seen as a future Prime Minister on his own merits. Yet Balfour did not shine – initially at least – in his new post. He lacked the patience to spend long hours attending to the minutiae of parliamentary debates, nor did he devote himself with conspicuous energy to the endless task of reconciling the views and prejudices of the various personalities and factions making up the House of Commons, in particular neglecting too often currents of opinion within his own party. While he had been Irish Secretary he had seen a clear purpose to his work, to which he felt totally committed. Playing party games in the House of Commons was a different matter, and he resented having to subordinate his other wide interests to the daily drudgery of leading the House. It may have been with some personal relief that he greeted the result of the election in July 1892 which brought the Liberals back to power. Although he subsequently devoted himself to leading the Tory opposition in the Commons, he also returned to his earlier love of philosophy, writing perhaps his most significant book, *The Foundations of Belief*, which appeared in 1895.

The collapse of Lord Rosebery's Liberal government in the same year saw his return as Leader of the House in Salisbury's third and final government. He again made heavy weather of the post, but gradually buckled down and became the ageing Salisbury's indispensable prop and partner, substituting for him on numerous occasions when he was indisposed. He was eventually seen as his uncle's inevitable successor, partly, it is true, because there was no obvious alternative. Lord Randolph Churchill had died in 1894, and neither Joseph Chamberlain nor the Duke of Devonshire, both Liberal Unionists, would have been readily acceptable at the head of a Tory government.

As Salisbury declined, Balfour took over more and more responsibility, providing much-needed leadership after the early disasters of the Boer War and taking personal charge of the highly controversial Education Bill which seemed doomed because of the strength and width of opposition, led by the Nonconformist churches which did not want public money to be spent on Anglican schools. It was finally enacted shortly after he replaced his uncle as Prime Minister in July 1902.

Balfour's inheritance in 1902 seemed to be full of promise. The return of peace after the hard-won victory in South Africa, and the succession of Edward VII to the throne had created a new atmosphere of optimism. Moreover, the 'khaki' election of October 1900 had given the Tories a crushing parliamentary majority, while the Liberals, torn apart by their differences over the Boer War, seemed hopelessly divided.

Yet there was one glaring gap. Balfour himself had no programme in mind for the government he was about to lead. Always in the past he had been guided by his uncle, and he had shown a high level of competence in carrying through the tasks which had been assigned to him. Now the onus of steering the ship of state was upon him, and – apart from completing the passage of the Education Bill – he had no particular destination in mind.

Others did know where they wanted to go – notably Chamberlain who had surprised both Salisbury and Balfour in 1895, when he had opted to become Colonial Secretary rather than Chancellor of the Exchequer. He retained this post under Balfour, and his belief in the importance of maintaining and expanding the British Empire was stronger than ever. Following a conference in August 1902, at which all the British colonies, notably Canada and South Africa, were represented, he became convinced that the best way of binding the empire together was to give trade preferences to all its members. He therefore demanded, as a first step, that import duties on corn, imposed as a temporary measure under the last Salisbury government, should be retained, but remitted in the case of empire suppliers. He saw this as the beginning of a process of 'tariff reform', which would be based on a generalised system of imperial preferences.

Chamberlain's advocacy of tariff reform was resisted by a no less determined group within the Cabinet, who strongly believed in the virtues of free trade. They were led by the Chancellor of the Exchequer, C.T. Ritchie, and the veteran Duke of Devonshire, who as Lord Hartington had defected from the Liberal Party with the great majority of the Whig faction two decades earlier. Chamberlain had succeeded in converting a large section of the Tory Party to his views, and neither he – nor his free trade opponents – were in any mood to compromise.

In the circumstances, any Prime Minister would have had difficulty in holding the Cabinet together, and it was fairly predictable that one wing or the other would be driven to resignation. Balfour's achievement was to lose both of them. Four free trade ministers (Ritchie, Devonshire, Lord George Hamilton and his own cousin, Lord Balfour of Burleigh) resigned because they believed he was leaning too far in Chamberlain's direction, while Chamberlain himself left because he did not lean far enough.

In truth, Balfour had no strong views on the issue one way or the other, a position which was neatly summed up by a piece of doggerel composed by a Liberal MP, Sir Wilfred Lawson:

I'm not for Free Trade, and I'm not for Protection.
I approve of them both, and to both have objection.
In going through life I continually find
It's a terrible business to make up one's mind.
So in spite of all comments, reproach and predictions,
I firmly adhere to Unsettled Convictions.

(quoted by Young, 1963, p. 214)

Balfour's attempt at compromise was to seek to commit the government
to a policy of 'retaliation'; that is, that it should continue a general policy of
free trade, while reserving the right to impose import duties against countries
which pursued protectionist policies. Although he recognised the strength of
support within the Tory Party for Chamberlain's views, he believed that tariff
reform, which implied a tax on imported food, would be deeply unpopular
in the country as a whole. He therefore concluded that it was not 'practical
politics', at least in the short run. His rational approach was shared by few of
his party colleagues. In the grip of ideological fervour, both sides continuously
fuelled the dispute – uncannily foreshadowing the contortions over Europe of
the Major government in the 1990s – and gravely damaging party unity.

A more tactically aware politician would have sought to divert the attention
of his supporters by spectacular initiatives in other directions. Yet Balfour
appeared to have no shots in his locker. He did not believe that social engineering was the business of government. Profoundly conservative in outlook, he
would certainly have subscribed to the tenet that 'he who governs least governs
best'. Despite his resourcefulness in pushing through the 1902 Education Act,
and his backing for several earlier bills designed to improve social conditions in
Ireland, he did not in general believe in the virtues of legislation. If an Act of
Parliament did no actual harm, that was a bonus in his view: most attempts to
legislate only made matters worse.

Although devoted to the Conservative Party, Balfour had little understanding of its psyche and, unlike his Uncle Robert, was not prepared to
immerse himself in matters of party organisation and patronage. Nor did he
have any respect for the views of the party rank and file. 'I would as soon be
guided by the views of my valet as by the Conservative Party conference', he
said on a famous occasion. This patrician indifference to the growing democ-
ratisation of British politics, which was even affecting the Conservative Party
under the influence of Joe Chamberlain, made Balfour an inappropriate figure
to lead a political party in the twentieth century. Moreover, his own lack of
raw ambition led him to underestimate the ambitions of others. He remained
on excellent personal terms with Chamberlain, and seemed never to have
suspected that the latter was at least partly motivated by his own desire for the
premiership, an aspiration which was only terminated by the massive stroke

which he suffered in July 1906 and which incapacitated him for the remaining eight years of his life.

Balfour became increasingly exasperated by the disunity of his party, but made only fitful attempts to overcome it, tending to withdraw 'to seek the solace of the golf course at North Berwick', as Mackay puts it. His government nevertheless lingered on for over two years after the resignations, by which time Balfour conceded that he had had enough. He was then guilty of a profound misjudgement. Instead of seeking a dissolution from the King, he meekly resigned on 5 December 1905, allowing a Liberal government, under Sir Henry Campbell-Bannerman, to take over in advance of a general election. This enabled the hitherto divided Liberals to present themselves as a united government, and combine the advantage of incumbency with the opportunity to blame the retiring government for all the current discontents. Balfour's private secretary, J.S. Sanders, attributed the stunning Liberal victory in the election which followed, in January 1906, to four causes: the swing of the pendulum, accentuated by the large Tory gains in 1900, the scandal over the importation of Chinese 'slave labour' into South Africa, the organisation of Labour and the Socialist vote, and Nonconformist campaigning against the 1902 Education Act (Mackay, 1985, p. 226).

Yet more important than any of these was probably the appalling picture of disunity presented by the Tories, and Balfour's maladroit handling of his own party. He himself was among the defeated candidates, but managed to get back to the Commons within two months when one of his supporters resigned a safe seat.

There was, however, more to Balfour's premiership than his failure to cope with the tariff reform issue. There were a number of achievements to his credit, many of which were of considerable long-term significance. Three, at least, stand out. The 1902 Education Act fell far short of matching the educational reforms in Germany which enabled its scientific and industrial development to exceed that of any of its European rivals. It did, however, put secondary education on a firm financial footing and opened up opportunities to a large number of (mostly lower middle class) children.

Secondly, Balfour, acutely aware of military failings and poor co-ordination between the services during the Boer War, was instrumental in establishing, and presiding over, the Committee of Imperial Defence (CID). For the first time, this enabled long-term military planning to proceed and provided a forum for mediating between the designs of the War Office and the Admiralty. Balfour was an extremely active chairman, and continued to take a keen interest in its work even after ceasing to be Prime Minister, writing far-seeing memoranda at their request, and unofficially rejoining the Committee in 1914 at the invitation of the Prime Minister, Herbert Asquith.

Thirdly, Balfour took steps to ensure that Britain's foreign and defence policies were properly co-ordinated, which all too often they had not been in the past. He also presided over the ending of Britain's long-standing tradition of 'splendid isolation', to use Salisbury's phrase. A treaty of alliance was signed with Japan, and the Anglo-French Entente was concluded in April 1904. This was not initially intended as a military alliance, but subsequent secret negotiations conducted by Asquith's Foreign Secretary, Sir Edward Grey, effectively converted it into one, making British participation in the First World War almost inevitable.

With the exception of Sir Alec Douglas-Home, who served as Foreign Secretary, Balfour was the only twentieth-century Prime Minister who continued to have a substantial political career after the end of his premiership. He was Leader of the Opposition for six years after 1906, acquiescing in, if not initiating, the use of the House of Lords ('Mr Balfour's Poodle', in Lloyd George's words) to frustrate the passage of the 1909 'People's Budget'. After King George V had agreed, following the two general elections of 1910, to Asquith's demand to create as many Liberal peers as necessary to secure the passage of the 1911 Parliament Act, which clipped the wings of the upper house, Balfour advised Tory peers to give up their die-hard opposition to the act. A large number of them defied his advice, though not quite enough to prevent the bill being passed. Balfour, in disgust, and already heartily sick of party political manoeuvring, threw in his hand. Not many in his party regretted his decision: they preferred a more partisan and less rational figure to lead them against the forces of radicalism and socialism which they saw closing in on them.

At that stage, Balfour almost certainly saw this as the end of his life in high politics, and joyfully returned to his study of philosophy, undertaking to give two major courses of lectures at the University of Glasgow. In the event, only one course had been given by August 1914, when Balfour, although a member of the Opposition, was immediately recruited to help the war effort. He was co-opted to the CID (henceforth renamed the War Council), and became First Lord of the Admiralty, in succession to Winston Churchill, when a coalition government was formed in May 1915. In December 1916, when Lloyd George replaced Asquith as Prime Minister, he was appointed as Foreign Secretary, provoking the lasting hostility of Asquith who previously had been a personal friend. Balfour had not intrigued against Asquith, who, however, was affronted by the alacrity with which Balfour had moved, in Winston Churchill's words: 'from one cabinet to another, from the Prime Minister who had been his Champion to the Prime Minister who had been his most severe critic ... like a powerful and graceful cat walking delicately and unsoiled across a rather muddy street' (Churchill, 1937, p. 249).

As Foreign Secretary, Balfour showed a sureness of touch which had eluded him as Prime Minister. His most significant contribution was in leading a mission to Washington, immediately after America's entry into the war in April 1917. He created an immensely favourable impression, and did much to persuade a still reluctant Congress and administration to devote themselves wholeheartedly to the war effort.

The Balfour Declaration of November 1917, expressing British support for 'the establishment in Palestine of a national home for the Jewish people' has undoubtedly become Balfour's greatest claim to posthumous fame. Although it resulted from a decision of the whole Cabinet (the one Jewish member, Edwin Montagu, being ironically the sole dissenter), it is unlikely that it would have seen the light of day without Balfour's enthusiastic advocacy. As a student of history, he had been fascinated by the survival over two millennia of this small and unimportant tribe, while great empires had perished. He had met with Chaim Weizmann a dozen years earlier and had been deeply impressed by his Zionist convictions. In his later years he often said that 'looking back on his life in politics, he felt that what he had been able to do for the Jews was the thing most worth while' (Young, 1963, p. 386).

In general, however, Balfour seldom took the lead in Cabinet, and normally strongly supported the views of Lloyd George. Yet on one occasion his influence was probably decisive, and may indeed have had the unfortunate effect of helping to prolong the war. In September 1917, the Austrian Foreign Minister, Baron Von Kühlmann, had sent a message through the Spanish government proposing peace talks. The war was going badly for the allies, with the Russians on the brink of collapse and mutinies in the French army, and Lloyd George and others were tempted to follow up the Austrian approach and to see whether Germany also would be interested in a negotiated peace. Balfour, however, after having first proposed unsuccessfully that the Austrian feelers should be discussed with all the other allied powers, rallied the War Cabinet into fighting on without responding to Von Kühlmann's approach.

Balfour's last important task as Foreign Secretary was to attend the Versailles Peace Conference as Lloyd George's deputy. According to eyewitness accounts, the business was despatched a great deal more expeditiously when he was substituting for his chief. In 1922 he accepted an earldom, but throughout most of the 1920s he continued as a Cabinet minister, as Lord President of the Council, representing Britain at the Washington Conference on naval limitation in 1921 and at the Imperial Conference in 1926. He continued to take a close interest in defence matters, being an assiduous attender of the CID, and took energetic steps to foster scientific and industrial research, creating the Committee of Civic Research (CCR) in 1925. Despite his age he remained one of the most influential members of the Cabinet, and Baldwin refused to allow him to resign, even when his health failed in 1928. He remained in office right up to the 1929 general election, when Baldwin was defeated, dying in the following year at the age of 81.

A long and distinguished political career thus came to an end, which contrasted sharply with his failure as Prime Minister. The simplest explanation is that he was lacking in leadership qualities, and that in particular he was deficient in man management. Despite his immense charm, and exceptionally wide range of friends and acquaintances, he did not find it easy to handle powerful and ambitious colleagues. His waspish wit was widely appreciated – except by its victims, who over the course of time became more and more numerous. On one occasion, for instance, he said of a Cabinet colleague, 'if he had a little more brains he would be a half-wit' (Douglas-Home, 1987, p. 170). His own lack of commitment not only prevented him from embracing political causes with enthusiasm, but blinded him from appreciating the passions and ambitions which drove many of his colleagues.

In human terms, his detachment undoubtedly had its redeeming features. In 1898, for example, when he was already number two in the Tory Party and the probable next Prime Minister, he performed an extraordinary act of friendship towards Herbert Asquith. At the bidding of the latter's wife, Margot, he wrote a letter to her wealthy father, Sir Charles Tennant, asking him to settle a large income on Asquith so that he could afford to give up his practice at the bar and assume the leadership of the Liberal Party. Tennant refused, but it was remarkable that Balfour had exerted himself to facilitate the choice by his political opponents of a man who promised to be a most formidable rival.

Many politicians undoubtedly take politics and themselves too seriously. With Arthur Balfour, the opposite was the case. The anonymous poet quoted above was writing about a carefree young man in his mid-twenties. His perceptive analysis could equally apply to the 54-year-old who became Prime Minister in 1902: 'Playful little Arthur, he/ Cannot take things seriously'.

Works consulted

Churchill, Winston, *Great Contemporaries*, London, Thornton Butterworth, 1937.

Douglas-Home, William, *The Prime Minister*: Stories and Anecdotes from Number 10, London, W.H. Allen, 1987.

Mackay, Ruddock F., Balfour: *Intellectual Statesman*, Oxford, Oxford University Press, 1985.

Ridley, Jane, and Clayre Percy, *The Letters of Arthur Balfour and Lady Elcho 1985–1917*, London, Hamish Hamilton, 1992.

Young, Kenneth, *Arthur James Balfour*, London, Bell, 1963.

34
Sir Henry Campbell-Bannerman – 'A Good, Honest Scotchman'

In December 1898, Lord Tweedmouth, a former Liberal Chief Whip, travelled to Scotland to meet Sir Henry Campbell-Bannerman at his residence at Belmont Castle. His mission: to offer him the leadership of the Liberal Party. Tweedmouth was confident that C.B., as he was universally known, would decline the offer, which was made as a courtesy to a popular and highly regarded but indolent colleague, already 62, who was believed to be without any ambition beyond becoming Speaker of the House of Commons. Once this formality was out of the way, Tweedmouth and the party's top brass, on whose behalf the offer was made, could get down to the serious business of choosing the man who was to lead their party into the next century. There appeared to be four possibilities. Former Prime Minister Lord Rosebery and former Chancellor of the Exchequer William Harcourt, both of whom had petulantly resigned the leadership in the preceding three years, complaining of lack of support by their colleagues. Could one, or the other, be tempted back? Former Home Secretary Herbert Asquith had ruled himself out, on the grounds that he could not afford to relinquish his prodigious earnings at the bar. Could his arm be twisted? And there was John Morley, the former deputy leader, who had somewhat hastily bracketed his own resignation with that of Harcourt, and now showed signs of regretting it. Any of these would cut a more impressive figure than the amiable but dull C.B., it was thought, and there was general consternation when Tweedmouth reported back that he had accepted the offer.

This is a plausible – but not necessarily accurate – account of how C.B. became the leader of his party. It was recounted by Austen Chamberlain 14 years later, on the authority of two Liberal Cabinet ministers, and is accepted by C.B.'s biographer, John Wilson, as possibly true (Wilson, 1973, pp. 287–8). Whether or not the offer to C.B. was genuinely intended, it is apparent that his appointment was originally seen only as a stopgap measure in the expectation that the 46-year-old Asquith would inevitably succeed him within a very short period. It was not to work out quite like that.

C.B., like Clement Attlee half a century later, was a prime example of a politician with apparently modest attainments outdistancing far flashier rivals. He was born plain Henry Campbell on 7 November 1836, the second son of a wealthy and self-made Glasgow businessman and local Tory leader, Sir James Campbell. His mother – Janet Bannerman – was the daughter of an equally wealthy Manchester merchant. Her own brother, Henry, was later to leave his nephew a life interest in his estate on condition that he 'assumed my surname of Bannerman either alone or in addition to his usual surname, but so that the name of Bannerman shall be the last and principal name' (Wilson, 1973, p. 46).

The young Henry Campbell had a happy and stress-free childhood. His parents, an earlier biographer, J.A. Spender, noted: 'had all the Scottish virtues: they were religious, dutiful, orderly and businesslike; in spite of their wealth, they lived simply and applied themselves seriously to the education of their children' (Spender, 1923, Vol. I, p. 7). At the age of 11 he was enrolled at Glasgow High School, and just before his 14th birthday was sent with his elder brother and a cousin on a ten-month tour through Europe (an upper-middle-class version of the Grand Tour). This left him with a lasting taste for continental travel, a good command of French, and a love of French life and literature. He subsequently studied at Glasgow University and at Trinity College, Cambridge, from which he emerged with a Third Class Honours degree in Classics. He was regarded as a pleasant and intelligent student, but indolent and failed to make much of a mark.

On leaving Cambridge, aged 22, he joined the family firm of J. & W. Campbell, warehousemen and drapers, run by his father and Uncle William, becoming a partner two years later without unduly exerting himself. At about this time he surprised his father and elder brother, both passionate Tories, by his conversion to liberalism, possibly influenced by Uncle William who had quit both the Tory Party and the Church of Scotland some years earlier to become a Free Churchman and a Liberal, while remaining on excellent terms with his brother who by then had become Lord Provost of Glasgow. C.B.'s own conversion was also accepted good-naturedly within the family, though it puzzled some of his later political colleagues. Augustine Birrell, for example, who was to be President of the Board of Education in C.B.'s government, wrote in his memoirs: 'How C.B. became a Liberal I never knew. Certainly not by prayer or fasting or by a course of hard reading' (Wilson, 1973, p. 38).

C.B.'s earliest major biographer, J.A. Spender, suggests the credit might belong to Daniel Lawson, one of the 200 clerks working in the family firm,

> a man of original character who read strange books and talked Radical and Chartist politics. The two had long, earnest and stubborn talks, and it was whispered that 'old Daniel' was getting great influence over Mr Henry. In

truth, he was rapidly becoming a Radical, not a Whig or Palmerstonian, but a really advanced politician. (Spender, 1923, Vol. I, pp. 20–1)

It was as a Radical that Henry Campbell contested a by-election in Stirling Burghs in April 1868 at the age of 31. It was an unusual contest: there was no Tory candidate and Campbell brashly offered himself in competition to the official Liberal nominee, a Whig. The Whig was victorious, but Campbell turned the tables later in the year in the general election, when the electorate was substantially enlarged as a result of the 1867 Reform Act, which provided for household suffrage.

No sooner elected, Campbell set himself the task of healing the divisions within the local Liberal Party, which he accomplished within a very short time. 'Praises of his tact, his geniality, his readiness to serve the humblest of his constituents, were soon in all mouths', Spender reports (1923, Vol. I, p. 30), and he represented the constituency for an unbroken period of 40 years, an unusual achievement at a time when even the longest-serving and most distinguished parliamentarians had frequently to change their seats. It was these same qualities, together with his evident disinterestedness and his strength of character, which quickly commended him to his parliamentary colleagues so that, without being regarded as in any way outstanding, he was soon accepted as a 'good House of Commons man', popular both in his own party and with his political opponents. Elected as a Radical, he moved imperceptibly within a few years to a position which could be described as slightly to the left of centre of his party, and remained there for the rest of his life. In personal terms, his loyalty was commanded, almost unquestioningly, by Gladstone.

Henry Campbell was excused his very light duties in the family firm, from which, however, he received a sufficient income to enable him to devote himself full-time to his new vocation and to live in considerable comfort. His elder brother, James Alexander Campbell, eventually took over the business, and much later became a Tory MP for Glasgow and Aberdeen universities. It was at James's wedding, in 1860, where she was a bridesmaid, that he met his own wife, Charlotte Bruce, the daughter of a Scottish general. Three years older than him, it was, in Spender's words, 'a case of love at first sight' (1923, Vol. I, p. 22), and they were married within a few months.

Thus began a partnership which was to endure until her death nearly 46 years later. It was a childless marriage, but one characterised by an unusual degree of mutual devotion. Shy, lacking in self-confidence, physically unattractive and later to become excessively fat and a semi-permanent invalid (probably due to diabetes, then an untreatable condition), she was hardly a social asset to her husband. Yet he depended on her judgement to a considerable extent, and her advice was almost invariably shrewd and to the point.

Campbell was in no hurry to make his maiden speech in Parliament, and indeed spoke rarely, but, Wilson notes, 'when he did speak – largely but not always on Scottish questions – he took trouble and was brief and effective, with the cheerful iconoclasm of a reformer' (Wilson, 1973, p. 45). At this early stage he seems to have made no impact on Gladstone, then at the height of his power during his first ministry, but he did come to the notice of Edward Cardwell. Cardwell was Secretary for War, and in 1871 requested his appointment to the new post of Financial Secretary to the War Office. In the same year, he inherited the estate at Hunton, near Maidstone, from his uncle, Henry Bannerman, and to his distaste, and even more that of his wife, was forced to hyphenate his name. As this was something of a mouthful, he encouraged his colleagues to refer to him as 'C.B.', and the sobriquet stuck.

Edward Cardwell was a reforming War Secretary, the most notable of the nineteenth century. His principal reform – carried through against the unrelenting opposition of a large proportion of the officer corps and the great majority of serving and retired generals – was the abolition of the ancient practice of selling commissions and promotions, clearing the way to promotion on merit. Equally significantly, he established the principle of civilian control over the military by ensuring that the Commander-in-Chief (an office held for 39 years by Queen Victoria's cousin, the Duke of Cambridge) should be subordinate to the Secretary of State. He also instituted the system of short-term service for the infantry, thus enabling an adequate reserve of trained men to be built up, and established the linked-battalion system whereby one battalion of a regiment remained at home while the other went abroad, while a regular interchange between the officers and men of both was provided for. He succeeded in providing Britain with a relatively small and economical professional army, and avoiding mass conscription, to which the continental powers were increasingly committed.

C.B.'s role as Financial Secretary was to prepare the estimates and supervise the funds of the War Office, which he succeeded in doing with a minimum of fuss and bother, releasing his superior to concentrate on weightier issues. Cardwell, with whom his personal relations were extremely cordial, was more than satisfied with his performance, while C.B.'s appreciation of Cardwell's achievements knew no bounds, and he became a role model for C.B. of how a reforming minister should be. As Wilson puts it,

> C.B. learnt from Cardwell that courage and determination and the will to do what seems right and to stand up to vilification and abuse are the qualities needed by statesmen whose work is to last. It was an experience he was never to forget. (Wilson, 1973, p. 54)

Disraeli's victory in the 1874 general election brought C.B.'s ministerial career to a temporary halt. The succeeding six years in opposition were relatively uneventful for him, and, as before, he took life easily, with long periods spent travelling in Europe and remaining in Scotland for several months of the year. Yet his weight in the House of Commons significantly grew, partly because, with Cardwell elevated to the Lords, he was the Liberal Party's chief spokesman on military affairs. He also gradually acquired the reputation of being the most influential MP from north of the border and his voice on Scottish affairs was always listened to with great respect.

When Gladstone formed his second government, in 1880, C.B. might reasonably have expected to be promoted, but he made no protest at being asked to resume his former post of Financial Secretary to the War Office. The evidence suggests that he had a very limited estimate of his own abilities, and did not, at that time at least, consider that he was fitted for anything more than junior office. C.B. remained for two years at the War Office, before transferring to an equivalent post at the Admiralty.

In 1884 it fell to C.B., in the absence in Egypt of the First Lord of the Admiralty, to advise the Cabinet on their response to a newspaper scare that the Fleet was being starved of funds and risked being overtaken by that of France. C.B. advocated a modest supplementary estimate which he argued was necessary more for political than naval reasons. The Cabinet responded by approving an increase three times greater than he had suggested. This succeeded in neutralising their opponents.

This was almost C.B.'s last action at the Admiralty. In October 1884 he left for a month-long holiday in Scotland with his wife, only to be summoned by telegram to meet Lord Spencer, the Viceroy of Ireland, in Edinburgh. He was taken aback to be told that Gladstone wanted to appoint him as Chief Secretary for Ireland, undoubtedly the toughest and most unpleasant job in the government. C.B. declined to accept, but being pressed, asked for a further day to consider. Within three hours, however, he had written to Spencer, stating categorically: 'I do not wish to undertake duties which I have reason to fear I should insufficiently discharge' (Spender, 1923, Vol. I, p. 59).

In the evening, however, he consulted his wife, and then proceeded to write a further letter setting out his reasons for refusal. What then transpired he recounted many years later to Augustine Birrell:

> I found a difficulty amounting almost to impossibility to get these excellent reasons into a letter. Then arose my domestic adviser and said 'See you not why you cannot write the letter. Your conscience is always telling you, as you write, that you ought to accept'. After a grand conseil de nuit, therefore, I telegraphed the next morning recanting my refusal. And this little manoeuvre remained a mystery to Spencer, and to a greater than he, Mr G. Thus is a woman ever a man's superior in intuition, and in self-sacrifice. (Wilson, 1973, p. 76)

C.B. remained as Irish Secretary for less than eight months. He was not a member of the Cabinet and was clearly subordinate, in practice if not in theory, to Lord Spencer, an old-fashioned Whig who was evidently uncomfortable – though less so than C.B. – with the coercive policies he was expected to carry out. C.B. himself continued very much in the same way as he had as a junior minister – fulfilling his duties with quiet efficiency, showing unremitting loyalty to his superior, but offering a flow of common-sense suggestions to meet the almost daily crises which arose. In the Commons he was a distinct success, largely deflating the spiked anger of Parnell's formidable Irish Party by his firm, unflustered but genial replies. At least one of the Irish members – T.P. O'Connor – became a committed fan of C.B.'s, publishing a eulogistic biography soon after his death. Neither Spencer nor C.B. had started out as supporters of Irish Home Rule. Yet both independently slowly became convinced of its necessity during their terms of office. When, in 1886, the majority of both Whigs and Radicals abandoned Gladstone, when he introduced the first Home Rule Bill, both stayed firmly in the Liberal camp.

C.B.'s Irish appointment came to an end in June 1885, when the Irish members joined with the Tories to defeat the Gladstone government on a vote on the Budget. The Salisbury government which followed did not last long, resigning soon after its disappointing result in the November 1885 general election. In the new government formed by Gladstone the following February, C.B. at last became – at the age of 49 – a member of the Cabinet. He became Secretary for War, which might seem to have been an obvious appointment following his two periods as Financial Secretary in the same department. Yet C.B. did not owe his promotion to Gladstone's appreciation of his earlier services. It was due rather to royal favour. Queen Victoria firmly resisted Gladstone's first choice of Hugh Childers, who was antipathetic to her cousin, the Commander-in-Chief. She indicated to Gladstone that C.B. would be a more acceptable alternative, and Gladstone reluctantly conceded. The Queen noted in her journal, 'Mr Campbell-Bannerman, a good honest Scotchman, to the War Office' (Wilson, 1973, p. 162). As for Gladstone, he warmly greeted C.B. at his first Cabinet meeting, waving his hand towards his colleagues, he said: 'You will get on all right with them. You will be canny and you will be couthy.' C.B later wrote: 'That he should address me in the patois of my own village put me at once at my ease, and enhanced my sense of his general omniscience.' J.A. Spender, in quoting this passage from C.B.'s papers, commented that ' "Couthy", as Campbell-Bannerman used to explain, was something more than the opposite of uncouth. It connoted affability, amiability, accessibility, and much more' (Spender, 1923, Vol. I, p. 100).

C.B. remained at the War Office for the whole of the 1892-95 Liberal government, continuing under Lord Rosebery when Gladstone retired in March 1894. He was not a great innovator, being mostly concerned to preserve the reforms introduced by Cardwell 20 years earlier. He once again impressed, however, by his steadiness, his good judgement and his ability to get on well with practically all his associates. Not all his Cabinet colleagues, however, were impressed by the amount of time which he spent away from London. Within two days of his appointment, he was off to Marienbad, where he went every year with his wife to take the waters, and he continued to insist on spending two months of the year abroad and at least three months in Scotland. Sir William Harcourt, who combined being Chancellor of the Exchequer with leading the House of Commons, where the government's majority was always precarious, bombarded him with sarcastic notes, including one in December 1894, saying: 'I really hope you will awake to the fact that there is an institution called H.M.'s Government, that there are such things as estimates, and that one day there will be a House of Commons' (Spender, 1923, Vol. I, p. 174).

His most notable achievement as War Secretary was, perhaps, finally to dislodge the Duke of Cambridge from the post of Commander-in-Chief. The latter, despite his 76 years, was most reluctant to go, having taken literally the pretence that his appointment was for life. It took six weeks, and the expenditure of a great deal of tact and resourcefulness, for C.B. to bring this about, using the good offices of the Queen herself to ease her relative out of his post. It was ironic that on the very day that the old buffer agreed to go, C.B. himself was the victim of a parliamentary ambush, the House of Commons voting by 132 votes to 125 to reduce his ministerial salary. The occasion for the vote was the so-called 'Cordite scandal', an alleged shortage of ammunition which later turned out to be a complete fabrication. C.B., however, insisted on standing down, and this led to the resignation of the whole Rosebery government, its chief having lost all stomach for continuing to govern without a secure majority.

Just a few months earlier C.B. had wanted to withdraw when a vacancy occurred for the Speakership of the House of Commons. The modest War Secretary, who had never thrust himself forward for any ministerial post, made a spirited bid for the position, for which he was eminently qualified as an experienced parliamentarian liked and respected on all sides of the House. The fact that his ministerial career would be ended after barely three years in the Cabinet appeared of no consequence to him. 'He was to his bones a House of Commons man, and a House of Commons man could, in his view, have no higher ambition' (Spender, 1923, Vol. I, p. 173). The Opposition would gladly have supported him, and he was deeply disappointed when Rosebery and his colleagues decided that he could not be spared from the government. Neither they nor he had the faintest idea they were thereby preserving him for a greater fate.

When the Rosebery government fell in 1895, Lord Salisbury formed his third administration and lost no time in calling an election which produced a large majority for the Tories and their Liberal Unionist allies, who were now included in the government. C.B., who had been knighted on Rosebery's recommendation, was now recognised as one of the senior figures in the Liberal Party, which, however, seemed weak, divided and thoroughly demoralised. Its two leading personalities – Lord Rosebery and Sir William Harcourt – found it almost impossible to work with each other. After each of them had successively flounced out of the leadership within three years, it must have come as a relief to many Liberals to serve under a leader who had no inflated idea of his own importance, who was genial, steady and imperturbable and had no enemies within his own party and precious few outside.

Yet although C.B.'s elevation was unanimously approved at a meeting of Liberal MPs in February 1899, his position was not strong. He was already 62, had only limited experience as a Cabinet minister and was almost universally seen as a transitional figure. Moreover, he was chosen specifically as leader of the Liberal Party in the Commons (as Harcourt had previously been) rather than leader of the party as a whole, and it was by no means a foregone conclusion that he would have become Prime Minister had the Liberals won the subsequent election.

Nevertheless, he made a solid start, shrewdly choosing Herbert Gladstone (the youngest son of the Grand Old Man) as his Chief Whip, and quickly smoothing over many of the differences between his colleagues. By the summer of 1899 a string of Liberal by-election victories had made the prospect of a triumph in the general election seem possible, or even probable. Then the Salisbury government, and more especially the Colonial Secretary, Joseph Chamberlain, blundered into the Boer War, which effectively removed this possibility. Instead, C.B. was placed in an almost impossible position, with his party split three ways, and personal antagonisms rising to new heights.

C.B.'s view was that the war could and should have been avoided, and he blamed Chamberlain for playing a dangerous game of bluff with President Kruger, despatching sufficient extra troops to South Africa to provoke the Boers but not sufficient to ensure victory in the event of hostilities. Once the war broke out, he was in favour of prosecuting it to a successful conclusion, but not in a vindictive manner, and of holding out to the Boers the prospect of reconciliation and an early return to self-government for the two Boer republics. On one flank of his party were the so-called Liberal Imperialists, notably Sir Edward Grey, H.H. Asquith and R.B. Haldane (with Lord Rosebery hovering in the background), who expressed wholehearted support for the government. They felt particularly committed to Lord Milner, the High Commissioner in South Africa (and a former Radical) who was the leading advocate of a fight to the finish with the Boers, with an insistence on unconditional surrender.

On the left wing of the Liberal Party were the so-called pro-Boers. These included Harcourt and Morley, and especially the young David Lloyd George, who braved severe public hostility and press vilification for their opposition to the war. Although C.B.'s own position was supported by the more thoughtful of his senior colleagues, and almost certainly by the bulk of Liberal activists, most of the more prominent and colourful figures had allied themselves with the two more extremist wings. He therefore appeared at times as a lonely and isolated figure, and few thought he would survive long as leader. The nadir seemed to have been reached when, on 25 July 1900, he recommended the party to abstain on a critical amendment to a government motion tabled by the pro-Boers. Only 35 Liberal MPs followed the leadership's advice, while 40 voted for the government and 31 supported the amendment. By this time, the early military setbacks had been reversed, and the war seemed to have been effectively won. Chamberlain seized the opportunity to press for a 'khaki' election, two years before the parliamentary term was up, and while the full force of jingoism in the country could be tapped. In the contest which followed, in October 1900, Tory candidates blatantly ran under the slogan 'A Vote for the Liberals is a Vote for the Boers'. The Liberal Imperialists fared no better than their pro-Boer or centrist counterparts, and though the Liberal Party was not routed, it failed to regain any of the ground it had lost in 1895.

Although their main centres had been overrun, the Boers stubbornly refused to surrender and their guerrilla operations continued for almost another two years, until May 1902. This provoked an increasingly ruthless response from the British forces, including the widespread burning of farms and the herding of thousands of women and children into 'concentration camps', where the death rate from disease was appallingly high. C.B. campaigned unceasingly against the government's demands for unconditional surrender and in favour of promising the Boers an early return to self-government. He was shocked to the core when a charity worker who had visited the camps, Miss Emily Hobhouse, gave him a first-hand account. In a forthright speech, in July 1901, he denounced the 'methods of barbarism' by which the war was being conducted. This speech caused outrage, and he was excoriated in the popular press and, notably, in *The Times*, and for some time there was concern about his personal safety. Among the torrent of abusive letters he received was one from a clergyman who wrote: 'You are a cad, a coward and a murderer, and I hope you will meet a traitor's or a murderer's doom' (Spender, 1923, Vol. II, pp. 9–10).

C.B. was apparently unfazed by this avalanche of abuse, kept steadily to his course and, while striving manfully to keep his deeply divided party together, made no attempt to trim his views which were now evidently closer to those of the pro-Boer wing of the party. He resented the activities of the Lib Imps, who formed an internal party pressure group, the Liberal League, which made strenuous efforts to obtain parliamentary candidatures for their own supporters. Wisely, however, he made no attempt to excommunicate them, and even cautiously attempted to reintegrate Lord Rosebery back into the party, while firmly resisting the condition which he set of repudiating Irish Home Rule. Rosebery, however, was determined to 'plough my furrow alone', as he put it in a speech in July 1901, and his once glittering political career sputtered out in increasing irrelevance.

By the time that peace was finally negotiated, in May 1902, the wave of jingoism had largely abated. More and more people concluded that if C.B.'s views had prevailed, the war could probably have been satisfactorily concluded a couple of years earlier. By this time it was evident that the great majority of Liberals outside Parliament had rallied to his side. His strength of character had won them over, and it was now evident that – so far from being a stopgap – he was the only conceivable leader to take them into the next election. This still, however, seemed several years ahead, and in the meantime his parliamentary colleagues were concerned at his limited debating skills in the House of Commons, where he was regularly worsted by Balfour, who, in August 1902, succeeded his uncle as Prime Minister.

Yet despite his parliamentary agility, Balfour proved an inept Prime Minister, and rapidly dissipated the large fund of goodwill he had built up as Salisbury's chief lieutenant. Moreover, the early actions of his government could almost have been designed to reunite the deeply divided Liberal Party. The introduction of a tax on corn was interpreted as a frontal attack on the free trade principles sacred to all Liberals, while the Education Bill, seen as forcing Nonconformist ratepayers to subsidise Church of England schools without these being submitted to public control, provoked the opposition of a large and influential section of the population, rekindling its traditional support for the Liberals. These two measures immediately brought C.B. and Asquith back together, greatly reinforcing Liberal firepower in the Commons, where Asquith was a formidable performer.

Moreover, the attempt by Joseph Chamberlain to follow up the corn tax with a fully fledged programme of protectionism fatally split his own party, leading to a series of ministerial resignations, including his own, and the defection to the Liberals of a number of prominent Unionists, notably the young Winston Churchill. Furthermore, it provided the Liberal Party with a potent electoral rallying cry in defence of cheap food.

With C.B.'s warm support, Herbert Gladstone negotiated an electoral pact with the nascent Labour Party, under which Labour candidates were given a free run in 31 constituencies in exchange for not opposing Liberals in many other sensitive seats. This act of opportunism probably damaged the Liberals in the long run as it enabled Labour to obtain a sizeable parliamentary bridgehead in 1906, thereby increasing its prospects of eventually supplanting its temporary allies. Yet there is little doubt that C.B., unlike some of his colleagues, was genuinely well disposed to Labour and positively welcomed the prospect of their increased representation at Westminster.

Despite C.B.'s reconciliation with the Lib Imps, they still distrusted him and as hopes for a Liberal government rose, they made a determined bid to circumscribe his influence should he become Prime Minister. In September 1905 a plot was hatched between Sir Edward Grey, Asquith and Haldane during a fishing holiday at Relugas in north-east Scotland. There, in Haldane's words,

> we agreed ... that if Campbell-Bannerman became Prime Minister he should take a peerage, and that Asquith should lead in the Commons as Chancellor of the Exchequer. Unless our scheme were in substance carried out we resolved that we could not join Campbell-Bannerman's Government. What we thus resolved on we used afterwards ... to speak of among ourselves as 'the Relugas Compact'. (Wilson, 1973, p. 427)

The three conspirators even, quite improperly, involved King Edward VII in their plot, persuading him personally to urge C.B. to go to the Lords on the grounds of his age and uncertain health.

It did not need a general election to put the Relugas Compact to the test. Balfour unwisely resigned in December 1905 rather than asking for a dissolution of Parliament. King Edward duly invited C.B. to form a government, coupling this with a plea to him to go to the House of Lords, which he firmly resisted. Within a few days the Compact had crumbled. Asquith, after unsuccessfully attempting to persuade C.B. to become a peer, succumbed to the offer of the Chancellorship and leadership of the House of Commons, which would make him the undoubted heir apparent. Haldane and Grey were more adamant, but in the end they too gave way – Haldane accepting the War Office and Grey becoming Foreign Secretary. This was a fateful decision, which may well have led to British involvement in the First World War. The probable alternative to Grey was John Morley, who became instead Secretary for India and who would have been highly unlikely to embark on the secret agreements which Grey made with the French which effectively committed Britain to ally itself with France in the event of war with Germany.

Campbell-Bannerman was the first person to be officially appointed as Prime Minister, all his predecessors being merely designated as First Lord of the Treasury. The government he formed contained the whole gamut of Liberal opinion, from Grey on the right to Lloyd George (who became President of the Board of Trade) on the left. This enabled the Liberal Party to go into the election, in January 1906, as a united force, whereas the Tories were bitterly divided. The result was the most dramatic turnaround since the 1832 Reform Act, the Liberals returning 379 MPs against only 157 for the Tories and their Unionist allies. In addition, there were 83 Irish Nationalists and 51 Labour members (21 of them 'Lib-Labs'), nearly all of whom would, on most occasions, vote with the government.

The reasons for the Liberal landslide and Tory debacle were enumerated by Balfour's secretary J.S. Sanders, in a letter written shortly afterwards (Mackay, 1985, pp. 226–7). In his view they were, as cited in the preceding chapter on

Balfour: the swing of the pendulum, accentuated by the large Tory gains in 1900, the scandal over the importation of Chinese 'slave labour' into South Africa, the organisation of Labour and the Socialist vote, and the Nonconformist campaigning against the 1902 Education Act. In fact, the Tory gains dated more from the 1895 election, and in retrospect, one would probably somewhat downgrade the importance of the Chinese labour issue and emphasise the effect of the Tory disunity which Sanders was loath to admit.

The Liberal victory led to a dramatic transformation in C.B.'s standing in the House of Commons. Previously, he had been a hesitant and inconsistent performer, now he succeeded in imposing himself on the House with great authority. On a notable occasion, he worsted Balfour in a parliamentary debate held shortly after the latter's return in a by-election in February 1906, having lost his former seat in the general election. With the cutting phrase 'enough of this foolishness', he succeeded in deflating the Leader of the Opposition who had made a clever-clever speech which totally failed to catch the mood of the new House.

In Cabinet, C.B. was equally dominant, though he allowed his ministers a very free rein, rarely intervening in their departmental concerns. His short period as Prime Minister did not, however, lead to a large volume of reforming legislation, although the King's Speech in 1906 foreshadowed a near record number of bills. This was, undoubtedly, due in part to his own lack of energy. Already 69 years old and in indifferent health when he became Premier, he exhausted himself in nursing his wife day and night for several months before her death in August 1906, which left him devastated. In June 1907 he suffered the second of several heart attacks, and though this did not prevent him making an effective speech the following day proposing that the House of Lords' powers should be trimmed, he was clearly weakened, and from then onwards Asquith increasingly assumed the day-to-day direction of government business.

The second reason was Balfour's cynical decision, taken early in the Parliament, to use the House of Lords ('Mr Balfour's poodle', in Lloyd George's words) to frustrate the will of the Commons. This tactic was first used, to devastating effect, to destroy the 1906 Education Bill, which sought to modify some of the provisions of the 1902 Bill which had so outraged Nonconformist voters. C.B. wondered later if he ought not to have used the occasion to provoke an immediate Peers versus People election, but the showdown did not come until after his death, when Lloyd George's People's Budget was thrown out. Until then the constant threat from the Lords undoubtedly inhibited the government's reforming zeal.

It could not, however, prevent Campbell-Bannerman's greatest achievement – reconciliation with the Boers in South Africa. Consistent with the position he had taken ever since the beginning of the Boer War, he insisted on granting immediate self-government to the Transvaal and Orange River colonies, overturning not only a provisional constitution introduced under Balfour, which gave only limited representational rights, but also a proposal from a committee of his own Cabinet which went only a little further. In what several of those present, notably Lloyd George, described as a masterly performance, he almost single-handedly persuaded the Cabinet to drop the proposals and to send out a commission to South Africa to prepare the way for full self-government. Asquith, who was also present, later questioned whether the Prime Minister's role had been all that great (Wilson, 1973, p. 482), but the weight of evidence points to his intervention being decisive. This was certainly the view taken by the Boer leaders, Generals Botha and Smuts, who became totally reconciled and who brought South Africa into both the world wars on the British side. Unfortunately, the settlement did not lead to the enfranchisement of non-European voters, which the government was advised was precluded by the terms of the Peace Treaty signed at Vereeniging four years earlier, and provisions written into the new constitution to prevent racial discrimination were subsequently violated by successive South African governments both before and increasingly after the Nationalist Party came to power in 1948. This casts a serious retrospective shadow over C.B.'s achievement, but it remained an outstanding act of magnanimity.

On several occasions, C.B. revealed himself to have more radical sympathies than most of his ministerial colleagues, and he showed particular sympathy with the new group of Labour MPs elected in 1906. This twice led him, on the floor of the House, to scrap government proposals, approved by the Cabinet, in favour of more radical measures proposed by Labour members. The first occasion – which caused great offence to Asquith and the government law officers, concerned the 1906 Trade Disputes Bill, which sought to restore trade union rights rescinded by the Taff Vale judgment of 1900. Then, in December 1906, having heard persuasive speeches from Keir Hardie and others, he accepted on the spot a Labour amendment to include domestic workers in the Workmen's Compensation Bill, after the Cabinet had resolved on their exclusion. Had C.B. lived a few years longer, it is quite conceivable that the fatal split between Liberals and Labour – which led to the Conservatives becoming the dominant governing party for most of the century – might have been averted, and that a broad left-centre party would have evolved. Such a possibility was effectively excluded by the attitude of Asquith, who did not share C.B.'s warm sympathy with working-class aspirations.

It is also possible that women's suffrage would have come sooner if C.B. had survived. As Prime Minister, he spoke – at the height of the Suffragette agitation – in favour of a Private Member's Bill to give women the vote, greatly to the irritation of King Edward. Another sign of his radical sympathies came when he addressed a conference of the Inter-Parliamentary Union, when news came in that the Tsar had dissolved the Russian Duma. C.B., who was speaking in French, added the words '*La Douma est morte – Vive la Douma*' to his speech, to the evident embarrassment of his Foreign Office advisors.

C.B.'s health began to deteriorate rapidly in November 1907, and by early April it was clear that he was a dying man. Bedridden at 10 Downing Street, he tendered his resignation on 5 April, and died 17 days later, still in Downing Street – the last Prime Minister to die 'on the premises'. He held the premiership for a mere two years and 122 days, and the balance sheet of his government's achievements – apart from the South African reconciliation – may appear slender. Yet his overall achievement was remarkable.

By holding together his fissiparous party, during the dark days of the Boer War, while continuing to give a principled lead to his party and his country, he, and almost he alone, made possible the great election victory of 1906, which paved the way for the foundations of the welfare state to be laid by his successors, Asquith and Lloyd George. He himself devised the strategy which led to the eventual curbing of the powers of the House of Lords by the Parliament Act of 1911. Not a bad legacy for a man who had been affectionately but patronisingly dismissed by a backbench colleague (Sir Alfred Pease), writing in his diary in 1886, as 'a jolly, lazy sort of man with a good dose of sense' (Wilson, 1973, p. 67).

Works consulted

Mackay, Ruddock F., *Balfour: Intellectual Statesman*, Oxford, Oxford University Press, 1985.

Spender, J.A., *The Life of Sir Henry Campbell-Bannerman*, GCB, 2 vols, London, Hodder & Stoughton, 1923.

Wilson, John, CB: *A Life of Sir Henry Campbell-Bannerman*, London, Constable, 1973.

35

Herbert Henry Asquith – Not Quite in the Gladstone Mould

Gladstone without the passion, and without the religiosity. That would be an inadequate but not altogether misleading description of the last person to head a Liberal government. A complex personality, he himself attempted a somewhat tongue-in-cheek assessment of his own qualities in an idle moment at 10 Downing Street during a critical period of the First World War, in March 1915:

> You were ... almost a classical example of *Luck*. You were endowed at birth with brains above the average. You had, further, some qualities of temperament which are exceptionally useful for mundane success – energy under the guise of lethargy; a faculty for working quickly, which is more effective in the long run than plodding perseverance; patience (which is one of the rarest of human qualities); a temperate but persistent ambition; a clear mind, a certain quality and lucidity of speech; intellectual but not moral irritability; a natural tendency to understand & appreciate the opponent's point of view; and, as time went on, & your nature matured, a growing sense of proportion, which had its effect both upon friends and foes, and which, coupled with detachment from any temptation to intrigue, and, in regard to material interests & profits, an unaffected indifference, secured for you the substantial advantage of personality and authority. The really great men of the world are the geniuses & the saints. You belonged to neither category. Your intellectual equipment (well cultivated and trained) still left you far short of the one; your spiritual limitations, and your endowment of the 'Old Adam', left you still shorter of the other. (Jenkins, 1978, pp. 334–5)

Though more than a little smug, this reveals a considerable degree of self-knowledge and it illuminates the reasons both for his many successes and his ultimate failure. Herbert Henry Asquith was a man uncertain of his own identity. This was superficially reflected in his inability to settle upon his own nomenclature. Publicly known as 'H.H. Asquith', which is how he signed his name, for the first 40 or so years of his life he was known to his family and his few intimate friends as Herbert. After his second marriage, to the fashionable Miss Margot Tennant, in 1894, and following her lead, Henry was substituted.

Born 12 September 1852, his family background was more modest than that of any earlier Prime Minister. His father, Joseph Dixon Asquith, was a weaver working in the woollen trade in the Yorkshire town of Morley. A cultivated man, he lacked ambition and, in the words of his son, was 'of a retiring and unadventurous disposition'. He was, however, a keen and active member of the Congregationalist church, as was his wife, Emily Willans, and Asquith's earliest years were strictly bounded by the activities of the Rehoboth Chapel in Morley.

Tragedy struck when Asquith was eight years old. His father died suddenly, at the age of 34, leaving a widow, two sons (of whom Herbert was the younger) and two daughters, one of them a month-old baby who died within five years. Emily, a semi-invalid who seldom rose from her couch, was nevertheless a strong character who had a considerable influence on her son's development. Her devotion to the Congregational Church was as strong as her husband's, but her puritanism was less rigid, and Asquith was eventually permitted to add card-playing to the voracious reading which had previously been the only permitted diversion in the household.

Emily's family, who were well entrenched in local Liberal politics and the Nonconformist churches, were more affluent than the Asquiths, and her father, William Willans, took responsibility for the education of the two young brothers. They were enrolled as day scholars at Huddersfield College, but were subsequently transferred to a Moravian boarding school in Leeds. Willans, however, died within a couple of years which led to a further family upheaval. Emily moved south with her two daughters to St Leonards-on-Sea, and the two boys were sent to live with their Uncle John in London, where they were enrolled (at his expense, though Asquith later insisted on reimbursing him) in the City of London School. Even this arrangement did not last long: John Willans returned to Yorkshire within a year, and the brothers were boarded out successively to families in Pimlico and Islington.

His arrival at the City of London School set Asquith firmly on the road to fame and fortune. The school did not then have much of a reputation, but it had dedicated teachers, in particular the new headmaster, Edwin Abbott. He quickly recognised great potential in Herbert Asquith and gave him every encouragement to develop his strengths, which lay particularly in English and the Classics. The young Asquith spent much of his leisure hours listening to sermons by Nonconformist divines and to trials in the Law Courts, as well as – a possibility denied him when he lived in the family home – theatre-going.

His interest in the sermons seems to have lain more in their rhetorical qualities than in the Christian message which they sought to convey. Asquith was quick to learn, becoming a star performer in the school debating society and declaiming a notable oration – far in advance of his years – in honour of the original founder of the school. Abbott himself disclaimed the credit for Asquith's brilliant progress at the school, which was crowned by his winning a classical scholarship to Balliol College, Oxford, one of only two awarded for the whole country. All he had done, he said, was 'to place before him the opportunities of self-education and self-improvement ... simply to put the ladder before him, and up he went' (Jenkins, 1978, p. 17).

At Balliol, between 1870 and 1874, Asquith continued his ascent, achieving a double First in Classics, and becoming President of the Union, where his outstanding debating achievements were remembered for many years after. He also acquired, to a marked degree, that aura of effortless superiority which was supposed to characterise a Balliol man. In 1874 he was elected to a fellowship, but he saw his future not in academic life but in the law, which, however, he regarded chiefly as a stepping stone to a political career. He obtained a pupillage in Lincoln's Inn, and was called to the bar in 1876.

His legal practice, however, was slow to develop. Briefs were few and far between, and he had to supplement his meagre income by lecturing, correcting examination papers and contributing to the *Spectator* and *The Economist*. This did not inhibit Asquith from getting married the following year, at the age of 26, to Helen Melland, the daughter of a Manchester doctor, whom he had known since he was 18 and she 15. She came from a higher social stratum and brought with her a small private income of a few hundred pounds a year. Yet it was undeniably a love match, and Asquith settled down to a calm family life in Hampstead, where five children were born over the following dozen years. Writing of this period, Roy Jenkins remarked on 'a surprising but strong streak of recklessness' in his character.

> It made him go to the bar instead of seeking a safer occupation. It made him marry before he had an assured income. It was later to make him enter Parliament before he had an established practice. And it made him, in the early eighties, when his briefs were still rare, spend nearly £300 (equivalent to at least £2,000 today) on a diamond necklace for his wife. (Jenkins, 1978, p. 39)

Asquith became active in Liberal politics, becoming in particular a member of the Eighty Club (so named to celebrate Gladstone's victory in the 1880 general election), a dining club and debating society which supplied speakers to Liberal branches throughout the country. The secretary was R.B. Haldane, a Scottish barrister four years younger than Asquith who became his most intimate friend. In 1883 Asquith's prospects at the bar suddenly improved when R.S. Wright, a fellow Balliol man, became Junior Counsel to the Treasury and invited Asquith to 'devil' for him. This work included preparing a detailed memorandum for the Attorney-General, Sir Henry James, on the Parliamentary Oath, which was at the centre of the prolonged and vexatious dispute concerning the right of Charles Bradlaugh, the Radical and atheist MP for Northampton, to take his seat in the Commons. This memorandum was sent on to Gladstone, who warmly commended it, and Asquith subsequently helped to draft the Corrupt Practices Act of 1883, and also wrote a guide to the Act which was distributed to Liberal election agents.

His friend Haldane, who belonged to a landowning family in East Lothian, was elected to Parliament for that constituency in December 1885. Six months later another general election followed the defeat of Gladstone's first Home Rule Bill. The Liberal MP for the neighbouring seat of East Fife had voted against the bill and was disowned by his local association. Haldane used his influence to secure the nomination for Asquith with only one week to go until polling day. The Tories withdrew in favour of the renegade Liberal, and Asquith squeezed home with a majority of 374. He was to hold the seat for the next 32 years.

Unlike most of his predecessors as Prime Minister, Asquith made an immediate impact in the House of Commons, and was soon marked out as a rising star. As J.A. Spender noted in his entry on Asquith in *The Dictionary of National Biography*, 'His speeches were brief, pointed, trenchant and admirably timed; it was said that from the beginning he spoke with the authority of a leader and not as a backbencher' (Spender, 1937, p. 29). He concentrated, initially, on the Irish question, becoming a vehement critic of Balfour's coercive policies as Chief Secretary.

Yet it was outside the House that Asquith first achieved fame and fortune. The occasion was the Statutory Commission set up in 1888 by the Salisbury government to investigate the case against Charles Stewart Parnell, the leader of the Irish Party, who, according to letters allegedly written by him and published in *The Times*, had approved the 1882 Phoenix Park murders of Lord Frederick Cavendish, the Irish Chief Secretary, and of Frederick Burke, the Permanent Under-Secretary of the Dublin administration. The Commission was established in 1886, and Parnell, who was being defended by Sir Charles Russell, one of the most brilliant lawyers of the day, chose Asquith as his junior counsel. In two days of relentless cross-examination, Russell totally destroyed Richard Pigott, who had forged the letters and who promptly decamped to Madrid, where he shot himself in a hotel.

There remained the responsibility of *The Times*, which had published the letters without taking the most elementary steps to verify their authenticity. Russell was due to cross-examine C.J. MacDonald, the newspaper's manager, but at the last minute turned to Asquith and said: 'I am tired: you must take charge of this fellow' (Koss, 1976, p. 29). Totally unprepared, Asquith rose to the occasion, and in the course of two hours completely demolished the witness.

This single event transformed Asquith's previously lacklustre legal career. He was soon overwhelmed by the number of briefs pouring in, decided to take silk, and within a year was admitted as a Queen's Counsel at the age of 37. He was soon enjoying an income of £5000 a year, not much less than the top barristers of the day.

Nor did this success do him any political harm. On the contrary, his role in the vindication of Parnell, and the discomforting of the Conservative government which had sought to blacken his reputation, greatly increased Asquith's popularity within Liberal ranks.

Asquith suffered a tragic loss in September 1891, when his gentle, unambitious, home-loving wife Helen died of typhoid fever while they were on holiday together on the Isle of Arran. He was left with five young children (four sons and a daughter), who had to wait a mere two and a half years before the arrival of a stepmother, in the form of Margot Tennant. By all accounts, she performed her duties in this regard admirably, though she was a very different character from Asquith's first wife. A brilliant society figure, known equally for her wit and her indiscretion, she was the younger daughter of a wealthy Scottish baronet, Sir Charles Tennant. Asquith was devoted to her, though their marriage undoubtedly had a negative effect on his political career. Her extravagant lifestyle (she once said: 'I hope to leave nothing but debts') meant that he had to maximise his earnings at the bar and this precluded him from seeking the leadership of the Liberal Party in 1898 – ten years before he eventually took over. She was also, in part at least, responsible for Asquith succumbing to the 'aristocratic embrace', which alienated him from some of his Nonconformist supporters and blunted his radical instincts.

By the time of his second marriage Asquith was already Home Secretary. When the Liberals won the 1892 general election, the 83-year-old Gladstone departed from his normal rule of appointing to his Cabinet only those who had previously served as junior ministers, and gave Asquith, at 39, one of the plum jobs in his administration, though one which has all too frequently proved an elephant trap for its holders. The government, as a whole, left few achievements to its credit. The centrepiece of its legislative programme – the second Home Rule Bill – was overwhelmingly rejected by the House of Lords in September 1893, and a disconsolate Gladstone finally retired six months later. His successor, Lord Rosebery, who had been a forceful Foreign Secretary, proved a languid and remote head of government and conducted a permanent feud with his Chancellor of the Exchequer and Leader of the House of Commons, Sir William Harcourt. The government's unhappy life was perhaps mercifully concluded by a parliamentary ambush over the 'Cordite scandal' (see p. 44), after which it resigned and lost the ensuing general election of 1895.

Asquith was one of few ministers to emerge with his reputation significantly enhanced. He was held to have handled a number of tricky Home Office issues, such as the demand for the release of convicted Irish terrorists and the right to hold meetings in Trafalgar Square, with firmness and good sense, and had established himself as a master of parliamentary debate. Less to his credit was his dispatch of troops to the Featherstone colliery in Yorkshire, where striking miners were rioting, and two of them were shot dead. This incident did some lasting damage to Asquith's standing with the working class. Many years later someone shouted at him at a meeting: 'Why did you murder the miners at Featherstone in '92?' Jenkins relates that his 'characteristic reply' was 'It was not '92, it was '93' (Jenkins, 1978, p. 69). Asquith had also been responsible for introducing two complex and important bills – the Employers' Liability Bill, which came to grief in the House of Lords, and the Factory Bill, which greatly extended protection for the workforce. As Spender noted, 'When Parliament was dissolved in 1895, he was generally seen as a future Prime Minister' (Spender, 1937, p. 30). He was also recorded as being 'the only man in the cabinet who had not quarrelled with anyone' (Iremonger, 1970, p. 228).

Thrust into Opposition, Asquith promptly broke a long-standing convention which prevented ex-Cabinet ministers from practising at the bar. For him it was a matter of economic necessity. There were no parliamentary salaries in those days (they were eventually introduced under his own premiership in 1911), and – unlike most prominent politicians of the day – he did not enjoy substantial private means. His wife Margot received an income of £5000 a year from her father, but this was by no means sufficient to maintain the Asquiths' lifestyle. Their home in Mayfair's fashionable Cavendish Square, for example, had a domestic staff of 14, plus a coachman and stable boy.

His professional labours, and the social whirl into which he was led, by no means reluctantly, by Margot, left him relatively little time for politics and he was often absent from the House of Commons. When Sir William Harcourt resigned the Liberal leadership in the Commons in 1898, only two years after the departure of Lord Rosebery, Asquith would probably have been the overwhelming choice as successor if he had not become virtually a part-time politician. In the event, he was not disposed to challenge the nomination of Sir Henry Campbell-Bannerman (see p. 537), partly it seems because he regarded him as a mere *locum tenens* and doubted whether he would in fact become Prime Minister if the Liberals were returned to power.

In any case, Asquith felt a peculiar personal loyalty to Rosebery and he was among those who clung most tenaciously to the hope that he might be lured back to the Liberal leadership. When, in the following year, the Boer War broke out, he – like Rosebery – strongly supported the Tory government and, together with his close allies, R.B. Haldane and Sir Edward Grey, became a leading figure in the Liberal Imperialist faction, on the right wing of the party. They were fratricidally opposed by the pro-Boers, led by Harcourt and the young Lloyd George, and Campbell-Bannerman – unhappily poised between the two camps – had the greatest difficulty in holding the party together. Had Asquith become the leader in 1898 it is highly probable that the party would have been split in two by the war.

Within the Liberal Imperialist camp, Asquith was one of the more moderate leaders and he quietly discouraged the schismatic activities of his more rabid followers. Nevertheless, his personal relations with Campbell-Bannerman became distinctly strained, especially after he had publicly criticised his leader for his use of the phrase 'methods of barbarism' to characterise the farm-burning activities of British troops in South Africa.

The coming of peace, and the provocative actions of the new Balfour government, restored harmony to the Liberal Party much sooner than anyone expected. The 1902 Education Act, which horrified Liberal Nonconformists, and Joe Chamberlain's passionate advocacy of protectionism, quickly put an end to Liberal divisions, with only Rosebery remaining disaffected. Asquith threw himself wholeheartedly into opposing the Tory initiatives, and rapidly emerged as Campbell-Bannerman's most effective lieutenant, both in the country and in Parliament.

On the surface, at least, his relations with C.B. were excellent, but Asquith's doubts about his chief's capacity, coupled no doubt with his own ambition, led him to plot with Haldane and Grey to deprive C.B. of the premiership, or at least to relegate him to the House of Lords, in the event of a Liberal election victory. The 'Relugas Compact', as recounted on p. 48–9 above, quickly collapsed in the face of C.B.'s firm resistance, but it was Asquith who proved the weak link in the conspiracy and who shied away from a trial of strength. It is clear that C.B. could fairly easily have formed a government without either Grey or Haldane: if Asquith had held out it would have been difficult, if not impossible.

Instead, he settled for the role of C.B.'s heir apparent, as Chancellor of the Exchequer and the dominant debating force on the government benches, and Haldane and Grey fell in line behind him. From that moment on, there was no real doubt that he would be C.B.'s successor, and he increasingly took over the load from his boss during the final year when C.B.'s health was visibly declining.

In the meantime, his record as Chancellor of the Exchequer had done nothing to diminish his claims to the succession. He was, in J.A. Spender's words, 'orthodox, thrifty and progressive' – reducing food taxes, overhauling local government finance, establishing a differential between earned and unearned incomes for income tax and, in his final budget, making the first provisions for old age pensions.

When C.B. finally resigned, 17 days before his death on 22 April 1908, there was so little doubt about who should succeed him that King Edward VII, holidaying in Biarritz, did not even return to London for consultations. Instead, he summoned Asquith to Biarritz to 'kiss hands' on 6 April. He returned the next day with his list of Cabinet ministers already approved.

Asquith revealed himself as shrewd and decisive in his choice of colleagues. He inherited a strong team from Campbell-Bannerman, but took immediate steps to shed its weaker members and was not afraid to promote his most able colleagues to the most influential posts where their talents could shine most brightly. He was, nonetheless, careful to achieve a good political balance in his Cabinet, making it clear that he intended to run it from the centre rather than from either wing of the party. This effectively meant that space had to be found for the more radical elements to offset what otherwise might have been seen as a government dominated by the former Liberal Imperialists. This was most spectacularly achieved by the promotion of Lloyd George to be Chancellor of the Exchequer, with Winston Churchill becoming, at the age of 33, President of the Board of Trade, and Reginald McKenna First Lord of the Admiralty.

Three ineffective peers – Lords Elgin, Tweedmouth and Portsmouth - were either ejected or demoted, without a word of warning or explanation. Elgin, who was replaced as Colonial Secretary by Lord Crewe, a close associate of Asquith, bitterly complained about his treatment in a letter to Lord Tweedmouth. 'I venture to think', he wrote, 'that even a Prime Minister may have some regard for the usages common among gentlemen ... I feel that even a housemaid gets a better warning' (Hazelhurst, 1977, p. 81).

Asquith's brutal treatment of these former Cabinet colleagues contrasted strongly with his subsequent dealings with his own ministers, whom he treated almost invariably with the utmost courtesy and consideration and to whom he showed great loyalty when they got into difficulty. Nevertheless, it accorded with Asquith's public reputation as a 'cold fish', lacking in human feelings and showing none of the spontaneous warmth of C.B. Asquith was widely admired for his intellectual qualities and his political judgement, but he was never regarded with great affection, even in his own party.

Like Campbell-Bannerman, Asquith left his ministers a pretty free run in their own departments, seldom interfering with their decisions. Neither did he play a dominant role in the Cabinet, preferring to act as a 'mediator rather than initiator' (Hazelhurst, 1977, p. 82). He seldom steered the course of discussion at Cabinet meetings, preferring to sum up after others had had their say. On most issues he seemed more concerned to reach decisions which would cause the least dissension rather than those which accorded most closely with his own preferences (Cassar, 1994, p. 32).

Where Asquith did show his leadership qualities was in the House of Commons, where he retained his eminence as a debater, with his Chancellor, Lloyd George, whose style was very different, his only serious rival. Asquith presented and defended government policies with polished skill, depending on his prodigious memory, his forensic training as a barrister and his ability to master the details of a brief with seemingly little effort to carry him triumphantly through many a dangerous encounter.

Outside the Commons, Asquith's routine as Prime Minister must appear astonishingly relaxed to modern readers, though perhaps no more so than that of most of his predecessors. A voracious reader of novels, and what Jenkins describes as a 'highly heterogeneous collection of books' (Jenkins, 1978, p. 262), he and Margot gave several luncheon parties each week, more often than not attended primarily by non-political personalities or society figures from Margot's own circle. The evenings were devoted to bridge, the theatre and smaller dinner parties often in the company of two or three of the more favoured of his younger ministers, notably Edwin Montagu and Winston Churchill. The guests usually included attractive and clever young women, with whom Asquith loved to gossip and chaff. The weekends were spent either at the Wharf, the Asquiths' country house near Abingdon, or at country house parties given mostly by Margot's aristocratic friends. In the midst of this social whirl, Asquith became rather too well acquainted with the demon drink, and he acquired the nickname of 'Squiffy' in political circles, though this was unknown to the general public. This occasionally led to embarrassment in the Commons where, during the Committee stage of the Parliament Bill, he was 'so drunk that he was barely able to speak and only the traditional discretion of the House averted a scandal' (Cassar, 1994, p. 34).

Although he was probably never unfaithful to Margot, Asquith acquired a reputation for enjoying the company of young women, with one of whom, Venetia Stanley, he became completely infatuated. The beautiful daughter of the Liberal peer, Lord Sheffield, she was less than half his age and was a close friend of his daughter Violet. Because of this her frequent visits to 10 Downing Street caused little comment. Asquith got into the habit of taking long drives in the country with her on Friday afternoons, and over several years wrote to her virtually every day.

Too buttoned up to confide to any extent with his male friends, Asquith undoubtedly found it a relief to be able to express himself candidly to a whole series of women correspondents, who subsequently included Venetia's elder sister, Lady Henley. Yet from around March 1914 his attachment to Venetia became something of a mania, and he increased the flow of his letters to two or even three a day, often writing during the course of Cabinet meetings. A large number of these letters were published in 1982, and according to the editors,

> Although Asquith knew that the letters were being kept, he filled them with personal, political and military secrets of every kind; and they include constant appeals for Venetia's counsel. They constitute the most remarkable self-revelation ever given by a British Prime Minister. (Brock and Brock, 1982, p. 13)

Asquith was Prime Minister for 8 years and 244 days, the longest consecutive period in this office since Lord Liverpool's 15-year stretch from 1812 to 1827, and only since surpassed by Margaret Thatcher's 11-year reign. The conventional verdict on Asquith was that as a peacetime premier he showed great sureness of touch, but that as a wartime leader he was seriously out of his depth. The reality was rather more complex.

The dominant events during Asquith's peacetime premiership were the laying of the first foundations of the welfare state, the struggle over House of Lords reform and the final unsuccessful attempt to implement the Gladstonian policy of Home Rule for Ireland. The main impetus for the welfare state reforms – which included old age pensions, National Insurance for unemployment and invalidity, wages boards and labour exchanges and the beginnings of town and country planning – came not from Asquith himself, but from ministerial colleagues, notably Lloyd George and Churchill. Yet Asquith strongly backed their initiatives, and the partnership which he formed with Lloyd George provided the essential equilibrium of his peacetime government, just as their mutual loss of confidence undermined his wartime administration.

The determining pre-war event was Lloyd George's so-called 'People's Budget' of 1909. This had been necessitated by the Cabinet's decision greatly to expand naval expenditure in the face of Germany's large ship-building programme, at the same time as it was committed to a major programme of social reforms. Lloyd George's response was to propose an extra £14 million in taxation, including new taxes on land which enraged the property-owning classes. Although it had been accepted for at least 250 years that the power of the purse belonged to the House of Commons, the House of Lords rejected the Budget, immediately creating a constitutional crisis of the first order.

It was clear to Asquith that an immediate general election must be held to achieve a popular mandate to override the peers' decision. He also realised that his party's patience with the upper house was at an end and a mandate should equally be sought to curb or remove the veto which the Lords had repeatedly applied to other Liberal measures. He therefore approached King Edward VII for an assurance that, should the election produce a majority in favour of the government, he would be prepared, if necessary, to create sufficient new peers to override the Tory majority if it refused to pass the necessary legislation. The King refused, saying that he would not 'feel justified in creating new peers until after a second general election' in which the veto would be the sole issue. (See Roy Jenkins, *Mr Balfour's Poodle*, 1964, which remains the definitive account of the struggle to reform the Lords.)

Asquith supinely accepted the King's decision, recoiling from the prospect of a People versus Monarch election. It is, however, arguable that he had the constitutional right as Prime Minister formally to advise the King to create the necessary number of peers, and he undoubtedly treated the King with greater deference than had been shown by his Tory predecessor, Arthur Balfour, some years previously, when he had resolutely refused to let the monarch see confidential Cabinet documents. The Prime Minister also blandly ignored the views of other senior ministers, including Grey, that a more thoroughgoing reform of the membership and powers of the upper chamber should be attempted.

The election which followed, in January 1910, produced a parliamentary majority of 124 in favour of overriding the Lords' veto. The Liberals, however, lost their overall majority and henceforth were dependent on the support of the Labour and Irish Nationalist parties to remain in power. This had far-reaching and largely unforeseen consequences.

After the election, the Lords let the Budget through without opposition, but adamantly refused to contemplate any trimming of their powers. The sudden death of Edward VII in May 1910 again led Asquith to hesitate and, rather than hold the new King, George V, to his father's undertaking concerning a second election, he attempted to arrive at a compromise through a conference of the leaders of both main parties. It was only after this proved abortive that he finally cornered George V, who reluctantly conceded in November 1910 that he would create sufficient peers if the situation arose, but did not wish this to become public unless it proved necessary to give effect to it in a new Parliament. Asquith immediately sought a new dissolution and a further general election was held in December 1910, which produced an almost identical result to the previous January.

The Lords did not give way even then, and it was only after the King's undertaking was revealed that a dissident group of Tory peers, led by Lord Curzon, decided to abstain, which just allowed the Parliament Act of 1911 to pass the Lords with a bare majority without the creation of additional peers. Asquith's role in this dispute was at best equivocal. While exerting himself sufficiently to ensure the passage of the Budget and the removal of the Lords' absolute veto, he missed the opportunity of more far-reaching reform and wasted the better part of two years, while putting the electoral survival of his government at unnecessary risk by acquiescing in the King's insistence on the holding of two elections.

During the course of the conflict over the Lords, Asquith had on several occasions appeared on the verge of exhaustion, and there is little doubt that the wear and tear of his long period in office was beginning to tell. While still capable of decisive action on occasion, his premiership was increasingly characterised by long periods of indecision, exemplified by the reply 'Wait and See', which he repeatedly gave when questioned about the government's intentions.

This was even more evident in his handling of the Irish Home Rule issue which dominated the last two years of peace. Never a passionate believer in the cause, Asquith had successfully avoided any action to give effect to the long-standing Liberal commitment until after the January 1910 election, which left him in hock to the Irish Nationalists for his parliamentary majority. The passage of the Parliament Act in 1911 removed the possibility of a permanent Lords' veto, and in April 1912 the government duly introduced a bill to transfer power over Irish affairs to an elected Parliament in Dublin. This was duly rejected by the Lords in 1912 and 1913, and was due to be passed for the third and final time by the Commons in the summer of 1914. Well before then it had become apparent that the Protestant majority in Northern Ireland was adamantly opposed to being governed from Dublin. Whipped up by the lawyer and Tory politician Sir Edward Carson (with the tacit approval of the Tory leader, Andrew Bonar Law), armed groups prepared to resist the transfer of power.

As the situation deteriorated, it became increasingly clear that only two alternatives were open to the government: firm action against those advocating and organising violent resistance or amending the Home Rule Bill to exclude, either permanently or temporarily, Protestant majority areas from the aegis of the projected Dublin Parliament. Yet Asquith temporised for month after month until March 1914 when, on the eve of the Third Reading of the Bill, he introduced an amendment which would allow the Ulster counties to opt out of Home Rule for a period of six years. This failed to appease the Protestants and was seen as too great a concession by the Nationalists. At the same time, Asquith decided on a show of force against the illegal arming of Protestant militias, only to be confronted by the so-called Curragh mutiny, when 60 British Army officers at a barracks near Dublin declared that they would resign their commissions rather than act against Protestant loyalists.

In the face of incipient civil war in Northern Ireland, Asquith initiated a series of inter-party discussions, culminating in a formal conference at Buckingham Palace. It opened on 21 July, but broke up three days later without any agreement. Asquith was at the end of his tether, and was only rescued from his dilemma by the greater crisis precipitated by the assassination in Sarajevo of the Austrian Archduke Franz Ferdinand. Writing to Venetia Stanley in March 1915, he admitted that 'the sudden outbreak of the Great War' had been the greatest stroke of luck in his political career (Brock and Brock, 1982, p. 111).

Asquith bore little direct responsibility for the outbreak of the war, though he was certainly instrumental in ensuring British entry. This was not a development which he welcomed, and his correspondence with Venetia suggested that he would have been happy for Britain to remain a neutral spectator (Brock and Brock, 1982, p. 123). His hands were forced, however, partly no doubt by the speedy build-up of jingoistic sentiment after the German ultimatum to Belgium, but more directly by pressure within his own Cabinet. This was, effectively, split three ways. A 'war party', led by Grey and Churchill, was adamant that Britain should enter the war on the French side. Grey, in particular, felt that this was the only honourable course, no doubt influenced by the strength and consistency of the undertakings (albeit only implicit) which he had given to the French leadership over the years, and which he and Asquith had long conspired to keep secret from the bulk of their Cabinet colleagues (Coogan and Coogan, 1985). On the other side was the 'peace party', led by John Morley and John Simon, who declared themselves opposed to British involvement 'in any circumstances'. Only a few months earlier they had rallied half the Cabinet, including Lloyd George, to resist Admiralty proposals for increased naval expenditure, and they probably represented a majority of Liberal MPs.

In the middle was a solid group of non-committed ministers, including Lord Crewe, Reginald McKenna and Herbert Samuel, who were ready to rally to any lead given by Asquith. He, however, was in no hurry to commit himself and, as usual, played a waiting game, carefully assessing the number and weight of potential resignations on either side before making a move. His overriding impulsion seemed to be to keep his Cabinet as united as possible. The intentions of two senior ministers, in particular, weighed heavily with him. One was Grey, to whom he felt a personal link of complicity; the other was Lloyd George, his only conceivable rival for the premiership. Grey had made it quite clear that he would leave the government if Britain remained neutral, but Lloyd George was desperately anxious not to resign and was furtively seeking a 'respectable' pretext to detach himself from the peace party. He seized on the German threat to Belgium, and as soon as it was clear that Lloyd George would not resign Asquith came down decisively on Grey's side. While four Cabinet ministers proffered their resignations, Asquith persuaded two (Simon and Lord Beauchamp) to change their minds, so only Morley and John Burns, the Lib-Lab President of the Board of Local Government, actually quit the government.

The British entry into the war went smoothly enough: the Expeditionary Force of six divisions was rapidly dispatched to France, and under the enthusiastic eye of Winston Churchill, the First Lord of the Admiralty, the Fleet assumed its battle stations. The appointment by Asquith of Lord Kitchener as War Secretary was a masterful stroke of public relations; it was only later that his military shortcomings became painfully evident. The immediate consequence was that Asquith's popularity soared and he was spoken of as a great war leader in the tradition of the Elder Pitt. This impression quickly faded. The deadlock on the Western Front and the failure of the Dardanelles campaign in the spring of 1915 led to growing disillusionment, which Asquith did little to dispel.

It should have been evident to him that, lacking a parliamentary majority, it was not practicable to conduct the war effort on the basis of a single-party government. Instead of actively seeking to form an all-party coalition in which the Tories – with virtually the same number of MPs as the Liberals – would certainly play a major role, he firmly resisted the idea, and it was only after the Dardanelles disaster, in May 1915, that he was forced to accept the inevitable. Unfortunately, this came at the very moment when his judgement was clouded by a crisis in his personal life. To his utter consternation, Venetia

Stanley announced her engagement to one of Asquith's favourite younger Cabinet ministers, Edwin Montagu, and that she was converting to Judaism in anticipation of the marriage. He took the news very hard, and broke off all communication with her.

What effect this blow had on his handling of the coalition negotiations can only be speculated, but it is undeniable that he conducted them in a stubborn, ungracious and ultimately self-defeating manner. His crucial error lay in his determination to deny the Tory leader, Andrew Bonar Law, one of the principal ministerial posts. Instead, he was fobbed off with the Colonial Secretaryship, one of a series of snubs he received at Asquith's hands. It seemed as if the Prime Minister was refusing to accept the fact that Law was the leader of his party, and that he was perversely determined to treat Balfour (who became First Lord of the Admiralty) as if he was still in command. It has been suggested that this arose from Asquith's intellectual snobbery (Hazelhurst, 1977, pp. 93–4). Bonar Law was a businessman, and not an intellectual or a member of the professional classes. Asquith had already shown a marked reluctance to include many of the large number of Liberal MPs with a business background in his peacetime government, which was made up almost exclusively of professional men together with a fair sprinkling of aristocrats. Whatever his motives, Asquith's disdainful treatment of Bonar Law cost him dear. As the American historian George Cassar shrewdly commented: 'in the long run ... Asquith's best chance of remaining Prime Minister would have been to turn the Unionist leader into a specially-trusted lieutenant and to have headed a genuine national ministry' (Cassar, 1994, p. 109). Instead, the Tory leader became deeply disgruntled and needed little encouragement to throw in his lot with Lloyd George in the crisis in December 1916, which led to his replacing Asquith as Prime Minister.

During the 18 months of the Asquith-led coalition, his reputation steadily declined. The progress of the war went from bad to worse, and the ill-fated Somme offensive, where the British casualties totalled 420,000, including Asquith's brilliant elder son, Raymond, killed off any lingering illusions of a cheap and easy victory. Yet it was not the military reverses or the terrible carnage which destroyed Asquith's standing as a war leader. It was the growing conviction that his heart was not in it. From the beginning he had given the impression that the conduct of the struggle should impinge as little as possible on the familiar routines of peacetime life, and he was far too rational and civilised a man to indulge in the hyperbole of war. His apparent lethargy was altogether too sharp a contrast with Lloyd George, whose dynamic energy as Minister for Munitions made him the inevitable candidate for War Secretary when Kitchener was drowned in June 1916. If Asquith was temperamentally incapable of waging war wholeheartedly, he showed very little inclination to work for a peace settlement. He consistently cold-shouldered mediation attempts by President Woodrow Wilson, and when his (Tory) Minister without Portfolio, Lord Lansdowne, circulated a Cabinet memorandum, in November 1916, urging the case for a negotiated peace, Asquith offered him no support.

The precise circumstances of Asquith's fall, in December 1916, have been the subject of great controversy, and need not concern us here, though they are discussed in broad outline in the next chapter, on Lloyd George. (For long the most authoritative account was believed to be that of Lord Beaverbrook, who was virtually a participant, being an intimate confidant of both Bonar Law and Carson. This appeared in the second volume of his *Politicians and the War*, published in 1932. It is challenged on several points by Jenkins (1978, pp. 422–61). The most judicious summing up is probably that of Cassar (1994, pp. 210–32).)

The situation was brought to a head by a memorandum compiled by Lloyd George and the former Tory Attorney-General, Sir Edward Carson, with the backing of Bonar Law. It did not seek Asquith's replacement as Prime Minister, but argued that the executive conduct of the war should effectively be removed from the Cabinet and entrusted to a small War Council of three or four, with Lloyd George as chairman. Asquith was not unsympathetic to this proposal, but was adamant that he himself should chair the new body, believing that otherwise he would be reduced to a mere figurehead. He met with Lloyd George and reached a partial compromise, which fell through, amid mutual recriminations, after a biased account had been leaked to *The Times*, probably by Carson. Lloyd George then raised the stakes by submitting his resignation, and the Tory ministers pulled the rug from under Asquith's feet by insisting that they would not remain in the government in the absence of Lloyd George. Asquith saw no alternative to submitting his own resignation, perhaps hoping against hope that neither Bonar Law nor Lloyd George could form an alternative government and that he would then be summoned back. In the event, the King first summoned Bonar Law, who declined, and then turned to Lloyd George, who had no difficulty in forming a government within 24 hours, despite the refusal of almost all the former Liberal ministers, as well as Asquith himself, to serve under him.

Asquith believed that he was the victim of a sordid intrigue between Lloyd George and the Tory ministers, and of an unscrupulous campaign by the Tory press, with Lord Northcliffe's papers, including *The Times*, to the fore. The reality was that his days were numbered, and it is hard to disagree with Cassar's verdict: 'It was Asquith's perceived inadequacies that ended his premiership. Simply put, he no longer possessed the requisite confidence of the nation and parliament to beat back a major challenge to his leadership.'

Asquith's pride was deeply hurt, though he characteristically made no public attempt to justify his wartime record. He became a sulky Leader of the Opposition, offering lukewarm support to the new government's conduct of the war, only challenging them on one ill-fated occasion. This was the so-called Maurice debate, in May 1918, when Asquith – to the fury of Lloyd George and Bonar Law – proposed a select committee to inquire into the preparedness of the British Army to meet the German spring offensive. In the ensuing vote he was supported by 98 Liberal MPs, while 71 voted with the government. The following November, when, immediately after the Armistice, a general election was called, Lloyd George wreaked his vengeance by refusing a coalition 'ticket' to virtually all the Liberals who had voted with Asquith in the Maurice debate.

The election result was a shattering defeat for the Liberals, from which they never fully recovered. Asquith himself lost his seat, and only 26 of his followers were elected, against 59 for the Labour Party (which became the official Opposition) and 474 for the coalition (338 Tories and 136 coalition Liberals).

Asquith continued as Leader of the Liberal Party until 1926, including a period in which Lloyd George uneasily served under him, following the eventual reunion of the two wings of the party. There were ups and downs during these years – Asquith got back into the Commons through a by-election at Paisley in 1920, only to lose the seat again in 1924, after which he accepted an earldom. In the interim, he had, as leader of the third party in the Commons, backed the appointment of a minority Labour government, under Ramsay MacDonald, in January 1924 – only to withdraw support eight months later, precipitating the 1924 election which effectively reduced the Liberals to minor party status.

Asquith died four years later, leaving a mixed legacy to his country. On the one hand, he has been remembered as a pioneer, whose achievements have reverberated down the years, paving the way for the welfare state legislation of the Attlee government in 1945–51, as well as Blair's constitutional reforms (especially concerning the House of Lords) after 1997. But he is also remembered as the last of the nineteenth-century Liberals, and certainly bears some responsibility for the eclipse of the once mighty Liberal Party. It is arguable, though far from certain, that it would have been replaced, in any event, by the nascent Labour Party. What is undeniable is that this process was greatly hastened by the vendetta between Asquith and Lloyd George, and their respective followers. The opportunistic Lloyd George may have been the more culpable, but this gifted, fastidious, proud yet ultimately indecisive man must also bear his share of the blame.

Works consulted

Brock, Michael, and Eleanor Brock (eds), *H.H. Asquith: Letters to Venetia Stanley*, Oxford, Oxford University Press, 1982.

Cassar, George H., *Asquith as War Leader*, London, Hambledon Press, 1994.

Coogan, John W. and Peter F. Coogan, 'The British Cabinet and the Anglo-French Staff Talks, 1905–1914: Who Knew What and When Did He Know It', *Journal of British Studies*, 24 (1985).

Hazelhurst, Cameron, 'Herbert Henry Asquith', in John P. Mackintosh (ed.), *British Prime Ministers in the Twentieth Century*, Vol. I, London, Weidenfeld & Nicolson, 1977.

Iremonger, Lucille, *The Fiery Chariot*, London, Secker & Warburg, 1970.

Jenkins, Roy, *Asquith* (revised edition), London, Collins, 1978.

Koss, Stephen, *Asquith*, London, Allen Lane, 1976.

Spender, J.A., article on Asquith in *Dictionary of National Biography* 1922–1930, London, Oxford University Press, 1937.

36
David Lloyd George – 'A Dynamic Force'

The child is father to the man, and in no case was this more true than with David Lloyd George – or Dafydd George, as he was first known. Brought up by an adoring uncle – Richard Lloyd – who persuaded him from an early age that he was an exceptional person, with no limits to what he could achieve, he unquestioningly accepted his destiny, and lived his whole life as if normal rules did not apply to himself, and that anything – or any person – that he desired was within his grasp.

Lloyd George was born in a dismal terrace house in Chorlton-upon-Medlock, Manchester, on 17 January 1863. His father, William George, was a dreamy, unsuccessful schoolmaster, who shortly afterwards resigned his post and returned to his native Pembrokeshire to rent a smallholding, but when Dafydd was only 18 months old caught pneumonia and died, aged 44. As well as Dafydd, he left a daughter, Mary Ellen, who was not yet three, while his widow, Elizabeth Lloyd, was expecting a second son, William, who was born seven months after his father's death.

Left penniless, and with no one else to depend on, Elizabeth sought help from her brother Richard, a village cobbler and unpaid Baptist pastor, who was living in Llanystumdwy, near Criccieth in North Wales. Without a moment's hesitation, Richard took his sister and her children into his household and devoted himself to their upbringing. All three children were bright and intelligent, but it was soon evident that he was absolutely enchanted by Dafydd, whose charm, amiability, vitality and vivid imagination knew no bounds. The others were relatively, if not absolutely, neglected. William, who lived to be 102, and when he was 92 published a memoir entitled *My Brother and I*, recalled somewhat caustically:

> He was the apple of Uncle Lloyd's eye, the king of the castle, and like the other king, could do no wrong ... Whether this unrestrained admiration was wholly good for the lad upon whom it was lavished, and indeed for the

man who evolved out of him, is a matter upon which opinions may differ. (George, 1958, p. 33)

The extraordinary extent to which William was discriminated against was personified by the fact that only Dafydd was permitted by his uncle to add 'Lloyd' to his name. When the two brothers qualified as solicitors and set up their own firm it was known as Lloyd George & George. It was William who devoted himself to the running of the firm, working long hours while Dafydd was freed to pursue his political career, which was heavily subsidised by his brother's toil.

That – coming from a modest but not impoverished background – they were able to become lawyers at all was due to the determination of Uncle Lloyd, as he became known. A self-educated Welsh moralist, he taught Dafydd everything he knew and made sure that he made the most out of the best education then available in rural Wales. When Dafydd left school at 13, he was articled to a local firm of solicitors in Portmadoc. William, who largely made his own way in Dafydd's slipstream, actually proved the more apt pupil, gaining First Class Honours in his law examination, while his brother only achieved Third Class.

The North Wales in which Lloyd George grew up had a distinctive political culture. An overwhelmingly agricultural society, it was deeply polarised. The upper and middle classes were dominated by English landowners, the Anglican Church and the Tory Party. Ranged against them were the rural poor, farm workers and small tenant farmers, predominantly Welsh-speaking, ardent chapel-goers and – at least since the Ballot Act of 1872, which protected them from the prying eyes of their Tory landlords – predisposed to vote Liberal. A further cause of dissension was the high level of drunkenness, which pitched a strong popular temperance movement against Tory publicans and brewers.

The main grievances of the mass of the population concerned the misdeeds of landowners and the privileges of the Church of England and especially its right to levy a tithe on Nonconformists. Lloyd George needed no special prompting from his uncle to determine whose side he was on, and already in his teens was taking an active part in the Portmadoc debating society and in local Liberal politics. Yet it was as a radical lawyer that he first made his name, as 'the People's David', by winning a series of local court cases, where his forensic brilliance won the day against the more pedestrian and often blundering advocates representing the establishment side. The most famous of these was the Llanfrothen burial case in 1885, when Lloyd George, having lost in a lower court, overturned the verdict on appeal and established the right of Nonconformists to be buried in parish churchyards.

Some years before this Lloyd George had already set his sights on a parliamentary career, recording in his diary following his first visit to the House of Commons, aged 17: 'I will not say but that I eyed the assembly in a spirit similar to that in which William the Conqueror eyed England on his visit to Edward the Confessor, as the region of his future domain. Oh, vanity!'

Lloyd George was brought up as a strict Baptist, though he lost his religious faith at the age of 12. Outwardly, however, he conformed to the prevailing Nonconformist culture, and he retained his enthusiasm for hymn-singing and Welsh preachers for the whole of his life. His uncle hoped that he would marry one or other of the girls from the Baptist community, but Lloyd George set his sights on Margaret Owen, the daughter of a prosperous Methodist farmer, who regarded the radical young lawyer as a far from appropriate suitor.

It was a long and difficult courtship, which was hardly helped by the brutal frankness with which he made it clear that their relationship would have to take second place to his political ambitions. 'I am prepared to thrust even love itself under the wheels of my Juggernaut', he wrote to her, adding: 'I must not forget that I have a purpose in life. And however painful the sacrifice I may have to make to attain this ambition I must not flinch.'

Yet whatever her misgivings, which were certainly augmented by early indications that he would not be the most faithful of husbands, Maggie Owen – like nearly every one else – succumbed to his charm and they were duly married in January 1888, when he was 25 and she 21. By the end of the same year, Lloyd George was selected as prospective Liberal candidate for the local constituency of Caernarvon Boroughs, which had been a Tory gain in 1886. Two months later he became an alderman on the Caernarvonshire County Council.

He did not have to wait long before getting into Parliament. In March 1890 the Conservative MP died, and in April, in a desperately close contest, he defeated the local squire, Ellis Nanney, by a mere 18 votes. He was 27, but had come within a hair's breadth of disaster a few weeks earlier when some leading Liberal supporters discovered that he had fathered a child on a widow in Caernarvon. Given the moral climate of the time – just before the Parnell divorce case – this could well have aborted his parliamentary career once and for all. Wealthy backers, however, succeeded in hushing up the affair, by settling an annuity on the widow on condition that not a word was to be revealed. So successful was the cover-up that nothing was ever known about it until many years later when Lloyd George's elder son Richard, already middle-aged, stumbled upon the truth through a chance meeting with a Caernarvon resident in South America (Lloyd George, 1960, pp. 41–4).

This was the first of a long series of extramarital scrapes in which Lloyd George, described by his son as 'probably the greatest natural Don Juan in the history of British politics', became involved, yet despite the incredible risks that he ran he never actually came a cropper. Although his predatory attitude to women later became notorious in political circles, where he was known as 'the Goat', the naturally discreet press of the time, coerced by draconian libel laws, seldom permitted itself more than the most oblique reference to his amatory activities. Nor did his 30-year-long relationship with his secretary, Frances Stevenson, which began in 1913 and eventually led to their marriage in 1943, following Margaret's death, ever make the public prints. In 1927, she bore him a daughter, Jennifer, who was successfully passed off as her adopted child.

L.G.'s waywardness as a husband was not entirely due to his uncontrolled libido. At least some of the blame should be attributed to his wife who, despite repeating urging, refused to come with their children to live with him in London, but chose to remain in Criccieth running the family home. The effect that this had on him can be inferred from a poignant letter which he wrote to her in August 1897:

> I have scores of times come home in the dead of night to a cold, dark and comfortless flat without a soul to greet me, when you were surrounded by your pets [that is, children] ... You have been a good mother. You have not – and I say this now not in anger – not always been a good wife. (Grigg, 1973, pp. 241–3)

Lloyd George's election for Caernarvon Boroughs began an unbroken term of nearly 54 years in the House of Commons. Re-elected in both the 1892 and 1895 elections, his parliamentary activities prior to 1899 were almost exclusively confined to Welsh issues. These included, notably, the campaign for disestablishment of the Church in Wales, demands for land reform, temperance legislation and opposition to subsidies for Church schools. These were subsumed in a general aspiration for Welsh Home Rule.

In pursuing these issues, Lloyd George showed scant respect for Liberal Party discipline, at one time putting the precarious Rosebery government at risk by threatening to withdraw support if priority was not given to a Disestablishment Bill. Lloyd George's aim was to achieve an autonomous existence for Welsh Liberal MPs comparable to that enjoyed by the Irish Party, an ambition which was largely frustrated by the divergent interests of North and South Wales. After ten years in the House, while he had undoubtedly established himself as the best known of the Welsh MPs, he was by no means universally accepted as their leader.

It was the Boer War, starting in 1899, which turned Lloyd George from a purely Welsh politician into a national figure. Without hesitation, he condemned it from the outset as an unjust war against a poor, brave, rural and God-fearing community, with which, as a Welshman, he instinctively empathised. Moreover, he did not flinch from accusing Joseph Chamberlain, the Colonial Secretary and chief architect of the war, of making personal profits through War Office contracts with a firm with which he had family connections He was the most prominent and most daring of the small group of Liberal MPs who took a 'pro-Boer' stance, and was the object of vitriolic attacks by the jingoistic press. He was physically assaulted on more than one occasion and barely escaped with his life when a mob broke up a meeting that he was addressing in Birmingham Town Hall. His popularity in Wales and even in his own constituency slumped, as did his standing in the Liberal Party, where the Liberal Imperialists, led by Rosebery, Asquith and Haldane, enthusiastically backed the Salisbury government, while the party leader, Campbell-Bannerman, struggled with great difficulty to maintain a middle position.

It was only after the war was over, and tempers had cooled, that Lloyd George was accorded respect for the courage he had shown and came increasingly to be recognised as the effective leader of the radical wing of the party. His attitude to the war, however, was widely misunderstood. It was not based on pacifism, nor on opposition to the maintenance, or even the expansion, of the British Empire. His essential objection was to the bullying of small nations by larger ones, and his attitude to the German invasion of Belgium in 1914 could therefore be seen as consistent with his position in 1899 rather than in conflict with it, as it has appeared to many.

In the years following the war, Lloyd George's parliamentary reputation grew steadily. He proved a resourceful opponent of Balfour's 1902 Education Act and – together with Asquith – led the Liberal attack against Chamberlain's tariff reform proposals which were the prime cause of the disintegration of the Balfour government. It was therefore no surprise that Campbell Bannerman chose him as a member of his Cabinet when a Liberal government was formed in December 1905. Most of the senior posts went to Liberal Imperialists, and C.B. sought to balance this by appointing Lloyd George, then aged 43, as President of the Board of Trade.

L.G. took to ministerial life like a duck to water. Within his department he proved a firm and decisive administrator, he carried a shoal of bills through Parliament at a time when other ministers had precious little to show for their labours, and he revealed remarkable powers as a conciliator in a series of industrial disputes, notably succeeding in averting a national rail strike in October 1907. He was clearly one of the success stories in C.B.'s government, and when Asquith succeeded to the premiership in April 1908 it was inevitable that he should follow him at the Treasury.

With this appointment, L.G. came to occupy the second place in the government. The partnership between him and Asquith – two fundamentally different but complementary talents – was to dominate British politics for most of the next decade. Given their subsequent hostility, it is remarkable how harmonious their relationship remained, and the depth of loyalty they showed to each other. Only the strains of war were to set them as under.

The first big challenge facing L.G. as Chancellor was to prepare the 1909 Budget. He was confronted with the prospect of the – for the time – enormous deficit of £16 million. This was caused by the necessity to finance a large naval rearmament programme (which L.G. had opposed in Cabinet) and the first old age pensions, of 5s. a week, which had been promised by the previous Budget, introduced by Asquith. Lloyd George was determined to show that he could close the gap without resorting to the tariff reform measures advocated by the Opposition and that the main burden would fall on the shoulders of the Tory landowners, who were using their domination of the House of Lords to frustrate the government's legislative programme.

Lloyd George was the outstanding parliamentary orator of his time – perhaps of all time – but by common consent his delivery of the speech presenting his 'People's Budget' on 29 April 1909 was the worst of his long career. Yet the impact of this speech surpassed all others. It provoked Balfour – the Leader of the Opposition – into denouncing it as 'vindictive, inequitable, based on no principles and injurious to the productive capacity of the country', and led to the most serious constitutional crisis in modern British history.

The actual Budget proposals must appear surprisingly mild to the modern reader. They involved increases in death duties (rising to 25 per cent for fortunes of over £1 million) and of income tax (6 per cent on unearned incomes) and the introduction of surtax, at 2.5 per cent, on incomes over £5000. What really stuck in the craw of the Tories, however, were three new land taxes, of which the most prominent was a 20 per cent levy on the 'unearned increment' on development land. (By a strange irony, these taxes raised very little by way of revenue, and two of them were actually repealed, on these grounds, when L.G. was Prime Minister in 1921.)

Opinions differ as to whether L.G. had deliberately set out to ensure that the House of Lords – which had not challenged a financial measure since 1678 – would fall into the trap of voting down his budget, but, if so, his plans could not have worked out better. The Lords rose to the bait with extraordinary insouciance, thus ensuring that the main political battleline over the next few years would be 'Peers versus People'. In this atmosphere nobody revelled more than Lloyd George who, in a series of ferocious speeches, notably at Limehouse and Newcastle, tore into the dukes 'who cost as much to keep up as two Dreadnoughts – and they are just as great a terror', and damningly characterised the House of Lords as 'five hundred men, ordinary men chosen accidentally from among the unemployed'.

These attacks horrified Edward VII, who vainly attempted to persuade Asquith to rein in his over-bellicose Chancellor, but they made Lloyd George a popular hero and the darling of the Liberal rank and file. They also made it impossible for the Liberal leadership to settle for any compromise which did not ensure the predominance of the Commons over the unelected upper chamber.

Strangely enough, however, it was Lloyd George who, when in June 1910 the new King, George V, proposed an inter-party conference to try to settle the dispute over the Lords, was prepared to go further than any other politician in seeking all-party agreement. The formal conference, consisting of four Liberals led by Asquith and Lloyd George and four Conservatives by Balfour and Lord Lansdowne got nowhere despite meeting over a dozen times. Lloyd George then composed a remarkable memorandum proposing the formation of a coalition government which would seek national consensus and, where it could not agree, would submit issues such as free trade, Irish Home Rule, Lords reform and Welsh disestablishment to non-partisan commissions. L.G. first showed the memorandum to his closest ministerial colleague and political friend, Winston Churchill, who responded enthusiastically and then approached opposition figures including F.E. Smith (later Lord Birkenhead) and Tory leader Balfour, both of whom expressed initial interest before subsequently backing off. Asquith was amused by the proposal which he did not think would get any Liberal backing, and was then disconcerted when both Foreign Secretary Edward Gray and Lord Crewe, the Lord Privy Seal, were favourably impressed. Writing in his *Memoirs*, 20 years later, L.G. claimed that several senior Tories, including Lansdowne, Curzon, Walter Long and Austen Chamberlain were also in favour. That nothing came of the proposal, which was not public knowledge at the time, was largely due to the fact that neither Asquith nor Balfour – no doubt with their own personal interests firmly in view – were prepared to take it any further. Its basic interest lies in showing that, not for the first time, L.G. attached relatively little weight to party political considerations.

So the Lords dispute followed its course, culminating in the passage of the Parliament Act in 1911, after two general elections and the reluctant agreement of George V to create sufficient new Liberal peers to carry the bill through the Lords if this proved necessary – as recounted in the previous chapter on Asquith. (The full story is most entertainingly told in Roy Jenkins, *Mr Balfour's Poodle*, first published in 1954.)

Despite its momentous aftermath, the 'People's Budget' was not central to Lloyd George's role as a social reformer. This owed much more to the National Insurance Act of 1911. It was the eventual fruit of the early discussions he had had with Churchill, shortly after the formation of the Asquith government, when they jointly agreed that, within the government, they should spearhead a great crusade against poverty and deprivation. In the summer of 1908 L.G. went on a visit to Germany where he was immensely impressed by the social security schemes and labour exchanges introduced by Bismarck two decades earlier. He resolved to introduce contributory insurance schemes against both sickness and unemployment as soon as the parliamentary timetable allowed.

In framing his legislation, Lloyd George had to overcome determined resistance from vested interests – the big insurance companies, the medical profession, and – in the first stages at least – the friendly societies and trade unions. Using the same mixture of coercion and charm which his fellow Welshman, Aneurin Bevan, was to employ 40 years later in introducing the National Health Service, L.G. managed to carry the day, though not without compromising on some of his original objectives. The most eye-catching feature of his bill was that lower-paid workers should pay 4d. a week for sickness benefit, which would be augmented by further payments of 3d. by the employer and 2d. by the state. This was successfully presented to the public with the slogan 'Ninepence for fourpence', and popular support was so strong that the Bill passed through all its parliamentary stages with virtually no opposition. The structures which it produced provided a firm basis for the much more comprehensive 'welfare state' provisions of the Attlee government of 1945–51. The passage of the bill, which came fully into effect in January 1913, marked the high-water mark of Lloyd George's pre-war reputation.

This suffered a heavy setback with the Marconi scandal of 1912–13 which, if it had not been for the firm support of Asquith, could well have ended his political career. In April 1912, at the suggestion of his friend and colleague, Sir Rufus Isaacs, the Attorney-General, who had himself made a larger investment, he bought shares on very favourable conditions in the American Marconi Company, in the hope of making a quick profit. This was at a time when the English Marconi Company was negotiating a profitable contract with the Postmaster-General Sir Herbert Samuel. Suggestions in the press, by, among others the xenophobic *Daily Mail*, which described them as 'the Welsh solicitor and the Jew barrister', that they had used private knowledge of the impending deal to enrich themselves was met by a disingenuous denial by Rufus, who said that neither he nor Lloyd George had any prior knowledge of the English Marconi Company deal, and that neither of them had had 'one single transaction in the shares of the company', making no mention at all of their investment in the associated American company.

After threats of libel action, the affair was referred to a select committee of the House of Commons, which revealed the whole story and from whose inquiries neither Isaacs nor Lloyd George emerged with much credit. The committee, however, split along party lines in drawing up its report, and the majority finding, supported only by the Liberal members of the committee, whitewashed the two ministers. Lloyd George felt constrained to offer his resignation to Asquith, who refused to accept it, and the majority report was adopted by the House of Commons in June 1913 after a tense two-day debate. Lloyd George's career was saved, but the distinct impression remained that, while he had not broken the law, he had been none too scrupulous in his business affairs. For those associated with him in his earlier unsuccessful and little publicised attempts to 'get rich quick', notably a gold-mining venture in Patagonia in the 1890s, this could hardly have come as a surprise

When war loomed in July–August 1914, L.G. probably believed until late in the day that Britain would, and should, keep out of the struggle. Yet he made no attempt to line up with the anti-war faction in the Cabinet, although he was assumed to be sympathetic to them, given his consistent opposition to naval rearmament and the construction of more and more Dreadnoughts, over which he had threatened to resign as recently as 1913. If L.G. had chosen to lead the 'peace party' – and *only* if he had done so – they might well have succeeded in keeping Britain neutral. Yet, given the rising jingoistic mood in the country, and to a lesser extent in Parliament, their stand could instead have led to the fall of the government, and its replacement by a Conservative-dominated coalition bent on war.

This was not something that L.G. was prepared to risk, nor it seems did he relish the prospect of resuming his lonely Boer War role as an anti-war militant. In fact, he was desperately anxious to avoid resignation and, in the words of one biographer, 'throwing away, in twenty-five seconds, a position which it had taken him twenty-five years to reach – perhaps surrendering it to Churchill' (Rowland, 1976, p. 282). Frances Stevenson, who some 18 months earlier had become both his secretary and mistress, gave the game away when she wrote in her memoirs 40 years later: 'the invasion of Belgium was, to be cynical, a heaven-sent excuse for supporting a declaration of war' (Lloyd George, 1967, pp. 73–4).

This was seized on by Lloyd George, and indeed by the majority of Asquith's Cabinet, as reason enough to stay on board, and the number of anti-war resignations was kept down to two – John Burns and John Morley. Lloyd George was nevertheless seen as a reluctant convert to British participation, and few could have foreseen the enthusiasm with which he would embrace the struggle.

His initial contribution was to take firm steps to steady the money markets and prevent the onset of a short-term financial crisis. His actions met general approbation, not least in the City of London which had previously entertained distinctly mixed feelings about the radical Chancellor. Yet nothing prepared them, or either Lloyd George's previous admirers or his critics, for the tremendous impact of the first major speech which he made after the outbreak of the war.

This was at a recruiting meeting at Queen's Hall, in London, on 19 September 1914, when L.G. pulled out all the stops in an emotional appeal to British youth to give their all in defence of national honour, freedom and the defence of small nations. The speech, of which 2.5 mil-lion copies were subsequently printed and distributed at government expense, was a mixture of deeply moving passages and of others of the sheerest demagogy appealing to the very jingoistic spirit which he had earlier opposed. Its reception changed L.G.'s persona overnight. Previously seen as a highly controversial and partisan figure, he now emerged as the voice of a united national determination to see the war through to its end, whatever the cost. Recruitment soared, and Lloyd George received an avalanche of admiring letters, many from previous Conservative opponents.

John Grigg neatly summed up the transformation in Lloyd George's standing: 'After the Queen's Hall meeting ... Lloyd George was Britain's war premier in waiting ... Unfortunately for the country, he had more than two years to wait' (Grigg, 1985, p. 174). During this time L.G. combined two roles: he was one of the government's leading actors, and its principal critic.

One persistent theme of L.G.'s criticism – expressed through a constant stream of memoranda addressed to his ministerial colleagues – was what he regarded as the over-concentration by the allies on the Western Front, in France and Flanders, where they were bogged down in a seemingly endless but bloody stalemate. He was repeatedly urging action on what most of his colleagues regarded as 'side-shows' against Germany's allies, Austria-Hungary and Turkey. He enthusiastically supported the ill-fated Dardanelles (Gallipoli) campaign launched in February 1915, though it was Churchill, as First Lord of the Admiralty, who initiated the venture and who took the blame for its failure. Lloyd George was also a vocal critic of the failure to mobilise the production and procurement of war material, which led to an allegedly serious shortage of shells for the British Expeditionary Force.

It was this, no doubt, that prompted Asquith to offer Lloyd George the post of Minister of Munitions, when the disappointing conduct of the war led to the formation of the first coalition government, in May 1915. He was reluctant to give up the Chancellorship, which went, not to one of the new Tory ministers, but to Reginald McKenna, his most bitter rival in the Liberal ranks. He was, however, promised sweeping powers, retained the use of 11 Downing Street, and relished the opportunity to make a direct contribution to the war effort.

It was his dynamic conduct of his new ministry, combined with the growing dissatisfaction at Asquith's apparent lethargy and ineffectiveness as a war leader, which paved the way for his assumption of the premiership 18 months later. The extent of his achievement is summed up in two sentences in Rowland's biography:

> The monthly output of shells ... increased from 70,000 in May to 120,000 in September and 238,000 in January 1916. By July 1916, when the time came for Lloyd George to leave the Ministry it had reached 1,125,660. (Rowland, 1976, p. 320)

Lloyd George left the Ministry of Munitions to become Secretary of State for War, when the impressive-looking but disastrously ineffective Lord Kitchener drowned when the ship on which he was sailing to Russia hit a mine off the Orkneys. His five months at the War Office were too brief for him to have a noticeable effect on the conduct of British military operations. Yet all the time his impatience was growing at the impasse which had been reached, as was his conviction that he alone had the vision and demoniac energy to carry the war through to a victorious conclusion. Despite this conviction, however, he did not at this time aspire to replace Asquith as Prime Minister. His objective was to replace the unwieldy War Council – made up of a large, fluctuating and quarrelsome group of ministers and officials which, under the meandering chairmanship of Asquith, had become a byword for indecision, with a small executive group of top ministers, shorn of departmental responsibilities, who would direct the war on a day-to-day basis, subject only to the right of the Prime Minister, at his own discretion, to refer particular decisions to the Cabinet as a whole. In L.G.'s view, he himself should be the chairman and chief executive of this committee.

L.G.'s dissatisfaction was shared by Bonar Law and by other leading Tories, notably Sir Edward Carson, who had become the leader of the Tory backbenchers. Together with Max Aitken (later Lord Beaverbrook), the Canadian newspaper owner and Tory MP for Ashton-under-Lyne, they joined with him in drafting a memorandum, which was sent to Asquith on 1 December 1916, proposing a reorganisation along the lines desired by Lloyd George. Asquith was not averse to the proposed arrangement, but insisted that he should have not just the right to attend the committee, but should preside over it, sensing that otherwise he would be reduced to a mere figurehead. Within two days, however, under strong pressure from Bonar Law, he climbed down and accepted a revised proposal of a supreme War Committee of three men, but then again changed his mind when press leaks convinced him – wrongly it appears – that the whole scheme resulted from a plot between Lloyd George and the newspaper proprietor Lord Northcliffe, owner of *The Times* and the *Daily Mail*.

Lloyd George then threw down a direct challenge by resigning and Bonar Law followed suit. Asquith, finding himself abandoned also by the other Conservative ministers, submitted the resignation of the whole government on 5 December, perhaps still hoping that his refusal to serve under a successor would prevent an alternative government from being formed.

In fact, the Conservative leaders, notably lacking in self-confidence, were far from eager to seize the reins of office for themselves, and neither Bonar Law nor Balfour – a possible compromise choice – was prepared to govern without Asquith's support. George V, having first approached Bonar Law, then invited Lloyd George, on 7 December, to form a government, which he succeeded in doing within 48 hours, despite the refusal of all of Asquith's Liberal ministers to serve under him. In practice, the coalition government which he formed consisted of the leading figures in the Conservative Party (with the exception of Lord Lansdowne), two Labour Party ministers and a 'second eleven' of Liberals, who commanded the support of fewer than half of their fellow Liberal MPs.

Asquith remained leader of the party. In the event, his downfall had been due, not to intrigues by Lloyd George, as his supporters and family continued to claim for many years, but to his own indecision and miscalculation. His greatest mistake had been to lose the confidence of Bonar Law, who played the decisive role in making L.G. Prime Minister, just as he was to be the key figure in his downfall six years later. Already, in February 1916, he had written a warning letter to Asquith, saying: 'In war it is necessary not only to be active, but to seem active' (Packer, 1998, p. 48). For L.G., his personal regard had had to struggle against the deepest suspicions of his motivations. He had told the newspaper proprietor, Sir George (later Lord) Riddell, in 1911: 'I like Lloyd George. He is a nice man, but the most dangerous little man that ever lived' (Rowland, 1976, p. 249).

What tipped the balance decisively for him was that he had become convinced that only L.G. could win the war, a conviction which was shared by Balfour, previously a friend and admirer of Asquith, who regarded it as an act of personal betrayal when he accepted the Foreign Office from Lloyd George. His niece reported him as saying:

> As you can imagine, I have no prejudice in favour of Lloyd George. I have opposed every political principle he holds – but I think he is the only one who can at the moment break down that wall of military red tape and see that the brains of the country are made use of. (Dugdale, 1936, p. 128)

L.G.'s accession to the premiership, at the age of 54, ensured his objective of creating a small executive body, with himself at the head, to prosecute the war effort. A War Cabinet of five, which met daily, was established, consisting of himself, Bonar Law – who became Chancellor of the Exchequer and effectively Deputy Premier – and three Ministers without Portfolio, Lords Curzon and Milner and Arthur Henderson, the leader of the Labour Party. A Cabinet Secretariat, headed by Lord Hankey, was set up, which for the first time ensured that minutes were kept and a note made of whose responsibility it was to carry out particular decisions.

The new arrangements certainly created the impression of a much more focused and effective concentration on the task in hand and Lloyd George himself continued to impress by his energy and passionate commitment, but one expert at least (George Cassar, author of *Asquith as War Leader* (1994)), doubts whether the change of leader made much difference to the actual conduct of operations. These remained largely in the hands of the generals – Sir Douglas Haig, the Commander-in-Chief in France, and Sir William Robertson, the Chief of the Imperial General Staff. L.G.'s wartime premiership was dominated by an increasingly bitter and frustrating struggle between the Prime Minister and the two leading commanders. He was unable to replace them because of the support they received from the King and from the Tory leaders, while they successfully blocked his efforts to divert men and resources from France to other theatres of operations – variously in Serbia, Greece, Italy, Romania, Russia and the Near East – where he was continually seeking, in vain, the 'knockout blow' which he believed would bring Germany and its allies to their knees.

Lloyd George had been determined to avoid a repeat of the appalling blood-letting of the 1916 Somme offensive, but, with deep reluctance, agreed to Haig's confident proposal for a heavy offensive in July 1917 whose purpose was to overrun the German U-boat bases on the Channel coast. This attack, which developed into the third battle of Ypres, ended at Paaschendaele in November 1917. In the words of his private secretary, Thomas Jones, it 'entailed terrible casualties, having gained no strategic advantage' (Jones, 1959, p. 521).

The Western Front then degenerated into a war of attrition with no likelihood of any resolution until the slow build-up of American forces (which followed the US entry into the war in April 1917) gave the allies a decisive numerical advantage. Before this could happen, however, the collapse of Russia and the acceptance of humiliating peace terms by the Bolshevik government gave the Germans the opportunity – which they took to only a limited extent – of a massive reinforcement of their own forces. The result was Ludendorff's last-fling offensive of March 1918, which only narrowly failed to achieve a decisive breakthrough. He could not capture Paris, but he almost brought down Lloyd George.

By April 1918, L.G. had at last succeeded in curbing the authority of Robertson and Haig. The former had been outmanoeuvred into resigning as Chief of the Imperial General Staff, and was replaced by the more amenable Sir Henry Wilson, while the latter was subordinated to the French Marshal Ferdinand Foch, who became Commander-in-Chief of all the allied forces in France.

Yet L.G. now faced charges that he had deliberately starved Haig of reinforce-ments after Paaschendaele, and that this had increased the danger from Ludendorff's attack, leading to heavy British casualties. A parliamentary challenge – led by Asquith – was mounted on the basis of accusations made in the press by General Sir Frederick Maurice, former head of Military Intelligence. Lloyd George dominated the debate with a rumbustious speech in which, with the add of a barrage of statistics (which were later shown to be dubious, though it is uncertain whether L.G. was aware of this), he comprehensively refuted Maurice's accusations and swept the floor with the Opposition. Asquith, however, unwisely maintained his demand for a select committee and divided the House. In the division, which the government won by 293 votes to 106, 98 Liberals voted against the government, while only 71 supported Lloyd George. This was to have dire consequences for the future of the Liberal Party.

The war ended six months later, and L.G. came to be known, with no show of reluctance on his part, as 'The Man Who Won the War'. It would, perhaps, be more accurate to describe him as the man who ensured that there would be no negotiated peace – either before or after America's entry into the war. It was his determination to go on to the bitter end – whatever the cost – that carried the greater part of the nation with him. As we have seen, he was unable to have much direct influence on the conduct of military operations. His main contribution was in mobilising the economy to meet the demands of total war, and it is certainly arguable that he had, in fact, already achieved this during his period as Minister for Munitions, and that this feat actually exceeded anything he did as Prime Minister.

During the last summer of the war, L.G. was much exercised about how he could continue his premiership into peacetime, and ensure victory at the general election which could not be long delayed. One possibility was to reunite the Liberal Party and resume his partnership with Asquith, though with himself in the senior position. This plan was stymied by Asquith's firm refusal to go to the upper house as Lord Chancellor. After toying with the idea, to which he was to return some years later, of creating his own 'centre party', L.G. concluded that his best bet would be to do a deal with Bonar Law under which the Conservatives and his own Liberal coalition supporters would fight the election together. Under an agreement negotiated by his Chief Whip, the Tories agreed to give a free run to 150 coalition Liberals, as well as a few Labour dissidents, in exchange for an endorsement from Lloyd George for their candidates in the remaining seats. The problem for L.G. was how to select the 150 individuals to whom the coalition 'coupon' would be sent, and he resolved this by denying the coupon to all the Liberals, including Asquith, who had voted against the government in the Maurice debate.

The plan worked out well – much too well for L.G.'s long-term interest. In the December 1918 election the government won 478 seats out of an effective House of 634 (73 Sinn Fein MPs declining to take their seats). Yet of the 478, only 133 were Liberals, and 10 coalition Labour. The rest were all Tories, who by themselves commanded an absolute majority in the Commons and to whom Lloyd George was now effectively a prisoner. It was, in reality, only a matter of time for the Tories to gain the self-confidence to ditch him and seize undiluted power for themselves.

Privately, L.G. realised that he had overdone it, and was distressed when the results showed that the independent Liberals were decimated, holding on to a mere 28 seats, with Asquith himself among the list of prominent losers. The Labour Party, with 63 seats, became the official Opposition for the first time. 'This is not what I intended at all', he said to Frances Stevenson (Lloyd George, 1967). Publicly, however, he gloried in the sweeping electoral victory, and his national prestige was at its apex as he left for the Versailles Peace Conference.

Here he was part of the dominant trio made up of himself, Woodrow Wilson and Georges Clemenceau, and his approach was pitched midway between the high-minded idealism of the former and the chauvinistic vindictiveness of the latter. While determined to secure what he regarded as British interests, such as the acquisition of former German colonies in Africa and mandates for

Palestine and Transjordan, he attempted, with little success, to moderate the harsh conditions imposed on the defeated Germans. He must share the responsibility for the terms finally agreed, including the quite unrealistic demands for punitive reparations which left Germany humiliated and bitterly resentful, undoubtedly playing a part in paving the way for Hitler's rise to power. L.G. himself was uneasily aware of what he had done, and felt chastened by the accusations made by J.M. Keynes, who resigned from the British delegation and subsequently wrote the Cassandra-like tirade, *The Economic Consequences of the Peace*.

If, at Versailles, he too often allowed his good intentions to be overridden by Clemenceau, a similar pattern soon appeared in domestic affairs, where he had to give more and more ground to the dominant Tory element in his coalition. This was seen most evidently in industrial policy, where his formerly good relations with the trade union movement were subjected to constant erosion, as the government consistently sided with the employers in a rash of disputes, while unemployment steadily mounted. Nor did the government live up to the high hopes raised by Lloyd George's election speech at Wolverhampton in November 1918 when he promised 'to make Britain a fit country for heroes to live in'. Its legislative programme did contain a number of important social measures, notably Christopher Addison's Housing Act of 1919. This enabled local councils to build good quality housing at low, controlled rents, the government making up the shortfall with subsidies. In the long term, this was a highly beneficial measure, leading to a substantial improvement, on a very large scale, of working-class housing standards, but Lloyd George took fright when the cost of the measure looked like getting out of hand, and – in the face of insistent Tory demands – forced Addison's resignation. Like many other left-wing Liberals at the time, the latter soon found a new home in the Labour Party. The housing programme, as well as other social reform measures, including notably the projected raising of the school-leaving age, was a casualty of the swingeing cuts in public expenditure, known as 'the Geddes axe', which were implemented in 1922. Perhaps not entirely fairly, L.G.'s peacetime government has been widely judged as among the most reactionary of the twentieth century. What was undeniable was that the Prime Minister, who pre-war had been the great hope of the left, was now regarded as being on the right.

The one big achievement of Lloyd George as a peacetime Prime Minister was the (partial and temporary) solution of the Irish problem, resulting in partition and the creation of the Irish Free State. This was the outcome of a masterly negotiation which L.G. concluded with the Sinn Fein leaders, Michael Collins and Arthur Griffiths when, against all expectation, he cajoled them into accepting self rule for only a part of their country. It was a bold move, but it brought little credit to Lloyd George. Most of his Tory ministers, and even more of their MPs, were highly reluctant to see independence ceded to southern Ireland, while he had already disgusted most Labour and Liberal opinion by his earlier repressive policies in Ireland and his tolerance of 'Black and Tan' atrocities.

In late 1919, L.G. returned to his earlier project of creating a new 'centre party' which he hoped would embrace all but the extreme left and the reactionary right. He found few serious takers, and instead proposed a fusion between the two coalition partners. With great reluctance, Bonar Law and his colleagues agreed to a merger with the coalition Liberals, who then – with a rare show of independence and to L.G.'s surprise and chagrin – turned the proposal down in March 1920. They were unwilling to surrender their principles on free trade and wanted to leave the door open for an eventual reunion with the Asquithians. Only Churchill, who was in any event to defect to the Tories within a couple of years, showed any enthusiasm for the proposed merger.

Lloyd George's position was now more vulnerable than ever, and it was further undermined, in March 1921, when Bonar Law resigned through ill health. His successor as Tory leader, Austen Chamberlain, was at least equally in awe of Lloyd George and loyal to him, but he had a far weaker control over his own party, which was becoming increasingly restless. L.G., however, comforted himself with the thought that he still held one trump card. This was the Lloyd George Fund, a treasure chest of perhaps as much as £3 million, built up through the sale of honours. Such methods had been used by both Tory and Liberal governments in the past to augment their party funds, and they continued subsequently at least until the Thatcher–Major era. Where Lloyd George differed was in the scale of the operation and the brazen way in which it was conducted, and because the money did not go directly to a political party but to a private fund entirely controlled by himself.

In the end the fund did him no good. It was the source of constant innuendo, and when – after 1923 – the Liberal reunion did in fact take place it was a major source of dissension. L.G. refused to transfer the fund to the Liberal Party, only doling out occasional contributions for projects which he personally approved and refusing to release a substantial amount for the 1924 election campaign, which would have enabled the Liberals to put up many more candidates. At the same time, the party was inhibited from making strenuous fundraising efforts on its own account by the widespread knowledge that its most famous figure was sitting on so large a nest egg.

Despite his growing isolation, Lloyd George made little effort to ingratiate himself with his Cabinet colleagues. He became more and more dictatorial, seldom consulting the full Cabinet about important decisions and being gratuitously rude to such senior figures as Churchill, Curzon and Milner. The extraordinary charm, which had become a byword, was now in distinctly short supply. Below Cabinet level, his credit with the Tories was now dangerously low, and it only required a *casus belli* and an alternative leader to trigger a revolt.

This eventually came, not over a domestic issue, but foreign affairs, which had remained L.G.'s main preoccupation long after the Versailles Treaty had been concluded. Both of his fellow triumvirs – Wilson and Clemenceau – had fallen from power, and Lloyd George was able to monopolise the international limelight. He was feted wherever he went – perhaps blinding him to his loss of popularity in his own country. Much of his time was spent preparing and participating in a series of international gatherings, some of which were intended – though with little success – to undo the worst consequences of Versailles.

L.G. was especially interested in the welfare of Greece, another small nation which attracted his instinctive sympathy. He unwisely skewed British foreign policy in favour of the Greeks in their post-war dispute with Turkey, encouraging their army to invade the Turkish mainland in the hope of seizing as much territory as possible in the wake of the disintegration of the Ottoman Empire. All went well for them initially, but in August 1922 Mustafa Kemal (later known as Atatürk) rallied the Turkish troops, who broke through the Greek lines, captured and sacked Smyrna and drove the Greek remnant into the sea. There was now nothing to stop the Turks from advancing on Constantinople, apart from a tiny British garrison guarding the Dardanelles, at Chanak. Lloyd George – backed by an ever-belligerent Churchill – telegraphed the British commander, General Harington, to deliver an ultimatum to the Turks to withdraw their forces or his own troops would attack. At the same time he appealed to France and Italy, and the British dominions, for military support, an appeal which met with no response.

A military disaster was averted by Harington, who ignored L.G.'s telegram and quietly negotiated a ceasefire with the Turks. Lloyd George's rash action was unanimously condemned by the press, and ominously for him, *The Times* published a letter from Bonar Law, now apparently restored to full health, adding his own weighty criticism. This was widely interpreted as a signal that he was ready and willing to take over the premiership if the opportunity arose.

He did not have to wait long. On 17 September, at a meeting in Chequers, the leading members of the government had agreed that a general election should be held, which the coalition parties would fight in tandem. There were immediate ructions within the Conservative Party, led by the party chairman, Sir George Younger, who wanted the Tories to conduct their own campaign. In an attempt to squash this challenge to his own authority, the Tory leader, Austen Chamberlain, summoned a meeting of all Tory MPs at the Carlton Club on 19 October.

At this meeting, despite the fact that most of the leading Conservative ministers – apart from Curzon, whose patience in the face of L.G.'s repeated snubs had finally cracked – wanted the coalition to continue, it was decided by 187 votes to 87 that the Conservative Party should fight the election with its own leaders and its own programme. In the debate, the most dramatic intervention had come from the previously little known Stanley Baldwin, who had recently been promoted to President of the Board of Trade. 'He is a dynamic force', he said of L.G.,

> and it is from this very fact that our troubles, in our opinion, arose ... It is owing to that dynamic force and that remarkable personality, that the Liberal Party, to which he formerly belonged, has been smashed to pieces; and it is my firm conviction that, in time, the same thing will happen to our own party. (Middlemas and Barnes, 1969, p. 123)

Yet it was Bonar Law's speech, hesitant and fumbling as it was, which swayed the greater number of votes, as he eventually made it clear that he believed that the coalition should come to an end.

Within hours the Conservative ministers had resigned, and at five o'clock L.G. drove to Buckingham Palace to tender his own resignation to George V, who immediately summoned Bonar Law to take his place. L.G. and his Liberal and Conservative supporters were not unduly downcast, being confident that Bonar Law would be unable to win an independent Conservative majority at the general election and that they themselves would soon be back in office – an outcome which Bonar Law himself half anticipated. In the event, it was not to be – the general election on 15 November 1922 produced a Tory majority of 75. Lloyd George's supporters, known as National Liberals, were reduced to 62 seats; the Asquithians won 54, while the Labour Party shot up to 142 and was now clearly the second party in the land.

At the age of 59 – still at the height of his powers – L.G.'s political career was effectively over, though a sad coda was to continue for another two decades, during which he repeatedly attempted, with much ingenuity but little consistency, to lever himself back into power. That he failed was mainly due to his lack of a firm party base, for which he himself was primarily responsible, but also because he had lost that essential basis of trust upon which all successful politicians must depend.

Lloyd George was probably the most gifted of all the Prime Ministers of the twentieth century, and he perhaps had a greater influence on people's lives than any other politician. His introduction of old age pensions and of National Insurance paved the way for the more comprehensive welfare state measures of the Attlee government, his 'People's Budget' led to the curbing of the powers of the House of Lords, while his institution of a Cabinet Secretariat brought order to government decision-making. His determination in the First World War to seek victory at whatever cost had incalculable consequences not only for his own country but for the whole world. With the benefit of hindsight, one may assert with confidence that it would have been far better if he had applied his energy and ingenuity to seeking a negotiated peace, as was urged by President

Wilson and by Lord Lansdowne in the stalemate which had been reached in 1916–17, instead of pursuing the struggle to the bitter end. Had he done so he would have been more worthy of the gratitude of succeeding generations, though he would not have achieved the enormous – if short-lived – popularity that he enjoyed as 'The Man Who Won the War'.

Great as were L.G.'s achievements, the abiding impression which one gains from a study of his life is the potential which remained unfulfilled. For he was brought down – or perhaps self-destroyed – at the height of his powers. This could be attributed to his crass underestimate of the importance of retaining a sound base of party support, but over and above this was the accumulated effect which his opportunism, demagogy, duplicity and cutting of corners – his failure to follow the rules – had on colleagues whose support he needed. In the end – as his brother William hinted – the inflated self-confidence which he imbibed from 'Uncle Lloyd' proved to be the source of his own destruction.

Works consulted

Cassar, G.H., *Asquith as War Leader*, London, Hambledon Press, 1994.

Dugdale, Blanche, *Arthur James Balfour, First Earl of Balfour*, 2 vols, London, Hutchinson, 1936.

George, William, *My Brother and I*, London, Eyre & Spottiswoode, 1958.

Grigg, John, *The Young Lloyd George*, London, Methuen, 1973.

Grigg, John, Lloyd George: *The People's Champion*, 1902–1911, London, Methuen, 1978.

Grigg, John, Lloyd George: *From Peace to War*, 1912–1916, London, Methuen, 1985.

Hattersley, Roy, *David Lloyd George: The Great Outsider*, London, Little Brown, 2010.

Hazelhurst, Cameron, *Politicians at War, July 1914 to May 1915*, London, Jonathan Cape, 1971.

Jones, Thomas, article in *Dictionary of National Biography 1941–1950, Supplement, London, Oxford University Press*, 1959.

Lloyd George, Frances, *The Years that are Past*, London, Hutchinson, 1967.

Lloyd George, *Richard, Lloyd George*, London, Muller, 1960.

Middlemas, Keith, and John Barnes, *Baldwin: A Biography*, London, Weidenfeld & Nicolson, 1969.

Packer, Ian, *Lloyd George*, London, Palgrave Macmillan, 1998.

Rowland, Peter, *Lloyd George*, London, Barrie & Jenkins, 1976.

Wrigley, Chris, *Lloyd George*, Oxford, Blackwell, 1992.

37
Andrew Bonar Law – Tory Puritan

Andrew Bonar Law has had the misfortune to be remembered – if at all – as 'the Unknown Prime Minister'. This was partly due to the brevity of his premiership – a mere 209 days – the shortest in modern times, but rather more to a bon mot attributed to Asquith, who attended his funeral in Westminster Abbey. The former Liberal Prime Minister, who had treated Law with disdain throughout his lifetime, was heard to remark how fitting it was 'that we should have buried the Unknown Prime Minister by the side of the Unknown Soldier'. This misfortune was compounded by Lord Blake, who chose it as the title of his highly praised biography (Robert Blake, *The Unknown Prime Minister*, 1955).

Law was a much more considerable figure than this epithet would suggest, leading the Conservative Party for ten years, playing a major role in the First World War and being responsible, as we saw in the previous chapter, for both the rise and fall of Lloyd George's premiership. He might, just as appropriately, be recalled as the only Prime Minister to have been born abroad, as the first Presbyterian to hold the office, the first businessman, or even, as Roy Jenkins has suggested, the first 'ordinary man'.

Bonar Law was born on 16 September 1858 in Kingston, New Brunswick, a small town later renamed Rexton. His father, the Rev. James Law, was a Northern Irish Presbyterian Minister, who spent 32 years ministering to his small, mainly Scottish immigrant, flock in what his son seems to have regarded in retrospect as a benighted Canadian backwater, before retiring to spend his last five years back in his native Ulster. The Rev. Law was a loving father, but was a manic depressive given to long periods of gloomy introspection punctuated by bursts of religious mania, and his household could hardly have been more austere. This was compounded by the death, at the age of 36, of his wife Elizabeth Kidston, leaving five small children, of whom the youngest, Andrew, was only two. It was she who had chosen Bonar as his second name, it having been the surname of another Presbyterian minister who had written a book about an eminent divine whom she much admired.

Throughout his life he was known as Bonar Law, and his family and few intimates addressed him as Bonar, but unlike Lloyd George he made no attempt to turn this into a hybrid surname for his family, and all his children were called plain Law. On the death of his mother, her spinster sister, Janet Kidston, came out to Canada from Glasgow to keep house for her brother-in-law and help bring up the children, four boys and a girl. This arrangement lasted for nine years, but – following the remarriage of the Rev. Law and his starting a new family – Janet returned to Scotland, taking the now 12-year-old with her to live near her wealthy cousins in Helensburgh, a prosperous town on the Clyde, 20 miles from Glasgow. James Law appears to have concluded that his youngest son would have better prospects in life in Scotland, and agreed to let him go.

The milieu that Bonar entered in Helensburgh resembled his father's in several respects, notably strict Presbyterian beliefs and austere personal habits and tastes. Yet it differed in one important detail, that it was under-pinned by very substantial wealth, which must have been an eye-opener to a penurious pastor's son. Bonar lived in his Aunt Janet's house, but nearby were two much grander mansions where four of his cousins – all well into middle age – lived. There were three brothers – Charles, Richard and William Kidston – who were partners in a firm of merchant bankers, and their sister Catherine. Only Charles was married, and he had no children, and it was not long before Bonar came to be seen as the heir that none of them had been able, or had bothered, to produce. Apart from material prosperity, Bonar owed another legacy to his cousins. Unlike the majority of the Scottish upper middle class at that time, they were staunch supporters of the Conservative and Unionist cause.

The Kidstons were kind to Bonar, but this was an inadequate substitute for the loving relationship with parents and siblings which he had been denied. He early learnt to be self-sufficient, and somewhat introverted, and appeared to have inherited a certain melancholy streak from his father. He got very little joy out of the normal pleasures of life, either then or later. A lifetime teetotaller, he had no interest in food, no appreciation of landscape or physical beauty, nor in music or the theatre, and a horror of social entertaining. He became, however, a voracious smoker, especially of cigars, a life-destroying habit which almost certainly contributed to his death from cancer at the age of 65. His enjoyment came mainly from indoor games – chess, at which he became a strong amateur player, bridge and billiards, and from tennis and golf which he played throughout his adult life.

He was sent to a boarding school at Hamilton, but at 14 was enrolled at Glasgow High School, where Campbell-Bannerman had been educated a generation earlier. He was a good, but not outstanding pupil, who was chiefly remembered for his extraordinarily good memory. No thought seems to have been given to his receiving a university education, though this could easily have been afforded, and at the age of 16 Bonar left school to join the family firm, travelling every day by commuter train from Helensburgh to Glasgow.

The Kidstons' merchant bank was mainly concerned with providing finance for the iron and steel industry. Joining the firm as a clerk, Law's work did little to expand his intellectual horizons, but he applied himself with assiduity, working long hours and quickly mastering all the details of his trade. After a few years, however, the work became less demanding, leaving him more leisure time in which to develop his own interests. He attended extramural lectures at Glasgow University, but most significantly became an extremely active member of the Glasgow Parliamentary Association, which ran a 'mock parliament' on a very elaborate scale. The experience, which continued for several years, was invaluable to Law in teaching him the elements of public speaking as well as the essentials of parliamentary procedure. Law was far from being an eloquent speaker, either then or later, but he impressed by his mastery of detail, and by the fact that his prodigious memory and careful preparation allowed him to speak without notes. This gave an enormous boost to his self-confidence, and implanted in him an ambition which was nevertheless to lie dormant for a great number of years.

This was because Law, extremely cautious by nature, was determined not to embark upon a political career until such time that he had established a firm, and independent, financial base. He continued to work for the Kidstons for 11 years, to their complete satisfaction, and in the normal course of events could have looked forward to eventually succeeding them in the direction of the bank. By 1885, however, their energies were waning fast, and they responded favourably to an approach from the much larger Clydeside Bank, proposing a merger. This might well have blocked Law's progress in the firm, but a lucky chance gave him an autonomous opportunity to advance in the business world.

In the 50-minute train journeys between Helensburgh and Glasgow, Law almost invariably passed the time by playing chess with fellow passengers, one of whom was a Helensburgh neighbour, William Jacks, a Glasgow iron trader who was anxious to cut down his business commitments upon his election as Liberal MP for Leith. He offered Law a junior partnership in his firm, for which he would have to contribute a capital sum of £7500, perhaps equivalent to £400,000 today. Very tentatively, he approached his cousins to enquire whether they would be willing to advance the money, which they were more than happy to do.

Law then effectively took over the management of William Jacks & Co., and became a leading trader on the Glasgow Royal Exchange, participating 'in two hectic daily sessions of two hours each which witnessed the exchange of millions of pounds weekly' (Adams, 1999, p. 13). With his quick reactions, mathematical abilities and cool judgement, Law became one of the most effective operators on the Exchange, while simultaneously acquiring a reputation for straight dealing. The firm's profits, and his own income, soared, and he was offered a clutch of non-executive directorships of other firms, including eventually the Clydeside Bank.

By the age of 30, Law felt able to establish his own bachelor household, inviting his unmarried sister Mary to keep house for him. Three years later, in March 1891, he married Annie Pitcairn Robley, aged 25, the daughter of a prosperous Glasgow merchant. It was undoubtedly a love match, and they went on to have six children over the next 14 years, four sons and two daughters.

Law subsequently received two legacies, worth in total £60,000 (over £3 million in current values) from the Kidston family, but it was not until he was 42 that he finally embarked on his political career. He was elected as Conservative MP for Glasgow, Blackfriars and Hutchesontown in the 1900 general election. It had been a Liberal seat, and when he was adopted as the prospective candidate two years earlier it had not seemed a likely prospect, but a split in the Liberal vote, following the sitting Member's rejection of Home Rule, together with the jingoistic sentiments unleashed by the Boer War, combined to give the seat to Bonar Law.

Law's first appearance in Parliament failed to cause a great stir. His maiden speech was totally overshadowed by that of Winston Churchill, made on the same day. Yet before very long he had secured a niche for himself as one of the very few Tory MPs with a practical knowledge of business and economics, at a time when the great majority of his colleagues were country squires or professional men. He was regarded as a pedestrian but knowledgeable speaker, who was able to discuss business affairs in a common-sense fashion, backed up with a wealth of detail. He did not have to wait long for his first appointment. Eighteen months after his election, in July 1902, Lord Salisbury resigned as Prime Minister to be succeeded by his nephew, Arthur Balfour, who immediately offered Law the post of Parliamentary Secretary to the Board of Trade.

Law proved to be an extremely competent if unflashy junior minister and, in particular, impressed the Colonial Secretary, Joe Chamberlain, who, following him in a debate, described his contribution as 'one of the most admirable speeches, short though it was, to which I have ever listened in the House of Commons'. This must have been especially encouraging to Law, who regarded Chamberlain as his political hero. When Chamberlain launched his campaign for tariff reform a year later, Law was among his most outspoken supporters, though unlike him he remained in the government, as did Chamberlain's own son Austen, with his father's approval.

Law continued as Parliamentary Secretary until the resignation of the Balfour government in November 1905, but both before and after this date became much in demand as a speaker in the country on tariff reform, the advantages of imperial preference and the fallacies of free trade. Indeed, following

Chamberlain's debilitating stroke in July 1906, which terminated his active political career, Law was seen, together with Austen, as the number one advocate of tariff reform.

Before then Law had suffered a setback, through the loss of his seat – together with those of Balfour and 175 other Tory MPs – in the general election of January 1906. He did not, however, have to wait long to get back into the House. A vacancy was created for him at Dulwich, and he was duly returned in a by-election in May 1906.

In May 1909 calamity struck Bonar Law, with the death of his wife, aged 43, following a gall bladder operation. Law was devastated, and a large part of the little joy that he had allowed to enter into his life was extinguished, never to return. Subsequently, there was no record of Law showing any interest whatever in any other woman, and he certainly never contemplated remarriage. Instead, in an echo of his Aunt Janet taking over his father's household in the aftermath of his mother's early death, his elder sister, Mary, moved in, taking charge of his six children and becoming his own closest confidante and advisor.

The void in his life was partly filled by an extraordinary friendship which he formed with a young Canadian businessman and self-made millionaire, Maxwell Aitken. He had first presented himself to Law, as a fellow migrant from New Brunswick and the son of a Presbyterian minister, with an investment proposition, from which Law was able to profit, but the relationship soon took on a far broader dimension. Twenty years his junior, Aitken (later the press magnate, Lord Beaverbrook) was everything which Bonar Law was not: brash, indiscreet, self-indulgent, mischief-making, witty and full of vitality. In a very short period of time, he became Law's principal counsellor, cheerleader and companion, a development not to the liking of Mary Law, who, confronting her brother, declared: 'I don't like the growing influence of Max Aitken here.' The lonely Bonar Law plaintively replied: 'Do let me like him', which melted her Calvinist heart and stilled for ever the resentment she felt against the threatened intruder (Beaverbrook, 1928, Vol. I, p. 59).

Aitken soon benefited from the relationship, as Bonar Law used his influence to secure him a Tory seat in the December 1910 election, but he more than repaid the debt by the generous and consistent support which he unceasingly gave to Law throughout the rest of his life. The December 1910 election proved to be a hiccup in Bonar Law's own career as, responding to an appeal from tariff reform supporters in Lancashire, he abandoned his Dulwich seat to contest the marginal Liberal constituency of North-West Manchester. He was unsuccessful, but this did him no harm, as he was compensated with the then safe Tory seat of Bootle, for which he was returned in a by-election in March 1911.

Eight months later, Balfour, exhausted by the prolonged struggle over the House of Lords and discouraged by the severe criticism to which he had been subjected by die-hard Tory peers and MPs over his eventual acquiescence in the passage of the Parliament Act, resigned as party leader. The Tories, for the first time ever, were faced with an open contest for the succession, which, moreover, threatened to be a bloody one. The two leading candidates – Austen Chamberlain, a former Chancellor of the Exchequer, and Walter Long, former Irish Secretary, appealed to different sections of the party. Chamberlain, son and heir to the famous Joseph, represented the more urban and liberal elements, was a strong tariff reformer and, perhaps surprisingly, was a die-hard over Lords reform. Long, a country squire *par excellence*, was a more traditional Tory, of limited intelligence but regarded as a great character, was lukewarm on tariff reform and an opponent of the die-hards. The personal relations between the two men were far from good, and those between their supporters positively hostile.

Nevertheless, it was believed that getting on for 90 per cent of Tory MPs were committed to one or other of them, and the prospects for a third candidate appeared bleak. This did not deter Aitken, who vigorously began canvassing on behalf of Law, who only finally decided to stand five days before the expected ballot. He had no great expectation of success, and his motivation appeared to be to put a marker down for the future.

He reckoned without the characters of Chamberlain and Long, neither of whom possessed the single-minded ambition which is often necessary to get to the top of what Disraeli described as 'the greasy pole'. In reality, each was more determined to deprive his rival of the crown rather than to claim it for himself, and when Chamberlain, fearing defeat, offered to withdraw in favour of Law if his opponent would do the same, Long, who harboured personal doubts as to his fitness for the leadership, readily agreed. So it was that when the scheduled meeting took place at the Carlton Club on 13 November 1911, Walter Long duly proposed Bonar Law's candidature, which was seconded by Austen Chamberlain. He was unanimously elected, and was astonished at the warmth and extent of the applause, so relieved were the mass of Tory MPs to have avoided a divisive contest.

Law had no illusions, however, that – with his relative lack of seniority and experience – he would not face severe difficulties in leading his party, and he felt genuine diffidence about the challenge which lay ahead. When Aitken sought to boost him by saying: 'You are a great man now. You must talk like a great man, behave like a great man', his response was: 'If I am a great man, then a good many great men must have been frauds.' He resolved to consolidate his leadership by giving his parliamentary supporters what they most wanted: bitter and unrelenting opposition to the Asquith government and all its works. He was as good as his word, and by most standards the Opposition which he led over the next three years was as partisan and uncompromising as at any period in British parliamentary history.

Law gave due notice to Asquith of what to expect. Walking back with him to the Commons after listening to the King's Speech in the Lords, opening the

1911–12 session, he said: 'I'm afraid I shall have to show myself very vicious this session, Mr Asquith, I hope you will understand.' To a large extent, Bonar Law's excessive partisanship was out of character. A man of little imagination, his approach to most issues was careful, calculating and commonsensical and he seldom allowed himself to get hot under the collar. Much later he told Austen Chamberlain that the only issues he cared intensely about were 'Tariff reform and Ulster; all the rest was only part of the game' (Blake, 1955, p. 96).

Unfortunately, it was Ulster which became the most hotly contested political issue in the three years leading up to the outbreak of war. The Asquith government, at the behest of its Irish nationalist allies to whom it now owed its parliamentary majority, introduced the third Home Rule Bill, and determined to force it through under the Parliament Act over the opposition of Tory peers. Bonar Law was less hostile in principle to Home Rule than many other Tories, notably Lord Lansdowne, the Tory leader in the Lords, who owned extensive estates in southern Ireland. On Ulster, however, he was adamant: it must be excluded from 'the imposition of a tyranny', that is, rule by a Dublin Parliament.

His feeling towards the Protestants of Northern Ireland can only be described as 'tribal'. He had never lived there, but knew the province well, as he had travelled there from Scotland almost every weekend for the last five years of his father's life, to visit him in his retirement. He identified completely with the Ulster cause, and went well beyond the constitutional duty of a Leader of the Opposition in encouraging armed resistance by the Ulster Volunteer Force organised by Sir Edward Carson. In July 1913, he sent a message to an Orange demonstration saying: 'Whatever steps they might feel compelled to take, whether they were constitutional, or whether in the long run they were unconstitutional, they had the whole of the Unionist Party under his leadership behind them.' He seriously contemplated using the Tory majority in the Lords to reject the annual Army Act and thus, in Roy Jenkins's words, 'deprive the government (and the state) for two years of the use of any military power' (Jenkins, 1998, p. 218). Dining with George V at Buckingham Palace, he tried to persuade the King to refuse the royal assent to the Home Rule Bill if it was passed under the Parliament Act, and thus attempt to apply a royal veto for the first time in 200 years. 'I think I have given the King the worst five minutes that he has had for a long time', he told Austen Chamberlain afterwards.

As the crisis deepened, Bonar Law somewhat reluctantly met with Asquith to seek a compromise solution, but he refused to contemplate the only formula which had a real prospect of being accepted by the Liberals, and more crucially, the Irish National Party. This was the so-called 'Home Rule within Home Rule' scenario, under which Ulster would have its own Parliament, which would, however, be subordinate to that in Dublin. Law was adamant that the total exclusion of Ulster – or at least the predominantly Protestant counties – was the only outcome that he would accept. By July 1914 total deadlock was reached, with the imminent threat of civil war. Both Asquith and Bonar Law were saved from the immediate consequences of their intransigence by the onset of a much wider war following the assassination in Sarajevo.

The outbreak of the war transformed Law from being a narrowly partisan leader to a statesman who put what he perceived to be the national interest before anything else. In a trice, his Ulster particularism was transmuted into a larger patriotism embracing the whole country and indeed the entire British Empire. Convinced that Britain should intervene on the French side, even before the German invasion of Belgium, he at once offered unconditional support to the Asquith government, and over the next nine months soft-pedalled any parliamentary opposition, despite growing Conservative concern at the conduct of the war effort. When the first wartime coalition government was formed in May 1915, he meekly acquiesced in his appointment as Colonial Secretary, even though he could and should have demanded a more major post, such as Chancellor of the Exchequer.

It is possible that his modesty on this occasion was affected by his acute embarrassment at the projected prosecution of his old firm, William Jacks & Co., for trading with the enemy. He had severed any executive connection with the firm when he was first elected to the House of Commons, but his brother John was still a partner, and Bonar Law resolved to withdraw altogether from public life if his brother was convicted. In the event, John Law was not implicated in the case – which was concerned with the failure of the firm to take sufficiently energetic steps to prevent a shipment of iron ore, already in transit from Canada to Amsterdam in early August 1914, from reaching its final destination in Germany. Two of the other partners in the firm were charged for what was, in reality, only a technical offence, and received short terms of imprisonment.

Although largely marginalised as Colonial Secretary, Law gradually emerged as one of the most influential members of the Cabinet. He was slow to make up his mind, and – initially at least – diffident in expressing his opinions, but once he had convinced himself about a particular issue was able to argue his case forcefully and consistently. This was most clearly seen over the endless discussions on whether, and when, to bring the costly and abortive Dardanelles expedition to an end. Law eventually forced the issue by threatening to resign if the troops were not withdrawn – an operation which was then carried out without a hitch and with hardly any casualties, despite the harrowing predictions of his senior Tory colleague, Lord Curzon. A comment made at the time by a Liberal minister helps to explain the respect in which he was held by his cabinet colleagues: 'Lloyd George is always threatening to resign and we don't believe him. Bonar Law said he would resign and we knew he would' (Beaverbrook, 1928, Vol. I, p. 171).

One colleague who did not share this respect was Asquith, whose Balliol-bred snobbery prevented him from assessing this relatively poorly educated Glasgow iron trader at his true worth He repeatedly snubbed him, and once complained to Lloyd George: 'He has not the brains of a Glasgow baillie.' By contrast, Law had perhaps exaggerated respect for Asquith, whom he regarded with awe. He had no greater desire than to serve him loyally, and his eventual disillusionment came only slowly and reluctantly. One turning point came in June 1916, when Law needed to see Asquith to discuss a matter of the highest urgency, and learning that he intended to extend his customary weekend in the country into Monday or beyond, motored down the 50 miles from London to Berkshire early on the Monday morning. He was shocked to find the Prime Minister playing a game of bridge with three ladies, and in no hurry to break off to discuss matters of state. (The veracity of this story, which appeared in Blake's biography in 1955, was challenged by Asquith's loyal daughter, Lady Violet Bonham Carter, in an angry letter to *The Times*. Blake's source, however, was Lord Beaverbrook, who said to his secretary: 'You can tell Blake that Bonar Law told me, and he always told the truth' (Adams, 1999, p. 214)).

Despite such episodes, it was no part of Bonar Law's plan to dislodge Asquith from the premiership during the government crisis of December 1916, described in the preceding chapter. Indeed, he regarded Asquith's continuation as essential, and he only submitted his resignation when Asquith had gone back on his earlier agreement to appoint a small war committee under Lloyd George's chairmanship. Law certainly erred by failing to hand over to Asquith a document which made clear that the other Conservative Cabinet ministers were also intending to resign unless Asquith yielded. It is possible that had he done so, Asquith would have again reconsidered his position, but Bonar Law, who was invariably straightforward in his dealings, can be acquitted of any Machiavellian intent. It was sheer inadvertence that during an unpleasant and tense interview, he forgot to produce the document from his suit pocket.

Bonar Law was invited by the King to form a new government, but he declined to do so unless Asquith was prepared to serve under him, which the Liberal leader refused to do. Lloyd George then took over the relay, and it was clear from the outset that he regarded Law as the key member of his new team. Law became Chancellor of the Exchequer, Leader of the House of Commons (the first time ever that this post had been held by anybody but the Prime Minister, except when the Premier was in the Lords), and the only departmental minister included in the small War Cabinet. As Conservative leader, he was consulted on all appointments, and effectively acted as party manager on behalf of the government. Nor was Lloyd George's deference to him purely on account of his party position. He evidently valued his counsel on a personal basis, and virtually every day the Prime Minister started his working day by going through the interconnecting door into 11 Downing Street and embarking on a wide-ranging discussion with his deputy on virtually every issue on the pending agenda (a practice he continued during his peacetime coalition after 1918).

This strange partnership between two very dissimilar personalities was the bedrock on which the Lloyd George premiership rested. Bonar Law was the workhorse of the government, devoting himself without stint to his manifold tasks, a devotion which even increased following the death in action of his two eldest sons in April and September 1917. As with the loss of his wife, eight years earlier, Bonar Law was inconsolable, and his only recourse was to bury himself deeper and deeper in his work. Religion was no help to him; indeed, he seems to have got the worst possible bargain from his Presbyterian upbringing. It had deprived him of most normal sources of enjoyment, but failed to bring him any consolation. Law did not believe in the after-life, and after the death of the sons, succumbed to a bleak pessimism which almost totally extinguished the flame of his once burning ambition.

Bonar Law readily agreed with Lloyd George that the wartime coalition should be continued after the Armistice, and the 'coupon' election of December 1918 delivered an overwhelming majority, of which the Conservatives formed by far the larger part. Bonar Law relinquished the Chancellorship, but retained the leadership of the House, and was effectively Deputy Prime Minister, substituting for much of the time for Lloyd George, who was abroad for long periods, both during the Versailles negotiations and afterwards. He continued to be a bulwark of strength for Lloyd George until March 1921, when his health collapsed under the strain, and he resigned from office, seeking rest in the south of France.

In retrospect, this can be seen as the beginning of the end for Lloyd George, as Law's successor, Austen Chamberlain, though equally loyal to the Prime Minister, had far less control over Conservative MPs, whose frustration was reaching a dangerous level. Law's health improved and he returned from France in the autumn in time to give his backing to the Irish treaty negotiated by Lloyd George.

It looked as though Law's career was over, but in October 1922 when Tory MPs rebelled against their leadership's decision to fight another general election under Lloyd George's leadership, they looked to Bonar Law as an alternative party leader. He reluctantly made himself available, having convinced himself that the Tories would be fatally split if they continued their alliance with the Lloyd George Liberals. This event was described in the previous chapter, and the sequel does not require lengthy retelling.

The government which Law formed on 23 October 1922 was singularly devoid of talent. Apart from Curzon and Baldwin, hardly any of the former Cabinet was willing to serve, and he had to make do with an evident second eleven, including an abnormally high number of peers. Nevertheless, on a programme of 'tranquillity and stability', he succeeded in obtaining a very comfortable majority of 75 in the election of November 1922. Subsequently, it was distinguished by only one event, and that was a stinging humiliation for the Prime Minister. Baldwin, who became Chancellor of the Exchequer, was sent to Washington to negotiate on British war debts, and finding a much more hostile reception than he had anticipated, came back with far less generous terms than Britain had been seeking, but nevertheless recommending acceptance on the grounds that this was the best settlement obtainable. When the Cabinet met, Bonar Law made it clear that he would resign if the terms were accepted, but only one of his colleagues supported his view. The meeting was hastily adjourned overnight, and on the following morning a letter, over the pseudonym 'Colonial', appeared in *The Times*, setting out the same arguments that Law had used in the Cabinet meeting – it subsequently emerged that Law himself had written the letter. Later in the day, in the face of entreaties from all his closest associates, Law climbed down, and at a five-minute meeting of the Cabinet withdrew both his opposition and his resignation threat.

It was, however, virtually the end of his brief premiership. Feeling utterly weary, and suffering from recurrent throat pains, he left on 1 May for a cruise to the Mediterranean and 'a complete rest'. The cruise did not last long: he left the ship at Genoa, and – joined by Beaverbrook – proceeded to Paris, where he was examined by an eminent doctor, Sir Thomas Horder. Diagnosing cancer of the throat, without actually telling the Prime Minister, Horder advised immediate resignation. Beaverbrook concurred, and later recalled that Law 'was almost light-hearted in his relief at the idea of laying down a burden which had been crushing his failing vitality'. Bonar Law resigned on 20 May, dying five months later on 30 October 1923. He declined to advise the King on who should be his successor, believing that it would be Lord Curzon, though he probably had a slight preference for Stanley Baldwin (see pp. 613–14).

Bonar Law was a man of considerable, if narrow abilities. At the end of his rather sad life, he could certainly claim, with Othello, to 'have done the state some service', though rather more to the Conservative Party, whose fortunes he did much to restore.

Works consulted

Adams, R.J.Q., *Bonar Law*, London, John Murray, 1999.
Beaverbrook, Lord, *Politicians and the War*, 2 vols, London, Hutchinson, 1928, 1932.
Blake, Robert, *The Unknown Prime Minister*, London, Eyre & Spottiswoode, 1955.
Iremonger, Lucille, *The Fiery Chariot*, London, Secker & Warburg, 1970.
Jenkins, Roy, *The Chancellors*, London, Macmillan, 1998.
Jones, Thomas, article in *Dictionary of National Biography* 1922–1930, London, Oxford University Press, 1937.

38
Stanley Baldwin – 'A Man of the Most Utter Insignificance'?

In June 1883 a Harrow schoolboy was flogged by his headmaster, and his adored father was summoned to the school to be warned of his son's moral wickedness. His offence? He had composed a piece of juvenile pornography and, apparently far worse, had injured the school's reputation by posting a copy to his cousin at Eton.

Fortunately, Stanley Baldwin's father, Alfred, took an indulgent view of his son's peccadillo, despite his own fervent High Church views. The effect on Stanley, however, was unfortunate. Previously, he had stood out as one of the school's brightest pupils, winning a string of prizes, but from that moment on he became demotivated, ceased to strive for academic excellence, and cruised through the remainder of his school career – and much of his subsequent three years at Cambridge – without bothering to exert himself unduly.

He emerged with a Third Class degree, occasioning the uncharacteristically sharp remark from Alfred: 'I hope you won't get a third in life.' In fact, the young Stanley's failure to live up to his earlier promise had a determining effect on his subsequent career, effectively forcing him to seek to follow in the footsteps of his remarkable father, a businessman and politician, rather than those of his more artistic mother, Louisa, which would have been more in tune with his own inclinations.

Alfred Baldwin came from a long line of Shropshire yeomen who gravitated to the iron trade in the mid-eighteenth century, later setting up a foundry at Stourport-on-Severn. Alfred was the youngest of 12 children of George Baldwin, who died eight months before he was born in 1841. It was George who had raised the family fortunes to a high level of affluence, but this was largely dissipated by Alfred's elder brothers who, by 1864, had brought the firm, then known as E.P. and W. Baldwin, to the brink of bankruptcy. In this year, Alfred asserted himself, took over control of the business and within six years succeeded in paying off all the debts and buying out his brothers' interest.

He moved into the ironmaster's house at Wilden, a mile away from Stourport and next door to the company's forge, and gained a reputation as a model employer who treated his workforce effectively as members of an extended family, Stanley, born on 3 August 1867, being his only child. His interests extended well beyond the family firm, and in 1892 he was elected as Conservative MP for the Worcestershire constituency of Bewdley. He became a highly respected if largely silent backbencher. He also became chairman of the Great Western Railway, one of the four large railway companies before nationalisation.

Alfred Baldwin, high-minded and a largely self-taught scholar as well as practical man of business, was to marry Louisa, one of the five gifted and artistic daughters of a Methodist minister, the Rev. George Browne MacDonald. Three of her sisters were to marry painters – Edward Burne-Jones, Edward Poynter and Lockwood Kipling. The undoubted highlights of Stanley Baldwin's childhood and youth were the times he was able to spend in the company of his lively young cousins on his mother's side, notably the poet, Rudyard Kipling. Louisa herself enjoyed some success as a novelist, ghost story writer and poet, but for 15 years of her life was confined to a couch suffering from a possibly psychosomatic illness which dated from the time of Stanley's birth.

Alfred and Louisa were affectionate parents, but with a busy father and a semi-invalid mother, the young Stanley was often left to his own devices. His was not, however, an unhappy childhood. A bookish boy, he immersed himself in the novels of Scott, in Malory's *Morte d'Arthur* and *The Pilgrim's Progress*, and he early fell in love with the Worcestershire countryside, taking long walks, the memory of which left a warm glow feeding the over-romantic view of England as a pastoral paradise which characterised many of his later speeches and writings.

Stanley's dreamy, artistic leanings might have led him into a very different career from the one he followed. While at Cambridge, he seriously considered going into the Church, and he had visions of becoming a writer and academic. Yet his poor examination results precluded this, leaving him with no practical alternative to following his father in the family business. Already when leaving Harrow, he had told his headmaster: 'I am going first into the family business and then to the House of Commons' (Middlemas and Barnes, 1969, p. 16). And so it was to be – after a long apprenticeship.

An imposing patriarchal figure with a long black beard, Alfred was nevertheless of a highly nervous disposition. A God-fearing man, whose conscience never gave him an easy time, he had a pronounced facial tic. He was worshipped by his son, who remained in awe of him, constantly measuring himself against his father and constantly finding himself wanting.

At the time he left Cambridge, in 1888, his personality remained largely unformed. Outwardly, he appeared relaxed and indolent, universally liked, but not regarded by his fellows as a man of any great consequence. In reality, he was a far more complex and sensitive young man than was apparent on the surface. With no enthusiasm, but with no great show of reluctance, he entered the family business and set himself conscientiously to master the secrets of the trade. Over the course of the next 20 years, he established himself as a thoroughly reliable but far from dynamic number two to his father, who undoubtedly derived great pleasure from their association. Meanwhile the firm steadily expanded, largely through amalgamations with other steel firms, eventually becoming part of the giant enterprise, Richard Thomas & Baldwins.

For the first four years, Baldwin stayed in the family home, but in 1892, on his marriage at the age of 25 to Lucy Ridsdale, he rented a Georgian house two miles away and cycled each day to the forge. Some years later he moved to a much grander house, Astley Hall, near Stourport, where he lived for the rest of his life. Baldwin had met his wife while staying with his Burne-Jones cousins. The daughter of the Deputy Master of the Royal Mint, she was an extrovert girl, fond of playing games; particularly cricket, of which she was notable exponent. She proved a loyal and supportive wife, though sharing none of his aesthetic or intellectual tastes nor his love of country walks. Yet she provided companionship and good advice, and bore him four daughters and two sons, the elder of whom later became a rather eccentric Labour MP.

During the 20 years that he worked alongside his father, Baldwin gradually extended his interests, becoming a Justice of the Peace and securing election successively to the parish, rural district and county councils. He early established the custom of taking long holidays, one month each year on winter sports in Switzerland and at least another month touring the continent in the summer. With his growing family, he appeared a thoroughly contented paterfamilias, taking part in country pursuits and basking in his reputation as a benevolent employer, more approachable because less formidable in appearance than his equally benevolent father.

If Baldwin was ever dissatisfied at having to play second fiddle to Alfred, he never showed it, and their relations remained excellent, though still somewhat hindered by shyness on both sides. When Baldwin contemplated heavy expenditure on Astley Hall, which he could ill afford, Alfred readily agreed to bear the cost, and then promptly forgot about it, and Stanley was too inhibited to remind him of it. In 1904 Alfred was delighted when Stanley became the prospective Conservative candidate for the neighbouring constituency of Kidderminster, regarded as being a totally safe Tory seat. Yet he was not fated to join his father in the Commons. In the 1906 general election, he was swept away by the Liberal landslide, though his father held on at Bewdley.

Baldwin had not much enjoyed the election campaign, but eagerly accepted an approach from Joseph Chamberlain, who was looking for a replacement for the Tory candidate who had been unseated at the City of Worcester because of corrupt practices. He later wrote:

I thought I was certain to be chosen at once, and I went before the selection committee holding my head high. And they chose an Irishman who I then thought, and still think, to be vastly my inferior. So I was turned down in my own county town in favour of a stranger and bang went all my hopes. (Middlemas and Barnes, 1969, p. 40)

It seemed unlikely that Baldwin, after these two rebuffs, would ever stir himself again to seek a candidature, but within two years his father died very suddenly, which proved, in his biographers' words, to be 'the greatest turning point in Baldwin's life' (Middlemas and Barnes, 1969, p. 41). Two days after the funeral, Baldwin was unanimously selected to replace his father and, as the Liberals decided not to contest the by-election, he was returned unopposed as MP for Bewdley on 29 February 1908, only 16 days after Alfred's death.

Baldwin was now 40 and for the next half-dozen years was content to remain an obscure and largely silent backbencher, speaking only five times in his first six years in the House. He was a wealthy man, vice-chairman of Baldwins Ltd and a director, like his father before him, of the Great Western Railway, and seemed entirely to lack political ambition. He was popular with his fellow MPs, was thoroughly 'clubbable' and was regarded as a 'good House of Commons man', content to spend many hours relaxing in the chamber, listening to the speeches of other members.

His attitude changed perceptibly at the beginning of the First World War. Thoroughly patriotic, he was too old to fight, but was acutely conscious that his almost entirely passive parliamentary service was making no contribution whatever to the war effort. He stirred himself to serve on several government committees of inquiry, and joined a ginger group of backbenchers critical of the Asquith government's conduct of the war. Yet by 1916 he was seriously thinking of relinquishing his parliamentary seat and concentrating on his local government responsibilities in Worcestershire. His wife, Lucy, dissuaded him, saying 'give it another two years' (Williams, 1965, p. 5).

It was in December 1916 that the second decisive turning point occurred in Baldwin's political life, when Andrew Bonar Law, newly appointed as Chancellor of the Exchequer in the Lloyd George government, invited him to become his Parliamentary Private Secretary (PPS). Perhaps he ought not to have felt flattered; he had apparently been recommended to Law as somebody who, in the opinion of the Conservative Chief Whip, Lord Edmund Talbot, was 'discreet enough to be safe and stupid enough not to intrigue' (Williams, 1965, p. 13).

Baldwin then had an extraordinary stroke of luck. A PPS is normally a silent, confidential advisor and general bag-carrier to his minister, but in this case it led to Baldwin's almost immediate translation to the front bench. The number two minister at the Treasury, Sir Hardman Lever, was unable initially to secure a parliamentary seat and was absent for long periods in the United States. With nobody else available to speak as his deputy in the Commons, Law asked Baldwin to substitute and for six months from February 1917 he regularly spoke from the front bench, creating a very good impression on MPs by his courtesy and the assiduity with which he replied to their questions. By July his position was regularised and he was appointed a junior minister with the title of Joint Financial Secretary.

In the December 1918 general election, Baldwin was returned unopposed, and was reappointed as Financial Secretary to the Treasury, now under Austen Chamberlain who took over from Bonar Law as Chancellor. Both of them regarded him as an adequate and agreeable colleague, without any great expectation that he would progress any higher in the ministerial hierarchy. He was, in fact, sounded out about becoming Governor-General, first of South Africa and then of Australia – basically consolation prizes for well-regarded politicians not expected to rise to the top – but he declined to be considered, and a suggestion that he might become Speaker of the House of Commons was not followed up.

In June 1919 a remarkable letter appeared in *The Times*, signed 'F.S.T.', though the significance of these initials, which referred obliquely to his ministerial post, was not recognised at the time. The writer appealed to the wealthy classes to tax themselves voluntarily to help reduce the burden of the war debts. 'I have made as accurate an estimate as I am able of the value of my own estate,' he wrote, 'and I have arrived at a total of about £580,000. I have decided to realise 20% of that amount or say £120,000 which will purchase £150,000 of the new War Loan, and present it to the Government for cancellation.'

Baldwin's self-esteem presumably benefited from his generous gesture, but its effect on the public finances was minimal. His hope that it would lead to a mass of similar donations by, amongst others, 'the hard-faced men who looked as though they had done very well out of the war' (his own description of the new Tory MPs elected in 1918), was to be sorely disappointed. Only about £500,000, including his own gift, was received by the Treasury (Jenkins, 1987, pp. 44–5).

In April 1921 Bonar Law resigned from the government due to ill health, and in the consequent reshuffle Baldwin was promoted to the Cabinet, on Law's recommendation, as President of the Board of Trade. He held this post for 19 months during which he continued to prove himself a competent administrator, but took few initiatives and seldom intervened in Cabinet discussions. Yet behind his silence lurked a growing sense of unease concerning Lloyd George's premiership. He viewed 'the Goat', as he habitually referred to him, with increasing distaste, feeling that he was continually undercutting the authority of his fellow ministers, was having a corrupting effect on public life and destroying the morale of Tory MPs, more and more of whom feared the consequences of fighting another general election under his leadership.

In September 1922, as the Chanak crisis (see Chapter 36) was building up, Baldwin and his wife left for their customary long holiday at Aix-les-Bains. It was here, while his wife took the waters, that during the course of several long and solitary hill walks, he came to the conclusion that it was his God-given duty to sacrifice his own political career to end that of the 'Welsh wizard'. He was summoned back by telegram to attend a Cabinet meeting on 1 October, and eight days later Chamberlain convened a meeting of all the Conservative Cabinet ministers to endorse his view that they should fight the forthcoming general election in alliance with the coalition Liberals and under the leadership of Lloyd George. Baldwin alone (though he was later supported by the Agriculture Minister, Sir Arthur Griffith-Boscawen), stood out, saying that he could not and would not fight the election as a coalitionist, would not serve again under Lloyd George and would shortly resign as a minister. When his wife returned from holiday a few days later, he met her at Victoria station and told her, as she reported in a letter to her mother:

> I have done something dreadful without consulting you. I have been fearfully worried, but I felt that it had to come. I am resigning from the Cabinet. I shall never get a job again. I do hope you won't mind fearfully, but I've said I cannot continue to serve under the G ['Goat'] any longer.' (Middlemas and Barnes, 1969, pp. 115–16)

So Baldwin prepared to go into the wilderness, but he was by no means as isolated as he feared. Both the Chairman of the Conservative Party, Sir George Younger, and the Chief Whip, Sir Leslie Wilson, wanted the Tories to fight the election as an independent force, a view that was fast gathering strength among Tory backbenchers and junior ministers, though all the Cabinet ministers except Baldwin and Boscawen continued to back Chamberlain (Lord Curzon was to defect at the last minute). Chamberlain summoned a meeting of all Tory MPs and ministers in the House of Lords at the Carlton Club on 19 October, and was supremely confident that he would crush any opposition.

Baldwin took the view that Chamberlain could only be defeated if an alternative candidate for the party leadership could be found. Ruling himself out as too junior and lacking in authority, he concluded that Bonar Law was the only feasible person to play this role. Together with Lord Beaverbrook (Law's most trusted and closest political friend), he began to apply pressure on the former party leader to attend the Carlton Club meeting and to make himself available. Law, worried about his health and feeling that he owed some loyalty to Chamberlain, was highly reluctant, but eventually persuaded himself (partly at the urging of his sister, Mary) that the future welfare of the Conservative Party depended on its being unhitched from the coalition.

This effectively sealed Chamberlain and Lloyd George's fate. As described in the earlier chapter on Lloyd George, the meeting voted by 187 votes to 87 to fight the election independently of Lloyd George, after a devastating eight-minute speech by Baldwin referring to Lloyd George as 'a dynamic force [which is] a very terrible thing; it may crush you but is not necessarily right' (Middlemas and Barnes, 1969, p. 123), and a more lumbering effort by Law, which nevertheless clinched the argument. Within hours, Chamberlain and the other Tory ministers resigned, followed by Lloyd George, and George V summoned Bonar Law to the Palace.

It was only after he had been formally elected as Tory leader that Law agreed to form a government, and his first act was to offer Baldwin the Chancellorship of the Exchequer. This was the one post which Baldwin coveted – he had been mildly disappointed not to have been appointed 19 months earlier – but now he declined, not wishing to seem to have profited from his part in unhorsing Lloyd George. He proposed instead that Law should appoint Reginald McKenna, who had been Chancellor under Asquith and was now a respected banker. Law duly approached McKenna, who was tempted, but foresaw difficulties as he was not then an MP. After three days mulling it over, he turned down the offer. Law again approached Baldwin who, having satisfied his conscience, gladly accepted and, as recounted by Roy Jenkins, 'went upstairs to his wife and said: "Treat me with respect; I am Chancellor of the Exchequer" ' (Jenkins, 1987, p. 54).

The most notable event in Baldwin's brief chancellorship was his handling of the American debt settlement. The British position, firmly held by Bonar Law and most of his Cabinet, was that all inter-allied debts should be cancelled, but that in any event Britain should not be required to repay its debt to America until comparable arrangements were in place for the repayment of its own loans to its European allies, notably France and Italy, and the achievement of a realistic deal on German reparations. The Republican-dominated US Congress was, however, demanding cash on the nail, and on 27 December 1922 Baldwin left for Washington, accompanied by Montagu Norman, the Governor of the Bank of England, with a firm mandate not to agree a settlement involving payments in excess of £25 million a year.

The best that Baldwin could achieve was a funding agreement providing for annual payments of £34 million for the first ten years, increasing to £40 million for the remaining 52 years of the agreement. This was unanimously rejected by the British Cabinet in his absence, and on 27 January 1923 Baldwin returned, ostensibly to seek a new mandate from his colleagues. On his arrival at Southampton, he gave a series of interviews to American journalists in which he revealed the details of the American offer, made it clear that he thought that they were the best available and should be accepted, and made disparaging remarks about the small-mindedness of the American senators who would have to approve the deal.

Baldwin's remarks were widely considered to be ill-judged and naive, and were attributed to his inexperience. This view was magisterially refuted by Harold Wilson in his book on British Prime Ministers. Wilson argued that Baldwin knew exactly what he was doing, and that his purpose was to cut the ground under Bonar Law's opposition to the projected deal. It was in connection with this episode that Wilson recalled Winston Churchill's judgement in his Memorial Address in 1947, that 'He was the most formidable politician I have ever known in public life' (Wilson, 1977, p. 9).

In any event, as recounted in the preceding chapter, Baldwin succeeded in undermining Law's opposition, and the consequence was not only a weakening of the Prime Minister's authority but an increase in that of his Chancellor, particularly among his Cabinet colleagues. This may have been a factor, though probably not the decisive one, influencing the choice of Baldwin, rather than the Foreign Secretary, Lord Curzon, as Bonar Law's successor four months later, in May 1923.

The general expectation, shared by Law, was that the choice would fall on Curzon. Law stubbornly refused to advise the King, but probably had a marginal preference for Baldwin. This was greatly magnified in a memorandum drawn up by his PPS, John Davidson, which was surreptitiously passed to Lord Stamfordham, the King's private secretary, by Ronald Waterhouse, an official in Law's office, with the evident implication that it faithfully represented the retiring Prime Minister's views. (This extraordinary episode is described in detail in Blake, 1955, pp. 516–27.) In the absence of direct advice from Law, the King chose to consult Balfour, as the only living former Conservative Prime Minister, which was bad luck for Curzon, whom Balfour keenly distrusted.

Balfour came down decisively against Curzon, whom the King had earlier favoured. Of the two contenders, Curzon had by far the longer experience of high office and was regarded as much the more distinguished figure, but suffered, probably decisively, from his membership of the House of Lords and from his reputation for arrogance and being a difficult colleague. It is hard not to believe that Baldwin was chosen less on his own merits than on his rival's defects.

It was a cruel disappointment for Curzon, who had received a telegram summoning him for a meeting with Stamfordham, which he not unreasonably assumed would be the preamble to an audience with the King. In fact, the intention was to break the news gently to him before the King saw Baldwin. Curzon was mortified, describing his successful rival as 'a man of the utmost insignificance'. Nevertheless, to Baldwin's relieved surprise, he swallowed his pride sufficiently to accept his invitation to continue as Foreign Secretary, and even to propose his rival as party leader at a meeting of all Conservative MPs and peers.

Baldwin was to remain leader of the Conservative Party for 14 years, during most of which time he was the dominant figure in British politics, serving three times as Prime Minister for a total length of seven years and 82 days. This was a sufficient length of time for all of Baldwin's qualities as well as his defects to be amply displayed. The first thing that should be said about Baldwin was that he was a thoroughly decent man, probably the nicest – apart from Campbell-Bannerman – of the 20 premiers of the 20th Century. He genuinely wanted to do good, was considerate to his colleagues and modest in his assessment of his own abilities, except that – like Gladstone, otherwise a very different character – he was convinced that he had been chosen by God for a special purpose.

He had a simple Christian faith in God, and after God he believed in England, and the English character and the essential goodness of Englishmen of all classes. After England, he believed in the Conservative Party, which he held to be the repository of national virtue, not the representative of any class interest. A natural conciliator, he hated violence and conflict, and wished for nothing better than that the world, and industrial relations in particular, should be run on the same benevolent lines as in his father's steel firm. Baldwin was often seen as a lazy man, which is not quite true. He had infinite patience, never seemed in a hurry and knew the value of waiting on events. He was capable of decisive action during a crisis, but it took a lot out of him, and he would then lapse into a period of passivity while he recovered his natural equilibrium. He took a close interest in the character and foibles of his colleagues, spending long hours in the Commons conversing with a surprisingly wide range of members, leading Attlee to remark: 'He always seemed more at home with our people, particularly the older trade union people, than his own lot' (Williams, 1965, p. 31).

He was not without guile in his dealings with other politicians, knowing how to exploit their vanity and ambitions in order to win their support. Because of his near universal benevolence, his disinterestedness and his apparent lack of ambition, Baldwin was liked and trusted by nearly everybody he met, and the aura of reassurance he conveyed became a potent electoral asset for the Conservatives.

Yet Baldwin himself was living in a dream world which bore little resemblance to reality, and this bred a dangerous complacency which in the end was to be his undoing and that of many who put their trust in him. The England in which he believed, and evoked so warmly in his speeches and writings, no longer existed, if in fact it ever had. A famous, but not untypical example, was the following:

> The sounds of England, the tinkle of the hammer on the anvil in the country smithy, the corn-crake on a dewy morning, the sound of the scythe against the whetstone, and the sight of a plough team coming over the brow of a hill, the sight that has been seen in England since England was a land and may be seen in England long after the Empire has perished and every works

in England has ceased to function, for centuries the one eternal sight of England. (cited in Williams, 1965, p. 46)

Few of the mine-owners and employers with whom he had to deal during the industrial troubles leading up to the General Strike shared the qualities of Baldwin's much admired father, nor was the Conservative Party quite the body of philanthropists that Baldwin believed it to be. Yet the biggest difference between reality and Baldwin's perception lay in foreign affairs, a field in which he took little interest; never flying in a plane, only once as Prime Minister meeting a foreign leader (French Premier Raymond Poincaré in 1923) and virtually confining his foreign visits to Aix-les-Bains. As late as 1936, when the barbaric nature of the Nazi regime in Germany was already abundantly evident, he was able to say in a speech that he had never come across a really 'malevolent' government – 'most governments seem to me to be not much better or worse than the people they govern'. So long as the dichotomy between Baldwin's beliefs and the real world remained unrevealed, he commanded a remarkable degree of trust and popularity. All this turned to dust at the very end of his career when he became the object of unparalleled loathing and contempt.

All this was far into the future when he became premier for the first time. His first term was extremely brief – a mere eight months – from 22 May 1923 to 22 January 1924. He was entirely responsible for bringing it to an end, in an ill-considered decision to call a premature general election. If the Conservative Party had not still been deeply divided and unable to agree on an alternative leader, this could well have been the end of Baldwin's political career. But luck, and his previously unsuspected survival skills, dictated otherwise.

On becoming Prime Minister, Baldwin became deeply worried by the high level of unemployment, which at 1.5 million amounted to more than 10 per cent of the insured working population. He saw no hope of reducing this figure except by adopting the Chamberlainite policy of tariff protection, which had split the Conservative Party 20 years earlier, but had since almost become party orthodoxy. Unfortunately, he was inhibited by a pledge which Bonar Law had given a year earlier that there would be no major change in fiscal policy in advance of a further general election.

Baldwin felt it would be dishonourable to disregard this pledge, but – as he explained some years later to his private secretary, Thomas Jones – he had an additional reason to act fast. He received reports, probably erroneous, that Lloyd George, currently on a lecture tour in the US, was about to declare for protection, and he feared that if he did so, he would scoop up the Tory coalitionists into a new centre party – and that, said Baldwin, 'would have been an end to the Tory Party as we know it' (Middlemas and Barnes, 1969, p. 212).

In the short run, Baldwin's electoral gamble proved a disaster. He threw away a comfortable Tory majority of 74, and finished up with a deficit of 50. The new House of Commons was split three ways, with the Conservatives on 258 seats, Labour with 191 and the Liberals (newly reunited under Asquith, with Lloyd George as his deputy) with 158. The formation of a minority Labour government, under Ramsay MacDonald, with passive Liberal support (see next chapter) was the optimum outcome for Baldwin of a distinctively messy situation. The alternatives, of a government led by another Tory (Stamfordham suggested Austen Chamberlain) or the inclusion of the Liberals in either a Tory- or Labour-led coalition, would have been far less acceptable to him. A Labour government in office, but not in effective power, would, he believed, help to 'house train' Labour without any risk of extreme Socialist policies being implemented. In the longer term, he much preferred the prospect of Labour being the main rivals of the Tories to any revival of the Liberal Party.

In the remaining nine months of the 1924 Parliament, Baldwin was, in Roy Jenkins's words, 'a gentle opponent to a weak government' (Jenkins, 1987, p. 80). He played little part in its downfall, which was occasioned by the withdrawal of Liberal support in a confidence motion in October 1924 on the Campbell affair (see next chapter). This was a hara-kiri operation by the Liberals, who, in the subsequent general election on 29 October 1924, were virtually destroyed as a major political force. The result was Conservatives 412 seats, Labour 151, Liberals 40, others 12. The total Labour vote actually increased, but the collapse in Liberal support was almost entirely to the Tories' benefit.

Baldwin waged an effective campaign, the highlight of which was that, for the first time, the party leaders were invited to make election broadcasts on the BBC. MacDonald, a powerful platform orator, chose to broadcast live from a mass meeting in Glasgow. The quality of reception was very poor, and he came over as an inconsequential tub-thumper. Baldwin settled himself comfortably into a chair in the BBC Director-General's office, and spoke softly and reassuringly, immediately establishing a rapport with his listeners. It was the beginning of the extraordinary reputation which he acquired as 'Honest Stan', the man who understood and was deeply involved in the concerns of the man in the street. Baldwin was a natural broadcaster, and used the new medium more effectively than any other democratic politician in the 1920s and 1930s, with the probable exception of Franklin Roosevelt.

His striking election victory put Baldwin in an exceptionally strong position. It enabled him to restore unity to the Conservative Party by bringing the main Conservative coalitionists back into the fold. Austen Chamberlain became Foreign Secretary, shattering the expectations of an almost choleric Curzon, who nevertheless agreed to become Lord President of the Council, while Birkenhead (F.E. Smith) went to the India Office. Curzon was to die within a year, and Baldwin then completed the work of reconciliation by bringing

Balfour into the government in his place. A surprise appointment was that of Winston Churchill, who had only just rejoined the Conservative Party 20 years after his defection to the Liberals, as Chancellor of the Exchequer.

Despite his many gifts, Churchill was out of his depth as Chancellor. One of his first decisions was to bring Britain back on to the gold standard, which by greatly strengthening the pound had a disastrous effect on exports, and especially on the already deeply troubled coal industry. This was, in effect, the beginning of the countdown to the General Strike of 1926, the dominating event of Baldwin's second premiership.

He emerged with his reputation greatly enhanced, the general impression being that he had done everything possible to prevent the strike from happening, while taking prudent steps to ensure that if it nevertheless occurred it would be unsuccessful, that he acted firmly during the nine days that it lasted and then exerted himself to ensure that it would not leave a heritage of bitterness and recrimination. The truth was somewhat more complicated and less flattering. During the year before the strike the government had failed to take any decisive initiatives to secure a reorganisation of the notoriously inefficient industry, and while Baldwin had certainly exerted himself to try to secure a compromise acceptable to the TUC in the final days before the strike, and actually negotiated an agreement with them, he failed to carry a majority of the Cabinet with him. The government then seized on the unofficial action of *Daily Mail* printers, who refused to set a provocative article criticising the strikers, as a pretext for going back on the agreement, even though this action was condemned by the TUC and by the printers' own union.

The strike then went ahead, despite the deep reluctance of the TUC leadership. During the strike itself, Baldwin suffering from nervous exhaustion, played little part, and subsequently his genuine attempts at reconciliation were largely frustrated by harder men in his own Cabinet, who forced through the vindictive Trade Disputes Act of 1927, and stood by imperviously while the miners were starved into submission at the end of their own strike which continued for a further seven months.

Baldwin, who campaigned on a platform of 'Safety First', confidently expected to win the 1929 general election, despite the continuing economic difficulties and the high level of unemployment. His government could claim a number of achievements, most of them due to Neville Chamberlain, Austen's younger half-brother, who had surprisingly chosen to be Health Secretary rather than Chancellor of the Exchequer and had proved the major success story of the administration.

Like that of 1923, the election produced an indeterminate result, but this time Labour was the largest party (Labour 287, Conservatives 260, Liberals 59), and there was no serious doubt that MacDonald would again become Prime Minister of a minority government. Baldwin's party took the result very hard, and there was a determined attempt during the following two years to drive him out of the leadership. For many Tories his moderate views on social policy and on India were anathema, as was his kid-glove treatment of the Labour government and his refusal to revive the tariff reform issue after his earlier rebuff by the electors in 1923.

Leading the campaign against Baldwin were the press lords, Rothermere and Beaverbrook, who not only used their newspapers constantly to snipe against him, but put up by-election candidates, under the label 'Empire Free Trade', against the official Tory standard-bearers. They had thought that the meek and mild Baldwin would be easy quarry, but like others before them they underestimated their man. *Cet animal est très méchant; quand on L'attaque, il se défend*, and in March 1931 Baldwin struck back at his persecutors in a memorable phrase, drafted by his cousin, Rudyard Kipling. 'What the proprietorship of these newspapers is aiming at is power, and power without responsibility – the prerogative of the harlot throughout the ages', he said of Rothermere and Beaverbrook, and went on to rub salt into their wounds by comprehensively routing their candidate in a by-election in the ultra-smart Westminster St George's constituency, which they had generally been expected to win. This marked the end of the campaign against Baldwin, and of efforts to replace him by the seemingly more dynamic Neville Chamberlain.

By then the Labour government was in deep trouble, with no idea of how to tackle the steeply rising unemployment, and suffering serious defeats in by-elections. It seemed only a matter of a few months before it would be forced out of office, leading to Baldwin's inevitable appointment as Prime Minister, followed by a general election which would produce a large Conservative majority. That this did not happen, and that he had to wait another four years before regaining Downing Street, was largely Baldwin's own fault.

In July Baldwin was informed of an indirect approach from MacDonald to discuss the formation of a National Government, but turned down the suggestion out of hand. Having destroyed one coalition government under Lloyd George, he had no desire to help in the formation of another one. His colleague, and effective number two, Neville Chamberlain, was, however, clearly attracted by the idea. He then made the decisive mistake of hurrying off to his customary lengthy holiday in Aix-les-Bains, leaving Chamberlain to deputise in his absence.

Though twice summoned back for urgent consultations, Baldwin played little part in the ongoing discussions provoked by the Labour government's inability to agree on the cuts necessary to achieve a loan sufficient to ride out the mounting financial crisis (see next chapter). The idea of a coalition, encouraged by Chamberlain, gained ground, particularly with George V, and when the King saw Baldwin on his second return to London and asked him outright if he would be prepared to serve under MacDonald in a National Government, he had little choice but to agree. The probability must be that, had he not insisted on going to Aix-les-Bains, the idea would have been nipped in the bud.

The National Government was meant to last just a few weeks to see out the crisis, but – after a snap election in November 1931 which saw the Labour Party almost wiped out – it continued under MacDonald's premiership for nearly another four years until June 1935, when Baldwin finally replaced him in 10 Downing Street.

Until then, he held the post of Lord President of the Council, leading the House of Commons. In the eyes of the Labour Party, and of many other observers, MacDonald was a mere puppet and front-man, with Baldwin pulling the strings. Yet it is questionable whether Baldwin was the dominant influence in the government. Neville Chamberlain, who became Chancellor of the Exchequer after the 1931 election, arguably carried greater weight and was perhaps unlucky not to succeed MacDonald as premier. According to Roy Jenkins, he would have been the majority choice of the Cabinet and of Tory MPS, but George V took it upon himself to appoint Baldwin without consulting them.

It might have been better if he had. Baldwin's third and last premiership did little good either to himself or his country. It was dominated by the defence issue, with which Baldwin had already been intimately concerned, as it came within his responsibilities as Lord President of the Council. The most deadly critic of Baldwin's premiership was Winston Churchill, who included the famous entry in the index of his Second World War memoirs: 'BALDWIN, Rt. Hon. Stanley ... confesses putting party before country'. The reference was to Baldwin's conviction that – though he had become convinced by 1934 that a major rearmament programme was necessary to combat the Nazi threat – it would be impolitic to mention this in advance of the 1935 general election, in view of the strong pacifist sentiments which he attributed to a large number of his fellow countrymen. Baldwin later admitted, in what he himself described as 'a speech of appalling frankness':

> Supposing I had gone to the country and said that Germany was rearming and we must rearm, does anybody think that this pacific democracy would have rallied to that cry at that moment? I cannot think of anything that would have made the loss of the election from my point of view more certain. (Hansard, vol. 317, col. 1144, 12 Nov. 1936)

Baldwin has since had his defenders, who argue that he did indeed initiate a rearmament programme, though he hardly pursued it with great energy. The most discreditable episode of Baldwin's last premiership was, without doubt, the Hoare-Laval Pact. It occurred only a month after the 1935 general election, in which he had proclaimed that 'The League of Nations is the keystone of

British foreign policy', and that sanctions would be continued against Italy for her aggression against Abyssinia (Ethiopia). The Foreign Secretary, Sir Samuel Hoare, visited Paris for discussions with Pierre Laval, who was then doubling up as France's Prime and Foreign Minister. Without having any mandate to negotiate, Hoare agreed a plan to partition Abyssinia, permitting Mussolini to annex half the country. Baldwin, who had been quite unaware of Hoare's initiative, strongly defended it in the House of Commons, only to abandon both his minister and the pact within a week, in the face of a storm of public and parliamentary protest. Hoare was forced to resign, and his place was taken by his junior minister, Anthony Eden.

Baldwin's reputation was badly damaged, but both it and his popularity were redeemed by the mixture of decisiveness and discretion with which he handled the Abdication crisis in 1937. He retired shortly afterwards, amid the plaudits of the nation, collecting an earldom and the Garter on the way.

His retirement to Worcestershire was not the happy epilogue to his career that he had imagined. As the clouds darkened, and the early disasters of the war developed, he became the almost universal scapegoat for the country's unpreparedness, receiving masses of hate mail and suffering the indignity of having the beautiful wrought-iron gates of Astley Hall forcibly removed as scrap metal for the war effort.

For a man who had bathed for long years in the warm glow of popular acclaim this was almost too much to bear, and he became more and more of a recluse. He survived the war, and died a largely forgotten man in December 1947. A public appeal to raise a simple roadside memorial to him near his home raised a pathetic amount, and was only saved by a large donation from Churchill. I do not know what epitaph it bears. 'Good intentions are not enough' might be the most appropriate.

Works consulted

Blake, Robert, *The Unknown Prime Minister*, London, Eyre & Spottiswoode, 1955.

Churchill, Winston S., *The Second World War*, Vol. I *The Gathering Storm*, London, Cassell, 1948.

Jenkins, Roy, *Baldwin*, London, Collins, 1987.

Middlemas, Keith, and John Barnes, *Baldwin: A Biography*, London, Weidenfeld & Nicolson, 1969.

Williams, Francis, *A Pattern of Rulers*, London, Longman, 1965.

Wilson, Harold, *A Prime Minister on Prime Ministers*, London, Weidenfeld & Nicolson, 1977.

39

James Ramsay MacDonald – An 'Aristocrat' among Plain Men?

No person ever did more to help build up a new political party than James Ramsay MacDonald. Few subsequently did more to damage their own creation. That was the essential tragedy of his life.

It began in the most obscure and discouraging of circumstances. He was born on 12 October 1866, the illegitimate son of a young servant girl, Annie Ramsay. She had been working on a farm near the fishing village of Lossiemouth on the Moray Firth. His father, John MacDonald, was a ploughman on the farm, who soon afterwards disappeared from the area and from all subsequent trace, though not before he and Annie had together confessed their sin before the local Kirk and been granted absolution. They had been engaged to be married, and it is probable that it was Annie herself who broke off the engagement, though whether this was of her own volition or because her formidable mother, Bella Ramsay, regarded him as an unworthy suitor is far from clear and will presumably never be known.

MacDonald grew up to be an exceptionally handsome and attractive man, which led to a great deal of speculation – particularly among the aristocratic women who took him up after he became Prime Minister – that his 'real' father must have been a Highland laird, or even, it was suggested, the Duke of Argyll. There was never the slightest justification for such a belief.

He was raised in a tiny cottage in Lossiemouth by his mother and grand-mother, both of whom scratched a living as seamstresses. The centre of their lives was young Jamie, who was lavished with care and attention, neither woman doubting for one moment that he was a superior being destined for higher things. Apart from them, the greatest influence on his young life was James MacDonald (no relation), the remarkable teacher, or dominie, of Drainie village school, four miles' walk from his home.

During the ten years that he attended the school, whose 70 pupils shared a single teacher, assisted by a student teacher and a sewing mistress, Jamie acquired a remarkably wide education. He became adept at Latin and Greek, devoured the works of Scott, Carlyle, Ruskin and Hazlitt and acquired a passion for science, which he fostered by reading university textbooks which he picked up at a second-hand bookshop. At 15 he left to work in the fields, but was rescued from manual labour, after a month or two, by the dominie, who eagerly recruited his prize student to replace the pupil teacher who had left for Edinburgh.

He brought to his new duties a lively intelligence, a soaring imagination and a burning ambition to succeed. He had a commanding physical presence and an appealing personality, though this concealed a darker side – he was suspicious, secretive and quick to take offence, a sensitivity perhaps related to his illegitimacy. As a child the only time he had been in any trouble was when he seriously injured a fellow pupil who had referred to him as a 'bastard', and as an adult he took pains to conceal his origins. When during the First World War he was viciously attacked as a 'traitor' and 'coward' by the right-wing jingoist Horatio Bottomley, he appeared unconcerned. Yet when Bottomley followed this up by publishing a facsimile of his birth certificate in the magazine *John Bull*, he was devastated, saying repeatedly: 'Thank God my mother is dead for this would have killed her' (Williams, 1965, p. 62).

MacDonald remained at the school for a further four years, deepening his own education and playing a full part in the social and intellectual life of the local community. Yet the wider world beckoned, and at 18 he began to scour the situations vacant columns of *The Scotsman*, and to apply for posts all over Britain. Eventually, he was successful and left in the summer of 1885 to take up a position in Bristol, assisting a clergyman to set up a Boys' and Young Men's Guild. Within six months he was back in Lossiemouth, though it is unclear whether he had left the job of his own accord or had been found wanting by his employer. While at Bristol, however, he had become a Socialist, joining the Marxist Social Democratic Federation (SDF) and playing a very active part in its local branch.

After a few frustrating months he left Lossiemouth again, this time for good. He headed for London, after hearing from a Bristol friend of a suitable post that might be available. On arrival he found that it had been filled only the day before, and he embarked on a dispiriting and increasingly desperate search for work, living in cheap lodgings in Kentish Town and surviving on a diet of oatmeal and hot water. Eventually he found a temporary job addressing envelopes for the National Cyclists' Union, at 10s. a week, and subsequently a more permanent post in the City as an invoice clerk, starting at 12s. 6d. a week.

His spare time was divided between Socialist activities – he abandoned the SDF in favour of the Socialist Union, a short-lived movement which adopted a much more moderate approach – and serious scientific studies at the Birkbeck Institute. These he hoped would lead to a scholarship at the South Kensington Museum. But his health broke down through over-work, before he was able to take the examination, and he abandoned his hopes of a scientific career. Instead, in 1888, he was fortunate to obtain a post as private secretary to Thomas Lough, a tea merchant and aspiring radical Liberal politician, who was to be elected as MP for West Islington in 1892.

This appointment substantially changed MacDonald's life. His income rose sharply, to £75 a year rising to £100, and the work was much more congenial, bringing him into contact with a wide range of radical Liberal circles, and introducing him into prosperous middle-class society. He joined the Fabian Society, the East London Ethical Society and even the Fellowship of the New Life, a Utopian Socialist group, from which the more down-to-earth Fabians had split off some years before. If the Fabians appealed to his practical sense, the Fellowship gave full rein to the high moral aspirations which were to characterise his speeches and writings throughout most of his political career. He became active in the Fabians, spending some time in 1892 as a paid lecturer touring the provinces on their behalf. By then he had resigned his post with Thomas Lough and was eking out a precarious existence as a freelance journalist.

Through his Liberal contacts, he had come into touch with the Labour Electoral Association, a body devoted to securing the election to Parliament of working men. Its favoured tactic was to obtain their selection by local Liberal associations as Lib-Lab candidates, particularly in two-member constituencies where they could balance the ticket by running in harness with more traditional middle-class candidates. Had the Liberals been more open to such arrangements it is possible that the movement towards founding an independent Labour Party might never have got off the ground. Yet time and time again, aspirant Lib-Lab candidates were turned down, and this was MacDonald's fate in 1894, when he responded to an invitation to offer himself as the second Liberal candidate in Southampton, then represented by one Liberal and one Conservative MP. He was rejected, and this prompted him to join the Independent Labour Party (ILP), which had been founded the previous year by Keir Hardie and others. He fought the 1895 general election in Southampton as an ILP candidate, coming bottom of the poll by a wide margin. His intervention, however, almost certainly led to the defeat of the sitting Liberal MP, the Tories capturing both seats.

His candidature had a momentous consequence for MacDonald. He received a cheque for £1 towards his election fund from an unknown sympathiser, signed 'M.E. Gladstone'. This turned out to be a 25-year-old social worker, Margaret Gladstone, who came from a distinguished and prosperous academic family. She had fallen at least half in love with MacDonald before she had even met him, and their courtship proceeded rapidly. They became engaged on the steps of the British Museum in July 1896, and married the following November.

It was an ideal partnership – Margaret, while sharing his basic values and commitment, was a much more outgoing personality, which did a lot to mitigate the aloofness which tended to surround her brooding Scottish husband. As well as bearing him six children, one of whom died in infancy from diphtheria, she threw herself wholeheartedly into all his activities, and their apartment in Lincoln's Inn, as well as their Buckinghamshire cottage, became an ever-welcoming meeting place for his growing number of political associates.

As well as her personal qualities, Margaret brought, for the first time, financial security to MacDonald. Though not conspicuously wealthy, she had a sufficiently large private income to enable him to devote himself full time to his political work. They were also in a position to undertake a series of lengthy overseas tours – to the United States, Canada, India, Australia and New Zealand, which stimulated MacDonald's interest and left him far better informed on foreign affairs than any of his Labour colleagues. Among European Socialist leaders whom he met and befriended was the notable German 'revisionist' Eduard Bernstein. He had a sure touch for international relations, and it is significant that when – in 1924 – he chose to combine the Foreign Secretaryship with being Prime Minister he was widely adjudged as a notable success in the former post, though hardly in the latter.

More immediately – and crucially for MacDonald's nascent political career – when, in February 1900, the Labour Representation Committee (LRC) (later the Labour Party) was set up by the trade unions, in conjunction with a number of Socialist organisations, principally the ILP and the Fabian Society, it was able to turn to MacDonald as its secretary. Not only was he in a position to accept the post without a salary (at least for the first few years), but until 1904 the offices of the LRC and practically all its meetings were located in the back room of the MacDonalds' flat.

Together with Keir Hardie, MacDonald had been one of the prime movers in creating the LRC. During the later 1890s, he had become increasingly prominent in the ranks of both the ILP and the Fabians. Paradoxically, in the ILP, of which by 1900 he had become one of the four leading figures, he was valued for his Fabian quality of being a first-class committeeman. In the Fabians, by contrast, where he fell foul of the Webbs, he was widely regarded as a woolly idealist, and was one of the minority of members who fiercely opposed the Boer War, which later led him to resign from the Society.

The green light for the creation of the LRC was a resolution from the Railway Servants' Union at the 1899 TUC calling for the convening of a 'conference of all the co-operative, socialistic and other working organisations ... to devise ways and means for securing the return of an increased number of labour members to the next Parliament'. It was only narrowly carried on a card vote, and it is improbable that it would have led to any permanent result had it not been for the skill of Hardie and MacDonald, both of whom were ILP delegates to the conference which took place in London at the Memorial Hall in Farringdon Street in February 1900. It was they who drafted the main resolutions to be put to the conference, which traced a careful middle way between the views of cautious trade unionists, most of whom were not Socialists, and the class-war objectives of the SDF. The outcome of the conference was the creation of a federal style party, which harnessed the weight of numbers and the financial resources of the trade unions (or at least the most advanced of them) to the campaigning vigour and idealism of the ILP and the pragmatic programme-making of the Fabians. The object of the party was defined as the establishment of 'a distinct Labour group in Parliament, who shall have their own Whips and agree upon their own policy'.

The new party put up 15 candidates in the 1900 general election, two of whom were elected – Hardie at Merthyr Tydfil and Richard Bell at Derby. MacDonald stood at Leicester – a two-member seat – where he substantially improved on his 1895 vote at Southampton, but again probably cost the Liberals the second seat, which was narrowly held by the Conservatives.

MacDonald was to continue as Secretary of the LRC, and subsequently of the Labour Party, until 1912, and then served a dozen years as Treasurer until he became Prime Minister for the first time in 1924. Even more than Keir Hardie, he could claim to be the dominant force in the rise of the new party. The first six years were the most crucial. In Marquand's words, 'Between 1900 and 1906 most of MacDonald's energies were absorbed by the wearing, repetitive and time-consuming tasks of party management' (Marquand, 1977). He had to deal with a series of awkward and argumentative colleagues, soothing the inevitable differences between trade unionists and Socialists (particularly the wilder spirits of the ILP) and to keep every one united behind limited but practical objectives without dimming their messianic hopes for the future.

He also had his own private agenda. While he was determined that the Labour Party should remain independent of the Liberals, his own electoral experiences in Southampton and Leicester had convinced him that only through an agreement that would prevent Liberals standing in Labour's most promising constituencies could the infant party hope to gain a significant foothold in the House of Commons. This was the reasoning behind the secret Lib-Lab pact, which he negotiated with Herbert Gladstone, the Liberal Chief Whip, in 1903, behind the backs of the LRC's executive committee, though he took Hardie into his confidence.

The result was that the Liberal Party agreed to give Labour a free run in a significant number of seats. In the event, of 27 LRC candidates chosen to fight single-member constituencies, 17 had no Liberal opponents, and of 11 chosen in two-member constituencies only one faced two Liberal candidates. In return, MacDonald gave no specific guarantees, but used his influence to prevent Labour candidates being chosen in seats where they had no realistic prospect of success. The short-term results of the agreement were a brilliant success. In the rout of the Tories in the 1906 election, Labour representation went up to 30, only five of whom had faced Liberal opposition. As the Liberals themselves won 400 seats, they too felt they had done well out of the deal. In the long run, however, they may have sown the seeds of their own destruction in helping to put a new and thrustful rival on its feet.

One of the new Labour MPs was MacDonald, who again contested Leicester, for which the Liberals nominated only one candidate. In the new Parliamentary Labour Party (PLP), MacDonald stood out as much the most impressive figure. By this time, he had evolved a most impressive speaking style, with a marvellously mellifluous voice, and he soon developed a mastery of parliamentary tactics. Hardie was chosen as the first Chairman of the PLP, but – though highly respected for his personal qualities and his pioneering role – he soon proved himself to be an unsatisfactory choice. He often neglected his parliamentary duties and tended to follow his own political interests rather than those of the party as a whole. MacDonald preferred to concentrate on his role as party secretary, and did not contest the chairmanship when Hardie resigned in 1908, to be succeeded first by Arthur Henderson and then by George Barnes. Only in 1911 did MacDonald take over, but after that it became clear for the first time that the Labour Party had effectively elected a leader, rather than a mere chairman of the party meeting.

By then, MacDonald through his writings had attempted to provide the Labour Party with its own ideology which, while respectful of Karl Marx, fundamentally rejected his conclusions. In three books – *Socialism and Society* (1905), *Socialism and Government* (1909) and *The Socialist Movement* (1911) – he set out a programme which, while collectivist in its approach, was essentially moderate in tone and rejected any belief in the class war. In place of Marx, he chose Darwin as his lodestar. As summarised by Marquand, he argued that

> Marx, in spite of his great achievements, had not absorbed the full implications of Darwinian biology; trapped as he was in Hegel's dialectic, he failed to realise that social evolution, like biological evolution, resulted from the slow emergence of higher forms of life out of lower forms, not from the clash of opposing forces ... In the 1840s, when Marx began his economic studies, it looked as though Britain was on the verge of revolution. No revolution had come, and 'The Marxian today still wonders why England fell from grace. England did not fall from grace. Neither Marx nor Engels saw deep enough to discover the possibilities of peaceful advance which lay hidden beneath the surface.' (Marquand, 1977, p. 89)

Six months after he was elected leader, MacDonald suffered a devastating blow, one from which he never really recovered. His wife, Margaret, still grieving from the death of their six-year-old son David, fell ill with blood poisoning and died on 8 September 1911. MacDonald was inconsolable, burying himself in his work, but appearing to derive little pleasure from it. He poured his sense of loss into an intensely moving memoir, which was first published privately, and then as a full-length book, *Margaret Ethel MacDonald*, in 1912. In later years, MacDonald turned to a number of women friends for emotional support at different times, one of whom – Mary Agnes Hamilton, later a Labour MP – his children thought he might marry, though nothing came of the relationship. Of close male friends, he had none – and his relations with his political and ministerial colleagues were notoriously distant.

In the two general elections of 1910, the Liberals lost their overall majority, and henceforth were dependent on the Irish Nationalists and on Labour to maintain themselves in power. MacDonald was convinced that the Labour Party should offer consistent support to the Liberal government, which as a quid pro quo pushed through a series of reforms – including the payment of MPs and the legalisation of trade union political funds – to which Labour was strongly committed. These tactics cost MacDonald much of his popularity with the ILP, many of whose members wanted him to show equal hostility to 'both capitalist parties', while his fellow Labour MPs resented what they regarded as his standoffish attitude. Marquand quotes a letter from W.C. Anderson, one of his strongest supporters, warning him that his followers found him 'too stern and intellectually cold', and urging him to 'rope some of your men nearer to you by a kind word and, when possible, by a confidential chat about their difficulties and misunderstandings' (Marquand, 1977, p. 151).

In government circles, MacDonald was by now held in the highest esteem and was twice sounded out – once by Lloyd George and once by the Liberal Chief Whip – on the possibility of joining the Cabinet in a senior post. MacDonald was evidently tempted, but felt that it would be difficult to persuade his own party, and replied that the time was not yet ripe. Despite his internal critics, there was by August 1914 a virtually universal acceptance that MacDonald, who towered over his parliamentary colleagues, was the only possible leader.

There was therefore general consternation within the party when, on 5 August 1914, he submitted his resignation. The cause was, of course, the British declaration of war on Germany, the previous day. MacDonald, who thought that Britain should have remained neutral, did not accept that German militarism was exclusively to blame for the outbreak of war. The real cause he believed was the policy of balance of power through the creation of two hostile alliances, and part of the responsibility lay with the secretive diplomacy of Foreign Secretary Sir Edward Grey, who had encouraged the French and Russian governments to believe that Britain was committed to intervene on their side, even though there was no formal agreement to this effect.

The majority of Labour MPs, carried away by public fervour for the war, resolved to support the government's request for war credits, and when MacDonald refused to reconsider his position, Henderson reluctantly took over as leader. Together with a group of radical Liberals, MacDonald set up a new organisation – the Union for Democratic Control (UDC) – which campaigned for a negotiated peace, with no annexations by either side, an international body to prevent future wars, general disarmament, and democratic control, through the British Parliament, of foreign policy. As the war progressed, the gap between MacDonald and the Labour leadership, which joined the coalition governments formed in April 1915 and December 1916, grew steadily wider. By contrast, he strengthened his links with the ILP, many of whose branches were militantly pacifist and who (especially after Hardie's death in 1915) increasingly looked to him for inspiration.

MacDonald unflinchingly maintained his position throughout the war, despite an avalanche of denigration from government supporters and the popular press. He maintained a correspondence with Bernstein, and placed his hopes on securing peace by contacts between the Socialist movements in the belligerent countries. This seemed a realistic possibility after the February 1917 Russian Revolution, when the Dutch Socialist Party proposed to convene a conference of the Socialist International in the neutral venue of Stockholm, a proposal strongly supported by Kerensky and the Petrograd Soviet. This effected a reconciliation between MacDonald and Henderson, and the two men travelled together to Paris, where they reached agreement with the French Socialist Party on attendance at Stockholm, which Henderson later successfully recommended to a special Labour Party conference. Stockholm was abruptly aborted, however, by the British government, which refused to issue passports to any British delegates, precipitating the resignation of Henderson from the War Cabinet.

So the war continued its bloody course until November 1918, when Lloyd George finally achieved his long-sought 'knockout blow', and went on to his overwhelming victory in the 'coupon' election the following month. This all but wiped out the Liberal Party as an independent force, and Labour, whose representation went up to 63 MPs, became the largest Opposition party, though the result fell far short of its hopes. Every one of its 'anti-war' MPs was defeated, including MacDonald who was resoundingly beaten at Leicester, and even Arthur Henderson lost his seat, leaving the Parliamentary Labour Party with no effective leader.

MacDonald made little effort to conceal his contempt for the feeble performance of Labour MPs during the 1918–22 Parliament, and devoted most of his energies to trying to restore the Socialist International and, in particular, to preventing the ILP from drifting off into the rival 'Third International' launched by the Russian Bolsheviks. He unsuccessfully fought a by-election at Woolwich East in March 1921, but did not get back into the Commons until November 1922, when he was returned for Aberavon in the general election won by Bonar Law's newly formed Conservative government.

Labour representation shot up to 142, including a large contingent of ILP members from what became known as the 'Red Clyde', the Glasgow region of

Scotland. Wrongly assuming from his anti-war record that MacDonald shared their left-wing views, the Clydesiders, led by Emanuel Shinwell, enthusiastically pushed his claim to the leadership, against J.R. Clynes, a somewhat colourless trade unionist and former minister in the Lloyd George coalition, who had been elected Chairman of the PLP the previous year.

In a closely fought contest, MacDonald prevailed by 61 votes to 56. Shinwell later wrote that only two men in the room were aware of the implications of the choice that was being made – himself and MacDonald. 'I was confident that we were not only electing the leader of one section of the Opposition for the duration of the new Parliament but also a future Prime Minister' (Shinwell, 1973, p. 25). What neither Shinwell nor MacDonald could have foreseen was that this distant prospect would become reality in little over a year, thanks to Baldwin's folly in calling a further general election in December 1923, resulting in a three-way split in the new Parliament (see previous chapter). The Conservatives won 258 seats, Labour 191, the Liberals 159.

In the post-electoral manoeuvring, the decisive element was the decision of the Liberal Party, briefly reunited under Asquith and Lloyd George, to put Labour into office, but without any guarantee of future support in the division lobbies. So on 22 January 1924, at the age of 57, MacDonald became the only Prime Minister of modern times to be appointed without any previous ministerial experience (until Tony Blair, 73 years later, in very different circumstances). He rose to the challenge with very little self-doubt, though he was only too aware of the paucity of talent from which to choose his ministerial team. He took the Foreign Ministry himself, Philip Snowden became an ultra-orthodox Chancellor of the Exchequer and Arthur Henderson, who had lost his seat in the election and had to be found another in an early by-election, was somewhat grudgingly made Home Secretary, after having turned down other less senior posts. Most of the other important portfolios went to ex-Liberals or even ex-Tories, such as Lord Parmoor (the father of Stafford Cripps), who became Leader of the Lords and, effectively, Deputy Foreign Secretary. This caused some resentment in the Labour Party, and particularly in the ILP, which was, however, thrown a sop by the appointment of the Clydesider John Wheatley as Health Minister and, incidentally, one of the few undoubted successes of the government.

Initially at least, MacDonald's reputation soared, both in Parliament and in the country, to which he appeared to offer commanding leadership. To his colleagues, however, he appeared less satisfactory. Most of them found him remote and uncommunicative; only with the affable but ineffectual railwaymen's leader J.H. Thomas, who became Colonial Secretary, did he enjoy anything approaching normal friendly relations. Nor did he attempt to ingratiate himself with the Liberal leaders, on whom he was dependent to remain in office. He greatly resented the patronising tone adopted by Asquith, and deeply distrusted Lloyd George. So far from viewing them as allies, he saw them as deadly rivals for the support of progressive voters, a perception which clearly also influenced their attitude to him.

MacDonald's most important work was undoubtedly done as Foreign Secretary, where he enjoyed a rare triumph at the London conference which he convened and chaired in August 1924. Successfully reconciling bitter French and German divisions over the punitive reparations clauses of the Versailles Treaty, he paved the way for the withdrawal of the French occupation of the Ruhr. He followed this up by a visit to the League of Nations in Geneva, where – together with the new French Prime Minister Edouard Herriot – he secured the adoption amidst great enthusiasm of the so-called Geneva Protocol, providing for international arbitration of disputes and general disarmament, which unfortunately was never ratified.

Despite his continuing anti-communism, MacDonald also opened diplomatic relations with the Bolshevik government, and began negotiations with them on two treaties concerning trade and compensation for British holders of Russian bonds, together with a possible loan agreement. Not only the Tories, but also Asquith and his fellow Liberals were opposed to the loan, and both Opposition parties determined to defeat the government if the treaties were offered for ratification, but before the opportunity arose the government fell because of the Campbell affair.

John Campbell had published an article in the Communist Party's *Workers' Weekly* calling on British soldiers not to turn their guns on their 'fellow workers'. The Attorney-General, Sir Patrick Hastings, initiated charges against Campbell for sedition, but these were later withdrawn when it was discovered that Campbell had an excellent war record and had been severely wounded.

Both the Tories and the Liberals put down motions challenging MacDonald's handling of the affair and alleging that he had overruled Hastings for political reasons. MacDonald declared that if either of them was passed he would call for a general election. In the event, the Tories rejected their own motion but voted for the Liberal amendment, and the die was cast.

The election campaign was notable for the extensive and exhausting speaking tour undertaken by MacDonald, who was hailed as 'the Gladstone of Labour', where he addressed vast and adoring crowds. The Tory campaign largely consisted of depicting MacDonald and his party as front-men for the Communists, in which endeavour they were assisted by the notorious Zinoviev letter. This purported to come from Grigori Zinoviev, the President of the Communist International and called for the 'revolutionising' of the British proletariat. The letter, later shown to be a crude forgery, concocted by Russian émigrés, but circulated with assistance from Conservative Central Office and blazoned across the columns of the *Daily Mail*, totally dominated the closing stages of the campaign. Whether or not it caused the government's defeat, it certainly provided MacDonald with an excellent alibi, and saved him from any serious recriminations in Labour's ranks. (See Lewis Chester, Stephen Fay and Hugo Young, *The Zinoviev Letter*, 1967.)

Apart from its foreign successes, the 1924 Labour government had little to show for its nine months in office. Yet it was an important milestone in Labour's onward march. It established it as the alternative party of government to the Tories, and – by its essential moderation (which even extended to its ministers, including MacDonald, donning court dress for their meetings with King George V, a subject for much mockery amidst the party's own ranks) – it went a long way to remove the irrational fears of many middle-class voters that it was unfit to govern. In fact, Labour substantially increased its vote at the 1924 election, though its parliamentary representation fell to 151 seats. The real losers were the Liberals, who returned only 40 members and were never again able to offer an effective challenge to Labour. The decline in Liberal votes disproportionately helped the Tories who, with 419 seats, dominated the new House of Commons.

As Leader of the Opposition for the next five years, MacDonald had a difficult time. No salary was attached to the post, and he incurred substantial expenses in carrying out his duties as party leader. The declining income from the Margaret Gladstone trust fund was barely sufficient to support his large family, and he was forced to undertake a great deal of hack journalism to make ends meet. He passed his 60th birthday in 1926, and the constant wear and tear began to tell. He was still an impressive speaker, but he had passed his prime, and no longer had the energy, or perhaps even the commitment, of earlier years. A severe illness in 1927 put him out of action for five months, and the strain on him was increased by constant struggles with the ILP, which became increasingly critical of his moderate stance.

The 1929 election again produced an indecisive result, though Labour emerged as the largest party, with 288 seats, against 260 for the Tories, with the Liberals on 59. This time, there was no question that MacDonald would become Prime Minister, though he again encountered difficulties in selecting his ministerial team. 'Indeed, I should rather fight half a dozen elections than make one cabinet', he confided to his diary. He havered between choosing J.H. Thomas as Foreign Secretary and again appointing himself, but finally yielded to an ultimatum from Arthur Henderson that he would not join the government unless he could have this post. This episode did not improve the already poor relations between the two men, and their mutual suspicion and rivalry steadily increased during the ensuing two years. Philip Snowden again became Chancellor, but there was no post for John Wheatley, despite his success in 1924. Wheatley, who was to die of a cerebral haemorrhage in May 1930, had been a consistent and virulent critic of MacDonald, and his place as the 'statutory left-winger' in the Cabinet went instead to George Lansbury.

Despite having ceded the Foreign Secretaryship to Henderson, much of MacDonald's energies were again expended in international relations. He made a highly successful visit to the United States in October 1929 – the first by a serving British Prime Minister – where he managed with difficulty to bridge Anglo-American differences over naval disarmament, paving the way for the five-nation London conference, over which he presided in January–April 1930. This produced only partial agreement, with Britain, Japan and the US agreeing parities for reduced naval strength over the following six years, but France and Italy refusing to comply.

In domestic policy, MacDonald was again handicapped by his lack of a parliamentary majority and the necessity of getting Liberal support – which did not come cheaply – for any legislative proposals. From the outset, the dominating issue was unemployment, which, following the Wall Street crash in October 1929, rose inexorably, from 1.53 million in January 1930 to 2.73 million in June 1931. Few of MacDonald's ministers had any grasp of economics, and they had no idea of how to cope with the 'economic blizzard' (MacDonald's term) which had struck them. The government's response was to increase rates of unemployment benefit (which stored up trouble for them later on) and to appoint a Cabinet Committee led by J.H. Thomas to consider solutions.

One of the members of the Thomas Committee was the Chancellor of the Duchy of Lancaster, Sir Oswald Mosley. In January 1930 he sent a memorandum to MacDonald, advocating a major public works programme along the lines suggested by Keynes and by Lloyd George. MacDonald referred the Mosley memorandum to another committee headed by his ultra-orthodox Chancellor, Philip Snowden. Snowden's hostility ensured that Mosley's proposals disappeared without trace, and with them any hope of Labour finding a solution to the unemployment problem. Mosley resigned in disgust, and though his stand was backed by some left-wing MPs, he was already so distrusted that he was unable to muster much support. Soon he had left the Labour Party altogether, and had plunged into the gutter politics, which culminated in his creation of the British Union of Fascists. A reluctant admirer of Mosley, at that time, was Beatrice Webb, who in her diaries compared him favourably to MacDonald, who, she wrote, owed his 'pre-eminence largely to the fact that he is the only artist, the only aristocrat by temperament and talent in a party of plebeians and plain men' (Cole, 1956, p. 243).

The final crisis which destroyed the Labour government was sparked by the failure of the famous Austrian bank, the Kreditanstalt, in May 1931. This immediately led to a run on German banks, and by July the pressure moved to Britain, where the Bank of England suffered heavy losses in defending sterling. At this time, MacDonald received a report from a committee of 'experts', the May Committee, predicting a budget deficit of £120 million (Snowden thought it would be £170 million), and insisting on heavy expenditure cuts, including £66 million on unemployment benefit, in order to balance the budget. MacDonald showed the report to Keynes, who advocated going off the gold standard, with an effective devaluation of 25 per cent. But neither MacDonald nor any of his Cabinet was prepared to contemplate going off gold, which Snowden told them would result in a 'ruinous fall' in the standard of living of the workers. Instead there followed a long series of tortured Cabinet meetings at which they attempted to balance the budget through a mixture of tax increases and spending cuts, in which unemployment benefits (which had sharply escalated as a proportion of total government expenditure) figured largely.

In the end, they were advised that bankers in New York and Paris would be prepared to bail them out if total economies of £76 million, including a 10 per cent cut in unemployment pay, were implemented, and if the two Opposition parties backed the deal. By this time nearly half the Cabinet, including Henderson (who was much influenced by the opposition of the TUC), was threatening to resign if the cuts were agreed. Finally, on 23 August, the Cabinet voted in favour by the bare majority of 11 to 9, but it was immediately clear that the government could not continue on that basis. The Cabinet agreed that MacDonald should see the King and inform him that all its members had placed their resignations in his hands. Their assumption, which MacDonald shared, was that the King would probably ask Baldwin to form an alternative government. Instead, George V asked Baldwin and Herbert Samuel, the acting Liberal leader in the absence of Lloyd George who was ill, whether they would be prepared to serve in a National Government under MacDonald, and then put heavy pressure on him to continue, saying that 'he was the only man to lead the country through the crisis'. MacDonald was taken aback, and there is little doubt that his first instinct was to decline, but to support what he was convinced were necessary if deeply painful cuts from the Opposition benches. He met Baldwin, Samuel and Neville Chamberlain, the deputy Tory leader, the following day to discuss the situation, and, according to Chamberlain's diary, told them that he would help them

> to get these proposals through, though it meant his death warrant, but it would be no use for him to join a Government. He would be a ridiculous figure unable to command support and would bring odium on us as well as himself.

It would have been far better for MacDonald's posthumous reputation, and for his own subsequent peace of mind, if he had kept to this resolve, but – flattered by the King's confidence in him and following what he persuaded himself was his patriotic duty – he allowed himself to be convinced. He formed a new government, which included only three other former Labour Cabinet ministers – Snowden, Thomas and Lord Sankey the Lord Chancellor – and attracted the support of a mere 13 Labour MPs. The new Cabinet also contained two Liberals and four Conservatives, though the Tories dominated the ranks of the junior ministers.

The government proceeded to implement the cuts which the Labour government had baulked at, but this did not prevent a further run on the pound within a few weeks, which led to the hurried decision – taken at an emergency Cabinet meeting held on Sunday 20 September – to go off the gold standard, an event which passed without any of the disastrous consequences against which the Labour government had been warned. 'Nobody told us we could do this', complained an aggrieved Sidney Webb, one of the nine Labour Cabinet ministers who had stood out against the cuts in unemployment benefit only a month earlier.

Within a few days of the formation of the National Government, MacDonald and his associates were unceremoniously expelled from the Labour Party, which elected Arthur Henderson as its leader. MacDonald had initially regarded the National Government as purely a temporary affair to see out the immediate financial crisis, and had assumed that normal party alignments would then be reconstituted, much as he and other anti-war MPs had been reunited with the Labour mainstream after 1918. He was, however, unable to resist overwhelming pressure from his new Tory allies to seek a popular mandate for the measures that the new government had taken, and the general election held on 27 October 1931 ensured that his break with Labour would be permanent.

During the course of the campaign he was bitterly attacked by the Labour leadership, and he and the sharp-tongued Philip Snowden retaliated in kind, which made any subsequent reconciliation impossible. On the Labour side the myth grew up – and was almost universally believed – that MacDonald had plotted from almost the outset of the 1929 government to betray his colleagues and link up with the Tories. It was spelled out with great conviction by his former Parliamentary Private Secretary L. Macneill Weir in *The Tragedy of Ramsay MacDonald* (1938), and, in fictional form, by Howard Spring in his novel *Fame is the Spur* (1940). Only the publication in 1977 of David Marquand's biography, with its very careful examination of the sources, notably MacDonald's own extensive diaries, showed this belief to have been erroneous.

MacDonald himself also believed in betrayal – but felt that the culprits were his former Labour colleagues. They had abandoned their Socialist principles, in his view, by becoming spokesmen for a sectional interest, that of the TUC. He fought the election hard, and held his north-eastern mining constituency of Seaham against a vigorous challenge from his former agent. What he had not anticipated – and did not at all welcome – was the staggering defeat inflicted on the Labour Party as a whole. It was reduced to 52 seats, against 554 for the National Government (including 473 Tories). Only one former Cabinet minister – George Lansbury – managed to hold his seat, and he subsequently took over the leadership from Henderson.

The new government was overwhelmingly Tory in its complexion, and MacDonald was increasingly seen as being a mere fig leaf, particularly after September 1932, when Snowden and the Free Trade Liberals resigned from the government. As during his previous governments, he played an active international role, heading the British delegation to the Geneva disarmament talks, and presiding over the Lausanne conference on phasing out German reparation payments. At least until early 1933, he remained the major influence on British foreign policy, though subsequently Baldwin, whose responsibilities as Lord President of the Council included defence, became more prominent. The Foreign Secretary, Sir John Simon, was little more than a bag-carrier.

On domestic policy, it was a different story. The leading Conservatives almost invariably got their way, and MacDonald found himself taken for granted. He bitterly resented this, and endlessly complained about his Tory colleagues in his diary, hinting in the entry for 27 December 1932 that he felt he had made a mistake in forming the National Government: 'Was I wise? Perhaps not, but it seemed as though anything else was impossible.'

Meanwhile, his physical and mental powers began an embarrassing decline. He suffered from glaucoma, necessitating debilitating eye operations, and his lapses in concentration became more and more frequent, which had a disastrous effect on his speeches, both inside and outside the Commons. Churchill woundingly said that his speeches 'compressed the largest number of words into the smallest amount of thought', while Francis Williams commented that 'he retreated into incoherency because incoherency had become less painful than lucidity' (Williams, 1965, p. 130). By 1933 MacDonald had become a standing embarrassment to the government, and there can be no doubt that if he had been a Conservative he would have been pushed into resignation. Instead, in order to maintain the fiction that it was still a National rather than a Tory government, he was pressed to stay on for at least two years after he had ceased to play an effective role.

It was only in June 1935 that, with a general election approaching, Baldwin at last took over the reins, though MacDonald lingered on, taking over Baldwin's post as Lord President of the Council. There were more humiliations to come. In the general election, which the government won with a large if inevitably reduced majority (Conservatives 432 seats, Labour 154, Liberals 21), MacDonald was heavily defeated at Seaham by his old sponsor for the Labour leadership, Emanuel Shinwell. There followed a desperate search to find him another seat in a by-election, and he was eventually returned for the Scottish Universities, despite his having been a passionate opponent of university representation. He continued to sit in the Cabinet – devoid of any influence – until Baldwin himself made way for Neville Chamberlain in May 1937. In November of the same year he died at sea, aged 71, during a voyage to South America which he had hoped would restore his health.

By any reckoning, MacDonald was a major historical figure, though he hardly rates as one of the more successful Prime Ministers. His essential achievement was in creating a new political party and leading it with exceptional skill and judgement so that, from small beginnings, it became one of the two great contending parties of state. This judgement failed him in 1931, and his character flaws – his vanity and inability to take others into his confidence – no doubt contributed to that failure.

The hard knocks he then inflicted on the Labour Party might, some feared, have proved mortal, but the construct he had built proved strong enough to survive. As Marquand suggested at the end of his biography, the Labour Party which triumphed in 1945 and transformed the face of British society was his true 'monument', though few Labour MPs at the time 'would have acknowledged a debt to MacDonald' (Marquand, 1977, p. 794).

Works consulted

Cole, Margaret, (ed.), *Beatrice Webb's Diaries 1924–1932*, London, Longman, 1956.

Cox, Jane, (ed.), *A Singular Marriage: Ramsay and Margaret MacDonald*, London, Harrap, 1988.

Elton, Lord, *Dictionary of National Biography, 1931–1940*, London, Oxford University Press, 1949, pp. 562–70.

Jeffreys, Kevin, (ed.), *Leading Labour: From Keir Hardie to Tony Blair*, London, Tauris, 1999.

MacDonald, J. Ramsay, *Margaret Ethel MacDonald*, London, Hodder & Stoughton, 1912.

Marquand, David, *Ramsay MacDonald*, London, Jonathan Cape, 1977.

Morgan, Kenneth O., *Labour People: Hardie to Kinnock*, London, Oxford University Press, 1992.

Shinwell, Emmanuel, *I've Lived Though it All*, London, Gollancz, 1973.

Spring, Howard, *Fame is the Spur*, London, Fontana, 1953 [1940].

Weir, L. MacNeill, *The Tragedy of Ramsay MacDonald*, London, Secker & Warburg, 1938.

Williams, Francis, *A Pattern of Rulers*, London, Longman, 1965.

40
Neville Chamberlain – A Family Affair

Many leading politicians come from political families which largely shape the course of their own political careers. Yet few have been so dominated, first by the presence, and then by the memory, of his remarkable father as Neville Chamberlain.

Joe Chamberlain was an epic figure. Sent from London at the age of 18 to run his family's screw manufacturing business in Birmingham, he became within a very few years one of the rapidly growing city's leading businessmen, and then the dominant force on the city council, serving as Lord Mayor in 1873–75, and building up a formidable Liberal political machine in the city. Elected an MP in 1876, he entered Gladstone's second Cabinet four years later as President of the Board of Trade and effective leader of the Radical faction of the party, but broke with Gladstone over Irish Home Rule in 1886, leading his 'Liberal Unionists' into a close alliance with Lord Salisbury's Conservatives, and subsequently serving as Colonial Secretary in two Conservative Cabinets. Having split the Liberal Party in 1886, he repeated the trick with the Conservatives in 1903, when his resignation from Balfour's Cabinet, over tariff reform, led to its premature demise.

Joe's marital career was no less remarkable than his political progression. Brought up a Unitarian, he married (twice) into one of Birmingham's main Unitarian families – the Kenricks. In 1861, aged 25, he married Harriet Kenrick, who gave birth to a daughter, Beatrice, the following year, but died in 1863, giving birth to his elder son, Austen. Five years later, he married her cousin, Florence Kenrick, and Neville was born the following year, followed by three younger sisters until, in 1875 Florence, too, died in childbirth. In 1888, after unsuccessfully wooing the young Beatrice Potter (later Webb), who was unwilling to accept his views on male dominance, Joe wed for the third time, a young American woman, Mary Endicott, who was actually a year younger than Austen and only five years older than Neville.

The young Neville grew up in the two successive houses which Joe acquired in the Birmingham suburbs – first at Edgbaston, and then, farther out, towards

611

Moseley. Here he built a rather grand but frightfully ugly house which he called Highbury, recalling his own youth in Islington. Neville's mother died when he was six, and the household was then presided over, in turn, by two of Joe's sisters, Caroline and Clara. Neville found his Aunt Clara cold and unresponsive, and was delighted that, when he was 16, her role was taken over by Austen's elder sister Beatrice, then aged 22. She herself gave way to Joe's third wife, Mary, three years later, who proved a devoted stepmother to Neville and, in particular, to his three younger sisters.

Joe frequently entertained at Highbury, where there was a constant flow of guests, many of them visiting politicians and important national figures, as well as local Birmingham dignitaries. Yet for long periods he was away in London, and never really got on intimate terms with his younger son. As Neville recalled much later in a letter to one of his sisters, 'For a good many years I respected and feared him more than I loved him ... the piercing eye ... few could face it with comfort.' Nor was he close to his half-brother – 'a certain deference', he wrote, entered into his relationship with Austen.

Nevertheless, Neville was supremely happy in the bosom of his family. He was devoted to his three younger sisters, Ida, Hilda and Ethel. The first two never married, and he unfailingly wrote to them, alternately, long, detailed letters almost every week from 1916, when he left Birmingham for London, until his death in 1940. These letters formed the principal source for his official biography, written by Keith Feiling. In addition to them, he had large numbers of mostly female cousins living nearby, who were always in and out of the house, and they became a close and loving family clan, of which Neville became the natural leader. Outside the clan, however, he was shy and withdrawn, and was bitterly unhappy at Rugby, despite being an above-average pupil. It was during the school holidays that he came into his own, romping with his younger kin in the spacious grounds of Highbury, and cultivating his passions for music, bird watching and botany, which in later life were supplemented by an equal devotion to fly fishing.

Austen had preceded Neville at Rugby, where he had achieved every distinction, but thereafter their paths were to diverge. The elder son was destined by his father for a political career; he was educated at Cambridge, Berlin and Paris, and was elected to the House of Commons, as a Liberal Unionist, before his 30th birthday. Neville, his father decided, should go into business and the question of a university education did not arise. Instead, he was sent as a day student to Mason College, Birmingham, where for two years he studied mathematics, engineering and metallurgy, and was subsequently apprenticed to a Birmingham firm of chartered accountants.

Joe Chamberlain had disposed of his interest in the firm of Nettlefold & Chamberlain in 1874, but was on the lookout for investment opportunities and in 1891, when Neville was 22, he bought part of the island of Andros, in the Bahamas, and sent his younger son out to establish a sisal plantation with a view to producing fibre for rope making. It was a singularly ill-considered venture. The soil on the island was poor and the local strain of the plant proved incapable of producing a commercial yield. Nevertheless, the young Neville threw himself into the enterprise with a fierce determination to succeed, not least to impress his father and his gilded half-brother.

He was desperately lonely, with only a white overseer, whom he did not consider his social or intellectual equal, and some 800 natives to supervise. He drugged himself with unceasing toil, and within four years had cleared 6000 acres of bush, planted it, built roads, houses, stores and shop and a wharf, imported machinery from Cuba and begun to lay a railway line to transport the fibre to the wharf. It was all in vain; the quality of the finished fibre was so poor it was impossible to find any customers to buy it. Yet Neville refused to face the facts, persevering long after there was any realistic hope of turning the venture round, and it was only after six years – in 1897 – that he returned to Birmingham and confessed that the operation was a total failure. By then, it had cost Joe more than a third of his fortune.

'It is not difficult to find in the young man on the island of Andros some of the virtues and defects that were later to be seen in the Prime Minister', was the perceptive comment of Francis Williams.

> The virtues of tenacity and courage, the defects of obstinacy and refusal to recognise any fact that did not fit in with his own hopes ... [his] increasingly exasperated contempt for the general incompetence of humanity, so incapable of appreciating what was good for it, so unwilling to do what it was told ... [he] was forced by the conditions of his life into a habit of inordinate dependence upon his own solitary judgment. (Williams, 1965, p. 139)

Yet Chamberlain blamed himself, perhaps unduly, for the Andros debacle, and determined to redeem himself, above all in the eyes of his father, by plunging into a business career in Birmingham. Family connections helped him secure controlling directorships in two medium-sized metal-making firms, but it was his clear if unimaginative mind, exceptional diligence and careful – even excessive – attention to detail which contributed to his success. He kept his head down, and after 14 years of steady if unspectacular growth by the two firms he had established himself as one of the city's leading businessmen and earned a sufficient competence to be able to consider wider horizons.

In 1911 he was 42 years old, and that year he took two decisive steps which were to determine the future pattern of his life. On 5 January, he got married to Anne de Vere Cole, the daughter of an army officer and country landowner. The marriage was to bring him great happiness, and the birth within three years of both a daughter, Dorothy, and a son, Frank. It did little to alter the public persona of a stiff, pernickety, obstinate character, whom many of his associates had regarded as an inveterate bachelor. In November, he was elected to the city council of Birmingham, which that year was greatly expanded by the absorption of many of its suburbs within the city boundaries.

Neville was already heavily involved in civic activities in Birmingham, becoming chairman of the General Hospital and a leading campaigner for the creation of a new university, which would absorb George Mason College. He had shown little public interest in politics, though he was a fully committed supporter of the Conservative Opposition to the Liberal government and of his father's tariff reform policies. By this time, Joe, who had suffered a devastating stroke in 1906, was totally incapacitated, though he remained an MP until his death in 1914. Austen had fulfilled his early promise, rising to Chancellor of the Exchequer under Arthur Balfour and was currently the favourite to succeed him as Tory leader, though – as described in Chapter 37 – he eventually stood down in favour of Bonar Law. Neville still appeared to be the ugly duckling of the family, and there were few indications that he would rise to a higher position in the state than his illustrious father and brother.

Joining Birmingham City Council was the making of Neville. He quickly revealed outstanding skills as a municipal administrator, and showed that he had inherited the radical instincts – at least as far as local government was concerned – of his father, who had first made his reputation as a reforming Lord Mayor four decades earlier. As chairman of the Town Planning Committee, he pioneered the first comprehensive town planning schemes ever to be adopted in Britain, and – against strong opposition from banking interests – he established the first and only municipal savings bank in the country, which proved a lasting success. After only four years on the council, he became Lord Mayor in 1915 – amazingly the 11th member of his family to hold the post, but the only one – apart from Joe – to leave a distinctive mark. The condescending description of him, often attributed to Churchill but actually by Lord Hugh Cecil, as 'a good Lord Mayor of Birmingham – in a lean year' was a considerable under-evaluation.

If it was not for his half-brother, Neville would probably have been content to continue serving his native city for many years, finally retiring amidst much honour as the great Panjandrum of British local government. But Austen, having joined Lloyd George's coalition government as Secretary of State for India, was asked by the Prime Minister if he could recommend a good administrator to take over the new post of Director-General of National Service, and had no qualms in suggesting his younger sibling.

Thinking it was his wartime duty to serve the government in whatever capacity was proposed, Neville immediately resigned as Lord Mayor and travelled to London to assume his appointment in March 1917, without any discussion of the extent of his responsibilities or even whether he would receive a salary.

Seven months later he resigned, feeling that the fiasco of Andros had been repeated, but this time he did not blame himself. He complained to his sisters of his 'd—d well-meaning brother', but his real ire was directed at Lloyd George, who he believed had utterly failed to give him the necessary backing to make a success of his assignment. This had been to organise voluntary recruitment both for military service, but above all for civilian work in war industries.

In fact, Neville was all at sea in Whitehall, whose ways were very different from those of Birmingham Town Hall. Not possessing a seat in the Cabinet, or even in the House of Commons, he was unable to defend himself from political attack, and was regularly outmanoeuvred by the War Office and the Ministry of Labour, which were in no mood to cede any of their responsibilities to the new department. Neville and his civil servants were subjected to a malicious campaign by Lord Northcliffe's newspapers (including *The Times*), which were anxious to abandon the voluntary principle in favour of compulsion. Stubborn as ever, Neville held on to his post for several months after it was clear that his position was hopeless, and finally threw in the towel in August 1917.

Neville drew two conclusions from this episode. One was that Lloyd George was fundamentally untrustworthy, and he resolved never again to have any dealings with him. The other was that he must get elected to the House of Commons if he was ever again to serve in a national post. Back in Birmingham, he tried – without success – to induce one or other of the sitting Tory MPs to resign in his favour, but he had to wait until the general election of December 1918, when he fought the newly created constituency of Birmingham Ladywood, to begin his parliamentary career at the age of 49. This was far older than any other twentieth-century Prime Minister, but once elected, Neville lost little time in making up for his late start.

His maiden speech, on the Rent Restriction Bill – in which he argued for more arduous conditions to be met by landlords before they would be permitted to raise rents – led to an immediate reversal of government policy. A rare achievement by a backbencher, which he followed up a few weeks later by successfully carrying an amendment against the government on the Electricity Supply Bill. These and other early parliamentary speeches were delivered with great clarity and authority, reflecting their author's formidable command of detail and the experience he had gained in local government. He introduced a Private Member's Bill to give protection to the children of unmarried mothers and was appointed to a number of influential committees, several of them as chairman. Little over a year after his election, he was offered a post in the government as Under-Secretary for Health. After some hesitation, he declined, not being able to bring himself to serve under Lloyd George.

At this time, Austen was Chancellor of the Exchequer, and in 1921 succeeded Bonar Law as leader of the Conservative Party. Though relations between the two brothers were generally good, they disagreed sharply in their views on the

Prime Minister. It was therefore fortunate that Neville, who was returning from a holiday in Canada, was absent from the famous Carlton Club meeting on 19 October 1922, when Austen vigorously defended Lloyd George at a meeting of Tory MPs, and saw his own leadership swept aside as they voted by 187 votes to 87 to withdraw from the coalition government. Bonar Law consequently became Prime Minister of a purely Conservative government, and on his return to Britain, Neville received a message offering to appoint him as Postmaster-General. He hastened to consult Austen, who, he reported to his sister Hilda, 'took the idea very badly, feeling that if I accepted it would be the last drop of bitterness in the cup' (Macleod, 1961, p. 87). Neville then declared that he would give up the post, and with it his political career because 'I cared more for our personal relations than for politics.' Austen, shamed or, perhaps, deeply moved, immediately withdrew his opposition.

Bonar Law, and his successor, Stanley Baldwin, were both immensely impressed by Chamberlain's judgements and administrative gifts, and his ministerial career took off like a rocket. Within little over a year, he had worked his way through three successive posts, including Minister of Health (where he passed an important housing bill). In August 1923 Baldwin wrote to him on holiday offering him the post of Chancellor of the Exchequer, which he promptly declined, writing to his sister Ida,

> I should be a fish out of water. I know nothing of finance; I like spending money much better than saving it; I hate blocking other people's schemes and – I only thought of this after I had written – I shall have to live in Downing St. instead of Eaton Square.

But Baldwin would not take no for an answer, and after a long interview in Downing Street Chamberlain reluctantly agreed to take the post, which Baldwin himself had been occupying on a temporary basis. Not that Chamberlain had any time to show his mettle. Barely three months after his appointment, Baldwin and his government went down to defeat in the 1923 election, before he was able to produce a single Budget. He could have resumed the chancellorship less than a year later, when the Labour government went down to defeat in the October 1924 election, but doggedly refused. 'I am likely to be a great Minister of Health,' he wrote, 'but am not likely to be more than a second rate Chancellor.' In choosing the lesser office, he was (consciously?) following in the footsteps of his father, who preferred being Colonial Secretary to Chancellor, under both Salisbury and Balfour.

Whether or not he was influenced by Joe's example, he was showing a clear-headed awareness of his own abilities and limitations which was not always typical of him. As Minister of Health he was the undoubted star of Baldwin's second government and clearly established himself as the number two in the

Conservative hierarchy. His determination and self-confidence were remarkable. Within a week of taking office, he had circulated his bemused Cabinet colleagues with a list of 25 bills which he intended to carry over the next four years. In the event, 21 of them reached the Statute Book, along with several others, which he had not originally foreseen.

They included a major reform of the rating system, and a comprehensive reform of local government, which also involved the abolition of the Poor Law Guardians. The general tenor of his reforms was in a socially progressive direction, which might have led to him being characterised as being well on the left wing of the Conservative Party, many of whose members resented his proposals. He averted this tag thanks to his cold public personality, which prevented him from showing any sympathy for the plight of the unemployed, and his studied contempt for the Labour leadership. Baldwin was to rebuke him for this, in June 1927 when, he wrote to one of his sisters, 'Stanley begged me to remember that I was addressing a meeting of gentlemen. I always gave him the impression, he said, when I spoke in the House of Commons, that I looked on the Labour Party as dirt.'

In the 1929 general election, Chamberlain shrewdly moved from the inner city constituency of Ladywood, which turned out to be a Labour gain, to the plusher seat of Edgbaston, which he represented for the remainder of his life. In Opposition, Baldwin appointed him as party chairman, and he instituted the Conservative Research Department and commissioned a study on the introduction of tariffs. When, in February 1931, rumbles of discontent about Baldwin's leadership reached him, he made no attempt to play them down, and passed on to his leader a savagely critical report from the Chief Agent, which implied that he should stand down in Chamberlain's favour. A shaken Baldwin agreed to go, but then changed his mind overnight and decided to fight back, excoriating the press lords, Beaverbrook and Rothermere, who had been campaigning against him, and routing the candidate whom they had put up against the official Tory in a crucial by-election in Westminster St George's. Chamberlain was now 61, only two years younger than Baldwin, and it looked as though he had blown his best chance of succeeding him.

Yet he continued to be the party's work-horse, and his assiduity was widely contrasted with Baldwin's apparent laziness. This stood him in good stead in August 1931, when he remained in London during the death throes of Ramsay MacDonald's Labour government, while Baldwin returned to Aix-les-Bains to conclude his holiday. Chamberlain favoured the formation of a coalition government, to which Baldwin was greatly averse, but when he finally got back to London for a meeting with George V on 23 August, he found that – with the Liberals already on board – it was almost a *fait accompli*. He did not have the temerity to refuse the King's request to serve under MacDonald and 'save the country'. As Roy Jenkins comments, had he returned to London earlier, 'he might have been asked a less direct question and been able to divert the pressure' (Jenkins, 1998, p. 344). For Baldwin, this meant that his return to the premiership was postponed for another four years; for Chamberlain it was confirmation of his still increasing authority within the Tory Party.

Chamberlain became Minister of Health in the new National Government, but after the election in October 1931, when it was returned with a huge (and predominantly Conservative) majority, he replaced Philip Snowden as Chancellor of the Exchequer. This time he had no hesitation in accepting the post, as he saw that the conjunction of the economic crisis and the massive Tory majority would give him the ideal opportunity to implement the protectionist doctrines he had inherited from his father, thus bringing an end to 90 years of free trade. It mattered little to him that, in so doing, he would drive Snowden and the free trade Liberal ministers to resignation. He announced the new policy – which included a general revenue tariff of 10 per cent, variable upwards to 100 per cent for industries, such as steel, needing special safeguards, and downwards to nil for reasons of Commonwealth preference – on 4 February 1932, which he described in a letter as 'the great day of my life'. He ended his speech with the following words:

> There can have been few occasions in all our long political history when the son of a man who counted for something in his day and generation has been vouchsafed the privilege of setting the seal on the work which his father began but was forced to leave unfinished ... I believe he would have found consolation for his disappointment if he could have foreseen that these proposals, which are the direct and legitimate descendants of his own conception would be laid before the House of Commons, which he loved, in the presence of one and by the lips of the other of the two immediate successors to his name and blood.

He was, of course, referring to Austen, whom he had long ago superseded as his father's principal political heir, and who was now languishing on the backbenches, from which he descended to give his brother a warm handshake. It was no accident that Neville, the late starter, had forged ahead in the political race. The elder brother was both the more pompous and the more soft-centred of the two; Neville had more iron determination in his character than Austen, who was the subject of a famous quip by F.E. Smith (Lord Birkenhead): 'Poor old Austen. He always played the game, and he always lost it.'

Neville was less lucky with the second half of his operation, which was to persuade the governments of the Dominions to offer reciprocal preferences to British exporters. The Ottawa conference on Commonwealth trade, which he attended with six other British Cabinet ministers in July 1932, was only a very partial success. According to Roy Jenkins, 'enough discrimination was achieved to give the Americans a running grievance, but not enough to produce any great stimulus of Empire trade' (Jenkins, 1998, p. 348).

Chamberlain proved an extremely efficient Chancellor, who probably achieved the best results possible from highly inappropriate policies. His Budgets, all very restrictive, succeeded in balancing the books, and by 1935 he had rescinded the last of the savage cuts imposed in 1931, and a partial economic recovery had taken place. Yet Chamberlain steadfastly refused to contemplate any Keynesian measures, and he was contemptuous of the public works programmes introduced by President Franklin Roosevelt as part of his New Deal.

Chamberlain retained the chancellorship when Baldwin succeeded Macdonald in 1935, and he held the office for nearly six years until May 1937, when he himself became Prime Minister, at the advanced age of 68, and two months after the death of Austen. Neither MacDonald nor Baldwin had shown the slightest inclination to interfere with his stewardship, and he was the undisputed master of Britain's economic policies throughout his tenure. As Prime Minister, he early showed that he had no intention of treating his own ministers with such a light hand, and – in particular – that he was determined to ensure that he was in complete command of foreign policy. His interest had been aroused in 1934, when there had been an attempt to make him Foreign Secretary to replace the ineffective Sir John Simon. Chamberlain successfully resisted the move, but he subsequently paid much closer attention to international affairs. He was more alarmed than Baldwin by the rise of Nazi military power, and less unnerved than him by the 1935 Peace Ballot which had inhibited Baldwin from embracing a full-hearted rearmament programme. It was Chamberlain who took the initiative by proposing a substantial increase in the air estimates in his 1934 budget. This may well have proved the decisive factor in the Battle of Britain six years later.

Chamberlain, too, was at first strongly in favour of backing League of Nations' sanctions against Italy, following Mussolini's invasion of Abyssinia, and it was only when these appeared to have failed, having been only partially applied, that he changed his tack. There was no point, he asserted, in continuing with ineffective sanctions, and he henceforth put his faith in appeasing first Mussolini and then Hitler, who he assumed were rational men, prepared to act reasonably if their legitimate grievances were met. The first obstacle to carrying out Chamberlain's intentions was his Foreign Secretary Anthony Eden – young, glamorous and vain – whom he had inherited from Baldwin.

Eden doubted the wisdom of Chamberlain's attempt to woo Mussolini by offering to legitimise his conquest of Abyssinia, and his nose was put out of joint by what he believed to be the Prime Minister's use of his sister-in-law Ivy Chamberlain, Austen's widow, who was visiting Rome, to negotiate behind his back. He was also shocked by Chamberlain's abrupt dismissal of a proposal by President Roosevelt to summon a peace and security conference in Washington.

Eden resigned on 20 February 1938, and was replaced by the more compliant Lord Halifax, leaving the still very junior R.A. Butler to answer Foreign Office questions in the House of Commons, though in the event Chamberlain himself took the major questions. Shortly before, he had shifted Sir Robert Vansittart, who was known to be anti-German and anti- appeasement, from his post as Permanent Under-Secretary of the Foreign Office. He then increasingly used his personal advisor, Sir Horace Wilson, an industrial relations expert who had no experience whatever of foreign affairs, as his chief diplomatic 'fixer'.

Chamberlain's commitment to appeasement (which was not then a 'dirty' word) was by no means an unworthy one. He hated the prospect of war, having been deeply scarred by the experiences of 1914–18, when, although he was too old for military service, he had been greatly affected by the death in action of his younger cousin, Norman Chamberlain, his closest ally on the Birmingham City Council, about whom this very unemotional man had published a moving memoir. He also shared the view, more widely held on the left, that the Treaty of Versailles had been unduly harsh on Germany, and that some restitution should be made. The tragedy was that what was withheld from a democratic Germany in the 1920s was willingly yielded, with interest, to the brutal Nazi dictatorship ten years later.

Chamberlain's error, and it was an egregious one, was in persisting with the policy long after it was apparent that, so far from placating the aggressive intent of the dictators, it was merely feeding their appetites for more and more outrageous demands. The refusal to confront Hitler's illegal military occupation of the Rhineland in 1936, or to react against the German and Italian inter-vention on Franco's side in the Spanish Civil War, led directly to his invasion of Austria in March 1938, to which Chamberlain made no serious protest and, indeed, replied to an urgent Russian request for Anglo-French-Soviet talks on joint resistance to any future aggression, that they would be 'inappropriate'.

Having swallowed up Austria, the Nazi dictator switched his attention to Czechoslovakia, where the large German minority in the Sudetenland had experienced a certain degree of discrimination, which fell far short of outright oppression. Czechoslovakia had a defensive pact with France, to which Britain was morally if not legally committed. The Soviet government was also pledged to come to the aid of the Czechs. Their government expressed its willingness to grant internal self-government to the Sudetens, but the Sudeten leader Konrad Henlein – egged on by Hitler – promptly upped his demands to the outright annexation by Germany of the whole region. On 12 September 1938, in a violent speech in Nuremberg, Hitler threatened imminent military action if the Czech government refused to cede the territory.

Edouard Daladier, the French Prime Minister, seemed ready to go to war in defence of the Czechs, provided Britain did the same, though his Cabinet was far from resolute. Chamberlain, who had earlier sent the British banker and former Liberal politician Lord Runciman to Prague, in an attempt to mediate, now sent a message to Hitler suggesting an immediate meeting to discuss a peaceful settlement. On 15 September he flew to Berchtesgaden – his first ever flight.

At Berchtesgaden, Chamberlain did little more than listen to a long rant by the Führer, who talked of the necessity of racial unity, boasted of his success in 'incorporating' the Austrian people into the Reich and stated that the 3 million Sudeten Germans must be similarly incorporated, and that Czechoslovakia must end its 'threatening military alliance' with Soviet Russia. Chamberlain made no attempt to counter Hitler's claims, saying merely that he would have to consult his Cabinet colleagues before giving a response. In the meantime, Hitler agreed to make no precipitate move. Chamberlain was not unduly impressed by the personality of Hitler, whom he later described to his Cabinet as 'the commonest little dog', and wrote to Ida: 'You would take him for the house painter he once was.' Nevertheless, he concluded, 'I got the impression that here was a man who could be relied upon when he had given his word.'

He returned to London in a complacent mood, confident that if the Czechs could be dragooned into accepting Hitler's demands all would be well. After assuring a somewhat restless Cabinet of his conviction that if Hitler was allowed to annex the Sudetenland that would mark the end of his ambitions, he met Daladier and his Foreign Minister, Georges Bonnet, who had travelled to London. It was a difficult encounter, lasting from before lunch until late in the evening, but finally the French duo was persuaded that they, too, should leave the Czechs in the lurch, despite their treaty commitments. At two o'clock the following morning the Czech President, Edvard Beneš, was summoned from his bed by the British and French ambassadors and was told that unless his government immediately agreed to Hitler's demands it would be abandoned to its fate. Faced with such overwhelming pressure, the Czechs felt they had no alternative but to give way.

Chamberlain returned for a second visit to Hitler, at Bad Godesberg on 22 September, confident of a warm reception, given that he was in a position to report acceptance of what he believed to be the Führer's demands. Not only the British, but the French and Czech governments were now agreeable, he said, to a peaceful and orderly transfer, under international supervision, of the territories with a German-speaking majority. He was appalled by Hitler's response, delivered in a tone of high hysteria. This was that there could be no question of international supervision: within a week German troops would enter an area marked on the map by Hitler himself (which would include 800,000 Czechs), and everything within the area must be handed over by the Czechs – not even a single cow might be removed. It was evident that Hitler was at least as much interested in a military triumph as in the acquisition of German-speaking territories. Chamberlain was shaken by Hitler's outburst, but undertook to transmit the terms to the Czech government, without recommending them. He returned to London to report back to the Cabinet.

Here he faced a rebellion, surprisingly led by the hitherto arch-appeaser Lord Halifax. The Foreign Secretary sharply contradicted Chamberlain's view that the Czechs should still be pressed to submit. He felt, he said, that Hitler 'was dictating terms as though he had won a war but without having to fight'. Halifax's arguments swung over a majority of the Cabinet, which was also influenced by mounting evidence that public opinion was swinging in favour of standing up to the German threats. The Cabinet reached no formal conclusions, but when it adjourned the general feeling was that if German troops were to enter Czechoslovakia Britain would have to join France in declaring war on Germany.

A naval mobilisation was ordered, and civil preparations for war proceeded apace, yet Chamberlain revealed just how little prepared he was to adopt the role of war leader by the hand-wringing broadcast he made on 27 September, when he said:

> How horrible, fantastic, incredible it is that we should be digging trenches and trying on gas masks here because of a quarrel in a far away country between people of whom we know nothing.

Yet even then, he did not give up trying. He dispatched Horace Wilson to Berlin to make a last despairing appeal to Hitler, and followed this up with a request to Mussolini to use his influence on his fellow dictator. In the midst of a fraught Cabinet meeting on 28 September, a relatively conciliatory message from Hitler was handed to Chamberlain, in which he insisted that German troops would march into the areas already conceded by the Czechs after the Berchtesgaden meeting, but that plebiscites should be held in the remaining areas. This was similar to a compromise plan already drawn up by Halifax, and it was agreed that Chamberlain should seek a further meeting with Hitler to clarify his intentions. Chamberlain then left for the Commons to address a House which fully expected that Britain would be at war within a few hours. In the midst of his speech, a further note arrived from Hitler announcing that he was convening a meeting in Munich the following day with Mussolini, and inviting Daladier and Chamberlain to attend. Chamberlain announced on the spot that he would accept the invitation, and the House responded with a great outpouring of relief and exaltation.

Early the following morning, Chamberlain, a tall incongruous figure, dressed in Edwardian clothing and clutching a rolled umbrella, boarded an aircraft at Heston aerodrome, to the west of London, accompanied by Horace Wilson, a clutch of officials and his Parliamentary Private Secretary, Lord Dunglass MP (subsequently rather better known as the Earl of Home or Sir

Alec Douglas-Home). The conference, from which the Czechs were rigorously excluded, started at 12.30 p. m. and continued, with lunch and dinner breaks, for about 14 hours. On paper, the agreement, which was eventually reached by the four leaders and signed in the early hours of 30 September, was less brutal than the terms laid down by Hitler at Bad Godesberg. The German occupation was staggered over ten days, instead of being effected on 1 October, and an international commission was to be set up to supervise the transfer of territories and to organise plebiscites in the disputed areas. In practice, it was to make little difference, as Hitler systematically flouted all the conditional elements in the agreement, which he tore up the following March when his troops occupied Prague and the rest of Czechoslovakia. The sole purpose of the agreement seems to have been to provide a figleaf for Daladier's and Chamberlain's sacrifice of Central Europe's only democratic state.

Chamberlain stayed on for a further meeting with Hitler, when he induced him to sign a vacuous declaration which stated that 'We regard the Agreement signed last night ... as symbolic of the desire of our two countries never to go to war with one another again.' This was the famous scrap of paper which he waved in the air on his arrival back in Heston, where he was greeted by an hysterical crowd, rejoicing that there would be no war.

Munich cost Chamberlain the resignation of the First Lord of the Admiralty, Duff Cooper, who joined the small band of anti-appeasement rebels led by Winston Churchill, but won him vast – if short-lived – popularity in the country. Munich subsequently became a dirty word in the English language, though Chamberlain continues to have his defenders, who argue that the agreement gave Britain a year's grace, and that it was in a better position to wage war one year later than it had been in 1938. This was no doubt true, but it is even more evident that the improvement in Germany's military might was far greater. The evidence is authoritatively examined by the historian Graham Stewart in *Burying Caesar: Churchill, Chamberlain and the Battle for the Tory Party*. His conclusion was that 'the justification for Munich seems threadbare' (Stewart, 1999, pp. 310–18).

The halo surrounding Chamberlain after Munich did not long survive. After the Kristallnacht pogrom in November 1938 it appeared quite tattered, and it was totally destroyed by the Nazi occupation of Prague four months later. The desperate and unrealistic guarantees that Chamberlain then gave to Poland and Romania were almost immediately negated by the failure to back them up with an agreement with the Soviet Union, whose signature of the Nazi-Soviet Pact on 23 August 1939 sounded the death knell for Poland, which was invaded by German troops nine days later. With evident reluctance, Chamberlain then declared war on Germany, after giving Hitler 48 hours to reconsider and withdraw his troops. He sought to enlarge his government by bringing in the Opposition Labour and Liberal parties, but they refused to serve under him. The inclusion of Winston Churchill, as First Lord of the Admiralty, and of Anthony Eden, as Dominions Secretary, was evidently intended as an assurance that the war would be conducted vigorously.

This was hardly the case; the period of 'phoney war' began, leading Chamberlain to make the unfortunate observation in April 1940 that Hitler had 'missed the bus'. Just over a month later, Chamberlain himself was forced to resign after a dramatic debate on a Labour censure motion. The government's majority fell from 240 to 81, with 41 Tories voting with the Opposition, and 60 others abstaining. Chamberlain made a final attempt to form a coalition government, but neither Labour nor the Liberals were prepared to serve, and he submitted his resignation, in the hope that Halifax would replace him (see next chapter). The censure debate had followed the disastrous Norwegian campaign, for which, ironically, Churchill bore the responsibility as First Lord. Chamberlain, however, attracted all the blame because of his utter failure to present himself as a convincing war leader.

He joined Churchill's government as Lord President, and proved a loyal and co-operative colleague, notably – though after some hesitation – joining Churchill and his two Labour colleagues in the five-man War Cabinet in rejecting Halifax's proposal to explore peace negotiations with Hitler. By then, cancer was creeping up on him and, after an unsuccessful operation in August, he resigned on 30 September. He died on 9 November, without any regrets, saying in one of his last letters, to Baldwin, 'Never for one instant have I doubted the rightness of what I did at Munich.'

It was as well for his peace of mind that he retained this certitude in his own judgement. For the appeasement policy was almost entirely his own project, pursued against the advice of top Foreign Office officials and without heed to occasional dissentient voices within his own Cabinet. Not that he was in the habit of seeking advice from his ministers, whom he regarded 'not as joint architects of policy but as executive officers called together from time to time to report what they were doing and to receive their instructions' (Williams, 1965, p. 161). Chamberlain was a true loner, who, according to his biographer, Keith Feiling, never had a single friend in whom he was able to confide. 'His family always excepted,' Feiling concluded, 'he did not depend on other human beings' (Feiling, 1946). Right up to the end, Chamberlain remained a man who communed only with his wife, his two adoring spinster sisters and the spirits of his dead father and brother.

Works consulted

Charmley, John, *Chamberlain and the Lost Peace*, London, Hodder & Stoughton, 1989.
Clarke, Peter, *A Question of Leadership*, Harmondsworth, Penguin, 1991.
Feiling, Keith, *The Life of Neville Chamberlain*, London, Macmillan, 1946.

Iremonger, Lucille, *The Fiery Chariot*, London, Secker & Warburg, 1970.

Jenkins, Roy, *The Chancellors*, London, Macmillan, 1998.

Macleod, Iain, *Neville Chamberlain*, London, Muller, 1961.

Stewart, Graham, *Burying Caesar: Churchill, Chamberlain and the Battle for the Tory Party*, London, Weidenfeld & Nicolson, 1999.

Williams, Francis, *A Pattern of Rulers*, London, Longman, 1965.

41
Winston Churchill – His Finest Hour

In all the other chapters of this book, the attempt has been made to deal, however briefly, with the main political events in the entire careers of the personalities discussed. In the case of Winston Leonard Spencer Churchill (1874–1965) this has proved impracticable – so long and varied was his career, and so many and great its vicissitudes, that such an approach would have been unrealistic within the tight space constraints of this volume. It has, accordingly, been decided to concentrate almost wholly on his wartime premiership, from 1940–45, and in particular on his contribution during the fateful year of 1940.

It is, however, necessary to consider the early circumstances of Churchill's life to understand the character of the man who became Prime Minister on 10 May 1940, at the age of 65. His father, Lord Randolph Churchill, a younger son of the 7th Duke of Marlborough, was a highly unstable figure and a demagogic politician, who became a youthful Chancellor of the Exchequer, only to resign from the post in a fit of pique after five months, in December 1886, dying nine years later at the age of 45 from syphilis. Lord Randolph was married to Jennie Jerome, the beautiful daughter of an American millionaire, whose fortune, sadly, proved to be insecurely based. A woman of easy virtue, who was to run through three husbands and a reputed 200 lovers, she was a glamorous but necessarily remote figure in the life of the young Winston, who was grievously neglected by both his parents.

This did not prevent him from idolising them. He doted on his mother from afar, and – as a young man – wrote a highly readable but unjustifiably laudatory biography of Lord Randolph. From his parents he inherited extravagant tastes, but not the financial means to support them – a gap he was largely able to fill by his amazing productivity as a journalist and author. An under-educated man, who was an indifferent pupil at his public school (Harrow), he nevertheless emerged with a deep love and knowledge of the English language, modelling his own style on the great rolling passages of the works of the historians Gibbon and Macaulay.

He also learnt early on that if he was to fan the flickering interest of his absent parents he must seize every opportunity to attract attention to himself. He grew up to be an exceptionally brash young man – a show-off, but one who was prepared to work diligently to obtain his objectives. He also became oblivious to personal danger, rushing round the world from one trouble spot to another in his search for glory and renown as a soldier and part-time journalist. This took him from Cuba to Sudan, the North-West Frontier and South Africa (where he escaped after being captured by the Boers) in the five years from 1895 to 1900, when he was elected for the first time as Tory MP for Oldham, at the age of 25.

The young Churchill had a pugnacious nature, but also a deeply romantic temperament. An ardent patriot, strongly committed to the British Empire, then straddling a quarter of the globe, he looked for inspiration to his warrior ancestor, John Churchill, the 1st Duke of Marlborough, of whom he was much later to write a four-volume biography, the success of which did much to ease the strain on his finances during the 1930s. Despite his traditional loyalties, he was by no means fixated on the past: he had an open, questing mind, which was ever seeking radical solutions to the problems of his own day. Intensely ambitious, he alienated many by his apparent self-absorption, though others were attracted by his vitality and zest for life. Among these was the 19-year-old Violet Asquith, whom he met at a dinner party in 1906, and who retained a vivid memory of their conversation nearly 60 years later, recalling that his final words were: 'We are all worms. But I do believe that I am a glow-worm' (Bonham Carter, 1995, p. 16). Beneath this braggadocio, however, lay a strong melancholy streak, which manifested itself in moods of dark depression, which he referred to as his 'black dog'.

Violet's father was also highly impressed by Churchill, bringing him into his Cabinet at the young age of 31, and promoting him to such senior offices as Home Secretary and First Lord of the Admiralty. Personally very fond of Winston, he was less uncritically admiring than his daughter and gradually lost his faith in his reliability, concluding in a letter to Lady Venetia Stanley in 1916:

> He will never get to the top in English politics, with all his wonderful gifts; to speak with the tongue of men and angels, and to spend laborious days and nights in administration, is no good if a man does not inspire trust.

Asquith's verdict in 1916 would surely have been repeated, in spades, by a large majority of politicians in the 1930s, particularly among his fellow Conservative MPs. A man who had changed his party affiliation twice, who was still widely if unjustly blamed for the Gallipoli disaster during the First World War, whose five-year term as Chancellor of the Exchequer during 1924–29 had been devoid of any lasting achievement, who had then wasted another five years of his life campaigning, in an unbridled way and alongside the most reactionary figures in his own party, against modest proposals to extend self-government in India, who had attacked his own party leaders with great ferocity, and had attempted a last-ditch stand in defence of King Edward VIII during the Abdication crisis, was regarded as 'unsound' if not completely off his head by all but a tiny group of admirers. Few observers would demur from the judgement of a later Tory MP and distinguished biographer, Robert Rhodes James, who entitled his book about his career up to 1939, *Churchill: A Study in Failure* (1970).

And yet one virtue of Churchill's was to weigh more in the scales than all his many failings – his clear-eyed view of the Nazi threat, which predated Hitler's rise to power in 1933, and which he tirelessly hammered home over the following six years to the great discomfort of his party leaders. This, despite the fact that he dearly wanted to resume his ministerial career, interrupted since 1929. Baldwin regretfully, but Chamberlain emphatically, refused to include him in their governments, even though the post of Minister of Supply, almost tailor-made for a man of his qualities, was created specifically to facilitate the rearmament programme.

When war broke out in September 1939, Chamberlain felt he had no choice but to broaden his government by bringing in Churchill, particularly as both the Labour and Liberal Parties had refused to serve under him. He became First Lord of the Admiralty, the post he had filled at the outset of the First World War, and a signal went out to all the ships of the fleet that 'Winston is back'. Chamberlain was pleasantly surprised to find him a co-operative and completely loyal colleague, who held himself aloof from any intrigue. It was, however, impossible to disguise the fact that he stood out as much the most combative member of the government, and his frequent and forceful broadcasts did much to rally national morale, while his personal popularity soared among the public at large, if not among Tory MPs.

He was virtually the only minister who pressed ideas for carrying the war forward aggressively against the enemy. As early as September 1939 he argued in favour of breaching Norwegian and Swedish neutrality by occupying or destroying the iron-ore fields in northern Sweden and cutting off vital supplies from the Germans through the Norwegian port of Narvik. His wider plans were not accepted, but the navy was eventually authorised to lay mines in Norwegian territorial waters, an action which was pre-empted by the German invasion in early April. Churchill then presided over a poorly planned and badly executed naval and military campaign to seize Narvik and other Norwegian ports. It was, ironically, the failure of this campaign which led to his replacing Chamberlain as Prime Minister.

Chamberlain's first reaction to the collapse of his majority in the censure debate on 7–8 May was to renew his invitation to the Labour and Liberal leaders to join a reconstructed government. Both again refused, but indicated that they would be prepared to serve under either Churchill or the Foreign Secretary, Lord Halifax. Halifax was a long-time opponent of Churchill, both as an appeaser and as an advocate of political reforms in India during his period as Viceroy, under the name of Lord Irwin, in 1926–31. He had overwhelming backing among Tory MPs and was the preferred choice of Chamberlain and of George VI. The fact that he was a member of the House of Lords was an inconvenience, but was not regarded as a serious obstacle, even by the Labour Party. It was, however, seized on by Halifax as the ostensible reason for declining the post. His real motivation was different – recalling the way in which the indecisive Asquith had been overshadowed and undermined by the more dynamic Lloyd George in the First World War, he feared that he would suffer the same fate if Churchill were to serve under him as Defence Minister, in fact if not in name. There is also some evidence that he thought that Churchill's tenure as Prime Minister would be short and unsuccessful, and that he would then be called upon to clear up the mess. For whatever reason, he bowed out when the premiership was his for the having, despite passionate entreaties from, among others, R.A. Butler, his Under-Secretary at the Foreign Office and Lord Dunglass (Alec Douglas-Home), Chamberlain's PPS, both of whom had been arch-appeasers.

Unlike Halifax, Churchill desperately wanted the premiership, and left a rather fanciful account in his war memoirs about how he had deliberately remained silent, when Chamberlain had asked him, during a quadripartite meeting with Halifax and the Tory Chief Whip, whether he saw any difficulty about the Prime Minister being in the House of Lords. Only when Halifax had definitely ruled himself out did Chamberlain decide that he should recommend Churchill to the King. This was on the evening of 9 May; on the following morning Hitler invaded Holland and Belgium, and Chamberlain tried to go back on his intended resignation – a move which was firmly squashed by senior ministers, notably the Air Minister, Sir Kingsley Wood, who was soon to be rewarded by Churchill with the post of Chancellor of the Exchequer.

At 6 p. m. on 10 May, Churchill was summoned to Buckingham Palace and accepted the commission to form a government. He returned to Whitehall, and worked, closeted with Attlee, until the early hours on the shape of his War Cabinet and other ministerial appointments. At 3 a.m., he at last went to bed, conscious, as he recalled in his memoirs, 'of a profound sense of relief' that he had obtained 'authority to give directions over the whole scene. I felt as if I were walking with destiny, and that all my life had been but a preparation for this hour and this trial.'

Lloyd George had said of Churchill: 'The two great qualities for a Prime Minister are patience and courage. Winston will be defective in patience.' It seemed a reasonable prediction, but was triumphantly refuted by Churchill's conduct during the first, difficult days of his premiership. In no respect was this clearer than in his handling of his dispossessed predecessor. Aware of the extreme weakness of his own position in the Conservative Party, Churchill set out to make a shield out of his former rival, and was determined to have him as a central figure in his small War Cabinet. Even in personal terms, he treated Chamberlain with great consideration, allowing him to continue to live in 10 Downing Street for a month while finding other accommodation. His first intention had been to make him both Chancellor of the Exchequer and Leader of the House of Commons, but this was vetoed by the Labour Party. In the end, Chamberlain settled for the most senior of the three sinecure offices – the Lord Presidency of the Council – in which capacity he was to chair important Cabinet committees and act as Churchill's deputy. Clement Attlee became Lord Privy Seal, and the deputy Labour leader, Arthur Greenwood, Minister without Portfolio. Halifax, who retained the Foreign Office, was the fifth member of this exclusive team.

Outside the Cabinet, senior posts were found for prominent Labour figures, such as Ernest Bevin, Herbert Morrison and Hugh Dalton, while A.V. Alexander succeeded Churchill as First Lord of the Admiralty. Most of the former Chamberlainite ministers were retained, though the least popular of them – Sir Samuel Hoare – was sacked and Sir John Simon was pushed up to the House of Lords as Lord Chancellor. The Liberal leader Sir Archibald Sinclair – a long-term associate of Churchill's – became Air Minister.

Churchill's first appearance in the House of Commons as Prime Minister underlined his lack of Conservative support. He was loudly cheered by Labour and Liberal members, but the Tories – who had a few minutes earlier given a hero's welcome to Chamberlain when he entered the Chamber – remained silent. They could not fail, however, to be impressed by the note of total defiance which he struck in the short statement he then made from the front bench – words which were to reverberate down the years:

> I would say to the House, as I said to those who have joined this government, that I have nothing to offer but blood, toil, tears and sweat. We have before us an ordeal of the most grievous kind ... You ask, what is our policy? I will say: it is to wage war, by sea, land and air, with all our might and with all the strength that God can give us: to wage war against a monstrous tyranny, never surpassed in the dark, lamentable catalogue of human crime. That is our policy. You ask, what is our aim? I can answer in one word: It is victory, victory at all costs, victory in spite of all terror, victory, however long and hard the road may be, for without victory, there is no survival.

The first fortnight of Churchill's premiership was filled with the most devastating news from the battlefronts in Belgium and France. The German army, superbly led, outflanked the Maginot Line and decisively broke through the

French defences at Sedan, while its panzer units raged through Belgium, reaching the Channel coast west of Dunkirk, cutting off the bulk of the British Expeditionary Force (BEF) and the French First Army. Then, on 24 May, Hitler – apparently unaccountably – halted General Guderian's forces which were rapidly advancing on Dunkirk. This fatal error probably cost him total victory in the war. Churchill and his government did not then believe that it would be possible to evacuate more than a tiny proportion of the troops who had been cut off, and thought that the bulk of the BEF would be carted off to prisoner of war camps.

At this moment – totally unknown to the British public – Churchill faced the greatest challenge to his leadership, as the War Cabinet debated – in nine meetings over three days (26–28 May) – whether, in effect, to seek a compromise peace with Germany. The initiative was taken by Halifax, who had had a lengthy interview with the Italian Ambassador, Giuseppe Bastianini. The ostensible purpose of the discussion was to determine what price, if any, Mussolini would demand to stay out of the war, instead of coming in on the German side, as was imminently expected. Yet behind this was a wider purpose – to seek to enlist the Italian dictator as a mediator with Hitler, with a view to a general settlement, which would enable Britain, as well as France, to withdraw from the conflict. Halifax proposed that a direct approach should now be made to Mussolini to assume this role.

Churchill was totally against making such a démarche, but – unsure of the balance of forces within the War Cabinet – made no attempt at the outset to squash Halifax's proposal, and allowed it to be argued out at length. It soon transpired that the two Labour men – Greenwood more volubly than Attlee – were on his side, whereas Chamberlain hovered on the fence, initially appearing to tend more towards Halifax. Churchill realised that a three-to-two division in his favour would not be sufficient, as in any open split Halifax and Chamberlain would be certain to carry with them the bulk of Conservative MPs, who them-selves constituted a sizeable majority in the Commons, leaving Churchill's position untenable. He gradually won Chamberlain round, and attempted to reinforce his stand by co-opting the Liberal leader, Archibald Sinclair, to join the discussions in the War Cabinet. When the Cabinet adjourned after the second of its three meetings on 27 May (the day the Belgians surrendered), the issue was still very much in doubt, with Halifax threatening to resign if he did not get his way. Churchill then took Halifax for a walk in the garden of 10 Downing Street, and used all his charm in a bid to keep his Foreign Secretary on board.

Churchill's crucial – and perhaps unpremeditated – move was his address to a meeting the following day of the most senior ministers outside the Cabinet. He recounted what happened in his war memoirs, reporting that, after he had said 'Of course whatever happens at Dunkirk, we shall fight on',

There occurred a demonstration which, considering the character of the gathering – twenty-five experienced politicians and Parliament men, who represented all the different points of view, whether right or wrong, before the war – surprised me. Quite a number seemed to jump up from the table and come running to my chair, shouting and patting me on the back.

This enthusiastic reception was fully confirmed in the published diaries of two of the participants of the meeting – Hugh Dalton (Labour) and Leo Amery (Conservative) – and word of it soon filtered back to the Cabinet room, which led Halifax to throw in the towel at the ensuing meeting – the last of the nine – which lasted a bare 20 minutes. Churchill made no reference to Halifax's peace initiative in his war memoirs, in which he made the extraordinary claim that:

> Future generations may deem it noteworthy that the supreme question of whether we should fight on alone never found a place upon the War Cabinet agenda. It was taken for granted and as a matter of course by these men of all parties of the State, and we were much too busy to waste time on such unreal, academic issues. (Churchill, 1949, Vol. II, p. 157)

Roy Jenkins described this as 'the most breathtakingly bland piece of misinformation to appear in all those six volumes' (Jenkins 2001, p. 610), and the truth only emerged many years later with the opening of the War Cabinet minutes under the Thirty Year Rule. The full story was finally told, in riveting detail, by the American historian, John Lukacs, in a brilliant short book, *Five Days in London, May 1940*, published in 1999. Churchill's motive in concealing it may well have been a chivalrous desire to protect the reputation of Halifax, whom he prudently replaced as Foreign Secretary by Anthony Eden in December 1940, dispatching him to Washington as Ambassador, where he proved a loyal interpreter of Churchill's policies for the remainder of the war.

Yet this episode was by far the most important in Churchill's entire premiership. It strongly suggests that if Halifax had accepted the premiership there would have been a negotiated peace with Hitler, with devastating consequences for the freedom of the world. And despite Chamberlain rallying, in the end, to Churchill's support, he also might well have sought peace if he had managed to carry on as Prime Minister (he had, already on 10 May, told the American Ambassador Joseph Kennedy that he did not see how Britain would be able to carry on if France dropped out of the war).

Less than a week after these anguished discussions, Churchill's position was immeasurably strengthened by the successful conclusion of the Dunkirk evacuation, with more than 338,000 British and allied troops brought back, although all their heavy equipment was left behind. This was the occasion for

one of Churchill's major parliamentary triumphs. 'Wars are not won by evacu-
ations', he told the Commons on 4 June, but went on to evoke with matchless
eloquence the newly evolving determination of the British people not to submit
to Hitler's will. His closing words have etched themselves on the collective
memory of succeeding generations:

> We shall not flag or fail. We shall go on to the end. We shall fight in France,
> we shall fight on the seas and the oceans, we shall fight with growing confi-
> dence and growing strength in the air, we shall defend our island, whatever
> the cost may be. We shall fight on the beaches, we shall fight on the landing
> grounds, we shall fight in the fields and in the streets, we shall fight in the
> hills, we shall never surrender, and even if, which I do not for a moment be-
> lieve, this island or a large part of it were subjugated and starving, then our
> Empire beyond the seas, armed and guarded by the British Fleet, would carry
> on the struggle, until, in God's good time, the new world with all its power
> and might, steps forth to the liberation of the old.

Churchill strove mightily during the next fortnight to keep France in the war,
despite the fall of Paris on 14 June. His last desperate throw was the proposal,
emanating from Jean Monnet, and approved in a few minutes by the War
Cabinet at a Sunday afternoon meeting on 16 June, to amalgamate the British
and French states in an 'indissoluble union'. De Gaulle flew to Bordeaux to take
the written proposal to the French government (having already telephoned the
contents to Prime Minister Paul Reynaud). Reynaud failed to carry it through
his Cabinet the same evening, and promptly resigned, leaving Pétain to seek
an armistice with the Germans. Churchill's response was to make another of
his magnificent orations to the House of Commons, full of echoes of Henry V's
speech before Agincourt:

> The battle of France is over. I expect that the battle of Britain is about to
> begin. Upon this battle depends the survival of Christian civilisation. Upon
> it depends our own British life and the long continuity of our institutions
> and our Empire ... Let us therefore brace ourselves to our duty and so bear
> ourselves that if the British Commonwealth and Empire last for a thousand
> years, men will still say, 'This was their finest hour'.

Yet Churchill had not finished with France. The peace agreement which
Pétain negotiated did not contain cast-iron guarantees that the powerful
French fleet would not fall into German or Italian hands. Churchill regarded
this as a life-or-death matter, and ordered British naval commanders to present
ultimata to the French squadrons in Alexandria (Egypt) and Oran (Algeria) to
submit or face attack. The French admiral in Alexandria complied, but not his

colleague in Oran, whose force was then largely destroyed, with the loss of 1300 lives.

This ruthless decision, which understandably caused lasting resentment in France, had the unforeseen effect of firing the enthusiasm of Tory MPs. Previously the bulk of them had reacted lukewarmly to his parliamentary speeches, but on this occasion the whole House responded in what Churchill later described as 'solemn, stentorian accord'. From then on – having demonstrated that he was an iron man of action and not just a purveyor of brave words – he no longer had to contend with the sullen resentment of his own party. A dwindling group of irreconcilables remained, but the great majority now counted themselves among his supporters.

For several more months, the nation remained in daily fear of a German invasion, but by the end of October, with the daytime Battle of Britain giving way to the nocturnal Blitz, the threat was effectively over. The Battle of Britain (which was the occasion of yet another Churchillian flourish – 'Never in the field of human conflict was so much owed by so many to so few') may in Roy Jenkins's words have been a 'draw' – in terms of actual aircraft losses – rather than the stunning victory it appeared at the time. Yet its outcome meant that there was no question of Germany gaining aerial supremacy which, given its naval weakness, was an essential condition for a successful invasion. Other dangers remained – notably the U-boat onslaught on the Atlantic shipping routes – but by then it was reasonably certain that Churchill's gamble had come off. If Britain, on its own, could not hope to inflict defeat on the Germans, it now seemed unlikely that the enemy would be able to conquer Britain.

That it had been a gamble is incontrovertible. In the dark days of May and June a more rational man would have accepted that the war was lost, and that the only sensible course was to get the best terms possible out of Hitler. This was the judgement that King Leopold and Marshal Pétain made, and both of them were applauded – at least in the short-term – by the bulk of their fellow countrymen. Nor had Churchill any solid basis for his belief that things were likely to improve. Halifax was pretty sure that they would not, and fumed in his private diary about Churchill 'talking the most frightful rot'. His biographer, Andrew Roberts, accurately interpreted his view by choosing 'Churchill as Micawber' as a chapter heading in his book, *The Holy Fox* (Roberts, 1997). The only 'something that will turn up' in Churchill's rosy-tinted vision at that time was American intervention on Britain's side, which, despite Churchill's friendly correspondence with President Franklin Roosevelt, was a distinctly remote prospect, particularly at a time when Roosevelt was seeking an unprecedented third term and declaring at an election meeting that 'Your boys are not going to be sent into any foreign wars.'

In truth, the only 'secret weapons' which Churchill had to deploy in 1940 were the force of his personality and the eloquence of his tongue. The first was evidenced by the way he galvanised his ministers, the armed forces and the Civil Service by his constant insistence on the urgency of the task. Every day a mass of memoranda flowed from Churchill's hand, many of them headed by the imperious instruction: 'ACTION THIS DAY'. As for his speeches, overblown and Baroque as they now often seem, and already sounding rather old-fashioned at the time, they struck a curious resonance with people of all classes. Their immediate impact in the House of Commons was amplified many times when they were repeated in BBC broadcasts. On his 80th birthday, Churchill modestly disclaimed the suggestion that he had inspired the nation in 1940, saying: 'It was the nation and the races dwelling all around the globe that had the lion heart. I had the luck to be called upon to give the roar.' That was to understate his role, and he knew it. Without Churchill, it must be doubted whether the British would have summoned up the determination to resist after the disasters of May and June.

A serious argument could be made that Churchill's unique contribution was completed by the end of 1940, and that if he had then died or been replaced by a more run-of-the-mill leader, it would have made no more than a marginal difference to the outcome of the war. For it was not won by Churchill's leadership, nor primarily by feats of British arms, but by Hitler's megalomania and grievous errors of judgement which brought both Russia and America into the war against him, ultimately ensuring his defeat.

Essential or not, Churchill continued to play a prominent role, not quite until the end of the war, but up to and beyond the final defeat of Germany in May 1945. For him, it was an all-absorbing task, to which he untiringly devoted himself – as if in a trance – at any hour of the day or night, to the continual exasperation of his hard-pressed staff. Lord Alanbrooke, for example, the Chief of the Imperial General Staff, described him in his war diaries as 'the most difficult man to work for I have ever struck ... lives for the impulse and for the present'. He concluded, however, 'I would not have missed the chance of working for him for anything on Earth.' Churchill was forever pressing ideas on the general staff – many of them half-baked if not fantastical – for new initiatives and campaigns – and they often had the greatest difficulty in restraining his enthusiasm. He had no inhibitions in abruptly replacing unsuccessful field commanders, but though he argued fiercely with his general staff, he was never known – in contrast to Hitler – to overrule them. He assumed the title of Minister of Defence, and, after the first few months, the War Cabinet, the size of which was considerably expanded, had little influence on the political direction of the war. For all intents and purposes, Churchill was the man in charge.

In domestic affairs it was a different matter. Churchill took very little interest in day-to-day decisions, and, for the most part, it was the Labour members of his Cabinet that made the running, particularly Ernest Bevin, the Minister for Labour, and Home Secretary Herbert Morrison. Overall co-ordination was left to his highly efficient deputy premier, Clement Attlee, who presided over the Cabinet during his frequent absences abroad. Ellen Wilkinson, a Labour Party minister, left a graphic description of their contrasting styles:

> When Mr Attlee is presiding over the Cabinet in the absence of the Prime Minister the Cabinet meets on time, goes systematically through its agenda, makes the necessary decisions, and goes home after three or four hours' work. When Mr Churchill presides we never reach the agenda and we decide nothing. But we go home to bed at midnight, conscious of having been present at an historic occasion. (cited in Martin, 1969)

Throughout his premiership, Churchill attached exceptional importance to fostering his relationship with Roosevelt. He later told his private secretary, Jock Colville, 'No lover ever studied every whim of his mistress, as I did those of President Roosevelt.' His attempts to lure him to enter the war prior to the Japanese attack on Pearl Harbor, in December 1941, proved fruitless, but Roosevelt did approve the deal, in September 1940, to send Britain 50 old destroyers in exchange for base facilities in the West Indies, and after his re-election as President a steady stream of military supplies were sent across the Atlantic. Their first meeting, at sea in August 1941, led to the signing of the Atlantic Charter, a joint declaration of 'war aims', despite the continuing neutrality of the US. After December 1941 their correspondence became an almost daily affair, they met a further eight times, and spent a total of 120 days in each other's company. Jointly they planned the strategy for the war in the West, and it was only after D-Day, in June 1944, that it became clear that Britain was the junior partner, as the American military contribution was so much greater. Churchill's influence on the American President then declined as the latter began to give more weight to Stalin's views.

Churchill himself made strenuous efforts to establish the same rapport with the Soviet leader that he enjoyed with the US President – with only limited success. He flew to Moscow in October 1944, and reached an agreement with him on 'spheres of influence' in Eastern Europe and the Balkans. Under this agreement, Greece fell within the British sphere, and not a word of protest was received from Stalin when British forces suppressed a Communist-led uprising in Athens, in December 1944. In exchange, Stalin expected a free hand in Eastern Europe, despite giving undertakings that the right to free elections would be respected, notably in Poland, the borders of which were drastically redrawn, in Russia's favour, at the Yalta conference in February 1945. By then, Churchill was seriously alarmed at the prospect of Soviet dominance, and tried – without success – to persuade the allied commander, General Eisenhower, to abandon his plans for a broad advance and to make a dash for Berlin to seize the city in advance of the Soviet troops.

Great war leader though he was, Churchill was no master strategist, and the historian A.J.P. Taylor identified three major strategic errors in his conduct of the war. First was the decision to concentrate on heavy bombing of German towns and cities, which he was convinced would bring German war production to a halt. It had no such effect, despite the killing of over half a million Germans. The cost to the allied cause was, Taylor argued, even greater, with production being diverted to the construction of heavy bombers, and the substantial losses of aircraft and aircrew. Mistake number two was what he described as Churchill's 'obsession with the Mediterranean and the Middle East'. Essentially a sideshow, he argued, 'it postponed any landing in northern France for two years and so helped to prolong the war' (Taylor, 2000). His third major error was grossly to underestimate the risk of an attack by the Japanese, and to neglect to strengthen the defences of Singapore.

Churchill had his critics at the time, but there is no doubt that the vast majority of the British public heartily approved his conduct of the war, and an opinion poll in April 1945 showed 91 per cent support. Yet three months later, at the general election of 5 July, he was heavily defeated in a general election, and his party suffered its biggest setback since 1906. This was only very partially due to his maladroit election campaign, in which, during a broadcast, he caused widespread indignation by accusing the Labour leaders, who had loyally served with him throughout his premiership, of planning to introduce a 'Gestapo' if they were elected. What brought Churchill down was his association with the Conservative Party, which had become deeply unpopular and was blamed not only for the failed appeasement policy, but also for the unemployment and economic failures of the 1930s. It could also be argued that the British electorate showed rare discrimination in deciding that, though his leadership in war had been indispensable, he was not the best person to lead the country in post-war reconstruction.

Clementine Churchill, who normally gave her husband good advice, wanted him to retire at this point, but he insisted on carrying on as Leader of the Opposition, though he attended to his duties very spasmodically, preferring to devote his energies to writing his six volumes of war memoirs, and giving a series of set speeches to international audiences, in which he spelled out the danger of Soviet expansionism and preached the gospel of European unity. He became Prime Minister for a second time, at the age of 76, having narrowly won the 1951 general election. Little remained of his wartime dynamism, and he settled for a quiet life, making no attempt to reverse the widespread reforms introduced by the 1945 Labour government, even though they had – for the most part – been strenuously opposed by Tory MPs. His health was bad, and he might well have given up after a year or so, but the death of Stalin, in March 1953, persuaded him that the opportunity existed to assure world peace through a three-way summit between himself, President Eisenhower and

Stalin's successor, and that only he could bring this about. It was an illusion, but Churchill carried on until April 1955, despite having had in July 1953 a severe stroke, which had been carefully hidden from the public. He then, clearly reluctantly, made way for Anthony Eden, to whom he had originally promised the succession as long ago as June 1940.

He remained an MP until October 1964, dying, full of honours, three months later. By this time, this once highly controversial figure had long since been almost universally recognised as 'the greatest living Englishman', if not of all time. Nor has this view been greatly modified in the half-century since his death, despite the appearance in 1993 of a hostile 'revisionist' biography by the historian John Charmley. Churchill may have been a man of monumental faults, but without him it is open to doubt whether hundreds of millions of Britons and other Europeans would be living in liberty today.

Principal works consulted

Addison, Paul, 'Winston Churchill', in John P. Mackintosh (ed.), *British Prime Ministers of the Twentieth Century*, Vol. II, London, Weidenfeld & Nicolson, 1978.

Bonham Carter, Violet, *Winston Churchill as I Knew Him*, London, Weidenfeld & Nicolson, 1995.

Charmley, John, *Churchill: The End of Glory*, London, Hodder & Stoughton, 1993.

Churchill, Winston S., *The Second World War*, Vol. I, *The Gathering Storm*, Vol. II, Their Finest Hour, London, Cassell, 1948, 1949.

Clarke, Peter, *A Question of Leadership*, London, Penguin Books, 1991.

Gilbert, Martin, *Winston S. Churchill 1939–1941*, Vol. VI, London, Heinemann, 1984.

Gilbert, Martin, *Winston S. Churchill 1941–1945*, Vol. VII, London, Heinemann, 1986.

Jenkins, Roy, *Churchill*, London, Macmillan, 2001.

Lukacs, John, *Five Days in London*, May 1940, New Haven and London, Yale University Press, 1999.

Martin, Kingsley, *Harold Laski*, London, Cape, 1969.

Pearson, John, *The Private Lives of Winston Churchill*, New York, Simon & Schuster, 1991.

Roberts, Andrew, *Eminent Churchillians*, London, Weidenfeld & Nicolson, 1994.

Roberts, Andrew, *The Holy Fox*, London, Weidenfeld & Nicolson, 1997.

Stewart, Graham, *Burying Caesar: Churchill, Chamberlain and the Battle for the Tory Party*, London, Weidenfeld & Nicolson, 1999.

Taylor, A.J.P., *British Prime Ministers and Other Essays*, Harmondsworth, Penguin, 2000.

42

Clement Attlee – Quiet Revolutionary

Clement Richard Attlee was born nine years later than Winston Churchill, in 1883, and came from rather lower down the social scale. Instead of Blenheim Palace, he was born in a solid middle-class house near Putney Hill. Yet he had a better start in life than the man he was to succeed as Prime Minister 62 years later. He was raised in a loving and stable family which had no financial worries, as his father, Henry Attlee, was a prosperous City solicitor. A God-fearing man, who took family prayers each morning before breakfast, he was a Gladstonian Liberal of advanced views, who was a 'pro-Boer' during the South African War. Clement's mother, Ellen, was a cultured and educated woman, who apparently found complete fulfilment in looking after her husband and their family of five boys and three girls. Unlike her husband, she was Conservative, with both a large and a small 'c'.

Clem, as he became known, was the second youngest child. He was undersized (as he was to remain so as an adult), and was regarded as too fragile to go to school until the age of nine, being educated at home by his mother and a series of governesses. One of these, Miss Hutchinson, had, by an astonishing coincidence, earlier had charge of the young Winston. It soon became clear that Clem was a clever boy, who immersed himself in books and developed a great love for poetry, dreaming of one day becoming a poet himself. He was, in fact, to write quite a lot of poetry, none of it above the 'good amateur' level, but mostly leavened with a mordant wit. He early developed a passionate interest in cricket, which he was to retain throughout his life, though he was an indifferent player, and the only 'sport' in which he ever gained any proficiency was billiards.

Clem was always particularly close to his brother Tom, who was two years his senior. Both were sent to a public school, Haileybury, then notorious for its bullying, which made a misery of Tom's life. Clem, however, despite his puny stature, seems to have remained unscathed, and formed a lifelong affection for his old school. He was to follow Tom to Oxford, where he studied modern history, specialising in the Italian Renaissance, and narrowly missed getting a

First Class degree. He attended some debates in the Oxford Union, but, in his own words, 'was much too shy to try to speak there' (Attlee, 1954). If he had, it would have been as a Tory, and to all appearances he was a thoroughly conventional young man.

Attlee came down from Oxford in 1904, after what he described as 'three exceedingly happy years'. He began to read for the bar, while living at his parents' home in Putney, and, having passed his exams without difficulty, joined the chambers of Sir Henry Dickens, the son of the novelist. Like other young barristers, he found that few briefs came his way, and he passed his time, pleasantly enough, by learning to ride, practising billiards and taking part in a literary society founded by his brother Tom. 'This then', he recalled in his autobiography, 'was the pattern of my days when in October 1905, an event occurred which was destined to alter the whole course of my life' (Attlee, 1954, p. 18).

This was his discovery of the East End of London, then mired in the most abject poverty and misery. He went to work for one evening a week at Haileybury House, a centre in the Limehouse area of Stepney, maintained by his old school, which ran a boys' club and cadet corps for youngsters in one of the most deprived districts. The painfully shy Clem found that he could unwind in the face of the warm reception which he received from the boys and his fellow voluntary workers. Soon he was going there on two evenings a week, then three and then four, and it became the main focus of his life. In 1907 the club manager resigned and Attlee was invited to take his place, which involved living on the premises. He accepted, and, he recalled, 'Thus began fourteen years' residence in East London' (Attlee, 1954).

His brother Tom, an architect, was similarly involved in helping out at a hostel in nearby Hoxton, and the two brothers – influenced by reading the works of writers such as John Ruskin and William Morris, became declared Socialists. Attlee always claimed, however, that the reason why he became a Socialist was the conditions of life in Limehouse. He recalled an occasion when he passed a little barefoot girl in the street, who asked him: 'Where are you going, Mr Attlee?' He replied: 'I'm going home for tea', and she responded: 'Oh, I'm going home to see if there is any tea' (Attlee, 1954, p. 31).

Clem and Tom hastened to seek membership of the Fabian Society, and attended a meeting addressed by Bernard Shaw, Sidney Webb and other famous luminaries, including H.G. Wells, whom he found 'very unimpressive'. The others, however, 'all seemed pretty impressive', and Attlee was rather overawed. More to his taste was the local Stepney branch of the Independent Labour Party (ILP), to which he was taken by an East End wharf-keeper called Tommy Williams. What Attlee liked about the ILP – apart from their warm comradeship – was the essentially ethical appeal of the socialism they preached. It was, he recalled, 'a way of life rather than an economic dogma' (Attlee, 1954).

They were only about a dozen strong – all working men – but were highly active and organised three or four open-air meetings a week at street corners. Attlee, who was soon elected as branch secretary, threw himself into their work, performing all the most menial duties, including carrying round the tiny platform on which the street orators spoke.

He dreaded the day when he himself would be asked to perform, but when it came – on a dark night in March 1908 in Barnes Street, just off the Commercial Road – he finally overcame his shyness and got up to speak before an audience of five – all fellow members of the ILP. He was not very good, his voice carried badly, but finally about a dozen people turned up and asked questions, to which he was able to give well-informed and evidently sincere replies. He was soon much in demand, speaking at 53 indoor and outdoor meetings in 1909, and 88 in the following year.

During the daytime, he continued to go to his chambers, but he became progressively more bored with the law and hankered after doing more socially useful work. He quit the chambers in 1908, when his father died, leaving him a private income of £400 a year. He worked for some time as an organiser for Beatrice Webb's National Committee for the Break-Up of the Poor Law, and then as an 'official explainer' for the new National Insurance law introduced by the Liberal government. Then, in 1912, what he regarded as the ideal job became available, when he was appointed a lecturer in Social Policy at the newly established London School of Economics. His unsuccessful rival for the post was Hugh Dalton, whom he was to appoint as Chancellor of the Exchequer 33 years later. Attlee found the work intellectually satisfying, and it left him full freedom to carry on his work at Haileybury House and his political activities with the ILP. At this stage, he had no notion of a political career – his highest aspiration was to be elected to the Stepney Borough Council or the Limehouse Board of Guardians, for each of which he was twice an unsuccessful candidate.

In August 1914 he was on holiday in Devon with Tom and his wife. When war was declared both men decided unhesitatingly what they should do. Tom, who was a Christian Socialist, resolved to be a conscientious objector and served two harsh prison sentences during the war. Clem, an atheist though never a militant one, decided to volunteer at the earliest possible moment. Within a month, despite his age (31) and his slight stature, he was commissioned with the South Lancashire Regiment. He served throughout the war – in Gallipoli, from which he was evacuated with severe dysentery, but insisted on returning and commanded the rearguard which covered the final retreat, being the last person but one to leave the peninsula, in Mesopotamia, where he was seriously wounded by 'friendly fire', and finally on the Western Front.

Major C.R. Attlee was demobilised in January 1919, and within two days was back in Stepney discussing the political situation with a local Jewish chemist, Oscar Tobin, who had emerged as the *de facto* Labour leader in the borough. Much had changed in Attlee's absence, with the establishment of a strong Stepney Labour Party and Trades Council, to which the local ILP branch was now affiliated. Tobin, aware that Attlee's war record would make him electorally popular, while his independent status would make him equally acceptable to the rival Irish and Jewish factions within the local Labour Party, strongly urged him to run in the forthcoming election for the London County Council. Attlee fought the Limehouse seat and was narrowly defeated, but when, in the following November, the Labour Party swept to victory in the Stepney Borough Council elections, he was nominated as Mayor, and subsequently became an Alderman. Fifteen other Labour mayors were elected in London, and Attlee was chosen as their chairman and spokesman, his fame beginning to spread more widely in the Labour movement. His mayoral year – in which he provided strong intellectual and political leadership to the Council in all its activities – was regarded as an unequivocal success. In the meantime, he was adopted as Labour's prospective candidate for the parliamentary constituency of Limehouse, then a Tory-held seat.

The general election did not come until November 1922, following Bonar Law's replacement of Lloyd George as Prime Minister. By that time, Attlee was able to face the voters as a married man. In the summer of 1921, he had planned a holiday in Italy with an old Oxford friend of Tom's, Edric Miller, who asked if his mother and younger sister Violet could come as well. Within six months Clem and Vi were married. He was 39, she 26. It was a happy and successful union, though Vi had virtually no interest in politics. She nevertheless invariably acted as a 'teller' for Clem at his election counts, and much later acquired some notoriety as his chauffeur during his nationwide election tours.

Attlee was elected with a comfortable majority, and was one of 142 Labour MPs who were recognised as the official Opposition for the first time. Their initial task was to elect a new leader. Together with all the other ILP MPs, Attlee backed Ramsay MacDonald against the previous leader, J.R. Clynes, a choice they were later to regret. As leader, MacDonald chose two Parliamentary Private Secretaries, one of whom was Major Attlee, as he continued to be known for some time. A year later, after the 1923 election, in which he more than doubled his majority, he was appointed as Under-Secretary of State for War in the minority Labour government. This survived for less than a year, but long enough for him to acquire a reputation as one of its more effective junior ministers.

In Opposition for the next five years, he was appointed as one of two Labour members of the Commission led by Sir John Simon, set up to consider constitutional development in India, which involved two lengthy visits to the sub-continent. Before accepting, he sought and received an assurance from MacDonald that this would not preclude his inclusion in a future Labour government, and he was bitterly disappointed when MacDonald reneged on this promise when he formed his second administration in June 1929. Attlee had only just returned from India in time to fight the election, and for several months afterwards he was involved in writing the voluminous report of the Commission, of which he had been much the most active member, apart from the chairman. It proposed substantial advances towards self-government at the provincial level, but fell short of recommending full Dominion status. Attlee's membership of the Commission greatly stimulated his interest in both India and Burma and undoubtedly contributed to the decisiveness he showed in pressing forward with their independence in 1947.

In May 1930, Attlee finally entered the government, replacing Sir Oswald Mosley, who had resigned as Chancellor of the Duchy of Lancaster in protest against the government's lack of energy in tackling unemployment. In this sinecure office, Attlee's duties included organising the 1930 Imperial Conference, which produced the Statute of Westminster, formally recognising the independence of the Dominions, as well as piloting an agriculture bill through the Commons. In March 1931, he was appointed Postmaster-General, and amazed his colleagues by taking a crash course in management, the better to be able to administer his new department.

When, in the following August, the Labour government resigned and was replaced by a National Government under MacDonald's premiership, Attlee was emphatically not one of the handful of Labour MPs who were tempted to follow their former leader. Indeed, he characterised MacDonald's action as 'the greatest betrayal in the political history of this country' (Attlee 1954, p. 74). In the general election which followed, two months later, the Labour Party was all but destroyed, going down from 287 to 46 MPs. The new Labour leader, Arthur Henderson, was defeated, as was every other former Cabinet minister except the 72-year-old George Lansbury. Attlee just held on to his seat at Limehouse, in contrast to near contemporaries such as Herbert Morrison, Arthur Greenwood and Hugh Dalton, all of whom were senior to him in the party or ministerial hierarchy. The consequence was that, when the sadly diminished group of Labour MPs gathered together after the election, they unanimously chose Lansbury and Attlee as leader and deputy leader respectively.

During the next four years, Attlee carried a very considerable load. He often had to deputise for the ailing Lansbury, and their small flock was mostly elderly and undistinguished. Only Sir Stafford Cripps, the former Solicitor-General, and the youthful Aneurin Bevan were major forces in debate. Attlee had to acquire a total mastery of parliamentary procedure, and be prepared to speak on a large range of subjects with which he had previously been unfamiliar. 'In 1932', he recalled, 'I filled more columns of Hansard than any other Member and, as I am generally considered to be rather a laconic speaker, it can be judged that my interventions in Debate were numerous' (Attlee, 1954, p. 77). Then, in October 1935, shortly before the general election, Lansbury, who as a pacifist was unable to back the party's policy of armed sanctions in support of the

League of Nations, resigned, and Attlee was elected in his place. He was not expected to serve as leader for more than a few months: he stayed for 20 years.

The general election, held on 14 November, saw only a partial Labour recovery, but 154 Labour MPs were returned, including many leading figures defeated in 1931. It was generally expected that one of these would take Attlee's place. Two were nominated – Arthur Greenwood, who had been Health Minister in the 1929 government, and Herbert Morrison, the ex-Transport Minister, who had recently won greater renown as the energetic leader of the London County Council (LCC). The results of the two ballots were as shown in the table below.

Attlee	58	88
Morrison	44	48
Greenwood	33	–

It was generally supposed that Attlee won primarily because the survivors of the 1931 Parliament voted almost en bloc in his favour. Another explanation was given to me many years ago by John Parker, who was elected in 1935 as a 27-year-old new MP. Morrison, he recounted, was asked at the party meeting if he would give up the leadership of the LCC if he was chosen, and declined to do so. This went down badly, and in his opinion cost Morrison the leadership. Whatever the reason, Morrison subsequently nursed a lasting grievance against Attlee, which surfaced in 1945 when he attempted, without success, to deprive him of the premiership.

The 1935 leadership election was significant for sowing the seeds of a future alliance between Attlee and Ernest Bevin. Bevin, the most powerful trade union leader at the time, had treated Attlee somewhat patronisingly, referring to him as 'the little man', but he regarded Morrison with monumental distrust. When Greenwood, who had been backed primarily by trade union MPs, dropped out of the race, his supporters, many of them influenced by Bevin, nearly all switched their votes to Attlee.

Attlee was an assiduous Leader of the Opposition, but made little mark in the country. He firmly opposed Chamberlain's appeasement policy, but his position was undermined because of Labour's reluctance to support the government's rearmament programme. The party rebuffed Chamberlain's invitation to join his government in September 1939 and again in May 1940, but then indicated its willingness to serve under another Prime Minister, which provoked Chamberlain's resignation. Attlee joined the War Cabinet as Lord Privy Seal, and after Chamberlain withdrew from the government in September, became Churchill's deputy and chief co-ordinator of domestic policy throughout the remainder of the war until May 1945.

It was not an easy role to play, and Attlee was constantly caught between the fears of the more right-wing Tory ministers that he was using his position to foist socialistic policies on the government, and those of outside Labour critics, notably Aneurin Bevan, who thought he was not doing nearly enough in this direction. Insiders soon concluded that his was a rare voice of calm and common sense in a highly volatile team, and that he was an indispensable ally and support of Churchill in his prosecution of the war. He was, however, essentially a behind-the-scenes figure, and was far less in the limelight than other Labour ministers, such as Bevin, Morrison and Stafford Cripps.

In May 1945, when the coalition was dissolved after the German surrender, there were those – particularly among Morrison's supporters – who pressed the case for a more high-profile leader to take Labour into the general election campaign. They included Ellen Wilkinson (widely believed to be Morrison's mistress), who was the retiring chairman of Labour's national executive committee, and Harold Laski, who succeeded her in that position at the party conference held later in the month. Laski, a left-wing political science professor at the London School of Economics, promptly wrote a long letter to Attlee asking him to stand down 'for the good of the party'. This provoked one of his famous staccato replies: 'Dear Laski, Thank you for your letter, contents of which have been noted. C.R. Attlee.'

In the election campaign, while Churchill embarked on a triumphal procession with a vast train of followers, Attlee's sole entourage was his wife Vi, who drove him on a nationwide tour in the family Hillman saloon. Everywhere he went, he received a thunderous reception, but – like nearly all other senior Labour figures apart from Aneurin Bevan – Attlee never believed he had a chance of defeating the mighty Winston. This despite the fact that a little-noticed Gallup Poll, published in the *News Chronicle*, was predicting a Labour landslide. Even the *News Chronicle* itself ignored the poll, suggesting that the result would be 'a near stalemate'.

In direct exchanges with Churchill during the campaign, Attlee was generally judged to have come out best. In a wild election broadcast, Churchill had gone over the top, predicting that a Labour government would adopt 'Gestapo' methods. Attlee's quiet, dignified but highly effective reply won him many plaudits. When the votes were finally counted on 26 July (three weeks after polling day in order to allow votes to come in from servicemen overseas), they produced a stunning Labour victory and the worst defeat for the Conservatives since 1906. The new House of Commons was comprised as shown in the table below.

Labour	393
Conservative	213
Liberal	12
Others	22
Total	640

According to election expert David Butler:

> Labour had won not because of the campaign but because the visible success of planning and 'fair shares' during the war, together with the proven competence of Labour ministers during five years of coalition government, had already made Labour seem more appealing than the Conservatives. Many in the intellectual and middle classes were disillusioned with a party that was associated with unemployment and appeasement as well as the other real and supposed failures of the inter-war period. (Butler, 1989, p. 9)

Attlee and Churchill had been attending the Potsdam summit with Stalin and Harry Truman, which was adjourned to allow them to return to Britain for the election results. Prompted by Bevin, the Labour leader ignored a last-ditch attempt by Morrison to force a new leadership election by Labour MPs before going to Buckingham Palace to meet George VI, following Churchill's resignation. The King asked him if he had yet decided on his main ministerial choices. He replied that he had not, but was thinking of Dalton for the Foreign Office and Bevin for the Exchequer. The King, who, unknown to Attlee, had a deep personal prejudice against Dalton, suggested that he was not the best man for the job proposed. Attlee subsequently denied that he had been influenced by the King, but, nevertheless, reversed his initial intention. Morrison, who had threatened not to serve, accepted the Leadership of the House of Commons, with responsibility for controlling the enormous legislative programme foreshadowed by the Labour election manifesto, *Let Us Face the Future*. Stafford Cripps was appointed President of the Board of Trade. Rather to their surprise, Attlee also included in the Cabinet two of his most persistent critics, Bevan becoming Minister of Health and Ellen Wilkinson, Minister of Education.

The government formed by Attlee faced bigger and more extensive challenges than any other peacetime administration, before or since. They were, essentially, five in number:

1. post-war reconstruction
2. building the welfare state
3. extending public ownership
4. confronting the Soviet threat
5. decolonisation.

Mistakes, sometimes serious ones, were made, under all five headings, perhaps most seriously over Palestine, but the verdict of history seems to be that they succeeded beyond all reasonable expectations, and the general consensus (apart from a few far right commentators, such as John Charmley and Corelli Barnett) is that this was one of, if not the most, successful peacetime governments of the twentieth century. Many of the changes made were highly controversial at the time, and were fiercely opposed by the Conservative Party. But, when it returned to power, in 1951, it made no serious attempt to reverse them, and the pattern established by the Attlee government, of a mixed economy with universal welfare entitlements, remained essentially untouched until the Thatcher and Major years, more than a generation later.

The stereotypical view of Attlee as an insignificant figure who presided over a Cabinet of powerful personalities, his own personal contribution being confined to keeping them on speaking terms with each other, is a caricature. It is true that he allowed Bevin enormous latitude in his conduct of foreign affairs, that – conscious of his own ignorance in this field – he took a back seat to Dalton, Cripps and, later, Hugh Gaitskell in guiding economic policy, and that Morrison was the undisputed manager of the legislative programme. Yet he kept a tight grip over the Cabinet, making sure that decisions were taken in good time and in proper order and proved a ruthless 'butcher' of ministers who failed to match up to his exacting standards (as Dalton discovered when he was forced to resign over a trivial and completely harmless Budget leak). When he decided to intervene personally, he did so with great decisiveness. It was his decision to press ahead speedily with Burmese and Indian independence, and – less wisely – to build an 'independent' British atomic bomb when the US government went back on its wartime undertaking to share its nuclear secrets with Britain. He and Bevin forced the decision through, amidst great secrecy, and despite the formidable opposition of both Dalton and Cripps. When, at a critical juncture in the Korean War – in December 1950 – there was widespread apprehension that the US would resort to nuclear weapons or invade Chinese territory, he decided at short notice to fly to Washington (Bevin being too ill to fly) to try to exercise a restraining influence on President Truman. He received a warm welcome, and his wise counsel possibly played a part in emboldening the President to dismiss his insubordinate commander, General Douglas MacArthur, a few months later.

In the House of Commons it was widely anticipated that he would be no match for Churchill, but more often than not he got the better of their exchanges – his dry, authoritative, clipped responses regularly puncturing the overblown rhetoric of a master platform performer whose style was ill-adapted to the mundanities of parliamentary debate. Attlee was also valued for the strong and consistent support which he gave his ministers when they got into conflict with vested interests in implementing Labour policies. This was notably the case with Aneurin Bevan in his prolonged struggle with the British Medical Association over the introduction of the National Health Service. Attlee also showed good nerves and sharp tactical skills in seeing off plots, on two occasions in 1947, to replace him as Prime Minister by Ernest Bevin. Dalton and Cripps, with backing from George Brown on the back benches, were the chief conspirators. Morrison remained aloof: he would no doubt have welcomed a change at the top, but only if he were to be the beneficiary. If Bevin had been a willing participant, the plots might have succeeded, but he angrily repulsed his would-be sponsors, saying: 'What's Clem ever done to me? Who do you think I am? Lloyd George?'

Attlee's overriding preoccupation throughout his premiership was to ensure that every last proposal in Labour's 1945 election manifesto should be carried through. In the past, governing parties had almost invariably ignored most of the specific promises they had made, regarding their manifestos more as 'mood music' rather than as blueprints for action. This, Attlee regarded as a betrayal of the voters' trust, and he was determined to set a new and higher standard for the future – an objective which he triumphantly achieved, even at the cost of a certain desirable flexibility.

A fat slab of the Labour programme derived from the famous Beveridge Report, of 1942, which set out a prospectus for slaying what the author described as the five giants of Want, Disease, Ignorance, Squalor and Idleness. Three essential ingredients, Beveridge argued, were a free National Health Service, child allowances and full employment. The report was welcomed by all three parties in the wartime coalition. It must be doubted, however, in the light of the obstruction which Tory MPs mounted against many of the Labour proposals, whether Beveridge would have been implemented by a Conservative government if Churchill had won the 1945 election. Certainly, it is improbable that they would have carried it through with such enthusiasm, and in such amplitude, as was shown by Labour ministers, particularly in the four great pieces of legislation which came into force in July 1948 – the National Insurance Act, the Industrial Injuries Act, the National Assistance Act and the NHS Act.

Labour's welfare state legislation, together with its educational and taxation policies, were credited with going a long way to wiping out poverty and to fostering a peaceful social revolution which transformed the lives of the bulk of the British population. At the time, it established a level of public welfare clearly superior to that of other economically advanced societies, with the possible exceptions of Sweden and New Zealand. Unfortunately, subsequent governments failed to develop and refine the system, so that 50 years later it was still substantially unchanged, but was creaking along, grievously underfinanced and providing levels of service markedly worse than in most of Britain's partners within the European Union. It was also the subject of a biting attack by Corelli Barnett, who argued in his book, *The Lost Victory* (1995), that Britain in the post-war era simply could not afford to create a welfare state. The obvious retort is that it could not afford *not* to do so, and that – given the high hopes raised during the war, and the promises made – it was a political imperative to move forward. The financial cost was, of course, considerable, but it was met by substantially retaining, for most of the 1945–51 period, the high levels of taxation introduced during the war.

The other large element in Labour's domestic policy was the extensive nationalisation, which brought into public ownership the Bank of England, the railways, road transport, airlines, gas, electricity and the iron and steel industry. Here, again, the government had little choice but to act, given the run-down state and appalling labour relations in the coal and transport industries, the need to develop and integrate the public utilities which were natural monopolies and the evident need for a change of direction at the Bank of England. The case for nationalising steel and road transport was much weaker, and these were in fact the only industries which the Tories chose to denationalise when they returned to power in 1951. Otherwise, the mixed economy established by Labour remained in place for well over 30 years until the advent of Margaret Thatcher. The record of the nationalised industries was a mixed one, but there was no doubt that they became highly unpopular and that their association with the Labour Party became an albatross around the party's neck and was an important factor in the subsequent sapping of its electoral appeal. Nor was this counter-balanced by any significant contribution to the core values of Labour. As Anthony Crosland argued persuasively in his monumental work of 1956, *The Future of Socialism*, the ownership of industry had little direct bearing on the distribution of wealth, the ability of governments to control economic policy, the status of the worker or even the level of efficiency of the undertaking. It would be wrong to conclude from this that the Attlee government was mistaken in all its individual acts of nationalisation, but it was misguided to make them such a central part of its strategy, while subsequent Labour proposals to extend the public sector were highly counter-productive.

What was not foreshadowed in Labour's election manifesto was the desperate struggle which would face the new government in rebuilding the economy and greatly expanding exports in the face of severe wartime losses and the abrupt end of American Lend-Lease aid immediately after the end of the war with Japan in August 1945. Yet this was not the least of the achievements of the Attlee government. Thanks to a sustained austerity programme, led by Cripps who replaced Dalton as Chancellor in November 1947, the maintenance of rationing and many wartime controls for several post-war years, and the agreement of the trade unions to accept a large measure of wage restraint – together with the resumption of American aid under the Marshall Plan in 1947 – the situation had been restored by 1950. In that year there was a surplus of £300 million in the balance of payments, an extraordinary turnaround from the £443 million deficit recorded in 1947.

The single-minded pursuit of austerity provoked a wave of discontent which was sedulously fostered by the Opposition and the Conservative-dominated press. Nevertheless, the government enjoyed unprecedented success in defending its large parliamentary majority in the 35 by-elections held in Labour seats during the 1945 Parliament. Not a single one of these was lost. It was therefore with considerable confidence that Attlee and his colleagues faced the general election of February 1950. They were to receive a nasty shock. The result of the election, with a record turnout of 84 per cent, was as shown in the table below.

Labour	315
Conservative	298
Liberal	9
Others	3
Labour majority	5

This result reflected a relatively small swing of 2.7 per cent from Labour to Conservative, but the Labour losses were greatly swollen by constituency boundary changes which came into effect at the general election. These were intended to reflect population movements, but had the unintended effect of building a strong Conservative bias into the electoral system (which was eventually reversed in the 1990s). Without this effect, Labour would have been re-elected in 1950 with a comfortable majority: in the event, few thought that it would be able to survive for more than a few months with a single-digit majority.

The government, in fact, survived for much longer than expected, but February 1950 nevertheless represented a watershed in its fortunes. Its great achievements were in the past; thereafter things began to go badly wrong. If Attlee can fairly claim much of the credit for the earlier period, he was equally to blame – at least in part – for much of what was to follow. He was, of course, not responsible for the two great disasters which afflicted his government. The retirement and death of its two great bulwarks – Bevin and Cripps – and the sudden outbreak of the Korean War. Yet his reaction to these events certainly contributed to the eventual defeat of his government and for Labour's subsequent lengthy spell in Opposition. Indeed, it could be argued that Attlee squandered an excellent opportunity for Labour to build on its successes and establish itself as the quasi-permanent party of government, comparable to the Swedish Social Democrats.

He made three serious errors of judgement. The first was in his choice of successors to Cripps and Bevin, and in particular of his handling of Aneurin Bevan. Bevan, the architect of the National Health Service, was one of the great stars of the government and had won a large following in the Labour Party, which at that time extended well beyond its left wing. He justifiably felt that he had earned promotion to one of the more senior posts in government, but Attlee twice passed him over within a few months, when he appointed Hugh Gaitskell to succeed Cripps and Herbert Morrison in place of Bevin. All he was offered – and reluctantly accepted – was a sideways move to the Ministry of Labour. Both of Attlee's choices could readily be justified. Gaitskell had been an able number two to Cripps and had good qualifications as an economist, but he was a newcomer to the Cabinet and vastly junior to Bevan in his standing in the party. Morrison was Deputy Prime Minister and had been highly successful both as a wartime Home Secretary and more recently as Leader of the House of Commons. Attlee was later to characterise his appointment as Foreign Secretary as 'the worst I ever made', but his failure was not predictable, and at that stage nobody realised that this highly able man was getting 'past it'. Attlee does not seem to have seriously considered Bevan for either post, which makes it all the more remarkable that he subsequently said, in a television interview with Francis Williams, that he had always expected 'Nye' to succeed him, and indeed had wanted him to. If that was true, he hardly went out of his way to bring this about.

Attlee's second grave error – for which he shared the responsibility with his Chancellor, Hugh Gaitskell, and the majority of the Cabinet, with the exception of Bevan and Harold Wilson, the President of the Board of Trade – was to accept, under strong US pressure, an unsustainable commitment to step up Britain's rearmament programme as part of its contribution to the Korean War. This involved increasing defence expenditure from 7.5 per cent to 14 per cent of the national income (a figure which was never reached and was quietly abandoned by the newly elected Churchill government the following year). To help foot the bill, Gailtskell proposed to levy charges on the National Health Service for the supply of false teeth and spectacles, which immediately provoked a resignation threat from Bevan. Gaitskell insisted, and Bevan carried out his threat, being joined by Wilson and by John Freeman, a junior minister. Attlee was in hospital being treated for a duodenal ulcer at the time of the resignations, and always blamed Morrison, who was deputising for him at the time, 'for losing three of my ministers'. Yet he had been kept in touch with what was going on, and indicated that, if the choice was between Bevan's and Gaitskell's resignations, then it was Bevan who had to go.

The consequent split in the Labour Party gravely damaged its standing, while developments in the Korean War spurred inflation and put the balance of payments back into the red. Yet public support for the government remained strong, and it might still have had serious chances of increasing its parliamentary majority if Attlee had timed the next election more judiciously. This would have involved hanging on through the next winter, and probably going to the polls in the spring of 1952, when the economic situation was expected to improve (it did). Instead of this, Attlee effectively sacrificed the interest of his own party to the convenience of King George VI. The King was due to embark on an extensive tour of the Commonwealth in the New Year, and by September was already nagging Attlee to get the election out of the way before his departure. He consequently set the election date for 25 October 1951, which was just about the least optimum time for Labour.

Conservative	321
Labour	295
Liberal	6
Others	3
Conservative majority	17

Despite this disadvantage, the election was desperately close, and Labour would still have won had it not been for the bias in the electoral system. It gained over 200,000 more votes than the Tories, but the result, in terms of seats, was as shown in the table above.

Attlee was then 68, and worn out by ten continuous years of high office. The time had surely come to bow out, but he lingered on in the party leadership for four more years, including the 1955 general election, in the pious hope of mending the deep split in his party. It was also widely suspected that part of his motivation was to hang on until Morrison, only five years his junior, would be seen as too old to succeed him. If so, he succeeded in his objective, as his unfortunate deputy polled only 40 votes to 157 for Gaitskell and 70 for Bevan, when he finally stood down in December 1955.

He then retired to the House of Lords, where his reputation as a wise and benign, if taciturn, elder statesman continued to increase until his death 12 years later. For the Labour Party, he remains to this day an iconic figure, though – if truth be told – he served his country rather better than his party. In his quiet way, he was every bit as much a patriot as Churchill, as the final words of his typically low key autobiography, *As It Happened*, reveal:

> I have been a happy and fortunate man, in having lived so long in the greatest country in the world, in having a happy family life and in having been given the opportunity of serving in a state of life to which I never expected to be called. (Attlee, 1954)

A kindly, unassuming and extremely shy man, with an exceptionally well-organised mind and a quiet determination to pursue the issues in which he believed, Attlee was not the person to write his own epitaph. The best he could manage was a rather smug limerick which he composed for the amusement of Tom Attlee:

> Few thought he was even a starter
> There were many who thought themselves smarter
> But he ended PM

CH and OM
An earl and a knight of the garter.

More apposite was the judgement of Peter Hennessy, the author of the definitive work on the Attlee government, who concluded 'that 1951 Britain ... compared to *any* previous decade was a kinder, gentler and far, far better place in which to be born, to grow up, to live, love, work and even to die' (Hennessy, 1992, p. 454).

Works consulted

Attlee, C.R., *As it Happened*, London, Heinemann, 1954.

Barnett, Corelli, *The Lost Victory*, London, Macmillan, 1995.

Beckett, Francis, *Clem Attlee*, London, Richard Cohen Books, 1997.

Brookshire, Jerry H., *Clement Attlee*, Manchester, Manchester University Press, 1995.

Burridge, Trevor, *Clement Attlee*, London, Cape, 1985.

Butler, David, *British General Elections since 1945*, Oxford, Blackwell, 1989.

Clarke, Peter, *A Question of Leadership*, London, Penguin, 1992.

Donoughue, Bernard, and G.W. Jones, *Herbert Morrison*, London, Weidenfeld & Nicolson, 1973.

Foot, Michael, *Aneurin Bevan 1945–1960*, London, Granada, 1979.

Harris, Kenneth, *Attlee*, London, Weidenfeld & Nicolson, 1982.

Hennessy, Peter, *Never Again: Britain 1945–1951*, London, Cape, 1992.

Jenkins, Roy, *Mr Attlee: An Interim Biography*, London, Heinemann, 1948.

Morgan, Kenneth O., *Labour in Power*, Oxford, Oxford University Press, 1984.

Morgan, Kenneth O., *Labour People: Hardie to Kinnock*, Oxford, Oxford University Press, 1992.

Morrison of Lambeth, Lord, *Herbert Morrison: An Autobiography*, London, Odhams Press, 1960.

43
Sir Anthony Eden – Self-Destruction of a Prince Charming

It was said of the Roman Emperor Galba that everyone thought he was capable of being a ruler until he actually became one. It was Anthony Eden's great misfortune that the same came to be said of him. Born in 1897, he grew up in what he felt to be an earthly paradise – the beautiful Windlestone Hall and estate, in County Durham – but with impossible parents. He was the presumed third son, and fourth child, of Sir William Eden, 7th baronet, whose family had been prominent in the area since the eleventh century. Sir William combined the traditional pursuits of a country gentleman with being a talented amateur painter and discerning art collector, but he was most renowned for the appalling temper which led him into frequent and uncontrollable rages over the most trivial causes.

Anthony's mother, Sybil Grey, was a kinswoman both of Earl Grey, of the Reform Bill, and of Sir Edward Grey, the Liberal Foreign Secretary from 1905 to 1916. A famous society beauty, she was a woman of great extravagance, whose unthinking generosity and self-indulgence was eventually to spell ruin to her husband's not inconsiderable financial resources. Anthony grew up to hate his mother, but he loved Sir William, despite his evident deficiencies as a parent. As he grew older his physical appearance began more and more to resemble that of George Wyndham, Arthur Balfour's secretary and later a Tory Cabinet minister – a dark, handsome dilettante, with whom Sybil Eden was known to be infatuated. According to his official biographer, Anthony was well aware of the 'persistent rumours' about his parentage, and 'found them both amusing and interesting. But he did not really believe them' (Rhodes James, 1986, p. 18).

Like all his family, Anthony was sent to Eton, which he disliked, and where he failed to distinguish himself. From his school reports, he emerged as a highly strung boy who suffered from temper tantrums, but 'is a nice, bright, intelligent fellow, with much that is very likeable about him' (Rhodes James, 1986, p. 25). When war broke out in August 1914, he was 17 years old, and thereafter he became more serious minded and applied himself more diligently to his studies. Its effect on his family was immediate and grave. His eldest brother, Jack, a professional soldier, was killed in France as early as October 1914; his second brother Tim, was interned in Germany, where he had been studying, his father was slowly dying – he survived until February 1915 – and his beloved Windlestone was turned into a wartime hospital. Anthony's only ambition now was to join the army, but his poor eyesight led to his being rejected on several occasions. However, late in 1915, he was welcomed into a Yeoman's regiment, commanded by Lord Feversham, who was the brother-in-law of his married elder sister, Marjorie. The medical test, Eden later reported, 'was hardly more than a formality' (Rhodes James, 1986, p. 36).

In nearly three years of service on the Western Front, Eden, who was promoted to be the youngest Brigade Major in the British Army, saw much grim action and the death or injury of vast numbers of his comrades in arms, while his younger brother, Nicholas, a 16-year-old midshipman, was killed in the Battle of Jutland. He himself escaped injury, and was awarded the Military Cross for rescuing his wounded sergeant under enemy fire. At the end of the war, as a 22-year-old veteran, he was at a loss what to do, but without enthusiasm decided to take up a place he had been offered at Christ Church, Oxford, in October 1919. He studied Oriental Languages (Persian and Arabic), and proved an excellent student, gaining a First Class degree. His only recorded student activity was to co-found an art appreciation society, entitled the Uffizi Society, and he started to build up a modest art collection of his own, showing an excellent eye for selecting up-and-coming artists. He followed political events with close attention, but showed no interest in joining the Union Society.

On graduation, he thought of trying for the Diplomatic Service, for which his knowledge of languages – including good French and German – made him well qualified. He decided, instead, on a political career, and fought the local Durham constituency of Spennymore, losing to Labour in the November 1922 general election. In the following year, he was selected to fight a by-election in the safe Tory seat of Warwick and Leamington. His candidature, however, was overshadowed by that of the flamboyant Labour candidate. This was none other than the Countess of Warwick (a former mistress of Edward VII, famously known to him as 'My Darling Daisy'), who, to complete the embarrassment, turned out to be his sister Marjorie's mother-in-law, and a relative by marriage of Eden's fiancée. The by-election was aborted in its final stages by the unexpected dissolution of Parliament, but in the general election which ensued he was returned with a large majority, the Countess coming a poor third. He was 26, and was to represent the seat, without any difficulty, for the ensuing 33 years.

Just before the election, he had married the 18-year-old Beatrice, daughter of Sir Gervase Beckett, a wealthy and generous Tory MP, who was also the owner of a leading regional newspaper, the *Yorkshire Post*. They made a glamorous couple, and Eden was to benefit both financially and politically from the Beckett connection, but the marriage, though it produced two sons, was not a success. Beatrice was immature, and shared none of Anthony's political, artistic or intellectual interests, and it was not long before they began to drift apart, each having numerous affairs, though they divorced only in 1950.

Eden made an inauspicious start as an MP, breaching the custom of confining his maiden speech to uncontroversial matters, and it was some time before he found his feet in the Commons. He confined his occasional interventions to foreign policy issues, but eventually became Parliamentary Private Secretary to a junior minister at the Home Office. Then, in July 1926, he had a great stroke of luck. Austen Chamberlain was now Foreign Secretary, and his own PPS left on a six-month trip to Australia, and recommended Eden, whom Chamberlain hardly knew, to replace him.

He remained with Chamberlain until the Tory defeat in the 1929 general election, and they soon became immersed in mutual admiration. Eden strongly approved Chamberlain's policies, which notably included the negotiation of the Locarno treaties of December 1925, reintegrating Germany into the mainstream of European diplomacy, while Chamberlain found him a highly proficient and well-informed assistant. This somewhat stiff and remote man developed warm feelings for Eden, who also became something of a favourite of the Prime Minister, Stanley Baldwin, who openly talked to him about his future as a Cabinet minister. He intended to bring him into the government, as Under-Secretary at the Foreign Office, had he won the election.

In opposition, Eden frequently spoke on foreign affairs from the front bench, and helped to restore his shaky finances (as the younger son of an estate almost bankrupted by his mother's fecklessness), by joining a stockbroking firm. A fervent supporter of Baldwin against his many Conservative critics, he joined a dining club of left-wing Tory MPs, whose leader, Noel Skelton, coined the phrase 'a property-owning democracy', which Eden was later to make his own hallmark.

The formation of Ramsay MacDonald's National Government in August 1931 marked the beginning of his ministerial career. MacDonald had flirted with the idea of appointing his own talented son, Malcolm, as Under-Secretary for Foreign Affairs, but was persuaded by Baldwin to choose Eden instead. The Foreign Secretary was a Liberal, the Marquis of Reading, an arrangement which suited Eden very well, as it meant that he alone would speak for the Foreign Office in the Commons. It lasted for only two months: after the October 1931 election, Reading was replaced by another Liberal, who was well on the way to becoming a right-wing Tory, Sir John Simon. Eden found him to be a most uncongenial boss – irresolute, cantankerous and openly jealous of his much younger deputy.

Largely excluded from the policy-making loop, Eden was dispatched for long periods to Geneva for meetings of the League of Nations, where he was extremely active in the abortive disarmament conference which dragged on from 1932 to early in 1934. Nothing of value was achieved, but it did wonders for Eden's public image. As his official biographer put it:

> In a somewhat drab scene, populated by so many older and duller men, and with shadows looming everywhere, he stood out as an exciting exception. At the beginning of 1933 he was almost unknown; by the end of the year he was being hailed as a rising star, better known through photographs, films and press reports than most members of the Cabinet. Few such opportunities have occurred to a young politician. (Rhodes James, 1986, p. 123)

At the League of Nations, Eden established a reputation as a highly accomplished diplomat, and was particularly noted for two of his initiatives. One was his proposal that an international force, including British troops, should supervise the plebiscite in the Saarland, which led to the return of the territory to Germany after 16 years of French occupation. The second was his contribution as a mediator between Yugoslavia and Hungary, after the latter's government was suspected of complicity in the assassination of the Yugoslav King Alexander in October 1934. In reality, Eden's commitment to the League of Nations and to the concept of collective security was by no means unequivocal, but in the public eye he became their very personification, and this was the essential basis for his extraordinary popularity in the 1930s, which did not, however, extend very far within the Conservative Party.

Although he was promoted to Lord Privy Seal, still outside the Cabinet, in December 1933, he continued to chafe under Simon's overlordship. When Baldwin finally took over as Prime Minister, in June 1935, he had high hopes that he himself would become Foreign Secretary. Instead, Sir Samuel Hoare, whom he found only a marginal improvement, was appointed. His tenure, however, lasted a mere six months. He was forced to resign in the aftermath of the Hoare-Laval Pact (see chapter on Baldwin), and, at the young age of 38, Eden's hour had come.

Under Baldwin, he was given a pretty free hand, and had very little to show for his handling of the three major crises which occurred during his watch – Abyssinia (Ethiopia), the Rhineland and the outbreak of the Spanish Civil War. A careful examination of the evidence (Carlton, 1981, pp. 71–99) reveals little of the determination to resist, which he subsequently claimed in his memoir of the period, *Facing the Dictators* (1965). Against Mussolini, he was in no hurry to lift the partial and ineffective sanctions applied by the League of Nations, but – in the face of French indifference – made no attempt to press the case for oil sanctions which he had previously supported. Nor did he pursue the one course which he himself had identified as likely to halt the Italian aggression in its tracks – the closure of the Suez Canal. On Hitler's occupation of the Rhineland, which was a breach of the Locarno agreements as well as the Versailles Treaty, he confined himself to verbal protests, even though there was some indication that the French would have supported a more muscular joint response.

Over Spain, Eden fully supported the principle of non-intervention, which effectively deprived the legal government of access to arms supplies, while hardly impeding the considerable German and Italian support for Franco, nor the more limited help which the Soviet Union sent to the Republican side. It is not true, however, that Eden took the lead in forcing the same policy on the new French Popular Front government, nor is there any evidence that he shared the sympathies of a probable majority of his Cabinet colleagues with the Francoist uprising. In fact, he tried to make the arms embargo more even-handed by proposing a naval blockade of the eastern Spanish coast. This initiative, however, was voted down in the Cabinet – Baldwin for once taking a keen interest in the issue and coming down heavily on the side of Eden's opponents.

Baldwin's retirement, in May 1937, brought an end to Eden's relative contentment as Foreign Secretary. Neville Chamberlain was far less willing than his predecessor to leave a free hand to his Foreign Secretary and – while outward courtesies were usually maintained – the tension between them gradually built up during the succeeding seven months. Eden, despite his subsequent and largely successful efforts to suggest the contrary, was not at all opposed to Chamberlain's early attempts to appease Hitler. He sought to draw the line, however, so far as Mussolini was concerned, whom he appeared to regard as a more serious menace than his fellow dictator. Chamberlain's considered view was that, though he was determined to pacify Hitler, he would prove an extremely dangerous enemy of Britain if his efforts failed. He consequently sought to detach Italy from its German alliance, so that Britain would not have to face two powerful foes at the same time. He was, accordingly, anxious to arrange bilateral talks in order to settle outstanding Italian grievances. These included, notably, the British refusal to give *de jure* recognition to the annexation of Abyssinia.

Eden's view was that such recognition should not be given before Italy made significant gestures of its own – such as the withdrawal of Italian 'volunteers' from Spain and a reduction in the large Italian garrison in Libya, which constituted a potential threat to Egypt. He consequently embarked on a surreptitious 'go-slow' campaign, doing everything he could to delay or frustrate the opening of talks with the Italians, while, on the surface, agreeing to carry out Chamberlain's intentions. Chamberlain soon became aware of what was going on, and fumed against Eden in his private letters to his sisters, while attempting – behind Eden's back – to use his sister-in-law, Ivy Chamberlain (Austen's widow), who was living in Rome, as a supplementary channel of communication with Mussolini's circle. The climax came in December 1937 at a joint meeting which was held – at Chamberlain's insistence – with the Italian ambassador, Count Dino Grandi, at which Chamberlain made clear that he wished to expedite Anglo-Italian talks. An astonished Grandi sent a dispatch to Rome, containing the revealing passage:

> Chamberlain and Eden were not a Prime Minister and a Foreign Secretary discussing with the Ambassador of a foreign power a delicate situation of an international character. They were – and revealed themselves as such to me in defiance of all established convention – two enemies confronting each other, like two cocks in true fighting posture. (Carlton, 1981, pp. 127–8)

It was at this point that Eden decided to resign, and Chamberlain made no strenuous efforts to dissuade him. At the time – and later – many people were puzzled at Eden's resignation, and thought that the issues involved were hardly weighty enough to justify so extreme a step. (Eden did not make public his disagreement with Chamberlain's abrupt dismissal of Roosevelt's tentative peace-making initiative – see Chapter 40.) Certainly, no other Cabinet minister was tempted to follow suit. One theory is that Eden grossly overestimated his own standing and thought that Chamberlain would not be able to continue in office without his support. Others believed that he was playing a long game, in the belief that Chamberlain would eventually become discredited and that it was better to detach himself from him in good time. Some thought he had acted purely out of pique, comparing him to Lord Randolph Churchill, whose resignation as Chancellor of the Exchequer in 1886 wrecked his political career.

One explanation was not considered at the time, but was apparently advanced by Eden himself in conversation with his colleague and close friend, Malcolm MacDonald, then Dominions Secretary, who tried to dissuade him from resigning. According to a letter which he wrote over 40 years later to one of Eden's biographers (Carlton, 1981, pp. 129–30), Eden told him that 'he could not continue working as a Minister because he did not feel fit to do so; he felt physically unwell and mentally exhausted'. MacDonald continued: 'When he made that remark I decided that it would in fact be better if he did resign.' He told this to the Prime Minister the following morning, who, he recalled, 'smiled and said that he had "slept on the matter" and had come to the same conclusion'.

Whatever moved Eden to quit, and – as in the case of most major resignations – there were probably several different factors involved, the long-term effect was certainly to burnish his reputation as an anti-appeaser to a far greater extent than was justified by his actual record. Nor did he now play a very active role in opposing Chamberlain's policies, holding himself aloof from the small group surrounding Winston Churchill. Churchill, however, professed the greatest admiration for Eden, describing him in his memoirs as 'one strong young figure standing up against long, dismal, drawling tides of drift and surrender'. Despite his many admirers in the country, Eden had only a tiny following among Tory MPs, who were disparagingly referred to as 'the Glamour Boys'. Within the party, he was regarded essentially as a light-weight figure, and it is revealing that, in May 1940, when both Halifax and Churchill were widely regarded as unsuitable candidates for the premiership, there was absolutely no move to push Eden's claims. He had rejoined the government as Dominions Secretary in September 1939, and he was disappointed that Churchill excluded him from the War Cabinet when he became Prime Minister, switching him instead to the War Office. It was only in December 1940, when Halifax was packed off to the United States as Ambassador, that he was able to reclaim his place as Foreign Secretary.

During the remainder of the war he had a number of differences with Churchill, but for the most part acted as a skilful and hard-working deputy, whom Churchill recommended to George VI as his successor if he should die or be incapacitated. Nevertheless it was Clem Attlee whom he appointed as Deputy Premier, compensating Eden in 1942 with the leadership of the House of Commons. The double burden of combining this post with being Foreign Secretary undoubtedly contributed to the breakdown of his health, and by June 1945 he was seriously ill with a duodenal ulcer and consequently played virtually no part in the general election campaign. In the same month he suffered the terrible blow of the death in action of his elder son, Simon, in Burma.

On more than one occasion, Churchill had promised Eden that he would retire in his favour at the end of the war, and he was much put out when he lingered on in the party leadership after the election rout. Even so, his medium-term prospects looked good. He was immensely popular in the country, and had no credible rival for the Tory succession. Yet beneath that suave and glamorous exterior, he was a bundle of uncertainties and insecurities. In public, he was renowned for his affability and perfect manners – yet his junior ministers and civil servants were only too aware of his violent temper, vanity and recurring obsessions. He was also a man with a guilty conscience. The world may have acquitted him of appeasement, but he brooded on his own culpability in failing to respond to the German occupation of the Rhineland in 1936, especially as captured German documents later revealed that Hitler would have backed down if Britain and France had threatened a military response. Twenty years later he was to tell his private secretary, Sir Pierson Dixon, that if Britain had resisted in 1936 the Second World War might have been avoided and 'Millions of lives would have been saved' (Dixon, 1968).

In October 1951, when the Tories were finally re-elected, Eden became Foreign Secretary for the third time, at the age of 54. It was a fruitful period for his diplomacy. An armistice was concluded in Korea, and a ceasefire negotiated between France and the Vietnamese Communists, while disputes with Persia and Egypt were settled, at least temporarily. In all of these events, Eden was credited with a major role. In August 1952, moreover, he embarked on his second marriage – to Churchill's niece, Clarissa Churchill – a union which turned out to be a great deal happier than that with Beatrice Beckett. Only eight months later, however, disaster struck. He had two gallstone operations which went badly wrong, and his life was only saved by a third operation in Boston, which was successful, though he was out of action until the following October. In June 1953, Churchill had a serious stroke, which was kept secret, though if Eden had been fully fit he would most probably have taken over the premiership. R.A. Butler, the Chancellor of the Exchequer, was in charge of the government, but lacked the boldness to seize the top post for himself. So Churchill held on, and gave way to his 'crown prince', apparently restored to health, only in April 1955.

When Eden succeeded to the premiership, his reputation was at its peak. He was regarded as a master diplomat and – though his interventions in domestic politics had been minimal – he was seen as the very model of a progressive Tory, in whose hands the recently built welfare state would be totally safe. He immediately called a general election, and had no difficulty in defeating an ageing Attlee still at the head of a deeply divided Labour Party. He tripled the narrow majority which Churchill had won in 1951, giving the Tories a lead of 58 seats over all other parties.

It was a time of hope, but not for some of those who knew Eden well, who were full of foreboding. These, apparently, included Churchill himself, as well as Lord Swinton, a veteran Tory Cabinet minister who was asked by Churchill early in 1955 if he thought that R.A. Butler would do better as Prime Minister than Eden. Swinton replied that 'anybody would be better than Anthony [who] would make the worst Prime Minister since Lord North. But you can't think like that now – it's too late. You announced him as your successor more than ten years ago.' Churchill replied 'I think it was a great mistake' (Ramsden, 1996, p. 274).

In retrospect, it might appear that the Suez affair was solely responsible for wrecking Eden's government and ending his political career. It did not look like that at the time. Within months of his taking over, loud voices of discontent were being heard, particularly within his own party, and there was widespread speculation that he would not long survive as Prime Minister. The feeling grew that he was just not up to the job – he proved at the same time chronically indecisive, but ever ready to interfere in the minutest details of the departmental work of his colleagues; particularly, but by no means exclusively, in the Foreign Office. He also showed himself to be exceptionally thin-skinned and upset by the slightest criticism. The most painful shaft for Eden came from the normally ultra-loyal *Daily Telegraph* in an article which mocked his speaking style. To emphasise his points, Eden had the habit, it said, of punching his fist into the palm of his other hand, but stopping short of an audible impact. 'Most Conservatives', the paper opined, 'are waiting to feel the smack of firm government.' Eden reacted by issuing a quite unnecessary and highly counter-productive denial that he was going to resign, which only increased the speculation that he would not last for long. Early in 1956, a leading political journalist, Ian Waller, made a prescient prediction in a syndicated article: 'If the year goes on as it has begun it will not be Sir Anthony Eden but Harold Macmillan who reigns in Downing Street in 1957.'

Despite these misgivings, Eden might well have survived and served a successful term as Prime Minister, but he was driven by an obsession. This was that the Egyptian leader, Colonel Nasser, was becoming as great a menace as Hitler and Mussolini had been in the 1930s, and must on no account be appeased. Eden saw him as a lethal threat to the British position in the Middle East and as a pawn of the Soviet Union. Several months before the Suez crisis began – in March 1956 – Eden gave an early indication to his Under-Secretary, Anthony Nutting, of his irrational attitude. King Hussein of Jordan had just dismissed the British General John Glubb as the commander of his army. Convinced that Nasser was behind this move, Eden screamed down the telephone to Nutting: 'what is all this poppycock you've sent me about isolating Nasser and neutralising Nasser? Why can't you get it into your head that I want the man destroyed?' This conversation was later related by Nutting to the author Peter Hennessy, who linked it with indications that Eden might even have tried to use the Secret Service in an attempt to assassinate the Egyptian President (Hennessy, 2000, p. 61).

Suez proper began on 19 July 1956, when the US and Britain announced the withdrawal of their earlier offer to partially finance the Aswan Dam in southern Egypt. Nasser's response – one week later – was to order the immediate nation-alisation of the Suez Canal Company, indicating that he would use the income from Canal dues to pay for the construction of the dam. Eden was by no means alone in being horrified by Nasser's action, which was strongly condemned by Hugh Gaitskell, the Labour leader, in the House of Commons. However, Gaitskell made clear, and repeated this more emphatically in private letters to Eden, that he did not support the use of force against Egypt. Nor would this have been justified in terms of international law – Nasser offered full compen-sation on the basis of the market value of the shares, the majority of which were held by the British government, and the bulk of the remainder by private French interests.

Nevertheless, from day one Eden was determined on the use of force if Nasser refused to back down – ostensibly to achieve international control of the canal, but in reality to ensure Nasser's overthrow. The French government, led by the Socialist Guy Mollet, was equally willing to use military force. Its main motivation was to punish Nasser for his support of the rebels fighting against France in Algeria. Unfortunately for the British and French leaders, their military staffs advised them that it was not possible to launch an immediate strike, as an airborne assault was seen as too risky. A seaborne invasion, from a base in Malta, would take at least a month to prepare, they insisted.

Eden was therefore forced to try diplomatic means to resolve the dispute, while secretly liaising with the French to launch an attack on Egypt on or after 8 September. The secrecy was necessary because President Eisenhower, and his Secretary of State, John Foster Dulles, had made it crystal clear to Eden that the US would not support military action. With US backing, a conference of the leading maritime powers was held on 16–23 August, which deputed a five-man committee, led by Australian Prime Minister Robert Menzies, to visit Nasser and try to persuade him to accept an international board of control for the canal. He turned them down flat, and the British and French resolved to take their case against Nasser to the UN Security Council, in the expectation that Russia would veto any resolution requiring Egyptian compliance. They would then feel free to launch their attack, having failed to secure satisfaction from the UN.

This plan was thwarted by Dulles, who insisted on further negotiations, coming up with the idea of establishing a Suez Canal Users' Association (SCUA), made up of signatories to the 1888 Convention which guaranteed international access to the canal. The proposal was that the SCUA would be responsible for hiring pilots and collecting dues. The inaugural meeting of the SCUA was held on 19–22 September, Nasser skilfully avoided committing himself either for or against this plan, and negotiations at the UN continued in a desultory way, with the prospect of Anglo-French military action seeming to diminish with every day that passed. During this period, Eden remained in a high state of excitement. There is some evidence that he was suffering from recurrent bouts of fever, perhaps related to delayed effects of his operations in 1953. On 5 October, while visiting his wife in hospital, he had a serious attack, with his temperature rising to 105 °F (40.6 °C). His press officer, William Clark, who later resigned in protest against the Suez operation, wrote in his memoirs that Eden was 'mad, literally mad and that he went so on the day that his temperature rose to 105°' (Clark, 1986, p. 209). Eden himself admitted to Sir Gladwyn Jebb (British Ambassador in Paris) that he had been 'practically living on Benzedrine'. There can be little doubt that his judgement was seriously affected at this time, though his health did not break down until later and 'several contemporaries noted that in the later stages of the drama Eden displayed a calm serenity, in marked contrast to his usually excited and nervous demeanour' (Dutton, 1997, pp. 422–3).

By mid-October it seemed that the threat of war over Suez was all but over, but on 14 October two emissaries from the French government arrived at Chequers with a hare-brained scheme to involve Israel in a clandestine plot to provide a pretext for an Anglo-French attack on Egypt. It is difficult not to believe that, had Eden's judgement not been affected, he would have rejected the proposal out of hand. As it was, he travelled with Foreign Secretary Selwyn Lloyd to Paris two days later for secret talks with Mollet and his Foreign Minister, Christian Pineau, from which all officials were excluded. A week later a confidential agreement was signed in a villa at Sèvres that Israel would launch an attack towards the Suez Canal on 29 October, and that Britain and France would then issue an ultimatum to both combatants to cease fire and withdraw their forces from the canal area or the two powers would intervene to separate the two armies and secure the safety of the canal.

Eden persuaded his Cabinet – many of whose members were not informed of the details of the collusion with Israel – to back the plan, which they did with varying degrees of enthusiasm, with only one member (Sir Walter Monckton) registering disagreement, though he did not resign (he had been switched a few days earlier from his post as Defence Minister to Paymaster-General, because of his lukewarm attitude to military intervention). Although Eden bore the main responsibility for the folly about to be committed, his two leading Cabinet colleagues were also greatly to blame. Either of them could effectively have vetoed the project if they had come out strongly against. Instead, Harold Macmillan, the Chancellor of the Exchequer, backed it with great enthusiasm, and reversed his position (in the face of a run on the pound) only after the Anglo-French forces had landed in Port Said on 5 November. R.A. Butler, the unofficial deputy premier, was convinced of the madness of the scheme and told everyone so afterwards, but kept his mouth shut during the Cabinet discussions.

The Israeli attack duly took place, and the Anglo-French ultimatum was delivered. The Egyptians turned it down, and Anglo-French air attacks were launched against Egyptian air bases, in preparation for the landing by the amphibious force which had already steamed out of Malta two days before the Israeli attack. President Eisenhower, aghast at the deception employed against him by Eden and Mollet, immediately instructed the US delegate to the United Nations Security Council to table a motion demanding that Israel should withdraw from Egyptian soil and calling on all UN members to refrain from force or the threat of force. Britain and France vetoed the resolution, the first time that Western powers had ever had recourse to the veto. When a similar motion was submitted to the UN General Assembly, it was passed by 64 votes to 5, only Australia and New Zealand backing the three states waging an undeclared war against Egypt.

If Eden's actions provoked near unanimous condemnation at the UN, they succeeded in splitting British public opinion right down the middle. The House of Commons erupted in uproar when he announced the Anglo-French ultimatum and the Speaker was forced to suspend the sitting. The Labour and Liberal parties, the Churches, the bulk of the intellectual community and the *bien-pensant* press reacted in horror, while he enjoyed ecstatic support from most Conservatives and – according to the opinion polls – a large number of working-class voters. The dozen or so Tory MPs who opposed Eden got short shrift from their supporters, most of them being deselected as parliamentary candidates. Two junior ministers – Nutting and Sir Edward Boyle – resigned from the government, and Eden also lost his press officer, William Clark, for the same reason.

There was sullen resentment from senior ministers and officials who had been kept totally in the dark about the government's intentions. These included the British Ambassador to Cairo, Sir Humphrey Trevelyan; the First Lord of the Admiralty, Lord Hailsham, who later wrote: 'I was told nothing of the contingency plans, and when ships were actually beginning to move I was misled as to their true purpose'; and Sir Charles Keightley, the commander of the British troops about to go into action, who was given no forewarning of the intended Israeli attack. (Dutton, 1997, p. 28). The plan was misconceived in any case, but that it descended into total fiasco was at least partly due to the failure to consult, or even inform, so many key figures.

It took over a week for the allied troops to make it from Malta to Port Said, where they landed on 5 November, and began to advance southwards along the canal. But by then the pressure of the United States on the British and French governments had become irresistible. The US 5th Fleet made threatening movements against allied ships, while the American Treasury blankly refused to support the pound sterling which was under pressure in the exchange markets. This was the pretext – if not perhaps the cause – of Macmillan's abrupt change of stance, which forced Eden to declare a halt of military operations on 6 November. By Christmas, the British and French troops were forced to withdraw in humiliating circumstances, with Nasser acclaimed a hero throughout the Arab world and beyond.

Those who had lauded Eden now turned against him. The more jingoistic Tories roundly condemned him for halting the operation when it was (at least in terms of securing the physical control of the canal) in sight of success. 'Worse than a crime, a blunder', was the standard Tory verdict on Suez, echoing the famous judgement on Napoleon's execution of the Duc d'Enghien. It nevertheless was a crime – not least because it provided a cover for the brutal and simultaneous Soviet suppression of the Hungarian revolution.

Eden's premiership did not long survive the failure of his enterprise. His health broken, he announced on 21 November that he was flying to Jamaica to recuperate, staying at the house of the James Bond author, Ian Fleming, and leaving Butler in charge of the government. He returned on 14 December, and six days later told a direct lie to the House of Commons when he denied any foreknowledge of the Israeli attack on Egypt. He resigned on medical advice on 9 January 1957, to be succeeded not by Butler, as he and most other observers had expected, but by Macmillan, who was the choice of the overwhelming majority of his Cabinet. He was to live for another 20 years, as the Earl of Avon, and set out a lengthy justification in three volumes of memoirs. Yet he could never bring himself to admit the collusion with Israel. The conspirators at Sèvres had pledged themselves to eternal secrecy, but Eden's French and Israeli partners proved a great deal less discreet than his own tight circle of collaborators. Within a few months, two French journalists, Serge and Merry Bromberger, had already revealed the essential details in their book *Les Secrets de l'Expédition d'Egypte*, which were later confirmed both by Pineau and by General Moshe Dayan, the Israeli Chief of Staff.

One good thing did come out of Suez – the realisation in both Britain and France that they were no longer world powers – and could not hope, even acting together, to embark on major military operations without at least the acquiescence of their American ally. This lesson was learned more quickly in France, which within a few months signed the Treaty of Rome and committed itself to European integration. It took much longer for the British, who were to find that when they wished to follow suit they were blocked by their former partner, and were only able to join the European Community 15 years after it was established.

What should one think of Eden? For most of his life he had appeared the soul of honour, yet he was responsible for perhaps the most dishonourable episode in British history in the twentieth century – arguably even worse than Munich, which was a sin of omission, while this was one of commission. In truth, Eden was a tragic figure, who had too lightly chosen the wrong career path after the First World War. Behind his elegant exterior, he lacked too many of the qualities necessary for effective political leadership at the highest level. He proved himself incapable of taking big decisions on a rational basis, his temperament was too brittle and he was too thin-skinned to cope with criticism, while his character contained more than a dash of naivety. It was a great pity that he did not follow his initial inclination to try for the Diplomatic Service – he would have cut a glittering figure presiding over the embassy in Paris or Washington, faithfully carrying out the policies determined by his political masters, without suffering the agony of having to decide on them himself.

Works consulted

Carlton, David, *Anthony Eden*, London, Allen Lane, 1981.
Clark, William, *From Three Worlds*, London, Sidgwick & Jackson, 1986.
Dictionary of National Biography 1971–1980, Supplement, Oxford, Oxford University Press, 1986.
Dixon, Piers, *Double Dilemma: The Life of Sir Pierson Dixon, Don and Diplomat*, London, Hutchinson, 1968.
Dutton, David, *Anthony Eden: A Life and Reputation*, London, Hodder Arnold, 1997.

Hennessy, Peter, *The Prime Minister: The Office and its Holders since 1945*, London, Allen Lane, 2000.

Kyle, Keith, *Suez*, London, 1991.

Nutting, Anthony, *No End of a Lesson*, London, Constable, 1967.

Ramsden, John, *The Age of Churchill and Eden, 1940–1957*, London, Longman, 1996.

Rhodes James, Robert, *Anthony Eden*, London, Weidenfeld & Nicolson, 1986.

44

Harold Macmillan – Idealist into Manipulator

He used to boast that his grandfather was a Scottish crofter, which was being somewhat economical with the truth. The last crofter in his family had been his great-grandfather, as he well knew. Grandfather Daniel Macmillan had come south to become a booksellers' apprentice in Cambridge, where – with his brother – he founded what was to become the great Macmillan publishing empire. By the time that Harold Macmillan was born, in 1894, the family, already immensely wealthy, had long been established in one of the most fashionable quarters of London, and any Scottish connections were but a distant memory.

His father, Maurice, was Daniel's second son, a cultured, diffident man, who was totally in thrall to his American wife Nellie, a talented musician, but a bit of a harridan, with no inhibitions in expressing her strong views and prejudices, which included a large dose of Mid-Western Protestantism. Macmillan was the youngest of three brothers, but was soon selected by his ambitious mother as the one most likely to make his mark in the world, and she lost no opportunity to push him forward. In later life, Harold was to write: 'I can truthfully say that I owe everything all through my life to my mother's devotion and support.' As Prime Minister, he was to tell a friend: 'I admired her but never really liked her ... she dominated me and she still dominates me.'

A solitary and withdrawn child, who got more affection from his nanny than his parents, he was unhappy at Eton, from where he was removed at the age of 15 on the grounds of ill health. This was probably the actual reason, though his official biographer, Alistair Horne, refers coyly to 'inevitable rumours' that he left for the 'usual reasons' for boys to be expelled from public schools. He was highly inhibited and, according to Lord Blake, who knew him well, found it hard in later life 'to relate at all easily to his contemporaries, to his children and to women' (Blake, 1996, p. 276). After Eton, he was educated at home by tutors, with one of whom – Ronnie Knox – he was to to form a close and affectionate relationship. Knox, who much later was to gain renown as a leading Roman

Catholic theologian, was then a young Anglo-Catholic priest, who had been at Oxford with Harold's eldest brother, Daniel. Still trembling on the brink of conversion to Rome, he was to be unceremoniously ejected from the household by a furious Nellie Macmillan, who had no intention of seeing her son being corrupted by Popish doctrines, and who also feared the growing attraction between her 17-year-old son and his 22-year-old tutor.

Despite the loss of his formidable tutor, Macmillan was able to win an Exhibition to Balliol College, Oxford, where he spent a gloriously happy two years between 1912 and 1914, gaining First Class Honours in the first part of his Classics degree, which he was never to complete. At Oxford he renewed his friendship with Knox, who was now a chaplain at Trinity College, and – together with another close friend – strongly urged him to take the final plunge and convert to Rome. To Knox's consternation, however, Macmillan himself – fearful of his mother's reaction – decided to remain an Anglican, even if a High Church one, which he was to remain for the rest of his life. Macmillan played an active role in the Union, becoming successively Secretary and Treasurer, with a good chance of succeeding to the Presidency if the war had not intervened. He espoused radical causes, but seemed very unsure of his party affiliation – or perhaps was hedging his bets – as he became a member simultaneously of the Canning (Tory) and Russell (Liberal) clubs, as well as of the Fabian Society (Labour). He supported a motion 'That this House approves the main principles of Socialism', and in his maiden speech attacked the 'public school' system.

Like most of his Oxford contemporaries, Macmillan, aged 20, hastened to join up in the early days of the war, and was commissioned as a second lieutenant in the King's Royal Rifle Corps. His mother then used influence to get him transferred to the much smarter Grenadier Guards, and in the summer of 1915, Macmillan went to France, where he was to remain for most of the rest of the war, acquiring a reputation for gallantry (but no decoration) and being seriously wounded three times. He emerged from the war feeling a great sympathy with the largely working-class soldiers that he had commanded, and only just alive. He was rotting in a poorly equipped military hospital, but the determined and energetic Nellie got him transferred to a private hospital in Belgrave Square, just round the corner from his family home, an action which Macmillan thought saved his life.

Now aged 24, Macmillan could not bear the thought of returning to Oxford, so many of his contemporaries having perished in the war. He retained his army rank of captain, and in 1919 went to Ottawa as aide-de-camp to the Governor-General of Canada, the 9th Duke of Devonshire. This post was secured for him by his ever-scheming and social-climbing mother, who may perhaps have been partly influenced by the fact that the Duke had several daughters of marriageable age. If so, her foresight was rewarded, for Harold fell deeply in love with the youngest of them, the 19-year-old Lady Dorothy Cavendish. The wedding at St Margaret's, Westminster, on 21 April 1920, was the social event of the year. The bride's party was packed with the cream of the aristocracy, including the future King George VI, and the bridegroom's with the pride of Macmillan authors, including Henry James and Thomas Hardy.

By this time, Harold himself was already working as a senior editor in the family firm, then headed by his uncle Frederick, who was flanked by Harold's father Maurice and his cousin George as co-directors. Alongside Harold, in the second layer, was his eldest brother Daniel and another cousin, Will. He found he had a natural aptitude for the work, and greatly enjoyed his contacts with such eminent authors as Hardy, Kipling, Yeats and Sean O'Casey, and younger writers, including the economists John Maynard Keynes, G.D.H. Cole, Colin Clark and Lionel Robbins. Still very buttoned up, however, he did not, on his own admittance, succeed in making friends with any other of them, except O'Casey, a self-proclaimed Communist and atheist.

Despite his contentment at being a publisher, Macmillan – again influenced by his mother – now began to contemplate a political career. Still harbouring radical views, and fervently admiring Lloyd George, his logical political home would have been one of the two branches of the Liberal Party, but opportunism gained the upper hand, and sensing that the Liberals were a busted flush, he approached Conservative Central Office, offering his services to fight a 'tough seat'. A wealthy, rather cerebral young publisher, with a fine war record, the Tories lost no time in despatching him to Stockton-on-Tees, a predominantly working-class constituency in the north-east, represented by a Liberal. What the average Stockton elector made of this earnest, rather uptight young man, with a duke's daughter at his side, may only be conjectured, but he came very close to winning the seat, a mere 73 votes behind the Liberal, with Labour a close third. The following year, aged 30 – in the 1924 election – he came out on top, 3000 votes ahead of Labour, with the former Liberal MP in third place.

Macmillan was appalled by the high level of unemployment in Stockton, and by the hardship and poverty of many of his constituents, feeling the same sympathy for them that he had for the men he had commanded on the Western Front. Their plight was the main theme of the periodic speeches he made in his early years in the Commons. Ponderous and poorly delivered, they soon won him the reputation of being a parliamentary bore, though few doubted the sincerity and disinterestedness of his views. More influential was a short book which he wrote with three other young MPs, entitled *Industry and the State* (1927), setting out the case for unorthodox measures (described as 'Socialistic' by more mainline Tories) to mitigate the effects of unemployment. Macmillan followed this up by a number of unsolicited memoranda which he sent to various ministers, one of which, addressed to Winston Churchill, the Chancellor of the Exchequer, was acknowledged by him to be the original source of the Derating Act of 1927, which, by relieving industrial enterprises of the burden of paying rates to local authorities, increased their profitability and thereby enhanced their prospects as employers. Macmillan and his three fellow authors became the nucleus of a Tory progressive group, mockingly referred to by fellow Conservative MPs as the YMCA. The group notably included Robert Boothby, Churchill's lively and mischievous PPS, who was to have a devastating influence on Macmillan's private life.

As an MP, Macmillan continued to work for his publishing house during the mornings while attending the House of Commons in the afternoon and evening. Three children – a son and two daughters – were born during the first six years of his marriage, and, while Harold was for the most part busily occupied in London, they were living with their mother at Birch Grove, the family's country residence in Sussex. Already a large Victorian pile, it was substantially extended in the 1920s by Nellie Macmillan, who ruled the roost as a materfamilias, with Harold's family allocated a large wing on the first floor. Nellie had persuaded her husband that – though Harold was the third son – he should be the sole heir of Birch Grove, though she should have the right to continue to live there during her lifetime.

This situation, of living under the same roof as her dominant mother-in-law, was undoubtedly oppressive for Dorothy, who had perhaps married Harold at a young age principally to get away from her own overbearing mother. Described by Horne as being 'neither clever nor intellectual, but shrewd', she soon became discontented, and increasingly bored by her worthy but unexciting husband. The arrival of the handsome, amusing and buccaneering figure of Bob Boothby in Macmillan's circle had the proverbial effect of applying a spark to dried tinder. Dorothy immediately fell head over heels in love with him, and started what proved to be a lifelong affair which she pursued with the absolute minimum of discretion. In 1930, she gave birth to a third daughter, Sarah, of whom Boothby was undoubtedly the father. Dorothy wanted a divorce, but Macmillan refused. A proud man, deeply hurt by his wife's infidelity, he suffered a nervous breakdown, but – determined to keep up appearances – resigned himself to a lonely and bleakly unhappy existence. He retreated into his books, reading widely in history and the classics, and returning repeatedly to the novels of Trollope and Jane Austen. Dorothy never let go of Boothby, but – particularly after Macmillan became Prime Minister in 1957 – provided companionship if not conjugal love to her husband. As for Boothby, who had been seen as a much more likely political prospect than Macmillan, his career spluttered out in the early 1940s after he was found to have used undue influence to enrich himself while a junior minister. While he remained an MP and later a life peer, he was to be remembered mostly for his rumbustious performances in television discussion programmes.

In the same year – 1929 – that Dorothy began her liaison with Boothby, Macmillan suffered another disaster – the loss of his Stockton seat in the general election which brought Ramsay MacDonald back to the premiership. He subsequently narrowly avoided a far worse fate – that of becoming a close associate of Sir Oswald Mosley. In May 1930 Mosley resigned as a minister in the Labour government because of its failure to tackle unemployment. Macmillan immediately fired off a letter to *The Times*, warmly supporting Mosley's action. When Mosley subsequently founded his New Party, pledged to a planned economy, this strongly appealed to Macmillan who seriously considered defecting from the Tories. He drew back at the last moment, saving himself from probable electoral humiliation at the subsequent general election and from the taint of having been a fellow traveller of Mosley in the early stages of his headlong flight into fascism. Instead, Macmillan, having unsuccessfully flirted with the possibility of fighting a safe Tory seat in the south-east, stuck to Stockton, which he easily regained in the landslide election of October 1931.

Throughout the 1930s, Macmillan was probably the most unorthodox of all the Tory MPs, rebelling against the party line on a wide range of issues. His main concern was still unemployment, and he persistently argued for Keynesian remedies, especially in his book, *The Middle Way*, published in 1938, which also advocated the nationalisation of the mining industry. It was not surprising that his views proved more acceptable in Labour circles than within his own party. Indeed, Frank Pakenham (later Lord Longford), a Tory who had switched to Labour, attempted to persuade Macmillan to follow suit. He replied: 'When I consider the prospect of associating with your wild young men of the Left, I have to remember that I am a very rich man' (Horne, 1988, Vol. I, p. 119). Nevertheless, Macmillan was far more willing than most other dissident Tories to consider joint action with Labour MPs to oppose the policies of his own government, and in a newspaper article in 1936 had floated the idea of a centre party which, he suggested, should be led by Labour's Herbert Morrison.

Apart from Churchill, he was also the most consistent and determined opponent of appeasement. In 1936 he had been one of only two Tory MPs to vote against the government in a foreign affairs debate following the fiasco of the Hoare-Laval Pact, and actually resigned the party whip for a while. He also backed A.D. Lindsay, the Popular Front candidate, in the Oxford by-election following the Munich agreement, against the official Conservative nominee, Quintin Hogg. (Another Tory who supported Lindsay was Edward Heath, who was then an undergraduate at Oxford University.) As Horne commented, 'It is difficult to see how [Macmillan] could have stood as an orthodox Conservative candidate if a general election had been held in 1939 or 1940' (Horne, 1988, Vol. I).

Macmillan's estrangement from the Conservative leadership was only brought to an end when it was replaced in May 1940, with Churchill succeeding Chamberlain as Prime Minister. Macmillan was one of the 41 Tory MPs who had voted to ensure Chamberlain's downfall, and his immediate reward was the ministerial office which had previously eluded him during 16 years as an MP. Even then, it was far from being a grand appointment – Parliamentary Secretary to the Ministry of Supply. He was 46 and was to remain a junior minister for nearly three years, under a series of senior figures including Herbert Morrison and the press baron, Lord Beaverbrook. He was to prove competent and highly resourceful, and in December 1942 his big opportunity arose. Following the successful US-led occupation of French North Africa, Churchill decided to appoint a Resident Minister at the headquarters of the allied commander, General Dwight Eisenhower, as a counterweight to Robert Murphy, President Roosevelt's personal representative. He was only Churchill's second choice, but he accepted with alacrity. The post was of Cabinet rank, but though he was not a member of the War Cabinet he was to report directly to Churchill.

Soon established in a luxury villa in Algiers, Macmillan visibly flowered under the warm Mediterranean sun. Eisenhower greeted his arrival with suspicion, but Macmillan played up his half-American ancestry for all its worth, and all his previous stiff formality fell away from him in the more relaxed atmosphere of a largely American military headquarters. Before long he was playing a major political role, brokering the agreement under which General de Gaulle and the former Vichy General Giraud reluctantly shared the leadership of the French Committee for National Liberation, a provisional government in embryo. He also played a significant supporting role in the Casablanca summit meeting between Churchill and Roosevelt in March 1943. The focus later moved to Italy, with the invasion of Sicily and the secret negotiations for Italy to change sides in the war, in which he played a part as a go-between with representatives of the new Italian government which had replaced Mussolini. With Eisenhower's departure for England to prepare for the Normandy landings, Macmillan was attached to the headquarters of the British General Alexander, who commanded the allied forces in Italy. In effect, he became a viceroy in charge of civil government in Italy, as the Acting President of the Allied Control Commission. The nominal president was Alexander, who was far too busy with military matters to play any part. Macmillan contrived to include Greece, from which German troops retreated in the autumn of 1944, and even Yugoslavia, within his sphere of influence. This aroused the bitter hostility of Anthony Eden, who resented his poaching on the Foreign Office's and his own competence. Eden conspired unsuccessfully to have Macmillan recalled, while – for his part – Macmillan cast envious eyes on the Foreign Office, unwisely hinting to one of Eden's senior officials that he thought he could do the job better.

Macmillan even fancied himself as a strategist, helping Alexander to devise a plan, known as 'Operation Armpit', for a major thrust through Northern Italy and the 'Ljubljana Gap', which, he argued would bring Anglo-American forces into Vienna and Prague well ahead of the Russians. Churchill responded with enthusiasm, but it was vetoed by the Americans who insisted on proceeding instead with the already planned 'Operation Anvil' – the invasion of southern France. Macmillan always insisted that if his plan had gone ahead the Iron Curtain would have been 250 miles further east than it actually was, but subsequent military opinion has been sceptical about its feasibility. What is certain is that his advocacy did him no harm with Churchill, who was also mightily impressed by his handling of the situation in newly liberated Greece, in December 1944, when, with the country plunging into civil war, Macmillan's proposal to install Archbishop Damaskinos as Regent may well have thwarted a Communist takeover.

The final wartime episode involving Macmillan – in May 1945 – was the sending back to almost certain death or torture of thousands of Russian and Yugoslav combatants and civilians who had been assisting the Germans and were captured by British forces in Austria. The decision to do this had been taken, in principle, at the Yalta summit the previous February, and Macmillan's responsibility was confined to advising the army commanders on the spot to proceed accordingly. His final years were clouded by accusations made much later, notably in a book published by Count Nikolai Tolstoy, and which featured in a sensational libel action, that Macmillan was personally responsible for sending back White Russian émigrés not covered by the Yalta agreement, for deceiving his friend General Alexander and for conspiring to delude the Yugoslavs into believing that they were being evacuated to Italy. None of these accusations was ever substantiated, despite detailed investigation. Macmillan must share the general guilt of those who carried out the policy, but the specific responsibility rests with Churchill and Roosevelt who agreed it with Stalin at Yalta. The repatriation of large numbers not strictly covered by the Yalta undertaking was due to the excessive zeal, or carelessness, of individual British officers, and cannot be placed at Macmillan's door.

Before the repatriations were carried out, Macmillan had been recalled to Britain, where – on the collapse of the coalition government – Churchill invited him to join his new 'caretaker' Cabinet, offering him the post of Air Minister, which he assumed on 25 May 1945. Two months later he was out of office, having lost his seat at Stockton by a majority of nearly 9000. Within another four months he was back in the Commons, a by-election vacancy having occurred in the safe south London suburban constituency of Bromley. The Harold Macmillan who took up his seat in November 1945 was a changed character from the Tory rebel of the 1930s. It would be an exaggeration to say that the young idealist had been transformed into a cynical middle-aged manipulator, but there is an element of truth in that. He was certainly a great deal more self-confident and extrovert, more concerned about the pursuit of power and less scrupulous about the means to be employed. He was also much less *boring*. He had become an accomplished conversationalist, and his speeches, while still tending to be over-long and over-prepared, were much better delivered and were spiced with occasional flashes of wit. He was now a force to be reckoned with, and though few foresaw his rise to the premiership nobody doubted that he would be a senior figure in any future Tory government.

During the next six years, Macmillan proved to be one of the most pugnacious critics of the Attlee government, despite the fact that many of its policies closely resembled those he himself had advocated during the 1930s. He was now extremely partisan in his approach, even, on the occasion of his daughter Catherine's marriage to Julian Amery, crossing off from the invitation list the names of several prominent Labour politicians, including Clement Attlee, who had been closely associated with Amery's father, Leo, in the wartime coalition government. Macmillan played only a limited role in the widespread reforms adopted within the Conservative Party, struggling to make itself re-electable after its landslide defeat. It was Macmillan's long-term rival, R.A. Butler, who oversaw the reshaping of Conservative policy involving the acceptance of all the major reforms introduced by Labour, while the parallel changes to the party's organisation and electoral machine were the work of Lord Woolton, the party chairman, and of the lawyer, Sir David Maxwell-Fyfe (later Lord Kilmuir). Nevertheless, Macmillan certainly expected to be offered a major post when Churchill formed his government in October 1951, and was deeply disappointed to be made Minister of Housing and Local Government, subjects on which, in his own words, he 'knew nothing'.

It was this appointment, however, which was to be the real making of Macmillan. The Tories' annual conference, normally a placid affair, had got out of hand in 1950 when the delegates, against the wishes of the platform, had insisted on setting a target of building 300,000 new houses per year, a figure which the party leadership regarded as quite impracticable (the current level was not much more than 200,000). Now Churchill challenged Macmillan to achieve it. 'It is a gamble' he said, 'which will make or mar your political career. But every humble home will bless your name if you succeed.'

On 1 December 1953, Macmillan was able to make a triumphant announcement: the target had been reached. It had been achieved through his own tireless energy – and ceaseless bullying (with Churchill's full support) of other ministers to release scarce supplies and financial resources desperately needed for other urgent purposes, such as school-building, road construction and industrial expansion. It had been achieved, in part, through the efforts of his junior minister, Ernest Marples, a professional builder, and of his remarkable Permanent Under-Secretary, Dame Evelyn Sharp. And it had been reached through a savage reduction of the minimum standards for public housing set by his predecessor, Aneurin Bevan. Never mind, the target had been reached, and Macmillan shamelessly took all the credit for it and was rewarded with standing ovations from subsequent Tory conferences. He was the hero of the hour, and he waited impatiently for promotion to one of the senior offices of state. But this had to wait on Churchill's retirement, which would release the Foreign Office on Eden's promotion to Number 10, and Churchill was in no hurry to go. He clung on until April 1955, and in the meantime, Macmillan had to make do with the Ministry of Defence to which he was appointed in October 1954. He did not enjoy the experience, finding that Churchill, whose powers in general were rapidly waning, still retained a close interest in defence matters and was constantly interfering.

It was an immense relief to Macmillan when Churchill finally retired and, as expected, Eden appointed him Foreign Secretary. The relief did not last long. The new Prime Minister wanted to conduct his own foreign policy, and was reluctant to give Macmillan his head. After only eight months, and much to Macmillan's chagrin, he replaced him by a much junior figure, John Selwyn Lloyd, who he rightly judged would be more compliant. Macmillan was made Chancellor of the Exchequer, replacing Rab Butler, who became Leader of the House of Commons. Macmillan made a mighty fuss and tried to impose conditions; one of which, that Butler should not formally be designated as Deputy Premier, he was granted, though Butler continued to preside at Cabinet meetings in Eden's absence.

Macmillan started off with the ambition of becoming a great reforming Chancellor, but is remembered in that role for a single gimmick, the introduction of Premium Bonds, in the only Budget he was to present. The truth is that, for the greater part of the year that he held the office, he neglected his duties – especially during the Suez dispute – to concentrate his attention on foreign and defence issues. Thus he failed, unlike his French opposite number, to draw on credits from the International Monetary Fund, which would have helped prevent any subsequent run on the pound.

Of all Eden's ministers, he was the most gung-ho in urging the use of military force, and even submitted a memorandum suggesting that Israel should be associated with an Anglo-French attack several weeks before the French came up with their own plan to collude with the Israelis. He also, perhaps unintentionally, seriously misled Eden into believing that Eisenhower would support British military action, after a meeting with the President in mid-September, a meeting from which the British Ambassador, Sir Roger Makins, who was present and took detailed notes, drew precisely the opposite conclusion. Then, when the Anglo-French invasion had just started, he took fright at the fall of the pound, which he had done nothing to guard against, and demanded an immediate cessation of activities. Macmillan was dubbed as 'First in, and first out' by Harold Wilson in a devastating critique of the Suez operation, but his performance did him no apparent harm, despite the presumption that his first stance would have alienated the anti-Suez Tories, and his later one the much more numerous pro-Suez element.

Two months later, when Eden resigned, the Queen failed to ask his advice as to whom to call on as his successor, though he went out of his way to express his appreciation of the way in which Butler had led the government during his absence. She did consult Churchill, but the choice was effectively made by the retiring Cabinet, who were interviewed one by one by their two senior colleagues in the House of Lords, Lord Salisbury and Lord Kilmuir. Salisbury (grandson of the Prime Minister) had difficulty in pronouncing his 'r's, and said to each in turn: 'Well, which is it, Wab or Hawold?'

Of the members of the Cabinet, only one, Patrick Buchan-Hepburn, the Minister for Works, plumped for Butler. Macmillan's appointment came as an almost total surprise to the general public, virtually all the newspapers having predicted that Butler would be chosen. Had the vacancy occurred six months earlier, there is very little doubt that he would have won the prize, but the Suez episode was a disaster for him. He was seen as weak and indecisive, and the constant talk of appeasement had cruelly revived memories of his pre-war record as a close collaborator of Neville Chamberlain. Macmillan, by contrast, was seen as strong and determined, even if his judgement left a great deal to be desired.

Macmillan's appointment looked remarkably like a poisoned chalice, and he himself told the Queen that he doubted whether he would survive for more than six weeks. Yet he took immediate steps to calm the situation, starting by subtly emphasising the contrast between his own and Eden's more febrile approach by pinning to the Cabinet office door a notice with the words 'Quiet calm deliberation disentangles every knot'. This was a quotation from W.S. Gilbert's *The Gondoliers*, and thus began the enduring legend of Macmillan's 'unflappability'. Nevertheless, during his first year in office he had a distinctly rocky ride. Already in March 1957, he suffered his first Cabinet resignation when Lord Salisbury, the Leader of the House of Lords, quit in protest against the release from captivity of the Cypriot independence leader Archbishop Makarios, who had been deported to the Seychelles a year earlier. Salisbury had a substantial following among right-wing Tories, and was later to be the focus of resistance to decolonisation in Africa, but his departure from the government had little immediate impact. More serious, in the short-term, for Macmillan was a rebellion of right-wing MPs, eight of whom resigned the party whip in May, when the Cabinet, in a final acknowledgement of the futility of the Suez operation, recommended British shipowners to use the canal and pay dues to Egypt. Throughout the year, the government was dogged by appalling opinion poll figures, giving a large lead to Labour and poor by-election results. Then, in January 1958, he lost his entire Treasury team when Peter Thorneycroft, the Chancellor of the Exchequer, and his two junior ministers, Enoch Powell and Nigel Birch, resigned, claiming that the expansionist economic policies which Macmillan was pursuing would have disastrous inflationary consequences. Macmillan, who was about to depart on an extensive Commonwealth tour, airily dismissed the resignations as 'little local difficulties', and was widely admired for his aplomb.

Almost the first, and certainly the most important, step that Macmillan had taken to put the Suez disaster behind him, was to meet with President Eisenhower in Bermuda in March 1957. The purpose was to restore the close Anglo-American relationship, which – aided by his wartime association with Eisenhower, and it must be admitted a generous helping of obsequiousness – Macmillan succeeded in doing. Also at Bermuda, Eisenhower agreed that the US would supply Britain with guided missiles, which allowed the fiction of an 'independent' British deterrent to be maintained. Soon after this the first British hydrogen bomb was exploded, conscription was abolished, defence expenditure sharply cut, and the era of excessive dependence on nuclear weapons in British defence policy began.

By the spring of 1958 the worst was past, and – though opinion polls and by-elections continued to go badly – Macmillan had succeeded in consolidating his government and binding up the wounds in his own party. Equally importantly, he had impressed his own personality on the consciousness of the voters. No grey, anonymous figure, he: what the public saw was 'a bit of a card'. Elements of Macmillan the showman had already been revealed as Housing Minister; as Prime Minister he was to undergo a substantial makeover. In Horne's words,

> Gone were the little commissar-like spectacles, the 'Colonel Blimp' moustache had been ruthlessly pruned, the disarrayed teeth fixed – which somehow transformed the toothy, half-apologetic smile; the hair had assumed a more sophisticated shapeliness. Here was a new, almost dapper figure, with instant authority; the television 'personality had arrived'. (Horne, 1989, Vol. II, p. 145)

It was not, however, a very modern persona. He still wore Edwardian clothes, went shooting on ducal grouse moors, and stuffed his government with Etonians (half the Cabinet), and other aristocrats, many of them his relations by marriage. In the short term, at least, this image did him no harm. It coincided with the last flourish of deference voting by a section of the working class. Moreover, at least until 1960–61, he was far more popular than his Labour opponent, Hugh Gaitskell, who came over to the public as too earnest and too cerebral (a little like the pre-war Macmillan, in fact). Attempts to mock Macmillan's image only rebounded on his critics. Epithets such as 'MacWonder' and 'Supermac', applied to him ironically by Aneurin Bevan and the left-wing cartoonist Vicky, were taken at face value by many people and added to his growing renown. In July 1957, Macmillan made a speech at Bedford, when, drawing on an earlier slogan used by the Democrats in the 1952 US elections, he said: 'Let us be frank about it: most of our people have never had it so good.' He was referring to the growing prosperity, as post-war shortages had come to an end and more and more people were owning motor cars, television sets and washing machines for the first time. The general sense of well-being which this engendered disguised the fact that it was precisely at this period that Britain began to fall seriously behind its continental neighbours, with lower growth rates and higher inflation. Never mind, most people were better off than before, and the Tories claimed – and duly received – the major credit for it.

It took time, however, for this feeling to work through to their political advantage, and it was only in early 1959 that the Labour lead in the opinion polls disappeared, and confidence began to grow in the prospects of a Tory victory. Macmillan was in no hurry to put this to the test. In order to bolster his image as an international statesman, he undertook two initiatives. One was to invite himself to Moscow, where, wearing an outsize fur hat (which unknown to his Soviet hosts he had acquired in Finland in 1940, where he had gone on an abortive mission to organise western help against the Russian invasion), he was able to achieve unprecedented media coverage, despite the relative paucity of the results of his talks with Nikita Khrushchev. Then followed his master-stroke – an invitation to the tremendously popular US President 'Ike' Eisenhower to visit him in London, where he allowed himself to be shamelessly exploited for electoral purposes by agreeing to appear in a relaxed television discussion with Macmillan, which turned out to be an exercise in mutual admiration. The Labour Party, whose leader, Hugh Gaitskell, had been refused any contact whatever with the American President, fumed, but could do nothing about it. A few months later, in October 1959, Macmillan faced the electorate, with the slogan 'Life is Better with the Conservatives – Don't Let Labour Ruin it', and was returned with a sharply increased majority of 100 seats. Gaitskell, who put up a spirited fight, was widely blamed for rashly promising that a Labour government would not put up income tax. This probably was counter-pro-ductive, but even if he had fought an impeccable campaign the odds would still have been stacked against him.

The 1959 election was Macmillan's greatest triumph, but it marked a watershed in his premiership. Before then virtually everything had gone right for him; afterwards almost everything went wrong. His main political initiative during his second term concerned the European Economic Community (EEC) (then usually known as the Common Market), and it cannot be denied that he made a botch of it, as he himself recognised in his memoirs. 'I shall never cease to blame myself', he wrote, for not having acted earlier and more decisively to pursue British membership, first of the European Coal and Steel Community (ECSC) and then of the EEC. He wasted his first term of office in promoting the European Free Trade Association (EFTA), essentially a spoiling tactic, which it rapidly became clear was in no way an adequate substitute for EEC membership. Then he hesitated for the best part of two years, before, on 31 July 1961, announcing a rather half-hearted application. He exerted himself, with no little skill and ruthlessness, to maximise support within his own party – only 40 out of some 4000 delegates opposed the application at the Conservative conference in October 1961 – but made no attempt at all to secure cross-party support. This undoubtedly was a factor in pushing the Labour leader, Hugh Gaitskell, who was initially believed by his friends to be mildly pro-EEC, into the hostile camp, thereby undermining the force of the British application.

Edward Heath was appointed to conduct the membership negotiations. He acquired an impressive mastery of the details of a very complex process, stubbornly holding out for the best deal obtainable in every chapter of the negotiation. In retrospect, this, too, can be seen as a mistaken tactic, as it only added to the delay in bringing the proceedings to a conclusion. (Later applicants for EEC membership – notably Greece – found that they did better to agree quickly to whatever was offered, knowing that their bargaining power would be much greater once they were *inside* the Community.) In the event, it was the accumulated delays which proved crucial in the failure of the application. It had always been suspected that de Gaulle was at best lukewarm to British entry, but French public opinion was broadly in favour, and the General was in a weak position to enforce his will. Then, in October 1962, he won a crushing majority in a referendum on the presidency, following this up with a sweeping electoral victory one month later, and his authority was transformed. Peeved by Macmillan's behaviour at his meeting with President Kennedy at Nassau in December 1962, when he won the US leader's reluctant consent to bolstering Britain's nuclear deterrent, while not securing equivalent assistence for France, he announced the French veto on 29 January 1963, only two days after his Foreign Minister, Maurice Couve de Murville, had told Heath that 'nothing can now stop these negotiations from being a success'.

The normally ebullient Macmillan was shattered by this setback, confiding to his diary, 'All our policies at home and abroad are ruined.' De Gaulle's rebuff was only one of a series of setbacks to Macmillan during his second term of office. His economic policies started to go seriously awry, and not only the Tories', but his own personal opinion poll ratings plunged, leaving him far behind Gaitskell, and after his death, Harold Wilson. There followed a series of by-election disasters, after one of which, in July 1962, Macmillan promptly sacked one-third of his Cabinet, including Selwyn Lloyd, the Chancellor of the Exchequer and the Lord Chancellor, Lord Kilmuir. The 'night of the long knives' was widely seen as a panic reaction, the Tory Chief Whip, Martin Redmayne, remarking to Rab Butler that 'For once the unflappable actually flapped.' A cartoon in the pro-Conservative *Sunday Express* showed a battered Macmillan, as the captain of the ship Never Had It So Good, saying 'Members of the crew, I have driven the ship on the rocks. For such striking incompetence, you're fired.'

The remaining months of his premiership were blighted by the twin scourges of satire and scandal. The satire boom, which began with the Cambridge Footlights review *Beyond the Fringe*, was followed by the BBC programme *That Was The Week That Was*, which portrayed the formerly dynamic leader as a clapped out anachronism. The damage to his image was compounded by his handling of the Vassall and Profumo affairs. He emerged badly from the Vassall spy scandal, in November 1962, when he over-hastily demanded the resignation of a junior minister who was later revealed as blameless. Then came the much more damaging Profumo affair, in which the War Minister was discovered to have shared the favours of a call girl with a Soviet agent, and in which Macmillan was revealed as being gullible and out of touch. He was severely shaken by the subsequent confidence debate, on 17 June 1963, when the normal Tory majority of 97 fell to 57 due to a spate of abstentions. The heaviest blow was a devastating speech by Nigel Birch, one of the three Treasury ministers who had resigned in 1957. He quoted Browning's poem *The Lost Leader* (originally written as an attack on Wordsworth for abandoning his youthful idealism):

> ... let him never come back to us!
> There would be doubt, hesitation and pain,
> Forced praise on our part – the glimmer of twilight,
> Never glad confident morning again!

'Never glad confident morning again' undoubtedly reflected the view of the majority of Tory MPs, who now saw Macmillan as an electoral liability and – though lacking the will to push him out – earnestly hoped that he would make way for another standard-bearer to take them into the general election, now possibly only a few months away. Macmillan, now nearing 70, agonised for several months over whether to continue, deciding – only on the night of 7–8 October 1963 – that he would do so and would lead the Tories at the general election. He announced this to the Cabinet the following morning, only to be stricken by severe pains, which led him to adjourn the meeting early. He had an inflamed prostate gland, necessitating an immediate operation. Macmillan, known for his hypochondria, convinced himself that he had cancer, and decided he must resign forthwith – a decision he was to regret for the rest of his life.

He made one other decision: that, come what may, he would not be succeeded by Rab Butler, who was the obvious choice. His motives for doing down the man who had served him loyally and efficiently as a deputy for nearly seven years were complex. He no doubt despised him as a Man of Munich, but both the rival contenders whom he sought to promote were equally tarred with the same brush. Lord Hailsham (Quintin Hogg) had been the pro-Munich Tory candidate in the Oxford by-election in October 1938, while Lord Home had actually attended the Munich conference as Neville Chamberlain's PPS. Whatever drove him to it, Macmillan, who supervised the whole selection process from his sickbed, was utterly unscrupulous in his methods. He got the Chief Whip and the Lord Chancellor to conduct highly suspect soundings of Cabinet ministers and Tory MPs, and then 'cooked the books', according to the then Tory Chairman, Iain Macleod, before reporting to the Queen that Lord Home had more support than any other candidate. It is arguable that had the Queen, or her advisors, been less guileless, they ought to have taken other soundings before sending for Lord Home, but Macmillan had really put her in an impossible situation. It is also true that if Butler, who undoubtedly would have been the majority choice if there had been a proper ballot either of the Cabinet or of Tory MPs, had had the guts to refuse to serve under Home, he could probably have forced the issue in his own favour (see next chapter). As it was, Macmillan did a serious disservice to his own party by landing it with the leader who was least well qualified to be Prime Minister and least likely to be a successful vote-winner at the subsequent general election.

Macmillan was prime minister for six years and 281 days – the fourth longest tenure in the century, after Thatcher, Wilson and Asquith. Technically, he was rated as one of the more effective Prime Ministers, but his long period in power was notably barren in its achievements. He pushed ahead with decolonisation, but not in the territories with a substantial settler population, though he prodded the South Africans to abandon apartheid in his 'Wind of Change' speech. Not a single parliamentary bill passed by his government has reverberated down the years as a landmark piece of legislation, unless it was the introduction of life peerages. The truth is that by the time he became Prime Minister, Macmillan had long ceased to be a reformer. He was the complacent leader of an essentially complacent country. Apart from wanting to increase British influence in the world, which led him to support both an 'independent' nuclear deterrent and British entry into the EEC, he had no deeply felt objectives. Instead, he was determined to put on a good show, and for a long time he succeeded in this, adding greatly to the gaiety of the nation. He attracted a variety of theatrical nicknames, including 'Mac the Knife', the 'Actor-Manager', and the 'Old Poseur'. But like most old troupers, he went on rather too long, the audience got bored, and he ended up being likened to *The Entertainer* in John Osborne's play. By 1963, it was time to leave the stage, as he subsequently conceded in his memoirs. He was to live another 23 years, refusing to take a peerage until his 90th birthday, when he became Earl of Stockton. This, apparently, was in part because he periodically harboured the (quite unrealistic) hope that he would be summoned back to lead a government of national unity. In his old age, he acquired a new reputation as a fount of wit and wisdom, and became something of a national treasure. It was rather a lonely life – his wife had died in 1966, and he lived virtually alone with his books in the cavernous house at Birch Grove, occupying himself with the affairs of his publishing firm and his duties as Chancellor of Oxford University, to which he had been elected while still in Downing Street. Consulted by Mrs Thatcher during the Falklands War, he later fell out with her when he likened her privatisation projects to 'selling off the family silver'. He died in 1986, and the most apt verdict on him was probably that of Lord Blake who, commenting on his lifelong admiration for Disraeli, wrote in the *Dictionary of National Biography*: 'It is arguable whether Disraeli was a great prime minister, but he was certainly a great character. The same can be said of Harold Macmillan' (Blake, 1996).

Works consulted

Blake, Robert, article in *Dictionary of National Biography 1986–1990*, Supplement, Oxford, Oxford University Press, 1996.

Bond, Martyn, Julie Smith and William Wallace (eds), *Eminent Europeans*, London, Greycoat Press, 1996.

Butler, David, and Richard Rose, *The British General Election of 1959*, London, Macmillan, 1960.

Howard, Anthony, Rab, *The Life of R.A. Butler*, London, Macmillan, 1987.

Horne, Alistair, *Harold Macmillan, Vol.I, 1894–1956*, London, Macmillan, 1988.

Horne, Alistair, *Harold Macmillan, Vol.II, 1957–1986*, London, Macmillan, 1989.

Ramsden, John, *The Winds of Change: Macmillan to Heath 1957–1975*, London, Longman, 1996.

Sampson, Anthony, *Macmillan: A Study in Ambiguity*, Harmondsworth, Penguin, 1968.

Young, Hugo, *This Blessed Plot: Britain and Europe from Churchill to Blair*, London, Macmillan, 1998.

45

Sir Alec Douglas-Home – Right Man, Wrong Century?

The 14th Prime Minister of the twentieth century was a 14th Earl, an improbable occurrence and one never likely to be repeated. Alexander Frederick Douglas-Home was born on 2 July 1903, the eldest of seven children of the 13th Earl of Home (pronounced *'Hume'*). He himself was to undergo several name changes, becoming successively Lord Dunglass, Earl of Home, Sir Alec Douglas-Home and, finally, Lord Home of the Hirsel. According to his official biographer, D.R. Thorpe, his 'upbringing was privileged even by the standards of the upper classes of the time' (Thorpe 1996). He was descended from two of the most powerful and wealthy families in Scotland. The Douglases, famous robber barons, had been the scourge of the English for several centuries; the Homes had betrayed their own countrymen to collaborate with their English oppressors, and, in 1603, the first Earl came down to London with King James I, as one of his most trusted advisers. The Douglas and Home families were united by marriage in 1832, and, when Alec was born, his grandfather, the 12th Earl, owned well over 100,000 acres, with estates in Berwickshire and Lanarkshire – the latter containing valuable coal deposits – as well as several grouse moors, valuable fishing rights over a long stretch of the River Tweed, and castles at Douglas and the Hirsel, near Coldstream.

Alec's family environment was a happy one. His father Charlie– reportedly an exceptionally nice man – was a conventional landowner and part-time banker in Edinburgh. His mother, the former Lady Lilian Lambton, daughter of the Earl of Durham, was a more radical influence. Known teasingly in the family as 'the well-known socialist', she was to vote Labour in the 1945 election, even though her son was by then a junior Conservative minister. Alec was educated at home by a governess until the age of ten, when he was despatched to a prep school in Hertfordshire, where he stayed until 14, the school having contrived to retain him for an extra year because of his prowess on the cricket field. By then, already known as Lord Dunglass (a courtesy title he assumed when his father became the 13th Earl), he arrived at Eton on the same day as a boy called Eric Blair

(George Orwell), though their careers, both at school and later, were sharply to diverge. In every respect, except academically, where he was – at best – no more than average, Alec's time at Eton was an outstanding success. Elected a member of Pop, an elite society of senior boys, the literary critic Cyril Connolly included a remarkable vignette about him in his own autobiographical essay, originally published in 1938:

> The other important Pop was Alec Dunglass, who was President and also Keeper of the Field and Captain of the Eleven. He was a votary of the eso-teric Eton religion, the kind of graceful, tolerant sleepy boy who is showered with favours and crowned with all the laurels, who is liked by the masters and admired by the boys without any apparent exertion on his part, without experiencing the ill-effects of success himself or arousing the pangs of envy in others. In the eighteenth century he would have become Prime Minister before he was thirty; as it was he appeared honourably ineligible for the struggle of life. (Connolly, 1938, p. 245)

From Eton, in 1922, Dunglass proceeded to Oxford, where he enrolled in Christ Church, the most socially exclusive college, where the ambience, espe-cially among his own group of friends, resembled that recounted by Evelyn Waugh in *Brideshead Revisited*. It was, according to Home's biographer, 'a carefree world of hunting, cricket, bridge and champagne, though racing was becoming one of Dunglass's interests at this time' (Thorpe, 1996, p. 32). He also began to take an interest in politics, and attended meetings of several political clubs, while steering clear of the Union. He studied history, obtaining only a Third Class degree, possibly, in part, because of a mysterious illness which afflicted him at the time of his finals, though, according to one of his tutors, it 'did not really matter to him what sort of academic label he would bear on leaving Oxford' (Thorpe, 1996, p. 31). He came down in 1925, and made no attempt to seek employment, even as the manager of the family estates, which his father would have been pleased for him to do. Instead, he decided to 'swan around' for a couple of years, devoting his time to an endless round of cricket matches, point-to-point meetings, shooting parties, salmon fishing and country house visits. He went on a cricket tour to South America with the MCC, and played for a variety of clubs including the local Coldstream side, the Eton Ramblers, the Free Foresters and I Zingari. He had a natural talent for the game, had been coached by top-class professionals at Eton, and was probably good enough to play regularly for an English county side if he had had the inclination.

He had, however, more serious interests in view, one of which was to become an MP – not, his biographer insists, because of *noblesse oblige*, but through a genuine ambition to hold senior office. Because of his social background, he had no difficulty at all in getting selected as a Conservative (or Unionist, as they were known in Scotland) candidate. He just mentioned to Sir John Gilmour, the Secretary of State for Scotland, and to Noel Skelton, MP for Perth, that he would like to contest a seat at the 1929 general election, and an immediate invitation arrived to fight Coatbridge and Airdrie, a predominantly industrial seat close to the family estates at Douglas. The 25-year-old Dunglass, who had led such a cloistered life, had a rude awakening when he faced the working-class electorate of the constituency. One of them – a miner – recalled him, 44 years later in a BBC programme, as being 'Probably the rawest and most immature candidate I have ever seen at any time.' Another recalled him as being 'pathetic on the platform, absolutely pathetic' (Thorpe, 1996, p. 44). Dunglass was easily defeated by the Labour candidate, but was not put off by the experience and in 1931 eagerly accepted an invitation to fight the Lanark constituency, formerly held by a leading Scottish Tory, Walter Elliot, which had been a narrow Labour gain in 1929. As part of the landslide victory won by Ramsay MacDonald's National Government, Dunglass easily defeated his Labour opponent with a nearly two-to-one majority. He was 28, and his foot was on the first rung of the political ladder.

No sooner was the election over than he reached the second, when he was invited to become PPS to Noel Skelton, who was Under-Secretary at the Scottish Office. Skelton, who was to die of cancer only four years later, was regarded as one of the most promising of younger Tory politicians and was the unofficial leader of a group of progressive MPs, including Anthony Eden. Working as Skelton's 'eyes and ears', Dunglass became familiar with the very wide range of economic and social issues for which the Scottish Office was responsible. This familiarity was extended to English and Welsh affairs in 1935 when he transferred to become PPS to Anthony Muirhead, the Under-Secretary at the Ministry of Labour. Home impressed people equally by his great courtesy and by the conformity of his views. Very much on the 'respectable' wing of the party, he firmly rebutted overtures from such subversive characters as Winston Churchill. Nevertheless, as a PPS to junior ministers, he remained a minor player on the Westminster stage. In 1936, however, he received a notable step up when he was asked to perform the same duties for the Chancellor of the Exchequer, Neville Chamberlain. Chamberlain liked his protectionist views, and another factor which they had in common was their love of bird-watching. The same year, at the age of 33, he had married Elizabeth Alington, six years his junior and the daughter of his former headmaster at Eton. The marriage, which was to last almost 54 years, was a happy one, and was to produce a son and three daughters. Dunglass remained with Chamberlain when he became Prime Minister, a few months later, and was a wholehearted participant in his appeasement policy.

He accompanied Chamberlain to the Munich conference with Hitler, and for ten days afterwards, Chamberlain, who was exhausted physically and mentally, went with his wife and the Dunglasses to the Hirsel to recuperate, at the invitation of the 13th Earl. Subsequently, Dunglass was heavily involved in the by-election which took place in Kinross and West Pethshire, in December 1938. The sitting MP, the Duchess of Atholl, had been deselected by the local Conservatives because of her criticism of Chamberlain, and promptly resigned her seat to fight a by-election on an anti-Munich platform. Described by a later Tory MP, Robert Rhodes James, as 'one of the dirtiest by-election campaigns of modern times, from which only the duchess emerged with any distinction', Dunglass's participation did him little credit, and he makes no reference to it in his autobiography. He, in fact, was the star speaker on behalf of the Tory candidate, who was narrowly elected, and the posters advertising his meetings read: 'COME AND HEAR THE TRUTH ABOUT MUNICH FROM THE MAN WHO WAS THERE WITH THE PRIME MINISTER.'

An unconditional admirer of Chamberlain, Dunglass remained with him to the bitter end, even declining office as a junior Scottish Office minister in September 1939 in order to continue as his parliamentary aide. On the day war was declared – 3 September – Dunglass was involved in a bizarre incident, which does much to explain his subsequent image as a comic character out of P.G. Wodehouse. He had driven down to the South Downs with his brother Henry to search for a rare species of butterfly. Arrested in some woods by a suspicious Special Constable, who, when Dunglass claimed to be the Prime Minister's PPS, replied: 'Yes, and I'm the Queen of Sheba', it required a hurried phone call to 10 Downing Street before he was prepared to release his captives. Amazingly, he was again to be arrested, by the Oxfordshire police, in similar circumstances a year later.

Dunglass was appalled when Churchill replaced Chamberlain as Prime Minister in May 1940, and joined in a last-ditch effort to persuade Lord Halifax to take over, describing Churchill and his associates as 'gangsters'. A month later, he was reported as having told the wife of a Tory whip that 'since W[inston] came in, the H of C had stunk in the nostrils of decent people' (Stewart, 1999, p. 426). It was unsurprising that Churchill found no place for Dunglass in his coalition government. Instead, Dunglass intended to join up, as did his four younger brothers, one of whom was killed in action. He already had a commission in the Lanarkshire Yeomanry, but his plans were thwarted by a breakdown in his health. He had tuberculosis of the spine, and in September 1940 underwent a vital operation, and was then incarcerated in a plaster cast for two years, during which he was unable to leave his home. It was only in July 1943 that he was well enough to resume his work as an MP. He made the most of his period of inactivity, which seemed to have the effect of focusing his mind on serious issues and maturing his personality. He read very extensively, notably historical and biographical works, and was the only British Prime Minister known to have read Marx's *Das Kapital* from cover to cover. The only effect this had on him was to strengthen his already fervent anti-communism, which was further reinforced by his contact with Polish soldiers billeted at Douglas Castle. One of these, Count Starzenski, a former private secretary to the Polish foreign minister, Colonel Beck, gave him a first-hand account of the horrors of the Russian occupation of eastern Poland between 1939 and 1941.

In the spring of 1945, Dunglass emerged as one of the fiercest critics of the Yalta agreement, which effectively put Poland at Russia's mercy. He made a powerful speech in the Commons, and was one of 21 Tories to vote against the government when the House was divided on a backbench motion regretting the transfer of 'the territory of an Ally' to 'another Power'. The former appeaser of Hitler was not prepared to bend the knee before Stalin. Churchill was probably not best pleased by Dunglass's repudiation of what he had agreed at Yalta, but nevertheless when a Conservative 'caretaker' government was formed three months later, at the end of the war in Europe, he was appointed as joint Under-Secretary at the Foreign Office. This was almost certainly due to the influence of the Tory Chief Whip, James Stuart, who effectively selected all the junior members of the government. A fellow Scottish aristocrat, and a descendant of King James V of Scotland, he was to continue to be Dunglass's mentor and protector for the best part of a decade.

Dunglass remained a minister for just two months, at the end of which he was heavily defeated in his Lanark constituency in the July 1945 general election, which swept Labour into power. He regained the seat with a narrow majority in 1950, but in July 1951 his father died, and he entered the House of Lords as the 14th Earl of Home. Three months later the Conservatives won the 1951 general election, and James Stuart was appointed Secretary of State for Scotland. He immediately asked for Alec Home to become his number two, as Minister of State. For the next four years he was the man on the spot, supervising the work of the Scottish administration from its headquarters in Edinburgh, and every now and then making a viceregal style tour throughout the country, almost invariably staying in the castles or country houses of various grandees, often his own relatives. Stuart, who was one of Churchill's closest associates, spent nearly all his time in London, leaving Home to operate on a very loose rein. The disadvantage for him was that he himself was very seldom in the national capital, and thus remained fairly unknown to the great majority of political actors, let alone the general public outside Scotland. This position only marginally improved in April 1955, when Eden brought him into his Cabinet as Secretary of State for Commonwealth Relations. In this post, he was largely invisible because of his membership of the upper house, while he was frequently away on visits to Commonwealth countries and territories.

He was confirmed in this post, in January 1957, when Macmillan succeeded Eden, and after another couple of months combined it with the leadership of the House of Lords, when Lord Salisbury resigned over the Cyprus issue. Altogether, he held the Commonwealth Relations portfolio for a record period of over five years. During this time he became very close to Macmillan, who valued his traditional background and relatively right-wing views as a counterweight to the younger, more radical figures he was bringing into his Cabinet, such as Iain Macleod, Edward Heath and Reginald Maudling. Then, in May 1960, he gave Home a staggering promotion, making him Foreign Secretary in place of Selwyn Lloyd, who became Chancellor of the Exchequer. The appointment went down almost universally badly. This was not primarily because of doubts over Home's capacity, but because of a very widespread feeling that it was inappropriate, and an affront to the House of Commons, to have a Foreign Secretary in the House of Lords. The *Daily Mirror* opined that it was 'the most reckless political appointment since the Roman Emperor Caligula made his favourite horse a consul', and the Labour Party put down a censure motion in the Commons. Macmillan recorded in his diary that 'Gaitskell made the cleverest and most effective speech I had heard him make. My reply was not too good, but the Party rallied round.' In fact, criticism within the Tory Party was almost as great as from the Opposition, and it made for a difficult beginning for Home. In the event, he made an adequate if far from outstanding Foreign Secretary, and was actually aided by not having to spend time nursing a parliamentary seat. He was also greatly helped by the appointment, as his deputy, of Edward Heath, as Lord Privy Seal, who took over complete responsibility for European issues and proved a highly effective number two.

Home became a popular figure among foreign diplomats because of his old world charm and congenial manner, and they respected him for his straight talking. Even the Soviet Foreign Minister, the dour Andrei Gromyko, was known to thaw in his presence. He was also easily the best-liked member of the Cabinet, with no known enemies, with the single exception of Iain Macleod. He had become Colonial Secretary in 1959, with a brief to speed up decolonisation, and he resented what he regarded as obstructionism by his colleague at the Commonwealth Relations Office. Macleod, who had famously been attacked as 'too clever by half' by Home's friend and predecessor as Leader of the Lords, Lord Salisbury, had a low opinion of Alec Home's intellectual capacity and regarded him as a reactionary of the deepest hue.

Home thoroughly enjoyed being Foreign Secretary, and no doubt regarded himself as being exceptionally fortunate to have reached what must have seemed the peak of his career at the age of 57. Yet in November 1960 an event occurred which was eventually to give an altogether unexpected twist to his destiny. This was the death of the Labour peer, Lord Stansgate, which had the immediate effect of disqualifying his eldest surviving son, the prominent Labour MP, Tony Benn, from sitting in the House of Commons. The same fate had affected Home himself, in 1951, and he had uncomplainingly complied, as well as Quintin Hogg (Lord Hailsham), who had impotently raged against it, in 1950. Benn was made of sterner stuff, fighting a by-election in his Bristol South-East constituency, and winning it handsomely with a majority of 13,000 over his Conservative opponent, who was nevertheless awarded the seat by an election court. Public opinion was clearly on Benn's side, and the government was eventually forced to introduce a bill enabling hereditary peers to disclaim their titles during their lifetime. Under the original draft, this would only have come into effect after the ensuing general election, but a Labour amendment was accepted in the Lords that it would apply as soon as the bill received royal assent. Within hours of this happening, Benn disclaimed his title; Home and Hailsham did not, but the passage of the amendment in July 1963 was to transform the outcome of the Tory leadership contest three months later.

As recounted in the preceding chapter, this was triggered by Macmillan's mistaken belief that he had cancer, and the announcement that he was to resign was made on 10 October to the annual Tory conference by Lord Home, in his capacity as President of the National Union of Conservative Associations. The febrile atmosphere of the conference was hardly calculated to ensure that there would be a calm and judicious assessment of the merits of the competing candidates, which it was not then generally known would include Home. Indeed, two days earlier he had privately offered his services, along with the Lord Chancellor, Lord Dilhorne, as an impartial 'collector of voices' within the Cabinet, from which his colleagues quite naturally concluded that he was not himself in the running. Earlier in the year, when it had looked as though Macmillan would be forced to resign in the wake of the Profumo affair, the hot favourite was seen to be Reginald Maudling, the youthful Chancellor of the Exchequer. Yet his star inexplicably faded during the summer, and neither he nor two other younger potential candidates – Heath and Macleod – were now seen as likely contenders. The effective choice seemed to be between Rab Butler and Lord Hailsham, who had become eligible since the passage on 31 July of the Peerage Act, which gave existing peers a six-month window of opportunity to disclaim. Butler had much the stronger claim in terms of experience and ministerial achievement, and was far ahead in the opinion polls; Hailsham was known to be very popular among the Conservative rank and file and was believed to be Macmillan's preferred choice. Yet Home was evidently holding himself in reserve as a compromise candidate. He had arranged to have a medical check-up to see if he was fit enough to bear the strains of the premiership, and a number of highly influential supporters, including Selwyn Lloyd, Heath and John Morrison, chairman of the 1922 Committee of Conservative backbenchers, were already canvassing on his behalf.

When he went to see Macmillan in hospital before his operation on 9 October, he was strongly urged to make himself available. The PM was perhaps having second thoughts about Hailsham, who a day later effectively blew his chances by the theatrical way in which he announced he was disclaiming his peerage, and by parading himself around the Tory conference with his baby daughter and her bottle in his arms. This upset the more decorous Tories, who, according to Home's biographer, believed 'that the proper person to be dispensing such attention was the nanny – and in private' (Thorpe, 1996, p. 525). After this, Macmillan switched his support to Home and set in motion a series of soundings (invariably conducted by Etonians, as Macleod later observed in a biting article in *The Spectator*, when he alleged that a 'magic circle' had fixed the selection on the orders of Etonian Macmillan for the benefit of Etonian Home). There can be little doubt that the soundings (of Cabinet members, Tory MPs and peers and of constituency representatives) were deeply flawed, and that the way in which the questions were put strongly skewed the answers in favour of Home. The overall effect was to give more weight to negative opinions rather than positive expressions of support. It was only on this basis that it was possible to conclude that Home 'enjoyed more support than any other candidate'. There is no serious doubt that Butler would have emerged on top, at least as far as the parliamentarians were concerned, if a straightforward ballot had been arranged, while Hailsham was clearly the favourite of the constituency associations. Home may have emerged as 'the lowest common denominator', but that is hardly a way to choose a party leader in the approach to a difficult election, let alone a Prime Minister. Even on this basis, the poll was later shown to be wildly inaccurate. The scorecard which Lord Dilhorne kept of Cabinet members' preferences, which was published much later, showed both Macleod and Sir Edward Boyle plumping for Home (Ramsden, 1996, pp. 205–6). Both indignantly denied this, and said that their votes had been cast for Butler. Macleod's accusation that Macmillan and his henchmen had 'cooked the books' was never effectively refuted.

When Macmillan received the soundings on 17 October he decided to recommend the appointment of Home when the Queen came to see him in hospital the following morning to receive his resignation. Word leaked out of what was intended, and the supporters of the other candidates reacted in fury. Eight Cabinet ministers were strongly opposed to Home, and at a late-night meeting held at Enoch Powell's flat both Hailsham and Maudling agreed to back Butler for the premiership and to refuse to serve under Home. If Butler's nerve had held, the crown was his. As Powell later graphically put it in a television interview, he and his colleagues had, in effect, given Butler a loaded pistol. He replied, according to Powell, 'Will it go off with a bang?' 'Well, Rab,' they responded, 'a gun does make rather a bang when it goes off.' Butler's response, in Powell's fanciful account, was 'Well, thank you very much, I don't think I will. Do you mind?' (Thompson and Barnes, 1971, p. 219). Home got to know of the opposition to him and suggested to Macmillan that he should delay his recommendation to the Queen, only to be told, impatiently, 'Go ahead. Get on with it' (Ramsden, 1996, p. 204.) So Macmillan railroaded it through, but when Home saw the Queen later in the day, he declined to 'kiss hands' on his appointment, merely saying that he would try to form a government and then report back. His first, highly tricky interview was with Butler, and he handled it with great tact, dangling before him the prospect of being Foreign Secretary, a long-standing ambition which Macmillan had twice refused him. Butler asked for some hours to consider, and then, to the despair of his supporters, meekly accepted. Maudling and Hailsham then agreed to serve under Home; only Macleod and Powell, whose weight was insufficient to make a crucial difference, deciding to boycott the government which Home was able to form on the following day. Macleod objected to Home because he thought he was utterly unsuitable; Powell for a more fastidious reason. He believed that Home had been less than straight in letting his Cabinet colleagues believe that he had no intention of becoming a candidate.

So Home became Prime Minister on 19 October 1963. His first task was to disclaim his peerage and secure election to the House of Commons. Fortuitously a vacancy existed due to the death of the Tory MP for Kinross and West Perthshire, where he had campaigned in the earlier by-election in 1938. The Tory candidate obligingly stepped down in his favour, and Home was duly elected on 7 November. Even now, he did not become plain Mr Home, which would have been more in tune with the modernising message which the Tories were planning to make the basis of their electoral appeal, but chose to be known as Sir Alec Douglas-Home (having been made a Knight of the Thistle in 1962). This was only the first of a string of tactical errors which Home was to make during the 363 days of his premiership, which was aptly described as 'a twelve-month election campaign against the odds' (Ramsden, 1996, p. 214). He had the great misfortune to be pitched against Harold Wilson. Opinions differ about Wilson's record as Prime Minister, but nobody disputes that he was the outstanding Leader of the Opposition of the twentieth century. He established a total domination over Home in the twice-weekly duels at Prime Minister's Question Time, and completely outclassed him as a television performer. Home had given a terrible hostage to fortune when, in September 1962, in an interview with the *Observer*, he said that he doubted whether he would ever become Prime Minister because 'When I have to read economic documents I have to have a box of matches and start moving them into position to simplify and illustrate the points to myself.' This interview was mercilessly recalled, and Home was caricatured as the 'matchstick man' and unfavourably compared to Wilson, who had a formidable reputation as an economist and was impressing many people with his speeches invoking the 'white heat of the technological revolution'.

Home, probably wisely, declined all invitations to debate directly with Wilson on television, but the contrast between their performances was telling. Occasionally, Home was able to score points, as when he commented that his opponent must be 'the 14th Mr Wilson', but the satirical TV programme *That Was The Week That Was* got it about right when it dubbed the contest 'Dumb Alec versus Smart Alec'. Occasionally Wilson overdid the mockery and viewers began to feel sorry for Home, but this was hardly a reassuring basis for building support. Home wryly accepted that he was ineffective on television, and recounted in his memoirs a conversation which he had had with a make-up girl:

Q. Can you not make me look better than I do on television?
A. No.
Q. Why not?
A. Because you have a head like a skull.
Q. Does not everyone have a head like a skull?
A. No. (Home of the Hirsel, 1976, p. 203)

As Prime Minister, Home was calmness itself, and it has been suggested that he, rather than Macmillan, merited the epithet 'unflappable'. He set himself a leisured pace, and I well remember a conversation I had a few years later with Sir Derek Mitchell, his principal private secretary, who went on to fulfil the same role with Harold Wilson. 'Harold', he said 'was the complete professional, working non-stop at the job. Alec would spend a couple of hours being Prime Minister, and would then disappear for a while to the upstairs flat to get on with his own life.' He probably exaggerated the contrast, but it had the ring of truth. Home showed himself singularly devoid of ideas for political initiatives. His electoral strategy consisted basically of hanging on like Mr Micawber, waiting for something to turn up. Possible election dates, first in March and then in June, were passed up because of Labour's continuing lead in the opinion polls, and Home resolved to go on almost to the bitter end, eventually choosing 15 October as polling day (the last possible date, under the five-year rule, would have been 5 November, and Home subsequently regretted that he had not waited until then). Nor did his government have much of a legislative record during his premiership. The only significant bill passed was the abolition of retail price maintenance, a measure insisted on by Edward Heath who, as Secretary for Trade and Industry, was determined to make his own personal mark as a radical reformer. It was fiercely resisted by Tory MPs and within the Cabinet as a likely vote-loser among small traders, even though it meant lower prices for the consumer, and Home only persisted with the bill because he feared that Heath would resign if it were withdrawn.

The decision to delay the election almost paid off, as by August the Labour opinion poll lead had evaporated. Yet it managed to pull ahead again during the actual campaign, when Home made what Thorpe described as 'probably the worst mistake of his entire premiership' (Thorpe, 1996). Questioned in a television interview about pensions, he replied that 'we will give a donation to the pensioners who are over a certain age', the use of the word 'donation' appearing to confirm the Labour assertion that the Conservatives, and Home in particular, were patronising and remote from the concerns of ordinary people. In the event, Labour finished up with an overall majority of only four, the result being as shown in the table below.

Labour	317
Conservative	303
Liberal	9
The Speaker	1

Some of Home's supporters claimed that this result justified his selection as leader, and that it had been a great achievement of his to pin back Labour to such a slender lead. The opposite view that the Tories would have done better under another leader, and especially Rab Butler, carried more conviction. It was not only Home's shortcomings, and his evident inability to personify the Tories' modernising themes, which made his task so difficult, but the whole manner of his selection, and the widespread belief that Macmillan had cheated, that fatally undermined public confidence. Harold Wilson, for one, was convinced that he would have lost the election if Butler had been his opponent.

Home himself blamed Macleod and Powell for the Labour victory and for a brief moment shed his normal gentlemanly manner, and to the amazement of his entourage let loose a flood of expletives against them when the last results trickled in on the afternoon of 16 October. Yet for the most part, he took the defeat philosophically, assuming it meant the virtual end of his political career and that he would soon be able to resume his beloved country pursuits in Scotland. He stayed on, however, as Leader of the Opposition, and – accepting the view that the Tory tradition of 'evolving' a leader had been irremediably discredited – appointed a committee to produce proposals for a direct election by MPs. By February 1965, the new system was ready, and five months later it was brought into effect when Home resigned the Tory leadership. He was not exactly pushed out, but criticism had been building up of his failure to put the new Labour government under pressure in what was expected to be a short period before another election. One damning set of opinion poll findings, which put Home well behind Wilson on every one of a long list of attributes including 'sincerity', was sufficient to persuade him that the time had come to bow out, and Heath duly defeated Maudling in the subsequent poll of MPs on 27 July. Heath insisted that Home remained in his Shadow Cabinet, and when, against expectations, he won the 1970 general election, appointed him for a further term as Foreign Secretary. This continued until the February 1974 general election when the Tories, in turn, were unexpectedly defeated. Home remained as an MP until the following September, and re-entered the House of

Lords as a life peer with the title Lord Home of the Hirsel in January 1975. He lived for another 20 placid years, dying, aged 92, on 9 October 1995, just a few months after Harold Wilson.

When Lord Dunglass came down from Oxford with his mediocre degree in 1925, a reasonable expectation might have been that he would one day become chairman of Berwickshire County Council or, more likely, Lord Lieutenant of the county. Instead, he was to rise to the highest post in the state, where, sadly, he proved to be out of his depth, without however committing the egregious errors of a Neville Chamberlain or an Anthony Eden. Cyril Connolly was perhaps right to conclude that he was born in the wrong century. Two hundred years earlier, he would never have made a Walpole or a Chatham, but might well have held his own with the likes of the Earl of Wilmington and the Duke of Portland.

Works consulted

Butler, D.E. and Anthony King, *The British General Election of 1964*, London, Macmillan, 1965.

Connolly, Cyril, *Enemies of Promise*, London, Routledge & Kegan Paul, 1938.

Dickie, John, *The Uncommon Commoner*, London, Pall Mall, 1964.

Home of the Hirsel, Lord, *The Way the Wind Blows*, London, Collins, 1976.

Ramsden, John, *The Winds of Change: Macmillan to Heath, 1957–1975*, London, Longman, 1996.

Stewart, Graham, *Burying Caesar: Churchill, Chamberlain and the Battle for the Tory Party*, London, Weidenfeld & Nicolson, 1999.

Thompson, Alan and John Barnes, *The Day before Yesterday*, London, Panther, 1971.

Thorpe, D.R., *Alec Douglas-Home*, London, Sinclair-Stevenson, 1996.

Young, Kenneth, *Sir Alec Douglas-Home*, London, Dent, 1970.

46

Harold Wilson – Master – or Victim – of the Short Term

He was only the third person of what used to be known as 'humble origins' to become Prime Minister, and his family background was markedly more comfortable than that of Ramsay MacDonald, and also of David Lloyd George. Yet Harold Wilson could claim to have been the first 'meritocratic' Prime Minister, coming up through a public education system which enabled him to compete with, and outshine, his contemporaries from upper- and middle-class backgrounds. Like his four predecessors – Attlee, Eden, Macmillan and Home – and four of his successors – Heath, Thatcher, Blair and Cameron – he was an Oxford graduate, but his academic achievements surpassed all of theirs.

According to Philip Ziegler, his 'authorised' biographer, Wilson's family were 'low church, low-living, lower middle class and proud of it' (Ziegler, 1993). He was born in Huddersfield on 11 March 1916, seven years after his sister Marjorie, who was later to become a headmistress, and who proved to be a notably bossy if affectionate sibling. Their parents, both active in the Congregationalist Church and the Scouts and Guides movements, and with ties to the fledgling Labour Party, had migrated from Manchester some years earlier. Harold's father, Herbert Wilson (who bore a remarkable physical resemblance to the novelist C.P. Snow, who was quite unexpectedly included, as a life peer, in Wilson's 1964 government) was a skilled industrial chemist who had missed out on a university education because of lack of means. Herbert's elder brother, Jack, had twice been election agent to Keir Hardie, the first leader of the Labour Party. A man credited with an 'extraordinary memory', for which Harold was also to be famous, Herbert had to uproot himself and his family several times in search of work, and was to suffer two prolonged periods of unemployment. His wife, the former Ethel Seddon, also had a brother – Harold – who was an active Labour Party worker. He emigrated to Australia, and was to rise to the level of Speaker of the West Australian Parliament, though by then he had abandoned his Labour affiliations.

The young Harold grew up in a frugal household, and his first interests closely mirrored those of his family and its immediate circle. He became a fanatical Boy Scout, an activity for which he was later to be much mocked – behind his back – by his more sophisticated political associates, and a fervent supporter of Huddersfield Town football team, the Manchester United of its day. At primary school he was more noted for his memory and tenacity than for his brilliance, but he won a scholarship to the local grammar school, and later – when Herbert was forced to move his family to Cheshire in search of employment – became the star pupil, and only sixth-former, in the newly established Wirral Grammar School, from which he won an Open Exhibition to Jesus College, Oxford.

Three events, in particular, were to be remembered from his childhood. At the age of eight, his father took him on a sightseeing trip to London, where he was photographed outside the front door of 10 Downing Street. This was to be reproduced many times 40 years later when he became Prime Minister, leading to the perhaps mistaken assumption that this had been a serious childhood ambition. A more significant influence on him was probably a visit to Australia, which he made with his mother, at the age of ten, to visit her Seddon relatives. This seems greatly to have expanded his horizons. Third, at the age of 14, was his apparently miraculous cure from typhoid, which killed six of his fellow Scouts on a camping trip, and from which he narrowly survived after three months in hospital, during which his weight went down to four and a half stone. His grandfather commented 'The lad is being saved for something', and his entire family was convinced that Harold was a special child and would go on to do great things.

He did not disappoint them. At Oxford, where he lived an exceptionally frugal life – not wishing to make more than the minimal demand on his family's straitened resources – he concentrated almost exclusively on his work, eschewing the social charms of the University which had largely occupied the time of his predecessor as premier, Alec Douglas-Home. Wilson studied Politics, Philosophy and Economics, and achieved one of the highest First Class Honours ever awarded, going on to win two of the grandest essay prizes in the University – the Webb Medley prize for economics and the Gladstone history prize, an extraordinary achievement for a non-historian. He was immediately snapped up by the Master of University College, Sir William Beveridge, to assist him on his research on unemployment and the trade cycle, and was elected to a junior research fellowship at the College. During his time as a student, he had taken only a peripheral interest in politics, never speaking at the Union, and soon migrating from the Labour Club, dominated by public school Marxists, to the Liberals, becoming the club treasurer, though not showing any deep or lasting commitment to Liberalism. It was not until 1939 that, under the influence of G.D.H. Cole, an Economics Fellow at University College and the leading Oxford Socialist of his generation, he joined the Labour Party in Oxford, without playing a very active role.

At the age of 18, when still at school, Wilson had met his future wife, Gladys Mary Baldwin, the daughter of a Congregationalist minister, at a tennis club in the Wirral. Within three weeks, he announced to her (a) that he was going to marry her, and (b) that he would become Prime Minister, the second of which assertions she did not take seriously. The marriage only took place six years later, on 1 January 1940. By this time, Harold, who had been supporting his parents during a lengthy period of unemployment for Herbert, now forced to resettle in Cornwall to find another job, felt at last in a position to establish his own household. Mary, who had been a shorthand typist, was entranced by Oxford, and felt that there was no better fate than to become the wife of a don. She little knew what to expect from her future life, despite Harold's forecast to her in 1934.

In fact, their life together in Oxford was extremely brief. Wilson had registered for military service, but as an economist was instead ordered to work as a temporary civil servant. By April he was transferred to London, where he undertook a series of demanding jobs related to the economic planning of the war effort, working under the supervision of such eminent economists as John Jewkes, Lionel Robbins and, again, William Beveridge. Wilson found Beveridge, a notably cold and self-centred man, an uncongenial boss, but professionally they were an extraordinarily good match. Inveterate workaholics, they both scorned theory and worshipped facts, the careful collection of which they saw as the starting-off point for the framing of policy. In June 1941, Beveridge, who was seen by ministers and senior officials alike as a disruptive influence, was eased out of his job as Chairman of the Manpower Committee of the War Cabinet Secretariat, and asked to chair an inter-departmental inquiry into the co-ordination of social insurance. It was meant to be a backwater, but the Beveridge Report, when it appeared in 1942, was a political sensation. and became the blueprint for much of Labour's post-war social legislation. Beveridge had asked Wilson to become the secretary of this committee, but he declined because he was already fully stretched by his other responsibilities. Thus did he narrowly avoid becoming one of the founding fathers of the welfare state.

Instead, he accepted a post in the Board of Trade concerned with the mining industry, whose poor levels of production were threatening the war effort. Wilson revolutionised the collection of statistics in what was universally seen as a chaotic industry, and created a much firmer base for policy planning. Among the many officials he impressed was Hugh Gaitskell, another temporary civil servant, who was a personal assistant to Hugh Dalton, the President of the Board of Trade. Asked to assess the personnel of the Mines Department, he wrote a glowing encomium on Wilson, whom he described as 'extraordinarily able. He is only twenty-six, or thereabouts, and is one of the most brilliant younger people about.' Seeing how the government machine worked from the inside reignited Wilson's dormant political ambitions and, encouraged by Dalton, he decided to seek a parliamentary constituency. At his second attempt, in September 1944, he won the nomination at Ormskirk, a sprawling constituency on the outskirts of Liverpool, and not regarded as a good prospect for Labour. Yet, aided by a split right-wing vote and the overwhelming national swing to Labour, he was duly elected in July 1945, at the age of 29.

On polling day he published a book, *New Deal for Coal*, which he had written in five weeks, drawing on his experience at the Mines Department. This provided a practical blueprint for the nationalisation of the industry to which the Labour Party had long been committed, but had devoted very little thought to its implementation. Wilson's book proved a godsend to the incoming Minister of Fuel and Power, Emanuel Shinwell, and, together with the formidable reputation which Wilson had gained as a civil servant, may have been the reason why – almost alone of the newly elected Labour MPs – he was given an immediate post in the government, of which he was the youngest member. He became Parliamentary Secretary to the Minister of Works, George Tomlinson.

He served for 18 months, without making any great splash. He was regarded as forceful and effective, but lacking any sort of profile, either with the general public or within the Labour Party, while, according to his biographer, Ben Pimlott, his 'ministerial speeches notoriously emptied the House', being 'technical, repetitive, excessively detailed, over-prepared and lacking in humour' (Pimlott, 1992). Nevertheless, he succeeding in attracting the favourable notice of senior members of the government, notably Sir Stafford Cripps, the President of the Board of Trade, and in March 1947 he became one of his junior ministers, as Secretary for Overseas Trade. He remained in this post for only six months, during which time he distinguished himself as a tough negotiator with Soviet ministers in two rounds of trade talks in Moscow, in which he was pitted against the formidable Armenian, Anastas Mikoyan. In late September, Cripps took overall charge of economic policy, becoming Minister for Economic Affairs, a post he soon combined with that of Chancellor of the Exchequer, when Hugh Dalton resigned in November following a trivial Budget leak. Cripps relinquished the Presidency of the Board of Trade, and Wilson was promoted to take his place on 29 September. He was 31 years old, the youngest Cabinet minister since 1806, and a good ten years younger than any of his new colleagues.

Still, like other economic ministers, under the overlordship of Cripps, he nevertheless enjoyed a fair degree of autonomy, and basked in the aura of success which the rapidly improving trade figures cast upon him. He made a big impact as the man who made a 'bonfire' of wartime controls, most of which were shed under his stewardship, starting with a large batch which were consigned to the flames on Guy Fawkes Day 1948. The choice of this date was one of many indications that the previously technocratic minister was rapidly learning the techniques of public presentation. Only one event marred Wilson's otherwise triumphal tenure of the Board of Trade, and this was totally unknown to the public. Its was his role in the 1949 devaluation of the pound.

This was forced on the government by heavy pressure on sterling and a subsequent drain on the reserves, which built up during the first half of the year. Many economists began to believe that devaluation was a necessary corrective, and that the sooner it was applied the better. This view was strongly resisted by Treasury officials, and in particular by the Chancellor, who felt that it was a moral imperative to maintain the value of the pound, especially because of the faith put in it by Commonwealth and other governments, who kept their foreign reserves in sterling. Meanwhile, Cripps's health was causing increasing concern, and, in July, he left to stay at a clinic in Zurich, leaving three relatively young ministers, all of them professional economists and former wartime temporary civil servants, in charge of economic policy, under the notional control of the Prime Minister, a self-confessed economic ignoramus. These were Hugh Gaitskell, Minister of Fuel and Power (though still outside the Cabinet), Douglas Jay, Economic Secretary to the Treasury, and Wilson. In the course of the next few weeks, both Jay and Gaitskell became convinced of the necessity to devalue and put the case strongly at a series of meetings with Attlee, Herbert Morrison and senior officials. Wilson was much more hesitant, appeared to change his stance erratically, and was suspected of playing politics with the issue in the hope of strengthening his position as Cripps's likeliest successor in the event of the latter's early resignation.

If this was his objective, it failed disastrously. On the contrary, he created a bad impression, both on Attlee and other senior ministers, and within the Treasury, whereas Gaitskell, who had previously not been viewed as a possible Chancellor, won high marks for his clarity and decisiveness. The devaluation was effected in September 1949, and was seen as a grave blow to the government's standing, though it went on to win the general election, the following February. Its majority, however, shrank to five seats, and it was regarded as inevitable that a further election would be held within a very few months. In fact, the government held out for another 20 months, during which it suffered a series of hammer blows. The first of these was the resignation of Cripps due to ill health in October 1950. Gaitskell, who already after the election had been made Minister of State at the Treasury, effortlessly moved up to take his place. Wilson was visibly put out, and so was another – more senior – member of the Cabinet, Aneurin Bevan, who felt that his great success in launching the National Health Service should have earned him promotion to one of the senior posts in the government. Bevan's dissatisfaction grew, five months later, when that other bulwark of the Attlee government, the dying Ernest Bevin, was replaced as Foreign Secretary by Herbert Morrison, while he himself was fobbed off with a sideways move to the Ministry of Labour.

Meanwhile, the Korean War was still raging, and under pressure from the United States the government decided, in early 1951, sharply to increase its rearmament programme. This decision brought Bevan and Wilson together, both arguing that the proposed level of expenditure was unrealistic and would gravely weaken the economy. They failed to convince their Cabinet colleagues, but in mid-March, Hugh Gaitskell, as Chancellor of the Exchequer, proposed a Budget which, alongside other economies, sought to rein in expenditure on the National Health Service, including making charges for false teeth and spectacles which had previously been supplied free of charge. The amount of money to be saved was trivial in relation to the Budget as a whole, but Gaitskell held his ground in the face of a threat by a furious Bevan to resign if the proposal went through.

In the event, two other ministers resigned along with Bevan – John Freeman, a promising junior minister, and – to general astonishment – Harold Wilson. Bevan's resignation was widely regretted, but understood. Many Labour MPs regarded it as quixotic, but few questioned his motives. It was seen as a principled action by a deeply emotional man who did not always calculate his moves wisely. The reaction to Wilson was quite different. His was seen as an act of pure opportunism, particularly on the right wing of the party. They saw it as an attempt to ingratiate himself with the left, with whom he had not previously been identified, and to attach his star to that of Nye Bevan, who was widely seen as a future Labour leader and Attlee's successor.

Even on the left, Wilson's motives were questioned, but he was quickly accepted as Bevan's number two in the developing rebellion which secured overwhelming support among Labour's rank and file, though alienating opinion in the trade unions and among a majority of Labour MPs. Bevan and Wilson were excoriated for splitting the party, and paving the way for defeat in the October 1951 general election. On the other hand, it soon became apparent that they had been right, and their colleagues wrong, in their judgement about the feasibility of the rearmament programme, which was quickly dropped by the incoming Conservative government.

In personal terms, Bevan's resignation undoubtedly damaged his career, and, together with a number of subsequent ill-judged actions, helped to destroy his previous excellent chances of succeeding to the party leadership. In Wilson's case, however, it is arguable that it proved an essential step on his way to the top. Nevertheless, it represented a considerable gamble at the time, and his subsequent path was far from smooth. One early effect of his resignation was to round him out as a politician. He received an avalanche of invitations to speak at meetings organised by constituency Labour parties. This took him to venues all around the country, and helped to familiarise him with a Labour movement previously almost unknown to him. He became a great deal more assured as a platform speaker. Always much respected for his knowledge and authority on economic issues, he broadened his canvas and began to speak in a more punchy and partisan way across the whole political spectrum. He inserted a previously unsuspected strain of wit into his speeches, and became increasingly adept at handling hecklers.

At the 1952 Labour Party conference at Morecambe, where the Bevanites made an almost complete sweep in the elections to the constituency party section of Labour's National Executive Committee (NEC), he and Richard Crossman succeeded in displacing two great stalwarts, Herbert Morrison and Hugh Dalton, who had sat on the committee since the 1920s. This gave him a valuable foothold in Labour's national organisation. He had less success in running for the Shadow Cabinet, elected by Labour MPs, gaining only 13th place in a ballot for 12 members in November 1953.

During this time, though publicly seen as Bevan's chief lieutenant ('Nye's little dog', as Dalton contemptuously put it), Wilson grew increasingly impatient with him, deploring his unpredictability and his unwillingness to consult with his allies. Temperamentally, they were very dissimilar, and Wilson's views on many current issues were, in fact, far closer to Gaitskell's than to Bevan's. He seems to have privately concluded that Bevan had blown his chances of ever becoming leader, and that Gaitskell was more likely to be Attlee's successor. He was unwilling, however, to break with Bevan, and was put in a quandary when the Welshman impetuously resigned from the Shadow Cabinet in April 1954 after a disagreement with Attlee over policy in the Far East. As runner-up in the ballot, Wilson was entitled to take the place vacated by Bevan, an action which most of the Bevanites regarded as rank disloyalty. Wilson hesitated long and hard, but eventually agreed to join the Shadow Cabinet, an action which perhaps foreshadowed his decision to vote for Gaitskell rather than Bevan or Morrison when Attlee finally resigned the leadership in December 1955.

Wilson was still only 39, ten years younger than Gaitskell, and no doubt reckoned that he stood an excellent chance of serving as Chancellor in a future Gaitskell government and eventually succeeding him in the leadership. He accordingly assured Gaitskell of his total loyalty, and was as good as his word in the four years up to the 1959 general election, by which time he was already Shadow Chancellor. Had Labour won the election, Wilson would almost certainly have become Chancellor and, with the death soon after of Nye Bevan, the most powerful figure in the government after Gaitskell, with every prospect of being his eventual successor. Instead – against his instincts – he found himself pitched into a struggle against his party leader which threatened to destroy all the goodwill built up during their previous four years of close co-operation.

Labour had entered the election campaign with high hopes of victory, and were shocked by the ease with which the Tories, only three years after the Suez fiasco, swept back to power with a greatly enhanced majority. The major reason for their success was undoubtedly the national sense of material well-being after the ending of wartime and post-war shortages. Gaitskell and his closest associates, however, concluded, with some justification, that a subsidiary cause was that Labour was widely seen as a doctrinaire nationalising party, even though this perception was hardly justified by the party's current policies. They fixed their attention on the Labour Party's constitution, dating from 1918, in particular on its Clause Four, which called for the common ownership of 'the means of production, distribution and exchange', and decided that it must be repealed or amended to emphasise that the party was not bound by ancient shibboleths. It was an ill-considered move, which ran up against deeply held sentiments in many sections of the party, particularly in the trade union movement, and was subsequently abandoned in a humiliating about-turn. Wilson, who had not been consulted, thought it was ludicrously inappropriate, believing that not one voter in a thousand knew about Clause Four and that to make a fuss about it would only draw attention to its provisions.

His other clash with Gaitskell was much more serious. At the party conference at Scarborough, in October 1960, a resolution in favour of unilateral nuclear disarmament was carried, despite a passionate speech by Gaitskell, in which he had pledged himself 'to fight, fight and fight again to save the party we love'. Gaitskell refused to accept his defeat, and resolved to continue the struggle in the hope of reversing it the following year. Wilson, whose own views on defence policy were very similar to Gaitskell's, thought that the differences should be papered over and a compromise document should be prepared by the NEC. He was taken aback when his former comrades from the Bevanite group decided to challenge Gaitskell's leadership at the beginning of the new parliamentary session the following month, and strongly pressed Wilson to be their candidate. He resisted their importunity, and only consented to stand when another prominent former Bevanite, Anthony Greenwood, put his hat into the ring. Wilson did not want a contest, but if there had to be one he was determined that no one else should be the left-wing candidate. In the ballot of Labour MPs, he secured the respectable but somewhat disappointing total of 81 votes, against 166 for Gaitskell.

Wilson's action revived all the old charges of opportunism which had been levelled at the time of his ministerial resignation, and he grievously offended the Gaitskellite wing of the party, now in the ascendant. He was regarded as thoroughly untrustworthy and feelings akin to hatred were freely expressed. Wilson feared that he would be dropped from his post as Shadow Chancellor, and exerted himself to bolster his position. For the time being, he managed to hold on, but a year later Gaitskell triumphantly succeeded in reversing the Scarborough conference decision, and was riding high. Wilson was then switched to Shadow Foreign Minister, hardly a demotion, though not a change that he welcomed. His position in the party and his rising reputation as one of the foremost debaters in the House of Commons made him an indispensable member of Gaitskell's team, but though he tried hard to ingratiate himself with the leader the distrust remained. His attempt to become deputy leader of the party, in November 1962, by challenging the erratic George Brown, who had succeeded to the position on the death of Bevan in 1960, was unsuccessful. He was almost universally regarded as the more able man, but lost by 103 votes to 133, due to the continuing hostility of the Gaitskellites. His long-term prospects for the leadership did not look good at that point. While guaranteed senior office in the event of a Labour victory in the forthcoming election, it seemed likely that he would subsequently be overtaken by a trio of slightly younger Gaitskellites of outstanding ability, Roy Jenkins, Tony Crosland and Denis Healey.

Everything changed with the sudden death of Gaitskell in January 1963. As deputy leader, George Brown was the favourite to succeed him, but, alarmed by his unpredictability and his alcoholism, several leading Gaitskellites refused to back him. 'It's a choice between a crook [Wilson] and a drunk', Crosland remarked, and together with Douglas Jay and others promoted the candidature of James Callaghan, who had succeeded Wilson as Shadow Chancellor. Brown proceeded to alienate many of his potential supporters by his bullying tactics, while Wilson projected a calm and statesmanlike air. He led on the first ballot by 115 votes, to 88 for Brown and 41 for Callaghan, and easily beat Brown by 144 to 103 in the run-off.

Wilson continued on his statesmanlike course as Leader of the Opposition, confirming all his Shadow Cabinet colleagues in their posts, even though only one of them had voted for him in the leadership ballots. The former Bevanite group had, of course, been his own core supporters, and he justified his favoured treatment of the Gaitskellites to them by saying that he was forced to run 'a Bolshevik revolution with a Tsarist Shadow Cabinet'. In his final year, Gaitskell had not only triumphed over his enemies in the Labour Party, but had also established a commanding position lead in the opinion polls, now being the preferred choice of a majority to the rapidly fading Harold Macmillan. All this would now be lost, Labour feared, but to their delighted surprise, Wilson's succession was followed by a further increase in the Labour lead. His somewhat dubious reputation in certain Labour political circles had never communicated to a wider public, and he started off with a virtual clean slate with the mass media exposure, which began with his election as leader. Young (46 – 22 years younger than Macmillan), energetic, forceful yet moderate in his views, with an easy manner and a classless appeal, he seemed to many to be the British answer to John F. Kennedy, then at the height of his renown, three months after his successful handling of the Cuban missile crisis. He built assiduously on the good initial impression which he had created, making virtually no serious mistakes in the unexpectedly long period – 21 months – before the 1964 election. He was helped, of course, by the self-inflicted wounds of his Tory opponents, from Macmillan's maladroit handling of the Profumo affair to the questionable circumstances in which Douglas-Home acceded to the premiership. During this period, he established a greater domination, as Leader of the Opposition over the Prime Minister, than any of his predecessors or successors, though Tony Blair perhaps came close in 1995–97. Yet despite Wilson's Herculean efforts, he was unable completely to dispel long-standing fears of what a Labour government might do, and in the final weeks before the election the Labour lead in the opinion polls shrank to nil. The election, after all, became a closely fought affair, and on 15 October 1964 Labour was elected with a majority of only four seats.

Nevertheless, the election of Labour after 13 years in opposition, and with Wilson, at 48, easily the youngest Prime Minister of the century so far, raised high expectations. Most of these were to be dashed by a decision taken within the next 24 hours, without proper consideration or consultation with their colleagues, by three exhausted men – Wilson, James Callaghan, who was appointed Chancellor of the Exchequer, and George Brown, First Secretary and Minister for Economic Affairs. The Tories had left the economy in a parlous state; Reginald Maudling, the Chancellor of the Exchequer, having introduced a giveaway Budget the previous March, in anticipation of an early election, and then failing to take any remedial action during the summer as the balance of payments position sharply deteriorated. Treasury and Bank of England officials advised the trio that immediate action was imperative, with three options available. These were devaluation of sterling, import quotas or temporary tariff surcharges.

The pound was clearly overvalued, and opprobrium for a new devaluation could easily have been shifted on to the outgoing government, but Wilson – with painful memories of his involvement in the 1947 devaluation – was determined not to go down the same route again. He had little difficulty in persuading his two less experienced colleagues to choose the third option – temporary import surcharges. It is easy, with the advantage of hindsight, to condemn the decision, as many have done. In the circumstances, however, it was an understandable choice to make, and Wilson should not be unduly blamed for his misjudgement. What is less easy to condone was his absolute refusal to reconsider the issue, which became the 'great unmentionable' until the eve of the final humiliating debacle of November 1967. According to Sir Alec Cairncross, the government's economic advisor, 'There was no meeting between 1964 and 1967 between ministers and officials on whether, when and how devaluation should be done' (Pimlott, 1992, p. 474).

Despite this initial mistake, Wilson's government got off to a tremendous start, impressing the country with its dynamism and wealth of ideas. Wilson himself completely dominated the political landscape, enjoying an unprecedentedly good press for a Labour leader, and maintaining his mastery in the

Commons, where he continued to worst Douglas-Home in their twice-weekly confrontations at Question Time. The Tories changed leader, in August 1965, choosing Edward Heath on the assumption that he would be able to hold his own with Wilson, but it made very little difference.

It was a government of near beginners. Apart from Wilson himself, only the veteran James Griffiths (Welsh Secretary) and Patrick Gordon Walker (Foreign Secretary) had ever served in a Cabinet before. Gordon Walker was an early casualty. He had lost his seat in the general election, but had still been appointed by Wilson, only to lose again in a by-election vacancy created for him, in January 1965, and promptly resigned, being replaced by the able, but unexciting, Michael Stewart. Wilson's key colleagues – George Brown and James Callaghan – had served as junior ministers in the Attlee government. Wilson hoped to provoke 'creative tension' between them by installing both in economic departments – Callaghan in the Treasury and Brown in the newly created Department of Economic Affairs, with a mandate to produce a National Plan which was intended to transform the British economy. Neither man was perfectly fitted for his job. Brown was highly intelligent and full of energy and drive, but was erratic, undisciplined and only intermittently sober. Callaghan was a much more controlled individual, with sharp political antennae, and seemed by contrast 'a safe pair of hands'. Yet he had only a limited grasp of economics, did not get firmly in control of his department and was too ready to defer to the judgement of his Prime Minister who was regarded, at least initially, as an economic as well as a political wizard.

Wilson early recognised the potential of his three slightly younger Gaitskellite rivals, giving each of them important posts. Denis Healey went straight into the Cabinet as Defence Secretary. Tony Crosland, much the most economically literate minister, became number two to George Brown, and began by having a furious row with him over his agreement with Wilson not to devalue. He soon moved on, becoming Education Secretary, in succession to Stewart, in January 1965. Roy Jenkins started off as Aviation Minister (outside the Cabinet), turned down the Education post, but became Home Secretary 11 months later.

The 1964 Labour government had its ups and downs, but its overall impact was extraordinarily positive, and Wilson got great credit for his skilful handling of his knife-edge majority. The highlight was undoubtedly the launch, in September 1965, of George Brown's National Plan, which – based largely on copying the successful French experience of indicative planning – confidently predicted that the notoriously sluggish British growth rate could be raised to the dizzy level of 3.5 per cent over nine years, enabling the social and economic life of the nation to be transformed. Wilson then cruised to an easy victory in the general election of March 1966, which increased his majority to 98 seats.

Wilson seemed at the height of his power, but it was not long before the chickens released by his refusal to devalue began to come home to roost. An ill-considered Budget introduced by Callaghan in April, followed by disap-pointing balance of payments figures and a strike by the National Union of Seamen, which seriously disrupted the export trade, led to a run on the pound in July. Wilson was absent on a visit to Moscow, and was disconcerted to find on his return that both Brown and Callaghan had been converted by Crosland, Jenkins and other ministers to the necessity for devaluation. Wilson, who suspected a plot against his own leadership, quickly won over Callaghan, who agreed to the alternative of a major deflation, involving severe cuts in expenditure, the statutory restriction of prices and wages and the virtual aban-donment of the National Plan targets. A furious Brown was determined to resign, but was bought off by the offer of the Foreign Office, the post he had always coveted. The hapless Michael Stewart was stripped of his responsibilities, and was compensated by Brown's title of First Secretary of State and the now sharply downgraded Department of Economic Affairs.

These events marked a watershed in Wilson's premiership. The almost universal esteem in which he had previously been held began to fade. The press, which hitherto had shown excessive admiration, now swung to the opposite extreme, and he became the butt of increasingly intemperate and often viciously personal attacks. Within the Labour Party, and particularly among Labour MPs, his critics began to multiply, both on the right and on the left. This became far worse a year or so later, when, in November 1967, a renewed run on sterling forced the devaluation against which he had for so long set his face. Wilson's humiliation was made even worse by his complacent – and widely mocked – television broadcast, in which he assured viewers that 'the pound in your pocket' would not lose 14 per cent of its value. Callaghan insisted on resigning as Chancellor, proposing Crosland, by then President of the Board of Trade, as his successor. Wilson demurred, and instead chose Jenkins, partly because he was anxious to keep Callaghan in the government, and the easiest way to achieve this was by a straight swap of jobs with the Home Secretary. There were other reasons, too, one perhaps being that whereas Crosland was the better qualified economically, he found Jenkins a more congenial colleague. He was, however, taking a risk, as Jenkins, who had already attracted widespread support among MPs for the progressive reforms he had backed as Home Secretary and for his commanding speeches in the Commons, would be a formidable rival if his leadership came under challenge.

Initially, however, it appeared as though Jenkins had been handed a poisoned chalice. For devaluation, if inevitable, was no easy option. It had to be bolstered by an even more severe deflation than in the previous year, and four major government policies were reversed. The British military presence east of Suez was abandoned, a large order for F-111 fighter planes was cancelled, prescription charges were re-introduced into the National Health Service and the raising of the school leaving age to 16 was postponed. Despite these radical measures, there was an exceptionally long and nerve-shattering wait until the gaping deficit in the balance of payments began to improve. In the meantime, the government became increasingly unpopular and lost a long series of by-elections, many of them in normally ultra-safe seats. Wilson himself became deeply unpopular, but respect for Jenkins continued to grow as he played a cool and steady hand and retained his parliamentary dominance over the Opposition.

Wilson had come to depend, to a perhaps excessive extent, on his 'Kitchen' Cabinet for moral support and political advice. Chief among them was his political secretary, Marcia Williams (later Baroness Falkender), who had served him throughout the long years of Opposition and continued to do so up to and beyond his final retirement in 1976. The two were extraordinarily close, and there was much speculation about the nature of their relationship. This was probably not – and certainly not primarily – a sexual one. On the whole, she gave him good advice, but she was something of a loose cannon and – according to the published accounts of other members of the Kitchen Cabinet – was given to hysterical outbursts, particularly in later years. Wilson was accused of paranoia, in suspecting imaginary plots against his leadership, and his tight group of advisors was believed to be fanning his fears. Not all the plots were imaginary: the supporters of both Jenkins and Callaghan periodically schemed to supplant him, but no overt move was ever made. This was because the two men were rivals, and neither was prepared to subordinate his own claims to the other. 'Willing to wound, but afraid to strike' best summed up the attitude of a fair number of Labour MPs during this period, and later again, in opposition, in 1970–74.

Much of Wilson's attention during his first premiership was focused on international affairs, three issues in particular predominating: Rhodesia, the European Community and Vietnam. There can be little argument that Wilson seriously mishandled the illegal declaration of independence by the white settler regime of Southern Rhodesia in October 1965, and was subsequently repeatedly outmanoeuvred by the settlers' leader, Ian Smith. It may not have been a crucial error to rule out in advance any resort to military force – the arguments for or against were finely balanced – but it was certainly a mistake to publicise this decision. The evidence is that the Rhodesian military was reluctant to fight British military forces and might very well have restrained Smith and his Cabinet from UDI (unilateral declaration of independence) if they had thought it was a possibility. Wilson subsequently grossly overestimated the prospect of economic sanctions bringing Smith to heel, saying that it would 'take weeks rather than months'. In fact, it took 14 years – and a prolonged guerrilla war – before the settler regime finally backed down, and negotiated an agreement with Margaret Thatcher's government which led to majority rule and independence for Zimbabwe.

Wilson had backed Gaitskell in 1962, when he had opposed the first British application to join the European Economic Community, but five years later, in tandem with his Foreign Secretary, George Brown, he launched a further application, which the two men energetically pressed forward in visits to the capitals of the six member sates. They received some encouragement from French Premier Georges Pompidou, and they were received in Paris with much courtesy by President Charles de Gaulle. A formal application was tabled in May 1967, after a positive vote of 488 to 62 in the House of Commons, but in the following November – before the negotiations began – de Gaulle pronounced his second veto. Wilson had announced that he 'would not take no for an answer', and soon after de Gaulle resigned as President, in 1969, he resolved to have another try, though he insisted that 'the terms must be right'. Negotiations, the government decided, would begin soon after the forthcoming general election.

On the Vietnam War, Wilson was seriously cross-pressured. A vigorous protest movement, largely made up of Labour Party supporters, called for him to dissociate himself from the American intervention. At the same time, President Lyndon Johnson was constantly pressing him to join in the war on the US and South Vietnamese side, as Australia had done. Wilson was acutely aware of the importance of US financial help to back up sterling, and was willing to offer moral but not material support to the US effort. He made several attempts to mediate in the dispute, once through an aborted Commonwealth mission, and another time in conjunction with the Soviet Union, but the Vietnamese Communists were not prepared to accept him as an honest broker, and nothing came of his efforts to achieve a ceasefire. The most that can be said is that he did well to avoid sending even a token military force to Vietnam, but the sum total of his endeavours had no visible effect on the outcome.

One of Wilson's boldest ventures was to attempt to reform industrial relations in Britain through legislation which would have clipped the wings of the increasingly unpopular trade union movement and forced it to behave in a more socially responsible manner. The occasion was the report, in 1969, of the Royal Commission on Trade Unions, chaired by Lord Justice Donovan. This produced a number of commonsensical but unexciting proposals for reform, but the Employment Minister, Barbara Castle, thought that something more emphatic was called for. With Wilson's strong support, she produced a White Paper, *In Place of Strife*, which proposed that ministers should be given powers to order pre-strike ballots and impose a 28-day 'conciliation pause', while a new Industrial Board would have powers to impose fines on unions and individuals who breached the new rules. Compared to the legislation later imposed by the Heath and Thatcher governments, this was pretty mild stuff, but it caused uproar among the trade unions. They exerted immense pressure on Labour MPs to oppose the bill which Castle subsequently introduced. Resistance within the Cabinet was led by the Home Secretary, James Callaghan, who infuriated

Wilson by using his position on Labour's National Executive Committee openly to oppose the bill.

This got bogged down during several months' struggle in the Commons, during which the government abandoned an important measure to reform the House of Lords in order to free more parliamentary time. Finally, the Chief Whip, Robert Mellish, informed the Cabinet that there was no prospect of success, and one by one the members of the Cabinet abandoned a humiliated Castle and Wilson. They had rushed into the venture without proper consultation and completely misjudged the mood of their own party. What was meant to be evidence of the government's ability to control the unions turned into a demonstration of its impotence. It would have been far better to have gone ahead with Lord Donovan's modest reforms. At this stage – mid-1969 – the government was still doing abysmally in opinion polls and by-elections, and hopes of a recovery before the next general election had been all but abandoned.

Yet during the summer of 1969 the balance of payments position dramatically improved, and by the following spring it was showing a substantial surplus, while Labour was rapidly catching up in the opinion polls. Jenkins was under some pressure to produce a pre-election giveaway Budget, but resisted the temptation and followed his judgement that only a mildly expansionist one was justified. Soon after, however, Labour went into the lead in the polls, and good local election results in May 1970 stampeded Wilson into calling an early general election for 18 June, rather than waiting until October, by which time the Labour advantage might well have consolidated.

Throughout the election campaign, Labour led in the polls and there was an almost universal expectation that Wilson would pull off his third consecutive victory. Unwisely, however, Labour based its claim for re-election almost exclusively on its success in restoring the balance of payments. Disaster struck three days before polling day, with the publication of the monthly trade figures for May, showing a large deficit. This was almost certainly the main reason for Edward Heath's remarkable victory, when he succeeded in turning a Labour majority of nearly 100 into a Tory one of 30. The May trade figures later turned out to be aberrant, due to the chance inclusion of a hefty bill for the order of fighter planes from the US. Had the election been a week earlier or a month later, Labour would most probably have won, but its recovery had been too recent and too shallow to withstand the shock.

Both Wilson and his party were devastated by the unexpected defeat, and embarked on nearly four unhappy years in Opposition, wracked with recriminations and disputes. There was no doubting the sense of disappointment at the record of Wilson's first government, after the exceptionally high hopes entertained in 1964. The biggest let-down – inevitably linked to the refusal to devalue during the first three years in power, though it is far from certain that it would otherwise have been achieved – was the failure to transform the economy and jack up the lagging growth rate through the aborted National Plan. This central failure overshadowed the otherwise notable achievements of the government, particularly in the field of education. The years 1964–70 saw the largest ever expansion in higher education, including the establishment of the Open University, and an end to the 11-plus examination through the widespread introduction of comprehensive schools. Equally important was the rash of 'Home Office' reforms, including the abolition of capital punishment, homosexual law reform, the ending of theatre censorship, divorce reform and the decriminalisation of abortion. Each of these long-overdue measures was effected by Private Members' Bills, but none of them would have been passed without government encouragement and, crucially, the provision of parliamentary time. The minister most directly involved was Roy Jenkins, but Wilson could also justifiably claim much of the credit for making Britain a more civilised country than he had found it in 1964.

Yet Wilson had lost much of his bounce and self-confidence, and signally failed as Leader of the Opposition to repeat the dominance he had shown in his earlier period in this role. He also found it impossible to stand out against the left-wing tide of anti-Europeanism which swept through the party and the trade unions as the Heath government successfully negotiated membership of the EEC on terms which most of Wilson's former ministerial colleagues believed he would have found acceptable as Prime Minister. Throughout the summer of 1971, he gave more and more ground to the anti-EEC elements in the party, while assuring the pro-EEC minority that they would have the right to a free vote when the terms were put to the Commons, a promise which in the end he was unable to keep. Eventually, 69 Labour MPs (including the present author) felt compelled to vote, in defiance of a three-line whip, in order to ensure that British membership would go ahead. The episode did immense damage to Wilson's reputation, as he was widely accused of cowardice and inconsistency.

He was deeply hurt by the criticism, maintaining that his overriding duty was to prevent the Labour Party from splitting in two over the issue, and that in consequence it was necessary for him to subordinate his own feelings. On one occasion his patience snapped, and he said to a meeting of his Shadow Cabinet: 'I've been wading in shit for three months to allow others to indulge their conscience.' Although he had been unwilling or unable to prevent the majority coming out against Heath's membership terms, he subsequently exerted himself to prevent an irrevocable Labour decision to withdraw from the EEC. Clutching at a proposal originally advanced by Tony Benn for a referendum to decide the issue, he managed to secure agreement that Labour would first attempt to renegotiate the terms before putting the final decision before the British people.

Few people (not including Wilson himself) seriously believed that Labour would have much chance of winning the next general election, but this was reckoning without Edward Heath. Locked in a struggle with the National Union of Mineworkers, who were in an all-out strike (see next chapter), he rashly called a general election in February 1974 on the issue of 'Who governs Britain?' and then badly mishandled his campaign. The result was a 'hung Parliament' – the first since 1929 – with Labour four seats ahead of the Tories, even though it polled fewer votes. The result gave Wilson an unexpected, and many believed undeserved, chance to redeem his reputation. This he was able to achieve, at least partially. He re-entered Downing Street as a chastened man, with none of the overconfidence he had shown in 1964. Once again, he inherited a precarious economic situation, largely due to the oil shocks following the Yom Kippur War of 1973, which had released ferocious inflationary pressures. Wilson's team this time round was a much more collegiate affair, with the Prime Minister showing little disposition to interfere in his colleagues' ministerial fiefs. The key figures were Denis Healey, as Chancellor of the Exchequer, Michael Foot – the left-wing veteran and Nye Bevan's political heir – brought in to pacify the unions as Employment Secretary, and – above all – James Callaghan, as Foreign Secretary, but *de facto* deputy premier. Roy Jenkins, who had hoped for the Treasury or the Foreign Office, reluctantly accepted a further stint as Home Secretary, but was no longer a central figure in the government. As soon as it was formed, Wilson hastened to settle the miners' strike on giveaway terms, and the following October invited the electorate to form a judgement on his new government, contrasting the calm which it had brought about with the 'chaos' left by the Heath administration, with Britain working only a three-day week, because of the shortage of coal supplies. If he had hoped to repeat his triumph of 1966, he was to be disappointed, but he did manage to secure a parliamentary majority for his previously minority government, though its overall lead was only three seats.

The key event of Wilson's second premiership was the referendum in June 1975 on British membership of the EEC. Shortly after his return to office, he instructed Callaghan to begin a renegotiation of the terms obtained three years earlier by Heath. Britain's European partners, especially German Chancellor Helmut Schmidt, were sympathetic, and he managed to secure a number of concessions. Several of these were of a cosmetic nature, but in the end he managed to cobble together a deal which could be plausibly presented as an improvement on what Heath had achieved. Wilson's difficulty was that a large number of people in the Labour Party, and within his own Cabinet, remained hostile. He solved this problem by a brilliant stroke, calling upon a precedent from 1932, when the members of Ramsay MacDonald's National Government agreed to suspend collective Cabinet responsibility on the issue of tariff reform. Wilson proposed that Cabinet members should be free to support either side in the referendum campaign, even though the government would be recommending a 'yes' vote. The Cabinet split 16 to 7 in favour, though a special

Labour Party conference came down emphatically on the 'no' side. Six months before the referendum, the antis had a strong lead in opinion polls; in the event the pros won by 2 to 1. The reason was almost certainly the greater public confidence in the judgement of the leaders of the 'yes' campaign. Wilson, Callaghan, Heath, Jenkins and the new Tory leader, Margaret Thatcher, were all vastly more popular than the leading antis – Enoch Powell, Tony Benn, Michael Foot, Barbara Castle and Ian Paisley. The real victor, however, was Wilson, who had been so much despised for his earlier tergiversations over the EEC. As the journalist Peter Jenkins put it, he had obtained his three objectives: 'to keep his party in power and in one piece and Britain in Europe'. Now there was nothing left for Wilson to do but retire with honour.

The following March he would be 60 years old, and Wilson had long planned to withdraw at about this time. He was an exhausted man; his wife, Mary, desperately wanted him to quit, and he was perhaps already detecting early signs of the waning of his mental powers which was to culminate some years later in Alzheimer's disease. So, secure in the belief that his elected successor would be the four-years-older Callaghan, with whom, despite their earlier rivalry, he had worked in close harmony throughout his second premiership, he announced his resignation on 16 March 1976. It was an impressive exit – the only voluntary resignation by a Prime Minister in the twentieth century who was still relatively young, in reasonably good health and under no political pressure to stand down. Then he went and spoilt it, by producing a resignation honours list containing a number of distinctly dicey characters. This led to a vast amount of speculation that there must be some other hidden, and discreditable, reason for his departure. This had come as a complete surprise to most people, despite the fact that Wilson's lawyer and confidant, Lord Goodman, had for several months past been dropping gentle hints, which were mostly ignored, to quite a number of leading political figures. However, no skeleton has ever emerged from Wilson's cupboard, and a generation later one must conclude that he gave up for the reasons suggested above. Wilson lived for a further 19 years after his retirement, wrote several more books, presided over a committee of inquiry into the City of London and became a life peer in 1983. Thereafter he gradually faded from public view, and his once famous memory sadly deteriorated. He died on 24 May 1995, aged 79.

Wilson was not a great Prime Minister, but he was much better than many people, including myself, were willing to concede at the time. He had strengths and weaknesses. The strengths included a very quick mind, good tactical sense, immense resourcefulness, an ability to manage a difficult and often querulous party and probably a better understanding of the gut feelings of ordinary voters than any other contemporary politician. He was a cautious man, who disdained any form of extremism, and regarded doctrinal disputes on such issues as public ownership as tedious 'theology'. He was accused of having no deep beliefs – a mistaken view. He was strongly committed to greater equality, the breaking down of class barriers, and the importance of planning. He abhorred racialism, and was a strong believer in sexual equality. He was a moderate believer in European integration, but was not prepared to give it priority over keeping the Labour Party together, though in the end he was instrumental in ensuring that Britain remained within the EEC.

His greatest weakness was his tendency to adopt short-term expedients, which often undermined his longer term goals. One of his most famous sayings was 'A week is a long time in politics', and he was accused of having no strategic vision. A kindly and considerate man, he was a natural conciliator who shied away from conflict, and constantly sought to avoid difficult decisions by seeking compromises where no happy mean actually existed. 'A master of fudge and mudge' was David Owen's damning description. Some of his opponents in the Labour Party regarded him as being exceptionally devious, a charge which was undoubtedly exaggerated. He was vain, ambitious and sometimes opportunistic, but probably no more so than the generality of politicians. He was the first – and only – professional economist to become Prime Minister, but he had no more success in solving the problems of Britain's economic decline than any other post-war premier. He did at least succeed, in very trying circumstances, in keeping the Labour Party together and winning four out of the five elections which it fought under his leadership. This was no mean achievement, and one which his immediate successors were quite unable to emulate. No sooner was he gone than the party began to split apart, and condemned itself to 18 years in Opposition.

Works consulted

Butler, D.E., and Anthony King, *The British General Election of 1964*, London, Macmillan, 1965.

Butler, David, and Michael Pinto-Duschinsky, *The British General Election of 1970*, London, Macmillan, 1971.

Clarke, Peter, *A Question of Leadership: From Gladstone to Thatcher*, Harmondsworth, Penguin, 1992.

Donoughue, Bernard, *Prime Minister: The Conduct of Policy under Harold Wilson and James Callaghan*, London, Cape, 1987.

Jeffreys, Kevin, *Leading Labour: From Keir Hardie to Tony Blair*, London, Tauris, 1999.

Morgan, Austen, *Harold Wilson*, Pluto Press, London, 1992.

Morgan, Kenneth O., *Labour People: Hardie to Kinnock*, Oxford, Oxford University Press, 1987.

Pimlott, Ben, *Harold Wilson*, London, HarperCollins, 1992.

Wilson, Harold, *The Labour Government 1964–70*, Harmondsworth, Penguin, 1971.

Ziegler, Philip, Wilson: *The Authorised Life of Lord Wilson of Rievaulx*, London, Weidenfeld & Nicolson, 1993.

47

Edward Heath – Cheerleader for Europe

In 1916, within four months of each other, were born the two men who, half a century later, were to face each other for ten years as rival party leaders and contest four general elections. They came from similar social backgrounds, but different geographical regions which were strongly to mark their characters – Wilson from Yorkshire, Edward Heath from Kent, where he grew up in the seaside town of Broadstairs, from where, on a clear day, he could see the coast of France. Continental Europe was a living reality to him from his earliest days.

Heath, who was known as a child, and still as a young man, as Teddy, was born on 9 July 1916. His father, William Heath, was a carpenter, who later set himself up as a builder and decorator. His mother, the former Edith Pantony, had worked as a lady's maid. Teddy had a younger brother, John, born in 1920, but was much the brighter of the two children, and became his dominant mother's favourite, and the focus of the family's hopes. William Heath was a skilled craftsman and became a well-respected local small businessman. Fiercely anti-trade union, the mild Liberalism of his youth was to evolve into firm Conservatism. Something of a ladies' man, he was an easygoing congenial character with few intellectual interests. His influence on his elder son seems to have been limited, and Teddy grew up very much a mother's boy. The qualities and habits which she instilled in him – the exceptional importance of cleanliness and tidiness, the necessity for hard work, for taking responsibility for others and a decent ambition to advance his own position in life – early marked him out as exceptional among his schoolfellows at the local Church of England primary school, where he always seemed old for his years. He also showed a precocious talent for music, which his parents encouraged, buying him an upright piano, which they could scarcely afford. The cost, Heath recorded in his autobiography, was £42, which they paid for in 24 monthly instalments of £2 each. Just before his tenth birthday, he sat for the scholarship examination for the local fee-paying grammar school, Chatham House School, at which he won a free place.

Heath was regarded as an ideal pupil at his school, where he won virtually every honour, except in sport, though he was felt by some to be almost unnaturally self-contained. His father wanted him to become an accountant, but Heath set his heart on going to a university, though, as he was to recall, 'I knew that my family would never be able to provide the money to fund me for three years' (Heath, 1998, p. 20). He sat a scholarship examination for Balliol College, Oxford, but did not do sufficiently well to win an Exhibition. He was, however, offered a fee-paying place, which he was able to take up only because Kent County Council offered a loan of £90 a year, repayable when he graduated. So he arrived in Oxford, in October 1935 – one year later than Wilson – to read Politics, Philosophy and Economics at Balliol. He was not there for long before an opportunity arose which transformed his financial situation and gave him a prominent position in the college. The college organ scholarship, worth £100 a year, became vacant, and Heath successfully applied for it. His duties were to include playing the organ in the college chapel at eight o'clock every morning and on Sundays, while also giving him opportunities for conducting choirs and orchestras and even composing. It was to run for three years beginning the following October, which meant that he was able to spend four years in Oxford rather than the normal three.

Heath worked selectively hard at his studies, but, in contrast to Wilson, they did not monopolise his activities. Apart from music, these were centred on the Oxford Union and on the Oxford University Conservative Association, of both of which he became President, as well as of the Federation of University Conservative Associations, and of the Junior Common Room in his own college – Balliol. Heath did not commit himself to the Tory cause without due consideration. In his autobiography, *The Course of My Life*, he admits being attracted to the Liberals, who, he said, 'remained committed to an open society, and to freedom in both the social and economic spheres ... but it was already clear to me that they were a spent force in British politics' (Heath, 1998, p. 28). He wrote that he never considered joining the Labour Party, but – before going up to Oxford – attended the 1935 TUC conference at Margate, out of curiosity. He witnessed there the savage attack by Ernest Bevin, then leader of the Transport and General Workers' Union, on George Lansbury, the pacifist Labour Party leader, who shortly afterwards resigned. He wrote:

> I was pleased that the trade unions were finally committing themselves to tackling fascism, but still considered that socialism smacked too much of state control. I concluded that a moderate form of Conservatism offered the best foundation for a free society, and that the best course for me was to campaign for that brand of thinking within the Conservative Party. But I continued to believe in fairness and deplored the snobbishness of many Conservatives. (Heath, 1998, p. 29)

Heath thus established himself from the outset as being firmly on the progressive wing of the Conservative Party, and soon became a strong opponent of Neville Chamberlain's appeasement policies, in relation to both Germany and Spain. He was one of very few Conservatives who wholeheartedly committed themselves to the Republican cause in Spain, travelling to Barcelona with a student delegation, and narrowly escaped death when the cars in which they were travelling were machine-gunned by a Francoist plane. He also visited Germany, where his conviction of the deadliness of the Nazi threat was only strengthened by his attendance as a spectator at a Nuremberg rally, and a subsequent unexpected encounter at a cocktail party with several Nazi leaders, including Goebbels, Goering and Himmler.

After the Munich agreement, in August 1938, Heath successfully moved a motion in the Union that 'This House deplores the Government's policy of Peace without Honour'. There happened to be a by-election vacancy at Oxford, and Heath proposed himself to the local Tories as their candidate, while making it clear that he was opposed to the Munich agreement. He was turned down, and the young Tory barrister Quintin Hogg (later Lord Hailsham) was brought in to defend the seat and also Chamberlain's appeasement policy. Heath then threw himself wholeheartedly into the campaign for the Independent candidate, running on an anti-Munich ticket, and in whose favour both the Labour and Liberal candidates had withdrawn. This was A.D. Lindsay, the Master of Balliol, whom Heath greatly admired and was much influenced by, despite his being a strong Labour supporter. Lindsay's campaign attracted enormous attention, and he succeeded in halving the Tory majority, without, however, preventing Hogg (later to be Lord Chancellor in Heath's Cabinet) from making his parliamentary debut at the age of 31.

Heath, who was still universally known as Teddy, was a popular figure at Oxford, and mixed easily with Labour supporters, such as Denis Healey, Roy Jenkins and Tony Crosland, who were friends and rivals in the Union. From their subsequent accounts, he appears to have been much more relaxed than the rather buttoned-up character they later confronted across the floor of the House of Commons. Yet Heath apparently felt some social insecurity in a pre-war Oxford, where the vast majority of his fellow students were public schoolboys from far more affluent backgrounds. His biographer, John Campbell, suggests that this was to blame for the 'curious accent' he developed, 'with its tortured and artificial vowel sounds which later attracted such mockery' and was 'markedly different from the soft Kentish burr of his father or – more significantly – of his brother John, who went to the same school but not to Oxford' (Campbell, 1994, p. 18).

Heath graduated in the summer of 1939 with a Second Class degree. He was disappointed not to get a First, but considering the range of his non-academic activities this was as good a result as he could reasonably have expected. He was then faced with a career choice, and hesitated between music and politics, to which he saw the law as a stepping stone. He consulted the Professor of Music, Sir Hugh Allen, who appears to have told him that, though he was a good musician, he was unlikely to reach the very top as a conductor. 'On the other hand, if you go into politics, you will always have music as an amateur to enjoy for its own sake', Heath recorded him as saying (Campbell, 1994, p. 38), and – without undue disappointment – he prepared to take up a scholarship to Gray's Inn to read for the bar. Meanwhile, in August 1939, he left for a visit to Danzig and Warsaw, and was hitch-hiking home through Germany when the Nazi-Soviet pact was announced. He got out of the country only just in time, and returned to London on 1 September, the day of the German invasion of Poland.

He hastened to register for military service, but was not actually called up until the following July, after the fall of France. In the meantime, he was encouraged by the Foreign Office to depart on a lengthy student debating tour of the United States, which was regarded as a good opportunity to project the British viewpoint to American audiences. Like other young budding British politicians, Heath was greatly impressed by much of what he saw in America, without, however, being bowled over by the experience; nor did it, Campbell observed, 'diminish the primary commitment he instinctively felt to Europe' (Campbell, 1994, p. 41). When Heath was eventually called up, he was given a commission as a second lieutenant in the Heavy Anti-Aircraft Artillery. By the time he was demobbed, six years later, he had risen to Lieutenant-Colonel.

Heath took his army duties exceptionally seriously. He saw relatively little action, but proved himself an outstanding administrator and a firm but fair commanding officer. He was noted for the assiduity and speed which he showed in getting to the root of any problems which arose. Campbell comments that 'this is characteristic at each successive stage of his career – and in his private pursuits too – Heath has set himself quickly and thoroughly to learnt the ropes. He had always been a formidably quick learner' (Campbell, 1994, p. 48). Heath ended the war in Germany, where he had been on the eve of its outbreak, and stayed on for a year as part of the army of occupation. He travelled extensively round the country, and was deeply affected by the extent of the destruction. The moral he drew from this is that Europe must never again be torn apart by internecine conflict. He later wrote:

> only by working together had we any hope of creating a society which would uphold the true values of European civilisation. Reconciliation and reconstruction must be our tasks. I did not realise then that it would be my preoccupation for the next thirty years. (Heath, 1998, p. 106)

Heath returned to civilian life in July 1946, and the Broadstairs home of his parents. He had lost the desire to read for the bar, but his inclination to follow a political career was as strong as ever. He was determined to find a parliamentary seat, but in the meantime had to earn his living. He took the Civil Service examination and finished equal top, with another former Balliol man. He was assigned to the Ministry of Civil Aviation, being disappointed not to be chosen for the Treasury. As a civil servant, Heath greatly impressed his colleagues by his administrative qualities and resourcefulness, many of them believing that he would rise to the very top of the service. He was, however, only a bird of passage, resigning in October 1947, as soon as he had been selected as a prospective parliamentary candidate.

This was his fourth try: the first three times he was beaten by rivals with a traditional public school background. The Tories in Bexley, however, a Labour-held marginal seat in the Kentish suburbs with 'a large homogeneous population of the lower middle class and upwardly mobile skilled working class' (Campbell, 1994, p. 60), were specifically on the lookout for a candidate who had risen successfully from a similar background. Heath sailed through the selection meeting, and plunged himself into the work of nursing the constituency with enormous energy and careful military-style planning of all his activities. Meanwhile, he needed a job, and took the first one which was offered – news editor of the *Church Times*, a weekly Anglican newspaper. It was not a happy choice – Heath soon became bored, though he carried out his duties with his customary efficiency. After some 18 months, he took a large salary cut and went to work for a city bank, Brown, Shipley, which undertook to teach him the banking business, while encouraging his political activities. He stayed on with them, on a part-time basis, after he became an MP.

He won the Bexley seat in the general election of February 1950, when the Labour government's previously large majority was cut to five seats. He had two strokes of luck. The sitting Labour MP, Ashley Bramall, had been an old associate of his in the Oxford Union, and happily agreed to an extensive series of debates with Heath. This was a great help to Heath in getting himself known throughout the constituency, and Bramall no doubt later regretted his magnanimity. Even more helpful to Heath was the intervention of a Communist candidate, whose votes – more than three times the size of Heath's majority of 133 – must have come almost exclusively at Bramall's expense. This enabled Heath to squeeze in, and once elected he was never to be shifted. He remained the MP for Bexley, and its successor seat, of Old Bexley and Sidcup, for 51 years, retiring at the age of just under 85 at the 2001 election.

The 1950 class of new Tory MPs was regarded as a vintage crop, including notably three young men who had already distinguished themselves in the Conservative Research department, under the aegis of Rab Butler – Iain Macleod, Reginald Maudling and Enoch Powell. The 33-year-old Heath, now known as Ted, was not seen as an equally promising figure, but made something of a mark by calling for British membership of the European Coal and Steel Community in his maiden speech. He then briefly associated himself with the One Nation Group of socially conscious Tory MPs before disappearing for eight years into the anonymity of the Whips' Office, first in Opposition, and, after the Tory victory in the 1951 general election, as a paid government whip, the most junior form of ministerial Office. The Whips' Office was traditionally a place where less bright but diligent MPs, with little hope of further promotion, were parked. Heath lost no time demonstrating that he was in a different category. He threw himself into the work of the office with the same enthusiasm and application that he had shown throughout his army career. He soon devised a complex card index system cataloguing every conceivable piece of information about Tory MPs, including their peccadilloes, and where they might be found at any time during the day or night. The Chief Whip, Patrick Buchan-Hepburn, a languid Scottish aristocrat, was mightily impressed and soon made Heath his deputy, devolving to him the greater part of his own responsibilities. In December 1955, eight months into Eden's premiership, he became Minister of Works, and Heath was promoted to take his place.

The following year he faced his first great challenge, with the eruption of the Suez crisis. Heath's closest friends believe that he disapproved of the Anglo-French invasion, but he kept his private views to himself, both at the time later. He saw his job as being to hold his party together during a period of extreme turbulence, and he devoted himself to ensuring that party revolts, on either the pro- or anti-Suez side, were kept to minimal proportions. This he was able to achieve through Herculean efforts, and a mixture of tough and tender methods. Macmillan, who replaced Eden in January 1957, regarded it as essential to retain Heath's services during the first difficult months and years of his own premiership. During this time the relationship between the two men was extremely close. Macmillan consulted him on a very wide range of issues – going well beyond parliamentary management, the traditional activity of Chief Whips – and on the whole received excellent and wholly loyal advice from him. Under Eden, Heath had been the first Chief Whip ever to attend Cabinet meetings on a regular basis, and Macmillan continued the practice, which has continued ever since. For his part, Heath had an unprecedented opportunity to build up personal links within the party. This compensated him for the greater public exposure of his contemporaries – Macleod, Maudling and Powell – all of whom preceded him into the Cabinet, and were seen, as he at this time was not, as future contenders for the leadership.

It was only after the 1959 election that he was to enter the Cabinet, as Minister for Labour, replacing Macleod, who became Colonial Secretary. He did not stay long in the post. In July 1960, Macmillan chose the Earl of Home as Foreign Secretary, and sought to balance this by appointing a second Cabinet minister as his deputy, and to answer for the Foreign Office in the House of Commons. Heath hesitated to accept what was technically a demotion, but was reassured when he was rewarded with the office of Lord Privy Seal and given special responsibility for relations with Europe. When, a year later, the government agreed to apply to join the European Economic Community, he was the natural choice as chief negotiator, a task on which he embarked with total enthusiasm, being instantly awarded the title of 'Mr Europe' by the popular press. In the event, it ended in failure – thanks to the veto of President de Gaulle, but it was a venture from which Heath emerged with tremendous credit. During 18 arduous months, he devoted himself single-mindedly to the task in hand, showing extra-ordinary stamina, resourcefulness and mastery of detail, stubbornly defending what he deemed to be essential British or Commonwealth interests, but always seeking a way through to the desired objective, which he was able to present with a rare passion, belying his reputation as a cool pragmatist. His efforts went down particularly well in his own party, where he – perhaps more effectively than Macmillan – played a decisive role in winning round the great majority of those who had initially harboured doubts.

It also turned Heath, who previously had been strictly a behind-the-scenes operator, into an instantly recognisable public figure. This was reflected by his appearance for the first time in newspaper cartoons as one of the small group of leading Tory figures. Even so, Heath had not quite reached the point where he was seen as a credible contender for the party leadership. He recognised this himself, and when Macmillan's resignation was announced at the Tory conference in October 1963 (see Chapter 14), he quickly emerged as one of Alec Home's strongest supporters. He was no doubt influenced by his esteem for Home, under whom he had worked amicably in the Foreign Office, but it cannot have escaped his notice that there was a serious risk of Reginald Maudling, the Chancellor of the Exchequer and one year younger than himself, being chosen and effectively blotting out his own chances in any future contest. In the event, Maudling's candidature faded, and it was Rab Butler who was pipped at the post by Macmillan's blatant manipulation, but the outcome was very much to Heath's advantage. Home appeared, from the outset, as only a stopgap leader, and all the other actual or potential contenders had been damaged in one way or another by the contest. Butler and Hailsham were effectively out of the running for the future, Maudling was seen to have failed, while Macleod and Powell offended against the Tory code of party loyalty by their refusal to join Home's government.

Heath probably hoped to become Foreign Secretary in the new government, but that post was reserved for Rab Butler, as his non-negotiable price for agreeing to serve under Douglas-Home, as the new premier chose to be called. Instead he was appointed to head a beefed-up Trade and Industry department, with a brief to promote economic modernisation and competition. Determined to make his mark, he promoted the only major piece of legislation to be passed in the remainder of the Parliament. This was the bill to abolish retail price maintenance (see Chapter 45), which was introduced and forced through against the resistance of a powerful group of Tory MPs, including several senior ministers. Heath certainly made an impact as a forceful and reform-minded minister, but in the process revealed a hitherto unsuspected streak of authoritarianism and a lack of consideration for the feelings of his colleagues, including junior ministers in his own department, notably Edward Du Cann, who became a lasting enemy.

After the Tory election defeat in October 1964, Heath was appointed Shadow Chancellor, and favourably impressed Tory MPs by the vigour and mastery of detail which he showed in leading the opposition to James Callaghan's first Budget, in the Finance Bill proceedings in the following spring. This may have the deciding factor in his victory over the more languid Reginald Maudling in the first ever leadership ballot, when Douglas-Home resigned in July 1965. He polled 150 votes to 133 for Maudling, and 15 for Enoch Powell. Tory MPs were comparing him not only with Maudling, but also with Wilson, whose toughness and mental agility they thought he would emulate. An unspoken comparison was also with Douglas-Home; they wanted a new leader who was as little like a 14th Earl as possible, and Heath's modest background was undoubtedly seen as an advantage. What was not considered an asset was Heath's bachelor status at the age of 49, a source of endless speculation in political circles. The general consensus was that he was a repressed homosexual, which may not actually have been the case. In fact, as a young man, he had courted – though in a spasmodic way – a local doctor's daughter in Broadstairs, Kay Raven, and apparently expected to marry her, though he never got round to proposing. He refers to this cryptically in his autobiography, saying: 'One day she suddenly let me know that she was marrying someone else. I was saddened by this … maybe I had taken too much for granted' (Heath, 1998). He was never known subsequently to take any sexual or romantic interest in any other woman, though he had a number of close female friends. He seems to have sublimated his feelings in music and – at a later stage – sailing, which he took up only in his fifties with conspicuous success, winning the famous Sydney–Hobart yacht race at his first attempt. His single status may have been an electoral handicap, though there is no firm evidence of this, but it liberated him to apply himself full-time to politics; indeed, he expected the same commitment from his associates and subordinates, seemingly oblivious of the conflicting claims of their wives and families. This undoubtedly proved an asset to Heath in his rise to the top: the downside was that he had nobody to unburden himself to when the going got rough.

It was not long before many Tory MPs began to regret the choice they had made. Heath proved no match for Wilson, who regularly ran rings round him in their parliamentary encounters, while on television he often appeared wooden and ill at ease. It is doubtful whether any other Tory leader would have done much better in the March 1966 general election, when Labour stormed back with a majority of 97, but it was Heath who was blamed by his party, and a whispering campaign against his leadership soon got under way, which was never completely silenced until his unexpected victory in June 1970. During most of the 1966 Parliament the government was highly unpopular, falling far behind in the opinion polls and performing abysmally in local elections and by-elections, where it lost a string of normally safe seats. This meant that Tory morale remained high and there was no overt movement to dislodge Heath from the leadership, despite the fact that his own poll rating fell well behind that of his party. However, when the election campaign got under way in May 1970, Labour leapt into a strong lead in the polls which was maintained right up till polling day, and the almost universal expectation was that it would win. The dismayed Tories were quick to blame their own leader, and it was an open secret that a high-level party delegation would wait on him immediately after the election and demand his resignation.

It is doubtful if even Heath himself believed that the Tories would win the election. During the previous four years he had presided over a comprehensive rethink of the party's policies, and its election manifesto was far more detailed than ever before, with the emphasis on three main themes – lower taxation, trade union reform and membership of the European Economic Community. During the campaign, however, Heath concentrated on a single issue – rising prices – which he hammered home continuously, promising that the Tories would take action to cut them 'at a stroke'. This struck a responsive chord among voters, though the principal reason for Labour's defeat was almost certainly the release just before polling day of monthly trade figures which appeared to undermine its claim to have solved the balance of payments problem (see Chapter 46). The election result was as shown in the table below.

Conservative	330
Labour	287
Liberal	6
Others	7
Conservative majority	30

This unexpected triumph put Heath in a very strong position and imme-diately silenced his many critics. It also had the unfortunate effect of making him surer than ever of his own judgement and even less inclined to seek advice from colleagues. Five of these would have carried sufficient weight to be able to force their views on him in other circumstances, but for one reason or other were not in a position to do so during the period of his government. Iain Macleod was appointed to the key post of Chancellor of the Exchequer, but died within a month of his appointment, a body blow to the new government. His successor, Anthony Barber, was in no sense an adequate replacement. Macleod's death cost Heath not only the shrewdist tactician in his team, but also incomparably the best performer, both in the House of Commons and on television – a particularly serious loss given Heath's own deficiencies in these departments. Reggie Maudling, the Tory Deputy Leader, became Home Secretary, but was now too laid back to make his views strongly felt, and resigned office in July 1972 when questions were asked about his unwise business associations. Enoch Powell, who had been dismissed by Heath from the Shadow Cabinet in 1968, following his notorious 'rivers of blood' speech on immigration, was left out of the government, and became a persistent critic from the back benches. Quintin Hogg was again despatched to the Lords, as a life peer, to become Lord Chancellor, and subsequently regarded his role as strictly non-political, while Alec Douglas-Home, who became Foreign Secretary for the second time, also largely abstained from intervening in domestic affairs. So Heath was effectively on his own, and though other ministers such as William Whitelaw, Robert Carr, Lord Carrington and James Prior subsequently became quite close to him, none of them was able to speak to him on a basis approaching equality.

Heath was also unlucky to come to power at a time of world economic disorder, when the post-war Keynesian consensus was coming to an end, the Bretton Woods agreement on fixed exchange rates was collapsing and strong inflationary pressures, culminating in a quadrupling of oil prices in the last months of his premiership, combined to blight his best endeavours. The consequence was that he had one historic achievement to his credit – British adhesion to the EEC – but that most of his other endeavours ended in failure. On Europe, his own personal contribution was central, and it is doubtful whether any other Prime Minister, in the circumstances of the time – and with the Labour Opposition coming down heavily against him – could have pulled it off. From the outset, Heath made two crucial decisions. One was to restrict the negotiations, ably conducted by Geoffrey Rippon, to an absolute minimum number of crucial issues, of which the continued access of New Zealand farm products to the British market was perhaps the most difficult. The other was to stake everything on winning the goodwill of the French government and its Gaullist President, Georges Pompidou, and to persuade him that Britain would be a constructive member of the Community rather than a Trojan horse on behalf of the United States. Despite Rippon's best efforts, the talks appeared to be bogged down by May 1971, and Heath went to Paris to hammer out the differences face to face with Pompidou in a two-day summit. Pompidou, a tough but relatively open-minded man, who did not share the prejudices or God-given sense of mission of his predecessor, was impressed by Heath's sincerity, straightforwardness and deep European commitment, and at the concluding press conference announced that the main issues had been resolved. Within a few days, the roadblocks in the membership talks were lifted one by one, and by mid-June the negotiation was virtually over.

Heath then faced the daunting prospect of getting the membership terms approved by the House of Commons, where his nominal majority was 25, but where up to 40 Tory MPs were anti-EEC. Thanks to the positive votes or abstentions of 89 Labour members (see Chapter 46), he achieved the surprisingly high majority of 112 in the vote on principle on 28 October 1971. Thereafter it was a hard slog to get the bill incorporating the terms through the Commons, where the committee stage was taken on the floor of the House. A single defeat would have killed the bill, and the process was a protracted and precarious affair, with the bulk of the Labour rebels, having satisfied their consciences by their act of defiance to their party whips in October, now doing what they were told. Altogether there were 105 divisions on the bill between February and July 1972, with the government's majority falling to as low as four, but it emerged unscathed thanks to a small number of Labour veterans not standing for re-election who abstained on the most crucial occasions, and to a masterly performance by Francis Pym, the Tory Chief Whip.

Heath showed courage and fortitude in his handling of the rapidly deteriorating situation in Northern Ireland, where he unhesitatingly followed the policy pursued by his Labour predecessor of pressurising the Protestant-dominated Stormont government to remove discriminations against the Roman Catholic minority. When they failed to do so, and with violence increasing both from the IRA and from Loyalist paramilitaries, he acted, in March 1972, to suspend Stormont and institute direct rule from London, appointing Willie Whitelaw as Northern Ireland Secretary. This was a brave decision for a Tory Prime Minister, half of whose parliamentary majority was made up of Ulster Unionist MPs, traditionally allied to the Tories, but vehemently opposed to direct rule. The appointment of Whitelaw proved an inspired choice. In less than two years, he not only achieved a steady fall in the level of violence, but coaxed Unionists and Nationalists into participating in a power-sharing executive to rule from Belfast. Led by the Unionist Brian Faulkner, with Gerry Fitt of the Social Democratic and Labour Party as his deputy, it was created under the Sunningdale agreement reached in December 1973. Sadly, however, Faulkner did not succeed in carrying the bulk of Unionists with him, and the new agreement was fatally undermined by the February 1974 general election when anti-Sunningdale candidates made a clean sweep of the Unionist-held seats. It collapsed three months later in the face of massed Loyalist demonstrations, which the new Labour government and its Northern Ireland Secretary, Merlyn Rees, were unable to counter. The Sunningdale agreement was, perhaps, premature, but it paved the way for more successful power-sharing initiatives launched by the Major and Blair governments a generation later.

Yet it was by his domestic policies that he would stand or fall, and in these he was singularly unsuccessful. He had grown to loathe and despise Harold Wilson, and determined from the outset that his government would be as dissimilar as possible from its predecessor. He began by repudiating the statutory incomes policy of the Wilson government and its interventionist approach to industry, saying that in future such decisions would be left to market forces. He then hastened to show that he would succeed where Labour had failed by introducing an Industrial Relations Bill which bore more than a passing resemblance to the trade union reforms which Barbara Castle had humiliatingly failed to enact a year earlier. Heath was no crude anti-union agitator, and genuinely believed that his bill would offer new opportunities and benefits for unions which registered under its provisions. This would be a fair quid pro quo, he felt, for the creation of an Industrial Relations Court, which would help ensure a more rational and orderly system of settling disputes. This intention was certainly shared by his Employment Minister, Robert Carr, who was in charge of the bill. Yet Carr made the fatal mistake of rushing its introduction, without allowing adequate time for consultation with the interests involved, which convinced even moderate trade union leaders that the government was utterly unwilling to take account of their views. They therefore mounted a concerted attack on the bill, browbeating Labour MPs into resisting it root and branch at every stage of the parliamentary process. The bill reached the Statute Book, with no serious amendment, by August 1971, but it was a pyrrhic victory. The Industrial Relations Act soon became a dead letter. Most unions refused to register, thus losing the privileges offered to them, while both the government and employers soon became unwilling to apply its penal clauses for fear of creating 'martyrs' among trade unionists sent to prison for 'contempt of court', against the intentions of the authors of the Act.

So the battle to get the bill through had been in vain, and had seriously compromised the prospect of trade union co-operation in the government's anti-inflation policies. These were its number one priority, certainly during its first two years. In place of Labour's statutory approach, Heath depended on a policy of voluntary wage restraint, which initially proved surprisingly successful. The big exception was the miners' strike in February 1972, which the government firmly resisted, but which – thanks largely to the 'flying pickets' tactics employed by a new young miners' leader, Arthur Scargill – rapidly threatened to close the nation's power stations. The government was forced to back down and acquiesce in an arbitration award of 27 per cent, far above the norm, and which threatened to open the floodgates to inflationary claims from many other unions. An even greater shock for the government was the rapid rise in unemployment, which the previous month had breached the highly symbolic 1 million mark, easily the highest total in post-war Britain, and representing an increase of almost 50 per cent during Heath's premiership. Henceforth reducing unemployment became his overriding priority, and he resolved on a policy of all-out growth. He accordingly performed what his critics (initially confined to Enoch Powell and his small group of supporters) lost no time in characterising as U-turns. He abandoned the market, in favour of government action, to control unemployment, and substituted statutory for voluntary restriction of wage increases. The Chancellor, Anthony Barber, was instructed to aim for an annual growth rate of 5 per cent, and the government, which had already shocked its right-wing critics by nationalising the ailing Rolls-Royce firm, proceeded to bail out United Clyde Shipbuilders and other 'lame ducks' threatened with closure, while steeply increasing investment in the nationalised industries. In November 1972, Heath announced a three-stage statutory control of prices and incomes, beginning with a pay, price, rent and dividend freeze.

For almost a year, these measures largely attained their objectives: unemployment fell rapidly and wage inflation was contained. There were, however, adverse side-effects – interest rates soared, and property prices rocketed as a result of the 'Barber boom'. Yet by the autumn of 1973, when the pay policy was due to move into its milder Stage Three, there seemed an excellent prospect that Heath would have a success story to tell when he faced the general election expected in late 1974 or early 1975. All this was changed by the Yom Kippur War of October 1973, which was followed by a cutback of oil supplies and the quadrupling of oil prices. This meant that coal, a declining industry for many years, suddenly became highly competitive with oil, and relatively underpriced. The miners seized the opportunity to put in a substantial pay claim – far greater than could be accommodated under Stage Three – and when this was refused, began an overtime ban with the evident intention of running down coal stocks to improve their bargaining position if they later moved to strike action.

Probably the only way the government could have saved Stage Three was by declaring that – because of the oil crisis – the miners were a special case, and that their pay claim, and theirs alone, would be settled outside its framework. This course was actually argued by Enoch Powell, who in other circumstances might have been expected to oppose surrender to a blind union threat, but was turned down by Heath and his colleagues. Believing that they could not afford to give way a second time to the miners, and mistakenly believing that they were now in a stronger position to stand up to them than 18 months earlier, they stood their ground. In order to conserve both oil and coal stocks, Heath announced on 13 December that a three-day week for industry would be enforced from 31 December. The public seemed to be on the government's side, and several ministers, notably Lord Carrington, the newly appointed Energy Secretary, began urging Heath to call an immediate election on the issue 'Who governs Britain?' Much evidence suggests that had Heath taken this advice and called an election for January or early February, he would indeed have won. Yet he was highly reluctant to do so, and for another month tried desperately to seek means to persuade the miners to back down and call off their threatened strike, which was due to start on 1 February. The TUC intervened and made the extraordinary offer that all other unions would undertake to conform to Stage Three if the miners were accepted as a special case. The government turned down the offer, the strike duly began, and Heath called an election for 28 February. A Tory landslide was predicted, and the opinion polls seemed to back this up. Yet the election campaign failed to go the government's way. Wilson fought a more skilful campaign than had been expected, and the Tories were unable to confine it to the single question of 'Who governs?' To their dismay, the issue of rising prices, with which they had made so much play in 1970 with Heath's promise to cut the rise in prices 'at a stroke', came back to haunt them, as inflation had, in fact, substantially increased. The most damaging event of the campaign was the publication of a report by a body called the Relativities Board, to which the government had referred the miners' claim, which appeared to show that it had got its sums wrong and that the miners were much less better off in relation to other workers than had previously been believed. A further setback to Heath was the defection of Enoch Powell, who resigned his candidature and urged voters to support Labour in order to ensure that there would be a referendum on the EEC. Another surprise factor in the campaign was a strong surge in support for the Liberals, very largely at the government's expense, though it did not win the Liberals many new seats. Despite their setbacks during the campaign, the overwhelming expectation was still that the Tories would win, and the inconclusive result, which gave them more votes but fewer seats than Labour (a reverse of the 1951 result). came as a devastating shock. The new Parliament's composition was as shown in the table below.

Labour	301
Conservative	297
Liberal	14
Nationalists	9
Others	14

The 14 others included 11 Ulster Unionists, who normally would have been included in the Conservative total, putting them ahead of Labour and in striking distance of an overall majority. Those elected on this occasion, however, wanted to have nothing to do with Heath, whom they blamed for the imposition of direct rule in Ulster. Nevertheless, Heath made one last desperate throw by offering a coalition to the Liberals, with its leader, Jeremy Thorpe, joining the Cabinet, probably as Home Secretary. Thorpe was tempted, but aware that his own party was unwilling, and that in any event, without the Ulster Unionists, Heath would still be several votes short of a parliamentary majority, declined. Heath's attempt to hold on to power collapsed over the weekend following the election, and was seen as a major misjudgement. It showed him up as a 'bad loser' and even worse tactician. Yet it was a true reflection of his stubborn character. In the face of defeat, he never contemplated for a moment resigning the Tory leadership or even of offering himself for a vote of confidence by his party. He just hung on and, even more remarkably, attempted to do so again the following October, after a further general election defeat, when Wilson's minority government (just) succeeded in gaining an overall majority.

This time, however, he faced an open revolt. He had now lost three elections out of four, and many Tories – including, most damagingly, Edward Du Cann, now chairman of the influential 1922 Committee of Tory backbenchers – were determined that he should be challenged in a leadership ballot. There was no obvious rival, and if Heath had willingly offered himself up for re-election he might well have succeeded, despite the discontent. As it was, he resisted for several months, which only spurred his more fervent critics to find a challenger – *any* challenger – to put up against him. Their first choice was Sir Keith Joseph, the former Social Services Secretary, who was known to have harboured doubts about Heath's policies and U-turns, though he had never considered resigning. He ruled himself out, as did Du Cann, who was facing public criticism because of his business affairs. It was only then that – in the absence of any more heavy-weight alternative – the former Education Secretary, Margaret Thatcher, threw her hat into the ring (see Chapter 49).

Neither Heath nor his supporters took her candidature seriously. Nor indeed, perhaps, did the majority of those Tory MPs who voted for her, seeing her only as a stalking horse who would do Heath just enough damage to enable more senior figures, notably Willie Whitelaw, a Heath loyalist, to offer themselves in the second ballot. Hardly anybody expected her actually to poll more votes than Heath, which immediately knocked him out of the running and gave her sufficient momentum to see off Whitelaw and three other contenders in the second ballot. The tragedy for Ted Heath was that he was largely responsible for his own undoing. He had led a remarkably loyal and harmonious Cabinet, which had not suffered a single resignation on policy grounds despite its change of direction. Yet over the years he had offended a high proportion of Tory MPs by his gruffness and insensitivity to their views. It had not always been so. As Chief Whip under Eden and Macmillan, he had been a popular figure, going out of his way to be agreeable to his charges and being much readier to use carrots rather than sticks to ensure their compliance. He evidently regarded this as being an essential part of his job. As Prime Minister and party leader, however, he felt no such compulsion: his task now was to run the country, and he had no time for small talk with 'bit players' such as backbenchers.

If Ted Heath had been a 'bad loser' to Labour in February 1974, he was an even worse one to Thatcher, never reconciling himself to her victory during the whole 15 years that she led her party, an attitude which won him the epithet of 'the longest sulk in history'. She, for her part, did not make it any easier for him, systematically rubbishing his government at every turn, despite the fact that she had been a compliant member and only became a critic retrospectively. Heath, who had made his own predecessor, Alec Home, Foreign Secretary, hoped that she would offer him the same courtesy, and was not amused when she instead proffered the Washington embassy, making it crystal clear that she saw this as an opportunity to get him out of the way. It was not surprising that he became her most trenchant critic, subjecting her monetarist policies and seemingly heartless indifference to rising unemployment to withering criticism while saving his most savage barbs for her failure to consolidate his European achievements, and for instead pursuing the elusive path of the so-called 'special relationship' with the US. The force of his criticism was, however, blunted by the widespread assumption that it was motivated by sour grapes.

In return, Thatcher's supporters mounted a formidable indictment against him, maintaining that his government had started out with similar intentions to hers – to destroy the post-war consensus of a mixed economy and to replace it by a resurgent capitalism. On this basis, they argued, Heath had failed while Thatcher had triumphed. This was fundamentally to misinterpret Heath's intentions. He had never been a prophet of untrammelled capitalism, had never preached monetarism or advocated widespread privatisation. On the contrary, he wished to bolster the mixed economy by making it more efficient. When the early policies of his government failed to achieve their objective, he changed tack; 'When the facts change, I change my mind, what do you do, Sir?' The words were spoken by J.M. Keynes, but they might well have come from Heath. He was a true pragmatist, whose approach to economic issues was in truth rather similar to Wilson's, though he would not have approved the comparison.

Heath can claim to have been the most intellectually honest premier of the second half of the century, seldom hiding behind the half-truths and evasions which were the stock-in-trade of too many of his rivals. It could equally be said of him that he was a poor politician – with a weak tactical sense, and a limited ability to communicate his message. In many ways, he would have been more suited to a career as a senior civil servant, and it was noticeable that as Prime Minister he formed closer relationships with mandarins, such as Sir William Armstrong, the Head of the Home Civil Service, than with his political colleagues. One of his more important innovations was to form the Central Policy Review Staff, or Think Tank, to provide independent but non-party-political advice to ministers.

On one issue Heath never changed his mind – that of the fundamental virtues of the European Union (as the EEC became). He continued to laud it throughout the 30 years or more following his negotiation of British entry. It was a great sadness to him that his view gained ever-diminishing support from his own party, though paradoxically the majority of his Labour opponents subsequently swung round to his side, with varying degrees of enthusiasm.

Heath remained in the House of Commons for 27 years after losing the premiership, finally retiring at the 2001 election, having been an MP for 51 years. He never accepted a peerage, but became a Knight of the Garter in 1992. He died on 17 July 2005, aged 89 years and eight days.

Works consulted

Butler, David, and Dennis Kavanagh, *The British General Election of February 1974*, London, Macmillan, 1974.

Butler, David, and Michael Pinto-Duschinsky, *The British General Election of 1970*, London, Macmillan, 1971.

Campbell, John, *Edward Heath, a Biography*, London, Pimlico, 1994.

Heath, Edward, *The Course of My Life*, London, Hodder & Stoughton, 1998.

Hurd, Douglas, *An End to Promises*, London, Collins, 1979.

Ramsden, John, *The Winds of Change: Macmillan to Heath, 1957–1975*, London, Longman, 1996.

48

James Callaghan – Labour's conservative[1]

Born in obscurity, raised in hardship, a long hard struggle in the trade union movement ... This was the life story of a long list of leading Labour Party figures in the first half of the twentieth century, the most outstanding being Ernest Bevin. The last of the line was to be James Callaghan, born in Portsmouth on 27 March 1912. His father, also James, was a Chief Petty Officer in the Royal Navy. He came from an Irish Catholic background, and had run away to sea in his teens, changing his name from Gargohan. This, together with the fact that he was half-Jewish, was quite unknown to his son until the *Sun* newspaper researched his genealogy after he became Prime Minister in 1976. Callaghan's father married a very young widow, Charlotte Cundy, whose first husband had died in a naval accident. She was a strict Baptist, and the elder James gave up his religion to marry her. Their children were brought up in his new faith. There were to be two of them – Dorothy, born in 1904, and Leonard James, eight years later. He was always known as Leonard, or Len, only adopting his second name in his early thirties, when he entered politics.

When Leonard was four his father was wounded in the Battle of Jutland, and after the war was transferred to less strenuous work as a coastguard at Brixham, in Devon. Here the family lived a relaxed and happy life, which came to an abrupt end in 1921 when the old sailor, still only 44, collapsed and died from a heart attack. Charlotte was devastated, and the family descended into near poverty, as she received only a small lump sum and no pension from the Board of Admiralty. She moved the family back to Portsmouth where they lived a life barely above subsistence level in a bleak series of furnished rooms. There was some relief in 1924 when the newly elected Labour government awarded her a pension of 10s. a week. This was sufficient, Callaghan later recalled, to turn her into an enthusiastic Labour voter; he himself, under the influence of

---

[1] This was the title of a profile I wrote for *The Economist* in the last week of his premiership, in April 1979. Thirty-five years later, I see no need to revise this judgement.

732

their Scottish landlady, was already from the age of 11 running errands for the Labour committee rooms during general elections. Politics, however, played little part in the family's life, which was centred on the local Baptist church, in whose varied activities the young Leonard willingly participated, becoming in due course a Sunday school teacher. A tall, bright and good-looking boy, he attended Portsmouth North Secondary School, where he was far from being a star pupil, being particularly poor at mathematics, and not taking his studies very seriously. He was, however, keenly interested in English and history and became a voracious reader at the local public library. His headmaster, he recalled in his autobiography,

> decided I should enter the Senior Oxford Certificate, which I passed easily enough, with exemption from matriculation. I was told that this would qualify me for entrance to a university, though such a far-fetched idea had never entered my calculations. (Callaghan, 1987)

Instead, he sat an examination to become a Civil Service clerk.

> This was an occasion for rejoicing at home, for I had fulfilled my mother's ambition that I should secure a permanent job offering a pension at sixty. I suppose she was influenced by her own past insecurity. (Callaghan, 1987)

So in the autumn of 1929, aged 17, he left home to work in the tax office at Maidstone, in faraway Kent, at a salary of £52 a year, plus a cost-of-living allowance. In comparison with many of his fellow school-leavers who faced the prospect of life on the dole, he felt himself to be exceptionally privileged. The local Baptists put him in touch with their co-religionists in Maidstone, who arranged lodgings for him. For a time he continued to take part in church activities, notably in the Sunday school, where he very soon met his future wife, Audrey Moulton. She was the daughter of a local businessman and deacon of the Baptist church, who for Callaghan was the acme of the middle-class respectability and security that his mother had craved. He was 17 and she 16 when they met, and they subsequently embarked on a lengthy engagement, marrying only in 1938 when he had attained some financial security and she had completed her higher education, becoming a domestic science teacher. It was to be a long and happy marriage, with three children, the eldest of whom – Margaret – was, as Baroness Jay, to be a Cabinet minister and Leader of the House of Lords under Tony Blair. Callaghan was soon to lose his Baptist faith, but he retained many of the puritanical attitudes with which he had been imbued.

It was not long before Callaghan began to get bored with his largely routine work as a tax official. He carried out his duties conscientiously, but reserved his enthusiasm for his trade union activities. He joined the Association of

Tax Clerks (AOT), a small union which succeeded in recruiting 95 per cent of its potential membership without the aid of a closed shop. He soon became branch secretary, and made a name for himself as a rebel who wanted the union leadership to adopt a far more militant stance against the employers. He was especially active in campaigning for better conditions for new entrants to the profession, and in attacking its rigid class structure, under which the administrative grade was reserved for public school and university men, the executive grade was for grammar school products, while only the clerical grade (to which Callaghan belonged) was open to those who had been educated at ordinary secondary schools. He was soon marked down as a trouble-maker by the union's general secretary, Douglas Houghton (later a Cabinet colleague of Callaghan's), who, however, took a more benign view after his election in 1932 to the union's national executive at the early age of 20. He was to detect in Callaghan a basic moderation and pragmatism, which was often concealed by the forcefulness with which he expressed his views. Four years later, when the union – now known, after an amalgamation, as the Inland Revenue Staff Federation (IRSF) – decided to elect an assistant general secretary, Houghton backed him against 31 other candidates. Len Callaghan, as he was known, was successful, and at the age of 24 became the number two official of the union, at a salary of £350 – far more than he had been earning as a tax clerk.

Over the next three years, Callaghan developed into a highly effective union negotiator and built up an extensive network of contacts in other unions besides his own. He also met Harold Laski, the Professor of Government at the London School of Economics and a leading figure on the National Executive Committee of the Labour Party, whose book, *The Grammar of Politics* (1925), had already greatly influenced his own political thinking. Laski, for his part, was much impressed, and wanted Callaghan to enrol as an external degree student at the LSE under his personal supervision. Callaghan could not spare the time from his union work, but Laski also encouraged him to consider a parliamentary career, recommending him to Labour headquarters as a likely candidate. When war was declared, in 1939, Callaghan attempted to join up, although his union post was held to be a reserved occupation. He was accepted for the army but vigorously protested, saying that both his father and his maternal grandfather had been sailors, and he wanted to join the navy. The union insisted on retaining his services until March 1943, however, when he finally got his way and joined the Navy as an ordinary seaman, subsequently being promoted to sub-lieutenant. He had a relatively quiet war, seeing no action except during the later stages in 1945, when the battleship in which he was serving in the Far East set off in pursuit of two Japanese cruisers which were, however, too speedy to be caught.

A year or so earlier a decisive event occurred in his life when he was selected as prospective Labour candidate for the Cardiff South constituency, for which he was nominated by contacts in the IRSF. It was a close-run thing: he won the selection by a single vote over the pacifist schoolteacher George Thomas, who was instead chosen for the neighbouring seat of Cardiff West, and ended his career as Speaker of the House of Commons. Callaghan attributed his success to having turned up in a glamorous naval uniform, but perhaps equally helpful had been his reply to a question asking if he was a Catholic. 'No, a Baptist', he replied, which enabled the many chapel-goers in the audience to vote for him in good conscience. Cardiff South was a good prospect, the defending Tory MP's majority being a mere 541 votes. Callaghan had no trouble in reversing this in the Labour landslide of July 1945, with a majority of more than 11,000. On becoming a candidate he had dropped the name of Len, and chose henceforth to be known as James, or more usually Jim. When he reached the House of Commons, there was a further change in his nomenclature. Previously, he had always been known as '*Callagan*', with the 'h' left silent. Tory MPs addressed him instead as '*Callahan*', with a silent 'g'. He liked the sound of it, and this is how he has been known ever since.

Callaghan arrived at Westminster with something of a reputation as a left-winger. At the Labour Party conference the preceding December, he had made a powerful speech supporting a resolution endorsing a large-scale programme of nationalisation, which was passed against the wishes of the party leadership. It had been moved by Ian Mikardo, later a leading light in the left-wing Tribune group, and, like Callaghan, a native of Portsmouth, though the two men were never close associates. Following the vote, Herbert Morrison, Labour's deputy leader, approached Mikardo and Callaghan and said: 'Do you realise that you have just lost us the general election?' As soon as the government was formed, Callaghan was invited to become PPS to a junior minister, John Parker, the Under-Secretary for the Dominions. He resigned after a few months when he voted – together with 22 other Labour MPs – against the terms of an American loan. For the next 22 months he was a backbencher, but one with independent views, though he was careful to keep his rebellions against the party whips to minimal proportions. He associated with the Keep Left group of Labour MPs, but declined to sign a report which they published calling for more Socialist-oriented policies. He did, however, lead a revolt in a parliamentary committee, which led to the government reducing the period of national service from 18 months to 12.

Then in October 1947 he was appointed to his first government post as Parliamentary Secretary for Transport, being switched to a similar position in the Admiralty, where as an ex-sailor he felt more at home, in March 1950. In both posts he made his mark as an energetic and competent minister, well able to take care of himself in the House and a good publicist outside. At the Admiralty, his senior minister, Viscount Hall, was in the House of Lords, and he made the most of his opportunity as spokesman for the department in the Commons. In March 1951, Hall left the government and was replaced by Lord

Pakenham (later Lord Longford). Callaghan had hoped to be promoted in his place, and had the temerity to write to the Prime Minister complaining that he had been overlooked. Somewhat surprisingly Attlee, who was usually pretty short with unsolicited applicants for office, did not take it amiss and sent an emollient reply.

Seven months later, Labour was to lose the October 1951 general election and to embark on what turned out to be 13 dreary years in Opposition. They were years, however, in which Callaghan's political career took a sharp upward turn. He was only one of perhaps 50 junior ministers in the Attlee government, and not the most prominent of them. Yet he took to Opposition like a duck to water, was immediately elected in the annual ballot for 12 members of the Shadow Cabinet (elected by MPs), and was the only MP to be re-elected every year throughout the years of Tory power. Equally remarkable was his performance in the ballot for the constituency party section of Labour's NEC, usually dominated by left-wingers. He polled well every year he stood, and on six occasions was one of the seven MPs elected.

One key to his success was the quality of his speeches, both in the House of Commons and at party conferences and meetings throughout the country. He was not a brilliant orator, but a highly confident and forceful speaker, with an almost unerring ability to gauge the feeling of an audience and to tell them what they wanted to hear. He was also one of the first British politicians to master the art of television, where he was a frequent performer in political discussion programmes. Equally important, however, was the assiduity with which he cultivated his fellow MPs, even the most obscure and undistinguished of them – they all had votes for the Shadow Cabinet! I well remember, as a young delegate to the annual Labour conference in the mid-1950s, spending an evening in his company and that of another Shadow minister, Michael Stewart. Callaghan challenged him to come up with some information about every member of the Parliamentary Labour Party. Stewart, who embarked on the game with some reluctance, gave up after about 200, but Callaghan was able to provide details about all 277 of them. Popularly known as 'Sunny Jim', Callaghan exuded an air of amiability, which concealed the fact that he was also on occasion capable of being a bully. He had few, if any, enemies in the party, carefully avoiding committing himself in the growing rivalry between Nye Bevan and Hugh Gaitskell, though he ended up as a supporter of the latter in the 1955 leadership election. What was important, he loudly proclaimed, was the unity of the party.

Callaghan's ascent was helped by the portfolios he was given to shadow. He started off with transport, where his three years as a junior minister enabled him to speak with authority, but in 1956 Gaitskell switched him to the colonies, where he was a great success over the next four years. He led a united party in its opposition to the government's attempt to force a settler-dominated federation on Southern and Northern Rhodesia and Nyasaland against the wishes of the African population. During this period he met virtually all the nationalist leaders (and future rulers) of British colonies and formed a good relationship with many of them. He was rewarded by topping the poll for the Shadow Cabinet in 1960, but in the same year failed to win the deputy leadership of the party on the death of Bevan, coming third to the right-winger George Brown and the left-wing Fred Lee. The following year, Callaghan received a crucial promotion, when Gaitskell, anxious to move the less than totally loyal Harold Wilson from the Shadow Chancellorship, shifted him to Foreign Affairs and appointed Callaghan in his place. The party leader had some misgivings. Callaghan had proved himself an effective parliamentary performer and had achieved a prominent position in the party, but lacked economic credentials. At Tony Crosland's prompting, Nuffield College, Oxford – of which Callaghan was already an Honorary Fellow – assembled a distinguished cast of economists to offer him guidance. Gaitskell was not entirely satisfied, and there was much speculation that, if he formed a government, the actual job of Chancellor would go to somebody else. This might well have been Crosland, whose economic expertise was held in the highest regard by Gaitskell, or, just possibly, Douglas Houghton, Callaghan's old boss and a formidable authority on taxation matters. The unexpected death of Gaitskell in January 1963 put paid to such prospects. Callaghan himself was a candidate for the succession (see Chapter 46), achieving a respectable third place behind Wilson and George Brown, and almost certainly casting his own vote for Wilson in the second ballot. He was immediately confirmed in his position as Shadow Chancellor, though Wilson planned to reduce his potential powers as Chancellor by creating an economic diarchy between him and George Brown, who was pencilled in to take over a new and powerful Department of Economic Affairs (DEA).

So it transpired, in October 1964, when Labour secured its narrow majority in the general election. Wilson's intention had been to produce a 'creative tension' between the two men, to prevent either from becoming so powerful as to constitute a challenge to his own leadership, but also to clip the wings of the Treasury, which Labour had long regarded as a baleful influence on the innovative intentions of reforming governments. It did not work out exactly as planned. There was tension, certainly, but it was hardly creative and caused a maximum of frustration to both men. Callaghan was gradually to achieve the upper hand, largely due to the Treasury's control over spending and Brown's volatility and unpredictability. By the time of the July 1966 crisis, which culminated in Brown's removal to the Foreign Office and the effective collapse of his much vaunted National Plan, Callaghan's victory was almost complete. Michael Stewart, who succeeded Brown, inherited a much diminished DEA. The triumph over Brown, his senior in party terms, did not mean that Callaghan was a successful Chancellor. His former occupation as an Inland

Revenue official had left him with a sure touch on taxation matters, and he was responsible for introducing some successful innovations. Yet on economic policy he was sadly out of his depth, though he nearly always put up a good show in defending his policies in parliamentary debates. He offered no resistance to Wilson's determination not to devalue in October 1964, though the pound was clearly seriously overvalued, and – more reprehensibly – acquiesced in his insistence that it should thenceforward be an unmentionable subject. He had a momentary wobble in July 1966, but thereafter was himself adamant that there should be no devaluation until the last moment before the inevitable occurred in November 1967. He had one considerable achievement as Chancellor – the negotiation by the Group of Ten industrial countries, under his chairmanship, of Special Drawing Rights (SDRs), which greatly expanded international liquidity. Yet his own sense of failure when the devaluation was announced was almost complete, and he insisted on resigning, and prepared to leave the government. Wilson, however, was desperate that he should stay, and proposed that he should swap jobs with the Home Secretary, Roy Jenkins, to which Callaghan agreed. His own recommendation that Crosland should succeed him was ignored.

Callaghan went to the Home Office as a much chastened man, and for some time afterwards kept a low profile. Yet his spirits soon began to recover and he established a firm control over his new department, where he proved a much less liberal figure than his predecessor. This was most clearly reflected in his introduction of the Commonwealth Immigration Act of 1968, which was rushed through Parliament in three days and was described by *The Times* as 'Probably the most shameful measure that Labour members have ever been asked by their whips to support.' It took away from Kenyan Asians with British passports the right to enter the United Kingdom, and went flatly against firm assurances given to them at the time of Kenyan independence by the then Colonial Secretary, Iain Macleod, who forcefully pointed this out in the parliamentary debate. Thirty-five Labour MPs voted against the bill, but Callaghan was able to claim that most Labour MPs representing constituencies with large immigrant populations were strongly supportive of him, and that public opinion was predominantly on his side.

While at the Home Office, Callaghan was quietly consolidating his position within the Labour Party and building up a power base for any future contest for the party leadership. In October 1967, while still Chancellor, he had contrived, through discreet lobbying of trade union leaders, to get himself elected to the Treasurership of the Labour Party, defeating the left-wing candidate, Michael Foot, by more than 2 to 1. This post was of great symbolic significance as it was the only position in the party chosen by all sections of the annual conference, but as the unions commanded 80 per cent of the votes their influence was predominant. From then on, they tended to think of Callaghan as *their* representative in the leadership of the party, and Callaghan increasingly saw himself as playing this role.

The crunch came, in early 1969, when the Employment Secretary, Barbara Castle, produced her proposals for trade union reform in the White Paper, *In Place of Strife*. As a former trade union official, Callaghan was horrified. Unions were voluntary bodies who should be left to control their own affairs, he believed. This was not an appropriate matter for legislation. His view was widely supported within the Parliamentary Labour Party and by the great mass of trade union activists. If Callaghan had restricted himself to arguing against Castle's proposals within the Cabinet nobody could reasonably have objected. He went much further – by breaking collective Cabinet responsibility and casting his vote against the proposed measures in the Labour NEC, on 26 March, when a motion to reject the projected bill was carried by 15 votes to 6. Wilson was outraged, and seriously considered dismissing Callaghan from the Cabinet, but in the end decided instead to exclude him from meetings of the so-called 'inner Cabinet' of senior ministers. Callaghan's conduct made him the hero of backbench opponents of the proposed bill, and of many trade unionists, but alienated most of his Cabinet colleagues who thought he had behaved shabbily. The ill feeling, particularly with Wilson, persisted for some time, but Callaghan's position was largely vindicated the following June when the government withdrew the bill in the face of a declaration by the Chief Whip, Bob Mellish, that there was no chance of getting it through the Commons.

In August 1969, Callaghan's action, as Home Secretary, of sending troops to Northern Ireland to head off the threat of sectarian violence did a lot to restore his reputation. He was hailed by both sides of the divide as a conciliator, but unfortunately his handling of Northern Irish affairs had little beneficial effect in the long term, the province descending into large-scale terrorist violence during the succeeding year. It was left to the incoming government of Ted Heath to impose direct rule. For Callaghan, however, Ulster remained a distinct plus on his CV, and the episode also helped to heal his relations with Harold Wilson.

Labour's unexpected defeat in the June 1970 general election left Callaghan vying with Roy Jenkins as probable contenders for the succession if Wilson should stand down, which he quickly demonstrated was not his intention. The Labour Party was about to be plunged into violent controversy over its attitude towards the renewed British application for EEC entry, and it was this dispute which enabled Callaghan decisively to overtake Jenkins who previously had appeared the favourite. Callaghan, a confirmed Atlanticist, was lukewarm about Europe, but was far from being a doctrinaire opponent. Nevertheless, his fine political antennae soon detected that Labour and trade union opinion was shifting in an anti-EEC direction, and he decided to help it on its way in a speech of breathtaking cynicism, which he delivered in Southampton in

May 1971. Seizing on an off-the-cuff remark by President Pompidou that he would like French to be the language of Europe, he expatiated on the virtues of the 'language of Chaucer, Shakespeare and Milton', and concluded, in a passage drafted by his Eurosceptic son-in-law, Peter Jay: 'If we are to prove our Europeanism by accepting that French is the dominant language in the Community, then the answer is quite clear, and I will say it in French to prevent any misunderstanding: *Non, merci beaucoup.*'

Few observers doubted that Callaghan was offering himself as an alternative leader to Wilson if he did not oppose the membership terms being negotiated by Ted Heath, and this is certainly how Wilson himself interpreted the speech. He was determined not to be outflanked by Callaghan, and in the following weeks decisively shifted his position in an anti-EEC direction. By the autumn both men had settled on a common position, which won majority support at the TUC and Labour conferences, and within the Parliamentary Labour Party. This was to oppose the Heath terms, but to seek to renegotiate them and then submit the result to a popular referendum. This prevented an immediate party split, and left the pro-European minority within the PLP with the invidious choice of voting either against their party or their convictions. As described in earlier chapters, 69 decided to vote in favour of the terms, and another 20 abstained, enabling British entry to go ahead.

After this episode, Callaghan seems to have concluded that he no longer had a realistic prospect of succeeding Wilson, who was four years his junior. Some years before, he had bought a farm in Sussex, which gave him a great deal of pleasure, and he even contemplated leaving politics altogether when Anthony Barber, the Chancellor of the Exchequer in the Heath government, proposed to nominate him as managing director of the International Monetary Fund, a proposal which was effectively stymied by Valéry Giscard d'Estaing, the French Finance Minister. Callaghan also had a serious prostate operation in early 1972, and though this was completely successful, it brought with it, in the words of his biographer, Kenneth O. Morgan, 'the first intimations of mortality [and] had its psychological impact on Callaghan as for many men his age' (Morgan, 1997, p. 376). Wilson, too, probably sensed a slackening in Callaghan's ambition, and his more relaxed approach, and this enabled the two men to work together in unaccustomed harmony for the remainder of their years in Opposition, and in government after the February 1974 general election.

Following the election, Callaghan went to the Foreign Office, the only person, other than R.A. Butler, to have filled all of the three senior ministerial posts of Chancellor, Home Secretary and Foreign Secretary. As in his earlier posts, his record was mixed. He was generally judged to have fallen too much under the influence of his US colleague, Henry Kissinger, and he badly mishandled the Cyprus crisis in April 1974. He failed to act decisively as the representative of one of the three countries named as guarantors of Cypriot independence and must bear a heavy responsibility for the subsequent Turkish invasion, which led to the partition of the island. But the crucial task handed to Callaghan in his new post was to renegotiate British membership of the EEC, and on that he played a blinder. Despite his earlier opposition to British membership, he and Wilson were agreed – implicitly, if not in as many words – that the best outcome of the renegotiation was one which would enable Britain to remain within the Community. He embarked on the negotiation in the style of a trade union leader pursuing a major wage claim, banging his demands down heavily on the table, and then involving himself in prolonged haggling over the details before emerging and claiming that he had got the best bargain available – even though it bore little relation to his opening bid. It worked. Although many of the concessions which he won turned out in the long-term to be merely cosmetic, the package he brought back appeared substantial enough to persuade many doubters that it was a marked improvement on the Heath terms. As recounted in Chapter 46, it enabled the government to win a sweeping 2 to 1 majority in the June 1975 referendum, prevented a split in the Labour Party and closed the issue of British membership, not unfortunately for all time, but at least for half a decade.

Wilson concluded that Callaghan was a safe pair of hands, and at the end of the year – through a Cabinet colleague, Harold Lever – sent him a confidential message that he intended to resign in three months' time and that Callaghan should prepare himself for the succession. He was as good as his word, and when, on 16 March 1976, he announced his decision to the Cabinet, Callaghan was the best prepared of the six contenders who emerged. Two of these – Michael Foot and Tony Benn – were from the left, and three – Roy Jenkins, Denis Healey and Tony Crosland – from the centre-right. Callaghan himself was bang in the centre, but his real strength lay in the fact that he had made very few enemies during his long political apprenticeship. His two strongest rivals were undoubtedly Foot and Jenkins, but each suffered from the weaknesses of the very qualities which had brought them to prominence. Foot had been the political heir of Nye Bevan, and much the most eloquent advocate of left-wing policies – this had brought him many admirers, but as many critics. The same was true of Jenkins, whose passionate support of the cause of European integration had been triumphantly vindicated in the 1975 referendum, but had left him in a minority within his own party, and it was only the pro-Europeans who were now ready to support him. Callaghan had never stood out strongly for any political objectives (other than his opposition to trade union reform) and so had avoided alienating any significant bloc of Labour MPs. He was to be elected *faute de mieux*, on the third ballot, by 176 votes to 137 for Foot, after Foot had led him on the first ballot by 90 votes to 84. Callaghan had succeeded in picking up a large majority of the second preference votes for the four other candidates who had withdrawn or been eliminated.

On forming his government, Callaghan made a number of personnel changes. He kept Healey on as Chancellor, but preferred Crosland to Jenkins as Foreign Secretary, which prompted the latter to accept an invitation to become President of the European Commission. Callaghan let it be known that he intended that, at a later date, Healey and Crosland would swap jobs, a plan which was thwarted by Crosland's sudden death, in February 1977, when he was succeeded by the much younger David Owen. The other key appointment was Michael Foot, as Leader of the House of Commons, who became – with Healey – Callaghan's closest collaborator. Much to her chagrin, Barbara Castle was peremptorily dropped. From the outset, Callaghan created a good impression as Prime Minister. If he had not been a conspicuous success in his earlier posts, he had at least accumulated a great deal of experience, and he presented himself as a tried and trusted servant of the state, firmer and more straightforward than Wilson, and oozing avuncular charm and reassurance.

Yet the legacy he took over from Wilson was a forbidding one: a tiny parliamentary majority and a host of economic problems. The most serious of these appeared to be inflation – down from the horrendous 26 per cent recorded the previous summer, but still a stubborn 13 per cent, and expected to rise again. Fresh pressure was also building up on the pound sterling, which the government desperately hoped to reverse. The twin policy on which it embarked was to combine wage restraint with cuts in government expenditure. In July 1976, agreement was reached with the TUC and the CBI (Confederation of British Industry) for a 5 per cent limit on pay increases, with a maximum of £4 a week. This resulted in a considerable decline in living standards, and a year later the unions were not prepared formally to agree on a limitation. The government, however, set a target of 10 per cent for wage increases, and largely imposed it within the public sector, while sanctions were imposed on private firms which breached the guidelines. On public expenditure, the government believed it had done as much as anybody could reasonably expect, when, in July 1976, Healey announced cuts of £1 billion, in addition to those he had already made in his two previous Budgets. Despite the fact that both the inflation rate and the balance of payments were improving, however, international confidence remained low, and the slide in the pound continued. By September, it had fallen to $1.56, from $1.93 when Callaghan had taken over. Healey concluded that the only way to staunch the flow was to seek a massive loan from the International Monetary Fund – $3.9 billion, the largest that the IMF had ever been asked for. The IMF demanded further spending cuts of £1.4 billion, to which the Cabinet reluctantly agreed, after a long series of meetings at which Crosland, the Foreign Secretary, had cogently argued that cuts on this scale were unnecessary. He persuaded the majority of his colleagues, but Callaghan eventually came down on Healey's side, and Crosland backed down on the basis that the Prime Minister and Chancellor could not be seen to be overridden on a central issue of economic policy. In the event, less than half the loan was taken up and the balance of payments rose rapidly into surplus, which retrospectively corroborated Crosland's judgement, but by then he was already dead. By then, too, Labour had lost its parliamentary majority through by-election losses and defections, and in March 1977 faced the imminent prospect of defeat on a confidence motion tabled by Margaret Thatcher, which would have precipitated an immediate general election.

At the last minute, Callaghan, using all his skills as a trade union 'fixer', negotiated the Lib-Lab pact with Liberal leader David Steel, which guaranteed Liberal backing in key parliamentary votes in exchange for policy consultations. This was a master stroke: the pact not only provided him with security of tenure, but increased his ability to resist left-wing demands for more socialistic legislation. He and his government used the period of respite well, and by the summer of 1978 they had built up a strong position for themselves, with their economic policies working well, while Callaghan had established himself as an influential figure in world affairs, being treated as a respected partner by Presidents Carter and Giscard d'Estaing and by Chancellor Helmut Schmidt. It was then that Callaghan threw it all away, by what can only be described as a serious loss of nerve.

He made two crucial errors of judgement – in both cases without adequate consultation with his Cabinet or even his closest political advisors. The first concerned the continuation of the government's incomes policy, which, in the view of the authors of the 1979 Nuffield Election Study, had 'worked far better than expected' (Butler and Kavanagh, 1980, p. 22). The union leaders, aware that pressure from their members was building up fast after several years of restraint, were unwilling to agree a voluntary limit for wage settlements. Furthermore, both Jack Jones, of the Transport Workers' Union, and Hugh Scanlon, of the Engineers, powerful left-wing figures who had co-operated with the government over wage restraint, had retired and had been succeeded by weaker figures less inclined, and less able, to be co-operative. Inflation was now down to 8 per cent, but there was little confidence that it would not rise again. Callaghan unilaterally insisted on a limit of 5 per cent, with another 2 per cent for 'anomalies'. Even his Chancellor, Denis Healey, a hawk on incomes policy, thought this too rigid and inflexible, and few Cabinet members thought that it could be sustained in the face of mammoth pay claims expected in the autumn. A 10 per cent target would have been more feasible, most felt. In terms of public relations, however, a 5 per cent limit had much to commend it, as it would suggest to the electors that a reduction of inflation to 5 per cent or less was in the offing. This would have gone down well if Callaghan had held an election in October 1978, before the wage round began; it was tempting providence to delay the poll until after it had been put to the test.

The objective case for holding the election in October was overwhelming. All the evidence was that the economic indicators had greatly improved, but were likely to deteriorate by early in 1979. Labour had regained the lead in the opinion polls, and the fact that Callaghan made no effort to persuade the Liberals to extend the Lib-Lab pact when it expired at the end of July led to the almost universal expectation that the election was imminent. This was reinforced by unofficial briefings given – in good faith – by Callaghan's political advisor, Tom McNally, that polling day would be on 5 October. The probability is that this was Callaghan's intention in early August, when he left for a short month on his Sussex farm, but subsequently changed his mind without, however, telling anybody. He did make a ritual effort to consult his Cabinet, asking them to send him by post their preferred election dates. The majority wanted an early poll, though Michael Foot, and to a lesser degree, Denis Healey, favoured delay.

Callaghan bluntly announced to the Cabinet, when it met on 7 September, that there would be no autumn election, and repeated the message to an incredulous nation in a television broadcast the same evening. It was possible, in party terms, to make a reasonable case for delay, as a Labour victory was by no means assured, though it would probably have entered the campaign as favourite, given Callaghan's high standing in the country and his large personal lead over Margaret Thatcher in the polls. What was highly imprudent was to dispense with the safety belt of a renewed pact, either with the Liberals or alternatively with the Ulster Unionists or the Scottish Nationalists (both of whom might well have been open to offers), to see him through the winter and guard against the possibility of a surprise parliamentary defeat. The responsibility for taking this risk was Callaghan's alone, and was his second major error.

The sequel was far worse than anybody predicted, and has gone down in history as the 'winter of discontent'. Pay restraint was voted down by large majorities at the annual TUC and Labour Party conferences, and an avalanche of pay claims greatly exceeding the 5 per cent limit were tabled. The floodgates opened in early December, when the Ford Motor Company, after a three-week strike, settled for 17 per cent – a figure far higher than public sector employers could possibly afford. This did not prevent their unions, notably the National Union of Public Employees, from demanding parity and launching a series of highly damaging strikes by lorry drivers, oil tanker drivers, and, above all, local government and health service workers which effectively destroyed any hopes of a Labour victory in an early election. It was not the economic effects of the strikes which hurt Labour, but the psychological impact of 'human interest' stories reported on television: stories of the dead remaining unburied and the sick being refused admission to hospitals. In a few short weeks Labour's main electoral asset – its ability to get on well with the trade unions – was cruelly mauled, and the Tory lead in the opinion polls shot up to a massive 20 per cent by early February.

Callaghan contributed to his own discomfiture by his response to reporters when he was interviewed at London's Heathrow airport, on his return from a summit conference on the lush French Caribbean island of Guadeloupe. Asked to comment on the 'crisis', he unwisely replied that no crisis existed, and the pro-Tory newspapers were not slow to draw the contrast between the Prime Minister sunning himself on West Indian beaches and the suffering British public. The first direct evidence that the industrial strife was hurting Labour came on 1 March, when Welsh and Scottish electors voted in a referendum on whether to establish devolved parliaments in Cardiff and Edinburgh. The Welsh proposals had long been given up for lost, but the Scottish ones had enjoyed strong public support, with a consistent majority of nearly 2 to 1 in opinion polls. In the event, they scraped through by the tiny margin of 51.6 per cent to 48.8 per cent – not enough to enable the proposals to go through under the terms of the Scottish Devolution Act. It was immediately clear that the disappointing result was due to the deep unpopularity of the Government following the January strikes. The Scottish Nationalist MPs, in their frustration, turned against the government and suicidally decided to support a no-confidence motion tabled by Margaret Thatcher, which would precipitate them into a general election which they were ill prepared to fight. The Liberals too – no longer beholden to the pact – prepared to vote against the government, as did the bulk of the Ulster Unionists.

The result was bound to be desperately close, but Callaghan – devastated by the conduct of the trade unions – seemed to have lost the will to fight on. He vetoed three separate initiatives proposed by his fellow ministers to stave off defeat, including concessions to the Ulster Unionists, and the offer by the wife of a dying Labour MP to bring her husband to the environs of the House in an ambulance, so that he could be 'nodded through' the division lobby by the whips, as was allowed by the Standing Orders of the House. Any one of these would almost certainly have saved the day, as the motion was lost on 28 March by a single vote – 311 to 310 – and Callaghan found himself to be the first British Prime Minister in more than 50 years to be trapped into fighting a general election at a time not of his own choosing. Many of his ministers privately felt that he was more concerned with his reputation than with the survival of his government. The influence of his self-effacing but strong-minded wife, Audrey, was suspected. She was determined, they felt, that her husband should be remembered as a man of principle rather than as a wheeler-dealer.

Had Labour won the vote, the government could probably have held on until the following October when its general election chances would have been rather better, as the rawest memories of the winter of discontent began to fade. It is improbable, however, that it could have won – the damage had been too great. As it was, Callaghan fought a highly dignified campaign in April, drawing strength from his massive lead over Thatcher in public esteem, as measured by the polls. He succeeded in making up some ground during the campaign, but the Tories won a comfortable majority on 3 May, when the result was as shown in the table below.

Conservative	339
Labour	269
Liberal	11
Others	16
Conservative majority	43

Callaghan's premiership was the end of an era. He represented the best – and some of the worst – of 'Old' Labour. Fixated on the triumphs of the 1945 government, he had no vision of the future and no strong political convictions, other than to improve the lot of working men (he was not much of a feminist). Deeply conservative (with a small 'c'), he was not, despite his many qualities, the person to lead his party down fresh paths, as it desperately needed to be. He seems to have sensed this himself, remarking to his political advisor, Bernard Donoughue, during the 1979 campaign:

> There are times, perhaps once every thirty years, when there is a sea-change in politics. It then does not matter what you say or what you do. There is a shift in what the public wants and what it approves of. I suspect there is now such a sea-change – and it is for Mrs Thatcher. (Morgan, 1997, p. 269)

Callaghan would have been well advised to give up the party leadership immediately after the election, when, almost certainly, he would have been succeeded by Healey, his evident preferred choice. Instead, he hung on for a further year, fighting a forlorn rearguard action against left-wing forces for the control of the party. Healey was then narrowly beaten by Michael Foot, a distinguished parliamentarian but who was to prove an ineffectual leader, and whose election was soon followed by a party split leading to the creation of the Social Democratic Party. Callaghan remained in the Commons until 1987, when he took a life peerage, and settled comfortably into the role of an elder statesman. He died on 26 March 2005, at the age of 93 years and ten months – the longest lived of all the British Prime Ministers.

Works consulted

Butler, David, and Dennis Kavanagh, *The British General Election of 1979*, London, Macmillan, 1980.
Callaghan, James, *Time & Chance*, London, Collins, 1987.
Coates, Ken (ed.), *What Went Wrong*, Nottingham, Spokesman, 1979.

Kellner, Peter, and Christopher Hitchens, *Callaghan: The Road to Number Ten*, London, Cassell, 1976.

Morgan, Kenneth O. *Callaghan: A Life*, Oxford, Oxford University Press, 1997.

Penniman, Howard R. (ed.), *Britain at the Polls, 1979*, Washington, American Enterprise Institute, 1981.

49

Margaret Thatcher – Grocer's Daughter to Iron Lady

When Alfred Roberts, a Grantham grocer, and his wife, Beatrice, had their second and last child on 13 October 1925, they apparently hoped to have a son, rather than a sister for their four-year-old daughter, Muriel. Beatrice, indeed, may never have got over her disappointment, and seems to have failed to develop a warm, loving relationship with the child, who was named Margaret Hilda. Alfred reacted differently, treating her exactly the same as if she were a boy, and the young Margaret grew up doing everything she could to meet her father's expectations, always declaring that he was the role model for her life.

Alfred Roberts was a formidable figure. The son of a Northampton shoemaker, he left school at 13 to work in the tuck shop at Oundle, the boys' public school, moving on to a series of jobs in grocery shops before becoming, at the age of 21, the manager of a grocery store in the Lincolnshire market town of Grantham. After six years, he had saved enough to take out a mortgage and buy his own shop, with living accommodation upstairs, on the outskirts of the town. Working immensely hard, he and Beatrice were soon able to expand by taking over two neighbouring shops, and opening a sub post office as well as a branch in another part of the town. By the time that Margaret was born the family was already prosperous, but the household was conducted in a highly parsimonious manner, with no labour-saving devices and all the girls' clothes being made by Beatrice, a skilled dressmaker. The frugality of their lifestyle was attributed to Alfred's strong religious principles. A Wesleyan Methodist local preacher, and strict Sabbatarian, his daughters attended church four times each Sunday, and were discouraged from participating in frivolous entertainments. Alfred also became a leading local government figure in Grantham, being elected to the town council in 1927, reaching the aldermanic bench in 1943, and serving as Mayor in 1945–46. Originally a Liberal, he was elected as an Independent, which in Grantham as in many other small towns at that time, effectively meant Conservative.

Margaret's most thorough biographer so far, John Campbell, casts doubt on whether she was quite so devoted a daughter to Alderman Roberts as she later claimed, pointing out that, after she left Grantham for good at the age of 18, she only returned on very rare occasions to visit her parents. (Nor, according to the political scientist, Sir Bernard Crick, was the alderman quite such an estimable character as she makes out. In 1997, he recounted in *Punch* magazine (21 June 1997) how he had been told by elderly Grantham residents that he had a reputation for paying low wages and groping his female shop assistants.) Nevertheless, Campbell identified in her three qualities which she clearly owed to her father's precepts and example. First, he argues, it was he 'who instilled in her the habit of hard work, as something both virtuous in itself and the route to self-advancement'. Second, he gave her a powerful impulse towards public service – 'her restless belief in her duty to put the world to rights was only a projection on a wider stage of the same missionary impulse which took Alfred from the pulpit of Finkin Street church to the council chamber'. His third, 'and perhaps most important legacy' was, he argues,

> an exceptionally powerful moral sense. More than anything else in her polit-ical make-up, it was her fierce confidence that she knew right from wrong – even if what was right was not always immediately attainable – which marked Margaret Thatcher out from contemporary politicians ... This rare moral certainty and unreflective self-righteousness was her greatest political strength in the muddy world of political expediency and compromise; it was also in the end her greatest weakness. (Campbell, 2001, pp. 30–1)

What she did not get from her father, Campbell asserts, was her anger and aggression, the root of which he believes was an internalised revolt against the narrow provincialism in which she was brought up and to which she outwardly conformed.

Apart from her father, the greatest influence on the young Margaret Roberts was growing up during the Second World War. This made her immensely patriotic, spurred by the nationalistic poetry of Rudyard Kipling and the lead-ership of Winston Churchill, whom she hero-worshipped. It also helped to shape her later attitudes both to Europe and the United States. Europeans, she grew to believe, lacked backbone – they had supinely succumbed in the face of the Nazi threat. Americans, on the other hand, of whom there were many in the Grantham area, which was surrounded by US Air Force bases, had come to Britain's aid, and the two countries had then gone on together to liberate the feckless West Europeans. Margaret Roberts attended a local grammar school, the Kesteven and Grantham Girls' School, where she was noted for her diligence and serious attitude. She was usually at or near the top of the class, but was regarded as lacking in imagination and a sense of humour. She early decided to aim at university, and perhaps already in her teens dreamed of a political career. She was offered places at Nottingham University and at Bedford College, London, but – against the advice of her headmistress – decided to sit the scholarship examination for Somerville College, Oxford. She did not win a scholarship, but was offered a place, and in October 1943, just 18, she went up to Oxford to study for a degree in chemistry.

She did not fit in very well at Somerville, where the ambience – personified by the principal, Dame Janet Vaughan – was frankly left-wing and imbued with the spirit of wartime idealism and egalitarianism. Margaret Roberts not only loudly proclaimed herself a Tory, but one with stridently right-wing views, which did not go down well even with the bulk of her fellow Conservatives, who were mostly on the progressive wing of the party. This did not prevent her from becoming a keen member of the Oxford University Conservative Association, of which she eventually became president. On Sundays she attended the Wesley Memorial Church, and she was active in student Christian groups, even to the extent of preaching – like her father – in local village churches. Yet her primary commitment was clearly to politics, and in the 1945 general election campaign she hastened back to Grantham, where – at the age of 19 – she acted as a warm-up speaker at meetings held by the local Conservative candidate. Despite the best efforts of what the local paper described as 'the very youthful Miss M.H. Roberts, daughter of Alderman A. Roberts of Grantham', the candidate unexpectedly went down to heavy defeat against the sitting Independent MP, who had snatched the seat from the Tories in a wartime by-election.

Margaret came to regret studying chemistry, which was not very relevant to a political career, but at least it would enable her to earn a living while she sought to put her feet on the lower rungs of the political ladder. She left Oxford in June 1947, with a good Second Class degree, to work as a research chemist for a plastic company in Colchester. She joined the local Young Conservatives, and the following year attended the annual Conservative conference at Llandudno, where she was introduced to the chairman of the Dartford Conservative Association, who was looking for a candidate for his constituency, a Labour stronghold in East Kent. Aged 23, she faced competition from four male opponents at the subsequent selection conference, in January 1949, but made an astonishingly favourable impression and was chosen unanimously. She also missed the last train back to London, and a local businessman in the audience gallantly offered her a lift in his car. His name was Denis Thatcher.

She was to fight two general elections at Dartford – in 1950 and 1951 – and proved an immensely popular candidate among the Tory rank and file, who were entranced by her enthusiasm, boundless energy and the ferocity with which she excoriated the Labour government. Two months after the second contest, she was to marry Denis Thatcher, who became, in her own words, the 'rock' on which she was to build her career. A divorcee, whose first wife had also been called Margaret, he was the head of a family paint-manufacturing business, which was subsequently taken over by Burmah Oil, of which he was to become a director. An affable, sport-loving man, with strong but unsophisticated political views which chimed in well with Margaret's own, his wealth was sufficient to enable her to drop her work as a chemist and read for the bar, where she was to qualify as a tax lawyer. Her 'bachelor girl' digs were exchanged for a luxury flat in Chelsea, and when their twin children, Mark and Carol, were born two years later there was no difficulty about paying for childcare and, later, expensive school fees. It would be unjust to suggest that Margaret married Denis for his money; there was a strong basis of love and affection in the marriage, but it undoubtedly greatly reduced the pressures on her as she single-mindedly pursued her way up the 'greasy pole'.

Margaret Thatcher was now determined to land a safe Tory seat, and hoped to use the contacts which she had built up with Kent Tory MPs to help her on her way. These included Ted Heath, elected in 1950 for Bexley, a neighbouring seat to Dartford, but her highest hopes were fixed on Sir Alfred Bossom, the elderly and enormously rich MP for Maidstone, who took a fatherly interest in this attractive young woman who he hoped would be his successor. It was not to be, and Thatcher encountered a marked resistance to selecting a woman candidate in several other seats which she sought. It was only in 1958 that she enjoyed better luck – in Finchley, a north London suburban constituency where she was narrowly chosen, despite strenuous efforts by the retiring MP, Sir John Crowder, to prevent her selection. As at Dartford, Thatcher threw herself wholeheartedly into the task of nursing the seat, and had built up a large and enthusiastic local following by the time of the 1959 general election, when she was returned with the very comfortable majority of 16,260. She was five days short of her 34th birthday.

The 1959 election was the apogee of the Macmillan premiership, and Thatcher was one of no fewer than 365 MPs who crammed the Tory benches. Much remarked as the youngest and most glamorous of the dozen Tory women MPs, few if any observers noticed her most significant characteristic. This was that she was not – as she herself confirmed much later – a 'consensus politician'. This marked her out as different from the vast majority of Conservative MPs. Though for electoral reasons, they deliberately exaggerated the differences which separated them from their Labour counterparts, in their hearts and in their private conversations, they recognised that these were, in reality, only marginal. They were fully signed up to the welfare state, enacted by their political opponents, and to the mixed economy, where the only serious difference was whether the steel industry should be in the private or the public sector. This apparent unity of approach was personified by the term 'Butskellism', conflating the names of Rab Butler and Hugh Gaitskell, coined by a journalist on *The Economist*, but in wide circulation in the 1950s and 1960s. Thatcher did not go along with this – the Manichean world view she had inherited from her father led her to believe that she was engaged in an unending struggle with evil, which she interpreted as 'socialism', making precious little distinction between the Labour Party and Soviet communism. Nevertheless, she was intensely ambitious and was shrewd enough to recognise that if she wanted to get on she must suppress her instincts and conform to the prevailing view. At Westminster she was seen as a typical moderate Conservative; in her speeches in Finchley, however, reported only in the local press, she gave vent to much more full-blooded language, which was also reflected – though more obliquely – in her Conservative conference speeches. Looking round among her fellow Tory MPs, she recognised few kindred spirits. One of these was Enoch Powell, but he was controversial, and she avoided getting too close to him.

She had an immediate stroke of luck in drawing third place in the ballot for Private Member's Bills, which meant that, very unusually, her maiden speech was devoted to introducing her own piece of legislation. This was a relatively minor bill to improve the access of the press to local government committee meetings, but it was duly passed and she won widespread and highly flattering coverage in the national press. Within two years she had joined the government, the first MP elected in 1959 to be promoted and the youngest ever woman minister. She served for three years as Joint Parliamentary Secretary for Pensions and National Insurance until the Conservative election defeat in October 1964. Here she won high marks for her efficient conduct of business and her confident and highly combative parliamentary performances. On the debit side was the widespread feeling, in her own party as well as the Opposition, that she was instinctively unsympathetic to the welfare claimants who were her department's main responsibility. She was also felt to be rather too ready to upstage her minister, the aristocratic and retiring Richard Wood, later Lord Holderness.

After the general election she became something of a workhorse for the Tory Opposition, filling a succession of junior Shadow posts, and – with her tax lawyer's expertise – excelling herself by exposing a whole series of ill-thought-out measures in James Callaghan's Budgets of 1966 and 1967. When Ted Heath was elected as Tory leader in 1965, he decided that he should have a token woman in his Shadow Cabinet, and James Prior, his PPS, suggested Thatcher. In his memoirs, he recounts Heath's response:

> There was a long silence. 'Yes', he said, 'Willie [Whitelaw, the Chief Whip] agrees she's much the most able, but he says that once she's there we'll never be able to get rid of her. So we both think it's got to be Mervyn Pike'. (Prior, 1986, p. 42)

Miss Pike, also a former junior minister, was regarded as an agreeable but unambitious colleague whom nobody seriously expected to rise much above her present level. The fact that she was preferred to Thatcher strongly suggests that the latter was regarded as altogether too pushy and opinionated. In fact, by 1967, Pike withdrew on the grounds of ill health, and there was then no alternative to appointing Thatcher, who was strongly backed by the Shadow Chancellor, Iain Macleod. She then became in rapid succession the Shadow Minister for Power, for Transport, and, finally, for Education.

After the June 1970 election, Heath duly appointed her Education Secretary, and she soon became one of his most controversial ministers, notorious for her early move to abolish free milk in primary schools. This earned her the tag 'Margaret Thatcher, milk snatcher', and she was described by the *Sun* as 'The most unpopular woman in Britain'. In fact, her record at Education was, on balance, a creditable one. Her decision on free milk was taken in the face of enormous pressure from the Treasury for spending cuts, which she largely fended off, offering only this small token so as not to make any economies which would damage *educational* needs. In particular, she preserved the infant Open University, which the incoming Chancellor, Iain Macleod, who died soon after, had earmarked as a prize candidate for the chop. Later she was able to win additional funds for raising the school leaving age and expanding the newly established polytechnics. She was hardly an enthusiast for comprehensive schools, and infuriated many local authorities (including some under Tory control) by the pernickety way in which she considered their changeover plans, but more plans were approved during her period than under any other minister, Labour or Conservative. Within the department, civil servants found her excessively impatient and abrasive, and there were many rows with senior officials, usually sparked off by her attempts to exceed her statutory powers. This was, to some extent, offset by her personal concern for the welfare of her staff, and she came to be admired for the forceful way in which she stood up for the interests of the department.

Thatcher's relations with the Prime Minister were formally correct, and, indeed, somewhat fawning on her part. At no time did she emerge as a critic of his policies, even if, in retrospect, she claimed to have misgivings. It is clear, however, that he found her a somewhat tiresome colleague. He instinctively reacted against her gushing manner, and her adopted persona as a prosperous, middle class, Home Counties lady. He thought that she talked too much in Cabinet, and took care to seat her at the far end of the table, out of his eye-line. He did not take her seriously as a contender, when she challenged him for the party leadership after his second successive general election defeat in October 1974, reportedly telling her 'You'll lose', when she, out of courtesy, informed him of her decision. Thatcher's emergence as a candidate owed much to opportunism, but also to her natural combativeness and a newly developed conviction. Although, as we have seen, she had never inwardly subscribed to the consensual approach of her colleagues, she had hitherto lacked an ideological basis for challenging it. This was now provided for her by Keith Joseph, who had been Health and Social Security Minister in the Heath government, and the only Cabinet minister known to have had serious doubts about the direction of his policies. A high-minded Jewish baronet, who was given to agonising about the effects of policies which he had agreed, he gradually became converted to the monetarist ideas previously championed by Enoch Powell and the right-wing think tank, the Institute of Economic Affairs. Strongly influenced by the Chicago economist, Milton Friedman, they repudiated Keynesian ideas for running the economy and proclaimed that the rampant threat of inflation could only be combated by strict control of the money supply, that is by deflating the economy. Heath's attempts to control prices and wages by a statutory policy and direct intervention in industry only made the situation worse, in their view. Joseph prepared to challenge Heath for the Tory leadership in the autumn of 1974, but effectively destroyed his chances by an 'over the top' speech in Birmingham, in which he suggested that 'our human stock' was threatened by the birth of too many children to adolescent mothers 'in social classes four and five'. In the face of the anger and ridicule which this provoked, Joseph withdrew from the battle, and when Edward Du Cann, the leader of the Tory backbenchers, also ruled himself out, Thatcher leapt into the fray, with Joseph's blessing.

It required guts for her to do so, but perhaps she was not risking all that much. Only if she polled a derisory vote would she have been seriously damaged, and she would surely have advanced her standing in the party, and won the gratitude of the new leader, if she sufficiently undermined Heath to make him vulnerable in the second ballot, when weightier candidates, notably Willie Whitelaw, could be expected to make themselves available. Hardly anybody at that stage saw her as anything more than a 'stalking horse'. She owed her actual election to the Machiavellian tactics of her campaign manager, Airey Neave, a former intelligence officer. He deliberately underestimated her support, telling enquirers that she was 'doing well but not well enough', so as to encourage anti-Heath MPs who wanted the chance to vote for another candidate to support her in the first ballot. Neave later admitted to having 120 firm promises, but put it about that she was sure of only 70 votes. In the event, she polled 130 against 119 for Heath, and such was her momentum that there was nothing to stop her in the second ballot (see Chapter 47).

Thatcher did not shine as Leader of the Opposition against either Wilson or Callaghan. The latter, in particular, patronised her to an appalling extent in their clashes in the House, and nearly always came out on top. Nor did she make a positive impact in the country: her opinion poll ratings remained poor, even though her party was ahead for most of the period between 1976 and 1978. After Callaghan had bolstered his position through the operation of the Lib-Lab pact, it began to look as though her chances of leading the Tories to an election victory were slipping away. It is, indeed, highly unlikely that she would have succeeded if Callaghan – as everyone expected – had seized the favourable opportunity of an election in October 1978. If that had happened, and she had gone down to defeat, she would most probably have been dumped in short order by the Tories, and would have rated no more than a footnote in the history books. As it was, the 'winter of discontent' which followed Callaghan's miscalculation (see Chapter 48), opened the way for her to be the longest-serving Prime Minister of the century and one of those who had the greatest impact on the country's destiny.

Elected with a majority of 43 seats, on 3 May 1979, her new Cabinet appeared to be dominated by former associates of Ted Heath, few if any of whom had voted for her in the leadership election three years earlier. Thus Lord Carrington became Foreign Secretary, with Ian Gilmour as Foreign Affairs spokesman in the Commons; Willie Whitelaw, Home Secretary; James Prior, Employment Secretary; Norman St John-Stevas, Leader of the Commons; Lord Soames, Leader of the Lords; Francis Pym, Defence Secretary; Peter Walker, Agriculture Secretary, and so on. They were the most prominent figures in the party and she could not afford to leave them out, especially as she had refused to include Heath. From the outset, however, the new Prime Minister was determined to keep the main economic portfolios in the hands of people sympathetic to her recently acquired monetarist convictions, people she habitually referred to as 'one of us'. She would have liked to make Joseph Chancellor of the Exchequer, but regarded him as too unstable, and instead chose Sir Geoffrey Howe, the former Solicitor-General, who had been a key figure in the Heath government, but was, like her, a convert to monetarism. John Biffen, formerly a close associate of Enoch Powell and a monetarist of long standing, became Chief Secretary to the Treasury, and John Nott, a merchant banker, President of the Board of Trade. These three, together with the Energy Secretary, David Howell, formed a sort of 'inner Cabinet' on economic policy, from which Prior was ostentatiously excluded.

It was the successive Budgets of Geoffrey Howe, and after 1983 of his successor, Nigel Lawson, that were the main instruments of Thatcher's monetarist policies. The first of these, in June 1979, made a resounding impact. Trailed as a tax-cutting Budget, it reduced the standard rate of income tax from 33 to 30 per cent, and the maximum marginal rate from 83 to 60 per cent. Projected cuts in public spending, of 3 per cent or more, by no means made up for the loss in revenue, which was made good by a near doubling of value added tax, which was consolidated at a single rate of 15 per cent. Thatcher seemed oblivious of the fact that this would have a devastating effect on inflation, still just under 10 per cent when she was elected but soon to rise above 20 per cent, nor that the public spending cuts would boost the unemployment figures. This was not, however, lost on some of her Cabinet ministers, including Prior (who privately described the

Budget as 'a disaster'), Gilmour and Walker. Thatcher quickly dubbed colleagues who queried her policies as 'wets'. As well as these three, their numbers grew over the next year to include Stevas, Pym, Soames and Carrington, though the latter spent so much time abroad that he was seldom around to support his colleagues when their fears were expressed in Cabinet meetings. Whitelaw also broadly sympathised with the wets' approach, but he had determined from the start to be a super-loyal colleague of Thatcher and her main buttress of support, so he usually refrained from weighing in on their side.

Howe's second Budget, in March 1980, added a further sharp twist to the deflationary screw, pitching the country into a deep recession. In Hugo Young's words:

> A uniquely painful experiment was being made ... By the date of its second anniversary, the Government had presided over the biggest fall in total output in one year since 1931, and the biggest collapse in industrial production in one year since 1921. Unemployment, up by a million in the past twelve months, was rising towards the once unimaginable total of three million. (Young, 1993, pp. 232–3)

Moreover, despite the deflationary policy, inflation had leapt to 20 per cent, while high interest rates and an overvalued pound were having a severe effect on exports and dealing a body blow to manufacturing industry. To all, except its most uncritical supporters, the government's policy appeared to be a ghastly failure. Thatcher was unshaken, saying 'After almost any operation, you feel worse before you convalesce. But you do not refuse the operation when you know that without it you will not survive.' Nevertheless, by the autumn of 1980 the almost universal expectation was that she would soon abandon the policy and perform a U-turn, as Heath's government had done at a similar stage in 1972. Thatcher defiantly rejected this course in her speech to the 1980 Tory conference. In words deftly chosen by her speechwriter, the playwright Ronald Millar, she alluded to the title of a once well-known play by Christopher Fry (*The Lady's Not for Burning*), saying: 'You turn if you want to. The lady's not for turning.'

Howe went on to introduce yet another deflationary Budget in April 1981, but the following July, when he presented a paper to the Cabinet proposing further spending cuts of £5 billion in the following year, the Cabinet exploded in open revolt. Leader of the rebellion was the Environment Secretary, Michael Heseltine, appalled by widespread rioting in the Toxteth area of Liverpool, which he believed to have been the consequence of the mounting unemployment which Howe's policies had produced. Not only all the leading wets, but even Biffen and Nott joined in the criticism, and Joseph and Leon Brittan (now Chief Secretary) were the only ministers to back Howe up. He was instructed to go away and do his sums again. This effectively marked the end of the extremist phase of monetarism. Henceforth it was applied in a gentler, more sensitive and attenuated form by Howe, and by his successor, Nigel Lawson. Thatcher acquiesced in the change, while refusing to admit that any alteration had occurred. She vented her anger, instead, on the leading wets, three of whom – Gilmour, Soames and Education Secretary Mark Carlisle – were purged from the government in a reshuffle two months later. Stevas had already been sacked the previous January, and henceforth she steadily filled the Cabinet ranks with her own 'placemen' to ensure that the July revolt would never be repeated. Prior she judged to be too big a fish to be chopped: instead he was sent to be Northern Ireland Secretary – well away from her main political concerns.

As Employment Secretary, Prior had implemented the Tories' election pledge to introduce a trade union reform bill, providing public money for union ballots on strikes and leadership changes, banning secondary picketing and making it more difficult for unions to obtain a 'closed shop'. Unlike the earlier efforts by the Wilson and Heath governments, Prior's bill was not only legislated but was put into effect, being reluctantly accepted by the trade unions. The Tory right wing were disgusted that Prior had not introduced a more full-blooded measure, and were encouraged by Thatcher in their criticisms, though formally she supported Prior's position. Prior was succeeded by the much more right-wing Norman Tebbit, and his bill was to be followed by two far harsher measures.

During its first three years in office, the Thatcher government's successes were few and far between. One of them was the settlement of the Southern Rhodesian conflict, which had festered on since Ian Smith's declaration of independence in 1965. The protracted effect of sanctions, pressure from neighbouring states and the continuing guerrilla war had finally brought the illegal regime to its knees, and at the Lancaster House Conference in December 1979, it agreed to transfer control back to Britain, which would conduct multiracial elections leading to independence for Zimbabwe the following April. The success of the conference was largely due to the diplomacy of Lord Carrington, but Thatcher deserves credit for letting him go ahead, despite her own deeply held suspicion of African nationalist leaders. Less obviously successful was Thatcher's handling of the dispute over the excessive British contribution to the Budget of the European Economic Community. She was totally justified in taking a firm stand, but she went about it in the wrong way. Her hysterical behaviour at the second EEC summit she attended, at Dublin Castle in December 1979, when she thumped the table and demanded 'my money back', unnecessarily antagonised her fellow heads of government, notably German Chancellor Helmut Schmidt and French President Valéry Giscard d'Estaing. Despite agreements on temporary palliatives, the dispute lingered on until the Fontainebleau summit in June 1984 when, due to the initiative of a new French President, François Mitterrand, a satisfactory settlement, involving substantial rebates, was finally reached. Thatcher probably gained popular support by her over-robust tactics, but it seems probable that a comparable deal could have been reached several years earlier if she had shown more subtlety in her approach.

By the spring of 1982, after almost three years in power, it looked as though the Thatcher government was completely washed up, and few observers gave it any hope of winning re-election. Both the government, and Thatcher personally, had the worst record ever in opinion polls. The Tories were then running a poor third behind Labour, and very far behind the alliance of Liberals and the newly created Social Democratic Party (SDP), which had established an impressive lead, and took three by-election seats from the Tories in quick succession between October 1981 and March 1982. Then the government was rescued by the folly of one man – General Leopoldo Galtieri, the Argentine dictator.

His invasion of the Falklands in 1982 could, and perhaps should, have been the final *coup de grâce* for Margaret Thatcher. For she had inadvertently provoked the invasion by withdrawing, as an economy measure and against the repeated advice of the Foreign Secretary, Lord Carrington, the British naval vessel which had been patrolling Falklands waters as a deterrent against Argentine threats. Yet when the Argentines launched their almost bloodless occupation of the Falklands on 2 April 1982, and the House of Commons erupted in anger on the following day, it was Carrington and his fellow Foreign Office ministers who resigned, while Thatcher stayed put. She then showed tremendous energy and determination in ordering the assembly of a naval task force to sail, within three days, to the South Atlantic, with the declared intention of ousting the Argentine invaders. Most observers, including the majority of her Cabinet, assumed that the real objective was to back up diplomatic pressure on Argentina to agree to a peaceful withdrawal to be followed by negotiations through the United Nations. In retrospect, it seems clear that both Thatcher and her closest military advisors – the Chief of the Defence Staff, Sir Terence Lewin, and Admiral Sir Henry Leach – were determined on a military reconquest, despite the enormous risks involved. When the US Secretary of State, General Al Haig, embarked on a marathon round of shuttle diplomacy between London and Buenos Aires, the British Prime Minister, overruling her new Foreign Secretary, Francis Pym, insisted on a considerable tightening up of what the Americans regarded as eminently reasonable conditions and the Argentine junta turned them down. The baton was then taken up by the UN Secretary-General, Javier Peres de Cuellar, and by the Peruvian President, Belaunde, who produced a revised version of the Haig proposals which appeared to meet both British and Argentine demands, and which he was confident that Galtieri would accept.

This plan was effectively torpedoed by the most controversial action of the war – the sinking of the Argentine cruiser, the *General Belgrano*, with the loss of 368 lives. The ship was well outside the 'total exclusion zone' which the British had proclaimed, and was actually steaming away from it. Thatcher announced to the Commons that it was sailing towards the zone, a fiction which she endeav-oured to maintain for some years afterwards, well after any possible operational reason for dissembling had passed. When the Labour MP Tam Dalyell accused her of 'lying', he was suspended from the House for using 'unparliamentary language', but Thatcher, who, with her War Cabinet, personally ordered the sinking, knew very well that his stricture was justified. The sinking of the ship and the enormous loss of life, provoked popular outrage in Buenos Aires, and Galtieri felt compelled to repudiate the Belaunde plan, despite his earlier assur-ances to the Peruvian President. So the undeclared war proceeded, and the British proved victorious, partly due to US assistance personally ordered by President Reagan, which was far more extensive than was realised at the time. Even so, it was a victory dearly bought – 254 British servicemen were killed and another 777 wounded. Argentine losses were at least twice as great, so the total number of casualties was undoubtedly higher than the Falklands' population of 1800.

For the Thatcher government – and even more for herself personally – the Falklands War proved a watershed. Hitherto, all their efforts appeared to be dogged by failure, and they were mired in the deepest unpopularity. From then onwards – right up almost to the last year of her premiership, with only a few blips – it appeared to be a non-stop success story. The initial boost came from the wave of jingoism, fanned by the popular press, which was reflected in the extraordinary swings in the opinion polls recorded between April and July 1982. The Tories shot up in the Gallup poll from 31 to 46 per cent, while the Liberal-Social Democrat bubble was well and truly burst, their support going down from 37 per cent to 24 per cent. The Prime Minister herself did everything she could to inspire a mood of national triumphalism, 'We have ceased to be a nation in retreat,' she boasted, 'doubts and hesitation were replaced by confidence and pride that our younger generation too could write a glorious chapter in the history of liberty.' Not everyone accepted the gloss which she had put on the struggle. One writer in the *Guardian*, for example, tellingly quoted Voltaire's *Candide* on the 'folly' of British and French soldiers 'fighting over a few acres of snow on the borders of Canada, and that they spend more money on this glorious war than the whole of Canada is worth'. Yet this was very much a minority view.

As well as boosting Thatcher's popularity, the Falklands had an extraordinary effect on her self-confidence. She saw herself as walking in Churchill's footsteps, and subsequently had no hesitation in evoking the name of 'Winston' to justify her every initiative. As one Cabinet minister said to Hugo Young at the time, the victory 'fortifies her conviction that she is right on every subject' (Young, 1993, p. 280). Henceforward, she acted as a virtual dictator, reducing the role of the Cabinet to that of a supporters' club. Ministers were appointed or dismissed at will; those who were not sacked were ruthlessly briefed against when they threatened to step out of line, and controversial decisions were seldom discussed in Cabinet, the Prime Minister preferring to settle them on a one-to-one basis with the minister most concerned. Peter Walker, who eventually became the only surviving 'wet' in the Cabinet, privately compared her approach to that of the Duke of Wellington, who wrote after the first meeting of his Cabinet: 'An extraordinary affair! I gave them their orders and they wanted to stay and discuss them.' Walker would conclude his account by saying: 'I'm so glad we don't have Prime Ministers like that today.' Francis Pym did not long survive his defeatism during the Falklands War, being dropped immediately after the 1983 election. Whitelaw was dispatched to the House of Lords at the same time, becoming its leader until his retirement in 1986. Until then, he remained the one minister whose views – usually expressed in private – she listened to with any regularity. Treating her with the softest of kid gloves, he largely fulfilled the role which Bagehot attributed to the monarchy – 'the right to be consulted, the right to encourage and the right to warn'. A wise old bird, he was credited with having saved her from many a rash venture, though there were also frequent occasions when his advice was disregarded.

The Falklands transformed Thatcher's standing not only in her own country, but also abroad. She was not universally admired for her wartime leadership – the feeling in West European countries, which had rather reluctantly agreed to apply sanctions against Argentina, was that her reaction had been somewhat 'over the top' – but all recognised that she had brought a new decisiveness and assertiveness to the direction of British foreign policy. In the US, the reservations were far fewer and her popularity soared. She was seen – and saw herself – as a natural partner for Ronald Reagan, who had described the Soviet Union as 'the evil empire' and who welcomed her as a rumbustious ally in the fight to extend the frontiers of 'freedom' around the world. The prolonged 'love-in' between Margaret and Ron was somewhat incongruous – she an inveterate workaholic who devoured every official paper put in front of her and peppered it with sharp comments; he, the nearest approach to a part-time President that the US has had in modern times. Yet both shared the same ideological approach and their personal chemistry worked like a dream. As for the Soviet Union, its leaders acquired a healthy respect for the British leader, whom they christened the 'Iron Lady', a description which she took as a compliment.

It was as the Iron Lady that Thatcher presented herself in the general election of June 1983, one of the most one-sided contests of the century. On the face of it the Tories should have had little chance – unemployment had soared to 3 million, and though inflation was now down to not much more than the European average, very few of the promises they had made in 1979 were kept. Yet their opponents were in near total disarray. The Labour Party had split, with many of its more modern-minded and attractive figures defecting to the newly formed SDP, and it was saddled with unrealistic and unpopular policies. Furthermore, it had, in Michael Foot, a leader who had fought his first parliamentary election in 1935, at the age of 22, and had done very little to adapt his electioneering style in the intervening period. As for the Liberal-SDP alliance, it polled astonishingly well for a third party, but not nearly well enough to overcome the handicaps imposed by the British electoral system. It polled 25.4 per cent against 27.6 for Labour, but it won not many more than one-tenth the number of seats. Altogether the Tories polled 700,000 fewer votes than in 1979, but their majority shot up from 44 to 144 (see table below).

Conservative	397
Labour	209
Liberal-SDP	23
Others	21
Conservative majority	144

Safely re-elected, Thatcher pressed forward, less cautiously than before, on her self-appointed mission to undo the post-1945 consensus. An extensive reshuffle brought Geoffrey Howe to the Foreign Office, and Nigel Lawson, a much younger and very self-confident monetarist ideologue, to the Treasury. These two ministers were to be her loyalest and most industrious supporters until 1989–90, when she fell out with both of them, with disastrous consequences for herself. The dominating event of Thatcher's second term was the miners' strike of 1984–85. Once again, she was lucky in her opponent. Arthur Scargill, the charismatic but hot-headed President of the National Union of Mineworkers, impulsively brought his members out to resist pit closures which he believed were imminent, but made the cardinal error of refusing to allow a strike ballot. This led to the loss of much of the public sympathy which the miners could normally rely on, and, crucially, provoked the defection from the union of a substantial slice of its membership, which formed the Union of Democratic Mineworkers, and carried on working. After a whole year – often marked by violent scenes between pickets and the large number of policemen mobilised to protect miners continuing to work – the strike finally collapsed, and the National Coal Board proceeded to implement a closure programme even more drastic than Scargill had predicted. Thatcher was triumphant, insensitively bracketing her victory over the miners with that over the Argentines in the Falklands. The symbolic significance was huge – after the two previous miners' strikes which had defeated the Heath government – and it graphically confirmed Thatcher's success in taming the trade union movement. This owed as much to the high unemployment as it did to the three bills which she had pushed through to reduce their powers. The weakening of the unions was reflected in a sharp decline in their membership – over 13 million when she was elected, down to 6.7 million when Labour finally regained power in 1997.

Apart from the miners' strike, the most dramatic event of the 1983–87 Parliament was the Westland affair in December 1985 and January 1986. This was provoked by a dispute between two Cabinet ministers, Trade and Industry Secretary Leon Brittan, and Defence Secretary Michael Heseltine, over whether the American helicopter company Sikorski should be permitted to take over the smaller British firm, Westland. This was vehemently opposed by Heseltine, who actively championed a rival bid by a European consortium in order to keep control this side of the Atlantic. Thatcher backed Brittan, as did a majority of the Cabinet, but was unwilling to face a showdown with Heseltine and resorted to 'dirty tricks' to discredit him. She was caught out, and Heseltine resigned in protest, dramatically stalking out of a Cabinet meeting. The hapless Brittan was fingered as the 'fall guy' and reluctantly resigned, but Thatcher then faced a Labour motion of censure, and was seen to be extremely vulnerable, she herself warning her private secretary on the way to the debate: 'This may be my last day as Prime Minister.' In the event, the opposition leader, Neil Kinnock, made a hash of his speech, as he himself readily acknowledged, and let her off the hook. In the long term, however, it did her immense harm. Her reputation for truthfulness was severely damaged, and the highly ambitious and vengeful Heseltine was released to the back benches from where he prepared his slow-burning campaign to replace her.

It was during Thatcher's second term that another of her more distinctive policies got into its stride. This was privatisation, hardly mentioned in the Tory election manifesto in 1979, but gradually building up into a crescendo as one by one the great state corporations were sold off, yielding an additional revenue, which grew from a mere £377 million in 1979–80 to over £7 billion in 1988–89, despite being offered at knock-down prices. The policy proved highly popular, particularly among the investors, many of whom were able to make instant capital gains by selling on their shares. Largely as a result, the number of individuals owning shares grew from 3 million to 9 million in ten years, a major step towards the Tory ideal of a 'property-owning democracy'. Alongside this, more than 1 million council houses were sold to their sitting tenants – again at very favourable prices – which was an even more popular measure, appealing as it did to many working-class electors and helping to lure them away from their previous Labour sympathies. Apart from housing, altogether two-thirds of the public sector was sold off during Thatcher's premiership, and the proceeds helped to move the budget into a large, though temporary surplus, enabling substantial further cuts, in both the higher and standard rates of income tax, to be made in Nigel Lawson's Budgets preceding the 1987 election. This promised to be a more closely fought contest than 1983, partly because Michael Foot had been replaced by the younger and more energetic Neil Kinnock, who had persuaded his party to jettison some of its more unpopular policies and had shown great courage in facing up to the extreme left. However, he was seen as inexperienced and lacking in *gravitas*, and succeeded only in reducing the Tory majority from 144 to 102 seats, although he decisively beat off the Liberal-Social Democratic challenge for second place. Thatcher became the first Prime Minister in more than 150 years to win an overall majority in three successive elections, and her standing and reputation, not to mention her arrogance, reached unprecedented heights. Angrily dismissing suggestions that she might retire half-way through her third term, she announced her intention of 'going on and on'.

Thatcher and her ministers talked a lot about 'taking government off people's backs' and 'setting the people free', but many of their policies had a centralising effect and increased the power of the national government. This particularly applied to their health service reforms and to local government, where the abolition of the Greater London Council and the other Metropolitan authorities, the removal of powers from elected education authorities and the progressively tighter control over local government finance all led to a strengthening of Whitehall at the expense of local representatives. Nor were civil liberties increased by this supposedly libertarian government. Hugo Young mounted a formidable indictment in his biography:

> Where the citizen's liberty met state power, the citizen experienced new deprivations. The Police and Criminal Evidence Act 1984 created large police powers. The reach of the security service was extended. A new Official Secrets Act rendered a bad law worse, criminalizing whistleblowers in government and editors who so much as mentioned certain secret activities of the state. The Home Secretary claimed executive power to impede normal reporting, in the name of anti-terrorism in Ireland. This was a government that incessantly interfered with individual liberties in this way. (Young, 1993, p. 612)

The third term did not go particularly well, with Lawson beginning to lose control of the economy and inflation shooting up to 10 per cent, more than it had been when Thatcher was first elected. The Thatcherite claim to have produced a British 'economic miracle' comparable to West Germany's began to appear risible. Thatcher had always been seen as an exceptionally lucky politician, but it is of the nature of luck that at some time it begins to run out. In the summer of 1989 she celebrated her tenth anniversary as Prime Minister, the longest uninterrupted premiership since Lord Liverpool's 15-year tenure in 1812–27. In retrospect, she would have been well advised to bow out at this stage, as Whitelaw and other leading Tories privately thought at the time, in which case her reputation as a successful if highly controversial Prime Minister would have been assured. As it was, she clung to power, became progressively more unpopular and steadily lost support within her own party, becoming the only Prime Minister in modern times to be ejected from office at the behest of her own party. For this to happen, however, required the interaction of three distinct factors – her stubborn pursuit of a deeply unpopular policy, her growing anti-European obsession and her appalling treatment of her Cabinet colleagues.

The unpopular policy was, of course, the poll tax, or Community Charge, as it was officially known – a highly regressive tax designed to replace the domestic rates. The rating system was far from perfect, but it had the great advantage of being easy to collect, and because it was long established it was not an active source of complaint against the government currently in power. Thatcher decided to abolish it for no better reason than that she had promised to do so more than ten years earlier, when she had been Shadow Environment minister before the October 1974 election; though she also saw the poll tax as a means of curbing expenditure by local authorities, particularly those under Labour control. The tax was introduced in Scotland in 1989, and in England and Wales in 1990, and provoked enormous discontent, leading to riots in the streets of London and a widespread refusal to pay. More damaging to Thatcher was the plunge in support for the Conservatives, who fell over 20 points behind Labour in the opinion polls and lost a string of by-elections, both to Labour and the Liberal Democrats. Large numbers of Tory MPs were terrified that they would lose their seats if the tax was not withdrawn; a smaller number was convinced that the only way to avoid electoral disaster was to change their leader. In December 1989, they availed themselves of the (hitherto unused) provision for an annual poll on the leadership by putting up a 'wet' backbencher, Sir Anthony Meyer, as a 'stalking horse' candidate. He polled 33 votes, against Thatcher's 314. This was not enough to undermine her, but another 27 MPs abstained, which meant that she had lost the support of more than one-sixth of the party. It was a warning shot which she did not heed.

Meanwhile, the Chancellor of the Exchequer had become convinced that the solution – both to rising inflation and to high interest rates – lay in bringing the pound sterling into the Exchange Rate Mechanism of the European Monetary System. The official position had long been that Britain would join 'when the time was right', but Thatcher had set her face against ever naming the day, even though a large majority of her ministers had long been in favour. Lawson decided that the next best thing would be to obtain exchange rate stability by 'tracking the Deutschmark', and using the resources of the Bank of England to ensure that the floating rate remained at or near three Deutschmarks to the pound. It took some time for Thatcher to realise what was going on, but when she found out she ordered Lawson to desist, publicly humiliating him in the process. Lawson did not give up, and before the EU summit in Madrid, in June 1989, he and Geoffrey Howe went to see the Prime Minister and threatened to resign unless she gave a clear indication at the summit that Britain would in fact join at an early date. Thatcher was furious, but nevertheless produced a form of words to satisfy them at Madrid, but took her revenge a month later when she quite unexpectedly removed Howe from the Foreign Office. Howe was devastated and seriously considered resigning, but reluctantly agreed to become Leader of the House, with the additional title of Deputy Premier, which Thatcher's spokesman, Bernard Ingham, promptly assured the press was purely honorific. Lawson did not long survive his colleague, resigning in October 1989 because of what he regarded as intolerable interference by Thatcher's part-time economic advisor, Sir Alan Walters. The new Chancellor was Thatcher's young protégé, John Major, who had already been made Foreign Secretary three months earlier, and was now replaced in this role by Douglas Hurd. These two men were now irreplaceable, and together finally persuaded Thatcher that Britain should join the EMS the following October, when, however, the crucial error was made of entering at an unrealistically high level.

A more immediately lethal error was made by Thatcher later the same month when she attended yet another EU summit, in Rome, discussing Economic and Monetary Union, and reported back to the House of Commons with a statement laced with bitter anti-European rhetoric. This so incensed the long-suffering Geoffrey Howe that he resigned from the government, and then astonished the House with a blistering resignation speech which was televised live. In total contrast to his normal soporific style, he dissected Thatcher's record with consummate forensic skill. Within 24 hours, Michael Heseltine, who had been waiting almost five years for an opportune moment, threw his hat into the ring and challenged Thatcher in the annual leadership ballot. It was immediately clear that she was in deadly peril – although it was her anti-Europeanism which had provoked the challenge, it was the raging discontent over the poll tax which threatened to sap her support. Under the Tory election rules, she required not only a majority of the votes cast but a lead of 15 per cent over her nearest challenger to win on the first round. Although she fulfilled the first requirement, she was four votes short of the second, polling 204 votes to 152 for Heseltine. She defiantly announced that she would carry on into the second ballot, but her position soon proved untenable. She conducted one-to-one interviews with her Cabinet ministers, a clear majority of whom told her that she had no chance of winning and recommended that she should withdraw. 'This was treachery,' she later said in a television interview, 'treachery with a smile on its face.' It was the end of her premiership, but not of her political activity. She intervened in the second round, personally telephoning many of the MPs still loyal to her, asking them to vote for John Major rather than Douglas Hurd or Heseltine, and then announced that she would be 'a good backseat driver' during Major's premiership. In fact, she soon became disillusioned with him and gave strong moral support to his anti-EU critics within the party (see Chapter 50), and then went on to back both William Hague and Ian Duncan Smith in subsequent leadership ballots. Increasingly embittered, she ended up as a considerable embarrassment to her successors and to the more moderate elements within her party, while retaining a fanatical following among the ageing rank and file.

Thatcher was – by a wide margin – the most divisive Prime Minister in the period covered by this book, and the division survived her death, following a stroke, on 8 April 2013, aged 87 years and 176 days. She was granted a full ceremonial funeral at St. Paul's Cathedral, and was praised to the skies by her supporters and much of the popular press. But her opponents paid her only grudging respect, and there were widespread celebrations in former mining villages and in deprived inner city areas whose inhabitants believed their lives had been blighted by the policies she pursued. There are very few 'don't knows' when people are asked their opinion of her. To her admirers, she is the greatest premier since Churchill, a leader who restored Britain's greatness, reversed a long-running economic decline, put the unions in their place, promoted a spirit of enterprise and fought to resurrect old and trusted values. To her critics, she was an uncaring power maniac, who deliberately fostered unemployment, decimated British industry, redistributed incomes in favour of the rich, neglected public services and left Britain dangerously isolated in Europe. What both sides might agree on is that she was *effective*, and that her apparent insensitivity probably made her more so. For good or ill, she made more difference to the country that she led for 11 years and 209 days than did the great majority of the other 52 politicians (all men) who have held the office of Prime Minister.

Works consulted

Campbell, John, *Margaret Thatcher: Vol.I, The Grocer's Daughter*, London, Pimlico, 2001.
Campbell, John, *Margaret Thatcher: Vol. II, The Iron Lady*, London, Cape, 2003.
Clark, Alan, *Diaries*, London, Phoenix, 1994.
Clarke, Peter, *A Question of Leadership: From Gladstone to Thatcher*, Harmondsworth, Penguin, 1992.
Dalyell, Tam, *One Man's Falklands*, London, Cecil Woolf, 1982.
Maddox, Brenda, Maggie, *The First Lady, London*, Hodder & Stoughton, 2003.
Prior, James, *A Balance of Power*, London, Hamish Hamilton, 1986.
Thatcher, Margaret, *The Downing Street Years*, London, HarperCollins, 1993.
Thatcher, Margaret, *The Path to Power*, London, HarperCollins, 1995.
Young, Hugo, *One of Us*, Final Edition, London, Pan, 1993.
Young, Hugo, *This Blessed Plot: Britain and Europe from Churchill to Blair*, London, Macmillan, 1998.

50
John Major – 'Thatcherism with a Human Face'

It has become customary to think of the premiership of John Major as a mere transitional interlude between the dominant figures of Margaret Thatcher and Tony Blair. In fact, Major was one of the longer-serving Prime Ministers of the twentieth century. He spent seven and a half years in 10 Downing Street – longer than Attlee, Macmillan, Lloyd George or Stanley Baldwin. Often described, rather unfairly, as a 'grey man', he came from a more exotic background than any of his fellow Prime Ministers of the century. Born on 29 March 1943, his father, Tom, was already almost 64, and his mother, Gwen, 38. Tom had had a varied and adventurous life. Brought up in the United States, where he won but did not take up a scholarship to the West Point Military Academy, and played junior league baseball, he returned to Britain with his family in his late teens and worked on a London building site before embarking on a long theatrical career, including a spell as a circus trapeze artist, before opening a business as a manufacturer of garden gnomes. His original name was Abraham Thomas Ball, and he had adopted Major as a stage name, eventually hyphenating himself to Major-Ball. Twice married, each time to partners in his theatrical acts, he also had many affairs, which meant that the future Prime Minister had at least two half-siblings, one of whom, a sister, he only became aware of after he became Prime Minister.

Tom Major, who had spent most of his theatrical life touring in music halls on both sides of the Atlantic, retired in 1930, aged 51. He had recently got married for the second time, and rapidly fathered three children, the eldest of whom, a boy, was stillborn, but Patricia, born in 1930, and Terry, in 1932, both survived. There was then an eleven-year gap until their younger brother, John, was born in 1943. Tom and Gwen went to live in Worcester Park, a prosperous south London suburb, where they rented, and later bought a bungalow, and Tom ran his business, known as Major's Garden Ornaments, from his back garden. It was a successful enterprise: the family bought a car, sent the two children to private schools and employed domestic help. When war broke out, however,

767

demand for his products dwindled, and Tom, who was feeling his years and whose health was declining, closed down the business. Their standard of living collapsed, but Gwen went to work in the local library, and earned just enough to keep the wolf from the door. After the war the business was restarted, with both Gwen and Terry playing an active part, but the pre-war prosperity was never regained and life became an unending struggle. John attended the local council school, passing the 11-plus examination and going on to the nearest local authority grammar school, Rutlish School, three miles away at Merton. This was a school with relatively low academic standards, but which consciously aped public schools, with its own cadet force, and so on. John was repelled by the school's ambience, was thoroughly demotivated, showed no signs of distinction throughout his school career, except on the cricket field, and left at 16 with very poor GCE results. Writing in his autobiography, 40 years later, he expressed bitter regret for having let his parents down and for failing totally to take advantage of what the school had to offer. He did, however, strongly criticise them for insisting that he should be registered at the school as John Major-Ball, despite his vehement objections at the time. He evidently foresaw that he would be constantly mocked and bullied because of the 'Ball', which was confirmed by one of his classmates when he was interviewed by his biographer, Anthony Seldon, in 1996. A deeper reason for his alienation was almost certainly the final collapse of the family business in 1955, which led to the sell-off of their home and abrupt removal to rented rooms in the depressed working-class area of Brixton, in inner London, As John Major was to recall:

> It was a sad comedown, part of the top floor of a four-storey Victorian building in Coldharbour Lane. We had two rooms for the five of us ... Dad, Terry and I slept in one room, and Mum and Pat in the other. This second room was used as a dining room and lounge during the day. We shared a cooker on the landing with the other top-floor tenant, a middle-aged bachelor. The lavatory, two floors below, was used by all the tenants. There was no bathroom. We washed at the sink or in a tub. (Major, 1999, pp. 15–16)

Their landlord, Tom Moss, a man in his mid-fifties, was a mystery to John and his brother and sister. It was only later that they discovered that he was, in fact, their half-brother, the offspring of an affair between Tom Major and a young dancer in 1901. The removal to Brixton meant that John now had a journey of an hour and a half each way to his school, which, added to his sense of shame and the stress of having to live in such cramped circumstances with ageing and increasingly ailing parents, was another contributory factor to his turning in on himself. On leaving school, he started work as a clerk for an insurance firm, which he greatly disliked. He soon left to work as a labourer, making garden gnomes, with his brother Terry, for the small company which had taken over his father's failed business. Soon after, his father died, at the age of 82, and his mother's health being poor, he left his work to look after her for a time, and then found it impossible to get another job, being unemployed ('unemployable, I feared', as he later wrote (Major, 1999)), for six months in 1963. One job he failed to get was as a bus conductor, being turned down, he recounted, because he was too tall. He eventually landed a job with the London Electricity Board, which he found 'mind-numbing', but it was a 'cheerful, happy place'. 'So far,' he was to recall, 'I had not made much of my life. School – a failure; career – I had none; sport – not good enough; politics – I was only playing at it. I needed a career and qualifications' (Major, 1999, p. 30). He began to take correspondence courses to get more O levels.

It was, in fact, politics which gave the young Major the motivation which he had previously lacked. Given a ticket to attend a House of Commons debate by the local Labour MP, Marcus Lipton, when he was 13, he immediately fell in love with the place and formed the ambition to become an MP. At 16, he signed up to the Brixton Young Conservatives, perhaps influenced by his parents who were both 'gut instinct' Tories. His biographer, Anthony Seldon, remarks that 'many of his embryonic views – on privilege, authority, social advance and race – put him closer to Labour', but

> he chose to see Labour as the party that denied individual expression and treated people as groups ... The Conservatives offered him the passport out of the ghetto; their emphasis on individuality and personal freedom struck a deep chord in the young man. They were also the party of prosperity, of a world he aspired to join. (Seldon, 1997, pp. 19–20)

The Brixton Young Conservatives soon became the main focus of the young Major's life; he joined in all their activities, in particular becoming their star soapbox speaker at meetings they held regularly outside Brixton pubs, and rose to become the branch chairman. His father died when he was 19, and shortly afterwards he began a relationship with a divorcee 13 years his senior with two young children, which caused his mother much distress. It could, however, be argued that his affair with Jean Kierans, a leading Brixton Conservative, was the making of John Major. A woman of sophisticated tastes, she smartened John up, greatly boosted his self-esteem, and gave him the stimulus to improve himself which his own family had not provided.

At the age of 21, Major stood for election to the Lambeth Council, but was heavily defeated in a strong Labour ward. The same year – 1965 – he left the LEB, and started work at a local branch of the District Bank (later taken over by NatWest). He now formed serious ambitions of becoming a banker, and studied to take the first of what proved to be a long series of banking exams. After a year, he left to take a more senior post at Standard Chartered Bank, on the understanding that he would have to serve for a lengthy period in an overseas branch of the bank. This turned out to be in Nigeria, six years after the country achieved independence in 1960. Major was posted to Jos, a small town in the northern region, where he settled in happily, though feeling acutely uncomfortable about the colonialist attitudes of many of his fellow expatriates. Major, who had freely mixed with the black population of Brixton, had no difficulty in accepting his African colleagues as equals, and insisted on being on first-name terms with them, which soon marked him out as not being a 'racialist'. In the event, his stay in Nigeria lasted barely five months: he was severely injured in a car crash and had to be flown back to London for lengthy restorative treatment, especially to his kneecap which had been shattered by the accident. Major was appalled by the likely consequences of the accident, saying 'This has ruined everything', not least lamenting the fact that he would be unlikely ever to play cricket again, a sport which he loved and at which he had shown distinct promise. In fact, the dramatic shortening of his overseas posting made possible an early blossoming of the political career for which he hankered.

The bank treated him very decently, slotting him into a job in their investment and international division, where his working hours were 9.15 a.m. to 4.45 p. m., enabling him to get off early for the evening's political activities. In May 1968 – aged 25 – he stood for the Lambeth Council for a second time, again in what was normally regarded as a safe Labour ward. But this was the nadir of the Wilson government's unpopularity, following the forced devaluation of the previous November, and the Tories swept to an overwhelming victory, winning 57 out of the 60 seats on the Council. Major immediately specialised in housing policy, becoming, in short order, Vice-Chairman and then Chairman of the Housing Committee. He was to prove himself exceptionally vigorous and innovative in this role, forging a formidable partnership with the Director of Housing, Harry Simpson, who later went on to be Director of the Northern Ireland Housing Authority, and subsequently of the Greater London Council.

In the spring of 1970 an incident occurred which showed just how strong was Major's belief in racial equality. The local Tory parliamentary candidate, James Harkess, was a right-wing lawyer with Powellite views. In his autobiography, Major recalled the events of the annual general meeting of the Conservative association:

> Harkess made a speech that was strongly anti-immigrant. I was appalled at his intolerance, and embarrassed, too, as we had a new West Indian member present, who must have been mortified. I replied angrily from the chair, rebutting Harkess's remarks, and the atmosphere turned sulphurous. (Major, 1999, p. 46)

Convinced that Harkess's views would damage race relations in Brixton, as well as the Conservative cause, Major subsequently went ahead with a motion to consider the adoption of a new candidate. This was, however, overtaken by Harold Wilson's sudden decision to hold a general election, and it was felt to be too late to consider a change. Harkess remained the candidate, being roundly defeated by the defending Labour MP.

Major's personal situation was transformed during his three years on the Lambeth Council. His mother died in September 1970, aged 65, and a few weeks later he got married to Norma Johnson, a teacher and fanatical opera-lover, whom he had met while canvassing during the GLC election, the previous April. Norma invited him to an opera performance: Major promptly fell asleep, but they got engaged ten days later. His relationship with Jean Kierans, which had lasted seven years, had gradually been winding down and Major now gently broke it off. He and Norma started their married life in a small bachelor flat he had bought in Streatham, but, in 1971, when Major lost his seat on the council, they moved to a three-bedroomed house in suburban Beckenham, where they lived more comfortably with their two children, Elizabeth, born in 1971, and James, 1975.

Meanwhile, Major had successfully completed his banking exams, and felt that the time had come to seek a parliamentary seat. He stood twice for St Pancras North, a working-class inner London constituency, in February and October 1974, where his experience as a Lambeth Councillor stood him in good stead, and his progress was favourably noted by Conservative Central Office. It was a different matter being selected for a safe Conservative seat, where his humble birth and upbringing was not held to be a recommendation by many members of selection committees. He did his best to burnish his CV, describing himself as an 'international banker', which did more than justice to the junior management position he had reached at the Standard Chartered Bank. After several rejections, he finally struck lucky in 1976 at Huntingdonshire, a cast-iron Tory seat, which blended lush rural areas with an overspill population from London. He then had a three-year wait until the 1979 general election, but threw himself into nursing the constituency with enormous energy, speaking to an estimated 450 meetings, and treating the constituency as if it was a super-marginal. His efforts were to be rewarded with a majority of over 21,000, in place of the 9000 achieved by his predecessor, one of the best Tory performances in the election which brought Margaret Thatcher to power.

When Major arrived in the Commons, he was regarded as unremarkable by most of his new colleagues. Yet he showed exceptional diligence in familiarising himself with the procedures of the House, and – while not seeming to push himself – was very ready to take on any chore, however menial. He decided, at first, to specialise in two areas where, he rightly believed, he had more experience than most – housing and local government. His work on the committee of the 1980 Housing Bill attracted favourable notice from his party whips, and Seldon records his growing popularity with his fellow Tory MPs. One described him as 'Hard working, very keen and not at all bombastic. Everyone liked him', and another said:

> I'd have listed John Major among my five best friends. Probably there were ten of us who would have said the same thing! But he probably wouldn't have listed any of us as his close friends. He had that knack of making people feel you were precious to him. (Seldon, 1997, pp. 50, 53)

Major carefully avoided identifying himself with any particular faction in the party, but was regarded as being mildly on the left wing, largely because of the exceptional concern he showed for the effect of policies on people who were handicapped or were on low incomes. After a while, Major began to chafe on the back benches, as one by one the more prominent of the new Tory MPs elected in 1979 were appointed to junior ministerial office. He had to wait until January 1983 before the call came, and this was to be an assistant whip, in Seldon's (1997) words 'the lowest form of ministerial life', but it was the first step on the ladder. With his assiduity and his gift for getting on with his colleagues, Major took to the Whips' Office like a duck to water, but feared he had irredeemably blighted his chances of further promotion when he had a fierce argument with Margaret Thatcher, after he had, tactlessly but honestly, reported to her on backbench grievances. In the event, it did him no harm – within weeks he was appointed to his first post in a ministerial department, as Parliamentary Under-Secretary for Social Security, the same position which Thatcher herself had occupied 25 years earlier. Within a year, he was promoted to Minister of State in the same department, and soon established a reputation as a competent, hard-working and sensitive minister, without being seen in any way as a high-flyer. Nevertheless, nine months later, he made it into the Cabinet, an unusual achievement after only eight years in the Commons. When he was summoned to see the Prime Minister, he expected and hoped that she had him in mind as Chief Whip, a post for which his personal qualities would have made him an excellent choice. Instead, he was made Chief Secretary to the Treasury, in charge of keeping public spending down. He owed his appointment to the advocacy of the Chancellor of the Exchequer, Nigel Lawson, who wanted somebody who was good at sums, and ideally would have preferred an accountant. Major was the next best thing: he looked and sounded like an accountant, and his background as a banker (though probably a more junior one than Lawson supposed) seemed an ideal qualification. He made an inauspicious start in his new post, fearing he was out of his depth, and Lawson recalled how he would 'come and see me at Number 11, ashen-faced, to unburden himself of his worries and seek my advice' (Lawson, 1992, p. 719). Yet by making an enormous effort – for some time his working day extended from 6 a.m. to midnight – he mastered his brief, and proved himself a remarkably skilful negotiator in his encounters with spending ministers, many of whom were far senior to him. Generally, he got his way in sharply reducing their bids, though he was adept at sugaring the pill by making exceptions for particular pet schemes. Thus he was able to keep expenditure pretty rigorously under control without unnecessarily alienating his colleagues. There were two notable exceptions. One was the Health and Social Security Secretary, John Moore, seen for a time as a special favourite of Thatcher's and rumoured to be groomed by her for the succession. The other was the right-wing Environment Secretary, Nicholas Ridley. Both became sworn enemies, but Major had the last laugh. Moore soon disappointed his sponsor's hopes, and was quickly demoted and then left the government because of ill health, while Ridley was later forced to resign after expressing outrageously anti-German sentiments in an interview with the editor of (Lawson's son, Dominic), which he claimed was meant to be 'off the record'.

Thatcher was well-pleased with Major's performance, and he appeared to many to have replaced Moore as her favourite. At the same time her relations with Lawson were sharply deteriorating, and by early in 1989 she probably had marked him down as a likely replacement for the Chancellor. She was not yet ready, however, to dispense with Lawson's services, but after the June 1989 Madrid summit of the European Union, when Foreign Secretary Geoffrey Howe had joined with Lawson in pressurising her to name a date for entry into the European Monetary System (see Chapter 18), she promptly sought revenge by unexpectedly dropping him from the Foreign Office in a reshuffle a few weeks later. The obvious replacement for Howe would have been Douglas Hurd, a foreign policy specialist who was then Home Secretary, but Thatcher did not want somebody with independent views in the Foreign Office, and instead chose Major who she correctly surmised would offer no threat to the dominant role she sought for herself. In fact, Major – still technically the most junior figure in the Cabinet – was perplexed to be promoted to an office for which he had no relevant experience or qualification. He took it to heart when Charles Powell, the Prime Minister's foreign policy advisor, jokingly asked him what was the capital of Ecuador. It was painfully obvious to an embarrassed Powell that he hadn't the faintest idea.

Major's tenure of the Foreign Office lasted a mere 94 days – long enough for the staff to learn to appreciate him as a thoughtful, considerate and notably unstuffy boss, but not for him to have any discernable influence on foreign policy, though an article in *The Times* did contrast his anodyne approach to European Community affairs with the 'ferocious rhetoric of the Prime Minister'. Only one episode excited much comment. This was his semi-public humiliation by Thatcher, when, after Major had negotiated a joint statement on sanctions against South Africa with other foreign ministers at a Commonwealth conference in Malaysia, she had insisted on issuing a separate communiqué setting out a far harder British line.

Yet within a day of their return from Malaysia – on 26 October 1989 – Major was able to swap the Foreign Office for a post which attracted him a great deal more, and to which – at least on paper – he was far better suited. Goaded beyond endurance by his own treatment from the Prime Minister, Nigel Lawson handed in his resignation (see Chapter 18), and Thatcher happily turned to Major to take his place. Less happily, she felt she now had no alternative but to make Douglas Hurd Foreign Secretary. Major was now 46, and had achieved the post which, a decade earlier he had confided to other newly elected MPs, was his ultimate ambition. He looked forward to a lengthy spell as Chancellor, but in the event stayed only for 13 months. He introduced one Budget, the most notable feature of which was the introduction of Tessas (Tax Exempt Special Savings Accounts), whose impact was increased by the fact that this was the first Budget Speech ever to be televised live. The Budget was, however, widely criticised, notably in the City of London, for not doing enough to combat inflation, which was again moving into double figures. Major undoubtedly felt much more at home at the Treasury than he had at the Foreign Office, but did not regain the authority which he had eventually achieved as Chief Secretary. He was handicapped by his ignorance of economics, and suffered (in his own oversensitive mind, at least) by constant comparisons between his hesitant approach and the much more self-confident manner of his predecessor, Nigel Lawson. He also, for the first time, experienced the resentment and envy of Tory MPs convinced that he had been promoted beyond his merits and inclined to view him as 'Mrs Thatcher's poodle'.

The most important decision taken during his chancellorship was entry into the Exchange Rate Mechanism (ERM) of the European Monetary System. By the time of his appointment, Thatcher was virtually in a minority of one in her Cabinet in her reluctance to take this step, which was strongly urged by the Bank of England, the City of London and overwhelmingly by the serious press. It still took nearly a year before the partnership of Major and Hurd (which replicated the earlier alliance of Lawson and Howe) was able to argue her round. Major's role was later described by the Permanent Secretary to the Treasury, Sir Peter Middleton:

> Major went out of his way to be sensitive to what the PM wanted to do, and the fact that he was sensitive meant they got on pretty well. It also meant that he got his way on most issues. He played her with all the skill of a fly fisherman after a big and suspicious salmon. He would raise the subject, then drop it when she objected, then come back to it from a different angle at their next meeting. (Seldon, 1997, p. 112)

The decision was long overdue, but the way in which it was implemented meant that Britain failed to obtain the benefits expected, and which the other members of the ERM had enjoyed during the previous 11 years. Despite warnings from economists, Major made no attempt to negotiate entry at a lower level than the current market rate of DM2.95, which was a serious overvaluation of the pound. This blunder came back to haunt him with a vengeance, and was the principal reason for the shipwreck of his own government.

Within weeks of this decision being taken, Thatcher was ousted from the premiership (see Chapter 18), and – on 28 November 1990 – Major became Prime Minister at the age of 47, the youngest thus far of the century. In retrospect, it may seem surprising that he was chosen, as he was clearly the least experienced and least qualified of the three contenders. Yet he enjoyed marked advantages over his rivals. Heseltine was seen as too adventurous, too disloyal and too left-wing by the majority of Tory MPs, and his large score in the first round was more a measure of Thatcher's unpopularity than of his own support. Had she contested the second round, he might well have won, but once she withdrew, his prospects sharply declined. In reality, the real contest was between Major and the Foreign Secretary, Douglas Hurd, and five factors weighed strongly in his favour. First was his genuine popularity among his fellow members, as Nigel Lawson later observed: 'He never let up on his instinctive networking; he became a near universally liked figure in the party' (Seldon, 1997, p. 83). Allied to this was his detachment from any clearly defined faction within the party. This was most notable concerning Europe – at around this time Major had candidly confessed to a sympathetic journalist that he revelled in the fact that both the pro- and anti-Europeans believed that he was on their side. Third was what could only be described as a class factor. His modest background – which had told against him when he was seeking a safe Tory seat – was now seen as a trump card in the coming electoral campaign against Labour, much to the chagrin of the old Etonian, Douglas Hurd. Fourth, Thatcher threw her considerable weight on his side, enabling him to scoop up practically the whole of her loyalist support. Lastly, he had a much more efficient election team, shrewdly led by Norman Lamont, the Chief Secretary to the Treasury, whom Major unwisely rewarded by promoting him to be Chancellor of the Exchequer. The result was as shown in the table below.

John Major	185
Michael Heseltine	131
Douglas Hurd	56

Technically, there should have been a third round, as Major had just failed to secure an absolute majority, but both the other candidates promptly withdrew.

Not wishing to be seen as a surrogate for Thatcher, who had already announced that she would be 'a very good backseat driver', Major lost no time in implicitly distancing himself from her when he told a small crowd gathered outside Downing Street, when he returned from his meeting with the Queen, 'I want us to build a country which is at ease with itself.' Apart from Lamont, Major's first ministerial appointments were well judged, and helped to secure an early closing of party ranks. Hurd was confirmed as Foreign Secretary, and Michael Heseltine rejoined the government as Environment Secretary, with a brief to find a replacement for the highly unpopular poll tax in double-quick time. Chris Patten, who vacated the Environment Department, was appointed Chairman of the Conservative Party, where he was to prove himself a skilled electoral tactician. Within the Cabinet, Major made a diffident start, wondering aloud at his first meeting whether he was up to the job. Yet nearly all his colleagues found him a breath of fresh air, after having suffered from Thatcher's authoritarian ways for the previous eleven years. 'Major has restored Cabinet government', several of them delightedly announced, welcoming the fact that he allowed important decisions to be argued out, if necessary at length, around the Cabinet table rather than being settled by diktat or by bilateral deals between the PM and the minister most directly concerned. The general public, also, seemed pleased by Major's early moves – the enormous Labour lead in the opinion polls disappearing overnight, and the Tories gaining a narrow lead which they kept for three months. Most observers, however, credited this more to the demise of Thatcher than to Major's positive impact. The inheritance that he came into was an unenviable one. He benefited from the impact of the first Gulf War, which – unlike its successor 12 years later – was generally popular, and Major was able to exploit this by getting himself photographed addressing the troops in the desert and mixing with them informally. Otherwise, however, the outlook looked distinctly bleak, as Britain was entering the longest recession since the Second World War, with unemployment again approaching the 3 million mark.

By mid-March 1991, Heseltine was able to deliver on his pledge to produce a realistic, and obviously fairer, alternative to the poll tax. This was the Council Tax, effectively a revamped version of the former rating system, but less regressive, and its introduction was to be smoothed by the transfer of a great wodge of local expenditure to the national budget. The proposal was well received, but in the same month Labour again went ahead in the opinion polls, scotching any idea that Major might call a snap election to cash in on the Gulf War victory. In June, Major produced his own distinctive policy initiative, with the publication of the *Citizens' Charter*, which aimed to improve public services by providing consumers with more choice, information and opportunities to lodge complaints. Otherwise, Major's main preoccupation during his first term in office was the sorry state of Britain's relations with the European Community. He immediately set out to improve them by making an early visit to Chancellor Helmut Kohl, in Bonn, where he was warmly received, and made an excellent impression on his hosts, giving a widely publicised speech, of which the opening words were:

> My aims for Britain in the Community can be simply stated. I want us to be where we belong – at the very heart of Europe, working with our partners in building the future. This is a challenge we take up with enthusiasm. (11 March 1991)

This speech greatly heartened the pro-Europeans in the Conservative Party, who were then still in a majority. Yet it was not long before Major began to back-pedal to appease the so-called Eurosceptics, a small but growing force, who were encouraged, privately at first but then increasingly openly, by Margaret Thatcher. So far from seeking to put Britain at the heart of Europe, he ensured at the Maastricht summit, in December 1991, that it would remain on the sidelines, by obtaining opt-outs, from two of its main projects, the Social Charter and, especially, Economic and Monetary Union. Major returned triumphantly from Maastricht, saying he had won 'game, set and match' in his negotiations with the other EU leaders, but all that he had done was to store up future trouble for himself (and his successor). Despite the opt-outs, the Eurosceptics reacted violently against the Maastricht agreement, which Thatcher was later to characterise as 'a treaty too far'.

Labour continued to lead in the polls, and there were further by-election losses to both Labour and the Liberal Democrats (though not as sweeping as in Thatcher's time), so Major was discouraged from seeking an early dissolution, and the 1987 Parliament continued until March 1992, when polling day was set for 9 April. The general expectation was that Major would lose, but not heavily. His low-key leadership style was favourably compared to that of his predecessor, and Ken Clarke's description of his approach as 'Thatcherism with a human face' rang favourable bells with many electors. On the other hand, the Labour opposition was in a far healthier state than in 1987, with Neil Kinnock having succeeded in junking many of its unpopular and unrealistic policies and winning growing respect for standing up to left-wing extremists. Yet Major's personal standing in the polls was far higher than Kinnock's, and the government's main problem was its perceived failure in combating the recession. The Tory strategists, guided by Chris Patten, therefore decided that their best hope of staving off defeat was not to offer positive proposals but to stake everything on casting doubt on Labour's economic competence, coupling this with a fierce assault on its spending plans. The cost of these was grotesquely exaggerated, with horror stories of enormous tax increases being enthusiastically taken up by the tabloid newspapers, all of which, apart from the *Daily Mirror*, were on the Tories' side. Major himself was seen to fight a plucky campaign in the face of an almost universal expectation of defeat, which was, however, hardly justified by the very narrow Labour lead in the opinion polls. Against the advice of party professionals, he insisted on augmenting his carefully controlled programme of ticket-only meetings, with a series of impromptu open-air gatherings in marginal constituencies, which he addressed from a soapbox, recalling his early days in Brixton. It was a risky venture, but it seemed to pay off.

In the event, the polls had got it wrong – the Tories led Labour by the apparently comfortable margin of 7.5 per cent, which, however, yielded them an overall majority of only 21 seats. It was a triumph for Major, but it would probably have been better for his subsequent reputation if he had narrowly lost. He would then have been credited with having led his government with some skill, and away from the electoral abyss which it appeared to be facing in the last days of Thatcher.

As it was, it was downhill almost all the way after he regained Downing Street on the morning after the election. Within five months, his government suffered a devastating and largely self-inflicted blow on Black Wednesday (16 September 1992), which demolished its own claims to economic competence, and from which it was quite unable to recover over the remaining four-and-a-half years that it stayed in office. The genesis of Black Wednesday was Major's own decision, as Chancellor of the Exchequer in October 1990, to take the pound into the ERM at too high a level against the Deutschmark. In early September the pound was under enormous speculative pressure, and at a meeting of EU Finance Ministers in Bath, presided over by Norman Lamont, he refused to allow any discussion of an ordered realignment of currencies. Instead, he repeatedly harangued the President of the Bundesbank, Helmut Schlesinger, who was present as an observer, to reduce German interest rates in order to reduce pressure on the pound and other currencies, notably the Italian lira. Schlesinger, whose constitutional position as head of the bank precluded him from taking advice from any politicians, let alone foreign ones, angrily refused, and threatened to leave the meeting, when Lamont returned to the attack for the fourth time. Major, who fully supported Lamont's tactics, then compounded the blunder by making an ill-advised speech in Glasgow, despite warnings from two of his closest advisors, Sarah Hogg, the head of his Policy Unit and Sir John Kerr, the UK Permanent Representative to the EU. Speaking in the most personal terms, he ridiculed any idea of devaluation or of changing the parities within the ERM. Three days later, the Italians decided to revalue and temporarily to leave the ERM, and Prime Minister Giulio Amato telephoned Major to enquire whether Britain would follow suit. Major firmly declined, but within three days, after a harrowing few hours in which he had agreed with Lamont to raise interest rates to 15 per cent and billions of pounds had been lost by the Bank of England in a vain effort to halt the speculative flow, he agreed with Lamont and three other senior colleagues to let the pound float and to leave the ERM.

Major, who was badly worsted by the new Labour leader, John Smith, in the subsequent parliamentary debate, felt humiliated by the disaster and seriously contemplated resignation, though he was persuaded by colleagues to stay on. Yet much of his authority was gone, and he was widely regarded thereafter as one of the 'walking wounded'. Throughout the whole remainder of his premiership, Labour was leading in the opinion polls by a margin of 20 per cent or more, the government set a new record by losing every single by-election during the Parliament, while his own poll ratings fell to unprecedentedly low levels. Black Wednesday was also the occasion of a serious falling-out between Major and Lamont, who years later were still exchanging bad-tempered recriminations about each other's conduct during the affair. Lamont half-heartedly offered his resignation, which Major refused, but eight months later peremptorily sacked him, offering the Environment Department as a face-saver. Lamont indignantly refused, and insisted on making a highly damaging personal statement to the Commons, in which he asserted that the government gave 'the impression of being in office but not in power'. Thereafter, he became a consistent and bitter critic, who effectively put himself at the head of the Eurosceptic rebels on the back benches.

If Major's second administration had otherwise been seen as competent, it might have been able, with time, to overcome the disaster of Black Wednesday which, objectively, was no worse than that suffered by Wilson's government at the time of the 1967 devaluation. Yet it was only one, if much the most serious, of a whole series of self-inflicted wounds that were to beset Major and his ministers. Many of these derived from their increasing divisions over Europe, and they were exacerbated by his seeming inability to act decisively. This was most apparent over the long delays in seeking ratification of the Maastricht Treaty. Formally signed in February 1992, it was finally approved by the House of Commons in a confidence vote only on 23 July 1993, a day after it had been defeated in a division in which 23 Tory MPs voted against the government. After Maastricht only seven Tory MPs, led by Norman Tebbit, had opposed the government on a motion approving the outcome, and the majority was 86. There would have been no difficulty at all in ratifying the treaty (including the British opt-outs) before the general election in April. But Major put if off until the summer, and then for a further year, following the first Danish referendum, which narrowly rejected the treaty in July 1992. In the meantime, the strength of the Eurosceptics, now openly backed by Thatcher and surreptitiously encouraged by Cabinet ministers such as Michael Howard, Michael Portillo, John Redwood and Peter Lilley, steadily grew. Asked by a television interviewer, Michael Brunson, whether he ought not to sack his disloyal ministers, Major replied that he did not want 'three more of the bastards out there'. These words were meant to be 'off the record', but were accidentally picked up by a BBC sound-line, and became widely known. Major's Cabinet opponents were subsequently invariably referred to as 'the bastards' by the press.

The ratification of Maastricht did not end the agitation of the Eurosceptics, who were now strongly backed by most of the pro-Tory press, including the normally ultra-loyal, *Daily Telegraph* and by the mass of Tory supporters in the country. Major now set himself on a course of appeasement, but like the original payers of Danegeld found that every concession was met by further demands. British ministers became increasingly obstructive at EU meetings, and the nadir was reached at an EU summit in June 1994, when Major vetoed the appointment of Belgian Prime Minister Jean-Luc Dehaene as President of the European Commission, even though he was the preferred candidate of all the other member states. This was intended as a 'macho' demonstration of strength, but in fact only underlined Major's weakness. The ostensible reason for Major's veto was Dehaene's supposedly 'federalist' views, but the falsity of this excuse was exposed a month later when Major accepted the appointment of Luxembourg Prime Minister Jacques Santer, who went out of his way to explain that his views were identical to Dehaene's. The net result was that the EU finished up with a less effective President than it otherwise might have had. Nor did this irresponsible action lead to any letting up of the Eurosceptics' demands. These were now stepped up to include an assurance that Britain would 'never' join the single currency or, at the very least, not during the course of the next Parliament. This demand won widespread backing throughout the party, and might well have been acceded to by Major if it had not been for the resolute opposition of senior Cabinet ministers, notably Michael Heseltine, who became Deputy Premier in July 1995, and Ken Clarke, who had replaced Norman Lamont as Chancellor of the Exchequer in May 1993. Eventually, Major did pledge that a Conservative government would not enter the single currency without securing a mandate to do so in a referendum, an undertaking which was subsequently also made by Labour.

The most ill-considered initiative undertaken by Major was his 'Back to Basics' campaign, which he launched in his speech to the Conservative conference in 1993. It was meant to emphasise the issues of law and order and education, but was given a moralistic twist by Tory spin-doctors, who linked it to the maintenance of 'family values'. To their undisguised horror, the tabloid press took this as an invitation to launch a veritable witch-hunt against ministers whose personal conduct did not match up to the highest moral standards. Altogether 15 ministerial resignations occurred during the 1992 Parliament, an unprecedented total, of which only three were on policy grounds. Nearly all the rest were linked to sexual or financial scandals, and Major himself was severely damaged by his apparently equivocal response, first resisting and then demanding resignations in several cases, including the high-profile case of David Mellor, a personal friend and a rising figure within the Cabinet. Major was almost certainly more embarrassed than he otherwise would have been, as he was nursing his own guilty secret. For several years he had conducted an affair, which continued after his promotion to the Cabinet, with the prominent Tory MP, Edwina Currie. She eventually revealed the details only in 2002, when she published her diaries. Major then acknowledged the affair, saying it was the thing about which he had been 'most ashamed' during his entire political career. The scandals concerning ministers and Tory MPs were linked by the press to others involving dodgy contributions to Tory funds, and the attempt to cover up ministerial responsibility for illegal arms sales to Iraq. The result was that the government acquired an unenviable reputation for 'sleaze', which was to dog it up to and throughout the 1997 election campaign. By the summer of 1995, dissatisfaction with Major had spread to all sections of the Conservative Party, and there were increasing calls in the press for his replacement by a more competent and more decisive leader. There was intense speculation that in the autumn he would be challenged by a 'stalking horse' candidate who would sufficiently undermine his position so that more heavyweight challengers could emerge. Those most favoured were Michael Portillo, the Employment Secretary and darling of the Eurosceptics, and Michael Heseltine, the Trade Secretary, who was now seen as the main hope of the party mainstream. In a rare moment of decisiveness, Major launched a pre-emptive strike, and in June suddenly resigned the party leadership, inviting his opponents to 'put up or shut up'. Neither Portillo nor Heseltine (who was promoted to the Deputy Premiership) responded to the challenge, though both reserved the right to contest a second round if one was required, but John Redwood, the Eurosceptic Welsh Secretary, resigned his post to enter the contest, hoping to cream off the support which otherwise would have gone to Portillo. Technically, Major needed only 165 votes (an overall majority and a lead of 15 per cent over the nearest challenger) to win on the first round, but privately decided that this would not be enough to restore his authority and that he would withdraw if he polled less than 215 votes (Major, 1999, pp. 608–47). In the event, he narrowly exceeded this target, polling 218 votes to 89 for Redwood and 20 abstentions or spoiled ballot papers. The result cleared the air to a certain extent, and ensured that there would be no further contest before the general election, but was not nearly decisive enough to put an end to the internecine strife within the party.

More difficulties lay ahead, including the privatisation of two industries which even Thatcher had left alone – coal and the railways. Both exercises were handled badly. In preparation for selling off coal, Heseltine announced a further massive programme of pit closures, which then had to be extensively modified in the face of overwhelming criticism, though most of the closures eventually went ahead, leaving only a skeletal remnant of a once mighty industry to be disposed of. Even less popular were the proposals to dismantle

British Rail and lease off franchises to a wide variety of private contractors who would be ill prepared to provide a co-ordinated service. Privatisation, which had undoubtedly been an electoral asset to the Tories throughout the 1980s, now became a liability. A final misfortune which hit the Major government, and which they were generally seen to have very badly mishandled, was the outbreak of 'mad cow disease' (BSE), which also led to a renewed dispute with the European Union.

On the positive side, however, and very much to Major's personal credit, was his patient handling of the Northern Irish question, leading to the signing, with the Irish Prime Minister Albert Reynolds, of the Downing Street Declaration in December 1993, and the declaration by the IRA of a ceasefire in August 1994, which lasted for 18 months. Hopes of turning this into a permanent peace settlement foundered, however, despite the valiant efforts of the American mediator, Senator George Mitchell. In the end, neither the IRA nor the Ulster Unionists were prepared to make the minimum concessions necessary, and later on Major did not feel in a position to apply maximum pressure on the Unionists, as he depended on their votes (or abstentions) for parliamentary survival, after by-election losses and defections to both Liberal Democrats and Labour had deprived him of a majority.

Paradoxically, after the humiliation of Black Wednesday, their handling of the economy should also be seen as a success story for the Major government. Under the skilful guidance of Ken Clarke, who replaced Lamont as Chancellor of the Exchequer in May 1993, economic recovery soon set in, and by 1997 nearly all the indicators were looking good, with unemployment well down and interest rates and inflation both low. Yet the government was so discredited that it got little benefit from it. John Major wryly referred in his memoirs to a maxim formulated by Chris Patten, 'There is no such thing as a voteless economic recovery' (Major, 1999, p. 609). Yet as the final date for a general election approached, the Tories still remained 20 points adrift in the opinion

Labour	419
Conservative	165
Liberal Democrat	46
Others	29
Labour majority	179

polls. The gap was slightly narrowed during the campaign, but the result of the election, which took place on 1 May 1997, could hardly have been more conclusive as shown in the table above.

It was the worst result for the Tories since the 1906 election, or possibly that of 1832. There were other reasons for the spectacular defeat, notably the transformation of the Labour Party and the extraordinary popularity of Tony

Blair, who had been leading it since the death of John Smith in May 1994. But it is the considered opinion of the leading pollster, Robert Worcester, that a landslide defeat was already 'inevitable' after Black Wednesday and Major's mishandling of the Maastricht ratification (Worcester and Mortimore, 1999). After 18 years of Tory rule, the argument that it was time for a change was extremely strong, and any Tory leader would no doubt have had great difficulty in retaining power. Yet Major's own shortcomings must have been, at least in part, responsible for the scale of the defeat. He was not the weak nonentity that is sometimes pictured. Hard-working and intelligent, he had clear ideas of his own about the direction in which he wanted to lead his party and his country, which could be summarised as broadly following Thatcherite economic polices, though applying them with a more sensitive hand, while adopting a much more liberal approach to social issues. He emphatically did not share Thatcher's view that 'there is no such thing as society' – when he sought the premiership in 1990 he declared that it was his aim to make Britain a 'classless society' by the year 2000. In less stressful times, he might well have led a successful government as a Tory social reformer, in the Shaftesbury–Disraeli tradition. A born conciliator, he was ill prepared to counter the venom and the self-destructive instincts of the Eurosceptic wing of his party. Had a more forceful leader been chosen in 1990, such as Michael Heseltine, or even Douglas Hurd, there might have been a happier outcome. But perhaps not: a death wish had entered the soul of the Tory Party, comparable to that which afflicted Labour a decade or so earlier. The closest parallel, however, was the Balfour government, riven by dissension over tariff reform in 1903–05, and which went down to a similar calamitous defeat in the 1906 election.

Unlike Balfour, who clung to the Tory leadership for another six years after his defeat and then went on to serve for a further dozen years in senior Cabinet posts, Major lost no time in bowing out, which he did with considerable dignity. On the morrow of the election, he announced his resignation as party leader on the steps of Downing Street, with the words 'When the curtain comes down it is time to leave the stage', and then went off to watch a cricket match at Lords. He reserved any recriminations for his autobiography, published two years later, a thoughtful and well-written volume, which is less self-serving than the great majority of political memoirs. Unfortunately, he proved to be rather better as an author than as a politician. A man of evident decent instincts, but limited abilities: as Prime Minister he pushed these abilities to the limit. It was not enough.

Major remained an MP until the 2001 general election, and then retired from active politics, declining a life peerage, but becoming a Knight of the Garter in 2005.

Works consulted

Butler, David, and Dennis Kavanagh, *The British General Election of 1992*, London, Macmillan, 1992.

Butler, David, and Dennis Kavanagh, *The British General Election of 1997*, London, Macmillan, 1997.

Clark, Alan, *Diaries*, London, Phoenix, 1994.

Currie, Edwina, *Diaries 1987–1992*, London, Little, Brown, 2002.

Lawson, Nigel, *The View from Number 11* , London, Bantam, 1992.

Major, John, *The Autobiography*, London, HarperCollins, 1999.

Major-Ball, Terry, *Major Major: Memories of an Older Brother*, London, Duckworth, 1994.

Seldon, Anthony, *Major: A Political Life*, London, Weidenfeld & Nicolson, 1997.

Worcester, Robert, and Roger Mortimore, *Explaining Labour's Landslide*, London, Politico's, 1999.

51
Tony Blair – Fallen Idol

Tony Blair enjoyed greater and longer-lasting popularity than any other British Prime Minister in modern times. He won three elections, two of them with landslide victories, and it is certainly conceivable that, had he not led Britain into the Iraq War, he might have gone 'on and on', in Margaret Thatcher's words, and rivalled the longevity in office of such early giants as Walpole (nearly 21 years) and the Younger Pitt (nearly 19). As it was, he fell somewhat short of Thatcher's twentieth-century record of 11½ years.

'I was not born into the Labour Party', he famously told his party conference in 1995. This simple statement goes some way to explain both the successes and the failures which he experienced in the 13 years following his election as Labour leader in 1994. What he *was* born into, on 6 May 1953, was a somewhat tangled family tree. His father, Leo, was the illegitimate son of an actor, Charles Parsons (stage name: Jimmy Lynton) and Celia (Gussie) Ridgeway, an actress, who came from a wealthy landowning family but was living a vagabond life with two early marriages and numerous affairs to her name. Three years after Leo was born, now divorced from her second husband, she and Parsons legitimized their liaison, but had already passed on the infant Leo to foster parents in Glasgow: James Blair, a shipyard worker, and his wife Mary, a dedicated Communist. Leo, who was brought up in a council tenement block, left school at 14 to work as a clerk for the Glasgow City Corporation, and for three years was secretary of the Scottish Young Communist League. In 1942, aged 18, he joined the army as a private, but by the time he was demobilized, in 1947, he had risen to the rank of major, with a fierce determination to make his way in the world. He got a job as a junior tax inspector, while studying law by night at Edinburgh University, becoming a law tutor and subsequently a lecturer in administrative law at the University of Adelaide. Before departing for Australia in 1954, however, he had established a family of his own, marrying Hazel Corscaden, the step-daughter of a Glasgow butcher, of Protestant Northern Irish origin, in 1948. They had three children, the eldest of whom, William, was born in 1950. When the second son followed, three years later, he was named Anthony Charles Lynton Blair, but was given no indication of the significance of his second and third names until 1994, when the *Daily Mail* dug up the details about his grandparents during the Labour leadership election. In the words of Blair's first biographer, Jon Sopel, 'Tony Blair had known that his father had been adopted, but it was something Leo did not speak about, and equally something the children didn't ask about' (Sopel, 1995, p. 6). The family was completed with the birth, in Australia, of Sarah, in 1956.

They stayed in Australia for three years, by which time Leo Blair, who had long since shed his Communist affiliations, had formed a firm ambition to become a Conservative MP, and returned to Britain with the primary intention of pursuing this aim. He successfully applied for a job as a law lecturer at Durham University, read for the English Bar and began to practise as a barrister in Newcastle-upon-Tyne, while becoming chairman of the local Conservative Association, where he was remembered as being full of charm and intensely ambitious. The young Tony was sent, as a day-boy, to the Durham Choristers' School, where he was renowned for his ever-present smile, as well as being a very good pupil, who took part in all the school activities, playing cricket and rugby for the school teams, singing in the choir and acting in school productions. From a toddler onwards, he had shown marked extrovert tendencies, always ready to put himself on show. Meanwhile, his father, who later confessed to having nursed ambitions to be Prime Minister, was all set to take the first important step in his own political career, being the hot favourite to secure the nomination for the safe Conservative seat of Hexham, in rural Northumberland. Then, on 4 July 1964, disaster struck. He suffered a devastating stroke, from which he was not initially expected to recover, and which left him without the power of speech for three years. The 11-year-old Tony went down on his knees and prayed with his headmaster, Canon John Grove, for his father's recovery. Their prayers were answered, but it took an unconscionably long time, and it permanently put paid to his hopes for a parliamentary career.

A further misfortune was to follow: Tony's younger sister Sarah fell seriously ill with Still's disease, a form of infantile rheumatoid arthritis, which necessitated her hospitalization for two long years, after which she emerged only partially cured. Tony's mother, Hazel, exhausted herself looking after her sick husband and daughter, and possibly neglected her second son in the process, while her own mother, who was suffering from Alzheimer's disease, came to live with them, and proved an additional burden. The family income sharply declined: the University kept open Leo's job and paid him throughout the three years that he was out of action, but his earnings at the Bar fell away. Blair himself was later to recall: 'Don't get me wrong, it was a happy childhood, but it also seemed as though I was spending every spare minute in Durham hospital, visiting either my father or sister…and there was a lot of worry and uncertainty attached to that' (Sopel, 1995, p. 12). Tony was yet to reject his father's chosen party, and just before leaving the Choristers' School, at the age of nearly 13, he stood as the Tory candidate in a mock election timed to coincide with the 1966 general election.

He left to go to Fettes, the 'Scottish Eton', where the majority of the pupils were the sons of wealthy Scottish businessmen, and this experience was to turn him into a rebel, though never an extreme one. Tony won a scholarship to go to the school, which was necessary as his father was no longer in a position to pay the full fees. One of the worst examples of an unreconstructed Victorian-age 'public' school, it had a culture of bullying and a host of petty restrictions, including firm rules about exactly how many buttons of the boys' blazers must be kept done up at all times. Blair particularly objected to the custom of fagging, and the fact that senior boys were entitled to cane the younger ones, almost at will. Blair was thrashed many times, ran away on one occasion and on another narrowly escaped expulsion. His rebellion did not appear to have any political overtones, but was manifested by a consistent flouting of authority. As earlier, he was noted at Fettes for his ever-present smile, and often devastating charm, so that he remained popular even with those to whom he caused offence. Blair's greatest distinction at Fettes was as an actor: he got rave notices in the school magazine for his performance as Mark Antony in *Julius Caesar*, and for playing the lead part in the R.C. Sherriff play, *Journey's End*.

After a gap year, spent in London, where, with other 'public' school types, he scratched a living as an impresario for rock bands, he went to St John's College, Oxford, to study law. Unlike most other future politicians of his generation who found themselves at Oxford or Cambridge, Blair had nothing to do with the Union or with student political clubs. Initially, at least, he devoted himself to having a 'good time', his main interests being rock music and girls, for whom, as a good-looking young man, over six feet tall and with an open, friendly manner, he had a ready attraction. He became the lead singer for a group called The Ugly Rumours, modelling himself very much on Mick Jagger, and being much remarked for the androgynous nature of his performances. There was, however, a more serious side to his three years at Oxford. He fell in with a group of high-minded, quasi-Marxist students, mostly from Commonwealth countries, led by an Australian priest and Christian Socialist, Peter Thomson. Blair maintains that Thomson converted him to both Christianity and Socialism. He was already a nominal believer, despite the atheism of his father, while from his mother, who was to die of cancer at the age of 52, shortly after his graduation, he had acquired much of her social conscience but little of her Presbyterianism. Under Thomson's influence, Blair was confirmed into the Church of England, and for some time considered taking Holy Orders. Thomson introduced him to an elderly, and once quite well-known, Scottish theologian, John Macmurray. Macmurray was the prophet of a 'communitarian' form of Christianity, whose effect, according to Blair's second biographer John Rentoul, 'was to invert Adam Smith's dictum "Social and self-love are the same". Smith said that if we follow our self-interest, we benefit the whole community. Macmurray said that by pursuing the community's interests we benefit the individuals within it, including ourselves' (Rentoul, 2001, pp. 41–2). Blair was bowled over by Macmurray's teaching, and proclaimed that it had become the basis of both his religious and his political beliefs.

Blair graduated in June 1975, with an upper second class degree, and, moving to London, where he shared a flat in Earl's Court with an Oxford friend, signed on for a one-year Bar course at Lincoln's Inn. He also joined the Labour Party, becoming secretary of his local ward branch at the first meeting he attended. He then applied for a pupillage at the chambers of Derry Irvine, a QC with strong Labour Party connections. Irvine had already selected another young prospect, called Cherie Booth, who had graduated with first class honours in Law at the London School of Economics, and had come top of the year in the Bar exams, well ahead of Blair. Irvine had intended to take on only one pupil, but was so impressed by Blair's enthusiasm that he accepted him as well. Irvine found Blair a quick and willing worker, and assigned him to handle a sheaf of trade union cases, which put him in touch with leading figures in the trade union movement. He also got to know John Smith, who was to be his predecessor as leader of the Labour Party, and who was a close personal friend of Irvine's. He and Cherie were initially wary of each other, being rivals for promotion within the chambers (Blair eventually won out, and Cherie left to join another firm). By then, however, the personal chemistry between them was well developed, Cherie subsequently saying 'Once you succumb to Tony's charm, you never really get over it.' On 29 March 1980, they were married at his college chapel in Oxford. Like Tony, Cherie had had a difficult childhood, and her family situation somewhat mirrored that of Tony's father, Leo. Her father was the well-known actor Tony Booth, an Irish Catholic and strong Labour Party supporter, who claimed to be related to the actor John Wilkes Booth, who had assassinated President Lincoln. For Cherie, however, he had been very much an absentee father, abandoning his first wife Gale, and leaving her to bring up Cherie and her younger sister Lyndsey alone, earning a living in the Lancashire town of Crosby by working in a fish and chip shop and other menial jobs. Booth then went on to have another five marriages or serious liaisons, which produced five half-sisters for Lyndsey and Cherie. Unlike Blair, Cherie had deep roots in the Labour movement, joining the party at the age of 16.

In May 1982, Blair put himself forward to be the Labour candidate for a by-election in Beaconsfield, a normally solidly Tory home counties seat, but which it was thought that the Social Democratic Party (SDP) might well win, in the light of its three successive by-election victories in Croydon, Crosby (where Cherie had unsuccessfully tried for the Labour candidature) and Glasgow

Hillhead. The Falklands war intervened, puncturing the SDP challenge, and the Tories held on comfortably enough, Blair coming in a poor third, and losing his deposit. He then embarked on a long search to find a safe Labour seat to contest at the forthcoming general election, and when the election was declared he had still not made it. Yet, there was one remaining seat which had not made its selection – Sedgefield in County Durham. Blair headed off for the constituency with only a vague hope of picking up a nomination, and, more by luck than judgment, succeeded. He was duly selected on the fifth ballot by the constituency Labour Party. The election itself was a virtual formality: he had a majority of over 8,000 over his Tory opponent, with the SDP/Alliance candidate coming in third.

The overall election result was a disaster for Labour, which polled its lowest percentage vote since 1918, and saw Thatcher's majority rise from 44 to 144. Blair, aged 30, was the youngest of the 209 Labour members elected. Soon after he was asked to share a room in the Commons with the new MP for Dunfermline East – Gordon Brown. Two years older, Brown had vastly more political experience than his new room-mate. A former chairman of the Scottish Labour Party, he had contested the 1979 general election for Edinburgh South, and already had behind him a distinguished academic career, as well as having worked as a television editor and reporter. Brown took Blair under his wing, and, on Blair's own account, taught him all the basic political and communication skills which he had previously lacked – how to draft a press release, the importance of bullet points and sound-bites, and the difference between a punchy political speech and a reasoned appeal to judges sitting in the High Court. Blair regarded Brown with something approaching awe, and shared the common view (certainly held by Brown himself) that he was a future leader of the party. The two men, who grew extraordinarily close, agreed on the fundamental necessity of modernizing the Labour Party, stripping it of all its unelectable policies and undemocratic structures so that it could present a much more appealing face to the voters. This aim was shared by the new party leader, Neil Kinnock, who, within a few months of their election, promoted both of them to be junior frontbench spokesmen. At Kinnock's prompting, Peter Mandelson, the Labour Party's new communications director, used his considerable manipulative skills to ensure that the two men achieved maximum exposure on radio and television programmes, estimating that they would make a far more favourable impression than most of their rivals on the opposition benches.

Over the next dozen years, with Brown always one step ahead, they worked their way steadily up the Labour Party's hierarchy, achieving election to the Shadow Cabinet and filling successively more senior shadow portfolios. In July 1992, following Labour's disappointing election defeat, John Smith succeeded Kinnock as leader, appointing Brown as Shadow Chancellor and Blair as Shadow

Home Secretary. This was an enormous challenge for Blair, and he took it with both hands. Identifying the popular belief that the Tories were the 'law and order' party, and that Labour was 'soft on crime', he set out to change this public perception and to turn a vote-losing into a vote-winning issue. Few people would have given him much chance of success, but the opinion polls recorded a remarkable turnaround. In 1992, according to the Gallup Poll, the Tories enjoyed a 21-point advantage over Labour on the issue. Two years later, Labour had established a five-point lead. Nobody doubted that Blair was responsible. He had shifted Labour's focus from explaining away the sociological causes of crime to a deep concern for the plight of victims, and had conspicuously refrained from opposing the ever more draconian measures introduced by the new Tory Home Secretary, Michael Howard. Above all, however, he had pulled off the trick by utilizing a brilliant sound-bite, which in fewer than a dozen words succeeded in encapsulating both the traditional Tory and traditional Labour approaches: 'Tough on crime, and tough on the causes of crime.' This he endlessly repeated in television debates, and neither Howard nor any other Tory spokesman was able to find an effective riposte.

By this time, and largely unremarked by most of his colleagues, including Brown, Blair had emerged as by far the most persuasive political performer on television. His over-ready smile may have put off a small minority of viewers, but most responded positively to his youth, charm, conviction and well-presented arguments. By contrast, Brown came over as formidably well-informed, but dour and more obviously repetitive. This was the underlying reason why it was Blair and not Brown who was chosen to succeed John Smith, after his sudden death on 12 May 1994. The immediate reaction of some observers was that Brown, who had proved a highly effective Shadow Chancellor, would be a 'shoo-in', but within a few hours it became clear that Blair had overtaken him in terms of support among Labour MPs, and was determined to put himself forward. Even worse for Brown was the publication within three days of opinion polls showing that Blair was far ahead of any potential rivals as far as public opinion was concerned. The MORI poll, for example, showed Blair with 32 per cent, John Prescott with 19 per cent, Margaret Beckett 14 per cent, Brown 9 per cent and Robin Cook 5 per cent. This was immediately sufficient to put Cook, Labour's best debater (who would have been a formidable challenger if the choice had been restricted to Labour MPs instead of an electoral college made up of parliamentarians, trade unionists and Labour Party members), out of the running. After 15 years in opposition, the party was desperately anxious to choose the person best placed to win a general election, and the opinion polls gave an enormous boost to Blair's chances. Although Brown was widely regarded as a more heavyweight figure and more intellectually distinguished than Blair, he seemed less well placed to win back voters in the south of England, which was the key to Labour's electoral success. The facts that he was a Scotsman and, unlike Blair, not a family man were probably seen as additional handicaps. Two years earlier, at the time of John Smith's election, the two men had agreed that they would not oppose each other in the event of a future contest, in order not to split the modernizers' vote. At that time, it had been clear that Brown would be the stronger candidate, and he regarded this agreement as a guarantee that Blair would not run against him. He was irate that Blair was now intent on supplanting him and was putting enormous pressure on him not to declare his own candidature. What probably made it all the more galling for Brown was that it was he who had suggested the famous 'tough on crime' sound-bite which had been so effective in furthering Blair's dizzy ascent. Eventually, he concluded that he couldn't win, and agreed to meet Blair at an Islington restaurant, the Granita, to strike a bargain. Blair agreed that Brown would become Chancellor if Labour won the election, with much more sweeping powers over both economic and social policy than any previous Chancellor had enjoyed. He also suggested that, if Labour were to win two successive elections, he would make way for Brown some time during the second term. Brown took this as a firm promise, yet it is doubtful whether Blair intended it as such. Brown then participated in a photo-opportunity with Blair, and declared his support for Blair's campaign. Blair went on to win the contest convincingly, with majorities in all three sections of the electoral college. The overall result, in percentages, was:

Blair	57.0
Prescott	24.1
Beckett	18.9

Although they continued to cooperate closely, and the government formed after the 1997 election was almost a diarchy, this episode marked the end of the intimate friendship between Blair and Brown. The latter was badly bruised and continued to harbour resentment, which he was scarcely able to conceal. It would probably have been better to have cleared the air, and for both to have contested the leadership election. Blair would almost certainly have won, and – as it was an exhaustive ballot – there was no serious risk of letting in a more 'traditionalist' candidate, such as Prescott.

The new party leader set himself single-mindedly to achieve one objective – to make Labour electable. He was able to build on the steps already taken by Neil Kinnock and John Smith, but he was to reveal a ruthlessness and determination which went far beyond anything they had shown. The fact that he had come to the party as an 'outsider' was a positive advantage, as he had no scruples or inhibitions about sweeping aside policies, attitudes and institutions which had become part of the mindset of most of those who were more rooted in the party. This was quickly evidenced by his assault on Clause Four, the famous article in the Labour

Party constitution which called for the 'common ownership of the means of production, distribution and exchange'. This nearly 80-year-old provision was at odds with the actual practice of Labour governments, but it allowed their Tory opponents to picture the party as doctrinaire nationalizers. Hugh Gaitskell had come a cropper when he tried to delete the clause after the 1959 general election defeat, and at least four of his five successors had been embarrassed by its provisions but had felt powerless to do anything about it. Blair used his first speech as party leader to announce to the 1994 party conference that he would be proposing a replacement clause, which would be submitted for approval to a special party conference in March 1995. Many thought he was heading for a humiliating rebuff, but he threw himself into the campaign, addressing Labour Party meetings throughout the country in shirtsleeves, and, when the vote was taken at the special party conference, Blair's innocuous re-wording, which excised any mention of 'public ownership' or even 'equality' from the party's aims, was approved by a 2–1 majority. It was a triumph, and Blair drove home the message even further by effectively re-naming the party New Labour, even though there was no official change of name. The Tories were nonplussed, as John Major acknowledged in his autobiography: 'They pronounced themselves "new" Labour, and with that single word denied their past... Effective it certainly was. It did us untold damage' (Major, 1999, p. 694).

Blair, clearly influenced by Bill Clinton's success in winning election in 1992 by driving the Democratic party sharply to the right, consolidated his New Labour makeover by re-drawing 'its policies on tax, inflation, the minimum wage, exam league tables, opted-out schools, Northern Ireland, regional government and the House of Lords... in each case, policy change moved Labour closer to the Conservatives' (Rentoul, 2001, p. 264). He even, daringly, spoke admiringly of Mrs Thatcher, and clearly regarded her as some sort of role-model, in her methods, if not her objectives. Blair's greatest coup was to help rid Labour of its reputation as a 'tax and spend' party. In agreement with Gordon Brown, he made a firm commitment not to increase either the standard rate, or – more controversially – the maximum rate of income tax, which had been reduced by the Tories to 40 per cent, lower than in most other western countries, where 50 or 60 per cent was the norm. Brown followed this up by pledging not to increase expenditure during the first two years of a Labour government beyond the levels currently planned by the Tory Chancellor, Kenneth Clarke. These moves pre-empted any attempt by the Tories to repeat their scare tactics of the 1992 election, when Labour was accused of planning massive tax increases; they were already inhibited by the fact – well publicized by Labour – that they themselves had introduced no fewer than 22 tax increases, despite their pledges at the previous election.

Blair also revolutionized Labour's presentation and handling of the media, under the tutelage of Peter Mandelson and the political consultant Philip Gould, whose 'focus groups' became an essential tool in trying out new initiatives.

Alastair Campbell, a talented tabloid journalist, was recruited as Blair's press adviser, and initiated a much more focused and pro-active approach to the media. This even extended to pro-Tory newspapers, which no previous Labour leader had contemplated wooing, regarding their hostility as a badge of their own rectitude. Particular attention was paid to Rupert Murdoch's newspapers, one of which, *The Sun*, had vilified Kinnock during the 1992 election and had – not implausibly – claimed to have been the crucial factor in ensuring Major's victory – 'It Was The Sun Wot Won It,' declared its post-election headline. Campbell's efforts certainly paid dividends. *The Sun* endorsed Labour at the outset of the 1997 election campaign, while both Lord Rothermere's *Daily Mail* and Conrad Black's *Daily Telegraph* notably softened their approach.

Consciously or otherwise, Blair was running not so much against the Tories, but against 'old Labour', abandoning, if not always attacking, most of the policies with which it had recently been associated. Indeed, what Blair was against was much clearer than what he favoured; he tended to speak in vague generalities, evoking mood music rather than setting out detailed policy proposals, thus denying his opponents concrete targets to attack, and earning himself the nickname 'Tony Blur'. What Blair was offering the country, however, was not so much new policies as a new man – himself. Largely through his television appearances and his platform speeches – less so his performances in the House of Commons, where he usually, but not invariably, came out on top in his encounters with John Major – he had created an astonishingly favourable impression, which was reflected in a massive lead in the opinion polls. He came over as fresh, youthful, energetic and eloquent – a beacon of hope and optimism, very much as John F. Kennedy had done in his presidential campaign three decades earlier. He also evoked more contemporary comparisons with Bill Clinton, though, as one Tory minister wryly remarked, he was even more effective 'because he kept his trousers zipped up'.

It was not only Blair's popularity, however, that set the stage for the sweeping Labour victory on 1 May 1997. At least equally responsible was the bitterly divided state of the Tory party, which must have made it highly probable that Labour would win, even if John Smith had not died three years earlier. He lacked Blair's charisma, and would not have gone nearly so far in reforming the Labour Party, but he was a highly respected figure who had already opened up a wide lead in the polls before his death. Had he survived, the Tories might well have done rather better, but it is improbable that, never having lived down 'Black Wednesday' (see Chapter 50), they would have been able to escape defeat. As it was, Labour under Blair's leadership won a majority of 179 seats, eclipsing even their famous victory of 1945, when Clement Attlee led by 146.

Blair, who had established close behind-the-scenes relations with the Liberal Democrat leader Paddy Ashdown, had secretly intended to form a coalition government, with Ashdown joining the Cabinet as Home or Foreign Secretary.

This would have effectively re-created the broad progressive alliance which had existed prior to World War I, the collapse of which had led – in the view of Roy Jenkins, with whom Blair was also in close contact – to the Tory dominance throughout the greater part of the twentieth century. Yet so overwhelming was Labour's victory that any thoughts of coalition soon evaporated, Blair realizing that even he would not be able to persuade his own party to give up part of the fruits of victory, when there was no pressing need to do so. The cabinet he formed was one of beginners – after 18 years of Tory rule neither he nor any of his colleagues had ever served in a cabinet before, and only three of them had experience of junior ministerial office. Nevertheless, none of them appeared lacking in self-confidence, and the general level of competence was high, though there were few obvious heavyweights, apart from Brown, the new Chancellor, and, to a lesser extent, Robin Cook, the Foreign Secretary. The other major offices were filled by John Prescott, who became Deputy Premier and headed an unwieldy department combining Environment and Transport, Jack Straw, Home Secretary, and Lord Irvine, Blair's legal mentor, as Lord Chancellor. David Blunkett, universally admired for overcoming the handicap of blindness, was to prove an energetic and resourceful Education Secretary.

Yet the government was dominated, from first to last, by two men, Blair and Brown, who made a formidable combination, though not always a harmonious one. Blair certainly consulted with Brown on all important matters, but hardly at all with the cabinet as a whole. The long, detailed discussions which had characterized Major's cabinets rapidly became a thing of the past, and Blair quickly reverted to the Thatcher model of short and relatively infrequent meetings, with most decisions taken at *ad hoc* meetings with individual ministers or in small groups. More influential than any cabinet minister, other than Brown, were Blair's three closest advisers. Peter Mandelson was appointed, initially, as Minister without Portfolio, outside the Cabinet, but was constantly at the Prime Minister's beck and call. Jonathan Powell, a former Foreign Office official who had resigned to run Blair's office while in opposition, became his Chief of Staff, taking over many of the normal responsibilities of the Principal Private Secretary, though he was denied the actual title after Civil Service protests. A younger brother of Charles Powell, who had been one of Thatcher's closest advisers, he was entrusted by Blair with many delicate tasks, including overseeing the Northern Ireland Office, much to the chagrin of the Secretary of State, Mo Mowlem. The third, and most influential, of the triumvirs was Alastair Campbell, appointed to head the government's information services, but so close to Blair that he was popularly known as 'the real deputy Prime Minister'.

The new government was fortunate in having been bequeathed a healthy economic situation by its predecessors, thanks largely to the stewardship of Ken Clarke as the last Tory Chancellor. All previous Labour governments had entered office in less favourable circumstances, and had had to contend with almost immediate financial crises. This time it was different, and Blair's team lost no time in consolidating and, indeed, improving on the hand which it had been dealt. Within days of taking office, Brown took the bold step of handing over to the Bank of England the regulation of interest rates, within the limits of an inflation target set by the Government. This meant that interest rate policy was no longer subject to crude political manipulation, and the change was warmly welcomed by most economic commentators. Brown kept to his promise of keeping spending down over the first two years to the limits set by the Tories, despite pressure from his own backbenchers. 'Prudence with a purpose' was his motto, holding out the prospect for considerable expansion at a later date, when much of the debt accumulated by the previous government would have been paid off. He was then able to announce very substantial increases in the money available for schools and the National Health Service. In the meantime, he embarked on a sustained 'welfare to work' programme, designed to take large numbers off the unemployment register and to provide them with productive jobs or training opportunities. The programme was largely financed by a 'windfall tax' levied on privatized firms which had been sold off cheaply by the previous government, and were making excessive profits. The government kept its promise not to raise income tax, but succeeded in increasing its revenues by a series of 'stealth taxes', which had no visible effect on the incomes of most taxpayers. The most controversial of these was the abolition of tax relief on the investment income of company pension schemes. Brown used the yield from these taxes to increase benefits skewed towards people on low incomes, and the redistributive effect was probably as great as it would have been if he had been in a position to raise the maximum income tax rate. Although he was criticized for attempting too much 'fine tuning' in his budgets and welfare policy changes, few would question that Gordon Brown was one of the most, if not the most, successful post-war Chancellors of the Exchequer. His record was summarized in the following terms by the authors of the 2001 Nuffield Election survey, normally regarded as impartial observers:

Inflation stayed below 3 per cent, GDP grew annually by about 2.5 per cent over the next four years. Opposition prophecies of doom were refuted regularly by the monthly economic statistics. Unemployment fell from 1.9 million in 1997 to under 1 million in 2001. Gordon Brown was able to boast of his achievement in paying off a sizeable proportion of the national debt, helped by buoyant tax revenues and by £22bn from the sale of digital channels in 2000. £34 bn of government borrowing was paid off and debt servicing fell from 44 per cent to 32 per cent of government expenditure. (Butler and Kavanagh, 2002, p. 2)

In addition, and for the first time ever, Britain's economic performance, as measured by the usual indicators, was better than that of the European Union as a whole.

If economic and social policy had largely been sub-contracted to Brown, Blair himself certainly kept close control over the various constitutional changes which figured prominently in his first term. Devolution to Scotland and Wales was quickly legislated, and was approved by a large majority in a referendum in Scotland, but by only a slender one in Wales. In the subsequent elections, conducted under proportional representation, Labour emerged as much the largest party, but without an overall majority, and Lab–Lib coalitions were formed in both countries. Labour also legislated to set up a Greater London Authority, with its own elected mayor, and this too was approved in a referendum by London voters. Blair, however, who was already being accused of 'control freakery' because of the tight discipline he sought to exercise over the Labour Party, seemed unwilling to accept the logic of these reforms and to leave the choice of leadership to the local populations. He manipulated trade union block votes (which he had previously sought to curb) in order to impose less popular candidates to lead the new assemblies in Wales and London, instead of Rhodri Morgan and Ken Livingstone, respectively. He just pulled it off, but in each case it ended in tears. In London, Livingstone refused to accept what he dubbed a 'rigged vote', stood for Mayor as an Independent and was very easily elected, with the unfortunate Labour candidate, Frank Dobson, who had resigned as Health Secretary to contest the election, reduced to a poor third place. The outcome in Wales was only marginally better: Blair's choice, Alun Michael, was only able to secure a mediocre victory in the election, and was soon forced out by the Assembly members to make way for Morgan.

A notable achievement of the Blair government was to incorporate the European Convention of Human Rights directly into British law, which was effected by the Human Rights Act of 1998. Less praiseworthy was the Freedom of Information Act, which was a pale shadow of the measure which Labour had trailed while in opposition, and which was regarded as a betrayal by many supporters of open government, both inside and outside the Labour Party. Blair himself, however, felt he had gone much too far, and later described himself as 'a naive, foolish, irresponsible nincompoop' for introducing the measure (Blair, 2010, p. 516). He also disappointed his party over House of Lords reform. A bill to replace the great majority of hereditary peers was duly passed, after a compromise was struck with Lord Cranborne, the Tory leader in the upper house. Cranborne had failed to consult William Hague, who promptly sacked him, though the deal went through. It allowed some 92 'hereditaries' to remain in the House pending a more thorough-going reform. No progress was made on this, however; Blair wished to proceed to an entirely nominated upper house, while a majority of Labour, Liberal and even Conservative MPs wanted at least a partially elected chamber.

Labour had had discussions, before and after the 1997 election, with the Liberals on the question of electoral reform, and had promised in its election manifesto to hold a referendum on whether to change over to proportional representation for elections to the House of Commons. Although an independent commission was appointed, presided over by Roy Jenkins, which produced a report in favour of a hybrid system with a strong proportional element, no referendum was in fact held, a rare example of a specific manifesto commitment by Labour not being honoured. Blair, in fact – unlike his predecessor Neil Kinnock – had never been convinced that PR would be desirable, and the promise had been made as an inducement to the Liberal Democrats, when he expected to be in need of their support. When this transpired not to be the case, he soon lost interest. For their part, the Liberal Democrats, though naturally disappointed, failed to kick up any sort of fuss about the broken promise. PR was adopted for the Euro-elections, as well as in those for the devolved assemblies.

In Northern Ireland, Blair followed up Major's earlier initiative, with rather greater success, partly because of his superior negotiating skills, but also because he was not dependent on Unionist support to maintain his parliamentary majority. The climax came in April 1998, when – with much assistance from the US mediator George Mitchell, and with President Clinton helpfully available at the other end of a phone – he and Irish Premier Bertie Ahern were able to conclude the Good Friday Agreement with the main Northern Irish political parties (except for Ian Paisley's Democratic Unionists). Under this agreement, the Nationalist parties (including Sinn Fein) agreed that Northern Ireland should continue to be part of the United Kingdom as long as this was the wish of the majority of the population, while the Irish Republic agreed to amend its constitution, renouncing its claim on the six Northern counties. In exchange the Unionists agreed to form a power-sharing executive with the Nationalist parties. Provisions were made for the release of convicted Republican and Loyalist prisoners provided that their organizations maintained a permanent cease-fire, and for the 'de-commissioning' of arms held by para-military groups on both sides. The agreement was to be underpinned by referenda on both sides of the Irish border, which took place a month later, producing a positive majority of 94 per cent in the Irish Republic, but only 71 per cent (including a bare majority of Unionists) in the North. Other people besides Blair and Ahern were responsible for the success of the negotiation, including the Northern Irish Secretary, Mo Mowlem, and Jonathan Powell, but few people would deny that Blair's contribution, which involved three long days of hard bargaining and the trading of subtle compromises, during which he showed enormous patience, intellectual agility and stamina, was crucial. An exhausted Blair told the concluding press conference that the negotiators had felt 'the hand of history' on their shoulders as they reached the end of their transactions. This was not the end of the rocky road in Northern Ireland, and the process continued to have its ups and downs, including one particularly bloody outrage in Omagh, in August 1998, in which 29 civilians were killed by Republican extremists, but since then there has been relative peace and security in the North, and hope has replaced despair. A power-sharing executive was sworn in, led initially by Ian Paisley, with Sinn Fein's Martin McGuinness as his deputy, which proceeded to govern with surprising harmony, though there have been occasional blips.

If Blair achieved more than most people expected in Northern Ireland, his record concerning the European Union was a frank disappointment, at least to Europhiles. Proclaimed as the most pro-European premier since Ted Heath, he made a good start by adopting a cooperative attitude during the Amsterdam summit, in June 1997, ending the growing isolation in which Britain had found itself during at least the latter half of the Major premiership. He did not, however, succeed in his aim of breaking into the tight Franco-German alliance, which had long been the driving force behind European integration. He did hold an important bilateral summit with President Jacques Chirac at Saint-Malo in 1998, when they agreed a measure of Anglo-French defence cooperation which helped to launch the beginnings of a European Defence and Security Policy (EDSP). On other issues, though, the French President and his German Socialist partner, Gerhard Schröder, kept him at arm's length. Blair responded by attempting to organize a rival power bloc within the EU by cosying up to the centre-right leaders of the other two large member states, Spain's Jose-Maria Aznar and Italy's Silvio Berlusconi.

Yet Blair's hopes of providing constructive British leadership for the EU were blighted, largely because of his own hesitancy and irresolution. He had formed the view that it was essential for Britain to join the single currency, due to be established in 1999, but had reluctantly agreed, in 1996, to promise a referendum on the issue, when Major had conceded this to his euro-sceptic critics. Boldness would have counselled holding an immediate poll after his election in May 1997, when the honeymoon period was in full swing and his own enormous popularity would most likely have produced a favourable result, despite the fact that the opinion polls were showing a majority in favour of keeping the pound. He passed up the opportunity, and later allowed himself to be consistently outmanoeuvred by Gordon Brown, a relative sceptic on the issue. Brown bounced him into agreeing an announcement, in October 1997, that Britain was unlikely to be one of the founding members of EMU in 1999, and that a decision to join was improbable during the course of the current Parliament. He also acquiesced in linking the ultimate decision to five largely subjective 'tests' on the effect on the British economy, which the Treasury, under Brown's direction, would be responsible for carrying out. The long delay involved in making these assessments, which continued until March 2003 – when only one of the five was judged to have been met – made it impossible to launch a wholehearted campaign to convince public opinion. In the meantime, the opposition in the polls, stirred up by a great deal of mendacious reporting in the Murdoch, Black and Rothermere press, grew greater and greater, so that the prospects of winning a referendum, even if the tests were judged to have been passed, grew increasingly bleak. Sadly, Blair's own words, spoken in 2001, could well be applied to himself: 'The history of our engagement with Europe is one of opportunities missed in the name of illusions – and Britain suffering as a result' (Stephens, 2004, p. 207).

Blair's hesitancy over Europe was not reflected in his broader approach to foreign affairs, where, fortified by his Christian faith, he hastened to give a marked moralistic twist to British policy. There was no doubt that Blair took his religious beliefs seriously. He was the first British premier since Gladstone known to be a regular Bible-reader, but his approach is somewhat eclectic, as he has also read the Koran three times, and described Islam, in an interview with *Muslim News* in March 2000, as 'a deeply reflective, peaceful, very beautiful religious faith' (Rentoul, 2001, p. 351). Although ostensibly an Anglican, he regularly attended Roman Catholic services with his wife and children, who have been educated in Catholic schools. (In 2008, after he had left the premiership, he was himself received into the Catholic faith.) The medley of religious influences to which he had exposed himself convinced him that Britain has a moral duty, where circumstances permit, to use its influence, and where necessary its armed strength, to intervene in defence of justice and democracy throughout the world. This put him in the direct line of succession from Lord Palmerston, the mid-nineteenth-century Premier, who did not share his Christian faith, but who proclaimed a Pax Britannica, and used gunboat diplomacy to promote it. Britain's military strength was insufficient to give Blair the same scope for international intervention, but, as a book published in early 2003 pointed out, it was 'some feat to go to war five times in six years' (Kampfner, 2003, p. ix). Three of these, the air strikes against Saddam Hussein in 1998, the Kosovo war a year later, and the despatch of British troops to Sierra Leone in 2000, occurred during his first term of office. Although there was some vocal opposition, especially to the Kosovo operation, he also attracted much admiration and support, and had little difficulty in carrying public opinion along with him. This perhaps added dangerously to his self-confidence, leading him into a much rasher, and infinitely less popular, venture in 2003.

Blair was fully aware of how damaging the repeated accusations of 'sleaze' had been against his Tory predecessors, and was determined that his own administration should not be tarred with the same brush. 'We must be whiter than white,' he told his MPs on the morrow of their election victory. It was hardly to be – though the number and the seriousness of the scandals which arose were far less, his government was unable entirely to escape criticism on this score. The most serious incident concerned a Labour promise to ban advertising and sponsorship by tobacco firms. Six months after the election, Blair received a visit at Downing Street from Bernie Ecclestone, the head of Formula One motor racing, who argued persuasively that the sport would suffer grievous harm if tobacco sponsorship was brought to a sudden end. Blair listened sympathetically to his case, and then sent a memo to the Health Secretary asking him to look for a way 'to protect the position of sports in general and Formula I in particular'. It then transpired that Ecclestone had earlier given a £1 million donation to Labour, and – in the face of press criticism – the party referred the matter to the incoming chairman of the Committee on Standards in Public Life, who advised that the donation be returned, which it was. Blair angrily denied in a television interview that his decision on sponsorship had been affected in any way by a knowledge of Ecclestone's gift, saying: 'I think most people who have dealt with me think I'm a pretty straight sort of guy.' His public standing was still very high, and most people seemed prepared to give him the benefit of the doubt. There were to be three cabinet resignations during Blair's first term, including two by Peter Mandelson, the first of which reflected on his personal judgment and the second on the Prime Minister's, but – on the whole – Labour escaped being bracketed with the Tories over 'sleaze'. It was another monosyllable – 'spin' – which came to be seen as its Achilles' heel.

The high priest of spin was seen to be Alastair Campbell, who had wrought wonders for Labour in opposition, and continued to render signal service to Blair for several years subsequently. His most notable coup was to compose Blair's 'spontaneous' reaction to the death of Princess Diana, whom he described as 'the People's Princess', striking a chord with the British public and adding enormously to Blair's own, already high, reputation. Yet eventually the law of diminishing returns began to set in. Campbell repeatedly made excessive claims on behalf of the government, for example by double-counting the amount of money being spent on successive education and health service initiatives. His own relations with the media also began to deteriorate, as he upset more and more journalists by his bullying manner, and by his frequent and often unjustified complaints to radio and television producers and executives about their political coverage.

The first Blair government was able to deliver on the great majority of its specific promises, but, as the end of the twentieth century loomed, there was no doubting the widespread sense of disappointment about its performance. Yet Labour continued to enjoy a massive opinion poll lead over the Tories, with no sign of a mid-term revolt, and only one very temporary blip, in September 2000, at the time of the fuel tax protests. One reason for this was the almost total failure of the Tories to regain public confidence, which in turn was partly due to their choice of William Hague as leader in 1997 in preference to the vastly more experienced and more popular Kenneth Clarke. Although Hague was a good performer in the House of Commons, and often had Blair in difficulty at Question Time, his political judgment was poor, and he never established a rapport with the general public. His choice of 'defending the pound' as his major campaign theme was a crucial error: although a majority of voters remained sceptical about changing to the euro, this was never a salient issue for more than a minority. When the voters returned to the ballot boxes in June 2001, their verdict was almost identical to that of 1997, with Labour gaining an overall majority of 165, and the Tories winning precisely one more seat than four years earlier. There was, however, one significant difference: the turnout was down by over 12 per cent, and, at 59.4 per cent, was the lowest since 1918. One contributory factor was clearly the widespread perception that Labour was certain to win, but it was widely seen as a measure of the disillusionment with the whole political process, which had set in during Blair's premiership, and a stark warning for the future.

The re-elected government lost no time in indicating that its top priority would be to match the large additional spending on public services with reform measures which would make a qualitative difference and ensure that the money would not be dissipated on inessentials or spent in pursuit of producer interests. Unfortunately, however, Blair and his ministers failed to consult widely within the Labour Party before launching their reforms, which led to two major rebellions by Labour MPs, on foundation hospitals and top-up fees for universities, which could well have toppled Blair if they had been supported by just a few extra dissidents. Greater consultation was promised for the future after the 'top-up' debate in February 2004, but many remained sceptical, feeling that the government had got into the habit of taking adequate backbench support for granted.

For Blair, however, these were mere sidelines to his main preoccupations during his second term, which were concentrated on international affairs and, in particular, on his relationship with President George W. Bush. He demoted his independent-minded Foreign Secretary, Robin Cook, to be Leader of the Commons, appointing the more pliable Jack Straw in his place. Straw had been a notably illiberal Home Secretary, sometimes even being compared unfavourably with his Tory predecessor, Michael Howard. There was no reason to doubt, however, that he was faithfully following Blair's intentions, and his own successor, David Blunkett, was an equal disappointment to penal reformers and human rights campaigners. Blair's fixation on Bush began on the day of the latter's election, in November 2000, when he put out immediate feelers to ensure that he would be the first foreign leader invited to the White House after the inauguration in January 2001.

Blair's immediate bonding with Bush seemed odd, after his apparently warm relationship with Bill Clinton, a fellow Oxford graduate who shared many of his political views and with whom he had launched the so-called Third Way initiative to unite centre-left leaders across the world. But Blair had a sharp eye for power, and a singular lack of sentiment, in choosing his associates, and seems to have concluded that the over-riding priority for Britain was to forge a close link with the US President, whoever he might be. Despite his vaunted pro-Europeanism, it soon became clear that this meant more to him than keeping in step with other EU leaders. His burgeoning relationship with Bush was cemented by the outrage of 11 September 2001, when Blair hastened once again to Washington to pledge unconditional support in the war against terrorism. On 20 September, seated next to Laura Bush in the visitors' gallery, he listened to Bush's speech to both houses of Congress. Gesturing towards him, Bush said that America had 'no truer friend than Great Britain', and Blair was given a standing ovation.

Britain was the major ally of the US in the war against the Taliban, and, despite some anti-war opposition, Blair had little difficulty in carrying his country, and his party, with him, notably in a barnstorming speech to his party conference in October. The speech went well beyond justifying the war in Afghanistan, pleading for a new world order which would come to the aid of victims of oppression wherever they were – 'The starving, the wretched, the dispossessed, the ignorant, those living in want and squalor from the deserts of northern Africa to the slums of Gaza, to the mountain ranges of Afghanistan: they too are our cause.' The quick and relatively cost-free victory in Afghanistan, despite the failure to capture or kill Osama Bin Laden, helped to convince Blair of the realism as well as the moral justification of his cause, and he began to lend a sympathetic ear to US plans for regime change in Iraq. He was anxious, however, that any action should be under UN auspices. He set out to persuade Bush to follow this path, despite the contrary advice he was getting from Vice-President Dick Cheney and Defence Secretary Donald Rumsfeld, who favoured unilateral US action. Blair's view reinforced that of Secretary of State Colin Powell, and Bush agreed to take the problem of Iraq's non-compliance with the UN disarmament resolutions to the Security Council. Blair may well, however, have unwisely left Bush with the firm impression that, if the UN route failed, Britain would still support a war. What was to prove even more damaging was that he was to base his case for going to war almost entirely on the 'imminent threat' of Iraq's weapons of mass destruction (WMD) rather than the evil nature of Saddam's regime, which, it appears, was what really motivated him. The sequel does not need to be recapitulated in detail here – how the UN agreed to send inspectors back into Iraq on an 'intrusive' basis; how the inspectors found no such weapons even though they had been guided to hundreds of sites by the 'best intelligence' the US and Britain were able to provide; how on US insistence the inspections were cut short even though the chief UN Inspector, Hans Blix, and his team thought that the job could be properly completed within another two to three months; how no UN resolution permitting an invasion was even put to the vote; how the invasion went ahead with only US, British and Australian forces involved, with striking military success, at least in the short run; and how, after a further year's search by a US-led team, no WMD were discovered.

From first to last, Blair remained convinced of the rightness, indeed the righteousness, of his decisions, though even his powers of persuasion were insufficient to convince a majority of his countrymen. A massive revolt, of 139 Labour MPs, occurred in the Commons, and, on the eve of the war, the biggest ever protest demonstration was held in London and other towns and cities. Though the opinion polls showed majority support while British forces were directly involved in action, this soon slumped when the large-scale fighting concluded. Allegations, broadcast on the BBC by the journalist Andrew Gilligan, that Blair and his entourage had deliberately exaggerated the threat of WMD led to a bitter dispute between the government and the Corporation, and the suicide of Dr David Kelly, the arms inspector who had been the source of Gilligan's story. Blair then did himself no favours by appointing an ultra-Establishment judge, Lord Justice Hutton, to conduct a one-man enquiry into the events leading up to Kelly's death, with very narrow terms of reference. Hutton's report came down so heavily on the government's side, and was so critical of the BBC, that the public saw it as a 'whitewash'. A large majority in the opinion polls concluded that Blair had lied and had deliberately deceived the nation over the WMD threat. From that time onward, Blair was dogged by demonstrators carrying placards captioned 'B.Liar'. Several other enquiries, notably one presided over by former Cabinet Secretary (Lord) Robin Butler, probed Blair's role in the lead-up to the Iraq War, and criticized his decision-making practices, without, however, condemning his actions or questioning his integrity. A much wider public enquiry into Britain's role in the Iraq War, chaired by Sir John Chilcot, and ordered by Gordon Brown after he became Prime Minister, began work in July 2009 and completed its hearings in February 2011, but had still not reported nearly three years later.

What Blair lost through the Iraq war was the instinctive feeling of trust which he had built up with the British public, who had seemed to regard him as more than a cut above 'ordinary' politicians. This led to a catastrophic fall in his opinion poll ratings, though much less in those of his party. Pressure then began to build up within the party for Blair to stand down in Brown's favour before the next general election. Blair became acutely depressed, and – distracted and worried by family problems – accepted an invitation from Deputy Prime Minister John Prescott to a private dinner with Brown. Prescott then withdrew to allow them to talk frankly together, and, when he returned, Blair, according to his own account, said to him:

I have made it clear I won't serve a full term and will go before an election, but I need Gordon's full and unconditional support. John said he thought that was sensible. We parted. (Blair, 2010, p. 497)

But no sooner had he made this promise than he reconsidered, and – pressed by his wife and several Cabinet Ministers – he decided to stay on, justifying the decision to himself by Brown's failure to cooperate fully in the new range of New Labour policies he was now pursuing. These included, notably, the provision of new 'academy' schools, outside local government control, and the creation of 'foundation' hospitals within the NHS, with increased possibilities of cooperation with the private sector. He did not communicate his change of mind to his Chancellor, who was understandably devastated when, several months later – on 30 September 2004 – he made a dramatic announcement, while Brown was abroad attending an IMF meeting. This was to the effect that he would fight the next general election, with the intention of serving another full term if Labour won, but would not then contest a fourth election campaign. When Brown returned, they had a stormy meeting, at which Brown allegedly declared that he would never again believe anything Blair said to him. Brown contemplated resignation, but clenched his teeth and chose to stay on, deciding, in effect, that his pathway to No. 10 would now be determined by intrigue rather than an open challenge. For his part, Blair was pressed strongly by many of his advisers to sack, or attempt to re-shuffle, his Chancellor, but decided that this would be too risky a venture.

The election was held on 5 May 2005, with the following result:

Labour 355, Conservative 198, LibDems 62, Others 31.

Labour secured an overall majority of 67 seats, which ordinarily would have been regarded as a highly satisfactory result. Yet this was in comparison to a majority of 167 in the previous election, so it was seen as a marked setback. Polls taken during the campaign revealed that the Iraq war and the consequent unpopularity of Blair were the principal reasons for the fall in Labour support. They also suggested that the much greater popularity of Gordon Brown – who, against Blair's original intention, had been brought in to front the campaign in a 'double act' with the Prime Minister – had possibly saved Labour from defeat, or, at least, from a much smaller majority. So Blair emerged much weakened, with few people now believing that he would be able to serve out another full term. In fact, he was able to survive for another two years before Brown finally succeeded in winkling him out of No. 10. In the meantime, Blair made ineffective attempts to find a plausible candidate to run against Brown for the party leadership, his hopes resting mainly on David Miliband, then the Environment Secretary. But Miliband took the view that Brown was unbeatable, and declined to stand, as did all other likely contenders (see Chapter 52). So, when Blair finally announced his forthcoming resignation, on 2 May 2007, he coupled it with a recommendation to elect Brown as his successor. Brown was duly elected unopposed at a special Labour Party conference on 24 June, and Blair's premiership ended three days later. He had served for ten years and 56 days.

Blair was still only 54 years old, and full of energy, when he left Downing Street, anxious to continue to play an important public role. He would have liked to be chosen as the first President of the EU's Council of Ministers, and Brown duly nominated him. But the other EU leaders were unenthusiastic, partly because of his role in the Iraq War, but – evidently – also because they did not want to be over-shadowed by someone who was already a major international figure, so the post went to Belgian Premier Herman Van Rompuy. President George W. Bush was instrumental in securing him the role of Middle East Peace Envoy of the 'Quartet' group (the UN, US, EU and Russia), and he energetically pursued this role, but with little success, largely due to inadequate support from Bush, lack of cooperation from Israeli Prime Minister Binyamin Netanyahu, and the intransigence of Hamas. In fact, he has never been seen by the Arabs as an 'honest broker', due to his previous unswerving support for Israel.

He published a memoir, *A Journey*, in 2010, including a well-argued defence of his Iraq policy, which – unlike the majority of his Cabinet – he still felt was justified. He made a lot of money advising companies and foreign governments on international issues, and devoted himself to a range of 'good causes', including climate change, development work in Africa, and establishing a Faith Foundation to encourage collaboration between people from different religions. So, lots of activity, but he still exuded the air of an unfulfilled man.

How will he be viewed by history? He should be credited with modernizing both the Labour Party and the country through a series of (incomplete) constitutional reforms and presiding over a period of steady economic growth and the improvement of public services, especially health and education. His government made good progress on reducing child poverty, but did not reach its ambitious targets, and its record on transport and on housing left much to be desired. Overall, the balance of his record on domestic policy is likely to be a favourable one, but, as a force for change in British society, he will be seen as a distant third to Clement Attlee and Margaret Thatcher among post-World War II premiers. In international affairs, he reached 'superstar' status, and arguably increased British influence in the process. But his reputation was punctured by Iraq, and he seems doomed to be remembered more as a 'fallen idol'.

Works consulted

Leo Abse, 2003, *Tony Blair: The Man Who Lost His Smile*, London, Robson Books.

Tony Blair, 2010, *A Journey*, London, Hutchinson.

Hans Blix, 2004, *Disarming Iraq*, London, Bloomsbury.

Vernon Bogdanor, 2010, *From New Jerusalem to New Labour: British Prime Ministers from Attlee to Blair*, London, Palgrave Macmillan.

David Butler and Dennis Kavanagh, 1997, *The British General Election of 1997*, Basingstoke, Macmillan.

David Butler and Dennis Kavanagh, 2002, *The British General Election of 2001*, Basingstoke, Macmillan.

Nick Cohen, 2003, *Pretty Straight Guys*, London, Faber.

Philip Gould, 1998, *The Unfinished Revolution*, London, Little Brown.

John Kampfner, 2003, *Blair's Wars*, London, Free Press.

Dennis Kavanagh and David Butler, 2005, *The British General Election of 2005*, London, Palgrave Macmillan.

John Major, 1999, *The Autobiography*, London, Harper Collins.

James Naughtie, 2001, *The Rivals*, London, Fourth Estate.

Andrew Rawnsley, 2000, *Servants of the People*, London, Hamish Hamilton.

John Rentoul, 2001, *Tony Blair: Prime Minister*, London, Little Brown.

Steve Richards, 2010, *Whatever it Takes: The Real Story of Gordon Brown and New Labour*, London, Fourth Estate.

Anthony Seldon, 2004, *Blair*, London, Free Press.

Anthony Seldon, 2007, *Blair Unbound*, London, Simon & Schuster.

John Sopel, 1995, *Tony Blair: The Moderniser*, London, Michael Joseph.

Philip Stephens, 2004, *Tony Blair: The Making of a World Leader*, New York and London, Viking.

Jack Straw, 2012, *Last Man Standing*, London, Macmillan.

52
Gordon Brown – Dominant Chancellor, Uncertain Premier

Gordon Brown was the eighth Scotsman to become Prime Minister of the United Kingdom, after the 3rd Earl of Bute, the 4th Earl of Aberdeen, the 5th Earl of Rosebery, Arthur Belfour, Sir Henry Campbell-Bannerman, James Ramsay MacDonald and Sir Alec Douglas-Home. Some would argue that he was the ninth, advancing the claims for inclusion in the list of Harold Macmillan. Yet he was, at best, only a 'notional' Scot: apart from being half-American, he was part of the second generation of his family to be born and raised in England, as members of the anglicized 'ruling class'. Brown, however, is very much the real thing. He was born in Govan, a working-class suburb of Glasgow, on 20 February 1951; his father, the Rev. John Ebenezer Brown, was descended from a long line of shepherds and tenant farmers from Fifeshire, while his mother, the former Jessie Elizabeth Souter, was the daughter of a builder and ironmonger from west Aberdeenshire. Named James Gordon Brown, he was the second of three sons, the eldest, John Souter Brown, being born in 1948, and the youngest, Andrew, in 1959. Three years after he was born, the family moved to the Fife seaside (and mining) town of Kirkcaldy, where the Rev. Brown was minister of the St Brycedale Church, or Kirk, as it is known in the Church of Scotland.

The Rev. Brown's parishioners were predominantly miners and factory workers and their families, lowly paid, and often living under the threat of unemployment. Yet – largely due to legacies which Gordon's mother had received – the Brown family were able to maintain a middle-class standard of living, though their lifestyle was austere. They lived in a commodious house, the doors of which were always open to those in need, and the message which the minister preached each Sunday was very much a social gospel. As Gordon was to recall in an interview many years later, in 1993:

> I was very much impressed with my father. First, for speaking without notes in front of so many people in that vast church. But, mostly I have learned a great deal from what my father was able to do for other people. He taught

me to treat everyone equally, and that is something I have never forgotten.
(Routledge, 1998, p. 25)

At four, a year younger than all his classmates, Gordon was enrolled at the local
primary school, Kirkcaldy West, and was soon outstripping all his compet-
itors, being particularly quick at sums. He excelled at all subjects, and was
also outstanding at sports, particularly football, forming an early ambition
to become a professional footballer, becoming, alongside his father, an avid
supporter of Raith Rovers, in the Scottish Football League. At 10, he left – again
a year early – to proceed to Kirkcaldy High School. Here he was one of the
'guinea pigs' selected for a remarkable experiment, designed to fast-forward the
most intelligent boys and girls through the school. Some 11 boys (including
his closest school friend from Kirkcaldy West, Murray Elder) and 25 girls were
chosen for an 'E-Stream', which was subjected to a pressure-cooker regime
designed to ensure that they would achieve outstanding examination results
at an earlier age than usual. For Gordon, it appeared to be a complete success:
he took his O levels, in eight or nine subjects, at the age of 14, and his 'highers'
(the Scottish equivalent of A levels) at 15. He sat five subjects, and achieved
an A in all of them. Gordon, however, considered that the whole E-Stream
experiment had been a cruel failure. Aged 16, he wrote in an essay:

> I watched as each year one or two of my friends would fail under the strain.
> I saw one girl who every now and then would disappear for a while with a
> nervous breakdown. I stood by as a friend of mine, who I knew was intel-
> ligent enough, left school in despair after five years of strain with no uni-
> versity or higher qualifications. I thought continually of how it could have
> been for these young guinea pigs, how the strain of the work, the ignominy
> and rejection of failure could have been avoided. All this, I thought I saw
> better than any educationalist in his ivory tower. (Ibid., p. 12)

Even for himself, the outcome had been less than satisfactory. He felt he had
no alternative to starting university at the age of 16, two years younger than
his fellow students. There was no point in staying at school for a further year,
as there was nothing more for him to learn there; the only prospect was that
of becoming Head Boy. Nor had the concept of a 'gap year' yet caught on, at
least in towns like Kirkcaldy. So, in the autumn of 1967, he reluctantly joined
his elder brother John at Edinburgh University, where he was to read history.
Six months earlier, during a rugby match between his school and its 'Old Boys',
he had been injured in a scrum, and emerged from the match with impaired
vision. Assuming it would soon rectify itself, he never bothered to consult a
doctor, but during his first weeks at university he headed a ball during a football
match and his sight worsened. This time he did see a doctor, who discovered

detached retinas in both eyes. Despite four operations at the Edinburgh Royal Infirmary, and being ordered to lie immobile for six months in a darkened hospital ward, he lost the sight of his left eye, and for a time it was feared that he would go completely blind. The right eye was eventually saved, and he was discharged with orders not to play contact sports. Gone was his aspiration to become a professional footballer, but more significant were the lasting physical and psychological effects. The former included a certain rigidity in muscles on the left side of his face, which made it difficult for him to smile and contributed to the dour reputation which he was later to acquire. The latter greatly reinforced his existing determination to push himself, to work harder than anyone else, and to prove that it was not only in the country of the blind that the one-eyed man is king. As a student at Edinburgh this ambition was to be more than amply fulfilled.

Professor Henry Drucker, at that time a junior politics lecturer at Edinburgh, described Brown as:

> an important figure, even as an undergraduate. He was hugely popular, a natural politician: totally self-assured. He was good to everybody, and everyone wanted to know Gordon Brown. He was a bit like a Bill Clinton figure. (Routledge, 1998, p. 43)

It was a time of great unrest and agitation in universities throughout Europe and North America, and Gordon Brown emerged as the most effective, but far from the most extreme, student leader in any British university. Not for him the excitement of leading 'sit-ins' and mass street demonstrations. His method was the careful accumulation, and presentation, of facts calculated to embarrass the University authorities and to bolster the legitimate, and sometimes not so legitimate, claims of the student body. Brown soon became chairman of the University Labour Club, but his main forum, initially, was his editorship of the student newspaper, through which he launched a series of campaigns which infuriated the ultra-conservative Principal (or Vice-Chancellor), Sir Michael Swann. Swann was an office-holder in the Anti-Apartheid Movement, and assured the University Court that none of the University's investments were in companies known to be active in support of Apartheid. Brown obtained a copy of a secret stockbroker's report which revealed extensive financial involvement in such companies, and he rushed out a special issue of the paper demanding that the University should dispose of its holdings. He launched a petition to this effect, signed by 2,500 students and 300 staff, and Swann was forced to change stockbrokers and liquidate the shares. Brown's next target was the Rectorship of the University, which had become a largely honorific post, though the Rector was legally entitled to chair meetings of the governing body, the Court. Elected by the students for a three-year term, in earlier times the

Rectors had been leading politicians, including Gladstone, Disraeli, Churchill, Lloyd George and Baldwin. More recently, however, the candidates had usually been figures from the media or show business, who did not take the take the job very seriously. As Paul Routledge comments:

> This absentee-rector situation suited the authorities admirably. The Principal presided over a group of establishment yes-men, who simply rubber stamped his wishes. (Routledge, 1998, p. 48)

In 1971, Brown, then aged 20, put himself at the head of a campaign to elect a student as Rector, who would go on to chair the meetings of the University Court and ensure that issues of concern to the student body were properly considered. Brown proposed that Jonathan Wills, his flatmate and close collaborator, then a postgraduate student, should be the students' candidate. Wills went on to defeat the satirist Willie Rushton, and – to the horror of Swann – proceeded to take the chair at meetings of the Court, but after only one year, anxious to pursue his own career, resigned his post. Brown was the overwhelming choice of the student body to succeed him, but the University authorities sought a heavyweight figure to oppose him, and came up with Sir Fred Catherwood, a leading industrialist, who had acted as an advisor to Harold Wilson's Labour government and chaired the National Economic Development Council (or 'Neddy'), a forum for consultation between the government, industrialists and trade union leaders. Brown emerged as victor, with more than 60 per cent of the votes, and proved to be a much more active and resourceful Rector than his predecessor, pressing a series of far-reaching reforms on a reluctant University administration. When the Principal high-handedly dismissed an assessor appointed by Brown, and forbade his attendance at the Court, Brown took him to a court of law, which ruled in Brown's favour; the assessor was restored to office and all business transacted in his absence was declared void. Swann and his colleagues next tried to take away the right of the Rector to chair the Court's meetings, and appealed to the University's Chancellor, the Duke of Edinburgh, who previously had played only a ceremonial role. They were astonished when he turned them down, unaware that Brown's then girlfriend, Princess Margarita of Romania, who was studying sociology and politics, was the Duke's god-daughter, and had presumably lobbied him on Brown's behalf. This was the last straw for Swann, who shortly afterwards left Edinburgh to become Chairman of the Governors of the BBC.

Brown graduated in 1972, reputedly having scored the highest marks ever recorded in his final examinations, and embarked on a PhD, his chosen subject being the development of the Labour Party in Scotland between 1918 and 1929. He had hoped to secure a full-time academic post in the University, but he had made so many enemies in the administration through his activities as

Rector that this proved impossible, and he was fobbed off with a small amount of part-time teaching. In 1976 he moved to Glasgow to take up a lectureship in politics at the City's College of Technology, and also became a tutor for the Workers' Educational Association. After four years he resigned to become a producer and investigative journalist for Scottish TV. His spare time, however, was taken up almost completely by Labour Party activities, his over-riding objective being to secure election as an MP. He had narrowly missed selection as Labour candidate for Edinburgh South, a Tory-held marginal, in the October 1974 general election, when he was 23, but was adopted as its prospective candidate two years later.

Brown was living in a large but chaotically organized apartment – with about six flatmates – the scene of many a raucous student party, of which Brown was the life and soul. Yet, as a beer rather than a spirits drinker, he was never seen to be the worse for wear, and, as a 'son of the manse', kept well clear of drug-taking, not even succumbing to the occasional whiff of 'pot'. In almost permanent attendance was his glamorous girlfriend, Princess Margarita of Romania, a great-great-granddaughter of Queen Victoria, and 53rd in succession to the British throne. As a matter of form, she kept her own flat, and, when Brown was visited by his strait-laced mother, they took care to ensure that the intimacy of their relationship was concealed from her. It lasted for five years, and most of Gordon's friends assumed that they would get married, but it was not to be. Margarita often felt neglected because of the all-consuming nature of Gordon's political activities, while he might perhaps have feared that his reputation as a campaigner for the poor and dispossessed might have been compromised by marriage to a princess. Eventually, Margarita's patience snapped, and she upped sticks and began an affair with a handsome fireman – also a Labour activist, but less single-mindedly so than Brown – which was to last for six years. Much later, she said in an interview: 'It was a very solid and romantic story. I never stopped loving him, but one day it didn't seem right any more. It was politics, politics, politics, and I needed nurturing' (*Harpers & Queen* magazine, August 1992). Brown was devastated, and confessed after a long drinking session with his tutor, Owen Dudley Edwards: 'It's the greatest mistake of my life. I should have married Margarita' (Bower, 2004, p. 31). He was then in his mid-20s, and, though he went on to have several other serious relationships, did not marry until he was 49, in 2000. Margarita also appears subsequently to have found it difficult to commit herself – she only married (a Romanian actor, Radu Duda) in 1996, at the age of 47.

Meanwhile, Brown's commitment to the Labour Party took up more and more of his time. Alongside his PhD thesis, he wrote and published a highly regarded biography of James Maxton (1885–1946), a famous Clydeside Labour MP, and leader of the left-wing Independent Labour Party (ILP). In 1975, aged 24, he also edited *The Red Paper on Scotland*, a 368-page collection of essays by the youngest and brightest left-wing figures in Scotland. This set out an agenda to modernize and radicalize the country and its institutions, including, notably, the Scottish Labour Party. He became a member of its Executive Committee, and later its chairman, and was responsible for organizing its campaign in favour of devolution in the 1978 referendum called by the Callaghan government. Earlier that year he had been strongly urged to run in a by-election in the safe Labour seat at Hamilton. It would have been a tremendous opportunity for him, but he hesitated, and finally declined to put his name forward, on the grounds that he felt committed to stick to Edinburgh South, a far less promising seat, where he was the prospective candidate. This was not the full story, however; the 'frontrunner' for the nomination was George Robertson, who was backed by the powerful Municipal and General Workers' Union, of which he was a senior official. The cautious Brown was unwilling to risk defeat and in the process make influential enemies (Robertson went on to become Defence Secretary in the Blair government, and Secretary-General of NATO). This episode prefigured his refusal to fight against Tony Blair for the Labour leadership in 1994. It was less understandable that Brown went on to turn down the candidature for another good constituency – Leith – where he would not have faced a powerful rival. So he stayed with Edinburgh South, where – in the 1979 general election – he trimmed the Tory majority, but still lost by 2460 votes. He had to wait to get into Parliament until the 1983 general election, when, aged 32, he was returned with a majority of over 11,000 votes for Dunfermline East, the neighbouring constituency to Kirkcaldy, where he had grown up.

Brown made an immediate impact in the Commons, making a highly praised maiden speech, highlighting the unemployment figures in his constituency and generally throughout Scotland. He became a close friend and collaborator of another new Member, Tony Blair, two years his junior and vastly less experienced in Labour Party politics, with whom he shared a small office. Within two years, Brown was appointed a frontbench spokesman on trade and industry, and in 1987 was elected as the youngest member of the 'Shadow Cabinet', with the task of 'shadowing' John Major, then the Chief Secretary to the Treasury. Blair also became a shadow spokesman, for Energy, and both of them benefited enormously from the activities of Peter Mandelson, who in 1985 was appointed as Labour's Director of Communications. An important part of his job was to recommend to the BBC and other broadcasting organizations suitable persons to present the Labour viewpoint in television and radio broadcasts. With Kinnock's encouragement, he repeatedly called on the services of Blair and Brown, whom he saw as the most personable and persuasive of the younger generation of Labour politicians. In the process, he became a close friend and collaborator of the two men, particularly Brown. In the many discussions between the trio at this time, many of the ideas which went into the later launch of New Labour were thrashed out.

Brown's big moment came in October 1988, when the Shadow Chancellor, John Smith, had a serious heart attack and was ordered to take at least three months' complete rest from politics. The Labour leader, Neil Kinnock, asked Brown to deputize for Smith during his absence, and his first great test came on 1 November, when the Chancellor, Nigel Lawson, presented in his autumn statement a rosy picture which hardly coincided with the underlying economic situation. In Paul Routledge's words, 'Brown fell upon Lawson like a wolf on the fold' (Routledge, p. 148), and with a wealth of statistics cast serious doubt upon virtually all the assumptions on which the Chancellor had based his statement. Lawson was seriously discomfited, and the Labour benches erupted with delight. Later the same month, when Labour MPs held their annual vote to choose the Shadow Cabinet, he topped the poll, rising from 11th place the previous year. Somewhat to his embarrassment, he even eclipsed Smith, who was pushed down into second place. From that moment on, he began to be seen, and talked about, as a future leader of the Labour Party. However, when a vacancy in that post occurred four years later, with Neil Kinnock's resignation after Labour's defeat in the 1992 general election, he was not among the candidates who opposed the favourite, John Smith, whom he strongly backed. He would have liked to contest the deputy leadership, but thought that the party would not accept two Scotsmen in its most senior posts. Blair himself considered running; though born in Edinburgh, he was clearly of English stock. He decided against, partly through fear of losing, but also so as not to upset Brown, who would not have enjoyed seeing his 'junior partner' leapfrog him in the party hierarchy. Smith, however, lost no time in appointing Brown as Shadow Chancellor, which gave him a dominant position in the new leadership team. His friend Tony Blair, who was still seen at the time as being much junior to him, was also given a big promotion, becoming Shadow Home Secretary.

The general expectation, backed by most opinion polls, had been that Labour would win the 1992 election, or at least emerge as the largest party. In the event, the Tories, led by John Major, were returned with an overall majority of 21. Their victory was universally attributed primarily to their success in painting Labour as a 'tax and spend' party, with fearsome predictions of massive tax increases if Labour won. The new 'Shadow Chancellor' determined that this would never happen again, and that under his aegis Labour's economic policies would always be marked by fiscal prudence. In particular, he determined that Labour should be in a position to give cast-iron assurances before the next election that there would be no increase in the basic rate of income tax. In pursuit of this objective, he ruthlessly vetoed virtually every policy proposal by his fellow 'shadow' ministers which would involve additional expenditure. This made him highly unpopular with many of his colleagues, including, notably, David Blunkett, the blind 'Shadow Education Minister', who was bristling with ideas for expensive educational reforms.

The sudden death of John Smith on 12 May 1994 was a devastating event for Brown. He undoubtedly saw himself as the heir apparent, but genuinely grieved over the loss of his friend, and, thinking it unseemly to begin campaigning before the burial of the Labour leader, he devoted himself to writing heartfelt tributes to him. He was appalled to discover that Blair had immediately thrown his hat into the ring, and was pressuring him not to split the modernizing vote by standing against him. He felt he had been betrayed by Blair, who, he believed, was committed to supporting him by an agreement they had made two years earlier. He was even more upset by Peter Mandelson, who was privately backing Blair's bid, and giving television interviews in which, without naming names, he implied that Blair would be a better prospect as a vote-winner. This view appeared to be corroborated by opinion polls, which showed Blair with a commanding lead, and Brown coming only fourth among five projected candidates. Blair undoubtedly owed his large lead to his skill as a performer on television, and the assiduous efforts he had made to court the press, which Brown had failed to do. Brown also suffered from his rough treatment of his fellow Labour MPs, among whom his support was now far from overwhelming. Nevertheless, his two brothers strongly urged him to run, as did his band of close parliamentary supporters, led by his namesake, Nick Brown, an influential trade unionist MP. They were convinced that if he launched a vigorous campaign he would rally sufficient support to overhaul Blair. Brown was sceptical, believing that his only hope of beating Blair was to run a ruthless and highly demagogic campaign, branding Blair as a toff and a closet Tory, appealing to the serried ranks of Leftists and backward-looking trade unionists in the party. This would have destroyed his own reputation as a modernizer, and Brown reluctantly concluded that he had no alternative but to seek a deal with Blair which would maximize his own power and influence in the party, in exchange for his endorsement.

So, after covert negotiations with Blair and his entourage, Brown met his rival on 31 May at an Islington restaurant, The Granita, and agreed a deal, subsequently confirmed in writing, that he would become Chancellor with effective control over not only the economy but virtually the whole range of domestic policy, and be consulted on all important appointments. Not included in the written agreement was a promise by Blair to relinquish the Prime Ministership in Brown's favour during the course of a second term, if any, of a Labour government. Blair appeared to have a guilty conscience about his treatment of his former close friend, and offered this as a sop to Brown's feelings, probably not taking his own words very seriously. Brown, however, took them at face value, and clearly regarded them as a firm commitment.

Despite his severe disappointment, Brown buckled down and worked closely and constructively with Blair to build up New Labour in the three years leading up to the 1997 election. He successfully concealed the bitter sense of betrayal which he felt against Blair, and focused it instead on Peter Mandelson, with whom he broke off all personal relations for more than a dozen years. Yet he was a changed man, as Robert Peston, then the political editor of the *Financial Times*, observed:

> The change that came over him in that period, compared with his personality before he decided not to challenge Tony Blair for the leadership of the Labour Party in June 1994, was startling. He became manifestly less relaxed. Every thought and deed was controlled. He retreated into himself and became much duller. (Peston, 2005, pp. 21–2)

As Shadow Chancellor, Brown built up his own little 'court' of advisers and core supporters. His main adviser, whom he recruited from the *Financial Times*, was the economist Ed Balls, whom Brown relied on very heavily, not only for economic advice but as a general sounding board for all his ideas and projects. He was later joined by Ed Miliband, son of a leading Marxist academic and the younger brother of David Miliband, who was advising Blair, and by Charlie Whelan, his press adviser. He was also assisted by Geoffrey Robinson, a millionaire Labour MP, who permanently rented a suite of rooms at the Grosvenor House Hotel, overlooking Hyde Park. Here he lived when staying in London, and it was here that Brown met almost daily with his close collaborators to plot his every move and to plan his future Chancellorship, when Robinson was scheduled to join him as a senior Treasury minister. They agreed on three major policy commitments, which would be announced in advance of the 1997 general election, in order to secure public confidence that a 'New Labour' government would be fiscally prudent. The first was to promise that Labour would keep to the very tight spending plans already announced by the Conservative Chancellor, Ken Clarke, for the first two years of government. The second was a commitment not to raise either the standard rate of income tax – then at 23 pence in the pound – or even the higher rate of 40 pence. Brown had considered this too low compared with other countries and wanted to raise it to 50 pence, but this had been vetoed by the even more cautious Blair. Third, Brown sought that rare commodity – a popular tax – in order to raise sufficient revenue to finance his ambitious plans to reduce unemployment ('Welfare to Work'). He hit upon a one-off 'windfall' tax on the public utilities, which had been privatized by the Thatcher and Major governments. They had been sold off far too cheaply, and then used their quasi-monopoly status to make enormous profits and pay very high salaries to their top managers. Robinson, a former chief executive of Jaguar Cars, was set to work on a draft Bill that would be legally watertight. He consulted the accountancy firm of Arthur Anderson, and did such a good job that the public utility bosses eventually withdrew their loud threats to challenge the legal validity of the ensuing legislation.

Brown's pledges undoubtedly contributed to the massive Labour landslide in the general election of 1 May 1997. On 2 May, he was duly installed as Chancellor of the Exchequer, and – unlike all his other Cabinet colleagues – with the right to nominate his entire team of junior ministers. These included Alistair Darling as Chief Secretary to the Treasury and Geoffrey Robinson as Paymaster General. Both Ed Balls and Ed Miliband joined them in the Treasury as special advisers, and Charlie Whelan as press spokesman. Brown hit the ground running. His first action, when he entered the Treasury for the first time on the afternoon of 2 May, was to present the deeply surprised Permanent Secretary, Sir Terence Burns, with a letter addressed to Eddie George, the Governor of the Bank of England. The letter announced that henceforward the Bank would be responsible for setting interest rates, thus depriving governments of the possibility of manipulating them for political purposes. When the news was announced it was very widely welcomed, and was greeted by the press as restoring the independence of the Bank of England. The Bank, however, lost its role of supervising and regulating commercial banks. Brown announced the creation of a new regulating body, the Financial Services Agency. This also was widely welcomed, but not by George, who was initially inclined to offer his resignation in protest. He resented not having been consulted in advance, but swallowed his pride and agreed to stay at his post.

Despite enormous pressure from within his own party, Brown kept to his pledge to adhere to Tory spending limits during his first two years in office. He defended this policy as 'prudence with a purpose', and made it clear that once financial security and a healthy budget surplus had been achieved more ambitious policies could be anticipated. What was the 'purpose' he had in mind? In a very perceptive book (Richards, 2010, *Whatever it takes*), the journalist Steve Richards seeks to unravel Brown's intentions, and the difficulties he faced in carrying them out. His over-riding passion, Richards argues, was to fight against poverty, both in Britain and in the developing world, and to achieve a more equal society. Brown, however, was convinced, by Labour's experience during the 1992 general election campaign, that the British electorate was viscerally opposed to tax increases, and that he would have to proceed with the greatest circumspection. He determined, therefore, to 'do good by stealth' by raising additional revenues by apparently 'painless' measures. By and large, he was successful in this endeavour, and by the end of his Chancellorship, in 2007, he was a popular figure, widely seen as the most successful Chancellor in modern times. He was also seen as a tax-cutter rather than a tax-increaser, cutting the standard rate of income tax from 23 per cent to 20 per cent, and corporation tax from 33 per cent to 28 per cent. The only 'visible' tax increase during his Chancellorship was in his 2002 budget, when National Insurance contributions were raised to pay for a major expansion in public spending in health and education. Other than this, and a range of 'stealth' taxes, Brown relied on a steady growth in tax revenues arising from economic growth, which averaged 2.7 per cent a year, compared with 2.1 per cent in the Eurozone. A great admirer of Anthony Crosland, the author of the highly influential *The Future of Socialism* and a senior minister in the Wilson and Callaghan governments, Brown was thus able to carry out Crosland's preferred policy of financing redistribution through the proceeds of growth. He also benefited from another 'windfall' wheeze, netting £22.5 billion through the auction in 2000 of telecoms spectrum licences. Brown made only one obvious error in his tax strategy, but it was an egregious one. In his 1999 budget, he announced a new, low starting rate of income tax, of 10p in the pound, replacing the basic rate of 23 per cent for the first £2230 of taxable income. Commending it, the Chancellor said:

> The 10p rate is very important because it is a signal about the importance of getting people into work and it's of most importance to the low paid. This is not about gimmicks. This is about tax reform that encourages work and families.

The move proved very popular, and Brown received much praise, but in his last budget in 2007 he insensitively abolished the rate, to help him achieve a 'masterstroke' of reducing the basic rate from 22p to 20p, the lowest level since 1930. The change was not due to come into effect until 2008, when Brown was no longer Chancellor, but when it did it provoked massive protests, not least within the Labour Party, which gravely damaged the standing of the government which he had formed only a few months previously (see below). Despite this, his overall record as Chancellor was highly successful, though it led him, hubristically, to claim to have finally banished the cycle of 'boom and bust' which had long afflicted the British economy. This claim came back to haunt him during his later premiership.

From 1997 to 2007, Brown was not just Chancellor, but also effectively co-leader of the government with Tony Blair. This could have been a source of enormous strength if their dissimilar qualities had been able to combine in a symbiotic relationship. Instead, their mutual distrust and resentment led to constant disharmony, which undermined, though it did not destroy, the effectiveness of the government. It had many achievements to its credit, but fewer than it might have had if their previous close friendship had not degenerated into almost open enmity. This was kept relatively under control during the first Parliamentary term which ended with the 2001 general election. There were, however, constant rows over 'turf wars', as Brown tried to muscle in on more and more of his cabinet colleagues' responsibilities, and concealed from Blair, until the very last minute, major policy initiatives, including the contents of his budgets. Blair retaliated in his first Cabinet reshuffle, in July 1998, when he purged several of Brown's leading supporters from ministerial posts, demoting Nick Brown from Chief Whip to Minister for Agriculture. He also installed his own close ally, Stephen Byers, as Chief Secretary to the Treasury in place of Alistair Darling, who was promoted to Social Security Secretary. Brown greatly resented this, regarding Byers as a 'spy' installed at the very centre of his own Treasury. Both Blair's and Brown's 'spin doctors' thought nothing of anonymously briefing the press about their respective masters' faults, most notoriously when Brown was described as having 'psychological flaws'. It was widely assumed at the time that Alastair Campbell had been responsible for this, though he indignantly denied it. It was later suspected that Blair himself was the author of these incriminating words (Peston, 2005, p. 15).

Despite the serious disharmony between the two men, which was largely concealed from the general public, there was only one serious policy difference between them during the first parliamentary term. This was over British entry to the Eurozone, of which Blair was a strong advocate. He was little inhibited by an electoral commitment to hold a referendum on the issue, being convinced that the high popularity of the government would ensure a successful outcome, despite opinion poll evidence that a majority (though at that time not a large one) were opposed. Brown, greatly influenced by Ed Balls and by cautious Treasury officials, was much less optimistic, and outmanoeuvred Blair over the issue, ensuring that entry would not be sought in advance of the following general election, and that the Treasury would be the arbiter of when, if ever, entry should be sought (see Chapter 51). For better or worse, it was Brown who decided that Britain should not adopt the euro, at least for the foreseeable future.

On 3 August 2000, the long bachelorhood of Gordon Brown finally came to an end. Aged 49, he married the 36-year-old Sarah Macaulay at a small ceremony in the living room of his Fife home, conducted by the Rev. Sheila Munro, a Church of Scotland minister. They had been together for around five years, but their courtship had been conducted with great discretion. They had first met in 1994, when Sarah, who had founded her own small public relations firm, Hobsbawn-Macaulay, with Julia Hobsbawn, daughter of the Marxist historian Eric Hobsbawn, was undertaking a project on behalf of the Labour Party. It was clearly a love match, and Gordon's friends noted that he became notably more relaxed and outgoing after the marriage. Then, in January 2002, they suffered the tragedy of losing their prematurely born baby, Jennifer Jane, when she was only 10 days old. Their sorrow turned to joy with the birth of a healthy son, John, in October 2003, followed by his younger brother, Fraser, in July 2006. The parents were again devastated some months later, when Fraser was diagnosed with cystic fibrosis, and the news was insensitively splashed on the front page of the Murdoch newspaper, *The Sun*. Unlike some other leading politicians, Gordon Brown and his wife have taken exceptional care to protect their children from public exposure.

With scarcely a blip in its high popularity levels, the Blair government successfully concluded its first Parliamentary term with a second landslide majority in the general election of June 2001. Any illusion that Blair might have held that his Chancellor was satisfied with his current lot was rudely shattered on the Monday after the election, when Brown abruptly demanded that Blair should give him a date when he would resign as Prime Minister (Richards, 2010, p. 184). Blair temporized, but Brown continued to confront him with the issue at regular intervals during the second parliamentary term. It did him little good: Blair had no intention of making an early withdrawal, and instead started to think of alternative leadership candidates, fixing initially on David Blunkett, the blind Home Secretary, and Alan Milburn, Health Secretary. At one stage, in December 2001, during a dinner at Downing Street, Blair allegedly offered Brown a deal: he would stand down in Brown's favour if Brown fully backed Euro entry (Seldon, 2007, p. 206). Brown declined, and two months later explained to a Cabinet colleague, Clare Short, that he

> could not conceive of recommending that Britain join the Euro to advance his own prospects at the expense of the economic interests of the country. (Ibid., p. 207)

If Blair's offer had been sincere, he soon regretted it, and it seems likely that around this time he privately decided that he would not keep to his promise to stand down during the course of the second term. Yet his position was greatly weakened by the disastrous consequences of the Iraq War (see Chapter 51), and in December 2003 he made a conditional promise to Brown that he would stand down by the time of the Labour Party conference in September 2004. He backtracked on this, to Brown's evident fury, and was able to survive to fight a third general election, in May 2005, when his parliamentary majority was more than halved. Thereafter he was clearly a 'lame duck' Prime Minister, with poll ratings inferior to Brown's, yet it took another two years for the latter, 'willing to wound', in Alexander Pope's words, 'and yet afraid to strike', to eject him from Downing Street. In his last few months as leader, Blair's strongest supporters desperately sought to find a candidate who could contest the leadership against Brown. The most plausible was the Environment Secretary, David Miliband, but, concluding he could not win, he refused what he considered to be a poisoned chalice. Several other less likely people were approached, even including Jack Straw, then the Leader of the Commons, who claims he was approached at least twice by Blair himself, saying 'You could do it, you know, Jack' (Straw, 2012, p. 490).

None could be found to contest the ballot, and on 24 June 2007 Brown was elected unopposed as Labour leader at a special conference in Manchester, having been nominated by 313 out of 356 Labour MPs. A left-wing Labour

MP, John McDonnell, had hoped to run against him, but failed to win the requisite number of nominations. Harriet Harman, who had fought off four rivals, narrowly beat the favourite, Alan Johnson, for the deputy leadership. Three days later, on 27 June, Brown succeeded Blair as Prime Minister. His new government was carefully balanced between leading 'Blairites' and his own long-standing supporters. The most senior appointments were Alistair Darling as Chancellor of the Exchequer, David Miliband as Foreign Secretary, Jacqui Smith, the former Chief Whip, as Home Secretary and Jack Straw as Justice Secretary. Ed Balls was sent to head the new Department for Children, Schools and Families, with a private understanding with Brown that after he had gained experience of running a large department he would be promoted to Chancellor (an understanding not communicated to Darling). Ed Miliband became Cabinet Office Minister, and was later promoted to Energy Secretary, while Douglas Alexander became Secretary of State for International Development, and was named as Labour's election co-ordinator. Sue Nye, who had been an adviser to Brown since 1992, was made Director of Government Relations, while Damian McBride, an abrasive civil servant, became his press secretary. Six former Cabinet Ministers – John Prescott, John Reid, Margaret Beckett, Patricia Hewitt, Lord Falconer and Hilary Armstrong – left the government, not all of them voluntarily. Brown, who wished to be seen as a national rather than a mere party leader, made strenuous efforts to create a 'government of all the talents'. His most daring move was to invite the former Liberal Democrat leader, Paddy Ashdown, to join the Cabinet as Secretary of State for Northern Ireland. Ashdown was keen to accept, but felt constrained to ask permission from his party leader, Menzies Campbell, who promptly vetoed the idea. So Brown had to content himself with appointing a number of junior ministers from outside the ranks of the Labour Party, though all but one of them subsequently joined the party. Appointed life peers, they included the distinguished surgeon Professor Ara Darzi, Admiral West, a former First Sea Lord, and Mark Malloch Brown, formerly Deputy Secretary General of the United Nations. The most curious appointment was that of Digby Jones, a former Director-General of the CBI, who had high Tory and Euro-sceptic views. He became Minister of State for Trade and Industry, but resigned in high dudgeon after only 15 months, saying that being a junior minister was 'one of the most dehumanising and depersonalising experiences' any one could have (*The Guardian*, 15 January 2009).

Some of Tony Blair's closest associates had expressed privately, and sometimes publicly, the view that Brown would not be up to the premiership. In his first few months in office, he appeared to have triumphantly refuted these fears, and his opinion poll ratings, and those of the Labour Party, soared upwards – too much, in fact, for his own good. In just a few weeks a Conservative lead of 4–6 per cent had been turned into a Labour lead of 6–9 per cent. Moreover,

Brown was receiving an excellent press – including, notably, from the normally Tory-supporting *Daily Telegraph*, *Daily Mail* and *Spectator* – for the calm and effective way in which he dealt with three crises which arose in quick succession. These were a terrorist attack at Glasgow airport, widespread flooding in England and Wales, and an outbreak of foot and mouth disease. It had been no part of Brown's plans to hold a general election so soon after his arrival at No. 10. Indeed, he had pencilled in the late spring or early summer of 2008, by which time he hoped to have a record of solid achievement.

Yet newspaper speculation soon built up that he would capitalize on his spiralling popularity and opt for an autumn poll. In late August, one of Brown's advisers, Spencer Livermore, sent him a memo setting out the case for an immediate general election. Brown showed little interest, and left the memo lying on his desk for three weeks. Then, in September, the crash of the Northern Rock Bank caused widespread panic, which led to a further rise in Brown's poll ratings. Although his immediate response was hesitant, he was seen as a safe pair of hands to deal with the crisis, due to the high reputation for economic competence which he had built up as Chancellor. By the end of the month, when the Labour lead in the polls had reached 10 per cent, most of Brown's closest associates and advisers had become convinced of the case for holding an early election, as had many Labour MPs representing marginal seats. Older (and wiser?) hands in the party were more sceptical. On the Friday before the annual Labour conference, Brown lunched at Chequers with Livermore, Douglas Alexander, Ed Balls, Ed Miliband, Damian McBride and an American polling expert and speech-writer, Bob Shrum. With varying degrees of enthusiasm, they all urged him to fire the starting gun. Brown remained reluctant, but agreed to commission a poll in marginal constituencies to make a more informed assessment of Labour's prospects. The news of the marginals' poll soon leaked out, along with a series of steps taken by the Labour Party to prepare for a campaign, and the speculation in the media broke all bounds. The atmosphere at the Labour conference in Bournemouth was euphoric, as enthusiasm built up day by day. At the end of the week, the normally down-to-earth Cabinet Minister, John Denham, summed up the general feeling by saying:

> We could turn a majority of 60 with two and a half years to run into a majority of 100 with five years to run. (Rawnsley, 2010, p. 504)

Brown ended the week in high good humour. He had not firmly decided on an election, but was excited by evidence that the Tories were panic-stricken at the prospect of a crushing defeat, and concluded that he should 'stir the pot' in the hope of provoking widespread recriminations at their own conference the following week in Blackpool. He also resolved to steal the thunder of the first day of their conference by a lightning visit – his first – to the British troops serving in Iraq.

It was a major miscalculation. The threat of annihilation at the polls united the Tories rather than exacerbating their differences. David Cameron kept his head and rose to the occasion, showing a confidence which he did not feel, and delivering a defiant address, without notes or autocue, and ending with the words:

> So, Mr. Brown, what's it to be? ... Let the people decide ... call that election ... we will fight. Britain will win. (Elliott and Hanning, 2012, pp. 340–1)

Speaking earlier in the week, the 'Shadow Chancellor' George Osborne dropped a bombshell, when he brought forward a proposal which the Tories had intended to announce during the actual election campaign. This was to abolish inheritance tax on all estates of less than £1 million, which effectively excluded most middle-class families from paying the tax. His announcement was greeted with thunderous applause throughout the hall, and an overwhelmingly positive response in the press. It chimed in with public fears that the apparently never-ending rise in house prices was bringing more and more people over the existing tax threshold. Brown's visit to Iraq also went awry: he was roundly condemned at the conference and in the media for involving British soldiers in what appeared to be an election stunt. By the end of the conference, three opinion polls revealed a sharp fall in the Labour lead. One poll showed a drop from 11 per cent to 4 per cent, another from 10 per cent to 3 per cent. The third poll showed that the Tories had closed an eight-point gap and were now level-pegging (Rawnsley, 2010, p. 507).

On the Friday – 5 October – Brown met his closest advisers in 10 Downing Street to discuss the findings of their own poll in 150 marginal seats. These were presented by the Labour Party's American pollster, Stan Greenberg. The message was not very optimistic. 'The balance of risk', Greenberg said 'was a small win', perhaps a 20-seat majority. But, he added, 'I can't guarantee what your majority will be.' Some of Brown's team felt that they had gone so far it was impossible to pull back, Livermore arguing strongly that 'If we don't do it, the only people who will be celebrating are Tory Central Office' (Ibid., p. 508). Others, including Brown himself, were disheartened. Later in the day Brown called a further meeting, and:

> asked each of them in turn – Alexander, Balls, Livermore, [Ed] Miliband, McBride and Nye – what they thought. No-one expressed a clear view. No-one wanted responsibility for the decision. 'So we are not going to do it then?' asked Brown morosely. Everyone avoided his gaze. (Ibid.)

Brown had only his own hesitation to blame. He should have made a firm decision, one way or the other, at least a week earlier. If he had decided on an election, he should have announced it at the Labour conference, which would have given him an excellent launching pad. If not, he should have put an end to the speculation before it became uncontrollable, by stating firmly that there would be no election in 2007. Either way, he would have remained in control of the political agenda.

It is impossible to be certain what the result would have been had he decided on an election. Most likely, it would have yielded a small Labour majority, but it is understandable that – having waited so long to attain the premiership – Brown was unwilling to put it at risk after barely four months. Had he lost he would have been the second shortest-serving Prime Minister in British history, after only Canning, who died in office after 119 days. Brown added to his humiliation by the cack-handed way in which he explained his decision. Asked at a press conference whether he had been deterred by adverse poll figures, he vigorously denied it, even saying that he would have called the election off even if the polls had predicted a majority of 100 seats. This exposed him to the devastating rebuke by David Cameron, at Prime Minister's questions two days later, that:

> He's the first prime minister in British history to flunk an election cos he thought he was going to win it.

Brown's reputation was severely damaged by the whole episode. The Tory claim that he had 'bottled the election' was very widely accepted, and he was henceforward seen, and was repeatedly described in the press, as a 'bottler' or a 'ditherer'. The verdict of his very sympathetic biographer, Steve Richards, was:

> The three weeks of election fever, followed by an announcement that there would be no election, destroyed Brown's premiership … He was now doomed to stumble on without a personal mandate and without a strategy for dealing with the long and precarious journey that lay ahead before an election could be called. (Richards, 2010, pp. 285 and 303)

It was 'long and precarious' because the Tories established an immediate lead in the polls, which they maintained, with fluctuations, almost continuously throughout the following three years. There was not a moment during this period when Brown could have called an election with any realistic hope of winning. Another serious consequence was a breakdown in the mutual confidence of Brown and his entourage. There were recriminations and resignations, and the spirit of *camaraderie* which had previously held them together was gravely weakened. This only exacerbated the chaotic state of the internal organization of 10 Downing Street under Brown. Used to the tidy and smooth-running organization of the Treasury, Brown seemed incapable of imposing an effective structure on the Prime Minister's Department. He failed to appoint a chief-of-staff to succeed the enterprising and highly efficient Jonathan Powell, who had acted for Tony Blair, nor did he find a press spokesman of the calibre of Alastair Campbell, or of Bernard Ingham, who had served, respectively, Blair and Thatcher. There was no clear hierarchy among his staff, and Brown's organization of his own time was far from optimal. As ever, he worked fanat-ically hard, and for very long hours, but he was a poor delegator, and his 'people management', both of his staff and his ministers, left very much to be desired.

'The election that never happened' was followed by another self-imposed disaster four months later, in the run up to Alistair Darling's first budget. The abolition of the 10p tax rate, announced the previous year in Brown's last budget, was due to come into force, and Darling warned Brown that as many as one-fifth of voters would be adversely affected by the change, though the remaining four-fifths would benefit by the reduction of the standard rate from 22 to 20 per cent. Brown flatly denied that anybody would be worse off, saying that the introduction of working tax credits and other budget changes would more than cancel out the losses. Brown was wrong, as a growing number of Labour MPs, alerted by anxious constituents, soon suspected, and he was confronted at an angry meeting of the Parliamentary Labour Party. Brown stubbornly insisted he was right, and invited MPs who thought otherwise to send him their evidence. The anti-poverty campaigner and former junior minister, Frank Field, then tabled an early day motion demanding that the 10p rate be maintained until a compensation package was worked out for those who would be net losers. Forty Labour MPs promptly signed up, enough to defeat the government if they voted against the budget proposals. At the last moment, Brown gave way, and instructed Darling to introduce compensatory measures, costing the Exchequer £3.5 billion, whereupon Field withdrew his motion. It was too little and too late, and disaffected Labour voters took their revenge in the May 2008 local elections, one week later. They were Labour's worst results in 40 years, the party came in third place nationally, and in the London mayoral election the inexperienced and buffoonish Tory candidate, Boris Johnson, defeated the Labour incumbent, Ken Livingstone. In the same month, the Tories won the Crewe and Nantwich by-election from Labour with a swing of 17.6 per cent, the first Tory by-election win from Labour in 26 years.

These dire results sparked off the first of three attempts to overthrow Brown as party leader, and displace him from the premiership. The leader of the first, in the autumn of 2008, was the former Home Secretary, Charles Clarke, who had been sacked by Blair in May 2006 after a scandal about the failure to deport foreign prisoners who had served sentences for serious crimes. Clarke, despite being a long-time critic of Brown's, had been severely disappointed when Brown made no move to bring him back into the government when he succeeded Blair. In September 2008 Clarke publicly called on the party to repudiate Brown, who, he claimed, was leading the party to 'utter destruction'. Meanwhile, David Miliband wrote an article in *The Guardian*, which was widely interpreted as a disguised leadership bid, and a number of Labour MPs promptly called for Brown's resignation, in the hope of provoking a revolt in the Cabinet. This did not materialize, but a group of three ministers, Justice Minister Jack Straw, Chief Whip Geoff Hoon and Work and Pensions Secretary James Purnell, started to meet periodically to monitor the developing situation. Of the three, Straw was the most influential, and if he had chosen to lead a cabinet coup against Brown it would have had a high probability of succeeding. But Straw, who clearly aspired to the leadership himself, knew that he was only, at best, the third favourite – after Alan Johnson and David Miliband – and sat tight. Meanwhile, Brown took steps to bolster his own position. He made an effective speech at the Labour conference in late September, and his implied rebuke – to both Cameron and Miliband – that 'this was no time for a novice' to take over – went down well. He then proceeded to a masterly cabinet reshuffle, in which he surprised the world by bringing back his old friend-turned-enemy, Peter Mandelson, from Brussels to become Business Secretary and unofficial Deputy Premier. Henceforward, Mandelson became Brown's closest associate in government, and one of the few to whom he would listen if they proffered critical advice.

Nevertheless, Brown continued to receive a bad press, with repeated stories of 'dithering' and of his bad temper and disloyalty towards colleagues. He was particularly damaged by reports that his former press adviser, Damien McBride, was implicated in a failed attempt to set up a website devoted to spreading scurrilous stories about leading Tory politicians. Brown denied any knowledge of the affair, and promptly dismissed McBride, but this did him little good. Then, in May 2009, a veritable tsunami hit the government in the form of the 'exposure' by the *Daily Telegraph* of details of MPs' expenses claims over the previous five years. Brown himself had nothing to hide, though the paper focused on a trivial sum which he had claimed for his share in cleaning expenses for a flat he had jointly occupied with his brother. It was entirely legitimate, and the *Telegraph* was later forced to withdraw its innuendos and publish an apology. Yet the damage to the government was considerable: although Labour MPs had collectively been no more avaricious than Tories, the paper featured them more prominently, and two ministers, Home Secretary Jacqui Smith and Communities Secretary Hazel Blears, resigned from the Cabinet in the wake of the allegations, though claiming loudly that they had done nothing wrong. Their departure coincided with the June 2009

European elections, in which Labour was badly mauled, coming in third place with less than 16 per cent. On polling day itself, Purnell, despairing of any hope for the government while Brown remained as leader, submitted his own resignation and wrote to the Prime Minister suggesting that he should do the same. It was a moment of maximum danger for Brown, and for once the alleged 'ditherer' acted decisively to shore up his position. In a lightning reshuffle, he promoted his main putative rival, Alan Johnson, to be Home Secretary, while Mandelson's responsibilities were greatly expanded and he was given the title of First Secretary of State. The first thing that Mandelson did, in the middle of the night, was to phone David Miliband and other cabinet ministers to persuade them not to follow Purnell into resignation. If they had done so, it would undoubtedly have been the end of the Brown government. Purnell, a hopeless conspirator, had made no attempt to co-ordinate his resignation with any prospective allies, and neither Straw nor Hoon made any move to support him. Yet Brown was frustrated in his intention to replace Alistair Darling with Ed Balls, as Chancellor of the Exchequer, which he had long planned to do. Darling refused point-blank to take any other post in the government, and Brown did not feel strong enough to sack him, and face his criticisms from the backbenches.

Even Brown's strongest supporters were bitterly disappointed at his performance as Prime Minister, which was now widely seen as a total failure. Yet his reputation was boosted by the onset of the world financial crisis in 2008–9, when, in the words of the leading economic journalist William Keegan, he proved to be 'the right man, in the right place, at the right time' (Keegan, 2012, p. 47). In September 2007, when there was a run on the Northern Rock Bank, he had been slow to acknowledge that temporary nationalization was the inevitable prerequisite to its rescue, but a year later he was well ahead of the game. When three of the largest banks – the Royal Bank of Scotland, Lloyds and Halifax-Bank of Scotland (HBOS) – were on the brink of collapse, and their bosses had no idea where to turn, Brown (advised by former investment banker and junior minister, Baroness Shriti Vadera) immediately stepped in. The solution, he insisted was two-fold: emergency measures to increase liquidity, combined with a massive re-capitalization of the banks, which only the government could provide. In return, the government would take an equity stake in the banks, which would eventually be sold off, hopefully making a profit for the taxpayer. During a hectic weekend, the Chancellor Alistair Darling wrestled with the largely uncomprehending bank bosses, finally convincing them that unless they accepted the government's offer their game was up. Meanwhile, Brown had been desperately trying to convince French President Nicholas Sarkozy and German Chancellor Angela Merkel that they too should re-capitalize their banks if the whole international banking system was not to seize up. Sarkozy, at least, was persuaded, and invited Brown to attend a meeting of the 15 heads of state of the Eurozone, where he delivered an extraordinary address, which convinced almost all his listeners. 'My friend Gordon has the right plan, we must do it in Europe,' Sarkozy said, and recapitalization of the French and German banks followed almost immediately. In America, too, the newly elected President Obama and his incoming Democratic administration were highly impressed, and worked closely with Brown in preparation for the G20 summit of world leaders, which Brown was due to chair in London in April 2009. Brown totally dominated this meeting, the result of which was

> nothing less than an agreement on what Brown dubbed 'a $1 trillion rescue plan for the world's economy', via a huge boost in the resources of the IMF (principally) and the World Bank, aimed at stabilising the system after the biggest decline in GDP, industrial production and world trade since the Great Depression of 1929–32. (Keegan, p. 74)

In addition, Brown later claimed, some $3 trillion was injected into the budgets of national economies in anti-recessionary measures. Brown was rewarded with international acclaim for his efforts. Nobel Prize winner for Economics, Paul Klugman, suggested in the *New York Times* that he might have 'saved the world financial system', a *Time* magazine headline ran 'Gordon Brown goes from zero to hero' and a leading American peace foundation proclaimed him World Statesman of the Year. In Britain, there was also a positive reaction, with the Labour deficit in the polls narrowing from 16 to 7 per cent, but the improvement was not sustained.

The Tories were undecided whether to react by attacking Brown's moves as irresponsibly increasing British debts, or to rally round as a patriotic gesture. In fact, they simultaneously tried both approaches, with Osborne taking one tack, and Cameron the other. Finally, they settled on the former, attacking Brown for reckless profligacy, and demanding severe expenditure cuts to reduce the fiscal deficit. Brown wanted to follow a Keynesian course of massive investment to lift Britain out of the recession, going into the next election offering the alternative of Tory cuts or Labour investment. He was restrained by Darling and the Treasury, who insisted on the necessity of having a plan to pay off the debt in a finite period. So Labour entered the election campaign with a commitment to pay off half the debt within five years, but not to implement cuts until economic recovery was well under way. In retrospect, this appears quite a reasonable approach, but it cut little ice during the election campaign, which terminated on 6 May 2010. A still unpopular Brown, who seemed to have lost all the *élan* and presentational skills of his earlier days, abandoned by most of the press, and heavily outspent by his opponents, went down to defeat, in an election which produced a 'hung' Parliament. The result was Conservatives

306, Labour 258, Liberal Democrats 57, others 29. As recounted in Chapter 53, the Liberal Democrats chose to go into coalition with the Conservatives, despite a bid by Brown (who offered to give up his Prime Ministership in the process) to form a 'progressive alliance' with them, with support from some of the smaller parties.

So, Brown's premiership came to end after two years and 321 days. Brown retained his parliamentary seat, but retired to the backbenches and virtually disappeared from Parliament. When Dominique Strauss-Kahn resigned as Director-General of the International Monetary Fund in May 2011 he would have been a strong candidate for the succession, but the new Cameron government rushed to nominate France's Christine Lagarde instead, with Cameron making mean remarks about Brown being a 'deficit denier'. Instead, Brown has devoted much of his time to charitable work, particularly concerning overseas development, while accepting an honorary role as Special Envoy to the UN Secretary-General for Global Education.

Despite his great abilities, and his stellar performance over the banking crisis, Gordon Brown's premiership was undoubtedly a disappointment. Some, particularly his Blairite critics, have argued that he was temperamentally unsuited for the role. Yes, he was a good strategist, they concede, and able to rise to the big occasion, but he was ill-prepared to meet the daily challenge of a constant stream of unexpected events. There is something in this, but the more likely explanation is that the opportunity came to him much too late. If he, rather than Blair, had succeeded John Smith back in 1994, he might well have made a better fist of the top job. As it was, he had to wait 13 long years, full of raised hopes and crushing disappointments, before he was able to take over the helm. For understandable reasons, he was burned up with resentment, and became increasingly paranoid and distrustful of his colleagues, and profoundly risk-averse. So it was a badly bruised and hesitant figure who took over the premiership in 2007, in contrast to the supreme self-confidence which he had shown on becoming Chancellor. Moreover, the years of grindingly hard work had taken their toll, and at 56 he appeared no longer capable of communicating effectively either with his colleagues or with the electorate as a whole. He fought a dogged election campaign in 2010, but, compared not only with Clegg but also with Cameron, he appeared a rather lumbering figure, somewhat slow on the uptake. It was a sad end to a career that had begun full of promise.

Works consulted

Francis Beckett, 2007, *Gordon Brown: Past, Present and Future*, London, Haus Books.
Tom Bower, 2004, *Gordon Brown*, London, HarperCollins.
Gordon Brown, 2010, *Beyond the Crash: Overcoming the First Crisis of Globalisation*, London, Simon & Schuster.

Alistair Darling, 2011, *Back from the Brink*, London, Atlantic Books.

Francis Elliott and James Hanning, 2012, *Cameron: Practically a Conservative*, London, Fourth Estate.

Dennis Kavanagh and Philip Cowley, 2010, *The British General Election of 2010*, London, Palgrave Macmillan.

William Keegan, 2004, *The Prudence of Mr. Gordon Brown*, London, Wiley.

William Keegan, 2012, *'Saving the World'?: Gordon Brown Reconsidered*, London, Searching Finance.

Peter Mandelson, 2010, *The Third Man: Life at the Heart of New Labour*, London, Harper Press.

James Naughtie, 2001, *The Rivals: The Intimate Story of a Political Marriage*, London, Fourth Estate.

Robert Peston, 2005, *Brown's Britain*, London, Short Books.

Giles Radice, 2010, *Trio: Inside the Blair, Brown, Mandelson Project*, London, I.B. Tauris.

Andrew Rawnsley, 2000, *Servants of the People: the Inside Story of New Labour*, London, Hamish Hamilton.

Andrew Rawnsley, 2010, *The End of the Party: The Rise and Fall of New Labour*, London, Viking.

Steve Richards, 2010, *Whatever it Takes: The Real Story of Gordon Brown and New Labour*, London, Fourth Estate.

Paul Routledge, 1998, *Gordon Brown, The Biography*, London, Simon & Schuster.

Anthony Seldon, 2007, *Blair Unbound*, London, Simon & Schuster.

Anthony Sheldon and Guy Lodge, 2010, *Brown at 10*, London, Biteback.

Jack Straw, 2013, *Last Man Standing*, London, Macmillan.

53

David Cameron – Plausible 'Front Man'?

When David Cameron was a schoolboy at Eton, he was surrounded by the busts of many of the 18 Etonians who had been British Prime Ministers (more than a third of the total) and perhaps wondered whether there would ever be another one. Twenty-five or so years later, he resolved any doubts by becoming, at the age of 43, the youngest Premier since Lord Liverpool in 1812.

There are some (perhaps even including himself) who believe that he was born to rule. He is the great-great-great-great-great-grandson, through an illegitimate line, of King William IV, which makes him a distant cousin of Queen Elizabeth II. Through both his parents, he is descended from several generations of Etonians: on his father's side, mostly wealthy stockbrokers, and on his mother's, baronets and Tory MPs. Born on 9 October 1966, he had an elder brother, Alexander, and sister, Rachel, and was to have a younger sister, Clare, five years his junior. His father was Ian Cameron (1932–2010), a senior partner, like his father and grandfather before him, of the stockbroking firm Panmure Gordon. Ian had been born with deformed legs, which were amputated late in life, and he was widely admired, not least by his younger son, for his fortitude and determination not to allow his disability to prevent his leading an active and constructive life. Cameron's mother, the former Mary Fleur Mount (born 1934), had several distinguished relatives, including Alfred Duff Cooper, a leading Tory Cabinet minister and close associate of Winston Churchill. Her cousin, Ferdinand Mount (a baronet, though he does not use his title), is a well-known author and served as Head of the Downing Street Policy Unit under Margaret Thatcher. 'Ferdy' Mount, himself a somewhat unconventional character, described his family in the following terms:

> The Mounts are very old fashioned, slightly stiff, you might say…They had a very comfortable upbringing. They were churchgoing, I don't think any of them have ever been divorced. They are straitlaced and full of a sense of duty. (Elliott and Hanning, 2012, p. 8)

Mary Cameron may be less forbidding than this suggests, but certainly inherited the sense of duty. She served as a Justice of the Peace in Berkshire for many years, as did her mother and grandmother before her.

When David was born, the family were living in Phillimore Place, Kensington, but three years later moved to the idyllic village of Peasemore, six miles north of Newbury, Berkshire. Their new home was a spacious Queen Anne mansion, the Old Rectory, with its own swimming pool and tennis court. There was also a live-in nanny, a family retainer of the Mounts, who had helped to bring up Mary a generation earlier. At the age of seven, David was dispatched to Heatherdown, near Ascot, perhaps the most exclusive preparatory school for boys in the whole country. It was determinedly old-fashioned in its methods; pupils were required to learn by rote the names and dates of all the Kings and Queens of England, as well as the names and order of the books in the Old and New Testaments. David Cameron's capacity to learn speeches by heart, so that he could deliver them without notes, which served him so well on at least two crucial occasions much later in life, perhaps owed something to his 'prep school' experiences. These were not uniformly happy. Corporal punishment was freely administered by the headmaster, and the young David was thrashed several times for such offences as talking in chapel and stealing strawberries from the headmaster's garden. On the whole, David settled down well at the school. He is remembered by contemporaries as being very well adapted, 'always smiling, very social and chatty' and 'with a good ability to get on with people'.

Although his family was wealthy, David apparently came from near the lower end of the social scale represented at the school. His biographers record that among the 80 or so sets of parents of his contemporaries were:

> eight honourables, four sirs, two captains, two doctors, two majors, one brigadier, one commodore, two princesses, two marchionesses, one viscount, one lord (unspecified) and one queen (*the* Queen). (Ibid., p. 20)

David did not particularly excel academically at Heatherdown, where his results were no better than average. Nevertheless, he did well enough at the end of his course to win admission to Eton, which was the ultimate objective of sending him to the school. He was to be one of its last pupils. It closed its doors in 1982, the super rich having apparently concluded that it was no longer the fashionable thing to send their children away from home at such a tender age.

At Eton, Cameron initially acquired the same reputation he had enjoyed at Heatherdown, of being bright, amiable, but of no more than average ability. Then, at the age of 16, he had a nasty shock, coming within an ace of being expelled from the school. In a scandal which reached the national newspapers, a number of his fellow pupils were thrown out of the school for smoking, and dealing in, cannabis. Cameron had not done any dealing, and was let off with being fined, 'gated' and having to copy out 500 lines of Latin verse. Much later, on the eve of the 2010 general election, he recalled in a newspaper interview the effect this had had on him:

> When I was 16 I was definitely going off the track a bit, losing interest in school and study and doing things wrong...I remember thinking, 'Hold on a minute, if you carry on like this you're not going to get any decent grades, you're not going to make much of your life'. (*Daily Mail*, 10 April 2010)

So, he buckled down, paid much more attention to his classes, broadened his interests, and, when he took his A-levels in 1984, scored three As – in History of Art, History and Economics with Politics. He then sat the entrance exam for Oxford University, and was awarded an Exhibition at Brasenose College.

Cameron's time at Eton coincided with the early years of Margaret Thatcher's premiership, and she became a heroine to the vast majority of Eton schoolboys, all but a tiny proportion of whom came from Conservative family backgrounds. Cameron was no exception, and became a strong admirer of the 'Iron Lady', though the Conservatism which he came to embrace was of a more compassionate and moderate brand than hers. There was one exception: his Euroscepticism. His biographers interviewed several of his close associates at the school, who recalled that 'his real passion was reserved for railing against the iniquities of the "Common Market"' (Elliott and Hanning, 2012, p. 40). While at Eton, Cameron, who expressed a preference for being known as 'Dave', was generally regarded as being very friendly and approachable. Some of his contemporaries, however, regarded him as arrogant, and thought the charm was only put on for people he wanted to impress, while he treated others with disdain. Several of them claimed to have detected an inner determination and ruthlessness behind the surface charm. For whatever reason, Cameron failed to be elected to the elite Eton Society, or 'Pop', which was evidently a disappointment for him. Opinions differ as to whether Cameron had already decided on a political career while still at school. Elliott and Hanning noted that, though he attended meetings of the school's prestigious Political Society, he made no attempt to be elected to its committee, which would have entitled him to meet the speakers, who included senior cabinet ministers, more informally over dinner. 'Unlike', they add, 'Boris Johnson, a year his senior' (Ibid., p. 41).

Nevertheless, for the first three months of his gap year before Oxford, he worked in the House of Commons as an intern with Tim Rathbone, the very 'liberal' Conservative MP for Lewes, who was his godfather. He then left for Hong Kong to work for another three months for the Jardine Matheson shipping agency, whose chairman, Henry Keswick, was a close associate of his father.

Cameron arrived in Oxford in October 1985 to read Politics, Philosophy and Economics. He was later described by his tutor, Professor Vernon Bogdanor, as 'one of the ablest students he had taught' (BBC News programme, 6 December 2005). His contemporaries remember him as someone who was extremely well organized, dividing his time very efficiently, and presenting his views, both in writing and in discussion, extremely clearly and with great good humour. He mixed in well with his fellow PPE students, but his social life revolved mostly around Old Etonians, and he joined the exclusive Bullingdon Club of wealthy young men, renowned for their heavy drinking and loutish behaviour. Also prominent in 'the Buller', as it was known by its members, was Boris Johnson, who by all accounts joined more enthusiastically in their destructive orgies than the more self-disciplined Cameron. Nevertheless, he was once summoned by his college authorities to explain why the furniture in his rooms had been systematically vandalized. Cameron declined to name the culprits, and footed the bill for the damages. Cameron had strings of girlfriends while at Oxford, and at least one serious relationship, with a diplomat's half-German daughter, Francesca Ferguson. It lasted for 18 months, and she took him to Kenya for a safari and to visit her parents, her mother remarking to her: 'That chap is going to be Prime Minister one day.' Soon after returning to Oxford, however, Cameron 'dumped' her rather abruptly, apparently more keen on working hard to secure a First in his degree than on spending his time courting (Ibid., pp. 64–5).

While at Oxford, Cameron played no part in the Union, and did not join the Conservative Association. There was no doubt, however, that he was a convinced Tory, and Vernon Bogdanor remembered him as having 'moderate and sensible Conservative political views' (*Sunday Times*, 25 March 2007). In the summer of 1988, Cameron sat his finals, and – as predicted by Bogdanor – duly obtained a First. This virtually assured him a smooth entry into whatever career he chose. At the time, he was still divided in his mind between business and politics. He had already applied for a number of management consulting and banking jobs, and also to *The Economist*, but nothing had come of them. He now decided to apply for a post at the Conservative Central Office, and was invited for an interview. Waiting to interview him was the deputy director of the party's research department, Alistair Cooke (later Lord Lexden). He was surprised to receive a telephone call from a man who announced, in a 'grand' voice, that he was calling from Buckingham Palace. He said:

> I understand that you are to see David Cameron. I've tried everything I can to dissuade him from wasting his time on politics, but I have failed. I am ringing to tell you that you are about to meet a truly remarkable young man. (Elliott and Hanning, p. 73)

According to Cooke, this 'unsolicited testimonial' had no effect, either way, on the decision to offer Cameron an appointment. He was 'clearly outstanding', Cooke reported years later when the story emerged in the press. Cameron himself was puzzled, believing that the caller was probably Sir Alastair Aird, then the Comptroller of the Queen Mother's Household, and the husband of Cameron's godmother. But Aird vehemently denied it, as did Sir Brian McGrath, Secretary to Prince Philip, a family friend and neighbour of the Camerons. Perhaps, after all, it was an anonymous hoaxer.

Cameron started work at the Conservative Research Department (CRD) on 26 September 1988. He was to remain there, or on secondment to a series of Cabinet ministers, for six years. He soon established a reputation as a keen, quick and highly efficient worker and by 1990 had been promoted to Head of the Political Section, under the overall direction of Andrew Lansley, who 20 years later was to serve under him as Secretary of State for Health, and later as Leader of the Commons. Among his colleagues at the CRD were several young researchers who later became his close associates as Leader of the Opposition and Prime Minister. These included Steve Hilton, whom he appointed as Director of Strategy at 10 Downing Street, and who was reputed to be his most influential adviser. Others, including George Osborne, became important politicians in their own right. Also working at the CRD was Laura Adshead, whom Cameron had known at Oxford, and with whom he now started a passionate affair, which lasted a year and apparently ended badly. Cameron resolved never again to date anyone in politics, and Adshead asked for 'compassionate leave' from her work, and subsequently, in a complete change in her life-style, became a nun.

Soon after John Major succeeded Margaret Thatcher as Prime Minister, he asked the CRD for help in preparing for the very testing and, at that time, twice weekly sessions of Prime Minister's Questions. Cameron was selected for this role, and every Tuesday and Thursday he had to get up very early in the morning to report to 10 Downing Street, where he was set to go through all the daily newspapers with a fine-tooth comb in preparation for briefing the Prime Minister on any tricky issues which were likely to come up, and to suggest suitable lines of response. He met with Major at 9 a.m., and then again over lunch, where the PM rehearsed his lines and took away a more detailed brief which Cameron had prepared during the morning. He performed his task well. The *Sunday Times* reported, on 30 June 1991: 'John Major's performances have become sharper of late', and attributed the improvement by name to the previously unknown 24-year-old researcher. In the 1992 general election, which the Tories were expected to lose, Cameron was given the crucial task of briefing Major every morning before his daily press conference. This involved him getting into Conservative Central Office by 4.30 each morning, having seldom gone to bed before midnight, and working all day scouring the papers and television programmes for negative points to use against Labour. The entire Tory campaign was built around two themes – to paint Labour as an irresponsible 'tax and spend' party and to undermine public trust in the Labour leader, Neil Kinnock. Cameron provided much of the 'ammunition' needed for these purposes, and, together with his sidekick Nick Hilton, he got much of the credit within the party for Major's surprise success. Not all senior Tories, however, were enamoured with Cameron. Lord McAlpine, for example, a former Tory Treasurer and close friend of Lady Thatcher, excoriated him in a press article, referring to his 'obvious arrogance' (Elliott and Hanning, 2012, p. 111). Some younger Tories also were clearly envious of his success, and fearful that he would leapfrog over them in his ascent up the party hierarchy.

At the election, Major's political adviser, Judith Chaplin, was elected Tory MP for Newbury, and Cameron was greatly disappointed that Major did not choose him as her successor. Instead, he was chosen by Norman Lamont, the Chancellor of the Exchequer, as the more junior of his two policy advisers. Cameron reluctantly agreed, complaining that the salary offered was below his expectations. Within a few months he probably regretted taking the job. He was pictured in all the newspapers, lurking in embarrassment behind the Chancellor on 'Black Wednesday', 16 September 1992, when Lamont announced Britain's humiliating withdrawal from the European exchange rate mechanism (ERM). Worse was to come a few months later, when Lamont was abruptly sacked as Chancellor and refused to accept demotion to a more junior cabinet post. Meanwhile, Judith Chaplin had suddenly died, and Cameron briefly contemplated offering himself as candidate for her Newbury constituency, which included his family home at Peasemore. Fortunately for him, he thought better of it: in the ensuing by-election the Tory majority of over 12,000 votes was converted to a Liberal Democrat majority of the same dimensions. At about this time, however, he took steps to ensure that he was included in the Conservative list of recommended candidates.

The incoming Chancellor, Kenneth Clarke, did not retain Cameron's services. He was instead chosen to assist the new Home Secretary, Michael Howard, to counter the challenge from his Labour 'opposite number', Tony Blair, To the chagrin of the Tories, Blair had succeeded in appropriating their mantle as the 'law and order party' with his 'tough on crime, tough on the causes of crime' message, and Howard was determined to win it back. Cameron himself became fascinated by Blair, whom he met in the course of his duties, and struck up a friendship with his adviser, Tim Allan, arranging occasional dinners with him at which they discussed the merits and faults of their respective bosses. This did not deter Cameron from helping Howard devise a series of ferociously tough measures, which he unveiled at his famous 'Prison works' speech at the 1993 annual Conservative conference . One of Howard's junior ministers, Sir Peter Lloyd, whose own views were distinctly 'liberal', doubts whether Cameron fully shared 'the determinedly right wing views of his boss'. 'I remember thinking in ministerial meetings', he recalled, 'he is a bright chap – does he really believe all this nonsense?' (Ibid., pp. 158–9).

While working for Lamont, Cameron had started a new relationship. This was with Samantha Sheffield, who had been a schoolfriend of his younger sister, Clare. Clare had invited her to join in a Cameron family holiday in Tuscany, and the pair were instantly attracted. Five years younger than her new admirer, Samantha was a rather wild art student in Bristol, frequenting 'rave' parties, and hanging out with a very Bohemian crowd at her local pub, described by one of her friends, the hip-hop star Tricky (Adrian Thaws), as a place where:

> bikers mixed with drug dealers, hippies, students and guys from the ghetto. It was a cool pub but ... there were always fights. (Ibid., p. 137)

But Samantha came from a very grand family: her father, Sir Reginald Sheffield, 8th Baronet, has large estates in both Yorkshire and Lincolnshire, and her mother, Annabel, who had divorced 'Reggie' when Samantha was still a small child, was now Viscountess Astor. She could also eclipse Cameron's royal connections, as a descendant of Charles II and Nell Gwynne, and was a distant cousin of Princess Diana. Less intellectual than his previous girlfriends, she enchanted David, who soon proposed marriage. But she thought she was much too young, at 20, and – perhaps recalling that her mother's early marriage had collapsed after barely five years – decided that they must wait, so they became only 'secretly engaged'.

By 1994, however, Cameron, now very keen indeed to become an MP, thought it would be advantageous to get some experience in business, and also to earn more money, as his income as a party 'apparatchik' had fallen far behind those of most of his Etonian and Oxford friends, who were virtually all engaged in commerce or the more high-paying professions. His future mother-in-law came to his aid. Annabel Astor, herself a highly successful businesswoman, was a close friend of Michael Green, the chairman of Carlton Communications, which had extensive interests in advertising and in television, including the London weekday franchise on ITV. Green hired him at almost double his salary as an aide to Michael Howard, and he eventually became the company's Director of Communications, essentially a PR and lobbying job. Cameron made it clear at the outset that his overriding priority was to became a Tory MP in the shortest possible time, and Green, anxious to curry favour with the Conservatives, acquiesced. Cameron started working for Carlton in September 1994, and his search for a safe Tory constituency began in earnest. He had unsuccessful forays at Ashford, Epsom and Reading, but in January 1996 he was selected at Stafford, a newly redistributed constituency, which was projected to have a Tory majority of around 8,000. Six months later, on 1 June 1996, he and Samantha, who was now working as Creative Director at Smythson's, the upmarket stationers in New Bond Street, were married at St Augustine's Church, East Hendred, Oxfordshire. All seemed set fair, but John Major's government was deeply unpopular, and 'New Labour' under Tony Blair's dynamic leadership was soaring in the polls. When the general election took place on 1 May 1997, there was a swing to Labour in the Stafford constituency of 10.8 per cent, slightly larger than the national average. Cameron lost by over 4,000 votes, and returned disconsolately to resume his job at Carlton.

His search for a parliamentary seat continued. He narrowly missed out on the selection for the West Sussex seat of Wealden, but had a stroke of luck a year later, in 2000, when Shaun Woodward, the Tory MP for Witney, the Cotswolds constituency adjacent to Newbury and where his mother-in-law, Annabel Astor, had her country home, defected to the Labour Party. Cameron seemed a natural for the seat, and was duly selected. He went on to be elected, in this very safe Conservative seat, in the 2001 election with a majority over Labour of just under 8,000. The first decision he had to take on election was whom to back as party leader, William Hague having resigned following the heavy Tory election defeat. He decided to vote for Michael Portillo, who – despite his earlier record as a fervent right-winger – presented himself as the modernizing candidate, and was seen as the favourite. He led on the first two ballots by MPs, but was squeezed by a single vote into third place in the third ballot, as other candidates were eliminated. Had he made it into the run-off between the two top candidates, he would almost certainly have been elected, as he was by far the most popular among the wider party membership, to whom the decision was now referred. What probably cost him the chance was his admission during the campaign that he had 'experimented' with homosexual relations when he was a student. So the final choice was between the former Chancellor of the Exchequer, Kenneth Clarke, and the almost unknown Iain Duncan Smith, an ardent Thatcherite. Clarke lost by a three-two margin, undoubtedly because of his pro-European views. Cameron gave his final vote to Duncan Smith, despite being far closer to Clarke in his views on everything except Europe.

Cameron was fortunate as a newly elected MP to be invited to serve on the Home Affairs Select Committee. At its first meeting, he successfully proposed that it should launch an investigation into heroin addiction and 'options for changing the law towards cannabis'. He rapidly revealed himself as one of the most 'liberal' members of the committee, advocating the decriminalization of cannabis and the downgrading of Ecstasy from a Class A to a Class B drug. He also soon formed a close association with George Osborne, the newly elected MP for Tatton, whose background was not dissimilar to his own. Nearly five years younger, the heir to a baronetcy, he was not an Etonian but had been educated at St Paul's school, and studied at Oxford, where he was a member of the Bullingdon Club, and subsequently worked at the Conservative Research Department, as a ministerial aide, and as speechwriter to William Hague as Leader of the Opposition. He had been a much earlier committed 'modernizer' than Cameron, and their views gradually merged, with Osborne generally leading the way. They were neighbours in the Notting Hill area of west London, and soon got into the habit of driving together daily between their homes and the House of Commons. Gathering round them was a smallish group of mostly young and newly elected members, nearly all of them wealthy and public-school educated, and committed modernizers. They frequently dined together, and were generically known as the 'Notting Hill set'.

On 8 April 2002, the birth of their first son, Ivan, gave great joy to David and Samantha, but a week or so later they learnt the devastating news that he was severely disabled, and would be unlikely ever to walk or talk. He was diagnosed with Ohtahara syndrome, an extreme form of epilepsy. He lived for nearly seven years, during which he required constant round-the-clock care, was often in great pain and was in and out of hospital. His parents' lives were greatly disrupted, but they lavished love and affection on him, and were heartbroken when he died following a series of uncontrollable seizures at St Mary's Hospital, Paddington, early in the morning of 25 February 2009. They had been told that there might be a one in four chance that any subsequent children would suffer from the same condition, but were brave enough to take the risk, and had three further children, all completely healthy – Nancy, born in January 2004, Arthur Elwen, in February 2006, and Florence, born after Cameron had become Prime Minister, in August 2010. The experience of having Ivan had a marked effect on Cameron. He was so deeply impressed by the care and devotion that his son received from the National Health Service throughout his short life that he became a passionate advocate on its behalf. This undoubtedly helped to improve the Tory Party's image, as it had long lagged behind Labour in the public's estimate of the two parties' support for the NHS. More personally, his friends noticed that he became much more patient and sympathetic about other peoples' misfortunes, and shed some of the blandness and self-satisfaction which he had previously radiated.

The newly elected party leader, Ian Duncan Smith, was finding it extremely difficult to match Tony Blair at Prime Minister's Questions, and before long both Cameron and Osborne, together with Boris Johnson, the newly elected MP for Henley, were drafted in to help prepare for the, now weekly, encounter, every Wednesday. Despite their help, Duncan Smith showed little improvement, and the party became more and more dissatisfied with his parliamentary performances. In July 2003, Cameron was given his first frontbench job – as 'Deputy Shadow Leader of the House' – and made a conspicuous début, with several newspapers identifying him as a possible future party leader. Duncan Smith's own leadership had not much further to run. In October, the requisite number of Tory MPs – 25 – formally demanded a vote on whether there should be a leadership ballot. Friends of Duncan Smith pressed him to stand down, fearing that he would suffer a humiliating defeat, but he insisted on holding his ground. In the event, he was defeated, but by a narrower margin than had been expected – 90 votes to 75.

A contest for the leadership was then expected, with the likely candidates being Michael Howard, who had established himself as the most effective debater on the Conservative side of the House, and David Davis, who was regarded as having done an excellent job as chairman of the all-party Public Accounts Committee, and who was widely seen as the carrier of the Thatcherite flame. Yet Davis was pressured not to run, and probably calculated that, if, as seemed highly likely, the Tories lost the next general election, he would be chosen to pick up the pieces. So Howard was elected unopposed, without the necessity of holding a ballot of party members. He performed much better as opposition leader than his predecessor, but did no more than dent Labour's majority at the general election, held on 5 May 2005. The Tories made 35 gains, winning 197 seats, against 355 for Labour and 62 for the Liberal Democrats.

Howard announced his intended resignation on the morrow of the election, but agreed to carry on until the party conference in October. In the meantime, he reshuffled his 'Shadow Cabinet' to give much greater prominence to younger MPs. He offered the Shadow Chancellorship to Cameron, who declined, perhaps because he was leery of facing the formidable Gordon Brown across the dispatch box. Instead, he chose the Education portfolio, and Howard appointed Osborne as Shadow Chancellor, at the same time encouraging him to run for the party leadership. Osborne accepted the post, but after reflection concluded that he was too young, at 33, to be a viable leadership contender. Cameron, however, quickly decided, with strong support from his wife, that he would like to run, and in early June summoned a secret meeting of the Notting Hill group of MPs, of whom 14 attended, including Osborne, Boris Johnson and Michael Gove, a former journalist on *The Times*, who had only just been elected to the House. Most agreed to back his candidature, though some wished he had rather more fire in his belly, and others feared that he would be seen as 'too posh'. Cameron's campaign did not take off, and by early September the number of his supporters had shrunk to nine. Meanwhile, it was generally assumed that the contest would effectively be between David Davis and Ken Clarke, though the thrusting young right-winger Liam Fox and former Foreign Secretary Malcolm Rifkind also entered the lists. As the party conference approached, Cameron took two vital steps to revive his flagging fortunes. He spent £20,000 on promotional activities, including an American-style launch meeting at the Royal United Services Institute in an auditorium specially jazzed up for the occasion. This was very favourably received by the assembled journalists, who contrasted it with a similar event held by David Davis the same day 'in the fusty oak-panelled surroundings of the Institute of Civil Engineers' (Elliott and Hanning, 2012, p. 293). The speech which Cameron made was reported as inspiring, while Davis's was dismissed as 'disappointing', so the young challenger received an excellent press. He also sought to ingratiate himself with the growing anti-European section of the party by matching Liam Fox's promise to take the Conservative Group out of the European People's Party, to which most of the main centre-right parties in the EU belonged. He thereby risked marginalizing the British Conservatives in the European Parliament, but felt the step was necessary to avert the threat of Fox overtaking him in the race for votes.

The Party Conference opened in Blackpool, and all the five candidates were given a specific day on which they could address the conference (and, through the television coverage, the party membership). First off was Rifkind, whose speech kindled little enthusiasm, and he shortly afterwards withdrew from the contest in favour of Clarke. It was Clarke's turn the following day, and, though he made a lively and witty speech, it was received with little warmth. On Wednesday, 4 October, Cameron's moment arrived, and he took the conference by storm. Speaking without any notes and wandering freely round the platform with microphone in hand, he made a passionate appeal to change and modernize the party, saying he wanted people to 'feel good about being Conservatives again'. Approaching his peroration, he continued:

> There is a new generation of people taking on the world, creating the wealth and opportunity for our future. We can lead that generation... Changing our party to change our country. It will be an incredible journey. I want you to come with me.

It was the speech of a lifetime, and the conference responded with great enthusiasm. In 20 minutes, Cameron had moved from being a rank outsider to a leading contender. He was halfway home, and his success was virtually assured on the following day, when Davis made a dull and uninspiring speech which shattered the hopes of his previously large band of supporters. Then Cameron was thrown out of his stride by press speculation, particularly in the *Daily Mail*, about his alleged drug-taking while at Oxford. He refused to give a direct answer, but said that he led 'a normal student life', and was profoundly relieved when after a few days the story died a natural death. Two weeks later, when Parliament resumed, the 198 Tory MPs proceeded to an exhaustive ballot to reduce the four candidates to two, with the following result:

	1st ballot	2nd ballot
Davis	62	57
Cameron	56	90
Fox	42	51
Clarke	38	–

Although Davis led on the first ballot, the margin was much narrower than expected, and when Clarke was eliminated Cameron won almost all his votes, while Davis's score actually fell. The two leading candidates were then submitted to a postal ballot of the party membership, with Cameron winning by a margin of more than 2:1:

Cameron 134,446 votes
Davis 64,398.

On 6 December 2005, he was declared elected as party leader, and, consequently, Leader of the Opposition. It was an amazing achievement after less than five years as a Member of Parliament. It was a great gamble for the party to turn to somebody so young and inexperienced, and it was a reflection of how desperate they had become after losing three elections in a row under three different leaders.

As leader, Cameron had no doubt as to what his mission should be. It was to 'detoxify' the image of the Conservative Party, which was now widely seen, in the words of his colleague Theresa May, as 'the nasty party'. During the leadership campaign, he had – perhaps unwisely – proclaimed himself to be the 'heir to Blair'. Now, he and his entourage, largely made up of youngish former employees of the Conservative Research Department, consciously modelled themselves on the Labour leader and his 'New Labour' colleagues. They pored over the book written by Blair's strategy adviser Philip Gould, *The Unfinished Revolution* (1998). This painstakingly spelled out every inch of the journey which the Labour Party had taken from the depths of 1983, when it was seen as a backward-looking, ideologically obsessed party, tied to outdated doctrines of nationalization and punitive levels of taxation, to the all-conquering 'New Labour' which had swept to power in 1997. Andrew Cooper, who was to become Cameron's Director of Strategy in 10 Downing Street, handsomely acknowledged the debt the Tories owed to Gould in a memorial volume published after his premature death in 2011 (Kavanagh, ed., 2012, pp. 132–51). His chapter is entitled 'How Philip Gould Helped to Save the Conservative Party'. It was not just that the Tories under Cameron adopted the *methods*, particularly the extensive use of focus groups, employed by Gould; they also adapted the *tone* of their message, particularly in the speeches and television appearances of their leader. These were consistently moderate, reasonably argued, open-minded and optimistic – or 'schmoozing the public', as less friendly observers might put it.

By no means all the Tories welcomed Cameron's new approach, and there was much resistance within the party to many of his initiatives. These included his attempts to ensure that the party in Parliament – overwhelmingly made up of white, public-school educated males – should be broadened by the adoption as candidates of many more women, ethnic minority and state-educated candidates. His efforts in this direction had some effect, despite the sullen opposition, but even after the 2010 general election the party's representation was still heavily weighted towards the privileged classes. Cameron also went out of his way to bury Conservative hostility to the gay community, announcing himself in favour of civil partnerships, and under his leadership – for the first time – a number of Tory MPs 'outed' themselves as homosexual. Cameron also placed great emphasis on environmental issues and the threat of global warming, travelling to Northern Norway, and being photographed sledging with husky dogs to dramatize his concern about the issue. He was also widely pictured cycling each day from his home to the House of Commons, but the effect of this was somewhat undermined when it was revealed that he was followed on his route by his official car carrying his shoes and papers. This did not prevent him from using the slogan 'Vote Blue Go Green' in the 2006 local elections. In the House of Commons, he was able to at least hold his own in his weekly confrontations with Tony Blair, now a somewhat diminished figure in the aftermath of the Iraq War and with rumblings of discontent within his own party.

The public response to Cameron's leadership was generally favourable, and by the summer of 2006 the Tories overtook Labour in the polls for almost the first time in 14 years and steadily increased their lead until mid-2007, when Brown replaced Blair as Prime Minister. There was then a sharp reversal during the new Prime Minister's honeymoon period, and by October 2007 the Tories appeared to be facing a heavy defeat in the general election which now appeared imminent. Yet Cameron kept his nerve (see Chapter 52), and defiantly rallied his party in a speech – again without notes – at the Conservative Party Conference. This, together with a desperate pledge by George Osborne to raise the inheritance tax threshold to £1 million, led to a sharp narrowing of Labour's poll lead, and Brown, humiliatingly, called off the election which he had been about to announce. In retrospect, this appears to have been the decisive event in Cameron's rise to power, and thereafter it seemed highly probable that he would overtake Labour at the next election, the main uncertainty being whether he would obtain an overall majority. The Tories immediately went into a lead in the polls, which they maintained, with fluctuations, right up till polling day in 2010.

The remaining two-and-a-half years of Brown's premiership were something of an anti-climax, except for his deft handling of the banking crisis, which resulted in some improvement in his polling position, which was not, however, sustained. He became deeply unpopular, not least because of the scandal over MPs' expenses; this hit all parties, but Labour as the government party was the more damaged. This was partly because the *Daily Telegraph*, which broke the story, gave the greatest prominence to Labour 'delinquents', and also because Cameron proved more adroit in handling the issue and acted more promptly in seeking to discipline his MPs. Nevertheless, his continuing efforts to 'decontaminate' his party achieved only partial success. Although his own standing with the public became increasingly positive, he never rivalled Blair's earlier charisma, and deep reservations about the Conservative Party persisted among many uncommitted voters. Nevertheless, the Tories entered the 2010 general election campaign with high hopes of success. The Labour Party appeared in disarray, it had lost almost all its support in the press, with the sole exception of the *Mirror* group (even *The Guardian* had abandoned ship), and it was heavily outspent by the Tories, whose normally ample funds were augmented by massive donations from Lord Ashcroft, the controversial billionaire and former vice-chairman of the party. Yet the Conservative campaign was blown off course by the apparent surge of support for the Liberal Democrats, following the first of three television debates in which Nick Clegg comprehensively outperformed his two rivals. Consequently the Tories turned all their fire on the LibDems, in particular by launching a sustained attack on their proposal of a partial amnesty for illegal immigrants. They also, in great secrecy, held a top-level meeting at which they discussed in detail the terms of a coalition agreement which might be offered in the event of a 'hung' Parliament. It was a prudent step. Although the Tories emerged from the election as the largest party, they were 20 seats short of a parliamentary majority. The overall result of the election of 6 May 2010 was:

Conservatives 306, Labour 258, Liberal Democrats 57, Others 29, Total 650.

No party was in a position to form a majority. There would have to be either a minority government or a coalition. The salient fact about the figures was that, whereas Conservatives plus Liberal Democrats could produce a majority, Labour plus Liberal Democrats could not. Any left-centre coalition would have to seek additional support from among the minority parties – Scottish and Welsh Nationalists, Northern Irish Members and one Green.

The election result was a bitter disappointment to Cameron, and threatened to put his leadership in question, but he acted with great speed and determination to extract the maximum advantage from the situation. In the early afternoon of 7 May, he called a press conference, at which he made a 'big, open and comprehensive offer to the Liberal Democrats' to form a coalition. Some of his colleagues had argued instead that he should form a minority government, asking the Liberal Democrats to reach a 'support and supply agreement' enabling him to get urgent legislation through, but with no guarantee of support for other government policies. Yet Cameron decided to go for what he considered the 'jackpot'. It seemed a long shot. The LibDems presented themselves as a left-of-centre party, and during the election campaign they had sided with Labour on the crucial issue of whether to begin with expenditure cuts before the fragile economic recovery had been consolidated. Yet Cameron was fortunate that Nick Clegg, unlike all previous leaders of his party, was right-of-centre, and, moreover, had developed a very marked aversion to Gordon Brown. So he responded with alacrity to Cameron's offer, and the first meeting between negotiating teams of the two parties was held on the same day. Brown responded by ringing Clegg and proposing a 'progressive alliance', with a pledge of immediate legislation on electoral reform, and promising, at the very least, a referendum on the Alternative Vote (AV). Clegg held him at arms' length, though he later agreed to parallel talks with a Labour team. These never really took off, and were effectively used by the Liberal Democrats to improve their bargaining position with the Tories. Several Cabinet ministers were less than enthusiastic about a deal with the LibDems, but Brown was very determined, and, when it appeared that his own leadership would be an obstacle, offered to stand down within a few months of a government being formed. His gesture came too late, the talks with the Tories went very well, and when Cameron reluctantly agreed, as a 'final offer', to a referendum on AV, which the Tories would be free to campaign against, it was clear that an agreement would soon be reached. Brown threw in his hand and drove to the Palace to resign on the afternoon of 11 May, and within an hour Cameron had kissed hands on his appointment.

On the following afternoon, he and Clegg gave a joint press conference in the rose garden of 10 Downing Street to present their government and the coalition agreement which underpinned it. There was much comment about the evident good feeling between the two men. They had much in common: the same age (43), the same wealthy background, 'public' school and Oxford education. Cameron had used all his ample charm on his LibDem partner during the previous days, and had been generous in his offer of ministerial positions. Clegg was offered, and accepted, the post of Deputy Premier, and four others of his colleagues were included in the Cabinet, rather more than they were mathematically entitled to, given their representation in Parliament. Fourteen other Liberal Democrats became junior ministers.

For Cameron, the coalition agreement was undoubtedly a good deal. He had preserved all the policy options which were important to him, and the only substantial concession he had been forced to make was over the AV referendum. It also enabled him to shed policy commitments which, while popular among Tory backbenchers, were embarrassing and/or unrealistic, such as the massive raising of the threshold for inheritance tax and attempting to repatriate powers from the European Union. For the Liberal Democrats it was to prove a great deal less satisfactory. They were forced to reverse their policy on expenditure cuts, and had made a major error in not making any attempt to secure concessions over the raising of student tuition fees, which they had very loudly campaigned against, all their candidates publicly signing a pledge to vote against any increase. One part of the agreement was equally satisfactory to both parties. This was the institution of a fixed parliamentary term, which virtually guaranteed the continuation of the government for a full five years. Provided the two parties stuck together, the next election would not be held until Thursday, 7 May 2015.

The cabinet which Cameron formed had 23 Members. The Tory appointments included George Osborne as Chancellor of the Exchequer, William Hague as Foreign Secretary, Theresa May as Home Secretary, Andrew Lansley as Health Secretary and Michael Gove as Education Secretary. David Davis was not included. The Liberal Democrat appointees included Vince Cable as Business Secretary, Chris Huhne as Energy Secretary and David Laws in the key post of Chief Secretary to the Treasury. He was forced to resign after less than three weeks because of serious irregularities in his expenses claims, and was replaced by Danny Alexander. At the rose garden press conference, Cameron had hailed not just a new government, but a 'new politics', with two parties giving up their distinctive preoccupations in the national interest. It was, indeed, a dramatic change over recent practice, effectively the first peacetime coalition government since Lloyd George's administration in 1918–22. (The so-called 'National Government', formed in 1931, was to all intents and purposes a Tory administration, with the ageing and ineffective Ramsay MacDonald merely a figurehead Prime Minister.)

Cameron's government has had at least one thing in common with Tony Blair's. It has been dominated by the relationship between the two most powerful ministers. Yet, whereas Blair and Brown were suspicious and resentful of each other, relations between Cameron and Osborne appear to be harmonious. This may be because the relatively laid-back Prime Minister has been happy to allow his hyper-active and hyper-political Chancellor to dominate the government's agenda. He has readily deferred to his judgment, and Osborne has been both the government's strategist and chief tactician. He had already assumed these roles in opposition, when he had, with considerable success, sought to blame the recession not on the greed and imprudence of bankers but on the alleged profligacy of Gordon Brown. He had committed the Tories to an immediate programme of expenditure cuts in a bold attempt to pay off the accumulated debts within the course of a single Parliament. This became the centrepiece of the new government's programme, and its success or otherwise came to be seen as its lodestar. Osborne began his austerity blitz with an emergency budget in June 2010, imposing immediate expenditure cuts of £6.2 billion, together with a steep rise in VAT. He followed this up, in October, with a spending review which fixed very tight spending limits for each government department up to 2014–15, with only health, education and international development ring-fenced to protect them from real expenditure cuts. Other measures included wage freezes for the public sector, deep cuts in benefit payments, the tripling of university tuition fees and a purge of 'quangos', with 192 to be abolished and another 118 merged. The screw was progressively tightened in subsequent budgets, and, though Osborne repeatedly claimed that 'we are all in this together', the brunt of the burden was clearly being borne by the less well off. Virtually the only sacrifice demanded of the wealthy was the withdrawal of child benefit from those whose incomes exceeded £40,000 (later amended to £60,000, with a partial reduction for those earning more than £50,000).

Initial reactions were largely favourable, with international economic organizations praising Osborne's policy, the press being broadly supportive, and opinion poll findings reassuring. Meanwhile, the Labour Party had made rather a meal of its choice of a leader to succeed Gordon Brown. This process involved five candidates, and lasted over four months, before the result was announced at the Labour Party conference on 25 September 2010. During this period, arguably, the Labour Party virtually threw away its chances of winning the next general election, not due for another five years. Government ministers, both Tory and LibDem, following the lead of George Osborne, continually emphasised in all their speeches that they had inherited a 'mess' of epic proportions from the Labour government, often adding that it was as bad – or even worse – than in Greece, and that they were in the process of 'clearing it up'.

'They crashed the car last time. Do you want to give them the car-keys again?' became the doorstep canvassing version of their refrain. The Labour leadership candidates, with Ed Miliband to the fore, were so anxious to distinguish themselves from New Labour that they made no attempt to defend the record of the Brown government. By the time that the leadership contest was over, the Tory narrative was already widely accepted as accurate, and Labour attempts to discredit it were largely unsuccessful. The flat denials of any Labour responsibility for the economic crisis fell on disbelieving ears. It would have been far better to admit, with the benefit of hindsight, that there had been a degree of over-spending in the years before 2008, but that this was only a relatively minor cause of what was a world-wide recession, whose origins were in the United States. The leadership election itself was deeply embarrassing for Labour. Ed Miliband's decision to run against his brother, David, who was the front-runner, was portrayed in the press as an act of fratricide, and the fact that his narrow victory was secured by the votes of trade unionists, while a majority both of MPs and party members backed David, was seen as undermining his legitimacy. This was a golden opportunity for Cameron, who had an easy time in Parliament, repeatedly scoring points off the new Labour leader, Ed Miliband, who started off very much on the back foot.

By May 2011, the Conservatives actually won additional seats in the local elections, which normally result in opposition gains. The Liberal Democrats, however, suffered severely for their about-turn on tuition fees and for flouting the wishes of large numbers of their former voters who did not approve of their siding with the Tories. They lost 747 seats, their worst performance in 30 years. In the opinion polls Cameron had established a large personal lead over Miliband, while Clegg's support had crumbled. In one year he had dropped from being the most to the least popular of all the main political figures. This proved to be the high-water mark of Cameron's popularity. Soon after, things began to go seriously wrong for him on a number of fronts.

These included relations with his Liberal Democrat allies, who were seriously put out – not only by the 2–1 margin by which they lost the AV referendum (which took place on the same day as the local elections), but by the way the Tories had conducted themselves during the campaign. Cameron reneged on his promise not to get personally involved, and the Liberals were appalled by the fact that the official literature of the 'no' campaign, paid for by Tory donors, contained a large photograph of Nick Clegg and accused him of breaking his election promises. This did not shatter the coalition, but thereafter there was a steady worsening of relations between the two partners, and none of the complicity which had marked the early days. Within the Conservative Party, and particularly in the Tory press, which had never liked the coalition, there was growing hostility towards the LibDems. This was especially evident among backbench MPs, fuelled by the frustration of a large number who thought, not necessarily correctly, that they would themselves have become ministers had a coalition not been formed. They blamed the LibDems for the government's failure to carry out 'real' Tory policies. Their constant pressure had its effect on Cameron, who was pushed notably to the right, both in the appointments he made in a number of small government reshuffles and in his policy choices, which undermined to some extent his earlier efforts to 'detoxify' his party. A later contretemps with the LibDems came in 2012, when Cameron announced the dropping of a Bill to reform the membership of the House of Lords, following a rebellion by right-wing MPs. Clegg took the opportunity to withdraw support for another Bill redistributing seats and reducing the size of the House of Commons. The LibDems had foolishly committed themselves to this Bill, only to discover later that it would have a devastating effect on their own representation. The Tories had expected to make a net gain of at least 20 seats from the same measure and saw its now inevitable defeat as a heavy setback to their objective of obtaining a majority in the 2015 poll.

Perhaps the most damaging development for Cameron was the introduction, in January 2011, of the Health and Social Care Bill by Andrew Lansley. This provided for a comprehensive structural re-organization of the NHS, with greatly increased opportunities for private sector interests to be involved. It had not been foreshadowed in the Conservative election manifesto or in the Coalition Agreement, and it ran into a storm of criticism, with all the leading medical associations in violent opposition. It was repudiated at the LibDems' spring conference in March 2011, and Cameron halted parliamentary consideration of the Bill for a re-think. Re-introduced with a number of amendments to placate the LibDems, it was still fiercely opposed by all the professional medical associations, who were – according to the polls – strongly supported by public opinion. It passed into law in March 2012, and Cameron lost little time in revealing his dissatisfaction with Lansley by switching him to another post in his next reshuffle, in September 2012. The passage of the Bill had undone all his previous efforts to present the Conservatives as friends of the NHS, and Labour's traditionally large lead on health issues had been fully restored.

Almost as damaging was the long-running 'phone hacking' saga, which principally involved the Murdoch press. Cameron had already been heavily criticized for hiring the former editor of the *News of the World*, Andy Coulson, as the Government's Director of Communications. In 2007, Coulson had quit his newspaper job following an earlier phone hacking scandal. He denied knowing anything about 'hacking' under his editorship, but successive *exposés* in *The Guardian* undermined his credibility, and he resigned his Downing Street post in January 2011, much to the embarrassment of Cameron. Coulson was subsequently charged with corruption, hacking, perverting the course of justice and perjury. Rebekah Brooks, the chief executive of News International, was also arrested on various charges, as were a large number of Murdoch journalists, and, much later, a couple from the *Mirror* Group. Within a few months the scandal went nuclear with the revelation that the *News of the World* had hacked the phone of child murder victim Milly Dowler. This led to the abandonment of News Corporation's bid to take over BSkyB, just as the Culture Secretary Jeremy Hunt was on the brink of approving it. Cameron felt constrained to set up a public enquiry, led by Lord Justice Leveson, into the culture, practices and ethics of the British press. The enquiry examined no fewer than 337 witnesses, including Cameron and three preceding Prime Ministers. Highly embarrassing revelations emerged about the closeness of Cameron to Murdoch and his chief lieutenants, notably Brooks, whose home was in Cameron's constituency, and with whom he and Samantha socialized a great deal. Cameron promised in advance to accept whatever Leveson recommended 'unless it is bonkers', but when the judge produced his voluminous report, in November 2012, he started to back-track. Leveson recommended the appointment of a new Press regulatory authority, independent of the newspaper proprietors, with powers to impose heavy fines, and to direct the publication of retractions, giving equal prominence to the original offending articles. The new authority should be backed up by legislation, Leveson insisted. Cameron accepted the proposal for a new authority, but baulked at the suggestion of statutory regulation, saying that it was a 'Rubicon' he would not cross. He was taken aback when not only Ed Miliband, but also Nick Clegg, insisted that the Leveson recommendations should be accepted in full. Inter-party negotiations were then initiated, but were abruptly terminated by Cameron on Friday 15 March 2013. He said that the government would table its own recommendations, which would be submitted to the Commons the following Monday. Clegg and Miliband then agreed on a joint amendment, on which they proposed to divide the House. Frantic efforts by government whips revealed that at least 20 Tory MPs would support the amendment or abstain, and a government defeat seemed inevitable. To avoid humiliation, Cameron dispatched his Cabinet Office Minister to negotiate with the other party leaders and with representatives of the hacking victims during the course of Sunday. A 'compromise' motion was agreed, which, however, could not disguise the fact that the Prime Minister had made a last-minute climb-down, and had given way on all significant points. Under this agreement, the Government was committed to the appointment, under a Royal Charter, of an independent press commission with greatly extended powers. The great majority of press proprietors then flatly refused to recognise the appointment of such a body, and proceeded to create their own regulatory body, the Independent Press Standards Organisation (IPSO), presided over by an eminent judge, Sir Alan Moses. The Government then effectively acquiesced, and made no moved to proceed with a Royal Charter.

Like other Tory Prime Ministers before him, Cameron faced difficulties over Europe, largely of his own making. He kept his promise to withdraw British MEPs from the European People's party, but faced much derision when he aligned them instead with a collection of extreme right-wing and oddball parties, some tainted by homophobia and anti-Semitism. He then pushed through the European Union Bill, which requires a referendum to be called before any additional powers whatsoever can be transferred to the EU. In December 2011, in what his biographers describe as 'a bungled too-clever-by-half diplomatic manoeuvre' (Elliott and Hanning, p. 485), he vetoed a proposed new EU treaty designed to help Eurozone countries co-ordinate their response to the recession. Twenty-five of the then 27 member states promptly signed their own treaty and won the right to use EU institutions for implementing it, but leaving Britain without a voice in their deliberations. Finally, after much hesitation, he made a long-delayed speech, in January 2013, saying that if the Conservatives won the 2015 election they would seek to renegotiate the terms of Britain's relationship with the EU, and then hold an 'in-out' referendum. All of these actions owed something to Cameron's own Eurosceptic views, but much more to his desire to placate the right wing of his own party, and to head off the growing electoral threat from the United Kingdom Independence Party. They appeared to have precisely the opposite effect – the more UKIP was appeased the greater demands it made, and the more support it got from the voters. The biggest shock to the Tories came in the Eastleigh by-election, in February 2013, caused by the resignation and imprisonment of the former Liberal Democrat minister Chris Huhne. The Tories had expected to capture the seat, but were devastated when the UKIP candidate came from nowhere and pushed them down into third place, narrowly failing to win the seat, which the LibDems retained with a reduced majority.

Cameron took a largely successful gamble in March 2011 when, together with French President Nicholas Sarkozy, he led the way in seeking a UN mandate for a no-fly zone over Libya in the face of a threatened massacre of the inhabitants of rebel-held Benghazi. Other nations, including a reluctant US, joined in, but after the first few days, in which the American input was crucial, it was the British and French who led the operation and made the largest contributions to the allied efforts. These enabled the rebel forces to triumph, with the final overthrow and death of Colonel Gadhafi some seven months later. The exercise, which involved no British casualties, was widely acclaimed, and brought much credit to Cameron, whose role was compared highly favourably to that of Blair over Iraq. Later, when Libya descended into chaos and effectively became a 'failed state', he himself was subjected to widespread criticism for his failure to provide effective aid to the democratically elected Libyan government. When, in September 2013, however, Cameron took the lead in urging a British military contribution to the punitive attack on Syria which President Obama projected, in response to the use of poison gas by the Assad régime, he made a bad miscalculation and was defeated in a vote in the House of Commons. This indirectly led to the abandonment of the American action, and the US-Russian agreement to force Assad to surrender and destroy his chemical weapons. Most people concluded that this was a good thing, but the episode hardly reflected well on Cameron's judgement.

Yet it is on his and Osborne's economic policy that Cameron's premiership will largely be judged, and this did not go well – at least, not for the first three years. As predicted by their critics, the early expenditure cuts blocked off the incipient recovery, with large job losses in the public sector not being compensated by a more modest growth of private employment. There was little, if any, economic growth, with a double-dip recession being recorded in early 2012 (though the figures were later revised to show it had been narrowly avoided). At the beginning of 2012 Britain registered the largest trade deficit since 1955, and the highest unemployment – at 8.4 per cent – for 17 years. Osborne conceded that there was now no prospect of paying off the debts by 2015, and revised his target to 2017–18. Leaders of the world's main economic bodies, the International Monetary Fund (IMF), the World Bank, the World Trade Organisation (WTO) and the Organisation for Economic Co-operation and Development (OECD), who had originally welcomed the government's strategy, now called for a halt to austerity and for economic policies which would foster growth. There were widespread calls for a 'Plan B', but ministers ploughed stubbornly on, repeating Thatcher's mantra of the mid-1980s, 'There is No Alternative.' Then, in March 2012, Osborne committed a major political error, with what became known in the press as 'the omnishambles budget'. As well as a series of petty taxes which raised little money, but caused great upset respectively to charity donors, grandmothers, hot pastry eaters and caravan owners, the budget reduced the marginal tax rate for incomes of over £150,000 from 50 to 45 per cent. This was immediately seized on by the Labour Party, which claimed that Osborne was effectively sending a cheque averaging £100,000 to each of 13,000 millionaires, at the same time as he was cracking down on the poorest elements of society. It appeared to make nonsense of Osborne's claim of 'all being in it together'. The public seems to have agreed: in the local elections two months later, the Tories lost 328 council seats in England alone, and the already seriously depleted LibDems another 190. In Parliament, Cameron had by now lost his easy mastery over Miliband, whose performances had greatly improved, and who frequently put the Prime Minister in difficulties. By the beginning of 2013 the position looked even worse, with Britain losing its AAA rating with Moody's credit agency, which Osborne had repeatedly claimed as the justification of his austerity policy.

Osborne's strategy was now widely condemned as a comprehensive failure, and the polls showed that even most Tory voters expected their party to lose the next general election. Moreover, the prospects of the Liberal Democrats agreeing to continue the coalition in the event of another 'hung' parliament seemed increasingly bleak, and the UKIP threat of stealing Tory votes appeared greater than ever. Yet all was not lost: Cameron still had a healthy lead over Miliband in his personal ratings, many voters still blamed Labour rather than the Tories for Britain's economic difficulties, and the Labour poll lead, at 10–12 per cent, was no greater than the 'normal' opposition lead in mid-Parliament. Moreover, renewed cuts in welfare benefits, which came into force in April 2013, seemed to go down well with many voters, who responded to Osborne's scarcely disguised attempt to paint the beneficiaries as work-shy layabouts (Continued in Postscript on page xv).

Appendix

Prime Ministers of the Eighteenth Century

Name	Party	Age at First Appointment	Dates of Ministries	Total Time as Premier
1. Sir Robert Walpole, first Earl of Orford, born 26 Aug. 1676, died 18 Mar. 1745. Married (1) Catherine Shorter, 30 Jul. 1700, (2) Maria Skerritt, Mar. 1738, 3 sons, 4 daughters	Whig	44 years, 107 days	3 Apr. 1721 to 11 Feb. 1742	20 years, 314 days
2. Spencer Compton, first Earl of Wilmington, born 1673, died 2 Jul. 1743. Unmarried, may have had illegitimate children	Whig	c. 69 years	1 Feb. 1742 to 2 Jul. 1743	1 year, 136 days
3. Henry Pelham, born 25 Sep. 1694, died 6 Mar. 1754. Married Lady Catherine Manners, 29 Oct. 1726, 2 sons, 6 daughters	Whig	48 years, 336 days	27 Aug. 1743 to 6 Mar. 1754	10 years, 191 days
4. Thomas Pelham-Holles, Duke of Newcastle, born 21 Jul. 1693, died 17 Nov. 1768. Married Lady Henrietta Godolphin, 2 Apr. 1717, no children.	Whig	60 years, 288 days	16 Mar. 1754 to 11 Nov. 1756, 29 Jun. 1757 to 26 May, 1762	7 years, 205 days
5. William Cavendish, fourth Duke of Devonshire, born 1720, died 20 Oct. 1764. Married Charlotte Boyle, Baroness Clifford, 17 Mar. 1748, 3 sons, 1 daughter	Whig	c. 36 years	16 Nov. 1756 to 29 Jun. 1757	225 days
6. James Stuart, third Earl of Bute, born 25 May 1713, died 10 Mar. 1792. Married Mary Wortley Montagu, 24 Aug. 1736, 5 sons, 6 daughters	Tory	49 years, 1 day	26 May 1762 to 8 Apr. 1763	317 days
7. George Grenville, born 14 Oct. 1712, died 13 Nov. 1770. Married Elizabeth Wyndham, May 1749, 4 sons, 5 daughters	Whig	50 years, 14 days	16 Apr. 1763 to 10 Jul. 1765	2 years, 85 days

Continued

Name	Party	Age at First Appointment	Dates of Ministries	Total Time as Premier
8. Charles Watson-Wentworth, second Marquess of Rockingham, born 13 May, 1730, died 1 Jul. 1782. Married Mary Bright, 26 Feb. 1752, no children.	Whig	35 years, 61 days	13 Jul. 1765 to 30 Jul. 1766, 27 Mar. to 1 Jul. 1782	1 year, 113 days
9. William Pitt, the Elder, first Earl of Chatham, born 15 Nov. 1708, died 11 May, 1778. Married Hester Grenville, 16 Nov. 1754, 3 sons, 2 daughters	Whig	57 years, 257 days	30 Jul. 1766 to 14 Oct. 1768	2 years, 76 days
10. Augustus Henry Fitzroy, third Duke of Grafton, born 28 Sep. 1735, died 14 Mar. 1811. Married (1) Anne Liddell, 29 Jan. 1756, (2) Elizabeth Wrottesley, 24 Jun. 1769, 7 sons, 9 daughters	Whig	33 years, 16 days	14 Oct. 1768 to 28 Jan. 1770	1 year, 106 days
11. Frederick North, styled Lord North, second Earl of Guilford, born 13 Apr. 1732, died 5 Aug. 1792. Married Anne Speke, 20 May, 1756, 4 sons, 3 daughters	Tory	37 years, 290 days	28 Jan. 1770 to 27 Mar. 1782	12 years, 58 days
12. William Petty, second Earl of Shelburne, 1st Marquess of Lansdowne, born 2 May 1756, died 7 May 1805. Married (1) Lady Sophia Carteret, 3 Feb. 1765, (2) Lady Louisa Fitz Patrick, 19 Jul. 1779, 3 sons, 1 daughter	Whig	45 years, 63 days	4 Jul. 1782 to 26 Mar. 1783	266 days
13. William Cavendish-Bentinck, third Duke of Portland, born 14 April 1738, died 30 Oct. 1809. Married Lady Dorothy Cavendish, 8 Nov. 1766, 4 sons, 2 daughters	Whig, then Tory	44 years, 353 days	2 Apr. 1783 to 18 Dec. 1783, 31 Mar. 1807 to 4 Oct. 1809	3 years, 82 days
14. William Pitt, the Younger, born 28 May 1759, died 23 Jan. 1806. Unmarried.	Tory	24 years, 205 days	19 Dec. 1783 to 14 Mar. 1801, 10 May 1804 to 23 Jan. 1806	18 years, 343 days

Continued

Prime Ministers of the Nineteenth Century

Name	Party	Age at first appointment	Dates of Ministries	Total time as Premier
15. Henry Addington, 1st Viscount Sidmouth, born 30 May 1757, died 15 Feb. 1844, married (1) Ursula Hammond, 17 Sep. 1781 (2) Mary Anne Townsend, 1823, 4 sons, 4 daughters	Tory	43 years, 291 days	17 March 1801–10 May 1804	3 years, 54 days
16. William Grenville, 1st Baron Grenville, born 24 Oct. 1759, died 12 Jan. 1834, married Anne Pitt, 18 Jun. 1792, no children	Whig	46 years, 110 days	11 Feb. 1806–25 March 1807	1 year, 42 days
17. Spencer Perceval, born 1 Nov. 1762, died 11 May 1812, married Jane Spencer-Wilson, 10 Aug. 1790, 6 sons, 6 daughters	Tory	46 years, 338 days	4 Oct. 1809–11 May 1812	2 years, 221 days
18. Robert Banks Jenkinson, 2nd Earl of Liverpool, born 7 Jun. 1770, died 4 Dec. 1828, married (1) Lady Louisa Hervey, 25 Mar; 1795, (2) Mary Chester, 24 Sep; 1822, no children	Tory	42 years, 1 day	8 Jun. 1812–9 April 1827	14 years, 305 days
19. George Canning, born 11 April 1770, died 8 Aug. 1827, married Joan Scott, 8 Jul. 1800, 3 sons, 1 daughter	Tory	57 years, 1 day	12 April 1827–8 August 1827	119 days
20. Frederick John Robinson, 1st Viscount Goderich, 1st Earl of Ripon, born 30 Oct. 1782, died 28 Jan. 1859, married Lady Sarah Hobart, 1 Sep. 1814, 2 sons, 1 daughter	Tory	44 Years, 305 days	31 Aug. 1827–8 Jan. 1828	130 days
21. Arthur Wesley (Wellesley), 1st Duke of Wellington, boirn 1 May 1769, died 14 Sep; 1852, married Lady Kitty Pakenham, 10 April 1806, 2 sons	Tory	58 years, 266 days	22 Jan. 1828–16 Nov. 1830, 17 Nov. 1834–9 Dec. 1834	2 years, 320 days

Continued

Name	Party	Age at first appointment	Dates of Ministries	Total time as Premier
22. Charles Grey, 2nd Earl Grey, born 13 March 1764, died 17 Jul. 1845, married Mary Ponsonby, 18 Nov. 1794, 10 sons, 7 daughters (one illegitimate)	Whig	66 years, 254 days	22 Nov. 1830–9 Jul. 1834	3 years, 229 days
23. William Lamb, 2nd Viscount Melbourne, born 15 Mar 1779, died 24 Nov. 1848, married Lady Caroline Ponsonby, 3 Jun. 1805, 1 son	Whig	55 years, 123 days	16 July 1834–14 Nov. 1834, 18 April 1835–30 Aug. 1841	6 years, 255 days
24. Sir Robert Peel, born 5 Feb. 1788, died 2 July 1850, married Julia Floyd, 8 Jun. 1820, 5 sons, 2 daughters	Conservative	46 years, 308 days	10 Dec. 1834–8 April 1835, 30 Aug. 1841–29 June 1846	5 years, 57 days
25. Lord John Russell, 1st Earl Russell, born 18 Aug. 1792, died 28 May 1878, married (1) Lady Adelaide Ribblesdale, 11 April 1835, (2) Lady Frances Elliot, 20 July 1841, 3 sons, 3 daughters	Whig, Liberal	53 years, 316 days	30 Jun. 1846–21 Feb. 1852, 29 Oct. 1865–26 Jun. 1866	6 years, 111 days
26. Edward George Stanley, 14th Earl of Derby, born 29 Mar. 1799, died 23 Oct. 1869, married Emma Bootle-Wilbraham, 31 May 1825, 2 sons, 1 daughter	Conservative	52 years, 331 days	23 Feb. 1852–17 Dec. 1852, 20 Feb. 1858–11 June 1859, 28 Jun. 1866–25 Feb. 1868	3 years, 280 days
27. George Gordon, 4th Earl of Aberdeen, born 28 Jan. 1784, died 14 Dec. 1860, married (1) Catherine Hamilton, 28 July 1805, (2) Harriet Hamilton, née Douglas, 4 sons, 4 daughters	Peelite	68 years, 326 days	19 Dec. 1852–30 Jan. 1855	2 years, 42 days

Continued

Name	Party	Age at first appointment	Dates of Ministries	Total time as Premier
28. Henry John Temple, Viscount Palmerston, born 20 Oct. 1784, died 18 Oct. 1865, married Emily, Lady Cowper, 16 Dec. 1839, no legitimate children	Liberal	71 years, 109 days	6 Feb. 1855–19 Feb. 1858, 12 Jun. 1859–18 Oct. 1865	9 years, 141 days
29. Benjamin Disraeli, Viscount Beaconsfield, born 21 Dec. 1804, died 19 April 1881, married Mary Anne Wyndham Lewis, 28 Aug. 1839, no legitimate children	Conservative	63 years, 68 days	27 Feb. 1868–1 Dec. 1868, 20 Feb. 1874–21 April 1880	6 years, 339 days
30. William Ewart Gladstone, born 29 Dec. 1809, died 19 May 1898, married Catherine Glynne, 25 Jul. 1839, 4 sons, 4 daughters	Liberal	58 years, 340 days	3 Dec. 1868–17 Feb. 1874, 23 April 1880–9 Jun. 1885, 1 Feb. 1886–20 July 1886, 15 Aug. 1892–2 March 1894	12 years, 126 days
31. Robert Arthur Cecil, 3rd Marquess of Salisbury, born 3 Feb. 1830, died 22 Aug. 1903, married Georgina Alderson, 11 Jul. 1857, 5 sons, 3 daughters	Conservative	55 years, 140 days	23 Jun. 1885–28 Jan. 1886, 25 July 1886–11 Aug. 1892, 25 Jun. 1895–11 July 1902	13 years, 252 days
32. Archibald Primrose, 5th Earl of Rosebery, born 7 May 1847, died 21 May 1929, married Hannah de Rothschild, 20 Mar. 1878, 2 sons, 2 daughters	Liberal	46 years, 302 days	5 Mar. 1894–22 Jun. 1895	1 year, 109 days

Prime Ministers of the Twentieth Century

Name	Party	Age at first appointment	Dates of ministries	Total time as premier
33. Arthur James Balfour, born 25 Jul. 1848, died 19 March 1930, unmarried	Con.	53 years, 352 days	12 Jul. 1902– 4 December 1905	3 years, 145 days
34. Sir Henry Campbell-Bannerman, born 7 Sep. 1836, died 22 April 1908, married Charlotte Bruce, 13 Sep. 1860, no children	Lib.	69 years, 89 days	5 Dec. 1905– 5 April 1908	2 years, 122 days
35. Herbert Henry Asquith, born 12 Sep. 1852, died 15 Feb. 1928, married (1) Helen Melland, 23 Aug. 1877, 4 sons, 1 daughter, (2) Margot Tennant, 10 May 1894, 1 son, 1 daughter	Lib.	55 years, 198 days	5 April 1908– 25 May 1915, 25 May 1915–5 Dec. 1916	8 years, 244 days
36. David Lloyd George, born 17 Jan. 1863, died 26 Mar. 1945, married (1) Margaret Owen, 24 Jan. 1888, 2 sons, 3 daughters, (2) Frances Stevenson, 23 Oct. 1943, 1 daughter	Lib.	53 years, 325 days	6 Dec. 1916– 19 Oct. 1922	5 years, 317 days.
37. Andrew Bonar Law, born 16 Sep. 1858, died 30 Oct., 1923, married Annie Robley, 24 Mar. 1891, 4 sons, 2 daughters	Con.	64 years, 37 days	23 Oct., 1922–20 May 1923	209 days
38. Stanley Baldwin, born 3 Aug. 1867, died 14 Dec. 1947, married Lucy Ridsdale, 12 Sep. 1892, 3 sons, 4 daughters	Con.	55 years, 292 days	22 May 1923–12 Jan. 1924 4 Nov. 1924– 4 Jun. 1929 7 Jun. 1935– 28 May 1937	7 years, 82 days
39. James Ramsay MacDonald, born 12 Oct. 1866, died 9 Nov. 1937, married Margaret Gladstone, 23 Nov. 1896, 3 sons, 3 daughters	Lab. Nat. Lab.	57 years, 102 days	22 Jan. 1924– 4 Nov. 1924 5 Jun. 1929– 24 Aug. 1931 24 Aug. 1931–7 Jun 1935	6 years, 289 days
40. Neville Chamberlain, born 18 Mar. 1869, died 9 Nov. 1940, married Anne de Vere Cole, 5 Jan. 1911, 1 son, 1 daughter	Con.	68 years, 71 days	28 May 1937–10 May 1940	2 years, 348 days

Continued

Name	Party	Age at first appointment	Dates of ministries	Total time as premier
41. Winston Churchill, born 30 Nov. 1874, died 24 Jan. 1965, married Clementine Hozier, 12 Sep. 1908, 1 son, 4 daughters	Con.	65 years, 163 days	10 May 1940–26 Jul. 1945 26 Oct. 1951– 5 April 1955	8 years, 240 days
42. Clement Attlee, born 3 Jan. 1883, died 8 Oct. 1967, married Violet Millar, 10 Jan. 1922, 1 son, 3 daughters	Lab.	63 years, 205 days	26 July 1945–26 Oct. 1951	6 years, 92 days
43. Anthony Eden, born 12 Jun. 1897, died 14 Jan. 1977, married (1) Beatrice Beckett, 5 Nov. 1923, 2 sons, (2) Clarissa Spencer-Churchill, 14 Aug. 1952	Con.	57 years, 299 days	6 April 1955– 9 Jan. 1957	1 year, 279 days
44. Harold Macmillan, born 10 Feb. 1894, died 29 Dec. 1986, married Lady Dorothy Cavendish, 21 April 1920, 1 son, 3 daughters	Con.	62 years, 335 days	10 Jan. 1957– 18 Oct. 1963	6 years, 281 days
45. Sir Alec Douglas-Home (14th Earl of Home), born 2 Jul. 2003, died 9 Oct. 1995, married Elizabeth Alington, 3 Oct. 1935, 1 son, 3 daughters	Con.	60 years, 109 days	19 Oct. 1963– 16 Oct. 1964	362 days
46. Harold Wilson, born 11 Mar. 1916, died 24 May 1995, married Mary Baldwin, 1 Jan. 1940, 2 sons	Lab.	48 years, 219 days	16 Oct. 1964– 19 Jun. 1970 4 Mar. 1974– 5 April 1976	7 years, 279 days
47. Edward Heath, born 9 Jul. 1916, died 17 Jul. 2005, unmarried	Con.	53 years, 259 days	19 Jun. 1970– 4 Mar. 1974	3 years, 259 days
48. James Callaghan, born 27 May 1912, died 26 March 2005, married Audrey Moulton, 28 Jul. 1938, 1 son, 2 daughters	Lab.	64 years, 9 days	5 April 1978– 4 May 1979	3 years, 29 days
49. Margaret Thatcher, née Roberts, born 13 Oct. 1925, died 8 April 2013, married Denis Thatcher, 13 Dec. 1951, 1 son, 1 daughter (twins)	Con.	53 years, 204 days	4 May 1979– 28 Nov. 1990	11 years, 209 days
50. John Major, born 29 Mar. 1943, married Norma Johnson, 3 Oct. 1970, 1 son, 1 daughter	Con.	47 years, 245 days	28 Nov. 1990– 2 May 1997	7 years, 155 days
51. Tony Blair, born 6 May 1953, married Cherie Booth, 29 Mar. 1980, 3 sons, 1 daughter	Lab.	43 years, 361 days	2 May 1997– 27 June 2007	10 years, 56 days

Continued

Name	Party	Age at first appointment	Dates of ministries	Total time as premier
52. Gordon Brown, born 10 Feb. 1951, married Sarah Macaulay, 3 Aug. 2000, 1 daughter (decd.), 2 sons.	Lab.	56 years, 134 days	27 Jun. 2007–11 May 2010	2 years, 321 days
53. David Cameron, born 9 Oct. 1966, married Samantha Sheffield, 1 Jun. 1996, 2 sons (1 decd.), 2 daughters.	Con.	43 years, 183 days	11 May 2010–	

Index

Note: Page numbers in bold refer to chapter titles